The Mitchell Beazley Illustrated Biographical Dictionary **WHO DID WHAT**

EMBLEM

The Mitchell Beazley Illustrated Biographical Dictionary

WHO DID WHAT

5000 men and women who have
shaped the world's destiny.

EMBLEM

© Mitchell Beazley Publishers
Limited 1974
Revised edition 1975
ISBN 0 85533 080 5
Printed in the Netherlands by Smeets
Offset B. V. Weert

The Book of Kells
The unknown monks who illuminated the
Book of Kells—an account of the
Gospels, and local records – in the 6th
century were members of an Irish
community which helped keep alight the
flame of Christianity at a time when the
survival of the religion was in doubt. They
left for posterity not merely a priceless
artefact, but a beacon of hope for
humanity and a lasting testimony to
individual achievement

STOP PRESS

For the latest events in our fast-changing
world and the way they have affected the
destinies of leading personalities, see
the special stop-press section beginning
on Page 385.

Edited and designed by
Mitchell Beazley Publishers Ltd.,
14-15 Manette Street, London
W1V 5LB

General Editor
Gerald Howat, B.Litt., M.A., F.R.Hist.S

Project Editor Victor Stevenson
Designer Nick Eddison
Text Editors Ian Grant, Yvonne
McFarlane **Editorial Assistants**
Sue Farr, Helen Varley
Design Assistants Malcolm
Smythe, Aean Pinheiro
Picture Researchers Kate Parish,
Jackie Webber

Editorial Director
Bruce Marshall
Managing Editor Frank Wallis

Consultant Editors
Don E. Fehrenbacher, M.A., Ph.D.,
D.H.L., Coe Professor of American
History, University of Stanford,
Calif.;
Douglas Harvey, M.Sc., Financial
Director, Texaco Ltd.;
D. W. Lomax, M.A., D.Phil.,
Professor of Spanish, University of
Birmingham;
M. J. MacLeod, M.A., Ph.D.,
Professor of Latin American History,
University of Pittsburgh;
Patrick Moore, O.B.E., F.R.A.S.,
author, astronomer and broadcaster;
L. G. R. Naylor, M.A., author and
historian;
J. R. L. Southam, M.A., Barrister-
at-Law, Legal Adviser, Gas Council.

Principal Advisers
Bronwyn C. Bennett; Michael J.
Bennett, B.Sc., Ph.D., D.I.C., A.R.C.S.,
A.E.A.; Nicolas Bentley, F.S.I.A.,

author and artist; J. D. Boreham,
D.L.C., A.S.I.A.; Ronald Burrow, B.A.,
F.R.C.O.; Hugh D. B. Clarke, B.A.;
D. B. Clegg, M.A.; Richard Cooper,
M.A.; Diana de Deney, LL.B.; Rev.
P. Doble, M.A.; J. T. Enticott, B.A.;
W. G. Fuge, M.A.; P. M. Gardner,
M.A.; M. R. Heafford, M.A., B.Litt.;
P. E. Heafford, M.A., B.Sc.; Anne
McG. Howat, M.B., Ch.B.; D. B.
Howat, B.Sc.; H. Frank Humphris;
M. P. James, M.A., Dip. Arch.; Francis
King; Graham Marchant, M.A.;
J. N. Mattock, M.A., Ph.D.; P. Mitter,
M.A., Ph.D.; R. G. Newey, M.A.;
Rawhide C. Papritz; A. P. Paterson,
N.D.H., M.Ed.; D. E. Pollard, M.A.,
Ph.D.; H. M. Radford, B.A., M.Litt.;
G. B. Rattray, B.Sc., A.I.C.T.A.;
David Robinson; R. T. Rowley,
B.A., B.Litt., F.S.A.; T. T. B. Ryder,
M.A., Ph.D.; James Shepherd, B.A.,
M. H. Shotton, M.A.; John
Skorupski, M.A., Ph.D.; A. Wyn
Lloyd, M.A., A.B.Ps.S.

A

Aalto, Alvar (born 1898) Finnish architect who was already developing the international modernist style during the late 1920s. Major works by him include the early Library at Viipuri and convalescent home at Paimio, and, later, a Hall of Residence at Massachusetts Institute of Technology, Cambridge, Mass.

Abbas, abu-al- (c. 721-54) Arab caliph who was the first of the Abbaside dynasty, under which Islam reached its peak. Although Abbas was titular head of the Arab empire, the real power lay with his brother and successor al-MANSUR. The accession of Abbas, and his transfer of the capital from Damascus to Kufa and then to Anbar, marked the displacement of Syria and Arabia by Persia and Turkey as the empire's focal points.

Abd-al-Malik ibn-Marwan (c. 646-705) Fifth and greatest caliph of the Umayyad line of Damascus, who restored and reorganized the Arab Muslim empire after a period of civil war (680-92). Recognized at first only in Syria and Egypt, Abd-al-Malik faced strong opposition from the Shi'ites of Iraq and even a revolt in his own stronghold of Syria (689), whilst the Byzantine empire threatened intervention. The Caliph made a truce with Byzantium in 689, agreeing to pay tribute to the Emperor, and then began active military operations against his enemies, crushing the Shi'ites (691) and capturing Mecca, where the rival caliph fell in battle. He restored order in Arabia and Persia (692-7), built the new garrison centre of Wasit (702) to maintain firm control over Iraq, and established bases for further Arab advances elsewhere. Abd-al-Malik centralized the administration, made Arabic the official language of his empire, and minted a new Islamic gold coin, the dinar.

Abd-er-Rahman I (731-88) Arab Emir of Cordoba (756-88), founder of the Omayyad dynasty that ruled Spain for three centuries. He escaped the slaughter accompanying the overthrow of the Omayyad dynasty in Syria (750) and made his way to Spain, where he defeated the deposed Amir Yusuf (756). Making Cordoba his capital, he ended near-anarchy and instituted governmental and other reforms. He enriched it with hospitals, schools and a mosque.

Abd-er-Rahman III (891-961) Emir and caliph during whose reign Muslim control of Spain was centralized. His fleets gained control of the western Mediterranean.

Abdul-Hamid II (1842-1918) Sultan of Turkey (1876-1909), who was largely responsible for the Armenian Atrocities (1895-6) (the massacre of Armenian subjects by Kurdish irregulars). Brought to power by a liberal movement which had deposed his brother Murad V, Abdul-Hamid suspended the constitution in 1878 and ruled as a dictator. In 1908 he was forced to call a parliament by the Young Turk Movement, which at that time was supported by Mustapha KEMAL. Abdul-Hamid attempted an unsuccessful counter-revolution (1909) and was deposed and subsequently exiled.

Abel, Niels Henrik (1802-29) Norwegian mathematician, who made fundamental contributions to the study of functional equations, elliptic functions and integrals of algebraic functions. His work shows the influence of the new and rigorous analytic work that began in the 19th century.

Abel, Rudolph (1902-72) Russian master-spy in the US, who sent top secret information to the Soviet Union from his Brooklyn photography shop. Apprehended and sentenced to a long gaol term, Abel was exchanged with the American pilot Gary POWERS in 1962.

Abraham (c. 2000 BC) Traditionally the first Hebrew Patriarch, the 'father of a multitude of nations'. He left his native Ur to settle in what is now southern Israel, where he founded the line that was to produce the twelve tribes of Israel.

Abramovitch, Shalom see MENDELE, Mocher

abu-Bakr (573-634) First Muslim caliph and founder of the Arab Empire. An early convert to the teachings of MOHAMMED, he succeeded him as Arab leader and by means of brilliant desert strikes subdued the Arab tribes which, united for the first time under Mohammed, had begun to revolt. Later expansionist moves into Syria and Iraq founded the empire that reached its peak under MUAWIYAH I.

abu-Nuwas (c. 760-c. 810) Persian poet featured as a character in the *Arabian Nights*. He developed new verse forms, and light-heartedly criticized and ridiculed the work of earlier poets, such as Imru' al-QAYS. Abu-Nuwas was a great favourite at the court of Caliph Harun al-RASHID, though his free speech and mordant wit frequently got him into trouble.

Acheson, Dean Gooderham (1893-1971) American lawyer and statesman who, as Secretary of State under President TRUMAN, was a principal architect of United States foreign policy after the Second World War.

Acheson, Edward Goodrich (1856-1931) American industrial chemist, who in 1891 discovered silicon carbide ('Carborundum'). In 1899 Acheson used the electric furnace to manufacture synthetic graphite, which has important applications in the electronics industry.

Adam de la Halle (c. 1230-c. 1287) French trouvère and one of the most famous of the medieval musician-poets. Adam's works have largely survived, including his pastoral *The Game of Robin and Marion*, made up of dialogue interspersed with songs.

Adam, Robert (1728-92) Scottish architect and interior designer who led the Classical Revival in English domestic architecture. Not only the designs of his buildings, but every detail of their furnishings and decoration influenced 18th-century architecture throughout the world. His father, William Adam, and his brothers James and John were also

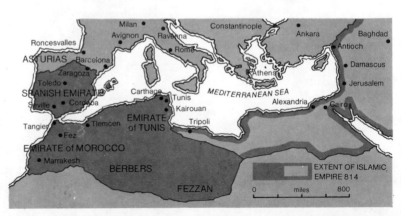

The map above shows the range of Arab domains at the time of their dominance of the Iberian peninsula.

Abd-er-Rahman I founded one of Islam's great dynasties of western Europe, and many traces of it remain in Spain

Much of Robert Adam's outstanding 18th-century architecture is still to be seen. Above, Kenwood, London

architects. Robert lived in Rome for three years where his intensive study of Roman architecture proved a lasting inspiration to the development of his own elegant and restrained Neo-Classicism. He designed many country houses, and his work in London included the screen and gateway of the Admiralty in Whitehall.

Adamantius see ORIGEN

Adamov, Arthur (born 1908) Russo-French dramatist and pioneer of the Theatre of the Absurd. He began his literary career as a Surrealist poet, but went on to write *The Confession* (1938-43), an autobiographical work in which he reveals the profound sense of alienation to be seen in his early plays, of which *The Parody* (1945) and *The Invasion* (1950) are two of the best known.

Adams, Brooks (1848-1927) American historian, who, in *America's Economic Supremacy* (1900), predicted that within 50 years the US would become supreme in world economics and that the world would be dominated by Russia and the US.

Adams, John (1735-1826) Second President of the United States (1797-1801) and one of the authors of the Declaration of Independence. Vice-President under WASHINGTON, he was elected President in 1796. His distrust of younger politicians and an authoritarian manner made him hard to work with. Adams stood for a second term, but was defeated by JEFFERSON and devoted the rest of his

life to writing. Adams, a barrister, was the first American ambassador to Britain (1785).

Adams, John Couch (1819-92) English astronomer, joint discoverer with LEVERRIER of the planet Neptune. In 1841 he investigated variations in the observed positions of the planet Uranus, and deduced from them the presence of an undiscovered planet. By 1845, he had completed his investigations. Meanwhile Leverrier had reached the same conclusion and his predictions led to the discovery of Neptune from the Berlin Observatory in 1846.

Adams, John Quincy (1767-1848) Sixth President of the United States (1825-9), son of John ADAMS, the second President. He drafted the Monroe Doctrine and was a leading campaigner for the abolition of slavery. In 1817, President MONROE appointed Adams Secretary of State, in which office he formulated the isolationist Monroe Doctrine in an attempt to prevent any further colonial encroachment of the European nations upon the American continent.

Adams, Samuel (1722-1803) American revolutionary politician and one of the most formative influences on American opinion in the years before the War of Independence (1775-83). He was leader of the radicals in the Massachusetts legislature (1765-74), and author of many revolutionary documents, including *Massachusetts Resolves*. Adams was also a leader of the agitation which led to the Boston Massacre (1770) and the Boston Tea Party (1773), and called and managed the first Continental Congress (1774), which marked the start of united colonial opposition to Britain. He was a signatory of the Declaration of Independence (1776).

Adams, William (1564-1620) The first English navigator to visit Japan.

After serving the Barbary Company for about 11 years, Adams joined the Dutch marine and in 1600 reached Kyushu in the *Charity*. His knowledge of shipbuilding and nautical mathematics commended him to IYEYASU, who gave him an estate. Adams spent the rest of his life in Japan, helping the English East India Company to establish a factory there.

Addams, Charles (born 1912) American cartoonist, responsible for the introduction of 'black humour' into the single-picture cartoon.

Addington, Henry (1757-1844) British Prime Minister, who succeeded his close friend PITT the Younger. His ministry negotiated the short-lived Treaty of Amiens with France (March 1802-May 1803) but Addington lacked incisiveness when war was resumed and he resigned in 1804. From 1812 to 1821 he was Home Secretary in the ministries of Lord LIVERPOOL. During a period of industrial and social unrest his policies were severe, though not unduly repressive by the standards of the time.

Addison, Joseph (1672-1719) English poet and essayist and co-founder with Sir Richard STEELE, of the *Spectator* (1711-12). Addison found a growing number of readers eager for periodicals and set out, in his magazine, to give them a genteel review of art, philosophy, manners and morals.

Adenauer, Konrad (1876-1967) German statesman, Chancellor of the German Federal Republic (West Germany) from 1949 to 1963. A Catholic Rhinelander and Lord Mayor of Cologne (1917-33), Adenauer supported the French plan for an autonomous Rhineland in 1919. A member of the Centre Party during the Weimar Republic (1918-33), he was a consistent anti-Nazi. When HITLER visited Cologne (1933) Adenauer had the

With the collapse of Hitler's Reich, Konrad Adenauer led Germany's post-war recovery. Behind him are the war ruins of Cologne, the city which, as chief burgomaster, he rebuilt, creating a new harbour, green belt and university

Nazi flag taken down and consequently was removed from office. During the Nazi régime he was twice arrested. In 1945, he became Mayor of Cologne again and founded the Christian Democrat Party. He was elected to the Bundestag in 1949 and became Federal Chancellor.

Adler, Alfred (1870-1937) Austrian psychiatrist and psychologist, originator of the concept of the inferiority complex. Each child, he thought, becomes conscious of smallness, dependence and possible weakness of some organ. To compensate for this the child strives either consciously or unconsciously for specific goals that will offset his feelings of inadequacy. An excessive sense of inferiority or the failure to achieve his self-imposed objectives may give rise to anxiety and aggression.

Adler, Larry (born 1914) American harmonica player whose virtuosity has given the 'mouth organ' new status. MILHAUD and VAUGHAN WILLIAMS have written for him. He has composed film scores.

Adrian, or **Hadrian, IV (c. 1100-59)** The only English pope (1154-9), who crowned FREDERICK BARBAROSSA Holy Roman Emperor, an act so unpopular that Adrian had to leave Rome for several months. His insistence on Church overlordship over all monarchs and their realms led to increasing conflict with Barbarossa and to the refusal (1156) to grant Ireland to England's HENRY II.

Adrian, Lord (born 1889) English physiologist who, with Sir Charles Sherrington, unravelled the mechanism by which nerves carry messages to and from the brain. Until this mechanism was known, it was impossible for anyone to understand disorders of the nervous system. In 1932 the two men were jointly awarded a Nobel Prize for their work.

Ady, Endre (1877-1919) Hungarian lyric poet, the outstanding innovator in 20th-century Hungarian literature, which he enriched with new forms and new imagery. He opposed the Hungarian right-wing régime, using his verse as a weapon against the nationalists.

A. E. (1867-1935) Pen-name of George Russell, Irish poet and essayist, who was an important figure in the Irish literary revival. He was a talented painter, and a student of mysticism, an interest he shared with W. B. YEATS. The theosophy of Madame BLAVATSKY and the Celtic mythology of Ireland both inspired Russell, who contributed poems to the *Irish Theosophist* and the *Irish Homestead*. His best poetry blends mysticism with the love of Ireland and her traditions.

Aelfric (c. 995-c. 1020) English abbot and writer, author of *Homilies*, the first Christian texts in the English vernacular. He is considered to be the greatest prose writer of Anglo-Saxon times.

Aeschylus (525-456 BC) Greek dramatist, who wrote the *Oresteia* trilogy – *The Agamemnon, Choephori* and *Eumenides*. Aeschylus transformed the essentially choric works

Aeschylus's drama is recreated more than two thousand years after his death

of the Athenian tragic drama festival – then characterized by a single actor and a chorus responding to each other in lyrical alternation – into drama, by introducing a second actor and reducing the chorus. He also introduced the trilogy into the tragic festival, which took the form of a competition. Of his 90 or so plays, only seven survive. The *Oresteia* trilogy is concerned with offences against the Gods by Agamemnon's family, and the Gods' revenge. *The Suppliant Women* is the first play of a trilogy, the other two being lost, as is *Prometheus Bound* (460 BC). *Seven Against Thebes* is the surviving third play of a trilogy. *The Persians* (427 BC) is a play on its own about contemporary events and inspired by the author's experience in the Greek army against the Persians at Marathon.

Aesop (6th cent. BC) Greek author of the oldest and most famous collec-

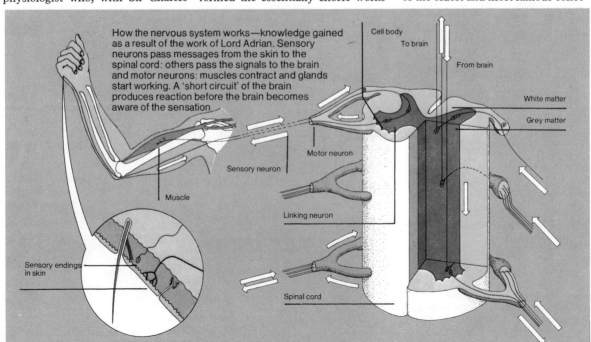

How the nervous system works—knowledge gained as a result of the work of Lord Adrian. Sensory neurons pass messages from the skin to the spinal cord: others pass the signals to the brain and motor neurons: muscles contract and glands start working. A 'short circuit' of the brain produces reaction before the brain becomes aware of the sensation

Cell body
To brain
From brain
White matter
Grey matter
Motor neuron
Sensory neuron
Linking neuron
Muscle
Sensory endings in skin
Spinal cord

tion of animal fables, whose aim was to point a moral or highlight basic human weaknesses and foibles. Originally used as references by orators and writers, they were not read widely until medieval times.

Aga Khan I see HASAN, Ali Shah

Agasias of Ephesus (2nd cent. BC) Greek sculptor of the late Hellenistic period, creator of the marble *Borghese Warrior*, now in the Louvre. The warrior appears to be a close copy of the earlier work of the school of LYSIPPUS. Agasias's warrior is important since it has for many centuries served as a standard for exact anatomy.

Agassiz, Jean Louis (1807-73) American naturalist and geologist of Swiss origin, who pioneered the study of geology and zoology in America and founded the Museum of Comparative Anatomy at Harvard. One of the ablest biologists of his day, he published prolifically on both living and fossil fish and his epoch-making *Researches on Fossil Fishes* (1833-44), which classifies nearly 1000 extinct species, became the springboard for the scientific study of extinct life in general. In 1836 Agassiz made an important contribution to geological knowledge by revealing that Switzerland was once covered by sheet ice. He then went to America, where he taught geology to both lay and specialist audiences.

Agesander (1st cent. BC) Rhodian sculptor who was mentioned in PLINY's *Natural History* as being the co-creator, with Athenodoros and Polydoros, of *Two Sons of Agesander*, the Hellenistic statue, in marble, depicting the death of the Trojan priest Laocoön and his two sons. This work, found in Rome (1506), greatly impressed MICHELANGELO, and was an important influence on the sculpting of the human form from the 16th century onwards.

Aghlabid see IBRAHIM IBN-AL-AGHLAB

Agnew, Spiro Theodore (born 1918) American Republican Party politician, who was nominated by Richard NIXON as his Vice-President in 1968 and again in 1972. He resigned the Vice-Presidency in October 1973, after he pleaded 'no contest' (guilty) to a charge of tax evasion, committed in 1967, while he was Governor of Maryland.

Agnon, Samuel (1888-1970) Polish-born Hebrew novelist and the first Israeli to win a Nobel Prize for Literature. His chief work is an epic trilogy of novels: *The Bridal Canopy* (1922), *Guest for the Night* (1945) and *The Day Before Yesterday* (1947). It deals with the decline of eastern European Jewry from the golden age of Hasidism to the disintegration that followed the First World War.

Agostino di Duccio (1418-81) Florentine sculptor, architect, and possibly goldsmith, who carved the marble altar in Modena Cathedral. His best-known work consists of tombs and low-relief panels of great linear beauty which form the decoration for the interior of the Tempio Malatestiano in Rimini.

Agricola, Georgius (1494-1555) German scholar and physician, known as the father of mineralogy. His work, the first to be based on practical knowledge and direct observation, initiated the development of modern geology and the study of metals. In *De Re Metallica* (1555), he summarized all that was then known of mining and smelting.

Agricola, Gnaeus Julius (c. 37-93) Roman general who pacified Britain. As its governor (78-84) he continued the invasion begun by Julius CAESAR and CLAUDIUS, using force and conciliation to extend Rome's frontiers. He conquered North Wales, northern England and lowland Scotland, achieving his northernmost victory at Mons Graupius (probably near Aberdeen) over the Caledonians. Agricola was the father-in-law of the historian TACITUS and the subject of his informative, if flattering, study *Agricola*.

Agricola, Johannes (c. 1494-1566) German religious reformer and advocate of Antinomianism, a doctrine which claims that salvation depends on faith alone, and in no way on moral laws (as, for example, the Ten Commandments).

Agrippa, Cornelius (c. 1486-1535) German scholar, magician and cabalist, author of *Three Books on Occult Philosophy*, first published in 1531 (written c. 1510). This compendium of astrology, music, geometry and necromancy attempted to provide a rationale for all the occult sciences and became a handbook for students of the occult. In 1529, Agrippa published *On the Vanity of the Arts and Sciences*, refuting his earlier beliefs.

Agrippa, Marcus (c. 63-12 BC) Roman general and statesman, and close friend of AUGUSTUS, who has been called the 'architect of the Roman empire'. Agrippa planned the campaigns of 44-30 BC, which brought Augustus to supreme power and ended the old republic. After suppressing disorders in Gaul and Germany (38 BC), he fought against POMPEY, defeating him first at Mylae (36 BC), and again decisively at Actium (31 BC). From 27-15 BC Agrippa was virtually Augustus's deputy, alternating with the Emperor between Rome and the provinces. A brilliant engineer, he built aqueducts, the Pantheon, and prepared a map of the known world.

Ahmes (11th cent. BC) Egyptian mathematician and possible author of a papyrus summarizing the state of the science at his time, called *Directions for Knowing all Dark Things*.

Aiken, Conrad (born 1889) American poet and novelist who drew upon contemporary psychological theories for his themes, and whose style was as much concerned with the sound of words as with their everyday meaning. One of his more important novels is *Blue Voyage* (1927), in which he tried to set down the wanderings of a playwright's mind (the 'stream of consciousness' technique). Aiken was in the famous Harvard class of 1911, which included T. S. ELIOT, Walter LIPPMANN and Robert BENCHLEY.

Airy, Sir George Biddell (1801-92) English astronomer, who determined the mass of the Earth. During his long tenure as Astronomer Royal (1835-81), he modernized the equipment of Greenwich Observatory, and brought order to the quantities of astronomical data that had accumulated since the mid-18th century. He instituted the regular recording of sunspots in 1874 and observed the transit of Venus. Airy was a disciplinarian and a hard worker, whose stubbornness occasionally hampered the work of his colleagues, who included John Couch ADAMS and FARADAY.

Akbar the Great (1542-1605) Mogul emperor of India. At the age of 13 he inherited the territories conquered by his grandfather, BABER, and within 50 years, through his military genius and personal energy, had established a powerful empire covering the whole of northern India. The unification of this vast area was supported by his deliberate policy of toleration towards conquered subjects, allowing freedom of worship to non-Muslims. As a patron of the arts, Akbar introduced a new epoch, the greatest achievements of which were the architectural masterpiece of Fathepur Sikri, his temporary capital, and a splendid series of manuscripts.

Akhmatova, Anna (1888-1966) Russian poet and one of the founders of the Acmeist group, whose members sought to replace the vagueness and affectations of Symbolism with compactness, simplicity and clarity of style. Among her many volumes of love poetry are *Beads*

(1914) and *The White Flock* (1917). In 1946, her poetry was banned, it having been declared socially non-constructive, but in 1959 she was 'rehabilitated' and by the time she died had been proclaimed as the greatest woman poet in Russian literature.

Akimov, Nikolai (born 1901) Russian theatrical director, stage and costume designer whose radical reinterpretations of classic, period plays, performed in modern dress made the Vakhtangov theatre in Moscow a centre of experiment and controversy in the 1920s. The peak of his fame, or notoriety, was his eccentric interpretation of *Hamlet* in 1932. In 1936, he became director of the Leningrad Theatre of Comedy.

Alain (1868-1951) French philosopher, teacher and essayist and author of the famous *Propos*. Originally published (from 1906) as newspaper articles, these reflective essays (seldom more than 600 words long) on subjects ranging from 'education' to 'happiness' appeared in book form, filling several volumes, under the title *Les Propos d'Alain*. He combined the Cartesian notion that men should be both capable of doubt and of making a choice, with the Socratic aim of provoking thought by stimulating men's minds.

Alaric (c. 370-410) Visigothic king (395-410) who conquered Rome (410). At first a general of Gothic auxiliaries for the Emperor Theodosius I, Alaric was elected king of the Visigoths and ravaged southern Greece until halted by the pro-Roman Vandal Stilicho. After Stilicho's death in 408, his army joined Alaric who, after three sieges of Rome, became the first foreigner for 800 years to capture the city.

Alba, Duke of see ALVA, Duke of

Alban, St (4th cent.) The first English martyr, converted to Christianity by a persecuted priest whom he sheltered in his Verulamium (St Albans) home. Alban was later arrested and executed at a site which subsequently attracted veneration, and in 429 became the location for St Alban's Abbey.

Albee, Edward (born 1928) American dramatist who wrote *Who's Afraid of Virginia Woolf?*, a success on both stage and screen. He began his career with contributions to the Theatre of the Absurd in *The Zoo Story* (1958) and *The American Dream* (1961). A later success was his adaptation of Carson MCCULLERS's novel, *The Ballad of the Sad Café* (1963). His subsequent work included *Tiny Alice* (1964) and *A Delicate Balance* (1966).

Albemarle, 1st Duke of see MONCK, George

Albéniz, Isaac (1860-1909) Spanish composer who was among the first to use traditional Spanish idioms. As a pianist he was a child prodigy. He stowed away on a ship bound for Puerto Rico at the age of nine, working his passage by giving recitals, and for years continued touring until he was about 30, when he went to Paris to study composition with D'INDY and DUKAS. He wrote operas and much keyboard music, and is probably best remembered for his suite for piano, *Iberia* (1906-9), the movements of which represent the musical traditions of various Spanish provinces.

Albers, Joseph (born 1888) German pioneer of abstract painting and one of the most influential artists in the Bauhaus group. While at the Bauhaus, Albers worked chiefly in the field of design in glass and ceramics. In 1933 he emigrated to the US and taught at Black Mountain College, North Carolina, for 16 years, then at Yale and Harvard, influencing a whole generation by his teaching.

Albert I (1875-1934) King of the Belgians (1909-34), whose military efforts hampered the German invasion and contributed to the Allied offensive of 1918. An energetic leader, who patronized the arts and initiated legal and social reforms, Albert was killed while rock climbing near Namur.

Albert, Prince Consort (1819-61) German-born husband and adviser to Queen VICTORIA who, despite his political competence, never managed to overcome popular disapproval. Marrying Victoria in 1840, Albert quickly became an informal but powerful member of government. He was insistent on developing the Crown's influence as an impartial force in domestic affairs and he repeatedly clashed with Lord PALMERSTON over foreign policy. In addition to his lasting influence on Victoria's reign, Albert was a devoted patron of the arts and a prime organizer of the Great Exhibition of 1851.

Alberti, Leone (1404-72) Early Renaissance Italian architect, playwright, musician and painter. Alberti designed the Tempio Malatestiano at Rimini and also worked in Florence and knew BRUNELLESCHI. There he completed the façade of the church of Sta Maria Novella (1470) with a design executed in polychrome marble and based upon the system of 'harmonic proportions'. His 10-volume treatise *De Re Aedificatoria* dealt with painting, sculpture and education as well as architecture.

Pioneered by men like Albuquerque, Portuguese ships reached Japan by the mid-16th century

Albertus Magnus (c. 1200-80) German philosopher, scientist, theologian and teacher of AQUINAS. The importance of Albertus Magnus lies largely in his use of observation as an aid to research and his defence of Aristotelianism against debased Platonism.

Albuquerque, Affonso d' (1453-1515) Portuguese governor of India (1509-15) who extended Portugal's influence far to the east. His first achievement was the capture (briefly) of Ormuz in the Persian Gulf (1507), a principal trading centre of the East. As Governor of India, he captured Goa (1510) and made it the capital of Portugal's eastern empire, seized Malacca (1511), reconquered Ormuz (1515), sent expeditions as far east as the Spice Islands (Moluccas), and extended Portuguese tradeship routes to China and Siam.

Alcibiades (c. 450-404 BC) Athenian politician and general who persuaded the Athenians to join an alliance against Sparta (421 BC), which provoked the last of the Peloponnesian Wars and led to the collapse of the Athenian Empire (404 BC). While leading an unsuccessful attack on Sicily (415 BC), Alcibiades was recalled to stand trial for mutilating statues of Hermes. He escaped and joined the Spartans, giving them advice ruinous to Athens and persuading the Ionian allies of Athens to revolt. He soon lost the confidence of the Spartans and conspired with the opposition in Athens. He finally regained short-lived favour in Athens when he attached himself to the fleet, and helped to defeat the Spartan navy and recover Chalcedon and Byzantium (411-409 BC). His defeat at Notium (407 BC) brought his dismissal from command. After the collapse of Athens, he fled to Phrygia where he was murdered at the instigation of the Spartans.

Napoleon's 'model hero', Alexander the Great was a military genius. His empire ranged from Greece to the Indus

Alcock's twin-engined Vickers Vimy had a laden weight of 12,500 lb. Today's jumbo jets weigh up to 820,700 lb

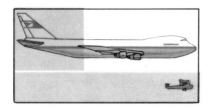

Alecsandri, Vasile (1821-90) Rumanian dramatist, lyric poet, and collector of Rumanian popular songs.

Alemán, Mateo (c. 1547-c. 1614) Spanish author who wrote *Guzman from Alfarache* (1599-1604), an account of a delinquent's descent into crime and his religious conversion, establishing a century-long vogue for picaresque novels in Europe.

Alembert, Jean le Rond d' (1717-83) French mathematician, philosopher and co-editor (until 1758) with DIDEROT of the *Encyclopédie*, for which he wrote the *Discours préliminaire* (1751).

Alexander (1888-1934) King of Yugoslavia (1921-34), who succeeded his father, Peter Karadjordjevic, as ruler of the united kingdom of Serbs, Croats and Slovenes set up in 1918. Animosity between Serbs and Croats led Alexander to proclaim a royal dictatorship in 1929, and in the same year the triune state was renamed Yugoslavia. His policies favoured the Serbs at home, and a Balkan peace based on a treaty between Yugoslavia, Rumania and Czechoslovakia abroad. In October 1934, on a state visit to France, he was murdered at Marseille by an assassin hired by the Ustase, a Croatian nationalist secret society.

Alexander I (1777-1825) Tsar of Russia (1801-25) who entered the War of the Third Coalition against France in 1805. After the defeat of the Russians at Friedland (1807), Alexander made peace with NAPOLEON at Tilsit, but the latter's economic, German and Polish policies and his Hapsburg marriage prejudiced the Treaty and led to the French invasion of Russia (1812). Alexander joined the War of the Fourth Coalition and took part in the invasion of France by the allies in 1814 and the overthrow of Napoleon. At the Congress of Vienna (1815) he obtained a kingdom of Poland under his own protection, and at home initiated a domestic policy of reform based on the partial alleviation of serfdom and the reorganization of the central administration of the Empire. In European affairs Alexander sought to provide for the collective security of the major powers (Austria, Prussia and Russia) by sponsoring the Holy Alliance, which ultimately became identified with the doctrine of coercive intervention against actual or threatened revolution.

Alexander II (1818-81) Tsar of Russia (1825-55). After succeeding his father, NICHOLAS I, during the Crimean war (which exposed the inadequacies of the Tsarist régime), he sanctioned a policy of modernizing reform. Polish unrest in 1863 and an

Alcock, Sir John (1892-1919) English aviator, who, with Sir Arthur Whitten Brown (1886-1948), completed the first non-stop transatlantic flight (1919). Their twin-engined biplane aircraft took 16 hours 27 minutes to fly 1936 miles from Newfoundland to Ireland. Alcock's flight was complicated by instrument failure, fog and turbulence. Brown repeatedly had to climb on the wings to hack off thickening ice.

Alcuin (735-804) English scholar, adviser on education to CHARLEMAGNE and defender of orthodoxy against the Adoptionist heresy (the view that JESUS was not born divine but became the Son of God at His Baptism). He contributed a detailed refutation of the heresy to the Council of Frankfurt in 793 and in 800 again took up the dispute with the heretic Bishop Felix of Urgel. Abbot at Tours from 796, his school became an influential educational centre.

Aldington, Richard (1892-1962) English poet, one of the founders of the 20th-century school of poetry known as 'imagism'. Following the lead of the philosopher T. E. HULME, Aldington and his American wife, Hilda Doolittle, aimed to write 'cheerful, dry and sophisticated' poetry which would render particulars exactly and not deal in vague generalities. His *Collected Poems* appeared in 1928 and he wrote one of the outstanding novels of the First World War, *Death of a Hero* (1929).

attempt to assassinate him (1866) caused him to resume despotic rule at home, and to initiate an aggressive policy abroad, leading to war with Turkey (1877-8) and imperial conquest in Central Asia. He refused to call a Constituent Assembly to prepare for parliamentary government, and was condemned to death by a secret revolutionary society, The People's Will and was assassinated.

Alexander III 'The Great' (356-323 BC) King of Macedon (336-323 BC) whose conquests culturally cross-fertilized Europe and Asia. He acquired Greek culture from his tutor ARISTOTLE and political power from his murdered father, PHILIP II. The youthful king first proved his military genius in lightning strikes on Thessaly, Thrace, Illyria and Thebes and by 335 he had gained ascendancy over all Greece. He then struck at the gigantic Persian empire founded by CYRUS THE GREAT and ruled by DARIUS III and his troops crushed the Persian armies at Granicus and Issus before overrunning Tyre and Gaza, occupying Egypt and turning east to Persia and India. In less than ten years, weaving 21,000 miles through southwest Asia from the Bosporus to the Indus Valley, Alexander seized intact an empire as big as the US and quadrupled the size of the world known to the Greeks. Alexander conserved the civilization he conquered, linking two great cultures of Greece and Persia in one Greek-speaking civilization that ran from India to Spain. On his death his generals, PTOLEMY, SELEUCUS and others divided up his empire. Culturally, Alexander's Hellenistic world endured – helping Greek art and architecture to enter India, and the Asian faiths founded by ZOROASTER and JESUS to penetrate Europe.

Alexander III (1845-94) Tsar of Russia (1881-94). His reign was marked by the persecution of the Jews and the repression of liberal ideas, as a result of which the first Russian Marxist group was formed (1883). To counter the expansion of Germany, Alexander concluded the secret Franco-Russian Alliance (sometimes referred to as the Dual Alliance) of 1894, which played an important part in the balance of power before the First World War. During the last years of his reign Russia's Far Eastern territories were developed under the guidance of the Minister of Finance and Communications, WITTE.

Alexander Nevski (c. 1220-63) Russian national hero, who kept the nucleus of what is now Russia intact against Mongol, Swedish and German pressures. Recognizing the futility of opposing the all-powerful Mongols, he held them off with tribute payments. Alexander earned the name Nevski by defeating Swedish troops near the river Neva (1240). Two years later he crushed the Teutonic Knights in a battle on frozen Lake Peipus.

Alexius I Comnenus (1048-1118) Byzantine emperor (1081-1118) and founder of the Comnenus dynasty. He ended anarchy, set in order Byzantium's legal and financial affairs, and defeated or bought off enemies besetting the empire (notably Normans, Scythians and Seljuk Turks). His appeal for West European aid to win back eastern Anatolia from the Seljuks and to take Jerusalem from Muslim hands, caused Pope Urban II to preach the First Crusade. Alexius was startled to receive 30,000 troops under powerful leaders instead of the mercenaries he had expected. They won back for him most of Asia Minor and many important cities, but the western world had now seen the wealth of Byzantium, and its downfall followed.

Alfonso I (of Sicily and Naples) see ALFONSO V (of Aragon)

Alfonso I (of Leon and Castile) see ALFONSO VI

Alfonso I (1112-85) Burgundian prince who established Portugal as an independent state and became its first king (1128). He freed Portugal from the sovereignty of Leon by seizing the throne from the troops and allies of his mother (who had acted as regent for her father, the King of Leon). Alfonso won many battles against the Moors, often with the help of crusaders, and eventually doubled Portugal's size.

Alfonso V (1396-1458) King of Aragon (1416-58), called the Magnanimous, ruler of an Italian-based

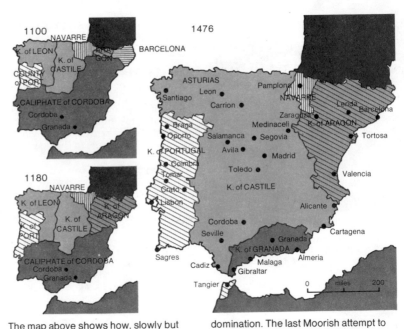

The map above shows how, slowly but surely, the grip of Islam was loosened on the Iberian peninsula after centuries of domination. The last Moorish attempt to regain lost control was defeated by Alfonso XI, in alliance with the Portuguese

Mediterranean empire and patron of learning. He enlarged the scattered empire founded by JAMES I, mastering southern Italy by diplomacy and force and ruling as Alfonso I of Sicily (1416-58) and Naples (1443-58). An ardent admirer of Renaissance Italy, he patronized poetry and scholarship at Naples, which he made his capital. By founding a strong central government, he helped to prolong Spanish rule (which persisted in southern Italy until 1707 and in Sicily until 1713).

Alfonso V (1432-81) King of Portugal (1438-81), whose expansionist reign (which included voyages inspired by Prince HENRY THE NAVIGATOR) produced Portugal's first great law code. Called the *Ordenaçoes Affonsinas*, the code (1446) incorporated features of traditional, Roman, and Visigothic law. Alfonso's military exploits included a successful Moroccan campaign (1458-71), and a failed attempt (which led to his retirement to a monastery) to defeat FERDINAND V and ISABELLA I of Castile (1476).

Alfonso VI (c. 1042-1109) King of Leon (1065-1109) and of Castile (as Alfonso I), who effectively started the Christian reconquest of Muslim Spain. He reunited kingdoms which his father had split among his sons, then seized Toledo from the Arabs and, helped by the CID, virtually ended Moorish control in Spain north of the Tagus.

Alfonso VIII (1155-1214) King of Castile whose victory at Las Navas de Tolosa broke the power of Spain's Muslim rulers for good and assured Christian supremacy in Spain.

Alfonso X (1221-84) King of Castile and Leon (1252-84), who was known as el Sabio (the Wise) for his encouragement of learning (particularly astronomy) and for his poems. His *Fuero Real* and *Siete Partidas* were the foundation of Spanish jurisprudence.

Alfonso XI (14th cent.) King of Castile (1312-50) who defeated the last Moorish invasion of Spain from Africa when, in alliance with Alfonso IV of Portugal, he won the Battle of Rio Salado (1340), near Tarifa in southern Spain. The ferocity with which he suppressed rebellious nobles earned him the name 'the Avenger'.

Alfred the Great (849-99) West Saxon king (871-99), who halted the Danish conquest of England. During the whole of his brother ETHELRED's reign and much of his own, he fought off successive invasions of Wessex, ending in his victory at Ethandune (878) when he forced the Danes to sue for peace. The Danes were cleared from Wessex and the western half of Mercia but were granted north and eastern England. In 885-6 Alfred fought off the East Anglian Danes and took London, and later repelled another invasion attempt in a series of land and naval engagements. During periods of peace he built a strong defensive system and set up a permanent national militia. As a civil administrator, Alfred drew up a code of laws, reorganized finance and promoted learning, attracting scholars from western Europe to his court. A scholar himself, he translated BEDE's

History, BOETHIUS's *Consolations*, and Pope GREGORY's *Pastoral Care*. He also inspired the *Anglo-Saxon Chronicle*.

Algardi, Alessandro (1602-54) Italian sculptor with a special gift for portraiture. His principal works were the marble tomb of Pope Leo XI (1645) and a relief of Leo driving ATTILA from Rome.

Ali, Mohammed (born 1942) American boxer who won the World Heavyweight Championship in 1964. His title was rescinded in 1967 because he refused to be drafted into the United States Army. He was subsequently permitted to return to boxing and, by 1973, had only been defeated twice in 43 contests. During his career he became converted to the Muslim faith and changed his name from Cassius Clay to Mohammed Ali.

Allenby, Edmund, Viscount (1861-1936) British cavalry general who, in the First World War, conquered Palestine by defeating the Turks. He captured Jerusalem in 1917.

Allston, Washington (1779-1843) American painter, who evolved a subjective landscape idiom, later developed by Cole and the Hudson River school.

Almagro, Diego de (c. 1475-1538) Spanish soldier, prominent among the conquistadors who served with PIZARRO in Peru. Almagro later led an expedition to conquer Chile and became the first European to travel overland far to the south as he made his way through the Andes from Cuzco to near Concepción (1535-7), and reached the Pacific coast by crossing the Atacama Desert. Immediately

Greatest of England's Saxon kings, Alfred the Great broke the power of the Danes in Southern England at the Battle of Ethandune in Wiltshire (marked above, with Alfred's West Saxon kingdom)

after this expedition, Almagro led a revolt against Pizarro and was captured and executed.

Almeida-Garrett, João Baptista da Silva Leitão de (1799-1854) Portuguese statesman and writer. While exiled in England and France (1823) (having been involved in the

'I float like a butterfly, sting like a bee' Mohammed Ali pounds Jerry Quarry

uprising of 1820), he assimilated the new Romanticism, and on returning to Portugal with the victorious Liberals (1833), he introduced Romantic styles and attitudes into Portuguese literature. He founded an academy of dramatic art and began to compose nationalist plays, such as *Frie Luiz de Sousa* (1843) and the traditional *Ballads* (1843), and wrote a semi-autobiographical work *Journeys in My Own Land* (1846).

Almoravides see IBN-TASHFIN

Almquist, Carl (1793-1865) Swedish poet, novelist, dramatist, essayist and educational reformer, who wrote the exotic romance *The Book of the Wild Rose* (1832-51), a collection of stories and plays. The diversity of his beliefs and career is reflected in his writings, which include wild, romantic poetry, propagandist pamphlets on progressive education, and school texts, and studies in linguistics. In 1851, he became involved in a scandal and fled to America, where he wrote some nostalgic verse. Later he returned to Sweden under an assumed name and died shortly afterwards.

Alp Arslan (1029-72) Sultan of the Seljuk Turks (1063-72), who ended Byzantine power in Asia Minor, and – by giving the Turks a lasting foothold there – laid the ethnic basis for modern Turkey. He inherited Khurasan from his father Chagri Beg and western Iran and Mesopotamia from his uncle Tughril Beg, and thus ruled Persia from the Oxus to the Tigris. He extended his territory by conquering Armenia and Georgia and

defeating the Byzantine Emperor, Romanus Diogenes, at Manzikert (1071). He was killed in a campaign to expand his rule into Turkestan.

Altdorfer, Albrecht (c. 1480-1538) Bavarian artist, who produced many religious woodcuts, but is best known for his small landscapes. His paintings are mostly of the Danubian region and the Austrian Alps, and the human figures in them are usually only incidental (e.g. *St George in the Forest*). His imaginative studies of pine forests and mountains anticipate modern 'pure' landscape. Altdorfer was also one of the first artists to produce landscape etchings.

Alva, Duke of (1508-82) Spanish general whose skill at arms was matched only by his brutality. Alva was sent by PHILIP II of Spain to the Spanish Netherlands (1567) to suppress growing nationalism and the Protestant heresy. Alva executed the Flemish ringleaders Egmont and Horn, ruthlessly punished, by the new Council of Blood, thousands of dissidents, permitted atrocities by Spanish troops, and announced unpopular tax demands. Protestants and Catholics united under WILLIAM OF ORANGE and seized four provinces. Alva retook all except the provinces of Holland and Zeeland before returning to Spain (1573).

Amenhotep IV (14th cent. BC) Egyptian Pharaoh of the 18th dynasty, who founded the world's first monotheistic faith. A fanatical worshipper of the sun god, whose high priest he had been, he rejected traditional polytheism for belief in a sole, benevolent sun god, Aton, and forbade worship of any other gods.

Amici, Giovanni (1786-1863) Italian astronomer who invented the first direct-vision spectroscope (a device for splitting up white light into a spectrum) and improved the optical microscope. He was the first man to examine the pollen tube in flowering plants and to recognize its role in plant reproduction.

Amis, Kingsley (born 1922) English novelist, associated with the literary aggression aimed at life in Britain in the 1950s. Among many other works, he wrote *Lucky Jim* (1954).

Ammianus Marcellinus (c. 330-400) The last great Roman historian, author of *Rerum gestarum libri*. This continuation of the *Histories* of TACITUS covered the period 96-378, but only the part covering the years 353-378 survives.

Amos (8th cent. BC) Hebrew prophet, whose picturesque and gloomy predictions were compiled, probably long after him, to form the Old Testament Book of Amos. A semi-nomadic shepherd from the pastoral area near Bethlehem, Amos was the first Hebrew prophet to declare that there is only one God.

Ampère, André Marie (1775-1836) French physicist. Within a week of OERSTED'S announcement in 1820 of his discovery that an electric current affects a nearby magnet, Ampère reported major extensions of Oersted's results, and by 1824 had established a full physical and mathematical description of the static interaction of currents with magnets and with each other.

Amundsen, Roald (1872-1928) Norwegian polar explorer, first man to reach the South Pole and to navigate the North West Passage. Sailing in the small sloop *Gjöa* with six companions, Amundsen succeeded where FROBISHER and many others had failed, in forcing a complete northwest sea passage from Europe to the Pacific through the Davis Strait and the Victoria Strait (1903-6). On this expedition, Amundsen also fixed the position of the magnetic North Pole. He was beaten to the geographical North Pole by PEARY, but successfully raced SCOTT to the South Pole. Starting 60 miles nearer than Scott, Amundsen's party reached the South Pole in 53 days, on 14 Dec. 1911. With ELLSWORTH and Nobile, Amundsen made the first air crossing of the Arctic over the North Pole in the airship *Norge* (1926). Amundsen died in a North Sea flying accident while searching for Nobile's lost balloon expedition to the North Pole.

Anastasia, Albert (c. 1902-57) American gangster and founder of 'Murder Inc.' Anastasia himself was reputed to have killed 31 men. Underworld enemies shot and killed him in a New York barber's shop.

Anaxagoras (c. 500-428 BC) Greek philosopher who taught that all matter contains elemental particles; an entity is defined by the predominance of one element.

Anaximander (6th cent. BC) Greek philosopher who taught that the universe evolved from the interaction of mutually repulsive and mutually attractive elements.

Andersen, Hans Christian (1805-75) Danish writer, celebrated for his *Fairy Tales* (1835). After various crises in his career he was befriended by Jonas Collin, the Director of the Royal Theatre in Copenhagen, who sent him to school and then to Copenhagen University. Under the personal patronage of King Frederick VI, he went to Italy. Soon afterwards, his first novel *The Improvisatore* (1835) appeared and was immediately successful. In the same year the first of the fairy tales appeared. Although they sold slowly at first, they brought him international fame.

Anderson, Carl David (born 1905) American physicist who discovered the positron and the first meson. Observing tracks of cosmic rays in a cloud chamber, Anderson found some identical to those of electrons but oppositely curved in a magnetic field. These positrons (positive electrons) had been suggested by the theories of DIRAC. In 1935 Anderson observed a mu-meson, a particle whose mass lay between those of the electron and the proton. Such a particle had been predicted by YUKAWA, but the predicted particle (the pi-meson) was different and not found until 1947.

Anderson, Elizabeth Garrett (1836-1917) English physician who was the first woman to qualify in medicine in Britain. In 1883 she became Dean of the London School of Medicine for Women.

Anderson, Maxwell (1888-1959) American dramatist, who restored verse drama to the American repertoire, but is best known for *What Price Glory?* (1924). His verse dramas on modern subjects include *Winterset* (1935), *Knickerbocker Holiday* (1938) and *Key Largo* (1939). His *Lost in the Stars* (1950), with music by Kurt WEILL, was based on Alan Paton's novel *Cry the Beloved Country*.

Anderson, Sherwood (1876-1941) American short story writer and novelist, best known for naturalistic books depicting the American as a disorientated man, as in the successful *Winesburg, Ohio* (1919), sketches of puzzled people in a small midwestern town.

Andrade, Antonio de (c. 1580-1634) Portuguese Jesuit missionary who, in 1624, set out from India for Lhasa to ascertain the truth of a report that Christians were living in Tibet. He did not reach Lhasa, but was the first European to discover one of the principal sources of the Ganges in the Himalayas.

Andrea del Sarto (1486-1531) Florentine painter, whose works are characterized by a subtle modelling of forms similar to LEONARDO's and a compositional balance like that of RAPHAEL. Some of his most important paintings are frescoes, as in the churches of the Scalzi and the Annunziata, Florence. He also painted a number of panels which include holy families and portraits. The beauty of his work lies mainly in his development of a colouristic technique, as distinct from the more traditional linear approach of Florentine painters.

Andres, Stefan (born 1906) German novelist. The basic theme of his books, the conflict between morals and worldly interests, is best expressed in his major work *We are Utopia* (1942). Though primarily a novelist, he has also published poems and plays for stage and for radio.

Andreyev, Leonid (1871-1919) Russian dramatist, whose symbolic play *He Who Gets Slapped* (1920) was successful in both Europe and America as well as in Russia. His first major success, also symbolic, was *The Life of Man* (1906). His early work foreshadowed the Theatre of the Absurd.

Andros, Sir Edmund (1637-1714) English colonial governor who, in 1686, became James II's governor of the newly created union of colonies, Dominion of New England. He enraged the hitherto largely self-governing and Nonconformist colonists by trying to enforce Anglican religious uniformity and English government taxes. Hearing that James II had been deposed, the New Englanders arrested Andros (on a charge of trying to seize the Connecticut charter) and dissolved the union. Andros was sent to England for trial but was immediately released. He later became Governor of Virginia (1692-8), Maryland (1693-4) and Guernsey (1704-6).

Angelico, Fra (c. 1387-1455) Italian Dominican friar, who is best known for a series of frescoes in the cells of the Florentine monastery of San Marco (c. 1440). These were intended as aids to contemplation and reveal a narrative directness and spatial order similar to MASACCIO's work.

Anne of Cleves see HENRY VIII

Anne (1665-1714) Queen of Great Britain and Ireland (1702-14), the last Stuart to rule Britain, during whose reign Britain became a great power. The era was dominated by the War of the Spanish Succession (1702-13), but at home England and Scotland were united (1707), political parties became more clearly differentiated, and writers like ADDISON, DEFOE and SWIFT made the age important in literature.

Anouilh, Jean (born 1910) French dramatist whose work dominated the theatre in the 1940s and 1950s. Particularly noteworthy were his plays on classical themes, rewritten in modern terms, *Eurydice* (1942) and *Antigone* (1944).

Anselm (1033-1109) Italian-born Benedictine monk and philosopher, who developed the 'ontological argument' for the existence of God in his treatise *Proslogiàn*. Anselm became Archbishop of Canterbury in 1093, and was canonized in 1494.

Anson, Admiral George (1697-1762) English naval commander and administrator, nicknamed 'father of the navy', for his reforms which improved naval efficiency. His heavy loss of men through scurvy on a voyage round the world (1740-4) led to James Lind's discovery that lime juice cures the complaint.

Antelami, Benedetto (mid-12th cent.) Sculptor, architect, and a key figure in early Italian sculpture whose work is best seen in *The Deposition* (1178), and in the reliefs of the doors of the Baptistry of Parma Cathedral. Little is known about his origins, although stylistically his sculpture appears to be linked with Provence.

Anthemius of Thralles (6th cent.) Greek mathematician who advised on the mathematical bases for the design of the masterpiece of Byzantine architecture, the domed church of Sta Sophia at Constantinople (532-7).

Antoine, André (1859-1943) French theatrical manager and director, who pioneered naturalistic drama at the turn of the century and was the first to produce plays by STRINDBERG, IBSEN, Becque and Verga in Paris. He produced plays at the Odéon until 1897, when he started the Théatre Antoine company to present plays by young or *avant-garde* writers.

Antonescu, Ion (1882-1946) Rumanian general and right wing dictator, who aligned Rumania with the Nazis in the Second World War after forcing the abdication of King Carol (1940). He was executed in 1946 for war crimes.

Antonius, Marcus (c. 82-30 BC) Roman leader, whose defeat by OCTAVIUS established rule by emperors. Under the patronage of Julius CAESAR, whom he supported in the civil war, Antonius became a leading soldier and politician. In 44 BC he was consul with Caesar and his oratory drove out Caesar's republican assassins. He enraged Octavius, Caesar's heir, by his affair with CLEOPATRA and by apparent plans to appropriate the Eastern Empire. In the ensuing civil war, Antonius and Cleopatra were defeated by Octavius at Actium (31 BC) and fled to Egypt, where Antonius committed suicide.

Antonius Pius (86-161) Roman emperor (138-161) whose patronage of learning, protection of Christians, legal and tax reforms, new aqueducts and baths, and 'welfare state' provisions marked a period of peace and prosperity throughout the Roman Empire. His name was given to the Antonine Wall built between the firths of Forth and Clyde (142) to protect Roman Britain from the warlike Picts and Scots.

Antony, Mark see ANTONIUS, Marcus

Ape (1839-89) Pseudonym of Carlo Pellegrini, British caricaturist of Victorian high society. His work, which appeared mainly in the journal

Vanity Fair (1862-80), represented 'not only what he saw but what he knew' (Sir David LOW) and later influenced Max BEERBOHM.

Apollinaire, Guillaume (1880-1918) French poet and art critic who participated in various *avant-garde* movements that flourished in France at the turn of the century. Friend of painters such as PICASSO, BRAQUE and others, Apollinaire was influenced by their art and himself experimented in his later poetry with verse forms in an attempt to bring Cubism, with its new vision of the world, to poetry. His best known poems appeared in the collections *Alcools* (1913) and *Calligrammes* (1918). He was also the author of the play *Les Mamelles de Tirésias* (1918), for which he is said to have coined the term 'drame surréaliste'.

Apollonius (3rd cent. BC) Greek mathematician, known as 'The Great Geometer', whose treatise, *Conic Sections*, deals with fundamental geometrical concepts. Apollonius's work formed the basis for further studies of conic sections, which are the geometrical figures (such as the ellipse, parabola and hyperbola) obtained when a plane cuts a cone at various angles.

Apollonius Rhodius (c. 295-c. 240 BC) Alexandrian scholar and epic poet who had a fiery quarrel with CALLIMACHUS, his teacher, on the nature of poetry. Claiming that epic poetry was not obsolete, Apollonius attempted to prove his point with a vast epic, the *Argonautica*. Its four books contain many passages of high poetic quality, notably in their portrayals of romantic love as expressed by Medea in her passion for Jason.

Appert, Nicholas (1752-1841) French pastrycook who in 1809 won 12,000 francs offered by NAPOLEON in 1795 for a practical process for preserving food. The method was to heat the food in glass bottles and then seal it from the air with corks while it was still hot.

Appia, Adolph (1862-1925) Swiss dramatic theorist and stage designer, who pioneered the use of lighting to create a specific atmosphere. He worked out the theory of producing the required effect through the play of light and shadow on stylized objects, without realistic scenery.

South Pole

Amundsen's route

Scott's route

Bay of Whales

McMurdo Sound

An earlier start, a shorter route and the use of husky dogs enabled Amundsen to reach the South Pole before his rival, the ill-fated Scott. Scott had chosen ponies as pack animals and was forced to kill them when their unsuitability was proved

Appleton, Sir Edward Victor (1892-1965) English physicist who revealed the presence of layers of charged particles in the atmosphere. In 1923, he suggested that some radio signals bounce off layers of ions at a height of about 65 miles (HEAVISIDE-KENNELLY layer) and 150 miles (Appleton layer). His investigations were of the greatest importance to broadcasting, and the techniques he originated paved the way for the development of radar.

Apuleius (2nd cent.) Roman writer, author of *The Golden Ass*, the only Latin novel surviving in its entirety. An imaginative and witty work, it tells the story of Lucius who, too curious about the black arts, is turned into an ass.

Appleton and Heaviside layers in the Earth's atmosphere. Long waves bounce off lower, Heaviside, layer and short-wave signals from the upper, Appleton, layer

Some of Fred Archer's contemporaries may well have sought to keep him safely caged, for he was a formidable rival on the racetrack. In his most successful year he won 147 of 530 races he entered

Aquinas, Thomas (1225-74) Catholic philosopher and theologian. Aquinas joined the newly founded Dominicans, immersed himself in academic life, and eventually became a professor, although much of his life was spent in wandering around Europe's universities. He adapted ARISTOTLE's philosophy to Christian dogma, carefully distinguishing faith from reason, and arrived at his 'Five Ways', which argue from man's experience of the world to the existence of God. His greatest works are the *Summa Theologica* and the *Summa contra Gentiles*. He was canonized in 1323 and declared a Doctor of the Church in 1567.

Aragon, Louis (b. 1897) French poet, novelist and journalist who founded, with Breton, the surrealist review *Littérature* (1919). After visiting Russia (1930) he became an ardent Communist. *La semaine sainte* (1958), a Marxist novel, is his best-known work.

Arany, Janos (1817-82) Hungarian poet, author of the epic trilogy *Toldi, Toldi's Love* and *Toldi's Evening* (1847-54), whose hero, a violent, self-defeating man, symbolizes Hungary itself. One of Hungary's major poets, he began as a teacher and itinerant actor and fought in the War of Independence of 1848. He became a professor of Hungarian language and literature at Nagykörös Gymnasium and translated SHAKESPEARE and ARISTOPHANES into Hungarian.

Arbuthnot, John (1667-1735) Scottish doctor, essayist and satirist, best known as the creator of John Bull, the famous archetypal Englishman.

Archer, Frederick Scott (1813-57) English inventor, in 1850, of the wet collodion photographic process. Though a cumbersome portable laboratory was necessary for outdoor photography, Archer's process superseded both daguerrotype (invented by DAGUERRE) and calotype (invented by TALBOT), being more sensitive to light and producing good quality glass negatives. For 30 years it continued to be widely used until replaced by gelatine-based emulsion.

Archer, Fred (1857-86) English jockey who won 147 out of the 530 races which he entered in his most successful year (1874).

Archimedes (c. 287-212 BC) Greek mathematician and inventor, and the most important scientist of antiquity. He invented various mechanical devices and engines of war, but his chief fame rests on mathematical and physical inventions. In geometry, Archimedes greatly extended the

method of exhaustion invented by EUDOXUS for calculating areas. His method of finding the area of a parabolic segment resembles the much later technique of integration. He gave a systematic account of the determination of centres of gravity, and laid the foundations of the science of hydrostatics. The Archimedes principle was his discovery that submerged bodies displace their own volume of liquid and have their weight diminished by an amount equal to the weight of liquid displaced. Using this principle he was able to determine whether the gold in a crown belonging to the King of Syracuse in Sicily had been alloyed with baser metals. Archimedes was killed by a Roman soldier when Syracuse fell to the Romans.

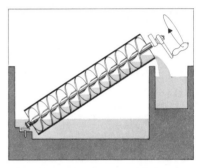

Archimedes's screw is said to have been invented to remove water from the hold of a ship for the King of Syracuse

Archipenko, Alexander (1887-1964) Russian sculptor who worked chiefly in wood, stone and bronze (from plaster originals). He went to Paris in 1908, where he was closely associated with the Cubist movement and is important for the explorations he made into the relationship of concave and convex areas, and his use of holes to open up the plastic form, creating a new idiom in modern sculpture.

Ardashir I (3rd cent.) King of Persia (c. 224-40), who revived Persian nationalism and built a new Persian empire extending from the Euphrates to Seistan and Herat. Ardashir established a unified state from a loose confederation of vassal kingdoms, founded or rebuilt many cities, and made Zoroastrianism the state religion.

Arden, John (born 1930) English dramatist, author of *Sergeant Musgrave's Dance* (1959). His prize-winning radio play *The Life of Man* made his name.

Ardrey, Robert (born 1908) American anthropologist, who lays particular emphasis on aggressiveness as a basic trait in primitive man, and accepts without hesitation the transfer of this instinct from animals to man.

Aretaeus the Cappadocian (1st-2nd cents. AD) Greek physician whose discovery that a lesion on the right side of the brain causes paralysis on the left side of the body was a great step forward in understanding the action of the brain. He also wrote clear descriptions of such diseases as diabetes, tetanus and pneumonia.

Aretino, Pietro (1492-1556) Italian humanist and satirist, whose castigation of his contemporaries earned him the name 'The Scourge of Princes'.

Argand, Jean Robert (1768-1822) French mathematician, who, in 1806, reintroduced a geometrical method of representing complex numbers. The numbers are formal solutions of algebraical equations involving the square roots of negative numbers. Argand diagrams are now extensively used in mathematics, theoretical mechanics and electricity.

Arghezi, Tudor (1880-1967) Rumanian poet, novelist and monk who won fame with experimental poems published in the journal *Liga Ortodoxa* (1896).

Argyll, 1st Duke of see CAMPBELL, Archibald, 1st Duke of Argyll

Ariosto, Lodovico (1474-1533) Italian poet second only to DANTE and author of satires, lyrics and comedies as well as the masterpiece, *Orlando Furioso*. This recounted the wars between CHARLEMAGNE and the Saracens, the adventures and loves of the Christian knights, Orlando and Ruggiero, and the mock-heroic deeds of the English knight, Astolfo. The language is elegant and harmonious, the result of frequent polishing and revision before the definitive edition of 1532. His seven letters, known as the *Satire*, contain a subtle and vivid portrayal of the times, whilst his five comedies, especially the *Cassaria* (1531), mark the beginning of Renaissance theatre.

Aristarchus of Samos (3rd cent. BC) Greek astronomer, the first to suggest that the Earth revolves about the Sun. His treatise, *On the Sizes and Distances of the Sun and Moon*, though inaccurate, was an important step forward in mathematical astronomy.

Aristides (c. 530-c. 468 BC) Athenian general and statesman, chief organizer of the Delian League, from which the Athenian Empire grew. He was instrumental in persuading some Spartan-dominated Ionian city-states to transfer their allegiance to Athens (478 BC), resulting in the Delian League. In earlier years he was ostracized for opposing the naval policy of THEMISTOCLES, but when Athens was attacked by the Persians (480 BC) he returned and was a successful commander at Salamis, Plataea, and off the coast of Byzantium.

Aristophanes (c. 448-c. 380 BC) Greek dramatist pre-eminent in the Old Comedy genre. Eleven of his 40 or so comedies survive. In the early group (425-410 BC) – *The Acharnians, The Knights, The Clouds, The Wasps, The Birds, Lysistrata* and *Thesmophoriazusae* – he retained the traditional chorus as an important element whose nature often gives the play its title. In the later group (405-388 BC) – *The Frogs, The Parliament of Women, Ecclesiazusae* and *Plutus* – the chorus is less in evidence and the play more liberated from traditional formalism. Aristophanes was a brilliantly intelligent conservative with the greatest contempt for democracy and the solemnities of such establishment dramatists as AESCHYLUS, EURIPIDES and SOPHOCLES, of whom he made savage fun in *The Frogs*.

Aristotle (c. 384-322 BC) Greek philosopher who was a student at PLATO's Academy and later a teacher there. Aristotle covered an enormous range in his work and was the inventor of logic (he called it *analytics*) as a separate systematic discipline. His best-known work in this field is his theory of the syllogism – for example, All men are mortal; Socrates is a man; therefore Socrates is mortal. Aristotle's influential theory of causality (in *Physics*) states that every event has four causes: *material*, the matter involved; *formal*, the way this is placed; *efficient*, what triggers off the change; and *final*, what the event tends towards. His theory of categories sets out the 10 different elements that Aristotle recognizes in any situation such as place, time, quality, quantity and the like.

Arius (4th cent. AD) Alexandrian priest who held that Christ was a created, not a divine, being. The controversy initiated by the Arian heresy raged until his death (c. 335).

Ariwara no Narihira (825-80) Japanese court poet, whose work appears in *Kokinshuh*, the first Imperial Anthology (c. 905). Ariwara is thought to be the principal author of *The Tales of Ise*, a collection of *tanka* (short poems, linked by descriptive passages of prose). This work deals with a variety of amorous adventures, many of which are probably autobiographical.

Arkwright, Sir Richard (1732-92) English inventor and industrialist, who, possibly with the help of others, developed the first practical way of mechanical spinning using rollers, which he patented in 1769. At first these machines were powered by animals, then at Cromford, Derbyshire, by water (1771) and, finally, by steam (1790). Arkwright invented, or introduced, machinery to carry out the remaining preparatory processes. His mill at Cromford was one of the wonders of the age, resulting in his being one of the first 'capitalists' of the Industrial Revolution.

Arminius, Jacobus (1560-1609) Dutch Protestant theologian. He opposed the Calvinist doctrine that God had predestined everyone to salvation or damnation, putting forward the less harsh view that salvation was open to all believers and penitents. His ideas, set out in the *Remonstrance* of 1610, had a liberalizing effect on Protestant theology.

Armour, Philip (1832-1901) American meat industrialist who expanded the pork-packing firm, founded by his brother Hermian, into the giant Armour Company. Philip Armour pioneered freezing and canning ('we freeze what we can and what we can't we can') the use of waste products ('everything except the squeal') and assembly-line handling of carcases: innovations which helped to decrease gluts, diminish scarcities and stabilize prices.

Armstrong, Daniel Louis (1900-71) American negro trumpet virtuoso, bandleader and vocalist, whose influence on the stature of jazz internationally was, perhaps, greater than that of any other musician. Armstrong's roots, in every sense, were in New Orleans, his home town. He sang for money as a child and, committed to an orphan's home at 13, learned there to play the cornet. His first and only mentor, Joe 'King' OLIVER, took him to Chicago where, in a few years, he was being billed as 'The world's greatest trumpet player'. He made his first of many trips to Europe in 1932, toured Japan, Ghana and the West Indies during the fifties. In his later years he had ceased the innovation on which his early fame had rested, but he remained the complete entertainer.

As a child, Louis Armstrong sang for money in the streets of New Orleans

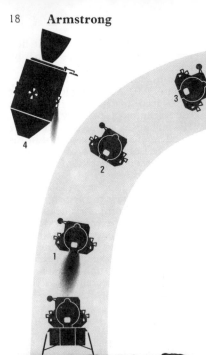

Mission completed; after the 'giant stride' on the surface of the moon Neil Armstrong, in Apollo 11's lunar module, begins the long journey home. 1. Blast off! 2/3. Into orbit. 4. The command module rotates. 5. Rendezvous. 6. Lunar module jettisoned into space.

Armstrong, Neil (born 1930) 'That's one small step for a man, one giant leap for mankind' were the words spoken by Armstrong, an American astronaut, who commanded the Apollo 11 spacecraft and was the first man to walk on the Moon, at 2.56 pm on 21 July 1969.

Arnauld, Antoine (1612-94) French Jansenist theologian who led an anti-Jesuit reform movement. His *L'Art de penser* known as the 'Port Royal Logic', remained a textbook on elementary logic until the 19th century.

Arne, Thomas Augustine (1710-78) English composer whose most famous work *Rule Britannia* formed part of the music he wrote for the masque *Alfred*. He is remembered also for his settings of Shakespeare in songs such as *Where the bee sucks* and *Blow, blow, thou winter wind*. Arne's reputation was greatest for his music for the contemporary theatre, which included plays, operas and masques.

Arnold, Benedict (1741-1801) American army officer, who deserted to the British during the War of Independence (1775-83). He acquitted himself with honour in the early Revolutionary battles, but later joined the British as a spy, for which he was scorned by the British public when he visited England at the war's end.

Arnold of Brescia (c. 1100-55) Italian ascetic priest who opposed the holding of temporal powers and possessions by the papacy and clergy, and led a Roman revolt against the Pope. Driven in turn from Brescia, France and Zurich for his religious unorthodoxy and protests against Church corruption, he went to Rome (1145) and became leader of the revolt that had already ousted the Pope (1143) and established republican rule in Rome. ADRIAN IV quelled the rebellion with the aid of BARBAROSSA and Arnold was hanged.

Arnold, Matthew (1822-88) English poet, critic and educationalist. Son of Thomas ARNOLD, he accepted an Inspectorship of Schools in 1851 and strove to introduce true national education and foster the spread of culture. He studied European education, reporting to the Newcastle and Taunton Royal Commissions (1861, 1868). In *Culture and Anarchy* (1869) and *Essays in Criticism* (1865, 1888) he attacked British complacency and materialism. Poetry played a central role in his life – 'The Scholar Gypsy' and 'Thyrsis' exemplify his romantic, nostalgic poems, while 'Sohrab and Rustum' is in restrained epic style.

Arnold, Thomas (1795-1842) English educationalist who, as headmaster of Rugby School (1828-42), established the ideal of the English public school concept of education. His use of the prefect-system, encouragement of personal responsibility and emphasis upon a religious basis all became associated with the public school system. He introduced modern history into the curriculum and was concerned to educate boys who would serve Church and State in the context of the 19th-century British Empire.

Arnold of Villanova (c. 1235-c. 1312) French or Spanish physician, astrologer and alchemist. His treatise, *Of the Distillation of Wine* (c. 1300), described its use (then widespread) in medicine, and gave recipes for the distillation of wine with spices and herbs to make liqueurs.

Arnolfo di Cambio (c. 1245-c. 1302) Italian architect and sculptor who, it is generally agreed, was architect of the first cathedral of Florence (begun 1294). Little of his decorative work remains there now. A pupil of Nicola PISANO, Arnolfo worked with

him on the Pulpit at Siena (1265-8). He struck a new note of innovation in his wall-tomb for Cardinal de Braye in S Domenico, Orvieto (c. 1282), in which the body lies on a bier below the Madonna in glory.

Arp, Jean (1887-1966) French sculptor and abstract painter, who, in 1912, exhibited with the *Blaue Reiter* group with KANDINSKY and others and later was one of the leading exponents of Dadaism.

Arpad (9th-10th cent.) Magyar founder of Hungary and the Arpad dynasty (c. 896-1301), which reached its peak with STEPHEN I. Son of a tribal chieftain, Arpad united the Magyars (the leading tribe of the nomadic Ugro-Finns) and by 896 brought them, under attack from Asian peoples, from southern Russia to the middle Danube basin. He mastered it by defeating Bulgars, Khazars, and Vlachs, and raided west to Bavaria. In Hungarian ballads and romances he is a hero round whom history and legend are woven.

Arrabal, Fernando (born 1932) Spanish dramatist and novelist, pioneer of the Abstract Theatre and exponent of the Theatre of the Absurd, after the manner of BECKETT. His plays and novels portray the grotesque aspects of life; in *Picnic in the Country* (1952) the countryside is a battlefield where the picnickers have all been shot and *The Car Cemetery* (1962) is a derisive satire in which life is lived in a used-car dump. Arrabal's work has never been accepted in Spain. He writes in French and lives and works in France.

Arrhenius, Svante August (1859-1927) Swedish chemist who developed the ionic theory of electrolytes. In 1887 he proposed that electrolytes (substances whose solutions conduct electricity) split up in solution into electrically charged particles, called ions, which conduct current. After years of controversy, his theory was accepted and in 1903 he was awarded the Nobel Prize for Chemistry.

Artaud, Antonin (1896-1948) French director, dramatist and theorist, who was the first to produce (1925) Surrealist plays. With Roger VITRAC he founded the Theatre Alfred Jarry. Their Surrealist productions included Vitrac's plays and one act of CLAUDEL's *Partage du Midi* as a farce.

Jean Arp used simple motifs, like this marble torso, to capture the essence of the female form

Arthur (c. 6th cent.) British king, perhaps legendary, the hero of an enormous cycle of mythological romances. In the fanciful 12th-century chronicle of Geoffrey of Monmouth, Arthur is said to have defeated the invading Saxons at Mt Badon and died at the Battle of Camlan (537). In Arthurian legend Arthur founded the Knights of the Round Table, but took little part in their exploits. The legend-cycle, which emerged principally in medieval French verse and prose romances, especially the verse of CHRETIEN DE TROYES, was later retold by MALORY and TENNYSON.

Arthur, Chester (1830-86) Twenty-first President of the United States (1881-5). He supported reform of the civil service (Pendleton Law, 1883). Arthur was nominated to the vice-presidency in support of GARFIELD and became President after Garfield's assassination in 1881. His administration was noted for its honesty and efficiency and saw the introduction of protective tariffs and the strengthening of the navy.

Ashbee, Charles (1863-1942) English architect who designed elegant and sparsely decorated furnishings for late 19th-century interiors. The restrained and rhythmic elegance of his domestic architecture owes something to the Art Nouveau movement, although Ashbee himself was more specifically associated with the English arts and crafts movement, taking the work of William MORRIS as his model.

Ashikaga Takauji (1305-58) Japanese warrior who rebelled against Emperor DAIGO II, and became actual ruler of Kyoto. He was officially appointed Shogun in 1338, the first of the Ashikaga shogunate.

Ashurbanipal (ruled 669-26 BC) Assyrian king, whose library helped modern scholars to reconstruct Mesopotamia's ancient history. He was a grandson of SENNACHERIB, and ruled Babylonia, Persia, Egypt and Syria, the most powerful and cultured monarch of his time. His library at Nineveh (rediscovered by LAYARD, 1845-7) held 22,000 clay tablets inscribed in cuneiform with Assyrian, Babylonian and Sumerian historical, literary, religious and scientific texts. Bilinguals and syllabaries in the hitherto unknown Sumerian tongue helped DE SARZEC and WOOLLEY to rediscover sites of Mesopotamia's (and the world's) first civilization. Ashurbanipal's Assyrian Empire died with him and was supplanted by the Chaldean Empire, the greatest king of which was NEBUCHADNEZZAR II.

Asoka (3rd-2nd cents. BC) Indian emperor of the Mauryan Dynasty, whose empire embraced two-thirds of the Indian subcontinent. Revolted by the bloodshed of his expansionist wars and converted to Buddhism, Asoka proclaimed the Buddhist code of toleration, truthfulness and abstention from killing in edicts inscribed throughout his empire on pillars and rocks. Asoka put his edicts into practice with reforms that enriched the empire, sent Buddhist monks overseas, and embarked on 'morality tours' through his domains. But though he gave his brahmanical subjects freedom to worship, within 50 years of his death Brahman opposition to his Buddhist tenets had helped to crush the Mauryan Dynasty – India's last great ruling house till BABER founded the Mogul Dynasty, 17 centuries later.

Aspdin, Joseph (1779-1855) English bricklayer who in 1824 invented 'Portland' cement, a preburnt mixture of powdered limestone and clay, which after the addition of water achieves rock-like hardness. Portland cement is one of the principal modern building materials as a constituent of mortar and concrete.

Asplund, Gunnar (1885-1940) Swedish architect who designed the Forest Crematorium near Stockholm (1935-40), a work of great solemnity. After evolving into a severe Neo-Classic style, exemplified by his Stockholm Library (1920-8), Asplund changed direction and became an important and original contributor to international modern architecture.

Asquith, Herbert Henry (1858-1928) British Liberal statesman and Prime Minister (1908-16). From 1905 to 1908 he was Chancellor of the Exchequer in the government of CAMPBELL-BANNERMAN, whom he succeeded as Prime Minister, and in office had to deal with the Suffragette movement, industrial unrest and Irish Home Rule. He was in power at the outbreak of the First World War and from May 1915 headed a coalition government until ousted in December 1916 by a combination of LLOYD GEORGE and the Conservatives, after disputes over the war leadership. The subsequent feud between the Asquithian Liberals and the supporters of Lloyd George seriously weakened the Liberal Party.

Astaire, Fred (born 1899) American dancer whose career has spanned musical comedy, vaudeville and the cinema, in which his partners have included Ginger Rogers, Judy Garland and Rita Hayworth. Astaire took the tap dance (born of clattering British clog dances and syncopated negro dance rhythms) and spiced it with ballet movements and Yankee humour. He created a new form of musical film in the 1930s, perfected by 'shooting' each dance sequence up to 30 times, then drastically editing, itself a new cinema technique. His many films include *Top Hat*, *Funny Face*, and *Broadway Melody*.

Astor, John Jacob (1763-1848) German-born American multi-millionaire whose fortune was based on the fur trade and, later, New York real estate. Astor founded and endowed the Astor Library, New York. At his death his personal estate was $20 million, but increases in land values in New York had raised it to about $250 million by the end of the century.

Lady Astor was a tireless champion of women's rights and an influential political hostess between the wars

Astor, Nancy Witcher, Viscountess (1879-1964) American-born British MP who succeeded her husband as the Unionist member for Plymouth in 1919 and was the first woman to take her seat in the House of Commons. She was an active political hostess between the wars and it was said that much government policy in the 1930s was decided at her house parties at Cliveden in Buckinghamshire.

Atahualpa (1500-33) Last Inca emperor, who was murdered by PIZARRO, the Spanish conquistador. At a supposedly friendly meeting at Cajamarca (1532), Pizarro demanded Atahualpa's conversion to Christianity and submission to Emperor CHARLES V. When Atahualpa refused, Pizarro massacred the Inca retinue and imprisoned the emperor. Atahualpa was strangled (1533) for alleged complicity in an anti-Spanish plot, even though Pizarro had accepted a room filled with gold and silver as a ransom payment.

Athanasias the Great (c. 293-373) Alexandria-born saint who was one of the four great Greek Doctors of the Church and helped to frame the basis of present-day Christianity at the Council of Nicaea in 325. Athanasias's unswerving idealism and lifelong opposition to the Arian heresy inspired both fierce loyalty and violent hatred, and his life swung between the extremes of public veneration and rejection. Although he became Primate of Egypt and was Bishop of Alexandria for 46 years, Athanasias spent 17 of those years in enforced exile in the Arabian desert, owing to the Arianism of Emperor Constantius and his successors. He wrote many polemical pieces against Arianism, and commentaries on the Scriptures. The Creed named after him is thought to have been written by St AMBROSE.

Attar (1119-c. 1229) Persian mystic poet, famous for his long poem, 'The Bird Parliament', an allegory of man's search for mystic union with the divine, a masterpiece of Sufist writing.

Atterbom, Per (1790-1855) Swedish Romantic poet whose greatest work was 'The Isle of the Blessed' (1824-7), a long, dramatic poem with fairy and folk-tale motifs, and many haunting lyrics. Its political symbolism and Atterbom's conservatism alienated an increasingly liberal public, and Atterbom spent the rest of his life a cool, aloof figure, engaged in literary and political polemics. His only later work was a series of nostalgic studies of Swedish writers, *Swedish Seers and Poets 1-6* (1841-55).

Attila (c. 406-53) King of the Huns (433-53), called the 'Scourge of God', who overran Europe from the North Sea to the Caspian and terrorized the crumbling Roman Empire. After consolidating his loosely organized Hun kingdom, he crossed the Danube with his multi-national cavalry, ravaged the Eastern Roman Empire (447-50) as far as Constantinople, and forced Theodosius II to make huge protection payments. Next he thrust west through Gaul (451), demanding half the Western Roman Empire and reaching Orleans before suffering his only defeat, by Roman and Visigothic troops at Châlons-sur-Marne. Attila next devastated northern Italy (452), but quickly left, probably forced out by famine. He died suddenly just before a second invasion of Italy, and his empire, lacking stable institutions, fell apart.

Attlee, Clement Richard, Earl (1883-1967) British Prime Minister (1945-51) during whose period of office the Welfare State was implemented. From 1922 to 1924 he was Parliamentary Private Secretary to the Labour leader Ramsay MACDONALD, and held office in the Labour administrations of 1924 and 1930, becoming party leader in 1935. From 1943 to 1945 Attlee was deputy Prime Minister to CHURCHILL in the Second World War coalition government and Prime Minister after Labour was returned to power in 1945. His ministry put through a programme of nationalization (railways, coal mines, road transport) and social reform (National Health Service and an extension of National Insurance). Though quiet and modest, Attlee was a shrewd politician, holding together and in balance the mutually hostile left and right wings of the Labour Party. During his premiership India was granted independence (1947).

Attwood, Thomas (1783-1856) British radical politician, currency reformer and Chartist leader. He was MP for Birmingham from 1832 to 1840 and one of the founders of the Birmingham Political Union (1829) whose agitation helped to secure the Parliamentary Reform Act of 1832. As a Chartist organizer Attwood represented the more moderate and constitutional section of the movement.

Aubrey, John (1626-97) English antiquary and the author of *Brief Lives*, a collection of amusing, slightly scandalous biographical portraits.

Auden, Wystan Hugh (1907-73) English-born poet, who was one of the most versatile and technically accomplished of all modern poets, and the most important of a group of English poets who were influenced by Marxism in the 1930s. His first published works were *Poems* (1930) and *The Orators* (1932). After teaching and making documentary films, he left England for Spain and drove an ambulance for the Republicans in the Spanish Civil War. Auden emigrated to America in 1939, and became a citizen and a university professor. He moved away from political and economic preoccupation, and his verse became more meditative and lyrical. In *The Age of Anxiety* (1947), *Nones* (1952) and *The Shield of Achilles* (1955) he began to write on moral and religious themes from a Christian viewpoint. He wrote also verse plays and critical essays.

Lord Attlee. He ousted Churchill in Britain's 1945 General Election

Auenbrugger, Leopold (1722-1809) Austrian physician who pioneered the use of percussion (tapping with the finger) to diagnose diseases of the heart and lungs. His simple discovery, that the chest of a patient, when it is tapped, sometimes sounds different when healthy than when diseased, is one of the cornerstones of modern medicine.

Augustine of Canterbury (6th-7th cent.) Saint, evangelizer of Saxon England, first Archbishop of Canterbury and the founder of the bishoprics of London and Rochester. In 596 he led a band of 40 missionary monks sent by GREGORY THE GREAT to convert the pagan Saxons and come to terms with the Christian Britons. In the first assignment he had considerable success, beginning with King Ethelbert of Kent: in the second he failed, the British bishops in Wales, Devon and Cornwall refusing to recognize him as Archbishop.

Augustine of Hippo, St (354-430) The most outstanding theologian in Christian antiquity, who successfully welded New Testament thought with Neoplatonism.

Augustus (63 BC-AD 14) First Roman Emperor (27 BC-AD 14), born Gaius Octavius, great nephew and heir of Julius CAESAR. After Caesar's death, Augustus sought to be dictator but compromised with his rival (ANTONIUS Marcus), and with Lepidus, they became joint rulers of the empire (Triumvirs), defeating the republicans at Philippi (42 BC). Enraged by the conduct of Antonius with CLEOPATRA and believing them to be about to take the Eastern Roman Empire, Augustus fought and defeated them at Actium (31 BC) to become sole ruler of the Empire. He restored all the constitutional forms of the republic but was invested by the senate with the power of *imperium* and designated Augustus, 'Exalted' (27 BC). Augustus's reign was marked by constitutional reforms, a growth in wealth, economic stability and able administration of the provinces.

Augustus II (1670-1733) Elector of Saxony and King of Poland (1697-1704 and 1709-33) whose attempts at territorial gain led to Polish subservience to Russia. Encouraged by success in his war in Turkey, Augustus joined Russia's PETER I in attacking Swedish-held Livonia (1700). This provoked CHARLES XII of Sweden to begin a devastating war on Polish soil, and Augustus was deposed (1704) by his nobles. When Peter I defeated Charles XII at Poltava in the Ukraine (1709), Augustus regained his throne, but his attempts to make the elective crown hereditary caused a civil war, which further weakened war-torn Poland and enabled Russia to interfere at will with his successors.

Aurangzeb (1618-1707) Last great Mogul emperor of India (1658-1707), during whose reign the Muslim Hindustan empire attained its greatest extent and wealth. Aurangzeb grasped power by imprisoning his father and murdering his three brothers, and by conquest extended his rule over all of northern and central India. Aurangzeb's religious bigotry undermined the empire he had built and provoked revolts and unsuccessful wars with the Hindu Marathas led by SHIVAJI (1689-1705). The founding of the Maratha kingdom started the erosion of Mogul power and, ultimately, the seizure of India by Britain.

Aurelius, Marcus (121-180) Roman emperor (161-80) and Stoic philosopher. Aurelius held equanimity to be the supreme goal in life, achieved by living in tune with nature, and requiring the virtues of wisdom, justice, fortitude and temperance, dictated by reason. His philosophy is outlined in *Meditations*, which also indirectly reflect his practical concern with his position as a statesman and general.

Aurelius Prudentius Clemens see PRUDENTIUS

Austen, Jane (1775-1817) English novelist, who wrote on the life and manners of comfortable country society with delicate wit and subtle characterization. With her quiet, ironic style Austen illuminates common hopes, desires and frictions. Her books, the best known being *Pride and Prejudice, Sense and Sensibility* and *Emma*, were published between 1811 and 1818. She spent an easy, uneventful life of security in the south of England and in her books there is no violence, little outward passion and few incidents, but she perfected the art of the novel of ordinary life, a tradition begun by Fanny BURNEY.

Austin, John (1790-1859) English jurist who has had a lasting influence on English jurisprudence and legal education. Suspecting BLACKSTONE of confusion, and (in his *The Province of Jurisprudence Determined* 1832) incorporating the utilitarian principles of his friends BENTHAM and MILL he clarified the distinction between law and morality. In later lectures, published in 1863, he analysed the fundamental ideas underlying all mature legal systems and demonstrated the need for the constant critical analysis of legal concepts.

Austin, John Langshaw (1911-60) English philosopher and leading figure in 'linguistic philosophy'.

Avicenna (980-1037) Persian philosopher and physician, who absorbed and developed Greek philosophy, science and medicine. He was chief physician to the hospital at Baghdad and court physician to a number of caliphs. His influence on medical practice was considerable.

Avila, Pedro Arias de see PEDRARIAS Davila

Aviles, Pedro Menendez de see MENENDEZ de Aviles, Pedro

Avogadro, Amadeo (1776-1856) Italian physicist who, in 1811, advanced the hypothesis, now named after him, that at standard pressure and temperature equal volumes of all gases contain the same number of molecules. When the quantity of gas involved is the molecular weight in grams this number is Avogadro's constant $(6 \cdot 025 \times 10^{23})$. He was one of the first scientists to distinguish between molecules and atoms, and his ideas play a fundamental role in the theory of gases and in physical chemistry.

Awolowo, Obafemi (born 1909) Nigerian politician of Yoruba origin. A graduate in law and commerce of London University, Awolowo led the opposition in the Nigerian Federal Parliament and was arrested and imprisoned (1962). Following GOWON's military coup he was released (1966) to secure Yoruba and Western Region support for the new régime, was made Vice-Chairman of the federal Executive Council and Commissioner for Finance, and became a member of Gowon's Cabinet in the Biafran War.

Aylward, Gladys (1903-70) English missionary, who travelled overland through Russia to China, where she took Chinese nationality and was known as Ai-weh-deh, 'the virtuous one'. In 1938, during the Sino-Japanese war, she led almost 100 refugee children away from the advancing Japanese, travelling for a month by foot, over the mountains from Yangcheng to Sian. She returned to England in 1949, but later settled in Taiwan, where she ran an orphanage.

Azaña, Manuel (1880-1940) President of the Spanish Republic at the outbreak of the Civil War (1936-9). Twice Prime Minister, he took a leading part in the organization of the Popular Front, but the Socialist, anti-clerical measures of his government strengthened the growing Fascism of the right wing. The Republicans threw down the gauntlet: 'In its relations with Fascism, the Government is a belligerent.' The army, led by General FRANCO, mutinied and the

Civil War began. Azaña resigned after the Nationalists broke the last Republican resistance in 1939.

Azikiwe, Dr Nnamdi (born 1904) Nigerian financier and politician, Prime Minister of Nigeria's Eastern Region (1954-9), who became Governor-General when Nigeria gained independence (1960), and President in 1963. Three years later he was deposed by GOWON's military coup.

Azo (c. 1150-1230) Italian jurist whose comprehensive exposition of Roman law was the main source used by Henry de BRACTON in his book *The Laws and Customs of England*.

Azorin (1873-1967) Spanish writer, whose impressionistic novels and essays, such as *The Villages* (1905) and *The Route of Don Quixote* (1905) convey the essence of the Castilian past.

Azurara, Gomez Eannes de (c. 1410-74) Portuguese historian and chronicler of the early Portuguese voyages of discovery, especially those sponsored by HENRY THE NAVIGATOR.

B

Babbage, Charles (1792-1871) English originator of the modern computer, who spent most of his life trying to eliminate errors in mathematical and astronomical tables by having them automatically calculated and printed by machines. He used much of his own fortune on this work and received financial help from the British Government. Babbage's first computer or 'difference engine' (1827) compiled and printed tables of logarithms from 1 to 108,000. His more complex 'analytical machine' was to be capable of undertaking any type of calculation. It would have been steam-driven and programmed by means of machined cards, but was never completed.

Babel, Isaak (1894-c. 1941) Russian author whose major work, *Red Cavalry* (1926), was based on his experiences in Poland during the Cossacks' campaign. His short stories are powerful works of pathos and irony, outstanding for their descriptive comments on war. Babel fought with the Tsarist army in the First World War, and during STALIN's purges he was sent to a concentration camp, where presumably he died. His reputation was officially restored in 1957.

Baber (1483-1530) Muslim Turkish conqueror of northern India and founder of its last major ruling family, the Mogul (i.e. Mongol) dynasty, which reached its peak under his grandson AKBAR. Having lost Ferghana, his inherited kingdom, and Samarkand, which he had conquered, Baber crossed the Hindu Kush and captured Kabul. Defeat by the Uzbegs (1514) ended his attempts to regain his kingdom and he turned to northern India, which he mastered after victories at Panipat (1526) and Kanwaha (1527). An effective administrator, he improved the road taxation and land measurement systems.

Babeuf, François Emile (1760-97) French egalitarian socialist and conspirator against the Directory who organized a left-wing movement of former Jacobins into the 'Society of Equals'. Babeuf propagated egalitarian socialism in the belief, that, in the words of his manifesto, 'Nature has given each man the right to enjoy an equal share in all property'. Babeuf was arrested (May 1796) and killed himself before he could be executed.

Bach, Carl Philipp Emanuel (1714-88) Influential German composer, third son of J. S. BACH, who contributed to the early evolution of the symphony. HAYDN said of him, 'Everything I know I have learnt from Emanuel Bach'; and MOZART: 'He is the father, we the children.'

Bach, Johann Christian (1735-82) German composer, the eleventh of

J. S. BACH's sons. He came to be known as 'the English Bach' after settling in London in 1762. Bach's ability as melodist and orchestrator is shown in his operas, symphonies, concertos and songs. He was music master to GEORGE III's family, a friend of GAINSBOROUGH and an influence on the young MOZART.

Bach, Johann Sebastian (1685-1750) German composer who brought European music to one of its highest peaks of achievement. During his lifetime Bach was known mainly as a fine organist who composed music as part of his duties as town organist, court musician and (from 1723) as Cantor (musical director) at St Thomas's Church, Leipzig. It was only when his work came to light again in the 19th century (largely through the efforts of MENDELSSOHN) that he was recognized as being among music's towering geniuses. Early in his career Bach declared his intention to write 'A properly regulated church music dedicated to the glory of God', and composed chorale preludes and fugues for organ and cantatas to Lutheran texts for use in church services. The expression of his strong Protestant faith was to culminate in his choral masterpieces, the *St Matthew Passion* (1729) and the *Mass in B Minor*. Some of his secular works were written to specific commissions: the set of six *Brandenburg Concertos* (1721) for the Margrave of Brandenburg; the 30 *Goldberg Variations* for harpsichord for the patron of one of Bach's pupils; the *Musical Offering* (1747) for, and based on a theme provided by, FREDERICK THE GREAT. Another work dating from Bach's last years, and uncompleted at his death, is *The Art of Fugue*, a set of studies in counterpoint probably intended for harpsichord. Bach married twice and fathered 20 children. Several of his sons continued the family's musical tradition and themselves became distinguished figures. The most notable among them were C. P. E. BACH and J. C. BACH.

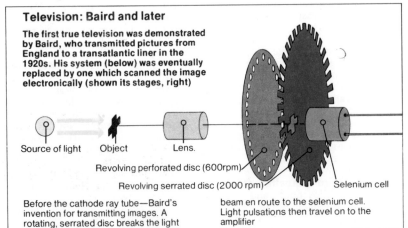

Television: Baird and later

The first true television was demonstrated by Baird, who transmitted pictures from England to a transatlantic liner in the 1920s. His system (below) was eventually replaced by one which scanned the image electronically (shown its stages, right)

Source of light   Object   Lens.

Revolving perforated disc (600rpm)

Revolving serrated disc (2000 rpm)   Selenium cell

Before the cathode ray tube—Baird's invention for transmitting images. A rotating, serrated disc breaks the light

beam en route to the selenium cell. Light pulsations then travel on to the amplifier

Image   Lens   Photoelectric cell

Light beams   Amplifier

The modern camera. Impulses of light are transformed into impulses of electric current, travelling in waves

Backhaus, Wilhelm (1884-1969) German virtuoso of the piano and the leading exponent of the classical repertoire during the first half of the 20th century.

Bacon, Francis (1561-1626) English philosopher, lawyer, statesman and author who was the first important writer of essays in English. Bacon rose to high legal office: he was Attorney-General (1613), Lord Keeper (1617) and Lord Chancellor (1618). He was made Viscount St Albans in 1621, but was convicted of bribery, and banished from Parliament. It was Bacon's ambition to reinterpret phenomena on rational rather than Aristotelian principles, and his philosophical works are an exposition of the state of knowledge at the time.

Bacon, Francis (born 1909) British painter, whose work is characterized by the individuality of his style and by amorphous malformations of the human figures, portrayed invariably in isolation, to a sinister, somewhat repulsive effect.

Bacon, Nathaniel (1647-76) English-born Virginian planter who led Bacon's Rebellion (1676). His marriage to Governor William BERKELEY's cousin Elizabeth helped Bacon gain a voice in Virginia's governing council. Although a democrat, he condemned BERKELEY's toleration of the American Indians and led an unauthorized attack against them as potential threats to Virginia's settlers. Denounced by BERKELEY as a rebel, Bacon turned on the Governor and, backed by settlers aggrieved by BERKELEY's aristocratic régime, captured and burned Jamestown and mastered most of Virginia before his death abruptly ended the revolt.

Baden-Powell, Robert, 1st Baron (1857-1941) English founder of the Boy Scout movement. Drawing on his experiences as a professional soldier and scout in India and Africa, he stressed the need for character development rather than military disci-

pline. British youth hero-worshipped Baden-Powell after his 215-day defence of Mafeking (1899-1900) during the Boer War, and after 1908, scout troops sprang up throughout the country, and the movement gradually became international. In 1910 Baden-Powell left the army to devote his life to scouting and, with his sister founded the Girl Guides.

Badoglio, Pietro (1871-1956) Italian soldier who formed a government and declared war on his former allies, the Germans, when MUSSOLINI resigned and Italy collapsed (1943) during the Second World War. Badoglio, who commanded the victorious Italian Army in its Ethiopian campaign (1935-6), resigned following defeats inflicted by the Greeks in the Albanian theatre (1940).

Baedeker, Karl (1801-59) German publisher, bookseller and writer of travel guides. In 1829 he issued a guide book to Coblenz and followed it with a series of books which would enable travellers to dispense with paid guides. The first was a guide to the Rhine from Mainz to Cologne.

Baekeland, Leo Hendrik (1863-1944) Belgian-born American chemist who invented the first major industrial synthetic plastic, Bakelite.

Baer, Karl von (1792-1876) Estonian embryologist whose work, showing the fundamental similarities between all vertebrate embryos, made an important contribution to evolutionary theory. He showed that in all vertebrates there are potential or 'germ' layers that give rise to the various organs and tissues. These and other similarities between foetuses of different species led him to postulate that individuals of different species diverge during their embryonic development from a primary or archetypal form. He also discovered the mammalian ovum.

Baffin, William (1584-1622) British explorer who was among the first

to study magnetic variation, which had long troubled mariners dependent on the magnetic compass. He piloted several expeditions seeking a northwest passage around America, reaching Greenland (1612) and Spitsbergen (1613), the east of North America and the west of Greenland (1615-16), and discovered Baffin Bay. On the voyage during which he discovered Baffin Bay (1615-16), he went as far north as 77°45', which remained for 236 years the record northerly latitude reached. His careful magnetic observations led to the making of the first magnetic chart.

Baird, John Logie (1888-1946) Scottish-born pioneer of television. In 1922, he began research into a system which depended on scanning the scene with a rapidly moving spot of light (the flying spot system). Four years later he gave the first demonstration of a television picture. The British Broadcasting Corporation adopted Baird's system for their first television programme in 1929, but in 1937 it was abandoned in favour of an electronic scanning system.

Baker, Sir Samuel White (1821-93) English explorer, who, with his wife, searched for the headwaters of the Nile, and discovered Lake Albert and the Murchison Falls.

Bakr, abu- see ABU-BAKR

Bakst, Leon Nikolayevich (1866-1924) Russian painter-designer who worked with DIAGHILEV and whose ballet decors set new trends in theatre design.

Bakunin, Mikhail (1814-76) Russian anarchist aristocrat and guards officer who resigned his commission over Russia's maltreatment of the Polish nationalist rebels. His pamphlet *Reaction in Germany* (1842) and his revolutionary ideas led to his permanent exile. He was involved in the February Revolution (Paris 1848) and helped to inspire the Czech rising (Prague 1848) and the Saxony revolt

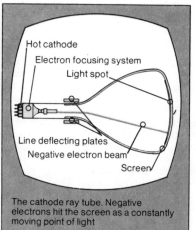

The cathode ray tube. Negative electrons hit the screen as a constantly moving point of light

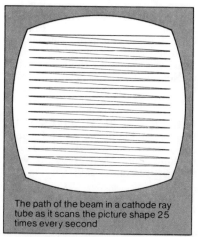

The path of the beam in a cathode ray tube as it scans the picture shape 25 times every second

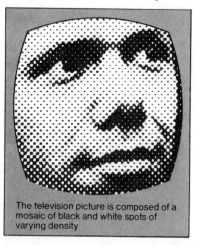

The television picture is composed of a mosaic of black and white spots of varying density

(1849). In 1849 he was arrested in Dresden, but though condemned to death by the authorities in both Berlin and Vienna, he was not executed but imprisoned in Austria, then handed over to the Russians and sent to Siberia (1855). After six years he escaped and devoted the rest of his life to West European revolutionary movements.

Balakirev, Mily Alexeyvich (1837-1910) Russian composer who founded and led the important group of Russian nationalist composers known as 'The Five' or 'The Mighty Handful', including RIMSKY-KORSAKOV, MUSSORGSKY, BORODIN and Cui. 'The Five' aimed to establish a musical standpoint in Russian music that looked to Russia's history, folk-music and literature rather than to the West. Balakirev wrote two symphonies and a symphonic poem, *Tamara* (dedicated to LISZT), though he composed little after a nervous breakdown in the 1870s.

Balanchine, George (born 1904) Russian-born choreographer and pioneer of the American 'classic' ballet. DIAGHILEV's last main choreographer, he founded the School of American Ballet, later the New York City Ballet, in 1934. Balanchine helped form a new American style of ballet which combined exuberant athletic movements with classical Russian dance. Balanchine collaborated for many years with STRAVINSKY on works such as *Agon* and *Orpheus*.

Balboa, Vasco Nuñez de (1475-1517) Spanish explorer, the first European to see the Pacific. He was a Spanish settler in Hispaniola (now Haiti and the Dominican Republic), where he joined a fleet taking provisions to San Sebastian settlement in Panama (1510). Finding the settlement deserted, Balboa continued to Darien where he later became Governor. He conquered the surrounding areas and, hearing of an ocean and rich lands over the mountains, led an expedition (1513) that reached the Pacific, which Balboa claimed for Spain. PEDRARIAS DAVILA, a bitter rival of Balboa, was sent out to replace him as Governor of Darien and had him tried for treason and beheaded.

Baldwin I (1171-c. 1205) First Latin emperor of Constantinople (1204-5), born in Valenciennes. By inheritance Count Baldwin IX of Flanders and Count Baldwin VI of Hainault, he was a leader of the Fourth Crusade which seized Constantinople and dethroned Alexius V. A council of crusaders and Venetians declared Baldwin Emperor and allotted to him the region round Constantinople, dividing the rest of the Byzantine (still largely unconquered) empire among themselves. Baldwin was murdered, but his successors ruled Constantinople until 1261.

Baldwin, James (born 1924) American negro novelist whose work is primarily concerned with the plight of the negroes in his country. Baldwin's novels, including *Go Tell It on the Mountain* (1953) and *Nobody Knows My Name* (1961), give a moving, pathetic account of the struggles of black urban families, and his essays, such as *The Fire Next Time* (1963), attack the sins of white society.

Baldwin, Stanley, 1st Earl of Bewdley (1867-1947) English statesman, three times Prime Minister (1923-4, 1924-9 and 1935-7). In 1926 Baldwin's government outmanoeuvred the General Strike, but subsequently had to contend with the beginning (1929) of the depression and mass unemployment. Baldwin served in RAMSAY MACDONALD's National Government of 1931 as Lord President of the Council and became PM again in 1935. He failed to appreciate the dangers of Nazi resurgence and his ministry was tainted by appeasement of the dictators MUSSOLINI and HITLER. He was instrumental in the abdication of EDWARD VIII (1936).

Balfour, Arthur James, 1st Earl of (1848-1930) English statesman who, as Foreign Secretary in 1917, was responsible for the declaration committing Britain to support the establishment of a Jewish national home in Palestine on condition that the rights of 'existing non-Jewish communities' in Palestine were guaranteed. The Balfour Declaration was ratified by the other Allied governments and resulted in Britain being given the League of Nations Mandate in Palestine (1920).

Baliol, John de (c. 1250-1313) King of Scotland (1292-6), during whose short reign Scottish national resistance against EDWARD I of England began. Chosen as a vassal king by Edward, Baliol was forced to rebel and make an alliance with France when Edward interfered actively in Scottish affairs. Easily defeated, Baliol was deposed and died in exile in Normandy. His deposition paved the way for ROBERT I to emerge as the champion of Scottish independence.

Balmat, Jacques (1762-1834) French mountain guide from Chamonix, who, with PACCARD, was the first to climb Mont Blanc (1786), to win the prize offered by SAUSSURE.

Balmer, Johann Jakob (1825-98) Swiss physicist who found the first mathematical formula describing the wavelengths of spectral lines. Balmer's simple formula fitted part of the hydrogen spectrum, but could not be explained without quantum theory.

Balsamo, Giuseppe see CAGLIOSTRO, Count Alessandro di

Baltimore, George Calvert, 1st Baron, see CALVERT, George

Balzac, Honoré de (1799-1850) French novelist of world stature and architect of the massive *Comédie Humaine*, which comprises over 50 volumes depicting every aspect of contemporary society, and an enormous range of human types. Despite obvious imperfections in style and technique, Balzac's exceptional powers of observation enabled him to transpose the raw material from notebooks and memory into lasting fictional works. The portraits of his main protagonists are etched brilliantly and boldly – the miser Grandet, the naïve Birotteau, Gobseck, cousin Pons, Vautrin and the student Rastignac. Balzac's lifelong struggle to keep his creditors at bay is reflected in his novels, whose themes are dominated by financial intrigue and the corrupting power of money, which he recognized as one of the dynamic forces in society. The principal titles of the *Comédie Humaine* include: *La Peau de Chagrin* (1831); *Le Curé de Tours* (1832); *Eugénie Grandet* (1833); *Le Père Goriot* (1834); *César Birotteau* (1837); *La Cousine Bette* (1846) and *Le Cousin Pons* (1847). Balzac was also the author of some memorable short stories (e.g. *Facino Cane*) and of the *Contes drôlatiques* and *Un Episode sous la Terreur* (1832-7).

Bancroft, George (1800-91) American historian and diplomat, who wrote the first full account of the emergence of the United States, the *History of the United States* (1834-74). It remained the most widely read work on the subject for 50 years. As a diplomat, Bancroft served in Berlin, and played a major role in the arbitration of the Oregon boundary dispute between the US and Britain.

Banda, Hastings Kamuzu (born 1905) First Prime Minister of Malawi. While practising medicine in London, Banda organized opposition to the Federation of the Rhodesias and to Nyasaland, where he took up politics (1958). In 1959 he was arrested for belonging to the illegal Malawi Congress Party, but was released in 1960 and appointed Prime Minister of Nyasaland in 1963. When independence was conceded by Britain in the following year he became

Roger Bannister (GB) 3 min 59·4, May '54
John Landy (Aus) 3min 58, June '54
Doug Ibbotson (GB) 3min 57·2, July '57
Herb Elliott (Aus) 3min 54·5, Aug '58
Peter Snell (NZ) 3min 54·4, '62
Peter Snell (NZ) 3min 54·1, Sept '64
Michel Jazy (France) 3min 53·6, June '65
Jim Ryun (USA) '65 3min 51·3, July '65
Jim Ryun (USA) '67 3min 51·1, June '67

The less-than-four-minute milers, since Bannister broke the 'barrier'

the first Prime Minister of Malawi, and President in 1966.

Bandaranaike, Solomon (1899-1959) Prime Minister of Ceylon, now Sri Lanka, from 1956 until 1959, when he was assassinated by a Buddhist monk. His policies were continued by his wife, Sirimavo, who entered politics on her husband's death and became Prime Minister (1960-5), being the first woman in the world to hold such office.

Bannister, Roger (born 1929) English athlete who was the first person to run a mile in under four minutes. At Oxford, in 1954, he ran the distance in 3 min. 59.4 secs.

Banting, Sir Frederick (1891-1941) Canadian doctor, who with Charles BEST discovered a treatment for diabetes. With the help of J. J. R. Macleod they discovered that small clumps or islands of cells in the pancreas secrete a hormone known as insulin and went on to show the key role of insulin in regulating the level of sugar in the blood. Insulin therapy is now a standard treatment for diabetes. In 1923 Banting and Macleod were awarded a Nobel Prize.

Bao-Dai (born 1911) Last Emperor of Vietnam (effective rule 1933-45). For much of his reign he was subservient to the French and in 1945, under pressure from the Japanese, who then controlled Vietnam, he repudiated treaties which had been made with France and set up a supposedly independent government. Later in the same year he abdicated after Hanoi was seized by the Viet-Minh and he acted as adviser to HO CHI-MINH. In 1949 he accepted the French proposition that he should head the associate state of Vietnam, a position he held until 1955 when he was deposed by Ngo Dinh-diem.

Barbarossa see KHAIREDDIN PASHA

Barber, Samuel (born 1910) American composer best known for his *Adagio for Strings* (1936). He has

written two symphonies, the first of which, cast in a condensed, single-movement form, is among the best by any American composer. He has also completed a series of song cycles in which his gifts have probably found their most effective expression.

Barbirolli, Sir John (1899-1970) English conductor and cellist of Italian and French descent who made the Hallé Orchestra of Manchester one of the world's finest when he was resident conductor from 1943 to 1968.

Bardot, Brigitte (born 1934) French actress who gained worldwide fame as the 'sex kitten' in such films as *And God Created Woman* and *Heaven Fell· That Night* (1957), directed by her then husband, Roger Vadim.

Barents, Willem (16th cent.) Dutch navigator who explored the waters north and northeast of Norway, later called the Barents Sea, in an attempt to find a North East Passage to eastern Asia. On his third voyage, he sighted Bear Island and West Spitsbergen, which he mistook for Greenland. His team rounded Novaya Zemlya but was trapped by ice and wintered ashore – the first Europeans to do so that far north. Barents died on the return journey.

Baring, Sir Francis (1740-1810) English founder of Baring Brothers and Company (1806), one of the world's strongest financial houses. He combined opportunism, expertise and integrity, qualities which successive Baring generations cultivated and maintained. Directly engaged in overseas developments, especially in America, he was a key figure in government finance, notably during the Napoleonic Wars, when he was a principal negotiator in the Louisiana Purchase (1802).

Barlow, William (1845-1934) English crystallographer, whose work on

crystal structure extended BRAVAIS's classification of the various types of structure to include the symmetry of crystals whose molecules do not have identical orientations in space.

Barnard, Christian (born 1922) South African surgeon, the first man to transplant the human heart (1967). One of his early patients, Philip Blaiberg, survived for 20 months after a heart transplant.

Barnard, Edward Emerson (1857-1923) American astronomer who discovered 16 comets. Barnard was a pioneer of astronomical photography, and at the Lick Observatory, California, made an important series of photographs of the Milky Way. He discovered Jupiter's fifth satellite by direct observation, and photographed a nebulous ring of matter ejected from Nova Auriga. In 1895, while at Yerkes Observatory, he showed that the dark 'lanes' in the Milky Way are caused by dust obstructing starlight.

Orphans were a common sight in the slum streets of London's East End during the 19th cent. Dr Barnardo gave them homes

Barnardo, Thomas (1845-1905) English physician and philanthropist, founder of the Dr Barnardo Homes for destitute children. While a medical student at the London Hospital, Barnardo determined to devote himself to the care of homeless orphans he had seen abandoned in the streets of London's East End. By 1870 he had raised enough money to found the first home for boys in Stepney. The number of homes grew rapidly, and they still flourish today, providing shelter and education for orphans.

Barnes, Thomas (1784-1841) British lawyer and journalist, whose editorship of *The Times*, from 1817 until his death, made it Europe's leading newspaper. After practising law for 10 years he turned to literature, writing articles on the theatre and politics. On becoming Editor of *The Times* he quickly established its independence from political parties. Vigorous editorial support of the Reform Bill (1832) earned the paper the nickname of the 'Thunderer'.

Barnum, Phineas T. (1810-91) American showman who, in the 1880s, with James Bailey, staged the world-famous circus known as 'The Greatest Show on Earth'.

Baroja, Pio (1872-1956) Leading 20th-century Spanish novelist, who belonged to the 'Generation of 1898', a group of ex-anarchist and ex-Marxist writers who attacked Spanish traditions and tried to arouse Spain from its alleged decadence. Baroja was its most sceptical member and all his novels (he wrote over 100) show a total hostility to any values other than that of vigorous action. Some deal with Basque and Spanish history, notably the Carlist wars; others, such as the *Struggle for Life* (1904), portray anarchist plots, endless debates about Spanish regeneration or are simple adventure stories, such as *The Restlessness of Sandy Andia* (1911).

Barras, Vicomte Paul François (1755-1829) French revolutionary politician. An aristocrat by birth, Barras became a Jacobin after the outbreak of the Revolution in 1789 and helped NAPOLEON, then captain Bonaparte, to organize the defence of Toulon, and to put down the royalist Vendémiaire rising in Paris (1795). He connived at the coup of Brumaire (November, 1799) which overthrew the Directory and enabled Napoleon to become First Consul. As the most powerful member of the Directory he had secured Napoleon's appointment as commander in Italy, and arranged his marriage to his own former mistress, Josephine de Beauharnais, thus setting Napoleon on the road to supreme power.

Barrault, Jean-Louis (born 1910) French actor, director, mime and leading exponent of 'total theatre', in

which light, sound, sets, costumes, movement and direction are given as much prominence as text. The film *Les Enfants du Paradis* made him internationally famous.

Barrie, Sir James Matthew (1860-1937) Scottish dramatist, who wrote *Peter Pan* (1904), *Dear Brutus* (1917) and *Mary Rose* (1920), sentimental fantasies for children. Among his other plays were *The Professor's Love Story* (1895), *Quality Street* (1903), *The Admirable Crichton* (1903) and *What Every Woman Knows* (1908).

Barrios, Eduardo (1884-1963) Chilean novelist, whose work is distinguished in Latin American literature by its emphasis on psychology rather than on social problems. His most successful novel, *Gentleman and Hell-raiser* (1948), portrays life on a Chilean farm. Clarity of style and a stimulating use of language characterize all Barrios's work, which also includes short stories and plays.

Barry, Sir Charles (1795-1860) English architect of the Houses of Parliament, London (1839-52). His designs for the Travellers' Club and the Reform Club, London, draw their inspiration from Italian Renais-

sance palatial architecture. His small Gothic churches, designs for castles and his conception of the Palace of Westminster are characterized by a controlled, balanced medievalism.

Barry, Comtesse du see DU BARRY, Comtesse

Barry, Sir Redmond (1813-80) Irish-born supreme court judge in Australia. In 1853 he was appointed the first Chancellor of Melbourne University and later assisted in the establishment of the Victorian Public Library, of which he was the first president. He died shortly after he had tried and convicted the bushranger, Ned KELLY.

Barrymore, John (1882-1942) American actor and film-star, famous for his interpretation of Hamlet (1922 and 1925) and his 'great profile'. He was the brother of Ethel and Lionel Barrymore, who both performed in films and plays.

Barth, Heinrich (1821-65) German explorer and geographer of North Africa. With his compatriot Adolf Overweg, Barth joined James Richardson's British expedition to the Western Sudan, organized by the government to open up trade with the

An outstanding figure in the world of big band jazz, Count Basie conducts from the piano

Sudan. The expedition left Tripoli (1850) and travelled south across the Sahara to Kano. Barth took control of it when Richardson died at Bornu, and – dogged by sickness – reached the Benue River from Lake Chad. The expedition then swung west and travelled more than 1000 miles to Timbuktu (previously reached by CAILLIÉ). Barth returned to Europe in 1855. His published account of the five-year marathon, *Travels and Discoveries in North and Central Africa* (1857-8), described the 10,000-mile journey and included the first description of the Middle Niger (previously reached by Mungo Park) from Timbuktu to Say.

Barth, Karl (1886-1968) Swiss Protestant theologian, who revolutionized 20th-century religious thought by breaking with rational theological systems and putting the humanity of JESUS and the concrete reality of God back into the centre of religious belief. His *Commentary on the Romans* (1922) marked the beginning of what is called dialectical or crisis theology. His violent opposition to the HITLER régime later cost him his professorship at Bonn University.

Bartholin, Rasmus (1625-98) Danish mathematician and physicist, who discovered the property of light now known as double refraction. He found that light passing through a crystal of Iceland spar (a type of calcite) split into two rays, and that images seen through it were double. On turning the crystal, one image remained still while the other rotated about it.

Bartlett, Sir Frederick (1886-1968) English anthropologist and experimental psychologist primarily concerned with the nature of thought processes, memory and perception. He rejected altogether the idea of memory as a 'storage' system, and saw it instead as a social learning 'construct' – an active process of reinterpretation, adapted to accommodate whatever new material is to be absorbed. Creative and systematic thinking, according to Bartlett, are learned skills in which symbols come to represent actions.

Bartók, Béla (1881-1945) Hungary's foremost 20th-century composer. The main influences on Bartók as a young composer were LISZT, BRAHMS and Richard STRAUSS. From 1905, in collaboration with KODALY, he began to collect Balkan folk music. His discoveries influenced his composition and much of the 'modernism' in his own work which so attracted hostility during his lifetime was a result of his synthesizing the melodic and rhythmic elements of folk music. Bartók's most important compositions are the opera *Bluebeard's Castle* (1911) and the balletic mime play *The Miraculous Mandarin* (1919); his three piano concertos and his second violin concerto; *Mikrokosmos*, the set of 153 piano studies; the *Music for Strings, Percussion and Celesta* and the *Sonata for Two Pianos and Percussion*.

Basawan (16th cent.) Hindu painter to the Emperor AKBAR, and a major influence on Mogul painting after the death of DASWANTH.

Bashoh see MATSUO BASHOH

Basie, William 'Count' (born 1904) American negro pianist and composer and leader of one of the few 'big bands' to survive the impact of small group jazz music.

Basil II (c. 958-1025) Eastern Roman Emperor during whose reign the Byzantine Empire reached its medieval apogee. He was called 'Bulgaroctonus' (Slayer of the Bulgars) for subduing the Bulgarians (986-1014) when, to regain control of the whole Balkan peninsula, he wiped out the whole of the Bulgarian army at Balathista (1014), brutally blinding 15,000 of his prisoners. Basil waged war for 50 years, suppressing feudal rebellions in Asia Minor, making some gains against the Saracens, and annexing Armenia to give the empire a strong highland frontier in the east, as well as defeating the Bulgarians. He was supposedly joint ruler with his brother Constantine, but Constantine was powerless until after Basil's death.

Basil the Great (c. 330-79) One of the four great Greek Doctors of the Church. After visiting monastic centres all over the Eastern Empire, he settled at Annesi in Cappadocia and formed a monastic community of his own. Here he formulated a rule which is still the basis of monastic life in the Greek Orthodox Church, which enjoins both manual work and hours of liturgy.

Baskerville, John (1706-75) English printer and a major innovator in typography. In 1750 he began experiments in type-founding and set up his own printing house. In 1758 he published his edition of MILTON's works and was appointed printer to Cambridge University, where he printed the Bible, The Book of Common Prayer and the works of many Latin authors. The Baskerville typeface is commonly used today.

Bassano, Jacopo (c. 1510-92) Italian painter, of the Venetian school, whose work was at first much influenced by that of TITIAN. Later he developed a more individual style. He painted night scenes, rustic subjects and religious works, all of which tend to contain a large number of figures and animals. Genuine paintings by Bassano are rare.

Bateman, Henry (1887-1970) British humorous artist, who specialized in caricaturing the habits and manners of the upper and middle classes. His work, usually in sequence form, dealt largely with social gaffes or with trivial events that led to disaster; they were often depicted in colour, e.g.

The Man who Lit his Cigar before the Royal Toast. Bateman's work, frequently represented in *Punch*, was popular in the 1920s and 1930s.

Bates, Henry Walter (1825-92) British naturalist who explored the Amazon Basin studying South American fauna. Bates travelled 1400 miles up the Amazon and collected 8000 previously unknown insect species. He published his discoveries in *The Naturalist on the Amazon* (1863). Bates's other principal contribution to biology was to perceive and explain the phenomenon of mimicry among separate insect species.

Bateson, William (1861-1926) English biologist who coined the term 'genetics'. His work on plant inheritance, based upon that of Gregor MENDEL, led him to conclude that certain characteristics are not inherited independently but invariably go together. This was later explained as gene linkage.

Batista y Zaldivar, Fulgencio (1901-73) Cuban dictator overthrown by Fidel CASTRO. He participated in the army revolt against President Machada in 1931-3, then led the coup that deposed Cespedes, the provisional President. He was elected President of Cuba (1940-4) and became provisional President again in 1952 after deposing President Prio. He was re-elected in 1954 and assumed dictatorial powers. His régime, noted for its harshness and brutality, was overthrown in 1959 and he fled to the Dominican Republic.

Batu Khan (13th cent.) Mongol Khan of the Western Kipchaks (the Golden Horde), whose realm, centered on the lower Volga, dominated Russia for two centuries. Sent to invade Europe by the Great Khan OGADAI, Batu, aided by General Subotai, conquered Russia, Poland, Hungary and Bohemia (1237-41).

Baudelaire, Charles (1821-67) French poet and art critic, prosecuted for obscenity on the appearance of his volume of poems, *Les Fleurs du Mal* (1857). The subtle power of his language and his use of striking associations (*correspondances*) paved the way for the Symbolist movement and established Baudelaire among the greatest of French poets. He was an admirer of the works of Edgar Allan POE, and translated many of the American's works into French.

Baxter, Richard (1615-91) English Puritan scholar and churchman, a notable and influential model of pastoral devotion and toleration. Baxter was involved in all the contemporary religious controversies and suffered for 20 years for his dissenting views, being forced out of the Church of England by the Act of Uniformity (1662). For the Savoy Declaration (1656), a statement of moderate dissent, he prepared a Reformed Liturgy and Exceptions (objections) to The Book of Common Prayer. Some of these were incorporated in the revised edition of 1662.

Baybers I (1223-77) Mameluke Sultan of Egypt and Syria (1260-77), who made Egypt the most powerful Muslim state in the Middle East. Of Turkish origin, Baybers distinguished himself fighting against the crusade of Louis IX of France in 1249-50, and in 1260 led the vanguard of the Mamelukes when they finally repelled the Mongol menace at Ayn Jalut. After seizing the throne, Baybers overran most of Christian Syria and waged several campaigns against Lesser Armenia (1266-75). He legitimized his position by establishing a shadow caliphate at Cairo. His successful reign enabled the Mamelukes to establish the strongest kingdom since the pharaohs.

Bayer, Adolf von (1835-1917) German chemist and industrialist noted for his synthesis of organic chemicals, especially indigos and arsenical compounds. He was awarded a Nobel Prize for Chemistry in 1905.

Bayle, Pierre (1647-1706) French philosopher and lexicographer, who is regarded as the founder of 18th-century rationalism. His major work, the *Dictionnaire historique et critique* (1697), a collection of essays on topics ranging from philosophy and history to religion, is particularly important for its undermining of traditional beliefs, by the use of critical footnotes which occupy far more space than the main text. In this work, Bayle foreshadows the sceptical, ironical style of the French *encyclopédistes*.

Baylis, Dame Lilian (1874-1937) British theatre manager, who founded the Old Vic and Sadler's Wells companies. As manager of the Victoria Theatre, later known as the Old Vic, she planned and presented opera, ballet and drama at popular prices, but her range of Shakespearean productions (1914-23) established the Old Vic's tradition of pure drama.

Baysunghur, Mirza (15th cent.) Timurid prince and patron of Persian learning and art. He ruled Herat for his father, Shah Rukh, from 1414, and there established a book academy under the direction of his chief calligrapher, Ja'far. The paintings of his artists, using brilliant colour and idyllic backgrounds, marked the flowering of the 'classic' period of Persian art.

Bazna, Elyesa (1904-70) Albanian, who under the code name 'Cicero' spied for the Germans during the Second World War. As a valet to the British Ambassador in Ankara, 'Cicero' obtained complete details of the Teheran Conference and Operation Overlord, the planned Allied invasion of Europe. However, the Nazi command disregarded the information, believing it to have been fabricated by British Intelligence, and paid 'Cicero' with counterfeit money.

Beardsley, Aubrey (1872-98) English illustrator, who was influential in the evolution of Art Nouveau, the international decorative style of the 1890s. His output was extensive and he had achieved an international reputation before his early death. His use of a flowing line with strongly contrasting blacks and whites was combined with a sensitive gift for decorative motifs. Among his best-known illustrations are those for WILDE's *Salomé*, POPE's *The Rape of the Lock*, and JONSON's *Volpone*.

Beaumarchais, Pierre de (1732-99) French dramatist, two of whose plays were the bases of operas by MOZART and ROSSINI. His first success, *The Barber of Seville* (Mozart), was presented at the Comédie Française in 1775. *The Marriage of Figaro*, a social satire, appeared in 1784.

Beaumont, Francis (c. 1584-1616) English dramatist, who, in collaboration with John FLETCHER, wrote ten plays. On his own, Beaumont wrote two comedies, *The Woman Hater* and *The Knight of the Burning Pestle*.

Beaumont, William (1785-1853) American army surgeon whose *Experiments and Observations on the Gastric Juice and the Physiology of Digestion* (1833) is often called the greatest single contribution to the history of gastric physiology. Beaumont's approach was practical to a degree; he made his classic observations directly through a large unhealed fistula, or opening, in the stomach of a wounded patient. He was thus able to give an accurate and complete description of the gastric juice, including the identification of hydrochloric acid present.

Beauvoir, Simone de (born 1908) French novelist and essayist, concerned mainly with the Existentialist concept of the importance of freedom in a life subject to laws and controls. Together with SARTRE, she founded the literary review *Les Temps Modernes* (1946) and is the author of the treatise *Le Deuxième Sexe* (1949)

A graceful decadence and morbid atmosphere characterize Beardsley's work

and *Les Mandarins* (1954). Perhaps her most interesting works are the volumes of reminiscences – *Mémoires d'une Jeune Fille rangée* (1958) and *La Force de l'Age*.

Beaverbrook, William, 1st Baron (1879-1964) Canadian-born British politician and proprietor of mass-circulation newspapers. He became a financier (1900) and in 1910 moved to England to become first an MP and then Minister of Information in 1918. He gained control of the *Daily Express* (1916), the *Sunday Express* (1918) and the *Evening Standard* (1923), and set new standards in popular journalism, using the papers for his Empire Crusade (1930). In 1936 he tried to prevent EDWARD VIII's abdication. A member of CHURCHILL's government throughout the Second World War, he became Minister of Aircraft Production (1940-1), Minister of Supply (1941-2) and Minister of War Production (1942). As a supporter of the British Empire, he backed the Suez campaign in 1956 and opposed Britain's entry into the European Economic Community.

Beccaria, Cesare (1738-94) Italian jurist and economist, who wrote the influential work on criminal law reform, *Crimes and Punishments* (1764). He denounced the savagery of contemporary trials and punishments, condemned torture, criticized the death penalty, urged that punishment should be commensurate with crime and stressed that it should aim to prevent it. In economics Beccaria pioneered the application of mathematics to economic analysis.

Becher, Johann Joachim (1635-82) German chemist who originated the phlogiston theory of burning. He

was interested in alchemy and this study led him to suggest, in 1669, that every substance contains within its make-up the agency behind combustion. This erroneous theory was later developed by Georg STAHL.

Becket, Thomas à (c. 1118-70) English saint, Archbishop of Canterbury, whose murder at Canterbury Cathedral after quarrelling with the king dramatized England's medieval Church-versus-State conflict. When HENRY II, whose friend he had been, made him Archbishop (1162), Becket angered Henry by zealously upholding the rights of the church against secular authority. In particular he refused to approve the Constitutions of Clarendon because they allotted to secular authorities the punishment of clerics convicted by ecclesiastical courts. Becket went into exile in France (1164-70), returning after a reconciliation with Henry, but within a month the quarrel was renewed. An unguarded expression of rage by Henry was acted on by four of his knights, who murdered Becket on the steps of the altar at Canterbury.

Beckett, Samuel (born 1906) Irish dramatist, novelist and poet who was awarded the Nobel Prize for Literature in 1969. He received international recognition with his play *Waiting for Godot* (1953), which is concerned with the absurdity of mankind's situation and has become a key work in the Theatre of the Absurd. Beckett's themes are characterized by a preoccupation with the misery of man even in sophisticated societies. Death, decay and a vision of society bent on helpless self-destruction are themes which are found in *Endgame* (1957), *Krapp's Last Tape* (1960), *Happy Days* (1961), *Play* (1963), *Come and Go* (1965). Beckett ignores conventional dramatic structure and development and creates a static form made up of a loose series of images. Apart from his first novel, *Murphy* (1938), written in English, he mainly writes in French (he has lived in Paris since 1937). His other novels include *Malone Dies* (1951) and *The Unnamable* (1953).

Beckford, William (1759-1844) English collector and novelist, whose strange oriental tale *Vathek* (1786) is a prime example of the English exotic and 'Gothic' romance.

Beckmann, Max (1884-1950) German Expressionist artist, influenced by Fauvism and Cubism, whose work usually embodied a social message. He left Germany in 1938 for New York, where he died.

Bécquer, Gustavo (1836-70) Spanish poet, who introduced a new

austerity and simplicity into Spanish Romantic love poetry and exercised strong influence on the poets of the 1930s.

Becquerel, Antoine Henri (1852-1908) French physicist who discovered radioactivity. In 1896, following ROENTGEN's discovery of X-rays, Becquerel investigated whether fluorescent substances give off X-rays as well as visible light and in 1901, after painstaking research, found an entirely new kind of radiation coming from within the uranium atoms in the fluorescent uranium salts. His colleague, Marie CURIE, named the phenomenon radioactivity.

Bede 'The Venerable' (673-735) English historian, theologian and scholar, whose *Ecclesiastical History of the English People* is the main source of knowledge of early English history. Bede, a Northumbrian priest, wrote more than 30 books, including a prose and a verse life of Cuthbert, theological commentaries, and works on grammar and physical science.

Beerbohm, Sir Max (1872-1956) British caricaturist and satirist of intellectual and political society, who was at his most active during the 1890s. His best-known work is in *The Poet's Corner* (1904) and *Rossetti and his Circle* (1922). Although Max (as he signed himself) was only moderately talented as a draughtsman, his ability to catch a likeness and his sense of the ridiculous compensated for his technical limitations. He usually worked in line and wash, with or without colour. He was also a skilful literary parodist.

Beethoven, Ludwig van (1770-1827) German composer who brought the symphony to its peak as a form of musical expression. Beethoven first made his mark as a piano virtuoso, but in 1800 the opening performance of his First Symphony began the cycle that was to culminate in the great Ninth ('Choral') Symphony in 1824. Despite the handicap of growing deafness he sustained a remarkable output until 1812, the main works of this period including the Third ('Eroica', dedicated to NAPOLEON), Sixth ('Pastoral'), Seventh and Eighth Symphonies and the Fourth and Fifth ('Emperor') Piano Concertos. The opera *Fidelio* also belongs to this period (1804), its theme of the individual triumphing over despotism expressing Beethoven's political ideals. From 1812-17, the composer wrote little, but later he began work on the Mass in D (1824) and the Ninth Symphony. Beethoven, brought up as a Roman Catholic, abandoned this religion for an individual, pantheistic 'deism' of the kind expressed in SCHILLER's 'Ode to Joy'. It was a setting of this poem which constituted the last choral movement of the Ninth.

Behaim, Martin (c. 1459-1507)
German navigator and merchant who made the oldest surviving globe. He advised JOHN II of Portugal on navigation techniques, sailed as far as West Africa, and stayed in the Azores. Then, with the painter Glockenthon, he made a segmented map as the basis for his terrestrial globe, produced in 1492 for Nuremberg City Council. The globe draws heavily on old Ptolemaic notions of geography, omits America, and even shows the contemporary Portuguese discoveries, albeit inaccurately.

Behan, Brendan (1923-64)
Irish dramatist, who wrote *The Quare Fellow* (1954), based on his experiences of Borstal, prison and the IRA. His next play, *The Hostage* (1958), was originally written in Gaelic. He started, but did not finish, a third, *Richard's Cork Leg*.

Behrens, Peter (1868-1938)
German architect and pioneer of industrial design, the most influential and renowned of whose buildings is the Turbine Factory, Berlin (1909), which is completely lacking in ornament and has side walls of glass and steel. He first worked as an Art Nouveau painter-designer in Germany but his later involvement in industrial design led him to favour a severely functional approach. This he applied at all levels, from the design of miners' lamps to his vigorous and bold industrial buildings for the German AEG Electrical Company. His non-industrial work, exemplified by the German Embassy, St Petersburg (Leningrad), demonstrates his strong and forceful Neo-Classicism.

Behring, Emil von (1854-1917)
German immunologist and winner of a Nobel Prize for Medicine in 1901, who with his Japanese colleague Shibasaburo Kitasato, demonstrated immunity to diphtheria and tetanus in animals. They showed that blood serum from animals that had been challenged by the toxins of either disease contained antitoxins which could confer a short-lived resistance when injected into man. In 1913 he found that a mixture of toxins and antitoxins gave more lasting immunity – a discovery that is the basis of modern immunization therapy.

Beiderbecke, Leon 'Bix' (1903-31)
American jazz cornetist, pianist and composer. Self-taught, Beiderbecke was one of the first white

Places to live, work and worship
Architecture: the mud huts of the ancients; the glorious temples of the Middle Ages; the monuments to 20th-century technology—all express the qualities and aspirations of the cultures from which they sprung. Ancient buildings, the fossils of civilization, are often our primary source of information about early cultures. The buildings below mark the ages of man, starting in the Neolithic period with his first crude attempt at building shelter. Then, in 2000BC, the crescendo of creative invention in which real architecture imaterialized. From then on it flourishes, changing and growing—a monumental expression of the burgeoning creativity of man

musicians to achieve a status in jazz accorded normally to negro artistes, but wide recognition of his talent did not come until after his death.

Békésy, Georg von (1899-1972)
Hungarian physicist who won the Nobel Prize for Medicine (1961) for his research into the mechanism of stimulation of the human inner ear. His work has made it possible to differentiate between various types of deafness and thus to apply more accurate treatment.

Bekr, abu- see ABU-BAKR

Bel Geddes, Norman (1893-1958)
American stage designer who, by introducing the ideas of APPIA and CRAIG and by his own contributions, transformed stage design in the US.

Belínsky, Vissarión Grigórievich (1811-48)
Russian critic and journalist, whose writings formed the basis of Russian literary criticism. He was largely responsible for the Russian

conviction that literature should express ideas, and his anti-imaginative opinions still persist in Russia.

Belisarius (c. 505-65)
Commander of the Byzantine army, who recovered much of the Western Roman Empire for the Eastern Emperor JUSTINIAN. He saved Justinian's throne by suppressing a revolt in Constantinople (532); crushed the Vandal kingdom in North Africa (534); drove THEOdoric's Ostrogoths from Italy (535-40); and fought Persia's KHOSRAU I in the east (541-2).

Bell, Alexander Graham (1847-1922)
Scottish-born American physicist and inventor who, in 1876, developed the first telephone. Bell's invention grew out of research in speech mechanics he had conducted while training teachers for the deaf. Among his other inventions were an electric probe for detecting bullets in the human body and the grooved wax cylinder with spiral sound track for Thomas EDISON's phonograph.

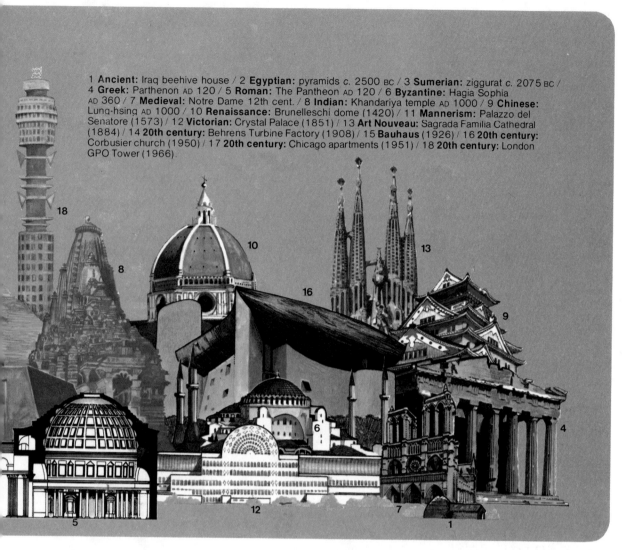

1 **Ancient:** Iraq beehive house / 2 **Egyptian:** pyramids *c.* 2500 BC / 3 **Sumerian:** ziggurat *c.* 2075 BC / 4 **Greek:** Parthenon AD 120 / 5 **Roman:** The Pantheon AD 120 / 6 **Byzantine:** Hagia Sophia AD 360 / 7 **Medieval:** Notre Dame 12th cent. / 8 **Indian:** Khandariya temple AD 1000 / 9 **Chinese:** Lung-hsing AD 1000 / 10 **Renaissance:** Brunelleschi dome (1420) / 11 **Mannerism:** Palazzo del Senatore (1573) / 12 **Victorian:** Crystal Palace (1851) / 13 **Art Nouveau:** Sagrada Familia Cathedral (1884) / 14 **20th century:** Behrens Turbine Factory (1908) / 15 **Bauhaus** (1926) / 16 **20th century:** Corbusier church (1950) / 17 **20th century:** Chicago apartments (1951) / 18 **20th century:** London GPO Tower (1966).

Bell, Andrew (1753-1832) Scottish-born clergyman and educationalist. As superintendent of a Madras orphanage (1789), he was prompted by a shortage of teachers to initiate his monitorial system by which pupils

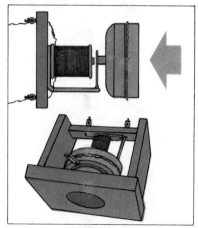

The prototype Bell telephone: the same diaphragm was used both for sending and receiving speech

taught each other. He published his *An Experiment in Education* in London (1797). Joseph LANCASTER aroused interest in Bell's educational system, which was adopted by the Church of England. Bell was appointed to organize a system of church schools (1807) and became superintendent of the National Society for Promoting the Education of the Poor under the Principles of the Established Church (1811).

Bell, Sir Charles (1774-1842) British anatomist and surgeon, the first man to describe paralysis of the facial nerve, or Bell's palsy. He was also the first to show the difference between sensory and motor nerves and to prove that they sprang from different roots in the spinal column.

Bellingshausen, Fabian Gottlieb von (1778-1852) Russian naval officer and explorer who made the first land sightings in the Antarctic Circle. He commanded the sloops *Vostok* and *Mirny* on a voyage (1819-

21) which circumnavigated Antarctica south of Cook's course. He sighted Alexander I Island and Peter Island and an unidentified land which may have been man's first glimpse of the Antarctic continent.

Bellini, Giovanni (c. 1430-1516) One of the leading artists of the Venetian school of painting, and an outstanding influence on classical painting in general. He maintained a large workshop and had many pupils, among them TITIAN, GIORGIONE and, briefly, TINTORETTO. Much of Bellini's work consists of altar-pieces and paintings of the Madonna and child, in both of which he evolved compositional formulae that were adopted by many later Venetian painters. His mature work is remarkable for its colour harmonies, which were of marked originality in their day. At the end of his life Bellini undertook a large-scale mythological picture (*The Feast of the Gods*, 1514), which was the starting point for Titian's later works in this grandiose and colourful genre.

Bellman, Carl (1740-95) Swedish writer, famous for his tavern and street songs and as the author of *Fredman's Epistles* (1790) and *Fredman's Songs* (1791). His serenades and townscapes are peopled by a motley collection of comic drinkers and dancers, but behind the revellers' alcoholic search for happiness lies a poignant awareness of death.

Belloc, Hilaire (1870-1953) Naturalized English writer, born in France, who with CHESTERTON represented a view of the world which admired tradition and opposed the social ideas of SHAW and WELLS. Belloc was a poet, historian, social commentator and novelist; he handled serious subjects in a sprightly, paradoxical way.

Bellow, Saul (born 1915) American novelist, who has a particular sympathy for lonely, intelligent men, usually Jews, at grips with the problems of the contemporary world. In his early novels, *Dangling Man* (1944) and *The Victim* (1947), Bellow showed an awareness of psychology and a subtle understanding of relations between Jew and Gentile. *The Adventures of Augie March* (1953) and *Henderson the Rain King* (1959) are picaresque novels employing rich, colloquial language. *Herzog* (1964) is a brilliant portrait of a modern intellectual Jew.

Bely, Andrei (1880-1934) Russian Symbolist poet and novelist, whose *Symphony* (*Second Dramatic*) applied the principles of musical composition to prose narrative. Fascinated by both science and mysticism, he saw Symbolism as a bridge between the two.

Bembo, Pietro (1470-1547) Italian cardinal and scholar whose works were influential in establishing Italian as a literary language. A typeface bearing his name was cut to print one of his works.

Benavente y Martinez, Jacinto (1866-1953) Spanish dramatist and Nobel Prize winner (1922), who translated SHAKESPEARE, MOLIÈRE and IBSEN into Spanish.

Ben Bella, Mohammed (born 1916) Algerian politician who led resistance to the French, was twice arrested by them, escaped and directed the Algeria National Movement from exile (1952-6). Following independence, Ben Bella became Premier of Algeria, and President, by national referendum, in 1963. After overcoming a revolt in 1964, he was deposed in a bloodless army coup led by Colonel Houari BOUMEDIENNE in June 1965 and some years later was still in custody, his whereabouts unknown.

Benchley, Robert Charles (1889-1945) American journalist and humorist who wrote for various New York publications and acted in successful Hollywood film shorts. His humour was urbane, wry, and frequently self-directed.

Benedict of Nursia (c. 480-c. 547) Italian saint, founder of the monastic order known by his name. Early in life, Benedict became disgusted by Roman dissipation and lived as a hermit. Although he had never been ordained, a community of monks asked him to become their abbot. This he accepted but was driven back to his hermitage, when, angered by his strict rule, the monks tried to poison him. He went on to organize a number of other small monastic communities and finally, in about 529, a monastery at Monte Cassino, where he founded his Benedictine Order.

Benedict, Ruth (1887-1948) American anthropologist, who demonstrated that the values adopted by different cultures may produce totally dissimilar psychological types. In *Patterns of Culture* (1934) she compared and contrasted the characteristics admired and fostered by certain tribes of New Mexico, Vancouver and New Guinea. *The Chrysanthemum and the Sword* (1946) was published as a result of her researches into Japanese culture carried out at the request of the US government after the Second World War.

Beneš, Eduard (1884-1948) Czech statesman and co-founder of Czech independence. Of peasant birth, he was educated at the universities of Prague, Dijon, Paris, Berlin and London, and in 1915 joined MASARYK in Paris to work for Czechoslovakian independence. Success at the Paris Peace Conference resulted in his becoming Foreign Minister of the new State (1918-35). Beneš was President of his country when, in 1938, by the Munich Agreement between HITLER and CHAMBERLAIN, Britain and France abandoned it to the Nazis. As a result, Beneš resigned. He became President of the Czechoslovak government-in-exile in London (1941-5), after which he returned to Prague. He had, however, lost the confidence of STALIN, and consequently lost control of the government to the communists, who were protected by Russia, and was finally forced to resign. He died shortly afterwards.

Benet, Stephen Vincent (1898-1943) American poet, who wrote 'John Brown's Body' (1928), a long narrative poem about the American Civil War. Most of his major works in poetry and prose explored American National character, history and legend. Benet's historical short stories achieved more popularity than his five novels.

Ben Gurion, David (1886-1973) Israeli statesman and politician and architect of the independent state of Israel. Polish-born, he settled in Palestine in 1906 and was exiled by the Turks in 1915. As a Zionist and an Allied sympathizer, he helped to organize the Jewish Legion in America and fought in it under ALLENBY. In 1930 he became leader of the Mapai (Labour) Party, and Chairman of the Jewish Agency for Palestine (1935-48), proclaiming independence of Israel in 1948. He was Prime Minister and Minister of Defence of the new state, 1949-53, and again 1955-63, when he resigned, though remaining in the Knesset, the Israeli Parliament.

Bennett, Arnold (1867-1931) English novelist whose reputation rests mainly on his regional novels, depicting the life of his native area, the Potteries, an area of Staffordshire, England. His best-known work is *The Old Wives' Tale* (1908), a finely detailed, naturalistic novel depicting the lives of the daughters of a draper. *Anna of the Five Towns* (1902) offers a picture of life in a provincial Wesleyan community; Bennett also depicted Potteries life in short stories. As well as novels, Bennett wrote a mass of prose for magazines.

Benois, Alexandre (1870-1960) Russian painter and theatrical designer. As co-founder, with DIAGHILEV, BAKST and others of the review *World of Art*, his previous experience of ballet prompted new ideas for integrating decor with the other elements in ballet.

Bentham, Jeremy (1748-1832) English philosopher, legal and economic theorist and reformer, and one of the chief proponents of Utilitarianism, whose central doctrine states that all human action must be aimed at producing the greatest happiness for the greatest number. It is by this criterion, Bentham said, that a man must judge the law and all other social institutions and practices that he might wish to reform.

Bentley, Nicolas (born 1907) British humorous artist and author, whose work is known for its allegedly anti-clerical bias. It is characterized by a fine, flowing line used in contrast with substantial areas of black. Among the many authors whose works Bentley has illustrated are Hilaire BELLOC, Lawrence DURRELL, T. S. ELIOT and Damon RUNYON.

Benz, Karl (1844-1929) German pioneer of the internal combustion engine designed specifically for the propulsion of vehicles, and, hence, of the modern automobile. After some success with an earlier two-stroke engine, Benz built a four-stroke in 1885 which, first applied to a tricycle, achieved great success when installed in a four-wheel vehicle in 1893. Benz was the first man to make and sell light, self-propelled vehicles built to a standardized pattern. Hundreds had been built by the turn of the century.

Berenguer, Ramón see RAMÓN Berenguer

Berg, Alban (1885-1935) Austrian composer and one of SCHOENBERG's leading disciples. He met Schoenberg in 1904 and won recognition with his opera *Wozzeck*, first performed in 1925, which vindicated the new atonal methods of his teacher. The progression of his style may be traced from the opera through the *Chamber Concerto* (1925) and the *Lyric Suite* (1925-6), to the unfinished but powerful 12-note opera *Lulu* (1937), taken from WEDEKIND's play *Pandora's Box*.

Bergius, Friedrich (1884-1949) German chemist, who developed a method of treating coal or heavy oil with hydrogen to produce petrol. The Bergius process was introduced in 1912 and allowed German industry to produce gasoline independently of imported crude oil.

Bergman, Hjalmar (1883-1930) Swedish novelist and dramatist whose best-known work, the novel *Thy Rod and Thy Staff* (1921), is a mixture of grotesque humour, satire and tragedy. These characteristics are common to many of his works such as *God's Orchid* (1919) and *The Swedenhielm Family* (1925). Bergman was the leader of the Bourgeois Writers, a group which satirized the mores of the bourgeoisie.

Bergman, Ingmar (born 1918) Swedish director of the theatre and cinema whose international reputation rests mainly on his work for the latter. Bergman is singular among film makers for his use of 'repertory' actors, giving his work a rare homogeneity. Stylistically he is best known for his mystical, expressionist, heavily symbolic films, including *The Seventh Seal* (1956), a medieval allegory with its famous personification of a chess-playing Death, which first established him internationally. More recent films by Bergman include *The Hour of the Wolf* (1968), *The Touch* (1971) and *Cries and Whispers* (1972).

Bergson, Henri (1859-1941) French philosopher and author of many works, including *Creative Evolution* (1906). A revolutionary and influential study of experience, it stressed intuition as the source of experience and saw the evolution of matter as affected by the *élan vital*, a disorderly, constantly diverging life-force, producing new from old. An important influence on Marcel PROUST, Bergson too was concerned with the nature of time, which he saw as an inner 'duration' – the true reality. He was awarded the Nobel Prize for Literature in 1927.

Beria, Lavrenti Pavlovich (1899-1953) Soviet politician and police chief, notorious for his harsh methods as STALIN's deputy. A Georgian of peasant stock, he was made Commissar for Internal Affairs (1938), and engineered the execution of his predecessor Yezhov, who had organized Stalin's 'purge' trials. He became deputy Prime Minister in 1941, and Stalin's principal Minister during the Second World War. Following Stalin's death (1953) he ruled briefly with MALENKOV and MOLOTOV and tried to use his secret police organization to make himself dictator, but was arrested, tried and executed.

Bering, Vitus Jonassen (1680-1741) Danish navigator who showed that Asia and America are separated by sea and discovered Alaska. He served in the Russian Navy and was commissioned by PETER THE GREAT to determine whether Siberia and North America were linked by land. Sailing from Eastern Siberia's Kamchatka River (1728), Bering pushed north through the sea and strait (later named after him) to latitude 67°18′, and concluded that the strait separated Asia from America.

Berio, Luciano (born 1925) Italian composer who, with STOCKHAUSEN, pioneered spatial effects in modern music. The pieces in an orchestral or vocal cycle may be switched round to create new relationships, or the order of certain groups of notes may be varied. Much of his music, including his simpler *Folk Songs*, has been written for Cathy Berberian, the American soprano who was for a time his wife.

Berkeley, George (1685-1753) Irish idealist philosopher who held that material phenomena exist only in so far as we perceive them; the universe is a constant perception in the mind of God. *Treatise concerning the principles of Human Knowledge* (1710) and *Three dialogues between Hylas and Philonous* (1713) expound his doctrine.

Berkeley, Sir William (1606-77) English colonial governor of Virginia (1642-52 and 1659-76) who provoked Nathaniel BACON's revolt (1676). Ruling for CHARLES I, Berkeley enriched Virginia's economy, fought off Dutch and American Indian enemies, and expelled Puritans. After being deposed by CROMWELL in 1652 he was reinstated by CHARLES II, but failed to take action against American Indian frontier attacks and economic disasters. These failures and his aristocratic absolutism led to Bacon's revolt.

Berlin, Irving (born 1888) American of Russian birth and self-taught composer of some of the most popular songs ever written. Berlin, whose real name is Izzy Baline, began as a singing waiter in bars in New York's Bowery. 'Alexander's Ragtime Band' (1911) was his first big hit. His many other songs include 'I'm Dreaming of a White Christmas', 'Cheek to Cheek' and 'How Deep is the Ocean?' He wrote the Broadway musical *Call Me Madam* (1950).

Berlioz, Hector (1803-69) Leading French composer of the Romantic era. Berlioz was intended by his father, a provincial doctor, to study medicine, but soon switched to music. One of the most likeable personalities in the history of Romantic music, Berlioz composed almost always on a large scale, often demanding massive forces. His structural weaknesses were more than offset by his vitality, subtlety of orchestral tone colour and originality. Berlioz's choral works include *The Childhood of Christ*, *The Damnation of Faust* and a fine setting of the *Requiem*. He wrote overtures, including *Les Francs Juges* and *Roman Carnival*. His symphonies were the *Symphonie Fantastique*, *Harold in Italy* (after BYRON) and *Romeo and Juliet* (after SHAKESPEARE). His operas include *Benvenuto Cellini*, *Beatrice and Benedict* as well as his masterpiece, *The Trojans*, of which complete performances are rare owing to its scale and production demands.

Bernadette (1844-79) French saint whose visions of the Virgin Mary resulted in the establishment of Lourdes as a healing shrine and one of the greatest places of pilgrimage in Christendom. She was born in Lourdes, and her 18 visions of the Virgin Mary (who appeared to Bernadette as a beautiful lady) in 1858 occurred in a cave on the River Gave. Admitted to the Convent of the Sisters of Charity at Nevers, she died in 1879 and was canonized in 1933.

Bernadotte, Jean Baptiste (1763-1844) French-born King of Sweden (1818-44), as Charles XIV. After joining the French army he gained rapid promotion and was an army commander at Austerlitz and Wagram. NAPOLEON made him a Marshal in 1804, and Duke of Ponte Corvo in 1806. When the heir to the Swedish throne died in 1810, the Swedish Parliament elected him Crown Prince of Sweden. Later he changed sides and led an army of 120,000 Swedes against Napoleon in the Leipzig Campaign. This was followed by the annexation of Norway by Sweden, which had been agreed to by Britain and Russia and confirmed in the Treaty of Vienna (1813). His rule was liberal and enlightened.

Bernanos, Georges (1888-1948)
French novelist and polemical writer of uncompromisingly Catholic views. His best-known novel, *Journal d'un curé de campagne* (1936) is an account of a relentless struggle against evil and corruption. Other notable works include *Sous le soleil de Satan* (1926), *La joie* (1929) and *Les grands cimetières sous la lune* (1937).

Bernard of Clairvaux (1091-1153)
French religious reformer, who rallied his fellow countrymen to the Second Crusade (which began in 1147). Under his influence the Cistercian Order of monks grew so rapidly that by the time Bernard died, there were 388 Cistercian monasteries in existence, 68 of them direct foundations from his own abbey at Clairvaux. As his reputation as an orator grew, Bernard was invited to intervene in important Church matters of administration and policy. In theology, he advocated the worship of the Virgin Mary and is said to have originated Christocentrism. He was canonized in 1174.

Bernard, Claude (1813-78) French physiologist, who was the first to show that the pancreas had a function in the digestion of sugar and protein, and that the liver could take the sugars that were broken down in digestion and build them up into a more complex sugar known as glycogen. This was the first time that anyone had shown that the body could actually build up substances on its own. He also discovered the existence of vasomotor nerves (the nerves that control the diameter and tension of the blood vessels and so direct the blood supply to various parts of the body).

Bernhardt, Sarah (1844-1923)
French actress, often considered the outstanding tragedienne of the late 19th century. She first became known through her Cordelia in *King Lear* (1872). Her most famous role was Phèdre; among her other outstanding roles were Marguérite in *The Lady of the Camelias* and the Queen in *Ruy Blas*. She also played Hamlet and other male roles, such as NAPOLEON's son in Rostand's *L'Aiglon*.

Bernini, Gianlorenzo (1598-1680)
Italian sculptor, mostly in marble, who influenced the Italian Baroque style. In the Vatican, Bernini worked as an architect as well as a sculptor and designed the Piazza of St Peter's. The intensity of Bernini's religious feelings made him a suitable interpreter of the upsurge of religious emotion during the Counter-Reformation, as can be seen in the *Ecstasy of St Teresa* (1645-52).

Bernoulli, Daniel (1700-82) Swiss doctor and mathematician, whose most important work, *Hydrodynamica* (1738), deals with the theory of statics and the motion of fluids. He found practical uses for his theories; for example, their relation to the propulsion of ships. He was the son of Johann BERNOULLI.

Bernoulli, Jakob (1654-1705)
Swiss mathematician, who worked on the theory of infinite series, studied various special curves and laid the foundations of the calculus of variations. This he developed after LEIBNIZ had discovered infinitesimal calculus and about which they corresponded.

Bernoulli, Johann (1667-1748)
Swiss mathematician and the first to use 'g' to denote acceleration due to gravity. He worked on various problems of calculus, particularly the properties of curves, his work overlapping with that of his brother Jakob BERNOULLI, whom he succeeded at Basel University in 1705.

Bernstein, Leonard (born 1918)
American composer and conductor whose best-known work is his score for the musical *West Side Story* (1957), with its choreography by Jerome Robbins. Bernstein's compositions show widely ranging influences, from atonality and the Jewish liturgy to jazz and various forms of popular music. His other works include a symphony *The Age of Anxiety* (1944), the operetta *Candide*, based on VOLTAIRE's story, and another musical *On the Town* (1944). As a conductor, Bernstein has shown himself to be an outstanding interpreter of the music of IVES and COPLAND, and of MAHLER.

Berruguete, Alonso (c. 1489-1561)
Spanish architect and artist who, as court painter to CHARLES V, undertook a number of altars which incorporated painting, carved reliefs and statues in architectural settings. The pre-eminent contemporary Spanish sculptor, Berruguete was the founder of the Mannerist style in Spain.

Berthelot, Pierre (1827-1907)
French chemist who showed that fairly complex organic compounds

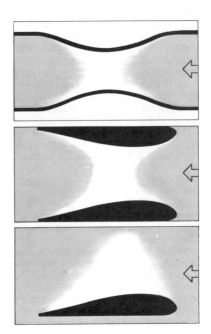

Daniel Bernoulli's *Hydrodynamica* of the 18th century propounded principles which hold good today in explaining the theory of flight. Top, constricted air is speeded up. Centre, pressure drops on the upper surfaces of aerofoils when placed in the stream. Bottom, the same applies to a single aerofoil, producing the lift conditions that give rise to a plane's flight

can be synthesized from simple compounds. In this way, Berthelot disproved the contemporary belief that organic compounds occur only in substances derived from living things. For example, in the mid-1800s, he made benzene and other aromatic hydrocarbons from acetylene.

Berthollet, Claude Louis (1748-1822) French chemist, who established the 'Law of Mass Action', the basis to the control and understanding of chemical reactions. In 1803, he suggested that the readiness with which two substances react together depends on their masses. But it was not until 1863 that another chemist, Guldberg, showed that concentrations (not masses) determine the rate at which substances react.

Bertillon, Alphonse (1853-1914)
French criminologist and pioneer of forensic science, who, despite strong opposition, devised the first scientific system for identification of the individual. Based on the recording of certain measurements of the human body (anthropometry) which taken together distinguish one individual from another, his system was replaced by the fingerprint method of identification by 1914.

Berzelius, Jöns (1779-1848) Swedish chemist who prepared the first accurate lists of atomic weights by analysing compounds. He used oxygen as the standard to which all other weights were referred. His many other contributions to chemistry included work on electrolysis, organic radicals, catalysts and chemical nomenclature and notation.

Bessel, Friedrich (1784-1846) German astronomer and mathematician, who was the founder of modern precision work in observational astronomy. His important work on HALLEY's comet in 1804 led within six years to his appointment as Director of Königsberg Observatory. In 1838, he was the first man to calculate accurately the distance of a star from Earth.

Bessemer, Sir Henry (1813-98) English metallurgist, who pioneered the large-scale manufacture of steel by decarbonizing iron. The underlying principle of his invention, announced in 1856, was that carbon could be removed by blowing air through the molten metal. Bessemer's process, and subsequent improvements by SIEMENS, began the era of cheap steel.

Best, Charles (born 1899) Canadian physiologist who, with F. G. BANTING, discovered insulin treatment for diabetes.

Betancourt, Romulo (born 1908) Venezuelan politician whose opposition to dictatorships in his country led to many years of exile. When the dictator, Jimenez, was overthrown by a popular rising (1958) Betancourt returned, and was elected President (1959).

Betjeman, Sir John (born 1906) English poet who writes with affection of out-of-the-way places, odd views, old Victorian buildings and the little formalities and pretensions of suburban living. His poems show neat observation expressed in clear, witty language, and often have a pleasantly nostalgic tone. In 1972 he was appointed Poet Laureate.

Betti, Ugo (1892-1953) Italian dramatist, who wrote *The Burnt Flowerbed* (1953). His other plays, *Corruption in the Palace of Justice* (1949), *Crime on Goat Island* (1950) and *The Joker* (1951), although performed in Italy, were unknown in Britain and America until after his death.

Bevan, Aneurin (1897-1960) Welsh Labour politician of mining stock and architect of the National Health Service, introduced in 1948 when he was Minister of Health (1945-51). After a brief period as Minister of Labour in 1951, he resigned because of the Health Service charges introduced by GAITSKELL, and thereafter,

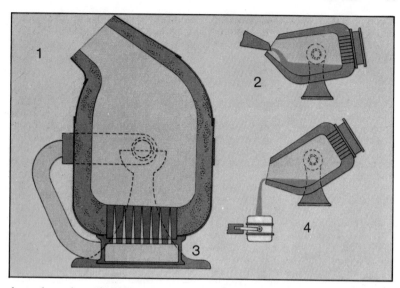

Hinged so as to tilt (1) the Bessemer converter is loaded with molten pig iron (2). Air blasted through vents (3) burns out impurities; after 12 minutes molten steel is poured out (4)

throughout the early 1950s, the rivalry between the two was tense and often bitter. In 1956, however, he reached agreement with Gaitskell and after supporting him in opposition to unilateral nuclear disarmament in 1957, they grew closer together. Bevan was a brilliant, and often colourful and irreverant orator. He became deputy leader of the Labour Party after the election of 1959.

Beveridge, William Henry, 1st Baron Tuggal (1879-1963) English economist and founder of the British 'Welfare State'. An authority on unemployment insurance, he was responsible for much of the thinking behind the sócial legislation introduced by LLOYD GEORGE. Under his directorship (1909-16) labour exchanges were established. In 1941 Beveridge was appointed Chairman of the Committee on Social Insurance and Allied Services. Practically all the major recommendations embodied in the Committee's report, known as the 'Beveridge Report' (1942), were adopted by the 1945 administration.

Bevin, Ernest (1881-1951) English Labour politician and former trade union organizer who rose to be his country's Foreign Secretary. A farm labourer at first, he became a docker and, in 1911, assistant general secretary of the docker's union. By 1921 he had combined about 50 unions into the world's largest, the Transport and General Workers' Union. He became a member of the Trades Union Congress General Council in 1925 and its Chairman in 1937, playing a considerable part in organizing the General Strike of 1926 and in the negotiations which concluded it. An outspoken opponent of Fascism, Bevin was appointed Minister of Labour in CHURCHILL's 1940 Second World War government and Foreign Secretary in ATTLEE's government (1945-51).

A Foreign Minister to be: Ernest Bevin, the young trades union leader (left)

Bewick, Thomas (1753-1828) English engraver, famous for his vignettes of birds and mammals. He specialized in the use of the reverse wood block, engraving white lines on a black background.

Beyle, Henri see STENDHAL

Bhave, Acharya Vinoba (born 1895) Indian philosopher. An ardent disciple and pupil of GANDHI, he founded the *Bhoodan* ('land-gift') and *Sarvadoya* ('welfare for all') movements in 1951 as his answer to the problem of malnutrition and hunger riots. What started as a barefoot mission throughout India to persuade the wealthy to give up their land resulted in the donation to the poor of over five million acres. Bhave is regarded in India as the most notable ascetic and 'saint' since Gandhi.

Bialik, Hayyim (1873-1934) Russian-born Hebrew poet, who was largely responsible for the revival of Hebrew culture in the state of Israel. His poetry deals mainly with his childhood sufferings and inner struggles about tradition, most movingly evoked in the long poem 'The Talmud Student'. Poems he wrote in reaction to the Kishinev pogrom (1903) made him the Hebrew poet of revolt, but equally he condemned the Jews themselves for their inactivity in the face of persecution. In 1924, he settled in Palestine and became the leader of Jewish cultural life there, writing stories, fairy tales and essays.

Bichat, Marie François (1771-1802) French anatomist, pathologist and physiologist, who founded the science of histology (the study of tissues).

Biddle, John (c. 1615-62) English schoolmaster and theologian, called the 'Father of English Unitarianism'. He refuted the deity of the Holy Ghost in a tract known as *Twelve Arguments* (1647), for which he was imprisoned, issued two further tracts on the subject, but was released under surveillance after CHARLES I's death. After the Act of Oblivion (1652) gave him complete freedom, he held Sunday meetings of his followers, who were called Biddellians or Unitarians. Biddle's later attacks on the doctrines of the established Church resulted in more spells in prison, where he ultimately died.

Bierce, Ambrose (1842-c. 1914) American satirist and short story writer who wrote with a sardonic, cynical wit, mixing the graphic descriptive powers of the newspapermen with the gloom of his own nature. His stories from the Civil War, *Tales of Soldiers and Civilians* (1891), are authentic records of the grimness of the conflict. He disappeared on a visit to Mexico, which was in the grip of civil war.

Biffen, Sir Rowland (1874-1949) British agricultural botanist who discovered that yellow rust, a disease of wheat, was caused by an inherited recessive gene. He developed a hybrid strain that did not exhibit the disease and was instrumental in replacing traditional plant-breeding with more scientific methods.

Binet, Alfred (1857-1911) French psychologist who produced an early set of scales for measuring intelligence and educational attainment and who pioneered the use of pictures and inkblots to detect emotions and prejudices. Rejecting the emphasis which his German contemporaries were placing on the study of elementary reactions and sensations, he devised ingenious experiments to test the higher mental processes.

Bingham, Hiram (1875-1956) American explorer-archaeologist whose discovery, in 1911, of the Inca mountain city of Machu Picchu in the Peruvian Andes, helped historians to retell the story of Peru before PIZARRO.

Birdseye, Clarence (1886-1956) American industrialist and inventor who developed a technique for deep-freezing foods. The first Birds Eye commercial pack was placed on the market in 1929. With most foods, the thawed-out items prove to be more palatable, and often more nutritious, than canned foods.

Birkenhead, F. E. Smith, 1st Earl of (1872-1930) English barrister, politician and law reformer, a brilliant orator and wit. In the House of Commons he supported CARSON in opposing Home Rule for Northern Ireland, but as Lord Chancellor (1919-22) negotiated the Irish Treaty (1921). He initiated a major reform and simplification of English land law, which achieved lasting form in the Law of Property Acts of 1922 and 1925 and other statutes.

Birney, Earle (born 1904) Canadian poet and critic, who is known for his vivid descriptions of Canadian life and for generous help and encouragement to other Canadian writers. His first poems, *David*, were published in 1942, and he has since written novels and a famous radio play, *Trial of a City* (1952). Perhaps his best poems deal with the features and the history of the land.

Bismarck, Prince Otto von (1815-98) German statesman and creator of a united, imperial Germany. Bismarck came from a Junker family, an ultra-royalist who favoured a powerful army, a strong Protestant church and the suppression of democracy. He believed in German unity, but only if it could be achieved under Prussian leadership. He served as ambassador to Russia and France (1859-62) and on his return to Prussia was appointed Chancellor. Bismarck concentrated on strengthening the Prussian army, despite parliamentary opposition, and turned his attention to making Prussia the dominant force in Europe. His ambitions were realized in the successful war against Denmark (1864) and in the Austro-Prussian and Franco-Prussian wars (1866 and 1870). He became Chancellor of Germany when the Empire was proclaimed in 1871, was created a prince and for the next nineteen years dominated European diplomacy. In domestic policy the codification of the law, nationalization of the railways and a continuing emphasis on military efficiency were means by which Bismarck reinforced the German state. After the accession of the youthful WILLIAM II (1888), Bismarck's régime was challenged by the new expansionist Pan-German movement and he was dismissed by the Kaiser in 1890.

Bizet, Georges (1838-75) French composer who wrote the opera *Carmen* (1875), based on a story of romantic passion and death in Spain by MERIMÉE. All his life he strove for recognition as a composer of opera, and in addition to *Carmen* wrote *The Pearl Fishers* (1863) and *The Fair Maid of Perth* (1866). But apart from

Tête-à-tête with Churchill in a railway carriage, Birkenhead leans forward. A leading advocate and orator of his times, Birkenhead was, with his fellow lawyer Carson, one of the architects of the partition of Ireland into a loyalist north and a southern free state

Carmen, almost his only music remembered today is the two orchestral suites based on incidental music to DAUDET's *L'Arlésienne* and the early *Symphony in C*.

Bjerknes, Vilhelm (1862-1951) Norwegian physicist and meteorologist who, with his son Jakob (born 1897), developed weather forecasting based on the concepts of air masses and polar fronts. In 1897, he discovered the circulation theorems which led to the development of physical hydrodynamics. This, in turn, made possible the scientific study of wind and water movements on a global scale. After the First World War they showed that cyclonic depressions (which largely determine weather in middle latitudes) are made up of two air masses: one warm and moist (from the tropics), and the other cold and dry (from the polar regions). The two are separated by a sloping interface which they called a polar front – a zone of fast-changing weather conditions.

Bjørnson, Bjørnstjerne (1832-1910) Norwegian dramatist, novelist, poet and orator, whose comedy *The Newly Married Couple* (1865) and the historical play *Mary Stuart in Scotland* (1864) are regarded as landmarks in Norwegian drama.

Black, Joseph (1728-99) Scottish chemist and physicist who originated the ideas of specific and latent heat. In the 1760s, he found that as ice is heated, it melts with no immediate temperature rise. He explained this by introducing the concept of latent heat, the heat absorbed by a substance changing state, such as from solid to liquid, without a temperature rise.

Blackstone, Sir William (1723-80) English jurist whose *Commentaries on the Laws of England* (1765-9) are the most influential work in the later development of the common law in England and America. The four volumes concern the rights of persons, the rights of things, public wrongs and private wrongs. Although oversimplified and antiquarian, his work was a law book both comprehensible to the layman and of exceptional authority to the lawyer. He was the first professor of law at Oxford (1758), a Member of Parliament and a Judge of the Court of Common Pleas (1770).

Blackwell, Elizabeth (1821-1910) American physician, the first woman to qualify as a doctor of medicine. In the face of tremendous opposition, she finally gained admission to Geneva Medical School, New York, where she was ostracized by her fellow students and the public. She gradu-

ated in 1849 at the head of her class, but the loss of an eye forced her to abandon her ambition of becoming a surgeon, and she established a hospital run entirely by women in New York in 1857.

Blackwood, Algernon (1869-1951) English novelist and short story writer, most widely known for his tales of the supernatural, beginning with his first collection *The Empty House* (1906), which was followed by others in the same genre. Later, Blackwood turned to the short story, published in collections such as *The Dance of Death* (1927) and *Tales of the Supernatural* (1949).

Blair, Eric see ORWELL, George

Blake, Robert (1599-1657) English admiral and general outstandingly successful against four separate enemies. In the English Civil War, Blake destroyed RUPERT's Royalist squadron off Spain (1650) and captured 17 treasure ships of the Portuguese, who had sheltered Rupert. During the Dutch War (1652-3) he repeatedly clashed with Dutch fleets and ended their naval supremacy. In 1654 he scoured the Mediterranean exacting from North African pirate states reparations for damage done to British merchants and severely damaged Tunis for resisting. During the Spanish War he sank a Spanish treasure fleet in the strongly defended harbour of Santa Cruz (Tenerife). Meanwhile he did much to improve English naval tactics and discipline.

Blake, William (1757-1827) English artist, engraver and poet of the Romantic movement who, using his own process of engraving from etched copper plates, which he called 'illuminated printing', produced volumes of his own verse, illustrated and coloured by hand. In 1789 he published *Songs of Innocence* and in 1794 *Songs of Experience*, among the best known of his lyrical poems. In 1793 he wrote *The Marriage of Heaven and Hell*, a prose work, heavy with mysticism and etched with symbolic and mythological designs. He is most famous for his brilliant series of original illustrations of the Book of Job (1825), and, at the time of his death, was working on a set of engravings to illustrate DANTE. Almost unrecognized in his own day, Blake's poetry later influenced RUSKIN and the Pre-Raphaelites. As an artist, he achieved recognition only towards the end of his life, though he is now remembered for his engravings rather than for his poetry.

Blanc, Jean Charles Louis (1811-82) French socialist, writer and politician, and publisher of *L'Organisa-*

tion du Travail (1840), in which he denounced the capitalist principle of competitive industry and proposed both a theory of equal wages and a system of state-subsidized workshops. His *L'Histoire de Dix Ans*, was a criticism of the régime of LOUIS PHILLIPE and contributed to the unrest which led to the Revolution of 1848. In that year he became a member of the Provisional Government and headed an industrial commission to consider the problem of unemployment. His idea of 'National Workshops' was unpractical in the turmoil of the revolutionary situation, and he was forced to flee to England after the left wing of the Revolution was suppressed in June 1848. He did not return to France until 1871.

Blanchard, Jean Pierre (1753-1809) French pioneer balloonist who in 1784, with the American aeronaut John Jeffries, became the first to measure air temperatures from a manned balloon. In this way, he extended the meteorological experiments of Alexander WILSON and anticipated those of HERMITE. In 1785 Blanchard and Jeffries made the first air crossing of the English Channel (Dover–Calais) and delivered the first international airmail consignment. Blanchard's other aeronautical 'firsts' included the first parachute drop (of a cat or a dog) from a balloon in 1785, and the first balloon ascents in England (1784) and America (1793).

Blanqui, Louis August (1805-81) French socialist who took part in the French Revolution of 1830. After attempting insurrection in 1839 Blanqui suffered numerous terms of imprisonment. Having served a ten-year sentence imposed by the Provisional Government after the Revolution of 1848 on a fabricated charge of treason, he led the working class and socialist Central Republican Party and formulated his ideas about socialism and the dictatorship of the proletariat as the only means of achieving Communism. Blanqui was active in the downfall of NAPOLEON III and inspired the leaders of the Paris Commune in 1871, though he himself was kept in custody.

Blasco Ibañez, Vicente (1867-1928) Spanish naturalist writer and republican politician, author of *Blood and Sand* (1908) and *The Four Horsemen of the Apocalypse* (1916).

Blavatsky, Helena (1831-91) Russian spiritualist, founder of Theosopy (a mystical philosophy loosely based on Indian religious thought) and co-founder, with Colonel Henry Olcott, of the Theosophical Society, in 1875. Madame Blavatsky claimed

A thousand years of insularity ended for England with the flight of Bleriot. Top, his 'plane crash-landed at Dover: below Bleriot (right) with another intrepid French birdman, Pegoud

direct access to 'divine truth' by psychic communication with invisible Indian 'masters' and outlined her revelations in two popular textbooks of the occult: *Isis Unveiled* (1877) and *The Secret Doctrine* (1888).

Blaxland, Gregory (1778-1853) English-born pioneer in Australia who (with William Lawson and William Wentworth) first crossed the Blue Mountains of New South Wales. In 1810 he explored up the Warragamba River and three years later crossed the many gorges of the Blue Mountains, discovering Mount Blaxland and the Bathurst Plains.

Blériot, Louis (1872-1936) French aircraft designer and aviator who, in 1909, became the first man to fly across the English Channel. The flight from Calais to Dover took 37 minutes. As a designer Blériot was responsible for a number of design innovations, including a system by which the pilot could operate elevators and ailerons by remote control.

Bligh, William (1754-1817) British naval officer, captain of the mutinous crew of the 220-ton *Bounty*. As Captain COOK's master, Bligh discovered breadfruit on Tahiti and his voyage in the *Bounty* was to introduce breadfruit trees to the West Indies. His crew, led by the mate, Fletcher CHRISTIAN, were disenchanted with his leadership and sought to end the voyage and settle on a Pacific island with their Tahitian mistresses. They seized the ship near the Friendly Islands and cast Bligh adrift with 18 sailors in the open longboat. After a 45-day voyage of 4000 miles, Bligh reached Timor in Indonesia. A master seaman and navigator, Bligh later distinguished himself at the Battles of Camperdown and Copenhagen.

Bliss, Sir Arthur (born 1891) English composer, once regarded as an *enfant terrible*, who reached the peak of the English musical establishment by becoming Master of the Queen's Musick (1953). Bliss developed an early reputation for unorthodox combinations of instruments, but a strong sense of pageantry revealed itself in his *Colour Symphony* (1922). His choral symphony *Morning Heroes* was performed in 1930, and in 1935 he wrote the score for the film *Things to Come*. His ballet scores include *Checkmate* and *Miracle in the Gorbals*.

Bloch, Ernst (1880-1959) Swiss-born American composer. His finest compositions *Piano Quintet* (1923) and the second two of his four string quartets rank among the most distinguished 20th-century chamber works. Bloch's Jewish ancestry was acknowledged in his best-known works, which include a rhapsody for cello and orchestra, *Schelomo* (1916), and the *Sacred Service* (1933) for baritone, chorus and orchestra for the Jewish Sabbath morning service.

Blok, Aleksandr Aleksandrovich (1880-1921) Russian poet whose poem 'The Twelve' (1918) is a mystical, Symbolist story of twelve Red Guardsmen, analogous to the Apostles, and an apologia for the Bolshevik

Revolution. Blok was the outstanding poet of the Symbolist school who felt that his poetry could be understood only by those who were in sympathy with his mystical experience. His best work was written between 1908 and 1916 and is contained in the third volume of his collected poems *Verses about Russia*.

Blondin, Charles (1824-97) French equilibrist, who became the world's most famous tightrope walker for his crossing of Niagara Falls in 1859. He repeated this feat many times, with startling variations: crossing blindfolded, on stilts, in a sack, pushing a wheelbarrow, carrying a man, and even stopping to cook and eat an omelette.

Blood, Col. Thomas (c. 1618-80) Irish adventurer who, in 1671, planned and carried out the theft of the Crown Jewels from the Tower of London. Arrested while trying to escape, he was imprisoned in the Tower, though later pardoned by King CHARLES II.

Bloomer, Amelia (1818-94) American women's rights campaigner. She founded and edited the *Lily*, the first American magazine for women, and wrote articles on education, unjust marriage laws and female suffrage. As part of her campaign for the emancipation of women she popularized the full trousers which became known as 'bloomers'.

Bloomfield, Leonard (1887-1949) American linguistics scholar and author of *Language* (1933), which has exercised an important influence on the American approach to linguistics. Bloomfield was one of the Structuralist school of linguistic theorists, using the strictly scientific approach which is now considered his main contribution to linguistics.

Blücher, Gebhard von (1742-1819) Prussian field-marshal who acted as commander-in-chief in the final stages of the Napoleonic wars. He commanded the army of the Lower Rhine and after NAPOLEON's return from Elba, was wounded and defeated at Ligny two days before Waterloo (1815). Nevertheless, he succeeded in joining forces with WELLINGTON, and ensured the defeat of the French armies.

Blum, Léon (1872-1950) French politician and socialist leader in the inter-war years. The DREYFUS affair (1898-9) helped to form his socialist convictions and brought him into contact with JAURÈS, whose disciple he became. He became Prime Minister when, in 1936, the Popular Front government of Left and Centre parties, opposed to Fascism, took office. His economic policy was based on the Keynesian idea of invigorating the economy by stimulating purchasing power, but inflation and financial crises prevented its application. His government was sabotaged by pro-Fascist industrial and financial interests, and his resignation was forced, but he was again Prime Minister for a short time in 1938. In 1942 he was tried at Riom by the Vichy government of PÉTAIN, charged with being responsible for France's military unpreparedness, but defended himself so ably that he fixed the responsibility for that failure on his accusers. Blum was interned in Germany until 1945, but on his release became head of France's brief caretaker government of 1946-7.

Blunden, Edmund (born 1896) English poet whose best work has been his sad, pitying reflections on his experiences in the First World War, yet drawing strength from a love of nature. *Poems 1914–30* and the prose work *Undertones of War* (1928) are moving recollections of that time. He admired poets like HARDY and John CLARE, whose works he edited.

Boadicea (1st cent. AD) British queen of the Iceni tribe who rebelled against the Romans after they had seized the lands of her late husband, Prasutagus, King of the Iceni. All East Anglia, and southeastern Britain rose under Boadicea while the Roman governor Paulinus was in Wales. TACITUS said that Boadicea burnt Roman Colchester and St Albans, killing 70,000 Romans and British collaborators before Paulinus annihilated her army near Fenny Stratford. Boadicea either died of shock or poisoned herself, but her revolt supposedly persuaded NERO to ease conditions for the British. Her statue at the reins of her chariot, looks across Westminster Bridge towards the Houses of Parliament in London.

Queen Boadicea led the Iceni of eastern England in revolt against the Romans

Boas, Franz (1858-1942) American anthropologist and pioneer of American-Indian studies, whose *Changes in Bodily Form in Descendants of Immigrants* (1911) demonstrates that cranial proportions previously considered as a racial characteristic, adapt according to environment. His *Handbook of American-Indian Languages* (1911) marks the start of structuralist linguistics, by proposing that a specific language should be studied according to its particular structure, rather than as part of the Indo-European language system.

Bobadilla, Francisco de (15th-16th cent.) Spanish soldier, who succeeded COLUMBUS as Viceroy of the Indies in 1499. He imprisoned Columbus in 1500, but exceeded his instructions in sending the explorer to Spain in irons. Bobadilla had earlier acquired a military reputation when fighting against the Moors of Spain and in the siege of Granada (1492). Recalled under arrest to Spain, he perished on the voyage from the Indies.

Boccaccio, Giovanni (1313-75) Italian writer and poet, whose *Il Decameron* is one of the world's acknowledged masterpieces. Its episodes, which are short and dynamic, range from bawdy farce to tragedy. Boccaccio studied commerce and law at Naples, where he mixed with courtiers and poets and perhaps met Fiammetta, a woman whom he immortalized in his writings. He met PETRARCH in 1350, while he was working on the *Decameron*, and the two remained friends until the latter's death in 1374. Other works of Boccaccio include a study of DANTE and the Latin treatises which first established his reputation.

Boccherini, Luigi (1743-1805) Italian cellist and composer who holds an important place in the development of chamber music. A relatively lightweight talent beside his contemporaries HAYDN and MOZART, Boccherini concentrated mainly on the 102 string quartets and the 125 string quintets, a form he virtually invented and which makes up the major part of his considerable output of chamber works. He also wrote 20 charming, if slight, symphonies, and a *Stabat Mater*.

Boccioni, Umberto (1882-1916) Italian sculptor and co-founder (1910) of the Italian Futurist movement, the aims of which were a break with the past and the embodiment in art of the speed and dynamism of the 20th century. In his sculpture, wire, glass, cardboard and wood express the energy beneath the surface of volume and the actual motion of an object in its environment.

Böcklin, Arnold (1827-1901) Swiss portrait and landscape artist whose paintings reflect the preoccupation with death of the late Romantics and Symbolists. His best-known work is *The Island of Death*.

Bode, Johann (1747-1826) German astronomer, who published a mathematical relation to express the distances of the planets from the Sun (Bode's Law), a formula first suggested in 1772 by J. D. Titius.

Bodley, Sir Thomas (1545-1613) English diplomat in Denmark, France and the United Provinces (1585-96), who refounded the library (begun by Cobham and Humphrey, Duke of Gloucester) at Oxford University, now world famous as the Bodleian Library.

Bodoni, Giambattista (1740-1813) Italian printer and outstanding typographer. The son of a printer, he became a compositor and later the head of the Duke of Parma's printing house. He issued editions of the Greek, Latin, French and Italian classics, which became famous for their typography.

Boehm, Theobald (1794-1881) German jeweller, inventor and flautist who developed the 'Boehm system' of finger control for the flute. This was a radical innovation which extended the flute's range and remains in use today. The principle was applied, less successfully, to clarinet, oboe and bassoon.

Boehme, Jakob (1575-1624) German mystic who contended that insight is obtained by direct divine revelation. His speculations had considerable influence on non-conformist sects and on later existentialist thinkers like KIERKEGAARD.

Boerhaave, Hermann (1668-1738) Dutch physician who introduced bedside teaching in medical schools.

Boethius (480-524) Roman philosopher and statesman who held high office under THEODORIC but was imprisoned for conspiracy in 522. Awaiting his execution, he wrote *On the Consolations of Philosophy*, a poetic work extolling stoicism, Neoplatonism and self-knowledge.

Bogart, Humphrey (1899-1957) American stage and screen actor who established himself in hoodlum roles in gangster movies of the 1930s, beginning with *The Petrified Forest* (1936). He later matured into a fine dramatic actor in some of the best films of the period, including *The Maltese Falcon* (1941), *Casablanca* (1942) and *To Have and Have Not*

Bogart made his name in the gangster movies of the 1930s. Later, he starred in some of Hollywood's greatest films

(1944), in which he first starred with Lauren Bacall, whom he subsequently married. Bogart's talent for comedy was rewarded by an Oscar for the Best Actor for his performance in *The African Queen* (1954).

Böhm-Bawerk, Eugen von (1851-1914) Austrian economist, Minister of Finance, and critic of MARX. In his *Capital and Interest* (1884-9) and *Positive Theory of Capital* (1891) he used the marginal utility theory of value, the satisfaction yielded by the last increment of consumption, to develop his theory of interest as the measure of individual preference for goods at the present as against at some future time. He stressed also that the employment of capital increases the 'roundaboutness' of production, and although this process is eventually subject to diminishing returns with respect to time, the end product is of better quality.

Bohr, Niels (1885-1962) Danish physicist who devised a new model of the atom which effectively combined the RUTHERFORD model of the atom with PLANCK's quantum theory of radiation. The model was able to account for the known patterns of atomic radiation as seen in spectra. The theory led to later systems of quantum mechanics which start from more general principles and correct certain limitations of Bohr's model. Bohr was awarded the 1922 Nobel Prize for Physics.

Boiardo, Matteo Maria (1441-94) Italian lyric poet, who, in the *Orlando Innamorato* created the Italian Romantic epic. The first poem to combine the Arthurian and Carolingian traditions of romance, it was the point of departure for ARIOSTO's *Orlando Furioso*. Early in life, Boiardo became a favourite at the court of Ferrara,

acting as diplomat and administrator. In 1469 he went to Reggio, where he fell in love with Antonia Caprera, who inspired his *Canzoniere*.

Boileau-Despréaux, Nicolas (1636-1711) French poet, satirist and critic whose work *L'Art poétique* (1674) laid down the principles of classical French literature. Regarded as one of the doyens of French literary criticism, Boileau was the author of a number of satires on contemporary literature (1666-8) and also published a translation of LONGINUS, as well as other works of criticism and a mock epic, *Le Lutrin*. In 1669, he received a pension from LOUIS XIV and eventually became, with RACINE, a royal historian. It is perhaps for his biting epigrams and sayings that Boileau is best remembered.

Boldrewood, Rolf (1826-1915) Pen name of T. A. Browne, Australian novelist, born in London, who was one of the first writers to give an authentic picture of pioneering life in Australia. *Robbery Under Arms* (1888) is the story of a bushranger, Captain Starlight. Boldrewood's appreciation of life in the wilds, and his intimate knowledge of squatters and miners (he was magistrate and commissioner of goldfields), appeared also in *The Squatter's Dream* and *The Miner's Right* (both 1890).

Boleslav I (11th cent.) First King of Poland (effectively 992-1025), called 'Chrobry' (the Mighty), who built his principality into a great power reach-

ing from the Bug to the Elbe and from the Baltic to the Carpathians. Boleslav founded a national administrative system, established an independent Polish Church and built a strong army. He was able to expand his territories largely at the expense of the Holy Roman Emperor Otto III, seizing eastern Pomerania, by which he gained a seaboard along the Baltic; taking Cracow, Moravia, and Silesia and gaining Lusatia and Bohemia. Three wars against Otto's successor, Henry II, during which Poland lost some large western gains, ended with the peace of Bautzen (1018), by which Poland kept Lusatia. In the same year Boleslav took Kiev (1018) and won overlordship of Russia. He was officially crowned King of Poland only in the year of his death.

Boleyn, Anne see HENRY VIII

Bolívar, Simón (1783-1830) Venezuelan revolutionary leader, who liberated much of South America from Spanish rule. Bolívar travelled in Europe, where he became influenced by the ideas of John LOCKE and the philosophers of the 18th-century French Enlightenment. His early attempts at revolt ended when, after hard fighting, he was driven out of Venezuela and Colombia (1815) by the royalist forces, and fled to exile in Jamaica. He returned in 1818 with British volunteers, raised an army, crossed the Andes and established the independence of Colombia and later Venezuela. In 1822 he liberated Ecuador and took over command of

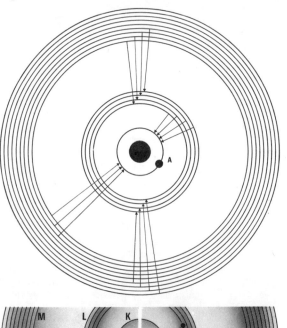

Bohr's atom resembles a miniature solar system with a central nucleus and planetary electrons. Right, Bohr's model of the hydrogen atom. It has one electron (A), the fundamental unit of negative electricity circling the nucleus, which bears one unit of positive electricity. It must move in one of several well-defined orbits or energy-levels, known, in order of distance from the nucleus, as the K-shell, L-shell and so on. When the electron moves from one energy level to another, it emits or absorbs radiation. If the jump is inward, energy is emitted; if the jump is outward, energy is absorbed.

the Peruvian army from San Martín. With his army, Bolívar conquered and liberated the territory now called Bolivia (1825). His overall plan for his country was that of a republican confederation, but he came up against the narrow-minded regionalism of his fellow countrymen. Betrayed by the separatism of his own lieutenants Bolívar died a disappointed man.

Böll, Heinrich (born 1917) German novelist and story writer, author of *Group Portrait with Lady* (1971) in which an imaginary author builds up a portrait of a woman through interviews with people who knew her. The novel is remarkable for its often satirical mini-biographies of Böll's contemporaries from the inter-war years to the 1970s. Böll's early writings were concerned with the problems of those involved in war and its aftermath, among which *Acquainted with the Night* (1953) is outstanding as an exposé of Germany's post-war 'economic miracle'. *Traveller, if you come to Spâ* (1950), a collection of stories, is one of his major achievements. Böll was awarded the Nobel Prize for Literature in 1972.

Bollstädt, Count Albert von see ALBERTUS MAGNUS

Bologna, Giovanni (c. 1529-1608) Flemish-born sculptor who worked in Florence, and was the prime exponent of the Mannerist style. His works were designed to be seen from a variety of viewpoints. Among the best known are his *Rape of a Sabine* (completed 1583), and, in Florence, *Venus of the Groticella* (c. 1575-6), the bronze *Flying Mercury* (1564) and the equestrian statue of Cosimo I (1587), set on a low plinth in the new style inaugurated by MICHELANGELO. His *Apennine* (1580-2) in Pratrolino, a giant 30-feet high representing the River Nile, came to be regarded as the eighth wonder of the world.

Bolyai, János (1802-60) Hungarian mathematician, who was one of the pioneers of non-Euclidian geometry. He showed that a consistent system (that is, one not leading to internal contradictions) could be set up without EUCLID's postulate of parallels, which states that only one parallel to a given line can be drawn through a point. His work was published in 1831, and duplicated ideas of GAUSS and LOBACHEVSKY.

Bondfield, Margaret Grace (1873-1953) First woman cabinet minister in Britain. She became a trade union official and Chairman of the General Council of the Trades Union Congress in 1923, and the first woman to hold cabinet office when appointed Minister of Labour (1929-

31) by Ramsay MACDONALD. She was attacked by the left wing of the Labour Party as she had opposed the General Strike of 1926, and in 1927 had supported the lowering of unemployment insurance benefits.

Bonhoeffer, Dietrich (1906-45) German Protestant theologian who saw his own role as that of uniting Christians and non-Christians and establishing a 'church of the world', for which traditional theology and the established church are superfluous. Bonhoeffer's non-religious interpretation of the Gospels, and his attempts to free Christianity of metaphysics and the supernatural, have guided the churches in the Communist bloc and provoked much radical thinking. His critics claim, however, that what he is advocating is not Christianity at all, but simply social involvement. An active member of the anti-Nazi resistance movement in Germany, Bonhoeffer was killed by the Gestapo in a concentration camp.

Boniface (c. 680-755) English saint, and evangelizer of the Germans. Author of the first Latin grammar written in English, he lived as a monk in England until he was 40 and was created first Bishop of Mainz and then Archbishop of Western Germany. After reorganizing the West German and Frankish Churches he set out in his 70th year to evangelize the Frieslanders, but was killed by them near Dokkum in Holland.

Bonington, Richard P. (c. 1802-28) British watercolour painter, whose technique and use of colour derived from a study of the Venetians and was much influenced by DELACROIX.

Bonnard, Pierre (1867-1947) French painter in the *intimisme* manner, a recorder of quiet interiors and bourgeois domesticity, expressed in muted tones. He also worked as a designer for the state, as an illustrator and a poster artist. After 1900 his palette brightened, though in landscape he did not seek an Impressionist's truth to natural effects, but truth to a poetic 'idea' in accordance with which the painter might modify nature.

Bonner, Neville (born 1918) The first Australian aboriginal MP.

Bonney, William H. (1859-81) American outlaw who, as Billy the Kid, became one of the most infamous gunmen of the American southwest – ranking in Wild West history with figures like Jesse JAMES and Sam Bass. Caught in 1880, and sentenced to be hanged for three murders, he escaped from gaol in 1881

after killing two deputies, but was tracked down and shot by the Lincoln County sheriff, Pat Garrett.

Bonnie Prince Charlie see STUART, Charles Edward

Boole, Georgè (1815-64) English mathematician and logician who developed an algebra of logic which allowed a variety of logical problems to be dealt with as algebraic operations. Of humble origin, Boole was appointed Professor of Mathematics at Cork University at the age of 34.

Boone, Daniel (1734-1820) American frontiersman and folk hero. As a hunter and trapper, he gained unique knowledge of the largely unexplored Kentucky region after crossing the Appalachians from the settled seaboard colonies. In 1769 he was engaged to explore the country beyond the mountains, carve a road through the Cumberland Gap, and escort settlers to three projected settlements. He did this, showing great enterprise and courage in his struggles with the Indians. He established fortified border-posts (one of which is now Boonesboro), and effectively began the colonization of Kentucky.

Booth, Charles (1840-1916) English social reformer, who introduced new and improved standards of statistical measurement in *Life and Labour of the People in London* (1891-1903). This book, which contains a series of coloured maps showing income levels street by street, demonstrates the relationship between poverty and depravity on the one hand, and between economic security and decent standards of living on the other. He was a member of the Royal Commission on the Poor Law (1905-9), and published his ideas on poverty among the old in *Poor Law Reform* (1910).

Booth, Edwin (1833-93) American actor and founder of the New York Players Club. His actor brother, John Wilkes BOOTH, assassinated LINCOLN.

Booth, John Wilkes (1838-65) American actor and assassin of Abraham LINCOLN. Booth was a Confederate sympathizer with an insatiable thirst for notoriety and shot President Lincoln at Ford's Theatre, Washington, during a performance on 14 Apr. 1865. He escaped to Virginia but was pursued and died, possibly by his own hand, while resisting arrest. The theory that Booth was implicated in a wider conspiracy has not been proved.

Booth, William (1829-1912) British religious leader, founder of the Salvation Army. His early contact with poverty as a pawnbroker's assistant aroused a passion for social justice, which he allied to a strong evangelical faith. As a Methodist preacher in London, he attracted a large following, which he organized into a Christian Mission for saving souls and relieving distress. In 1878 the movement was reorganized on military lines as the Salvation Army. Recognition and support for General Booth's crusade came with the publication of *In Darkest England and the Way Out* (1890).

Bopp, Franz (1791-1867) German philologist, the first to attempt the scientific comparison of the grammars of the Indo-European languages.

Borchert, Wolfgang (1921-47) German short story writer, dramatist and poet whose work is a condemnation of war. He used his experiences in the Second World War to produce plays of intense realism, one of which was *The Man Outside* (1947).

Bordet, Jules (1870-1961) Belgian bacteriologist who discovered that the serum of an animal immunized against a disease could be used to ascertain its presence in other animals. He was awarded a Nobel Prize for Medicine in 1919.

Borelli, Giovanni (1608-79) Italian mathematician, astronomer and biologist who first explained the action of muscles in mechanical terms. His theories of muscles and bones acting as systems of levers and pulleys were substantially correct.

Borges, Jorge Luis (born 1899) Argentinian poet, essayist and novelist, who invented the *ficción* (fiction), an extended analogy of a metaphysical theme which, when applied to everyday experience, can lead to nightmarish conclusions, as in the works of POE and KAFKA. A selection of his works was published in English in 1962 under the title *Labyrinths*.

Borgia, Cesare (c. 1475-1507) Son of Pope Alexander VI and his clever, unscrupulous chief tool for building BORGIA fortunes in Italy. Cesare, a cardinal at 17, enlarged his personal power by reputedly murdering his elder brother; seizing and terrorizing central Italy; attempting to loosen the Spanish hold on Naples by contriving the murder of the King of Aragon's nephew (Cesare's own brother-in-law); and murdering members of Italy's powerful, rebellious ORSINI family. Imprisoned by his enemies after Alexander's death, Cesare escaped, but died fighting in Navarre. His deeds won the admiration of MACHIAVELLI, who falsely portrayed Cesare's selfish schemes as far-sighted plans for uniting Italy.

Borgia, Lucrezia (1480-1519) Italian aristocrat, popularly renowned as a scheming poisoner, but in reality the victim of her father, Pope Alexander VI, and brother, Cesare BORGIA, who had her make four political marriages: first by proxy to the Spanish Count of Aversa (annulled by her father); secondly to Giovanni SFORZA (also annulled by her father); thirdly to Alfonso of Aragon, Duke of Bisceglie (ended by Alfonso's murder, arranged by Cesare); and finally, when she was 22, to Alfonso of Este, later Duke of Ferrara. After Alexander's death, Lucrezia helped to make Ferrara a centre for Renaissance artists and writers, including TITIAN and ARIOSTO.

Boris I (10th cent.) King of Bulgaria, who established his country's national language and religion. He became a Christian probably from political motives and made Eastern Orthodoxy Bulgaria's state faith, using force where necessary. By favouring a Slavonic Church Liturgy (pioneered by CYRIL and Methodius), he helped to establish Slavonic as Bulgaria's official tongue. Boris retired to a monastery in 889 but emerged to blind and depose his incompetent successor – his eldest son, Vladimir.

Borodin, Aleksandr (1833-87) Distinguished Russian professor of chemistry who, in his spare time, became one of the influential group of Russian composers known as 'The Five'. His work ranged from the attractive symphonic poem, *In the Steppes of Central Asia* (1880), to one of the finest of Russian operas, *Prince Igor* (1890, completed posthumously by RIMSKY-KORSAKOV and Glazunov). His important *Second Symphony*, with its atmosphere of medieval pageantry, was made up of material prepared for the opera.

Borovský, Havel see HAVLIČEK, Karel

Borromini, Francesco (1599-1667) The chief exponent of the Baroque in Italian architecture. His first Roman work, S Carlo alle Quattro Fontane (1634-44), has an elliptical rather than a circular ground plan and a honeycomb dome. Borromini achieved an illusion of movement by a clever placing of concave and convex curves. His architectural style was too personal to be immediately popular with his own contemporaries, and he was dismissed in the middle of his work on Sta Agnese in the Piazza Navona, although his designs were used in the construction of the façade. His final work, the Collegio di Propaganda Fide, is uncompromisingly austere.

Borrow, George (1803-81) English writer of robust, original works notable for their sympathetic portraits of the nomadic gypsy life. Borrow lived as a wandering journalist and, as an agent for the Bible Society in Russia and Spain, he gathered the material for *The Gypsies of Spain* (1841) and *The Bible in Spain* (1843). *Lavengro* (1851) and *The Romany Rye* (1857), born out of his dislike for Anglo-Catholicism and his interest in gypsies, mix biography, adventure and erudition.

Boru, Brian see BRIAN BORU

Bosch, Hieronymus (c. 1450-1516) Netherlandish painter, whose inventive fantasies, although no longer fully understood, are still regarded with deep interest. Many of his paintings are religious allegories on the theme of man's sinfulness, the best known often depicting nightmarish hell scenes or landscapes with fantastic creatures, as in the *Garden of Delights* (c. 1510). Bosch's work, which may be said to anticipate that of BRUEGEL, was immensely popular in the 16th century and often copied.

Bosch, Karl (1874-1940) German chemical engineer and industrialist. Until the early part of the 20th century the main sources of nitrogenous chemical fertilizer were the Chilean nitrate deposits and ammonium sulphate, a coal by-product. As these could be limited in supply, scientific effort was directed to the fixation of nitrogen, which constitutes 80 per cent of the atmosphere. Bosch, working for the German chemical company, BASF, successfully developed HABER's process to an industrial scale. By 1930 two and a half million tons a year of synthetic nitrogen was being produced, principally as fertilizer. Haber was awarded the Nobel Prize for Chemistry in 1919; Bosch in 1931.

Bose, Subhas Chandra (1897-1945) Indian nationalist who supported the Japanese in the Second World War. Originally a supporter of GANDHI's civil disobedience policy, he spent three years in Europe (1933-6), during which time he moved to a more extreme position, advocating a form of totalitarian militancy in order to secure India's independence. Making the most of Britain's precarious position in the early years of the Second World War, he went to Berlin in 1941 to persuade HITLER publicly to announce his support for India's independence. In this he failed, but in 1943 formed a Provisional Government of Free India and a Japanese-supported Indian National Army. A sincere nationalist, he was unsuccessful in shaking

Two examples of allegories: above, the nightmarish work of Bosch; below, the gentle grace of Botticelli

Africa (1910-19). An opponent of both KRUGER and of war with Britain, he nevertheless joined his country-men on the outbreak of the Boer War and eventually became commander-in-chief of the Boer force at Lady-smith (1900) and defeated the British at Colenso. During his premiership Botha followed a policy of economic expansion and racial harmony. His support of Britain and the Allies in the First World War alienated HERT-ZOG, and he had to crush a rebellion against this policy before beginning the campaign which ended in the conquest of German South West Africa (1915).

Botta, Paul Emile (1802-70) French pioneer of archaeological ex-cavation in Mesopotamia. At Khor-sabad, he found the remains of a huge Assyrian palace built by Sargon II (721-705 BC), providing evidence of a civilization hinted at in the Bible.

Bottger, Johann Friedrich (1682-1719) German alchemist to AUGUSTUS II, and the first European to redis-cover (1710) the method of making true hard porcelain, then only known from oriental samples. In 1710, Augustus established the famous porcelain works at Meissen, near Dresden. The manufacturing pro-cesses, involving the fusion of kaolin (china clay) with calcareous (and later felspathic) flux at 1300-1400°C, were closely guarded secrets. Dres-den-ware remained supreme until 1768, when kaolin was also used to produce hard porcelain at Sèvres.

Botticelli, Sandro (c. 1445-1510) Florentine painter, who was a favour-ite artist of the MEDICI circle. His celebrated mythological pictures painted for a member of the Medici family (e.g. *The Birth of Venus*, *c.* 1478-86) are characterized by deli-cate colouring, shallow modelling of the human form, and an emphasis, derived from the work of POLLAIUOLO, on outline. *The Birth of Venus*, which reveals Botticelli's preoccupation with antiquity, includes the first monumental image of a naked god-dess that had been seen since Roman times. The picture has, nevertheless, a quasi-religious meaning. In his later years Botticelli became a follower of the religious reformer SAVONAROLA, and his religious paintings reverted to an archaic style which is often in-tensely emotional. Botticelli pro-duced a complete set of drawings illustrating DANTE's *Divine Comedy* which are remarkable for their sensi-tivity of line and their gentle grace.

Gandhi's ascendancy over India and in imposing a more militant pro-gramme on Congress.

Bossuet, Jacques-Bénigne (1627-1704) French theologian and moral-ist, renowned for his pulpit oratory, particularly his *Oraisons funèbres*. His *Discours sur l'histoire universelle* (1681), an educational work written for the Dauphin (whose tutor he was at the time) is regarded as the first attempt at a philosophy of history.

Boswell, James (1740-95) Scottish lawyer, biographer and man of letters, who wrote *The Life of Samuel Johnson* (1791), one of the world's outstanding biographies. Boswell first met JOHN-SON in 1763 and saw him at intervals for the next 20 years. At Johnson's death (1784) he began to work on the

Life with indefatigable energy, and keen, minute observations of the character of his subject. Boswell was also a highly individual diarist and memoir writer; some of his indiscreet and amusing papers, such as his *Lon-don Journal*, and his travels in Europe, have been rescued from obscurity by 20th-century scholarship.

Botev, Khristo (1848-76) Bul-garian poet and revolutionary, whose 20 surviving poems show a true lyric genius and profound patriotic senti-ment. He devoted his life to the fight to liberate Bulgaria from the Turks and was killed by them after invading occupied Bulgaria with 200 men.

Botha, Louis (1862-1919) South African soldier and statesman and first Premier of the Union of South

Bottomley, Horatio (1860-1933) English financier, MP and promoter of fraudulent companies. He was also the founder of the weekly journal *John Bull* and printer of *Hansard*. For 20 years, he managed to frustrate numerous attempts to convict him of fraud. In 1922, however, he was prosecuted for fraudulently advertising in his magazine, and was sentenced to seven years' penal servitude. He died in poverty.

Boucher de Crêvecoeur de Perthes, Jacques (1788-1868) French pioneer of Palaeolithic (Old Stone Age) archaeology, who was largely responsible for establishing the existence of prehistoric man. After finding chipped-flint hand-axes beside the bones of prehistoric animals in the Somme valley in 1837, he claimed that the men who made the tools were contemporary with the animals, and that, therefore, man's origins were 'antediluvial'. French scientists rejected his arguments until they were upheld by a group of British scientists who visited the sites in 1859.

Boucher, François (1703-70) French Rococo artist and protégé of Madame de POMPADOUR. Boucher became Director of the Academy and chief painter at the court of LOUIS XV, and in addition designed tapestries, stage sets and vignettes for the Sèvres porcelain factory. His subject matter ranges from the sensual delights seen in his interpretations of mythology, to pastoral and landscape scenes, portraits and genre paintings. Boucher's versatility, together with his technical virtuosity, were qualities much admired in his day, appealing to the senses rather than the mind with whimsical, lighthearted and often witty subjects.

Boucicault, Dion (1822-90) Irish dramatist and actor, who adapted many French works, and wrote *The Corsican Brothers* (1882) and *The Colleen Bawn* (1860).

Boudicca see BOADICEA

Boulanger, Georges (1837-91) French soldier-politician, who plotted to overthrow the Third Republic. As War Minister (1886) his introduction of military reforms, his patriotism and handsome appearance made him widely popular, and when a change of government (1887) relegated him to a provincial command, right wing dissidents and royalists persuaded him to mount a *coup d'état* to seize power for the so-called 'League of Patriots'. At the critical moment when all was prepared (March 1889), he lost his nerve and failed to act, fled to Brussels and then to Jersey, and was convicted *in absen-*

tia of high treason. In 1891 he committed suicide.

Boulanger, Nadia (born 1887) French composer and one of the most influential teachers in 20th-century music. Taking her inspiration from STRAVINSKY, she has included among her pupils Lennox BERKELEY as well as the important American composers HARRIS and COPLAND. Her sister was Lili Boulanger (1893-1918), who was, in 1914, the first woman to win the Prix de Rome, for which Nadia had been runner-up in 1908.

Boulez, Pierre (born 1925) French composer and conductor who made his reputation with *Le Marteau sans Maître*, a song cycle for contralto and chamber orchestra and a key-work in post-war European music. He has had considerable influence on contemporary music through his interpretations of the most important 20th-century composers, and through his own works. Boulez was a pupil of MESSIAEN, and BARRAULT's musical director (1948).

Boulton, Matthew (1728-1809) English engineer, a pioneer of engineering technology at the outset of the Industrial Revolution. In 1775 he went into partnership with James WATT to manufacture steam engines. Boulton had the engineering skills which, after 18 uncertain years, made Watt's invention a commercial and financial success and one of the cornerstones of the Industrial Revolution. Boulton was the centre of an influential group of scientists and industrialists, the Lunar Society of Birmingham, which included among its members Joseph PRIESTLEY, Josiah WEDGWOOD and James KEIR.

Boumédienne, Houari (born 1927) Algerian soldier-revolutionary, who established a socialist state in Algeria. Boumédienne worked with BEN BELLA to drive the French out of Algeria and to establish its independence. By 1956 Boumédienne was in command of the militant rebellion in Algeria, and in 1960 went to Tunis to train and command the 60,000 strong National Liberation Army assembled there ready to invade Algeria. Following the independence granted by DE GAULLE, and finding the government of President Ben Khedda insufficiently socialist, he used his army to march on Algiers, depose Ben Khedda and install Ben Bella as Prime Minister and President. Boumédienne himself retained the position of Minister of Defence and used the army to crush all opposition to socialization of the country. In 1963 he became the First Deputy Premier, and in 1965 ousted Ben Bella to become virtual dictator.

Bourguiba, Habib (born 1903) Tunisian politician and first President of the Republic of Tunisia. As a founder and leader of the nationalist Neo-Destourian Socialist Party (1934), he campaigned for Tunisia's independence, and was exiled and imprisoned by the French, from 1934 to 1936, 1938 to 1943 and again from 1952 to 1954. When independence was conceded in 1955 he returned to become Tunisia's first Prime Minister in 1956 and Minister of Foreign Affairs and Defence. In 1957 Bourguiba became President of the Tunisian National Assembly.

Bournonville, August (1805-1879) Founder of Danish Ballet, who studied in Paris with the great teacher Vestris, then returned to Denmark in 1829 and was appointed ballet master. The most famous of his 36 ballets is *La Sylphide*.

Bouts, Dieric (c. 1410-75) Dutch painter, who was influenced by Rogier van der WEYDEN, but whose homely religious scenes have much less intensity of feeling.

Bowen, Elizabeth Dorothea Cole (1899-1973) Irish novelist, who has been described as a 'poet working in prose'. Her sensitive, quiet books, the best known of which is *Death of the Heart* (1938), analyse states of mind and conflicts of emotion.

Bowen, Norman (1887-1956) Canadian-born American geologist, a pioneer of experimental petrography (the science of rock composition). His research was on the structure and chemical composition of igneous rocks (those cooled from a molten state) and metamorphic rocks (those altered by heat or pressure or both).

Bowman, Isaiah (1878-1950) American geographer who prompted major geographic studies of large areas. His *Forest Physiography* (1911) was the first detailed study of the physical geography of the United States. As director of the American Geographic Society of New York (1915-35), he made it an immensely useful tool for international geographic studies – mapping all of Central and South America, and exploring polar and other aspects of world geography. His broad grasp of international affairs, revealed in *The New World: Problems in Political Geography* earned him the post of adviser to presidents WILSON and ROOSEVELT.

Boyce, William (1710-79) English composer and organist who, after deafness wrecked his career, edited the famous collection known as *Cathedral Music* (1760-78), a landmark in musicology. Boyce's own compositions included music for church and stage, but he was also a gifted instrumental composer, and his eight one-movement symphonies have continued to receive deserved hearings in the concert hall.

Boyle, Robert (1627-91) Irish-born physicist and chemist, who formulated a law governing the behaviour of gases. In 1660, he put forward his gas law which stated that, at a given temperature, the pressure of a gas is proportional to its volume. In chemistry, Boyle introduced the idea of elements, and distinguished between mixtures of elements and chemical compounds, in which the elements are combined together.

Bracegirdle, Anne (c. 1663-1748) British actress, who excelled in the plays of CONGREVE, notably as Millament in *The Way of the World*.

Bracton, Henry de (13th cent.) English jurist who wrote the first systematic treatise on English law, *The Laws and Customs of England* (unfinished; first published 1569). In it, he stressed the recorded practice and procedure of the English royal courts and cited decided cases as precedents. This work and the cases collected in his *Note Book* indicate the increasing importance of precedent in the development of common law. He was an ecclesiastic and sat as a judge.

Bradford, William (1590-1657) English Puritan and Pilgrim Father. An early Congregationalist, Brad-

Cross-section of an explosive volcano. Bowen helped unravel its mysteries

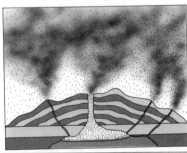

ford went to Leyden (1607) with the first English separatists. He helped to draw up the Mayflower Compact, was elected governor of Plymouth (1621), and re-elected 30 times at annual elections. Bradford was a strong administrator, coping with famine, Indian troubles and internal quarrels, and maintaining the independence of Plymouth against Massachusetts. He co-operated with other Puritans in the Pequot War (1637) and in the New England Confederation (1643).

Bradlaugh, Charles (1833-91) British politician, who, as a freethinker, was refused permission by the House of Commons to take his seat, because he declined to take the oath. In 1876, Bradlaugh was convicted of advocating birth control, and sentenced to imprisonment. The sentence was quashed on appeal. Elected as a Radical MP for Northampton (1880), he refused to take the oath, but offered to 'affirm'. A Select Committee ruled that he had no right to do so, and when Bradlaugh then offered to take the oath, this was objected to on the grounds that it would not be binding on a free-thinker. Though re-elected three times, he was excluded on each occasion. When he insisted on taking his seat, he was removed by the police (1881). A new Speaker decided (1886) that he had the right to take the oath and he was allowed to take his seat. In 1888 he promoted the Oath Act, which secured the right of affirmation in both the Commons and the law courts.

Bradley, Francis Herbert (1846-1924) British philosopher. His *Appearance and Reality* (1893) is a critical survey of the general categories of thought (space, time, causality, quality, relation and the like). He found them to be inconsistent with one another and representative only of the world of appearance. He concluded that there is a real world, which lies beyond thought, which is indivisibly One and Absolute.

Bradley, James (1693-1762) English astronomer who, in 1727, discovered the aberration of light (the apparent displacement of a star's position due to the movement of the Earth during the time it takes the light to travel from the star). In 1742 he succeeded HALLEY as Astronomer Royal. Bradley discovered the nutation (oscillation) of the Earth's axis, after observations lasting 20 years.

Bradman, Sir Donald (born 1908) Australian cricketer who was the most prolific scorer in the game. He played in 52 test matches and in his career made 117 centuries with a first class average of 99·94 runs. His score of

452 not out against Queensland in 1929-30 was a record for 29 years.

Bradstreet, Anne (c. 1612-72) American poet, whose *Tenth Muse* (1650) was one of the first works of poetry to be published by a woman in English. Born in Northampton, England, she settled in New England, and her introspective meditations on family life reflect the theological and moral preoccupations of the Puritan community.

Brady, Mathew (c. 1823-96) American photographer known principally for his Civil War battle pictures, but who was also a pioneer of the daguerreotype technique. Brady photographed 18 United States presidents, before dying penniless in a New York hospital.

Bragg, Sir William Henry (1862-1942) English physicist who with his son, William Lawrence, worked, using X-rays, on the determination of the structures of crystals. In 1915 the Braggs became intrigued by the distinctive patterns Max von LAUE had produced on photographic plates by passing X-rays through crystals. Their work showed how the structure of crystals could be deduced from the patterns they produced. Father and son were awarded the 1915 Nobel Prize for Physics.

Brahe, Tycho (1546-1601) Danish astronomer and mathematician, the most accomplished and systematic observer of the skies before the use of telescopes. His suggestion that comets are heavenly bodies, not exhalations of the Earth's atmosphere, was a refutation of the doctrine that planets were fixed to solid crystalline spheres, and struck a blow at the Aristotelian theory. However, he could not bring himself to accept a fully heliocentric Solar System, maintaining that the Earth remained still at the centre, with the Moon and Sun

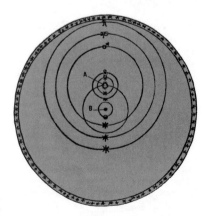

Brahe believed that while the planets moved around the Sun A, the Sun in turn orbited the Earth B

revolving around it, while the other planets revolved around the Sun. Brahe was assisted by his pupil KEPLER, who later used Brahe's observations of Mars to determine his three laws of planetary motion. In 1576 Frederick II gave Brahe the island of Hven, where he built the observatory of Uraniborg ('Castle of the Heavens'), equipped with the best instruments then available. He perfected the art of astronomical observation before the advent of the telescope, obtaining many remarkably accurate results, and calculating the length of the year to within one second and thus laid the basis of the Gregorian calendar.

Brahms, Johannes (1833-97) German composer, who, following in the tradition of BEETHOVEN, became the leading symphonist of the Romantic-Classical school, and was said to have destroyed many works which failed to satisfy his exacting standards. His four symphonies were composed between 1876 and 1885. His other most important compositions were the two piano concertos (1861 and 1882); the Violin Concerto (1879), written for JOACHIM; the Double Concerto for Violin and Cello (1888); the great *German Requiem* (1868), to a Lutheran text; and a large body of chamber music. As a lyric composer, Brahms represented an antithesis to WAGNER's dramatic Romanticism. LISZT and Joachim recognized his importance, and SCHUMANN's help and friendship firmly established his career.

Braidwood, Robert J. (born 1907) American archaeologist whose excavations in northern Iraq, in the 1940s, indicated that farming began between 9000 and 11,000 years ago, north of the territory bordering the Arabian desert.

Braille, Louis (1809-52) French inventor of the Braille system of read-

Braille's alphabet and numerals gave the blind a fingertip sight

ing for the sightless, who was himself blinded at the age of three. While a scholar, and later a teacher, at the Institute of Blind Youth in Paris, Braille developed a system of embossed dots to enable the blind to read by touch. This was published first in 1829 – and in a more complete form in 1837. In 1932, a form known as Standard English Braille became accepted for worldwide use.

Brain, Dennis (1921-57) English French horn player who became the outstanding horn soloist of his day. He was descended from a family of distinguished wind instrumentalists. The unique roundness of his tone inspired BRITTEN and HINDEMITH, among others, to write specially for him. He died in a car accident.

Bramah, Joseph (1748-1814) Prolific English inventor of the ball-valve and syphon system water closet (patented 1778), which is the basis of the flushing system still in use. This was the first of many inventions that brought him fame and wealth. His factory in Pimlico was an important training ground for engineers and inventors of machine tools.

Bramante, Donato (1444-1514) Influential Italian architect of the High Renaissance, who was influenced by ALBERTI and LEONARDO. He first worked in Milan where he evolved an individual classical style, using central plans for churches and chapels, and re-introducing coffering on domes, a popular feature in Roman architecture. In 1499 he went to Rome, where he built the cloisters for Sta Maria della Pace (1500), whose perfect detailing and use of the classical architrave are reminiscent of Roman buildings. His Tempietto di S Pietro in Montorio is a circular building, the form and details of which closely resemble those of a classical temple.

Brancusi, Constantin (1876-1957) Rumanian sculptor who arrived in Paris in 1904, having walked across Europe. Brancusi's original style was classical and academic, but from 1907, influenced by RODIN, his forms became simplified. Brancusi's considerable importance for the development of 20th-century sculpture is in the sense of the freedom which emanates from the simplicity and monumental grandeur of his work; e.g. *Bird in Space* (1925), his rare pierced work in wood, *King of Kings* (1937) or his *Colonne sans Fin* in steel (also 1937).

Brando, Marlon (born 1924) American film actor whose first big success in the cinema was as the incoherent Kowalski in *A Streetcar*

Named Desire (1952). He has since starred in many different roles, including that of Mark Antony in *Julius Caesar* (1953), the Englishman Fletcher CHRISTIAN in *Mutiny on the Bounty* (1962), the title role in *The Godfather* (1972) and the American in Bertolucci's controversial *Last Tango in Paris* (1972).

Brandt, Willy (born 1913) West German politician, born Karl Frahm, the first socialist Chancellor of the Federal Republic. His socialist writings forced him to seek refuge in Norway when the Nazis came to power (1933). He worked as a journalist in Sweden and after returning to Berlin in 1945, was elected to the Berlin Chamber of Deputies in 1950. He became its President (1955-7) and, in 1957, Burgomaster of West Berlin. He became West German Minister of Foreign Affairs and Vice-Chancellor (1966-9) in Kiesinger's coalition government, and was elected Chancellor in 1969. The Ostpolitik policy of non-aggression and friendship pacts with USSR and countries of eastern Europe, which Brandt pursued as Minister of Foreign Affairs, and then as Chancellor, earned him the Nobel Peace Prize.

Braque, Georges (1882-1963) French painter, one of the founders of the Cubist movement. In 1907 he met PICASSO and soon afterwards began to study CÉZANNE's paintings, two events of fundamental importance to the development of Cubism, with its concern with the nature of pictorial space. Braque's work at this time was cool and somewhat detached. Its characteristic subject-matter was the still-life. Later, he reintroduced more sensuous and formal elements into his paintings, but retained the sense of discipline.

Braun, Wernher von (born 1912) German-born rocket engineer who pioneered the V2 rocket used to bombard Britain in the Second World War. The first missile was launched from the rocket research site at Peenemunde on the Baltic in 1942. Von Braun's rockets came too late to influence the course of the Second World War, but their political and military significance has been considerable. Von Braun and many of his associates later went to the US, where he led the group which put America's first satellite into orbit on 31 Jan. 1958. Von Braun was later responsible for the Saturn rocket developments for the Apollo lunar programme.

Bravais, Auguste (1811-63) French crystallographer, who devised a system for classifying crystals.

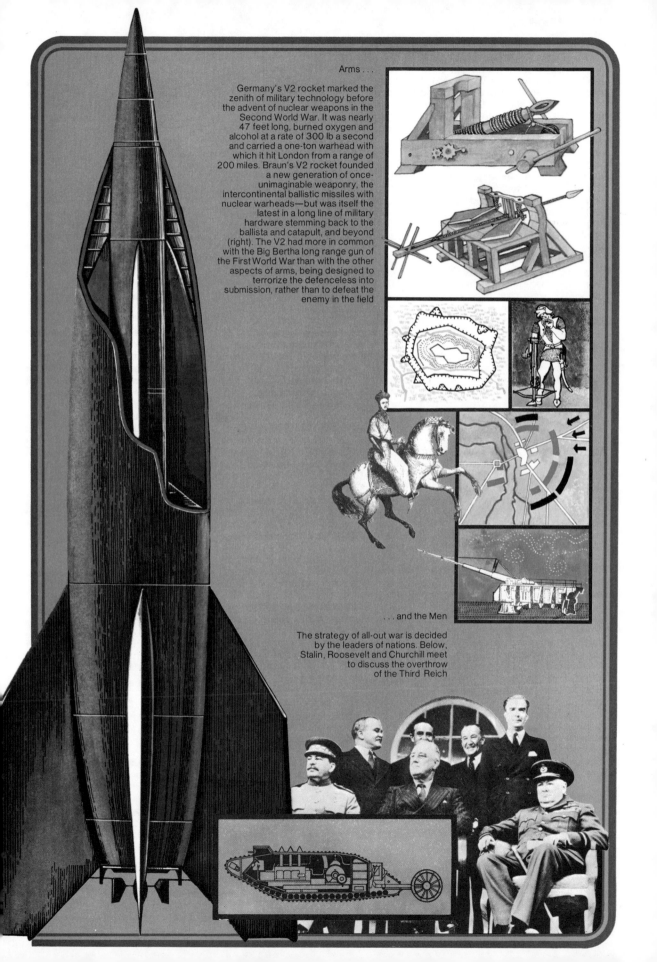

Arms . . .

Germany's V2 rocket marked the
zenith of military technology before
the advent of nuclear weapons in the
Second World War. It was nearly
47 feet long, burned oxygen and
alcohol at a rate of 300 lb a second
and carried a one-ton warhead with
which it hit London from a range of
200 miles. Braun's V2 rocket founded
a new generation of once-
unimaginable weaponry, the
intercontinental ballistic missiles with
nuclear warheads—but was itself the
latest in a long line of military
hardware stemming back to the
ballista and catapult, and beyond
(right). The V2 had more in common
with the Big Bertha long range gun of
the First World War than with the other
aspects of arms, being designed to
terrorize the defenceless into
submission, rather than to defeat the
enemy in the field

. . . and the Men

The strategy of all-out war is decided
by the leaders of nations. Below,
Stalin, Roosevelt and Churchill meet
to discuss the overthrow
of the Third Reich

Brecht, Bertolt (1898-1956) German dramatist, director and the most widely influential theorist in the modern theatre. His Expressionist work, represented by *Baal* (1923) and *A Man's a Man* (1926), create imaginary, romantic worlds. His Marxist and didactic period began with *The Threepenny Opera* (1928) and includes *Saint Joan of the Stockyards. Mother Courage* and *The Caucasian Chalk Circle* belong to his third period, which is more concerned with character and the complexity of human relationships. From 1949, he ran his own company, the Berliner Ensemble, and developed his dramatic theories in writings.

Brentano, Franz (1838-1917) German philosopher who claimed in his theory of mind that psychical processes are distinguished from physical ones by being intentional. His work influenced MEINONG and HUSSERL. Brentano became a Catholic priest in 1864 and taught at Wurzburg from 1886, but, when Pope PIUS IX declared the dogma of infallibility in 1870, he became estranged from the Church and left it and his post in 1873, to become Professor of Philosophy at Vienna (1874-80).

Breton, André (1896-1966) French essayist, novelist, critic and one of the founders of the Surrealist movement, the basis of which he established in his *Manifeste du surréalisme* (1924) and *Second manifeste du surréalisme* (1930). His novel *Nadja* (1928) came to be regarded as a masterpiece of Surrealist writing.

Breuil, Henri (1877-1961) French priest and archaeologist whose studies shed new light on the Old Stone Age cave paintings of Europe and Africa. During the early 1900s he published a number of books to prove the antiquity of the prehistoric cave paintings in western Europe, notably the Palaeolithic animal paintings at Altamira in Spain and Lascaux in France, many of them 20,000 and some possibly 60,000 years old. Equally important was his influence on the rejection of the old system in which one 'epoch' followed another, to the more accurate and complex sequence of 'cultures', showing how some had flourished simultaneously. He also copied and publicized the mysterious rock paintings of southern Africa.

Brewer, William Henry (1828-1910) American scientist and an assistant in the geological survey of California. Brewer and others gained a collective fame for climbing, for the first time, many major mountains of the western United States, using only the crudest of climbing gear.

Brezhnev, Leonid Ilyich (born 1906) Soviet politician who succeeded KHRUSCHEV as First Secretary of the Central Committee of the Communist Party of the Soviet Union in 1964. A Ukrainian, he trained as a metallurgist and engineer, and became prominent in 1952, the year before STALIN's death, when he was appointed to the Central Committee of the Communist Party. Brezhnev was effectively head of state from 1960, when he succeeded Voroshilov as Chairman of the Praesidium of the Supreme Soviet, and in 1964 took over Russia's top political office when he replaced Khruschev as First Secretary (title altered to 'Secretary General' in 1966) of the Party. It was Brezhnev, the strongest member of the collective three-man leadership (with KOSYGIN and Podgorny), who ordered the invasion of Czechoslovakia in 1968 and who formulated the doctrine of limited sovereignty, by which the USSR claims the right to intervene whenever it considers that socialism in the 'satellite' countries is threatened from within. He has since adopted a rapprochement policy with the United States and the West.

Brian Boru (926-1014) King of Ireland (1002-14), whose victory in the Battle of Clontarf (1014) crushed Viking attempts to conquer all Ireland. Succeeding to the kingdom of Munster (978), he conquered the provincial kings and was recognized by them as king of all Ireland. Some of the resentful, displaced rulers allied with leaders of the Danish and Norse invaders, and although Brian defeated them at Clontarf, his death in the battle reduced Ireland to political anarchy, the cause of later invasions.

Brian, Havergal (1876-1972) English symphonist, who completed 32 symphonies, 22 of them after his 76th birthday. Although his qualities were early recognized by such musicians as TOVEY and Henry J. WOOD, Brian faced a hard struggle to get his work heard: his enormous *Gothic Symphony* (composed 1919) was not performed until 1961. Brian was a natural symphonist and what has been played of his late work shows him doggedly pursuing a strongly individual, if isolated, path.

Briand, Aristide (1862-1932) French statesman notable for his efforts on behalf of international peace and Franco-German reconciliation, for which he was awarded the Nobel Peace Prize in 1926. He was 11 times Prime Minister of France, between 1909 (when he succeeded CLEMENCEAU) and 1929, though he held office for a total period of less than 5 years. As Foreign Minister from 1925 to 1932, his influence on French foreign policy was supreme. With STRESEMANN Briand formulated the Locarno Treaties of 1925, which confirmed Germany's frontiers with France and Belgium and the demilitarized Rhineland zone. In 1928 he concluded the Kellogg-Briand Pact with Frank Kellogg, COOLIDGE's Secretary of State, renouncing the use of war as an instrument of national policy.

Bridges, Robert (1844-1930) English scholarly poet who made some interesting metrical experiments. He was an intelligent, retiring man who was not well known, even when he became Poet Laureate in 1913. He was the friend and encourager of Manley HOPKINS, though a stern critic of Hopkins's more daring work. Bridges's long 'Testament of Beauty' (1929) is a major poem.

Bridgewater, Francis, 3rd Duke of (1736-1803) The founder of Britain's canal system. In 1759 Parliament authorized the Duke to build a canal to link the collieries on his estates at Worsley with Salford and Manchester. He employed the engineer James BRINDLEY, who in two years built the 10-mile long canal, including the famous aqueduct across the Irwell. The efficiency of the canal as a means of transporting coal lowered its price and started a canal-building boom in Britain.

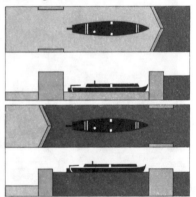

Pioneered by men like Bridgewater and Brindley, a canal depends on its locks. The pressure of the river race holds the angled gates shut, while the water level rises, bearing the craft upward

Bridie, James (1888-1951) Scottish dramatist, who wrote *Daphne Laureola* (1949) and founded the Glasgow Citizens' Theatre. He was a practising physician, and had reached 40 before the first of his plays was produced. The theme of his best-known works is the conflict between puritanism and the flesh, as in *The Anatomist* (1930), his first success.

Bright, John (1811-89) British orator and Liberal statesman whose political career began in the campaign of the anti-Corn Law League, which he led in collaboration with COBDEN. He was an MP almost continuously from 1843 until his death, representing Durham, Manchester and Birmingham. In the 1850s Bright opposed the Crimean War and pressed for the transfer of Indian administration from the East India Company to the Crown (India Act, 1858). He supported the admission of Jews to the House of Commons and was influential in the campaign which led to the Parliamentary Reform Act of 1867. Bright was President of the Board of Trade (1868-70) in GLADSTONE's first Liberal ministry, but opposed the Liberal government's intervention in Egypt in 1882 and Gladstone's crusade for Irish Home Rule. His independent provincialism and serious mind were representative of the mid-19th-century reformer.

Bright, Richard (1789-1858) English physician and medical researcher who discovered that kidney disease could be diagnosed from the presence of albumin in the urine. The condition, formally known as Bright's disease, is now known to be a number of separate diseases, including acute and chronic nephritis.

Brindley, James (1716-72) Pioneer English canal builder. Although illiterate and without any kind of formal education, he was an inventor of genius. In 1752 he devised a water-driven pump for draining a mine, and later designed a silk mill. These works led the Duke of BRIDGEWATER in 1759 to engage Brindley to build the Bridgewater canal. The success of the canal (part of which went by aqueduct over the River Irwell) led to a career in canal building which included the Grand Trunk, Birmingham, and Chesterfield canals – 365 miles in all.

Britten, Benjamin (born 1913) English composer, one of the foremost of his generation. In 1945 he wrote the score that became the *Variations and Fugue on a Theme of Purcell* (*Young Person's Guide to the Orchestra*) for an educational film. The same year, his opera *Peter Grimes* (based on CRABBE's poem 'The Borough') was produced at Covent Garden, and its success was directly responsible for the revival of opera in post-war England. Britten's gift for subtle empathy between words and music has made him one of the finest song writers of his day and is seen equally well in his HARDY settings, *Winter Words* (1953), the opera *Billy Budd* (1951), and *War Requiem* (1962), which intersperses the Latin text with poems by Wilfred OWEN. He has written works for many distinguished soloists, particularly the

tenor, Peter Pears. He has composed most effectively for children, as in the church opera, *Noye's Fludde* (1959). With Pears, Britten founded the annual music festival at Aldeburgh, Suffolk, where his most recent opera, *Death in Venice*, was first performed in 1973.

Broch, Hermann (1886-1951) Austrian novelist and poet whose major work is *The Death of Virgil* (1945). In 1938 he emigrated (with the assistance of friends, among them James JOYCE) to the US where he established his reputation as a writer.

Broglie, Prince Louis de (1892-1970) French physicist, who extended the notion of dual wave-particle behaviour to matter. This duality, in which particle-like properties are shown in some circumstances, and wave-like properties in others, had been accepted in the case of light and incorporated in the quantum theory based on the work of PLANCK. In 1923 de Broglie suggested it should also appear in material particles such as electrons, a prediction that was subsequently verified, paving the way to a more general quantum theory.

Brongniart, Alexandre (1770-1847) French geologist who established the sequence of the rocks of the Tertiary period in France on the basis of their fossils. Brongniart also made his mark on theoretical palaeontology; his broad classification of living and fossil reptiles is still basically used today. With a group of colleagues, he also laid the foundations of the chemistry of ceramics.

Bronstein, Lev Davidovitch see TROTSKY, Lev Davidovitch

Brontë, Anne (1820-49) English novelist, who wrote *Agnes Grey* (1847) and *The Tenant of Wildfell Hall* (1848), novels of less dramatic qualities than those of her sisters, Charlotte and Emily.

Brontë, Charlotte (1816-55) English novelist, author of *Jane Eyre* (1847), the eldest of three precocious sisters, all novelists. Brought up by their eccentric father at Haworth, his bleak Yorkshire parsonage, all three fashioned their own worlds of the imagination. Charlotte wrote, with her sisters, the *Poems of Currer, Ellis and Acton Bell* (1846), which were the pseudonyms under which the sisters wrote. She then wrote *Jane Eyre*, which, despite some faults, was a new departure in the novel, mixing romantic love with grim realism and, for the first time, analysing the world of emotion from the woman's point of view. Charlotte, the longest lived of the sisters, spent some time in

Brussels and wrote of her life in Yorkshire and Belgium in the novels *Shirley* (1849) and *Villette* (1852).

Brontë, Emily (1818-48) English novelist, who wrote *Wuthering Heights* (1847), one of the most powerful 19th-century novels. Writing in an elemental world far from the daily life of Victorian England, Emily presented evil as a disinterested force of nature; her characters are buffeted by passions they can no more control than they can the storms of the Yorkshire moors. She was the second of the Brontë sisters.

Bronzino, Agnolo (1503-72) Florentine painter, well known for his family of the MEDICI portraits (e.g. *Eleanora of Toledo and her son, c. 1550*). These are elegant but cold works in which more attention is paid to textures than to the sitter's personality.

Brook, Peter (born 1925) Considered by some to be the most original and dynamic British producer and director of his generation. While in his twenties, he directed at the Shakespeare Memorial Theatre, Stratford, and made his name in London with *Doctor Faustus* (1943). Since 1956 he has worked in France as much as in Britain. Since 1962, he has directed the Royal Shakespeare Company productions, including *Marat/Sade* and *A Midsummer Night's Dream*.

Brooke, Rupert (1887-1915) English poet, who was one of a number of young, talented writers who died during the First World War. He had grown up in the prosperous idyllic years of the first decade of the century, and his early poems, like 'Grantchester', spoke nostalgically of stability and enduring values. He welcomed the war with a patriotic flourish, but seemed to foresee his own death in 'The Soldier', an impressive sonnet. The *Letters from America*, introduced by Henry JAMES, containing fresh reports from a journey there, appeared in 1916.

Broschi, Carlo see FARINELLI

Brosse, Salomon de (c. 1565-1626) French architect who designed a number of French châteaux, notably Coulommiers and Blérancourt. He also worked as an architect in Paris, where he built the Palais de Luxembourg and probably the façade of the church of St Gervais.

Brougham and Vaux, Henry, 1st Baron (1778-1868) English jurist who played a significant part in governmental reforms. In 1828 his speech in Parliament on law reform led to far-reaching changes in civil procedure, through him slave-trading became a felony, and as Lord Chancellor (1830-4) he helped the great Reform Bill through the House of Lords (1832). Brougham was also responsible for the reform of the Privy Council's judicial committee and for the establishment of London's Central Criminal Court (Old Bailey).

Brouwer, Adriaen (c. 1605-38) Flemish artist, who specialized in pictures of drinking or brawling peasants in tavern settings, which are in the tradition of BRUEGEL's depictions of peasant life and have a similar ironical humour. He spent the first half of his working life in Holland, where he may have been a pupil of Frans HALS.

Brown, Sir Arthur Whitten see ALCOCK, Sir John

Brown, Ford Madox (1821-93) British painter, a follower, though not actually a member, of the Pre-Raphaelites. He shared the social ideals of RUSKIN and MORRIS.

Brown, John (1735-88) Scottish physician who advanced the then-revolutionary proposition that diseases can be caused by weakness in the system rather than by a positive predisposition to contract disease. Brown strenuously opposed such treatment as bloodletting, but used instead doses of stimulating drugs.

Brown, John (1800-59) American anti-slavery crusader, who led a raid in Kansas in which five alleged slave-owners were killed. In an attempt to provoke a slave rebellion in Virginia he raided a government arsenal at Harper's Ferry, Virginia (18 Oct. 1859), but was captured by a company of marines commanded by Robert E. LEE. After being tried for insurrection, treason and murder, he was convicted and hanged at Charleston, Virginia (2 Dec. 1859). He is commemorated in 'John Brown's Body', one of the most popular marching songs of the American Civil War.

Brown, Lancelot (1715-83) British landscape gardener and architect, known as 'Capability Brown', who developed the natural style of landscape gardening, transforming tens of thousands of acres into landscape 'pictures'. Born in Northumberland, he went south to work under William KENT, from whose basic ideas his own style evolved. Believing that house and grounds should be a unity, he became an architect, and built several houses in the Palladian style. The chief elements of Brown's landscapes were winding drives, serpentine rivers, large lakes, broad sweeps of undulating lawn or pasture stretching up to the house, and groups of mainly deciduous trees, of which he planted hundreds of thousands. Vestiges of his work survive in 25 English counties and more complete examples are to be seen at Kew Gardens, Harewood House and Blenheim Palace. Brown was called 'Capability' because of his habit of referring to the potential of the estates on which he was working as 'capabilities'.

Browne, Robert (c. 1550-c. 1633) English separatist clergyman, the pioneer of Congregationalism, which holds that congregations should govern themselves. In the US, Congregationalism is honoured for its connection with the Pilgrim Fathers.

Browne, Sir Thomas (1605-82) English doctor and author, whose rich, ornate and solemn style is typified by the *Religio Medici* (1643), a work of personal reflection on religious and philosophic themes, showing delight in the paradoxes and mysteries of Christianity.

Browning, Elizabeth Barrett (1806-61) English poet, who married Robert BROWNING against her father's wishes.

Browning, Robert (1812-89) English poet, who analysed character and states of mind, particularly in his unique dramatic monologues. His verse displays a fund of invention and a love of unusual incidents, words and rhymes, and he devised the dramatic monologue for his needs.

Broz, Josip see TITO, Marshal

Bruce, James (1730-94) British explorer who rediscovered the source of the Blue Nile and was the first European to trace it to its confluence with the White Nile. His five-volume *Travels to Discover the Source of the Nile in the Years 1768-73* (1790) recorded his journey down the Red Sea and through Ethiopia to its capital, Gondar, and Lake Tana, the beginning of the Blue Nile, and from there down the Blue Nile to the confluence at Khartoum, and on to Aswan.

Bruckner, Anton (1824-96) Major Austrian symphonist whose works are characterized by broad, slowly expanding themes drawn across an often enormous canvas; the slow movement of his *Seventh Symphony* (1883) is an outstanding example. Shortly before he was 40, he heard

For years a wreck in the Falkland Is., the *Great Britain* has returned to Bristol, where it was built by Isambard Brunel

Tannhäuser, and thenceforth WAGNER became a dominant influence on him. Between 1865 and 1896 he composed nine symphonies which became progressively more powerful in their expression. Bruckner's church music, including a *Te Deum* (1884), conveys a deep sense of unity with a God-created world.

Bruegel, Pieter (c. 1525-69) The most important Flemish painter of the 16th century. His best-known works are genre scenes depicting the life and customs of peasant communities – pictures which earned him the nickname 'Peasant Bruegel'. He was, however, an educated man and his interest in such subjects was detached and frequently satirical. Paintings like *The Peasant Wedding* (*c.* 1565) are not so much descriptions of specific events as thinly veiled comments on the coarse appetites of mankind in general. Others, which satirize mankind's follies, are based on popular proverbs, as in *The Blind Leading the Blind* (1568). On his return from a journey to Italy, Bruegel made a series of drawings of alpine scenery which he used in several landscape compositions, some of which contain unobtrusive religious incidents. The motifs of these alpine scenes also recur in some of the five landscapes painted in 1565 which illustrate the seasonal cycle.

Brugmann, Friedrich (1849-1919) German philologist whose *Foundations of the Comparative Grammar of Indo-Germanic Languages* (1886-93) surveyed the whole field of Indo-European linguistics and organized the material clearly. Brugmann stressed the fact that phonetic laws are fixed and apply without exceptions.

Brulé, Etienne (c. 1592-1633) French explorer of much of the Great Lakes system of North America. He first went to Quebec with Samuel de CHAMPLAIN (1608) and became the first European to travel in the Michigan and Ontario areas, and explored Lakes Huron (1611), Ontario (1615), and Superior (1621). Brulé learned to speak the Algonquin language and lived with the Huron Indians, who eventually boiled and ate him.

Brunel, Isambard Kingdom (1806-59) Great English engineer of the 19th century. Son of Marc Isambard Brunel (1769-1849), who designed and built the Thames tunnel from Wapping to Rotherhithe (1825-43), Brunel first designed the Clifton suspension bridge in 1829 (it was completed in 1864). In 1833 he became chief engineer of the Great Western Railway and constructed all its viaducts, bridges and tunnels, including the Royal Albert Bridge across the River Tamar into Cornwall. In 1838 he designed the *Great Western*, the first wooden steam ship built to cross the Atlantic, followed in 1845 by the *Great Britain*, the first large iron-hulled screw-driven steam ship. Then in 1853 he began the construction of the *Great Eastern*, the largest ship of its day. Although not a success as a passenger ship it was used in 1866 to lay the first transatlantic telegraph cable.

Brunelleschi, Filippo (1377-1446) Italian architect and pioneer of the early Florentine Renaissance. His first work in Florence was to design a dome to span the enormous crossing of its cathedral, an unprecedented feat of engineering. His characteristic use of grey and white surfaces was first evident in the miniature Pazzi chapel in Florence. Later, he built the two important and finely proportioned Florentine basilicas of S Lorenzo and S Spirito, and, in 1421, designed the elegant arcade of the Foundling Hospital, Florence. Of his secular works, the most famous is the Pitti Palace, Florence.

Bruno (c. 1030-1101) German saint and founder of the Carthusian Order of monks. In 1084, some eight years after being dismissed from his university teaching post in France, he and six companions formed a community with a very harsh Rule of Worship, penitence and work at the Grande Chartreuse, a remote and wild spot in the Massif Central. Later, they founded two further houses, La Torre in Calabria and the Charterhouse at San Stefano-in-Basco. Bruno was never formally canonized.

Bruno, Giordano (1548-1600) Italian Dominican who posited that the universe was made up from single indivisible particles, or 'monads'. This theory greatly influenced LEIBNIZ. Bruno opposed Aristotelian logic and was burnt at the stake for heresy in 1600.

Brunton, Sir Lander (1844-1916) Scottish physician and one of the founders of modern pharmacology, whose classic textbook, *The Action of Medicines* (1887), focused students' minds on the biochemical effects of medicines at the level of cells and tissues. He also pioneered the use of amylnitrate for angina pectoris (heart-centred chest pains).

Brush, Charles Francis (1849-1929) American inventor of electric devices. In 1879 he devised a method of stabilizing the electric arc between carbon electrodes and so made the arc lamp possible.

Brutus, Marcus Junius (c. 85-42 BC) Roman, leader of the republican conspirators against Julius CAESAR. He sided with POMPEY against Caesar, but after defeat at Pharsalus (46 BC), was pardoned by Caesar and given the governorship of Cisalpine Gaul. He was praetor in Rome (44 BC) and was to have been Caesar's governor in Macedonia but joined the conspirators who stabbed Caesar to death (44 BC). Lacking any effective plan to re-establish republican rule, Brutus fled to Macedonia where his army was defeated at Philippi (42 BC) by Octavius (later AUGUSTUS) and Marcus ANTONIUS. After the defeat Brutus committed suicide.

Bryce, Lord James (1838-1922) British historian, lawyer, politician and diplomat, whose *Holy Roman Empire* (1864) was a scholarly study establishing its author's name while he was still a young man. He held office in various Liberal governments and was British ambassador to the United States before the First World War.

Buache, Philippe (1700-73) French geographer who developed new theories in physical geography and a new technique in map-making. He divided the Earth's surface into four great basins separated by mountain chains – a physiographic system which enabled him accurately to predict the discovery of Alaska and the Aleutian Islands. He also developed the use of contour lines to show relief in maps.

Buber, Martin (born 1878) Austrian philosopher. He was born in Vienna where he studied, but later moved to Frankfurt to lecture in Jewish theology. His most influential work was *I and Thou* (1923), which expounded in mystical terms the differing relations between man and things (I – it) and interpersonal or man to God relations (I – Thou). HITLER's rise led to Buber's moving to Jerusalem.

Buch, Christian von (1774-1853) German geologist and geographer who made the first detailed geological map of Germany.

Buchan, John (1875-1940) Scottish historian and novelist, author of dashing popular adventures such as *Prester John* (1910), *The 39 Steps* (1915) and *Greenmantle* (1916). He was created 1st Baron Tweedsmuir.

Buchanan, George (1506-82) Scottish humanist, poet and political philosopher. Educated at the Universities of Paris and St Andrews, Buchanan divided his time during the years 1520-60 between Scotland and

France, according to the existing political climate, teaching (one of his pupils was MONTAIGNE), translating Greek literature and writing poetry. A definite Calvinist by 1560, he turned against MARY STUART in 1567 and became tutor to JAMES VI. His most important political work *De Jure regni spud scotos* (1579) is a plea for limited monarchy.

Buchanan, James (1791-1868) Fifteenth President of the United States (1857-61) whose equivocal attitude on the slavery question encouraged the establishment of the Southern Confederacy. Although he believed slavery to be morally wrong, he was strongly against Congress interfering in the slave states. As the slavery question grew more acute, his answer was to enforce the fugitive slave law and prevent Northern agitation. The election of LINCOLN in 1860 led South Carolina to call for secession and, as 'a Northern man with Southern principles', he declared that, although the state had no legal right to secede, the federal government had no right to use force to prevent it from doing so.

Buchman, Frank Nathan Daniel (1878-1961) American evangelist, founder and leader of the Moral Rearmament movement. This was a campaign for moral reform and the promotion of international harmony which aimed at a world 'governed by men governed by God' and the practice of the virtues of honesty, purity, unselfishness and love. The Movement grew out of Buchman's 'world-changing through life-changing' Oxford Group in the 1930s. With the end of the war it resumed its crusade against materialism, particularly Communism.

Büchner, Georg (1813-37) German dramatist, who wrote *Woyzec*, the basis of Alban BERG's opera *Wozzeck*. This melancholy study of the life and death of an illiterate soldier was written in reaction to Romanticism and foreshadows the work of such playwrights as TOLLER and BRECHT. His only other important play, *Danton's Death* (1835), is about the French Revolution.

Buck, Pearl (1892-1973) American novelist, many of whose books are about life in China, where she was brought up and to which she returned as a missionary teacher. In her trilogy *The Good Earth* (1931), *Sons* (1932) and *A House Divided* (1935) she showed a sympathetic understanding of the Chinese. *The Good Earth* gained for her a Pulitzer Prize, and in 1938 she became the first American woman to receive the Nobel Prize for Literature.

Buddha see GAUTAMA BUDDHA

Budding, Edwin (1795-1846) English inventor of the first practical lawn mower, which he patented in 1830. Budding's 19-inch roller mower was basically similar to that used today and worked on the same principle of rotating cutters operating against a fixed cutter. His other notable invention was the adjustable screw or shifting spanner.

Buffon, Comte George (1707-88) French naturalist, the first to attempt a fully comprehensive work of natural history. His massive *Histoire naturelle, générale et particulière* (1749-1804) resulted from his job as keeper of the Jardin du Roi, Paris.

Bugaev, Boris see BELY, Andrei

Bukharin, Nikolai Ivanovich (1888-1938) Russian journalist and politician who, after escaping from exile in Siberia in 1910, joined LENIN in Austria. As a member of the Politburo (1918-29) and president of the Third International (1926-9), he was one of the major ideologists of the Communist Party. After Lenin's death in 1924, Bukharin supported STALIN against TROTSKY in the belief that Stalin was Lenin's political heir, but in 1929 he was expelled from the Communist Party as a Trotskyite. He was readmitted and appointed editor of *Izvestia* in 1934, but in 1937 he was tried for anti-Soviet activities and betraying the cause of Communism. He was executed in March 1938.

Bulgakov, Mikhail Afanasyevich (1891-1940) Russian novelist and playwright, whose finest prose work *The Master and Margarita* was published abroad in the 1960s. He first achieved fame with his novel *The White Guard* (1924), which enjoyed great popularity in the Soviet Union, in spite of its sympathetic portrayal of White Russian officers. It was dramatized as *The Days of the Turbins* and staged with great success by the Moscow Arts Theatre, until banned by the Soviet authorities. After official attacks on two of his later plays – *Zoyka's Apartment* (1926) and *The Crimson Island* (1928) – Bulgakov found it impossible either to publish or stage many of the plays he wrote in the 1930s.

Bulganin, Nikolai Alexandrovich (born 1895) Soviet politician and soldier, one of the leaders of the USSR after STALIN's death in 1953. He joined the Communist Party in 1917 and served in the secret police (Cheka) from 1918 until 1922, when he became involved in economic affairs and in industry. During the Second World War he became a

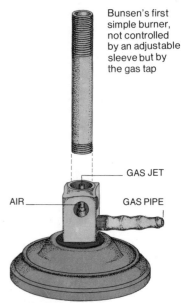

Bunsen's first simple burner, not controlled by an adjustable sleeve but by the gas tap

GAS JET

AIR   GAS PIPE

general, and was promoted to Marshal of the USSR in 1947, and held the post of Defence Minister from 1947 to 1949 and again from 1953 to 1955. He became Deputy Chairman of the Council of Ministers in 1949 and Chairman following Stalin's death, from 1955 until 1958, when he was replaced by KHRUSCHEV.

Bull, John (1563-1628) English composer and organist, one of whose virginal pieces may have been the basis for the British national anthem, 'God Save the Queen' (known in America as 'My Country, 'tis of Thee'). By his compositions for the virginal Bull became a pioneer of keyboard repertory and contrapuntal keyboard style, an ingenious professional rather than an inspired composer. He spent the last 11 years of his life as organist at Antwerp Cathedral.

Bülow, Hans Guido von (1830-94) German conductor and pianist who promoted the music of WAGNER and BRAHMS and who was the first international celebrity of the baton. Bülow's wife (LISZT's daughter Cosima) left him for Wagner.

Bunch, Ralph Johnson (1904-71) United Nations diplomat; one of several American negroes appointed to senior administrative posts by President Franklin ROOSEVELT. He was awarded the Nobel Peace Prize (1950). He began his career as an academic specializing in philosophy and social anthropology at various American, British and South American universities. He was appointed adviser to the US Government on colonial and international affairs and conferences 1941-5; US Commissioner, Caribbean Community 1945-7; Principal Director, United Nations

Trusteeship Department (1947-54), and UN Mediator in Palestine 1948-9. In the civil war following independence of the Belgian Congo (now Zaïre) in 1960, he was the UN representative on the spot.

Bunin, Ivan Alexeyevich (1870-1953) Russian prose writer and poet, one of Russia's finest stylists, whose novels reflect the poverty and darkness of pre-revolutionary Russia. His major works, *The Village* and *A Grammar of Love*, deal with rural life. Bunin was awarded a Nobel Prize for Literature in 1933.

Bunsen, Robert (1811-99) German chemist and pioneer of modern spectroscopy. He is best remembered for inventing the Bunsen burner, which allowed him, with Gustav KIRCHHOFF, to make a careful study of the light emitted by compounds heated to incandescence. They found that compounds emit light with wavelengths characteristic of the elements they contain.

Buñuel, Luis (born 1900) Spanish writer and film director whose first films were the Surrealist fantasies *Un Chien Andalou* (1928, made with DALI) and *L'Age d'Or* (1930), which at first shocked the public. Buñuel continued to provide shocks in later films such as *Viridiana* (1961), outraging religious feeling with a parody on The Last Supper, and in *Belle de Jour* (his first film in English), an effective study of sexual fantasy. Throughout his career, working in Europe and Mexico, Buñuel has followed his obsession with satirizing the fantasies and hypocrisies of sex and religion in middle class society, in such films as *Tristana* (1970) and *The Discreet Charm of the Bourgeoisie* (1972).

Bunyan, John (1628-88) English non-conformist preacher and author of *Pilgrim's Progress*. Besides its religious interest as a moral allegory, *Pilgrim's Progress* is a model of narrative and descriptive skill. Bunyan was a man of little education and his art sprang from the Bible and folk-tales. Among his other notable works, always on religion or morality, are *Grace Abounding* (1666), a spiritual autobiography, and *The Life and Death of Mr Badman* (1680), a vivid picture of a misspent life.

Burbage, Richard (c. 1567-1619) English actor, who was considered the finest tragedian of his time. He played, among other roles, Lear, Othello, Hamlet and Richard III. He was the son of James Burbage, the actor-manager who built the Blackfriars Theatre, and the brother of Cuthbert, who built and managed the Globe Theatre on Bankside.

Burckhardt, Jakob (1818-97) Swiss cultural historian, who, in his masterpiece *The Civilisation of the Renaissance in Italy* (1861), took the Italian Renaissance as the birthdate of modern man.

Burghley, 1st Baron see CECIL, Sir William

Burgoyne, John (1722-92) British general whose defeat at Saratoga in the American War of Independence encouraged France openly to join the colonists' side, which ultimately cost Britain the war. In 1777 he thrust south from Lake Champlain as part of a three-pronged drive to isolate New England, but was outnumbered at Saratoga and surrendered. Burgoyne was also a successful dramatist: *The Maid of the Oaks* (1775) was produced by GARRICK, and a comedy, *The Heiress* (1786), ran to 10 editions and was translated into several languages.

Burke, Edmund (1729-97) Irish-born Whig politician and political theorist, who attacked American governments, criticized the power of George III and the Indian administration of HASTINGS. He opposed the French Revolution in *Reflections on the French Revolution* (1790) and was a leading supporter of Wilberforce's fight against slavery.

Burke, Robert O'Hara (1820-61) Irish-born Australian explorer who led the first south-north crossing of Australia. He left Melbourne (1860) with 17 men, and provisions on 26 camels and 28 horses. With a small advance party he laid food dumps at Cooper's Creek, Queensland, then pushed north with W. J. Wills, Charles Gray and John King. They reached the Gulf of Carpentaria (1861), but were weakened by

Triumph marred by tragedy: the first south-north crossing of Australia, 1860-1

hunger, and on the return journey Gray died. The others regained Cooper's Creek, but it was deserted. Burke and Wills died of starvation, but King was saved by aborigines.

Burke, William (1792-1829) Irish mass murderer, who, in association with William Hare, sold his victims' bodies for illegal dissection at Edinburgh Medical schools. The two men lured travellers to Hare's rooming house, where they were suffocated. In ten months Burke and Hare sold the bodies of at least 15 victims, receiving £8 to £14 per corpse. After their arrest, Hare turned King's evidence, but Burke was convicted and hanged. Hare spent the rest of his life in England under an assumed name.

Burne-Jones, Sir Edward (1833-98) English painter of medieval, romantic and chivalrous themes, reflecting the interests he shared with his friends MORRIS and D. G. ROSSETTI. His style was strongly influenced by BOTTICELLI.

Burnet, Sir Frank Macfarlane (born 1899) Australian immunologist, who shared a Nobel Prize with MEDAWAR in 1960 for their work on the body's tolerance of skin grafts. He put forward the forbidden clone theory of immunological development, which describes how organisms develop tolerance to their own tissues but reject those of others.

Burney, Charles (1726-1814) English scholar, musicologist and man of culture who wrote one major work, *A General History of Music* (4 vols., 1776-89), which is still a standard. To obtain material he first made his musical 'Grand Tours' to France and Italy in 1770 and the Low Countries and Germany in 1772. The journals of those travels with snippets of information and anecdotes of musicians are still delightful entertainment.

Burney, Fanny (1752-1840) English novelist and diarist, who first made popular the social novel of domestic life, enlivened with comedy. Her early novels, *Evelina* (1778) and *Cecilia* (1782), catch the tone of the everyday events of her own social world. She wrote a memoir of her father, a historian of music, and under her married name, D'Arblay, published a lively diary which contained good sketches of Dr JOHNSON and GARRICK. She wrote a biography of her father, Charles BURNEY.

Burns, Robert (1759-96) Scottish poet, who broke through the formal artificiality of 18th-century verse with a lyricism which grew from the ballad poetry of the border. He was an unsuccessful farmer, but after the publication of his dialect *Poems* (1786) he prospered and lived an amorous, dissipated life. The pungent diction of his dialect, his unusual metres, and his humanity and passion helped to revivify English poetry. The range of his satiric and humorous lyrics was wide, from the acid scorn of 'Holy Willie's Prayer' to the wild energy of 'Tam o'Shanter' and 'The Jolly Beggars'.

Burroughs, William (born 1914) American writer noted for his experiments in fictional form. Among his innovations is the 'cut-up', a mosaic of phrases drawn from widely disparate sources, then recombined in novel patterns. His most widely known works are *The Naked Lunch* (1959) and *The Soft Machine* (1968).

Burroughs, William Seward (1855-98) American inventor, who in 1892 patented the first commercially successful adding machine. Numbers, selected by means of a typewriter-type keyboard, were stored and added by means of sets of toothed gears, similar to the modern mechanical adding machine.

Burt, Sir Cyril (born 1883) English psychologist who pioneered the use of psychology as a means of solving social problems. The intelligence tests and methods of statistical analysis which he devised are significant in their own right, but also have led to important contributions to the study of juvenile delinquency.

Burton, Sir Richard Francis (1821-90) British explorer and writer, translator of the 'Arabian Nights' tales. He travelled in India; made a pilgrimage to Mecca disguised as a Pathan; explored Somaliland, the lakes of central Africa (discovering Lake Tanganyika with SPEKE while trying to trace the sources of the Nile) and the Gold Coast. He recounted his travels in a number of vividly in-

formative books, including *Pilgrimage to Al-Medinah and Meccah* (1855) and *First Footsteps in East Africa* (1856).

Burton, Robert (1577-1640) English scholar and divine, and the author of the *Anatomy of Melancholy* (1621), in part a serious work on abnormal psychology and in part a sceptical survey of human pretensions.

Busch, Wilhelm (1832-1908) German artist, whose unconventional calligraphic techniques and characters, often created as if from the realms of fantasy, introduced into cartoon drawing a style that was comic in itself. His verse-and-picture story *Max und Moritz* (1865) was one of the first examples of the comic strip. It inspired W. R. HEARST to commission the American artist, Rudolf Dirks, to produce *The Katzenjammer Kids* for Hearst's King Features Syndicate in the American newspapers.

Busoni, Ferrucio (1866-1924) Italian composer of *Dr Faustus* (1925). The opera, based on a pre-GOETHE version of the Faust legend, was completed by one of his students after his death. Through his anti-romantic temperament, he pioneered the return to classicism in 20th-century music. He was also the first composer to conceive a choral piano concerto (1903-4). Busoni's importance lies in the intellectual integrity which is reflected in all his work. As a pianist, he ranked with the greatest virtuosi of the last 100 years.

Bustamente, Sir William Alexander (born 1884) Jamaican politician, who withdrew his country from the West Indies Federation in 1962. Bustamente founded the Jamaican Labour Party in 1943 and was elected to the House of Representatives, where he held various offices, including that of Chief Minister (1953-5). When the Federation was established (1958) he became leader of the Democratic Labour Party, but resigned in 1960 to draw attention to his policy of quitting the Federation. He was vindicated by a referendum and in 1962 was elected Prime Minister (1962-7).

Butler, Joseph (1692-1752) English theologian. Butler entered the Church of England, went to Oxford, and shortly showed his ability as a preacher and apologist. His greatest work, *The Analogy of Religion* (1736), is a classic statement of natural theology and its congruity with revealed religion. His reasoning, taut and demanding, has exercised great influence. On his death, his manuscripts were destroyed on his instructions.

Butler, Josephine (1828-1906) English social reformer, a dedicated campaigner for the rehabilitation of prostitutes. In Britain, as in other countries, prostitution was tacitly tolerated although restricted by law. To Mrs Butler, this implied acceptance of prostitution, and her unremitting concern and agitation led to the eventual repeal of the Contagious Diseases Acts of 1864-9, which permitted the arrest and medical treatment of prostitutes in garrison towns.

Butler, Samuel (1612-80) English verse satirist, whose *Hudibras* was the English judgement of the abortive religious and political experiments of the Commonwealth period.

Butler, Samuel (1835-1902) English satirist and novelist, who attacked most of the Victorian attitudes towards life. He refused to enter the Church and went instead to farm sheep in New Zealand; he drew on this experience in *Erewhon* (1872), an inventive satire on progress, with some touches worthy of SWIFT. On his return to London in 1865 Butler was a persistently mocking critic of scientists, music critics and teachers. He liked odd attitudes and insisted that HOMER was a woman. In *The Way of All Flesh* (1903) he attacked the Victorian family and education.

Butterfield, William (1814-1900) English High-Church Victorian architect who employed original detail and polychrome, or many-coloured brickwork. His Gothic-revival church, All Saints, London, with its geometric patterns and horizontal bands of black brick and stone, was much praised by RUSKIN in his book *Stones of Venice*. Other works by Butterfield include Keble College, Oxford, and buildings for Rugby School.

Butterick, Ebeneezer (1826-1903) American tailor and shirt-maker who, in the 1840s, devised a technique for printing and cutting paper dressmaking patterns. They could be used by anyone with one of the new sewing machines, such as that of SINGER.

Buxtehude, Diderik (1637-1707) Danish organist and composer who helped to found the public concert with a series of musical evenings in Lübeck from 1673. Although Buxtehude was among the founding fathers of organ playing and composition, much of his music is now lost. The surviving church cantatas and organ compositions prove him to have been a major composer.

Buys Ballot, Christoph (1817-90) Dutch meteorologist who stated the law named after him. In 1857, while Director of the Royal Netherlands Meteorological Institute, he announced the law, which states that, if you stand with your back to the wind in the northern hemisphere (outside the equatorial zone), there is low atmospheric pressure to your left and high to your right; the opposite is true in the southern hemisphere. Unknown to Buys Ballot, the American William Ferrel had already independently deduced this law months before.

Byng, John (1704-57) British admiral, shot for neglect of duty. Just before the Seven Years' War he was sent to protect Britain's base on the Mediterranean island of Minorca, but failed to drive off an attacking French fleet. Believing himself seriously outgunned and outmanned, he withdrew to Gibraltar, where he was court-martialled, found guilty and given the mandatory death sentence. Despite a recommendation for mercy Byng was shot to appease the enraged public. This provoked VOLTAIRE's celebrated remark that the English sometimes shot an admiral *pour encourager les autres* (to encourage the others).

Byrd, Richard Evelyn (1888-1957) American naval officer, polar explorer, and pioneer in scientific research on Antarctica. Abandoning the traditional land transport methods of SCOTT and AMUNDSEN, Byrd explored both Poles by aeroplane, becoming with his pilot, Floyd Bennett, the first to fly across the North Pole (1926). With the pilot, Bernt Balchen, and five others aboard, he was the first to fly across the South Pole (1929). Byrd led several major Antarctic scientific expeditions (1928-47), and, for the Department of the Navy, led 4700 men in an Antarctic programme (1946-7) which mapped a land area as big as France and Germany combined.

Byrd, William (c. 1542-1623) English musician who became the

Byrd in the cockpit of the plane he flew on his second Antarctic expedition

greatest composer of the Elizabethan period. A lifelong Roman Catholic, Byrd was appointed by ELIZABETH I to be joint organist of the Chapel Royal with TALLIS, who may have been his teacher. With Tallis, he was granted a monopoly to print music, though the first printing of his *Gradualia* (1605) was suppressed under JAMES I as politically subversive. Byrd was master of all the musical forms of his day, important for his madrigals, the body of distinguished church music that he wrote for both Catholic and Anglican services, and for helping to lay the foundations of a future keyboard style.

Byron, Lord George Gordon, (1788-1824) English poet, whose scandalous, colourful conduct and popular poetry made him, especially on the Continent, one of the leading figures of the Romantic movement. Byron's 'Childe Harold' (1812-18) and his many verse-tales gave poetry the movement, historical stories and foreign landscapes that SCOTT had introduced to the novel. In *Don Juan* (1819-24), satire, cheerful cynicism, colloquial diction, imagery and descriptive writing cover a sure understanding of psychology and a bleak, sometimes despairing, view of human nature. Byron died of fever at Missolonghi, Greece, in the fight for Greek independence.

C

Cabot, John (1425-c. 1500) Venetian immigrant to England (*c.* 1484), the first of England's ocean explorers. Seeking a sea route to Asia he sailed from Bristol (1497) and reached Cape Breton Island, Canada, which he mistook for northeastern Asia. The following year, backed by HENRY VII, he reached south Greenland (the first European known to do so since Viking times), then crossed to North America and followed its coast southward to the Delaware.

Cabot, Sebastian (c. 1476-1557) English explorer who accompanied his father, John CABOT, on one or both of his voyages and, while seeking the North West Passage, reached Hudson Bay (1509). He was in HENRY VIII's army sent to aid FERDINAND V of Castile and was appointed Pilot Major of the Spanish Navy. While leading an expedition to find the Spice Islands, Ophir, and Cathay, he entered and explored far up the River Plate, in South America. He returned to England, where he founded and became Governor of the Merchant Adventurers.

Cabral, Pedro Alvares (c. 1460-c. 1526) Portuguese discoverer of Brazil. At the head of 13 trading vessels which set out for India (1500), Cabral's route took too westerly a course and he sighted the Brazilian coast of South America, which he claimed for Portugal. After four of his fleet (including the ship carrying Bartholomeu DIAS) sank in a storm, the rest continued to India, traded successfully, and returned laden with spices, porcelain, aromatic woods and pearls.

Cadamosto, Alvise da (c. 1432-c. 1511) Venetian navigator who explored the West African coast for HENRY THE NAVIGATOR of Portugal. On his first voyage (1455), Cadamosto went to the Madeiras and Canaries, and down the Sahara coast to Senegal and Gambia. During his second voyage down the African coast (1456) he was blown out to sea and claimed to have discovered the Cape Verde Islands. His long account of his voyages describes Portuguese settlements, trading and tribal customs in Africa.

Cade, Jack (15th cent.) English, or possibly Irish, landowner, who led a Kentish revolt against corrupt courts, government maladministration, and heavy taxation. In 1450 he led a force from Ashford, Kent, to the outskirts of London. Cade's rebels retreated briefly before Henry VI's army, but defeated it at Sevenoaks and then entered London, killing the Lord Treasurer and the Sheriff of Kent. The rebels dispersed after an amnesty had been arranged, but Cade was hunted down and killed.

Cadillac, Antoine de la Mothe (1658-1730) French founder of Detroit. He went to America as a soldier (1683) and became commander of the post at Mackinac (1694). Eager to build personal wealth and further the French fur trade in North America, he gained a land grant, and in 1701, with 100 French settlers and soldiers, founded a colony consisting of a civil settlement called Ville d'Etroit (Detroit) enclosed by Fort Pontchartrain. Recalled to France in 1711 by LOUIS XIV he was later made governor of Louisiana (1713-16).

Caesar, Gaius Julius (100-44 BC) Roman general and dictator of the Roman empire. After gaining popularity by public displays of democratic feeling and by vast expenditure on public entertainments, Caesar arranged and joined the First Triumvirate (60 BC) with POMPEY and CRASSUS. This ruled in place of the discredited but constitutional oligarchic party. Caesar was elected consul the following year. He built his military reputation on campaigns in northwest Europe (58-51 BC), during which he isolated and crushed Gaul, and made brief forays into Britain (55 and 54 BC). These victories, recounted in his *On the Gallic War*, brought northwest Europe into the orbit of Rome's Mediterranean civilization, so shaping the future of Europe. After these victories, the Senate, prompted by Pompey, demanded that Caesar disband his armies or be declared an enemy. Caesar crossed the river Rubicon into Italy with his army and defeated Pompey at Pharsalus (48 BC). Now dictator of Rome, Caesar unified the empire by equitable reforms and extended citizenship to subject peoples. He refused the offer of the crown (44 BC), but his rule became more absolute. He was killed by Republican conspirators led by BRUTUS.

Cage, John (born 1912) American composer who pioneered the concepts of chance and indeterminacy in modern music. In this he has had a considerable influence over such European composers as STOCKHAUSEN and BERIO. Cage studied with SCHOENBERG and COWELL. In the 1930s he invented the 'prepared piano', an instrument modified to produce an unfamiliar range of sound.

Cagliostro, Count Alessandro di (1743-95) Italian bogus magician and alchemist who travelled Europe earning fame and wealth by predicting the future and selling love potions and elixirs of youth. In 1791, he was condemned to death in Rome for establishing an order of freemasons. Although his sentence was commuted to life imprisonment, Cagliostro was eventually strangled by his jailer.

Caillié, René Auguste (1799-1838) French explorer, the first European in recent times to reach and return alive from Timbuktu. He spent three years in Senegal (1824-7) learning Arabic and studying Islam, then, passing as an Arab on his way to Egypt, joined a Muslim caravan. He reached Timbuktu (1828), where he joined another caravan going north across the Sahara, and reached Fez in Morocco.

Calamity Jane See CANARY, Martha Jane

Calder, Alexander (1898-1973) American sculptor who invented the mobile and became a leading figure in the school of sculptors who work in metal. His *Mobile* (1934) consists of a variety of objects suspended in a black frame; *Red Petals* (1942) is made of metal and wire, transformed into boughs and leaves.

Calderón de la Barca, Pedro (1600-81) Spanish dramatist who succeeded LOPE DE VEGA as playwright to the court of PHILIP IV. A follower of GÓNGORA, the theme of many of his dramas was the rejection of the materialism of 17th-century Spain. *Life's a Dream* (1635), a symbolic play, emphasized the transient qualities of life. Calderón wrote dramas for the Church, the court and the public theatre, and the wide range of his subjects gave a valuable picture of a great nation in decline. *The Mayor of Zalamea* (1642) is one of the most famous of his tragedies about the rigorous code of honour of his times and *King Balthazar's Supper* is one of the best known of his *autos sacramentales* (allegorical religious plays specially written for performance on the Feast of Corpus Christi).

Callaghan, Morley (born 1903) Canadian novelist who has written on a wide range of contemporary topics with humanity and tolerance. He worked for a time with HEMINGWAY, in Paris, where he met FITZGERALD and JOYCE, remembered in *That Summer in Paris* (1963). He has often chosen difficult subjects; *Strange Fugitive* (1928) deals with bootlegging, *It's Never Over* (1930) concerns the family of a murderer, and *More Joy in Heaven* (1937), a reformed prisoner.

Callas, Maria (born 1923) American soprano of Greek parentage who combined personality and musical skill to become the leading operatic soprano of her day.

Calne, Roy (born 1930) English surgeon who, in 1968, after several years of successfully transplanting human kidneys, became the first surgeon to transplant the human liver.

Calvert, George, 1st Baron Baltimore (c. 1580-1632) English colonizer associated, with his son Cecilius (1605-75), with the founding of Maryland (named after CHARLES I's queen, Henrietta Maria). Calvert was granted a charter to colonize Newfoundland (1623), but found the land too cold and was granted another (1632) to colonize and govern between the Potomac and the 40th parallel. He died before the charter was issued but his son sent the first colonists to found St Mary's City at the mouth of the Potomac.

Calvin, John (1509-64) French theologian and religious reformer, founder of the Calvinist branch of the Protestant church. The *Institutes of Christian Religion*, was the most systematic Protestant theological treatise of the Reformation. Although few Protestants now believe in predestination, Calvin's somewhat austere doctrine has greatly influenced the reformed religions, especially the state Protestantism of northern Europe and the Puritan movement in both Britain and North America, although some of the harsher features have softened with time.

Cambyses II (6th cent. BC) Achaemenid King of Persia (530-522 BC), who continued the conquests of his father, CYRUS THE GREAT, by adding Egypt to his empire. In 525 BC he invaded Egypt, and after defeating the Egyptians at Pelusium, captured Thebes and Memphis. The submission of the Greeks of Libya and Cyrene which followed gave him control of their wealth. Cambyses planned expeditions against Ethiopia and Carthage; but although he occupied North Ethiopia, he was forced to withdraw for lack of supplies. He died mysteriously, perhaps by his own hand.

Camerarius, Rudolf (1665-1721) German botanist and physician, who identified the role of pistils and stamens in the reproduction of flowering plants.

Camões, Luís Vaz de (c. 1524-80) Portugal's outstanding literary figure and lyric poet. His masterpiece, *The Lusiads* (1572), is an epic poem exalting Portuguese history and the voyages of Vasco da GAMA. Camões's collection of lyric poems *Rhymes* was published posthumously in 1595. A master of every verse form, his sufferings and philosophical meditations in these anguished and deeply felt works express the uniquely Portuguese *saudade-soledade* (a yearning, with overtones of loneliness) as no other Portuguese poet has ever done.

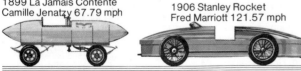

1899 La Jamais Contente
Camille Jenatzy 67.79 mph

1906 Stanley Rocket
Fred Marriott 121.57 mph

1927 Sunbeam
Henry Seagrave 203.92 mph

Campbell, Archibald, 1st Duke of Argyll (c. 1651-1703) Scottish soldier responsible (with John Campbell, 1st Earl of Breadalbane, and Sir John Dalrymple) for the Massacre of Glencoe. He supported William of Orange in the Revolution of 1688 and was deputed to offer him the Scottish crown (1689). In February 1692, Campbell clan troops quartered with the Macdonalds in the Argyllshire pass of Glencoe, and butchered some 40 of their hosts, including the Macdonald Chieftain MacIan. The pretext was the Macdonalds' suspected disloyalty to WILLIAM III, but the massacre also struck a blow at the Campbells' traditional clan enemies.

Campbell, Colen (1673-1729) Scottish architect who introduced the Palladian style into England. Mereworth Castle, Kent, modelled on PALLADIO's Villa Rotunda, is the most correct example of this style. In 1715, he published *Vitruvius Britannicus*, a collection of designs of buildings mainly by contemporary British architects which first aroused Lord Burlington's interest in architecture. Burlington House, London, which he remodelled in 1718-19, and Compton Place, Eastbourne, are other examples of Campbell's works still in existence.

Campbell, John (1653-1728) Scotsborn journalist and publisher, who emigrated from Scotland to Massachusetts in 1695 and became a postmaster in Boston. In 1704 he first published the *Boston Newsletter*.

Campbell, Sir Malcolm (1885-1948) English racing driver who became one of the most successful speed record-breakers on both land and water. Between 1924 and 1935 he broke the land speed record nine times raising it to 301·13 mph. When he turned to boats, he broke the water speed record three times, raising it to 141·75 mph. His son, Donald Campbell (1921-67), continued Sir Malcolm's record-breaking attempts and reached 328 mph in a last, fatal attempt on the water speed record.

Campbell, Roy (1901-57) South African descriptive poet and satirist, whose best writing is of the outdoor life. Campbell gained notoriety by fighting on FRANCO's side in the Spanish Civil War. 'The Flaming Terrapin' (1924) and the satiric 'Georgiad' are his best known poems.

Campbell-Bannerman, Henry (1836-1908) English Prime Minister and head of the Liberal government which came to power in 1905 after ten years of Conservative and Unionist rule. As Liberal leader in the Commons (1899) he advocated conciliation of the Boers during the South African War of 1899-1902 and criticized the more extreme tactics (concentration camps) used by Britain during the campaign. He became Prime Minister on the resignation of BALFOUR, and his party gained a sweeping victory in the election of 1906. His government began the policy of reconciliation in South Africa which led to the grant of self-government (1909).

Campen, Jacop van (1595-1657) Dutch 17th-century architect who was influenced by PALLADIO. Probably his best building is the Mauritshuis (1633-5), in the Hague, a mellow brick building in which the giant pilasters and pediment are combined with the Dutch type of hipped roof. His other works are the Amsterdam Town Hall, now the Royal Palace, and the Nieuwe Kerk in Haarlem.

Campion, Edmund (1540-81) English Jesuit martyr who was tortured, convicted of treason and hanged at Tyburn for encouraging the Catholic community outlawed by ELIZABETH I after her excommunication in 1570. Unable to accept Anglicanism, Campion, a brilliant scholar and orator, left England for Rome in 1573, when he became a Jesuit priest, returning to his country as head of the first Jesuit mission to England in 1580. He was canonized in 1970.

Campion, Thomas (1567-1619) English lyric poet and musician, who, amongst a series of books of songs, published *Observations in the Art of English Poesie* (1602), which questioned formalized conventional notions on the art of writing verse.

Camus, Albert (1913-60) Algerian-born French novelist, dramatist and essayist, winner of the Nobel Prize for Literature in 1957. His early sympathy with Existentialist ideas is reflected in philosophical essays like *Le mythe de Sisyphe* (1942) and symbolic novels such as *L'Etranger, La Peste* (1947) and *La Chute* (1956). They explore the nature of action in an absurd world, the problem of suffering,

and the reconciliation of the claims of art with those of political responsibility. In the postwar years, the rift with SARTRE's Existentialist views became more marked as Camus argued against cynicism and nihilism, vealing his compassion and humanitarian outlook. Among his other notable publications were his treatise *L'Homme revolté* (1951) and a number of plays – *Le Malentendu* (1944), *Caligula* (written 1938, produced 1946), *Les Justes* (1949) and *L'Etat de siège* (1948). He died in a motor accident.

Canaletto, Antonio (1697-1768) Italian artist and etcher, who is celebrated for his views of Venice and Rome. His early style was impressionistic, but Canaletto's colours sharpened and his technique became crisp, with an emphasis on detail facilitated by the use of the *camera obscura*. In *Ascension Day at Venice*, which depicts the city during one of its most important festivals, Canaletto captures the essential vitality of the scene and contrasts it with the timelessness of the buildings, which are particularly Venetian.

Canary, Martha Jane (1852-1903) American frontierswoman who became a flamboyant legend in her own lifetime. Nicknamed 'Calamity Jane', she usually dressed in men's clothes, and worked heroically nursing the sick during the 1878 smallpox epidemic at Deadwood, South Dakota.

Canning, George (1770-1827) English statesman who supported the revolt of the Spanish American colonies (1823). A Foreign Secretary in 1807, Canning initiated the Peninsular War policy. A quarrel and duel with CASTLEREAGH in 1809 restricted him to a series of minor offices until 1822 when, as a result of Castlereagh's suicide, he was reinstated as Foreign Secretary and appointed Leader of the House of Commons. He continued the later policy of Castlereagh in abandoning the Congress system and the policy of non-intervention, and his support of independence movements in Europe anticipated the extension of British trade. Canning became Prime Minister and Chancellor of the Exchequer in 1827, for the last five months of his life.

Cannizzaro, Stanislao (1826-1910) Italian chemist who champ-

1935 Bluebird
Malcolm Campbell 301.129 mph

1964 Proteus Bluebird
Donald Campbell 403.10 mph

1970 The Blue Flame
Gary Gabelich 630.388 mph

THE BLUE FLAME

ioned AVOGADRO's hypothesis that equal volumes of all gases (at the same pressure and temperature) contain the same number of atoms or molecules. Cannizzaro saw it could be used to determine atomic weights and establish chemical structures, and successfully convinced science of its importance.

Cano, Sebastian del (16th cent.) Spanish navigator who completed the first circumnavigation of the globe. He sailed on one of MAGELLAN's five ships (1519) and, after Magellan's death and heavy casualties among senior officers, rose to command the *Vittoria*, the only one of the five ships fit for the long journey home from the Spice Islands. The homeward voyage, by the route already known through the Indian Ocean and round the Cape of Good Hope, took nine months. Few of the crew survived.

Canova, Antonio (1757-1822) Italian Neo-classic sculptor, chiefly in marble, who was often inspired by the erotic myths of Greece, as in *Cupid and Psyche* (1793). His *Tomb of Maria Christina* (1798), which treated the figures in the round, was revolutionary for tomb sculpture.

Cantor, Georg (1845-1918) German mathematician, whose most famous work deals with the theory of infinity and the theory of sets. He extended the numerical series introduced by FOURIER. His set theory was a new departure in mathematics, and forms the basis of much modern mathematical analysis.

Canute II (c. 994-1035) Danish king of England (1016-35), who ruled a short-lived northern empire. Successfully finishing his father SWEYN's fight with Ethelred II, he was elected king of all England by the Witan (the English Saxon Parliament) in 1016 and married Ethelred's widow. Canute pursued a policy of reconciliation, respecting local customs, sending back to Denmark his Danish fleet and soldiers except for a bodyguard of house carls and a fleet of 40 ships. In 1026 he inflicted a major defeat on a Norwegian-Swedish attack on Denmark and was able to take over Norway and became its king (1028). There are many stories about Canute, including the one that he tried in vain to stop the incoming tide to show his sycophantic followers the limitations of his powers.

Cão, Diogo (15th cent.) Portuguese mariner who first pushed the exploration of Africa's west coast far south of the Equator. On his first voyage (1482-4), he discovered the mouth of the Congo and sailed on to Cape St Mary (13°26′S). On his last known

voyage (1485-6), he reached Monte Negro (15°41′S) and beyond that Cape Cross, within 150 miles of the Tropic of Capricorn. At each of the four points he set up commemorative pillars, found by later travellers.

Capa, Robert (1913-54) Hungarian-born photographer who covered five wars in the space of 18 years. Capa was killed by a land mine during the Indo-China conflict.

Capek, Karel (1890-1938) Czech dramatist, who wrote *R.U.R.* and *The Insect Play* in 1921. *Rossum's Universal Robots* is a science-fiction play in which robots take over the world. In *The Insect Play*, Capek satirizes humanity in the guise of insects. His work belongs to the Expressionist school of TOLLER and WEDEKIND.

Capet, Hugh see HUGH CAPET

Capone, Alphonso, 'Al' (1895-1947) Italian-born American gangster, who built up a criminal organization during the Prohibition era (1919-33). Running the illicit liquor trade, gambling saloons and brothels in Chicago, Capone maintained his position by wholesale elimination of his rivals and is said to have been responsible for over 500 murders. In 1930, the FBI attempted to convict him, but lacked sufficient evidence to obtain his impeachment. He was eventually sentenced to 11 years' imprisonment in 1931 for tax evasion.

Capote, Truman (born 1924) American novelist, whose work centres frequently on lonely people fighting against society in the Southern States of America. His book *In*

King gangster Al Capone rose from the ranks of petty villainy to dominate crime in prohibition Chicago

Cold Blood (1966), a detailed reconstruction of a particularly mindless and brutal murder, was hailed as a new type of prose narrative. His earlier work, especially *Other Voices, Other Rooms* (1948) about the painful development of a homosexual boy, is more Gothic in style.

Capp, Al (born 1909) Creator of the American comic strip *Li'l Abner* (1934). His work, which deals with the tribulations of an eccentric mountain community, satirizes American national institutions.

Caragiale, Ion (1852-1912) Rumanian playwright and short story writer, whose satires on contemporary social and political institutions give a vivid picture of Rumanian society in transition from East to West European and from an agrarian to an urban way of life.

Caran D'Ache (1858-1909) French cartoonist, who worked mostly in line. He frequently depicted domestic events or military scenes, but was also a caricaturist, political satirist and illustrator.

Caravaggio, Michelangelo Merisi da (1573-1610) Italian artist, with whom the development of *chiaroscuro* (contrasts between light and shade) is chiefly associated. It is apparent even in his earliest important commission: a series of large pictures of the life of ST MATTHEW for a chapel in S Luigi dei Francesi in Rome. In one of these, *The Calling of St Matthew*, the darkness of the scene is dramatically relieved by a shaft of light which falls directly on the saint. The original altar-piece of *St Matthew and the Angel* in the same chapel was rejected. Exception was also taken to another radical innovation by Caravaggio: an uncom-

promisingly realistic interpretation of religious scenes conceived as contemporary events, biblical characters being depicted as peasants with dirty feet and sweating faces. Caravaggio's aim was to bring his religious scenes closer to ordinary experience and this he attempted to do partly by eschewing reverential poses and by bringing sharply-lit figures close to the picture plane, where his realistic treatment of his characters could not be ignored. Caravaggio's influence was greatest outside Italy, where it spread both to France, in the painting of LA TOUR, and the Netherlands (Utrecht school).

Cardano, Geronimo (1501-76) Italian physician and mathematician, who produced the first accurate account of typhus fever, and was the first to publish solutions to cubic and quartic equations, and calculations on the theory of probability. Among his many publications were an attack on the medical practices of his day, a work on the treatment of syphilis, and some notes on the teaching of deaf, dumb and blind people. His most important mathematical publication was *The Great Art, or The Rules of Algebra* (1545), a fundamental text in the study of algebra. It contained his solutions of cubic equations and work done by his former servant, Lodovico FERRARI, on quartic equations. Cardano's other principal mathematical work was *The Book of the Game of Chance*, which sets out a theory of probability not fully formalized until the work of PASCAL a century later.

Carducci, Giosuè (1835-1907) Italian critic, poet and Nobel Prize winner who advocated a return to classicism in fiction and attempted to introduce classical metrical schemes into contemporary Italian poetry. The patriotic evocation of Italy's past and the visions of her future which permeate his poetry, notably *Primitive Odes* (1877-89) and *Rhymes and Rhythms* (1899), have caused him to be hailed as the national poet of modern Italy.

Carey, Joyce (1888-1957) English novelist, whose many books have a buoyant optimism rare in 20th-century writing. His first novels, *Aissa Saved* (1932) and *The African Witch* (1936), showed remarkable sympathy for African character and problems. His chief works are contained in two trilogies. The first, including *The Horse's Mouth* (1944), is a study of closely interrelated lives, full of skilful characterization. The second, starting with *A Prisoner of Grace* (1952), links English politics, social history and religion. He also wrote poetry, stories and political studies, including *The Case for African Freedom* (1941).

Carlson, Chester (born 1906) American inventor of the dry copying process called xerography (1937). The process uses electrostatic charges to form a copy of an original in fine carbon powder.

Carlyle, Thomas (1795-1881) British historian and journalist whose work offers a powerful social and political commentary on his times. He was concerned with the role of the 'hero' in history and most of his writing depicts events through the lives of men and women. He also examined the drabness and bitterness occasioned by social structures. His works included *The French Revolution* (1837), *Frederick the Great* (1865) and *Chartism* (1839), all distinguished by a dramatic use of dialogue and imagery.

Carman, Bliss (1861-1929) Canadian poet, who wrote expansive, descriptive verse extolling the virtues of an open-air, country life.

Carnegie, Andrew (1835-1919) Scottish industrialist who expounded a 'Gospel of Wealth' theory (1889) in which half a man's duty was to get wealth and the other half to redistribute the surplus for the general welfare. Carnegie emigrated to America in 1848 and worked for the Pennsylvania Railroad before concentrating (from 1873) on steel manufacture and founding the US Steel Corporation (1901). Notable beneficiaries of his philanthropy were educational institutes in Pittsburgh and Washington and American and Scottish universities.

Carnot, Nicolas Léonard Sadi (1796-1832) French physicist whose work on the theory of heat engines led directly to the discovery of the Second Law of Thermodynamics. In 1824, he showed that the maximum efficiency attainable by any engine from a given source of heat depends only on the temperatures of that source and of the 'sink' to which waste heat is released. This is very close to the Second Law, but Carnot's work was largely ignored

In Carracci's 'Flight into Egypt' the Holy Family is placed in a landscape over which the eye is invited to travel

for 25 years until rediscovered and generalized by CLAUSIUS and KELVIN.

Carothers, Wallace (1896-1937) American chemist who led the research team at the Du Pont Company, which, in 1935, developed nylon, the first completely man-made fibre.

Carpaccio, Vittore (c. 1460-c. 1523) Venetian painter, whose work often depicts the ceremonial pageantry of his native city. His most famous work is the early narrative cycle, *The Legend of St Ursula* (1490-8).

Carpeaux, Jean-Baptiste (1827-75) French sculptor of the Second Empire, whose best-known work is *The Dance* (1865-8) on the façade of the Paris Opera House.

Carpenter, Nathanael (17th cent.) English geographer who published the first geographical study to be written in English. It was ahead of its time in stressing the spatial relationships between geographical phenomena, and in the scientific spirit in which he described them.

Carpini, Giovanni de Piano (c. 1182-c. 1252) Italian Franciscan monk and one of the first Europeans to explore the Mongol empire. In 1245, Carpini led a delegation to the Khan of Tartary at Karakorum to protest about the invasion of Christian lands by Mongol hordes. The journey, across what is now eastern Europe and central Asia, was documented in his *Liber Tartarorum*.

Carracci, Annibale (1560-1609) Italian artist, who was one of the first eclectic painters, absorbing elements from a number of sources, notably MICHELANGELO, RAPHAEL, TITIAN and antique art. His most famous work, the ceiling fresco in the gallery of the Farnese Palace, Rome (1597-1604), combines narrative mythological scenes with a scheme of simulated architecture and sculpture evolving from Michelangelo's Sistine Chapel ceiling. The work was influential in the development of 17th-century illusionistic decorative schemes.

Carrier, Willis Haviland (1876-1950) American engineer, who initiated the scientific approach to air-conditioning systems. His paper *Rational Psychometric Formulae* presented to the American Society of Mechanical Engineers in 1911 was based on ten years' work, and is the basis of all modern air-conditioning practice.

Carroll, Lewis (1832-98) English mathematician and writer, whose imaginative fantasies are among the most original prose works of the 19th century. The famous 'nonsense' books, *Alice in Wonderland* (1865), *Through the Looking-Glass* (1871), and the poem, 'Hunting of the Snark' (1876), do not lack sense, but are parodies of sense which, following an idiosyncratic logic, point out the absurdities in apparently normal behaviour.

Carson, Edward (1854-1935) Anglo-Irish barrister and politician who, in 1912, was instrumental in raising a force of 80,000 men (Ulster Volunteers) to resist Home Rule for Ireland. From 1905 he led the Protestant movement against Home Rule and established (1911) the Ulster Unionist Council and a draft Constitution for Ulster. In 1915-16 he helped LLOYD GEORGE and the Tories to remove ASQUITH from office as PM, and became a member of Lloyd George's war cabinet. He was created a life peer in 1921 and sat as Lord of Appeal from 1921 to 1929. After the war, in contrast to his earlier intransigence, he tried to find a compromise solution to the Irish problem.

Carson, Kit (1809-68) American frontiersman famous for pioneering west of the Mississippi (as Daniel BOONE was famous east of it). He became successively teamster, trapper, Indian fighter, hunter, and army scout and ranged from Texas to Oregon during a hectic career that helped to extend westward settlement.

Carter, Howard (1873-1939) English Egyptologist who discovered the tomb of Tutankhamun (14th century BC), the first royal tomb to be found almost intact. Sponsored by Lord Carnarvon, he began, in 1917, a five-year hunt for Tutankhamun's tomb in the Valley of the Kings at Luxor. He was on the point of abandoning the search in 1922, when he found the flight of rock-cut steps leading to the tomb, which contained the undis-

turbed mummy of the king with an array of funerary equipment.

Cartier, Jacques (1491-1557) French explorer, who discovered the St Lawrence River. After exploring the North American Atlantic seaboard south to Labrador, he took a small fleet up the St Lawrence as far as modern Quebec city, and went on by boat as far as modern Montreal, which he named.

Cartwright, Edmund (1743-1823) English clergyman, who invented a power-driven loom from which modern counterparts have been developed. After building improved handlooms, he installed the first power looms in mills at Doncaster (1786) and Manchester (1791), thus doubling a weaver's output, and, by 1809, they were in general use. Cartwright also patented a wool-combing machine (1789, 1790), a rope-making machine (1792) and improved various agricultural machines.

Caruso, Enrico (1873-1921) Italian operatic tenor who was the first singer to owe world-wide fame to the gramophone. By the time of his death he had made 154 recordings. His most popular roles were Carnio in *Pagliacci*, Rodolpho in *La Bohème* and the duke in *Rigoletto*.

Carver, John (c. 1576-1621) English merchant and first governor of Plymouth Colony, in what is now Massachusetts. After joining the Pilgrim Fathers in Holland (1609), Carver obtained a charter to settle in the New World, raised money for the *Mayflower* and collected the London pilgrims. He sailed with some 100 colonists, including English Puritans seeking religious freedom. When they reached Cape Cod (1620), Carver became governor of new-born Plymouth Colony in accordance with the Mayflower Compact, an improvised agreement for democratic self-government devised off-shore. Carver and half of the colony died in the first severe winter.

Casals, Pablo (1876-1973) Spanish virtuoso cellist whose interpretations, particularly of the unaccompanied cello suites of J. S. BACH, combined great technical skill with philosophical and humanitarian depths. In 1905 he formed a legendary trio consisting of himself, the violinist Jacques Thibaud and the pianist Alfred Cortot. From 1940 Casals remained in exile to show his dislike for the Spanish régime.

A narrow flight of steps led Howard Carter into the entrance gallery of the tomb of Tutankhamun. In the burial chamber he found a wealth of treasure

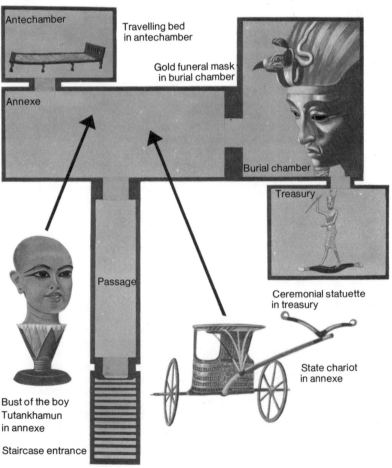

Antechamber

Travelling bed in antechamber

Gold funeral mask in burial chamber

Annexe

Burial chamber

Treasury

Ceremonial statuette in treasury

Passage

State chariot in annexe

Bust of the boy Tutankhamun in annexe

Staircase entrance

Casanova, Giovanni Jacopo (1725-98) Italian adventurer whose exploits and guises dazzled European high society. After expulsion from a seminary for scandalous conduct, Casanova was variously a preacher, alchemist, and violin player. In 1755, he was jailed for sorcery, but quickly engineered a daring escape. Casanova fled to Paris, where he introduced a lottery, accumulated a fortune, and mixed with the Empress CATHERINE II, VOLTAIRE, Madame de POMPADOUR and CAGLIOSTRO. After a brief career in espionage, Casanova settled down as a librarian and wrote his bawdy memoirs. It was not published in unexpurgated form until 1960.

Casement, Roger (1864-1916) Irish nationalist and British consular official. Casement joined the British Consular Service in 1892 and won fame and a knighthood (1911) through his reports on the exploitation and maltreatment of rubber-tapping workers in the Congo (1903) and in Brazil (1910). During his consular career he canvassed the cause of Irish nationalism, and on retiring from the Service became an active Irish Nationalist. When war broke out in 1914 he went to Germany and tried – unsuccessfully – to raise a brigade of Irish prisoners of war to fight against Britain. He landed in Ireland from a German submarine in 1916, just before the Easter Rising, but was caught, taken to London, tried for high treason and hanged. His remains were subsequently disinterred from Pentonville gaol and taken to Ireland, where he is regarded as a patriot and martyr by Irish republicans.

Casey, Richard Gardiner (born 1890) Governor-General of Australia (1965-9) who was Australia's minister to the United States from 1940 to 1942 and, from 1942 to 1943, a member of the War Cabinet in Britain. In 1944 he was appointed Governor of Bengal.

Casimir III (1310-70) King of Poland (1333-70), called 'the Great'. Succeeding his father LADISLAS I, Casimir made peace with the Teutonic Knights and Bohemia, and formed an alliance with Hungary which helped him to acquire Galicia (1340) and, with it, much trade. Casimir's domestic measures checked aristocratic oppression of the peasants, founded towns, reformed administration and currency, built national defence and supported industry and commerce. He founded Cracow University (1364), later to become Eastern Europe's intellectual capital.

Casimir IV (1427-92) King of Poland (1447-92), who made his country a great Central European power. Inheriting both Poland and Lithuania, he worked to preserve the union and to restore Polish lands lost to the Teutonic Knights. Helped by Prussian towns, he regained the lost western and northern territories (1454-66), restoring Poland's Baltic outlet, absorbing western Prussia, and gaining overlordship of Eastern Prussia. To preserve the Polish-Lithuanian union he adopted an anti-German policy which he maintained only by granting to his nobles wide privileges and the right to elect the monarch. As a result of his enlightened approach to the freedom of opinion, Poland became a refuge of scholars and a centre of culture.

Caslon, William (1692-1766) English printer, noted for the distinction and legibility of his type. He established a type foundry and his work soon became known throughout Europe. The Caslon type-face is still used in book printing.

Caso y Andrade, Alfonso (born 1896) Mexican archaeologist whose excavation of the ancient city of Monte Alban made a major contribution to the reconstruction of Mexican prehistory. In 1930 he began 18 years' work on the large ceremonial complex above Oaxaca in southern Mexico and revealed that development began in about 500 BC, culminating in the superb Zapotec temples, altars and tombs of about AD 600.

Cassidy, Butch (1866-1910) American cowboy and rustler, who became a leader of the Wild Bunch, a group of outlaws operating mainly from 'Hole in the Wall' in the wilds of Wyoming. In 1902, Cassidy and his companion Harry Longabough, the Sundance Kid, fled the West and sailed for South America accompanied by Etta Place, who had joined the outlaws. Several robberies were committed by the trio before Cassidy and Longabough were killed by soldiers in Bolivia.

Cassini, Giovanni (1625-1712) Italian-born French astronomer, who greatly extended knowledge of the Solar System. While Professor of Astronomy at Bologna (1650-69), Cassini calculated the rotation periods of Venus, Mars and Jupiter. In 1669 he was appointed Director of LOUIS XIV's new Paris Observatory. In the following years he discovered the division that separates the rings of Saturn (the 'Cassini Division') and calculated the eccentricity of the Earth's orbit. He began the work, carried on by his son Jacques, which confirmed that the Earth was not a perfect sphere. Between 1671 and 1684 he discovered four satellites of Saturn and estimated the distance from Mars to the Sun.

Castagno, Andrea del (c. 1423-57) Florentine painter, whose early work (e.g. Last Supper, c. 1445-50) was influenced by MASACCIO's and later by that of DONATELLO. He painted a celebrated series of Famous Men And Women.

Castelo Branco, Camilo (1825-95) Portuguese author of novels and short stories. His life was that of the prototypical Romantic, full of amorous and literary intrigues, including an attempt to become a priest, and culminating in blindness and suicide. His most popular work Disastrous Love (1862) was based on an adventure of his own. All Castelo Branco's works deal with Romantic passion, though with a redeeming irony and vitality, which together with his richly vernacular style, make him still readable today.

Castiglione, Baldassarre (1478-1529) Italian courtier and author of one of the 16th century's most popular books, The Courtier (1528) – an illuminating but idealized picture of Italian Renaissance court society. Born of an aristocratic family, he served the Duke of Urbino as a diplomat, eventually becoming Papal Nuncio in Spain.

Castlereagh, Robert Stewart, Viscount (1769-1822) Anglo-Irish statesman, who was responsible for the Fourth Coalition, consisting of Britain Russia, Austria and Prussia, which defeated NAPOLEON. Among the causes he espoused were the union of Britain and Ireland, and Catholic emancipation, the rejection of which (1801) by George III caused his resignation and that of PITT. He also served at the India Office (1802) and was War Secretary (1805-6; 1807-9). His duel with CANNING (1809) led to his enforced retirement for some years. After becoming Foreign Secretary in 1812, he sought to establish the balance of power and diplomatic order in Europe which became known as the 'Congress System', though Castlereagh became progressively disillusioned with its reactionary pretensions. He committed suicide in 1822.

Castriota, George see SCANDERBEG

Castro, Fidel (born 1927) Cuban revolutionary politician who overthrew BATISTA's dictatorship (1959) and made Cuba a socialist state. Son of an immigrant from Spain, he became a militant socialist, and was captured in 1953 while leading an attack on the Moncada Barracks with the purpose of seizing arms and ammunition. He was sentenced to 15 years' imprisonment by the Batista régime, but was released under an amnesty in 1955. He went to Mexico where he organized a Cuban revolutionary movement, and returned secretly to the island with a small force, including 'Che' GUEVARA. He took to the Sierra Maestra mountains and recruited more men (1956). After inflicting a series of defeats on government forces, he took Havana on 1 Jan. 1959 and seized political power. In 1961 he declared himself Marxist-Leninist and requested Russian aid. Missile sites were installed and missiles and other equipment shipped to Cuba by Russia, which provoked the United States and resulted in the major international 'Cuba crisis' of October 1962.

Cather, Willa (1873-1947) American novelist, who wrote affectionately about immigrant and pioneer life in the agricultural West. *O Pioneers!* (1913) and *My Antonia* (1918) are set in the frontier world of the Nebraska prairies where she spent her childhood. Nearly all her work is imbued with a sense of history coloured by Roman Catholicism.

Catharine of Aragon see HENRY VIII

Catherine II 'the Great' (1729-96) German-born Empress of Russia (1762-96) who continued PETER I's work of westernization and expansion. After forcing her unpopular husband Peter III to abdicate, she made St Petersburg rival Paris as a cultural showplace, by patronizing Italian opera, painting, sculpture and architecture, and popularizing French etiquette, literature, and liberal philosophy. Catherine corresponded with VOLTAIRE and the French *encyclopédistes* and favoured social reforms proposed by MONTESQUIEU and BECCARIA, but she also extended serfdom (forced by the powerful Russian nobles) and suppressed liberalism. Under Catherine's brilliant generals (who included Suvorov and one of her numerous lovers, Potemkin) Russian troops seized Byelorussia from Poland (in and after 1772) and the Crimea from Turkey.

Cato, Marcus Porcius (234-149 BC) Roman statesman and writer, author of the first important Latin prose works, including a history of Rome and a treatise on agriculture.

Cattell, Raymond (born 1905) American psychologist known for his multi-factorial approach to the analysis of personality. Like EYSENCK, he believes that personality can be broken down into common character traits (factors) and then measured, the overall personality being the sum of common traits.

Latest in a long line of American revolutionaries, Cuba's Fidel Castro

Catullus, Gaius Valerius (c. 84-c. 54 BC) The first Roman personal poet whose works survive. His many short poems, in lyric, iambic and elegaic metres, though written with great care and an attention to Greek models which delighted his sophisticated circle, convey a deep sincerity, rising to passion, especially when he writes of his love for Lesbia. His four longer poems, and especially No. 64 on the Marriage of Pelius and Thetis, more clearly show his learning and the influence on him of Alexandrian poetry.

Cauchy, Augustin Louis (1789-1857) French mathematician, who wrote three main treatises on analysis and calculus between 1821 and 1828. At the same time, he developed the theory of functions of a complex variable, which is fundamental to many fields of applied mathematics.

Causley, Charles (born 1917) English poet, whose verse, telling of his life in Cornwall, in the navy and as a schoolteacher, continues the tradition of folk poetry.

Cavafy, Constantinos (1863-1933) Greek lyric poet whose few poems are among the finest in modern Greek literature, evoking regret for unfulfilled desires and capturing fleeting moments of happiness or beauty.

Cavallini, Pietro (c. 1250-c. 1330) Roman painter and mosaicist. His works (e.g. mosaics in the church of Sta Maria in Trastevere, in Rome; frescoes in Sta Cecilia, also in Rome), although dependent on the stylized forms of Byzantine art, echo the classical spirit of antique painting.

Cavell, Edith Louisa (1865-1915) British nurse, shot by the Germans for aiding the escape of Allied soldiers from Belgium. Matron at the Berkendael Medical Institute, Brussels, she helped some 200 English, French and Belgian soldiers to escape to the Dutch frontier. For this she was arrested in August 1915 and shot on 12 October.

Cavendish, Henry (1731-1810) English chemist and physicist who calculated the Earth's mass. Isaac NEWTON had stated his famous law of gravitation in an equation involving the Earth's mass and an undetermined constant called the gravitational constant. Cavendish performed a delicate experiment to measure the gravitational force of attraction between two metal balls and from this calculated the constant. He used the constant in Newton's equation to calculate the Earth's mass. His result, nearly 7000 trillion tons, was about 10 per cent higher than modern estimates.

Cavour, Count Camillo (1810-61) Italian statesman who, with GARIBALDI, accomplished the union of Italy. With Count Cesare Balbo, he started the nationalist newspaper *Il Risorgimento* (The Resurrection) in 1847, advocating a representative system of government for Piedmont, which in 1848 was granted a constitution by Charles Albert (King of Savoy and ruler of Piedmont-Sardinia). Cavour entered politics in 1848 and, after holding several portfolios, he became Premier in 1852, and developed and modernized his native Piedmont's agriculture, industry, communications and army. Believing that he could unite Italy by bringing her onto the international stage, he took Piedmont into the Crimean War, and in 1858 signed a secret treaty with NAPOLEON III (Plombières) whereby France and Piedmont were to make war on Austria. He resigned (1859) when Napoleon III made a premature peace with Austria without consulting him, but returned to office in 1860 to accomplish the union of Tuscany, Parma, Romagna and Modena with Piedmont. Garibaldi, meanwhile, recruited and led a patriot army to victory in Sicily and Naples. He advanced on Rome and met Cavour, at the head of the Piedmontese army, at the River Volturno. The two leaders proclaimed a united Kingdom of Italy on 17 Mar. 1861, with VICTOR EMMANUEL II as king.

Caxton, William (c.1422-91) England's first printer, who produced the works of MALORY, GOWER and CHAUCER as well as translations of VIRGIL's *Aeneid* and French romances. In 1476, he set up his press at Westminster, after a successful career as a merchant and printer in Bruges, where his first press was established.

Cayley, Arthur (1821-95) English lawyer and mathematician, who, with J. J. SYLVESTER, originated the theory of algebraic invariants. Cayley's work covered the whole range of pure and applied mathematics, but his major work is a series of ten papers on algebraic forms, developing the theory of algebraic invariants.

Cayley, Sir George (1773-1857) English engineer and inventor who was the founder of the science of aerodynamics and a pioneer in aerial navigation. His paper *On Aerial Navigation* (1809) defined the problem of heavier-than-air flight. The culmination of his aeronautical career came in 1853, when a large glider he had constructed carried his coachman on a flight of about 500 yards across a valley. This was the first successful manned heavier-than-air flight.

Cecchetti, Enrico (1850-1928) Italian dancer who vastly improved classical ballet dancing technique and taught the greatest ballet dancers of the early 1900s. Formulator of the strict Cecchetti Method of dancing, based on logically progressive exercises, smoothly linked sequences of steps, and harmony of line in the static poses called *arabesques*, Cecchetti taught FOKINE, KARSAVINA, NIJINSKY and PAVLOVA and future teachers such as De VALOIS.

Cecil, Sir Robert, Earl of Salisbury (c. 1563-1612) English statesman, who was the vital link between the Tudor government of ELIZABETH I and the Stuart government of JAMES I. Trained by his father, Sir William CECIL, in statecraft, he became Secretary of State in 1596 and was mainly responsible for the smooth accession in England (1603) of James VI of Scotland, who made him an earl (1605). An able administrator, he negotiated peace with Spain (1604), dealt with the Gunpowder Plot and endeavoured to improve the royal finances. His last act was to arrange the marriage of James's daughter Elizabeth to Frederick, Elector Palatine; their descendant, George of Hanover, became King of Britain in 1714.

Cecil, William, 1st Baron Burghley (1520-98) English statesman who steered his country through its golden Elizabethan age. A courtier by birth, he took a prudent middle course in politics and religion which enabled him to gain influence, survive MARY I's anti-Protestant purge, and become ELIZABETH I's most trusted minister. As administrative head of government he increased economic and cultural growth by keeping England at peace until 1585 and supported the establishment of the Church of England. Cecil possessed Elizabeth's confidence to a remarkable degree but opposed her dynastically undesirable wish to marry the Earl of Leicester.

He hired spies to foil Catholic plots and executed those who threatened the throne, including MARY, Queen of Scots.

Cellini, Benvenuto (1500-71) Florentine sculptor and goldsmith, whose fame rests largely on his semi-scandalous autobiography, *The Life of Benvenuto, the son of Giovanni Cellini written by himself in Florence*. Dictated as he worked to a young scribe (1558-66), this work presents him as an archetypal Renaissance figure. The best-known piece of Cellini's few remaining works is a salt-cellar (1540-3) made for King Francis I, now in Vienna. Most of his sculptures are in Florence; the largest, the *Nymph of Fontainebleau* (1543-4), an elegant and sophisticated relief, is in the Louvre.

Celsius, Anders (1701-44) Swedish astronomer who devised the centigrade temperature scale, now used by scientists throughout the world. In 1742 he proposed a temperature scale that divided the difference between the freezing and boiling points of water into 100 equal intervals.

Celsus (2nd cent. AD) Platonist philosopher and opponent of the emergent Christianity which, he argued, cut across the traditional values of humanity. There was, he said, little evidence to support the miracles of JESUS.

Celsus, Aulus (1st cent. AD) Roman nobleman and landowner whose book *On Medical Matters* was one of the first medical texts to be printed (1478). It collated all contemporary knowledge of human and veterinary medicine and agriculture and stressed the importance to health of diet and a regular way of life.

Cervantes Saavedra, Miguel de (1547-1616) Spanish novelist and

Don Quixote dies of disillusionment. Cervantes's book has been more widely translated than any but the Bible

dramatist, who, elderly, disgraced and in debt after a lifetime of adventure, wrote *Don Quixote* (Part I, 1605, Part II, 1615), one of the most widely translated works of all time. The story may be said to have paved the way for the novels of FIELDING, SMOLLETT and DICKENS, and in its treatment of madness and illusion, directly influenced DOSTOEVSKY. Cervantes followed Part I of Don Quixote with the short romantic adventure works *Exemplary Novels* (1613) and some one-act farces and plays. His final work, *Persiles and Sigismunda* (published posthumously, 1616) is a long, heroic romance whose prologue contains Cervantes's farewell to life.

Cesalpino, Andrea (1519-1603) Italian physician and botanist who compiled the first major work of plant classification based on reproductive organs, fruit and seeds.

Ceulen, Ludolph van (1540-1610) German mathematician, who devoted almost his whole life to finding a numerical approximation for the value of π, and eventually obtained it, correct to 35 places of decimals. Some German textbooks of the 16th century refer to π as 'Ludolphische Zahl' (Ludolph's number).

Cézanne, Paul (1839-1906) French artist, who was a leading influence on the Impressionists. His early work betrayed strong passions: romantic, indeed erotic, in subject, the paint rich and sensuous in both colour and texture. Contact with Impressionism not only brightened his palette, but above all focused his attention on nature and away from romantic visions. From then on he attempted to realize a comprehensive vision of nature through the media of still-life, landscape and portrait. This change in his outlook is exemplified by the painting of *Bathers* made towards the end of his life, in which the female nude is no longer erotic, but an architectonic element. Unlike the Impressionists, Cézanne did not seek to render nature's surface and her fluctuations, but to discover her permanent qualities. To this end he developed a technique of modelling forms, defining space, and indicating tones, all in terms of coloured strokes placed on the canvas with infinite care. His revolutionary use of colour, which emphasized the structure and volume of objects, slight distortions in the interests of higher truth, and his demonstration that the technique of painting could still evolve, made him highly influential on innumerable later painters, notably the Cubists.

Chabrier, Alexis Emmanuel (1841-94) French composer who

created the rhapsody *España* (1883).
With its brilliant orchestral colouring
and lively use of Spanish themes, it has
remained an ever-popular piece in the
concert repertoire. Later Chabrier
composed several pieces including an
opera, *King Despite Himself*. In his
harmonic and orchestral experiments he was the forerunner of
DEBUSSY and RAVEL.

Chadwick, Sir Edwin (1800-90)
English lawyer and social reformer,
author of one of the classics of social
medicine, *Report on the General Sanitary Condition of the Labouring
Classes in Britain* (1842). This was a
masterly inquiry into the working of
the Poor Law in England and Wales,
and drew attention to the urgent need
for reforms.

Chadwick, Sir James (born 1891)
English physicist who in 1932 discovered the neutron, a particle similar
in mass to a proton but without an
electric charge. Being neutral it pene-
trates atoms easily and is therefore an
efficient means of splitting nuclei. The
greater splitting ability of neutrons
was important in developing the
technical processes required for making atomic power, for bombs and
nuclear reactors.

Chagall, Marc (born 1887) Russian-born painter, whose colourful
fantasies and strange juxtapositions of
objects strongly influenced Surrealist
painters. He studied in St Petersburg
under BAKST, the stage designer, and
in 1910 went to Paris where he met
APOLLINAIRE, LÉGER, DELAUNAY and
MODIGLIANI. He returned to Russia
1917, but found the authorities'
preoccupation with social realism incompatible with his own ideas. The
rest of his life has been spent largely
between Paris and New York, illustrating books, designing stage sets,
painting pictures and working in
glass, as well as designing tapestries
and mosaics. Chagall's designs decorate, among other buildings, the
Knesset (the Israeli parliament building), and the Paris Opéra.

Chain, Ernst (born 1906) British
biochemist of German origin who
shared a Nobel Prize with Sir Alexander FLEMING and Lord Florey in
1945. His systematic investigation of
antibacterial substances produced by
fungi and other micro-organisms led
to a reinvestigation of penicillin and
proved to be the foundation of the
antibiotics industry.

Chaka (c. 1773-1828) Zulu chieftain
and founder of the Zulu empire. He
became chief of his own tribe in 1816
and, by the incorporation of other
tribes, united the Zulus into a powerful nation by the mid-1820s, when he

is thought to have ruled 50,000
people. At the time of his assassination in September 1828 he dominated
an area as large as France. Those of
the surrounding tribes who would not
swear allegiance to Chaka were obliged to flee, and it is estimated that
approximately one million people
were killed during his chieftainship.
He developed a new battle formation
for his *impis*, or regiments, and
equipped them with a new weapon,
the short stabbing assegai, which
compelled his warriors to fight at
close quarters.

**Chaliapin, Feodor Ivanovich
(1873-1938)** Russian, the most famous bass of his time, who came from a
peasant family. When DIAGHILEV
brought him to Paris, his rich, powerful voice and impressive physique
made a major impact on Western
audiences. An outstanding interpreter
of the great operatic bass roles,
Chaliapin was also an actor, and
starred in a film of *Don Quixote*.

**Chamberlain, Houston Stewart
(1855-1927)** English philosopher,
who refined the theory of the superiority of the so-called Aryan race,
which became the Nazi creed. His
theory of 'Germanism', which embodied all that he conceived as being
the best in European history, appeared in his *The Foundations of the
19th Century* (originally written in
German, 1911). The book was not
simply a glorification of the German-

Top: Pagoda at Kew Gardens, London:
a departure for architect Chambers

Right: Rabbi with Tora: Chagall's Jewish
background reflected in his art

Below: Greatest of film comedians,
Charlie Chaplin at peak of his fame

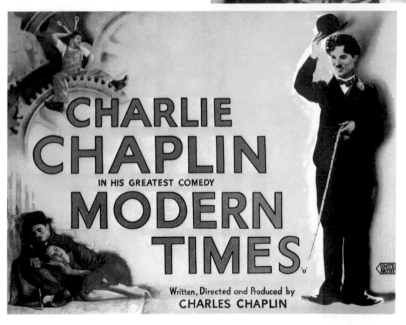

CHARLIE
CHAPLIN
IN HIS GREATEST COMEDY
MODERN
TIMES

Written, Directed and Produced by
CHARLES CHAPLIN

ic, but a broad survey of European culture. Nazi anti-Semitism can also be traced to Chamberlain, whose writings were, however, largely derived from those of Gobineau. He supported Germany against England in the First World War, and became a naturalized German in 1916.

Chamberlain, Joseph (1836-1914)
English statesman who laid the economic foundations of the British Commonwealth. He was made President of the Board of Trade by GLADSTONE in 1880, and was responsible for the Bankruptcy Act of 1883 and other financial and economic reforms. He resigned from the Government in 1886 over his opposition to Gladstone's Irish Home Rule policy, and his defection split the Liberal Party and toppled the Government. From 1891 he was leader of the Liberal Unionists. In 1895 he joined SALISBURY's Conservative-Unionist coalition as Colonial Secretary. As part of his imperialist theories he supported the idea of Imperial preference, by which the British Dominions and Colonies were to become a self-contained economic unit. He resigned from the Government in 1903, in order to campaign for an extension of Tariff Reform, which was intended as a form of moderate protection for British industry. His campaign embarrassed and divided the Conservative-Unionist government of BALFOUR and was largely responsible for the defeat of the Party in the 1906 election.

Chamberlain, Neville (1869-1940)
Son of Joseph CHAMBERLAIN, and Prime Minister whose term was noted for its policy of appeasement of MUSSOLINI and HITLER, culminating in the infamous Munich Agreement (1938). Chamberlain became Prime Minister in 1937 in succession to BALDWIN. Ill-informed about foreign affairs, he believed he could negotiate personally with the dictators, while realizing that Britain was ill-prepared for war. His apparent political myopia caused the resignation (1938) of his Foreign Minister, EDEN, who was replaced by HALIFAX. Chamberlain persisted in appeasement until the Germans occupied Prague, when he belatedly guaranteed the integrity of Poland. He was forced to declare war on Germany (3 Sept. 1939) when the Nazis invaded Poland, and upon their occupation of Norway, criticism of his lack of war leadership by a hostile House of Commons compelled him to make way for CHURCHILL.

Chambers, Ephraim (c. 1680-1740) English pioneer of modern encyclopaedias with his *Cyclopaedia* (1728). Chambers covered the arts and the sciences so comprehensively that he was elected a member of the Royal Society. It clearly influenced DIDEROT's *Encyclopédie* (1751-77) and the first *Encyclopaedia Britannica* (1771).

Chambers, Sir William (1723-96)
English architect whose work is a combination of English Palladianism and the Neo-Classicism of SOUFFLOT. His best-known work, Somerset House (1776-86) in the Strand, has an impressive river front and a portico facing the Strand. He also built the Casino at Marino, a villa at Roehampton and Duddingston House, Edinburgh, and wrote *A Treatise on Civil Architecture* (1759). The only testimony of his early voyages to India and China is the Pagoda in Kew Gardens, but Chambers retained links with France, begun when he trained under BLONDEL.

Champaigne, Philippe de (1602-74) Belgian painter whose masterpiece is an austere full-length portrait of Cardinal RICHELIEU.

Champlain, Samuel de (c. 1567-1635) French explorer and colonizer in Canada who founded the city of Quebec (1608), the first permanent European settlement in America north of Florida. From there he explored south to Lake Champlain (1609), making allies of the Huron Indians. He explored the Ottawa River (1613) and probed Lakes Huron and Ontario with BRULÉ (1615).

Champollion, Jean François (1790-1832) French Egyptologist whose deciphering of Egyptian hieroglyphics helped historians to read scripts up to 5000 years old. He spent years studying the Rosetta Stone – a black basalt slab found in Egypt by French troops in 1799 – which bore three seemingly identical inscriptions: one in (readable) Greek, and two in undecipherable Egyptian scripts – demotic (cursive writing) and hieroglyphic ('picture' writing). It was Champollion who, in 1822, made the first full translations after discovering that hieroglyphic script consisted of both phonograms (sound-signs) and ideograms (sense-signs).

Chancellor, Richard (16th cent.) English navigator who inaugurated trade between England and Russia. He commanded a ship in Sir Hugh Willoughby's fleet to find a northeast passage to India (1553), was separated from the others by bad weather, rounded North Cape and the Kola Peninsula, and crossed the White Sea, before travelling overland to Moscow, where he negotiated a trade treaty. Chancellor died in a shipwreck while returning from a second Moscow visit.

Chandragupta I (4th cent.) Indian Rajah of Magadha who founded the Gupta dynasty (320-480), the golden age of Hinduism. By conquest and marriage he dominated the Ganges valley and began a period of peace and prosperity during which Hindu culture embraced most of the Indus and Ganges valleys, with art, literature, music, sculpture, painting and scientific studies all flourishing.

Chang Ch'ien (2nd cent. BC) Chinese emissary of emperor Su Ti, who explored the area between the Hindu Kush mountains and the Amu Darya River. His further travels to the west led to direct trade contacts between various Mediterranean states and China.

Chao K'uang-yin (10th cent.) Chinese emperor (960-76) who, as T'ai Tsu (Grand Progenitor), founded the Sung dynasty (960-1280), during which Chinese culture enjoyed one of its most creative periods, especially in painting and pottery, but also in literature and philosophy. An ambitious general, Chao K'uang-yin used military power to seize the throne. China had been deeply divided among war lords since the decline of LI YUAN's T'ang dynasty in the 9th century, but Chao built a strong, centralized government with a reformed civil service structure in northern China. When he died, he had mastered most of the south.

Chao Meng-fu (1254-1322) Chinese poet, scholar, calligrapher and painter, who rose to high office under the Mongol rule of the Yüan dynasty, and eventually became Secretary of State for War to KUBLAI KHAN. His famous equestrian and figurative paintings were suited to official tastes, but his landscapes and bamboos, painted in a lucid, calligraphic manner, are in the style practised by the literati. The technique of creating solid form with a single brush movement, at which Chao excelled, was later adopted by other artists.

Chaplin, Charles (born 1889) English director-writer who has become probably the best-known actor in the history of the cinema. He first went to America in 1910 with Fred Karno's company and on a second tour, in 1913, was persuaded to join Mack Sennett at Keystone, where he began in one-reelers. The tramp character – the 'little man' who somehow always won through – made him world famous. Chaplin's early films contain some of his best work, demonstrating his gift for mime. Later, he not only starred in films, but also directed them, including classics such as *The Gold Rush* (1924), *City Lights* (1931) and *Modern Times*.

Charcot, Jean (1825-93) French physician who, in his pioneering psychiatric work at the neurological clinic of the Silpêtrière (where FREUD studied for a time), discarded the sexual theory of hysteria and studied its relation to hypnotism. He also made important contributions by identifying diseases which had previously been lumped together.

Chardin, Jean Baptiste (1699-1779) French painter, of still-life and everyday scenes (genre paintings), whose appeal lay in their honesty and simplicity, pervaded as they are by a reflective calm devoid of sentiment or didactic moral purpose. The objects in his pictures, however commonplace, are subjected to intense scrutiny, and forms, surfaces and textures are realized with great fidelity. His distinctive greys, creams and rusts thickly but delicately applied, show that Chardin possessed the virtuosity, characteristic of his age, in the handling of his materials.

Chardonnet, Hilaire Comte de (1839-1924) French founder of the artificial silk industry. In the 1880s, after studying silk worms as an assistant to PASTEUR, he discovered a method of making a silk-like thread from nitrocellulose which he called rayon. Developments of this process by British chemists led, in 1892, to viscose rayon, on which most modern artificial silk is based.

Charlemagne (742-814) King of the Franks (768-814), and Western (Holy Roman) Emperor, who built the biggest empire in western Europe since that of Rome. Inheriting the Frankish kingdom, Charlemagne fought to unify all Germanic peoples in one Christian empire by seizing Saxony, Bavaria and Lombard Italy and fighting Avars, Moors and Slavs in border battles which pushed his empire's boundaries east to the Elbe and Danube and south into Spain. He gained Pope Leo III's support for refounding the Western Roman Empire, but on Christian, Germanic lines, with centralized government on a feudal basis. Charlemagne revived Latin learning, established reading schools and cathedral and monastic schools throughout the empire, and was a patron of the arts and sciences.

Chard, John Rouse Merriott (1847-1897) English soldier whose defence of Rorke's Drift in 1879 marked the turning point of the Zulu War. Fresh from their success at Isandhlwana, where they had surprised and wiped out a British force, the Zulu *impis* repeatedly attacked Rorke's Drift, held by 140 men, a third of whom were invalids. After six assaults the Zulus withdrew.

Charles I (1288-1342) King of Hungary and the first of the Anjou line, which gave the nation power and prosperity. He ruled as an absolute monarch, discarding dissident feudal lords as his councillors and making use of men from the middle classes. He granted privileges to towns to encourage their growth and reformed the fiscal system.

Charles I (1600-49) King of Great Britain and Ireland (1625-49), son of JAMES I, who was beheaded as a 'tyrant, traitor, murderer and public enemy' when his claims to absolute rule brought to a head the power struggle between Crown and Parliament. Dominated at first by his minister, BUCKINGHAM, he waged costly and inconclusive foreign wars with Spain and France, for which he kept demanding money from Parliament. This, and his High Church leanings, caused clashes with the predominantly Puritan Parliament; for 11 years (1629-40) Charles, invoking the doctrine of the divine right of kings, tried to rule without Parliament, raising money by forced loans, and other means. Eventually his need of money with which to go to war with Presbyterian Scotland (1639) led him to seek help from Parliament, which demanded increased powers in return. The long struggle, marked by the Petition of Right of 1628 (which attempted formally to curb the king's powers) and the Grand Remonstrance of 1641 (which listed the grievances against Charles), ended in deadlock and outbreak of the English Civil Wars (1642-6, 1648). CROMWELL's Parliamentarians defeated the Royalists and the Rump Parliament instigated Charles's trial.

Charles II (1630-85) King of Great Britain and Ireland (1660-85), nicknamed the 'merry monarch'. Exiled under the Commonwealth, Charles was invited by Parliament to return to the throne 18 months after Oliver CROMWELL's death. Determined 'Not to go on his travels again', Charles sought to strengthen the monarchy by an alliance with LOUIS XIV of France which might destroy England's chief commercial rivals, the Dutch, and free the king from financial dependence on Parliament, but the Dutch wars of the reign (1664-7 and 1672-4) were not successful. The

A TRUE RELATION OF THE Late Kings Death.

The passing of Charles II in 1685, reported in the contemporary account above, contrasted with the tumultuous exit on the headsman's block of his father, 36 years earlier. Charles I below was not the least worthy of English kings—there were others far more oppressive than he—but his reign brought to a head the clash of interests between the power of the Crown and that of Parliament

reign saw a reaction against Puritan
austerities. Restoration drama enlivened the theatre, experimental
science was encouraged through the
Royal Society (1662), art and architecture flourished, WREN producing
his masterpiece of St Paul's after the
fire of 1666, which largely destroyed
London. Tolerant in religion, Charles
failed to improve the lot of Catholics
and dissenters because of the opposition of his strongly Anglican parliament.

Charles II (1661-1700) King of
Spain (1665-1700), during whose
reign the problem of the Spanish
succession emerged. Charles's wish
was to keep the last Spanish empire
intact for his successor, and, resenting

the two partition treaties of 1698 and
1700 agreed between LOUIS XIV and
WILLIAM III, Charles willed the entire
empire to Louis's grandson, Philip,
and so helped to precipitate the War
of the Spanish Succession.

Charles IV 'The Fair' (1294-1328)
King of France (1322-8), whose re-
newal of hostilities with England
anticipated the Hundred Years' War
(1337-1453). He occupied most of
Guienne and Gascony, but restored
them to England, except for Agenais
and Bazadais in 1327. He intervened
also in Flanders to protect French
interests. Childless, Charles was the
last Capetian King of France, after
whom the crown passed to the House
of Valois.

Charles V (1337-80) King of France
(1364-80), who saved the nation from
the English in the first phase of the 100
Years' War. Becoming Regent (1356),
Charles agreed to the Peace of
Bretigny (1360), which granted a
third of France to Edward III of
England. After gaining support from
the factious States-General and the
provincial assemblies, and raising
money to buttress the army and navy,
Charles was ready to fight. Under
Bertrand du GUESCLIN, his troops
struck back at the English, forcing
them into a few pockets, principally
round Bayonne, Brest, Calais and
Cherbourg.

Charles V (1500-58) Hapsburg
King of Spain (1516-50) and Holy
Roman Emperor (1519) who ruled an
immense empire that far outstripped
the traditional Germanic limits of the
Holy Roman Empire by including the
Low Countries, Franche-Comté,
Spain, Naples, and soon vast New
World possessions, won by con-
quistadores such as CORTES and
PIZARRO. Charles had no real policy for
dealing with the disparate elements
of his Empire and was content to deal
piecemeal with problems as and when
they occurred. He altered little in
Spain, using it mainly as a source of
taxation revenue, and in the Netherlands welded all the loosely connected
provinces into a whole by applying a
common system of law, taxation and
parliamentary assembly. His eventual
domination of Italy was a by-product
of a long rivalry with FRANCIS I of
France. Hostilities between the two

ended with the Treaty of Crécy
(1544), which favoured the Empire.
In Germany, Charles led an army
against the Lutheran states and
defeated them, but gave Lutherans
equal rights with Catholics in the
Peace of Augsburg (1555).

Charles VII (1403-61) King of
France during whose reign the 100
Years' War ended. When he came to
the throne, England, under HENRY V,
held all northern and some of southwestern France. As the Dauphin,
Charles was a mere figurehead; it
was JOAN OF ARC who led the French
armies in their victories over the
English (1428-31).

Charles VIII (1470-98) King of
France (1483-98), who added Brittany to his kingdom when he married
Anne of Brittany (1491). He bought
neutrality from England, Spain and
the Holy Roman Empire (which had
all wanted to keep Brittany independent of France) with gifts of land and
treaties, while he pursued his ambition to reclaim the kingdom of
Naples for the house of Anjou. He invaded Italy in 1495, but was repulsed.

Charles X (1757-1836) King of
France (1824-30) who with his minister Polignac provoked the French
revolution of 1830 by the Ordinances
of St Cloud, a series of repressive
decrees. In 1789, as Comte d'Artois,
he had fled to Scotland, from which
he returned in 1814.

Charles XII (1682-1718) King of
Sweden (1697-1718), whose daring
military exploits ended in national
disaster. In 1700-2, he brilliantly
wrecked a Danish-Polish-Russian
alliance aimed at despoiling Sweden,
by crushing Denmark, driving Russian troops out of Swedish-held
Livonia, and ravaging Poland (deposing AUGUSTUS II). He then invaded
Saxony (1706), which became his
springboard for an attack on Moscow
(1707). Charles underestimated the
Russian winter and Russian scorched-
earth tactics. He lost the decisive
battle of Poltava (1709), which left
him, with MAZEPA, a temporary fugitive and finished Swedish supremacy
in northern Europe. Charles was
killed invading Norway.

Charles XIV see BERNADOTTE, Jean

Charles the Bold (1433-77) Duke of Burgundy, whose death ended the last great threat to royal supremacy in France. In an attempt to form an independent kingdom by linking his Burgundian and Netherlandish possessions, Charles repeatedly clashed with France's LOUIS XI and encouraged feudal anarchy among the other nobles. Louis's troops killed Charles at Nancy, enabling Louis to seize Burgundy for France and the remainder of Charles's possessions passed to the Hapsburgs.

Charles the Great see CHARLEMAGNE

Charles, Jacques (1746-1823) French physicist who studied gases. In 1787, he calculated that for every degree Centigrade rise in temperature, a gas expands proportionally to its volume at 0°C. This was later developed into what is now called Charles's Law. Charles was the first to use hydrogen in a balloon.

Charles Martel (c. 689-741) Carolingian Frankish ruler, known as Charles the Hammer, who established the basis of the empire ruled by his grandson CHARLEMAGNE. As effective ruler of the entire Frankish kingdom, he subdued Burgundy and Aquitaine (719), Provence and Septimania, and defeated the Arab invaders of Gaul (732). He also gained control of Frisia, Alemannia, Bavaria and Saxony. He instituted the assemblies of nobles known as *Champs de Mars*, and his gifts of Church lands to his nobles fostered the growth of the feudal system in his kingdom.

Chartier, Emile Auguste see ALAIN

Chasles, Michel (1793-1880) French mathematician, who was one of the founders of modern projective geometry. His works have become standard textbooks on the origins and development of geometry.

Chateaubriand, François René de (1768-1848) French novelist, poet and politician whose short novels, *Atala* and *René* (1801 and 1805), are sometimes said to mark the birth of the Romantic hero in French fiction. He was renowned for the exotic settings of his tales, some of which were inspired by his travels in the New World. Chateaubriand was in America when the Revolution began and returned to Paris to fight with the emigrés, but later fled to England in 1793, where he lived in great poverty until 1800, translating novels and teaching French in order to live. He was recalled to serve under NAPOLEON, but soon resigned and went abroad once more. After Waterloo, he became ambassador in Berlin and later in London and Rome, and in

1823 became Foreign Minister to LOUIS XVIII. Other notable works by Chateaubriand include his *Essai sur les révolutions* (1797); *Le Génie du Christianisme* (1802; of which *Atala* and *René* originally formed part), a rambling, historico-cultural work intended as an apologia for the Church; *Les Martyrs* (1809); *Les Mémoires d'outre-tombe* and autobiographies published posthumously.

Chatham, Earl of see PITT, William

Chaucer, Geoffrey (c. 1340-1400) English poet, 'Father of English literature' who wrote *The Canterbury Tales*, a collection of medieval stories, planned as part of a larger design of which only the Prologue and 22 tales were completed. Chaucer's pilgrims are drawn from many different spheres of medieval life and in the prologue each pilgrim is described in a series of vivid portraits which are by turn satirical, hostile, ironic or amused. In the main body of the work each character tells a tale, ranging from courtly romance to rumbustious ribaldry, comic anecdote to philosophical or religious fable. Between 1359 and 1372 Chaucer translated *Le Roman de la Rose* from the French, and in 1369 composed his earliest datable work, *The Book of the Duchess*, on the occasion of the death of Blanche, wife of John of Gaunt. After 1372, he was called upon to make several ambassadorial journeys abroad, to Flanders, France, Lombardy and Italy, where he gained an almost unique knowledge of DANTE and BOCCACCIO, and is thought to have met PETRARCH. *The House of Fame* and *The Parlement of Foules* were probably composed at this time, rich in descriptive passages and light in

mood, on the favourite medieval theme of love; and 'Troilus and Criseyde', a long, narrative poem modelled on Boccaccio's 'Il Filostrato', in which Chaucer used rime royal, a stanza of seven lines. During the 1380s Chaucer began *The Canterbury Tales*, in which foreign influences diminish and Englishness prevails.

Chauliac, Guy de (c. 1300-c. 1370) French surgeon, author of *Great Surgery* (1363), which catalogues all the surgical knowledge of medieval times. He devised operations for hernia and cataract, cauterized cancers, accurately described the treatment of fractures and dislocations, and described a number of ointments and plasters for surgical use.

Chavez, Carlos (born 1899) Mexican composer and founder of the Symphony Orchestra of Mexico. In works such as *Sinfonia India* (1936) he introduced Mexican Indian themes and rhythms, together with a use of original instruments, into a symphonic setting. The resulting colour and vitality are typical of a great deal of modern Mexican music.

Chekhov, Anton (1860-1904) Russian dramatist and master of theatrical tragi-comedy, whose work foreshadowed important trends in modern drama. It was, however, as an author of short stories that he first attracted attention. His early plays were one-act farces and tragedies. His first full-length plays, *Ivanov* (1887), *The Wood Demon* (1889) and *The Seagull* (1896), were all failures. He

Conversation piece: Shaw, Belloc and Chesterton in the 1930s

had decided to give up play-writing when he met NEMIROVICH-DANCHEN-KO, who wanted to revive *The Seagull* at the Moscow Art Theatre, then run by him and STANISLAVSKY. This production, which interpreted with proper feeling Chekhov's delicate poise between the tragic and the absurd, was the beginning of his success in the theatre. In 1898, he rewrote *The Wood Demon* as *Uncle Vanya*; then came *The Three Sisters* (1901) and *The Cherry Orchard* (1904). He lived the last years of his life in Yalta, where his house is maintained as his memorial.

Chelyuskin, Semyon Ivanovich (18th cent.) Russian explorer who first reached the most northerly point of the Asian land mass, a cape subsequently named after him.

Cheng Ho (15th cent.) Chinese admiral who made his country mistress of the Indian Ocean and of Indonesia. A Muslim eunuch at the court of Emperor Yung Ho, of the Ming dynasty, he was sent on seven expeditions (1405-34), which visited Indonesia, Ceylon, India, Arabia and East Africa. Cheng Ho's armadas (the first consisting of 63 junks carrying 28,000 men) traded with and cowed the states they visited. In 1415, 16 states made tribute payments to the Chinese emperor. Cheng Ho brought back foreign curiosities including zebras and giraffes, but with his last voyage (1430-34) China's unprecedented show of interest in the outside world came to an end.

Chénier, André Marie de (1762-94) French poet whose *Bucoliques* and *Iambes*, poignant and sometimes withering satires, written during imprisonment under the Terror, show him to be classical in spirit, though in lyrical fervour a precursor of the Romantics. Purged as a rebel, his execution robbed France of one of her greatest poets.

Cheops see KHUFU

Chernikhovski see TCHERNICHOW-SKI

Cherubini, Luigi (1760-1842) Italian composer of operas, whose *Medea* (1797) is a landmark in tragic musical drama. He spent his working life in Paris, becoming the most important operatic composer of his day. BEET-HOVEN acknowledged his influence, and Cherubini's opera *The Two Days* (1800) provided a model for *Fidelio*.

Chesterton, Gilbert Keith (1874-1936) English writer, who set his hand to all types of literature – poetry, novels, stories, essays and controversial pamphlets. Chesterton's attitudes

were Catholic, Romantic and traditional; together with BELLOC, he opposed the socialist ideas of SHAW. In his exuberant, fanciful novels, including *The Napoleon of Notting Hill* (1904), *The Man who was Thursday* (1908), *The Flying Inn* (1914), there is an element of social preaching behind the fancy.

Chiang Kai-Shek (born 1887) Chinese soldier-politician. A professional officer, he was training with the Japanese army at the outbreak of the Chinese Revolution of 1911. He returned to China and became chief of staff to SUN YAT-SEN. In 1923 he went to Moscow to study Red Army methods, but despite Sun Yat-Sen's broadening of the *Kuomintang* (Chinese Nationalist Party) to admit Communists, he remained an anti-Communist. In 1928, three years after Sun's death, he set up a Kuomintang government in Nanking, and thereafter fought local war-lords, Japanese invading armies and Communists led by MAO TSE-TUNG. He was captured by the Communists in 1936, but was released on the intervention of CHOU EN-LAI to continue fighting the Japanese. Chiang was head of the Chinese government and Commander-in-Chief of the armed forces throughout the Second World War and during the subsequent civil war with the Communists (1946-8). He was defeated in 1948 and forced to withdraw to Taiwan (Republic of China), where he still presides over a Nationalist government.

Chichester, Sir Francis (1901-72) English sailor and airman, who set a record for the single-handed passage of the Atlantic in 1962. In 1966-7 he circumnavigated the world in his yacht *Gipsy Moth*, sailing 29,000 miles in 226 days.

Ch'ien Lung (1711-99) Chinese emperor, under the name Kao Tsung (1736-96), whose reign saw Manchu (Ch'ing) China reach and pass its peak. A population explosion and great prosperity in China supported his ambitious conquests deep in Asia; for more than 40 years China dominated Tibet, Kashgaria, Burma and Nepal. Cochin-China and Korea, in addition, made tribute payments to him. Ch'ien Lung favoured limited friendly relations with the western world, and sponsored vast cultural projects. His achievements were weakened during the last years of his reign by the corrupt administration of his favourite, Ho-shen.

Chikamatsu, Monzaemon (1653-c.1725) One of Japan's outstanding dramatists, who wrote about 160 Joruri and Kabuki plays. These plays, based on popular myths and legends

or historical themes, involve the use of elaborate scenery, a revolving stage and stylized make-up. While retaining their traditions, Chikamatsu broke through their rigid formalism by using original characters and situations.

Childe, Vere Gordon (1892-1957) Australian archaeologist and prehistorian who is famous for his comprehensive writings in such books as *Man Makes Himself* (1936) and *What Happened in History* (1942). He explained both cogently and with authority how the Old World civilizations began, and initiated, by his stress on the links between primitive cultures, a new international approach to archaeology. Childe saw prehistory in terms of social and technological development, and he

Gipsy Moth IV, in which Sir Francis Chichester made his lone voyage around the world. He sailed at twice the speed of the next fastest small vessel. At the end of the journey the boat was put into dry dock at Greenwich

showed how the stages of Palaeolithic (Old Stone Age) savagery and Neolithic (New Stone Age) barbarianism led to the Bronze Age 'urban' revolution in Mesopotamia about 3000 BC.

Childers, Robert Erskine (1870-1922) Irish nationalist, author of the spy story, *The Riddle of the Sands* (1903), who, after involvement as a political agitator, was executed for arms possession.

Chirico, Giorgio de (born 1888) Founder of the Italian school of metaphysical painting, who later adopted an imitative, academic style.

Chomsky, Noam (born 1928) American linguistics theorist. In his *Syntactic Structures* (1957) he proposed that the sentence is the basic component of language and that, from a few basic sentence types, an infinity of actual sentences can be produced by a series of rules codified as transformational grammar. The computer, with its potential for translation and information storage, inspired this attempt to establish how sentences are generated. Chomsky has also published *Aspects of the Theory of Syntax, Language and Mind*, and works of a political nature.

Chopin, Frédéric François (1810-49) Polish Romantic composer and pianist who embodied his country's national aspirations, although he lived outside Poland from the age of 18, mostly in Paris; his father was French. Apart from his two piano concertos, he wrote almost entirely for solo piano. In his valses, nocturnes (invented by FIELD), preludes, studies, mazurkas and polonaises, he often achieved a small-scale perfection. For some time he lived with novelist George SAND, who took him to Majorca in an attempt to relieve his tuberculosis. The 1848 Revolution in France drove Chopin to Britain, and in the following year he returned to Paris, where he died.

Chou En-Lai (born 1898) Premier of the State Council of the Chinese People's Republic. Of Mandarin rank, he was educated at Nankai University and in Germany and Paris, where he became a Communist. Chou helped to found the Red Army in 1931 with MAO TSE-TUNG, whom he accompanied on the Long March (1934-5). As one of the Chinese Communist leaders in 1936 he was responsible for co-operation between the Communist forces and CHIANG KAI-SHEK's Nationalist Party in fighting the Japanese invaders. In 1949 Chou became Premier and Foreign Minister in the new Communist government. He has played a major role in leading China into close

co-operation with the Third World, and while remaining committed to Mao, helped to restrain some of the excesses of the Cultural Revolution of 1966. An experienced diplomat, Chou handled the negotiations which led to a *détente* with the West and culminated in China's re-admission to the United Nations as a member of the Security Council (1971).

Chrétien de Troyes (12th cent.) French poet and author of extravagant tales of courtly love, some of the earliest extant Arthurian romances, including *Erec et Enide* (*c.* 1170), *Lancelot, ou le chevalier de la Charette*, and *Perceval*.

Christian IV (1577-1648) King of Denmark and Norway (1588-1648), whose efforts to make Denmark the leader of northern Europe brought him defeats and loss of territory. Denmark's trading prosperity and control of the Baltic and North Sea inspired his aim and the attendant rivalry with Sweden, against whom he fought the indecisive War of Kalmar (1611-13). In the 30 Years' War, he intervened on the Protestant side, but was heavily defeated by Tilly and Wallenstein. His efforts to lessen Swedish influence in Germany brought him once again to war with Sweden (1643-5) and he was defeated and forced to yield Gottlan, Oesel, Norway, Herjedalen and Jemteland.

Christian, Fletcher (18th cent.) English leader of the *Bounty* mutiny (1789), in protest against the alleged brutality of Captain William BLIGH. Arms were seized and the ship's officers cast adrift. While Bligh succeeded in making his way back to England, the 25 mutineers sailed on to Tahiti. Christian is believed to have sailed to Pitcairn Island and there set up a colony. Whether Christian died there or made his way back to England is not known.

Christov, Boris (born 1919) Bulgarian bass-baritone and exponent of the great dramatic roles in Russian opera. His most famous characterization has been of MUSSORGSKY's *Boris Godunov*.

Chuh Teh (born 1886) Chinese Communist soldier, who became Commander-in-Chief of the armed forces of the Chinese People's Republic. He took part in SUN YAT-SEN's 1911 revolution, became a Communist in 1922, helped MAO TSE-TUNG to organize the Red Army after the 1927 split with the *Kuomintang* (Nationalist Party), and made the Long March (1934-5) with Mao. He held important commands in the war against Japan (1937-45), was Commander-in-Chief of the Chinese People's

Liberation Army (1946-54) during the Civil War against CHIANG KAI-SHEK's army (1946-8) and was appointed to the rank of Marshal in 1955. In 1959 Chuh became both Commander-in-Chief and Chairman of the Standing Committee of the National People's Congress.

Churchill, John, 1st Duke of Marlborough (1650-1722) One of England's greatest generals. He helped to stamp out MONMOUTH's rebellion (1685), backed WILLIAM III's accession, and survived ill-documented charges of treason. His career reached its climax when he was commander-in-chief of the Anglo-Dutch armies in the War of the Spanish Succession (1702-14). He drove the French out of Spanish Gelderland (1702) with victories at Kaiserwerth, Venlo and Liège. With Prince Eugène of Savoy, he defeated a Franco-Bavarian force at Blenheim, Bavaria (1704). He later routed the French at Ramillies (1706), so winning Brabant and Flanders and then, with Eugène, defeated the French at Oudenarde (1708). Victory was won also at Malplaquet (1709), but with greater losses than the French.

Churchill, Lord Randolph (1849-95) English Conservative statesman, and a son of the Duke of Marlborough, who advocated Tory democracy whilst leading the 'fourth party', a group of progressive Conservative MPs, from 1880 to 1885. As Chairman of the Central Union of Conservative Associations (1884) he demanded more power for constituency associations. He was Secretary for India (1885-6), and the youngest politician for over a century to become Chancellor of the Exchequer (1886). By resigning in protest against increased military expenditure he put an end to his political career.

Churchill, Sir Winston Leonard Spencer (1874-1965) British statesman, Prime Minister during Britain's 'finest hour' (Battle of Britain, 1940), historian and painter. The son of Lord Randolph CHURCHILL, he began his career as a soldier, serving with a lancer regiment at the battle of Omdurman (1898). As a war correspondent in South Africa (1899-1900) he was captured by Boers, but escaped. First elected to Parliament in 1900 as a Conservative, he joined the Liberals in 1904, largely on account of his Free Trade principles. As First Lord of the Admiralty (1911-15), when he thought war likely he laid on a 'practice mobilization' and then kept the Fleet at war stations. He was held responsible for the disaster of the Dardanelles expedition against the Turks in 1915, and resigned to

Soldier, historian, painter, Churchill was treated with reserve as a politician, but was among the greatest of war leaders

serve on the Western Front. Later he became Secretary for War (1918-21), the Colonial Secretary (1921-2). He joined the Conservatives in 1922 and, though Chancellor of the Exchequer from 1924 to 1929, was thereafter kept out of office by his insistence in warning the country – against his Party's beliefs – that Nazi Germany was a menace, and by his rejection of concessions his Party were making in India. On the outbreak of the Second World War public opinion forced Neville CHAMBERLAIN to make him First Lord of the Admiralty. After Chamberlain resigned he became

Prime Minister (10 May 1940), and Minister of Defence. He was leader of the Opposition during ATTLEE's Labour administration (1945-51) Prime Minister again (1951-55).

Churriguera, José Benito de (1650-1723) Spanish architect who, with his brothers Joaquín (1674-1724) and Alberto (1676-1750), developed a highly decorative baroque style concerned with surface detailing, partly as a result of their training as retable carvers.

Chu Yüan-chang (1328-98) Chinese emperor, known as Hung Wu (1368-98), who founded the Ming dynasty (1368-1644). A Buddhist priest who joined rebels seeking to end oppressive Mongol rule, he was a brilliant soldier and soon became leader. With untrained men, he seized Nanking and lands north of the Yangtze River (1356-64), and drove the enfeebled Mongols from the western provinces. Chu became emperor in 1368 and within 15 years put all China once more under Chinese leadership.

Ciano, Count Galeazzo (1903-44) Italian politician and son-in-law of MUSSOLINI, under whom he served as Minister of Propaganda (1935) and Foreign Minister (1936-43). In the Second World War he initiated Italy's annexation of Albania and invasion of Greece, but was dismissed after Italy's defeat in North Africa. When the Fascist Grand Council debated Mussolini's overthrow (1943), Ciano voted for it. He later went to Ger-

many, but was arrested and sent back to Mussolini, who ordered his execution.

Cibber, Colley (1671-1757) English dramatist and theatrical manager, who wrote *An Apology for the Life of Mr Colley Cibber, Comedian*, an autobiography. The most successful of his many sentimental comedies was *The Careless Husband*. He translated and adapted MOLIÈRE's *Tartuffe* as *The Non-Juror* (1717).

Cicero, Marcus (106-43 BC) Roman lawyer, politician and philosopher whose Latin treatises, based on PLATO, ARISTOTLE and their schools, and on the Stoics, introduced Greek philosophy to ancient Rome. A celebrated orator and advocate, he also wrote on rhetoric, and many of his speeches survive, as do many of his letters.

'Cicero' see BAZNA, Elyesa

Cid, El (c. 1040-99) Popular name (from the Arabic, Sayyid, 'Lord') for the Spanish warrior hero Rodrigo Diaz de Vivar. He fought brilliantly for Sancho II of Castile, then for Sancho's successor ALFONSO VI. Exiled (1081) for suspected treachery, he became a soldier of fortune and fought for the Moorish kings of Saragossa. Later (1089-94), El Cid used war and intrigue for personal gain, taking Valencia and Murcia (1094-9), until defeated by the Moors.

Cierva, Juan de la (1896-1936) Spanish aeronaut, who invented the

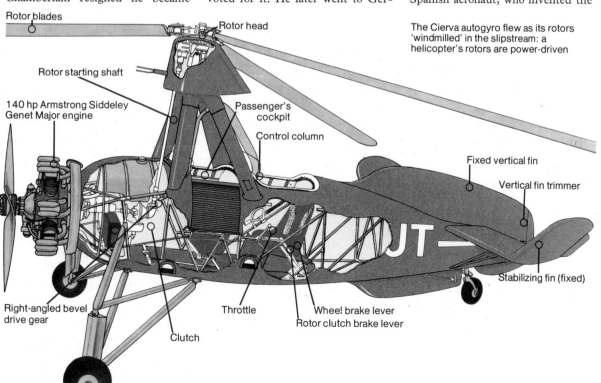

The Cierva autogyro flew as its rotors 'windmilled' in the slipstream: a helicopter's rotors are power-driven

Rotor blades

Rotor head

Rotor starting shaft

140 hp Armstrong Siddeley Genet Major engine

Passenger's cockpit

Control column

Fixed vertical fin

Vertical fin trimmer

JT

Right-angled bevel drive gear

Throttle

Wheel brake lever

Rotor clutch brake lever

Stabilizing fin (fixed)

Clutch

autogyro. In 1923 he showed that·an aircraft given forward power by a conventional propeller could gain lift from a large, horizontal, free-running rotor. The autogyro represented a significant advance in aeronautics and provided technical background for the development of helicopters.

Cimabue, Giovanni (c. 1240-1302) Florentine artist whom DANTE called the most famous painter before GIOTTO, whose teacher he may have been. His outstanding work, the huge *Madonna Enthroned* (c. 1285), departs from the tradition of Byzantine icons and mosaics in its size, architectural severity of design and tendency towards a more naturalistic description of the human form.

Cimarosa, Domenico (1749-1801) Italian composer of *The Secret Marriage* (1792), a highly successful comic opera with a theme of sharp social satire, which bears comparison with MOZART. Cimarosa, however, never achieved Mozart's psychological penetration, although in his lightness of touch he is a precursor of ROSSINI. He wrote about 60 operas. Cimarosa was imprisoned for having pro-French Revolution sympathies and died in Venice a short time after his release.

Clairaut, Alexis Claude (1713-65) French mathematician, best known for his *Théorie de la figure de la terre* (1743), which contains important theorems on the mechanics of rotating ellipsoids. He worked on astronomical problems and calculated the date of the reappearance of HALLEY's Comet.

Clare of Assisi (c. 1194-1253) Italian saint, follower of St FRANCIS OF ASSISI and foundress of the Poor Clares, a religious order living wholly on alms. She was canonized in 1255.

Clare, John (1793-1864) English poet, who wrote of rural life, experience as a farm worker, and was known as the 'Northamptonshire Peasant Poet'. *The Shepherd's Calendar* (1827) and *The Rural Muse* (1835) show his genuine lyrical talent. His most moving verse is that written later in his life, describing his solitude and desolation when confined to an asylum.

Clark, John (born 1907) British archaeologist whose discovery (1949-50) of a lakeside settlement of hunters and fisherfolk at Star Carr in Yorkshire threw light on life in Britain 10,000 years ago.

Clark, William (1770-1838) American explorer and soldier who, with Meriwether LEWIS, commanded the expedition which in 1804-6 first crossed North America from St Louis to the Pacific, exploring and mapping much of what is now the northwestern US. On the return journey Clark independently explored the Yellowstone River while Lewis explored Maria's River, and the two men rejoined each other near the Yellowstone-Missouri confluence. During the expedition, Clark mapped the land, sketched its wildlife, and wrote the records which provided the material for *History of the Expedition under the Commands of Captains Lewis and Clark* (1814).

Claude Gellée see CLAUDE LORRAINE

Claude, Georges (1870-1960) French engineer who is best known for perfecting a process for liquefying air (1902) and the separation of its constituent gases by distillation of the liquid. The process enabled oxygen and nitrogen to be prepared on an industrial scale.

Ancient times in medieval garb: Claude Lorraine's *Departure of the Queen of Sheba*

Claude Lorraine (1600-82) French landscape painter, who evolved a technique of dividing his landscapes, which usually embodied some mythological or historical incident, into receding planes, with features such as trees or classical ruins judiciously placed to help draw the eye into the distance. Although he made a number of drawings in the Roman *campagna*, his landscapes are not necessarily topographically exact, but rather ideal, attempting by means of atmospheric hazes, delicate lighting and a suggestion of infinite distance, more to evoke a golden age than portray specific places.

Claudel, Paul (1868-1955) French poet and playwright who was also a distinguished diplomat. His plays appeared regularly, from *Tête d'or* (1890) to *Le Soulier de satin* (1928-9) and, like his poetry, were informed by a devout Roman Catholicism.

Claudian (4th cent.) Greek-speaking Alexandrian and the last important classical Latin poet. His writings range from eulogies of his patrons the emperor Honorius and his adviser Stilicho to unrestrained satirical attacks on common enemies. He wrote vigorously and eloquently in the classical tradition and revealed himself as a master of description, particularly in the unfinished epic, *De raptu Proserpinae*.

Claudianus, Claudius see CLAUDIAN

Claudius I (10 BC-AD 54) Roman emperor (41-54), who, following Julius CAESAR's attacks, began the long-lasting Roman occupation of Britain (43). A coarse and deformed man, he was present at the triumphant crossing of the Thamesis (Thames) and at the capture of Camulodunum (now Colchester), where he founded a Roman colony. Claudius adopted a liberal policy in Rome's provinces, and advanced the organization of an imperial bureaucracy. Before his death, allegedly by poison, he made his adopted son, NERO, emperor.

Clay, Cassius see ALI, Mohammed

Clausius, Rudolph (1822-88) German physicist who in 1850 enunciated the second law of thermodynamics and introduced the concept of entropy. He gave the first systematic treatment to kinetic gas theory, and suggested a new theory of electrolysis, later taken up by ARRHENIUS.

Clemenceau, Georges (1841-1929) French statesman who led France to victory in the First World War. He began political life as Mayor of Montmartre. As a Radical deputy (1876-93) he earned his nickname 'The Tiger' by the ferocious wit of his speeches. Fiercely republican, anticlerical and anti-socialist, Clemenceau was among the most ardent defenders of DREYFUS during his trial, which shook many French institutions to their foundations. His denunciation of France's military incompetence during the first three years of the First World War led to his becoming Prime Minister when, in 1917, defeat seemed imminent. His courage and determination held France together through the defeats early in 1918 and made possible her recovery and the attack which led to victory in November 1918. But the French people's disgust with the results of the Paris Peace Conference of 1919, for which they held him responsible, and the French Parliament's resentment of his authoritarianism, led to his downfall in 1920. During his last decade, in retirement, he repeatedly warned of German military resurgence, and foresaw 1940 as the year in which Germany would strike back at France—a prophecy that was borne out completely.

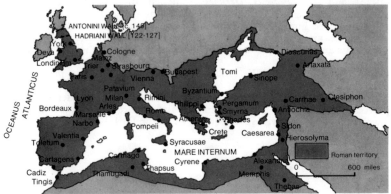

The Roman empire, at its height, encompassed nearly all of Europe. It stretched north to Scotland, south into Africa. Claudius helped extend its boundaries

Clement I (c. 30-c. 100) Italian pope, recognized as the first of the Apostolic Fathers (early Christian writers who were the associates of the apostles) and writer of the *Epistle to the Corinthians*. Written (*c.* 96) to the church at Corinth to calm a dispute there which had caused several presbyters to be dismissed, the epistle is chiefly important for stating the basis of the Christian ministry.

Clement VII (1478-1534) Italian pope (1523-34), whose refusal to sanction HENRY VIII's divorce of Catharine of Aragon initiated the break between England and the Roman Catholic church.

Cleopatra VII or VI (69-30 BC) Graeco-Macedonian Queen of Egypt, mistress of Julius CAESAR and Marcus ANTONIUS. Caesar met her when he pursued his rival POMPEY into Egypt, and restored her to her throne. She became Caesar's mistress and lived with him in Rome. After his assassination (41 BC), she returned to Egypt and bewitched Marcus Antonius, commander of the eastern Roman empire. Dreams of mastering the entire Mediterranean as a kingdom for Cleopatra and himself led Antonius to divorce Octavia for Cleopatra, provoking the disastrous war with Octavia's brother, Octavius (later the emperor AUGUSTUS), in which Antonius and Cleopatra were defeated at Actium (31 BC). Antonius committed suicide and Cleopatra, failing to charm Octavius, also killed herself.

Cleveland, Stephen Grover (1837-1908) American President who forced Britain to accept arbitration of the British Guiana-Venezuela frontier dispute (1897). His first term as President (1885-9) was marked by excessive use of the Presidential veto and his second (1893-7) by a Wall Street panic in 1893, which led to unpopular deflationary measures and the use of troops in strike-breaking. After winning the Presidential election in 1884 he became the first Democratic President of the United States for 28 years.

Clive, Robert (1725-74) English soldier and statesman who founded British India. Fighting for the British East India Company against its French counterpart for supremacy in India, he checked French power by seizing Arcot with a tiny force (1751), then ended it by taking Calcutta (1757). In defeating 50,000 enemy troops with 3200 soldiers and artillery at Plassey (1757), Clive mastered India's richest province, Bengal, and became virtually its ruler. He returned to Britain in 1760, but was sent out again, as Governor of Bengal (1764-7), to end disorder there. He obtained the document granting the East India Company full sovereignty over all Bengal, making it the secure nucleus for a British empire in India. Clive reorganized the civil and military service of the Company and raised salaries to end corrupt private trading and acceptance of gifts. He returned to Britain again (1767)

addicted to opium (perhaps to ease chronic illness) and committed suicide.

Clouet, Jean the Younger (c. 1485-c. 1545) French court painter, whose son, François, succeeded him. Both father and son made a number of precisely drawn portrait drawings in black, red and white chalk, of which Jean's are thought to be more psychologically expressive.

Clovis I (c. 466-511) King of the Salian Franks (481-511), who became ruler of all the Frankish tribes, founded the first powerful state in France with Paris as its capital, and drew up the Salic Law. Using murder, intrigue and war, he extended his Merovingian kingdom (centred at first on Tournai in western Belgium) into an empire comprising most of present-day France, Belgium, western Germany and the Netherlands. Clovis became a Christian and built a church at Paris, but his empire, divided between his four sons, did not survive his death.

Cnut see CANUTE II

Coates, Eric (1886-1957) English composer of the breezy *London Suite*, and other light orchestral pieces, such as *Sleepy Lagoon*, and of songs, including 'Bird Songs at Eventide'. Coates originally made his name as a viola player, having studied under TERTIS.

Cobbett, William (1762-1835) English politician, journalist and historian of rural life. His *Rural Rides* (1830) is an honest and vivid account of early 19th-century life. Cobbett was a soldier (1784-91) and spent many years in the United States. In 1800 he returned to England and began *Cobbett's Weekly Political Register*, in which he set forth his radical political views.

Cobden, Richard (1804-65) British radical publicist, who, with BRIGHT, secured the repeal of the Corn Laws (1846). The plight of cotton mill operatives in Manchester caused him to devote his time to campaigning for Free Trade. He was active in the Anti-Corn Law League (1839-46), and was elected MP for Stockport. He lost his seat (1857) largely as a result of his opposition to the Crimean War. Although re-elected in 1859, he refused Cabinet office under PALMERSTON in order to remain independent. In 1860 he secured a reduction of tariffs in trade between Britain and France. During the American Civil War (1861-5) he played a valuable role in easing the tense relations between LINCOLN's administration and the government of Palmerston.

Cochran, Sir C. B. (1873-1951) Britain's leading theatrical impresario of the 1920s and 1930s, famous for revues featuring 'Mr Cochran's young ladies' and for productions of Noël COWARD's *Bitter Sweet* and *Cavalcade*.

Cochrane, Thomas, 10th Earl of Dundonald (1775-1860) British naval officer who, after expulsion from the Royal Navy for fraud, commanded in turn the fleets of Chile, Brazil and Greece before receiving a pardon and reinstatement to the RN.

Cockcroft, Sir John Douglas (1897-1967) English physicist who, with Ernest Walton, was the first to split the atom, using artificially accelerated sub-atomic particles. In the 1920s Cockcroft and Walton built a voltage multiplier which could accelerate charged sub-atomic particles to extremely high velocities. In 1932, using protons as bullets for their 'atomic gun', they bombarded lithium. The alpha particles (helium nuclei) produced showed that the protons had reacted with the lithium nuclei to produce helium. Cockcroft and Walton were awarded the Nobel Prize for Physics in 1951.

Cockerell, Charles Robert (1788-1863) English architect who developed a highly original and forceful Neo-classical style based on studies of classical architecture in Greece and Italy, and also upon his study of WREN and the English baroque. His major works are the Ashmolean Building, Oxford, St George's Hall, Liverpool, and a number of branch offices of the Bank of England.

Cockerell, Sir Christopher Sydney (born 1910) English engineer who invented the hovercraft. In 1953 he began experimenting with ways of reducing the friction around the hulls of boats, in order to increase their performance. Cockerell discovered that a cushion of air was the best method of achieving this and, with the British government's backing, the pioneer SRN-1 hovercraft was built, and demonstrated its capability by crossing the English Channel in 1959. By 1965, the hovercraft industry was firmly established. The main uses for these transporters are for fast ferry and patrol duties.

Cocteau, Jean (1889-1963) French dramatist, poet, novelist, film direc-

tor and designer. In 1912, he met DIAGHILEV, for whom he created ballets and mimes. Like many writers of the period (e.g. GIDE, GIRAUDOUX, ANOUILH, SARTRE), he showed a predilection for refashioning ancient myths. His rewriting of classical themes in *Orphée* (1927) and *Antigone* (1928) was followed by melodramas such as *La Machine infernale* (1934), a revival of the Oedipus legend, and the heroic-romantic play *L'Aigle à deux têtes* (1946). One of his most outstanding films was *La Belle et la bête* (1945) and he was also author of two novels, *Thomas l'Imposteur* (1923) and *Les Enfants terribles*. Cocteau's remarkable versatility and talents enabled him to play a significant role in artistic and literary experiments during the inter-war years.

Cody, Samuel Franklin (1862-1913) Texas-born pioneer aviator who became a British citizen and played an important part in the development of flight. He experimented with man-lifting kites, helped to build the first British dirigible (steerable airship) and constructed an aeroplane of his own in 1908. The tree to which he used to tether his aircraft remains a memorial to him at the Royal Aircraft Establishment at Farnborough. He died when his aircraft crashed.

Cody, William Frederick (1846-1917) American frontiersman and showman who helped to create the popular image of the Wild West. He gained his nickname 'Buffalo Bill' as a bison hunter who reputedly shot 4280 bison in 17 months to feed men building a railroad through Kansas. In 1872, by then an experienced messenger, teamster, hunter and army scout, he starred with HICKOK and others in Wild West shows. In 1883, Cody formed the most famous of all, Buffalo Bill's Wild West Show, a spectacular circus that toured the United States and Europe, featuring, among others, Annie Oakley and the Sioux chieftain SITTING BULL

Coke, Sir Edward (1552-1634) English, the champion of common law against the royal prerogative and a great Chief Justice. As Attorney-General to ELIZABETH I (from 1594) he supported the authority of government and displayed a violent hatred for its enemies in his prosecutions of RALEIGH, ESSEX and the Earl of Southampton. But under JAMES I as Chief Justice, first of the Court of Common Pleas (1603-13) then of the

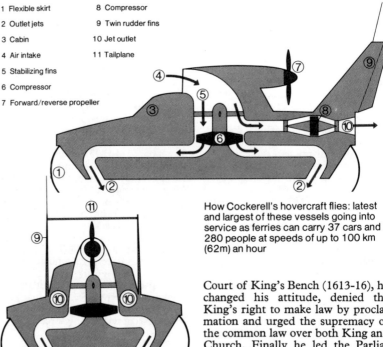

1 Flexible skirt
2 Outlet jets
3 Cabin
4 Air intake
5 Stabilizing fins
6 Compressor
7 Forward/reverse propeller
8 Compressor
9 Twin rudder fins
10 Jet outlet
11 Tailplane

How Cockerell's hovercraft flies: latest and largest of these vessels going into service as ferries can carry 37 cars and 280 people at speeds of up to 100 km (62m) an hour

Court of King's Bench (1613-16), he changed his attitude, denied the King's right to make law by proclamation and urged the supremacy of the common law over both King and Church. Finally he led the Parliamentary opposition to CHARLES I, especially by blocking his demands for subsidies. The Petition of Right (1628) was based on Coke's ideas.

Colbert, Jean Baptiste (1619-83) French statesman, Chief Minister of LOUIS XIV in succession to MAZARIN, whose agent he had been. Appointed officially Controller General of Finance (1665), he reformed the corrupt financial administration and widened direct and indirect taxation. He built up a major export trade based on state-sponsored industries employing foreign craftsmen, founded trading companies and colonies (notably in Canada) to encourage overseas trade and supported new communications projects, including a major road and canal system, and a substantial merchant navy. As Secretary of State for the Marine (from 1668), he created the French navy.

Coleridge, Samuel Taylor (1772-1834) English philosopher, critic and poet of fantasy and the supernatural. In the *Lyrical Ballads* (1798), written in collaboration with WORDSWORTH, Coleridge agreed to write of the supernatural, and his great success is in the strange, haunting realms of 'The Ancient Mariner', 'Kubla Khan' and 'Christabel'. The ode on 'France' (1798) and 'Dejection' (1802) are the best of his other poems. He was the main philosopher of the Romantic movement, although his criticism is interesting for its insights rather than its ordered system.

Coleridge-Taylor, Samuel (1875-1912) English composer who wrote the cantata *Hiawatha's Wedding Feast* (1898). This was later extended to form part of a trilogy, including *The Death of Minnehaha* (1899) and *Hiawatha's Departure* (1900), all based on LONGFELLOW's poem. He studied with Stanford, and his talents were recognized and praised by SULLIVAN and ELGAR, though his death occurred before he had attained full development.

Colet, John (c. 1467-1519) English scholar and theologian, promoter of the New Learning and founder of St Paul's School, London. Educated and ordained at Oxford, Colet's critical and original interpretation of the Bible profoundly influenced ERASMUS. Like MORE, Colet pressed for ecclesiastical reform, constantly deploring the ignorance and corruption of the clergy. He became Dean of St Paul's in 1505, founding the school with the fortune inherited from his father.

Colette, Sidonie Gabrielle (1873-1954) French novelist and foremost woman writer of her age, whose sensitive studies of a youth's love for an older woman in *Chéri* (1920) and *La Fin de Chéri* (1926) established her as a major writer. In the early sketches of the 'Claudine' series (e.g. *Claudine à l'Ecole*, 1900; *Claudine à Paris*, 1901) she collaborated with her first husband, the novelist and music critic Henri Gauthier Villars ('Willy'). But it was in the post-war years that she produced her best works, including *Le Blé en herbe* (1923), *La Chatte* (1933) and the famous *Gigi* (1943).

Collins, Michael (1890-1922) Irish republican who helped to organize the Dublin 'Easter Rising' of 1916.

His early working life was spent in London, but after his return to Ireland in 1916, he was imprisoned for his part in the Easter Rising, and again in 1918 for militant nationalism. In that year he was elected to the first Dail Eireann (Irish parliament) which declared for Irish independence and a republic. In the ensuing conflict with Britain, Collins played a major role in setting up the IRA, of which he became Chief of Staff. As one of the commissioners sent to London in 1921 to negotiate a settlement, he was instrumental in the establishment of the Irish Free State, of which he became Chairman (i.e. Prime Minister) and Minister of Finance. Dissatisfaction with the settlement which fell short of complete republican independence led to conflict within the IRA itself and Collins was assassinated by extremist republicans in 1922.

Collins, Wilkie (1824-89) English novelist and pioneer of detective fiction in England. His first mystery story, *The Dead Secret*, appeared in 1857. The best of its successors, all

very popular, are *The Woman in White* (1860) and *The Moonstone* (1868). Collins was a friend of DICKENS, and his descriptive and atmospheric writing has affinities with Dickens's style.

Collins, William (1721-59) English poet, adept at writing in the classical ode form, including such famous odes as 'The Evening' and 'To the Passions'.

Collinson, Sir Richard (1811-1883) English naval officer and explorer of the Arctic, who took part in the search for Sir John FRANKLIN.

Collot d'Herbois, Jean Marie (1749-96) French revolutionary and one of the most ruthless leaders of the Terror which followed the downfall of the French monarchy. He died in exile after the failure of the Jacobin rising in 1795.

The pensive Burgundian girl who was to become a legend in her own lifetime—Sidonie Gabrielle Colette

Colt, Samuel (1814-62) American gunsmith, who in 1836 patented his single-barrel, rotating breech pistol and later built the world's largest privately owned armoury. His hand guns were the principal artefacts of American western legend.

Colum, Padraic (born 1881) Irish poet, whose work was part of the flourishing of Irish literature in the early 20th century. His poetry is deeply rooted in Irish folk songs and ballads and he compiled *A Treasury of Irish Folklore* (1955). He helped found The Irish National Theatre, for which he wrote many plays, mainly depicting the dying Irish rural culture.

Columba (521-97) Irish missionary saint. The evangelizer of Scotland, he preached the gospel to the heathen Picts and founded a monastery on the island of Iona.

Columbus, Christopher (1451-1506) Genoese-born explorer for Spain, whose voyage to the Americas in 1492 achieved for him the credit for their discovery (although the Vikings had reached America centuries before). Columbus, who believed the Earth to be round, and that only the Atlantic separated Europe from eastern Asia, offered to find John II of Portugal a sea route to the Orient by sailing westward, but finally took his offer to FERDINAND and Isabella of Spain (1484), who agreed to back him. On 3 August 1492, Columbus sailed from Palos with the *Santa María*, the *Pinta* and the *Niña*, and on 12 Oct. reached San Salvador Island in the Bahamas. He went on to explore the north coast of Cuba, which he thought to be part of mainland Asia, and an island which he imagined was Cipango (Japan), and named it Hispaniola. Columbus received unprecedented honours on his return to Spain, and in 1493 led 17 shiploads of colonists to Hispaniola and discovered Dominica, Puerto Rico and Jamaica. On his third voyage (1498), he discovered Trinidad, and on a last

journey (1502-4), explored the east coast of Central America from Honduras to Panama, believing throughout that all his discoveries were in the Orient.

Comenius, Johann Amos (1592-1670) Moravian theologian, politician and educationalist who originated a scheme requiring universal education, a pooling of knowledge and reformed teaching methods. His own textbooks were revolutionary in their grading and use of pictures. *Gate of Language Unlocked* (1631), a Latin textbook, was translated into 16 languages, while *The Visible World in Pictures*

Columbus's route across the North Atlantic, and his tubby little carrack, the *Santa Maria*. The carrack never made the return journey—it was wrecked in the West Indies

was in use for 200 years. A visit by Comenius to England (1641-2) led to the founding of the Royal Society. LEIBNIZ and others were influenced by his ideas.

Commoner, Barry (born 1917) American biologist. His numerous articles in *Science and Survival* are concerned mainly with the effects of man's technology on the environment and the urgent need for measures to save it from irreversible changes.

Commynes, Philippe de (c. 1447-c. 1511) French chronicler, whose *Mémoires* provide eye-witness accounts of the reigns of LOUIS XI and CHARLES VIII.

Comnena, Anna (1083-c. 1153) Byzantine historian. When deprived of the throne by her younger brother, John, Anna Comnena turned to writing. Her *Alexiad* is an eight-volume history of the reign of her father Emperor ALEXIUS I COMNENUS.

Compton, Arthur Holly (1892-1962) American physicist who showed that X-rays sometimes behave like particles of matter. In 1923, while investigating the scattering of X-rays from a paraffin-wax target, Compton found that the scattering of the rays lengthened their wavelength (a phenomenon now called the Compton Effect). He was able to explain this by regarding the X-rays as a hail of tiny particles.

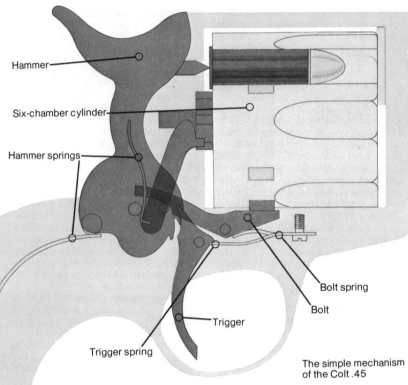

Hammer

Six-chamber cylinder

Hammer springs

Bolt spring

Bolt

Trigger

Trigger spring

The simple mechanism of the Colt .45

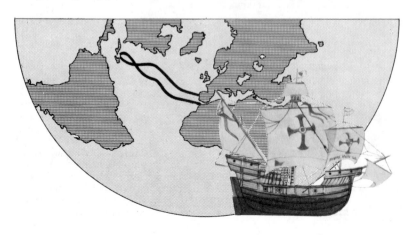

Comte, Auguste (1798-1857) French philosopher, inventor of the term 'sociology', who put forward a system of positivist philosophy based on the methods of science. Comte stated that human thought passes through a theological and metaphysical stage before becoming scientific, whence it evolves from the simple and general to the complex and special. For instance, in the sequence of mathematics, astronomy, physics, chemistry, biology and sociology, each branch of knowledge draws on the preceding one. Sociology, the scientific study of society, completes the series. He also advocated a positive social organization with a rational religion somewhat in the style of the Enlightenment and the French Revolution.

Compton-Burnett, Ivy (1892-1969) English novelist, who constructed her books almost entirely from dialogue. Her 19 novels achieve their effect by the calm way in which crime, cruelty and violence in eccentric families are revealed through the conversations of her characters.

Condé, Prince de see LOUIS II de Bourbon

Condillac, Etienne de (1715-80) French philosopher who claimed that all mental activity consists in sensations and their transformations, the senses contributing severally to the pleasures and pains that motivate men. He was a contemporary of ROUSSEAU and DIDEROT, with whom he associated.

Condorcet, Jean, Marquis de (1743-94) French philosopher, mathematician, politician and encyclopedist. Condorcet became President of the Legislative Assembly in 1792; he was arrested with other Girondists and died in prison.

Confucius (c. 551-479 BC) Chinese philosopher (K'ung Fu-tzu), who exercised more influence on Chinese culture than any other thinker. His *Analects* (collected sayings) do not constitute a religion or carry a profound intellectual message, but simply stress man's duty to man within social units from the family to the state. Confucius saw keeping to one's station as the surest way of curbing political anarchy, but also stressed the hereditary lord's obligation to set an ethical example by practising inner integrity, loyalty, altruism and love for his fellow men. While Confucian doctrines helped autocrats such as SHIH HUANG TI and WU TI to retain power, they also gave China's rulers a philosophy which put personal ambition in a social perspective.

Congreve, William (1670-1729) English dramatist, pre-eminent among Restoration comedy writers. His first play, *The Old Bachelor* (1693), was followed by *The Double Dealer* (1694) and *Love for Love* (1695), which took him to the height of his popularity. While his *The Mourning Bride*, in verse, was a success, *The Way of the World* (1700) was a failure. This so annoyed Congreve that he retired to live as a country gentleman. Now it is generally considered his best play and is frequently revived. It provides actresses with a fine comedy role in the part of the heroine, Millament.

Conn (2nd cent.) Irish king of Connaught who reputedly founded a northern Irish kingdom and a line of 'high kings', including the Cormac and Niall of the Nine Hostages.

Conrad II the Salian (c. 990-1039) King of Germany and Holy Roman Emperor (1024-39), who founded the Salian or Franconian dynasty and began Germany's great imperial phase. He crushed rebel factions in Germany (1025-30), added Lusatia (1031) and Burgundy (1033-4) to his empire, and did much to overcome northern Italy (1036-7).

Conrad III (1093-1152) King of Germany who founded the Hohenstaufen dynasty of Holy Roman Emperors (1138-1268). Lacking the statesmanship to keep Germany united, Conrad, a member of the Waiblinger family, was forced to cede Saxony (1142) to Henry the Lion, leader of the Welf (Guelph) family, which had formerly ruled the empire. Conrad's reign thus tortured Germany with struggles between Welfs and Waiblingers (better known as Guelphs and Ghibellines), and saw German expansion against the Slavs and the Scandinavians.

Conrad, Joseph (1857-1924) Polish-born English writer of short stories and novels that combine stirring adventure with profound analyses of human psychology. Conrad went to sea and became an English master mariner. His first novel, in English, was published in 1895. *Lord Jim* (1900), *Heart of Darkness* (1902) and *Nostromo* (1904) show a fluent and effective English prose style. In his works he often studied men put to the test in lonely places, using his novels to expound his view of human nature.

Conscience, Hendrik (1812-83) Belgian writer, whose outstanding historical novel *The Lion of Flanders* (1838) is an epic story of the revolt of the Flemish municipalities against France and their victory at the Battle of the Golden Spurs (1302). It was the first novel written in the Flemish tongue, giving the movement for the revival of the language its symbol of the lion.

Constable, John (1776-1837) One of the outstanding English landscape painters of the 19th century. His love for the mills and waterways of his native Suffolk and his acquaintance with Dutch Realist landscapes were at odds with his admiration for the order and clarity of the tradition of the 'ideal' landscapes of CLAUDE LORRAINE. He attempted to maintain the spontaneity of his oil sketches done in the open, while presenting an organized and digested experience of landscape. At the Paris Salon in 1824, Constable received the recognition he lacked in England. His influence on DELACROIX was profound and also important in the development of the Impressionist painters.

Constantine I 'The Great' (c. 280-337) Emperor of Rome (306-37), the first to embrace Christianity, who moved the imperial centre of gravity east from Rome to Constantinople, and made Christianity the religion of the Empire. He fought his way (306-14) to become undisputed western Emperor and reversed DIOCLETIAN's policies by reuniting the partitioned Empire. The position of the Emperor was henceforth to be absolute and hereditary. Constantine made Byzantium on the Bosporus his new capital, renaming it Constantinople. It was modelled on Rome but was more strategically placed at the crossroads of Europe and Asia, in the empire's richer and more secure eastern zone (later the Byzantine empire). Constantine called and presided over the first general Council of Nicaea (325), when the Nicene Creed was adopted.

Constantine XI Palaeologus (1404-53) Last Byzantine emperor (1448-53), who defended his weak and shrunken empire against MOHAMMED II's determined Ottoman attacks, but died defending Constantinople against the Turks. The capture of the city and death of Constantine ended the 1000-year-old Byzantine Empire.

Conway, Sir William (1856-1937) English art historian and mountaineer. In 1895 he was knighted for his survey and exploration achievements over 2000 square miles of the Karakoram mountains. During a later expedition to South America he climbed several mountains, including Aconcagua, Sorata and Illimani and also explored Tierra del Fuego. Conway produced several books on mountaineering, including a prototype handbook for climbers without guides.

Cook, James (1728-79) English sea captain whose voyages of exploration were among the greatest of 18th-century achievements. Cook accurately charted New Zealand and the east coast of Australia (1768-71). He correctly surmised the existence of Antarctica and discovered and mapped numerous tropical islands. He was murdered by natives in Hawaii on his third voyage in search of a northwest passage.

Cooley, Charles (1864-1929) American pioneer of sociology who showed how human values are formed from close relationships in 'primary' groups such as the family, which are fundamental in the social behaviour and ideals of individuals.

Coolidge, Calvin (1872-1933) Thirtieth President of the United States. He first gained public attention when, as Governor of Massachusetts in 1919, he broke a strike of the Boston city police. As HARDING's Vice-President, he succeeded to the office on Harding's death in 1923, and in 1924 was elected to serve a second term (1925-9). His irresolution in the face of business excesses and commercial profiteering led to the Wall Street crash and the beginning of the world-wide depression of 1929.

Cooper, Anthony Ashley see SHAFTESBURY, 7th Earl of

Cooper, James Fenimore (1789-1851) American novelist, who was the first to portray, in his Leatherstocking stories, a distinctively American way of life and thought. His best-known work is *The Last of the Mohicans* (1826).

Copeau, Jacques (1878-1949) French theatrical manager and director, who led the reaction against realism and introduced a new style of production and direction. His object was to be governed by the script of a play, conveying to the audience the author's intention as simply as possible. He reduced scenery and movement to a minimum, making his actors deliver their lines clearly and without fuss. His Vieux-Colombier company performed not only in Paris but in London and New York.

Copernicus, Nicolaus (1473-1543) Polish astronomer, who revolutionized theories of the motion of the planets and laid the foundations of modern astronomical studies. In his principal work, *The Revolutions of the Heavenly Bodies*, Copernicus refuted the theory propounded by PTOLEMY and went back to original Greek writers to discover that a heliocentric theory of the Solar System had been proposed, but not generally accepted. He adopted the assumption that the Earth was moving, and discovered that a simpler and more consistent theory of the Solar System arose from it. Copernicus's conclusions gained wide acceptance through the work and teachings of KEPLER and GALILEO, and are the basis for all later studies of the motions of the planets.

Copland, Aaron (born 1900) American composer and writer whose early work *Piano Variations* (1930) was marked by intellectual austerity and expressed the alienation of urban life. In humanizing his style, Copland turned increasingly to more 'pastoral' subjects, such as the cowboy tunes he used in the ballet *Billy the Kid* (1938) and the charming Shaker hymn-tune incorporated into *Appalachian Spring* (1944). Copland has also written film scores, notably for the film versions of WILDER's *Our Town* and STEINBECK's *Of Mice and Men*.

Corbett, James C. see SULLIVAN, John

Corelli, Arcangelo (1653-1713) Italian violinist and composer who established the *concerto grosso*, a musical form in which a small group of instruments is contrasted with a larger orchestral group. A pioneer in playing and writing for the violin, Corelli spent most of his musical life at the court of Cardinal Ottoboni in Rome.

Cori, Charles (born 1896) American biochemist of Czech origin who shared a Nobel Prize in 1947 with his wife, Gerty Cori, and Bernardo Houssay for their investigation of the process by which glycogen (animal starch) is converted into glucose, the main energy-yielding molecule in living tissues.

Cori, Gerty see CORI, Charles

Cornelius, Peter von (1783-1867) German painter, who was an influential member of the Nazarenes, a

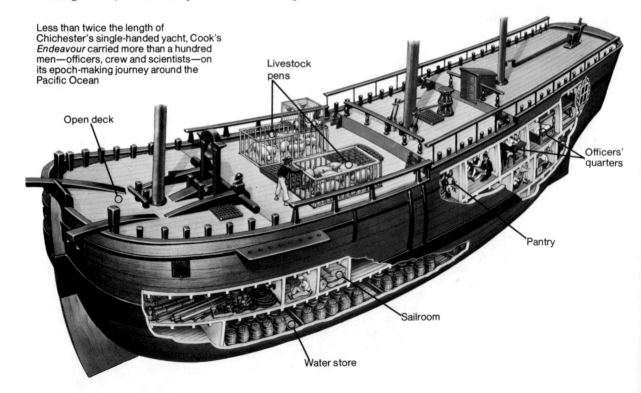

Less than twice the length of Chichester's single-handed yacht, Cook's *Endeavour* carried more than a hundred men—officers, crew and scientists—on its epoch-making journey around the Pacific Ocean

Livestock pens

Open deck

Officers' quarters

Pantry

Sailroom

Water store

group of German artists working in Rome. Emulating the primitive Italian and northern artists, they worked together on frescoes in the Casa Bartholdy and Casino Massimo. Cornelius himself was much influenced by the sophisticated composition and detailed technique of RAPHAEL. After returning to Munich in 1819, Cornelius embarked on a systematic programme for the revival of art in Germany, through his teaching and complex fresco cycles.

Cornell, Katherine (born 1898) American actress-manager. She made her debut in New York in 1916, but was relatively unknown until 1931 when she went into management. She achieved fame in three roles, SHAW's Candida, as Elizabeth in *The Barretts of Wimpole Street* and as Juliet.

Coriolis, Gaspard Gustave de (1792-1843) French mathematician and engineer who formulated laws to describe moving bodies. He showed that the ordinary equations of motion can be applied to a rotating system by including a special inertial force at right angles to the motion of the body and to the axis of rotation. This 'Coriolis' force is important in all problems of rotational dynamics.

Corneille, Pierre (1604-84) French dramatist and the first great writer of classical tragedy in France. He was inspired to write a comedy, *Mélite*, after seeing farces staged by a touring company that visited his birthplace, Rouen. Its success in Paris encouraged him to continue writing plays. His first tragedy, *Médée* (1635), led to his appointment as salaried playwright by RICHELIEU, with whom he later quarrelled. After returning to Rouen, he wrote *Le Cid* (1637), a new kind of romantic heroic comedy and his most frequently revived play. Although it fitted awkwardly into the classical style which was then *de rigueur*, it established Corneille as France's leading dramatist, until he was superseded by RACINE. His principal tragedies are on classical themes – *Horace* (1640), *Cinna* (1641), *Polyeucte* (1642), *La Mort de Pompée* (1643). His only comedy after his early period was *Le Menteur* (1643).

Cornwallis, Charles, 1st Marquess (1738-1805) British major-general whose defeat virtually ended the American War of Independence. During the War he seized New York, and forced WASHINGTON's retreat through New Jersey. Later, disobeying orders to avoid major risks, he entered Virginia, where Washington's troops, backed by a French fleet offshore, trapped Cornwallis and his lesser troops at Yorktown, forcing their surrender. Later, as Governor-

George Washington accepts the surrender of Cornwallis at Yorktown

General of India (1786-93; 1805), he pioneered major administrative reforms. Viceroy of Ireland (1798-1801) at the time of the Union, he resigned when Catholic emancipation was not granted. Cornwallis negotiated the 1802 Treaty of Amiens, which brought a brief pause during the Napoleonic wars with the French.

Coronado, Francisco Vasquez de (1510-54) Spanish explorer, discoverer of the Grand Canyon of the Colorado River. Inspired by the rumours of fabulous wealth which spread after expeditions into southwestern North America, he travelled across present New Mexico, northern Texas, Oklahoma and Kansas. One exploring party from his expedition reached northern Arizona, another discovered the Grand Canyon, and a third explored the Rio Grande.

Corot, Jean Baptiste (1796-1875) French classical landscape artist. His work falls into two main categories: firstly, the large synthetic landscapes painted for exhibition at the Salon, which are in the tradition of CLAUDE LORRAINE (e.g. *Souvenir de Montfortaine*, 1864); and secondly, the smaller, informal paintings which reflect his love of working out of doors, and influenced the Impressionists, notably PISSARRO, who was Corot's pupil. Corot's mature style is marked by a subtlety of tonal modulation which led BAUDELAIRE to describe him as a 'harmonist' rather than a colourist.

Correggio, Antonio (c. 1494-1534) Italian artist, who was an important forerunner of the 17th-century ceiling painters. His two greatest works are in Parma: the cupolas of S Giovanni Evangelista (1520-3) and the Cathedral (1526-30). In both of these are the formal types exemplified in the work of RAPHAEL and MICHELANGELO, but the main effect is of a mass of figures soaring into an illusionary space that denies the architectural solidity of the cupola itself. Correggio also painted a

number of pictures illustrating the loves of the gods, which are characterized by a delicacy of modelling of human forms that derives ultimately from LEONARDO.

Corte-Real, Gaspar (c. 1450-1501) Portuguese navigator, explorer of the northwestern shores of the Atlantic. He reached south Greenland in 1500 and the next year reached Labrador and Newfoundland, a journey from which he never returned.

Corte-Real, Miguel (16th cent.) Portuguese navigator, brother of Gaspar CORTE-REAL. In 1501, he left Gaspar in Newfoundland, hoping soon to see him again in Portugal. In May, 1502, when Gaspar's return was long overdue, Miguel sailed northwest in search of him, and vanished without trace.

Cortés, Hernando (1485-1547) Spanish conqueror of Mexico. Cortés emigrated to the West Indies (1504) and was appointed by Diego Velasquez, Cuba's governor, to lead an expedition to Mexico, where he landed (1519) with 500 men. MONTEZUMA, the Aztec monarch, believing Cortés to be the god Quetzalcoatl, sent him conciliatory gifts, but Cortés, surrounded by hostile Aztecs, took Montezuma hostage. The Aztecs revolted but, after heavy losses and a long siege, Cortés took Tenochtitlan, the capital, ended Aztec power (1521), and became Governor of Mexico. The king of Spain, alarmed by Cortés's success and ambition, gradually ousted him from authority.

Cortona, Pietro da (1596-1669) Italian Baroque architect, whose work is characterized by a verve and theatricality achieved by amassing shapes and using unusual surface details such as giant pilasters. His first church in Rome, SS Luca e Martina (1635-50), is a wildly exuberant building and the façade of his church Sta Maria della Pace (1656-7) provides a theatrical backdrop to the Piazza he designed in front of it.

Cosa, Juan de la (c. 1460-1510) Spanish navigator whose first-hand knowledge helped him to make the earliest surviving world map, which shows the New World discoveries of the 1490s. As Captain of the *Santa Maria*, he accompanied COLUMBUS on his first transatlantic voyage (1492-3), and later (between 1499 and 1508) piloted expeditions to explore northern South America, where he was killed by American Indians. His large, hand-drawn world map (made in 1500), which took account of the discoveries of Columbus, CABOT and others, can be seen in the Naval Museum, Madrid.

Cotman, John Sell (1782-1842) British painter, one of the leaders of the Norwich school. His watercolours rank with the best examples of this genre in England.

Cotta, Johann Friedrich (1764-1832) German publisher of works by GOETHE, Hegel and other leading writers, a proponent of freedom of the Press and revolutionary printing methods.

Cotton, John (1584-1652) English-born American clergyman, whose influence in the civil and ecclesiastical affairs of New England was greater than that of any other minister. Educated at Cambridge, where the Puritan ethic flourished, Cotton fled from his vicarage at Boston, England, to Boston, Massachusetts, in 1633. Speedily establishing himself as a religious and political leader, he successfully opposed 'liberals' like Roger WILLIAMS. A man of great learning, with a prolific pen, he wrote catechisms, commentaries on prayer and works on Congregationalism. His best-known book was *The Way of the Churches of Christ in New England* (1645).

Coulomb, Charles Augustin de (1736-1806) French physicist who discovered the inverse square law for the force between electric charges. The practical unit of charge is called after him. This law states that the force between two charges is proportional to their product and inversely proportional to the square of the distance between them. He found a similar law for magnetic poles. A full mathematical formulation of these results was later given by POISSON.

Couper, Archibald (1831-92) Scottish chemist who developed a method of depicting structures of chemical compounds. Couper was interested by Friedrich KEKULÉ's ideas of showing chemical structures by drawing the patterns of atoms making up molecules and added proposals for linking up the symbols for atoms by lines representing the chemical bonds between them.

Couperin, François (1668-1733) French harpsichordist and composer, among the first to use picturesque, or programmatic, titles for pieces of music and who wrote a classic on harpsichord technique, *L'Art de toucher le clavecin* (1717). Couperin was the most outstanding of a family of five generations of musicians. RAVEL paid him tribute in his set of six piano movements, *Le Tombeau de Couperin* (1917), four of which he later orchestrated.

Courbet, Gustave (1819-77) French realist painter, who believed resolutely that painting should be a democratic depiction of the life of the workers and the peasantry. He fulfilled this ambition in such famous works as *The Stonebreakers* (1849) and *The Burial at Ornans* (1850), the latter portraying a peasant funeral. His political convictions led him to identify himself with the Paris Commune of 1871, and he was forced to flee to Switzerland after his part in the demolition of NAPOLEON's memorial column in the Place Vendôme. Courbet was largely self-taught, and tried to free his landscapes from the compositional clichés of contemporary French art, thereby anticipating Impressionism. Although friendly with BAUDELAIRE and PROUDHON, the philosopher of socialism, Courbet remained wholly independent in spirit, and countered official neglect by mounting separate exhibitions of his work during the international exhibitions of 1855 and 1867.

Cournand, André (born 1895) American physician of French origin who, with Werner Forssman and Dickinson Richards, developed the technique of cardiac catheterization, for which they were awarded a Nobel Prize in 1956. The cardiac catheter is a fine tube that is inserted into a blood vessel in the arm or leg; guided by X-ray-assisted visual display, it is then worked upstream or downstream to the heart. It can be used to take direct pressure readings, withdraw blood samples for analysis, or inject dyes opaque to X-rays, and so assist in the diagnosis of cardiac conditions.

Cournot, Antoine (1801-77) French pioneer in applying mathematics to economics. His *Researches into the Mathematical Principles of the Theory of Wealth* (1838) laid foundations for subsequent work by WALRAS.

Court, Margaret (born 1942) Australian tennis player, who throughout the 1960s dominated women's tennis. She was three times women's champion at Wimbledon and in 1970 she achieved the grand slam, winning the Australian, French, British and American open championships.

Courtenay, Jan (1845-1929) Polish philologist who was the originator of the theory of phonemes. He showed that language can be broken down into single sound images or abstracts. Thus, for example, there is a phoneme 't' to which all 't' sounds approximate, though they differ according to speaker or occasion used.

Cousteau, Jacques-Yves (born 1910) French pioneer of underwater exploration and its techniques. Cousteau developed skin-diving gear, in particular the aqualung, to carry out free-diving exploration of shallow seas, and in the Mediterranean found enough sunken Greek and Roman wrecks to reconstruct ancient trade routes. He has also made a number of discoveries about underwater life in the Red Sea, Caribbean and Indian Ocean.

Couturat, Louis (1868-1914) French logician, who was the first French exponent of the new mathematical logic which arose at the end of the 19th century.

Covarrubias, Miguel (1904-57) Mexican archaeologist, who in the 1940s identified what may be the oldest civilization in Central America, the La Venta culture of southeast Mexico, which began about 1500 BC.

Coverdale, Miles (1488-1568) English translator, who ranks second only to TYNDALE in the story of the English Bible. Originally an Austin friar, he became a Reformer in 1528, henceforth dividing his time between England and Europe according to the religious situation at home. In 1529 he helped Tyndale translate the Pentateuch; in 1535, encouraged by CRANMER and Thomas CROMWELL, he published an English Bible, and in 1539 he edited the Great Bible. Edward VI made him a royal chaplain and Bishop of Exeter, but he fled to Switzerland in MARY I's reign, working on the Geneva Bible (1557-9). Though he returned to England under ELIZABETH I, he did not resume his bishopric, but remained a popular Puritan preacher until his death.

Covilhão, Pedro de (c. 1450-c. 1545) Portuguese explorer whose report of India's riches encouraged the search for a sea route to India. Covilhão went through the Mediterranean and the Red Sea, crossed the

Arabian Sea to India, returned to East Africa, and settled in Ethiopia. He sent home an account of his travels and said that if Portuguese pilots could round southern Africa they would find on its east coast pilots to lead them to India. DA GAMA used this information and reached India.

Coward, Sir Noël (1899-1973) All-round man of the English theatre, whose plays include *Bitter Sweet*, *Cavalcade*, *Private Lives* and *Blithe Spirit*. He also wrote and acted in revues and films and often appeared in cabaret.

Cowell, Henry (1897-1966) American composer and a leading experimentalist in US music. He introduced the tone-cluster in which whole blocks of piano keys are struck with fist or forearm. Cowell, self-taught, was a true original, exploring acoustic and percussive techniques, indeterminacy and random selection. He was an influential teacher, and CAGE was among his pupils.

Cowper, William (1666-1709) British surgeon and anatomist who first described the calcification (hardening) of the aorta and aortic valve, the chief outlet from the heart.

Cowper, William (1731-1800) English poet, who wrote the ballad 'John Gilpin' (1785). Cowper was a barrister, but his career was hindered by recurrent bouts of mania. He retired to the country and wrote the *Olney Hymns* (1779) and his longest work, *The Task* (1785), in which he shows his delight in country life and rural scenes.

Crabbe, George (1754-1832) 'Though nature's sternest painter, yet the best', wrote BYRON of Crabbe, whose principal narrative poems are grimly realistic pictures of the hardships of country life. In such typical works as 'The Parish Register' (1807) and 'The Borough' (1810), the harshness of the lives of the poor is set against the flat, grey countryside of the Suffolk fens. Crabbe was aided and encouraged by Edmund BURKE and Dr JOHNSON. *The Borough* was the inspiration for BRITTEN's opera 'Peter Grimes'.

Craig, Gordon (1872-1966) English director, stage designer and theorist, whose *The Art of the Theatre* (1905) influenced modern theatrical technique. One outcome of Craig's theories is 'total theatre', whose most successful exponent has been Jean-Louis BARRAULT.

Cranach, Lucas (1472-1553) German artist, and a friend of LUTHER, whose portrait he painted and whose

Noël Coward in an early production of one of his greatest successes, 'Private Lives'

doctrines he helped to spread by means of woodcuts. While court painter to the Electors of Saxony he produced, in addition to portraits, some small, slightly erotic pictures of subjects such as Venus and Lucretia.

Crane, Hart (1899-1932) American poet, who tried to assert the positive 'myth of America' against the disillusionment he saw in modern poetry, particularly in ELIOT's *Waste Land*. He wrote a long poem of the old and new America called *The Bridge* (1930), which takes Brooklyn Bridge as a symbol and WHITMAN as one of the heroes. After a short, turbulent, drunken life, Crane committed suicide by leaping from a ship.

Crane, Stephen (1871-1900) American short-story writer and novelist, who was a pioneer of naturalistic fiction. His main work, *The Red Badge of Courage* (1895), described the enormities of the American Civil War in raw, colourful prose.

Cranmer, Thomas (1489-1556) English archbishop who compiled the liturgies of the Church of England. Cranmer was appointed Archbishop of Canterbury by HENRY VIII for his assistance in the struggle with Pope CLEMENT VII for a divorce from Catharine of Aragon. In 1533 Cranmer annulled the marriage and accepted Henry as Supreme Head of the Church of England (1534). Cranmer extended the English Reformation by having English Bibles placed in all churches. He compiled Edward VI's prayer books (1549 and 1552), and evolved a church whose doctrines compromised between those of Rome and Geneva. Before it took root under ELIZABETH I, the Catholic Queen MARY condemned Cranmer as a heretic (1555), despite his admission of papal supremacy. He later retracted, and was burnt at the stake.

Crashaw, Richard (c. 1612-49) English poet, whose ornate, religious verse is the closest in English literature to the traditions of the continental Baroque style. His sacred poetry

is exotic, sometimes, as in 'The Flaming Heart,' a hymn to ST TERESA, showing mystical passion and a confident command of elaborate imagery. His main work, *Steps to the Temple* (1646), combines ecstatic devotional verse with graceful secular lyrics.

Crawford, Osbert (1886-1957) British pioneer of archaeological air photography and field work, whose discovery that air photographs showed traces of otherwise invisible settlements led to dramatic discoveries, including that of Woodhenge.

Crichton, James (c. 1560-c. 1582) Scottish man of letters, called the 'admirable (wonderful) Crichton'. He supposedly knew ten languages, had vast knowledge of the Schoolmen and the Church Fathers, was a great debater, and skilled in arms and horsemanship. The report of his murder (1582) may be incorrect, but he was dead by 1585.

Crick, Francis (born 1916) British geneticist who, with James WATSON, proposed the first model of a deoxyribonucleic acid (DNA) molecule. The DNA molecule has the basic structure of a double helix, and it is now known to carry inheritable genetic material. Crick and Watson showed how this material is replicated during cell division and how the DNA molecule has series of bases which serve as patterns for ordering the genetic material so that it can be reproduced accurately. With their colleague, Maurice Wilkins, they were awarded a Nobel Prize for Medicine in 1962.

Crippen, Dr Hawley (1862-1910) American doctor, who killed his wife with poison. Crippen, a US citizen, settled in London in 1900. Soon after, he began an extra-marital affair, and in January 1910 his wife disappeared. A search of Crippen's house revealed her remains. Crippen, who was traced aboard an ocean liner by wireless telegraphy (the first time it was used in criminal detection), was convicted of the murder of his wife and subsequently hanged.

Cripps, Stafford (1889-1952) English lawyer and politician, Chancellor of the Exchequer in ATTLEE's Labour government. In 1939 he was expelled from the Labour Party for advocating a Popular Front against Neville CHAMBERLAIN's policy of appeasement. As Ambassador to Moscow in 1940 he improved Anglo-Soviet relations considerably and, as Special Envoy to India in 1942, he offered the country dominion status, which was rejected by both GANDHI and JINNAH. He became President of the Board of Trade in 1945, and as Chancellor of the Exchequer (1947-50) introduced the policy of austerity for which his chancellorship is remembered. His were the first genuine attempts at economic planning, however, and his policy of income restraint was a pioneering one, A man of firm Christian principles, he believed they could be exercised through politics, and he brought moral stature and integrity to both the government and parliament.

Crispus, Gaius see SALLUST

Cristofori, Bartolommeo (1655-1731) Italian craftsman who in the early 18th century developed the first pianoforte (piano). Cristofori's principal contribution was replacing harpsichord jacks with hammers.

Croce, Benedetto (1866-1952) Italian philosopher who believed in the central role of history and aesthetics. Anti-positivist, he regarded the world as living spirit, manifesting itself through history and working at four levels – aesthetic, logical, economic and ethical. Art, he thought, manifests itself not in the objects produced, but in the prior intuition of the artist and the later one of the beholder.

Crockett, Davy (1786-1836) American frontiersman. In 1813, he scouted for Andrew Jackson against the Creek Indians, but as a Congressman subsequently opposed Jackson's Indian and land policies. Crockett died helping defend San Antonio's Alamo fort against 4000 Mexican troops trying to crush Texan independence.

Croesus (6th cent. BC) Last king of Lydia (560-546 BC), who by conquest dominated what is now the western half of Turkey and built a legendary personal fortune through trade. His kingdom was conquered and absorbed by CYRUS of Persia.

Le Petit Journal

ADMINISTRATION
61, RUE LAFAYETTE, 61
Les manuscrits ne sont pas rendus
On s'abonne sans frais
dans tous les bureaux de poste
5 CENT.   SUPPLÉMENT ILLUSTRÉ   5 CENT.
21ᵐᵉ Année   Numéro 1.030
DIMANCHE 14 AOUT 1910
ABONNEMENTS
SEINE et SEINE-ET-OISE ... 2 fr. ... 3 fr. 50
DÉPARTEMENTS .... 2 fr. ... 4 fr.
ÉTRANGER .... 2 50 ... 6 fr.

ARRESTATION DU DOCTEUR CRIPPEN ET DE MISS LE NEVE SUR LE PONT DU «MONTROSE»

Crippen is arrested, with his girl companion dressed as a boy

Crome, John (1768-1821) Leading artist of the Norwich school of English landscape painters. His work, which was much influenced by HOBBEMA, is characterized by a freshness of observation and a sensitivity to effects of light, noticeable especially in his delicate depiction of trees. He worked almost exclusively in Norfolk.

Crompton, Samuel (1753-1827) English inventor of the spinning mule, so called because it was developed from a hybrid of HARGREAVES's jenny and ARKWRIGHT's water frame spinning machine, both of which had serious limitations. He developed the mule secretly in 1779, after five years of work, and attempted to pass off the machine's product as his own. However, the superior quality and fineness of this yarn gave him away and he was tricked into revealing the mechanism of his (unpatented) spinner to the manufacturers of Bolton. Eventually he received a government grant of £5000, but this was insignificant compared to the financial benefits derived from his invention.

Cromwell, Oliver (1599-1658) Lord Protector of England and head of the republican Commonwealth that came to rule England, Scotland and Ireland between the execution of CHARLES I (1649) and the Restoration of CHARLES II (1660). During the Civil War, Cromwell's highly trained Puritan troops held together the Parliamentary supporters in eastern England and turned the Battle of Marston Moor (1644) against the Royalists. After the war, he supported the execution of Charles and became a member of the ruling Council of State. He re-conquered Ireland, massacring dissident citizens, and crushed Scotland, returning to London to eventually take the position of Lord Protector. Ruling as virtual dictator under the Instrument of Government (1653), Cromwell reorganized the Church along tolerant lines, made peace with Holland and Denmark, and successfully fought Spain in the West Indies and Spanish Netherlands (1655-8). Cromwell's protectorate did not long survive after his death.

Cromwell, Thomas (c. 1485-1540) English statesman who carried out HENRY VIII's Reformation to increase royal power at the expense of the Church. After trading successfully abroad, Cromwell became a financial adviser to nobles, an agent and favourite of WOLSEY and, by the early 1530s, a leading member of the House of Commons. He became the king's secretary (1534), drafted and engineered through Parliament most of Henry's Reformation Acts (1532-9), and ruthlessly carried out the dissolution of the monasteries and the confiscation of their property for the crown. His reward was a barony and the positions of Lord Privy Seal, Vicar General, and Deputy Head of the English Church. He lost the king's favour by negotiating his marriage with the unprepossessing Anne of Cleves (the 'Flanders mare') to win the support of Protestant German princes. Although Cromwell became Earl of Essex (1540), he was beheaded for heresy and treason.

Crookes, Sir William (1832-1919) English physicist, who by means of a vacuum tube established that cathode rays were streams of tiny charged particles. In the early 1900s his work was confirmed by J. J. THOMSON's discovery of electrons, the particles that make up cathode rays.

Cross, Charles Frederick (1855-1935) English chemist who, in 1892, together with Edward John Bevan, patented a method for producing viscose rayon from which the modern industry stems. Cellulose was dissolved in a mixture of carbon disulphide and sodium xanthate. The viscous solution was then squirted through fine holes to produce spinnable fibres. Cross was later involved in the development of thin transparent viscose films ('Cellophane').

Crowley, Aleister (1875-1947) English occultist notorious for the orgies which earned him the title of the 'wickedest man in the world'. Since his death, some of his books, notably *Confessions* and *Magick*, have considerably influenced the current occult revival. Apart from his occult activities, Crowley was a prolific writer of verse and a distinguished

mountaineer, leading the major Himalayan expedition of 1905.

Cruikshank, George (1792-1878) British caricaturist and illustrator, who was famous for his satires against the Prince Regent, later George IV, in *The Scourge*, a satirical journal. His very large output included the illustrations for DICKENS's *Sketches by Boz* and *Oliver Twist*, as well as for many other books. In middle age he became a teetotaller and produced a celebrated series of drawings (*The Bottle*, 1847) advocating temperance.

Cugnot, Nicholas Joseph (1725-1804) French military engineer, who in 1769-70 made a large three-wheeled carriage driven by a steam engine, which ran for about 20 minutes at two to three miles an hour. It was intended for military use and was the earliest forerunner of the motor-car.

Culpeper, Nicholas (1616-54) English physician and botanist whose herbal remedies described in *London Pharmocopeia* (1654) were widely used in the treatment of disease for many generations. He was a strong opponent of secrecy in medical matters and translated many learned works.

Cumberland, William Augustus, Duke of (1721-65) English military leader known as 'Butcher Cumberland' for the manner in which he crushed the 1745 Jacobite rising. Son of George II, he led an international force in Flanders in the War of the Austrian Succession, but returned to halt Prince Charles Edward STUART's Scottish invasion of England. Cumberland defeated Charles's 5000-strong Jacobite army at Culloden with the superiority of his firepower over the claymores of the clans. He later fought in the Seven Years' War, but suffered several defeats, losing Hanover.

Cummings, Edward Estlin (1894-1962) American lyric poet, who in his verse experimented with layout, typography and punctuation to suggest movement in time and space.

Curie, Marie (1867-1934) Polish-born French chemist who, with her husband Pierre, pioneered the earliest research into radioactivity. This remarkable husband and wife team worked for years in the late 1890s to establish that the uranium ore, pitchblende, owed much of its radioactivity to tiny quantities of highly active impurities. In 1898, the Curies discovered a new element which they named polonium (in honour of Marie's homeland). But Marie believed there was another still more

active element in the ore. After four more years of painstaking work, they isolated a tenth of a gram of another new element from the several tons of ore with which they had started. They called it radium. Its tremendous radioactivity was a first glimpse of the huge energies obtainable from atomic processes. Marie eventually died of leukaemia, brought on by constant exposure to radiation.

Marie Curie, joint discoverer of radium, received her early scientific training from her father at her home in Warsaw

Curie, Pierre (1859-1906) French physicist who studied the relationship between magnetism and heat. He showed that above a certain critical temperature (now called the Curie point) ferromagnetic substances lose their magnetism. He also established that the ease with which a substance becomes magnetized is proportional to its temperature, a principle now called Curie's law. With his wife Marie, he pioneered research on radioactivity.

Curnow, Allen (born 1911) New Zealand poet. In his work he describes the characteristics of New Zealand. He uses various forms of poetry, displaying technical versatility.

Currie, James (1756-1805) Scottish doctor who pioneered the use of cold water in the treatment of fever. Until Currie's time, it was widely thought that fevers were beneficial and it was the practice to let the fever burn itself out, the patient often being killed in the process. Currie saw that it was important to keep the patient's temperature as near to normal as possible. His success promoted water cures (hydrotherapy) for many diseases, and the use of clinical thermometers.

Curtis, Cyrus (1850-1933) American publisher and journalist who founded the *Ladies' Home Journal* (1879) and the Curtis Publishing Company. In 1897 he bought the *Saturday Evening Post*, and the *New York Evening Post*.

Curzon, George Nathaniel (1859-1925) British statesman and proponent of Britain's Imperial aspirations. He became Under-Secretary for India at the age of 32, for Foreign Affairs at 37, and Viceroy of India at 39. There he pursued a policy so independent that it was said of the government of India during his rule that it often behaved to Britain like that of a 'foreign and far from friendly power.' He held various offices under LLOYD GEORGE in the War Cabinet (1916-19), and as Foreign Secretary from 1919 to 1924 he arranged the British settlement with Turkey at the Lausanne Conference (1923). It was Curzon's ambition to be Prime Minister and a bitter disappointment to him when, in 1923, BALDWIN achieved the premiership, but a dedicated aristocrat and 'a most superior person', Curzon was hampered by his own personality throughout his political career.

Cushing, Harvey (1869-1939) American neurological surgeon who pioneered brain surgery. He wrote a monograph on the pituitary gland (1912) and gave his name to a disease of that organ. His experiences during the First World War led to his paper on wartime injuries of the brain.

Custer, Colonel George Armstrong (1839-76) American soldier who distinguished himself during the Civil War (1861-5) and was promoted to brevet Major General. His subsequent controversial career reached its climax in 1876, when, in command of the 7th Cavalry at Little Big Horn, Custer and the 108 troopers were annihilated by the combined Sioux and Cheyenne tribes. It was the most spectacular victory achieved by the Indians against the US troops.

Cuvier, Baron Georges (1769-1832) French naturalist, who in *The Animal Kingdom Arranged in Conformity with its Organization*, classified the animal kingdom on the basis of comparative anatomy. He is sometimes said to have founded the science of palaeontology (the study of fossils), since his research covered animals, both living and fossil.

Cyril of Alexandria (376-444) Greek saint who is said to have engineered the murder of the great neoplatonist philosopher Hypatia. The nephew of Theophilus of Alexandria, who had contrived the deposition of JOHN CHRYSOSTOM, he succeeded his uncle as bishop, and disgraced his office by his violent temper, intolerance of opposition, and persecution of the Jews. At the Council of Ephesus in 431, he defended the unity of CHRIST's person against the doctrine of NESTORIUS, Bishop of Constantinople, who held that Christ was two persons, the Son of God, and the man Jesus.

Cyrus II, 'The Great' (c. 600-529 BC) King of Persia (550-529 BC) who founded the Achaemenid dynasty (named after his ancestor Achaemenes), and built the biggest empire the world had then known. Cyrus united the Medes and Persians, defeating a coalition of neighbouring powers and extending Persian power to the Mediterranean. His army of mobile bowmen proved invincible, and in less than 20 years took much of Greece, Asia Minor, Mesopotamia and northern and eastern Iran, building a state that reached from India to the Aegean and the Egyptian border. A statesman as well as a soldier, Cyrus spurned the scorched-earth tactics of Assyrian war-lords such as SENNACHERIB, and treated the defeated peoples humanely, respecting their cultural traditions and taking them into the army and administration on an equal footing with the Persians. He was killed fighting the Massagetae east of the Caspian.

Czaczes, Shmuel see AGNON, Samuel

Czerny, Carl (1791-1857) Austrian composer and pianist remembered for his piano studies familiar to generations of keyboard students as practice pieces. A pupil of BEETHOVEN and a teacher of LISZT, Czerny also wrote many other kinds of piano music.

Cuyp, Aelbert (1620-91) Dutch painter, who is best known for his landscapes, which usually contain horses and riders, or cows, and sometimes both. He was one of the few Dutch exponents of the tranquil 'ideal' landscape, but his work has more of a pastoral character than that of CLAUDE LORRAINE, from whom he derived his poetic effects of golden evening sunlight.

Cyrano de Bergerac, Savinien de (1619-55) French dramatist (*Le Pédant joué*; *La Mort d'Agrippine*), author of satirical romances and model for ROSTAND's play, *Cyrano de Bergerac*.

D

Daguerre, Louis Jacques Mandé (1789-1851) French artist and inventor, who, in 1837, after a partnership with NIEPCE, perfected the process of heliography. The result of the 'daguerrotype' process was a single direct positive photograph, with the disadvantage that no copies could be made.

Dahrendorf, Ralf (born 1929) German sociologist who maintains that social conflict, not stability, is the basic condition of social life. In *Class and Class Conflict in Industrial Society* (1959) he contends that only through conflict can the changes occur which are necessary in industrial society.

Daigo II (1287-1339) Japanese emperor (1318-39) who ended domination of the emperors by the Kamakura shoguns, the leaders of the military class. Daigo was unable to maintain his domination and was driven out by ASHIKAGA TAKAUJI, who forced him from the civil capital, Kyoto. Daigo set up a rival court in the south, and dual rule in Japan lasted for 56 years.

Daimler, Gottlieb (1834-1900) German engineer who, together with BENZ, was one of the most important contributors to the development of the petrol engine automobile. After working for various engineering firms, in 1872 Daimler joined OTTO's firm where, during the next decade, in conjunction with MAYBACH and others, he improved the four-cycle gas engine. In 1882, he and Maybach resigned to set up a factory to develop a light, internal combustion engine, which ran at higher speeds than those of Benz's. In 1885 Daimler placed an engine on a wooden bicycle, creating the world's first motorcycle. Two years later he used the engine to power a four-wheeled vehicle, one of the first true automobiles. He founded the Daimler motor company in 1890.

Daladier, Edouard (1884-1970) Co-signatory with Neville CHAMBERLAIN of the Munich Agreement with HITLER. Having twice been briefly Premier of France (1933 and 1934), he became Prime Minister for the third time in 1938. He was a Socialist, a pacifist and a supporter of the policy of appeasement towards Hitler. Like Neville Chamberlain he believed that the Munich Pact, signed in September 1938, would ensure European peace, or at least buy time for rearmament. When war was declared DALADIER formed a war cabinet, but resigned in March 1940. After the collapse of France he was put under house arrest by the Vichy régime, where he remained until the end of the war. He played a prominent part in radical politics from 1945 until 1959, when he retired after DE GAULLE became President – an outcome which he had tried to prevent.

Dalai Lama, 14th (born 1935) Tibetan Buddhist leader and ruler *in absentia* of the world's last theocracy. After being named the reincarnation of the Buddha Chenrezi when only four years old, the Dalai became involved in a power struggle with the rival Panchen Lama. Although the Chinese conquest brought a temporary *détente*, the Dalai Lama fled to India in 1959, claiming China had failed to respect Tibetan autonomy.

Dale, Sir Henry see LOEWI, Otto

Dali, Salvador (born 1904) Spanish Surrealist painter, who credits himself with having invented 'paranoic-critical activity', described by him as 'a spontaneous method of irrational understanding based on the interpretative critical association of delirious phenomena'. After trying his hand at Cubism, Futurism and metaphysical painting, Dali joined the Surrealists in 1929. His painting is meticulously accurate, highly finished, and sometimes appears to be deliberately sensational.

Dallapiccola, Luigi (born 1904) Austrian-born Italian composer, the first in Italy to practise a note-row technique. Dallapiccola sought to humanize serialism in such works for chorus and orchestra as his *Songs of Prison* (1938-41) and *Songs of Liberation* (1955).

Expelled from the Academy of Fine Arts in Madrid, Dali was the enfant terrible of the Surrealist School of Painting

Dalton, John (1766-1844) English chemist who defined an atom as the smallest particle of a substance that can take part in a chemical reaction. He also stated that, because elements are in the form of atoms, they must combine together in definite proportions. He made the first tentative calculations of atomic weights, on a scale based on the atomic weight of hydrogen as one. Dalton also contributed to meteorology and physics, in which he formulated the law of partial pressures, which states that, in a vessel containing a mixture of gases, the total pressure is equal to the sum of the pressures that each gas would exert if it alone occupied the vessel.

Damocles (4th cent. BC) Greek courtier in Sicily remembered in the phrase 'the sword of Damocles'. According to CICERO, the sycophantic Damocles extravagantly acclaimed the happiness of his master, DIONYSIUS, who responded by inviting Damocles to a sumptuous feast, and seating him beneath a sword hung by a single hair, to symbolize the ever-present threat of peril, even amid good fortune.

Dana, Richard Henry (1815-82) American novelist whose realistic stories of the lives of sailors helped, with MELVILLE's later books, to bring about reform of conditions for ships' crews. His most famous work is *Two Years Before the Mast* (1840).

Daniel, Samuel (1562-1619) English poet, dramatist and critic, best known for his sonnet sequence *Delia* (1592), which ranks among the best Elizabethan works of its kind.

Daniell, John Frederic (1790-1845) English chemist who developed the first electric cell with a long working life. Alessandro VOLTA's earlier battery was a great innovation, but its current ran down quickly. In 1836, Daniell designed a cell that could produce a steady current for a considerable time.

D'Annunzio, Gabriele (1863-1938) Italian poet, dramatist, novelist and adventurer. After his early sensual poems and short stories he became a prolific writer of novels, of which the best known are *The Child of Pleasure* (1889), *The Intruder* (1892) and *The Flame of Life* (1900). The d'Annunzian hero, an egoist verging on the superman, immersed in sensuality and aesthetics, recurs throughout his works.

Dante, Alighieri (1265-1321) Italy's most famous poet and author of *The Divine Comedy*, one of the greatest European epic poems and a comprehensive survey of medieval theology, thought and literature. In this and other works he created a new, non-dialect poetic language which was to become the basis of modern Italian.

Danti, Vincenzo (1530-76) Italian sculptor whose art is best seen in the group depicting the execution of the Baptist, Baptistery, Florence (1571). Influenced by MICHELANGELO, Danti was asked to supply sculpture and painting for Michelangelo's funeral ceremonies in 1564, and the proximity of his style to that of Michelangelo is seen in the bronze figure of *Julius II* (1555), the *Venus Anadyomene*, and *Honour Overcoming Falsehood*. Danti's importance lies chiefly in his appointment as one of the first teachers in the newly founded Academia del Disegno, Perugia (1573). His treatise on proportion, published in 1567, was dedicated to the Grand Duke Cosimo de MEDICI.

Danton, George Jacques (1759-94) One of the principal leaders and greatest orators of the French Revolution. A lawyer by profession, he rose to become Administrator of Paris in 1791 and Minister of Justice in 1792. As Leader of the right wing of the Jacobins, he was not among the most dedicated of the Terrorists, and as a member of the Committee of

To scientists like Charles Darwin and Raymond Dart man owes the knowledge that he did not spring into being in a form indistinguishable from his present appearance, but evolved from ape-like ancestors. In fact, his history of development stems back for at least 70 million years. For the first half of this period various monkey groups evolved. About 35 million years ago the more advanced of these gave rise to the first hominoids, the primitive stock from which sprang today's pongids, or great apes, and hominids, the humans. Practically no fossil record survives of this period. Fragments exist of Ramapithecus, a kind of hominid of 14 million years ago. A gap follows until the first undeniable hominid group, Australopithecus, of three to five million years ago. It was Raymond Dart who discovered and established the existence of this group

EOCENE   OLIGOCENE   MIOCENE

Ramapithecus

Hominidae

Propliopithecus

Pongidae

36,000,000   25,000,000   13,000,000   10,000,000   3,000,000

Skull of the earliest hominid, found by Dart and dating from the Pleistocene— *Australopithecus africanus*

A later *Australopithecus, a. robustus,* has massive cheek teeth. Remains were found in South Africa

Most finds of *Homo erectus* were found in the neighbourhood of Peking, dating from about 450,000 years ago

Public Safety his speeches were more patriotic than revolutionary, notably in his use of the powers of oratory to rally the nation's courage following the Austrian invasion (1792). His carelessness in financial matters enabled ROBESPIERRE to indict him and his followers before the Revolutionary Tribunal, and he was guillotined in 1794.

Darboux, Gaston (1842-1917) French mathematician, whose most important treatise was on the differential geometry of surfaces, which applies infinitesimal calculus to the study of surfaces.

Darby, Abraham (1678-1717) English ironfounder who played a notable part in the Industrial Revolution. At Coalbrookdale, Shropshire, in 1709, he manufactured high-grade iron, ideal for casting, in a coke-fuel furnace. This was a major discovery, for the use of charcoal in blast furnaces had until that time imposed economic and technical limitations on the industry's growth. The Coalbrookdale works produced iron boilers for NEWCOMEN's steam engines, the world's first iron bridge over the nearby River Severn (1779), iron rails, an iron canal aqueduct, an iron boat (1788) and the first railway locomotive with a high pressure boiler (1802).

Darby, John (1800-82) English clergyman and theological writer who established the Plymouth Brethren in England. The Brethren originated in Dublin as a non-denominational group dedicated to Christian fellowship. Puritanical and fundamentalist, Darby's Plymouth Brethren recognized no official ministry but centred their worship on a commemorative 'breaking of bread'. In 1845 the movement began to split into the Open and the Exclusive Brethren, a more rigid wing led by Darby. There

have been more divisions since, but most modern Brethren, widely scattered over England, Ireland, the US and Europe, belong to open assemblies.

Darío, Rubén (1867-1916) Nicaraguan poet, journalist and diplomat. The publication of his poems *Blue* (1888) and *Profane Songs* (1896) introduced French Symbolism into Spanish poetry. Darío founded and led the literary Modernist movement which spread Parnassian aestheticism (as in the work of GAUTIER) throughout Latin American literature, and made himself the leading contemporary poet in the Spanish language. A friend of VERLAINE, MARTI, RODO and all the leading Parisian intellectuals, his later work synthesized French techniques and Hispanic nationalism, as in *Songs of Life and Hope* (1905).

Darius I (c. 558-486 BC) King of Persia, who ruled the Achaemenid Empire at its height, and pushed Persia's boundaries east beyond the Indus and west into Europe. His conquests were not principally to extend the empire but to reach natural frontiers which could be held against the enemies beyond. Like all rulers of the Persian Empire, he

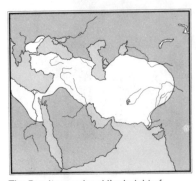
The Persian empire at the height of Darius's power, c. 500 BC

treated the conquered peoples humanely and on an equal footing with the Persians. Darius's only major failure was his defeat by Athens, when he attempted to punish the Greek states for aiding Persia's rebellious Ionian cities. His two expeditions against Greece failed, the second ending in defeat by Athens at Marathon (490 BC). He died preparing a third expedition.

Dart, Raymond (born 1893) Australian-born South African anatomist and anthropologist whose discovery of the remains of an upright-walking manlike ape in Africa bridged the evolutionary gap between man and the apes and established Africa as the cradle of man. The territory of Dart's 'southern apes' or 'australopithecines' is now known to have extended right through the eastern part of the continent, their time range spanning more than two million years.

Darwin, Charles Robert (1809-82) British naturalist and the main proponent of the modern theory of evolution in biology. *On the Origin of Species by Means of Natural Selection* (1859), based on the evaluation of his observations on a five-year scientific expedition to South America and the Pacific, outlined a theory according to which species develop by natural selection through survival of the fittest, and a gradual differentiation through adaptation. Darwin's other great work, *The Descent of Man* (1871), uses evolutionary principles to trace the development of man from a more primitive animal that gave rise also to the anthropoid apes.

Daswanth (16th cent.) Leading Indian painter, who, from humble Hindu origins, became the protégé of the Emperor AKBAR, and a favourite artist of the court. Daswanth's known work survives in three manuscripts, but one miniature is entirely

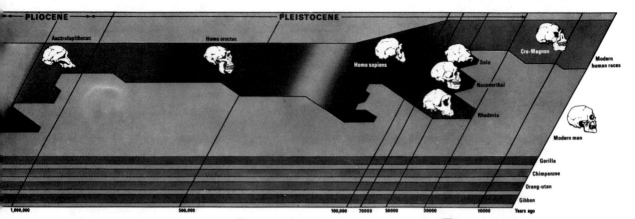

The oldest fossils that are likely to be those of *Homo sapiens* were discovered in parts of western Europe

Found in Italy, the skull of Neanderthal man is characterized by the very large size of the brain

A recent ancestor, Cro-Magnon man, lurked in caves. Many finds of Cro-Magnon man have been made in France

attributable to him. His work was an important influence on Mogul painting as a whole.

Daudet, Alphonse (1840-97) French author of picturesque tales and burlesque novels. Today, his best-known works are *Lettres de mon moulin*, tales of Provençal life (1866), and his novel *Tartarin de Tarascon* (1872) and its sequels, *Tartarin sur les Alpes* and *Port-Tarascon*. He also wrote *L'Arlésienne* (1872), a play for which BIZET composed the incidental music.

Daumier, Honoré (1808-79) French caricaturist, whose thousands of lithographs, made for the journals *La Caricature* and *Charivari*, are of both artistic and social interest. His earlier works were politically inspired, and he was imprisoned in 1832 for caricaturing LOUIS PHILIPPE. He was also a gifted painter and sculptor, achieving lively and suggestive *chiaroscuro* (light and shade) effects, and was drawn particularly to the theme of Don Quixote. He was much admired by the young CÉZANNE, and by VAN GOGH.

Davenant, Sir William (1606-68) English dramatist and theatre manager, who was a producer of masques at CHARLES I's court and, after 1638, Poet Laureate. During the Commonwealth (1649-60), the Puritans banned plays but not music. By making his *Siege of Rhodes* a play-with-music, Davenant evaded the ban, and incidentally initiated a vogue which developed into opera.

David, St (6th cent.) Patron saint of Wales. Traditionally of royal descent and the founder of numerous churches in South Wales, his shrine at St David's, Pembrokeshire, was a place of pilgrimage in medieval times. Very little else is known about his life or work.

David (10th cent. BC) Founder of a dynasty that ruled Judah for 400 years, until NEBUCHADNEZZAR conquered it. David, a Bethlehem shepherd, was summoned (either for his skilful harp-playing or for his slaying of the giant Philistine, Goliath) to the court of SAUL, King of Israel (north Palestine). On the death of Saul's son, David was accepted by the Israelites as their king, captured Jerusalem and made it his capital, beat off the Philistines from Israel, and conquered other hostile groups.

David, Gerard (c. 1450-1523) Netherlandish painter of religious scenes which are notable for their craftsmanship and simple piety. His style, based on that of the 15th-century Dutch painters, became dated once Italian painting achieved an influence in northern Europe.

David, Jacques (1748-1825) French artist, of the Neo-classical school. His painting, *The Oath of The Horatii* (1784), which proclaims the Roman civic virtues, is now recognized as the foundation stone of French Neo-classicism. Later, *The Death of Socrates* and *Brutus Condemning his Sons to Death* enhanced the esteem in which David was held by the public. David engaged in political activities during the 1789 Revolution, and his *The Dead Marat* was a powerful piece of revolutionary propaganda.

Davies, William Henry (1871-1940) Welsh poet who, as a young man, went to the United States and lived as a tramp and ranch-hand. His memoir of this time, *The Autobiography of a Super-tramp* (1908), is his most widely read work.

Davis, Dwight (1879-1945) American lawn tennis enthusiast (later a politician) who established the Davis Cup competition. In 1900, he donated a silver cup to be presented annually to the nation winning an international men's tennis championship. By 1914, the Davis Cup competition was established on a world-wide basis.

Davis, John (c. 1550-1605) One of ELIZABETH I's chief navigators, remarkable for the extent of his explorations, from Baffin Island to the Falklands. Davis made three voyages, from 1586, in a fruitless search for the elusive North West Passage, but his journeys drew attention to the abundance of fish and fur-bearing animals in the northeast section of America.

Davis, Stuart (1894-1964) American painter, a pioneer of Cubism and abstraction in America and an important precursor of Pop Art.

Davis, William Morris (1850-1934) American geographer who was Professor of Physical Geology at Harvard from 1893-1912, and is widely regarded as the 'father of modern geomorphology' (the study of the evolution of land forms). His influence on the study and teaching of geography has been immense – especially through his model, 'the Geographical Cycle' – in which Davis likened the evolution of such features as rivers and their valleys to the evolution of individual organisms – passing through stages of 'Youth', 'Maturity', 'Senility' and even 'Death'. The beauty of the system made it widely attractive to many disciples, but in recent years it has been under severe attack by modern scholars.

Davy, Sir Humphry (1778-1829) English chemist who studied the effects of electric currents on compounds. Davy became interested in William Nicholson's discovery that electricity passing through water splits it up into its component elements hydrogen and oxygen. In 1807,

Davy built a huge battery and by passing current through molten potash he isolated a metal he called potassium. From soda he produced another metal which he named sodium. At the same time, he worked on an electro-chemical theory in which he discussed the relationship between electrical and chemical actions on compounds. Much of his work was developed further by his brilliant young protégé, Michael FARADAY. In 1815, Davy invented the miner's safety lamp, in which a metal gauze surrounding the flame prevents it from igniting any inflammable gas.

Day Lewis, Cecil (1904-72) English poet and critic, born in Ireland, contemporary at Oxford with AUDEN and SPENDER, with whom he formed the core of the left-wing poetic movement of the 1930s. He showed his individual lyrical talent in works like 'Transitional Poem' (1929) and 'Overtures to Death' (1938). He translated VIRGIL and VALÉRY and was appointed Poet Laureate in 1968. He wrote outstanding criticism in *The Poetic Image* (1947), and an autobiography, *The Buried* (1960). He also wrote numerous detective stories under the pseudonym of Nicholas Blake.

Dayan, Moshe (born 1915) Israeli general and Minister of Defence in Golda MEIR's government, who headed the Israeli army forces during the Sinai campaign, the Six-Day War (1967), and again during the war of late 1973.

Debré, Michel (born 1912) French politician who drafted the Constitution of the Fifth Republic. During the Second World War he fought as a cavalry officer, was captured by the Germans, escaped and served in Morocco, then joined the Resistance (1942). On being elected to the Senate in 1948, he attacked the constitutional weakness of the Fourth Republic, and when DE GAULLE returned to power (1958) he was made Minister of Justice and given the task of drafting a new constitution. He was Prime Minister from 1959 to 1962, Minister of Economy and Finances (1966-8) and Minister of Foreign Affairs (1968-9).

Deburau, Jean (1786-1846) Czech-born French mime, who originated the tragi-comic character of Pierrot, a famous attraction of the Funambules circus-theatre in Paris.

Debussy, Claude-Achille (1862-1918) The leading Impressionist composer in French music, whose style has direct parallels with the techniques of Impressionism in painting. Debussy was influenced by

Davy's safety lamp gives miners visual advance warning of possible explosions

the work of the Symbolist poets, BAUDELAIRE and VERLAINE, but most of all by WAGNER, even though Debussy's own music was a profound reaction against the senior composer. *L'Après-midi d'un faune* (1894), a tone poem based on a poem by MALLARMÉ, was his first major work. His later compositions include the opera *Pelléas et Mélisande* (1902) and the three symphonic sketches, *La Mer* (1905). Debussy also wrote an early string quartet of distinction. His last chamber works – the sonatas for cello, flute, viola, harp and for violin – showed him exploring ever more deeply into harmonic originality.

Debye, Peter Joseph Wilhelm (1884-1966) Dutch-American physicist who developed the modern theory of electrolytes. Debye argued that ARRHENIUS's idea of salts only partly disassociating in solution into ions (charged atoms) did not go far enough, and by 1923 worked out a mathematical explanation of why disassociation does not always *appear* to be total, which at the same time provided a brilliant new picture of ions in solutions.

Dedekind, Julius (1831-1916) German mathematician, who did basic work on number theory, particularly

Defoe's Robinson Crusoe was wrecked on the island of Juan Fernandez

the theory of irrational numbers in terms of the notion of 'cuts' (which were later named after him, and are now in common mathematical usage). He also founded the modern theory of algebraic numbers.

Dee, John (1527-1608) English mathematician and philosopher. An erudite scholar and book-collector, he was deeply involved in magic and astrology and found favour with ELIZABETH I, who often sought his advice, including suggestions for reforming the Julian calendar. His numerous writings include a preface to the English edition of EUCLID, the *Monas Hieroglyphica*, and several books on navigation.

Defoe, Daniel (c. 1660-1731) English author of *Robinson Crusoe* (1719), one of the earliest English novels. He was a prolific and versatile writer whose political pamphlets, often attacking religious intolerance or the Jacobites, twice caused his imprisonment. He founded and largely wrote a well-known periodical, the *Review* (1704-13). Defoe wrote his outstanding full-length works, including *Robinson Crusoe, Moll Flanders, A Journal of the Plague Year* (1722) and *Roxana* (1724), quite late in life; their energy and crowded detail reflect his varied life as a merchant, traveller, soldier under WILLIAM III and secret agent in Scotland.

De Forest, Lee (1873-1961) American radio and television pioneer who held more than 300 scientific patents. In 1906, he modified and improved Sir John FLEMING's diode tube, thus speeding the development of the electronics industry. De Forest also invented the variable-intensity lamp that made possible the first motion pictures with soundtracks.

Degas, Edgar (1834-1917) Leading French Impressionist painter possessing the characteristic feeling for the instantaneous, for nature caught at a specific moment. Unlike MONET, PISSARRO and SISLEY, he cared little for landscape, preferring to concentrate on the human figure. He extended the traditional compositional disciplines beyond academic conventions, achieving seemingly arbitrary, but in fact carefully contrived, effects. He did not hesitate, for instance, to bisect a figure by the frame or to place major figures off-centre. He often used pastels, through which he achieved remarkable colouristic effects. Late in life, he made many wax models (later cast in bronze) of ballet dancers in motion which have an affinity with the work of RODIN.

De Gaulle, Charles André Joseph Marie (1890-1970) French soldier-statesman who rallied the 'Free French', persuading them to continue to fight after France's defeat by Germany in the Second World War. A general in 1940, he was appointed Under-Secretary of Defence in Reynaud's government, but, seeing French surrender as inevitable, he decided that England must become the base for continued French resistance. He commanded the 'Free French' forces until 1944 and was virtual head of a French government in exile, becoming recognized head of the Provisional French Government following liberation. In 1946 he chose to resign rather than meet opposition demands to reduce military expenditure. In 1958 De Gaulle was recalled to power by President Coty to deal with French Algerian opposition to the proposals for Algerian independence, and was elected President in December of that year. In 1960 he gave France an independent nuclear military force and tried to restore her status as a great power. During the 1960s he succeeded in stabilizing the economy, industry and social life of France, but at the expense of democratic liberties. In January 1966 he was re-elected President for another seven-year term, during which he took France out of the North Atlantic Treaty Organization (1966), formally rejected Britain's entry into the European Economic Community (1967) and openly supported French Canadian separatism in his Quebec speech of 1967. After a year of industrial unrest and student riots (1968) he appealed to the country for a fresh mandate, but was defeated in a constitutional referendum and retired in 1969.

De Havilland, Sir Geoffrey (1882-1965) English aircraft designer and manufacturer whose company produced the world's first commercial jetliner, the Comet, as well as many other famous aircraft, including the Tiger Moth, the Mosquito and the Vampire.

De la Beche, Sir Henry (1796-1855) English geologist who founded the Geological Survey of Great Britain. After an early career working on the geology of southwest England and, among other places, Jamaica, De la Beche turned to his main work, the recording of geological features on Ordnance Survey maps, which were then being published for the first time.

Delacroix, Eugène (1798-1863) French painter, who is usually considered as the great exponent of Romanticism, in opposition to the classical INGRES. His first Salon picture, *Dante and Virgil Crossing the Styx* (1822), depicts a morbid scene derived from GÉRICAULT's *Raft of the Medusa*. Delacroix was an eclectic artist who drew inspiration from such diverse sources as RUBENS, CONSTABLE, BONINGTON and Lawrence. These influences combined to produce the brilliant colour and free handling of *Death of Sardanapalus* (1829), a subject drawn from BYRON, who, with SHAKESPEARE and SCOTT, became Delacroix's principal source of inspiration. In 1832 he visited Morocco, where, for him, antiquity lived on in the Arabs he encountered in the streets, as depicted in *Femmes d'Algers* (1834). His water-colour sketchbooks reveal a proto-Impressionistic observation of the brilliance of light and the existence of complementary colours in shadows. From the mid-1830s, Delacroix received five public commissions for murals, which occupied him till the end of his life.

Echoes of De Gaulle's leadership on the wall of a London pub frequented by Free French Forces in the 1940s

De la Mare, Walter (1873-1956) English author whose poetry and other work concentrates on the themes of childhood, innocence and the magical. His language is often lyrical and haunting. De la Mare published some 50 volumes and was awarded the Order of Merit at 80.

De la Pasture, Rogier see WEYDEN, Roger van der

Delavay, Jean (1834-95) French Jesuit missionary and botanist, who was first to study and introduce into Europe the plants of Yunnan, China. He is commemorated by several plants that bear his name, among them *Paeonia delavayi*.

Délibes, Léo (1836-91) French composer of the music for the ballets *Coppelia* (1870) and *Sylvia* (1876) and a creator of light, melodic tunes. He also composed operas and operettas, but it is his ballet scores which are most often performed.

Delius, Frederick (1862-1934) Self-taught English composer of German descent whose famous works are *Appalachia* (1904), variations on a slave song, *Brigg Fair* (1908), based on an English folk song and the tone poem *On Hearing the First Cuckoo in Spring* (1913). Delius possessed a highly personal, impressionistic style, unique in English music. Influenced by GRIEG and DEBUSSY, he nevertheless worked in isolation at a time when music was not highly regarded in his homeland. After 1889, Delius lived in self-imposed exile in France.

Delorme, Philibert (c. 1515-70) French architect, whose work was greatly influenced by the three years he spent in Italy. His best-known work, which he began in 1547, is the tomb of Francis I in St Denis, Paris.

De Mille, Cecil Blount (1881-1959) American Hollywood producer-director and writer, famous for his Biblical spectaculars. His career centred around epic films, with 'a cast of thousands', including *The Ten Commandments* (1923, 1956), *Samson and Delilah* (1949) and *The Greatest Show on Earth* (1952).

Delcassé, Théophile (1852-1923) French statesman, who was largely responsible for both French colonial expansion in Africa and for the *entente* with the UK. As Minister for the Colonies (1892-5) he authorized MARCHAND's Fashoda expedition, which produced a crisis in Anglo-French relations (1898), but on becoming Foreign Minister in the same year he began to seek an *entente* between the two countries, which was agreed in 1904. Though forced out of office by a pro-German faction of his colleagues in 1905, he became Naval Minister (1911-13), and worked with the British Admiralty to co-ordinate French and British naval dispositions in the Mediterranean. As Foreign Minister (1914-15), he was instrumental in bringing Italy into the Second World War.

Democritus (c. 460-c. 370 BC) Greek philosopher who elaborated on the atomic theory put forward by his contemporary Leucippus.

De Moivre, Abraham (1667-1754)
Mathematician of French parentage, who, resident in England, greatly developed analytical trigonometry. He worked on probability theory and first discovered the normal distribution curve. A friend of NEWTON and HALLEY, he never gained a permanent post but lived by coaching and giving advice on the 'odds' at various gambling games.

Derain, André (1880-1954) French painter, a leading member of the *Fauves*, whose pure colour, bold brushwork and joyful response to landscape are all to be seen in the Thames views painted while on two visits to London. He flirted briefly with Cubism before reverting to a less adventurous, more elegant style.

Déry, Tibor (born 1894) Hungarian novelist and short-story writer, author of *Response* (1952), a study of pre-war Hungarian society, and *Niki* (1958), an exposé of Rákosi's régime. He was born of wealthy parents and through working in the family business he acquired a sympathy for the working classes which turned him towards Communism. He was actively involved in the 1956 uprising and became the leader of the Hungarian writers' fight for freedom of artistic expression.

Derzhavin, Gavril Romanovich (1743-1816) Russian lyric poet, who gained literary fame with *Felitsa* (1783), a humorous poem to CATHERINE II, and *Ode to God* (1780-4).

Desargues, Gérard (1593-1662) French mathematician and engineer, whose work was mainly on conic sections and perspective. PASCAL was influenced by him.

De Saussure, Ferdinand (1857-1913) Swiss linguistics theorist, the most influential of the Structuralist school of linguistics, whose theories were published posthumously under the title *A General Linguistics Course* (1916). He put forward the theory that language exists on two levels, the systematic structure and the actual speech. He also perceived distinctions between language studied diachronically (historically) and synchronically (at one stage), and between signs and what they signify.

Descartes, René (1596-1650) French philosopher, inventor of analytical geometry. His philosophic aim was to unify all science by means of the appropriate single method – namely that of geometry, which possessed the required properties of clarity and simplicity. His influence has spread throughout modern philosophy, to both rationalist and empiri-

cist. In *Discourse on Method* (1637) he set out his basic theory – that the method for the proper guidance of reason is the systematic doubt of everything until one arrives at clear and simple ideas that are beyond doubt. In this, the one fundamental certainty is reached, in his famous words *Cogito ergo sum* (I think therefore I am).

Deshnev, Semyon (c. 1605-73) Russian explorer of the extreme northeast of Asia. In 1647 he accompanied a large, but unsuccessful, expedition to the land of the Chukchi people on the Asian shores of the Bering Strait. One year later, Deshnev's ship was wrecked off the site of modern Anadirsk, in the extreme northeast of Siberia.

Des Prés, Josquin (c. 1440-1521) Flemish musician who became the leading composer of the High Renaissance and who was the first important modern composer. Apart from some secular songs, he wrote church music exclusively, including masses, motets and a *Stabat Mater*. He was among the first to develop a style which attempted to express in music the value and meaning of the words being set.

Deutsch, Erich see SCHUBERT, Franz Peter

De Valera, Eamon (born 1882) American-born Irish Republican statesman. During the Easter Rising of 1916 he commanded a body of Irish Volunteers and was captured and sentenced to death by the British, but was later reprieved. De Valera became Prime Minister when his party *Fianna Fáil* (founded in 1926) was able to form a government in 1932, and in 1937 the constitution of the Free State was revised naming it Eire. De Valera held the premiership until 1948. From 1951-4 and again 1957-9 he was Prime Minister of the Republic of Ireland (recognized by Britain in 1949). He was President of the Republic from 1959-73, when he was succeeded by Erskine CHILDERS.

Devereux, Robert see ESSEX, SECOND EARL OF

Devine, George (1910-66) British actor, theatre manager and director, who founded and directed the English Stage Company at London's Royal Court Theatre (1956-65). He began his career as an actor and in 1938 became director and manager of the London Theatre Studio. He made his West End debut as a director with Daphne du MAURIER's *Rebecca* (1940). After the war, Devine directed the Young Vic, a company of young actors at the Old Vic Theatre.

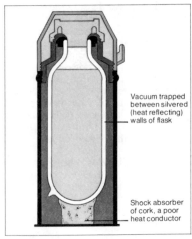

Vacuum trapped between silvered (heat reflecting) walls of flask

Shock absorber of cork, a poor heat conductor

Cross-section of a vacuum flask, a modern aid to living based on the Dewar flask invented in the 19th century

Dewar, Sir James (1842-1923) British chemist and physicist who invented the vacuum flask and, with Frederick Abel, the propellant, explosive cordite.

Dewey, John (1859-1952) American philosopher and educationist who believed that education should extend the child's experience in the light of contemporary social needs and goals, rather than past tradition.

Dewey, Melvil (1851-1931) American librarian and inventor of the decimal classification of books. His basically simple idea of using ten main classes, divided decimally into minor subjects, spread to many other countries. Dewey became Chief Librarian and Professor of Library Economy at Columbia University, the Director of New York State Library and a founder of the American Library Association.

Dewey, Thomas Edmund (1902-71) Governor of New York State, twice unsuccessful Republican Presidential candidate against ROOSEVELT (1944) and TRUMAN (1948).

De Witt, Jan (1625-72) Dutch Republican statesman who backed the States Party against the autocratic power of the House of Orange and was murdered by its supporters. De Witt became the Dutch leader during WILLIAM III's minority and made large concessions to end the first Anglo-Dutch war (1654); in the second (1665-7), helped by the admirals de RUYTER and TROMP, and his own brother, Cornelius, he secured the favourable Treaty of Breda. With peace restored he improved the nation's finances and strengthened the Dutch trading hold on the East Indies. He passed the Permanent Edict to ensure Republican administration (1667) and made the Triple Alliance with England and Sweden against LOUIS XIV (1668), but when Louis invaded Holland (1672), de Witt was forced to resign and, with his brother, was killed by Orangists.

Diaghilev, Sergei Pavlovich (1872-1929) Russian impresario whose ability to recognize talent led to a renaissance of Western ballet. After introducing shows of Russian painting and music to Paris, Diaghilev established his newly founded French- and Russian-backed Ballets Russes in 1908. His company deeply influenced Western ballet, using male dancers, striking costumes, vividly imaginative décor and new and startling music, in ballets such as *Scheherazade* and *L'Après-midi d'un faune*. The qualities of drama, vitality, colour and imaginative fantasy in works like *Petrouchka* and *The Firebird* were due entirely to Diaghilev's ability to exploit the talents of his artistes.

Dias, Bartholomeu (c. 1450-1500) Portuguese navigator who first rounded the southern tip of Africa as part of his country's search for a sea route to the Orient. Dias rounded the Cape of Good Hope, touching in at Mossel Bay, and continued round to the Great Fish River before turning back along the coast, discovering Table Mountain on the way home.

Diaz, Porfirio (1830-1915) Mexican general and dictator who fought against the US in the Mexican War of 1846-8 and with JUAREZ against MAXIMILIAN. As President (1877-80 and 1888-1911), he opened up Mexico to foreign investment principally from the US, but also adopted dictatorial methods of government. These abuses, exacerbated by his lack of concern for poverty among the peasants, ultimately brought about his downfall. In 1911 the peasants, led by Francisco MADERO, and his supporter, Pancho VILLA, rose and overthrew him. He died in exile in Paris.

Diaz de Vivar, Rodrigo see CID, El

Dibdin, Charles (1745-1814) English actor, song-writer and dramatist. He wrote the famous shanty *Tom Bowling* and a ballad-opera, *The Waterman* (1774).

Dicey, Albert (1835-1922) English jurist and expert in the constitutional law of England. His *Introduction to a Study of the Law of the Constitution* (1880) analysed and interpreted the fundamentals underlying the thought and life of the nation.

Dickens, Charles (1812-70) English novelist who wrote many of the outstanding social novels of the 19th century. He began as a journalist and his novels make extensive use of detailed documentary writing. Many of his works were written in monthly instalments, the first being *The Pickwick Papers* (1836-7), which showed his powers as a humorist. Dickens concentrated on the exposure of contemporary social evils: *Oliver Twist* (1837-8) depicted life in workhouses and in the violent criminal underworld; *Nicholas Nickleby* (1838-9) satirized tyrannical educational establishments. Such later works as *Hard Times* (1852), *Little Dorrit* (1855-7), *Our Mutual Friend* (1864-5) and *Great Expectations* (1880-1) deal with the social effects of money and the evil it can generate. Dickens was adept at creating grotesque, fantastic figures, like Quilp, the dwarf in *The Old Curiosity Shop* (1840-1). Two others, Mrs Gamp and Pecksniff, appear in *Martin Chuzzlewit* (1843-4), in which Dickens criticizes American life after a visit to the United States. Much autobiographical material appears in *David Copperfield* (1849-50). Dickens liked dramatics and undertook tours of personal readings, delivered to enthusiastic audiences, which earned him much money, but left him exhausted and helped to hasten his death, in the middle of his last serial, *The Mystery of Edwin Drood* (1870).

A reporter's eye for detail—for as a young man he had been a newspaperman—enabled Charles Dickens to describe accurately the social evils of his time

Dickinson, Emily (1830-86) American poet who wrote short, ecstatic lyrics, often about death and life after death. Her poems are notable for their simple, startling language, fresh imagery and occasional, whimsical humour.

Diderot, Denis (1713-84) French *encyclopédiste*, philosopher and writer. In 1745, he embarked with D'ALEMBERT on the 20-year task of editing the *Encyclopédie*, whose aim was to demonstrate the essential principles and application of every art and science. The first volume was published in 1751. Diderot was also the author of plays (e.g. *Le Fils naturel*, 1757), novels (e.g. *Le Neveu de Rameau*, 1762) as well as literary and art criticism.

Didot, François (1689-1757) Founder of the French family of printers, publishers and typographers. He began his career as a bookseller and printer and is famous for his edition of the works of the Abbé PRÉVOST.

Diem, Ngo Dinh (1901-63) President of South Vietnam whose policies exacerbated the Vietnamese conflict. He governed almost entirely through a small group of personal supporters and members of his own family. Being a Catholic, many of his measures were calculated to antagonize the Buddhists, and this, and his failure to control the Viet Cong guerillas, drove many of his countrymen to the rebel cause. In the last three years of his life, he was dependent mainly on US support. His religious policies and distrust of the army led to his deposition and murder while under arrest in 1963.

Diemen, Anton Van (1593-1645) Dutch colonial statesman who sent TASMAN to explore the Australasian seas. After a successful career with the Dutch East India Company, Van Diemen was made Governor-General of the Dutch East Indies (1636). There he enlarged Dutch holdings in Indonesia, took part of Ceylon from Portugal and established trade with China and Japan.

Diesel, Rudolf (1858-1913) German engineer and inventor of the internal combustion engine that bears his name. In 1890 he conceived the idea of compressing a fuel-air mixture so highly that it ignited spontaneously. Between then and 1897 (with KRUPP of Essen and Maschinenfabrik of Augsburg) he perfected the engine which, having no electrical ignition system, is simpler and more trouble-free than the petrol engine. It also uses a lower grade and, therefore, cheaper fuel. Diesels came into their own as the motive power for heavy transport vehicles, rail cars, boats and locomotives.

Dietrich, Marlene (born 1901) German actress and singer who first achieved fame as the night-club singer in Josef von Sternberg's *The Blue Angel* (1930), becoming a symbol both for destructiveness and for the decadence of Europe. Since the early 1950s, she has made an equally successful career in international cabaret.

Dillinger, John (1902-34) American bank robber whose exploits made him the Federal Bureau of Investigation's 'Public Enemy Number One' He was shot and killed by the FBI outside a Chicago cinema.

Dilthey, Wilhelm (1833-1911) German philosopher who sought to replace traditional, idealistic metaphysics with modern theory of knowledge, recognizing the place of the will, in addition to sensation and thought, in acquiring knowledge. Metaphysics could no longer claim to be the knowledge of reality, he said, but it was important in expressing an attitude to life, together with religion and art. Dilthey's main works, in which he stressed the historical and cultural relativity of all values, were *Das Erlebnis und die Dichtung* (1905); *Das Wesen der Philosophie* (1907); *Einleitung in die Geisteswissenschaften* (1883).

D'Indy, Paul (1851-1931) French musician who helped to found the Schola Cantorum in Paris. Although a composer, he is best remembered today as a teacher, promoter of concerts and operas and reviver of old music in France.

Diniz (1261-1325) King of Portugal, called Ré Lavrador (the farmer king) for his introduction of improved cultivation methods and the founding of agricultural schools. Diniz, who was a talented poet, was patron of literature and music, and founded Portugal's first university at Lisbon (1290). To enrich the economy, he promoted farming, forestry and shipbuilding, furthering trade with England, Flanders, France and Italy.

Diocletian (245-313) Roman emperor (284-305) who reorganized the administration of the Empire, ending all outward form of republicanism and local self-government, ruling as absolute monarch. Among other measures, Diocletian reformed taxation, and fixed wages and prices (with a death penalty for offenders) to curb inflation caused by bad harvests and commercial speculators, but the policy failed. He persecuted Christians severely, considering them a divisive force within the Empire.

Diogenes, Apolloniates (5th cent. BC) Greek philosopher and physician who held that air was the fundamental basis of all things. His belief that human intelligence emanated from air influenced HIPPOCRATES, who came to believe that diseases such as epilepsy occurred when the supply of air to the brain was hindered.

Dionysius the Elder (c. 430-367 BC) Greek tyrant (unconstitutional ruler) of Syracuse in Sicily 405-367 BC) whose successes made Syracuse the biggest and most powerful Greek city. Dionysius rose by demagogy from being a clerk to a dictator, crushing opposition, helped by secret police and troops, often mercenaries from Gaul and Spain.

Dionysius Exiguus (c. 500-560) Scythian scholar who made his calculation of CHRIST's birth date the basis of modern chronology. He calculated that Christ was born on 25th December in the year 753 of the Roman calendar, which dated from the traditional foundation of the city. By 1400 most Christian countries had adopted this date but it is now known to be between four and six years later than Christ's actual date of birth.

Dionysius Thrax (2nd-1st cent. BC) Greek grammarian, author of *Techné Grammatiké*, the first Greek grammar, the basis of all European grammars.

Diophantus (c. 3rd cent. AD) Greek mathematician, who wrote *Arithmetica*, a famous treatise on algebra. His name is particularly associated with problems requiring the solution of an equation containing up to four variables.

Dioscorides, Pedanios (1st cent. AD) Greek physician who wrote the first pharmacopoeia (a catalogue of drugs and their preparation) detailing the uses of plants as drugs. His five-volume work *De Materia Medica* was used for over 1500 years.

Dirac, Paul Adrien Maurice (born 1902) English physicist, co-founder of the modern theory of quantum mechanics. In his doctoral thesis of 1926, Dirac produced the formal theory that governs submicroscopic phenomena in essentially the form used today. Over the next four years, he extended the theory to embrace ideas of relativity and its implication that electrons, for example, must necessarily 'spin' in just the way they are observed. He received a Nobel Prize for Physics.

Dirichlet, Peter Gustave (1805-59) German mathematician, who contributed to the study of prime numbers in arithmetical series, and to problems in applied mechanics, such as the equilibrium of systems.

Disney, Walt (1901-66) American cartoon film producer. Although credited with the creation of Mickey Mouse, Donald Duck, etc, Disney was in fact a film entrepreneur and established an organization that produced some 340 short animated films and many full length cartoon features. He made his mark in 1928 with the first animated sound film *Steamboat Willie*. The style typified in the cartoons produced by his studios at Burbank, California, influenced all branches of the industry until the early 1950s when he began to produce conventional nature films, and later, drama and comedy films.

Disraeli, Benjamin (1804-81) British statesman, Prime Minister and author, who identified the Conservative Party with social reform and the promotion of Empire. He was Chancellor of the Exchequer (1852, 1858-9 and 1867) and as Leader of the Commons introduced the Reform Bill of 1867. He was Prime Minister for a brief period in 1868 and again from 1874-80. During his second premiership he advocated a forward foreign policy and gave imperialism a popular appeal by sponsoring the Royal Titles Bill of 1876 by which VICTORIA became Empress of India. At home the government codified and extended social legislation (slum clearance, public health and merchant seamen's conditions of service) but there was no move towards incisive government intervention. Defeats in the Afghan and Zulu wars (1878-9), GLADSTONE's moral condemnation of 'Beaconsfieldism', the recession in British commercial and industrial prosperity at the end of the decade and his own ill health, all contributed to Disraeli's defeat (1880).

Dixon, Jeremiah see MASON, Charles

Djilas, Milovan (born 1911) Yugoslav politician and political theorist who both criticized and influenced Yugoslav Communism. As a wartime partisan and close friend of TITO, Djilas was instrumental in guiding Yugoslav Communism along the road which led to the break with Moscow in 1948. He criticized a rigidly centralized régime which distorted the aims of the revolution by becoming a political bureaucracy. Though expelled by the Party and imprisoned (1956-66), he carried his criticism still further in his books *The New Class* (1957) and the autobiography, *Land Without Justice* (1958), in which he held that the owners and exploiters of the old order had been superseded by owners and exploiters whose authority was based upon absolute powers and tyranny.

Dodgson, Charles Lutwidge see CARROLL, Lewis

Doenitz, Karl (born 1891) German U-boat commander and HITLER's successor as Führer. As submarine commander in the First World War, he became a fervent believer in the efficacy of submarine warfare, and as Hitler's U-boat flag officer during the Second World War he was responsible for the wolf-pack system of U-boat operations and for sinking many millions of tons of Allied shipping. He succeeded Raeder as Grand Admiral in 1943, and on Hitler's death in 1945 surrendered to the Allies in May. Subsequently he was sentenced at Nuremberg to ten years' imprisonment.

Dohnanyi, Ernö (1877-1960) Hungarian-Czech pianist and composer of the *Variations on a Nursery Theme* (1913) for piano and orchestra, which was based on a well-known nursery rhyme tune. Dohnanyi travelled widely as a virtuoso pianist, and his many compositions include two piano concertos and two symphonies.

Dollfuss, Engelbert (1892-1934) Austrian politician, Chancellor and Foreign Minister (1932). Dollfuss headed a coalition of right-wing political groups. Not wishing to be dominated by either Nazi or Fascist policies, whose aims conflicted with his desire to maintain Austrian independence, and refusing to ally himself with the largest single party, the Social Democrats, Dollfuss was driven to rely on the next largest party, the Christian Socialists, which became increasingly dominated by its right wing. Under pressure, Dollfuss was forced, in 1933, to suspend parliamentary government, and proclaimed a dictatorship. In 1934 he was persuaded by MUSSOLINI to outflank the Austrian Nazis by crushing the socialists, and used artillery to destroy their housing estates in Vienna's suburbs. Later in the same year his murder was engineered by the Nazis.

Dolmetsch, Arnold (1858-1940) French instrument maker who pioneered the reproduction of 15th-18th century musical instruments and reconstructed the methods of playing them. He learned his craft at his father's workshop where pianos and organs were made, and studied music in Brussels and London. His study of the instruments collection in the British Museum in London led to his setting up his own workshops in Surrey, where he founded a festival (1925) to bring the instruments and their music to life again.

Domagk, Gerhard (1895-1964) German biochemist, who in 1932 established that a dye, prontosil red,

could control streptococcus infections. Subsequently, the antibacterial action was found elsewhere to be due to only part of the molecule, the sulphonamide group. This outstanding discovery led to the development of a range of drugs effective in the treatment of several highly pathogenic infections, including some varieties of pneumonia. Among those whose lives were saved was Domagk's daughter, who had been infected accidentally in the laboratory. Domagk was awarded a Nobel Prize for Physiology and Medicine.

Domenichino, Il (1581-1641) Italian decorative painter who studied under the CARRACCI family and worked with Annibale in the Palazzo Farnese, in Rome. The frescoes in S Andrea della Valle, Rome (1624-8), are his principal religious works, but he is best remembered for his landscapes with sacred or pagan themes.

Domenico, Veneziano (15th cent.) Florentine painter of Venetian origin. One of his most important works is the main panel of the Sta Lucia altarpiece, painted in about 1445 for a church in Florence.

Dominic (1170-1221) Spanish saint who founded the Order of Preaching Friars or Dominicans, a group of highly trained priests skilled in the arts of debate. In 1203, he was chosen to accompany Bishop DIEGO on a mission to convert the Albigensians of Languedoc. Dominic deprecated the use of threats or force, employing carefully prepared and persuasive public discussion. In 1207, the Albigenses murdered the papal legate, so Innocent III organized and launched a military campaign against their overlord, Count Raymund of Toulouse. During the consequent five years of massacre, Dominic continued his campaign of persuasion, and in 1216, based in Toulouse, he founded the Order of Preaching Friars to continue and enlarge his own activities.

Domitian (51-96) Roman emperor (81-96), who built a 300-mile line of forts and blockhouses called the *Limes Germanicus* from the upper Rhine (near Bonn) to the upper Danube (near Regensburg), the rivers themselves forming a natural defence between the North Sea and the Black Sea.

Do Nascimento, Arantes see PELE, Edson

Donatello, Donato Di Niccolo (c. 1386-1466) Florentine sculptor. His early Gothic style reflects the influences of GHIBERTI, MICHELOZZO and BRUNELLESCHI (with whom he

worked for a while), but Donatello soon developed an individual style of revolutionary boldness. The quality of Donatello's art was first seen in his two marble figures of *St Mark*, which showed a recognition of the individual human's worth, and *St George* (or *San Michele*), demonstrating the new development of perspective, creating with mathematical precision a definite space for the figures. His later style, examples of which are *St John the Baptist* in Venice, and the *Magdalen* in Florence, both carved in wood, is more dramatically expressive than his earlier work.

Donatus, Aelius (4th cent. AD) Latin grammarian, author of two school grammars, *Ars minor* and *Ars major*, the basis of all medieval grammatical study.

Donders, Franz (1818-89) Dutch oculist, who discovered the process by which the eye focuses on different objects, and, with VON GRAEFE, was a pioneer in the science of ophthalmology. The scientific formulation of glasses to correct short and long sight and astigmatism owes a great deal to the work of the two men.

Donizetti, Gaetano (1797-1848) Italian composer who wrote over 60 operas in a light, melodic style that also often shows a strong individual vein of comedy. The best known of his operas are *The Elixir of Love* (1832), the more dramatic *Lucia di Lammermoor* (1835), based on a novel by Sir Walter SCOTT, and *Don Pasquale* (1843).

Donne, John (c. 1572-1631) English poet and clergyman whose passionate, sharply-reasoned verse made him the outstanding poet of early 17th-century English literature. The principal figure of the metaphysical poets, his genius appeared in the *Songs and Sonnets* in which he made the love lyric conversational and dramatic, laced with obscure knowledge and strange metaphor.

Doppler, Christian Johann (1803-53) Austrian physicist who discovered a wave effect now named after him. In connection with the colour of double stars, he suggested that there is a change in colour depending on whether the star is moving towards or away from the observer. He drew upon the analogous effect of the pitch of sounds whose source is moving.

Doré, Gustave (1832-83) French artist and illustrator, who was enormously popular in England and America, as well as France. His output was prodigious: among the books he illustrated were the Bible, DANTE's masterpiece, *Inferno*, CERVANTES' *Don Quixote* and Honoré BALZAC's *Contes Drôlatiques*.

Doria, Andrea (c. 1468-1560) Genoese statesman and admiral. As captain of the Genoese fleet he roamed the Mediterranean fighting the Turks and Barbary pirates (*c.* 1513-24). When Genoa was captured by the Emperor CHARLES V, Doria aided FRANCIS I of France (1524-8) to recover it, but Doria joined Charles and expelled the French. He then set up a new aristocratic régime in Genoa, which he ruled until his death, so ending factional squabbles.

Dos Passos, John (1896-1970) American novelist who wrote principally about the brutal materialism and machinery of American civilization. The trilogy *USA* (1930-6) sets its story against a background of corruption, commercialism and vulgarity, using technical devices – headlines, biographies, popular songs, a commentary – to give the effect of a documentary.

Dostoevsky, Fyodor Mikhailovich (1821-81) Russian writer, whose major works tackle the great metaphysical, religious and philosophical themes. His last novel, *The Brothers Karamazov* (1879-80), was the crown of his literary achievement, a story of parricide and jealousy between brothers which deals with the problems of atheism and belief in the existence of God. Dostoevsky's first novel *Poor Folk* (1845) was an instant success, acclaimed by BELINSKY as a masterpiece. In 1849, however, he was arrested for subversive activities and condemned to death, only to be reprieved in the execution yard. The experience affected him deeply and aggravated the epilepsy from which he had begun to suffer. He was subsequently sentenced to four years' hard labour, and later wrote *The House of the Dead* (1860-2), based on his prison experiences. Dostoevsky was continually burdened by heavy debts and two of his major works, *Crime and Punishment* (1866) and *The Idiot* (1868) were written in an effort to stave off his creditors. With these novels and with *The Demons* (1871-2) his name became known and he was able to enjoy a more prosperous life.

Doubleday, Frank (1862-1934) American publisher, who, in 1897, founded the company now known as Doubleday and Company. Managing Scribner's Magazine he formed his own publishing company, which became Doubleday, Page and Company when Walter Hines Page joined it in 1900. In 1910 Doubleday founded The Country Life press at Garden City, New York, and established over 30 bookshops. Absorption of George H. Doran created Doubleday, Doran until 1946, when the company emerged as Doubleday and Company. Its authors include KIPLING, CONRAD and O. HENRY.

Doughty, Charles (1843-1926) English author whose *Travels in Arabia Deserta* (1888) was the most famous Victorian account of Eastern travel. It is notable for its unusual style – a compound of archaism, dialect and arabisms.

Douglas, David (1798-1834) Scottish explorer and plant collector, who introduced numerous species of trees and shrubs into Britain from North America where he had been sent by the Horticultural Society after training in the Glasgow Botanic Garden. From British Columbia and California he sent home nearly all their indigenous conifers and maples now familiar in Britain, as well as common mahonia, snowberry, red flowering currant, and many other species. The Douglas Fir is a tree of major importance to forestry.

Douglas, Norman (1868-1952) Scottish writer, whose famous novel *South Wind* (1917) celebrated the richness of Italian culture.

Douglas-Home, Sir Alec (born 1903) Scottish peer and politician who created a precedent by renouncing his hereditary peerage in order to become Prime Minister. He was Foreign Secretary when the Prime Minister, MACMILLAN, retired in 1963, and in order to succeed him Douglas-Home renounced his peerage and was later elected MP for Kinross and West Perthshire. As Foreign Secretary (1960-3) he signed the nuclear test-ban treaty in Moscow (1963). In July 1964, he presided at the Commonwealth Prime Ministers' Conference, but his short-lived premiership (1963-4) was overshadowed by the impending election and an economic crisis. He resigned after a narrow defeat in the 1964 General Election, but was later appointed Foreign Secretary by Edward HEATH when the Conservatives won the 1970 General Election.

Douwes Dekker, Eduard (1820-87) Dutch writer and moralist, whose novel *Max Havelaar* (1860), was an important precursor to the 1880 literary revival in Holland. In it he attacked the colonial government of Java in the Dutch East Indies and thus achieved fame as a champion of the exploited natives. Dekker also wrote the seven-volume *Ideas* (1865-77), in which he encouraged his contemporaries to think for themselves and be independent.

Dowland, John (c. 1563-1626) English lutenist whose songs for voice and lute accompaniment were the best of this period. His work was published throughout Europe and he was court lutenist to the king of Denmark for eight years. His songs are distinctive for their fresh beauty of vocal line and the subtlety of counterpoint in the lute part.

Doyle, Sir Arthur Conan (1859-1930) Scots-born author and doctor and creator of Sherlock Holmes, one of the most famous detectives in fiction. *A Study in Scarlet* (1887) was the first Holmes story. Over the next 40 years Doyle wrote a series of Holmes adventures and also historical and romantic novels, including *The White Company* (1891) and *The Lost World* (1912).

Doyle, Richard (1824-83) British humorous artist, who designed the original cover of *Punch*, where he was on the staff (1843-50). He produced several albums of linear sketches, depicting mainly middle-class society, with a fanciful wit and a marked sense of the absurd. He also contributed illustrations to three of DICKENS's *Christmas Books*.

D'Oyly Carte, Richard (1844-1901) British impresario and theatre manager, famous for his presentation of GILBERT and SULLIVAN's operas.

Draco (late 7th cent. BC) Athenian lawmaker who produced Athens' first known written code of law. It made trivial offences punishable by death, and so gave rise to the adjective 'draconian' to describe any savage edict or system. It aroused such hatred that SOLON repealed all but its laws on murder.

Drago, Luis (1859-1921) Argentinian jurist and statesman who opposed the British, German and Italian blockade of Venezuela (1902) and proclaimed the Drago Doctrine which made illegal European armed intervention in the Americas on the grounds of public debt.

Drake, Daniel (1785-1852) American physician and traveller in the United States, whose best-known book, *Diseases of the Interior Valley of North America* (1850-4), dealt with the geographical distribution of diseases and differing standards of living in the Mississippi Valley.

Drake, Edwin Laurentine (1819-80) American, one-time railroad constructor, who carried out the first drilling operations specifically for oil at Oil Creek, Penn. His strike in 1859 was small, but marked the beginning of the modern petroleum industry.

Drake, Francis (c. 1540-96) English explorer, adventurer, and naval captain who circumnavigated the world and served the Crown by harassing the treasure ships of Spain. Throughout the early 1570s, Drake was a celebrated privateer on the Spanish Main, his most legendary exploit being the attack on Nombre de Dios in 1572. After decimating a Spanish naval unit at Porto Bello, Drake sailed on to the Isthmus of Panama, where he saw the Pacific, and prayed for 'life and leave to sail once in an English ship in that sea'. During his next major voyage (1577-80), he not only crossed the Pacific but became the first Englishman to sail around the world. Drake lost two ships while attempting passage of the hazardous Strait of Magellan, but managed to steer his vessel, the *Pelican*, through safely, renaming her *Golden Hind*. Continuing up the west coast of the New World, Drake headed west to Java, rounded the Cape of Good Hope, and reached England in September 1580. He was subsequently knighted by the queen, despite Spanish protest. In 1587, Drake sailed into Cadiz harbour and attacked PHILIP II of Spain's Armada, a feat popularly known as 'singeing his Catholic majesty's beard'.

Draper, Henry (1837-82) American astronomer, the first to take a successful photograph of the spectrum of a star (1872).

Draper, John William (1811-82) English-American chemist and physiologist, who founded photochemistry by recognizing that chemical reactions could be brought about by molecules absorbing light energy. Draper also showed that all substances glow a dull red at about 525°C (called the Draper point), above which, in increasing temperature, more of the visible light region is added until the glow becomes white.

Drayton, Michael (1563-1631) English poet whose vast output was typical of the themes and attitudes of the Elizabethan age. He is best remembered for some of his sonnets and *Poly-Olbion* (completed 1622), a huge verse gazetteer of England.

Drebbel, Cornelius van (1572-1633) Dutch inventor who built the first 'submarine', which, in about 1620, was rowed successfully 12-15 feet under the Thames. The outer hull consisted of greased leather over a wooden framework and it was propelled either on or beneath the surface by eight oars sealed through the sides with leather flaps. The next significant stage in submarine development was over 250 years later.

Sir Francis Drake—"merry and careful" according to an enemy Spaniard

Drebbel also discovered a bright scarlet dye which was used with effect in the manufacture of Gobelin tapestries, and devised improvements in the microscope and telescope.

Dreiser, Theodore (1871-1945) American novelist who wrote dry, realistic fiction about the poverty and corruption of city life. In his principal works, *Sister Carrie* (1900), *The Financier* (1912) and *An American Tragedy* (1925), the characters act out thwarted lives with little positive satisfaction.

Dreyfus, Alfred (1859-1935) French army officer of Jewish blood who was the focus and victim of the 'Dreyfus Case' which split France into two hostile factions at the turn of the century. Dreyfus was a staff captain in the army in 1894 when, on flimsy evidence, he was unjustly convicted of giving military information to Germany and imprisoned on Devil's Island. After years of public agitation, in 1899 a new trial was finally forced, at which Count Marie Charles Esterhazy confessed that he had forged the documents that constituted the only real evidence against Dreyfus. Dreyfus was found guilty with extenuating circumstances and pardoned, which did not satisfy the Dreyfusards including ZOLA, who continued their agitation until the case went to the Appeal Court. There the sentence was quashed and the innocent Dreyfus reinstated and promoted. He went on to distinguish himself in the First World War and in 1919 received the Legion of Honour.

Dreyse, Johann Nikolaus von (1787-1867) German inventor, who perfected the 'needle' (i.e. firing-pin) gun. When the trigger was pulled, the pin pierced the propellent powder charge and struck the detonator at the bullet base. The gun was adopted by the Prussian Army in 1848 and was responsible for its resounding victories in the 1860s.

Drinker, Cecil (1887-1956) American inventor (1929) of the iron lung. This was the first machine to undertake one of the human body's vital functions.

Droste-Hülshoff, Annette von (1797-1848) German writer whose best-known work is the story *The Jew's Beech* (1842), the originality of which lies principally in its combination of realistic descriptions of the Westfalian countryside and its people with a subtle evocation of the mysterious and often evil motives which can determine human actions. Droste-Hülshoff also published poems during her lifetime, several of which were reprinted in a collection entitled *The Spiritual Year*, published posthumously in 1851.

Droysen, Johann (1808-84) German historian, who believed it to be Prussia's 'mission' to lead Germany. His views found fulfilment in BISMARCK's creation of the German Empire and personal expression in his *Political History of Prussia* (1855-86). He also wrote on ALEXANDER THE GREAT and on Hellenism.

Drummond of Hawthornden, William (1585-1649) Learned Scottish author whose principal work, *The Cypress Grove* (1623), is a philosophical prose meditation. His notes on a visit from Ben JONSON throw light on Jonson's character.

Dryden, John (1631-1700) English poet, dramatist and essayist who was the driving force of a literary movement that began with the Restoration in 1660. He followed the ideal of the Royal Society towards clarity and elegance, but retained the imaginative fire of the Elizabethans. In verse, he fashioned the heroic couplet into the perfect metre for the irony and bite of his satires, *Absalom and Achitophel* (1681), *The Medal* and *MacFlecknoe* (1682). His best-known plays are *Marriage à la Mode* (1673), a comedy, and *All for Love* (1678), the story of ANTONY and CLEOPATRA. His criticism, unsystematic but clearsighted, appeared in various essays and prefaces. The most famous is the *Essay of Dramatic Poesy* (1668), a model of the new lucid prose style, containing a vindication of English drama and a tribute to SHAKESPEARE.

Du Barry, Comtesse (c. 1746-39) French mistress of LOUIS XV, who dominated both the king and his court. Successor to the Marquise de POMPADOUR as the king's mistress (1768), Madame Du Barry became a patroness of artists and writers.

Du Bellay, Joachim (1522-60)
France's first poet to use the sonnet form. In 1549, he published *L'Olive*, 115 Petrarchan sonnets to an imaginary mistress. A visit to Rome inspired another sequence, *Les Antiquités de Rome* (1558), and, in the same year, his disenchantment with the city and homesickness for France resulted in *Les Regrets*, satirical elegies of melancholic beauty, which analysed his emotions. With RONSARD, he formed the Pléiade, a group of poets who advocated a rejection of medieval traditions and a return to the major 'genres'. Du Bellay's *Déffense et illustration de la langue française* (1549), setting out many of their precepts, became a landmark in the history of French literature.

Dubček, Alexander (born 1921)
Czechoslovak Communist politician who attempted to moderate the repressive orthodox Communism of his country. He was elected First Secretary of the Czechoslovak Communist Party in 1968, but his attempt to liberalize and democratize the country's Communist government provoked the USSR to invade Czechoslovakia, using tanks to suppress popular support for Dubček, and to bring about his resignation. His popularity made it dangerous to remove him from public life immediately, but the importance of his offices was reduced gradually until, in 1970, he was dismissed from public life, expelled from the Communists and forced to work outside Prague.

Dubois, Guillaume (1656-1723)
French statesman and cardinal who played an important role in the formation of the Triple Alliance against Spain in 1717. Dubois was originally tutor to Philippe, Duke of Orléans, and gained power by advising on foreign policy during the regency of the Duke (1715-23). He was responsible for the Anglo-French Treaty in 1716 which led to the Triple Alliance to exclude Philip V of Spain from the French succession. He was made archbishop of Cambrai in 1720, cardinal in 1721 and finally Prime Minister in 1722.

Dubois, Marie (1858-1940) Dutch anthropologist who, in 1891, discovered the remains of Java Man, or *Homo erectus*, who flourished about 500,000 years ago.

Duccio di Buoninsegna (c. 1255-c. 1318) Italian artist, who founded the Sienese school of painters and was one of the first artists to infuse the stylized forms of Byzantine art with a new naturalism and humanity. His masterpiece is the *Maestà*, painted for the high altar of Siena Cathedral (1308-11). The scenes originally on the reverse, depicting the life of Christ and the Passion, reveal a new narrative power, while the Madonna and Child on the front are figures of unprecedented weight and substance. The tenderness and grace of these figures were to become characteristic of the Sienese school.

Duchamp experimented with analytical Cubism, as can be seen in the fragmentation of *Nude Descending a Staircase*

Dubček's policy of liberalization in Czechoslovakia was not to be tolerated by the Russians. Military action was called for, and troops closed on Prague in a sudden, merciless 'pincer' action

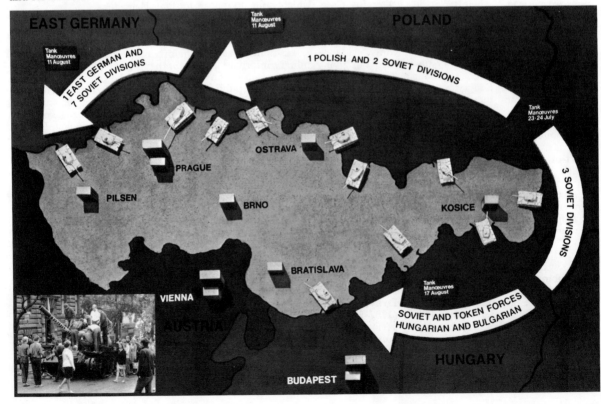

Duchamp, Marcel (1887-1968) French artist and aesthetic philosopher, who was one of the most influential figures in modern art. Developing from Post-Impressionism to Cubism, he painted *Nude Descending a Staircase* (1911), a landmark in the evolution of Cubism and Futurism. In 1914 he invented the 'ready-made', an object of normal daily use presented as a work of art, and thus challenging the accepted values and critical criteria of such works. Most famous of his 'ready-mades' are the *Bicycle Wheel*, mounted on a stool, and the *Fountain*, a urinal. From 1915 to 1923 he worked on another celebrated work *The Bride Stripped Bare by her Bachelors, Even*, a sexual allegory painted on glass. During the late 1920s Duchamp's interest in art was superseded by a preoccupation with chess, to which he devoted the latter part of his life.

Dudintsev, Vladimir Dmitriyevich (born 1918) Russian novelist, author of *Not by Bread Alone* (1956), one of the key works in the so-called post-Stalinist 'thaw' in Russian domestic politics. It describes the individual's struggle against bureaucracy.

Dudley, Robert, 1st Earl of Leicester (c. 1532-88) English courtier and favourite suitor of ELIZABETH I, whom he influenced for some 30 years. He became a privy councillor in 1559, and after the death in suspicious circumstances of his wife Amy Robsart (1560) became the suitor of Elizabeth, who finally refused him. She nevertheless made him Earl of Leicester and enjoyed his lavish hospitality at Kenilworth Castle. Forgiving his court intrigues and secret marriage to the widow of the Earl of Essex, she gave him command of English troops fighting Spain in the Low Countries (1585), and of the English forces gathered to resist the expected Spanish Armada invasion.

Dufy, Raoul (1877-1953) French artist, who was primarily a colourist but who also possessed an intuitive and calligraphic manner of drawing. An associate of the Fauve group of painters, his favourite subjects – racecourses, harbours and streets *en fête* – and the translucent gaiety of his style appeal more readily to the eye than to the intellect.

Dukas, Paul (1865-1935) French composer and music critic, known mainly for his vivid and lively symphonic scherzo, *The Sorcerer's Apprentice* (1897), which was used for one of the most successful sequences in DISNEY's film *Fantasia*. Dukas also wrote a ballet score, *The Péri* (1912), and an opera *Ariadne and Bluebeard* (1907), based on a play by MAETER-

LINCK. Shortly after 1905, he began to withhold his compositions from publication and, before he died, burnt everything hitherto unpublished.

Dulles, John Foster (1888-1959) American Secretary of State (1953-9) who conceived the theory of 'brinkmanship' in international relations: the idea that a statesman should, when necessary, take his country to the edge of war, but not beyond. Dulles negotiated and concluded the Japanese peace treaty (1950-1) in the TRUMAN administration and in 1953, as Secretary of State under EISENHOWER, adopted strongly anti-Communist policies which earned him a reputation for inflexibility in matters concerning the USSR and Communist China. An internationalist, Dulles became senior United States adviser at the United Nations founding conference in 1945 and was three times US delegate to the UN.

Dumas, Alexandre (Dumas père) (1802-70) French dramatist and novelist, best known for his swashbuckling historical romances such as *The Three Musketeers* and *The Count of Monte Cristo* (1844). He also wrote travel books, stories for children and memoirs. His son, Alexandre Dumas fils (1824-95), devoted most of his career to the stage. He wrote *The Lady of the Camellias* (1848), a popular romantic novel later transformed into his first play (1852). He enjoyed considerable success as a playwright during the Second Empire.

Dumas, Jean (1800-84) French chemist, who suggested that there are certain 'types' or families of chemical compounds that retain their chemical properties when hydrogen atoms in them are replaced by chlorine atoms. His theory was developed by his former pupil, Auguste LAURENT.

Du Maurier, George (1834-96) British artist, who joined the staff of *Punch* in 1865 and thereafter regularly contributed somewhat laboured drawings (and jokes) about high society, which enjoyed a tremendous vogue. In 1894 he published the semi-autobiographical novel *Trilby*, a story of bohemian life in Paris, the fame of which still survives.

Du Maurier, Sir Gerald (1873-1934) English actor-manager, who played the roles of Captain Hook and Mr Darling in BARRIE's *Peter Pan*. He also excelled in drawing-room comedy.

Dumont d'Urville, Jules Sébastien (1790-1842) French navigator and explorer of the southern hemisphere. He made three voyages between 1822 and 1840, visiting Australasia, Indonesia, and the Antarctic. On the last voyage, attempting to beat WEDDELL's record for Antarctic penetration and reach the magnetic South Pole, he discovered Adélie Land. On an earlier voyage in the eastern Mediterranean, he secured the preservation of a newly unearthed Greek statue.

Dunant, Jean Henri (1828-1910) Swiss founder of the International Red Cross. Having witnessed appalling suffering for want of medical attention on the battlefield of Solferino in 1859, he advocated the establishment of a permanent organization and an international convention for the aid of the wounded. The first international meeting was held at Geneva in October 1863, when the fundamental principles of the organization were laid down, and in August 1864 the Geneva Convention was adopted by a diplomatic conference of 26 nations. In 1901 Dunant shared the first Nobel Peace Prize with Frédéric Passy, a founder member of the International Peace League.

Duncan, Isadora (1878-1927) American-born English dancer, who disliked the distortions and artificiality of ballet and tried to restore simplicity, spontaneity and true

Isadora Duncan came from America to Europe. There she found international success as a dancer

emotion to dancing. Together with Edward Gordon CRAIG, she devised productions based on architectural forms, drapery and lighting effects with dancers dressed in simple Greek tunics. Her influence on modern choreographers from FOKINE to Martha GRAHAM is incalculable. A pioneer of Women's Liberation she campaigned against the use of corsets and petticoats and in favour of a less male-dominated view of marriage.

Dundee, 1st Viscount see GRAHAM, John

Dunham, Katherine (born 1914) American dancer, choreographer, and anthropologist who studied ballet and Caribbean dances based on West African and Spanish rhythms. These she combined into internationally performed ballets such as *Shango*, which retained the spirit of frenzied and sensuous improvisation of the Caribbean dances.

Dunlop, John Boyd (1840-1921) Scottish veterinary surgeon, who in 1888 patented his pneumatic bicycle tyre, which revived Thompson's earlier concept. He began experiments with an air-filled tyre to cushion his son's bicycle against the bumpy cobbles of the day, after the family's doctor had prescribed cycling to improve the boy's health. Together with W. H. Du Cros, Dunlop formed a company to exploit the tyre, but later sold his patent rights to Du Cros and derived only a small profit from his invention. The firm eventually developed into the Dunlop Rubber Company.

Dunsany, Lord Edward Plunkett (1878-1957) London-born Irish story-teller and playwright who invented fantasies, fairy tales, myths and fables. His main work was *Travel Tales of Mr Joseph Jorkens* (1931). He wrote many works of fiction and an autobiography, *Patches of Sunlight* (1938).

Duns Scotus, John (c. 1265-c. 1308) Scottish theological philosopher who, opposing the doctrine of AQUINAS, held that faith was divorced from reason. He emphasized the individuality of things and believed that will, rather than reason, was the ruling principle. Known as the 'Subtle Doctor', Duns Scotus was one of a line of Franciscan scholars whose views precipitated a schism in Catholic theology.

Dunstable, John (c. 1370-1453) English mathematician, astrologer and composer, who exercised a considerable influence on both English and continental music in the early 15th century. Dunstable's impor-

tance is that, working at a time when traditional counterpoint was a serious restriction, he introduced a new sense of flexibility and melodic invention.

Dupin, Lucile-Aurore see SAND, George

Dupleix, Joseph François, Marquis de (1697-1763) French colonial administrator, who sought to expel the British from India. He aimed to acquire territory as a basis for trade and empire and to utilize the internal Indian political situation to this end. After making a fortune from trade, Dupleix was made Governor-General of all the French settlements in 1742, and in 1746 took Madras (temporarily) from the British. In 1751 – when Britain and France were at peace – he attempted to exploit the situation by placing his own candidate on the throne of the Carnatic, but was defeated by CLIVE.

Durand, Peter (18th-19th cent.) English merchant, who in the 19th century introduced the idea of preserving food in tin-plate cans. He later sold his patent to a firm in London, and by 1830 canned food was being retailed in English shops.

Duras, Marguérite (born 1914) French novelist, born in Indo-China, where she spent her early childhood. She was the author of the scenario for Resnais's film *Hiroshima mon amour* (1960) and has also produced many novels, including *La vie tranquille* (1944), *Un Barrage contre le Pacifique* (1950) and *L'Amante anglaise* (1967). Passion, time and its parallel of events, developing and then passing, are important themes of her works, which recall PROUST in their rejection of traditional chronological narrative.

Dürer, Albrecht (1471-1528) The outstanding German artist of the Renaissance in northern Europe. While in Italy Dürer was influenced by the colours of BELLINI and became interested in the writings of LEONARDO. Not content with the traditional role of the northern European artist as little more than an artisan (unlike the artist in Italy), he tried to achieve a status for painters equal to that of scholars and humanists. One aspect of this preoccupation was his study of the theoretical basis of art, which resulted in an influential treatise on proportion (1528). Although he regarded himself primarily as a painter, his paintings are relatively few, his fame depending largely on his graphic work. This consisted of wood-cuts and copperplate engravings, some being single prints, such as the famous *Knight, Death and the Devil* (1513), but most of them forming a series illustrating religious themes such as the Passion, the Apocalypse or the life of the Virgin. These prints set new standards of technical perfection and during the 16th century their compositions and expressive qualities were imitated by artists throughout Europe. Dürer was among the first to produce water colours painted directly from the landscape.

Durkheim, Emile (1858-1917) French sociologist who attempted to apply scientific methods in social studies, but insisted that logical as well as purely statistical connections must be established. He stressed the importance of studying 'social facts', such as social customs or moral beliefs, which exist as a result of the feelings of the individual.

Dürer's fame rests largely on engravings but he was an outstanding watercolourist, a technique little used in his day

Durrell, Lawrence (born 1912)
English poet and novelist, whose
best-known work, the four novels of
the *Alexandria Quartet* (1957-60), are
typical of his recurrent theme of the
meeting of eastern and western cultures in the lands of the eastern
Mediterranean.

**Dürrenmatt, Friedrich (born
1921)** Swiss dramatist whose *The
Visit* and *The Physicists* became world
famous. *The Visit* (1955) concerns an
old woman's revenge on her former
neighbours. In *The Physicists* (1962),
three scientists have themselves
committed to a lunatic asylum to
save the world from their inventions.

Duse, Eleonora (1859-1924) Italian
actress, who rivalled BERNHARDT as
the greatest tragedienne of their era.
Though less spectacular than Bernhardt, Duse was more academic in
her creation of great roles. She made
her name in *Les Fourchambault*
(1878) and in D'ANNUNZIO's plays.
She was at her zenith in IBSEN's
Rosmersholm.

Dutton, Clarence (1841-1912)
American geologist who, in collaboration with J. H. Pratt, first publicized
the theory of isostasy, which states
that the continents and oceans are
maintained in equilibrium, floating
on the underlying rocks of the Earth.

Dutton, Edward (1831-1923)
American book publisher who be-
came associated with Dent, the
English publisher, in publishing the
Everyman's Library series, cheap
reprints of English classics.

Duvalier, François (1907-71)
Dictator of Haiti, known as 'Papa
Doc', who was regarded by his
people as the incarnation of the Voodoo god, Baron Samedi. A physician
by training, he was elected President
in 1957, obtained dictatorial powers
from the national assembly and
maintained them by means of a
private army of thugs, the *Tontons
Macoutes* (bogeymen), by voodoo,
and by deliberately keeping the population poor, primitive and illiterate.
His régime was condemned by the
International Commission of Jurists
(1966) for its 'innumerable excesses'.
He repulsed several attempts by
Haitian exiles to invade Haiti and
overthrow his government.

Dvořák, Antonin (1841-1904)
Czechoslovakia's leading symphonic
composer, who began his career as a
butcher's boy. Dvořák joined the
orchestra formed under SMETANA at
the Prague National Theatre as a viola
player, and meanwhile practised
composition. BRAHMS saw some of his
scores and became his friend and

Voodoo ritual in Haiti. The voodoo cult
was used by 'Papa Doc' Duvalier to
keep the island population under control

adviser. Czech folk music had always
been an underlying if indirect influence in Dvořák's work and after he
became head of the National Conservatory in New York (1892) the
negro spiritual came to play a similar
role. The theme of the famous slow
movement of his Symphony No. 9
(*From the New World*) is an original
tune by Dvořák, but clearly shows
where its influences lay. Besides his
nine symphonies, Dvořák composed
prolifically. His other orchestral
works include the sets of *Slavonic
Rhapsodies* and *Slavonic Dances*; a
violin and a cello concerto; and
several concert overtures, including
Carnival. He also wrote operas, songs,
a *Te Deum* and *Requiem* as well as a
good deal of chamber music.

**Dyck, Sir Anthony van (1599-
1641)** Flemish artist, who was Court
Painter to CHARLES I of England. At a
very early age he was RUBENS's most
gifted assistant in Antwerp. He
travelled widely in Italy, where he
produced some of the portraits for
which he is now best known. The
greatest period of his career began
in 1632, when he was appointed as a
painter to the court of CHARLES I in
London. Among his pictures for
Charles was the 'dismounted' equestrian portrait now in the Louvre.

E

Eakins, Thomas (1844-1916)
American painter, who founded a
school of American realist painting.
In his later years he concentrated on
portraits, whose realism is as much
psychological as visual.

Eannes, Gil (15th cent.) Portuguese navigator, who first ventured
beyond the limits of Arab navigation
in the Atlantic. The Arabs, who had
long monopolized the coastal waters
of northwest Africa, believed that
south of Cape Bojador the sea boiled.
HENRY THE NAVIGATOR commissioned
several mariners to round the Cape,
and Eannes succeeded in 1433.

Earp, Wyatt (1848-1929) American
marshal famous for law enforcement
by gun. Like his contemporaries the
'hanging' judge, Isaac C. Parker, and
Judge Roy Bean, who held court
in a saloon with a gun and a law book,
Earp represents the men whose crude
methods of law enforcement helped
to tame America's Wild West.

Eastman, George (1854-1932)
American inventor of the flexible roll
film system of photography. In 1884,
Eastman patented a photographic
film, consisting of paper smeared
with gel emulsion. Four years later,
he produced the famous Kodak (a
meaningless, but, as Eastman hoped,
a catchy trademark) camera, which
was quite light and used the new roll
film. The camera was shrewdly
marketed, with the slogan, 'You press
the button – we do the rest'. The
paper of the film was replaced first
by celluloid (1889) and later (1924)
by cellulose acetate.

**Eça de Queirós, José Maria de
(1845-1900)** Portuguese writer of
realistic novels, who was deeply concerned with the improvement of the
conditions of the under-privileged.

He wrote a number of novels exposing the complacency of the Portuguese Church and middle-class. Eventually, however, he became disillusioned, and his later works were little more than exercises in style.

Ecgberht see EGBERT

Eckener, Hugo (1868-1954) German dirigible pilot and aeronautical engineer. Eckener commanded the *Graf Zeppelin*'s global flight (1929) and designed the ill-fated *Hindenberg*, which exploded in 1937.

Eckert, John Presper (born 1919) American electrical engineer, who, in 1946, with John William Mauchly, made the first electronic computer, called ENIAC. This massive device used 18,000 radio valves and thus considerable electrical power. Removal of the resulting heat presented a major problem. The valves were also unreliable and the machine functioned only for short periods.

Eckhart, Johannes (c. 1260-c. 1327) German theologian and mystic known as Meister Eckhart, whose speculations on the infinite nature of God, condemned at the time, later influenced Protestant thinkers in both theology and philosophy, and find some echoes in KIERKEGAARD.

Eddington, Sir Arthur (1882-1944) English astronomer who discovered the relationship between mass and luminosity of stars. He was appointed Plumian Professor of Astronomy at Cambridge University in 1913, and three years later began investigating the interiors of stars, and showed how energy is transmitted through the body of a star, which he recognized to be made up of gas. Eddington was one of the first scientists to appreciate the importance of EINSTEIN's theory of relativity.

Eddy, Mary Baker (1821-1910) American religious leader and founder of the Christian Science Movement. Setting out her views in *Science and Health with a Key to the Scriptures* (1875) Mrs Eddy taught that disease and pain are evidence of mental error and can be cured by spiritual healing, that everything material is an illusion. She believed that God is the only reality and that as men learn the truth, so they will cease to sin. She founded the First Church of Christ, Scientist, in Boston in 1879 and also organized the publication of newspapers, notably the *Christian Science Monitor*.

Eden, Anthony, 1st Earl of Avon (born 1897) British statesman who as Prime Minister authorized military intervention in Egypt (November 1956) to recover control of the Suez Canal, which had been nationalized by the government of NASSER. As Foreign Secretary during the 1930s, he worked for League of Nations action against HITLER and MUSSOLINI, and opposed the policy of appeasement, over which he resigned in 1938. When CHURCHILL became Prime Minister in the Second World War coalition government, Eden was appointed Foreign Secretary and after the war led the British delegation to the San Francisco Conference (1945) which established the United Nations. When the Conservatives were returned to power he was again appointed Foreign Secretary (1951), and in 1955 he succeeded Churchill as Prime Minister. His health had been failing, however, and United Nations, United States and USSR condemnation of the Anglo-French intervention in Egypt led to his resignation and retirement from political life in 1957.

Edgeworth, Maria (1767-1849) Irish novelist who wrote of the manners and customs of her native land. Her best-known works are *Castle Rackrent* (1800), *The Absentee* (1812) and *Ormond* (1817). Sir Walter SCOTT acknowledged her influence in his writing.

Edison, Thomas Alva (1847-1931) American inventor, with more than a thousand patents to his credit. His professional life began at 12 when, as a railway newsboy, he printed and published his own paper (the first ever to be printed on a train). Later he became a telegraph operator and developed his interest in electrical technology through the acquisition of FARADAY's writings. With the proceeds from his development of an improved stock market ticker in 1870, he set up the world's first industrial research laboratory in Newark, New Jersey. He made major contributions to telegraphy (1874), the development of telephones (1877), incandescent light (1879), the phonograph (1877), electric generating equipment, motion photography and storage batteries (1900-10). His major contribution to cinematography (1891) was the introduction of 35 mm celluloid film with perforations along each edge, allowing sprocketed gear-wheels inside both the camera and projector to transport the film forward a defined distance and in precise alignment.

Edward the Confessor (c. 1002-66) King of England (1042-66) whose alleged promises to Duke WILLIAM of Normandy provoked the Norman invasion. Recalled from France, where he was brought up, by HARDECANUTE to be his heir, Edward became more monk than king (hence the name 'the Confessor'), allowing first Norman favourites and later his father-in-law Earl Godwin of Wessex to run the government. Lacking direct heirs, he reputedly named first his cousin William of Normandy, then Harold, Godwin's son, as his successor – so giving both a claim to the throne. He built the first Westminster Abbey, in which he was buried.

Edward I (1239-1307) King of England (1272-1307) whose reformist measures place him, with HENRY II, as one of the two greatest Plan-

Most prolific of inventors, Thomas Edison at work in his laboratory: inset, his electric bulb and prototype phonograph

tagenet kings. Leaning heavily on the new, monied middle class for financial support, he used Parliament to endorse plans to extend royal authority and promulgate reforms such as the weakening of feudalism, and thus began a new age in English government. England gained mastery of Great Britain under Edward's rule, by the crushing of Wales and Scotland. He died, leaving Edward II to deal with ROBERT THE BRUCE's Scottish revolt.

Edward III (1312–77) King of England (1327–77) who defeated the French at Crécy (1346). His long reign is notable for martial exploits against the Scots and the beginning of the 100 Years' War against the French. At home, his reign was remarkably peaceful, his court being regarded as Europe's most magnificent. Economic problems resulting from the Black Death and Edward's subjugation to his son, John of Gaunt, caused civil strife which marred the reign of Richard II.

Edward, 'The Black Prince' (1330-76) English leader of campaigns against the French in the 100 Years' War. At the battle of Crécy (1346) Edward, who was Prince of Wales, won the insignia still borne by his successors – ostrich plumes and the mottoes *homout; ich dene* (courage; I serve). He led the English troops who won the major battle of Poitiers (1356) and captured France's John II, whom England traded for a ransom payment of a large area of France. Prince Edward ruled from Bordeaux as Prince of Aquitaine (1362-72) but lost control in a revolt, and resigned Aquitaine to his father, EDWARD III. His nickname, supposedly from his wearing black armour, was not used until the 16th century.

Edward IV (1442-83) King of England (1461-70 and 1471-83), the first of the House of York (1461-85). As a great-great-grandson of EDWARD III he succeeded (where his father, Richard of York, had failed) in pressing his claim to the throne. Backed by Parliament, he unseated Henry VI and crushed his Lancastrian backers. In the relative peace that followed, Edward patronized trade and culture (befriending the pioneer printer William CAXTON) and left to his son Edward V a throne solvent for the first time since HENRY II.

Edward VII (1841-1910) King of Great Britain (1901-10). He was the eldest son of Queen VICTORIA and Prince ALBERT. The queen, jealous of her own position and distrustful of Edward's abilities, denied him experience of state business or access to

Cabinet papers until 1892, and he became the leader of fashionable society, enjoying racing, yachting, sport and continental travel. The personal influence and power of the monarchy declined during his reign.

Edward VIII (1894-1972) King of Great Britain (20 Jan.-11 Dec. 1936), whose abdication caused great consternation and public controversy. As Prince of Wales, his personal charm and preference for informality had made him widely popular. He became king on the death of his father, GEORGE V. The abdication crisis occurred because he wished to marry Mrs Wallis Simpson, an American, whose second divorce was pending and who was therefore unlikely to be acceptable as queen. The proposal of a morganatic marriage (one between a person of exalted status and a partner of inferior rank who does not share the dignities accorded to the partner, nor inherit his or her possessions) was rejected and after one of the shortest reigns in British history, the King renounced the throne, without having been crowned. He was created Duke of Windsor by his brother, GEORGE VI, who succeeded him. He lived for the rest of his life in Paris with Mrs Simpson, whom he married in 1937.

Edwardes, George (1852-1915) English theatrical manager, who popularized musical comedy. Among his famous productions at the Gaiety and at Daly's were *The Merry Widow* and *The Quaker Girl*.

Egerton, Francis see BRIDGEWATER, Third Duke of

Ehrenberg, Christian (1795-1876) German zoologist, whose work on micro-organisms led to the foundation of protozoology as a science.

Ehrenburg, Ilya Grigoryevich (1891-1967) Russian poet, novelist and journalist whose best works are considered to be his memoirs *Men, Years and Life* (1960-4) and his critical essays, collected in *Chekhov, Stendhal and Other Essays*.

Ehrlich, Paul (1854-1915) German bacteriologist, who founded chemotherapy, the science of the chemical treatment of disease. Previous chemical cures had been accidental. His most important discoveries, the compounds trypan red and salvarsan, were effective in the treatment of trypanosomiasis and syphilis respectively. Although it was hoped then that all infectious diseases could be so cured, the more common smaller bacteria remained resistant to chemical treatments until DOMAGK's discoveries 25 years later.

Eichendorff, Joseph von (1788-1857) German poet and novelist who epitomized the German Romantic movement. In his poems and in his story *Memoirs of a Good-for-Nothing*, he conveys the moods and longing of the individual, often contrasting the pettiness of day-to-day existence with the beauty and unfathomability of love, religion and nature. Many composers, including MENDELSSOHN and SCHUMANN, set his poems to music.

Eichmann, Karl Adolf (1906-62) German administrator of HITLER's Jewish extermination policy. As a Gestapo agent during the *Anschluss* (annexation) of Czechoslovakia in 1939, he was responsible for the deportation of 35,000 Jews. His sinister skills as an administrator were given free rein in 1941, when GOERING ordered the 'final solution of the Jewish question' to be carried out. Eichmann organized special extermination squads and was personally responsible for the logistics of the deportation and extermination of millions of Jews. He escaped to Argentina after the war, but was captured clandestinely by Israeli agents in 1960, tried in Israel in 1961, and executed.

Eichmann, the merchant of death, awaits his own execution at the hands of the Israelis in 1961

Eiffel, Alexandre Gustave (1832-1923) French engineer best known for his design of the tower built for the Paris Exhibition of 1889 and which bears his name. Eiffel's greatest interest was in bridges, and he also designed the framework for the Statue of Liberty in New York Harbour (1885), and the locks on the Panama Canal (1893). Eiffel founded the world's first aerodynamics laboratory at Auteuil, France, in 1912.

Eijkman, Christian (1858-1930) Dutch physician, who in 1896 showed that disease could result from the absence in a diet of trace quantities of essential components, now known as vitamins. Although Eijkman had misinterpreted his results, later workers proposed the correct explanation and the trace constituents were then called vitamins. Eijkman shared a Nobel Prize for Medicine (1929).

Einstein, Albert (1879-1955) German-American physicist who proposed the theory of relativity. In 1905 he announced four new and fundamental ideas in physics: the special theory of relativity (which seeks to account for the constant speed of light); the equation relating mass and energy; the theory of Brownian movement; and the photon theory of light. In 1916 he first presented his general theory of relativity, and spent much of his later life applying the theory to cosmological problems. At the other extreme of the scale of size, he never accepted as satisfactory the usual interpretations of the new quantum mechanics in terms of probabilities and conducted a long and lively (if unsuccessful) open debate in favour of determinism. These diverse but fundamental interests led Einstein to turn his attention to the problem of formulating a single theory to cover both gravitation and electrodynamics. Just as general relativity, based on the general geometry of RIEMANN, sought to explain gravitation as a property of space (whose geometry was a function of the matter contained in it), so this unified field theory sought to explain electrodynamics in addition to gravitation. This remains an

The atom bomb, sinister fruit of the researches of Einstein

unfinished line of investigation. In 1933, when the Nazis gained power in Germany, Einstein emigrated to the United States. Just before the Second World War, after uranium had been split (by HAHN in Germany), Einstein was prompted to contact President F. D. ROOSEVELT. This approach led to the establishment of the Manhatten Project to develop the atomic bomb. Einstein's contributions to science were vast. His general theory of relativity led to a new era in cosmological research and speculation. The equivalence of mass and energy, stated in his famous equation $e = mc^2$, was demonstrated with devastating effect in the atomic bombs.

Like earlier military heroes—Washington and Grant—Eisenhower became US President

Einthoven, Willem (1860-1927) Dutch physiologist, who developed electrocardiography. In 1903 Einthoven invented the string galvanometer, with which he was able to measure the varying electrical potentials of the heart. Subsequently, he improved the device and by 1906 was correlating variations in the patterns of the electrocardiograms with types of heart disorder. For the development of electrocardiography he was awarded the 1924 Nobel Prize for Physiology and Medicine.

Eisenstein chose as his subjects some of the great moments of Russian history

Eisenhower, Dwight David (1890–1969) American general and United States President (1953-61). During the early part of the Second World War, he was Chief-of-Staff, Operations Division, Washington, becoming Commander-in-Chief of the Allied Forces in North Africa in 1942. As Supreme Commander, Western Europe (1944-5) his ability to co-ordinate the activities of Allied staff was perhaps his most valuable contribution to the war. He was Supreme Commander of NATO forces in Europe (1950-2) when he resigned his commission to run for President as Republican candidate, and defeated the Democratic candidate, Adlai STEVENSON. He was elected for a second term, again defeating Stevenson, in 1956 by a margin of nearly 10 million votes. During Eisenhower's first presidential term, the US was occupied with a campaign against 'Communist subversion', and domestic legislation included an extension of the social security programme, with some support for civil rights. His popularity waned during his second term as a result of economic recession, the US spy plane incident on the eve of summit talks with Russian leaders (1960) and doubts about his health.

Eisenstein, Sergei (1898-1948) Soviet film director and theorist chiefly notable for his development of 'montage' (the cinematic art of editing and assembling pieces of film to give a new expressive force to the elements). A famous example was the Odessa Steps sequence in *The Battleship Potemkin* (1925), in which he cuts from the apparently mechanical advance of the soldiers to the disorganized panic of the citizens and specific images – a runaway pram, shattered spectacles. His films, *Strike* (1924), *October* (1927), *Alexander Nevski* (1938) and *Ivan the Terrible* (1942-6) are regarded as classics.

More than any other landmark, the Eiffel Tower symbolizes Paris. Built for the Paris exhibition of 1889, it was the outstanding achievement of engineer and bridge-builder Alexandre Eiffel. During his last years, Eiffel made use of the tower for experiments in aerodynamics

Eleanor of Aquitaine (c. 1122-1204) Queen of France (1137-52, when her marriage to Louis VII was annulled), and of England (1154-1204), who played a dominant role in French and English politics for many years. Her importance lay in her possession of the vast duchy of Aquitaine, which she brought to HENRY II of England. In 1173 she supported her sons in unsuccessful rebellion against HENRY II, after he had been continually unfaithful to her. After Henry's death she took RICHARD I's part against an attempt by her other son, JOHN, to displace him from the throne. She was a patroness of poets and troubadours, introduced chivalric courts of law into England and took part in the Second Crusade (1147-9).

Elgar, Sir Edward (1857-1934) English composer in the British musical renaissance of the early 20th century. He was self-taught, and worked as a local violinist and teacher until, in 1899, a performance of his orchestral set, the *Enigma Variations*, brought him overnight fame. This, and his oratorio *The Dream of Gerontius* (1900, to a text by NEWMAN), established him as a major figure at home and on the Continent. He went on to write two symphonies, a violin concerto and the *Introduction and Allegro* for strings, as well as the set of five *Pomp and Circumstance* marches (No. 1 containing the tune for 'Land of Hope and Glory'). His best works such as his cello concerto or the symphonic study *Falstaff*, display a remarkable introspective sensitivity. After the death of his wife in 1920, Elgar's creative drive seemed to break down, and he wrote little during the last 14 years of his life.

Elgin, Thomas Bruce, 7th Earl of (1766-1841) British diplomat famous for acquiring the so-called 'Elgin Marbles'. Between 1803-12, while envoy to Turkey, he shipped large portions of the Parthenon's sculp-

Born into a musical household, Elgar was 42 before his *Enigma Variations* made him famous

tured frieze to England from Athens, then controlled by the Turks.

Elijah (9th cent. BC) Hebrew prophet of Yahweh (Jehovah), who ranks with MOSES as a founder of Judaism and hence of Christian belief. Coming from Judah (southern Palestine), he opposed worship of the old fertility god Baal, enforced as a state religion in Israel (northern Palestine) by King Ahab's Phoenician queen Jezebel. Elijah insisted on unswerving obedience to the moral dictates of his 'God of Righteousness' even at the cost of the interests of the state.

Eliot, George (1819-80) Pen-name of Mary Ann Evans, English novelist, whose books are a realistic portrait of provincial, Victorian life. Her principal works, *The Mill on the Floss* (1860), *Middlemarch* (1871-2) and *Daniel Deronda* (1876), revolve around the theme of the value of human suffering in the creation of a contented, philosophical existence. She was commercially successful and gained a reputation for unconventionality. George Eliot began her literary career as a reviewer, translator and then assistant editor of the *Westminster Review*. The early *Scenes from Clerical Life* (1858) impressed the literary world, including DICKENS and THACKERAY.

Eliot, Sir John (1592-1632) English parliamentarian, who became the leading figure in the House of Commons in opposition to the royal policy between 1625 and 1629. Originally a follower of BUCKINGHAM, he turned against his patron after the disastrous Cadiz expedition and urged the Duke's impeachment (1626). Mistrusting CHARLES I's religious and financial policies, Eliot refused to pay a forced loan (1627) and supported the Petition of Right (1628). The climax of his career came in 1629, when his oratorical powers influenced the Commons to pass three famous resolutions condemning arbitrary taxation and religious innovations. Imprisoned in the Tower until his death, Eliot came to be regarded as a martyr to the Parliamentary cause.

Eliot, John (1604-90) English immigrant to Massachusetts (1631), the first Christian missionary to the American Indians of New England. He became known as 'the Apostle of the Indians' for his evangelistic work, including the founding of a village of American Indian Christian converts near Boston (1651), the first of 14 such villages set up by 1674.

Eliot, Thomas Stearns (1888-1965) American-born English poet, critic and playwright, who was the central figure in the modern English poetic tradition. The tone and rhythm of his language has influenced most of the poetry written in English since the Second World War. His early poetry, in *Prufrock* (1917) and *The Waste Land* (1922), was stern and anti-romantic, a picture of contemporary sickness built from myth, anthropology and older English poetry. He used an imagery drawn from popular songs, pub conversations and oriental mysticism. Later in life, Eliot described himself as royalist in politics, Anglo-Catholic in religion and classical in literature. In his poetry, especially in *Ash Wednesday* (1930) and *The Four Quartets* (1943), he writes of the great themes of the Christian tradition in a dry, ironic style, with dignity and great depth of emotion. Eliot was an influential critic, relating the poetic tradition to the new circumstances of the modern world. In his plays, he revived verse drama in the English theatre. His four modern tragi-comedies with religious overtones, especially *Murder in the Cathedral* (1935), reached a much wider audience than even his crowning poetic achievement, 'Little Gidding', in *The Four Quartets*.

Elizabeth I (1533-1603) Queen of England and Ireland (1558-1603), and last of the Tudor monarchs, who gave her name to an age of outstanding national achievement. She succeeded MARY I and, with the help of her minister William CECIL, disposed of a potential rival to the throne (1587), MARY, QUEEN OF SCOTS. She established a middle-of-the-road National Church aimed at preventing extremist revolts and, though at odds with Catholic France and Spain, kept clear of costly wars until 1585. In 1588 her navy scattered PHILIP II's great Armada, and her privateer-explorers, headed by Sir Francis DRAKE and Sir Walter RALEIGH, ravaged Spanish America. Under Elizabeth, new chartered companies (notably the East India Company) carried English trade and colonists overseas. The growing national prosperity helped to finance the first English theatres, for which SHAKESPEARE, MARLOWE and JONSON wrote their most famous plays. Elizabeth died a childless spinster.

Elizabeth II (born 1926) Queen of Great Britain. She succeeded her father, GEORGE VI, in 1952, and has continued to reign while most other monarchies have fallen out of favour. While retaining much of the tradition and ceremony associated with the British crown, she has, with the aid of her family, reinforced the institution of the monarchy and achieved worldwide popularity by international visits, informality, and the acceptance of television and press coverage of her activities.

Ellington, Edward Kennedy 'Duke' (born 1899) American composer, band-leader and pianist, and one of the most important influences on popular music in the 20th century. As the organizer and leader of a jazz orchestra, his reputation internationally is as great as that of Louis ARMSTRONG's as a soloist. To mark United Nations Day in 1973, Ellington and his orchestra performed a 'Sacred Concert', written by him, in Westminster Abbey, London.

Ellsworth, Lincoln (1880-1951) American polar explorer and civil engineer who made the first air crossing of Antarctica. With AMUNDSEN and Nobile, he made the first trans-Arctic flight over the North Pole in the airship *Norge* (1926) and, with pilot Herbert Hollick Kenyon, made the first aeroplane crossing of Antarctica (1935).

Elsevier, Louis I (c. 1546-1617) Dutch founder (*c.* 1581) of the family firm of booksellers, printers and publishers whose scholarly books set new standards in typography and design. Today Elsevier Ltd is one of Holland's leading publishers.

Elsheimer, Adam (1578-1610) German artist, who was much praised for his small, highly finished landscapes painted on copper. He was admired by REMBRANDT.

Eluard, Paul (1895-1952) French poet and leading member of the Surrealists (and one of the movement's founders, along with BRETON and ARAGON) from 1919-38. His poems of the period are striking for their mysterious images and sensuous language. In 1936, as a result of the Spanish Civil War, he proclaimed the need for greater commitment by poets to their fellow men. During the Second World War, he became known as the poet of the Resistance through war poems such as 'Poésie et vérité' (1942) and 'Au rendezvous allemand' (1944).

Emerson, Ralph Waldo (1803-82) 'Nature is the incarnation of thought', wrote Emerson, American philosopher and poet, who met COLERIDGE, WORDSWORTH and CARLYLE whilst on a tour of Europe. He blended the humanitarian nature-worship of Romantic Europe with a belief that America had unrivalled opportunities to create a new social and moral order. His ideas were set out in *Nature* (1836).

Eminescu, Mihail (1850-89) Rumanian poet, whose lyrical ballad, 'The Evening Star' (1883), won for him, after his death, the position of Rumania's national poet. In addition to his work on social and economic subjects, he wrote philosophical meditations, satires, romances, short stories and fragments of drama.

Empedocles (5th cent. BC) Greek philosopher, physician and democrat who originated the theory of four elements—fire, air, water, earth—as the basic substances from which all else is made. They are combined in varying proportions, according to the unifying and separating agency of the principles of Love and Strife, which in turn explains all change.

Empson, William (born 1906) English poet and critic whose work aims at a subtle, complex and rigorous analysis of experience. His principal critical work, *Seven Types of Ambiguity* (1930), is a linguistic study of shades of meaning.

Enders, John (born 1897) American microbiologist whose discovery, with Frederick Robbins and Thomas Weller, that the poliomyelitis virus could be grown in tissue other than nerve tissue was an essential step in the development of polio vaccines. In 1962 he produced the first successful measles vaccine. The three men were awarded a joint Nobel Prize for Medicine (1954).

Enesco, Georges (1881-1955) Rumanian violinist and composer of three symphonies, an opera, *Oedipus*, as well as two Rumanian Rhapsodies. Enesco studied in Vienna, absorbing the influence of BRAHMS and WAGNER, and later fused these influences with a study of Rumanian folk-song and a period of study with FAURÉ and MASSENET in Paris into a distinctive national style. He was a distinguished teacher of violin technique whose pupils included Yehudi Menuhin.

Engels, Friedrich (1820-95) German political writer and disciple of Karl MARX, with whom he collaborated in formulating the theory of dialectical materialism. As agent in England of his father's textile business (1842-4) he took an interest in the workers' conditions and, under the influence of the Chartist movement, wrote *The Condition of the Working Classes in England* (1844). This brought him into touch with Marx, then an exile in England, and together they wrote the *Communist Manifesto* (1848). While Marx was doing research and writing in London, Engels supported him, and from 1870 until Marx's death (1883) he helped Marx with his writings. He completed the latter's *Das Kapital* (1894), which Marx left unfinished.

Ennius, Quintus (239-c. 169 BC) Roman poet, known as the father of Roman poetry. His works, which survive only in fragments, range from tragedy and comedy to satire and didactic poetry, and reveal him as a poet who approached his Greek models in his originality. His pre-eminence at Rome was achieved by the rugged grandeur of his (probably) unfinished hexameter epic of Roman History, the 18-volume *Annales*.

Eötvös, Roland (1848-1919) Hungarian physicist who established accurately that the gravitational force on a body depends only on its mass, not on its constitution.

Epictetus (2nd-1st cent. BC) Greek philosopher and follower of the early Stoics, who emphasized the autonomy of the individual will. All men, he believed, share in divine rationality; the wise man attunes his will to that of God by viewing the universe in its totality. His pupil, Arrian, recorded his teaching.

Epicurus (c. 342-270 BC) Greek philosopher whose name has mistakenly become synonymous with luxury and an excessive love of pleasure. In fact, he taught that the supreme goal is the happiness which comes from peace of mind, achieved by banishing fear of the gods and fear of death, and by avoiding immediate pleasures that are outweighed by greater consequent pains.

Epstein, Sir Jacob (1880-1959) American-born British sculptor whose style and technique were highly original, and it became customary for any new work of his to be greeted with uproar. Among Epstein's more important busts are those of Somerset MAUGHAM, Albert EINSTEIN and George Bernard SHAW. Epstein's sculpture possessed a nervous tension, shown in one of his last works, *Christ in Majesty* (1957), cast in unpolished aluminium.

The work of Sir Jacob Epstein often caused a sensation. In 1907 it was declared by some to be obscene

Erasmus, Desiderius (c. 1466-1536) Dutch Renaissance theologian and scholar whose Greek versions of the New Testament showed for the first time that contemporary Latin translations were defective. As editor and commentator, he did much to publish the writings of the Christian Fathers, and generally promoted classical scholarship. His satire, *In Praise of Folly*, written for his friend Sir Thomas MORE, is the best remembered of his works. Although sympathetic to sources implicit in the Reformation movement, he had the scholar's dislike for violent political and religious upheaval and therefore never openly joined the reformers.

Erastus, Thomas (1524-83) Swiss theologian who maintained that even in ecclesiastical matters, supremacy belongs to the state. His doctrine has come to prevail in most civilized countries, where clerical authority is always ultimately subject to civil sanction.

Eratosthenes (3rd cent. BC) Greek astronomer and geographer who calculated the circumference of the Earth.

Erhard, Ludwig (born 1897) Architect of the West German 'Economic Miracle'. He was appointed Minister of Economic Affairs by ADENAUER in 1949, and retained the post until he became Chancellor of the Federal Republic in 1963. After 1965 his coalition government of Christian Democrats and Free Democrats proved increasingly difficult to control, and he resigned in November 1966 to be succeeded as Chancellor by Kiesinger. Erhard's policies as Economics Minister, and later as Chancellor, were fundamental with other factors, such as Marshall Aid, to the growth of the German economy to a position of almost unrivalled prosperity in Europe.

Eric the Red (10th cent.) Norwegian mariner and discoverer of Greenland (*c.* 982). Eric sailed west from Iceland and the landfall he made was so visually appealing compared to Iceland that he named it Greenland. In the following year, a number of Icelandic Vikings settled there.

Ericsson, John (1803-99) Swedish-American engineer and inventor who, in 1836, patented a screw propeller to replace paddle wheels for the propulsion of steamships. The propeller had rotating right- and left-handed screws on concentric shafts, which eliminated the tendency of a single screw to slew the stern. Ericsson's devices were fitted to a small, Birkenhead-built US Navy vessel which reached New York in May, 1839. In 1862, he launched the *Monitor*, an ironclad, self-propelled floating platform for two 11-inch naval guns in a rotating turret. Later that year *Monitor* defeated the Confederate Navy's ironclad *Merrimack*, a battle significant both in deciding the outcome of the Civil War and as a step forward in naval design.

Ericsson, Leif (10th-11th cents.) Norse mariner, son of ERIC THE RED, who, according to the Icelandic sagas, made a westward expedition on which he discovered Helluland ('Land of the Flat Stone'), Markland ('Woodland') and Vinland. These discoveries are thought to relate specifically to Labrador, Nova Scotia and New England, though the 1965 evidence of the Vinland map is now known to have been a post-1920s forgery. Impressed by the moderate weather and natural maritime resources, Ericsson's party set up a colony for the winter, and recent archaeological finds suggest that the site was on the Newfoundland Coast.

Erlanger, Joseph (1874-1965) American physiologist, who pioneered the technique of displaying nerve impulses on an oscilloscope and shared a Nobel Prize in 1944 with Herbert Gasser. They showed that nerves conduct impulses at a rate proportional to their diameter.

Ernst, Max (born 1891) German-born Surrealist painter whose technical innovations have had a considerable influence. Most notably, these were collage (compositions embodying scraps of paper, cloth or other material stuck onto the canvas), frottage (an impression of substances achieved by rubbing paper over a grainy surface), and automatic writing, a fundamental Surrealist technique (allowing the unconscious to rule the creative process). Ernst is one of the few Surrealist painters to achieve distinction in other media.

Eshkol, Levi (1895-1969) Israeli politician and the young state of Israel's third Prime Minister. Born at Kiev, he migrated to Palestine in 1913 and served in the First World War with the Jewish battalion of the Royal Fusiliers. He founded a number of kibbutzim, became Secretary of the Jewish Federation of Labour, and of the Jewish Labour Party. He was Minister of Agriculture and Development (1951) in BEN GURION's government and later Prime Minister (1963-9). During his Ministry Israel defeated the Egyptian Alliance in the Six-Day War of 1967.

Espronceda, José de (1808-42) Spanish poet, who studied the work of the English Romantics and introduced their style and outlook into Spanish poetry. After fighting at the Paris barricades in 1830, he returned to Madrid to participate in the liberal revolution after 1833 as an ultra-radical journalist. His long poems include an historical legend 'The Student of Salamanca' (*c.* 1840) and 'The Devilish World', an unfinished philosophico-didactic allegory, enlivened only by a section reproaching his mistress for abandoning him. His best poems are short, bitter protests against social injustices and the uncertainty of human life.

Essex, Robert Devereux, 2nd Earl of (1566-1601) English courtier, soldier, statesman and poet, successor to RALEIGH and the Earl of LEICESTER as favourite of the ageing ELIZABETH I. He led flamboyant military expeditions to Cadiz and the Azores, and gained political power as Earl Marshal of England (1597) and Lord Lieutenant of Ireland (1599). By his absences from court, his marriage, his feud with the Cecils, and his disobedience in making a truce with Tyrone in Ireland, he fell into Elizabeth's disfavour and was imprisoned (1599-1600). His plot to seize government control ended in failure and his ultimate execution.

Ethelbert (c. 522-616) English King of Kent, promulgator of the first Anglo-Saxon law code, the earliest known document in any Germanic language. He was baptized a Christian by St AUGUSTINE.

Etherege, Sir George (c. 1634-91) English dramatist and prime exponent of the Comedy of Manners, a type of play amusing for the foibles and mannerisms of its characters. While in exile in France during CROMWELL's time, he became familiar with the works of MOLIÈRE, from which he borrowed the mixed verse and prose form of his *The Comical Revenge; or Love in a Tub* (1664). His most famous play, *The Man of Mode* (1676), satirized the new dandyism in the character of Sir Fopling Flutter.

Euclid (3rd-2nd cent. BC) 'There is no royal road to geometry', said Euclid, Greek mathematician, to PTOLEMY I, who sought an easy way to learn the science. Euclid created the *Elements*, a fundamental geometric treatise, building up a number of theorems deduced from axioms and definitions and including the work of HIPPOCRATES and EUDOXUS. The *Elements*, in 13 books, was translated into Arabic in the 8th century and into Latin in the 11th. The first English version was published in the 18th century. Euclid was widely known as a teacher, and founded a school of mathematics in Alexandria during the reign of Ptolemy.

Eudoxus (408-347 BC) Greek mathematician, astronomer and geographer, known for his theory of proportions, later expounded by EUCLID. He also devised a method for calculating areas, a precursor of the integral calculus method of solving such problems. His star map was long in use, and his method of explaining planetary motion in terms of spheres foreshadowed the epicycles of PTOLEMY. He estimated the Earth's circumference, prepared a world map and wrote a treatise on geography.

Eugene of Savoy (1663-1736) French-born soldier, statesman and diplomat who raised Austria to the rank of a European power. A farsighted statesman, he advocated consolidation of the Hapsburg lands as a basis for imperial power in Germany. He was a patron of Baroque artists and an art collector.

Euler, Leonhard (1707-83) Swiss mathematician, who was the first great systematic expounder of the methods of mathematical analysis. His *Introduction to the Analysis of Infinite Numbers* (1748) was as fundamental to mathematical analysis as was EUCLID's *Elements* to geometry, and he wrote two other major textbooks on infinitesimal calculus. Euler's application of calculus to geometrical problems in a study of curves (1760) was the first successful attempt to combine these two aspects of mathematics. He first treated trigonometrical functions mathematically, and formulated and devised the notation for many other commonly used theorems.

Euripides (484-406 BC) Greek dramatist, one of the three outstanding tragic poets of the ancient Greek theatre. Euripides was more interested than AESCHYLUS and SOPHOCLES in character and the personal predicament, and less bound than they by the archaic rules of the ancient drama. He wrote about 90 plays, of which 17 tragedies and one satyr-play remain. His subjects were tragedies of passion, politics and war. *The Bacchae*, produced after his death, is generally considered his finest play. It shows Euripides at his most mature and depicts irrational emotion taking over from the newer, more precarious human attribute of reason and self-control.

Eusebius Hieronymus see JEROME

Evans, Alice (born 1881) American bacteriologist who, between 1917 and 1926, showed that the bacterium which causes contagious abortion (Bang's disease) in cattle can pass to human beings, particularly via milk, giving them undulant fever (brucellosis). She met considerable opposition from the dairy industry and the medical profession, but through her efforts, the pasteurizing of milk became compulsory in the late 1920s.

Evans, Sir Arthur (1851-1941) English archaeologist, who discovered Europe's oldest civilization. Evans began digging at Knossos in 1899, and excavated a magnificent, labyrinthine palace – arguably that of the legendary King Minos. Evans's finds showed that Crete's hitherto unknown civilization, which he named Minoan, flourished between 2500 and 1400 BC, and was transmitted to Europe by the Cretans.

Evans, Dame Edith (born 1888) British actress, who took the female leads in SHAW's *Heartbreak House* and *The Millionairess* and played most of the leading women's roles in SHAKESPEARE during several seasons at the Old Vic. Her genius for comedy, first praised by critics in DRYDEN's *All for Love* (1922), has shown itself to perfection in Restoration comedies.

Evans, Mary Ann see ELIOT, George

Evans, Oliver (1755-1819) American engineer often called the 'Watt of America'. In 1802, inspired by WATT's steam engine, he built an improved machine capable of operating at higher pressures and, thus, with improved efficiency. Two years later, he adapted it to work a bucket dredger in Pennsylvania harbour.

Evelyn, John (1620-1706) English gentleman and diarist who left a vivid record of the cultivated life of his time. The *Diary* is remarkable for its extent and its individual portraits. Evelyn became Secretary to the Royal Society, and his writings on engraving, architecture, navigation and gardening were popular and influential.

Ewald, Johannes (1743-81) Danish lyric poet and dramatist, who was a precursor of Danish Romanticism. In his work he achieves a remarkable blend of 18th-century rationalism and 19th-century emotionalism. Having studied SHAKESPEARE extensively, in 1770 he wrote *Rolfe Krage*, the first important Danish tragedy, and followed this with *The Death of Balder* (1773), the first blank verse tragedy in Danish. His poems, which range from solemnity to ecstatic lyricism, are considered his greatest works. He also wrote an autobiography.

Eworth, Hans (16th cent.) Dutch painter, whose portraits, which follow HOLBEIN in their precision of detail, are allegorical, e.g. *Juno, Minerva and Venus eclipsed by the Majesty and Beauty of Queen Elizabeth* (1569).

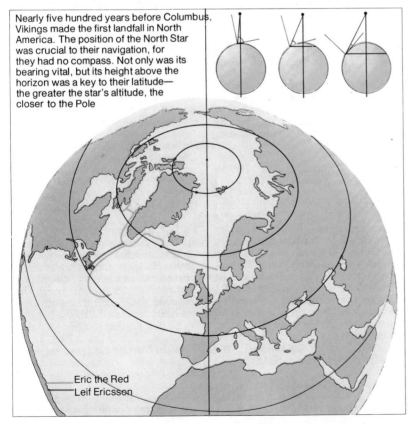

Nearly five hundred years before Columbus, Vikings made the first landfall in North America. The position of the North Star was crucial to their navigation, for they had no compass. Not only was its bearing vital, but its height above the horizon was a key to their latitude—the greater the star's altitude, the closer to the Pole

Eric the Red
Leif Ericsson

Exeter, David, 6th Marquess of, (born 1905) English athlete who won the 400 metres hurdles in the 1928 Olympic Games and was later an administrative figure in world athletics.

Eyck, Jan van (c. 1390-1441) Influential painter of the early Netherlandish school. In 1425 he was recorded as Court Painter to PHILIP THE GOOD, the Duke of Burgundy, for whom he also acted as a diplomat, travelling to Spain and Portugal. His most famous work (part of which has been attributed to his brother Hubert) is the *Adoration of the Lamb*, an altarpiece in St Bavon, Ghent, completed in 1432. It is remarkable for the realism with which van Eyck represented the various elements, the portraits of the donors, the nude Adam and Eve, and the central panel in which the adoration is seen against a detailed landscape, which appears to recede into the distance through its atmospheric perspective. The faithful detail, brilliance of colour and subtle effects of light found in this work and in private commissions, such as the *Arnolfini Marriage* (1434), were made possible by van Eyck's perfection of a fluid oil medium and varnish. A number of small-scale portraits mark the emergence in his work of easel painting as an activity as important as manuscript illustration.

Eyre, Edward John (1815-1901) British colonial Governor in Australia who explored much of southern Australia. He travelled widely in New South Wales, South Australia and Western Australia, and led an expedition (1840-1) to establish a land route along the barren coast of the Great Australian Bight.

Eysenck, Hans (born 1916) German-born British psychologist known for his insistence on a rigorously scientific approach to psychology and for his study of the human personality. His main concern in personality research has been to submit psychological data to experimental and quantitative assessment.

Ezekiel (c. 6th cent. BC) One of the major Hebrew prophets of the Old Testament. He believed that God ruled the destinies of all nations. While stressing individual moral responsibility, like JEREMIAH, he also described the worship of an ideal religious state centred on the reconstructed Temple. This vision of divine glory became the basis of a branch of Jewish mysticism. Scholars are divided about the date of the Book of Ezekiel, which is divided into two main parts, dealing first with the fall of Jerusalem and then with the return of the exiles from Babylon.

F

Fabius Maximus (3rd cent. BC) Roman general and consul, whose military delaying tactics and avoidance of decisive battles earned him the name 'Cunctator' (the Delayer) and inspired the adjective Fabian to describe any strategy based on attrition. Made dictator (217 BC) during the Second Punic War, he avoided pitched battles and instead harassed Italy's Carthaginian invaders by hit-and-run attacks on their supplies.

Fabre, Jean (1823-1915) French entomologist who meticulously observed insect behaviour, comparing it with that of humans. He was puzzled to see insects of apparently little intelligence and fixed habits using extremely complex behaviour patterns, for instance a wasp, paralysing its prey by stinging it in nerve centres, to keep it alive and at its most nutritious for the young to eat.

Fabricius, Hieronymus (1537-1619) Italian physician whose discoveries concerning the valves in veins were published in *On the little Doors of the Veins*. During a dissection demonstration, he showed the valves in limb veins to his pupil, HARVEY. It was this that aroused Harvey's interest in blood circulation, though Fabricius never understood the true function of valves.

Fahrenheit, Gabriel Daniel (1686-1736) German-Dutch physicist who was the first to use mercury in a thermometer. Fahrenheit's thermometer measured a wider range of temperatures more accurately than hitherto, encouraging him to devise the scale that took his name. The Fahrenheit scale places the freezing point of water at 32° and boiling point at 212°.

Fairfax, Thomas, 3rd Baron Fairfax of Cameron (1612-71) Scottish peer, Commander-in-Chief of the victorious Parliamentarian army in the English Civil War. He turned defeat into victory as a cavalry officer at Marston Moor (1644) then, as Captain-General of the New Model Army, welded it into the tool that won for the Parliamentarians the decisive Battle of Naseby (1645). Fairfax commanded CROMWELL's Commonwealth army until 1650 when he resigned because he opposed the invasion of Scotland. He opposed CHARLES I's execution and eased the way for the return of CHARLES II.

Faisal I (1885-1933) Comrade-in-arms of T. E. LAWRENCE and first King of Iraq. Accompanied by Lawrence, he advanced to Akaba in 1917 with his forces, which eventually formed the right wing of ALLENBY's army. Later that year he led his troops into Jerusalem and Damascus. He was acclaimed King of Syria by a national congress (1920), but was deposed by the French. After a plebiscite, he was placed on the throne of Iraq by Britain, who held the League of Nations mandate for that country. By steering a diplomatic course in a difficult period, he guided Iraq to independence and membership of the League of Nations (1932).

Faisal II (1935-58) King of Iraq, who was murdered in a military *coup d'état*. He succeeded to the throne at the age of four on the death of his father, Ghazi, and gained full power in 1953. He supported NASSER in the Suez crisis of 1956. Sharing the aims of his cousin, HUSSEIN of Jordan, in February 1958, he agreed to a federation of Iraq and Jordan in opposition to the United Arab Republic of Egypt and Syria. In July 1958, however, General Abdul Karim al-Kassem led a military revolt and Faisal and his entire household were assassinated.

Falconnet, Etienne-Maurice (1716-91) French sculptor and director (1757-66) of the Sèvres porcelain factory; at the height of his middle period, when he created works such as *Bathing Nymph* (1757), which embody in marble the essence of French Rococo. Invited to Russia by CATHERINE II, Falconnet worked there from 1766-9 on a Baroque-style equestrian statue of PETER THE GREAT. The statue is notable for its vigour and the technical brilliance of the rearing horse, and appears to have developed from an idea by BERNINI in a terracotta sketch of LOUIS XIV on horseback. It was later borrowed by DAVID for his portrait of NAPOLEON.

Falkner, John Meade (1858-1932) English historian and novelist who wrote romances in the manner of Robert Louis STEVENSON. The best known are *The Lost Stradivarius* (1895) and *Moonfleet* (1898).

Falla, Manuel de (1876-1946) Spanish composer who gave his country's music its international status. He spent some time in Paris, where he was a friend of DEBUSSY and worked for DIAGHILEV. Andalusian folk song was Falla's main influence, but he incorporated it into a personal style full of rhythm and colour in such works as the ballets *The Three-Cornered Hat* and *Love, the Magician*, and, for piano and orchestra, *Nights in the Gardens of Spain*.

Fallopius, Gabriel (1523-62) Italian anatomist who discovered the

Fallopian tubes (leading from the ovaries to the uterus). He also discovered and named many other parts of the human body, publishing his findings in *Observationes anatomicae* (1561) and his posthumous *Opera* (1584).

Faludy, György (born 1913) Outstanding Hungarian poet, whose lyricism and deep sensitivity are best seen in *A Keepsake Book of Red Bysantium* (1961).

Fangio, Juan-Manuel (born 1911) Argentinian racing driver, five times World Champion (1951, 1954-7). After winning 24 Grand Prix races, he retired in 1958.

Fantin-Latour, Henri (1836-1904) French painter, best known for his flower pieces and his portrait of the Impressionists, *Homage to Manet* (1870).

Faraday, Michael (1791-1867) English physicist, whose discovery of electro-magnetic induction revealed the principle of the electric motor and dynamo, the transformer and the telephone. He was the first to demonstrate continuous motion of a current-carrying wire in a magnetic field (a primitive motor) and the continuous production of current from a conductor moving in a field (a primitive dynamo). He developed the laws of electrolysis. His work on dielectric constants was independent of, though later than, the then unpublished work of CAVENDISH. He found that magnetic fields cause a rotation of the plane of polarized light, and was the first to investigate the behaviour of diamagnetic substances. Faraday knew little mathematics and therefore conceived the theoretical explanations of his discoveries in terms of graphic notions of lines of force. MAXWELL later developed a full mathematical treatment of electrodynamic theory.

Fargo, William George (1818-81) American co-founder of the West's most famous stagecoach company. Carrying gold, silver, mail, freight and passengers, the Wells Fargo stagecoaches became the quickest means of travel across the newly settled heartlands of the continent.

Farigoule, Louis see ROMAINS, Jules

Farinelli (Carlo Broschi) (1705-82) The most renowned of the Italian castrati singers. The male castrato voice was created by operating on the genitals during boyhood.

Farnese, Alexander, Duke of Parma (1545-92) Spanish soldier who recovered the southern provinces of the Netherlands for his uncle

With a battery, iron ring and galvanometer, Faraday made the first electrical transformer

PHILIP II. Alexander was the most distinguished member of a family which ruled the Parma duchies from 1545 to 1731. As a young man he joined Philip's half-brother, Don JOHN OF AUSTRIA, serving with him in Italy and Belgium (1571-8). As Regent of the Netherlands (1578), by military skill and astute diplomacy Farnese regained Ypres, Bruges, Ghent and Antwerp and their hinterlands by 1585. His later operations in the Netherlands were hindered by Spanish preparations for the Armada and intervention in France against HENRY IV.

Farouk I (1920-65) King of Egypt who succeeded his father Fuad I in 1936. His early years as king were marked by extensive agrarian reform schemes and projects for economic development. However, his involvement in the unsuccessful war with Israel in 1948, and his increasingly hedonistic and flamboyant way of life resulted in much popular dissatis-

faction, particularly on the part of the nationalist WAFD Party. In 1952 he was deposed by General Neguib, who was himself deposed two years later by Colonel NASSER. Farouk died in exile in Italy.

Farquhar, George (1678-1707) Anglo-Irish dramatist, who was the successor to CONGREVE as the leading dramatist of the period. His plays are less bawdy than most Restoration comedies. *The Recruiting Officer* (1706) and *The Beaux Stratagem* (1707) are the only ones that have been revived.

Farr, William (1807-83) English doctor who was a pioneer of preventive social medicine. He was one of the first men to realize that statistics, properly applied, could be an important weapon in the fight against disease. He was a leader in the 19th-century fight to improve public health and sanitary conditions.

Farrer, Reginald J. (1880-1920) British author and plant collector whose main source was in the Himalayas. He introduced many now well-known garden plants, including *Gentiana farreri* and *Vibernum farreri*, and described his experiences in his two works *On the Eaves of the World* and *The Rainbow Bridge*.

Faulkner, William (1897-1962) American novelist who produced a series of impressionistic, sometimes violent and brutal stories of life in the southern States of America. His later novels constituted a saga of the degeneration of family and community in the Deep South, called by the author Yoknapatawpha County. His main works were *The Sound and the Fury* (1929), *As I Lay Dying* (1930), *Sanctuary* (1931) and *Light in August* (1932).

Fauré, Gabriel (1845-1924) French composer, organist and the most influential teacher of French music of his generation. RAVEL was among his pupils. Fauré's own style was one of delicate elegance. His best-known

Once an Argentinian bus driver, Fangio became a star of the racing circuits

works are his *Requiem,* his *Pavane* for chorus ad lib. and orchestra, and the children's *Dolly Suite* for piano duet.

Fawcett, Percy Harrison (1867-c.1925) British explorer of the Matto Grosso region of South America. He vanished with his son, Zack, during an intended two-year search for the lost city of Atlantis in the Brazilian jungle. Search parties found no certain trace of father or son and it is thought they were killed by Indians.

Fawkes, Guy (1570-1606) English Roman Catholic conspirator in the unsuccessful Gunpowder Plot to blow up the House of Lords (1605) as a protest against the treatment of Catholics. This event is commemorated in England by the burning of effigies called 'guys' on November 5.

Fechner, Gustav (1801-87) German pioneer in psychophysics, who in 1860 formulated the law (first postulated by WEBER) that the intensity of a sensation is proportional to the logarithm of the stimulus. However, he thought more of his philosophic system, which attributed souls to all aspects of nature, including the plants and stars.

Fedin, Konstantin Aleksandrovich (born 1892) Russian author whose *Cities and Years* (1924) revived the pre-Revolutionary Russian realistic novel. The theme of the book, the problems of the intellectual in time of revolution, was continued in *The Brothers* (1928), in which Fedin explored the contrast between the pre- and post-Revolutionary Russias. Since 1945 he has produced two parts of an historical trilogy: *Early Joys* (1945), *No Ordinary Summer* (1950) and Part I of the final part, 'The Woodpile' (1962).

Félix, Elisa see RACHEL

Fellini, Federico (born 1920) Italian film director whose works often reflect his personal obsessions, either the fantasy world of the individual, as in 8½ (1963) or the degeneration of society as in *La Dolce Vita* (1959) and *Fellini Satyricon* (1969). His early films, sad comedies like *La Strada* (starring his wife Giulietta Masina), showed Fellini's concern with the values of modern society and his fascination with clowns and circuses which was to run through all his films, notably *I Clowns* (1970).

Fénelon, François de Salignac de la Mothe (1651-1715) French novelist and theologian. A priest, he became tutor to LOUIS XIV's grandson the Duc de Bourgogne, for whose instruction he wrote *Télémaque,* a tale of adventure which adds a chapter to

HOMER's *Odyssey.* In 1695 he was appointed Archbishop of Cambrai, but had become attracted to Quietism, a doctrine which holds that the way to Christian perfection is the way of inner contemplation. Fénelon was relegated to his diocese when Quietism was declared a heresy by the Pope. His other important publications included the *Traité de l'éducation des filles* (1687) and *Dialogues des morts* (1712).

Ferdinand I (1503-64) Austrian Holy Roman Emperor (1556-64) of the Hapsburg dynasty who succeeded his brother CHARLES V. Ferdinand claimed Bohemia and Hungary when his brother-in-law LOUIS II of Bohemia and Hungary was killed by the Turks at the battle of Mohács (1526). Ferdinand was elected King and established hereditary Austrian-Hapsburg rule in Bohemia and Hungary.

Ferdinand II (1578-1637) Holy Roman Emperor (1619-37), defender of Catholic and Hapsburg interests during the 30 Years' War, who was the true founder of the Austrian empire centred in Vienna. An ardent Catholic, with absolutist political ideas, Ferdinand's attempt as King to enforce his views in Bohemia (1617-18) led to rebellion and the temporary loss of the Bohemian crown. After his election as Emperor, Ferdinand recovered Bohemia (1620), which henceforth was a hereditary Hapsburg dominion. By the Edict of Restitution (1629), he tried to restore to the Catholic Church all lands lost since 1552, but was forced to abandon the Edict in 1635. Ferdinand finally crushed Protestantism in Austria, but was more tolerant in Hungary, where the Turkish threat impelled preferential treatment for the people. He was the last Emperor to attempt the unification of central Europe.

Ferdinand V of Castile (II of Aragon, III of Naples) **(1452-1516)** King whose marriage (1469) to Isabella of Castile united Spain. Together, the 'Catholic Kings' warred against Granada, expelling the Moors, restored order to the country and encouraged such notable voyages of discovery as that of COLUMBUS.

Ferdinand of Brunswick (1721-92) German soldier, whose masterful strategy in the Seven Years' War (1756-63) tied down large French forces in Germany, thus aiding Britain in her colonial conquests in North America and India. Brother-in-law and close friend of FREDERICK II, Ferdinand made his military reputation between 1757 and 1759, when he restored the shattered allied forces

and defeated the French at Crefeld (1758) and Minden (1759), thus relieving the pressure on Frederick in the East.

Fermat, Pierre de (1601-65) French mathematician, who contributed to number theory and partly anticipated both the analytical geometry of DESCARTES and the differential calculus of LEIBNIZ.

Fermi, Enrico (1901-54) Italian-American physicist who built the first nuclear reactor. In the early 1930s he established the theory of beta decay and discovered the statistical laws obeyed by such elementary particles as the electron. In 1938, during the rise of Fascism, he left Italy for the United States, where he began to search for a way of producing a controlled, self-sustaining nuclear fission reaction – the key to a new and virtually inexhaustible source of energy. Eventually, in 1942, in a squash court at Chicago University, Fermi's nuclear reactor was built and tested. Its success heralded the beginning of the age of nuclear power. A year later Fermi was in Los Alamos, New Mexico, helping to develop the atomic bomb.

Fernandes, Alvaro (15th cent.) Portuguese sea captain serving HENRY THE NAVIGATOR. His longest recorded voyage (c. 1446) reached about as far south as modern Freetown, Sierra Leone.

Ferrari, Lodovico (1522-65) Italian mathematician whose most famous discovery was the solution (named after him) of an equation of the fourth degree, published by CARDANO in *Ars Magna* (1545).

Ferrier, Kathleen (1912-53) English contralto, the beauty of whose voice brought her international fame before her early death from cancer. BRITTEN, in particular, wrote music for her – including the role of Lucretia in *The Rape of Lucretia.*

Fet, Afanasii Afanasyevich (1820-92) Russian lyric poet, friend of TOLSTOY and TURGENEV, whose most important volume of poetry was *Evening Fires* (1883).

Feuerbach, Ludwig (1804-72) German philosopher who gave an anthropological account of the idea of God – 'theology is anthropology'. He began from a Christian viewpoint, passed through a Hegelian phase, arriving at a position of humanistic materialism, experience which he described thus: 'God was my first thought, reason my second, man my first and last.' Feuerbach's ideas influenced participants in the conflict between Church and State in Germany and the thought of MARX, ENGELS and others.

Feydeau, Georges (1862-1921) French dramatist and past-master of the bedroom farce. His two best-known plays are *Le Dindon* (1889) and *Occupe-toi d'Amélie* (1908). His economy of style and theatrical expertise have led to some of his plays being included in the *Comédie Francaise* repertoire.

Feynman, Richard Phillips (born 1918) American physicist who developed the quantum approach to electromagnetic theory. In 1948, working with Julian Schweinger, he developed a means of avoiding the mathematical ambiguities in the original quantum electrodynamics of HEISENBERG and DIRAC, and produced a far more powerful theory than theirs.

Fibonacci, Leonardo (c. 1170-1230) Italian mathematician who introduced Arabic numerals into Europe where they soon replaced the Roman system, particularly among merchants and traders. Fibonacci, who was among the foremost mathematical scholars of Medieval Europe, was a champion in the mathematical tournaments which were popular at that time. He was the author of a number of books on arithmetic and geometry.

Fichte, Johann Gottlieb (1762-1814) German philosopher and exponent of ethical idealism who used a dialectic process later adopted by HEGEL, advocating a philosophical system in which the ego is free, within the constraints of its own moral law.

Ficino, Marsilio (1433-99) Italian philosopher and classical scholar whose translation into Latin of the works of PLATO and other Greek writers greatly influenced later scholarship, his texts remaining authoritative for three centuries. His own speculations are strongly Neo-Platonic, and he saw Platonism as compatible with Christianity.

Field, Cyrus West (1819-92) American businessman, who was responsible for initiating, organizing and financing the laying of the first Atlantic telegraph cable, opened in 1858.

Field, John (1782-1837) Irish composer and virtuoso pianist who invented the 'nocturne', a one-movement piece, usually for piano, evoking a night reverie. Field, a former pupil of CLEMENTI's, also wrote seven piano concertos. He settled in Russia in 1803 and died there, having toured Europe from his base, St Petersburg.

Field, Marshall (1834-1906) American merchant whose Chicago-based establishment, Marshall Field & Co., was the first department store and, for 25 years, the world's largest. High-volume sales were the key to Field's low prices and varied selection.

Fielding, Henry (1707-54) English author and magistrate who helped to establish the novel as a literary form in England. His main work, *Tom Jones* (1749), is a human comedy, influenced in its form by CERVANTES, in which energy, spirit and honesty are celebrated as the finest human virtues. It breaks from the tradition of the novel of conventional morals, particularly from the work of RICHARDSON, which Fielding satirized in *Joseph Andrews* (1742). In the 1730s Fielding supported himself and his wife by writing burlesques and comedies for the stage. He became a barrister in 1740, and was made Justice of the Peace for Westminster in 1748. He vigorously suppressed hooligans and petty criminals, whose world he depicted in his satire *Jonathan Wild the Great* (1743).

Fielding, Sir John (1721-80) English London-based police magistrate and social reformer. His work as a pioneer of police methods included attempts to educate the public to co-operate in the fight against crime, persuading the government to contribute to the expenses of his so-called Bow Street Runners and the founding of *Hue and Cry*, later renamed *The Police Gazette*. He was the half-brother of novelist Henry FIELDING.

Fields, W. C. (1879-1946) American screen comedian whose career began as a juggler in vaudeville. His screen character was lazy, dishonest and drunken, given to cheating and kicking children and lovable pets, an hilarious antidote to the contemporary sentimentality. Among his best known films are (with Mae WEST) *My Little Chickadee* (1940) and *Never Give a Sucker an Even Break* (1941).

Figg, James (c. 1695-1734) English prizefighter, swordsman and wrestler who, in 1719, became the first bare-fisted boxing champion of England. He opened a boxing academy which was called Figg's Amphitheatre.

Figgins, Jesse Dade (1867-1944) American palaeontologist whose discovery of flint tools near Folsom, New Mexico, established that man lived in America as far back as 10,000 years ago. Until the discovery of the so-called Folsom points, it was believed that man had lived in America for only a few thousand years before the birth of CHRIST.

Fillmore, Millard (1800-74) Thirteenth President of the United States (1850-3), and supporter of the slavery compromise of 1850. As a congressman, Fillmore gained something of an anti-slavery reputation by supporting the prohibition of the domestic slave trade and opposing the annexation of Texas as a slave state. But on becoming President after TAYLOR's death (July 1850), his signing of the Compromise of 1850, particularly the Fugitive Slave Law, made him unpopular in the North.

Finch, Heneage see NOTTINGHAM, First Earl of

Finsen, Niels (1860-1904) Danish physician, who won the Nobel Prize for Medicine (1903) for advances in the treatment of skin diseases. He published a paper on the treatment of smallpox pustules with red light (1893), and developed the treatment of lupus with ultra-violet light.

Firbank, Ronald (1886-1926) English novelist whose books were sophisticated entertainments for men of culture. His fantasies contain little plot, but Firbank was a master of comic dialogue and inconsequential incident. His novels include *Vainglory* (1915), *Valmouth* (1919), and *Concerning the Eccentricities of Cardinal Pirelli* (1926).

Firdausi (c. 930-c. 1020) Persian poet, author of the great epic masterpiece *The Book of the Kings*, which tells the history of the heroes of Iran from the early legends to the fall of the Sassanids, with long accounts of famous battles and warriors. Its stories included that of Sohrab and Rustam, later retold by Matthew ARNOLD.

'My little passion fruit, my little flower of the desert': comedian W. C. Fields and sultry comedienne Mae West

Fischer, Bobby (born 1943) American chess player who captured the world championship in 1972 by defeating Boris Spassky of the Soviet Union. Fischer won his first US championship at the age of 14.

Fischer, Emil (1852-1919) German organic chemist who pioneered the study of naturally occurring organic substances. His work founded the complex field of protein and carbohydrate chemistry.

Fischer, Johann Michael (c. 1692-1766) German Rococo architect, who was one of the masters of that style, although perhaps less talented than ZIMMERMANN or NEUMANN. He often used a central plan for his buildings and his use of lighting verges on theatrical. Major examples of his prolific output (23 monasteries and 32 churches) include the abbey churches of Ottobeuren, Zwiefalten and Alto-munster, as well as churches in Munich (St Anne) and Rott-am-Inn.

Fischer Von Erlach, Johann (1656-1723) Austrian architect, who with HILDEBRANDT was a leader of the Austrian Baroque. The Karlskirche in Vienna (begun in 1716), with its mighty dome, is his masterpiece. He studied in Rome before settling in Vienna, where he was appointed Court Architect. His Italian experiences, together with his training as a stucco-worker and sculptor, led to his developing a vigorously plastic style.

Fisher, John Arbuthnot, 1st Baron Fisher of Kilverstone (1841-1920) British admiral who was largely responsible for preparing the Royal Navy for efficient action in the First World War. He promoted the use of torpedoes, revolutionized training and tactics, and insisted on outbuilding the Germans in 'Dreadnought' class battleships. His forthright views made him many enemies, and in 1910 he retired after a dispute with the Commander-in-Chief, Channel Fleet. CHURCHILL, as First Lord of the Admiralty (1914), recalled him as his First Sea Lord, but Fisher would not tolerate Churchill's interference with his dispositions and resigned in 1915.

FitzGerald, Edward (1809-83) English translator and poet whose famous version of the *Rubáiyát of Omar Khayyám* is a recreation of the Persian original. The combination of melancholy and sensuality, and the rhythms of an original four-line stanza, have given the poem an enduring popularity.

Fitzgerald, F. Scott (1896-1940) American novelist and story writer

Ian Fleming and his creation, the masculine, amoral '007', James Bond

whose work portrays 'the Jazz Age', the time of social and economic change after the First World War. His early works, including *This Side of Paradise* (1920) and *The Beautiful and the Damned* (1922), are reflections of his generation's yearning for a sophisticated, hedonistic life. *The Great Gatsby* (1925) examines the division between wealth and youth, between possessions and ideals, written in meticulous prose.

Fitzherbert, Sir Anthony (1470-1538) English judge who helped to establish the importance of case law. His *Great Abridgement* (1516) summarized the most important medieval legal judgments suitable as precedents for future decisions.

Fizeau, Armand Hippolyte (1819-96) French physicist, who devised the first terrestrial method of measuring the velocity of light. In 1849 he set up a powerful lamp on a hilltop and a large mirror on another, five miles away, measuring the time it took a flash of light to make the round trip from lamp to mirror and back, by means of a toothed wheel which interrupted the beam.

Flaccus, Quintus Horatius see HORACE

Flagstad, Kirsten (1895-1962) Norwegian soprano, the leading international interpreter of WAGNER's heroines for two decades between the 1930s and the 1950s. She was probably among the finest Isoldes and Brünhildes there have been. She also excelled as a *lieder* recitalist.

Flaherty, Robert (1884-1951) American pioneer of documentary film whose early career as an explorer led him to his first film, the famous study of the Eskimo, *Nanook of the North* (1920). His later film, *Man of Aran* (1937), a study of the fishing community on the tiny island off the Irish coast, influenced the British documentary makers of the 1930s. Other films by Flaherty include *Elephant Boy* (1937) and *Louisiana Story* (1948).

Flamsteed, John (1646-1719) English astronomer, the first Astronomer Royal, and compiler of a star catalogue. Flamsteed's early observations were published in the Philosophical Transactions of the Royal Society, and gained him the attention of the scientific community. The influence of his colleague, Sir Jonas Moore, with CHARLES II, secured for Flamsteed the appointment of Astronomer Royal in 1675, and he was put in charge of the newly established observatory at Greenwich. Working alone, and paying for much of the necessary equipment himself, he recorded over 20,000 stellar observations.

Flaubert, Gustave (1821-80) French novelist, whose works have become masterpieces of world literature. His first novel, *Madame Bovary* (1857), for which he and his publisher were tried (for offences against public morals) and acquitted, is the story of a bored provincial woman's unfulfilled dreams of romantic love, her degradation and ultimate self-destruction. His painstaking documentation, shrewd observation and realist style put Flaubert in the front rank of European novelists. His other important novels were *Salammbô* (1862), an exotic and barbaric tale of ancient Carthage, and *A Sentimental Education* (1869), which explored a young romantic's disillusionment with contemporary Paris, partially reflecting the author's own life. However, it is in the *Trois Contes* (1877) that Flaubert's art is revealed in its purest form.

Flavius Anicius Justinianus see JUSTINIAN

Flavius, Claudius Julianus see JULIAN

Flecker, James Elroy (1884-1915)
English poet and dramatist who tried
to combine classical lucidity with a
strain of exoticism. His famous poem,
'The Golden Journey to Samarkand'
(1913), is sensuously evocative of the
romantic east, as is his best-known
play *Hassan*, first staged in 1922 with
music by DELIUS.

Flémalle, Master of (c. 1378-1444)
The most important Flemish artist
before VAN EYCK. His chief work is
probably the *Mérode Altar* (*c*. 1425),
an example of the early use of oil paint
instead of tempera. The various
domestic objects in the central panel
of this altarpiece, the Annunciation,
have a specific religious symbolism
and are painted with realistic detail.

**Fleming, Sir Alexander (1881-
1955)** Scottish bacteriologist, who, in
1928, discovered the bacteria-killing
properties of the fungus *Penicillium
notatum*. His discovery was quite accidental. Some *Penicillium* fungus had
fallen by chance into a preparation of
bacteria that Fleming was about to
throw away; he noticed that no bacteria had grown in the vicinity of the
fungus. He recognized the importance of this but did not isolate the
antibiotic substance. In 1945 Fleming
shared a Nobel Prize with Florey
and CHAIN who, during the Second
World War, isolated the antibiotic
and called it penicillin.

Fleming, Ian Lancaster (1908-64)
English writer, the creator of James
Bond. After service as a Naval Intelligence Officer, he began his series
of novels in 1953 with *Casino Royale*,
the debut of his super-spy hero who
featured in a number of works,
several of which have been made into
highly successful films.

**Fleming, Sir John Ambrose
(1849-1945)** English electrical engineer who developed the first electronic
valve after EDISON's discovery (1883)
that electricity will flow between a
heated filament and a metal wire
sealed in an evacuated glass bulb.
Fleming investigated the phenomenon and quickly discovered that the
heated filament was giving off electrons, an effect soon to be known as
thermionic emission. By 1904 he had
utilized it to produce a simple diode or
rectifying valve, to convert alternating current to direct current.

Fletcher, John (1579-1625) English
dramatist, famous for his collaboration with Francis BEAUMONT. Of the
50 plays attributed to their partnership, about 40 are believed to have
been written entirely by Fletcher.
The three most important products
of their collaboration were *Philaster*
(1610), *A Maid's Tragedy* and *A King*

and No King (1611). These were
written in the new romantic tragi-
comedy form perfected by SHAKE-
SPEARE, with whom Fletcher is
thought to have collaborated in the
writing of *Henry VIII*. Fletcher's
best-known plays were a pastoral,
The Faithful Shepherdess, and a farcical comedy, *The Wild Goose Chase*.

Floyer, Sir John (1649-1734) British physician who invented a watch
which ran for one minute, to measure
the pulse rate.

Foch, Ferdinand (1851-1929) Marshal of France, under whose leadership the Allies achieved victory in the
First World War. Foch joined the
army in 1870 and became the General
Staff's artillery specialist. He proved
to be a considerable military tactician
in the early battles of the war (Marne,
1914). In May 1917, he became Chief
of Staff to the French commander,
PÉTAIN, but it was soon clear that he
was abler than his chief, and as a
result, in April 1918, he was appointed
Supreme Commander on the Western Front. The Allied armies took the
offensive in July and by November he
had driven the Germans to seek an
armistice. Foch retired after participating in the Paris Peace Conference
(1919).

Fogazzaro, Antonio (1842-1911)
Italian novelist, most famous for his
cycle of four novels, *Little World of
the Past* (1896), set in Austrian Lombardy in the 1850s, which portray
the tension between reason and emotion in the religious and political context of 19th-century Italy.

Fokine, Michel (1880-1942) Russian-born dancer and choreographer,
whose integration of dancing, drama,
music and décor revolutionized ballet
in the early 1900s.

**Fokker, Anthony Herman (1890-
1939)** Pioneer Dutch, later naturalized American, aircraft designer and
industrialist. After building his first
aeroplane in 1911, and receiving little
support, he left Holland for Germany,
where he received financial backing.
Many fighter planes of his design
took part in the First World War.
Fokker perfected an interrupter
mechanism that allowed a machine
gun to fire through whirling propeller
blades without damaging them. After
1918, he established factories first in
Amsterdam and then in the United
States, concentrating on making
commercial aircraft.

Fonseca, Juan Rodriguez de see
RODRIGUEZ DE FONSECA

Fontane, Theodor (1819-98) German novelist, author of *Before the*

Greatest of France's First World War
generals, Marshal Foch led the Allied
Armies to victory in 1918

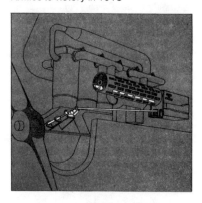
Air combat was revolutionized by
Fokker's device, enabling a machine-gun
to fire through a propeller

Storm (1878), an historical novel
about the Napoleonic age. A master
of realistic fiction, he wrote war
books, travel books and a volume of
lyrics in addition to his historical
novels, and many ballads from
English, Scottish and Prussian
sources. After the success of his first
novel, written at the age of 56, he
wrote a series of novels of contemporary life, notably *Trials and Tribulations* (1888) and *Effi Briest* (1895).

**Fontenelle, Bernard Le Bovier de
(1657-1757)** French philosopher and
writer, who was the first to present
scientific knowledge in literary form.
His *Entretiens sur la pluralité des
mondes* (1686), an elegant, religiously
sceptical 'conversation' on astronomy, the possibility of life on other
planets, and the relative smallness of
man and his world, did more to
awaken popular interest in astronomy
and to secure fashionable acceptance
of COPERNICUS's theories than any
other work.

Fonteyn, Dame Margot (born 1919) English ballerina whose performance as *The Sleeping Beauty*, when the Royal Ballet first performed in New York in 1948, established the pre-eminence of the company and her own international standing. Dame Margot helped to popularize ballet in Britain by her dancing with Robert Helpmann during the 1940s, and in the 1960s established a famous partnership with Rudolf NUREYEV. Her talent for controlled, expressive dancing won her recognition as prima ballerina of the Royal Ballet, and her world tours confirmed the quality of British ballet to international audiences.

Forbes-Robertson, Sir Johnston (1853-1937) British actor-manager, whose Hamlet was considered his finest performance. His other great roles were Romeo, which he played to Mrs Patrick CAMPBELL's Juliet (1895), and the Stranger in Jerome K. JEROME's *The Passing of the Third Floor Back*.

Ford, Ford Madox (1873-1939) English critic, novelist and editor, an influential figure in the London literary world, and an acute observer of his contemporaries. He founded *The*

English Review and *The Transatlantic Review*. As a novelist he is famous for a tetralogy, *Parade's End* (1924-8), about Western civilization approaching the First World War.

Ford, Henry (1863-1947) American industrialist and automobile manufacturer who invented and developed mass-production assembly-line techniques to provide cheap and reliable 'motoring for the millions', and pioneered high-wage, high-output labour utilization. The vehicle on which the fortunes of the Ford Motor company were built was the 'Model T', introduced in 1909 and produced continuously until 1927, by which time more than 15 million had been made. With his son, Edsel, he engaged in tractor manufacture (from 1915) and from 1924 steadily expanded the manufacture overseas of his vehicles. In 1940, he set up the Willow Run bomber aircraft plant which became vital to the Allied war effort.

Ford, John (c. 1586-1639) English dramatist, who wrote *'Tis Pity She's a Whore*, the only play by which he is widely known. This tragedy of a brother's incestuous passion for his sister was staged by Visconti in a spectacular revival in Paris (1961). Ford also wrote another violent tragedy, *The Broken Heart*, and an historical drama, *Perkin Warbeck*. *The Witch of Edmonton* was written by Ford in collaboration with Dekker and Rowley (1621).

Ford, John (1895-1973) British film director, noted chiefly for his Westerns which are marked by his involvement with the legend of the pioneering West. His films include the classic *Stagecoach* (1939), and two non-Westerns for which he received Academy Awards, *The Informer* (1935) and *The Grapes of Wrath* (1940).

Forrest, George (1873-1932) British explorer and plant collector who introduced into western horticulture hundreds of Chinese and Tibetan plants, including more than 300 species of rhododendron.

Forster, Edward Morgan (1879-1970) English novelist whose books explore human relationships with delicacy and intelligence, upholding the individual creative imagination as the most important quality of humanity. *Howard's End* (1910) examines with fine irony the limitations of the English sensibility and heart. *A Passage to India* (1924) is an account of the social, moral and political difficulties of British rule in India.

Forster, Georg (1754-94) German explorer, scientist, writer and politician who pioneered the scientific travel book. He emigrated to England in 1766, and accompanied his clergyman-scientist father Johann Reinhold Forster on COOK's second world voyage (1772). Both recorded their experiences, and Georg's *A Voyage Round the World* (1777), brilliantly combined science with good writing, setting a new fashion in travel books and influenced leading German writers and scientists from GOETHE to HUMBOLDT.

Fortescue, Sir John (c. 1394-1476) English judge, who wrote the first law book for laymen, *In Praise of the Laws of England*. In it he gave support to law based on cases decided by the English courts, rather than on canon or Roman law. It took the form of a dialogue between Fortescue and the exiled Prince Edward, son of Henry VI, and was a comparative study of English and French government, containing the earliest account of the Inns of Court and the legal profession. He was Chief Justice of the Court of King's Bench (1442-61).

Fortune, Robert (1813-80) British plant collector who smuggled tea plants out of China for the East India Co. to found the Indian tea industry. He first went to China as a plant collector for the Horticultural Society (1843-6) and sent back hundreds of new plants, including forsythia, Japanese anemone, winter-flowering jasmine, weigela and many rhododendrons, azaleas, peonies and chrysanthemums.

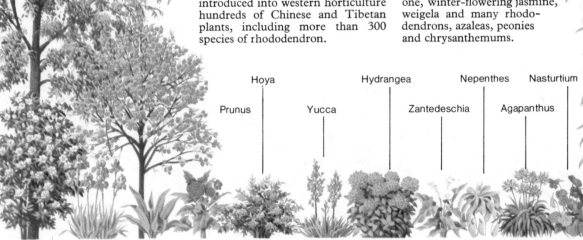

Gingko bileba

Hoya

Prunus

Yucca

Hydrangea

Zantedeschia

Nepenthes

Agapanthus

Nasturtium

Camellia   Iris   Begonia

Foscolo, Ugo (1778-1827) Italian novelist, critic and poet, whose sonnets were considered the best in Italian since those of TASSO. His poem 'The Tombs' (1807) expresses many of his compatriots' national aspirations, while the theme of his incomplete poem 'The Graces' is the civilizing effect of beauty and art on society. As a young man, Foscolo had revolutionary ideas, and admired NAPOLEON. The Treaty of Campoformio, which ceded Venice to Austria, disillusioned him and he went into exile where his writings voiced his despair.

Foster, Stephen Collins (1826-64) American writer of now traditional songs such as *Swannee River, My Old Kentucky Home* and *Camptown Races*, which were based mainly on the life of the negro in the southern United States. Virtually self-taught, Foster wrote more than 175 songs before his early death from alcoholism. His drawing-room ballads include *Jeannie with the Light Brown Hair*.

Foucault, Léon (1819-68) French physicist known for his researches on light and on precessional motion and who determined the velocity of light in various media. Suspending a swinging pendulum from the dome of a church, he found that the plane in which the pendulum swings twists gradually round in a clockwise direction. This proves that the Earth must turn in the opposite direction. He also invented the gyroscope (1852) and the Foucault prism (1857).

Fouché, Joseph (1763-1820) French revolutionary politician and chief of a secret political police and intelligence system. Though at first a supporter of ROBESPIERRE (1792-3) and the Terror, he changed sides and helped to bring down his master (1794) when Robespierre tried to establish his 'Cult of the Supreme Being'. As Minister of Police (1799) under the Directory, Fouché proved himself so useful that NAPOLEON retained him, with intermissions, in the same office. He survived the Restoration, maintaining contacts with METTERNICH and LOUIS XVIII, and became ambassador in Dresden.

Fouquet, Jean (c. 1420-c. 1481) French painter, whose self-portrait is the first work of its kind that is not part of a larger picture. His most characteristic works, such as the portrait of *Estienne Chevalier with St Stephen* (c. 1450), combine Flemish realism in the depiction of surfaces with an Italian preoccupation with classical architecture and the weight and solidity of the human figure.

Fourier, Jean Baptiste (1768-1830) French mathematician and physicist, best known for the Fourier Series, by which complex functions can be represented in terms of certain trigonometrical series. His most important work is *Analytical Theory of Heat* (1822), a mathematical study of heat transfer in which he developed the theory of the Fourier Series.

Fourneyron, Benoît (1802-67) French engineer, who in 1827 devised the first water-wheel turbine. It was more powerful than the water-wheel, from which it also differed in that the water under pressure flowed from the hub towards the rim. Following his successful demonstration in 1883 of an experimental 50 hp unit, over 100 of Fourneyron's turbines were built. He was frustrated by the inadequate materials and technology of his time in his efforts to drive turbines with steam. This was achieved about 50 years later by PARSONS.

Fournier, Pierre (1712-68) French engraver and typefounder who was the first typographer to devise the points system for measuring and naming sizes of type. His principal work was the *Typographic Manual* (1764).

Fox, Charles James (1749-1806) English liberal statesman and orator, champion of democratic government. Entering Parliament as a Tory (1768), he soon disputed the extent of royal authority and, proclaiming the sovereignty of the people, led Whig opposition to George III's Tory government. He supported the American colonists against Lord NORTH's repression, and after the American War of Independence, tried, as Britain's first Foreign Secretary (1782), unsuccessfully, to achieve Britain's unconditional recognition of American independence. Later he supported the French Revolution, opposing war with France as aiding despotism. He

An opponent of the hidebound establishment of his day, Charles James Fox was a popular subject for lampoons

The plants illustrated here are all 'exotics', collected by men like Forrest and Fortune, to be introduced and established in regions far from their native homes

Nothofagus

Lilium

Poinsettia Sprekelia Brunfelsia Pelargonium Cineraria Erica

Clianthus Strelitzia Canna Ficus Chrysanthemum

Gloriosa Rhododendron

secured Parliament's pledge to end the slave trade (1806) and urged full freedom for dissenters and Roman Catholics.

Fox, George (1624-91) English religious reformer who (c. 1648) founded the Society of Friends, commonly called the Quakers. Fox preached that God and the Bible could directly guide man's actions, opposed formalized religion and was often imprisoned for interrupting church services. He gained support in Britain, northern Europe, America and the West Indies, and his followers included William PENN. The monthly meetings begun by Fox became an enduring religious movement. The name Quaker reputedly comes from his telling a hostile judge to 'tremble at the word of the Lord'.

Foxe, John (1516-87) English martyrologist, a Protestant who went into exile to avoid MARY I's persecution, returning in ELIZABETH I's reign to complete his monumental *Actes and Monuments of these latter and perilous Dayes*, commonly called *Foxe's Book of Martyrs*. A graphic description of religious persecutions from WYCLIFFE to CRANMER, the book aroused widespread bitter hostility in England to Roman Catholicism, yet Foxe was a tolerant man and opposed the execution of Jesuits in 1581.

Fracastoro, Girolamo (1483-1553) Italian physician, poet, astronomer, geologist and mathematician, author of the important medical work *Concerning Infection* (1546), which contains a description of the process of infection. His poem 'Syphilis' (1530) gave the name to the disease.

Fragonard, Jean Honoré (1732-1806) French Rococo artist, in the tradition of BOUCHER, who developed considerable ability as a landscape artist. His 'Fantasy Portraits' of the late 1760s display an energy of brushwork reminiscent of RUBENS.

France, Anatole (1844-1924) French poet, novelist, critic and moralist. He was the author of highly successful novels *Le Crime de Sylvestre Bonnard* (1881), *Le Livre de mon ami* (1885) and *Thaïs* (1893), and of the *Histoire contemporaine* (1896-1901) – four satirical studies of French social and political life, with many allusions to the DREYFUS case. Perhaps his best novel was *Les Dieux ont soif* (1912), a story of fanaticism during the French Revolution. France was awarded a Nobel Prize in 1921.

Francis I (1494-1547) King of France (1515-47) who imported Italian Renaissance culture. He built splendid châteaux at Fontainebleau, Chambord and elsewhere, commissioning leading Italian sculptors and painters, including Benvenuto CELLINI and LEONARDO DA VINCI, to design and decorate his palaces and organize royal entertainments. Primarily to further Renaissance humanist studies, Francis founded the Collège de France (1530), where lecturers taught the classics, mathematics and medicine in a progressive spirit contrasting with the conservatism of the Sorbonne. Protestant aspirations of his support for the Reformation were dashed, and after 1534 he reverted to orthodox Catholicism. Francis strengthened royal power by centralizing the financial administration, largely to pay for four costly wars fought over Italy with the Emperor CHARLES V, who had outdone Francis by winning election as Holy Roman Emperor. In the first war Francis was taken prisoner and had to concede Burgundy to gain his freedom. After losing Italy in the second war he gained some successes which gave him Savoy and Piedmont. Francis finally conquered the Imperial forces in 1544.

Francis de Sales (1567-1622) French saint whose gentle example and goodness won back for the Roman Catholic church thousands of followers of CALVIN. His first mission was to the Chablais area, where for four years he worked, often in danger of his life, applying his rule that whoever preaches with love preaches effectively. Consecrated Bishop of Geneva, the city of Calvin's Presbyterian government, he set about reforming the dioceses while continuing to preach. In 1610 he founded the Order of the Visitation, with Jane de Chantal. He was canonized in 1665 and declared a Doctor of the Church in 1877. His best-known work is the *Introduction to the Devout Life* (1608).

Francis Joseph I (1830-1916) Emperor of Austria (1848-1916) and King of Hungary from 1867. After succeeding his uncle, FERDINAND I, who abdicated in 1848, he spent the first years of his reign dealing with revolts in various parts of his Empire. Subsequently, he waged a disastrous war against his former ally, Prussia (1866), but afterwards abjured intervention in the affairs of other nations. He survived a succession of family tragedies (among them the assassination of his wife and the suicide of his son) in a long and eventful reign of almost 68 years. Francis Joseph was always prepared for expansion in the Balkans – a cause of the First World War. The spark that ignited Europe was the assassination at Sarajevo of his nephew and heir, Francis Ferdinand in June 1914.

Francis, St, of Assisi (c. 1182-1226) Italian founder of the Franciscan Order of friars, based on JESUS CHRIST's teachings on the principles of poverty and charity.

Francis Xavier (1506-52) Spanish missionary saint, the evangelist of the East Indies and Japan. With St IGNATIUS LOYOLA he was one of the founders of the Society of Jesus, and went to the Far East as a Jesuit, where he worked for seven years in Goa, southern India and Ceylon, combating European ill-treatment of the natives, but winning converts only among the Untouchables. In 1549 he was sent to Japan and as representative of the King of Portugal was allowed to teach Christianity in Kyoto and Yamaguchi. After two years he left his Japanese mission to his native convert colleagues, revisited Goa, and in 1552 set out for China, which was closed to foreigners. He was secretly set ashore on the island of Shangchuan where he died. His body was taken back to Goa and enshrined there.

Franck, César Auguste (1822-90) Belgian organist and composer who lived in Paris, earning his living as a church organist and later becoming organ professor at the Paris Conservatoire. While his fame as an improvisor on the organ was well known, much of his music was little heard or understood during his lifetime. After his death, works such as the *Symphonic Variations* for piano and orchestra, and his Symphony, Violin and Piano Sonata and String Quartet came to be widely admired for their warm romanticism.

Franco, Francisco (born 1892) Dictator of Spain, who overthrew the Republican government in an armed rebellion and the bloody civil war that followed it. Disliking the Socialist and anti-clerical policies of the AZAÑA government, he used his position as army Chief of Staff to launch a military attack on it, employing both white and Moorish troops from Spanish Morocco. He received substantial Italian and German aid furnished by MUSSOLINI and HITLER. In a three-year civil war, in which the government was helped by an International Brigade of volunteers, he eventually gained control of the countryside and finally captured Madrid (March, 1930). His success in maintaining Spanish neutrality during the Second World War, the elimination by force of all opposition, and a measure of economic improvement (largely due to US rents for military bases in Spain), has reduced to some extent a widespread reluctance to his rule. In 1947, Franco intimated that Spain would again

Attended always by birds and animals, Francis of Assisi is one of childhood's favourite saints

become a monarchy after his death – this is still a source of speculation. He resigned as Prime Minister in 1973 but remains head of state, Commander-in-Chief of armed forces and leader of the National Movement, Spain's only official political party.

Frankland, Sir Edward (1825-99) English chemist who originated the theory of valence. After preparing the first organic compounds containing metal atoms, he speculated why the atoms linked together in the ways they did, and eventually suggested (1852) that all atoms have a certain fixed capacity to combine with other atoms – the theory of valence.

Franklin, Benjamin (1706-90) American statesman and scientist, one of the pioneers of electricity. A fierce supporter of America's struggle for independence, he also played an important part in the drafting of the Declaration of Independence (1776) and the United States Constitution (1787). His most famous electrical experiment was the proof, in 1752, that lightning is an electrical phenomenon. He flew a kite in a violent thunderstorm and a spark leaped from the key he had fastened to the kite's string. Charge from the electrified air had travelled down the thread and discharged through the key. On the basis of this experiment, Franklin designed the first lightning conductor. (The next two men to try the experiment were killed when lightning struck their kites.)

Franklin, Sir John (1786-1847) English commander of an ill-fated expedition to explore the Canadian Arctic region for the 'North West Passage'. In May 1845, the ships *Erebus* and *Terror* left London for Greenland, which they reached, and continued north. Neither crew was seen alive again. For the next 10 years, 40 expeditions tried to discover what had happened to the Franklin expedition, and as a result of the searches the North West Passage was found and traversed.

Frasch, Herman (1851-1914) German-American chemical engineer who devised a way of extracting sulphur from underground deposits. In the Frasch process, perfected in 1902, superheated water is pumped down a borehole into the sulphur beds. A froth of water and molten sulphur ascends through another pipe concentric with the borehole.

Fraunhofer, Joseph von (1787-1826) German optician and physicist who discovered dark lines in the Sun's spectrum. In 1814 he was testing the refractive indices of glass prisms in sunlight and noticed numerous thin dark lines crossing the spectrum formed by one of the prisms. He charted the positions of several hundred lines – later called Fraunhofer lines – but failed to grasp their significance as pointers to the elements present in the Sun.

Frazer, Sir James (1854-1941) Scottish anthropologist, classical scholar and student of primitive magic and religion. His major work was *The Golden Bough*, a study of sacral kingship and animism.

Frederick I (c. 1122-90) King of Germany (1152-90), Holy Roman Emperor (1152-90), King of Italy (1155-90), called 'Barbarossa' (Red Beard), who coined the term 'Holy Roman Empire'. He restored order in Germany by appeasing the nobles, then spent 30 years trying to subdue the cities of northern Italy, with some success, before the Lombard League defeated him in 1176. In 1184 Frederick arranged a marriage that gave his son, Henry, southern Italy and Sicily, surrounding the popes (at odds with the emperors since Emperor Henry IV) by imperial territories.

Frederick I (1657-1713) First King in Prussia (1701-13). He became Elector of Brandenburg as Frederick III (1688) and greatly enhanced his state's prestige by crowning himself 'King in Prussia' (not 'of Prussia' since West Prussia remained Polish). The title of king had been Frederick's chief aim and he achieved it by the sanction of the Emperor Leopold I, to whom he promised (and later gave) military aid during the War of the Spanish Succession (1702-14). He was renowned as a patron of scholarship.

Frederick II (1194-1250) King of Sicily (1198-1250), King of Germany (1212-50), and Holy Roman Emperor (1215-50), a brilliant lawmaker, administrator, warrior, multilingual diplomat and patron of the arts and sciences. He founded Naples University (1224) and then made Salerno Europe's leading medical school, and financed translations of major Greek and Arabic works. He also sponsored a veterinary handbook and wrote a book on falconry remarkable for its scientific observation. As Holy Roman Emperor he continued the power struggle with the popes, fought emergent German and Italian towns, and became King of Jerusalem (1227) by capturing the city in a crusade.

Frederick II (1712-86) King of Prussia (1740-86), called 'Frederick the Great', who made Prussia Austria's rival for the leadership of Germany. Rebelling against the rigid, uncultured militarism of his father, FREDERICK WILLIAM I, Frederick wrote poetry, published treatises on political philosophy, rejected Christianity, corresponded with French writers, and gained the admiration of VOLTAIRE for preaching rule by enlightened despotism. Determined to maintain the power and prestige of Prussia, Frederick maintained a strong economy by encouraging agriculture and industry, and increasing the army. Austria and Prussia regarded themselves as rivals for the mastery of Europe and a struggle between them became inevitable. Frederick reversed his father's pro-Hapsburg policy and seized Austrian-held Silesia in 1740, thus antagonizing MARIA TERESA, and helping to provoke the War of the Austrian Succession (1740-8) and the Seven Years' War (1756-63) in which Frederick's enlarged Prussian army fended off Austrian, then French, Austrian and Russian forces. He not only retained Silesia, but took part of Poland (1772).

Frederick III (1415-93) Last Holy Roman Emperor (1440-93) to be crowned at Rome by the pope. Frederick was elected German king (as Frederick IV) in 1440 and was crowned emperor in 1452 by Pope Nicholas V after the Concordat of Vienna (1448) had settled differences over State versus Church authority within the empire. The marriages he arranged for his children laid the foundation for the future power of the Hapsburgs in Europe.

Frederick William (1620-88) Elector of Brandenburg (1640-88), called 'the Great Elector', who laid the foundation of Prussian power. He became ruler during the 30 Years' War and immediately started to repair the damage the war had brought to his small state. By the Peace of Westphalia, which ended the 30 Years' War, he acquired new territories. His army enabled him to force Poland to cede Brandenburg the Duchy of Prussia (East Prussia) in 1657 and to defeat Charles XI's powerful Swedish forces at Fehrbellin (1675). By clever manipulation of his allegiance he utilized his position between Poland and Sweden to secure from each recognition as independent Duke of Prussia. Outside Brandenburg-Prussia, he generally supported the Hapsburgs, the Empire and Protestant causes, and his strong army made his support sought after. He founded the Prussian navy and promoted colonization of West Africa.

Frederick William I (1688-1740) King of Prussia (1713-40) who founded its characteristic, rigidly organized military and administrative systems. Ruling severely as an absolute monarch, Frederick William created a powerfully centralized government, in every department of which he scrutinized operations and had the final power of decision. He doubled his standing army to 80,000 men (recruiting a grenadier regiment of tall men – the 'Potsdam Giants' Guard'), and seized much of Swedish Pomerania.

Frege, Gottlob (1848-1925) German philosopher and mathematician who invented a new logical notation, developed modern mathematical logic and, like RUSSELL and WHITEHEAD, sought to derive mathematics from logic, based on the notion of a formal system, with axioms and rules.

Frei, Eduardo Montalva (born 1911) Chilean statesman, who was a founder member, in 1934, of the National Falange, later the Chilean Christian Democratic Party. He was Senator from 1949 to 1957, in which year the National Falange and the Social Christian Conservative Party merged to form the Christian Democratic Party in an attempt to get Frei elected as President. Although this move failed in 1958, it succeeded in 1964, when Frei was elected for a six-year term.

Fremont, John Charles (1813-90) American explorer, known for his extensive exploration of the lands west of the Mississippi, during the early 1840s.

Frescobaldi, Girolamo (1583-1643) Italian composer and organist whose colourful toccatas and other compositions for organ and harpsichord influenced French and German music.

Fresnel, Augustine Jean (1788-1827) French physicist who developed the theory that light is a transverse wave motion. In the 1800s, he worked, at first with Dominique Arago, on a mathematical formulation of the wave theory of light – that light waves oscillate perpendicularly to their direction of travel – confirming his theory by developing the first successful theory of diffraction. A special type of condensing lens is named after him.

Freud, Sigmund (1856-1939) Austrian psychiatrist and founder of psychoanalysis. At the heart of his work was the belief that a complex of forgotten or deliberately buried impressions underlies all abnormal mental states. A cure, he said, could often be effected by revealing these hidden impressions, and he replaced hypnosis by making the patient talk by free association of ideas. This technique remains the basis of psychoanalytical treatment today. Freud stated that children are not, as was supposed, unaffected by their sexuality until puberty, and frequently suffer from a desire to possess the parent of the opposite sex, based upon rivalry with the same sex parent – the Oedipus complex. Eventually he concluded that arrested infantile mental processes lay at the root of all serious personality disturbances in the adult. Freud saw four stages in the development of what he called the *libido* (which is often equated with sex, but which has a wider and more general significance). These are the oral stage, from birth, when the mouth is the organ of pleasure; the anal stage, beginning towards the end of the first year, the third (phallic) stage and the fourth (genital) stage, beginning at puberty. Failure of the libido to develop smoothly through these phases led, according to Freud, to aberrations of character or sexual perversion.

Friedel, Charles (1832-99) French chemist remembered for his discovery of the Friedel-Crafts reaction. In collaboration with an American, James Crafts, Friedel found that aluminium chloride is an excellent catalyst for the reaction which links chains of carbon atoms to rings of carbon atoms. The Friedel-Crafts reaction has important applications in the petroleum industry.

Friedrich, Caspar David (1774-1840) German Romantic landscape painter, who, like many Romantics, held pantheistic beliefs in the divinity of nature, and expressed its moods with great conviction and sensitivity. A favourite pictorial device of his was the setting of a single figure with his back to the spectator in a landscape whose distant horizons and aerial perspective are suggestive of the infinite (e.g. *The Capuchin Friar by the Sea*).

Frisch, Max (born 1911) Swiss author who, after working as a journalist and architect, devoted himself exclusively to writing novels and plays. His first plays, *Santa Cruz* and *Now Sing Again*, were completed in 1944-5, but the play which brought him wide recognition was *The Fire Raisers* (1958), originally produced as a radio play.

Frobisher, Sir Martin (c. 1535-94) English explorer who made pioneering attempts to find and sail through the North West Passage. In 1576, Frobisher sailed around the south tip of Friesland (now Greenland) looking for a short cut to the East and entered what is now known as Frobisher Bay. On his trip he met 'tawny coloured human beings wearing seal-skins' and found they used small seal-skin boats called 'kayaks'. Frobisher later served under DRAKE, and against the Armada. He befriended the Eskimos with displays of folk-dancing.

Fröding, Gustaf (1860-1911) Swedish poet, who became nationally famous when his humorous, delicate poems describing the people of his province of Varmland were published under the title *Guitar and Concertina* (1891). He suffered from schizophrenia which began to appear in his writings in *New Poems* (1894) and *Splashes and Rags* (1896). The latter contained 'En morgondrom', a glorification of sex which led to Fröding's prosecution for obscenity. Although acquitted, his schizophrenia worsened, and he spent the rest of his life under psychiatric supervision. *Grail-Splashes* (1898) is a collection of fragmented poems inspired by his strange, terrifying visions.

Froebel, Friedrich (1782-1852) German educator, who is particularly associated with the development of the 'kindergarten'. In 1840 he established the first of many at Blankenburg, and in 1849 he founded a training institution for kindergarten teachers. After his death, Froebel's influence continued to grow, fostered by his publications, in particular *The Education of Man* (1826), and the activities of his disciples. Believing, like ROUSSEAU and PESTALOZZI, that children should be able to grow up naturally, unfettered by superfluous adult constraints, Froebel valued highly play encouraged by a stimulating environment, believing that, through such free activity, the child would develop his thoughts and feelings in a spontaneous and genuine manner.

Froissart, Jean (c. 1337-c. 1400) French medieval chronicler and poet whose *Chroniques*, detailing events of the years 1325-1400 in Western Europe – and in particular the 100 Years' War – form a brilliant tapestry of 14th-century feudal life.

Fromentin, Eugène (1820-76) French novelist, painter and art critic whose travels are described in two volumes of travel notes and sketches, *Un Eté dans le Sahara* (1857) and *Une Année dans le Sahel* (1859). After writing *Dominique* (1863), a restrained but penetrating psychological study of renunciation and unfulfilled love, Fromentin – like his hero Dominique de Bray – abandoned his literary career and devoted himself almost entirely to painting.

Fromm, Erich (born 1900) German-born American psychoanalyst who adapted the theories of FREUD to allow for the special social and cultural demands on the individual in different societies. Fromm's concern with the problems facing man today is reflected in *Escape from Freedom* (1941), which analyses the roots of Nazism and the history and character of Western civilization.

Frontinus, Sextus Julius (1st cent. AD) Roman administrator who wrote technical manuals in a clear, straightforward style. His *On the Strategems* (c. 90), on the art of war, survives in four books. The *Aqueducts*, written for his own guidance as the administrator of the water system under Nerva, is a complete account of all aspects of the Roman supply.

Frost, Robert (1874-1963) American poet whose work is based on traditional forms, and is rooted in the land that he farmed. His rhythms are regular, his diction is colloquial and his characters are poor, labouring realists. He combines exact and beautiful descriptions of nature with humour and shrewd observation.

Froude, James (1818-94) British historian, who regarded the reigns of HENRY VIII and ELIZABETH I as critical periods in English history. His work, *History of England from the Fall of Wolsey to the Defeat of the Spanish Armada* (1856-70), reflected his Protestant outlook on history.

Froude, William (1810-79) English engineer and naval architect, who pioneered the science of ship hydrodynamics, by which the results of experiments with scale models in water tanks are used to assess performance of ships at sea.

Fry, Elizabeth (1780-1845) British social worker and prison reformer.

The daughter of John Gurney, a rich Quaker banker, she was herself a leading Quaker and a notable preacher. She married Joseph Fry (a London merchant) in 1800. She agitated for more humane treatment of women prisoners and of convicts sentenced to transportation to New South Wales, and later became active in other fields of reform, notably in raising the standards, skill, training and status of hospital nurses, and improvement in the facilities for women's education. Her fame extended far beyond Britain, and in 1838 she was requested by King LOUIS-PHILIPPE of France to inspect and report on French prisons. This led to penal reforms in France.

Fuchs, Klaus Emil Julius (born 1912) German-born British spy. As a fugitive from Nazi Germany, he came to England in 1933, and in 1942 became a British citizen. A brilliant physicist, he was sent in 1943 to work on the atomic bomb in America. In 1946, after returning to England, he became head of the theoretical physics division at Harwell atomic research centre. Two years earlier, he had started passing information to the Russians, and in 1950 was tried and convicted. Revelations during his trial led to the exposure of the ROSENBERGS in America. On his release from prison in 1959 he became an East German citizen.

Fuchs, Leonhard (1501-66) German physician and author of *Concerning the Description of Plants* (1542), a graphic botanical work of precise scholarship, illustrated with beautiful woodcuts. The fuchsia was named after Dr Fuchs. He is also remembered for his successful treatment of people suffering from plague.

Fuchs, Sir Vivian Ernest (born 1908) British geologist and explorer, leader of the first overland crossing of Antarctica (1957-8). His 12-man team covered the 2158 miles from Shackleton Station on the Weddell Sea to Scott Station on the Ross Sea in 99 days. They met Edmund

HILLARY's team from Scott Station at the South Pole base then followed the line of supply dumps laid by Hillary.

Fugger, Jakob I (15th cent.) German founder of a banking and merchant firm which, at its height, loaned money to popes and emperors, monopolized the silver and copper trades, and had a network of trading posts from the Baltic to the Mediterranean. Fugger's son Jakob II built the Fuggerei, 52 low-rent houses for poor Catholics near Augsburg, which still survives. The Fuggers also provided stocks of goods for maritime explorers like Magellan, to barter when they reached their destination.

Fujiwara Michinaga (966-1027) One of the great figures of Japanese history, who brought the power of the Fujiwara clan (858-1184) to its zenith. As Regent (998-1027) he proved an adroit statesman, retaining power by marrying five of his daughters to successive emperors. Fujiwara spent much money on decorating palaces, encouraging the arts and building Buddhist shrines. His rule witnessed a classical period of Japanese literature.

Fuller, Thomas (1608-61) English clergyman, historian and biographer, who wrote detailed, learned books including *The Holy State* (1642) and *Church History* (1655).

Fulton, Robert (1765-1815) Irish-American inventor who, after early training as an artist, devoted his life to engineering and built the first commercially practical steamboat. In 1786, he went to England where he studied methods of improved canal construction and navigation. Fulton then journeyed to France, where he drew up plans for a submarine. His *Nautilus* was launched in 1800, but although it behaved well, Fulton could not arouse official interest in it. He had more success in the United States when, in 1807, his *Clermont* steam paddleboat started commercial trips from New York to Albany. He followed this with 17 other steam-

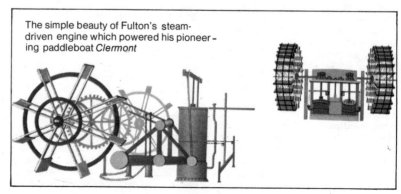

The simple beauty of Fulton's steam-driven engine which powered his pioneering paddleboat *Clermont*

boats, a ferry, a torpedo boat which rammed enemy vessels with torpedoes mounted on a long boom, and, in 1815, a steam frigate, unfinished when he died.

Funk, Casimir (1884-1967) American biochemist of Polish origin, who in 1914 coined the term vitamin, to describe the essential food factors discovered by F. G. Hopkins. He went on to make important studies of vitamins, diet, hormones and cancer prevention.

Fürtwangler, Wilhelm (1886-1954) German conductor and an outstanding interpreter of the German classics, particularly of WAGNER and BEETHOVEN. Much criticized for having stood by Germany during the HITLER régime, he had nevertheless worked to protect Jewish colleagues, and was cleared by a de-Nazification tribunal in 1946.

G

Gabo, Naum (born 1890) Russian sculptor and chief exponent of the Constructivist movement. His series of sculptures (e.g. *Head of Woman*, c. 1917-20) were mostly Cubist constructions in sheet steel or sheet steel and celluloid. In 1920, Gabo drew up the famous 'Realist Manifesto', which outlined the fundamental principles of Constructivism. That year Gabo made his first kinetic sculpture, a steel blade, circumscribing volume in space, which was set in motion by a motor. Later he adopted a style based on curved surfaces built up of slender tubes and plastic threads, as in the 85-ft-high *Construction* (1954-7).

Gaboriau, Emile (1835-73) French writer, pioneer of the detective novel and creator of the famous sleuth, Monsieur Lecoq, a forerunner of Conan DOYLE's hero, Sherlock Holmes.

Gabrieli, Giovanni (1557-1612) Italian Renaissance composer who was the first major musician to use polychoral effects and instrumental accompaniments. He succeeded his uncle Andrea Gabrieli, another major figure, as the chief organist at St Mark's, Venice (1585).

Gaddi, Taddeo (c. 1300-66) Florentine painter and worker in mosaic and marble, whose importance lies in his transmission of GIOTTO's style. He was probably Giotto's pupil and inherited his sober style of religious narrative painting. His best-known work is the *Life of the Virgin* cycle (c. 1332-8) in the Baroncelli chapel, Florence.

Height 360ft (110m)

Left to right:
Vostok 1, Mercury 3, Mercury 6, Voskhod 1, Gemini 3, Apollo 5, Soyuz 1 and Apollo 8

Gagarin, Yuri Alekseyevich (1934-68) Russian air force test pilot and cosmonaut. Gagarin became the first man in space on 12 April 1961. His spacecraft, Vostok 1, completed a single orbit of the Earth in 89·1 minutes, travelling at a maximum velocity of 17,400 mph at an altitude of 187·7 miles.

Gainsborough, Thomas (1727-88) English artist, who rivalled REYNOLDS as the most sought-after portrait painter in England. *Mr and Mrs Andrews* (1748) combines 'that branch of painting which they will pay for' (i.e. portraiture) with his own natural inclination for landscape. The discovery of RUBENS's landscapes led to a more grandiose style and a deeper palette of rich browns and greens, e.g. *The Watering Place* (1777). *The Hon. Mrs Graham* (1777) marked Gainsborough's entry into the London arena to compete with REYNOLDS, who, though he warned his students against Gainsborough's unlearned approach, later admitted the brilliance of his technique.

Gaiseric see GENSERIC

Gaitskell, Hugh Todd Naylor (1906-63) English leader of the Labour Party, who died with the Premiership almost within his grasp. He was a disciple of CRIPPS, whom he

Post-Gagarin rocketry: within ten years of the Russian's first space flight, man circled and landed on the Moon

succeeded as Chancellor of the Exchequer in 1950. His introduction of National Health Service charges in that year led to the resignations of BEVAN and Harold WILSON and a long-standing feud with the left wing of the Labour Party. Gaitskell's authority grew rapidly, however, and in 1955 he defeated Bevan in the election for the leadership of the Party, consolidating his position with attacks on EDEN's Suez policy the following year. He is perhaps best remembered for his vow to 'fight and fight and fight again' to reverse a narrow Party Conference vote for unilateral disarmament in 1960, a promise which he fulfilled in 1961. He attempted the modernization of the Party, particularly with regard to modifying the doctrine of the total nationalization of the means of production, proposing the 'shareholder state' as an alternative.

Gaius (2nd cent. AD) Roman jurist whose opinions, together with those of ULPIAN and others, were important sources of Roman law. His four-part *Institutes* was a layman's guide to Roman law and dealt with the status of individuals, the law relating to objects as possessions, intestacy and the different types of legal action. This work, which enables students to retrace the history of civil law, was one of the bases of JUSTINIAN's *Institutes*.

Gaius Sallustius Crispus see SALLUST

Galen (c. 131-200) Greek physician whose anatomical works formed the basis for medical teaching for more than a millennium. An indefatigable dissector of animals and an accurate observer and describer of what he found, his experiments in physiology resulted in many discoveries. His works remained the ultimate medical authority until VESALIUS.

Galilei, Galileo (1564-1642) Italian astronomer, physicist and mathematician, who established the scientific method of testing theories by rigorous and extensive experimentation, one of the first men to use a telescope for astronomy, and discoverer of the principles of motion stated later in NEWTON's first two laws. Galileo was the first man to perceive that mathematics and physics were parts of one and the same area of knowledge. In his astronomical work he greatly improved the telescope and promoted the cosmological theory of COPERNICUS. Galileo's lucid and elegant exposition of his views in his *Letters on the Sunspots* (1613) caused a wide and radical movement of opinion away from the Ptolemaic theory. When, in 1616, some scholars and the Church had the Copernican theory denounced as blasphemous, Galileo wrote the *Dialogue of the Two Great World Systems*, which was hailed throughout Europe as a literary and philosophical masterpiece. Galileo was convicted of heresy in 1633 and forced to recant his views.

Gall, Franz (1758-1828) German physiologist who discovered the difference between the grey (active) and white (connective) matter in the brain, and who pointed out the localization of brain function. He is also remembered as the founder of the now discredited science of phrenology, which seeks to relate the shape and bumps of the skull to character.

Gallup, George (born 1901) American public opinion statistician, the first to conduct polls based on scientific sampling methods. The founder and Director of the American Institute of Public Opinion (1935) and its British equivalent (1936), Gallup's 1936 national poll was the only one to forecast correctly ROOSEVELT's re-election.

Galois, Evariste (1811-32) French mathematician, who, although only 20 when he died, pioneered the theory of groups in connection with the theory of equations. Much of this was sketched in a letter he wrote on the evening before he fought the duel in which he was killed.

Galsworthy, John (1867-1933) English novelist and dramatist, best known for *The Forsyte Saga*, a trilogy that studied social change and middle-class acquisitiveness. It began with *The Man of Property* (1906) and ended with *To Let* (1921), and achieved great popularity, both in book form and as a television serial. He wrote two further trilogies about the Forsytes and a number of plays on moral issues. In 1932 Galsworthy was awarded the Nobel Prize for Literature.

Galton, Sir Francis (1822-1911) British geneticist, the founder of eugenics, the science concerned with producing finer types of human being by carefully controlled breeding. He also devised a method of identifying fingerprints.

Galvani, Luigi (1737-98) Italian anatomist who opened the way for the development of the first electric cell. Intrigued by the occasional twitching of a frog's leg during an experiment, he found that the leg always twitched if the copper hook from which it was hung was brought into contact with an iron plate. He believed this was an electric effect caused by the animal tissue. Another Italian, Alessandro VOLTA, realized that the contact between the dissimilar metals was generating the electric current.

Gama, Vasco da (c. 1469-1524) Portuguese navigator, commander of the first fleet to sail from Europe to Asia. He left Lisbon in July 1497, with four vessels, the *St Gabriel*, the *St Raphael*, the *Berrio* and a store ship. The fleet reached St Helena Bay, near modern Capetown, in November, and by Christmas Day had rounded the southern tip of Africa and sighted Natal. At Malindi, he found a Muslim pilot who conducted his ships across the Arabian Sea to Calicut (modern Kozhikode), which they reached on 21 May 1498. Although it reached its destination, da Gama's expedition was not entirely successful. Many of his men died of scurvy, and da Gama obtained few of the spices he had hoped for because his trading goods were too shoddy. Da Gama made a second voyage to Calicut in 1502 and returned home with shiploads of riches. He was made Viceroy of India in 1524.

Gambetta, Léon Michel (1838-82) French lawyer and republican politician who proclaimed the Third French Republic (1870). As an advanced liberal and leader of the Party in the Assembly, he opposed NAPOLEON III. He proclaimed the establishment of the Third Republic on receiving news of Napoleon's defeat by the Prussians at Sedan in September 1870, and later escaped from besieged Paris in a balloon. As Minister of War and of the Interior, he organized French resistance in the later stages of the Franco-Prussian War, and throughout the 1870s devoted his energies to protecting the new republic from monarchist influences. In 1879, he was instrumental in forcing President MacMahon to resign and for a few months (1881-2) was Prime Minister of a short-lived government.

Gandhi, Indira (born 1917) Indian stateswoman and one of the first women to become a Prime Minister. The daughter of Jawaharlal NEHRU, she joined the Congress Party in 1938 and was imprisoned for nationalist political agitation during the Quit India movement (1942). After holding several increasingly responsible offices, she was elected President of the Indian National Congress in 1959. When her father died in 1963 his successor, SHASTRI, appointed her to his government as Minister of Information. Following Shastri's death in 1966 she was elected Congress Party leader and thus became Prime Minister. The 1967 election confirmed her in office.

Gandhi, Mohandas Karamchand (1869-1948) The principal creator of India's independence and most notable exponent of 'passive resistance' as a political and social revolutionary tactic. Gandhi, later known as the Mahatma (saint), was educated in London and called to the Bar in Bombay. After practising there as a barrister, he went to South Africa and persuaded its Indian population to offer passive resistance to the Transvaal government's discrimination against Indians. By 1914 he had won assurances from SMUTS of just treatment for Indian South Africans. He returned to India to lead the Indian National Congress, which was demanding *Swarj* – home rule for India. Gandhi deprecated and discouraged terrorist methods, and used instead passive resistance, boycott of British goods, development of village industries and hunger strikes. As a result, he was imprisoned four times. By 1940, Gandhi's aim had become complete independence for India, which was granted by ATTLEE's Labour government after the Second World War (1947). His agreement to the partition of India and Pakistan was bitterly resented by Hindu extremists, one of whom assassinated him on 30 Jan. 1948. The spiritual content of Gandhi's political action should not obscure his considerable talents as an administrator and communicator of his views. His sponsorship of struggling and oppressed peoples made an international impact, and his campaign in India led to a moral reappraisal of British imperialism.

Garamond, Claude (c. 1480-1561) French publisher and designer of typefaces, whose designs, perfecting the work of JENSON, gradually replaced the universal Gothic typefaces and radically altered the appearance of printing in western Europe.

Garay, Juan de (c. 1527-c. 1584) Spanish soldier who became Governor of Paraguay and refounded Buenos Aires (1580), on MENDOZA's site, as a seaport for Asunción and as a strongpoint against the Portuguese.

Gardner, Gerald Brousseau (1884-1964) English author, who owned a witchcraft collection situated on the Isle of Man. He was the creator of the contemporary witchcult in both Europe and the US. His publications included *Witchcraft Today* (1954) and *High Magic's Aid* (1949).

Garfield, James Abram (1831-81) American President, who was assassinated after only four months in office. He was a self-made man and strongly antagonistic towards slavery. During the Republican search for a presidential candidate in 1880 – in which 28 ballots had been held without success – the need for a compromise candidate was acknowledged, and Garfield, known to be a hard worker and fine speaker, was declared the Party's candidate on the 36th ballot. In office he showed himself tactless, and his support of civil service reform antagonized both his opponents and a powerful section within his own party. He gave preferential treatment to members of the radical wing of the Republican Party, and was shot and mortally wounded by a disappointed office-seeker.

Garfinkel, Harold (born 1917) American sociologist who devised Ethnomethodology. This theory, as defined in his *Studies in Ethnomethodology* (1964), is indifferent to conventional sociology's concern to explain social order and focuses instead on how members of society accomplish that order.

Garibaldi, Giuseppe (1807-82) Italian patriot, who, with CAVOUR, helped to achieve the unification of Italy. A supporter of MAZZINI's Young Italy Movement, he was forced to take

refuge in South America (1834), where, during the war between Uruguay and Argentina, he commanded the troops defending Montevideo (1843). After returning to Italy in 1848 he commanded the defence of the Roman Republic against the French (1849), but was again driven into exile. Later he led guerillas against the Austrians in the region of the Italian lakes (1859). A year later he sailed from Genoa with his 'Thousand Redshirts' and eventually conquered Naples and Sicily, thus forming the nucleus of a united Italy. He then marched northwards and joined forces with Cavour at the Volturno. His conquests, united with those of the Piedmontese, largely achieved the united Italy he had dreamed of. He made two unsuccessful attempts to capture Rome (1862 and 1867) and in 1870 led a volunteer force in the Franco-Prussian War. Garibaldi was the supreme example of the romantic patriot-leader and was greeted with enormous enthusiasm when he visited England in 1864.

Garnerin, André Jacques (1769-1823) Early French aeronaut who, in 1797, was the first man to make a parachute descent in public, jumping over 2000 feet from a balloon. The first man to parachute from an aircraft was Captain Albert Berry at St Louis, Missouri, in 1912.

Garnier, Jean Louis Charles (1825-98) French architect whose Opéra in Paris illustrates the final stage of the evolution of the Baroque in the 19th century, while, at the same time, remaining light and unlaboured. The stage is placed like a jewel in its setting and great emphasis is placed on the richness of the auditorium and foyer.

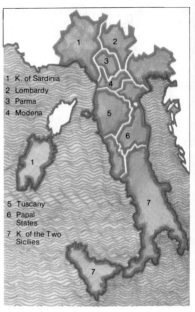

1 K. of Sardinia
2 Lombardy
3 Parma
4 Modena
5 Tuscany
6 Papal States
7 K. of the Two Sicilies

Italy, a jigsaw of small countries in the early 19th century, emerged as a unified nation after Garibaldi

Garrick, David (1717-79) English actor and theatre manager, who was one of the outstanding men of the theatre of the 18th century. He originated the easy, natural style of acting and made London's Drury Lane Theatre the European centre of dramatic art. His first acting success was as Richard III (1741) and he played all the leading tragic roles of SHAKESPEARE, JONSON and the Restoration dramatists. As manager of Drury Lane, from 1747, he pioneered the use of naturalistic landscape backdrops and concealed lighting.

Garrick ended the centuries-old practice of actors sharing the stage with spectators

Garrison, William Lloyd (1805-79) American abolitionist, who exerted great influence on the anti-slavery movement. A pacifist, he fought for the anti-slavery cause solely by moral means, his contribution being publicly recognized by LINCOLN. In 1831, he founded the *Liberator* in Boston, which held considerable sway until Garrison closed it down in 1865, after it published the amendment to the constitution abolishing slavery in the United States. He was often the object of mob violence and frequently subject to extreme personal danger.

Garvin, James (1868-1947) English journalist who renewed the vitality of NORTHCLIFFE's Sunday *Observer* when he was appointed editor in 1908. During the inter-war years the *Observer* urged co-operation with the League of Nations, supporting appeasement over Italy's invasion of Abyssinia, but finally took a stand against HITLER. In 1942 Garvin disagreed with the proprietor, W. W. Astor, and resigned.

Gaskell, Mrs Elizabeth (1810-65) English novelist who was brought up in Knutsford, a small northern town, whose way of life is described in her pastoral novels, such as *Cranford* (1853). Having married a Unitarian minister in Manchester, she was also able to give a first-hand picture of the hardships of industrial workers, in novels like *Mary Barton* (1848). She also wrote an important biography, *The Life of Charlotte Brontë* (1857).

Gassendi, Pierre (1592-1655) French philosopher and scientist who sought to explain mental activity in terms of mechanical change, producing material traces that manifest themselves in behaviour.

Gatling, Richard John (1818-1903) American inventor who perfected a rapid-fire machine gun which fired 1200 shots per minute. The gun, adopted for the US army, was put to use in the later stages of the American Civil War and was in use until the end of the century. As a boy, Gatling helped his father to devise a machine for planting cotton seeds, and also invented a screw propeller for steamboats.

Gaudi, Antoni (1852-1926) Spanish architect, who was one of the most brilliantly inventive of the exponents of Art Nouveau. He worked largely in Barcelona, which contains his enormous, unfinished cathedral La Sagrada Familia and a number of houses. His originality lay in his use of bizarre form and structure, and the brilliant collage of appliqué materials that ornament the surface of his forms.

Gauguin's studio: a rebel in art, he said of his work 'It does not stink of models, techniques or of pretended rules'

Gauguin, Paul (1848-1903) French Post-Impressionist painter, whose art was both a development of and a reaction to Impressionism. In 1883, he abandoned a career as a stockbroker to devote himself to painting, and learnt a great deal from PISSARRO and CÉZANNE. Becoming disenchanted with European society, he went to the tropics in 1887, visiting Panama and Martinique. In 1888, in Brittany, he painted the *Vision after the Sermon* in a new style which rejected Impressionist naturalism. Synthetism, as this style was called, was a means of trying to express the essence of emotion through the technique of painting, and may be said to have contributed to the development of abstract art. Gauguin visited Tahiti between 1891 and 1893, and returned there in 1895, living in native communities whose life and beliefs he made the subject of his paintings.

Gauss, Karl Friedrich (1777-1855) German mathematician, astronomer, and physicist. He contributed widely to various aspects of pure and applied mathematics: the study of elliptic functions, prime number theory, topology and differential geometry. He also worked in theoretical astronomy, mechanics, electricity and magnetism, optics, statistics and other subjects. Much of his most important work in mathematics was completed before he was 20, and his discoveries in number theory were published in *Disquisitiones Arithmeticae* (1801).

Gautama Buddha (c. 563-c.483 BC) Indian-born founder of Buddhism (Gautama was his family name, Buddha means 'the enlightened'). Many details of his life story are now held to be legendary, but the outline appears to be that of a well-born, married man, disenchanted and confused about life's meaning in the face of senility, disease and death, who went away in his thirtieth year to seek understanding. He tried the traditional Hindu paths of wisdom, then asceticism, and finding himself despairingly beneath a bodhi tree, vowed not to stir until the mystery of suffering and existence was yielded to him. There he was enlightened with the Four Noble Truths, the basis of Buddhism – that all existence means suffering; suffering follows from desire; suffering ends when desire is extinguished; and to achieve this end one must follow the Eightfold Path. The Buddha gathered a community (Sangha) of monks who, with him, travelled widely to enable others to find enlightenment. They rejected the caste system, and were agnostic about a Creator. The religion founded by Gautama Buddha now has about 70 million adherents.

Gautier, Théophile (1811-72) French novelist, journalist and a major Parnassian poet, who helped to transform the Romantic tradition of the early 19th century into the aestheticism and naturalism of later decades. *Emaux et Camées* (1852), his best-known collection of poetry, is a volume of lyrics, each perfectly-chiselled, a monument to Gautier's cult of beauty and purity of form. His famous poem 'L'Art', which claimed that art is the most important thing in life (*'l'art pour l'art'*: art for art's sake) became the keystone for the Parnassian poets.

Gay, John (1685-1732) English dramatist, who wrote *The Beggar's Opera* (1728), his only memorable work, which later became the basis of BRECHT's *Threepenny Opera*. His sequel, *Polly*, was politically offensive to the authorities and not produced until 1777. Gay wrote the libretto for HANDEL's *Acis and Galatea*.

Gay-Lussac, Joseph (1778-1850) French chemist who formulated the law of combining volumes, which showed that gases combine with each other in proportions by volume that can be expressed as small whole numbers (for example, two parts of hydrogen combine with one of oxygen to form water). The law was subsequently used by Jöns BERZELIUS to calculate accurate atomic weights.

Gedymin (14th cent.) Lithuanian grand duke, who made his state the most powerful in eastern Europe. He inherited large domains, including territories adjoining Lithuania, and secured them against the raiding Teutonic Knights and Livonian Knights of the Sword by fortifying key border areas, engaging the pope's protection, and giving privileges to immigrants from Wendish, Baltic and Hanseatic towns to empty Russian lands. He founded several cities, including Vilna, the capital.

Geiger, Hans (1882-1945) German physicist, inventor of the Geiger counter for detecting atomic particles. An assistant of RUTHERFORD, he developed the counter in 1913. A high voltage is applied to a chamber full of gas. The entry of an atomic particle causes an avalanche of ionization and clicking sounds in the headphones indicate the presence and level of radioactivity.

Geijer, Erik Gustaf (1783-1847) Swedish Romantic lyric poet and historian, whose lectures on Scandinavian history paved the way for Swedish Romanticism. His Gothic poems 'The Vikings' and 'The Yeoman Farmer' (1811) and his monumental histories *Annals of the Kingdom of Sweden* (1825) and the unfinished *The History of the Swedes* (1832-6) are generally considered his best works. He edited the first definitive edition of Swedish folksongs, *Swedish Ballads* (1814-16).

Genet, Jean (born 1910) French dramatist, novelist and chronicler of the underworld. The hardships of his childhood quickly led him into delinquency and crime. It is in his books such as *Our Lady of the Flowers* (1944) and *Thief's Journal* (1949) that he records his experiences of Europe's bars, brothels and prisons. His plays, among the best known of which are *The Maids* (1947) and *The Balcony* (1956), are concerned with an equivocal world of illusions, masks and mirrors.

Genghis Khan (c. 1167-1227) Mongol chief, one of the great conquerors in world history. He inherited a Mongol tribal chiefdom at 13, conquered nearby tribes, and renamed himself Genghis Khan (Very Mighty King). Embarking on a career of world conquest, he welded Central Asia's independent Mongol and Altaic nomads into a 250,000-strong well-drilled, well-armed, fighting machine. From his capital, Karakorum, in northeast Asia, Genghis Khan struck east south and west. He seized northern China (1211-15) and Korea (1218), then (1218-22) ravaged what are now Russian Turkestan, West Pakistan, Iran and southern Russia, razing towns and slaughtering their inhabitants. Ultimately his empire spanned 4000 miles.

Genseric (5th cent.) King of the Vandals (428-77) who seized North Africa from the Roman Empire. Helped by Bonifacius (a disaffected Roman governor in North Africa) Genseric shipped some 80,000 Vandals from southern Spain to what is now Morocco (429). Sweeping eastwards, his armies seized all northern Africa to Tunisia, taking Hippo in a two-year siege (430-1), and made Carthage his capital. Creating a navy, Genseric used Carthage as a springboard for capturing the Balearic Islands, Corsica, Sardinia and Sicily. He even plundered Rome (455) and threatened Constantinople's trade with Egypt before he died, undefeated.

Gentile da Fabriano (c. 1370-1427) Italian artist whose work reveals the decorative characteristics of the international Gothic style. The *Adoration of the Magi* (c. 1422) is typical of his work, with fragile figures and schematic natural forms painted in an archaic manner which was largely superseded during the 15th century.

George (4th cent.) Patron saint of England since 1349. He is said to have slain a dragon, but nothing factual is known about him, though attempts to prove that he is a myth are offset by references to him in 6th-century texts.

George IV (1762-1830) Regent (1811-20) and King of Great Britain (1820-30). He was the eldest son of George III, with whom he was on bad terms, partly on account of his friendship with FOX, SHERIDAN and the Whigs, and partly due to his extravagance and moral laxity. On becoming Regent due to his father's indisposition, he supported the existing Tory ministry of PERCEVAL, despite his earlier attachment to the Whigs, who thereafter upheld the cause of his estranged wife Caroline of Brunswick. On his accession, George attempted to divorce Caroline but was unsuccessful and attracted much public hostility by his conduct towards her. His acceptance of more liberally-minded ministers and of reform policies was given with a reluctance which did nothing to arrest the decline in the prestige of the monarchy. But although he was temperamentally difficult, he avoided direct confrontation with his ministers, unlike his father, and brother, WILLIAM IV. He was a notable patron of the arts, commissioning the portrait painter Sir Thomas LAWRENCE, the building projects of Regent Street and Regent's Park (1812-13) and the rebuilding of the Brighton Pavilion (1815) to the designs of John NASH.

George V (1865-1936) King of Great Britain and Emperor of India (1910-36). He succeeded his father, EDWARD VII. His reign was a difficult one which had to contend with the First World War and, at home, an increasingly democratic and socialist age, marked by industrial unrest, economic depression and the constitutional problems of Ireland. During the war he opposed extreme anti-German feeling but identified himself more closely with the country by adopting the family name of Windsor (1917). When he intervened in politics (as in the case of the Parliament Bill of 1911, or the appointment of BALDWIN as Prime Minister in 1923), he did so on the suggestions of his constitutional advisers. He had a particular attachment to his Indian Empire and was the only British Emperor to visit his territories.

George VI (1895-1952) King of Great Britain (1936-52) and Emperor of India (1936-47). In the First World War he was mentioned in dispatches at the battle of Jutland, but ill-health brought his naval career to an end. His strength of character was shown in his fight against poor health and a noticeable stammer, both of which he conquered. He succeeded to the throne on the abdication of his brother EDWARD VIII in 1936, and less than three years later Britain was at war. The King visited the major theatres of war and endeared himself to his countrymen by staying at Buckingham Palace throughout the worst of the Blitz and broadcasting to the nation. In 1947 he toured South Africa with the Royal Family. His last great public occasion was the opening of the Festival of Britain at South Bank, London, in 1951.

George-Brown, Lord (born 1914) English politician who, as George Brown was Foreign Minister (1966-8) in WILSON's Labour Government. He was elected MP for Belper, Derbyshire, in 1945 and held a number of offices in the ATTLEE administration. When Labour returned to office in 1965, he became first Secretary of State and Minister for Economic Affairs, then in 1966 Foreign Secretary and Deputy Prime Minister. His readiness to speak his mind with less than the customary measure of discretion earned him both affection and criticism. Following differences with Wilson in 1968, he resigned from the Cabinet.

George, Stefan (1868-1933) German poet whose verse is characterized by lofty poetic inspirations, aiming to impose a new classicism on German poetry by ridding it of the irregularities and impure rhymes of the Romantic movement. He was associated at first with MALLARMÉ and the Symbolists, but perfected his own aesthetic type of poetry in the descriptions of nature in *The Year of the Soul* (1897) his most famous book.

Gerard, John (1545-c. 1607) English gardener, apothecary and superintendent of Lord BURGHLEY's gardens, who had his own physic garden in Holborn, London. In 1596 he published a catalogue of the plants grown there, including American species such as the tomato and so-called African marigold. His *Herball, or Generall Historie of Plantes* (1597) listed native British plants and about 100 trees and shrubs already introduced from abroad.

Gerhard, Roberto (1896-1970) Spanish composer and pupil of SCHOENBERG, whose works include the ballet *Don Quixote* (1941), a setting of passages from CAMUS's *The Plague* (1964) and four symphonies. An *avant-garde* composer, he moved from atonality, through serialism to exploring patterns of pure orchestral sound. Like CASALS he remained in exile after the Spanish Civil War, and from 1938 lived and worked in Cambridge, England, where he was a research fellow at the university.

Gerhardt, Charles (1816-56) French chemist who developed a means of classifying organic compounds, called the theory of types. In collaboration with August LAURENT, he suggested that organic compounds could be classified by their relationship to four basic 'types': ammonia, hydrogen, hydrogen chloride and water.

Géricault, Théodore (1791-1824) French artist, best known for his boldly colourful sporting scenes and paintings with social themes. Géricault, unlike his contemporaries, painted directly on to the canvas, a technique which, in combination with his eye for detail, lends a dramatic realism to the compositions. Particularly noteworthy are his equestrian scenes and the celebrated work *Raft of the Medusa* (1819), based on a controversial shipwreck of the day.

Geronimo (1829-1909) Chiricahua Apache chief, who led one of the last serious Indian revolts against white supremacy in North America. His surrender in 1886 ended the history of Indian stands against the white man.

Gershwin, George (1898-1937) American composer and pianist who extended jazz into a concert idiom with his opera *Porgy and Bess*. This original material incorporated the spirit of jazz and negro blues. *Rhapsody in Blue* (1924), written to a commission from Paul Whiteman, was his first serious composition. Later Gershwin made his own orchestrations in such works as the *Piano Concerto* and the orchestral suite, *An American in Paris*.

Gesell, Arnold (1880-1961) American psychologist, known as the father of child psychology. His work emphasizes the constitutional aspect and cyclical nature of mental development in the child. He based his researches for the most part on the simple, accurate observation of children's behaviour (often using film cameras and two-way mirrors), and was able to establish norms, both in the ages at which specific developments occur, and in their order. His many books on the subject have helped to make child psychology popular among laymen.

Gesner, Konrad von (1516-65) Swiss physician, whose encyclopedic work, *A Catalogue of Animals* (1551-8), is considered by many to have been the starting point of modern zoology. A purely descriptive work, it reflects von Gesner's non-analytical approach to biology.

Gesualdo de Venosa, Carlo (c. 1560-1613) Italian madrigalist, whose work explored the possibilities of chromatic harmonies, involving violent switches of tempo and key.

Getty, Paul (born 1892) American oil magnate, reputedly one of history's richest men. He has been President of the Getty Oil Company since 1947.

Geulincx, Arnold (1624-69) Flemish philosopher whose theory of moral conduct stated that the ego is autonomous, but also subject to some extent to the occasionalism described by MALEBRANCHE.

Gezelle, Guido (1830-99) Belgian Romantic and mystical poet, whose most famous works, *Garland of Time* (1893) and *String of Rhyme* (1897), collections of lyrical poems in the western Flemish dialect, paved the way for a Flemish poetic renaissance.

Ghazali, Abu Mohammed al- (1058-1111) Influential Islamic mystic and theologian whose chief book, *The Revival of the Religious Sciences*, sets out, often in antagonistic terms, the religious heritage of Islam in a synthesis of orthodox dogma with Sufi mysticism. He also attacked the rationalist approach to theology in *The Incoherence of the Philosophers*, asserting that the religious life represented a higher form of understanding than that achievable by reason. In spite of AVERROES's counterattack, this denigration of Arabic philosophy led to its decline.

Gheorghiu-Dej, Gheorghe (1901-65) Premier of the Rumanian People's Republic (1952-5) and Head of State (1961-5). His position was an unusual one in Communist states in that in 1961 he was both President of the newly created Council of State (the supreme administrative body) and First Secretary of the Rumanian Communist Party. This gave him almost unprecedented power, which he used to establish Rumania's independence from Russia. By the time he died Rumania's economic independence was established and recognized by Moscow.

Ghiberti, Lorenzo (1378-1455) Florentine sculptor, much of whose career was spent on the ornamentation of reliefs for the doors of the Baptistry of Florence Cathedral. Ghiberti was engaged in many other activities and had a large workshop of assistants in which many famous Florentine painters and sculptors were trained, including DONATELLO.

Ghirlandaio, Domenico (1449-94) Florentine painter, in whose workshop MICHELANGELO spent three years as an apprentice. Important frescoes by him are in Florence (Sta Maria Novella and Sta Trinita); he also worked in the Sistine Chapel, Rome. The religious themes of his frescoes are offset by bourgeois Italian settings and details, and his scenes sometimes contain portraits of contemporary Florentines.

Giacometti, Alberto (1901-66) 'Space is hollowed to build up an object and, in its turn, the object creates space,' said Giacometti, Swiss sculptor and draughtsman. Between 1925 and 1930, he created objects largely from memory, giving sculptural expression to a world of dreams. His figures, often individually placed, or arranged in small groups, form a spatial texture derived from their visual relationships, as, for example, in *Project for a City Square*, 1932. To emphasize their fragility, he mounted his figures on a heavy base, as in *Female Figure* (1946-7).

Giap, Vo Nguyen (born 1912) North Vietnamese general, founder of the Vietnamese Communist Party in the early 1930s. As leader of the Viet-minh guerillas under HO CHI-MINH against France, his victory at Dien Bien Phu in 1954 forced the French to withdraw from Indo-China, and in 1959 Giap became the commander of the North Vietnamese forces. Fighting on home ground and on his own terms, with expendable troops and Viet Cong guerilla forces, he cost the US so much in terms of men and materials that the war became unacceptable to an increasingly large section of the American public.

Gibbons, Christopher see GIBBONS, Orlando

Gibbons, Edward see GIBBONS, Orlando

Gibbons, Ellis see GIBBONS, Orlando

Gibbons, Grinling (1648-1720) English sculptor, outstanding representative of the English decorative style of the Late Stuart Period (*c.* 1668 onwards) mainly through his wood carvings at Windsor, Hampton Court, Middlesex, and St Paul's, London.

Gibbons, John Heysham (born 1903) American surgeon, who developed the first artificial heart–lung machine, which was used in May 1953. This, and later developments, although not yet practical replacements for the heart, have been used widely during surgery. With the restoration of normal heart function and circulation, the patient's life expectancy is often comparable to that of a person with a normal heart.

Gibbons, Orlando (1583-1625) English composer of Anglican church music. Gibbons, organist of Westminster Abbey, was probably the finest keyboard player of his day, whose church music includes some 40 anthems and a single set of highly distinguished madrigals. Gibbons's brothers Edward and Ellis were also composers and a few of their works survive. His son, Christopher, organist at Westminster Abbey and private organist to CHARLES II.

Gibbs, James (1682-1754) Scottish architect, who designed St Martin-in-the-Fields and St Mary-le-Strand. The Radcliffe Camera at Oxford, one of his best-known buildings, reveals his debt to Christopher WREN.

Gibbs, Josiah Willard (1839-1903) American physicist, who founded chemical thermodynamics. Having studied the work on thermodynamics by Nicolas CARNOT, James JOULE and Lord KELVIN, Gibbs applied their approaches to chemical reactions. In the 1870s he identified the quantities, such as free energy and chemical potential, that underlie all chemical reactions, and worked out the mathematical basis of what was to become modern chemical thermodynamics.

Gibson, John (1790-1866) Welsh sculptor who revived the art of colouring in Neo-classical sculpture. In England he met opposition, mainly through his reintroduction of the tinting of marble, although his earlier work, *Psyche Borne on the Wings of Zephyrus*, was accepted by the Royal Academy, of which he was elected a member in 1838. His fortune was large and his bequest to the Royal Academy enabled the Diploma Gallery to be built.

Giddings, Franklin (1855-1931) American sociologist, whose writings drew together the ideas of many contemporaries in a systematic form and significantly influenced the teaching of sociology in America. In *Studies in the Theory of Human Society* (1922) he describes social behaviour as 'differential responses to stimulation', but accounts for the general overriding social co-operation by 'the consciousness of kind', or 'fellow feeling', a doctrine which he derived from Adam SMITH. Giddings believed that one of the benefits of social progress was the recognition by men of the advantages of diversity in society.

Gide, André (1869-1951) French novelist and literary critic renowned for his meditative *Journals*, covering the years 1889-1949. In his work, Gide is perpetually torn between the puritan and the pagan in himself, the Christian and the admirer of NIETZSCHE, whose influence is apparent in Gide's defiant exhortation to his readers to assert their personal freedom in *Les Nourritures Terrestres* (1897). Among his other well-known works are *L'Immoraliste* (1902), *La Porte Etroite* (1909), the farcical tale *Les Caves du Vatican* (1914), in which the hero commits murder, Gide's most famous example of the motiveless act (l'acte gratuit), and *Les Faux-Monnayeurs* (1926), an experiment in the art of fiction and an important landmark in the development of the French novel. Gide won the Nobel Prize for Literature in 1947.

Gielgud, Sir John (born 1904) English actor and director, considered the greatest Hamlet of his generation. He has played virtually every major English classical role.

Giffard, Henri (1825-82) French aeronautical engineer, who in 1852 made the first powered flight in an airship. It was fitted with a three horse-power steam engine driving a three-bladed propeller. The machine paved the way for the rigid, powered airships of the late 19th century. In 1859, Giffard invented an apparatus to inject feed water into steam engine boilers, which prevented them from running out of steam when not in motion.

Gilbert, Sir Humphrey (1539-83) English soldier and navigator who claimed England's first colony in North America, in Newfoundland. A half-brother of Sir Walter RALEIGH, Gilbert was granted a charter in 1578 to explore and colonize North America. His first expedition failed, but he eventually equipped another five ships, and reached Newfoundland (1583), where he claimed an area for ELIZABETH I, but did not found a permanent colony. He explored to the south, then sailed for England, but was drowned in a storm off the Azores.

Gilbert, William (1544-1603) English physician whose treatise *De magnete* (1600) is a model of scientific method. By studying the behaviour of freely suspended magnetic needles near magnetized iron spheres, he saw that the Earth behaves like a huge magnet whose poles do not quite coincide with its geographical ones. He also introduced the word electricity, from the Greek *electron*, meaning amber, a substance that becomes 'electrified' when rubbed.

Gilbert, Sir William Schwenck (1836-1911) English humorous poet and librettist who collaborated with Sir Arthur SULLIVAN on an immensely successful series of 14 comic operas. His lyrics reveal an exuberant, often macabre humour and a talent for inventive rhymes.

Giles of Rome (c. 1245-1316) Italian Augustinian monk, theologian and philosopher who first put forward the premise that the pope must have supreme political as well as spiritual power.

Giles, Carl (born 1916) English cartoonist, whose work, which has appeared in the *Sunday Express* and *Daily Express* since 1942, is characterized by his feeling for linear perspective.

Giles, Ernest (1835-97) English-born Australian explorer who crossed the deserts of southern and Western Australia. In the course of four expeditions (1872-6), he explored and named the Gibson Desert, and made a formidable round trip of about 3000 miles from Beltana along the 30th parallel to Perth in five months. He returned approximately along the 25th parallel and south to Adelaide.

Gill, Eric (1882-1940) English sculptor and typographer, who designed the widely used Gill Sans-Serif, Perpetua and Joanna typefaces. His engravings for the Golden Cockerel Press, notably the type and design for *The Four Gospels* (1931), brought him international fame.

Gillette, King Camp (1855-1932) American inventor who, in 1895, devised the modern safety razor which used throw-away blades and had a toothed guard, permitting the cutting edge to pass over the uneven surface to be shaved.

Gillray, James (1757-1815) English political and social caricaturist of the reign of George III and the Regency, whose savage and often coarse caricatures had an enormous vogue and a considerable influence on public opinion.

Ginsberg, Allen (born 1926) American poet regarded as a leading figure of the Beat Movement. He voiced the spirit of protest prevalent among the youth of the 1950s and 1960s, especially in *Howl and Other Poems* (1956), a cry of lamentation for the sickness of urban America. His poems have been politically moti-

Programme for an early production of *The Yeomen of the Guard*, one of the best-known of Gilbert & Sullivan comic operas

Beards passed into a half-century limbo after the introduction by Gillette of the modern safety razor

vated, attacking authoritarianism in such collections as *Reality Sandwiches* (1963) and *Planet News* (1969).

Giolitti, Giovanni (1842-1928) Italian statesman and Liberal reformer, who tried to keep Italy out of the First World War. Between 1892 and 1921, he was Premier five times, the last Italian Liberal Prime Minister before the advent of MUSSOLINI. Public opinion led him to declare war against Turkey in 1911, but the experience was such that he tried strenuously to keep Italy neutral in the First World War, a move which forced him out of office in 1914. Though a near-Socialist, he failed to gain Socialist support in 1920 during his last term of office, and Italian liberalism died when he retired.

Giono, Jean (1895-1970) French writer of regionalist inspiration, known for his anti-intellectual pan-

theistic novels concerning the Provençal peasants and countryside such as *Colline* (1928), *Un de Baumugnes* (1929) and *Regain* (1930). His pacifist views led to charges of collaboration during the Second World War and even imprisonment. His numerous publications since this ordeal, such as *Le Hussard sur le Toit* (1952), have demonstrated the range of Giono's talent.

Giordano, Luca (1632-1705) Italian painter, a pupil of RIBERA. He travelled widely in Italy and his work successively reflects the styles of CARAVAGGIO, PIETRO DA CORTONA and the Venetian painters. In 1692 he went to Spain, where he painted the ceilings in the Escoriál.

Giorgione (c. 1476-1510) Italian artist of the Venetian Renaissance, and pupil of Giovanni BELLINI, whose influence is found in Giorgione's first important religious work, the *Castelfranco Madonna* (1504). Only a few paintings can be definitely attributed to him, one of the most famous of which is the *Tempest*. This painting is historically important as it is the earliest picture in which the mood of a landscape is captured, and also because it is a small painting intended for a private collection rather than for a church. Giorgione's technique of 'trembling' brush strokes of fine disconnected lines and dots makes the entire image on the canvas appear to vibrate and focuses the attention of the onlooker on the relationship between individual objects as affected by colour and light. Giorgione's influence was extensive and his work with colour and light directly influenced TITIAN and the entire tradition of Venetian painting.

Giotto (c. 1266-1337) Florentine artist, who was the first painter whose works exhibit a concern for both naturalism and emotional content, the major preoccupations of artists

until recent times. His first important work was the fresco cycle of the *Legend of St Francis* in the Upper Church at Assisi (*c.* 1300), a series of murals which gave visual form to the humanity of the saint. His best-preserved and most characteristic works are, however, the scenes from the lives of Sts Joachim and Anne and the Virgin and the *Life and Passion of Christ* in the Arena Chapel, Padua (*c.* 1305). These important frescoes reveal his rejection of the flat stylized forms of the Byzantine tradition in favour of figures of solidity and weight whose relationship to each other contributes to a sense of space and have an unprecedented dramatic power. The emotionally charged content of frescoes such as the *Lamentation* are achieved with an economy and directness which was later admired by MASACCIO and MICHELANGELO.

Giovanni da Fiesole, Fra see ANGELICO, Fra

Girard, Jean-Baptiste (1765-1850) Swiss priest and educator who influenced educational practice by stressing the use of the vernacular.

Girardin, Emile de (1806-81) French political journalist who founded and edited the now-defunct *La Presse* (1836), a daily newspaper that pioneered cheap, popular journalism in France.

Giraudoux, Jean (1882-1944) French dramatist who wrote *Siegfried* (1928), *Amphytrion '38* (1929), *The Trojan War Will Not Take Place* (1935) and other plays. His success owed much to his collaboration with the director, Louis JOUVET, which began with *Siegfried*. *The Madwomen of Chaillot* was successfully produced in London and New York. *Tiger at the Gates*, *Duel of Angels* and *Judith* were translated by Christopher FRY for the London theatre.

Gislebertus (12th cent.) French Romanesque sculptor. The great imagination shown in his work, ranging from the tender to the powerful, and from small vignettes to the great tympanum relief of the *Last Judgement* (*c.* 1135) at Autun Cathedral, served as inspiration to generations of carvers working on Burgundian churches.

Gissing, George (1857-1903) English novelist whose work gives a grim, realistic picture of industrial poverty and despair. In his numerous novels he was influenced by DICKENS's technique. His principal work, *New Grub Street* (1891), portrays the jealousies and intrigues of the London literary world and the difficulty of artistic integrity. Gissing suffered from ex-

treme poverty and an unhappy marriage, and in *The Private Papers of Henry Rycroft* (1903) portrayed a man in similar circumstances, whose solace was bookish solitude.

Gladstone, William Ewart (1809-98) The greatest British reforming statesman of the 19th century. First elected an MP in 1832, he was appointed President of the Board of Trade by PEEL in 1843, but after Peel's defeat in 1846 he was kept out of office until 1852 by his belief in free trade. As Chancellor of the Exchequer (1852-5 and 1858-66), he began a series of reforms by cutting tariffs and government expenditure. He became Leader of the Liberal Party in 1866 and Prime Minister in 1868. His first administration (1868-74) reformed the legal system, education and the army, disestablished the Church of Ireland and passed the Irish Land Act, and established the secret ballot at elections. During his second ministry (1880-5) his government carried the Third Reform Act of 1884, but was discredited by GORDON's death and Britain's defeats in the first Boer War (1881). Gladstone's third ministry (1886) fell when the Liberal Party split over his proposals for Irish Home Rule, which were opposed by CHAMBERLAIN and his followers. His fourth ministry (1892-4) was preoccupied with a further unsuccessful attempt to procure Home Rule. Like his chief opponent DISRAELI, Gladstone was a great orator. His political career was founded upon strong religious principles.

Glanville, Ranulf de (12th cent.) English jurist and statesman who substantially changed the English legal system. As HENRY II's chief adviser, he strengthened the common law by re-establishing the royal courts, where cases were tried before a jury and not by 'ordeal' and by increasing the use of itinerant judges (Justices in Eyre) to try cases at local Assizes. Glanville is reputed to have written the *Treatise on the Laws and Customs of the Kingdom of England*, which described the procedure in the royal courts and extended the influence of common law as against canon and feudal law.

Glenn, John Herschel (born 1921) American experimental military test pilot, the first American astronaut in the Mercury capsule, Friendship 7, to orbit the Earth (20 Feb. 1962). This he did three times in just under five hours, covering a distance of 81,000 miles at an altitude of 160 miles.

The year after Gagarin first circled the Earth, John Glenn put America on terms with the Russians in a three-orbit flight

Glidden, Joseph Farwell (1813-1906) American farmer who, in 1873, devised a reliable machine for the manufacture of barbed wire in quantity. Barbed wire fencing played an important part in the ranching of the American West and became used increasingly in military defence and during the First World War. Entanglements stretched from Switzerland to the English Channel.

Glinka, Konstantin Dimitrievich (1867-1927) Russian soil scientist who revolutionized world soil studies (pedology). Glinka sent teams of soil scientists to survey Russia (1908-14), and published a soil map of the Soviet Union (1927). His pioneer textbook, *The Great Soil Groups of the World and Their Development* (1908), was translated into German (1914), English (1927) and eventually swept the scientific world. Modified by MARBUT, it gave economists new insight into the agricultural importance of soil and its conservation.

Glinka, Mikhail (1804-57) Russian composer of *Russlan and Ludmilla* (1842), which, based on a PUSHKIN fairy-tale, had a sense of colour and fantasy that made it the first Russian musical work to be recognized outside his country. He travelled in Italy and Germany to study European musical traditions, and his first opera, *A Life for the Tsar* (1836), while incorporating Russian folk elements, owed a great deal to Italian operatic models.

Gluck, Christoph von (1714-87) German composer who reformed opera by insisting, in the preface to his work *Alcestis* (1767), that opera return to one of its basic principles – the subordination of the music to the drama. He wrote many operas to Italian and French librettos, the most

William Ewart Gladstone was one of the giants of Victorian government

famous of which was *Orpheus and Eurydice* (1762).

Gnaeus Pompeius Magnus see POMPEY

Go-Daigo see DAIGO II

Godard, Jean-Luc (born 1930) French film director, at first associated with other directors such as Truffaut, Chabrol and Resnais in the Nouvelle Vague of 1959-60 and has since become one of the most influential and controversial figures in contemporary cinema.

Goddard, Baron Rayner (1877-1971) English judge, Lord Chief Justice (1946-58), whose administrative work paved the way for later reforms of the judicial system. His views on punishment highlighted the dilemmas of the penal system.

Goddard, Robert Hutchings (1882-1945) American physicist and pioneer of rocketry. The history of rockets as fireworks and in war dates back to the 13th century, but all early devices used solid, gunpowder-like fuel. In 1926, Goddard launched his revolutionary rocket on liquid fuels, the power on which modern rocketry is based. Goddard later pioneered the use of liquefied gases as propellants, rocket steering by the combination of gyroscopes and movable vanes in the exhaust gases, and instrument-carrying rockets. He also patented the multi-stage rocket.

Godunov, Boris Fedorovich (c. 1552-1605) Tsar of Russia (1598-1605). Godunov founded many towns to civilize the eastern regions, recovered lands lost to Sweden and encouraged cultural and trading contacts with western Europe. In his domestic policy, Godunov favoured the middle classes at the expense of the old nobility and peasants, and his binding of peasants to the life-long service of one landowner rigidly entrenched serfdom.

Goebbels, Joseph (1897-1945) German politician and Nazi propagandist. As one of HITLER's closest followers, he was put in charge of the National Socialist Party's propaganda in 1929, and was Minister for Propaganda and National Enlightenment from 1933 to 1945. His skill in arousing anti-Semitism and in exploiting the public's basest sentiments made Goebbels one of the most dangerous men ever to hold political office. When, in 1945, it became clear that Germany had lost the War, he shot his wife and children, then committed suicide.

Goering, Hermann (1893-1946) German Nazi leader and creator of the Luftwaffe. During the First World War he served with distinction as a pilot in the famous RICHTHOFEN squadron. Goering was one of HITLER's earliest associates and helped to foster Nazi party contacts with industrialists and politicians before Hitler achieved power in 1933. He laid the basis of the police forces later controlled by HIMMLER and authorized the detention camps for political, religious and racial suspects. He was chairman of Germany's four-year rearmament plan (1936). Following the early German victories in the Second World War, which were due largely to the Luftwaffe, he was made *Reichsmarschall* (1940). He remained important in the Nazi hierarchy until at least 1941, but thereafter the failure of the Luftwaffe to maintain its ascendancy in the air and Goering's own indolence reduced his prestige with Hitler. Towards the end of the war, as Hitler's successor-designate he attempted to negotiate an armistice with the Allies. As a result, and due largely to the influence of Bormann, he was accused of treason and defeatism. At Nuremberg, in 1946, he was tried and sentenced to death but poisoned himself.

Goes, Hugo van der (c. 1440-82) Flemish painter whose style, as seen in the central Adoration panel of the famous *Portinari Altarpiece* (c. 1476), reveals the painstaking realism of Flemish painting enhanced by a marked emotional intensity.

Goethe, Johann Wolfgang von (1749-1832) German poet, novelist, dramatist, critic, politician, scientist, painter and philosopher, who regarded as his province the entire range of human knowledge, and excelled in many fields. His central philosophical principle was the concept of organic growth, which emerges in his biological and zoological work and in his imaginative writings. His supreme dramatic achievement, *Faust*, completed in the last years of his life, is a representation of man's unceasing search for breadth and depth of experience. His outstanding novels are *Die Leiden des Jungen Werthers* (1774), which Goethe based upon the emotions of his characters, rather than on a rational, 18th-century system of values, and *Wilhelm Meister* (1812), which was based closely on events in his own life. Goethe also wrote treatises on botany and optics and was a pioneer of the theory of evolution. A journey to Italy (1786) gave him the inspiration for *Römische Elegien*, translated by W. H. AUDEN and E. Mayer, and the enthusiasm to express dramatically his humanistic ideals in *Iphigenie auf Tauris* (1787). At the same time he completed *Egmont*, an historical drama which expanded Goethe's fundamental

Last days of Goering: the Nazi leader faces his accusers at Nuremberg

belief in the external forces which motivate men's actions, a concept which found its ultimate and most compelling expression in *Faust*.

Goffman, Erving (born 1922) Canadian author of many detailed sociological analyses of face-to-face encounters in a wide range of different settings. His books include *The Presentation of Self in Everyday Life* (1956), *Asylums* (1961) and *Stigma: Notes on the Management of Spoiled Identity* (1964).

Gogarty, Oliver St John (1878-1957) Irish writer and politician who is best known for his appearance in JOYCE's *Ulysses* under the name of Malachi Mulligan. Some of his best poems are on classical themes, such as 'Leda' and 'Europa'. He was a senator in the Irish Free State, and wrote entertaining memoirs in *As I Was Going Down Sackville Street* (1937), which includes accounts of the Irish revolts of the 1920s.

Gogh, Vincent van (1853-90) 'I want to say something comforting, as music is comforting. I want to paint men and women with something of the eternal.' So wrote van Gogh, son of a Dutch pastor whose extremely popular work is unique in its powerful rhythmic drawing and expressive colour. He began to paint in 1880, after an unsuccessful period as an evangelist. His early pictures, before he went to Paris in 1886, are of peasants and the land they worked, e.g. *Potato Eaters* (1885), a picture of a peasant family's meal-time. In Paris, van Gogh met SEURAT, GAUGUIN and PISSARRO. The impact of Impressionism upon him was immediate: his palette brightened, he became technically more versatile. In 1888 he moved to Arles in Provence, and there, in a period of insanity after a quarrel with Gauguin, he cut off his own ear. Two years later, in July 1890, he committed suicide. It was during these two years, however, that van Gogh painted his best-known works, a series of portraits and landscapes that now, in reproduction, enjoy a huge popularity. Van Gogh's collected letters are highly informative about his life and work and are also a moving human document.

Gogol, Nikolai Vasilievich (1809-52) Russian novelist and dramatist, author of *The Government Inspector* (1836), a satirical drama about bureaucracy, and *Dead Souls* (1842), a novel about an adventurer, the purchaser of the souls of serfs who died after the last census but who exist in law until the next, thus achieving for himself a 'prosperous' status. *The Overcoat* (1842), another of Gogol's most celebrated works, is the story

of a poorly paid clerk in a government office, and is based on his own experiences. From his Ukrainian Cossack background, Gogol wrote many stories and sketches of Ukrainian life, collected in *Evenings on a Farm near Dikanka* (1831), which includes some *Cossack Tales* (enlarged and rewritten in 1842). After 1836 Gogol spent many years travelling, during which period he wrote *Selected Passages from Correspondence with Friends* (1847), a collection of essays in defence of the Tsarist régime and its institutions which provoked much criticism in Russia. Seeking comfort in religion he embarked on a pilgrimage to Palestine in 1848, but returned in the grip of a religious fanaticism, and later destroyed some of his manuscripts.

Golding, William (born 1911) English novelist whose books examine the primitive urges of man. *The Lord of the Flies* (1954) is a disturbing picture of children marooned on an island, producing 'evil as a bee produces honey'. His second novel, *The Inheritors* (1955), is an imaginative work concerning the extermination of Neanderthal man by *Homo Sapiens*.

Goldmann, Max see REINHARDT, Max

Goldmark, Peter Carl (born 1906) Hungarian-born engineer who developed a colour television system (1940) and the long-playing gramophone record (1948). The microgroove record, playing at $33\frac{1}{3}$ rpm and with 250 grooves to the inch, was made possible only by the development of suitable plastics.

Goldoni, Carlo (1707-93) Italian dramatist, whose work led to written parts replacing the fixed characters and improvisation by actors of the Commedia dell'Arte. He wrote more than 200 plays in Italian, French or Venetian dialect, many of them realistic comedies, mildly anti-aristocratic, reflecting contemporary life in Venice. Only a few of them are still performed today, notably *La Locandiera* (1753), which was one of Eleonora DUSE's favourite parts.

Goldsmith, Oliver (c. 1728-74) Irish author, best known for *The Vicar of Wakefield* (1766), one of the first novels to make a popular blend of sentiment, domesticity and middle-class morality. His poetry is classical, 'The Deserted Village' (1770) showing a moral concern about the effects of the Industrial Revolution. His most famous play, *She Stoops to Conquer* (1773), was a success, and is still revived. Always in dire need, Goldsmith did much hack work for booksellers and journals, and

tried, unsuccessfully, throughout his life, to set up as a physician. He was a member of JOHNSON's literary circle.

Goldwyn, Samuel (born 1884) American film producer who was for many years one of the most influential and powerful men in Hollywood, noted for paying extravagant fees to his stars. Goldwyn has become famous as the discoverer of Greta Garbo, whom he groomed for stardom and for his insistence on making family entertainment, including films such as *The Adventures of Marco Polo* (1938) and *Porgy and Bess* (1959). His Goldwyn Picture Corporation was one of the companies amalgamated to form M-G-M.

Gomes, Fernão (15th cent.) Wealthy Portuguese citizen who sponsored the exploration of 2000 miles of African coast (1469-74) in return for the profits reaped from any consequent trade.

Gomulka, Wladyslaw (born 1905) Polish Communist leader. After the Second World War, in which he was a leader of the Polish underground movement, Gomulka opposed collectivization and resisted Russian domination of his government's internal policies. In 1949 he was expelled from the Party and imprisoned (1951) for anti-Stalinist deviationism. After STALIN's death and the break-up of the Stalinist system, Gomulka was returned to power as First Secretary of the Party in October 1956, having declared his policy of taking an independent road to socialism. Although most collectives have been dissolved, and there is now some measure of freedom in Poland, Gomulka failed to live up to his early liberal promises, and reverted to the more traditional pattern of Iron Curtain government. Unrest over inept economic policies led to strikes and demonstrations, and to Gomulka's downfall in 1970. He was replaced as party leader by Gierek.

Goncourt, Edmond Louis Antoine de (1822-96) and **Jules Alfred Huot de (1830-70)** French novelists, historians and dramatists, authors of the famous *Journal*, an invaluable record of contemporary life. Begun in 1851, it was continued by Edmond after his brother's death, and provided a series of fascinating glimpses of French society and observations on leading artists and writers of the day, particularly FLAUBERT, ZOLA, DAUDET, TURGENEV and their circle. The Goncourt brothers produced some moving and original novels, including studies of psychiatric disorders, such as *Germinie Lacerteux* (1865) and *Madame Gervaisais* (1869).

Gongo Musa (c. 1307-c. 1332) Sudanese *mansa* (emperor) of Mali who, by inheritance and conquest, ruled over most of Africa southwest of the Sahara. A Muslim like his Sudanese predecessors, he made a pilgrimage to Mecca, debasing Egypt's coinage with the huge quantity of gold brought back by his splendid retinue. The effect of his personality led to the spread of Islamic culture to West Africa and to the making of the first European map of West Africa (1375).

Góngora y Argote, Luis de (1561-1627) Spanish poet, who has had an appreciable influence on contemporary Spanish poetry. His works are written in two styles, some consisting of short poems, romances, *letrillas* and sonnets. His other style was *gongorismo*, or *culteranismo*, a more obscure style, full of word-play, dislocated syntax and mythological allusion, as in *The Fable of Polifemo and Galeta* (1612-13). For three centuries his name was synonymous with obscurity and pedantry. Today, his work has been revalued and he is now considered one of Spain's most important poets.

Gonzalez, José see GRIS, Juan

Gonzalez, Julio (1876-1942) Spanish sculptor who, in the 1930s, found his most personal expression in welded iron. His best-known work, inspired by the Spanish Civil War, was *Mascarade Monserrat* (1937).

Goodnight, Charles (1836-1929) American pioneer rancher who did much to establish the cattle empire of the West. He established the first ranch on the Staked Plains and was noted for his efforts to improve beef production by importing Shorthorn and Hereford cattle.

Goodyear, Charles (1800-60) American inventor who developed vulcanized rubber. From about 1830 he started experimenting on methods to improve the properties of natural rubber and in 1844 patented the process of forming vulcanized rubber by heating rubber-sulphur mixtures at high temperatures. At the same time, MACINTOSH and HANCOCK were working on the same problem in Britain, where they took out key patents two months before Goodyear.

Goolagong, Evonne (born 1951) Australian tennis player, the first Australian aboriginal to play international tennis. In 1971 she won the Wimbledon Women's Singles Championship.

Gordon, Charles George (1833-85) English general, famous for his ten-month defence of Khartoum. He served in the Crimean War (1854), then entered the employment of the Chinese Manchu government (1860-5). His explorations, and his quelling of the Taiping rebellion (1864), earned him the nickname of 'Chinese Gordon'. From China he went to Egypt (1874) and became governor of the Sudan (1877-80), where he attempted to suppress slave-trading. After some time in South Africa he was sent to the Sudan again in 1884, to rescue Egyptian garrisons cut off by the forces of the Mahdi (the Muslim 'Messiah', who roused Sudan in revolt against Egyptian rule in 1882). He was besieged in Khartoum, and after ten months of resistance, was killed shortly before a relief force arrived. Gordon's character was complex. He was both a mystic and a man of action, with a marked sense of his own destiny. In England he was noted for his practical evangelical Christianity and was a hero of the Victorian public.

Gordon, Lord George (1751-93) Protestant extremist of Scottish descent who inspired the Gordon Riots in London. In 1780, he organized and led a march of Protestants to Parliament, petitioning for the repeal of the Catholic Relief Act, which freed Catholics from certain legal disadvantages. Reinforced by other disaffected groups, the Protestants began a riot which ravaged London for six days. Gordon was acquitted of treason but later imprisoned for libelling MARIE ANTOINETTE. He died in jail, converted to Judaism.

Gorenko, Anna Andreyevna see AKHMATOVA, Anna

Gorky, Maxim (1868-1936) Russian novelist and dramatist, whose best-known books are the autobiographical *Childhood, In the World* and *My Universities*, studies of life in pre-revolutionary Russia. His popularity, particularly with the Russian working class, stemmed mainly from his realistic, boisterous short stories, portraying tramps and social outcasts. His famous play, *The Lower Depths*, was popular more for its political content than its dramatic quality. He was arrested twice for his revolutionary views.

Gorton, John Grey (born 1911) Australian Prime Minister from 1968 to 1971. He entered the Federal Government in 1958 and held many ministerial positions in the Liberal Country Party government.

Gottwald, Klement (1896-1953) Leader of the Communist *coup d'état* in Czechoslovakia. After spending the war years in Moscow, he returned to Czechoslovakia in 1945 and the following year became Prime Minister of a coalition government, democratically appointed by BENES. Through the gradual infiltration of Communists into the organs of government, particularly the police, Gottwald ruled within the constitution for almost two years, until in February 1948 he gained complete control in a bloodless *coup d'état*, and Czechoslovakia followed in the path of Hungary, Bulgaria and Rumania. A firm supporter of the Moscow line, he became the dictator of a state constructed on the Stalinist model.

Goudy, Frederic (1865-1947) American printer and typographer, who founded the Village Press in Park Ridge, Illinois (1905). He designed all his own type, some of which is still used today, particularly Goudy Old Style.

Goujon, Jean (c. 1510-68) French Renaissance sculptor, whose reliefs are ranked among the best works of the period.

Gould, Jay (1836-92) American financier, speculator and railway tycoon. Having acquired capital from a leather tanning business he became notorious for the promotion, sale and manipulation of railway company stock. Particularly dubious were his dealings against Cornelius VANDERBILT in connection with the Erie Railroad (1867-72). In 1869 he and his associates tried to corner the gold market and in the 1870s he juggled for control of the Union, Kansas, Denver, Central and Missouri Pacific railroads. By 1890 he owned half the railway mileage in the southwest of

Gorky wandered Russia, searching for work. He educated himself as he went along, and became a writer

the US. He owned the *New York World* (1879-83) and controlled the Western Union Telegraph Co. His will disclosed a personal fortune of $77 million, but it was believed that the much larger real total had been concealed and was probably tied up in trusts for his six children.

Gould, Shane (born 1957) Australian Olympic swimmer. While still only 15 years old, she won three gold medals, one silver and one bronze at the Munich Olympic Games of 1972.

Gounod, Charles-François (1818-93) French composer and conductor remembered today for his opera *Faust* (1857), based on Part I of GOETHE's masterpiece, and for his *Ave Maria*, a 'meditation' on the first prelude of J. S. BACH's *Well-Tempered Clavier*. A pupil of Halévy, he won the Prix de Rome and wrote many church compositions. Gounod completed 13 other operas, and during a period in England (1870-5) was first conductor of the Royal Choral Society.

Gourgand, Françoise see VESTRIS, Madame

Gower, John (c. 1330-1408) English poet who, with CHAUCER, made English a literary language. He wrote poems in French, Latin and English. His *Confessio Amantis* (1390), written in English, is a huge collection of stories about love, taken from classical and medieval sources, and told in regular, polished couplets.

Gowon, Yakubu (born 1934) Nigerian soldier-politician, and Head of State, who crushed the Biafran secessionist revolt of 1967-70. As a member of the Angas tribe, Gowon was born a Christian. His education was completed at Sandhurst Military Academy in England, and in 1957 he was commissioned into the Nigerian army. While serving with a UN Force in the Congo during the war of 1960-1, he became a strong opponent of secession by member regions of African federal republics. In 1966, the government of Sir Abubaka Tafawa Balewa was overthrown in a coup which resulted in the establishment of a military government under General Ironsi. In July 1966 Ironsi (an Ibo) was himself deposed and murdered in an anti-Ibo counter-revolution. Gowon was appointed Supreme Commander of the military forces and head of the federal military government which was then set up.

Goya y Lucientes, Francisco José de (1746-1828) Spanish artist, whose portraiture combines Neo-classical control with realistic perception and a romantic feeling for form and colour, e.g. *The Maja Nude* and *The Maja Clothed*. He was court painter for 53 years and though political expediency played its part at times in the commissions he accepted, he never flattered his sitters, nor, like the Neo-classicists, idealized them, e.g. *The Portrait of Charles III in Hunting Dress* and that of *Josefa Bayeau*. Nevertheless the distinction in style and subject-matter between his commissioned and his non-commissioned works reveal the depth of Goya's own convictions. When the subject is war, e.g. *The Disasters of War* (1810-13), painted after the French invasion, realism and imaginative creation meet to expose the full horror to his audience. In 1792 Goya fell seriously ill: *The Flaggellants*, a group of 12 small paintings which concentrate on the terror of suffering; and the drawings for the 80 etchings, *Los Caprichos* (caricatures that savagely disclose the abuses in Church, Court and State), were the results of this period of illness and depression.

Goyen, Jan van (1596-1656) Dutch topographical painter, whose panoramic views of the Dutch countryside are characterized by their low horizons and effects of spaciousness, enhanced by features such as distant sailing boats, windmills or tiny figures.

Grace, William Gilbert (1848-1915) English cricketer who was the foremost influence on modern batting and bowling techniques. He scored nearly 55,000 runs and took nearly 2900 wickets in first-class cricket in a playing career of more than 50 years. He was also a medical practitioner.

Graebner, Fritz (1877-1934) German sociologist who studied ethnology from the point of view of the history of whole culture areas, and developed the notion of 'cultural links'.

Graham, John, 1st Viscount Dundee (c. 1649-89) Scottish soldier, known as 'Bonny Dundee', who led the first Scottish revolt against WILLIAM III. He helped James, Duke of York, to suppress Scotland's military Covenanters (1677-9), was created Viscount Dundee (1688), and became second-in-command of James II's Scottish army opposing the

1861

The demon doctor, W. G. Grace remains the greatest legend in cricket

accession of William of Orange. After James had fled, Dundee gathered an army of Highlanders and shattered the pro-William forces at the Pass of Killicrankie (1689), but he was killed in the battle and Jacobite resistance ended until 1715.

Graham, Martha (born 1895) American dancer and choreographer and one of the most influential figures in modern dance. She rejected classical Russian ballet and stressed bodily movements as expressions of states of mind, synchronizing breathing, movement, muscular co-ordination and balance in ways which permitted new fluid forms of dancing barefoot. Working with American composers,

including Aaron COPLAND, she wove more than 100 ballets around social, psychological and literary themes.

Graham, Thomas (1805-69) Scottish chemist who established a law describing the diffusion of gases. In the 1820s he studied the rates at which gases diffuse through various porous materials and in 1831 formulated his law, which states that the rate of diffusion of a gas is inversely proportional to the square root of its molecular weight.

Grahame, Kenneth (1859-1932) Scottish writer of children's stories. His chief work, *The Wind in the Willows* (1908), was dramatized by A. A. MILNE as *Toad of Toad Hall*.

Grainger, Percy Aldridge (1882-1961) Australian-born composer and pianist who wrote the perennial *Country Gardens*, based on a morris tune. The success of this and its companion pieces has tended to obscure his work in folk music. In 1912, Grainger recorded *Brigg Fair*, upon which DELIUS based his orchestral work. Grainger became a naturalized United States citizen and lived in America from 1915 onwards. During his later years he was much occupied with experimental compositions.

Granados, Enrique (1867-1916) Spanish conductor, pianist and composer whose best-known work is the opera *Goyescas*.

Grandier, Urbain (1590-1634) French parish priest, notorious for his love-affairs, who was falsely charged with bewitching a convent of nuns at

Loudun in France. Although the nuns co-operated with his accusers by pretending to go into convulsions and hysterics, the charge failed. Accused a second time, Grandier, who had provoked the enmity of Cardinal RICHELIEU, was tried for witchcraft, tortured and burned at the stake.

Grant, Ulysses Simpson (1822-85) US President who, as Commander of the Union army during the American Civil War, defeated the forces of the Confederacy under LEE. Grant fought in the Mexican War (1846-8), retired, then re-enlisted when the Civil War started and was appointed Major-General (1862). After receiving Lee's surrender at Appomattox (April 1865) he served for two years as Secretary for War and was then elected President, in which office he served two terms (1869-77). His second administration was disturbed by a business depression and financial scandals in which some of his Cabinet were involved. After his retirement, he was swindled out of his savings by a confidence trickster, but paid his creditors by selling his memoirs.

Grass, Günter (born 1927) German novelist, poet and dramatist, whose famous novel *The Tin Drum* (1959) is a grotesque survey of modern Germany, from the Third Reich to the 'economic miracle'. Other novels include *Cat and Mouse* and *Dog*

The main protagonists in the American Civil War, 1861-5. Grant became President of the US , Lee a hero in defeat. The intervening maps show the diminishing of Confederate territory in the bloody conflict between North and South. Grant took Lee's surrender at Appomattox

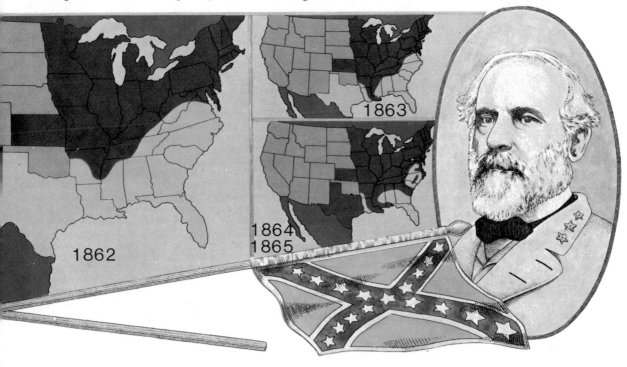

1862

1863

1864
1865

Years, and Grass has also written poems and short plays, in the manner of BECKETT, all of which embody his preoccupation with the 'absurd'.

Grassman, Hermann (1809-77) German mathematician, who discovered the calculus of extension, a kind of algebra of geometry, in which geometrical entities are represented by symbols, a notion going back to LEIBNIZ. From this work, later German mathematicians developed vector calculus, which was later widely used in various branches of pure and applied mathematics.

Gratian (early 12th cent.) Italian Camaldolese monk who has been called the father of canon (ecclesiastical) law. In his *Decretum* he collated nearly 4000 texts on Church discipline from earlier collections (notably one by DIONYSIUS EXIGUUS), and reconciled their discrepancies. This comprehensive and scholarly work became a vital part of the growing body of canon law taught in universities and cited by the popes. In 1917, Cardinal Gaspari completed an official codification of canon law using the *Decretum* as his major source.

Grattan, Henry (1746-1820) Irish statesman, champion of Irish independence and religious reform. Trained as a barrister, he entered the Irish Parliament, where his oratory helped to end Great Britain's veto over Irish legislation (1782). He demanded reforms to benefit Irish Catholics and peasants, but could not stop the Act of Union (1800), which helped Ireland's Protestant minority government to keep control over the Catholic majority. He continued the fight for Catholic emancipation after the Union.

Gravelet, Jean François see BLONDIN, Charles

Graves, Robert (born 1895) English poet and novelist who pursues an interest in myth and religion. His early verse reflects the effect of his service in the First World War. The poetry of his middle period, between the wars, avoids emotion, while the later poetry returns more to natural feelings. The prose works, *I Claudius* (1934) and *Claudius the God*, are imaginative recreations of the Roman mind. Reminiscences and social history in *Goodbye to All That* (1929) and *The Long Weekend* (1940) are graphically descriptive of the English society of the 1920s and 1930s.

Gray, Thomas (1716-71) English scholar and poet, most widely known for his 'Elegy Written in a Country Churchyard' (1750), a melancholy reflection on life and death, which achieved great popularity. Gray twice refused the Poet Laureateship.

Greco, El (1541-1614) Cretan-born artist, with a highly individual style, characterized by asymmetry of composition, acid colours, elongated figures and ecstatic expressions and gestures. He is believed to have trained under TITIAN, and lived, from 1577 until the end of his life, in Toledo, where he received two major commissions for altarpieces (S Domingo el Antiguo and the Cathedral), but his highly original style was not always acceptable to the Church. His best-known work, *The Burial of Count Orgaz* (1586), was commissioned to commemorate the burial of a benefactor. The occasion was depicted by El Greco in dazzling colours as a contemporary event, and it embodied the reception of Count Orgaz into heaven. This part of the picture is painted in an entirely different style, in which the colours, figures and relationships of scale are anti-naturalistic. El Greco's religious works must be seen against the background of the Inquisition in Spain and particularly the *Spiritual Exercises* of St Ignatius LOYOLA.

Greeley, Horace (1811-1872) American journalist whose editorial policies helped to rouse northern popular opinion against slavery. His liberal views gained him the editorship of the *Jeffersonian* (1838) and the *Log Cabin* in the presidential campaign (1840). In 1841, he founded and edited the New York *Tribune*, where his progressive Whig ideals of socio-economic reform and his powerful anti-slavery editorials were highly influential. He helped to organize the Republican Party (1854-5), and supported Abraham LINCOLN in his presidential campaign (1860). Greeley fruitlessly sought office, broke with the Republican Party and finally became the unsuccessful presidential candidate for the dissenting Liberal Republicans in 1872.

Green, John (1837-83) British historian, whose *Short History of the English People* (1874) was the first socio-economic description of Britain.

Greene, Graham (born 1904) English writer, author of *The Power and the Glory* (1940) and *The Heart of the Matter* (1948) which, like most of his major novels, portray a sad world of guilt and remorse. Greene was converted to Catholicism, and religion is a constant theme in his novels. His prose has a powerful atmosphere of misery and defeat, even in his 'entertainments', his literary thrillers, spy stories and historical fiction: *Stamboul Train* (1932), *Brighton Rock* (1938), *Ministry of Fear* (1943) and

Edvard Grieg remains one of the most popular light classical composers

The Third Man (1950). In his later work, Greene abandoned explicitly religious themes, and adopted a 'softer line' on the question of morality, achieving a compromise between the serious novels and the 'entertainments'. Thirteen of his novels have been filmed.

Greene, Robert (c. 1560-92) English poet, playwright and pamphleteer, whose works are most valuable for their picture of Elizabethan London. His autobiographical *A Groatsworth of Wit Bought with a Million of Repentance* (1592) contains an attack on the young, successful SHAKESPEARE.

Gregory, Lady Augusta (1852-1932) Irish dramatist, who helped to establish the Irish Literary Theatre (1898-9), and the Irish National Theatre Society (1902). She wrote two full-length plays, *The Pot of Broth* and *Cathleen ni Houlihan* (1902) in collaboration with W. B. YEATS, and some one-act plays and comedies, among them *The Workhouse Ward* (1908). Her work pioneered the revival of drama in Ireland at the turn of the century.

Gregory, Sir Augustus Charles (1819-1905) British-born explorer who crossed northern Australia from near the site of Darwin eastwards to the Pacific near Brisbane (1855), and sought traces of LEICHHARDT in a transcontinental journey down the Barcoo River through east-central Australia to Adelaide (1857).

Gregory the Great, Saint (c. 540-604) Roman magistrate turned monk who, as Pope Gregory I, made the papacy a power to be reckoned with. Last of the Church fathers (after saints AUGUSTINE, AMBROSE, JEROME), he strengthened Church administration, discipline and authority by proclaiming the pope head of all Christian churches. He reserved the Church's right to try and punish clerical offenders, enforced celibacy of the clergy, reformed the management of Church estates and sent Benedictine monks (notably St Augustine of Canterbury) to evangelize England, Italy and North Africa. His successors' claims to absolute power derive from Gregory's successes.

Gregory Nazianzus (329-389) Greek saint, one of the four great Greek Doctors of the Church. His preaching on the doctrine of the Trinity earned him fame and ensured the final rejection of Arianism by a general council in 381. But, consecrated Bishop of Constantinople, he could not face the political difficulties and retired to finish his life in contemplation.

Gregory of Tours (c. 538-93) French Bishop of Tours (from 573) whose *History of the Franks* contains an absorbing account of the Frankish invasions, and barbarian customs and rule in post-Roman western Europe to AD 575. He was later canonized, his feast day falling on 17 November.

Gresham, Sir Thomas (c. 1519-79) English merchant and royal financial agent. He worked largely in Antwerp as a private financier, and as financial agent to the English crown (1552), raising and repaying loans and organizing gold shipments to England. He established the Royal Exchange in London as a bankers' meeting house. Gresham was ahead of his time in proposing (unsuccessfully) a national equalization fund to stabilize the exchange rate of the pound sterling, which had dropped since HENRY VIII debased the coinage. He expounded what much later became known as Gresham's law, which stated that money of greater intrinsic value is hoarded while that of equal monetary but lesser intrinsic value is circulated.

Greuze, Jean (1725-1805) French painter, best remembered for his lachrymose, half-draped maidens. His most important works are generally considered to be his narrative pictures, inspired by ROUSSEAU, displaying the simple virtues of the poor, e.g. *The Paralytic Tended by his Children* (1763), which proclaimed the Neo-classical concern with morally elevating themes.

Grey, Charles, 2nd Earl (1764-1845) English Whig politician and Prime Minister whose ministry carried the 1832 Reform Bill through Parliament. Grey had long advocated parliamentary reform, and after forming a ministry in 1830, at the reluctant request of WILLIAM IV, the government produced a Parliamentary Reform Bill (1831). This was defeated and Parliament was dissolved, but the Whigs returned to power even more intent on reform. The House of Lords rejected a similar Bill the same year, and drastically amended a third in 1832. Grey resigned but WELLINGTON was unable to form a ministry, and Grey returned to power with an undertaking by William IV to create a sufficient number of peers to enable the Bill to pass through the Lords. The threat of this alone was sufficient to get it passed. In numerical terms the franchise was not greatly enlarged but the Act marked a distinct departure from the character of politics in the pre-Reform era. Grey's ministry also carried the abolishment of slavery in the colonies (1833). Disagreement within the government over Irish policy led to Grey's permanent retirement in 1834.

Grey, Sir Edward (1862-1933) English politician, who influenced Britain's decision to enter the First World War. He was Liberal MP for Berwick from 1885 to 1916. As Foreign Secretary (1905-16), he concluded the Anglo-Russian Entente of 1907 and was an advocate of the talks that took place between the British, French, Belgian and Russian general staffs in the period 1906-14. Despite his pacifism and belief in international arbitration, he was aware of the German threat. Although unwilling to declare war, he persuaded Parliament that Britain was bound to go to Belgium's aid when Germany invaded that country. He brought Italy into the war on the side of the Allies by the secret Treaty of London (1915), and by his awareness of the sensitivity of the US on the blockade issue, helped to secure her as an ally in 1917.

Grey, Lady Jane (1537-54) Queen of England for nine days (in 1553). Her father-in-law, the powerful Duke of Northumberland, had persuaded Edward VI to name her his heir. Northumberland was, however, unsuccessful in resisting MARY I's claim to the throne, and Jane was at first imprisoned, and later executed after the failure of Sir Thomas WYATT's rising against Mary.

Griboedov, Alexandr Sergeyevich (1795-1829) Russian dramatist, who achieved fame with *Woe from Wit* (1824), a satirical attack on the values of contemporary Moscow society. The play is remarkable for its vigorous, colloquial dialogue and was an early development in Russian realistic drama. Griboedov died at the hands of a Persian mob which stormed the Russian mission in Teheran in 1829.

Grieg, Edvard Hagerup (1843-1907) Norwegian composer, who, at IBSEN's request, wrote the incidental music to *Peer Gynt*, first performed in 1876. At a time when Norway was seeking its national identity and independence from Sweden, Grieg's originality and lyric gifts were inspired by Norway's folk music. His *Piano Concerto in A Minor* is one of the most popular piano concertos ever written. On his return to Norway after studying in Leipzig his style became conspicuously 'nationalist'. His best-known music after the Piano Concerto is the *Lyric Pieces* for piano and the *Holberg Suite* (1884) for strings.

Grierson, John (1898-1972) Scottish pioneer of the British documentary film movement, a key figure in the international development of realist cinema and director of *Drifters* (1929). Grierson gave documentary its name and the classic definition: 'the creative treatment of reality'. In 1938, he established the National Film Board of Canada.

Grieve, Christopher see MACDIARMID, Hugh

Griffith, David Wark (1875-1948) American director of films who revolutionized the entire language of movies. His two great silent works are *The Birth of a Nation* (1914) and *Intolerance* (1916). The first film, dealing with the Ku-Klux Klan, roused storms of controversy, but the huge cast, the great battle scenes and the sheer scale of the picture made it a triumphant box office success. *Intolerance*, intercutting a modern melodrama, the fall of Babylon, the story of Christ and the Huguenot massacre, bewildered its audiences and was a commercial disaster. Griffith's work subsequently declined and he rarely worked again after the early 1930s.

Griffith, John see LONDON, Jack

Grijalva, Juan de (c. 1489-1527) Spanish leader of an expedition along the Mexican coast from Yucatán to modern Vera Cruz, where he received gifts of gold sent by MONTEZUMA.

Grillparzer, Franz (1791-1872) Austrian writer, whose works combined elements of Classicism and Romanticism. His plays, which give a fine insight into the delicate and subtle feelings of the characters, are mainly concerned with individuals and their attempts to escape the role prescribed to them by divine law, nature or society. His best-known works include *Sappho* (1818), in which the heroine is torn between fulfilling her artistic calling and living life to the full, the trilogy entitled *The Golden Fleece* (1821), a tragedy based on the story of Jason and Medea, and the patriotic drama *King Ottocar, his Rise and Fall* (1825).

Grimaldi, Joseph (1779-1837) Anglo-Italian clown, who, as a singer, dancer, mime, actor and acrobat was a great attraction in Covent Garden harlequinades (1806-23). He created the archetypal clown known as Joey.

Grimm, Jacob (1785-1863) and **Wilhelm (1786-1859)** German philologists and mythologists most widely known for their collection known as *Grimm's Fairy Tales* (1812-15). Jacob's most important contribution to philology was *German Grammar* (1819-37), which included Grimm's Law, which first laid down the principle that language development is governed by regular phonetic laws and the correspondence of certain consonants within the Indo-Germanic languages. Jacob's other works include *German Legends* (1835), which traces the entire course of Teutonic myths and superstitions, and *Legal Antiquities* (1828), a study of Teutonic laws. Wilhelm collaborated with him on the *Fairy Tales*, on *German Legends* (1816-18), and on the only volume of the projected *German Lexicon* (1854) and on many editions of early literature. He also published his own translations and studies.

Grimmelshausen, Jacob von (c. 1625-76) German novelist who wrote *The Adventurous Simplicissimus* (1669), a long, picaresque story of the life and adventures of Simplicissimus. The humour and sympathetic understanding with which this expresses the Christian pessimism of the age reveal Grimmelshausen's love of life and his humanity. In his boyhood he was carried off by soldiers to fight in the 30 Years' War and fought on both sides before being converted to Catholicism in 1646.

Grindel, Eugène see ELUARD, Paul

Gris, Juan (1887-1927) Spanish Cubist painter who lived and worked in France. He developed a form of Cubism characterized by a stringently controlled composition and the inclusion of still-life motifs.

Grivas, George (1898-1974) Cypriot military leader and politician at the forefront of the struggle for *Enosis*, the union of Cyprus and Greece. Although Grivas's military efforts against the British were instru-

Son of a pantaloon player and an actress, Joseph Grimaldi grew up in a world of tumblers, tightrope walkers and buffoons

Nightmarish but enchanting, the stories of the brothers Grimm remain popular with children

mental in the formation of the Republic of Cyprus (1960), a rift developed between Grivas and Archbishop MAKARIOS concerning *Enosis*, and Grivas again took to guerilla strategy.

Grock (1880-1959) Stage name of Adrien Wettach, Swiss clown who achieved fame as the greatest of his kind since GRIMALDI.

Gromyko, Andrei Andreevich (born 1909) Russian, Foreign Minister of the Soviet Union, who has represented his country at nearly all the

important meetings with the West since 1945. An economist, he joined the Foreign Ministry at the outbreak of the Second World War and was made head of the American section. Later, he was sent to Washington as Counsellor at the Soviet Embassy and became Ambassador to the US in 1943. He was Soviet representative at the United Nations (1946-9), where he made extensive use of the veto, deputy Foreign Minister (1949-52), Ambassador to Britain (1952-3) and Foreign Minister in 1957, in succession to Shepilov. Although, in the earlier stages of his career, he pursued relentlessly the 'Cold War' against the West, his recent pronouncements have been in line with Russia's policy of coexistence.

Groot, Huigh de see GROTIUS, Hugo

Gropius, Walter (1883-1969) German pioneer of 20th-century architecture and design who founded the famous school of arts and crafts known as the Bauhaus (1919). Gropius studied under BEHRENS and his early works show that he was already turning his attention to industrial architecture, which demanded solutions in form, structure and materials which broke away from tradition. The Fagus factory at Alfeld and his pavilion for the Cologne Werkbund Exhibition of 1914 were also directly allied to the demands of industrialization. The Bauhaus embodied his idea that the arts should be subservient to and united in an architectural whole, with emphasis on the teaching crafts and on research into new materials. HITLER closed the Bauhaus in 1932 and Gropius fled first to England and then to America, where his works include Harvard Graduate Centre.

Grossmith, George (1847-1912) English humorist who, with his brother Weedon, contributed sketches of Victorian middle-class life to *Punch*. They were published as *The Diary of a Nobody* (1892).

Grosvenor, Gilbert Hovey (1875-1966) American geographer and editor who popularized the study of geography. In 1899 he became the director of the National Geographic Society, and was chief editor of the *National Geographic Magazine* for more than 50 years (1903-54). Grosvenor used his position to promote popular, but soundly scientific, expeditions which probed the oceans, atmosphere and polar regions. Their discoveries were published as lavishly illustrated accounts.

Grotefend, Georg Friedrich (1775-1853) German classical scholar who pioneered the decipherment of the cuneiform (wedge-shaped) script, first copied at Persepolis in Iran in 1802, deducing correctly that the inscriptions were in three languages.

Grotius, Hugo (1583-1645) Dutch lawyer, who wrote *On the Law of War and Peace*, a treatise on international law based on the view that natural law is a dictate of right reason, independent of any religion, and that even God cannot make good what is evil.

Grouchy, Emmanuel, Marquis de (1766-1847) French soldier of the Revolutionary and Napoleonic armies. Notwithstanding his aristocratic birth, Grouchy joined the revolutionaries and became one of NAPOLEON's most trusted generals. He fought with distinction in the Russian campaign of 1812. In June 1815 he defeated a detachment of BLÜCHER's army at Ligny, but did not prevent Blücher's main force from joining WELLINGTON at Waterloo.

Grove, Sir George (1820-1900) British civil engineer and musical scholar who founded and edited *Grove's Dictionary of Music and Musicians* (4 vols., 1879-99). Expanded and updated regularly, it remains a standard international work of reference. Among other varied activities, Grove built lighthouses in the West Indies and became the first director of the Royal College of Music, London.

Grünewald, Mathäus (c. 1475-1528) German painter, whose most famous painting is an altarpiece, the *Isenheim Altar*, completed *c.* 1515 and now in Colmar. The most striking part is a large crucified Christ, sombre in colour (unlike the other panels) and which is obsessed with physical pain.

Guardi, Francesco (1712-93) Italian artist, one of the major 18th-century painters of Venetian views. He collaborated with his brother Gian Antonio in painting religious pictures, but by the 1760s he was working almost exclusively on views of Venice. He could not command CANALETTO's high prices, but today Guardi's vivacity of touch, flickering light effects and poetic atmosphere are often preferred to his rival's precision.

Guareschi, Giovanni (1908-68) Italian novelist and journalist. In 1936 he went to Milan to edit *Bertoldo*, a humorous weekly. He founded another humorous weekly *Candido* (1945), and became world famous with the publication of *The Little World of Don Camillo* (1950), a collection of delightful, warm-hearted stories round the perpetual war of wits between the tolerant all-too-human parish priest Don Camillo and the Communist mayor Peppone. He followed this success with other Don Camillo books, as well as a humorous account of his own family life, *The House that Nino Built* (1953).

Guarini, Giovanni Battista (1538-1612) Italian pastoral playwright and author of the elaborate Arcadian drama *The Faithful Shepherd* (1590), which gained extensive popularity throughout Europe for 200 years.

Guarnerius see IRNERIUS

Guericke, Otto von (1602-86) German physicist who first proved the existence of a vacuum. This he demonstrated in 1650 when he removed water from a barrel with a pump. His later, successful evacuation of air from metal spheres resulted in a number of dramatic demonstrations.

Guesclin, Bertrand du (c. 1320-80) French soldier during the 100 Years' War, who fought for CHARLES V of France against the English. He brilliantly defended Rennes (1356-7) and organized defence in Normandy until 1364. As Constable of France from 1370, he harassed English troops by unconventional hit-and-run attacks, and although captured and held to ransom several times, Guesclin played a crucial role in pushing back the English from southern and western France.

Guettard, Jean-Etienne (1715-86) French naturalist and mineralogist, who drew up his findings on the distribution of minerals and rocks in the form of a map, one of the first of its kind.

Guevara, Ernesto (1928-67) Argentine-born Communist revolutionary, known universally as Che, whose theory and practice of guerilla warfare made him a hero among young left-wing revolutionaries. After being associated with revolutionary movements throughout Latin America, he joined CASTRO in Mexico (1956) and worked with him until the coup which brought Castro to power in Cuba (1958). Thereafter he served in Castro's administration, trained the militia which defeated KENNEDY's 'Bay of Pigs' adventure (a US-supported attempt to overthrow the Castro régime by Cuban exiles in 1961) and published a treatise on guerilla warfare. In 1966 he left Cuba to organize a revolution in Bolivia against the régime of President Barrientos. In October 1967 he was caught and shot by Bolivian government forces.

Guicciardini, Francesco (1483-1540) Italian statesman and historian whose *History of Italy* is one of the chief historical works of the 16th century. This vast, meandering account of Italy's history from 1492 to 1534 is a sceptical analysis of human corruption. Between 1512 and 1523 he held various Florentine and papal appointments. He retired in 1527 to write *Civil and Political Memoirs*, maxims on a theme similar to the earlier work. When the Florentines rose against the Medicis, he acted as counsellor, pleading the cause of Alessandro de Medici, though with the emergence of the absolutist Cosimo de MEDICI he retired once more.

Guilhem de Poitou (1071-1127) The first Provençal troubadour, whose surviving poems are the earliest lyrics in any European vernacular.

Guillotin, Joseph Ignace (1738-1814) French doctor and revolutionary who, in 1789, proposed the adoption of a beheading machine for administering capital punishment. His main arguments were that decapitation should not only be the privilege of the nobility, but be available to all candidates for capital punishment and, moreover, it should be as swift and as painless as possible. Similar machines had been used in medieval Europe. Guillotin's proposal was adopted in 1791 and the first

'Che' Guevara, more successful as a symbol of revolution than as a revolutionary, operates a clandestine radio from his guerilla base

machines, German-made, were used the following year. Soon they became known as *guillotines*. But the excesses of the French Revolution tainted their use, and they were never widely adopted outside the French-speaking world.

The invention of the guillotine arrived in time to serve the fell purposes of the French Revolution. The tumbril was the 'conveyor belt' by which thousands died during the Terror

Guiscard, Robert (c. 1015-85) Norman adventurer who founded Norman power in Italy and Sicily after joining his brothers, who had won most of Apulia. In a series of conquests, he drove the Byzantines out of southern Italy and began the Norman invasion of Muslim Sicily, which was completed by his brother, ROGER I of Sicily, so founding the Italo-Sicilian kingdom of Naples.

Guitry, Sacha (1885-1957) French actor and playwright who specialized in light comedy and farce, and plays about the private lives of eminent people, among them *Pasteur* (1919); *Mozart* (1928) and *Frans Hals* (1931). Of his early comedies *The Night Watchman* (1911) and *The Grand Duke* (1921) are two of the best. He later became known widely through films, which he wrote and directed, including *The Story of a Cheat* (1936), *They were Nine Bachelors* (1939) and several historical films.

Guizot, François Pierre (1787-1874) French historian and statesman. A professor of history at the Sorbonne (1812), Guizot became associated with the intellectual opposition to NAPOLEON and briefly held the post of Secretary-General of the Ministry of the Interior (1814) during the first restoration of LOUIS XVIII. After the final defeat of Napoleon he obtained a post in the Ministry of Justice and a seat on the Council of State (1815). Out of favour during the autocratic régime of CHARLES X he meanwhile devoted himself to historical writing. In 1830 he became deputy for Lisieux and became prominent in opposition. Following the Revolution of 1830 he became a minister and introduced innovatory legislation on primary education and teacher training. He became Minister of Foreign Affairs (1840) under Soult, whom he succeeded as Prime Minister in 1847. His policies were narrowly conservative and he refused to extend the franchise or reform the corruption of the political system. Ironically, by refusing political concessions to the lower classes who had benefited from his educational legislation, he helped to precipitate the Revolution of 1848 in which he was swept from power.

Gulbenkian, Calouste (1896-1955) Turkish-born financier and oil magnate, who founded the Iraq Petroleum Company. After admitting British, French and American participation in the company, Gulbenkian retained the share which earned him the international name of 'Mr Five Per Cent'. He left art treasures and a 70-million dollar fortune to the Gulbenkian Foundation.

Guldberg, Cato (1836-1902) Norwegian chemist who established the law of mass action. In 1863, Guldberg and his co-worker Peter Waage, incorporating the earlier work of Claude BERTHOLLET, announced their law, which states that the rate at which two substances react together depends on their concentrations.

Gull, Sir William (1816-90) British physician whose work on cretinism led him to identify myxoedema (a disease marked by thick, cold skin and thin hair), and to isolate thyroid deficiency as its cause. He also did important research on paralysis, cholera and abscess of the brain.

Gustavus I (1496-1560) King of Sweden (1523-60), who freed Sweden from Danish control and founded the Vasa dynasty (1521-1720). In opposition to Christian II of Denmark's suppression of Swedish nationalists, Gustavus led a popular revolt which ended Danish rule in

Sweden and left Gustavus the elected king of an independent state. To strengthen Sweden he ended the Hanseatic monopoly of Baltic trade, made Lutheranism the state religion (subject to royal authority), promoted trade, farming and mining and quelled opposition to his innovations.

Gustavus II Adolphus (1594-1632) King of Sweden (1611-32) who made his country a military power. Determined to make Protestant Sweden secure, he fought Denmark (1611-13) and won back lands in southern Sweden, fought Russia (1613-17) and excluded her from the Baltic, and fought Poland (1621-9), achieving recognition from her as King of Sweden and winning the Vistula delta in the last two years of his life. Gustavus Adolphus intervened in the 30 Years' War, principally to ensure that the Holy Roman Emperor did not take the Baltic seaports and become a danger to Sweden, but also to aid Protestant Germany against the Catholic armies of the Holy Roman Empire. He brilliantly defeated the Hapsburg generals, Tilly at Breitenfeld and Walltenstein at Lützen, but he died from wounds received there. Sweden's domination over the Baltic survived until PETER I of Russia defeated CHARLES XII.

Gutenberg, Johannes (1398-1468) German goldsmith, traditionally credited with the invention of printing from movable type. The process had its origins in techniques used for making playing cards and mass-produced woodblock prints. Others in Europe experimented with movable-type printing at about the same time as Gutenberg, but the first large printing house to use movable type was that of Gutenberg and his partner, Johann Fust, at Mainz. In 1448 they had cast enough type to set and print a whole Bible. In 1456 there was a printing of the Bible which is thought to be Gutenberg's work.

Gwynn, Nell (1650-87) British actress, who became CHARLES II's mistress. Her beauty and wit took her from being an orange-seller at Drury Lane Theatre on to the stage.

The modern printing presses, illustrated opposite against the background of a 16th-century printing shop, produce millions of copies where Gutenberg might have printed a handful. But Gutenberg's invention was one which was to change the face of the world. The book and literature generally became an object of mass production, albeit on a limited scale; the heretical beliefs of a handful of scientists and theologians, questioning dogma and the traditional order of things, gained ever-wider audiences. The modern processes as shown—letterpress, lithography and gravure—are now in general use

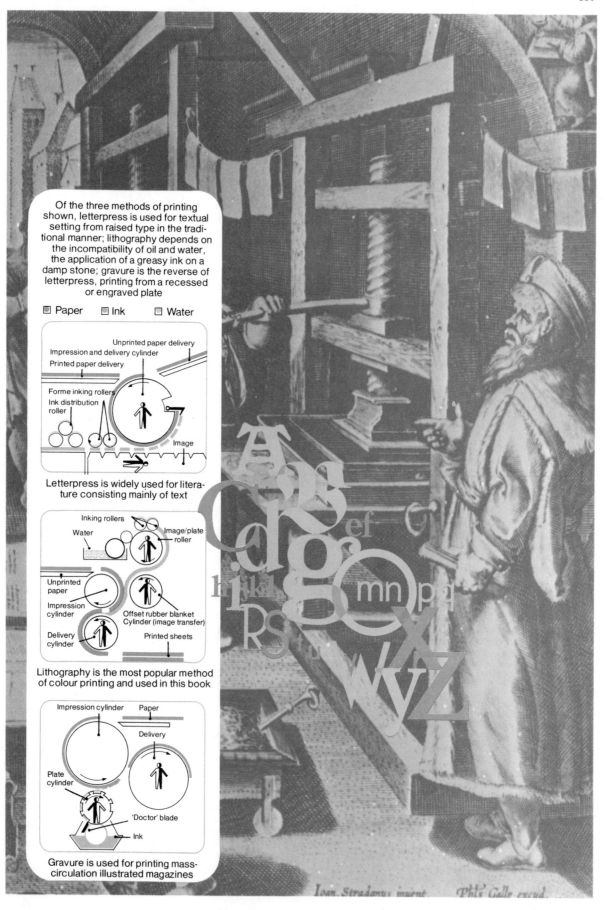

Of the three methods of printing shown, letterpress is used for textual setting from raised type in the traditional manner; lithography depends on the incompatibility of oil and water, the application of a greasy ink on a damp stone; gravure is the reverse of letterpress, printing from a recessed or engraved plate

☑ Paper   ☑ Ink   ☑ Water

Unprinted paper delivery
Impression and delivery cylinder
Printed paper delivery
Forme inking rollers
Ink distribution roller
Image

Letterpress is widely used for literature consisting mainly of text

Inking rollers
Water
Image/plate roller
Unprinted paper
Impression cylinder
Offset rubber blanket Cylinder (image transfer)
Delivery cylinder
Printed sheets

Lithography is the most popular method of colour printing and used in this book

Impression cylinder   Paper
Delivery
Plate cylinder
'Doctor' blade
Ink

Gravure is used for printing mass-circulation illustrated magazines

Ioan. Stradanus inuent   Phls Galle excud

Haakon IV Haakonsson (1204-63)
King of Norway (1217-63) who endeavoured to build an overseas empire for his country. He achieved some success and was acknowledged ruler of Greenland (1261) and Iceland (1262). He led a fleet to the Hebrides (1263) to make good Norwegian claims to rule the islands, but after an indecisive clash with the Scots, he sailed to Orkney, where he died.

Haakon VI Magnusson (1339-80)
King of Norway (1355-80) whose marriage to MARGARET OF DENMARK (1363) led to the union of the kingdoms and the subservience of Norway to Denmark until 1815.

Haber, Fritz (1868-1934) German chemist who discovered how to synthesize ammonia using the nitrogen in air. Ammonia is a basic material for making fertilizers and explosives. In the early 1900s, Haber found that, under certain conditions of temperature and pressure, and with a suitable catalyst (such as platinum), nitrogen and hydrogen combine to form ammonia. By 1913 his work had been developed by another German, Carl Bosch, into a full-scale industrial process. The Haber-Bosch process is still one of the chief ways of producing ammonia.

Hachette, Louis (1800-64) French bookseller and publisher whose textbooks and editions of the classics raised the standard of French educational publishing. He first published in 1833, when the creation of primary schools produced a demand for textbooks. He also produced dictionaries, scholarly editions of the classics, a cheap railway library and guide books. In 1855 he founded the weekly *Le Journal pour Tous*. Today the Hachette group controls major French newspapers, book publishers and booksellers.

Hadfield, Sir Robert Abbott (1859-1940) English metallurgist and industrialist who, following the steelmaking improvements of BESSEMER and SIEMENS, led research into new steel alloys. Although others had previously added manganese to steel and obtained tough alloys, they were also brittle. Hadfield discovered that this defect could be overcome when the manganese content was increased. His firm patented the alloy in 1883 and it found a wide range of applications, such as in rock-breaking and railway tracks. Hadfield later investigated additions of other elements, including vanadium and chromium to

steel, which enabled his company to produce a range of alloys for special purposes, among them springs and machine parts.

Hadley, George (1685-1768) British meteorologist, who formulated the currently accepted theory of trade winds. He showed that to understand the movement of the trades the Earth's rotation must be taken into account and that the different speeds of rotation (fastest at the equator and relatively slower at distances) govern the circulation of these winds.

Hadrian (76-138) Roman Emperor (117-138) under whom the empire enjoyed a golden age. Hadrian succeeded his cousin TRAJAN, whom he had served in Rome's provinces, and his first act was to abandon Trajan's untenable Parthian conquests and make the Euphrates the empire's eastern boundary. Hadrian strictly supervised the provincial governors, but set the provinces on an equal footing with Rome. In Palestine he put down a Jewish rebellion led by Simon Barchocheba and during his government in Britain, ordered the building of the 73-mile Hadrian's Wall to keep the troublesome Picts and Scots out of England. At home, Hadrian carried out numerous reforms, reorganizing the civil service, law, the financial administration and the tax system. He erected many fine public buildings and founded several cities.

Hadrian IV see ADRIAN IV

Haeckel, Ernst (1834-1919) German biologist, who contended that an organism's embryological stages reflect its evolutionary history. His work leading up to the formulation of this (in fact erroneous) 'biogenetic law' was the starting-point for much late 19th-century research into evolution and embryology. Haeckel was also the first man to recognize the importance of sexual selection in the evolutionary process.

Hafiz (c. 1325-90) Persian poet, who brought the form of the *ghazal*, the lyrical poem, to perfection. He was born in Shiraz and spent his early working life as an impoverished teacher, until his poetry brought him success. The *ghazals* are all that remain of his work.

Hahn, Otto (1879-1968) German chemist who discovered nuclear fission. In the mid-1930s, with Lise MEITNER, he bombarded uranium with neutrons, and saw that an extremely radioactive substance was formed in the uranium. In 1938 Hahn suggested that it was a radioactive form of barium, an element far lighter

than uranium, formed by the splitting of uranium atoms, each into two roughly equal parts.

Hahnemann, Samuel (1755-1843) German physician, the founder of homeopathy. This is a system of curing the sick by administering minute traces of the drugs which, in healthy people, would produce the symptoms of the disease involved. His observation that insoluble substances could be dissolved by prolonged rubbing in water, paved the way to an understanding of colloids (a solution of particles too fine to settle but too coarse to pass through a membrane that will pass pure liquids).

Haidar Ali (1722-82) Muslim ruler of Mysore (1759-82) who threatened the infant British Empire in India. A successful soldier-adventurer, he usurped the Mysore throne and seized nearby states. He twice threatened British-held Madras, first forcing an advantageous treaty (1769), then wiping out a small British force (1780), before Warren HASTINGS sent troops from Bengal to subdue him in 1781.

Haig, Douglas, 1st Earl (1861-1928) Scottish-born soldier, Commander-in-Chief of the British army in the First World War. Haig, who distinguished himself as a cavalry officer in the second Boer War (1899-1902), commanded the 1st Army Corps of the British Expeditionary Force in 1914, fighting at Mons, on the Meuse, and at Ypres. He succeeded Sir John French as Commander-in-Chief, Western Front, in 1915, but had neither imagination nor great talent, and was distrustful of innovations in warfare. The casualties suffered by Haig's armies led to antagonism between him and LLOYD GEORGE over strategy of attrition warfare, but his prestige in the higher ranks of the army enabled him to retain his command even after his severe defeat by the Germans in March 1918. He made a major contribution to victory by securing the appointment of FOCH as Supreme Commander of the Allied armies in France.

Haile Selassie (born 1892) Emperor of Ethiopia. He succeeded the Empress, Zauditu, in 1930 and introduced a new and more liberal constitution a year later. In 1936, after MUSSOLINI had invaded Ethiopia, he was forced to leave the country and took refuge in England. Subsequently he rallied Ethiopian patriots in Kenya and the Sudan and, in June 1941, he was reinstated in Addis Ababa after Ethiopia had been liberated by British forces. He pre-

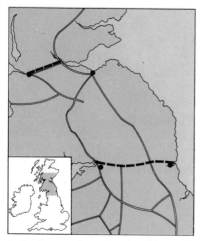

As the Romans marched north, Hadrian's Wall was superseded by the Antonine Wall, joining the Forth and Clyde

sides over the Organization for African Unity, established in 1963.

Haldane, John Burdon (1892-1964) British biologist, who tried to link the sciences with Marxist philosophy, especially with regard to the theory of evolution.

Haldane, Richard Burdon, 1st Viscount (1856-1928) English lawyer, philosopher and liberal statesman, who was forced out of public life by the popular press for his alleged pro-German leanings early in the First World War (1915). He was educated in Germany and became an authority on German philosophy. As War Secretary (1905-12) under CAMPBELL-BANNERMAN and ASQUITH he created the General Staff (1906), the Territorial Army (1907) and Officers' Training Corps in public schools.

Hale, George Ellery (1868-1938) American astronomer, responsible for the founding of the Yerkes and the Mount Palomar Observatories. In 1889 he invented an instrument called a spectroheliograph for studying the Sun, and in 1908 discovered the existence of magnetic fields in sunspots, which led (1919) to his discovery of the periodic reversal in the polarizing of their magnetic fields.

Hale, Sir Matthew (1609-76) English jurist whose *History of the Pleas of the Crown* (1685) was an influential work on English criminal law. He played a prominent part in the trials of political offenders during the Civil War and under the Commonwealth, when he achieved a great reputation for moderation and fairness. CHARLES II appointed him Chief Justice of the Court of King's Bench (1671). His *Analysis of the Law* was the most important precursor of BLACKSTONE's legal history *Commentaries*.

Hales, Stephen (1677-1761) English clergyman, botanist and chemist who, by inserting glass tubes into the veins and arteries of live horses, was the first man to measure the pressure and velocity of blood. His *Haemastaticks* (1733) is a classic of cardiac medicine. His experiments in plant physiology included measurements of the rate of plant growth and an explanation of the mechanism of transpiration.

Halifax, 1st Earl of see MONTAGU, Charles

Halifax, Edward, First Earl of (1881-1959) English statesman who, with Neville CHAMBERLAIN, was responsible for the Munich agreement of 1938. As Lord President of the Council (1935) with responsibility for foreign affairs, he held an appointment partly designed to enable the Prime Minister, Chamberlain, to counter the policy of his Foreign Secretary, EDEN, who disagreed with the appeasement of HITLER and MUSSOLINI. When Eden resigned (1938), Halifax took his place, carrying out Chamberlain's policy of appeasement, though he advocated a stronger line towards Germany from March 1939 onwards. He retained the same office after the Second World War broke out, but seven months after CHURCHILL became Prime Minister, Halifax was sent to Washington as Ambassador (January 1941), a post which he retained until 1946.

Hall, Charles Francis (1821-71) American explorer who made three Arctic expeditions between 1860 and 1871. The first two were in search of traces of Sir John FRANKLIN's vanished party; on the first, Hall, single-handed, landed in and studied Frobisher Bay; on the second, helped by Eskimos, he explored King William Land and discovered the fate of some of Franklin's party. On his third expedition, Hall failed in a government-backed attempt to reach the North Pole, but had already sailed farther north than any other explorer.

The Hale 200 in reflector telescope at Palomar can be directed to any point in the sky. The observer's cage allows photographs to be taken at prime focus; there is a Cassegrain arrangement, and

1 Primary mirror
2 Observer's cage
3 Cassegrain focus
4 Coudé focus
5 Southern end of the polar axis
6 Coudé and Cassegrain secondary mirror
7 Right ascension drive

in the Coude system light is reflected to a fixed position outside the telescope, avoiding the constant moving of any heavy equipment used. The telescope, was not completed until after Hale's death

8 Declination axis
9 Dome shutter (opening 30ft)
10 Dome (137ft diameter)
11 Primary focus (54ft)
12 Northern pillar
13 Southern pillar
14 Control panel

Hall, Charles Martin (1863-1914)
American chemist, who, in 1886,
developed an electrolytic process for
manufacturing aluminium. The
French metallurgist Paul Louis
Toussaint Héroult had independently also devised a similar method in the
same year. The Hall-Héroult process
founded the modern aluminium industry. Its wide uses have had significant results, particularly in such
applications as aircraft manufacture,
where the lightness of the alloy is
important.

Hall, Sir James (1761-1832) British
geochemist who discovered that
when rocks are heated until they
melt they form crystals if allowed to
cool sufficiently slowly.

Hall, James (1811-98) American
geologist and palaeontologist who
contributed greatly to the understanding of the geology of many parts
of the USA. Hall became state
geologist of New York and did much
field-work. His most important publication was a 13-volume monograph
on the palaeontology of New York.

Hall, Marshall (1790-1857) British
physician and physiologist, who carried out important work on the nervous system and saw that reflex actions
occur even when the nerve cord to
the brain is severed. He concluded
that the nerve cord must be made up
of sections that not only interact to
produce co-ordinated movements,
but also operate as autonomous reflex
systems. His name is given to a type
of artificial respiration.

Haller, Albrecht von (1708-77)
Swiss physiologist, anatomist, botanist, encyclopedist, historian of medicine and poet. His account of a
technique he devised for injecting
blood vessels with dyes so as to make
their course clear was so accurate and
comprehensive that it became the
basis for later cardiovascular anatomy. His were the first research
works to realize the importance of the
nerves in carrying sensations to the
brain, and commands to the muscles
from the brain. He also made pioneer
studies on the digestive juices, blood
clotting, the growth of bone and the
mechanism of breathing.

Halley, Edmond (1656-1742) English astronomer, after whom Halley's
Comet is named. While still a school-
boy, Halley became a skilled astronomer. In 1676 he went to St Helena
to catalogue the stars of the southern
hemisphere, and while there he observed the transit of Mercury across
the Sun (1677). On his return Halley
became friendly with NEWTON, and it
was his discussions with Halley that
encouraged Newton to write his

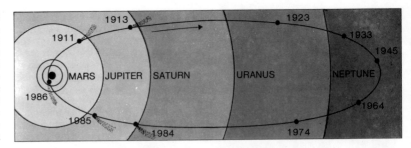

Due again in 1986, Halley's comet
was recorded in the Bayeux Tapestry

Principia, which Halley financed and
saw through the press. In 1721 Halley
became Astronomer Royal in succession to FLAMSTEED. Close study of
comets led him to the correct belief
that the comet of 1682 was the same
heavenly body as the comets of 1456,
1531 and 1607, and accurately predicted that it would reappear in
1758.

Hals, Frans (c. 1580-1666) One of
the greatest of all Dutch portrait
painters. His portraits were official
studies of civic dignitaries, of the
para-military groups which were
formed during the Dutch wars against
Spain, or less formal portraits of
cavalier or bourgeois types, of which
the most famous is the *Laughing
Cavalier* (1624). They give an impression of remarkable spontaneity,
though their liveliness also depends to
some extent upon brush-strokes
which appear to have been applied
with great speed – although in fact
the opposite is true. Hals's colours,
always muted, became more sombre
in his late works.

**Hamilton, Alexander (c. 1757-
1804)** US lawyer and statesman, who
advocated a strong central government rather than loose confederation
of states. In the War of Independence
he raised and organized artillery
regiments in New York, and from
1777 to 1781 was Washington's secretary and aide-de-camp. He drafted
the report which resulted in the
calling of the Constitutional Convention at Philadelphia in 1787 and in a
series of essays, later published as the
Federalist (1787-8), he advocated a
strong central government. His principal opponents were JEFFERSON and
Aaron Burr, who were provoked by
his appointment as Secretary to the
Treasury (1789-95), and by his
policies of a federal tax system and
the Federal Bank. His long quarrel
with Burr led to a duel in which Burr
mortally wounded him.

Hamilton, Sir William (1805-65)
Irish astronomer and mathematician,
who invented the theory of quater-
nions, a precursor of vector theory
and similar to GRASSMANN's calculus
of extension.

**Hammerskjold, Dag Hjalmar
Agne Carl (1905-61)** Swedish political economist, second Secretary-
General of the United Nations (1953-
61) and posthumous winner of the
Nobel Peace Prize. As Secretary-
General of the UN, he believed that
the smaller nations had greater need
of UN protection than the large, and
so, unlike his predecessor, Trygve
LIE, avoided involvement in great
power disputes as far as possible. It
was his personal integrity, however,
which guaranteed the acceptance of
the UN Emergency Force in Sinai
and Gaza after the Suez crisis of
1956, and of UN observers in
Lebanon in 1958. UN forces were
also sent to the Congo when Katanga
seceded in 1960, and while flying to
see TSHOMBE he was killed in a plane
crash at Ndola, Zambia.

Hammurabi (c. 1955-1913 BC)
Babylonian lawgiver. He unified and
pacified Babylonia and provided it
with a written code of laws which is
often regarded as the first major
legislative work of the forerunners of
western civilization.

Hampden, John (1594-1643) English leader of Parliamentary opposition to CHARLES I. In 1636, the king
demanded that all counties make
peace-time payments of ship-money,
which had formerly been levied only
on coastal counties in time of war, to
finance the fleet. Hampden refused to
pay on the grounds that the new tax
was not authorized by Parliament and
was therefore illegal. Charles narrowly won the consequent legal action
(1637) but lost face in doing so. The
incident helped to provoke the
English Civil War, in which Hampden died fighting for the Parliamentary forces.

Hamsun, Knut (1859-1952) Norwegian novelist, dramatist and poet,
who was the most considerable literary figure in Norway after IBSEN. He
was chiefly concerned to show the
corruption of the individual through
contact with society and explored
this idea in a series of ironic novels
depicting the wanderings of a root-
less man at grips with hunger,
physical labour and danger. The
best known of these is *The Growth of
the Soil* (1917), in which the wanderer

comes to rest. But *Pan* (1894) and *Children of the Age* (1913) are of greater literary merit.

Hancock, Langley George (born 1909) Australian mine owner and stock rancher. He has pioneered the development of the iron ore industry of Western Australia, doing much of his prospecting from small aircraft.

Hancock, Thomas (1786-1865) English inventor who patented (1820) a method of making various parts of clothing more elastic and invented a masticator for the production of solid rubber from the raw material. Hancock improved GOODYEAR's vulcanization process and was granted the first English patent.

Handel, George Friederich (1685-1759) German-born (naturalized British) composer and master of 18th-century oratorio. A four-year stay in Italy during his early twenties had a lasting effect on his style, which might be described as Italianate Baroque. An orchestral violinist, he also became a virtuoso harpsichordist and organist. Handel composed easily and quickly, but was not averse to using another's material without acknowledgement. His music has a vivid immediacy and a power to attract and had a considerable and long-lasting influence upon music in Britain. In 1732 he wrote *Esther*, the first English biblical oratorio. Of the series of oratorios which followed, the most outstanding was *The Messiah*. He also wrote Italian operas for the London stage. His anthem *Zadok the Priest* was written for the coronation of George II (1727). Handel's orchestral band suites, the *Fireworks Music* and the *Water Music*, were written for state or royal occasions.

Handley-Page, Sir Frederick (1885-1962) English aircraft designer and manufacturer of civil and military multi-engined aircraft, among the last of which was the Victor nuclear strike aircraft for the Royal Air Force.

Hannibal (247-183 BC) Carthaginian general and statesman who came near to overthrowing Rome. Dedicated to defeating Carthage's great rival, the 26-year-old Hannibal became Carthaginian Commander-in-Chief in Spain, where he began the Second Punic War (219 BC) by seizing pro-Roman Saguntum. In the following year he marched on Italy itself, leading 40,000 troops and 38 war elephants across the Pyrenees, southern France and the Alpine passes into Italy. Hannibal lost most of his elephants and perhaps one-quarter of his men in the early autumn

snow and from tribal attacks, but gained the psychological advantage over the astonished Romans. Inside Italy, Rome's troops outnumbered his, but he won (216 BC) the battles of Ticino, Trebia, Lake Trasimene and Cannae. Under Hannibal's brilliant leadership, and helped by local dissidents, the Carthaginians ravaged Italy for 15 years but did not attempt to take fortified Rome. Hannibal was forced to leave Italy in 203 BC to defend Carthaginian North Africa against SCIPIO's invasion and was defeated decisively at Zama (202 BC). After some years in civil administration, he was exiled from Carthage and eventually committed suicide to avoid falling into the hands of the Romans.

Hanno (5th cent. BC) Carthaginian navigator who made the first well-documented voyage round the West African coast. Leading 30,000 Carthaginian settlers in 60 multi-oared vessels, he sailed west from the Strait of Gibraltar (*c.* 480 BC); founded towns in what is now Morocco; reached Gambia; and probably touched Sierra Leone and Cameroon.

Hansard, Thomas (1776-1833) English printer of the official daily record of British parliamentary debates, originated by William COBBETT in 1803. He took over publication of the debates from Cobbett in 1809 and in 1823 established the Paternoster Row Press. *Hansard* is still the name given to the official verbatim report of debates in Parliament.

Hanslick, Eduard (1825-1904) Austrian music critic who promoted BRAHMS against WAGNER. He was caricatured as Beckmesser in WAGNER's *The Mastersingers*.

Han Yü (768-824) Chinese essayist, who is famous for the part he played in reviving the classical prose style. An active government official for most of his life, his profound belief

in Confucianism is expounded in his writings, which attacked the influences of Taoism and Buddhism. His essays were esteemed as models of prose till the end of the empire.

Harald Bluetooth (10th cent.) King of Denmark (*c.* 950-*c.* 986), who boasted of reuniting Denmark, converting its people to Christianity, and conquering Norway (*c.* 960). He recorded his achievements on the stone at Jelling, which he erected to the memory of his father, Gorm, and mother, Tyre.

Hardecanute (c. 1019-42) Danish king of Denmark (1035-42) and England (1040-42), whose death ended CANUTE's northern empire. Hardecanute alienated the English by levying heavy taxes to finance his fleet, and by devastating Worcester and the surrounding area in reprisal for the murder of two tax collectors. At his death, rule in England was restored to ETHELRED's line by his son, EDWARD THE CONFESSOR.

Hardie, James Kier (1856-1915) Scottish politician and Labour leader. In his twenties he organized miners' trade unions in Scotland, and in 1888 founded the Scottish Parliamentary Labour Party. Five years later he was elected Independent Socialist MP for West Ham (London) and the same year founded the Independent Labour Party (1893). For 15 years, from 1900, Hardie was MP for Merthyr Tydfil and became leader of the Parliamentary Labour Party in 1906. A temperance reformer, pacifist and a pious Nonconformist, he opposed Britain's entry into the First World War.

Harding, Warren Gamaliel (1865-1923) US President, who was responsible for America's isolationism between the two World Wars. As

Harding, whose Presidency was marred by corruption, on a whistle-stop tour

a Republican senator, Harding opposed Woodrow WILSON's attempts to give the US an international role through the League of Nations. Chosen by a lobby of influential businessmen as a pliable candidate for the Presidency, Harding was elected in 1920 on a 'return to normalcy' ticket. His administration (1921-3) was chiefly remarkable for political dishonesty on a vast scale and the gaoling for corruption of his Secretary of the Interior, Fall. Daugherty, the Attorney-General, was also implicated. Responsibility for the loss of prestige to the office of President rested as much on the Republican party and the nation as on Harding, whose mediocre talents were ill-suited to his office.

Hardy, Thomas (1840-1928) English poet and novelist whose creation of vivid, often humorous, characters, forced to live in a world of bleak, indifferent fate, won immense popularity. Almost all Hardy's work is set in Wessex, the central counties of the south coast of England, particularly Dorset, the region of Hardy's home. His characters are mainly country people, bound up with the land which governs their lives. Hardy divided his works into three categories: novels of character and environment, which include *Far from the Madding Crowd* (1874), *The Mayor of Casterbridge* (1886) and *Tess of the D'Urbervilles* (1891); romances and fantasies, including *The Trumpet-Major* (1880); and novels of ingenuity. He also published an epic trilogy of plays, *The Dynasts* (1904-8), and seven volumes of verse.

Hare, William see BURKE, William

Hargreaves, James (c. 1720-78) English weaver and textile engineer. KAY's shuttle had increased the speed of weaving, which was controlled by the production of spinning yarn, and Hargreaves's invention, the spinning jenny (1764), then speeded up the production of spinning yarn. It initially took eight, and in later models up to 120 spindles, though, as the drawing was done still by hand, the yarn produced was coarse and non-uniform. It was CROMPTON's mule which eventually was capable of providing the yarn required, and this invention embodied the principal features of Hargreaves's spinning jenny.

Harmsworth, Alfred see NORTH-CLIFFE, Lord

Harness, Henry Drury (1804-83) British engineer and cartographer who helped to pioneer statistical mapping techniques. In 1837, he published maps of Ireland, designed to show regional differences in population and traffic; they were among the first quantitative maps based on censuses.

Harold I Haarfager (c. 850-c. 933) First king of a united Norway, which he brought about by a series of conquests of petty kingdoms, defeating an alliance of their rulers at Hafrsfjord (*c.* 900). Those who submitted became his administrators, others (including ROLLO) fled abroad to settle Normandy, Iceland, the Faroes, Hebrides, Orkney and Shetlands. His kingdom's strength was wrecked by disunity among his successors.

Harold III Haardraade (1015-66) Warrior king of Norway (1047-66) whose invasion of England in 1066 made possible the unopposed landing in Sussex of WILLIAM. Haardraade fled to Russia in his youth, to become the best known of the Varangians (Russian and Scandinavian warriors serving the Byzantine emperors). He returned to Norway in 1046 and became king in the following year. He invaded England (1066) but died in the Battle of Stamford Bridge. His conqueror, Harold II of England, learned of the Norman landing two days after the battle.

Harper, James (1795-1869) American publisher, the founder of Harper and Brothers. Apprenticed to a printer in New York City, he set up a printing business with his brother John in 1817, and turned to publishing, in which they gained a high reputation.

Harriman, William Averell (born 1891) US millionaire businessman, who became a roving ambassador for his country. He was ROOSEVELT's personal representative in the UK (1941) and later Ambassador to the USSR and to the UK. He served as personal adviser to President TRUMAN (1951), then as Mutual Security Director until 1953, and in 1955 he was elected Governor of New York. In 1961 he became Ambassador-at-Large, and was chief US negotiator of the nuclear test-ban treaty, Moscow (1963). In 1968-9 he was the US representative at the Vietnam peace negotiations in Paris.

Harris, Benjamin (1673-1716) English journalist and publisher of the first newspaper printed in Am-

The works of Hardy, chronicler of Wessex, are enjoying a new popularity

erica. He worked as a journalist in London until 1686, and then emigrated to America, where he opened a bookshop in Boston. In 1690 he issued *Publick Occurrences Both Foreign and Domestick*. He returned to London in 1695 and published the newspaper *London Post* from 1699 until 1706.

Harris, Joel Chandler (1848-1908) American journalist and story-teller, and author of the tales of Uncle Remus, dialect fables of Brer Rabbit and other characters.

Harris, Roy (born 1898) American composer of whose works the *Third Symphony* and *Piano Quintet* are best known. He has extended his country's traditional music into a modern idiom. Harris, with his roots in American folk music and hymnody, was largely self-taught until studying with Nadia BOULANGER in Paris.

Harrison, Benjamin (1833-1901) Twenty-third President of the US (1889-93). The grandson of William HARRISON, and a fervent opponent of slavery, he served through most of the Civil War, distinguishing himself in SHERMAN's Atlanta Campaign. In the presidential campaign of 1889, he defeated CLEVELAND, thus achieving a victory for protection over free trade, signified by the passage in 1890 of McKINLEY's Tariff Bill.

Harrison, James (1816-93) Scottish-born Australian journalist and inventor of the first refrigerating plant used for a manufacturing process (1851). Harrison was the first to recognize the potential of meat export to the economy of Australia, which initiated the exportation of canned meat. A meat-freezing plant was first set up in 1861 by a fellow Australian, Thomas Sutcliffe Mort. First Harrison (1873), and then Mort (1876), attempted to ship frozen meat to England, but failed owing to plant breakdown at sea. By 1877, however, frozen mutton was shipped successfully from Buenos Aires to Le Havre, so establishing the frozen meat trade.

Harrison, John (1693-1776) English horologist, who invented (1735) the first chronometer which was accurate enough for use in long distance oceanic navigation. In 1726 he invented the constant-length pendulum, made of a 'gridiron' of brass and iron, so arranged that the thermal expansions of the metals counteracted each other. His chronometer, which lost less than two minutes on a return voyage to Jamaica, won an Admiralty prize of £20,000 for a timepiece accurate enough to allow longitude to be determined to within 30 miles.

Harrison, William Henry (1773-1841) Ninth President of the US, who held office for only one month. His father, Benjamin Harrison, was one of the signatories of the Declaration of Independence, and he himself became governor of the Indiana Territory 1801-13. As commander of the troops in the northwest, he inflicted several defeats on the British forces in the war of 1812-14. In 1840 he was chosen as Whig candidate for the Presidency and was elected overwhelmingly. He died of pneumonia a month after his inauguration.

Harsha (c. 590-647) Emperor of Northern India, whose reign (622-47) marked a transitional period between ancient and medieval India. The basis of Harsha's power was the union of the Punjab and Uttar Pradesh. He expanded his territory to bring most of northern India from Malwa to the Gulf of Bengal under his sway, but failed to conquer the Deccan. He revived imperial splendour, stimulated literature and the arts, and was himself a writer of ability. He is better known than most Indian kings because of a biography of his early life, the *Harshacarita*. His decentralized empire broke up after his death.

Harte, Bret (1836-1902) American humorist and short-story writer whose romantic tales of mining-camps created part of the mythology of the West.

Harthacnut see HARDECANUTE

Hartmann von Aue (12th-13th cents.) German poet, who was one of the masters of the courtly epic. His free versions of CHRÉTIEN DE TROYES's *Erec* and *Iwein* introduced the Arthurian legends into German literature. He also wrote love lyrics and two didactic poems, *Gregorius* and *Poor Henry*, flowing religious narratives preaching the ideals of restraint and moderation.

Harun-al-Rashid (c. 764-809) Abbasside caliph (786-809) who ruled, in a golden age of Islam, all southwest Asia and North Africa. He encouraged the free interchange of goods and ideas among Arabs and non-Arabs, and reportedly had contacts with CHARLEMAGNE and with China. Music, art and learning flourished under Harun, and his capital, Baghdad, became the cultural centre of the Islamic world. His reign was disturbed by many rebellions and what are now Morocco and Tunisia broke away, beginning the political disintegration of the Islamic Empire.

Harunobu Suzuki (c. 1718-70) Japanese print artist of Samurai origin, the first to exploit the full possibilities of the many-coloured print, raising it to a very high standard through delicate and subtle harmonies. His work, confined almost entirely to the depiction of slender and graceful women, was produced during the last ten years of his life.

Harvard, John (1607-38) English clergyman who gave his name to America's oldest university. A graduate of Cambridge University, England, he emigrated to Charlestown, Massachusetts, in 1637 as a Puritan minister. He died the following year, bequeathing his 260 books and £780 (half his estate) to the then unestablished college proposed in 1636 for Newetowne (renamed Cambridge in 1638).

Harvey, William (1578-1657) English physician who discovered the process by which blood circulates in the body. Until Harvey's time all anatomists thought that there were two blood systems in the body and that the blood flowed to and from the heart through each. Harvey published his epoch-making discovery that the blood flows from the heart in the arterial system, through the tissues, and then back towards the heart in the venous system in *The Movement of the Heart* (1628). His later work on embryology, summed up in *Of the Animal Species* (1651), was also important.

William Harvey first showed how the heart pumps blood around the body. The diagram below follows the blood as it is pumped from the left auricle *h* and ventricle *g* through the head and arms *m*, lungs *c*, trunk *n* and legs *o*. The blood then returns to the right auricle of the heart *a*

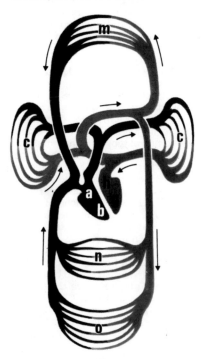

Hasan, Abu'l (16th cent.) Persian painter and protégé of JAHANGIR, Mogul Emperor of India. His refined and minutely observed portraits show the down-to-earth qualities favoured by his patron, often within the framework of elaborate regal symbolism borrowed from Europe.

Hasan, Ali Shah (1800-81) Persian religious leader and first holder of the hereditary title Aga Khan: spiritual head of the Nizari Ismaili sect of Shi'ite Muslims, who claim direct descent from MOHAMMED's daughter Fatima. His title was confirmed by the British administration in India when the Aga fled there after leading an unsuccessful revolt. Today most Nizaris live in India, Pakistan and Africa.

Hasan ibn-al-Sabbah (12th cent.) Persian founder of the Assassins, an Ismaili sect of Islam which believed murder of its enemies to be a religious duty.

Hašek, Jaroslav (1883-1923) Czech satirical novelist and short-story writer, author of the best-selling novel *The Good Soldier Schweik* (1928). Schweik is an ambivalent character, variously interpreted as the Czech patriot making fun of his Austrian rulers, as an anarchic, anti-social figure, and as the 'little man' struggling frustratedly against the massive powers of modern bureaucracy.

Hassan ibn-Ali see NIZAM-AL-MULK

Hastings, Warren (1732-1818) English colonial administrator, first Governor-General of India, who began his career as a clerk in Calcutta, with the East India Company (1750). He became a member of its Calcutta administrative council (1761) but resigned in protest against the corruption of his colleagues and returned to England (1766). Hastings rejoined the Company in 1768, became Governor of Fort William in Bengal in 1772 and Governor-General of India in 1773. After the British Government took over the running of India, numerous disputes arose between Parliament's representatives and the Company, and India became a political issue when Hastings retired in 1785. He was impeached for corruption by political enemies, but won acquittal in a seven-year trial which left him penniless.

Hauptmann, Gerhart (1862-1946) German dramatist, said to be the first to write a play in which the 'central character' is a crowd. *The Weavers* (1892) concerns a group of Silesian weavers who break into revolt. Hauptmann began by writing naturalistic plays in the manner of IBSEN and had a success with his first, *Before Sunrise* (1889), a study of human debasement in a Silesian village.

Haushofer, Karl (1869-1946) German general and political geographer whose theories of geopolitics helped to shape HITLER's strategy. Influenced by Ratzel, KJELLÉN and MACKINDER, he saw political states as biological units striving to dominate land masses, the control of which was crucial for their survival. He stressed the implied natural right of a dynamic, thrusting Germany to seize *lebensraum* (living space) at the expense of others, to grasp the whole of Eurasia, and hence to dominate the world's so-called oceanic countries. He committed suicide during Allied investigations into alleged war criminal activities.

Haussmann, Baron Georges (1809-91) French lawyer, civil servant and architect who was responsible for the design of modern central Paris. Haussmann was commissioned by NAPOLEON III to draw up plans for improving the city. His long, straight boulevards, intersecting each other at ronds-points, were designed for the huge state processions which celebrated the visits of foreign royalty, or the opening of international exhibitions. The Franco-Prussian War, which was followed by the setting up of the Republic, ended the Baron's plans. One of the famous *grands boulevards* in Paris is named in his honour.

Haüy, Abbé René (1743-1822) French priest and mineralogist, who showed that crystals are built up of units, so founding the science of crystallography. Accidentally dropping a crystal of calcite, Haüy noticed that it broke along certain definite planes and that the smaller fragments were identical with the parent crystal from which they had come.

Havlíček, Karel (1821-56) Czech satirist and author of the unfinished *The Conversion of St Vladimir* (1876), a work of liberal invective in which he attacked the Church and the despotic political régime. In 1848, he founded *Národni noviny*, the first Czech daily newspaper, and as a politician as well as a writer he spent his life fighting for national independence and constitutional reform.

Hawke, Edward, 1st Baron (1705-81) British admiral and pioneer of the naval blockade. He gained his reputation by defeating a French squadron protecting a convoy for the West Indies (1747), and during the Seven Year's War (1755-63) blockaded Brest, delaying a French supply convoy for French troops in Canada. He crushed a retaliatory French attempt to invade England by destroying their invasion fleet in the Battle of Quiberon Bay (1759).

Hawkins, Sir John (1532-95) English admiral, designer of the Elizabethan navy. Hawkins rebuilt, rearmed and modernized ELIZABETH's outdated fleet and by doing so, and by leading a naval squadron, helped to defeat PHILIP II's Spanish Armada (1588). Hawkins, who pioneered England's part in the Africa-America slave trade, died while raiding the Spanish West Indies with his cousin, DRAKE.

Hawksmoor, Nicholas (1661-1736) English architect destined in his lifetime to take second place to WREN and VANBRUGH, Hawksmoor nevertheless produced some of the most original early 18th-century architecture. As a young man he assisted Wren in his work on Greenwich Hospital, and Vanbrugh at Castle Howard and Blenheim Palace. Hawksmoor's own works range between a grave Roman style, inspired by BRAMANTE, and a capricious Gothicism.

Hawthorne, Nathaniel (1804-64) American short-story writer and novelist who is famous for *The Scarlet Letter* (1850) and *The House of the Seven Gables* (1851). His background was strongly Puritan, but although his chief works revolve around the themes of sin and retribution, suffering and compensation, his morality was not bound by convention – in *The Scarlet Letter*, Hester Prynne, the mother of an illegitimate child, is worthier of respect than her husband, who degrades himself in persecution of her lover.

Haydn, Franz Joseph (1732-1809) Austrian composer known as 'father of the symphony'. He took as his starting point the symphonies of C. P. E. BACH and from them evolved the classical form of a set of contrasting orchestral movements that were musically interrelated and balanced. Similarly, he evolved the classical form of the string quartet. Haydn was largely self-taught in composition and reached maturity slowly. In 1761 he entered the service of the Austro-Hungarian Esterhazy family and was able to compose and direct his compositions with an orchestra and choir always at his disposal. He wrote 104 symphonies, many of them known by popular nicknames such as *The Farewell* (45), *The Surprise* (94), *The Clock* (101), *The Drum-roll* (103) and *The London* (104). He wrote also over 80 string quartets and 20 operas, as well as the major oratorios of his later years, *The Creation* (1798) and

The Seasons (1801). Hadyn also wrote the national anthem of Imperial Austria, *The Emperor's Hymn*, later to be used in Germany as the tune to *Deutschland Uber Alles*. He visited England, where he enjoyed great popularity and received a musical doctorate from Oxford University. His brother, Michael Haydn, was also a gifted composer and, with MOZART's father, wrote the *Toy Symphony*, for long ascribed to Joseph.

Hayes, Rutherford Birchard (1822-93) Nineteenth President of the US (1877-81), elected on the contested returns of four states. He was twice Governor of Ohio, and his nomination as Republican presidential candidate in 1876 was followed by a close election. The result hinged on the disputed votes of four states, and a congressional commission of eight Republicans and seven Democrats eventually decided in Hayes's favour by a majority of popular votes. His opponent, Tilden, gained a majority of popular votes. Under his Presidency the US recovered much of the commercial prosperity it had lost in the crash of 1873, and his policy of conciliation towards the southern states, though arousing opposition within his own Party, was of benefit to the country as a whole.

Hazlitt, William (1778-1830) English essayist who was one of the central figures of English Romantic literature. His essays in criticism, principally the *Characters of Shakespeare's Plays* (1817-18) and *Lectures on the English Poets* (1818-19) are personal and clearly argued. His miscellaneous essays appeared in several collections, and he wrote frequently, propounding liberal arguments, in the *Edinburgh Review*.

Hearne, Samuel (1745-92) English employee of the Hudson Bay Company and explorer of large areas to the west of Hudson Bay.

Hearst, William Randolph (1863-1951) American newspaper publisher who expanded sensational journalism on lines begun by Joseph PULITZER, and built up a chain of 25 big dailies, starting with the *New York Journal* (1895). Hearst filled this paper with sensational reports on crime and scandal and with jingoistic foreign news reports, capped by banner headlines, and matched by lurid pictures. His organization was served by his International News Service (from 1909), and complemented by magazines like *Harper's Bazaar*. He was a member of the US House of Representatives (1903-7) and stood unsuccessfully for the mayoralty of New York City and for the governorship of New York.

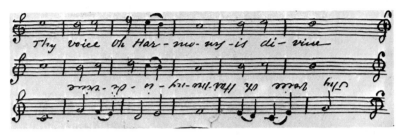

Typical of Haydn's happy approach to music, 'Thy voice, oh Harmony, is divine' can be played either forward or backward. One of his symphonies, the *Farewell*, was written as a hint to his patron to give Haydn's musicians a chance to see their families more often

Heath, Edward Richard George (born 1916) Conservative Prime Minister of Britain (1970). After war service, a short time in the Civil Service, and as news editor of *The Church Times* (1948-9), he was elected MP for Bexley (1950). After becoming assistant whip in 1951, he was appointed chief whip in 1955, Minister of Labour in 1959, Lord Privy Seal in 1960 and President of the Board of Trade and Secretary of State for Industry in 1963. From 1961 to 1963 he conducted Britain's initial and unsuccessful negotiations to join the European Economic Community (Common Market). In 1965, he was elected Conservative Party leader and became leader of the Opposition. He took office as Prime Minister after the Conservatives' unexpected victory in the General Election of June 1970.

Heaviside, Oliver (1850-1925) English physicist who predicted the existence of a conducting layer of ions in the upper atmosphere which made long-distance radio communication possible. This layer was independently suggested by KENNELLY. Heaviside created powerful but unorthodox mathematical methods which he applied to many other electromagnetic problems; he used them to show that long telephone lines must be 'loaded' with artificial inductance at intervals to avoid serious distortion.

Hebra, Ferdinand von (1816-80) Austrian physician, whose pioneer microscope studies of ringworm, eczema and scabies showed that many skin disorders were diseases in their own right. Until his time doctors had believed skin diseases to be symptoms of disorders elsewhere in the body. He founded one of Europe's earliest and most important clinics for the treatment of skin diseases in Vienna.

Hedin, Sven Anders (1865-1952) Swedish geographer and traveller who explored and mapped much of Central Asia. His first journey, at the age of 20, was to Persia and Mesopotamia, and in the 1890s he travelled in Khurasan and Turkistan, and crossed Tibet and China. In several expeditions between 1899 and 1908, he found ruined cities in Turkistan, crossed the Lop Nor Basin, explored central Asia's high plateau complex and crossed the Gobi Desert and Tibet.

Hegel, Georg Wilhelm Friedrich (1770-1831) German philosopher, the most influential thinker of the Idealist movement. Hegel derived his famous dialectical method from studying the history of Greek philosophy and saw the universe as a single system developing in time, in which the whole gives each part its own full meaning. The idea, in Hegel's terms, is like a prayer, recited first by a young child, hardly aware of what the words mean; and then once again when the child has grown into an old man who has seen life, and has come to grasp the deeper significance of the words.

Heidegger, Martin (born 1889) German philosopher and influence on contemporary Existentialism, whose analyses of Being and Time (from a standpoint which accepts the equal reality of the mental and the physical), seek to reveal man's place in his world in the way he actually deals with it throughout his life.

Heidenstam, Werner von (1859-1940) Swedish lyric poet, novelist and essayist whose poems *Pilgrimage and Years of Wandering* (1888) marked the beginning of the Swedish literary revival. These poems, together with his essay *Renaissance* (1880) and his novels, established him as the leader of the Nititalist group. The works of this circle of writers of the 1890s, which included LAGERLÖF, FRÖDING and KARLFELDT, are characterized by a pantheistic, naturalistic romanticism, whose subject matter was consequently concerned with the countryside (the Varmland) or with nostalgia for childhood.

Heine, Heinrich (1797-1856) German lyric poet and satirist whose reputation was established with the first two volumes of his *Pictures of Travel* (1826) and *Book of Songs* (1827). Many of these poems were set to music, notably by SCHUMANN in the song cycle *Poet's Love*. In 1831, fired by the ideals of the July Revolution, Heine went to Paris, where he remained for the rest of his life, and where he wrote *Remarks on the History of Religion and Philosophy in Germany* (1835) and *Conditions in France* (1832), intending to make the two nations familiar with each other's way of life and intellectual achievements. In Paris, too, he produced *Germany, A Winter's Tale* (1844) and *Atta Troll* (1841-6), two satirical mock-epics which served to reinforce his reputation.

Heinz, Henry John (1844-1919) American food manufacturer whose company, using such advertising slogans as '57 Varieties', pioneered the universal use of prepared, canned and bottled foodstuffs.

Heisenberg, Werner (born 1901) German physicist who developed the matrix mechanical version of modern quantum theory. His name is particularly linked with the uncertainty principle, according to which certain pairs of variables describing motion (such as velocity and position or energy and time) cannot be simultaneously measured with complete accuracy, because the measuring process itself interferes with the quantity to be measured. In 1932 he won the Nobel Prize for Physics.

Helmholtz, Herman Ludwig Ferdinand von (1821-94) German scientist who is best known for his statement of the first law of thermodynamics – that is, that energy can be converted from one form to another but cannot be created or destroyed. He studied acoustics and optics, making discoveries about hearing, harmony and colour vision and inventing the ophthalmoscope.

Helmont, Jan Baptista van (1579-1644) Flemish alchemist who originated the term 'gas'. He was the first to realize that there are, in addition to air, other air-like substances. It occurred to Helmont that this form of matter was best described as a 'chaos', the Flemish spelling of which yielded the word 'gas'.

Helvetius, Claude (1715-71) French philosopher who held that all mental activity could be reduced to physical sensation. Men, he said, act from self-interest, based on an assessment of pleasure gained and pain avoided. He also argued, against ROUSSEAU, that education is effective provided only that men chose to acquire it, for by nature they are all equally intelligent.

Hemans, Felicia (1793-1835) English poet, who wrote extremely popu-

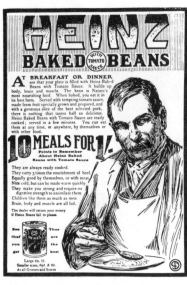

Wordy advertising ancestor of the modern 'Beanz Meanz Heinz' television jingle

lar sentimental verse. She is famous for 'Casabianca', which begins, 'The boy stood on the burning deck.'

Hemingway, Ernest (1899-1961) American novelist whose famous books, *A Farewell to Arms* (1929) and *For Whom the Bell Tolls* (1940), are about the personal dangers of war – the individual physical and emotional losses. His other novels deal principally with disillusioned characters who attempt to give meaning to their lives by a vigorous code of action. An ambulance driver in the First World War, Hemingway was a war correspondent during the Second World War.

Henderson, Arthur (1863-1935) English iron-foundry worker, who became one of the chief organizers of the British Labour Party in its early years, and the first Labour cabinet minister in ASQUITH's (1915-16) and LLOYD GEORGE's (1916-17) war cabinets. Although he was Home Secretary in the first Labour government (1924) under MACDONALD, he grew more and more internationalist in outlook. He acquired a high reputation among European statesmen, particularly as Foreign Secretary (1929-31), and was unanimously elected Chairman of the World Disarmament Conference, which position he held from 1932 to 1935. He was awarded the Nobel Peace Prize in 1934.

Henley, William Ernest (1849-1903) English journalist and poet, who wrote impressionistic and patriotic verse. Most of his series of poems entitled *In Hospital* (1888, 1903) concerns his experience of life as a cripple in an infirmary. Henley collaborated on four plays with R. L. STEVENSON,

who modelled his character Long John Silver on him and portrayed him as Burley in *Talk and Talkers*.

Henry I 'The Fowler' (c. 876-936) King of Germany (919-36) who founded the line of Saxon rulers (919-1024). He succeeded his father Otto as Duke of Saxony (912), and was chosen as King by the Franks and Saxons, reputedly while he was out hawking, hence his nickname. Other German dukedoms recognized his sovereignty, and, as uncrowned Holy Roman Emperor, he strengthened Germany by fortifying towns and reorganizing his army, which then extended his territory by defeating the Wends (929), Magyars (933) and Danes (934).

Henry IV (1050-1106) King of Germany, Italy and Burgundy (1056-1106) and Holy Roman Emperor, whose assertion that kings might disobey popes began a power struggle with the Holy See. Twice excommunicated by Pope Gregory VII, Henry induced his allies to depose the pope three times and set up, as antipope, Clement III, who crowned him Holy Roman Emperor (1084). Supporters of the legitimate pope rose against Henry, loosening his grip on Germany and Italy, where the Lombard towns became independent. The future division of Germany into principalities owed its origins to the struggle, which was known as the War of Investitures.

Henry II (1133-89) First Plantagenet King of England (1154-89), ruler of territories stretching from northern Scotland to southern France. His French possessions came through his father, Geoffrey of Anjou, his wife, ELEANOR OF AQUITAINE, and his son, Geoffrey of Britanny. He inherited England through his mother, Matilda, wrenched northern England from Scotland's Malcolm IV (1157); subdued Wales (1158-65); conquered southeast Ireland by 1171; and gained recognition as Scotland's overlord (1174). Henry's territorial expansion was at first supported by his chancellor, BECKET, but when Becket became Archbishop of Canterbury the two quarrelled over clerical privilege. Henry's reign was of great importance for constitutional and legal developments, which included the beginnings of Common Law.

Henry V (1387-1422) Lancastrian king of England (1413-22), and master of France. To restore English prestige he tried to acquire France, first by diplomacy, then by war, financed largely by parliamentary taxation. Henry set out to dominate the English Channel, and turn the towns of Normandy into English strongholds maintained by local taxes. His plan succeeded; after winning at Agincourt (1415), Henry conquered Normandy (1417-19), reached Paris (1419), and forced on the French the Treaty of Troyes (1420), which made Henry Regent of France and heir to the French throne. He died before acceding, but his son, Henry VI, became, for a time, king of France as well as of England.

Henry the Navigator (1394-1460) Portuguese prince who founded systematic sea exploration and paved the way for Europe's great age of discovery. Henry made exploration of the African coast his life's work, and founded an observatory and school of navigation at Sagres in Portugal, where he assembled cartographers, instrument-makers, astronomers, and pilots to train explorers and co-ordinate the results of their voyages.

Henry VI (1421-71) King of England, son of Henry V, who succeeded to the throne in his infancy, and whose reign culminated in the Wars of the Roses.

Henry VII (1457-1509) King of England (1485-1509) and first Tudor monarch. Henry was crowned after the death of RICHARD III at Bosworth Field (1485). Henry, Lancastrian claimant to the throne during the Wars of the Roses, ended hostilities and united the rival houses by marrying Elizabeth of York, heiress of EDWARD IV. He scotched two attempts, by Lambert Simnel and Perkin Warbeck, to usurp his throne and, to curb the power of the nobles to make civil war, established the Star Chamber and abolished private armies. Henry amassed a large fortune, at first to protect himself against conspiracies, later to gain prestige for England as the paymaster of Europe. He was a patron of the Renaissance, supported exploration by encouraging the CABOT family and, by marrying his daughter Margaret to James IV of Scotland, eventually brought about the union of England and Scotland (1603).

Henry VIII (1491-1547) King of England (1509-47), who, by making the Church of England independent of Rome, began the English Reformation. Henry was totally unscrupulous in bending to his own ends the constitutional forms which had by then become strongly centralized, and employed a number of able statesmen, among them Cardinal WOLSEY, Sir Thomas MORE, Archbishop Thomas CRANMER and Thomas CROMWELL. One of their tasks was to make or dissolve Henry's six largely unfruitful marriages (1) CATHERINE OF ARAGON, a marriage which ended

in divorce after the birth of a daughter (later MARY I) and caused the dispute between Henry and the pope which ended with the establishment of an independent Church of England; (2) Anne Boleyn, who also

Headstrong and volatile, Henry VIII remains the best-known of English kings. His popular fame rests more on his profligate use of marriage vows rather than the fundamental change in church-state relations by which the English Reformation was brought about

bore a daughter (later ELIZABETH I) and was beheaded; (3) Jane Seymour, who died after giving birth to the future heir, Edward VI; (4) Anne of Cleves who was divorced; (5) Catherine Howard, beheaded; and (6) Catherine Parr, who outlived him. Henry's break with Rome made him head of the ecclesiastical as well as the secular arm of state, but he allowed few Protestant innovations. Strengthened by the absolute supremacy that this gave him, Henry dissolved the monasteries (seizing their treasures and land), strengthened central government, and built a strong navy.

Henry IV (1553-1610) King of France (1589-1610), first of the Bourbons, who sacrificed his personal (Calvinist) religion in the national interest and became one of France's greatest kings. As King of Navarre (1572-89), he fought the War of the Three Henrys (1585-7) to enforce recognition that he was Henry III's rightful heir, and finally, at Coutras, defeated the Catholics under Henry III and the Duke de GUISE, Henry I of Lorraine. After inheriting Henry III's throne, he spent nine years fighting Spain and the Holy League to make good his claim to rule, and embraced Catholicism (1593) to heal the wounds of religious strife. The Edict of Nantes (1598) granted toleration to, and political equality for, Protestants. His foreign policy sought to counterbalance the power of the Hapsburgs by alliances with Germany, Sweden and Switzerland, and he aided the Dutch against Spain. Henry was assassinated by a Catholic extremist, François Ravaillac, who believed he was preparing war against the pope.

Henry I of Lorraine see GUISE

Henry, Augustine (1857-1930) Irish plant collector who made the first study of the flora of the Yangtze-Kiang gorges, China, from where he sent back 158,000 plant specimens to the Royal Botanic Gardens at Kew.

Henry, Sir Edward (1859-1931) English criminologist and originator of a system of classification of fingerprints which was introduced at Scotland Yard in 1901. By 1914, it had replaced the BERTILLON system of anthropometry and remains in use at Scotland Yard today.

Henry, Joseph (1797-1878) American physicist who studied magnetic induction and invented an electric telegraph. In 1831 he saw how an electromagnet can be used to send messages over great distances by connecting it by wires to a switch and turning it on and off. As he operated the switch, the magnet attracted and released a piece of iron, producing a pattern of clicks corresponding to the switch's movements. Henry did not patent this idea and in 1844 Samuel MORSE took credit for the first practical electric telegraph.

Henry, O. (1862-1910) Pseudonym of William Sydney Porter, prolific and successful American author of humorous and sentimental short stories. His ironic surprise endings were particularly effective, as in the famous story, *Gift of the Magi*.

Henry, Patrick (1736-99) American lawyer and orator who, with James OTIS and Samuel ADAMS, roused colonists against British rule. As a member of Virginia's legislature (1765), Henry urged the right of colonies to legislate for themselves, condemning the Stamp Act which was intended to finance British troops in America. Henry worked to arm Virginians for the American War of Independence (1775-83) and was Governor of Virginia (1776-9, 1784-6). He supported WASHINGTON during the war but afterwards opposed the proposed federal constitution, refusing many high offices.

Henze, Hans Werner (born 1926) German composer who has moved away from serialism to seek a new expression of humanism and social commitment. He wrote *Ode to the West Wind*, based on Shelley's poem, for cello and orchestra and the opera *Elegy for Young Lovers* (1961). More recently he composed the opera-cantata *The Raft of the Medusa*, after the painting by DELACROIX, and the song-cycle *El Cimarron* for baritone with flute, guitar and percussion accompaniment, based on the autobiography of a rebel Cuban slave.

Hepworth, Dame Barbara (born 1903) English sculptor whose work pays particular attention to subtleties of texture and surface movement, as in *Large and Small Forms* (1945), carved in Cornish elm. Her later work, not dissimilar to that of Henry MOORE, shows a concern with geometric construction and the achievement of a tighter structure through the pierced form, e.g. *Square with two circles* (1963).

Heraclitus (6th-5th cent. BC) Greek philosopher, the first to recognize the central role of 'logos', a word with a range of meanings: *word*; *explanation*; *account*; *proposition*. Aware of the connection between opposites ('the way up and the way down are one and the same') and seeing change as the pervasive principle, he likened the world to an eternal fire, in which part is set alight and part extinguished according to set 'measures' or proportions; there is constant change while the flame itself is unchanged.

Herbart, Johann (1776-1841) German philosopher who supported the work of PESTALOZZI. A pupil of FICHTE, he became professor of philosophy at Göttingen (1805-8 and 1833-41) and Königsberg (1808-33). At first a sceptic like HUME and KANT, he developed a method resembling that of HEGEL; he stressed experience and used logic to clarify uncritical notions. His psychology foreshadowed that of FREUD.

Herbert, George (1593-1633) English churchman and metaphysical poet. 'Herbert speaks to God', a clergyman said, 'like one that really believeth a God, and whose business in the world is most with God.' His religious verse is quiet and simple: *The Temple* (1633) contains about 160 poems on sacred subjects, many of them in irregular forms, some, such as 'The Altar', shaped like physical objects.

Herculano, Alexandre (1810-77) Portuguese historian, poet, novelist and politician, whose monumental *History of Portugal* (1846-53) and *History of the Origin and Establishment of the Inquisition in Portugal* (1854-9) were the first impartial, scholarly histories of Portugal. As a poet and novelist, with Almeida GARRETT he introduced Romanticism into Portuguese literature.

Herder, Johann (1744-1803) German philosopher and Lutheran theologian who was chiefly influential as the theoretician of the *Sturm und Drang* (Storm and Stress) movement, a movement away from sterile, foreign forms and establishing a new, national German literature inspired by SHAKESPEARE. He edited and contributed two important essays to the book which is regarded as the movement's manifesto, *On German Style and Art* (1773). His chief philosophical work is *Outlines of a Philosophy of the History of Man* (1784-91), an essay on humanism and historical evolution that anticipated HEGEL.

Heredia, José María (1803-39) Cuban romantic poet and national hero, exiled after an abortive attempt to free his country from Spanish domination.

Hereward (11th cent.), called Hereward the Wake, Anglo-Saxon landowner who led the last English resistance to WILLIAM I's Norman invasion. Hereward led Anglo-Saxon rebels who, with some Danish raiders, sacked Peterborough Abbey (1070). When the Danes withdrew, Hereward was forced to retreat to the fens round Ely. There he led Anglo-Saxon resistance to William's onslaught in 1071, but was driven finally into hiding as an outlaw, and died in obscurity.

Hermite, Charles (1822-1901) French mathematician, remembered chiefly for his development of the theory of algebraic forms and for his studies of elliptic functions.

Hero of Alexandria (1st cent. AD) Greek mathematician also called Heron, who wrote a series of treatises, based on his own and previous investigations, covering a wide range of mechanical, mathematical and physical subjects.

Herod the Great (c. 73-4 BC) King of Judaea, appointed by AN-TONIUS and OCTAVIUS. With Roman help, Herod made Judaea a powerful state, enlarging its territory, embellishing provincial cities, building great fortresses, including Masada, and lavishly rebuilding the Temple at Jerusalem. He is remembered most for his atrocities, notably the massacre of all male children in Bethlehem under the age of two, among whom he feared a claimant to his throne, JESUS.

Herodotus (c. 484-424 BC) Greek writer whose *History* described (within its major theme of the Greco-Persian struggle) the rise of Persia under CYRUS and DARIUS I, the development of the Greek city-states and Egypt, Babylon and other parts of the Greco-Asian world in the mid-5th century. Insatiably curious, he was over-credulous of tall stories, but could apply sound critical criteria and is justly called the Father of History.

Herrick, James (1861-1954) American physician who proved that sudden coronary artery blockage was not necessarily fatal and who stressed the little-suspected role of the coronary arteries in heart attack.

Herrick, Robert (1591-1674) English poet and clergyman, whose most famous work is the collection *Hesperides* (1648). He wrote lyrical verses of love and country matters in a great variety of metrical forms. Herrick was one of the 'sons' (disciples) of Ben JONSON.

Herschel, Sir John (1792-1871) English astronomer who continued the work of his father, Sir William HERSCHEL, on double stars and nebulae. He also made extensive studies of solar radiation and one of the first appraisals of the Earth's elliptical orbit upon its climate.

Herschel, Sir William (1738-1822) Hanover-born British astronomer, who discovered the planet Uranus (1781) and carried out extensive systematic observations of the stars. His major results, given in papers to the Royal Society from 1770 onwards, concerned the variable star Mira Ceti, the mountains of the Moon and the rotation of the planets and their several known satellites. He was the first to discover white spots on the surface of Mars, which he concluded were deposits of polar snow. By means of more powerful telescopes he observed and described double stars, measuring their relative distances over a number of years and discovered that many were true binaries revolving around each other. He also attempted to determine the relative distances of the stars from our own

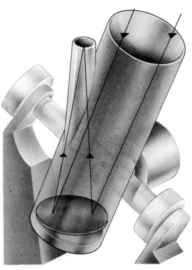

The main mirror in Herschel's reflector was tilted to form an image at the side

Sun, and compiled extensive catalogues of the results. Herschel was at first a musician, and made a successful career as an organist and a music teacher before devoting all his time to astronomy. Following his discovery of Uranus he accepted the position of private astronomer to George III.

Hertz, Heinrich Rudolph (1857-94) German physicist who discovered radio waves. Hertz conducted a series of experiments and demonstrated the existence of electromagnetic (radio) waves. He found their velocity to be the same as that of light and showed that, like light, they can be focused and reflected. This confirmed MAXWELL's theory.

Hertzog, James Barry Munnik (1866-1942) Advocate of South African independence and champion of Afrikaner nationalism. He was a general in the second Boer War (1899-1902) and in 1913 founded the

Nationalist Party in opposition to BOTHA, its main policy being to achieve South Africa's independence from Britain, whom he refused to support during the First World War. He was Prime Minister from 1924 to 1939 (from 1933 in coalition with SMUTS), during which time Afrikaans replaced Dutch as the official language and the racial segregation laws of 1936 were passed. Because of his continued opposition to involvement in 'Britain's wars', he was forced from office (1939) when Parliament approved Smuts's motion in favour of South Africa's participation in the Second World War. He was the true founder of Boer nationalism and Afrikaner culture, and MALAN and VERWOERD were his spiritual successors.

Hertzsprung, Ejnar (1873-1967) Danish astronomer, who discovered the relationship between a star's colour and brightness, and hence its magnitude. In 1905, Hertzsprung found that stars are divided distinctly into dwarf and giant classes, with the former far outnumbering the latter.

Herzen, Alexander Ivanovich (1812-70) Russian revolutionary theorist and writer who supported BAKUNIN and other Russian revolutionary militants out of his private fortune. He was forced to serve in the Tsarist civil administration from 1835 to 1842, but promotion was blocked because of his suspected liberalism. He resigned and, on inheriting a fortune, left Russia (1847) and went to live in Geneva and London alternately. As a political journalist he advocated a realistic appreciation of the revolutionary situation, in articles remarkable for their brilliance and clarity.

Herzl, Theodor (1860-1904) Father of modern Zionism, and an advocate of Jewish political autonomy. The outbursts of anti-Semitism in the late 19th century led him to publish his pamphlet *The Jewish State*, in which he argued that Jews had only two alternatives; either assimilation by intermarriage, or a separate national state. The latter course was his answer to the problem, and though his reasons were political and economic, not religious, the first Zionist Congress held at Basel in 1897 resolved to secure for the Jewish people a legally assured home in Palestine. Herzl negotiated for a Jewish homeland with the Sultan of Turkey, the Pope, and the British, French, German and Russian governments. He accepted a British offer of land in East Africa, but this was rejected by the 1903 Zionist Congress, and when Herzl died in 1904 the territorial question was still unresolved.

Herzog, Emile Salomon Wilhelm
see MAUROIS, André

Hess, Walter see MONIZ, Caetano
de Abreu Freire Egas

**Hess, Walter Richard Rudolf
(born 1894)** German politician, HIT-
LER's deputy, who flew to Britain
during the Second World War in
order to present his own peace proposals. After the Munich *putsch*
(1923) he was imprisoned with Hitler,
and *Mein Kampf* was probably
written by him at Hitler's dictation.
In 1934 he was appointed deputy
leader of the party and in 1939 Hitler's successor-designate after GOER-
ING. Just before Germany's invasion
of Russia in 1941, Hess flew on his
own initiative to Scotland with compromise peace proposals for CHURCH-
ILL. He was put in gaol, underwent
psychiatric treatment, and in 1945
was sentenced to life imprisonment
at Nuremberg. By 1966 he was the
only remaining inmate of Berlin's
Spandau prison.

Hesse, Hermann (1877-1962) German novelist and poet, whose main
preoccupation is the tension between
the material and the spiritual in man.
This idea is given clear expression in
Steppenwolf (1927), the story of a
lonely and withdrawn artist with a
split personality. In 1911 Hesse
settled in Switzerland, where he
wrote most of his major works, including *The Glass Bead Game* (1943),
considered by some to be his greatest
work. It is the story of a man who
seeks self-fulfilment through an
aesthetic game which develops into a
form of worship. Hesse was awarded
the Nobel Prize for Literature in
1946.

Heydrich, Reinhard (1904-42)
Deputy chief of the Gestapo and
'Protector' of Czechoslovakia. A protégé of HIMMLER, he participated in
the Röhm purge in 1933 and in 1935
was appointed second-in-command
to Himmler, head of the Gestapo and
overlord of the concentration camps.
After ruthless action against resistance in Norway and the Netherlands,
'the hangman', as Heydrich came to
be called, was made Deputy-Protec-
tor of Bohemia and Moravia in 1941,
an appointment which he celebrated
by having some 250 Czechs killed and
hundreds arrested. He was assassinated by Czech patriots in Prague in
1942 in reprisal for which the village
of Lidice was razed to the ground
and all its inhabitants murdered or
deported.

Heyerdahl, Thor (born 1914) Norwegian ethnologist whose 'drift voyages' in primitive craft showed how
ancient peoples may have crossed the
oceans. With five companions, Heyerdahl drifted on the single-sailed balsa
raft, *Kon-Tiki*, 4300 miles across the
Pacific from Peru to Polynesia (1947)
in an attempt to prove that the
Polynesians came from South America and not, as most ethnologists
believed, from southeast Asia. Pursuing his theory, Heyerdahl led
archaeological expeditions to the
Galapagos Islands (1953) and to
Bolivia, Peru and Colombia (1954).
In 1970, Heyerdahl sailed from Africa
to America in the papyrus boat *Ra II*,
based on Egyptian and American
Indian designs, demonstrating that
the ancient Egyptians could have
crossed the Atlantic in similar craft,
thousands of years earlier.

Heymans, Corneille (1892-1968)
Belgian physician, awarded a Nobel
Prize in 1938, who discovered the role
of mechanisms in the blood vessels
near the heart in regulating blood
pressure.

Hiawatha (16th cent.) Red Indian
chief remembered as the founder of
an Indian league. In 1570, he reputedly tried to end tribal strife by
organizing the Cayuga, Mohawk,
Oneida, Onondaga and Seneca tribes
into the Five Nations (Iroquois), a
union which became the most effective Amerindian grouping in North
America. LONGFELLOW's fictional
hero, Hiawatha, was not connected
with the real Iroquois statesman.

Hickok, James Butler (1837-76)
American frontiersman and gun-
fighter, better known as Wild Bill
Hickok.

**Hidalgo y Costilla, Miguel (1753-
1811)** Mexican priest and revolutionary. NAPOLEON's invasion of
Spain (1808) resulted in the formation of a number of revolutionary
groups in Mexico. Hidalgo's rising,
which occurred in 1810, soon became
a social and economic conflict between the masses and the privileged
conservative and higher clerical upper class. Hidalgo, a village priest
among the lower ranks of the clergy,
attracted a large following of mestizos
and Indians, on whose behalf he
sought the abolition of slavery and
the return of land. The racial composition and radicalism of his army
aroused the fears of the Creole or
Mexican-born Spanish class. After
considerable initial success, the rebellion failed to capture Mexico City
and in a subsequent engagement at
Guadalajara (1811) Hidalgo was
heavily defeated by a numerically
inferior Spanish force. He was degraded from the priesthood and shot.
The Hidalgo Rebellion has become
part of the martyrology of Mexican
independence.

**Hildebrandt, Lucas von (1668-
1745)** Italian-born architect who
became, with FISCHER VON ERLACH,
the leading exponent of Baroque
architecture in Austria. He trained in
Rome and his style was influenced
by both GUARINI and BORROMINI. His
work consists of magnificent palaces
and churches in and around Vienna,
notably the Upper Belvedere with its
grand staircase, built for Prince
Eugen.

Hill, Graham (born 1929) English
motor-racing driver who was world
champion in 1962 and runner-up for
the following three years. He has been
placed first in many grand prix races,
including the American Grand Prix
three years running (1963-5).

**Hillary, Sir Edmund Percival
(born 1919)** New Zealand mountaineer who, in May 1953, with the
Sherpa, TENZING Norgay, was first to
climb Mount Everest. They were
members of Sir John HUNT's British
Everest expedition, the eighth attempt on the mountain. Hillary, who
was knighted for the achievement,
was later a member of the New
Zealand Antarctic expedition (1957-
8) which reached the South Pole from
Scott Station at McMurdo Sound,
the first overland journey to the
South Pole since SCOTT.

Hillel (1st cent. BC-1st cent. AD)
Jewish rabbi and theologian descended from the family of DAVID,
whose reinterpretation of the Bible
introduced a new tone of tolerance.
His sayings in some ways anticipate
the attitude of JESUS and prepared the
way for the later acceptance of
Christian teaching.

Hillyarde, Nicholas (c. 1547-1619)
English miniature painter, whose
work is characterized by a languorous
quality which probably derives from
French painting. His work is typified
by *The Young Man among Roses* (c.
1588), probably intended as a lover's
gift and much less formal than
HOLBEIN's miniatures. Hillyarde, like
most early miniaturists, made little
attempt to model his forms, preferring a surface pattern painted with
exquisite delicacy.

Himmler, Heinrich (1900-45)
German politician, creator and chief
of the Gestapo, the Nazi secret police.
In 1927 he became deputy-leader of
HITLER's Storm Troopers (SS) and in
1929 was appointed their leader. In
1936 he assumed control of all German police forces, then, on the outbreak of war, became chief of Reich
Administration and in 1943 Minister
of the Interior. He was infamous for
the number and horror of his atrocities
and was feared even by his colleagues.

Everest
29,028 feet

1953 Hillary
and Tenzing Norgay

1933 Ruttledge
28,100 feet

1924 Mallory and Irvine
28,000 feet +

1922 Bruce expedition
27,300 feet

The greatest climb of all
Since 1953, when Edmund Hillary and Tenzing Norgay conquered Everest for the first time, assaults on the world's highest peak have taken place almost annually and have reached the stage where there is a 'booking list' for years ahead. The success of 1953 was achieved after seven previous attempts, and three reconnaisance expeditions. One of the most famous climbs was that of Mallory and Irvine, who climbed upward, never to be seen again. One of the strangest was that of Maurice Wilson in 1934, who died alone on the mountain after being refused permission to crash-land an aircraft on the peak.

On the defeat of Germany he went into hiding but was found and arrested by the British, and committed suicide.

Hindemith, Paul (1895-1963) German composer of symphonies, operas and chamber music. His early, dissonant music was replaced in the 1930s by a mellower style which informs his symphony *Mathis the Painter* (based on his score for the opera of the same name), the lyrical ballet suite *Noblissima visione* and *Symphonic Metamorphoses*. Hindemith, who was banned by the Nazis, settled in America before the Second World War.

Hindenburg, Paul von (1847-1934) German soldier and politician, who halted the Russian advance at Tannenberg (1914). He was President of the Weimar Republic (1925-34), and made HITLER Chancellor of the Reich in 1933. He was better served by luck, and the adulation of the popular press, than by talent, and his Tannenberg victory was really due to LUDENDORFF and Hoffman. His Presidency was largely sustained by right-wing nationalists' fears of the left wing, but such was Hindenburg's popular influence that Hitler was unable to overthrow constitutional government until after his death.

Hipparchus (2nd cent. BC) Greek astronomer and mathematician, who was one of the most accurate observers of stars in ancient times and

Hillary's feat in conquering Everest with Tenzing Norgay in 1953, ended 50 years of glorious endeavour and failure

Himmler, as much feared by his colleagues as by his enemies, greeted by Hitler. With them are Doenitz and Keitel

who discovered the precession of the equinoxes. His star catalogue listed over 850 stars, giving position and apparent brightness to six magnitudes.

Hippocrates (c. 460-377 BC) Greek physician, called the 'Father of Medicine'. The many writings attributed to him stress accurate observation and reject superstitions about diseases. His extensive descriptions are the bases of classical medicine, and the 'Hippocratic Oath' is the essential expression of medical ethics.

Hippocrates of Chios (5th cent. BC) Greek mathematician, who preceded EUCLID and compiled a now-vanished collection of mathematical elements. He calculated the areas of various figures bounded by circular arcs and showed how the problem of doubling the cube was equivalent to finding two mean proportionals between a number and its double.

Hirohito (born 1901) Emperor of Japan. In 1921 he became the first member of the Imperial family to leave Japan when he visited Europe on a goodwill tour. He acceded in 1926 and has ruled Japan during times of internal conflict and overseas aggression, although it is probable that he genuinely desired not to enter the Second World War, and

encouraged Japan's surrender in 1945. Now ruling under a modified constitution, he has attempted to break away from the traditional isolation of the Japanese Imperial Family and has made several visits abroad, including one to Britain in 1972. He is interested in marine biology and has written a number of learned works on the subject.

Hiroshige, Ando (1797-1858) Japanese print artist famous for the landscapes he developed as an independent genre. His numerous prints of Japanese scenery record particular landmarks in all weathers with a poetic objectivity, gentle humour, and sensitive feeling for atmosphere. His style was followed by later artists.

Hiss, Alger (born 1904) US civil servant, who was accused of espionage during America's anti-Communist period of the 1950s.

Hitchcock, Alfred (born 1899) English film director and master of the thriller, who once said 'I can't bear suspense'. In 1940, Hitchcock went to Hollywood, where his work lost some of its English character, though he still retained his particular brand of humour, creating suspense by his mastery of cinematographic techniques. Hitchcock manipulates ordinary situations to heighten their

Hitchcock, the master of suspense. His famous film *The Birds* is the epitome of his special talent. Hitchcock himself always appears, fleetingly, in his films

Relative strengths of European powers and the US, 1939. Hitler's Germany dominated on land, with 1.5m soldiers and, in the air, with 4,500 aircraft

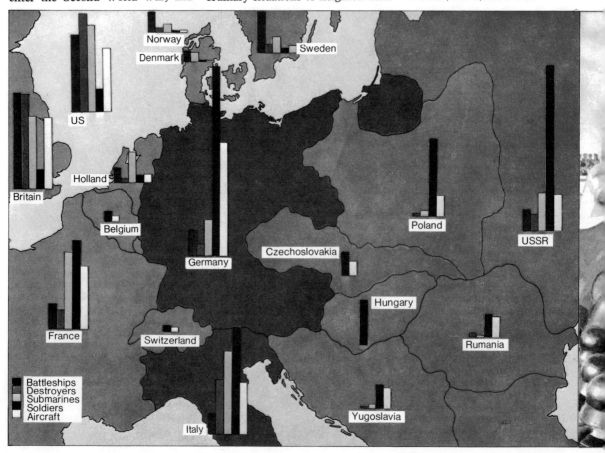

Battleships
Destroyers
Submarines
Soldiers
Aircraft

fear and menace, and tension is built up by his giving to the audience rather than the protagonists as many facts as possible as early as possible. Milestones in his repertoire include *The Lady Vanishes* (1939), *North by Northwest* (1959), *Psycho* (1960), *The Birds* (1963) and *Frenzy* (1972).

Hitler, Adolf (1889-1945) Austrian-born demagogue and Führer of the German Third Reich, whose policies plunged Europe into the Second World War. He died by his own hand in the flames of Berlin as the conflict drew to its close. At the end of the First World War, in which he served in the German army, he joined the insignificant National Socialist Workers Party, which he transformed and enlarged by his talent as a rabble-rousing orator, and in 1923 he tried, unsuccessfully, to overthrow the Bavarian government in a *putsch* at Munich. For this he was imprisoned and while in jail wrote *Mein Kampf*, in which he expounded his political and social theories. The great depression of the late twenties brought him millions of recruits from people disillusioned with other parties, frightened by inflation, workless and hungry. It also won him the support of business interests, fearful of Communism. By 1930 the Nazi Party was the second largest political organization in Germany, having

achieved much of its success by offering the Germans a scapegoat for all their sufferings – the Jewish people, who were to die in their millions by 1945, at the hands of the Nazis. In 1933 President HINDEN-BURG made Hitler Chancellor, and, by contriving the burning down of the Reichstag and blaming it on the Communists, Hitler was able to establish a dictatorship, having eliminated his main rival, Ernst Röhm. Hitler then set about re-arming Germany. In a series of increasingly aggressive acts, phased to coincide with the progressive re-militarization of Germany, he embarked on the gradual conquest of Europe by sending troops into the demilitarized Rhineland (1936), forming an alliance with MUSSOLINI (formally concluded 1939) and sending his troops into Austria and Czechoslovakia (1938). Finally, by invading Poland (Sept. 1939) he precipitated the Second World War.

Hitomaro see KAKINOMOTO

Hobbema, Meindert (1638-1709) Dutch landscape painter, a pupil of RUISDAEL, whose works, although less romantic, are similar to his teacher's in their detailed realism. His best-known painting is the *Avenue at Middleharnis* (1688), in which an avenue of trees leads the eye across a wide, flat landscape, but his most typical paintings are of watermills in wooded settings.

Hobbes, Thomas (1588-1679) English political theorist, lifelong controversialist and philosopher, often called the father of modern analytical philosophy. His principal work *Leviathan* (1651) argued that sovereignty is vested in a ruler when the people agree to limit their freedom in return for protection. Hobbes paved the way for SPINOZA, LOCKE, HUME, ROUSSEAU and BENTHAM to develop concepts of human co-operation, as opposed to ruling authority, as the basis for social order.

Hobhouse, Leonard (1864-1929) English sociologist, who regarded sociology not as a speciality, but as an interpretation of life as a whole. His four-part *The Principles of Sociology* (1918-24) is a study of comparative morals and social institutions, designed to show that throughout history a progressive development in moral and ethical ideas can be traced.

Ho Chi-minh (1890-1969) Vietnamese revolutionary politician, who organized and led resistance first to French colonialism and then to the US in Vietnam. He was founder and first President of the Democratic Republic of Vietnam (North Viet-

nam) from 1954 to 1969. He began his political career in Paris, where he preached revolution to Vietnamese in Paris. He was trained as a Communist agitator in Moscow (1923-5), then went to Canton, and with Mikhail BORODIN helped to organize the South East Asian Comintern. For 15 years he worked as a Communist agitator. In the Second World War, with General GIAP and Phan Van Dong, he organized and led the Viet-minh Communist-Nationalist alliance against the Japanese forces, and in 1945 his partisan army, after receiving the Japanese surrender, turned its attention to the Anglo-French-Nationalist Chinese army of occupation. The uneasy compromise between the Viet-minh and France soon broke down. Ho was in effective control of the North only, the South having been controlled by the anti-Communist BAO-DAI, backed first by France and, when France withdrew, by the US. Ho's attempts to gain control of all Vietnam led to US military intervention and the state of constant warfare between Ho's North Vietnam, and the South Vietnam-US alliance.

Hockney, David (born 1937) English artist, who achieved his first success with Pop Art. His early work was considerably influenced by American painters, but latterly his paintings have shown Surrealist tendencies.

Hodgkin, Thomas (1798-1866) British pathologist. Following his work on the diseases of the lymph glands, the name Hodgkin's disease was given to lymphadenoma.

Hoe, Richard Marsh (1812-86) American inventor of the rotary printing press (1846), which printed at far higher speeds than the traditional 'flat-bed' press. Later developments by William Bullock and Hoe further increased the pace by printing on a roll or 'web' of paper, rather than on single sheets. These webs were made by a machine developed in 1807 by two English paper makers, Henry Fourdrinier and his brother Sealy. The rotary press and the web feed are the foundations of the newspaper industry.

Hoff, Jacobus Henricus Van't (1852-1911) Dutch chemist who showed how laws governing the behaviour of gases could be applied also to solutions. In 1886, he suggested that molecules of a substance in a dilute solution could be likened to those of a gas and that some of the simple gas laws could then be used to describe such dilute solutions.

Hoffa, James Riddle (born 1913) American labour leader whose controversial leadership of the International Brotherhood of Teamsters was cut short by a criminal conviction, largely through the efforts of the then Attorney-General Robert F. KENNEDY. Hoffa's sentence was commuted in 1971 by President NIXON.

Hoffman, Ernst (1776-1822) German writer, composer, music critic and illustrator of the German Romantic period, author of *The Legacy* (1817), a short story *The Golden Pot* (1813), an allegorical fairy tale; and *The Devil's Elixirs* (1812-16), his only novel. Hoffman's talent for inventing bizarre and grotesque adventures in an exploration of the relationship between the natural and the supernatural influenced other 19th-century writers such as BALZAC, POE and SCOTT, and inspired OFFENBACH to write his famous opera, *The Tales of Hoffmann*. He also wrote an essay on MOZART's *Don Giovanni*, and *The Relationship between Artist and Society* (1819-21).

Hoffmann, Josef (1870-1956) Austrian architect connected with the Art Nouveau movement. Hoffmann studied under Otto Wagner in Austria and brought new clarity and restraint to continental Art Nouveau. In his major work, the Palais Stoclet in Brussels (1905-11), he uses rich materials in a rectilinear pattern which contrast sharply with the building's elaborate frieze, designed by Gustav KLIMT.

Hoffnung, Gerard (1925-59) British humorous artist and musician, known for his fanciful drawings of musical subjects. His work, which was somewhat Teutonic in character, shows a robust and eccentric sense of humour, though there was a profoundly serious side to his nature. His comic concerts, given at the Albert Hall, revealed his love of the absurd, combined with an extensive knowledge of serious music.

Hofmann, August von (1818-92) German chemist whose experiments with aniline and other coal-tar products helped to establish the aniline dye industry.

Hofmann, Hans (1880-1966) German-born American Abstract Expressionist painter. His influence on contemporary American painting was considerable.

Hofmannsthal, Hugo von (1874-1929) Austrian dramatist, poet and essay writer, author of *The Play of Everyman* (1911), a verse drama regularly staged at the Salzburg Festival, of which Hofmannsthal was one of the founders. Hofmannsthal was one of Richard STRAUSS's librettists and collaborated with him on *Der Rosenkavalier* (1911) and other operas. The importance of language to Hofmannsthal is clearly expressed in the *Chandos Letters* (1902), an imaginary correspondence between Lord Chandos and an Elizabethan nobleman, in which he gives his reasons for abandoning poetry, and describes a personal crisis in which language and reality seemed to have lost their meaning. Towards the end of his life Hofmannsthal turned to an elegant narrative prose as a means of expressing his ideas.

Hogan, Ben (born 1912) American golfer who won the American Open Championship on four occasions and the British Open once. In 1953 he scored a record 274 (14 under par) to win the US Masters' tournament.

Hogarth, William (1697-1764) English artist, famous through the enormous and lasting popularity of his engravings. Wishing to be judged as a moralist as well as an artist, he painted what he called 'modern moral subjects' in a number of pictorial cycles, subsequently engraved, the first of which was the *Harlot's Progress* (1731-2). Though he twice visited Paris, Hogarth was an extreme chauvinist and refused to recognize his debt to foreign masters. In his aesthetic treatise, *The Analysis of Beauty* (1753), he attacked the connoisseurs, the concept of ideal beauty, and the vogue for collecting Italian works at the expense of English ones. Nevertheless in *Sigismunda* (1759) he attempted, without much success, to outdo the Bolognese painters. He also made attempts at historical painting, recognizing that the practice of this genre had been an important element in the success of his father-in-law, the painter, Sir James Thornhill.

Hogg, Quintin (1845-1903) English educational pioneer whose successful administration of the Regent Street Polytechnic Institution in London led to the founding of public polytechnics which gave a broad industrial education.

Hohenheim, Theophlast von see PARACELSUS

Hokusai Katsushika (1760-1849) Japanese print artist famed for his highly original views of Mount Fuji. His dramatic landscape compositions betray European influences derived from his knowledge of Dutch engraved books, and make much use of Prussian blue, which he is credited with introducing into Japanese printmaking.

Holbach, Baron Paul d' (1723-89) French philosopher of German extraction, friend of the *encyclopédistes* and author, with DIDEROT, of *The System of Nature* (1770), in which he expounded a comprehensive materialism. Holbach's Paris home was a meeting place of all the great contemporary thinkers and scientists.

Holbein, Hans the Younger (c. 1497-1543) One of the most important German artists of the 16th century and court painter to HENRY VIII. He was trained by his father, also a painter, and from 1515 worked in Basel, where he painted portraits, received civic commissions and executed decorations for house façades, now known only through drawings. His reputation was enhanced by illustrations for LUTHER's Bible and two series of woodcuts on a medieval theme: the *Dance of Death* (1523-4) and the *Alphabet of Death* (1524). In 1523 he painted three portraits of the humanist ERASMUS and when, in 1526, the Reformation crisis forced Holbein to leave Basel, Erasmus gave him a letter of introduction to Sir Thomas MORE. One of the first commissions he obtained after arriving in England was a portrait group of More's family, of which only sketches and copies remain. By 1528, More was in disfavour and Holbein began painting portraits of German merchants in London. These pictures are characterized by an amazing virtuosity, best seen in the *Ambassadors* (1533), which led to his royal appointment.

Hölderlin, Johann (1770-1843) German lyric poet whose work in poems such as 'Hyperion's Song of Fate', 'Diotima' and 'Patmos' is considered to be among the finest verse in German literature. Influenced by KLOPSTOCK's vision of the poet as a seer, and, like Klopstock, writing in a consciously elevated, Neo-classical style, Hölderlin yearned for the golden age of Greece and its rebirth in Germany.

Holland, John Philip (1840-1914) Irish-born American inventor who developed the modern submarine. He devised the scheme of using electric motors for power under water and internal combustion engines on the surface and also introduced the method of submergence by water ballast. These systems were used in the *Holland*, the first modern submarine, purchased by the American Government in 1900.

Holmes, Oliver Wendell (1809-94) American author and academic, best known for *The Autocrat of the Breakfast-Table* (1858) and *The Professor at the Breakfast-Table* (1860), humorous philosophical discourses. He was a central figure in the cultural life of New England, and Professor of Anatomy at Harvard (1847-82).

Holmes, Oliver Wendell (1841-1935) American judge. Appointed to the Supreme Court (1902-32) by Theodore ROOSEVELT, he urged restraint in the use of judicial power, and maintained that law is not void merely because it seems to judges to be excessive, inappropriate, or based on a morality with which they disagree; latitude must be allowed for different views. Holmes stated in *The Common Law* (1881) that law is based not on logic but on experience, and his constant re-evaluation of legal concepts in the light of social change, although arousing fierce opposition, led to the abandonment of many obsolete doctrines.

Holst, Gustav Theodore (1874-1934) English composer who wrote the orchestral suite, *The Planets* (1914-16). Holst, formerly an organist and music teacher, associated closely with VAUGHAN WILLIAMS and, like him, was deeply influenced by English folk music. Holst also possessed a strong, original musical personality. He wrote equally effectively for brass band or school orchestra but moved always towards an increasing austerity of vision, as in his fine tone poem, *Egdon Heath* (based on the landscape description in HARDY's *Return of the Native*). Holst's other works include *The Hymn of Jesus*, an affirmative setting of a Byzantine text, and a comic opera, *The Perfect Fool*.

Holt, Harold (1908-67) Prime Minister of Australia (1966-7). Holt was the deputy-leader of the Liberal party from 1956 until becoming Prime Minister on the retirement of Sir Robert MENZIES. He was drowned while swimming off the coast of Victoria in 1967.

Homer (8th cent. BC) Greek legendary author of the *Iliad* and the *Odyssey*. Though the authorship of the poems was not doubted in antiquity, modern research has shown that they represent the culmination of several centuries of orally transmitted poetry about the war of the Greeks against Troy. The *Iliad* is concerned with the episode in the Trojan War of the wrath of Achilles; the *Odyssey* deals with Odysseus's return from Troy, after 10 years of wandering, to his native Ithaca and his wife Penelope. The two works had far-reaching effects on Greek and Latin literature and their expression of the heroic ideal formed the basis of ancient education.

Homer, Winslow (1836-1910) American painter, who began as a journalistic illustrator. His later seascapes, for which he is now best known, show virtuoso technique, and are often dramatic in content.

Honegger, Arthur (1892-1955) Swiss composer who sought to express the conflicts of humanity in his music. In a highly individual style, he wrote five symphonies depicting the struggle between beauty and evil, peace and war, and the stage cantatas *King David* and *Joan of Arc at the Stake* (text by CLAUDEL). He also wrote a symphonic movement *Pacific 231*, depicting a steam locomotive in motion.

Honnecourt, Villard de (13th cent.) French architect, none of whose buildings survive, but whose handbook, filled with sketches of architectural plans and details seen on his travels and with his own designs, still exists. Containing contemporary records of the cathedrals of Laon, Reims, Lausanne and Chartres, both from his designs and his sculptural drawings it is clear that he was one of the foremost architects and master masons of that period.

Hooch, Pieter de (1629-c. 1684) Dutch genre painter, whose typical interiors, usually with two or three figures engaged in domestic chores, and interest in the fall of light recall the painting of VERMEER, though his work tends towards a more 'photographic' form of realism.

Hood, Thomas (1799-1845) English journalist and poet, editor of comic periodicals such as *The Gem* and the *Comic Annual*, in which his own humorous poems appeared. He was also known for serious poems against social injustices, and was a friend of LAMB and HAZLITT.

Hooft, Pieter (1581-1647) Dutch poet, historian and playwright whose 20-volume *Dutch History* (1642-54) based on the work of TACITUS was a monument to his lifelong dedication to the ennoblement of the Dutch language. The most brilliant Renaissance figure in Dutch literature between 1607 and 1610, he wrote a series of Petrarchan sonnets, some tragedies based on SENECA, the pastoral play *Grandida* (1605) and the comedy *Warenar* (1616).

Hooke, Robert (1635-1703) English physicist who discovered a fundamental law describing the elasticity of springs. In 1678 he formulated what is now called Hooke's law, which states that stress is proportional to strain.

Hooker, Sir Joseph Dalton (1817-1911) British botanist commissioned to explore and collect plants in eastern Nepal and eastern Bengal (1848-51) and who introduced many Himalayan plants, including nearly 40 previously-unknown rhododendrons into European horticulture. Hooker had been assistant-surgeon on ROSS's Antarctic expedition (1839-43) and subsequently published zoological and botanical studies of Antarctica, New Zealand and Tasmania (1844-60). He succeeded his father as Director of the Royal Botanic Gardens at Kew (1865-85).

Hooker, Thomas (c. 1586-1647) English-born Puritan clergyman who fled to America to escape persecution and where his ideal of Christian democracy, embodied in the 'Fundamental Orders', became law for Connecticut.

Hooker, Sir William Jackson (1785-1865) British botanist, horticulturist and the first Director of the Royal Botanic Gardens, Kew (1840), which he made the finest botanic gardens in the world. He commissioned plant collectors to bring home new species, redesigned and extended the gardens, greatly increased the collection of hardy as well as tropical plants and initiated a series of botanical studies from British colonies overseas. Earlier in his career he made botanical expeditions to various parts of Britain, Iceland (1809) and France, Switzerland and northern Italy (1814). At his Suffolk home he built up a herbarium which became known to botanists throughout the world and was eventually bought for the nation.

Hookham, Peggy see FONTEYN, Dame Margot

Hoover, Herbert Clark (1874-1964) Republican, 31st President of the US (1929-33), in office during the Great Depression. He succeeded COOLIDGE as President in 1929, and his encouragement of big business led to a handful of companies, including Standard Oil, J. Pierpoint Morgan, and the US Steel Corporation, controlling a large proportion of the country's wealth. The Wall Street crash in October 1929 indicated the failure of this policy, however, and the subsequent depression revealed Hoover's lack of political acumen. Believing the setback to be temporary, and declaring at the height of the collapse that 'the fundamental business of the country . . . is on a sound and prosperous basis,' he opposed direct government aid to the unemployed and became one of the most hated men in the country. In the 1932 presidential election he was decisively beaten by F. D. ROOSEVELT, whereupon he retired to private life.

Hoover, John Edgar (1895-1972) American Director of the United States Federal Bureau of Investigation (FBI). In 1924, he took over the directorship of the Bureau of Investigation and began to reorganize this somewhat discredited agency. Later, Congress expanded the Bureau's powers and it became the Federal Bureau of Investigation. Hoover led the FBI for 48 years.

Hopkins, Sir F. G. see EIJKMAN, Christian

Hopkins, Gerard Manley (1844-89) English poet, who was a great technical innovator and a potent influence on the development of 20th-century English verse. Hopkins was a Jesuit and felt that publication of his poems would be contrary to his duty. He sent most of them to friends such as Robert BRIDGES, his executor, but the boldness of his verse experiments caused Bridges to delay publication of *Poems* until 1918. His language is condensed and uses the accentual pattern of Old English verse, seeking to capture the inward peace of Christian faith, and yet expressing tormenting doubts, as in the later 'terrible' sonnets.

Horace (65-8 BC) Roman lyric poet and satirist. A master of form and metre, he has been the supreme interpreter of Augustan culture to succeeding generations, and his popularity is undiminished today. His *Epodes* and *Satires*, written in a racy style, portray a variety of scene and character in contemporary life. The earlier *Epodes* are bitter in mood, but in the *Satires* and the later *Epistles* Horace's writing became more sympathetic. His sane philosophy and his gentle humour, coupled with skilful story-telling, show a depth of insight into life in general and his own in particular. The three books of lyric *Odes* which were published in 23 BC, and a fourth after 13 BC, range in subject matter from wine and women to patriotism and national purpose.

Horney, Karen (1885-1952) American psychoanalyst of German origin. Dissatisfied with the anti-feminism of much Freudian doctrine, she put forward the idea that many of the personality traits which FREUD thought of as universal were culturally and socially determined. She stressed the importance of early training, but suggested that later experiences could also influence character.

Horthy, Miklós de Nagybánya (1868-1957) Hungarian admiral, who became Regent and dictator of Hungary (1920-44). After service as a naval officer in the First World War, he became the last Commander-in-Chief of the Imperial Austro-Hungarian navy. When, in 1919, Béla KUN became dictator of Hungary, Horthy, with Rumanian assistance, organized and led a successful counter-revolution. He became Regent in 1920. In 1921, Charles Hapsburg returned to claim the throne, but Horthy refused to retire from office. Though he followed the Axis powers in the Second World War he was never a convinced supporter of HITLER and tried to extricate Hungary from the war in 1944. He was imprisoned by the Nazis, released by US troops in 1945 and later went to Portugal (1949), where he died.

Hotchkiss, Hazel see WIGHTMAN, Mrs George

Hotspur see PERCY, Sir Henry

Houdini, Harry (1874-1926) American escapologist and illusionist, who accepted seemingly impossible challenges. He extricated himself from ropes, chains and handcuffs and from prison cells and even escaped from a strait jacket while hanging upside down. His name imitates that of the French magician, Houdin. His real name was Ehrich Weiss.

Greatest of all escapers, Harry Houdini prepares to perform one of his seemingly impossible stunts

Houdon, Jean-Antoine (1741-1828) French portrait sculptor who won renown with his classical-style statue of *St Bruno* (1764). Among his best-known busts are those of DIDEROT (1771), GLUCK (1775), Benjamin FRANKLIN and VOLTAIRE (1778) and WASHINGTON (1785). They illustrate his skill in capturing characteristic traits of gesture and expression.

Housman, Alfred Edward (1859-1936) English classical scholar and lyric poet, author of delicate, melancholy poems, often about rural tragedies. He is best known for the poem 'A Shropshire Lad' (1896).

Houssay, Bernado see CORI, Charles

Houston, Samuel (1793-1863) American soldier and statesman, who helped join Texas to the United States. The first President of the Republic of Texas (1836-8 and 1841-4), he achieved union with the United States (1845), then served Texas as senator (1846-59) and Governor (1859-61). The biggest industrial city in the southwestern United States is named after him.

Howard, Catharine see HENRY VIII

Howard, Charles, 2nd Baron of Effingham (1536-1624) English admiral who defeated the Spanish Armada (1588). As Lord High Admiral on board the *Ark Royal*, he led DRAKE and HAWKINS to their victory over the Spanish fleet and saved England from threatened invasion. Howard of Effingham commanded both the army and the navy in 1598 and 1599 when there were further invasion threats, and, with ESSEX, captured Cadiz (1596). The following year he was created 1st Earl of Nottingham.

Howard, John (c. 1726-90) English prison reformer who first put forward the view that prisoners might be reformed by such methods as solitary confinement, regular work and religious instruction. Appalled to find that some gaolers existed on fees from prisoners, who, on discharge, had to pay for their release, Howard spent his life touring the prisons and hospitals of England, Ireland and the Continent, campaigning against the brutal treatment of the inmates. His findings, compiled in *The State of the Prisons* (1777), had considerable influence.

Howel the Good (10th cent.) Welsh ruler (915-50) who codified the Welsh tribal customary law. He was ruler of Deheubarth (south-central Wales), but by marriage and inheritance briefly united almost the whole of Wales under his rule (943-50) so that his sophisticated law code became nationwide.

Hoxha, Enver (born 1908) Albanian leader, supporter of China against Russia, and the last self-confessed Stalinist head of state in Europe. His policy is independent of Moscow's and occasionally openly hostile to it. His support of China against Russia has given MAO TSE-TUNG a European outpost, largely because of Russian attempts to persuade Yugoslavia, traditionally hated by the Albanians, to return to the Russian fold, and because of the violently anti-Yugoslav line adopted by Peking.

Hoyle, Edmond (c. 1672-1769) English card player who first systematized the game of whist. His *Short Treatise on Whist* (1742) regulated play until the revisions by leading clubs in 1864, which were followed by new rules made by the American Whist League (1893) and universally adopted in the US.

Hrolf see ROLLO

Hroswitha (932-83) German nun of the Benedictine order who wrote six religious dramas in Latin, modelled on TERENCE but with Christian historical themes. They have occasionally been revived in modern times and are of interest to historians of dramatic art because they form a literary bridge between late Roman and medieval drama.

Hsieh Ho (late 5th cent.) Chinese painter and art critic, author of the *Six Canons of Painting*. These rules, still fundamental to the study of Chinese painting, summarize the basic principles formed in previous centuries.

Hsüan-Tsang (c. 600-64) Chinese Buddhist pilgrim to India. From Kansu, in northern China, he crossed the Gobi Desert and Tien Shan Mountains, and passed through Samarkand and over the Hindu Kush to India. He described his travels in *Record of the Western Regions*.

Hsüan Tsung (685-762) Chinese Emperor (713-56) of the T'ang dynasty, whose reign marked a cultural zenith in Chinese history. He founded the Hanlin Academy of Letters (725) to compile histories, draft decrees and perform other literary work. He established schools throughout the empire, and attracted poets and men of the arts to the royal court. Sculpture, painting, true porcelain work and wood-block printing on paper all flourished. His reign ended disastrously when a rebellion forced him to abdicate.

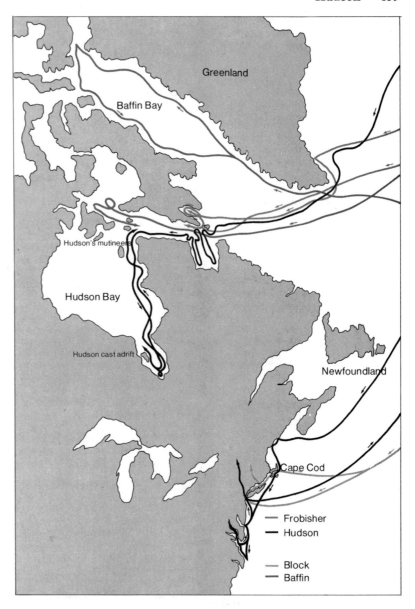

The search for a route to Cathay by a North West Passage around the Americas led to a series of fruitless attempts between 1576 and 1615

Hsüan T'ung see PU-YI, Henry

Hubble, Edwin Powell (1889-1953) American astronomer, who discovered that galaxies exist outside our own, all apparently receding at a speed that depends on their distance. In 1923 Hubble identified peripheral stars in the Andromeda galaxy and proved that its spiral nebulae are distant and separate from our own Milky Way Galaxy. By 1929 Hubble had proved that the more distant a galaxy is from us, the faster it seems to be receding.

Huber, Eugen (1849-1923) Swiss jurist who was the chief draftsman of the Swiss civil law. His four-volume study of the civil laws of the 25 Swiss cantons and a history of private law provided him with the necessary background for his codifications. Swiss civil law became a model for

other countries, including Brazil, China (until 1954) and Turkey.

Hudson, Henry (17th cent.) English mariner and explorer of Arctic and subarctic waters who vanished after being cast adrift by mutineers. His name is commemorated in the Hudson River and Hudson Bay, which he explored in his search for the North West Passage.

Hudson, William Henry (1841-1922) English writer and naturalist who wrote of the English countryside and of the forests of Argentina, where he was born, with equal success. His best-known works are *A Shepherd's Life* (1910) and a fictional romance, *Green Mansions* (1904).

Huggins, Sir William (1824-1910)
English astronomer, who pioneered
the use of spectroscopic photography
for investigating the chemical composition of stars. While investigating
Sirius in 1868 he discovered a shift in
its light towards the red end of the
spectrum ('the red shift'), which
enabled him to determine its velocity
and that of other stars.

Hugh Capet (c. 940-96) King of
France and founder of the Capetian
dynasty (987-1328). He was elected
king on the death of LOUIS V, so
ending the enfeebled Carolingian
dynasty, but throughout his reign his
authority was threatened by the
nobles who had elected him and he
had to buy their loyalty by large land
grants.

**Hughes, David Edward (1831-
1900)** Anglo-American inventor of
the teleprinter, which he patented in
1855. He later set out the basic
principles of the 'loose contact',
which underlies the various forms of
microphone, such as the telephone
and hearing aids.

Hughes, Howard (born 1906) American aircraft manufacturer, film-
maker and head of the $2 billion
Hughes Enterprises. A keen amateur
pilot, he won the land-plane speed
record in 1937, the US Transcontinental record in 1937 and the
round-the-world flight record in
1938.

Hughes, Langston (1902-67) American author, who was one of the
first negroes to win a literary reputation and to express the negro view of
America. He is admired for his poems
– 'The Weary Blues' (1926) attracted
readers by its attempt to introduce
the rhythms of jazz and folk music
into poetry. Since that time, he has
helped create a body of negro American writing, producing ballads, plays,
stories and two autobiographical
works, *The Big Sea* (1940) and *I
Wonder as I Wander* (1956).

Hughes, Richard (born 1900) English novelist and writer of stories for
children. After travels in America and
the Caribbean, he wrote *A High
Wind in Jamaica* (1929), a study of
amiable pirates and malevolent children.

Hughes, Ted (born 1930) English
poet, whose poems convey vividly
the existence of natural objects,
plants, animals and birds, alongside
industrial and urban life. His language and imaginative perception celebrate their survival, while the human
beings in his poems struggle to live.
Typical collections are *The Hawk in
the Rain* (1957) and *Lupercal* (1960),

while he has also written verse and
tales for children. He was married to
Sylvia PLATH.

Hugo, Victor Marie (1802-85)
French author and the leading apostle
of Romanticism. Hugo, a prolific
writer, revolutionized poetry and the
historical novel, which he developed
with *Notre Dame de Paris* (1831) and
in his social drama *Les Misérables*
(1862) about the victims of society.
Hugo had shown his passion for
liberty, as well as his skill in handling
technical innovations, in *Odes et
Ballades* (1828) and *Orientales* (1829)
and had shattered convention with
his dramas *Cromwell* (1827), *Hernani*
(1830) and *Ruy Blas* (1838). The
'Préface de Cromwell', setting out his
dramatic precepts, came to be regarded as a manifesto of the new
Romantic movement. In 1841, Hugo
was elected to the French Academy,
created a peer of France and began an
active political life. As a result of
vigorous opposition to NAPOLEON
III's *coup d'état* in 1851, Hugo was
obliged to live in exile in the Channel
Islands, a period which prompted his
scathing satirical poems *Les Châti-
ments* (1853). Napoleon's overthrow
in 1870 facilitated his return and
subsequent election to the National
Assembly. A national hero and a
popular symbol of humanitarian and
democratic ideals, he was buried in
the Pantheon in Paris.

Hui-Tsung (1028-1135) Last Emperor of the Northern Sung dynasty
in China and patron of a brilliant
academy of painters. A poet, calligrapher and painter of talent, Hui-
Tsung continued his role as arbiter of
taste until the sack of his capital by
Tatars in 1126. He died in captivity
in Manchuria, but the style which he
encouraged had a lasting effect on the
art of the East.

Hulagu (1217-65) Mongol founder
of the Il-khan (provincial khan) dynasty (1260-1353) in Persia. Ordered
by his brother, the Great Khan
Mangu, to crush dissidents in Islamic
lands, he left Central Asia (1256) and
swept through the southwest of the
continent. In Persia he defeated and
massacred the Assassins and took
Baghdad (1258), executing its last
Abbasside caliph, al-Mustasim. After
his advance on Egypt was blocked
(1260), Hulagu turned back to consolidate Mongol power in Persia,
ruling as Viceroy for his brother
KUBLAI KHAN, who had succeeded
Mangu.

Hull, Clark (1884-1952) American
psychologist whose reinforcement
theory of learning states that learning
occurs in view of anticipated rewards
and dies away when these are not

Exiled for 20 years, Victor Hugo (right)
was given a hero's funeral when he died

forthcoming. Habits are the bonds
that link stimulus and response, but
they acquire force only from some
drive, i.e. an unfulfilled need. Hull
also made a lifelong study of aptitude
tests and their validity. His findings
in both fields have served to reconcile
and integrate the work of PAVLOV,
THORNDIKE, TOLMAN, WATSON and
others.

**Humboldt, Baron Alexander von
(1769-1859)** German botanist and
explorer whose South American journeys helped to broaden the bases of
modern geography. After years of
travelling in Europe, Humboldt and
the French botanist, Aimé Bonpland,
set out on a scientific exploration of
South America (1799-1804). They
discovered the Casiquiare, a curious
natural canal linking the Amazon and
Orinoco rivers; visited Cuba and
Mexico; followed the Andes from
Colombia to Peru (reaching the then
record altitude of 18,893 ft on Mount
Chimborazo) and studied the cold
Pacific stream, rich in marine life,
now called the Humboldt Current.
Humboldt was the first scientist to
grasp relationships between certain
natural phenomena, correlating rise
in altitude with fall in temperature,
noting that some volcanoes are
aligned (hence structurally linked),
and discovering connections between
plant distribution and environment.
He thus virtually founded modern
physical geology, biogeography and
ecology. Humboldt presented his
new, integrated view of the universe
in his most important publication,
the five-volume *Kosmos* (1845-62).
His work was a significant influence
on DARWIN and WALLACE.

Humboldt, Karl von (1767-1835)
German philologist and writer who
first formulated the theory that
language is an expression of the inner
life and experience of man and that
languages differ one from another, in
accordance with the differences between the peoples who use them.
Humboldt pioneered the study of the
Basque language.

Hume, David (1711-76) Scottish
philosopher, essayist and historian.
As a philosopher, his empiricist ap-

proach went a step further than that of BERKELEY, who had denied LOCKE's assertion that there are material objects, while retaining the concept of the mind as that which has ideas. Hume denied the existence of mind as well, and allowed merely impressions and ideas (corresponding roughly with Locke's ideas of sensation and ideas of reflection respectively). Hume argued that the only justifiable attitude is scepticism. Hume's ethical theory is based on his observing men to have moral sentiments that are motivated on broadly utilitarian lines, not just self-seeking (as with HOBBES) but for the good of the whole, an approach that greatly influenced BENTHAM and J. S. MILL. Some of his views on economics may have influenced Adam SMITH.

Humphrey, Hubert Horatio (born 1911) American senator, President Lyndon B. JOHNSON's Vice-President (1964-8) and defeated Democratic candidate for the presidency in the 1968 elections. Humphrey failed to gain the Democratic nomination when he tried again in 1972.

Hung Wu see CHU YÜAN-CHANG

Hunt, Leigh (1784-1859) English journalist, essayist and poet, whose editorship of numerous periodicals brought the work of the Romantic poets such as KEATS and SHELLEY to the public. During a period in Italy, with BYRON, he produced *The Liberal* magazine (1822), which contained some of Byron's works. Hunt was a prolific essayist on an extensive range of literary topics. His main poetic work was 'The Story of Rimini' (1816).

Hunt, William Holman (1827-1910) English artist, a member of the Pre-Raphaelite movement, which included MILLAIS and ROSSETTI. Hunt alone remained faithful throughout his career to the moral and technical aims of the Brotherhood, as in such works as *The Awakening Conscience* (1853) and *The Scapegoat* (1855).

Hunter, John (1728-93) British physiologist and surgeon, who founded surgical pathology. His *Natural History of Human Teeth* (1771-8) influenced the development of scientific dentistry. Hunter studied a wide range of subjects, including gun-shot wounds, the constitution of the blood, embryology, venereal disease and the nature of inflammation. Most of his life was devoted to the study of comparative anatomy.

Huntingdon, Ellsworth (1876-1947) American geographer who held the view that climate influences civilization. His *Civilization and Climate* (1915) tried to show that hot climates encourage indolence, irritability and excessive self-indulgence; that cold climates use up all human energy in the sheer effort of survival; but that cool climates with rapid weather changes stimulate mental and physical activity. This theory attempted to account for the economic world dominance in the 20th century of peoples in and from the world's north temperate zone.

Hunyadi, János (c. 1387-1456) Hungarian national hero in his country's fight against the Turks. After a series of military successes he was made Lord of Transylvania (1440), which bore the brunt of Turkish onslaughts on Christian Europe. He won several victories in the Balkan Peninsula (1443) and marched on the Black Sea to push the Turks out of Europe, but was defeated at Varna (1444). He led a peasant army which freed Belgrade from a Turkish siege (1456), assuring Hungarian independence for 70 years.

Husayn, Mirza (15th-16th cents.) Timurid ruler of Khorasan (northeast Persia), soldier, poet, bibliophile and patron of the arts. He attracted the most talented men of the period to his court at Herat, including the poet Jami, the historian Khwandamir, and the painter Bihzad. His reign marked the end of Timurid power in Persia, but the high literary and artistic standards then set were to have a lasting influence on Persian cultural history.

Husein ibn-Ali (1856-1931) King of the Hejaz, an ally of T. E. LAWRENCE, and great-grandfather of HUSSEIN of Jordan. At first a supporter of Germany and Turkey in the First World War, he was persuaded by Lawrence to support the Allies, and in 1916 he proclaimed the independence of Arabia from Turkish rule. His army captured Yanbu, the port of Medina, in July 1916, and by the end of the year he was formally recognized as King of Hejaz, part of Saudi Arabia. Internal unrest and invasion by IBN-SAUD forced him to abdicate in 1924.

Huskisson, William (1770-1830) Tory reformer and pioneer of free trade and one of history's first victims of a railway accident. Secretary of the Treasury under both PITT (1804-5) and Portland (1807-9), his considerable reputation as a free-trade economist led LIVERPOOL to appoint him as President of the Board of Trade (1823), an office he held until 1827, when he was appointed Colonial Secretary. Huskisson, logical successor of Pitt in his attempts at fiscal reform, was killed by a train at the opening of the Liverpool and Manchester Railway in 1830.

Huss, Jan (c. 1369-1415) Bohemian theologian and religious reformer, whose criticism of the malpractices of the Catholic Church directly inspired LUTHER a century later. His followers, the Hussites, who supported all WICLIF's teachings, believed in freedom of speech, poverty of the clergy, and the punishment of notorious sinners and they campaigned for the expropriation of all church property. They were denounced as heretics for administering Holy Communion to the laity, and in 1415 Huss was burned at the stake in Constance. His martyrdom paved the way for the Reformation in Europe.

Hussein ibn-Talal (born 1935) King of Jordan. His rule began in 1952 and throughout his reign he has tried to follow a policy of compromise between friendship with the West and Arab nationalism, both within and outside Jordan. His expulsion of Sir John Glubb, commandant of the Arab Legion, in 1956 and the abrogation of Jordan's treaty with Britain was in response to Arab criticism, but he was opposed to the formation of the belligerent United Arab Republic and, in order to counteract it, established the short-lived Arab Federation with FAISAL II of Iraq. He is, however, an Arab nationalist himself, though moderate in his views, and has remained largely unreconciled to the creation of Israel. In the Arab war with Israel in 1967 Hussein was forced to take part on behalf of his Palestinian subjects but lost almost half of his territory. Nevertheless, his policy was not considered sufficiently extreme by Palestinian guerillas in Jordan, and he was faced with civil war in 1970, when they openly flouted his authority. The revolt was crushed, but Hussein lost the support of Egypt and the other Arab states as a result. Always under the pressure of extreme nationalism, he remains a key figure in the search for peace in the Middle East.

Husserl, Edmund (1859-1938) German philosopher and founder of phenomenology, a conceptual study of what is involved generally in outward appearances.

Hutton, James (1726-97) British geologist, who showed that in interpreting geological phenomena, the present is the key to the past. This came to be called the 'principle of uniformaterianism'. Hutton observed that geological features are produced as a result of slow change and not by a series of catastrophes. He also opposed one of the most influential of his colleagues, WERNER, denouncing the Wernerian doctrine of Neptunism (the belief that all the rocks of the Earth were originally precipitated from a solution in water). Hutton maintained that certain types of rock had once been in a molten state and had cooled down. This, the Plutonist school of thought, is now known to be correct.

Huxley, Aldous (1894-1963) English novelist, whose reputation rests on clever, witty novels giving a sardonic view of English intellectual life in the 1920s. After early successes like *Crome Yellow* (1921) and *Antic Hay* (1923) he grew more pessimistic and bitterly satirical in *Point Counter Point* (1928) and the prophetic *Brave New World* (1932). He was the grandson of T. H. HUXLEY.

Huxley, Sir Julian Sorell (born 1887) British biologist and evolutionist who has drawn the social and political implications of biology to public attention in books such as *Evolution: The Modern Synthesis*. His work has been notable for its interpretation of modern biological thinking in terms comprehensible to the layman. Sir Julian was the first Director-General of Unesco.

Huxley, Thomas H. (1825-95) English biologist, who suggested that evolutionary changes need not be gradual, as DARWIN thought, but might be step-like, foreshadowing the more correct view that genetic change is due to mutation. A mutation is a sudden change in the gene structure of germ plasm brought about by physico-chemical causes.

Huygens, Christiaan (1629-95) Dutch astronomer, physicist and mathematician, who discovered the nature of Saturn's rings and propounded the wave theory of light. In 1655 Huygens developed a new method of polishing telescope lenses and discovered markings on Mars and on Titan, Saturn's brightest satellite, and the ring of Saturn.

Huysmans, Joris Karl (1848-1907) French 'decadent' novelist and art critic, one of the first to appreciate the Impressionists. Among his chief novels were *A rebours* (1884) and *La Cathédrale* (1898).

Hyatt, John Wesley (1837-1920) American inventor, who in 1868 produced a cheap substitute for ivory for billiard balls. This material, which he called celluloid, was the first synthetic plastic. Although later utilized particularly for photographic films, its greatest drawback was its inflammability and consequent danger.

Hyde, Edward, 1st Earl of Clarendon (1609-74) English royalist and Restoration statesman, who helped to stabilize the monarchy after the Restoration. As an MP, Clarendon had sided with CHARLES I against Parliament's extreme reformers, believing that their demands would damage Church and State. He backed his decision with forceful arguments that won much support for Charles in the ensuing Civil War. Afterwards he was CHARLES II's chief adviser.

Hyder Ali see HAIDER ALI

I

Iaroslav see YAROSLAV

Ibarruri, Dolores (born 1895) Spanish Republican demagogue known as 'La Pasionaria', who became the symbol of resistance to Franco's nationalist campaigns throughout the latter stages of the Spanish Civil War (1936-9).

Ibert, Jacques (1890–1962) French composer who wrote the lively suite *Divertissement*, based on his incidental music to the well-known farce, *The Italian Straw Hat*. He was also director of the French Academy in Rome.

ibn-Batuta (1304-68) Moroccan traveller famous for his descriptive accounts of Mohammedan society of the Middle East and North Africa in the 14th century. He began his extensive travels when he was 22, visiting Egypt, Palestine, Mecca, Iraq and Persia. Later his travels took him to Asia Minor, Russia and, possibly, Siberia.

ibn-Hazm (994-1064) Leading Moorish scholar who is best known for two major works, a study of comparative religion and a work on romantic love, *The Dove's Necklace*.

ibn-Khaldun (1332-1406) Leading Arab historian. He held various official posts in North Africa and Spain, but his fame rests on one book, a general history of the Muslim dynasties and, more specifically, the *Muqaddima*, the introduction to this work, in which he theorized on the nature, significance and methodology of history. It was described by Arnold TOYNBEE as 'the greatest work of its kind that has ever yet been created by any mind in any time or place'.

ibn-Saud (1880-1953) Creator of the kingdom of Saudi Arabia. During the First World War, he refused to join the Arab revolt organized by T. E. LAWRENCE because the Allies had recognized Hussein of Hejaz as king of the Arabs. He went to war against Hussein (1919) and by 1925 had defeated him and his allies and seized Mecca, Medina and Jeddah. He was proclaimed King of Hejaz and Nejd (1926), and recognized as king by a series of treaties with the great powers, completed in 1932, when he renamed his kingdom Saudi Arabia. He made his country economically viable by negotiating concessions with American oil companies. During the Second World War, he remained neutral, though he maintained friendly relations with Britain. After the war, American finance and technical aid supported a large-scale programme of irrigation schemes and public works. A founder member of the Arab League (1945) he subsequently took Saudi Arabia into the United Nations.

Ibn Sinaobumi see AVICENNA

ibn-Tashfin, Yusuf (11th cent.) Berber chieftain, one of the founders of the Almoravid Empire of northwest Africa and Spain. He and his cousin ABU BAKR conquered Morocco, and ibn-Tashfin became its sole ruler in 1071, taking the title of amir. With Abu Bakr, he founded Marrakesh (c. 1069). When ALFONSO VI of Castile attacked Muslim Spain, ibn-Tashfin intervened, defeating him at Zallaga in 1086. He deposed (1090-1) the rulers of Granada and Seville and thus established an Afro-Spanish Empire in which African and Andalusian cultures gradually blended.

Ibrahim 'adil Shah II (1580-1627) Muslim sultan of Bijapur in southern India, and patron of the arts. For most of his reign he was involved in intrigues and alliances with the early Mongols, but he was also known to them as a talented painter, calligrapher and musician, who attracted men of similar gifts to his court. The school of painting which flourished under his patronage shows mixed cultural influences, being a rich combination of Indian opulence, Mongol realism and Persian elegance.

Ibrahim ibn-al-Aghlab (756-812) Arab founder of the Aghlabid dynasty (800-909) which ruled Ifriqiya (eastern Algeria and Tunisia) from Kairouan. He asserted Aghlabid independence from HARUN AL-RASHID, founding a line of 11 Aghlabid amirs who enriched Ifriqiya with fine buildings and irrigation works, and built fleets which dominated the central Mediterranean (seizing Sicily and Sardinia) until overthrown by the Fatimid dynasty.

Ibsen, Henrik (1828-1906) Norwegian dramatist who was one of the founders of naturalistic theatre. His first play, *Catalina*, a romantic drama, was produced when he was 22. It was a failure, but won him a position as literary assistant (*dramaturg*) at the Bergen theatre, and then in Oslo. He was, meanwhile, writing prose and verse plays. As a result of the publication of his verse-drama *Brand* he was granted a state pension to enable him to write. This ponderous work about a Protestant parson's relations with God and man foreshadowed the feeling, but not the literary tact, of his later, more important plays. Next came *Peer Gynt* (1867). After two verse dramas he turned to the realistic, small-town drama for which he is best known. These were written at the peak of his powers: *Pillars of Society* (1875-7), *A Doll's House* (1878-9), *Ghosts* (1881), *An Enemy of the People* (1882), *The Wild Duck* (1884), *Rosmersholm* (1886) and *Hedda Gabler* (1890). All these plays are on the levels of the manifest and the symbolic. In *Ghosts*, venereal disease is the symbol of spiritual corruption in family life, and in *The Wild Duck* the crippled bird symbolizes the social and moral crippling of the heroine. The symbolism is less well controlled in *The Lady from the Sea* (1888), *The Master Builder* (1892) and *Little Eyolf* (1894). In *John Gabriel Borkman* (1896) and *When the Dead Awaken* (1899) Ibsen returned to the overt symbolism of his early play, *Brand*.

Ictinus (5th cent. BC) Greek architect who achieved an immortal reputation for his masterpiece, the Parthenon, which he designed with Callicrates. Until the fall of his patron, PERICLES, he enjoyed a leading position in Athens. He is believed to have designed the Doric temple of Apollo Eupicurius at Bassae, in which all three Greek Orders of Architecture – Doric, Ionic and Corinthian – were introduced.

Idris ibn-Abdullah (8th cent.) Arab founder of the Idrisid dynasty

An eternal masterpiece of architecture, Ictinus's Parthenon in Athens

(788-974). He was a descendant of MOHAMMED and one of the rival claimants fighting for the caliphate, but fled from the struggle and settled in Morocco, where he founded the dynasty which ruled Morocco from Fez, until overthrown by the Miknasa Berbers.

Idrisi, al- (1100-66) Arabian geographer, cartographer and poet whose geography digest revealed the world as known to Muslim travellers. He studied widely in Muslim Mediterranean states, then settled in Sicily where he spent 15 years working for ROGER II to produce the *Book of Roger*. This was an ambitious compendium of world geography based partly on writings by PTOLEMY and the Spaniard Orosius, but chiefly on works by the Arabs al-Masudi and ibn-Hawqal and on Muslim travellers' tales. It abounded in geographical and mathematical errors, but contained a valuable, detailed account of Sicily.

Ieyasu see IYEYASU

Ignatius Loyola, St (1491-1556) Spanish founder of the Society of Jesus or Jesuit Order. Devoted to the papal service, this order came into being when Ignatius, with six other students, including Francis XAVIER, took an oath to become a missionary to the Muslims in Palestine. The seven would-be missionaries found however that war made the journey to Palestine impossible, and offered their services to Pope PAUL III. He had them ordained and later formed them into an order. Ignatius remained in Rome to direct its activities and by the year of his death there were 1000 active Jesuits in the known world. He was canonized in 1622.

Ihara Saikaku (1642-93) Japanese writer of prose and poetry, whose novel *Five Women Who Loved Love* (1686) is one of the literary masterpieces of the Tokugawa period. Saikaku began as a poet, and became famous for the quantity as much as for the quality of his output. At the age of 40, he turned from poetry to prose with his first novel, *Life of an Amorous Man* (1682). His books and stories are chiefly notable for his lively and robust style, and he is regarded as the founder of modern Japanese fiction.

Ikhnaton (14th cent. BC) Egyptian king of the XVIIIth dynasty, also known as Amenhotep III, famous for his brief establishment of the cult of Aten, the sun god. His correspondence survives.

Il Cavalier Marino see MARINO, Gianbattista

Illyés, Gyula (born 1902) Hungarian poet and author, whose main achievement is his heroic poetry in *Goes the Plough* (1945) and *Hunyadi's Hand* (1956), which is characterized by subtlety and precision. His autobiographical analysis of contemporary problems, *People of the Plains* (1936), is a Hungarian classic.

Imru' al-Qays (6th cent. AD) Leading pre-Islamic Arab poet. The poetry for which he is remembered is mostly in the form of the *qasida* or ode. It remained a popular verse form for centuries despite attacks from later poets such as ABU-NUWAS.

Ingres, Jean (1780-1867) French artist, and the foremost exponent of Classicism in 19th-century French painting. His training included a period in the studio of DAVID, the leading Neo-classicist in art. But Ingres's preoccupation with order and clarity was complemented by an innate sensuality, apparent in his rendering of silks, velvets, lace and gold braid in his portraits, and the languorous rhythms of his nudes (e.g. *Grande Odalisque*). His art was based on the distillation, by constant repetition of his own work and imitation of others, of a formal language which grew increasingly idealized and abstracted.

Ionesco, Eugène (born 1912) Rumanian dramatist, who was the initiator and remains the leader of the Theatre of the Absurd. His aim is to shock audiences by exposing the nihilism of the Universe and man's vulnerability and isolation. His best-known works include the one-act plays *The Bald Prima Donna* (1948), *Jacques, or Obedience* (1950), *The Lesson* (1951), *The Future is in Eggs* (1951) and *The Chairs* (1951). *Amédie, or How to Get Rid of It* (1953), was the first of a series of three-act plays, which include a cycle: *The Killer* (1957), *Rhinoceros* (1958) and *Exit the King* (1961).

Ipatieff, Vladimir Nikolaievich (1867-1952) Russian-American chemist, whose studies of high temperature catalytic reactions were fundamental to the petro-chemical industry. From 1930 he worked for an American oil company on the improvement of the octane rating of automobile fuel.

Ireland, John Nicholson (1879-1962) English composer for the piano, among the foremost of his generation. He also wrote (for orchestra) *The Forgotten Rite* (1913) and *A London Overture* (1936).

Irnerius (c. 1050-1130) Italian jurist who pioneered the study of Roman law in the Middle Ages. After studying in Rome he founded a law school at Bologna where lawyers, including AZO and Vacarius, collated ancient manuscripts and reconstructed the *Digest* of JUSTINIAN. Their summary and interpretation of Roman law made possible the development in Europe of the legal systems necessary to regulate its rapidly expanding commerce.

Irving, Edward (1792-1834) Scottish preacher, one of the originators of the Catholic Apostolic Church, whose teaching was dominated by the expectation of CHRIST's Second Coming. A Church of Scotland minister, Irving moved to London in 1822, where he joined a revivalist group gathered round Henry Drummond, from which evolved the Catholic Apostolic Church. Its following declined after the death in 1901 of the last of the original 'apostles' with powers of ordination.

Irving, Sir Henry (1838-1905) English actor-manager, who made his name overnight in a melodrama, *The Bells*, in 1871. Manager of the Lyceum from 1878, he had a long run of Shakespearean successes with Ellen TERRY as his leading lady. He was the first actor to be knighted.

Irving, Washington (1783-1859) American author, best known for his collection of essays, *The Sketch-Book* (1820), which includes the story of Rip van Winkle. He travelled widely, and many of his works, particularly on Spain and England, stem from his voyages. He also wrote a detailed *Life of George Washington* (1855-9).

Isabella I (1451-1504) Queen of Castile (1474-1504) and Aragon (1469-1504), whose marriage to FERDINAND II of Aragon (1469) united Spain's two most powerful kingdoms. Ruling jointly with her husband (who became Ferdinand V of Castile in 1474), she helped to strengthen royal rule and national prestige, promoted culture, and financed COLUMBUS's venture (1492). Her devout Catholicism made her work to reform national morality, and to introduce the Inquisition into Spain, forcing Jews and Muslims to embrace Christianity or emigrate.

Isaiah (c. 8th cent. BC) Hebrew Old Testament prophet who worked in Jerusalem and made easy contact with its rulers. The book of the Bible bearing his name is now thought to comprise at least two distinct works, the first containing material derived from the prophet himself. The second half of 'Book of Isaiah', chapters 40-66, is widely held to be the work of a man prophesying the end of the exile

of the Jews to Babylon in the 6th century, and is called *Deutero Isaiah*. The characteristic themes of the man Isaiah, the holiness of God and his demand for holy living, are found throughout the whole book.

Isherwood, Christopher (born 1904) English playwright and novelist, whose tales of Berlin before the Second World War, particularly *Goodbye to Berlin* (1939), are evocative of the period. The novel was made into a play, a film and the musical *Cabaret*. During the 1930s, he collaborated with AUDEN on three plays and a travel book. More recently he has turned to Indian mysticism and written *A Meeting by the River* (1967), about the pressures on an Englishman who enters a Hindu monastery.

Ismail I (1486-1524) Shah of Persia (1500-24) who founded the Safawid dynasty. In the confusion of power struggles following the end of unified rule of Persia by the Mongols, Ismail launched an onslaught on his Sunnite neighbours. He brought all Persia under his rule and enlarged it by conquests, including that of the Uzbegs (1510). Despite losses to Turkey's Sunnite Sultan SELIM I, he established the Persian state, which reached its zenith under ABBAS I.

Ismail Pasha (1830-95) Khedive of Egypt whose heavy borrowing to finance schemes for internal reform led to the sale of Suez Canal shares to Britain in 1875. In 1876 further financial difficulties led to joint Anglo-French financial control over Egypt and in 1878 British and French ministers were included in the Egyptian government. His new government was dismissed after only six months and Britain and France advised him to abdicate, which he refused to do. Dismissed by the Sultan of Turkey in 1879, he retired to Constantinople, where he died.

Isocrates (436-338 BC) Athenian writer important as a teacher of rhetoric and for political works which, though circulated as written pamphlets, took the form of speeches for public occasions, e.g. the *Panegyricus* (380), or of open letters, e.g. the *Philip* (346).

Ito, Hirobumi (1838-1909) Japanese statesman who helped to transform Japan into a modern, westernized, industrial power. Between 1894 and 1901 he was four times Prime Minister of Japan. His main achievements were the calling of the first Japanese parliament (1890), the establishment – with the help of Admiral TOGO – of the Japanese navy and the introduction

of modern fiscal and bureaucratic systems. He fell from favour through opposing the Russo-Japanese war, and was sent to Korea as Governor. At Harbin, China, he was assassinated by a Korean nationalist.

Iuvenalis, Decimus Iunius see JUVENAL

Ivan III Vasilievich (1440-1505) Grand Duke of Muscovy (1462-1505), better known as 'Ivan the Great', the first real ruler of Russia. Ivan enlarged Muscovy by force, marriage and purchase. He conquered Novgorod (1478), absorbing all northern Russia between Lapland and the Urals, and took the lesser principalities of Yaroslavl (1463), Rostov (1474) and Tver (1485), and part of Lithuania (1503). He refused to continue tribute payments to the Tatars and ended for ever their hold on Russia. Ivan refused to share his gains with his brothers and destroyed their semi-independent principalities by changing the Russian inheritance system, so that when these princes died their estates passed to the grand duke instead of being divided among their heirs. By this means, Ivan forged a united Russian Empire, whose first (self-styled) emperor was Ivan's grandson IVAN IV.

Ivan IV Vasilievich (1530-84) First tsar, or emperor, of Russia (1533-84, crowned in 1547). Ivan's ruthless and often murderous pursuit of national and personal aggrandisement earned him the name by which he is best known – 'Ivan the Terrible'. Orphaned as the child prince of Muscovy, Ivan grew up under the regency of hereditary nobles, the boyars, for whom he conceived a deep loathing. As tsar, his purpose was to strengthen royal rule at the expense of the hereditary dukes and boyars. His armies pressed east and south to wrest Kazan and Astrakhan from the Tatars, setting Russia astride the Volga with an outlet on the Caspian. He was less successful in the west, where he was defeated by the Swedes and the Poles and driven back from the Baltic. On the death of his wife, Ivan seems to have become unbalanced, subjecting his kingdom to a reign of terror, including systematic massacres in Novgorod. Four years before his death he struck and killed his favourite son in a fit of rage.

Ives, Charles (1874-1954) American composer, son of an organist and bandmaster, who was the first 'original' in US music. From about 1900-20 he wrote a wide range of songs, instrumental and orchestral works while pursuing a successful business career, and much of his work anticipated European composers in experimental techniques. He also made full use of childhood memories: two 4th July bands marching against each other in *Three Places in New England* and revivalist hymns at a camp meeting in *Violin Sonata No. 4*. Ives worked in isolation, his ideas misunderstood, his music unheard. It was only after a public performance of *Piano Sonata No. 2* ('*Concord*') in 1938 that he was recognized as one of the founding fathers of America's music.

Ives, Frederick Eugene (1856-1937) American inventor of the half-tone printing system, in which the tones of a picture are reproduced as small dots of varying sizes. He also invented a similar process for gravure printing in which the ink is carried, not by raised dots, but by minute pits etched into a metal plate. Among his other inventions are the photo-chromoscope, a device for optically reproducing objects in natural colour, and a binocular microscope. His son, Herbert Eugene, played an important part in developing television and a wire-photo system.

Iyeyasu (1542-1616) Founder of the Japanese Tokugawa shogunate (1603-1867), named after his family. As a prominent general, he helped NOBUNAGA and Hideyoshi to unify Japan, and became its effective leader by defeating rivals in the Battle of Sekigahara (1600). Ruling, with the puppet emperor's approval, until 1616 (as official Shogun 1603-5), he made Yedo (Tokyo) the new political, economic, and cultural capital of Japan.

Centuries of Tatar presence in Russia came to an end during the violent reign of Ivan the Terrible. He went out of his mind in later life

J

Jabir, ibn-Haijan (c. 721-815) Arabian alchemist credited with the first preparation of the poison arsenic (arsenious oxide). He was a prolific and influential writer on chemistry.

Jackson, Andrew (1767-1845) First Democratic President of the US. A veteran of the American War of Independence, Jackson was elected a senator in 1797, but a difference with JEFFERSON led to his temporary retirement from political life. He became a national hero when, in 1815, he drove off a British attack on New Orleans. In 1818 he led a force which occupied Florida and later became its first governor (1821-3). He was elected seventh President of the US in 1828 and was re-elected in 1832 as the nominee of the newly-styled Democratic Party.

Jackson, Thomas Jonathan (1824-63) American Confederate general, known as 'Stonewall' Jackson. During the American Civil War, after leading a successful campaign in the Shenandoah Valley, he joined LEE in the seven-day defence of Richmond and became Lee's most trusted subordinate, while in the Maryland campaign, he captured over 12,000 Federal troops at Harper's Ferry (Sept. 1862). The Confederate success at Chancellorsville (May 1863) was largely the result of Jackson's skill, but while returning from a reconnaissance after the battle, he was accidently shot by his own men and died a week later.

Jacobsen, Jens Peter (1847-85) Danish novelist and poet and exponent of naturalism in literature. After a scientific training he translated DARWIN into Danish, and his two novels *Marie Grubbe, a Lady of the 17th century* (1876) and *Niels Lyhne* (1880) both demonstrate his talent for the minute detail of nature and psychological insight.

Jacquard, Joseph Marie (1752-1834) French silk weaver who (1801-8) perfected a loom which could weave patterns automatically. As this dispensed with guidance by hand, it aroused bitter hostility from many silk weavers, fearing for their livelihood. However, its advantages soon began to be accepted, and by 1812 11,000 were in use in France. The looms were controlled by punched cards, which were the forerunners of those used in modern data storage systems.

Jadwiga (1373-99) Queen of Poland (1383-99), whose marriage to

LADISLAS II, Duke of Lithuania, united Poland and Lithuania and established Poland's second dynasty, the Jagellon.

Jagello see LADISLAS II JAGIELLO

Jahangir (1569-1627) Mogul emperor of India and patron of the arts. During his reign, Indian miniature painting reached its peak of refinement as a result of the personal interest he took in the work of his artists.

Jahiz, al- (c. 780-869) Persian writer, among the first to promote broad-based studies of arts and sciences among the educated public. His wide-ranging essays and works such as his *Book of Animals* have been popular and influential throughout the Arab world until the present day.

Jakai, Maurus see JOKAI, Mor

Jalal al-Din see RUMI

James I (1208-76) King of Aragon (1213-76), called 'el Conquistador' (the Conqueror). James founded a Barcelona-based Aragonese Empire in the Mediterranean after inheriting the powerful northeastern Spanish state established by RAMÓN BERENGUER IV. He enlarged it by conquering the Balearic Islands (1229-35) and Valencia (1238), establishing an empire based on Catalonian seamanship and Jewish finance.

James I (1556-1625) King of England (VI of Scotland). Although a believer in witchcraft, James was one of England's most learned monarchs, the author and sponsor of many books, including the Authorized Version of the Bible (1611). His partiality towards favourites and heavy-handed relationship with parliament made him unpopular and laid the foundation of the dispute which cost CHARLES I his head.

James, Henry (1843-1916) American novelist, who wrote subtle, complex novels which frequently examined American characters and their innocence, testing them against the established culture of Europe. James left America in 1875 and *Roderick Hudson* (1876) and *The Portrait of a Lady* (1881) pursued this theme. In *What Maisie Knew* (1897), a story of passion seen through the eyes of a child, and in the ghost story *The Turn of the Screw* (1898), his prose grew more subtle and complex, leading to the tortuous puzzles and delicate psychology of *The Wings of the Dove* (1902) and *The Golden Bowl* (1904). James wrote a considerable number of other novels and short stories.

James, Jesse (1847-82) American outlaw who, with his brother Frank, led a gang notorious for bank and train robberies. Jesse was shot dead by an associate and Frank, who surrendered, was tried and acquitted.

James, Montague Rhodes (1862-1936) English antiquary, biblical scholar, palaeographer, and outstanding writer of ghost stories. His *Collected Stories*, which combined suspense and scholarship, were published in 1931.

James, William (1842-1910) American philosopher and psychologist who put forward the theory of pragmatism: that the criterion for the truth of a concept is its successful use in practice. His *Principles of Psychology* (1890) helped to establish psychology as a separate discipline, drawing on natural science and adopting the functionalist approach of defining metality in terms of what it does. Along with this goes the theory that emotions are identical with bodily feelings and therefore subordinate to the bodily states that provoke them. This foreshadows modern behaviourism.

Jameson, Sir Leander Starr (1853-1917) Scottish administrator of the British South Africa Company, who in 1895 led 470 mounted volunteers from Bechuanaland into Transvaal in an attempt to help the non-Boer European miners (Uitlanders) to overthrow the government of Paul KRUGER in Johannesburg. His force was captured by the Boers and in the ensuing political repercussions RHODES, Premier of Cape Colony, who was implicated, was forced to resign and the conduct of the Colonial Secretary, Joseph CHAMBERLAIN, was subjected to Parliamentary inquiry. On his return to England, Jameson was imprisoned as a result of the raid. After his release, he returned to Cape Colony, became its Premier (1904-8) and, in 1911, a baronet.

Jameson, Storm (born 1897) English writer, critic and exponent of the 'family chronicle', whose first success was *The Lovely Ship* (1927).

Janáček, Leoš (1854-1928) Czech composer who wrote some of the most strongly individual humanist operas in the modern repertoire. The best known of these are *Jenůfa* (1904), *Katya Kabanova* (1921, based on OSTROVSKY's *The Storm*), *The Makropoulos Affair* (1926, from the play by CAPEK) and *From the House of the Dead* (1930, derived from the book by DOSTOEVSKY). Janáček matured late as a composer, but earlier studies he had made of peasant dialects deeply influenced his idiosyncratic settings of words. His other compositions include the *Glagolitic Mass*, to an ancient Slav ecclesiastical text; the Sinfonietta and the tone poem *Taras Bulba* for orchestra; two string quartets; and a song cycle, *The Diary of a Man who Disappeared*.

Janet, Pierre (1859-1947) French neurologist and psychologist, who saw the healthy personality as a well-knit integration of conscious and unconscious ideas and tendencies. Hysteria, according to Janet, was a weakness of the bonds holding personality together, so that it could split or alternate.

Jansen, Cornelius (1585-1638) French ecclesiastic who, within the Roman Catholic Church, initiated an anti-Jesuit reform movement which had much in common with Protestantism, except that Jansen rejected justification by faith and maintained the supremacy of the Roman Church. In the outcry which followed, ARNAULD and PASCAL were amongst his chief defenders. Exiled from France, Jansen lived mainly in Holland and contributed to the independent outlook of Dutch Catholicism today.

Jansky, Karl (1905-50) American radio engineer and pioneer of radio astronomy who discovered radio emission from the Milky Way. Jansky, an engineer with Bell Telephone Laboratories, was investigating the origin of 'static' when he found a new and distant source of interference originating beyond the Earth.

Janssen, Pierre Jules César (1824-1907) French pioneer of solar physics and of photography who, on 8 December 1874, made the first film recording the transit of Venus across the Sun.

Jarry, Alfred (1873-1907) French dramatist and Symbolist poet, whose work promoted the Theatre of the Absurd. His allegorical farce *Ubu Roi* (1896), a satire on bourgeois society, is generally considered his most important play. In it, the bourgeois Ubu makes himself a tyrant-king. His influence on the Theatre of the Absurd stems largely from his novel *The Deeds and Opinions of Dr Faustroll*.

Jaspers, Karl (1883-1969) German Existentialist philosopher who saw, in the experience of failure, material for positive conclusions about the nature of human existence.

Jaurès, Jean (1859-1914) French socialist politician, who tried to prevent the First World War by organizing a strike of German and French workers. Co-founder, with BRIAND, of the left-wing newspaper *L'Humanité* (1904), Jaurès was one of the greatest socialist writers and orators of his time, but he was never a doctrinaire Marxist and was frequently at odds with the socialist establishment. In July 1914 he went to Brussels and called on German socialists to strike against mobilization. On his return to France, he was murdered by a right-wing nationalist.

Javier, Francisco see XAVIER

Jeanneret, Charles-Edouard see LE CORBUSIER

Jean Paul see RICHTER, Johann Paul

Jeans, Sir James (1877-1946) English astronomer and physicist, and popularizer of astronomy. Though he was responsible for much original scientific work on the quantum theory, stellar radiation and the evolution of stars, Jeans was best known for books, including *The Universe Around Us* (1929) and *The Stars in their Courses* (1931), which made complex scientific theories comprehensible to laymen.

Jeffers, Robinson (1887-1962) American poet, whose verse is full of contempt for 'the animals Christ was rumoured to have died for'. He rejects rhetoric and speaks directly, passionately and brutally.

Jefferson, Thomas (1743-1826) Third US President, who drafted the Declaration of Independence (1776). Jefferson was born in Virginia and was its delegate to the Continental Congress in 1775 and 1776. After the revolution, while US Minister in Paris (1785-9), he helped to draft the Declaration of the Rights of Man and later, as Secretary of State (1789-93), resigned in protest against the federal centralization. Under ADAMS (1797-1801) he was elected Vice-President and President in 1800, serving two terms. During the first, Jefferson was responsible for the 'Louisiana Purchase' (1803) in which the US bought French colonial territory in North America. His second term of office was preoccupied with the problem of neutrality in the face of British and French wartime restrictions on trade. In retirement, he introduced English landscape gardening into America and popularized Neo-classical architecture.

Jeffries, John see BLANCHARD, Jean Pierre

Jekyll, Gertrude (1843-1932) British gardener, author and watercolourist. The essence of her garden style lay in a sophisticated, though apparently artless, re-use of cottage-garden motifs, arranging species in carefully graded associations of colour, shape and texture. Her work exists still in several gardens in Berkshire and Kent.

Jelal-ed-din-Mohammed see AKBAR the Great

Jenkins, Charles Francis (1867-1934) American inventor, who devised a ciné projector with intermittent motion (1895), a braking system for aeroplanes, an altimeter, the conical paper drinking cup, and a self-starter for cars. He was a television pioneer and was one of the first (1925) to transmit TV pictures, although his system was not commercially viable. He made several other inventions in the fields of radio, facsimile transmission and television.

Jenkins, Robert (18th cent.) English mariner whose ear was cut off by a Spanish sea captain, an incident which helped to cause Anglo-Spanish hostility to flare into the War of Jenkins's Ear (1739-48).

Independence—the unanimous declaration of the 13 States of America in 1776

Jenner, Edward (1749-1823) English physician who developed vaccination against smallpox, a discovery which stemmed from an 'old wives' tale' that dairymaids who caught cowpox never subsequently caught smallpox. Jenner investigated the various diseases called cowpox, and, isolating a pure strain of the true disease, brought it to the peak of its infective phase. In 1796 he achieved the experiment which proved the theory correct. Jenner's method of preventing smallpox by vaccination rapidly ousted the older use of inoculation.

Jenney, William Le Baron (1832-1907) American architect, who in 1884 designed the Home Insurance Company building in Chicago. Although only ten floors tall, it had a steel-frame construction, which made it the forerunner of the modern skyscraper.

Jensen, Johannes (1873-1950) Danish novelist and lyric poet. His epic six-volume novel cycle *The Long Journey* (1908-22), which was highly descriptive in style, with strongly mystical overtones, was concerned with man's moral predicament. Jensen defined his writings as 'myths', and they are almost all strongly symbolic tales with historical, anthropological or travel themes. In 1944 he won a Nobel Prize for Literature.

Jenson, Nicolas (c. 1420-80) French printer and designer of type-faces. In 1458 he went to Mainz to learn the art of printing from GUTENBERG and in 1470 he appeared in Venice as a publisher and printer. He became famous as the first printer to use purely roman letters (perfected by GARAMOND), which are substantially the same today.

Jeremiah (c. 650-c. 585 BC) Hebrew Old Testament prophet. Jeremiah bewailed the idolatry of the people of Judah, prophesying divine punishment by the destruction of Jerusalem. But, like ISAIAH, he preached a message of eventual redemption, proclaiming a new covenant between God and his people, based on moral virtue rather than outward observance. The Judean kingdom fell in 586 and Jeremiah was forced into exile in Egypt. Scholars question the dating and authenticity of much of the Book of Jeremiah, and also the rabbinic tradition that the prophet wrote the Lamentations of Jeremiah and the Book of Kings.

Jerome (c. 340-420) Dalmatian saint, one of the four Latin Doctors of the Church, and translator of the Bible into Latin (Vulgate). Brought up as a Christian, he spent some years as a hermit in Syria, learnt Hebrew and reluctantly accepted ordination. He then went to Constantinople, where he was influenced by GREGORY NAZIANZUS. In 382, he became Secretary to Pope St Damasus in Rome. Jerome's rudeness and austerity made him unpopular and when Damasus died he settled in Bethlehem, where he taught, worked on his Bible and other writings.

Jerome, Jerome Klapka (1859-1927) English author, who was most successful with *Three Men in a Boat* (1889), a picturesque, farcical and sentimental book, set in an innocent world of sunlit, idle hours on the Thames.

Jespersen, Jens (1860-1943) Danish philologist and authority on English grammar, whose *Growth and Structure of the English Language* (1905) and seven-volume *Modern English Grammar on Historical Principles* (1909-31) are basic texts for scholars. The *Philosophy of Grammar* (1924), his most popular work, and *Analytic Syntax* (1937), propound his view that grammar constantly evolves as language changes and that the rigid rules of grammar based on Latin categories are therefore irrelevant. His *Phonetics Textbook* (1904) long remained one of the best scientific treatises on general phonetics.

Jesus Christ (died c. AD 29) Founder of the Christian faith and, to its believers, the Son of God. He was born in Bethlehem, Judea, the son of Mary, by whom, according to Christian belief, he was conceived miraculously. Mary's husband, Joseph, taught the young Jesus his trade of carpenter, but beyond that little is known of his early life. His latter days are chronicled in the Gospels. After his baptism by his cousin JOHN, he gathered together 12 disciples and set forth on his missionary work. Loved by the common people for his compassion and skill with the sick, and for his attacks on the social conditions of the time, he earned the hatred of the Pharisees and the ruling classes. Their hostility culminated in Jesus's arrest by Roman soldiers, his trial and sentence of death as a blasphemer. Little more than 30 years of age, he was crucified and died, between two convicted thieves, on Golgotha – 'the green hill, far away'. His preaching of a God of Love, not of vengeance, and his emphasis on love, humility, meekness and charity gave to the world a faith that now numbers more than 900 million adherents – far more than any other religion.

Jiminez de Cisneros, Francisco (1436-1517) Spanish prelate and statesman, responsible for the *Complutensian Polyglot Bible* in Hebrew, Latin and Greek, Jiminez was an ardent patron of learning and in 1500 he refounded the University of Alcalá, where, at his invitation, a team of scholars compiled the polyglot Bible.

Jiménez, Juan Ramón (1881-1958) Spanish poet, author of the classic *Silver and I* (1917) and winner of the Nobel Prize for Literature (1956).

Jimmu (7th-6th cent. BC) Reputedly the first Japanese emperor, supposedly descended from the Sun Goddess, and founder of the nucleus of the Japanese state near what is now Osaka.

Jinnah, Mohammed Ali (1876-1948) Indian Muslim politician and Governor-General of Pakistan (1947-8). Jinnah opposed GANDHI's policy of civil disobedience and was distrustful of the Hindu element in the Congress Party. He organized the Muslim League and eventually directed its policy towards separate statehood for Indian Muslims, and opposed all schemes which tried to preserve Indian unity. His continued insistence that partition was the only way of solving the Indian problem succeeded and led to the creation of the Dominion of Pakistan in 1947. After founding a religious state, however, his policy became one of secular nationalism and co-operation with India.

Jippensha Ikku (1766-1831) Japanese comic novelist, author of *Travels on foot along the Tokaido*, a series of books describing the adventures of two travellers, Yaji and Kita. The stories are earthy and usually bawdy, but always good-natured.

Joachim, Joseph (1831-1907) Hungarian virtuoso violinist who founded the Joachim Quartet. BRAHMS's Violin Concerto is dedicated to him.

Joan of Arc (1412-31) French peasant girl who became a national heroine in the 100 Years' War with England. 'Voices' urged her to help the Dauphin (later CHARLES VII), whose kingdom was under severe English and Burgundian attack. Charles granted her wish to lead an army to free besieged Orléans, and, in armour, she spearheaded the assault which freed the city (1429). Joan fought in many battles and her inspiration turned the war in France's favour. In 1430, Joan was seized by Burgundians, who sold her to the English, and she was burned as a witch at Rouen. The Church exonerated her in 1455 and she was canonized in 1920.

John II (1455-95) King of Portugal (1481-95) who encouraged and organized Portugese exploration. Hoping to find a sea route to the Orient round the south coast of Africa, he sent out Bartholomeu DIAS in 1486.

John (1167-1216) Plantagenet king of England (1199-1216), whose reign is important in the development of the British constitution. Able, but selfish, unpopular and a poor soldier, John ultimately alienated barons, Church and people alike. His conflict with the papacy over the appointment of Langton as Archbishop caused a humiliating defeat at the hands of Innocent III, and after a further defeat of his allies, his opponents seized their chance. The Church and barons forced John to sign the Magna Carta (The Great Charter) at Runnymede, in 1215. It asserted the supremacy of the law over the king and granted rights which were eventually extended to all sections of society. The Magna Carta was to influence the democratic constitutions of Britain, and British-influenced nations, including the United States.

John IV (1604-56) King of Portugal (1640-56), founder of the Braganza dynasty (1640-1910). He was a leading claimant to the Portuguese throne, which had passed to the kings of Spain, in the reign of PHILIP II of Spain. John was the figurehead for a successful, bloodless revolution against Spanish occupation (1640), engineered by John Ribeiro, a professor at Coimbra University. The dynasty which John IV founded, though long-lived, ruled during a time of waning Portuguese power.

John of Arderne (1307-90) One of the first English surgeons. He practised among the nobility both in Newark and in London, and stressed the importance of cleanliness.

Joan of Arc and the Cross of Lorraine, symbol of Free French Forces, 1940-45

Augustus John lived the Bohemian life expected of an artist. His most distinguished work was as a portraitist

John, Augustus (1878-1961) British artist, who for the first quarter of the 20th century, represented all that was most rebellious, independent and original in English art. The archetypal bohemian, he painted in a style of great virtuosity that sometimes degenerated into bravura, and was also a fine draughtsman. He often portrayed the gipsy life of the Wales that he loved. Later in life he became a fashionable portrait painter.

John of Austria (1547-78) Spanish general known as Don John, victor at the Battle of Lepanto (1571). John led the Holy League's fleet formed to protect Venetian property against the Turks, whom he defeated at Lepanto. The battle, the last major conflict between oared warships, temporarily curbed Turkish aggression in the Mediterranean. John was made Governor-General of the Spanish Netherlands to suppress the insurrection of WILLIAM THE SILENT, but was forced to issue the Perpetual Edict (1577), accepting William's terms.

John the Baptist (c. 7 BC-AD 28) Hebrew preacher who urged people to repent their sins in readiness for the coming of the Messiah, and baptized JESUS and others in the River Jordan. John's ministry ended with imprisonment and execution, reputedly for condemning the marriage of Herod Antipas to his niece Herodias.

John of the Cross, St see JUAN de la CRUZ, San

John VI Cantacuzene (c. 1292-1383) Byzantine emperor (1347-55). Chief administrator of Emperor Andronicus III, he set himself up as emperor in Thrace while the supporters of John V, heir of Andronicus, ruled from Constantinople. In the ensuing civil war (1341-7) both sides sought help from Byzantium's strongest enemies – the Serbs (under STEPHEN DUSHAN) and the Ottoman Turks (led by Orkhan I). Although Cantacuzene took Constantinople (1347), he was forced to let Turkish troops inside Europe to ward off the Serbs, and so surrounded the imperial capital with its enemies. He was deposed by John V in 1355.

John, Chrysostom (c. 345-407) Syrian saint, one of the four great Greek Doctors of the Church. Brought up as a Christian he was intended to study law, but became a hermit and in 381 was ordained in Antioch, where his preaching made him famous. Elected Archbishop of Constantinople in 398, his reforming zeal and uncompromising tongue earned him the enmity of the rich and the opposition of Theophilus, Archbishop of Alexandria, who called a council of Egyptian and Syrian bishops in 403 and deposed him. Chrysostom was banished by the emperor, recalled, then banished twice more, first to Armenia and three years later to Iberia, dying on the way.

John, Don see JOHN OF AUSTRIA

John of Gaddesden (1280-1361) English physician, whose *Rosa Anglica* (1330) was the first book to deal with diseases systematically according to cause, symptoms, prognosis and cure.

John of Luxemburg (1296-1346)

King of Bohemia (1310-46) and founder of Bohemia's Luxemburg dynasty. He was elected king, but preferred fighting to ruling. He enlarged Bohemia, gaining overlordship of Silesia from Poland (1326) and acquired much of Upper Lusatia (1320-9). Seeking chivalrous adventure, he fought as a knight errant throughout Europe and died fighting for France at Crécy. The huge taxes levied for his exploits provoked civil strife in Bohemia.

John III Sobieski (1624-96) King of

Poland (1674-96), who saved Vienna from the Turks. A brilliant opportunist and self-seeking military leader, he fought against the Cossacks and Turks, fought with and against the Swedes, and plotted with and against the French. He ensured election to Poland's throne by a show of military strength. In 1683 he led Polish troops to aid Austria against the Turks and personally headed the cavalry charge that ended the siege of Vienna.

John I Zimisces (925-76) Byzan-

tine emperor (969-76), whose short but remarkable reign left the empire much strengthened. Securing the throne following the assassination of Nicephorus II Phocas, he proved himself a brilliant general, diplomat and statesman. After suppressing internal revolts he crushed the Kievan Russians, who were threatening Constantinople (970-1), subdued eastern Bulgaria and extended the imperial frontier to the Danube. He renewed the war against the Arabs, driving into Iraq, Syria and Palestine (974-5), but his sudden death saved Jerusalem from capture. During his reign, he won the support of the Church and established friendly relations with the Western Empire.

John XXIII (1881-1963) 263rd pope,

during whose brief pontificate (1958-63) Vatican councils initiated a number of reforming measures, and who convened the 21st Ecumenical Council to seek unity among the various Christian denominations. Born Angelo Giuseppe Roncalli, the son of a peasant, he was ordained in 1904 and during the First World War served as a military chaplain. He later held a series of increasingly important administrative and diplomatic posts, in one of which, as Papal Nuncio in France, he championed the controversial system of worker-priests. When he became pope, he broke with tradition by leaving the Vatican to visit hospitals and prisons

in Rome, and at the time of his death was held in regard and affection not only by those of his faith, but by many beyond it.

John, St (1st cent. AD) Palestine-

born Christian apostle and evangelist, disputed author of the fourth Gospel of the New Testament and of the three Epistles of St John. One of the greatest creative writers of early Christian literature, his Gospel differs from the three Synoptic Gospels of MATTHEW, MARK and LUKE (to which it was intended as supplement) in both content and form. Containing few parables and stressing the supernatural aspects of JESUS's life, it attempts to justify Christianity from the historical facts connected with the life of Jesus and interprets the life of Christ in mainly allegorical terms. John was a Galilean fisherman until he came under the influence of JOHN THE BAPTIST.

Johnson, Amy (1903-41) English

aviator who, in 1930, became the first woman to fly solo from England to Australia. She broke other records on flights to India and Japan (1931), Cape Town (1932) and, with her husband, to the US and India (1934).

Johnson, Andrew (1808-75) The

first US President ever to be impeached by the Senate. As LINCOLN's Vice-President, he assumed the presidency when Lincoln was assassinated (1865), and tried, against the policy of his powerful Minister of War, STANTON, to carry out Lincoln's policy of conciliating the defeated South. When the Senate passed the Tenure of Office Act (1867), which denied the President the right to dismiss high executive officials without consulting it, Johnson challenged that infringement of Presidential authority and dismissed Stanton. The House of Representatives called for Johnson's impeachment, but the Senate vote for his conviction fell short of the required two-thirds majority and he was acquitted.

Johnson, Lyndon Baines (1908-

72) US politician, who succeeded to the Presidency when John KENNEDY was assassinated in 1963. Johnson was elected for a second term in 1964 with an unprecedented popular majority, but his second term was marked by the escalation of the war in Vietnam and vastly increased American involvement. Despite a number of measures towards the 'Great Society', (civil rights, tax reduction, war on poverty) the conflict in southeast Asia so undermined his prestige that he decided not to seek renomination in 1968.

Johnson, Samuel (1709-84) Eng-

lish critic, essayist, lexicographer and scholar who was most widely known for his witty conversation and eccentric personality recorded by James BOSWELL, and for his *Dictionary of the English Language* (1755). The *Dictionary*, intended as the definitive record of the literary language, was distinguished mainly for its pithy definitions and liberal use of quotations to illustrate shades of meaning. The reputation for scholarship, which led to Johnson's selection (1747) to compile the *Dictionary*, was based largely on two anonymously published works, 'London' (1738), a

Heroine of the air-conscious world of the 1930s, Amy Johnson was celebrated in a popular song

poem imitating a satire of JUVENAL, and *Life of Savage* (1744), a masterpiece of biography. His reputation was increased by the *Rambler* essays (1750-2). Johnson was not a highly creative writer, but by his conversation and presence, honesty, panoramic knowledge and strict principles, rallied and supported literature for a quarter of a century.

Johnson, Sir William (1715-74) Irish-born administrator for Britain in the American colonies. Johnson emigrated to America in his twenties, settling in the Mohawk Valley. He was to become one of his time's richest colonists. Johnson held the American Indian in high regard, spoke their language and dressed as they did, receiving from the Mohawks a gift of land of 100,000 acres. He was instrumental in gaining the support of the Iroquois confederacy in the wars with the French, whom he defeated in the Battle of Lake George (1755). He was created a baronet that year.

Jókai, Mór (1825-1904) Hungarian popular novelist, whose books helped to sustain Hungarian morale after the War of Independence of 1848. His later novels, in which he attempted to tackle the problems of a mercantile society, are humorous fantasies.

Joliot-Curie, Frédéric (1900-58) French physicist who, in collaboration with his wife Irène, discovered artificial radioactivity. In 1934, they studied the effect of bombarding aluminium with alpha particles (helium nuclei) from a naturally radioactive source and found that after the bombardment the target had become radioactive and had turned into a radioactive form of phosphorus.

Joliot-Curie, Irène (1896-1956) French physicist and daughter of Pierre and Marie CURIE. With her husband Frédéric, she continued their researches into radioactivity.

Jones, 'Bobby' (1902-71) American golfer, who won the American Open championship four times, and the British Open Championship three times. In 1930, he achieved the 'grand slam', winning the British and US Open and Amateur championships.

Jones, Daniel (1881-1967) English linguistics scholar, whose most important works are *The English Pronouncing Dictionary on Phonetic Principles* (1917) and *An Outline of English Phonetics* (1918). His classification of vowel sounds established a set of so-called 'cardinal' vowels, later fixed in the International Phonetic Alphabet.

Jones, Ernest (1879-1958) British psychiatrist who introduced psychoanalysis into Britain in 1910. He was largely instrumental in bringing the aged FREUD to safety in England after the Nazi invasion of Austria.

Jones, Inigo (1573-1652) English architect, who revolutionized the English concept of what a building should look like, translating the vigour and sophistication of Italian mannerist buildings to the streets of London with his Doric St Paul's portico, Covent Garden, his lavish banqueting house in Whitehall, and his delicately elegant Queen's Chapel at St James's Palace, London. The perfectly proportioned Queen's House, at Greenwich, stands astride a covered path with no loss of compactness or restrained elegance. Jones was also famous for his stage designs.

Jones, John Paul (1747-92) Scottish-born American naval hero. He commanded a British merchant ship but (*c.* 1773) fled to Virginia and added 'Jones' to his original name 'John Paul' to escape a charge for murdering a mutineer. Fighting as a ship's captain for the colonists in the American War of Independence, he raided British coasts and attacked British shipping. After the post-war abolition of the American navy, he served briefly as rear-admiral in the Russian Black Sea fleet (1788-9).

Jones, Sir William (1746-94) English jurist and Oriental linguist who first perceived that Sanskrit, Greek, and Latin must have a common source. Jones's revelation and his description of Sanskrit, the first to the western world, started the study of Indo-European languages as the members of one family.

Jongkind, Johan Barthold (1819-91) Dutch artist, whose influence on Impressionism was considerable. He went from Holland to Paris in 1846 and developed a sensitive response to the nuances of light, especially in his water-colours. His oils often show an affinity with the Dutch school of the 17th century.

Jonson, Ben (c. 1572-1637) English playwright and poet, who wrote the comedies *Volpone* (1606) and *The Alchemist* (1610). Jonson was one of the central figures of the literary world of London under JAMES I, who conferred a pension on him, and for whom Jonson wrote many masques, or court entertainments for which the elaborate scenery, a theatrical innovation, was often designed by Inigo JONES. Jonson's plays were frequently performed – SHAKESPEARE was in the cast of *Every Man in his Humour* (1598). Jonson was also a consider-

able poet, who tried to make expression in English as clear and accurate as it was in classical languages. Around him formed a group of young poets, including HERRICK and Suckling, and his verse influenced such poets as MARVELL. His chief prose work, *Timber; or Discoveries made upon Men and Matter* (1640), is a literary miscellany which demonstrates Jonson's wide-ranging intellect and strong Neo-classical views.

St Paul's, Covent Garden, by Inigo Jones has a fame far beyond London. Shaw's *Pygmalion* (the musical *My Fair Lady*) has its opening scene set in the portico

Jordaens, Jacob (1593-1678) Dutch painter of portraits, genre scenes and religious and historical subjects, who early in life assisted RUBENS.

Jordan, Camille (1838-1922) French mathematician, who gave a full account of the theories of GALOIS on substitution groups and applied it to algebraic equations.

Joseph II (1741-90) King of Germany (1764-90), Holy Roman Emperor (1765-90), who introduced revolutionary social reforms. He was dominated by his mother and co-ruler MARIA TERESA until her death (1780), but then initiated radical change in place of her policy of slow progress. His beliefs were formed by reading VOLTAIRE and the *encyclopédistes*, but his instrument was an all-powerful state for which he was the sole spokesman, unhampered by any controlling laws. His measures to allow religious toleration, end the noble's stranglehold on local government, and to promote unity by compulsory use of the German language, were not popular: clergy and nobles opposed them and even the peasants rebelled in many of his states. When he died, the schemes typical of Joseph's 'enlightened despotism' were largely reversed by his brother, Leopold II, who succeeded him.

Joseph, Chief (c. 1840-1904) American Indian chief who led a 2000-mile retreat in the Nez Percé War of 1877. Joseph fought for five days before surrendering.

Joule, James Prescott (1818-89)
English physicist who established by
experiment that a given amount of
mechanical work produces a definite
amount of heat. Similar findings,
comparing electrical and chemical
effects, led him to formulate the first
law of thermodynamics (the law of
conservation of energy), which states
that energy can be converted from
one form to another but cannot be
created or destroyed. A unit of energy
was named after him.

Jouvet, Louis (1887-1951) French
actor-director, who applied COPEAU's
principles to the production of French
classics and was famous for his
direction of GIRAUDOUX's plays.

Joyce, James (1882-1941) Irish
novelist and one of the outstanding
writers of the 20th century. He moved
from the naturalistic short stories of
Dubliners (1914) to the literary realism of *Finnegan's Wake* (1939) in an
attempt to recreate an idea or feeling
in the reader's mind by rendering the
complexities of experience in the
sound, movement, associations and
derivations of words, as well as in their
meaning. His best-known work,
Ulysses (1922), marked an important
stage in this development. Stephen
Dedalus, one of the characters in
Ulysses, represents Joyce himself in *A
Portrait of the Artist as a Young Man*
(1916), a fictional, satirical autobiography of his early years and
aesthetic principles. Joyce was a
talented musician, an ability revealed
in his verses in *Chamber Music* (1907),
often based on the rhythms of
Elizabethan songs. He also wrote a
play, *Exiles* (1918), in the manner of
IBSEN. Joyce spent most of his life
abroad, but his novels are all intricate
reconstructions of Dublin, his home
city.

Joyce, William (1906-46) British
traitor. Before the Second World
War he was a member of Sir Oswald
MOSLEY's British Union of Fascists
and founded (1937) the British
National Socialist Party. In August
1939, Joyce left England for Germany
on a falsely-obtained British passport
and throughout the war broadcast
Nazi propaganda in English to
Britain, which came to call him 'Lord
Haw-haw', because of the affectation
of his speech. He was captured near
the Danish border in May 1945, tried
and found guilty of treason, and
hanged in 1946.

Juan de la Cruz, San (1542-91)
Spanish mystic and lyric poet. A
Carmelite friar, he joined St TERESA
in her drive to reform the Carmelite
order and to found new, reformed
convents. This task lasted him until
his death, bringing him imprisonment, torture and, in 1726, canoniza-
tion. His mystical experiences were
turned into eight poems, with prose
commentaries, in *The Ascent of
Mount Carmel* (1578-83), which
explains the stages of spiritual
development in simple metaphors.

Juarez, Benito (1806-72) Mexican
reformer and revolutionary leader.
He led the successful liberal revolution of 1855 against the régime of
President SANTA ANNA and, as a result,
became Minister of Justice (1855-7).
His radical reforms – judicial, educational and anti-clerical – precipitated
a violent reaction, and, during the
civil war which followed (1858-60),
he was declared provisional President, but was forced to abandon
Mexico City to his conservative
opponents. However, he reorganized
his forces in Vera Cruz and led them
to victory. On assuming power, he
suspended payment of foreign debts.
This gave NAPOLEON III of France,
acting ostensibly on behalf of French
capitalists, an excuse to invade
Mexico and set up a puppet empire,
with the Austrian Archduke MAXI-
MILIAN as emperor. Juarez and his
forces maintained their resistance,
encouraged by the promise of help
from the US. When, under US
pressure, Napoleon withdrew his
army, Juarez took the initiative and
Maximilian was caught and shot
(1867). Juarez was President until his
death, when he was succeeded by his
lieutenant, Porfirio DIAZ.

Judah ha-Nasi (c. 135-c. 220)
Jewish scholar and traditional compiler of the Mishnah, the first comprehensive codification of Jewish oral
law. The political and religious head
of Palestinian Jewry, Rabbi Judah devoted his wealth and influence to

'Germany calling, Germany calling' was
the parrot cry of traitor broadcaster Joyce

gathering earlier rabbinic teachings
into a unified and acceptable legal
code. Later scholars elaborated the
Mishnah, which was finally edited
into the vast encyclopedias of law,
learning and tradition known as the
Palestinian and Babylonian Talmuds.

Julian (331-63) Roman emperor
from 361 to 363. Traditionally known
as 'the Apostate', his policy was to
restore the pagan cults, deprive the
Christian Church of its privileges and
re-establish Roman prestige in the
East. His surviving writings, chiefly
speeches and letters, reflect the complexity of his make-up as scholar,
soldier, statesman and mystic.

Jung, Carl Gustav (1875-1961)
Swiss founder of analytic psychology. An early friend and disciple of
FREUD, he propounded his own theory
of the libido as something like 'life
force'. The Jungian psyche has three
levels: consciousness, the 'persona' or
mask; the personal unconscious, a
mirror image of the persona containing unrealized possibilities and forgotten experiences (female elements
of men and vice versa, extrovert elements of introverts, etc; and the collective unconscious, which contains
the whole psychological heritage of
the human race. Jung classified
characters as introverted or extro-
verted, subdividing them according
to the prevailing domination of feeling, intuition, sensation or thought.
He saw psychic troubles as the result
of unbalanced development, and
treatment consisted of putting the
patient into touch with his personal
and collective unconscious. An important Jungian concept is that of
'archetypes', the significance of any
actual person or object depending on
its resemblance to certain archetypes
stored in the collective unconscious.
He regarded the recurring themes of
myths in different cultures as evidence for this theory.

**Junqueiro, Abilio Manuel Guerra
(1850-1923)** Portuguese poet and
politician, best known for the verbal
ingenuity and satire of his collection
The Simpletons (1892). He had an
important influence on the Portuguese poetry of his day and was one
of the founders of the Portuguese
republic, the two spheres of his life
overlapping in the volume *The
Fatherland* (1896), which made him
the outstanding poet of the 1910
revolution.

Justinian (483-565) Roman
emperor and lawgiver. He initiated
the codification of the Roman law,
through a committee of ten jurists
under the direction of Tribonian.
They produced the *Codex* (529, and a
revised version in 534), the *Institutes*

(based on those of GAIUS), the *Digest* or *Pandects* (533), and supplementary volumes (*novellae*).

Juvenal (c. 50-c. 140) The greatest Roman satiric poet. In his 16 *Saturae* (100-130) he bitterly attacked contemporary stupidity while avoiding mention of living people. His vivid pictures of Rome at that time ranged from attacks on homosexuality and other vices to a diatribe against women and a great sermon on the 'follies of human ambitions'. Both amusing and cruel, his epigrams are memorable and his brilliant powers of parody, irony, innuendo and invective gave a new dimension to Roman satire. Juvenal had a profound influence in the Middle Ages and few modern satirists have not used him as their model.

Kabir see NANAK

Kádár, János (born 1912) Leader of the Communist régime in Hungary after the Russian invasion of 1956. As Minister of the Interior, he played a major part in the trial of Cardinal MINDSZENTY in 1948 and in the trial and execution of Rajk, the Hungarian Foreign Minister in 1949 on charges of supporting the deviationist line of TITO. He was a member of NAGY's government, but during the revolution of 1956, changed sides and subsequently headed a Russian puppet government. Under Kadar's administration, Hungary has achieved a greater measure of internal freedom and material progress (through the New Economic Policy of 1968, and Five-Year Plans), but Kadar has repeatedly stressed Hungarian commitment to the Warsaw Pact.

Kafka, Franz (1883-1924) Austrian novelist, whose nightmare-like parables reflect man's search for reality and identity. Only his essays and short stories were published in his lifetime, one of the most famous of which is *Metamorphosis* (1912), an early example of Kafka's dominant theme, man's predicament in an inexplicable and unsympathetic world. His major novels, *The Trial* (1925), *The Castle* (1926) and *America* (1927) were published posthumously by his friend Max Brod.

Kaiser, Georg (1878-1945) German dramatist, who originated Expressionist drama. His first, satirical comedies made no impression, but success came with *From Morn to Midnight* (1916), the story of a bank-clerk who stole a fortune, found it did not buy him happiness, and discovered the baseness of man when he threw the money to a mob. This initiated a series of plays showing how industrial civilization has enslaved and degraded mankind. Kaiser rejected character, using types instead.

Kaiser, Henry (1882-1967) American industrialist. He entered shipbuilding in 1940, pioneering prefabrication and welding techniques which enabled him to launch a million-dollar ship (the 'Liberty' freighters) a day, each taking less than five days to assemble. His companies built the Oakland-San Francisco Bay bridge, and the Bonneville, Boulder, and Grand Coulee dams. Kaiser's civil engineering and manufacturing ventures embraced more than 30 industries from the manufacture of dishwashers to airport construction.

Kakinomoto no Hitomaro (8th cent.) Japanese poet whose work appeared in the earliest surviving anthology, the *Collection of a Myriad Leaves* (c. 760), comprising over 4000 poems of two main types – the short 31-syllable *tanka*, and the long poems, *chohka*. Hitomaro wrote both, and although the *tanka* was to form the main model for Japanese poetry for many centuries, the *chohka*, as developed by him, showed itself to be a form of great potential. His work reflects his beliefs in Shinto (the native religion of Japan), and the elegies and love poems in particular have great depth and beauty.

Kalidasa (5th cent.) Indian dramatist and lyric poet, best known for *Sakuntala*, the third drama of the *Natyasastra* trilogy, a love story involving human and godly characters. One of the Hindu 'nine gems' he wrote the *Vikramorvasiya* and the *Malavikagnimitra*.

Kamal-al-din Bihzad (c. 1450-c. 1536) Leading Persian painter, who as court artist made no radical break with tradition, but introduced a new tendency towards naturalism and a subtle use of colour into his strong but effectively simple compositions.

Kamenev, Lev Borisovich (1883-1936) Russian revolutionary, who was shot for conspiracy on the orders of STALIN. He was director of the Bolshevik Party's activities in Russia in 1914, and was arrested in 1915 for advocating LENIN's policy of ending the war. He was exiled to Siberia, and on his return to Russia on the outbreak of revolution in February 1917, he was still an avowed follower of Lenin. By October that year, he had come to oppose him and advocated a coalition government of all Socialist parties. Though at first antagonistic to TROTSKY's heresies, by 1926 he (and ZINOVIEV) had become a firm supporter of his opposition to Stalin, with the result that in 1927 he himself was expelled from the Communist Party. He was readmitted in 1928, but expelled again in 1932, and arrested four years later, with ZINOVIEV, and shot for allegedly conspiring against Stalin.

Kamerlingh-Onnes, Heike (1853-1926) Dutch physicist, who was the first to liquefy helium and subsequently to discover the superconductivity of metals. In the late 1880s, interested by the work of Johannes van der WAALS, he began studying gases at low temperatures. In 1908, using a liquid hydrogen cooling system, he liquefied helium and found its temperature to be just four degrees above absolute zero. He discovered that at this very low temperature certain metals, such as mercury and lead, lose all electrical resistance and become what are now known as super-conductors.

Kandinsky, Wassily (1866-1944) Russian-born artist, who became a pioneer of abstract painting. From 1896 until 1914 he lived in Munich, where, with Franz Marc, he founded (1911) the *Blaue Reiter* (Blue Rider) group, which played an influential role in the German Expressionist movement. After the First World War he returned to Germany, where he taught at the famous Bauhaus school until it was closed by the Nazis. He then moved to Paris. At the Bauhaus he had developed a vocabulary of geometrical forms; but in Paris the organic quality of his early abstracts was revived, though now disciplined by a precise technique. Underlying all his work is the Expressionist theory, which emphasizes the metaphysical status of art and its expressive function.

K'ang-hsi (1654-1722) Chinese emperor (as Sheng-tsu, 1661-1722), the greatest of the Manchu dynasty. He campaigned deep in Mongolia, added three provinces in the north, made a treaty with Russia on the northern border (1689), conquered Yunnan and Formosa, and won control of Tibet. While he ruled as a conqueror, keeping the peace with strategically placed garrisons, he adopted Chinese culture, encouraging the arts and sponsoring collections of Chinese literary classics and major works of reference, notably a 5000-volume encyclopedia. He tolerated the Christians and actively encouraged the Jesuit scholar-missionaries, who brought to China their scientific skills.

Kano Eitoku (1543-90) Japanese artist, renowned for his forceful outline ink painting borrowed from the Chinese, which he combined with the native tradition of bright colour against gold or silver backgrounds. Having founded the Momoyama style of painting, his sons, Kano Mitsunobu (c. 1561-1608) and Kano Takanobu (1571-1618), and his adopted son, Kano Sanraku (1559-1635), continued the family tradition which lasted into the 19th century.

Kano, Jigoro (1860-1938) Japanese founder of judo. He studied the many clan techniques of ju-jitsu and combined them to create judo.

Kant, Immanuel (1724-1804) German philosopher, widely regarded as the greatest modern philosopher. A lifelong teacher at Königsberg and a prolific writer – originally on the physical sciences – his later philosophical works, such as the *Critique of Pure Reason* (1781) were so influential that he became an oracle on important questions of his day. His critical philosophy is the foundation of the subsequent history of the subject.

Kao Tsung see CHIEN LUNG

Karadžić, Vuk Stefanović (1787-1864) Serbian scholar and folklorist, who helped to establish Serbian as an official and literary language in place of the synthesis of Russian and liturgical Slavonic.

Karlfeldt, Eric Axel (1864-1931) Swedish lyric poet and follower of HEIDENSTAM's Nititilist school, whose *Songs of the Wilderness and of Love* (1895) captures the spirit of his native province, Dalecarlia. His fascination with ancient folk life is expressed in *The Songs of Fridolin*, published in two volumes (1898, 1901), the story of a learned man of peasant origin who returns to the countryside of his forefathers. In 1931 Karlfeldt was posthumously awarded the Nobel Prize for Literature.

Karlstadt, Andreas von (c. 1477-1541) German Puritan reformer. An early supporter, but later an opponent of LUTHER, he advocated clerical reforms which established the bases of German Puritanism.

Karsavina, Tamara (born 1885) Russian ballerina whose artistry helped to establish FOKINE's new school of expressive Russian dancing in the Western world.

Kasprowicz, Jan (1860-1926) Polish lyric poet, whose famous *Book of the Poor* (1916) is the first work to give Polish folklore poetic expression.

A master of dead-pan slapstick, Buster Keaton was second only to Chaplin

His 'Ballad of the Sunflower' is considered one of Poland's greatest poems.

Kästner, Erich (born 1899) German writer and satirist, best known outside Germany for his children's books, notably *Emil and the Detectives* (1929).

Kaunda, Kenneth David (born 1924) Zambian nationalist politician, the first President of the Republic of Zambia. A fervent nationalist in the years leading to his country's independence, he was Secretary-General of the North Rhodesian African National Congress. He started the break-away Zambian African Nationalist Congress in 1958, and, when it was banned, was imprisoned. On his release, he became President of the United National Independence Party (1960), Prime Minister of Northern Rhodesia in 1964 and, on independence later in the same year, President of Zambia. Although Kaunda's attitude to political change was inspired by the non-violent methods of GANDHI, he has increasingly supported the African liberation movements operating in Rhodesia and Portuguese Africa.

Kautsky, Karl (1854-1938) German Social-Democratic theorist, who denounced LENIN's concept of the 'dictatorship of the proletariat' as a betrayal of true Marxism. He was born in Prague, and was a friend of MARX. Though he supported the view that socialism could be accomplished only by violent revolution, he disliked and opposed Bolshevik authoritarianism and disassociated himself from the Russian Revolution. After settling in Vienna, he devoted himself to social-democratic writing and theorizing and achieved great influence among anti-Bolshevik socialist intellectuals.

Kavafi, Constantinos see CAVAFY, Constantinos

Kavanagh, Patrick (1905-67) Irish poet, who, in *The Great Hunger* (1942), and *A Soul for Sale* (1947), wrote wry, lyrical, indignant poetry about Irish history and rural life.

Kawabata Yasunari (1899-1972) Japanese novelist who was awarded the 1968 Nobel Prize for Literature. Kawabata was deeply influenced by the Japanese cultural tradition, and his novels, the most popular of which are *The Izu Dancer*, *The Snow County*, *A Thousand Cranes* and *Sound of the Mountain*, display the latent melancholy of Heian literature. President of the Japan Pen Club, Kawabata was a prominent critic and patron of new writers such as MISHIMA Yukio. Kawabata committed suicide in 1972.

Kay, John (18th cent.) English inventor of the flying shuttle (patented 1733), a weaving device for automatically moving the shuttle from side to side across the warp of a loom.

Kazantzakis, Nikos (1885-1957) Greek poet whose most widely known novel is *Zorba the Greek* (1946). His 24-volume epic poem, *The Odyssey* (1938), continues HOMER's story, embracing the whole of Kazantzakis's philosophical ideas in a tapestry of symbolism and rich imagery.

Kazinczy, Ferenc (1759-1831) Hungarian literary critic and leader (through his translations and correspondence) of its language reform.

Kean, Edmund (1787-1833) British actor, who was an outstanding tragedian and a romantic theatrical personality. HAZLITT and COLERIDGE were fascinated by his tragic genius, as were the audiences by his interpretations of villainy in such roles as Iago.

Keaton, Buster (1895-1966) American screen comedian who began his career in his parents' vaudeville act. His masterpieces of silent comedy include *The Navigator* (1924), *The General* (1926) and *Steamboat Bill Junior*, in which, like CHAPLIN, Keaton played the little man who always won through, though unlike Chaplin, he never slipped into sentimentality. In 1959, he was awarded a special Oscar for his contribution to the art of cinema.

Keats, John (1795-1821) 'Here lies one whose name was writ in water', were the words Keats wanted on his tomb. An English Romantic poet, he devoted himself to literature. Although befriended by Leigh HUNT and SHELLEY, his work gained little contemporary favour at first. His narrative poems had historical subjects: 'La Belle Dame sans Merci' (1819) is an evocation of medieval romantic mystery. In his last volume (1820), containing, among others, 'The Eve of St Agnes', 'Lamia' and 'Hyperion', he worked on the haunting theme that the transient quality of beauty can only be arrested in art, as stated in 'Ode on a Grecian Urn'. Soon after, Keats died of consumption, in Italy.

Keble, John (1792-1866) British clergyman and poet, originator of the Oxford Movement, which fought the erosion of Church authority by secular elements. The movement was launched by a Keble university sermon in which he criticized the abolition of ten Irish bishoprics. Its ideas were disseminated by John Henry NEWMAN's *Tracts for the Times*, to which Keble made nine contributions. He was also joint editor with Newman and Edward Pusey of a series of new translations of patriotic writings, for which they claimed absolute doctrinal authority. After Newman's conversion, Keble remained a loyal Anglican, but persisted in trying to 'Romanize' Church doctrine and practice.

Keir, James (1735-1820) Scottish founder of the Tipton Alkali Works (1780), where he developed a process for the commercial manufacture of caustic soda from waste sulphates. His work marked the beginning of the scientific chemical industry.

Kekulé von Stradonitz, Friedrich (1829-96) German chemist who discovered the ring structure of benzene. His work on chemical structures, especially in organic chemistry, led to an understanding of other compounds.

Keller, Gottfried (1819-90) Swiss poet and novelist, and Switzerland's foremost narrative writer of the Realist school. His kindly, ironic humour and sympathy for his fellow men are seen at their best in the collections of stories called *The People of Seldwyla* (Part I, 1856; Part II, 1874), ten stories of events in a fictitious Swiss town. He was also a notable lyric and epic poet. 'The Jesuit Procession' (1843) is a satirical poem on the theme of the petty intrigues of bourgeois society. Among his other major works *Green Henry* (1755) is an autobiographical novel.

Keller, Helen Adams (1880-1968) American social worker, who overcame the loss of sight, hearing, and speech, yet achieved distinction as a lecturer and scholar. Illness rendered her blind and deaf at the age of nineteen months, and later she became dumb. In Anne Sullivan, who taught her to speak within a month at the age of seven, she had a dedicated teacher, and Helen Keller's ability was such that she obtained a degree in 1904 and mastered several languages. She also won a reputation as a lecturer all over the world and worked extensively for the relief of the handicapped.

Kelly, Gene (born 1912) American dancer and actor who was one of the first to integrate dance with drama in motion pictures.

Kelly, 'Ned' (1855-80) Australian bushranger, whose daring crimes and outwitting of the police made him the most celebrated criminal in Australian history. In 1880, at Glenrowan, his gang failed to derail a train-load of police reinforcements sent to capture them and a gun battle followed. Kelly survived but was later arrested, charged with murder, and hanged.

Kelvin, Lord William Thomson, (1824-1907) Scottish physicist and inventor, who devised the absolute temperature scale and so put the second law of thermodynamics on a sound theoretical basis. In 1851 he gave a full account of thermodynamic theory, co-ordinating the findings of the previous 50 years. He drew attention to the dissipation of energy implied in the second law of thermo-

Blind and deaf from childhood, Helen Keller was a prize scholar at 24

Sinatra, Kelly and Williams star in a popular film musical of the 1940s

Ned Kelly without the iron helmet in which he was usually depicted

dynamics, and this 'running down' of the universe has figured largely in scientific speculation since. Also spectacular was his work on electrical theory and its application to submarine telegraph cables. He invented many instruments for use in electrical engineering (such as the mirror galvanometer). His investigation of the oscillating discharge of condensers was the basis for the later discovery, by HERTZ, of radio waves.

Kemal, Mustapha (1881-1938)
Turkish soldier-statesman, known as Kemal Ataturk, who westernized and modernized Turkey. He joined the army and the Young Turk Movement, but soon quarrelled (1908) with its leader, Enver. He fought against the Italians in Libya (1911) and in the Balkan Wars. As a divisional commander of the Turkish Forces at Gallipoli (1915) he successfully resisted the British invasion but was defeated by ALLENBY in Syria. He formed the Turkish Nationalist Party (1919) to resist Greek annexation of Smyrna (Ismir). Resistance turned into revolution, and in 1920 he set up a revolutionary government in Ankara. Within two years he had driven the Greeks from Smyrna. He abolished the caliphate (1924), set up the Turkish Republic (of which he was first President, 1923) as a wholly secular state, banned oriental in favour of European dress, emancipated women, enforced the use of the Latin alphabet, and ruled Turkey as a dictator until his death.

Kempis, Thomas à see THOMAS A. KEMPIS

Kennedy, John Fitzgerald (1917-63) First Roman Catholic US President, assassinated in Dallas, Texas, by Lee Harvey OSWALD, after less than three years in office (November 1963). Educated at Harvard, Kennedy served with distinction in the navy in the Second World War. In 1946 he was elected to the House of Representatives as a Democrat, and to the Senate, for Massachusetts, in 1952. He became President in 1961, defeating NIXON, the better-known Republican candidate. His attempt to restore a right-wing government in Cuba by backing an invasion of Cuban exiles to fight CASTRO (April 1961), was a failure. In 1962 US intelligence discovered Soviet missile sites in Cuba, and Kennedy announced that Soviet ships carrying weapons to the sites would be intercepted. The Prime Minister of the USSR, KHRUSCHEV, proposed to withdraw offensive weapons from Cuba if the US would withdraw theirs from Turkey. Kennedy refused to negotiate until work on the Cuban sites stopped, missile launch-

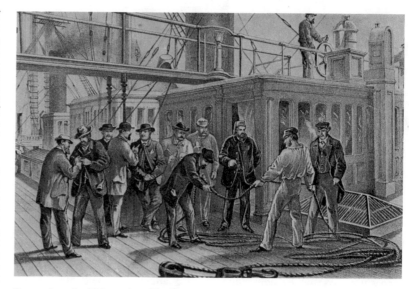

Scene aboard a 19th-century Atlantic cable-laying ship. Its success depended largely on the work of Kelvin

ers were rendered inoperable and shipment of weapons ceased. Among important elements of Kennedy's internal policy were the Civil Rights Bill, which made discrimination against negroes and racial segregation in schools and other institutions illegal. In the international field, his promotion of the General Agreement on Tariffs and Trade, signed at Geneva by many leading industrial powers, ensured a progressive reduction of tariff barriers. In Vietnam, the Kennedy administration in-

creased support of the South Vietnamese régime, increased US aid and the number of American economic, military and political advisers, a commitment which was subsequently to involve the US to a far greater extent, under JOHNSON his successor. Kennedy brought to the presidency an attractive presence, interest in art and literature and a youthful idealism which appealed to the young.

Kennedy, Joseph P. (1888-1969) American financier and diplomat whose ill-starred family became one of the most celebrated and potent forces in American politics. Serving

as Ambassador to the UK from 1938-40, Kennedy was instrumental in securing American support for Britain in the early stages of the Second World War. When his eldest son, Joseph Jr., was killed in the war, John KENNEDY inherited the family's political mantle and rose through the Democratic Party ranks to become President in 1961. During his tragically shortened term of office, John appointed his brother Robert (1925-68) Attorney-General and his career was equally spectacular and ended as violently. Elected senator for New York in 1964, Robert was campaigning for the Presidential nomination when assassinated by a Palestinian extremist. Edward, the youngest son, has been a Massachusetts senator since 1962.

Kennelly, Arthur Edwin (1861-1939) British-born American electrical engineer, who predicted the presence of electrically charged layers in the atmosphere. In 1902, after MARCONI's experiments with radio waves, Kennelly noticed that the waves could reach beyond the Earth's horizon. He suggested that they did this by bouncing off a layer of ions high in the atmosphere. Oliver HEAVISIDE, an English physicist, made a similar proposition and the layers are called Kennelly-Heaviside layers.

Kenneth I MacAlpine (9th cent.) First king of Scotland, who subdued the Picts and, from his capital at Dunkeld, claimed to rule all territories north of the Firth of Forth.

Kent, James (1763-1847) American jurist whose writings, notably his four-volume *Commentaries on American Law* (1826-30) had a great influence on the development of Anglo-American law. He made English common law the basis of court decisions, setting a pattern adopted by New York and other American states.

Kent, William (1684-1748) English architect who, under the sponsorship and guidance of Lord Burlington, began as a painter and turned to architecture at the age of 40. Kent became an important exponent of the English Palladian style. Among his best-known works are the Horse Guards, The Royal Mews and the Treasury Buildings, Whitehall. He also influenced the art of landscape gardening, turning against the formal patterns of the 17th century, emphasizing the potential harmony between a building and its setting.

Kenyatta, Jomo (born 1890) Kenyan politician of the Kikuyu tribe, first Prime Minister of his country (1963) and President the following year. A lifelong worker for the independence of his country, Kenyatta became secretary of the Kikuyu Central Association in 1928 and as its representative visited Britain. In 1947, he began a vigorous Nationalist campaign, was accused of

Jomo Kenyatta acknowledges the cheers of his supporters in Nairobi

being implicated in the Mau Mau disturbances in the early 1950s and was sent to prison for seven years (1953). Allowed complete freedom in 1961, he took the lead in Kenya's political affairs as President of the opposition party, the Kenya African National Union. After KANU victory in the election of May 1963, Kenyatta became the first Prime Minister of self-governing Kenya. He became President of the Republic of Kenya in December 1964. As head of state, he has shown a marked desire for moderation in African affairs, demonstrated by his caution in the Rhodesian crisis of 1966.

Kenyon, Kathleen (born 1906) British archaeologist who in the early 1950s, using LIBBY's newly developed carbon dating technique, showed Jericho (now named Ariha) in Jordan to be among the oldest walled towns in the world. Her finds proved that the twin bases of civilization,

Khruschev, John Kennedy and (some of) the Kennedys, led by Joseph P., father of the assassinated statesman. The family, whose forebears emigrated to the US in the 19th century, gained its first political power in Boston, most Irish of American cities. Joseph Kennedy became a multi-millionaire and supported F.D. Roosevelt during his 1932 campaign. Ambassador to Britain at the outbreak of the Second World War, his wealth and the ability and charisma of his sons were to take them to the forefront of American politics, culminating in the election to the Presidency of John in 1960. During his term of office, US commitment to aid South Vietnam began and confrontation of the US and Khruschev's USSR over Russian missiles in Cuba came near to nuclear war

farming and town life, had begun far earlier than was hitherto supposed.

Kepler, Johannes (1571-1630) German astronomer, who discovered the elliptical orbit of the Earth around the Sun, and formulated the laws of planetary motion. Kepler's religious faith convinced him that there was a harmony in the relationships of the planets. Attempting to resolve the apparent discrepancy between the observed motion of Mars and the theoretical motion as laid down in the Copernican system, Kepler formulated his major hypothesis that the orbits of the planets are elliptical. In order to account for the irregular velocities of the planets in their orbits, he sought some fundamental law of their motion, and found the solution in the discovery that the radius from a planet to the Sun describes equal areas in equal times.

Kerensky, Alexander (1881-1970) The first and last prime minister of a democratic, parliamentary Russian government. A lawyer by profession he was elected as a Social-Democratic member of the *Duma* in 1912, became Minister for War following the March Revolution of 1917, and by July was Prime Minister of the Provisional Government. His policy of continuing the war had no public support and he was swept aside by the October Revolution – LENIN and TROTSKY's *coup d'état* of 7 November. Kerensky tried unsuccessfully to rally resistance to the Bolsheviks but was forced to flee abroad to France and later went to the US (in 1946), where he died.

Kerouac, Jack (1922-69) American novelist, the best-known author of the Beat generation (a romantic movement of revolt against convention and authority), defined and described in such works as *Desolation Angels* (1965).

Keynes, Lord John Maynard (1883-1946) British economist who stressed the control of economic mechanisms to achieve desirable objectives. A government adviser during the Second World War, he favoured a world bank and international currency, and was one of the chief architects of the Bretton Woods Agreements in 1944 which set up the International Monetary Fund and the World Bank. In his *The General Theory of Employment, Interest and Money* (1936), he urged the government to stimulate consumption, encourage capital goods production and invest in public works, rather than waiting for automatic forces to revive employment. He resigned the leadership of the British Treasury team at the Versailles negotiations (1919) to write against imposing on Germany enormous reparation payments which, he foresaw, would upset the world economy.

Khaireddin Pasha (c. 1466-1546) Turkish corsair, known as Barbarossa, whose activities in Tunisia and Algeria influenced their political development for three centuries. Accepting Ottoman suzerainty, he built up Algiers as a stronghold of Mediterranean piracy, ended a Spanish threat to North Africa, and gave the Ottoman empire naval supremacy in the Mediterranean until the battle of Lepanto (1571).

ibn-Khaldun (1332-1406) Leading Arab historian. He held various official posts in North Africa and Spain, but his fame rests on one book, a general history of the Muslim dynasties and, more specifically, the *Muqaddima*, the introduction to this work, in which he theorized on the nature, significance and methodology of history. It was described by Arnold TOYNBEE as 'the greatest work of its kind that has ever yet been created by any mind in any time or place'.

Khan, Mohammed Ayub (born 1907) Pakistani soldier and politician. President of Pakistan, who was deposed in 1969 by a peasant revolt. He was the first Commander-in-Chief of the Pakistani army and a bloodless military coup brought him to the presidency in 1958, when President Mirza abrogated the constitution and martial law was proclaimed. Autocratic, yet paternalistic in his rule, Ayub Khan brought a measure of economic stability to Pakistan, but lack of both industry and development funds in East Pakistan led to demands for autonomy and a revolt of the peasantry in 1969. His presidency ended as it had begun, under martial law.

Khorana, Har Gobind (born 1922) Indian-American biochemist, co-winner of the 1968 Nobel Prize for Medicine, who in 1970 manufactured the first synthetic gene. Future developments could lead not only to the treatment of diseases caused by gene deficiencies but also to the possibility of reproducing people with defined characteristics by the manipulation of genes.

Khosrau II (7th cent.) Last major Sassanid King of Persia (590-628), called 'Parvez' (Victorious), who was helped to gain the throne by the Byzantine emperor, Maurice. When Phocas murdered and supplanted Maurice (602), Khosrau attacked the Byzantine Empire, plundering Syria and Asia Minor, taking Damascus, Jerusalem and Egypt, and penetrating to Chalcedon opposite Constantinople before Phocas's successor Heraclius hit back. Heraclius attacked by land and sea, invaded Mesopotamia, and routed the Persians at Nineveh (627). The disgruntled Persians murdered their leader.

Khruschev, Nikita Sergeyevich (1894-1971) Soviet politician and First Secretary, whose election to the Soviet Communist Party's leadership brought Stalinism to an end. He joined the Communist Party during the First World War, and served in the Red Army during the Civil War. A mineworker by trade, Khruschev studied engineering, meanwhile holding increasingly important political offices, until, in 1937, he was elected to the Supreme Soviet. As First Secretary of the Ukrainian Communist Party, he organized and led guerilla warfare against the Germans in the Second World War and was responsible later for the execution of a large number of Ukranians who had collaborated with the enemy. On STALIN's death in 1953, he was elected First Secretary, and a secret session of the Party denounced Stalin's abuse of power, judicial murder of his comrades, failure to prepare for the war, and other crimes. He became Chairman of the Council of Ministers in 1958, but was dismissed from both these offices in 1964, and replaced by the triumvirate of KOSYGIN, BREZHNEV and Podgorny. There was no State acknowledgement of his death or of his achievements in office.

Khufu or Cheops (26th cent. BC) King of Egypt, who built the Great Pyramid, largest of the pyramids at Giza.

Khwaja 'Abd al-Samad (16th cent.) Persian calligrapher and painter to Humayun and AKBAR, Mogul Emperors of India. He was co-founder of the Mughal school of painting with MIR SAYYID'ALI, whom he succeeded as head of the royal studio in 1574. Under Akbar's patronage, he changed his own decorative style to lead the trend towards a more realistic manner.

Kidd, William (c. 1645-1701) Scottish seaman, who, in 1696, sailed from England as a privateer officially authorized to suppress pirates, but who fraternized with Madagascar's pirates and attacked local vessels. He finally reached New England, but was seized and sent to London, where he was tried and hanged for piracy at Execution Dock on 23 May, 1701.

Kierkegaard, Sören (1813-55) Danish philosopher and theologian whose assessment of the human pre-

The astronomical watershed

Johannes Kepler (right) was the first man to prove that the Sun, and not the Earth, lay at the centre of the Solar System. He calculated that the orbit of Mars (below) was an ellipse, and that the area covered by the imaginary line from the Sun (A) to the planet moving from 1 to 2 was the same as that covered from 3 to 4.

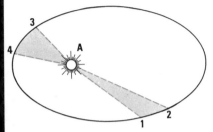

The Ptolemaic system (below)

At the centre lay the Earth. Around it moved the Moon (A), Mercury (B), Venus (C), the Sun (D), Mars (E), Jupiter (F) and Saturn (G).

In spite of his revolutionary mathematics, Kepler was obsessed with the idea that the orbits of the planets could be constructed around geometrical solids (below). However, the years he spent fruitlessly trying to prove that the cube (1), tetrahedron (2), dodecahedron (3), icosahedron (4) and octohedron (5) contained, and were enclosed by, spheres constructed on circular planetary orbits, succeeded in throwing up, almost by chance, the proofs that denied the authority of the theory of Ptolemy, venerated for over 1300 years.

In 1534, Copernicus had mapped the planets, with the Sun at the centre (right), in the correct order – Mercury (A), Venus (B), Earth (C), Mars (E), Jupiter (F) and Saturn (G), with the Moon (D) rotating about the Earth – but still believed that the orbits were perfect circles.

Sir Isaac Newton (below right), who consolidated the astronomical revolution, showed that the Moon is pulled towards the Earth by the force of gravity (bottom right), causing it to arrive at A_2 rather than at A_1, as it would if undisturbed by the Earth. The same fundamental principle proved correct Kepler's elliptical orbits.

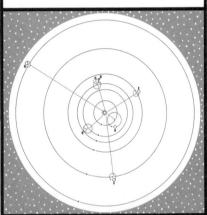

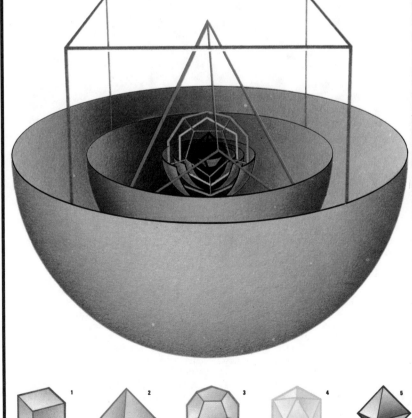

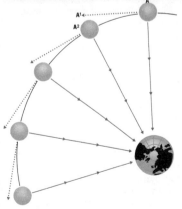

dicament makes him one of the sources of Existentialism. Opposed to the system building of HEGEL, Kierkegaard was impressed by the isolated and subjective life of the individual, and by the unbridgeable gap between sinful man and God. Kierkegaard saw the individual, filled with dread and overawed by the fact of being, taking refuge in a 'leap of faith' towards the religion of CHRIST.

King, Billie Jean (born 1943) American lawn tennis player who won her first title at the age of 15. Her subsequent successes included winning the American women's title in 1967 without losing a set, and the singles championship at Wimbledon three years in succession (1967-9).

King, Clarence (1842-1901) American geologist and mining engineer who laid the foundation of the geological survey of the United States. During the survey of California, he explored the Sierra Nevada and the southern Californian and Arizona deserts and later led the transcontinental survey of the 40th parallel, across the Rocky Mountains.

King, Martin Luther (1929-68) American civil rights leader, whose methods of non-violent demonstration and passive resistance, advanced the cause of the American negroes. A Baptist minister in Alabama, his leadership of a negro boycott of public transport (1956) resulted in a desegregation order enabling blacks to sit with whites in public vehicles. This success led him to organize and lead huge non-violent demonstrations and marches in Washington and elsewhere in support of KENNEDY's civil rights legislation. He became head of the Southern Christian Leadership and lent its weight and his personal influence to support of the National Association for the Advancement of Coloured People. He was awarded the Nobel Peace Prize in 1964 for his maintenance of non-violence in his political work. King was assassinated in Memphis, Tennessee.

King, William Lyon Mackenzie (1874-1950) Canadian statesman and Prime Minister of Canada for a total of 22 years (1921-6, 1926-30 and 1935-48). His policies for international trade and constitutional reform, and his handling of his country's contribution in the Second World War considerably raised Canada's standing in the international community.

Kingdon Ward, Francis (1885-1958) British geographer, botanist, and plant collector who discovered and introduced into cultivation the prized Himalayan blue poppy and

hundreds of other previously-unknown plants. He spent 50 years on constant botanical explorations to remote areas, including 25 journeys to the mountains of the eastern Himalayas.

Kingsley, Charles (1819-75) English author and clergyman, best known for his novels *Westward Ho!* (1855), *Hereward the Wake* (1866) and the children's story, *The Water Babies* (1863). An active campaigner and writer for social and national

causes, Kingsley's social conscience and impetuous nature brought him into controversy with Cardinal NEWMAN.

Ki no Tsurayuki (c. 880-946) Japanese poet, prose writer and calligrapher who was the main compiler of the *Collection of Old and New Poems* (c. 905), the first imperial anthology of poetry. Unlike OHTOMO no Yakamotchi's earlier compilation, this contains mainly the short 31-syllable *tanka*. The poems, written entirely by court officials, are sophisticated and aristocratic, with mainly romantic themes, setting the style and standard for *tanka* writing

for nearly 1000 years. The preface is the first example of Japanese literary criticism.

Kipling, Rudyard (1865-1936) English author, who is famous for his record of the spirit of England's Imperial expansion in India. From *Plain Tales from the Hills* (1888) onwards, his stories of India, the sea, the jungle and many other subjects brought him popularity. His verse, as in the *Barrack-Room Ballads* (1892), is skilful, and his stories for children, including

MARTIN LUTHER KING JR.   1929   1968

The Jungle Book (1894-5), display his principal quality as a storyteller.

Kipping, Frederick, Stanley (1863-1949) English organic chemist, best known for his work, starting in 1899, on the organic derivatives of silicon. These compounds, the silicones, have outstanding properties of water-repulsion and high temperature stability, and have come into widespread use particularly as greases, hydraulic fluids, synthetic rubbers and water repellents.

Kircher, Athanasius (1601-80) German Jesuit polymath who helped to pioneer new map-making techniques and the magic lantern. In 1643, he made one of the first maps to show magnetic variation, and in 1665 pioneered the making of maps showing ocean currents. In 1645, he discovered how to use a powerful light, a reflector and a lens to project an image of a picture painted on a glass slide onto a screen.

Kirchhoff, Gustav Robert (1824-87) German physicist who, in the 1850s (and working with Robert BUNSEN), constructed the first spec-

WEATHER Sunny and cool Friday with a high in middle 40s. See Page 50.

CHICAGO SUN-TIMES

FINAL

Vol. 21, No. 55   Phone 321-3000   FRIDAY, APRIL 5, 1968   128 Pages, 2 Sections—10 Cents

MARTIN LUTHER KING SLAIN

PHOTO

troscope. Kirchhoff realized that every element when heated to incandescence emits its own distinctive set of spectral lines, thus enabling it to be identified. He also pointed out that the dark lines observed by FRAUNHOFER were due to an equally characteristic absorption, making it possible to investigate the composition of the Sun and stars.

Kirkes, William (1823-64) British physician who showed that emboli (blood clots and other small solids in the bloodstream) may cause cerebral thrombosis or an acute pulmonary disorder. Priority for the discovery was disputed by VIRCHOW.

Kissinger, Henry (born 1923) German-born diplomat and consultant to four American presidents. In the 1950s, Kissinger's theories offered a moderate alternative to Secretary of State DULLES's Cold War 'brinkmanship'. As NIXON's top foreign adviser, Kissinger negotiated the settlement in Vietnam and helped build new links with China, and in 1973 he was appointed Secretary of State.

Kitasato, Shibasaburo see BEHRING, Emil von

Kitchener, Horatio Herbert, 1st Earl (1850-1916) Commander-in-Chief of the British army in the first half of the First World War. He served in the French army against Prussia in 1871 and in the same year was commissioned into the Royal Engineers. His first major command was as Sirdar (Commander-in-Chief) of the Egyptian army in the Sudan (1884-5). In the second Boer War (1899-1902) he was chief-of-staff to Roberts, whom he later succeeded as GOC, overcoming Boer resistance by controversial strategies which included the establishment of concentration camps. While Commander-in-Chief in India (1902-9) he assumed

control of the Indian army, despite CURZON's strong opposition. From 1911-14, Kitchener ruled Egypt, as British Agent, but was recalled to Britain to become War Minister when the First World War broke out. His inability to work smoothly with his Cabinet colleagues or to remain on good terms with his field commanders was already causing anxiety when, en route to Russia for secret talks in June 1916, he was drowned when HMS *Hampshire* was sunk by a mine.

Kivi, Alexis (1834-72) Finland's first internationally known novelist and dramatist. His *Seven Brothers* (1870) was the first novel in Finnish literature, and his plays, among them *Kullervo* (1860) and *Shoemakers of the Heath* (1864), laid the foundations of the Finnish national theatre.

Kjellén, Rudolf (1864-1922) Swedish political scientist who invented and explained the term geopolitics. Influenced by Friedrich RATZEL's work on political geography (which reflected DARWIN's teachings on evolution and natural selection), he declared in *The State as an Organism* (1916) that a political state is a biological organism, subject to growth and decay. Developed by HAUSHOFER in Germany and adopted by Fascist Italy and by Japan, this intellectually appealing fallacy became a pretext upon which the Axis powers justified their struggle for dominance in the Second World War.

Klaproth, Martin (1743-1817) German chemist who, recognizing that certain compounds contained hitherto unknown elements, isolated and named two of them as titanium and zirconium. A substance which he produced from pitchblende, and which he named uranium, turned out to be the oxide of that metal.

Klee, Paul (1879-1940) Swiss artist, who became a member of the *Blaue Reiter* circle in Munich before the First World War, and taught at the Bauhaus (1921-31). He was for many years in close contact with KANDINSKY. His art is remarkable not only for its small scale and its delicacy, but because Klee's creative process allowed him to achieve a new kind of harmony of formal and imaginative elements. Klee's published diaries (up to 1918) and his writings (published in English as *The Thinking Eye*) contribute to an understanding of his work.

Klein, Felix (1849-1925) German mathematician who worked mainly on geometry and the theory of functions. While a professor at Göttingen (1886-1913), he founded the *Encyclo-*

pedia of Mathematics (1895) and edited the *Mathematische Annalen* from 1872 to 1925.

Klein, Melanie (1882-1960) British psychoanalyst who developed and adapted FREUD's theories and practices for the treatment of children from the earliest years.

Kleist, Heinrich von (1777-1811) German dramatist and pioneer of psychological plays, the most important of which, *Penthesilea* (1808), is about the Amazon queen's hopeless love for Achilles. In the same year he wrote *The Broken Jug*, symbolizing the role of society as accessory before every crime. Subject to melancholia, he died by his own hand.

Klemperer, Otto (1885-1973) German conductor and leading interpreter of BEETHOVEN who was, in his early days, an advocate of contemporary music associated with the works of MAHLER, SCHOENBERG, HINDEMITH and STRAVINSKY. It was in the 1950s that Klemperer, after years of struggle with partial paralysis, emerged as a masterly exponent of Beethoven's symphonies.

Klenze, Leo von (1784-1864) German architect, whose major buildings in Munich, the Glypothek and the Propylaea (for King Ludwig I), testify to his enthusiasm for the Grecian style for public buildings. His Hall of Liberation at Kelheim, Bavaria, illustrates the restrained vigour with which he was able to assemble neo-Grecian elements to form a 19th-century temple.

Klimt, Gustav (1862-1918) Austrian painter and exponent of Art Nouveau. His work has its typical decorative emphasis, but is notable also for its symbolic iconography, usually concerned with the themes of Love or Death. Both these aspects are apparent in the mosaic frieze he designed for Josef HOFFMANN's Palais Stoclet in Brussels. He strongly influenced Schiele and the young KOKOSCHKA.

Klopstock, Friedrich Gottlieb (1724-1803) German lyric poet and dramatist, author of *The Messiah* (1748-73), a life of Christ beginning at the point when he ascends the Mount of Olives. The publication (1748) of the first three of its 20 cantos made Klopstock internationally famous. The work is written in a Neoclassical style in which Greek hexameters were used in German literature. In his odes (collected edition 1771) Klopstock used the various classical ode forms in verses about religion, nature and love. His poetry influenced HÖLDERLIN and RILKE.

Knoll, Max see RUSKA, Ernst August Friedrich

Knox, John (1505-72) Scottish writer, statesman and leader of the Scottish Reformation, a democratic religious revolution which, with English support, ended French political domination and abolished the authority of the pope, 'idolatry' and the Mass. The so-called Reformed Kirk adopted the Calvinistic *Scots Confession of Faith* and the non-episcopal Church Constitution of the *Book of Discipline*, both largely Knox's work. When Catholic MARY STUART returned as Queen in 1561, Knox and the new Church were strong enough to win the struggle for political and religious supremacy.

Koch, Robert (1843-1910) German bacteriologist, and discoverer in 1882 of the tuberculosis bacillus. As well as proving that each disease is caused by a specific bacterium, and that a bacterium of one type does not change into one of another type, Koch devised techniques for the culture of bacteria, and their identification under the microscope by the use of dyes. He identified the causative organism of cholera in 1883, and introduced an inoculation against anthrax.

Kochanowski, Jan (1530-84) Polish poet who gave Polish literature its first masterpiece, *Laments* (1580), a series of deeply personal lyrics on the death of his daughter. The volume was to establish the Polish language as a poetic instrument.

Kodály, Zoltan (1882-1967) Hungarian composer. Appointed a teacher of composition at Budapest Conservatory at 24, Kodály's earliest work was the collection and editing of Hungarian folk-songs, which he carried out partly in collaboration with BARTÓK. This material gave him the basis for the national idiom which is the hallmark of his style. His best-known works are the comic opera *Háry János* (1927), based on Garay's ballad of the tall stories told by a veteran of the Napoleonic Wars; the *Psalmus Hungaricus* (1923) for chorus and orchestra on an epic Old Testament theme; and a set of variations on *The Peacock* (1939), a Hungarian folksong.

Koestler, Arthur (born 1905) Hungarian-born English author and journalist, who has written numerous philosophical and fictional works on the split in the Western mind between technological expertise and adherence to any non-material code of behaviour. Among his novels are *Darkness at Noon* (1940), an account of the mental and physical tyranny of a Communist prison, and *The Call Girls* (1972), a tale of international philosophic congresses. His trilogy, *The Sleepwalkers* (1959), *The Act of Creation* (1964) and *The Ghost in the Machine* (1967), forms an attempt to understand the creative and destructive tendencies of the human mind.

Koffka, Kurt (1886-1941) American psychologist of German origin who with Wertheimer and KÖHLER developed the *Gestalt* theory of psychology, especially in relation to child development.

Köhler, Wolfgang (1887-1967) American psychologist of German origin who was largely responsible for developing the *Gestalt* theory of psychology, based on observable data. In the same way that a picture or a pattern is visible as colours or points are visible, so the mind can best deal with material when some pattern is perceived. In time, experiences are seen as organized events. Köhler also investigated the electrical activity which accompanies vision in the brain.

Kokoschka, Oskar (born 1886) Austrian Expressionist painter, whose early years were spent in the Art Nouveau atmosphere of Vienna. In 1938 he settled in England and concentrated on landscapes and portraits.

Koldewey, Robert (1855-1925) German architect and archaeologist who excavated the city of Babylon. Beginning in 1899, he spent 15 years excavating and mapping the city built by NEBUCHADNEZZAR II during the 6th century BC. He identified huge palaces, massive walls, the famous hanging gardens, and a ziggurat (possibly that recorded in the Bible as the Tower of Babel). Koldewey's thorough work showed that the Bible and HERODOTUS were almost certainly correct in their description of Babylon as the greatest cosmopolitan metropolis of the ancient world.

Kolff, Willem J. (born 1911) Dutch physician who, in 1944, produced the first successful clinical apparatus to take over the function of a human kidney and remove noxious waste substances from the blood.

Kollár, Jan (1793-1852) Slovak poet and scholar whose principal work, *The Daughter of Slava* (begun in 1824), a long lyrical sonnet cycle written in Czech, celebrated events of Slavonic history.

Komisarjevsky, Theodore (1882-1954) Russian theatrical director, who was the first great exponent of STANISLAVSKY's theories. He began in the theatre by working with his sister, Vera Komisarjevskaya, the famous tragedienne. He was a director at the Imperial Theatre and the State Theatre in Moscow until 1919, when he left for England. His productions of CHEKHOV enabled British audiences to appreciate that dramatist at his true worth.

Kooning, Willem de (born 1904) American painter and pioneer of Abstract Expressionism. Unlike most of his contemporaries, de Kooning has produced figurative paintings as well as abstractions.

Korneichuk, Theodore Alexander (born 1905) Ukrainian dramatist, one of the most popular writers in the Soviet theatre. His first success was *Wreck of the Squadron* (1934), in which Communist sailors scuttle a flotilla to prevent it falling into White Russian hands. In the 1930s his greatest success was *Truth*, a play about LENIN. *Mr Perkins in Bolshevik Land* (1944) is a satirical comedy about an American millionaire who visits the USSR to discover the truth about Communism.

Kornilov, Lavr Georgievich (1870-1918) Russian counter-revolutionary and leader of the Don Cossacks. Commander-in-Chief of the Russian forces in August 1917, he put forward proposals for enforcing discipline in the army. On these being rejected, he attacked the government and, after refusing to accept dismissal, marched on Petrograd with the intention of liberating the provisional government of KERENSKY from Socialist domination. Many soldiers defected, however, and Kerensky called on the Bolsheviks for support. Kornilov was defeated, but his leadership of the Don Cossacks in December 1917 marked the beginning of the Civil War. He was killed in action in 1918.

Kosciuszko, Tadeusz (1746-1817) Polish patriot, who provoked and led the Polish insurrection against Russian domination in 1794. He was trained as a soldier in the Prussian and French armies, and fought for the Americans in the War of Independence, for which he was given honorary US citizenship. In France, during the Revolution, he received verbal support for the Polish cause, but no practical help, though Russia and Austria were discussing a new partition of his country. He went to Warsaw, roused the people, and in April 1794, at Raclawice, overcame a Russian army sent against him. Six months later, the Russians defeated him outside Warsaw. He was captured and deported to the US, but throughout his subsequent exile in

France, continued to work for Poland's independence until his death.

Kossuth, Lajos (1802-94) Hungarian Nationalist revolutionary, who fought for Hungary's independence from Austria. A liberal pamphleteer in the 1830s, Kossuth's writings resulted in his being imprisoned (1837-40) for treason. From 1841, as editor of the nationalist newspaper *Pesti Hirlap*, he led the Hungarian nationalist movement and in 1847 he was elected to the Hungarian Diet. His leadership culminated in the revolution of 1848, when he organized a citizen's army to fight the Austrian and Croatian imperial armies. Such was his success that in April 1849, he was able to declare Hungary independent and the Hapsburg dynasty deposed. But NICHOLAS I sent Russian troops to help the Austrian government crush the rebellion and Kossuth was forced to flee. He died in America.

Kosygin, Alexei Nikolayevich (born 1904) Soviet administrator and politician, who joined the Communist Party in 1927 and became Chairman of the Council of Ministers (Prime Minister) following the dismissal of KHRUSCHEV (1964). Under his premiership Russia's foreign policy has been one of peaceful co-existence with the West, but attempts to heal the breach with China, widened by Khruschev's feud with MAO TSE-TUNG, have thus far been unsuccessful.

Koussevitsky, Serge (1876-1951) American musician of Russian birth, conductor of the Boston Symphony Orchestra (1924-49). Koussevitsky first became known as a virtuoso double-bass player and a publisher of contemporary music in pre-Revolutionary Russia. He encouraged contemporary composers by offering commissions (ROUSSEL and PROKOFIEV were both among the many beneficiaries). In 1942 he created the Koussevitsky Foundation in memory of his first wife, Natalie.

Krafft-Ebing, Baron Richard von (1840-1902) German physician and neurologist, author of *Disorders of Sexuality* (1886), a pioneering attempt at a scientific treatment of sexual problems. He also wrote papers on hypnotism, nervous diseases and criminal psychology.

Krasicki, Ignacy (1735-1801) Polish writer of *Fables* and *Tales* (1779), epigrammatic works that reveal a deeply pessimistic view of life and which are outstanding early examples of Polish satire. As Prince Bishop of Warmia, he wrote comic

epics ridiculing the monastic life, and also satires, epistles and didactic novels.

Kreisler, Fritz (1875-1962) Austrian violinist and the most widely known violin soloist of his day. His public success was world-wide and lasted for decades.

Kremer, Gerhard see MERCATOR, Gerhardus

Kretschmer, Ernest (1888-1964) German psychiatrist who revived the ancient idea that character is linked with body type. He distinguishes three basic types: *asthenic*, the tall, thin person; *athletic*, the square, muscular person; *pyknic*, the rounded person.

Kreuger, Ivar (1880-1932) Swedish industrialist, often called the 'match king'. Within 10 years of its foundation, his United Swedish Match Company owned 250 factories in 43 countries. After the First World War he made loans to various governments in return for trading concessions, but the economic recession of 1929 ended many of his enterprises. His suicide led to the discovery that he had engaged in extensive forgeries of securities for loans: his empire was bankrupt.

Krishna Menon, Vengalil Krishnan (born 1896) Indian barrister, diplomatist and nationalist leader. As secretary of the India League (1929-47), he was spokesman for Indian nationalism in Europe, and was India's first High Commissioner in London (1947-52). He played a leading part as an arbitrator during the Korean War (1950-3) and the Suez crisis (1956). As Defence Minister when India and China clashed in border conflicts during 1962, he resigned when the readiness and ability of the army was questioned.

Kritios (5th cent. BC) Greek sculptor whose 'Kouros', in the Acropolis Museum, marks a crucial change from the static Archaic to the organic Classical style. With his partner Nesiotes, Kritios produced a bronze group known as the 'Tyrannicides' (477 BC), depicting the slaying of the tyrant HIPPARCHOS in 514 BC by Harmodios and Aristogeiton, copies of which still exist.

Kroeber, Alfred (1876-1960) American anthropologist, who examined the interrelated structure of the culture, language and religion of North American Indians. His main interest lay in the discovery of cultural patterns in, for example, changes in women's clothes, art styles and sign language. Kroeber also made important contributions to the archaeology of Mexico and Peru, and his book *Anthropology* (1923) was the first textbook on the subject.

Krogh, Schack August Sternberg (1874-1949) Danish professor of physiology, who discovered the regulation of the motor mechanism of the capillaries. In 1920, he was awarded the Nobel Prize for Physiology and Medicine.

Krolow, Karl (born 1915) German poet and literary critic, whose early lyrical verse was later developed towards a surrealistic approach. He has also translated works of French literature into German, notably the poems of Guillaume APOLLINAIRE.

Kronecker, Leopold (1823-91) German mathematician, who was a forerunner of intuitionism – that is, he criticized existence proofs that did not actually construct the item in question (so-called non-constructive proofs). Kronecker also worked on elliptic functions, algebraic equations and numbers.

Kropotkin, Peter (1842-1921) Russian revolutionary who shares with BAKUNIN an important place in the history of anarchism. His career as a revolutionary is told in *Memoirs of a Revolutionist* (1899), but his doctrines and diagnosis of the ills of capitalist society are to be found in *Mutual Aid* (1902) and *Modern Science and Anarchism* (1912).

Kruger, Stephanus Johannes Paulus (1825-1904) Boer statesman who started the second Boer War (1899-1902) by invading Natal and Cape Colony. At the age of 11, he made the Great Trek (1836-7) with the Boers who migrated by waggon away from British rule in the Cape to found new republics – the Orange Free State, Natal and Transvaal. His aim in the Transvaal, of which he became President in 1833, was to keep it a simple, pastoral land. But the Witwatersrand gold strike of 1886 transformed it, despite his attempts to minimize the effects of mining by taxing the British miners heavily and refusing to give them Transvaal citizenship – acts that manifested his bitter anti-British feelings. Following the JAMESON Raid, Kruger bought German arms and invaded Natal and Cape Colony (1899). With the British successes in the second phase of the war he went to Europe (May 1900) for the help which he had been led to expect from Germany. It was refused, and Kruger never returned to South Africa. He died in Switzerland.

Krum (9th cent.) King of Bulgaria and one of its most forceful early leaders. He rose to power by military success against the Avars and gained domination over much of present Rumania, eastern Hungary and northern Bulgaria. He favoured his Slav subjects to undermine the Bulgar aristocracy and so strengthen royal power. Krum fought against Byzantium, killing the Emperor Nicephorus in battle (811), menaced Constantinople, seized Adrianople and devastated Thrace.

Krupp, Alfred (1812-87) German steelmaker and armaments manufacturer who expanded his father's small iron foundry into a giant industry. He was the first steelmaker to install the BESSEMER process and was one of the leaders in the industrial development of the Ruhr valley. His son Friedrich Alfred Krupp (1854-1902) expanded into shipbuilding and the manufacture of chrome and nickel steel alloys and armour-plate. Krupp had the monopoly of German arms manufacture during the First World War. Among its products was Big Bertha, a monstrous but inaccurate train-borne gun which shelled the Paris area from a distance of 70 miles. The firm played a major role in the economic recovery of West Germany after the Second World War.

Krylov, Ivan Andreyevich (1769-1844) Russia's foremost fable writer. He translated those of LA FONTAINE, and between 1809 and 1843 published nine volumes of epigrammatic cameos attacking the self-satisfaction, pretence and arrogance of the Russian upper classes. Many of his lines have

Brought up on the borderland between civilization and barbarism, constantly trekking, fighting and hunting, Kruger (left) received little formal education

passed into the language as proverbs. TURGENEV said of him that a foreigner studying Krylov's fables would gain a clearer understanding of the Russian character than by reading treatises on the subject.

Kuan Han-ching (c. 1220-c. 1300) Chinese dramatist, and leading exponent of *tsa chu* or Northern Drama, the first form of Chinese opera, best known of which is *Snow in Midsummer* (*The Tragedy of Tou E'*). An actor and a prolific dramatist, Kuan wrote tragedy, historical romances, social dramas, comedies and satire, and his libretti are notable for the way in which he brings great freshness and vitality to a form which too often suffered from stereotypes.

Kublai Khan (1216-94) Mongol founder of China's Yüan dynasty (1260-1368) and one of the great rulers of history. Grandson of GENGHIS KHAN, Kublai helped to subdue southern China. After his brother, Khan Mangu, died (1259), Kublai's troops acclaimed him Great Khan of the entire Mongol Empire. Kublai Khan remained in China, ending the Chinese Sung dynasty and reigned as undisputed emperor (1280-94). He founded Khanbalik (Peking) as his winter capital, restored prosperity to war-torn China, and encouraged unprecedented contacts with the West.

Ku K'ai-chih (c. 344-c. 406) The only important artist of the early period of Chinese painting to whom any surviving work can be attributed. He was also a poet, scholar, celebrated wit and author of *How to Paint the Cloud Terrace Mountain*, which explained his methods. He can be seen as a forerunner of T'ang figure painting in a hand-scroll which depicts rules, for the moral behaviour of court ladies, in a carefully controlled and dignified manner.

Kummer, Ernst Eduard (1810-93) German mathematician, who worked mainly on higher arithmetic and geometry. He discovered certain sets of numbers, called 'ideals', that obey ordinary rules of divisibility in the fields of algebraic numbers – that is, numbers generated by the roots of an algebraic equation with rational coefficients.

Kun, Béla (1886-1939) Hungarian Communist, who ruled Hungary as dictator for four months in 1919. Kun had been captured by the Russians in the First World War, had taken part in the Revolution, and was sent by the Bolsheviks to stir up revolution in his own country. After winning many converts, he overthrew Karolyi's government and seized power. Kun introduced badly needed reforms, but was discredited by atrocities committed by his followers. Military intervention by Rumania in support of the counter-revolution of Admiral HORTHY, brought down the Communist government and Kun fled to Russia. He reappeared in Vienna (1928), where he was imprisoned, and was later deported to Russia where he is thought to have died in the Great Purge of the 1930s.

Kurchatov, Igor Vasilevich (1903-60) Russian physicist who led the team that developed Russia's first nuclear weapon, exploded in 1949. They went on to develop the first Russian hydrogen bomb in 1952.

Kurosawa, Akira (born 1910) Japanese film director who, in *Rashomon* (1950), introduced the savage, bloodthirsty world of the Samurai warriors to Europe and America. The popularity of his genre was confirmed with *Seven Samurai* (1954), later remade by John Sturges as *The Magnificent Seven*. He has also made films in a modern idiom, notably *Living* (1952).

Kutuzov, Mikhail Ilarionovich, Prince of Smolensk (1745-1813) Russian general, whose 'scorched earth' policy caused NAPOLEON's retreat from Moscow. In 1812 ALEXANDER I appointed him Commander-in-Chief of the Russian army. After the battle of Borodino (September 1812) he retreated beyond Moscow, a large part of which the Russians deliberately destroyed by fire. By laying waste the countryside as he withdrew, Kutuzov denied food to the French army. With no supplies, little shelter, and no government with which to negotiate, Napoleon was forced to retire, the French army suffering meanwhile from the winter weather and incessant Russian attacks along its flanks. Although too cautious to attack and win a convincing victory, Kutuzov's strategy resulted in the decimation of Napoleon's army of invasion. Kutuzov, one of the founders of Russia's military science, led the pursuit of the fleeing French army, and died in Silesia.

Kyd, Thomas (1558-94) English dramatist, who wrote *The Spanish Tragedy* (c. 1587). This revenge melodrama started a fashion for such plays and influenced SHAKESPEARE in the writing of *Titus Andronicus*, in which some critics believe that Kyd collaborated. There is also a theory that he wrote versions of *Hamlet* and *The Taming of the Shrew*, on which Shakespeare based his own plays. *The Spanish Tragedy* is Kyd's only surviving play.

L

Laban, Rudolf von (1879-1958) Hungarian dancer, teacher, and inventor of a comprehensive system of choreographic notation which records almost any movement of the human body.

Labiche, Eugène (1815-88) French dramatist, who wrote, or collaborated on, over 150 farces. He was successful from the start with *Monsieur de Coislin, ou l'homme infiniment poli*. The penetrating social comment in his plays led to the inclusion of some of his plays in the repertoire of the Comédie Française and to his election to the Académie Française.

Labrouste, Henri (1801-75) French architect who popularized the use of iron in Paris. He handled the new material with great sensitivity, and the Bibliothèque St Geneviève in Paris is one of the first buildings in which iron and cast-iron were used on a large scale, in this case for the colonnades and domes.

Labrunie, Gérard see NERVAL, Gérard de

La Bruyère, Jean de (1645-96) French writer and moralist, famed for his sole work, *Les Caractères ou les moeurs de ce siècle* (1688). Written in an epigrammatic style, *Les Caractères* consists of a series of satirical portraits of contemporary characters, exposing the vices, follies and secret impulses of human nature.

Laclos, Pierre Choderlos de (1741-1803) French writer and soldier, whose licentious novel, *Les Liaisons dangereuses* (1782), is recognized today as one of the great works of French realism. It described, in the form of letters, the seduction of two women by an unscrupulous rake, Valmont. Though initially a *succès de scandale*, its characterization and psychological insight place it in a far higher category of fiction.

Ladislas II, Jagiello (1350-1434) Lithuanian-born king of Poland (1386-1434), who was the founder of Poland's Jagiellon dynasty (1386-1572). He was Grand Duke of Lithuania when he married Queen JADWIGA of Poland (1386) and became Poland's king. His Lithuanian duchy added to Poland an area three times its size and made it one of Europe's great powers. Jagiello greatly strengthened the new state by defeating the Teutonic Knights at Tannenberg (1410), bringing to an end their long-standing threat to Poles and Lithuanians.

Laënnec, René (1781-1826) French physician, who invented the stethoscope to further his studies of lung disease.

Lafayette, Marie-Joseph, Marquis de (1757-1834) French aristocrat and statesman who participated in the American War of Independence, and became a revolutionary soldier and politician in France. Lafayette was commissioned into the American revolutionary army in 1777 and, together with other French aristocrats, was given command in the decisive Yorktown campaign of 1781. On his return to France the following year, he pressed for social and political reform. He was elected to the Estates General and became Vice-President of the National Assembly (1789). He helped to draft the Declaration of the Rights of Man, the American precedent for which he fully appreciated. After the defeat of the French armies by the Austrians in the autumn of 1792, Lafayette returned to Paris in an attempt to protect the monarchy of LOUIS XVI, but was impeached for his alleged military failure and fled to Austria. He was subsequently held in custody by the Prussians, but returned to France in 1799. He played no active political role during the régime of NAPOLEON and after the restoration of the Bourbons, was elected Deputy (1818) and pressed for liberal reforms, a campaign which he pursued during the early years of LOUIS PHILIPPE's rule.

La Fayette, Marie Madeleine Pioche de la Vergne (1634-93) French writer, author of *La Princesse de Clèves* (1678), a novel about a woman whose marriage is shattered by a guilty passion. It is written in a sober, classical style and with a psychological insight that anticipates STENDHAL, Jane AUSTEN and PROUST. The first perfected short novel analyzing the complexity of human emotions, it broke the tradition that love stories must be involved, unreal and interminably long.

La Follette, Robert Marion (1855-1925) American politician and 'Progressive' senator for Wisconsin. He was active in railway legislation, advocating state control of the railways, and did much to reform Wisconsin politics during his period as Governor from 1900-6. As a senator (1906-25), he became leader of the Progressive movement and sponsored measures to subject industrial corporations, railways, and banks to effective public control, and to end corruption in municipal government.

La Fontaine, Jean de (1621-95) French poet, whose *Fables* published between 1668 and 1693, are among the masterpieces of French literature. La Fontaine, a meticulous craftsman, took his basic material from AESOP and the oriental fabulists, enriched and perfected it, and, mingling the animal and human worlds, satirized many aspects of French life and society. He also wrote scandalous short stories in verse, *Contes* (1664-74) (which he later repudiated), as well as plays, poems and opera libretti.

Laforgue, Jules (1860-87) French Symbolist poet, and an inventor of the free verse which revitalized European poetry by replacing lofty, 'poetic' sententiousness with the rhythms of everyday speech. The free association, puns and juxtapositions of his mocking, ironical fantasies *Les Complaintes* (1885) and *L'Imitation de Notre-Dame La Lune* (1886), can be seen as marking the beginnings of modern French poetry.

Lagerkvist, Pär Fabian (born 1891) Swedish Expressionist poet, dramatist and author of *The Dwarf* (1945) and *Barabbas* (1950), for which he won the Nobel Prize (1951). At once symbolic and naturalistic, both works concern the human predicament, the problems of good and evil and man's inherent bestiality. The collection of poems *Anguish* (1916) and the play *The Difficult Hunt* (1918) reveal a prevailing pessimism and his contemplation of a world deprived of the hope once provided by religious belief.

Lagerlöf, Selma (1858-1940) Swedish novelist and poet, the first woman to receive a Nobel Prize for Literature. Her novel *The Story of Gösta Berling* (1891) played an important part in the Swedish Romantic revival of the 1890s. Her story of a boy's flight on a goose, *The Wonderful Adventures of Nils* (1906), is an international children's classic.

Lagrange, Joseph (1736-1813) French mathematician, who, at the age of 18, was appointed Professor of Geometry to the Artillery school in Turin and the following year produced a solution to an isoperimetrical problem out of which grew the calculus of variations. This solution made him one of the leading mathematicians of Europe before he was 20. His writings covered a wide range of subjects, including partial differential equations, the theory of numbers, elliptic functions, calculus of variations and research into the propagation of sound.

La Guardia, Fiorello Henry (1882-1947) American municipal leader of Italian-Jewish origin who was Mayor

of New York (1934-45). He defeated both the Democratic and the Republican official candidates when he was elected Mayor for the first time in 1934. During his term of office, he was responsible for housing and labour schemes and released New York's administration from the corrupt control of the 'bosses' and the city machine. He was an outspoken critic of HITLER's anti-Semitism. After the Second World War, he became Director of the UN's refugee relief programme.

Laing, Alexander Gordon (1793-1826) Scottish explorer, the first modern European to see Timbuktu, where he was strangled by Arabs. He served as a soldier in Sierra Leone and was sent to the Mandingo country (1822) to build trade, end slaving, and find the Niger's source, a search blocked by hostile Africans. He crossed the Sahara from Tripoli on his last journey to Timbuktu.

Lamarck, Jean Baptiste de (1744-1829) French naturalist who was the first scientist to distinguish vertebrates from invertebrates. He followed the view of BUFFON that species were not fixed, but that the complex developed from the simple, and put forward the idea that new organs developed as a result of new needs, while those that were little used degenerated. He also thought that characteristics acquired by an organism in its lifetime are passed on as an inheritance to its offspring, a view since disproved by modern genetics.

Lamartine, Alphonse de (1790-1869) French Romantic poet and politician. His lyrical poetry, approaching WORDSWORTH in its vision of the affinity between man, the universe and the divine, rescued French verse from the stale abstractions of classicism and strongly influenced the Romantic movement in France. Some of his best-known poems are included in *Méditations poétiques* (1820), *Harmonies poétiques et réligieuses* (1830) and *Recueillements poétiques* (1839). Lamartine was a notable orator, and became one of the popular idols of the 1848 Revolution.

Lamb, Charles (1775-1834) English writer who, with his sister Mary, wrote *Tales from Shakespeare* (1807) for children. Lamb was a friend of COLERIDGE, and the latter published some of his poems. In 1820, Lamb began contributing essays, which he signed 'Elia', to the *London Magazine*. Written in an elaborate literary style, the essays were eventually collected as *Essays of Elia* (1823-33).

Lambert, Johann Heinrich (1728-77) Swiss mathematician and scien-

Black and white processing time

A pocket processing plant for pictures, an early Land Polaroid camera together with a modern version

tist, who was the first to show that π is not a rational number. He made many original contributions to mathematics, physics and astronomy.

La Mettrie, Julien (1709-51) French physician, materialist philosopher and author of *L'Homme machine* (1747), a treatise whose general atheist position caused a sensation at the time. La Mettrie stated that man is a complex mechanism like a machine, and saw the soul as the thinking part of the body, which perishes with it, the only pleasures being those of the senses. La Mettrie's views influenced the utilitarian thought of Jeremy BENTHAM.

Lampedusa, Giuseppe Tomasi di (1896-1957) Italian writer and author of an outstanding novel, *The Leopard*, published posthumously in 1958. It is a long, sensual story which evokes the decadence, intrigue, corruption and violent social contrasts of 19th century Sicily at the time of GARIBALDI's invasion.

Lancaster, Joseph (1778-1838) English educator who adapted the monitorial system of Andrew BELL. He converted its original purpose into an educational principle, in which teachers were merely overseers and learning was a form of drill. The Royal Lancasterian Institution (later the British and Foreign School Society) was formed to promote his work (1808), but he quarrelled with the trustees and emigrated to the USA, subsequently visiting Venezuela and Canada.

Lancaster, Osbert (born 1908) British cartoonist, satirist and theatrical designer. He began drawing his

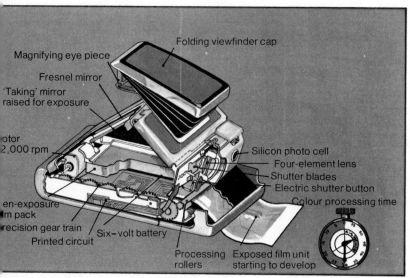

Magnifying eye piece
Fresnel mirror
'Taking' mirror raised for exposure
otor 2,000 rpm
en-exposure m pack
recision gear train
Printed circuit
Six-volt battery
Folding viewfinder cap
Silicon photo cell
Four-element lens
Shutter blades
Electric shutter button
Colour processing time
Processing rollers
Exposed film unit starting to develop

Pocket Cartoon, featuring his best-known character, Maudie Little-hampton, in the London *Daily Express* in 1939. He also worked for the *Architectural Review*, and has produced a number of illustrated books satirizing town-planning and development, among them *Draynefleet Revealed*, which traces the spoliation of an historic town.

Land, Edwin Herbert (born 1909) American inventor who, in 1937, produced a material known as 'pola-roid' which has been used in polarimeters, safety glass and particularly in spectacles to reduce reflected sunglare. Land's most ingenious and important later invention was the Polaroid camera (1947). This produces a positive print in less than a minute without a negative having to be removed separately from the camera. A colour system was later developed for the camera, and it has become a valuable aid to both the professional and amateur photographer.

Landa, Diego de (16th cent.) Spanish prelate who made possible extensive decipherment of Maya hieroglyphs. He went to Central America as a Franciscan friar, and became the first bishop of Yucatan. He destroyed every pagan Maya manuscript he found, but wrote *Account of the Facts of Yucatan*, an account of Maya life and history. This included an explanation of native numerals and day and month signs, making possible the decipherment of Maya hieroglyphs.

Landau, Lev Davidovich (1908-68) Russian physicist whose many contributions included the basic theories describing ferromagnetism and liquid helium. In the 1930s he calculated the way in which the atoms in small regions (called domains) of a substance like iron line up in a magnetic field, creating the strong effect

known as ferromagnetism. In the 1940s and 1950s he created the theory that underlies the strange ('superfluid') behaviour of liquid helium.

Landor, Walter Savage (1775-1864) English author, whose principal work was *Imaginary Conversations* (1824-48), a series of dialogues between historical characters, which were largely a vehicle for Landor's own views.

Landowska, Wanda (1877-1959) Polish virtuoso pianist and harpsichordist who re-established the harpsichord in the 20th century. No one who heard her play BACH's *Italian Concerto* on the harpsichord, said Albert SCHWEITZER, could 'imagine wanting ever again to hear it on the piano'. She also inspired modern composers, like FALLA, to write works for her.

Landru, Henri (1869-1922) French murderer, known as the 'modern Bluebeard'. When arrested in 1919, he was found to possess a notebook recording the names of 11 missing persons. Landru, protesting his innocence, was charged with their murder and guillotined in 1922.

Landsteiner, Karl (1868-1943) Austrian pathologist who distinguished four different blood types, later labelled A, B, AB and O, and paved the way for scientific blood transfusion. He showed that blood of some groups is incompatible with that of others and that, if incompatible bloods are mixed, they will form clot-like lumps. His findings explained why some transfusions of blood in the past had been beneficial, whilst others had been fatal.

Lane, Sir Allen (1902-70) British pioneer of paperback publishing. Apprenticed at the Bodley Head, Lon-

don, he became managing director and left the company in 1936 to found Penguin Books Ltd under whose imprint he published paperback editions of modern novels and later a wider range of literature at about two US cents each. Though booksellers were wary at first, other publishers soon followed suit, so revolutionizing book publishing.

Lang, Fritz (born 1890) Austrian film director whose early career in Germany included two masterpieces, *M* (1932), starring Peter Lorre as a psychopathic killer, and *Metropolis* (1926) a fantasy of the future. His later Hollywood films (post 1934) are remarkable for their superb photographic composition, but the images of chaos beneath normality – whether in the dreamed violence of Edward G. Robinson in *Woman in the Window* (1944) or the actual violence of *The Big Heat* (1953) – lift the films to a new, higher level.

Lange, Carl (1834-1900) Danish physician and psychologist who (independently of William JAMES) propounded the theory that the emotions we feel are the result of bodily reactions rather than their cause.

Langevin, Paul (1872-1946) French physicist, renowned for his work with Chilowski (from 1915), in the development of a method, using the reflection of ultrasonic waves, to detect the range and distance of submerged objects. The impetus for this device stemmed from the need to detect submarines in the First World War, which ended before it was operational, but it was widely used during the Second World War. The system, now known as Sonar, is used extensively in oceanography and in commercial fishing for the detection of fish shoals. Langevin also studied secondary X-rays, relativity theory, magnetism and Brownian movement.

Langland, William (c. 1332-c. 1400) English poet, who probably wrote *The Vision of Piers the Plowman* (three versions, 1362, 1377, 1392), an allegorical poem in Middle English alliterative verse. The poem mixes allegory, theology, homely morality and bitter satire against the vices and conditions of the time.

Langley, Samuel Pierpont (1834-1906) American astronomer who demonstrated the feasibility of mechanical flight. In 1881 he invented the bolometer, an instrument for accurately measuring minute quantities of heat, with which he studied the red region of the solar spectrum. He was appointed Secretary of the Smithsonian Institute in Washington (1887) and during the following decade become interested in the possibility of heavier-than-air flying machines. His large steam-powered model aircraft accomplished the most successful flights of their time (1896).

Langmuir, Irving (1881-1957) American chemist who found a way of extending the life of incandescent electric lamps. In early lamps, the glass bulb enclosed a vacuum and a tungsten wire filament. Langmuir's research showed that if, instead of a vacuum, a bulb enclosed an inert gas such as nitrogen or argon, the filament lasted far longer.

Lansbury, George (1859-1940) British Labour Party politician and pacifist. Lansbury acquired experience of municipal politics among the poor in the East End of London and became an MP in 1910. He was a pacifist during the First World War, edited the socialist *Daily Herald* (1919-23), was a member of the 1929-31 Labour government, but refused to have anything to do with the MACDONALD-BALDWIN coalition (National) government of 1931. Lansbury became Leader of the Labour Party (1931-5) largely because he was the one Labour politician of Cabinet rank to keep his seat in the 1931 General Election. His devout Christian view of socialism, however, alienated his tougher colleagues, including BEVIN, and he was forced to resign the leadership. His peace-seeking visit to HITLER in 1937 proved fruitless.

Lanston, Tolbert (1844-1913) American inventor of the Monotype typesetting machine. This was the first mechanical means of casting and setting type in lines, and was controlled by coded programme tape. Its introduction revolutionized the printing industry, and in 1885 the first patents for the Monotype machine were granted. Lanston spent the following years perfecting it before introducing it commercially in 1897.

Lao-tzu (c. 604-531 BC) Chinese philosopher and founder of Taoism (named from *Tao*, 'the way'). His philosophy was that to live harmoniously with the supreme universal power, man must relinquish the struggle for wealth and live for others, but follow his own inclinations as his best ethical guide. Later, Taoism degenerated into a religion of superstition, magic and hedonism.

La Pérouse, Count Jean-François de (1741-88) French explorer and navigator, chosen by LOUIS XVI in 1785 to lead an expedition to the Pacific and in particular to the waters around Australia. The voyage took him along the coast of America, west across the Pacific to China, then south through the strait which now bears his name, between Sakhalin and Hokkaido. His expedition was later lost and was probably wrecked off the islands of the New Hebrides.

Laplace, Pierre Simon, Marquis de (1749-1827) French astronomer and mathematician who developed the Nebular Hypothesis to account for the origin of the solar system from a shrinking gas cloud.

Lapparent, Albert de (1839-1908) French geologist who helped to draw up the geological map of France, mapping in the field and studying stratigraphy and mineralogy. He published *Treatise on Geology* (1882), a work on European stratigraphy which remains authoritative today.

La Ramée see OUIDA

Larkin, Philip (born 1922) English poet and novelist, whose verse is concerned with the problems and puzzles of personal affairs. In 'The Less Deceived' (1955) and 'The Whitsun Wedding' (1964) he developed a plain, reflective style, influenced by HARDY. He has written two novels, *Jill* (1964) and *A Girl in Winter* (1947), the former recapturing his own youthful experience at Oxford, and has edited the anthology *English Poetry of the Twentieth Century* (1973).

La Rochefoucauld, Duc François de (1613-80) French moralist and writer of maxims. His fame rests upon his *Réflexions ou sentences et maximes morales*, known as the *Maximes* (1665), a collection of 500 laconic, often finely constructed sentences analysing human conduct and aspirations.

Larousse, Pierre (1817-75) French lexicographer who compiled the 15-volume *Universal Dictionary of the 19th Century* (1866-76). This work was designed more for popular use than the scholarly earlier dictionaries and is a combination of lexicon and encyclopedia. A model for many later works, it defines common words, and contains many biographical entries, articles on history, geography and other subjects.

La Salle, St Jean Baptiste de (1651-1719) French founder of the teaching order of Christian Brothers which spread in Europe and America during the 19th century. He was canonized in 1900.

La Salle, Robert Cavelier de (1643-87) French explorer of much of the Mississippi River. He made the first complete voyage downstream to its mouth and also recorded the earliest description of the Niagara Falls (1678). In 1681, La Salle sailed down the Illinois River to the main stream of the Mississippi then on to the Gulf of Mexico. On his last journey he sailed from France to the Mississippi delta and landed in what is now Texas. During an overland march to find the Mississippi he was killed by members of his party and they, in turn, were killed by Comanche warriors.

Latimer, Hugh (c. 1485-1555) English Protestant reformer and martyr. With Thomas CROMWELL and CRANMER, he supported and advised HENRY VIII in the dispute with Rome, and his preaching as Bishop of Worcester (1535-9) did much to publicize Protestant doctrine. With Cranmer and RIDLEY, Latimer was condemned as a heretic in MARY I's reign, and was burned at the stake with Ridley.

La Tour, Georges de (1593-1652) French painter of religious and genre subjects, whose work is characterized chiefly by chiaroscuro, or contrasts between light and shade, popular among CARAVAGGIO's followers. La Tour's religious pictures, such as *St Sebastian Tended by St Irene* (c. 1650), are remarkable for the monumental scale of their figures, the simplification of forms, and the stillness which pervades even the most harrowing scenes – a quality due mainly to the subtle effects of light cast in predominantly dark interiors by a candle or torch. His paintings are comparatively rare, and until the 20th century his reputation was modest.

Laud, William (1573-1645) English, Archbishop of Canterbury (1633-45) who supported CHARLES I and STRAFFORD against the Puritans. He demanded religious uniformity based on the views of the High Anglican Church, and used prerogative courts such as the Star Chamber to subdue dissidents with severe punishments. His actions, together with Charles's concept of absolutism, antagonized both the Presbyterian Scots and the Puritan Parliament, who impeached and imprisoned Laud (1641), condemned him to death, and had him beheaded (1645).

Laue, Max Theodor Felix von (1879-1960) German physicist who showed that X-rays can be diffracted by crystals. In 1912 Laue passed an X-ray beam through a crystal and obtained a photograph of a complex but distinct diffraction pattern.

Laughton, Charles (1899-1963) English stage and film actor, internationally known for his screen performance in *The Private Life of Henry VIII*, and as Quasimodo in *The Hunchback of Notre Dame*.

Laurel, Stanley (1890-1965) English comedian, who with Oliver Hardy, an American, formed the cinema's greatest double act, whose popularity was at its height in the 1920s and 1930s. The long-suffering Hardy and the helpfully inept Laurel starred in films such as *Putting Pants on Philip* (1926), and in 1932 they won an Oscar in the Short Subjects category for *The Music Box*. In 1960, Stan Laurel was awarded a special Oscar 'for his creative pioneering in the field of cinema comedy'.

Laurent, Auguste (1807-53) French chemist who developed the idea of classifying organic compounds according to characteristic atomic groupings. Working from the ideas of his former teacher, Jean DUMAS, Laurent built up a body of experimental evidence to support his classification scheme.

Laurier, Sir Wilfred (1841-1919) First French Canadian to become Prime Minister of Canada, an office he held from 1896 to 1911. He was responsible for giving Britain preferential tariffs, for sending Canadian troops to the South African War (1899-1903) and for trying to improve trade relations with the US, which resulted in his defeat. In the First World War he opposed Prime Minister MACKENZIE KING's policy of conscription and refused to join a coalition government in 1917.

Laval, Carl Gustav Patrik de (1845-1913) Swedish inventor, whose two most important contributions were a centrifugal cream separator (1877), which was soon adopted by large dairies throughout the world, and the solution of major problems turbine with his 'windmill' device (1887) for small engines.

Laval, Pierre (1883-1945) French politician and leading collaborator with the Germans during the Second World War. He started in politics as a Socialist (1903) but lacked sincere convictions. Twice Prime Minister of France during the 1930s, he was

Charles Laughton in one of his roles as the emperor Nero. Laughton specialized in serio-comic parts

forced to resign (1936) through public indignation over his appeasement of MUSSOLINI. He supported PÉTAIN and was effective chief minister of Vichy France (1942-4), though he was careful to avoid military commitments to the Nazis. When he realized that the Allies were going to win the Second World War, he tried to rehabilitate himself by calling a National Assembly, but was arrested by the Germans. In 1945, he took refuge in Spain, but returned voluntarily to France to face charges of treason. Laval was convicted and shot.

Laver, Rod (born 1938) Australian lawn tennis player who won the All England singles championship at Wimbledon four times in the 1960s.

Lavoisier, Antoine Laurent (1743-94) French chemist who laid the foundations of modern chemical thought. His series of brilliant experiments in the 1770s demolished the prevailing phlogiston theory of combustion and established the basis of modern ideas. He showed that combustion is the combining of a substance with air (actually oxygen) and, with remarkable insight, linked it to the energy processes that generate heat within living organisms. Later, he showed that the air is made up mainly of two gases: oxygen and what he called azote (later named nitrogen). In the late 1780s, Lavoisier worked out the first logical system for naming chemical compounds and so founded the language of modern chemistry. He was guillotined during the French Revolution.

Law, John (1671-1729) Scottish financier who devised the disastrous 'Mississippi Scheme'. Law produced a scheme to enrich nations by substituting bank-notes for gold and silver coin, and France, impoverished by LOUIS XIV's wars, welcomed the scheme. Law opened France's first bank (1716), then founded the Louisiana Company to develop the French-held Mississippi Valley. The bank-note issues succeeded initially, but over-issue and misuse of them for speculative purchases of Louisiana stock led clients to demand gold for their notes. Unable to pay, the bank closed (1720), bankrupting thousands and forcing Law – then France's Director-General of Finance – into exile and obscurity.

Lawes, Sir John (1814-1900) British agriculturalist who founded the synthetic fertilizer industry by making superphosphate.

Lawrence, David Herbert (1855-1930) English poet and author, regarded by E. M. FORSTER as 'the

Lonely, legendary leader of the Arabs in their revolt against the Turks, Lawrence of Arabia in Bedouin dress

greatest imaginative novelist of our generation'. Lawrence combined detailed realism and social criticism with a lyrical, symbolic representation of man's condition, as shown in his first major work, the loosely autobiographical *Sons and Lovers* (1913) and again the *The Rainbow* (1915) and its companion *Women in Love* (1920). *The Rainbow* was at first suppressed for obscenity, and *Lady Chatterley's Lover* (1928) was banned in England until 1960. He also wrote short stories, powerful verse and criticism.

Lawrence, Ernest Orlando (1901-58) American physicist who invented the cyclotron, the nuclear accelerator which traps nuclear particles in a large magnetic field, in which they follow circular orbits. Twice in each orbit they are accelerated by a small electric field. After a large number of orbits the particles have high energies and are deflected out of the machine for use in nuclear experiments.

Lawrence, Thomas Edward (1888-1935) British soldier and writer known as 'Lawrence of Arabia', leader of the Arab revolt against the Turks in the First World War. A knowledge of the Arabs, acquired during archaeological research in the Middle East, led to his being sent (1916), with the rank of colonel, to Jedda to help HUSSEIN, who was trying to induce the Arabs to revolt against their Turkish masters. Lawrence organized and led raids on the Damascus-Medina railway, captured various key-points, and in 1917-18 fought his way through Palestine to Damascus on the right of ALLENBY's advance. He returned to Oxford (1919) as a Fellow of All Souls' and wrote an account of the revolt, *The Seven Pillars of Wisdom* (1926). He attended the Paris Peace Conference in Arab dress, and was disgusted by what he regarded as a betrayal of the Arabs by the terms of the peace treaties, and withdrew from public life. After changing his name to Ross, he joined the RAF as an aircraftsman. When his disguise was penetrated, he changed his name again, to T. E. Shaw. He was killed in a motorcycle accident.

Layard, Sir Austen Henry (1817-94) British archaeologist, whose spectacular Assyrian finds encouraged the search for lost civilizations in the Middle East. Between 1845 and 1851, he excavated at Nimrod and Kiyunjik (Nineveh) in Iraq, and discovered the remains of vast and magnificent palaces of the Assyrian kings.

Leacock, Stephen (1869-1944) Canadian writer and political economist who wrote a succession of popular humorous works, among which were *Nonsense Novels* (1911), *Sunshine Sketches of a Little Town* (1912) and *Winsome Winnie* (1920).

Leakey, Louis (1903-72) British anthropologist and palaeontologist whose finds added a million years to the history of man. In Olduvai Gorge, Tanzania, between 1960 and 1963, he found fossil bones and crude stone tools in a volcanic ash shown by potassium-argon dating to be 1,780,000 years old. Leakey reconstructed this tool maker, named *Homo habilis* (handy man), as a man-like animal four feet tall. *Homo habilis*, apparently the first known tool maker and so the first true man, predates the Java man found by Eugène DUBOIS, and may have been a direct ancestor of modern man.

Lear, Edward (1812-88) English painter, poet and fantasist, who wrote *The Book of Nonsense* (1846), verses in limerick form. Their slightly melancholy tone appears more strongly in 'The Owl and the Pussycat' and 'The Dong with the Luminous Nose'.

Le Bel, Joseph Achille (1847-1930) French chemist who proposed that the chemical bonds from a carbon atom are arranged in space as if they pointed towards the corners of a regular tetrahedron. This theory allowed chemists to work out the molecular structures of organic compounds.

Lebon, Phillipe (1769-1804) French pioneer of gas illumination, who from 1791 investigated methods for the production of inflammable gas from wood, which he then patented (1799). He also made notable contributions to the theory of gas lighting and fore-

saw most of the uses to which gas was to be put in the 19th century.

Le Brun, Charles (1619-90) French painter responsible for many of the artistic achievements of the reign of LOUIS XIV. Under the patronage of COLBERT, he became controller of most French decorative manufactures and, personally, the decorator of parts of the Palace of Versailles.

Le Châtelier, Henri Louis (1850-1936) French chemist and formulator (1888) of the law of chemical reaction known as Le Châtelier's principle. It states that if in any chemical system in equilibrium one of the factors in the equilibrium (such as temperature or pressure) changes, the system readjusts itself to minimize the change.

Leclanché, Georges (1839-82) French engineer, who, in 1867, invented an electrolytic cell which could provide an intermittent electric supply, as required. Millions of the familiar dry cells developed from this have been, and still are, used throughout the world.

Leconte de Lisle, Charles Marie (1818-94) French poet and leader of the Parnassians, a group of poets whose aim was to replace the subjective and sentimental effusions of the Romantics with a more impersonal approach. His best-known publications are *Poèmes antiques* (1852) and *Poèmes barbares* (1862). Inspired by the classical writers and attaching greater importance to craftsmanship than his Romantic predecessors, Leconte de Lisle wrote in a disciplined, formally perfect and restrained style. The pessimism of his work is relieved by exotic descriptions (some inspired by Réunion, the tropical island of his birth) and he is particularly renowed for his portraits of wild animals, e.g. 'Les Eléphants'; 'Le Rêve du Jaguar'.

Le Corbusier (1887-1965) Swiss architect who practised in France and was one of the pioneers of modern architecture. With GROPIUS and MIES VAN DER ROHE he was one of the chief influences on mid-20th century architecture. He studied under Auguste PERRET, the pioneer in reinforced concrete, and Peter BEHRENS, and designed furniture (as for the Pavillon de L'Esprit Nouveau at the Paris Exhibition of Decorative Art of 1925), and his activities eventually extended to town-planning and urban development. He conceived the cities of tomorrow as places where skyscrapers would rise up as mighty slabs of concrete, leaving the surrounding areas free for recreational parks and gardens. For Le Corbusier, a tradition of classicism comparable with that of

the Parthenon could be found in the functional architecture of a Citroën car or an American grain elevator. His concept of the individual house, which he said should be a 'machine for living in', was of a structure (often lifted off the ground on stilts) that remained quite distinct from its natural settings; examples include his houses at Garches and Poissy. Public buildings designed by him include a store in Moscow and the Pavillon Suisse at the Cité Universitaire in Paris. Of his later works, the Unité d'Habitation at Marseilles, a reinforced concrete apartment block, is conceived as a total community.

Le Douanier see ROUSSEAU, Henri

Ledoux, Claude-Nicolas (1736-1806) French architect of considerable originality whose projects for buildings based upon geometrical solids have gained him a reputation as one of the most imaginative and romantic 18th-century designers. An early influential work was the Neoclassical Pavillon de Louveciennes, built for Madame DU BARRY, in which the interior decoration and furnishings were all in this style. In 1773 he was made Academician and Architecte du Roi. His gift for stark, impressive silhouettes found expression in his public buildings such as the theatre at Besançon and the toll houses of Paris.

Lee, Ann (1736-84) British mystic, leader of the Shakers, or Shaking Quakers, a revivalist group that originated in France in 1688 and developed in England as a form of Quakerism, the name arising from their agitated ritual dancing.

Lee, Laurie (born 1914) English poet of pastoral and lyrical verse. Most of his poetry is quiet and intimate; his images often odd and striking. His volumes include *The Sun My Monument* (1944), *My Many-Coated Man* (1955) and *Poems* (1960). *Cider with Rosie* (1959) and *As I Walked Out One Midsummer Morning* (1969) are romantic autobiographies.

These charts trace the story of evolution from the emergence of marine life in Pre-Cambrian times (600m years ago) to the Age of Mammals, the Pliocene era (10m years ago). Coloured bands outline the history of the main species. The Ordovician period (500m years ago) marks the appearance of vertebrates; by Silurian times (450m years ago) marine flora began to invade land and in the Devonian (350m years ago) air-breathing creatures evolved. The Jurassic Period (c. 100m years ago) was the age of giant reptiles, lasting until the Palaeocene era (60m years ago) when mammals gained ascendancy. Leakey's *homo habilis* lived 1,780,000 years ago, but modern man is only 10,000 years old

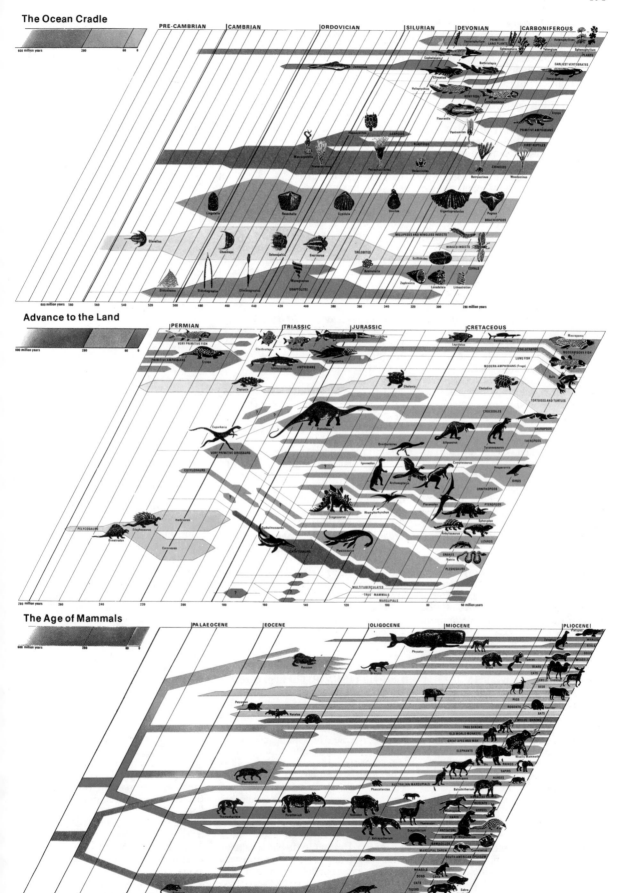

The Ocean Cradle

The Age of Mammals

Advance to the Land

Lee, Robert E. (1807-70) American general, Commander-in-Chief of the Confederate armies in the Civil War. Lee began his career as an engineer officer, and fought in the Mexican War (1846). On the outbreak of Civil War (1861), LINCOLN offered him a command, but his sympathies were Southern and he took command of the Confederate Army of North Virginia. He won a number of battles in 1863, but while advancing to invade Northern territory across the Potomac river, was defeated by Meade at Gettysburg. His subsequent defeat by GRANT at Appomattox in 1865 ended the war.

Lee, Tsung-Dao (born 1926) Chinese-American physicist and Nobel Prize winner (1957) who showed that among sub-atomic particles, the law of conservation of parity (that nature, in effect, makes no distinction between right- and left-handedness) does not always hold. For 20 years this law had seemed a basic and incontrovertible aspect of nature. But in 1956, working with Chen-Ning Yang, Lee suggested that in certain types of sub-atomic reactions, parity is *not* conserved, and this was subsequently verified by experiment.

Lee, William (16th-17th cent.) English clergyman, who in 1589 invented the first knitting machine. The device consisted of a stocking-knitting frame with an array of fixed hooks on which loops or stitches were lifted over the wool by a series of movable hooks. This is the basic action underlying all subsequent types of knitting machine.

Leech, John (1817-64) British humorous artist, whose pictorial satires on the rough designs for murals in the Houses of Parliament gave rise to the use of the word 'cartoon' to describe a comic drawing. He was among those who illustrated DICKENS's *Christmas Books* (1845) and also illustrated Surtees's *Mr Sponge's Sporting Tour* (1853) and à Beckett's *The Comic History of England* (1847). In 1841 he joined the staff of *Punch*, where he stayed until his death, producing more than 4000 drawings.

Leeuwenhoek, Anton van (1632-1723) Dutch microscopist and one of the chief pioneers of microbiology. Using a close-focus single-lens type of microscope, he was the first man to observe bacteria. He also described spermatozoa, blood corpuscles and the fine structure of muscle and skin.

Le Fanu, Sheridan (1814-73) Irish writer of supernatural tales, such as *The House by the Churchyard* (1863), *Uncle Silas* (1864) and *In a Glass Darkly* (1872).

Legendre, Adrien Marie (1752-1833) French mathematician, whose work on number theory and elliptic integrals was not properly appreciated until it received a new impulse towards the end of his life. In his study of quadratic residues, Legendre discovered the law of reciprocity much praised and used by GAUSS. He introduced the method of least squares, to calculate the paths of comets.

Léger, Fernand (1881-1955) French Cubist artist, a friend of PICASSO and BRAQUE. After the First World War, he began to incorporate simplified mechanical and human forms into his paintings, which reflected his belief that painting's function was essentially that of mural decoration. His proletarian sympathies are apparent in the *Leisures* series of his later years – paintings of cyclists, bathers and circuses.

Lehár, Franz (1870-1948) Hungarian military bandmaster born in the days of the Austro-Hungarian Empire, who wrote many Viennese operettas.

Leibniz, Gottfried (1646-1716) German philosopher, mathematician, historian and physicist. His main contribution to mathematics was the invention of differential calculus, although his claim to be the first to do so was disputed by NEWTON. In Leibniz's extensive philosophic work, he saw the world made up of a hierarchy of simple, self-contained and mutually mirroring units (monads), with the universe as an organic whole, its logical organization reflected in its greatest and smallest parts. He also sought to establish a universal and perfectly logical language, in which true propositions are at once seen as such, and false ones seen as absurd.

Leicester, 1st Earl of see DUDLEY, Robert

Leichhardt, Friedrich Wilhelm Ludwig (1813-48) German explorer who made one crossing of Australia, and disappeared on a second. After landing at Sydney (1842), he walked alone 600 miles north to Moreton Bay, Brisbane, then led a seven-man expedition some 2000 miles northwest across the continent to Port Essington near Darwin. Leichhardt vanished on the Cogoon River while leading a nine-man party in an attempted east-west crossing from Moreton Bay to Perth.

Lely, Sir Peter (1618-80) German-born Dutch artist, who was important in the development of English portraiture between van DYCK and GAINSBOROUGH. He arrived in England from Holland in the mid-1640s and by 1661 had become principal painter to CHARLES II. He was immensely productive throughout the Commonwealth and Restoration periods, and much of his work emulates the refinement of van Dyck's portraits.

Lemaître, Frédérick (1800-76) French tragedian and romantic figure of the 19th-century stage. He graduated from melodrama into the great tragic roles of classical drama.

Lemercier, Jacques (1585-1654) French architect best known today as the designer of the town of Richelieu, built for Cardinal RICHELIEU in 1631. Lemercier, who was influenced by the Italian mannerist style, was also patronized by Louis XIII. In Paris existing buildings by him include part of the Louvre Pavillon de l'Horloge, The Sorbonne and the dome of the Val-de-Grâce Church.

Le Nain, Louis (c. 1593-1648) French genre painter of the 17th century. The peasants in his rural scenes are notable for their contemplative dignity. His two brothers, Antoine and Mathieu, were also painters and worked in a similar vein.

Lenin, Vladimir Ilyich (1870-1924) Architect and leader of the Bolshevik revolution which created the USSR. Lenin became a revolutionary at 16 when his elder brother was hanged for involvement in a plot to assassinate the Tsar. He left Russia in 1900, living first in Germany, then Brussels, Paris and London, writing pamphlets developing Marxism, and editing *Iskra* (Spark), the Russian Social Democrat newspaper-in-exile. He emerged as left-wing leader of the Party when, at its congress in London in 1903, a vote on the composition of the paper's editorial board gave his group a majority (*bolsheviki*, members of the majority). In the revolution of 1905, Lenin returned to St Petersburg, but was again forced into exile, where he continued to prepare for the revolution. He returned to Russia following the March Revolution of 1917; attempting to take it over, he was forced to take refuge in Finland in July, but returned in October, organized the Boshevik *coup d'état* and seized power from the KERENSKY administration. He set up, as government, the Council of People's Commissars, nationalized the banks and the means of production, distribution and exchange, redistributed the land to the peasants and withdrew Russia from the war by signing the treaty of Brest-Litovsk. Meanwhile there was civil war, in which TROTSKY emerged as creator of the Red Army, on half a dozen fronts, and the strain of this fighting, combined with socialization of the whole country, caused the economy to collapse (1920). To restore it, the New Economic Policy – allowing a limited measure of capitalist enterprise – was introduced, to be abolished later by STALIN. Wounded in an attempt on his life by an anti-Bolshevik 'Social Revolutionary' in 1923, Lenin's health broke down and he died early the following year.

Lenz, Heinrich Friedrich Emil (1804-65) Russian physicist who formulated a law giving the direction of an induced electric current. In 1834 he summarized ideas on electrical induction in what is now called Lenz's law, which states that the direction of a current induced in a circuit by moving it in a magnetic field produces an effect tending to oppose the circuit's motion.

León, Luis de (1527-91) Spanish humanist, author and lyric poet, whose chief prose works are *Christ's Names* (1583-5), a treatise on the different names given to CHRIST in the scriptures, and *The Perfect Wife* (1583). His lyric poems celebrate the wonder of the universe. An Augustinian friar and professor of theology at Salamanca, he translated the Psalms, Proverbs, Job and the Song of Songs into Spanish, and was imprisoned by the Inquisition.

Leonardo da Vinci (1452-1519) Greatest figure of the Italian Renaissance. His significance as an artist lies in his scientific analysis of natural phenomena and the preparatory studies for his paintings, throughout which he rejects the traditional schematic depiction of matter such as rocks or the texture of clothing or drapery. This objective approach is found in the two versions of *Madonna of the Rocks*. Leonardo made further advances in multi-figure compositions based on geometrical principles: the central figures of *Adoration of the Kings* (1481) form a pyramidal group within a space constructed according to a mathematical perspective. He also broke away from the traditional portrait: the *Mona Lisa* (*c*. 1500-4) is an example of the half-length portrait in which the hands are exploited to complement the facial expression. Leonardo's most historically influential work, in High Renaissance style, is the *Last Supper* (*c*. 1497), a mural in the Sta Maria delle Grazie monastery, which was the first painting to examine systematically the attitudes and gestures of the subjects, and to analyse the psychological relationships between them. The *Battle of Anghiari* (*c*. 1503-5) is another important, though incomplete, work. As a scientist, his achievements are equally considerable, though his influence is limited since the bulk of his notebooks and drawings were not published until the 19th century. Written, with exceptions, in the last 30 years of his life, they reveal his true nature – that of a scientist who trusts nothing. His art reflects the empirical basis of his thought and his studies of nature can be seen as a fusion of imagination and science based upon observation and experiment.

Leonidas I (5th cent. BC) King of Sparta who was killed with all his 300 men in an attempt to hold the pass of Thermopylae against XERXES I's Persian army.

Leonov, Leonid Maksimovich (born 1899) Russian novelist and dramatist, author of *The Thief* (1927), which describes the degeneration and eventual redemption of a Red Army officer during the New Economic Plan period. His other works include *The Badgers* (1924), a novel about the early years of the Revolution; a carefully constructed, psychologically penetrating play, *Invasion* (1924) and *Tuatamur* (1924), a prose poem.

Leopardi, Giacomo (1798-1837) Italian lyric poet and scholar. An invalid almost from childhood, his studies convinced him that it was man's destiny to be unhappy. The best of his poems appear in *Centi* (1831), which includes 'All' Italia', the patriotic ode which first brought Leopardi to public notice. For feeling, musicality and simple diction, it is one of the finest books of poetry in Italian literature. Leopardi also wrote a commentary on PETRARCH's *Book of Lyrics* and several important philosophical works, notably the prose dialogues, *Philosophical Studies* (1924).

Leopold III (born 1901) King of the Belgians (1934-51) whose reign was marred by tragedy when his queen, Astrid, was killed in an automobile crash in 1935. Leopold was taken prisoner during the German invasion of 1940 and never ruled again. Shortly after his return to Belgium in 1950, Leopold abdicated in favour of his son, Prince BAUDOUIN.

Lepsius, Karl Richard (1810-84) German archaeologist who put Egyptology on a scientific basis. Spurning the tomb-robber methods of predecessors such as Belzoni, Lepsius made extensive drawings and plans of his discoveries on his major expedition (1842-5) and published his findings in the 12-volume *Monuments of Egypt and Ethiopia* (1849-59).

Lermontov, Mikhail Yurevich (1814-41) Russian Romantic poet, dramatist and author of the novel *A Hero of our Times* (1840). His *Masquerade* (1835) is one of the masterpieces of the Russian theatre. Lermontov achieved poetic fame with 'Death of a Poet', a poem which castigated court society for its ill-treatment of PUSHKIN. For this, Lermontov was banished to the Caucasus but later pardoned. He was a major influence on Russian writers, including TOLSTOY and CHEKHOV. Lermontov was killed in a duel.

Lescot, Pierre (c. 1510-78) French architect whose work reflects the change of style brought about by the Italian Renaissance. Lescot's work can best be appreciated today in the wings he built for the Louvre, with the sculptor GOUJON.

Leskov, Nikolai Semyonovich (1831-95) Russian novelist whose finest work, *Cathedral Folk* (1872), is a combination of passion, humour

Drawings of an ornithopter, a wing-flapping flying machine, by Leonardo, inventive genius and master artist

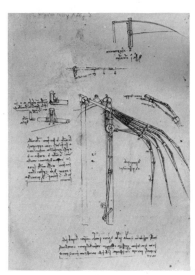

and fantasy, loosely formed but written in a rich, varied language. He came to fame in the 1860s with *No Way Out* and *At Daggers Drawn*, which were seen by some as reactionary attacks on the progressive political movements of the day.

Lesseps, Vicomte Ferdinand Marie de (1805-94) French diplomat and promoter of the Suez Canal. He first had the idea of a canal to link the Red Sea and the Mediterranean in 1832, but he did not gain the initial concession until 1854. Digging began in 1859, using 30,000 Egyptian forced labourers, who, for political reasons, were withdrawn in 1863. The work was finished with mechanical equipment from Europe. The canal was opened by the Empress Eugénie in November 1869. In 1879, de Lesseps headed a French company which began work on the Panama Canal, which he had to abandon nine years later, owing to political and financial troubles.

Lessing, Doris (born 1919) English novelist, whose work concentrates on the difference in attitude of two generations, and on social and political reform. Much of her writing is set in Africa, where she was brought up. Her series of novels with Martha Quest as the heroine (1952-8) is strongly autobiographical. *In Pursuit of the English* (1960) describes her early days in London, and *The Golden Notebook* (1962) examines her central themes in a number of variations.

Lessing, Gotthold Ephraim (1729-81) German playright and dramatic theorist. His first success was a naturalistic tragedy of middle-class life, *Miss Sarah Sampson*, but his real quality emerged in comedy of intrigue, *Minna von Barnheim* (1767). While *dramaturg* (literary reader-manager) of the Hamburg Theatre, he wrote 'Dramatic Theory of Hamburg', a study which draws heavily on ARISTOTLE.

Lethaby, William Richard (1857-1931) English architect, whose restrained but lively style, exemplified by All Saints' Church, Brockhampton, Hertfordshire (1901-2), illustrates an emphasis upon materials and direct knowledge of the skills of production.

Lettsom, John (1744-1813) English physician, who helped to found the Medical Society of London (1773), the Royal Humane Society (1774) and a system of dispensaries enabling poor patients to be treated throughout London.

Le Vau, Louis (1612-70) French architect who trained in Paris as a master mason. He became a successful architect and head of the vast body of artisans who produced monuments for LOUIS XIV. He was also responsible for the Château of Vaux-le-Vicomte, the sumptuousness of which may have led to the downfall of its owner, Fouquet, and also for the king's château at Versailles. His gift for the grandiloquent was encouraged to the full by Louis XIV, though his work at Versailles is marred by later alterations.

Le Verrier, Urbain (1811-77) French astronomer, joint discoverer (with John Couch ADAMS) of the planet Neptune. Like Adams, he realized that anomalies in the orbit of Uranus could be due only to the gravitational influence of a hitherto undiscovered planet, but he was luckier than Adams in that notice was taken of his theory, which was proved correct by the Berlin Observatory in 1846.

Levi, Carlo (born 1902) Italian novelist and painter who exposed the plight of southern Italy in his deeply moving *Christ Stopped at Eboli* (1945), a portrayal of the misery of the peasants of Gagliano. He has since returned to a similar theme in another novel *Words are Stones* (1955).

Levi-Civita, Tullio (1873-1941) Italian mathematician, who, with his one-time teacher RICCI, developed absolute differential calculus (tensor analysis), which has many applications in relativity and general unified field theory.

Lévi-Strauss, Claude (born 1908) Belgian anthropologist who in his best-known book, *A World on the Wane* (1955), explains his view that, ideally, an ethnologist should only analyse the differences between himself and the people he is studying; he should not condemn or try to change them. His writings include *Elementary Structure of Kinship* (1949), a study of human kinship practices, *Totemism Today* (1962), a study of preliterate classification systems, *The Savage Mind* (1962), which contains an attack on SARTRE's existentialist view of history and progress, and *Le Cru et Le Cruit* (1964), in which Lévi-Strauss discusses the significance of cooking and the things people eat. He has become established as a leader in European structuralist thought.

Levni (18th cent.) Turkish painter who reinterpreted 17th-century Persian style. His most famous work is a series of paintings of elegant, fashionable women.

Lévy-Bruhl, Lucien (1857-1939) French philosopher who described

the psychology of primitive societies in *Les Fonctions mentales dans les sociétés inféríeures* (1910), and propounded his view that primitive thought was 'pre-logical', differing in nature from that of civilized societies. From DURKHEIM, he took the concept of 'group ideas', which led him to stress the formative influence of tradition and the psychology of the society rather than the individual.

Lewin, Kurt (1890-1947) American social psychologist of German origin who applied the *Gestalt* theories of KÖHLER to the study of groups. He devised numerous ingenious experiments to test and measure various kinds of group activity, making studies of authority, social influence, frustration and regression, memory in real-life situations and motivation to complete or substitute tasks. Lewin's descriptions are in terms of field theory, i.e. a system of pressures operating on personality in a perceived life-space. They provide valuable insight into group behaviour and indicate how it may be modified.

Lewis, Clive Staples (1898-1963) British scholar, critic and author, best known for his novels on religious and moral themes, including *The Screwtape Letters* (1942). He also wrote children's books and critical works, and was Professor of Medieval and Renaissance English at Cambridge University from 1954 until his death.

Lewis, John Llewellyn (1880-1969) American labour leader who helped found the AFL-CIO, presided over the stormy attempts to unionize the automobile and steel industries, and headed the United Mine Workers Union for 40 years (1920-60). Lewis's controversial calling of miners' strikes during the Second World War was largely responsible for the passage of the Taft-Hartley Act (1947) which curtailed union power.

Lewis, Meriwether (1774-1809) American explorer who, with William CLARK, commanded the expedition that first crossed America from St Louis to the Pacific (1804-6). The expedition sought to find out whether the Gulf of Mexico and the Pacific

De Lesseps's Suez Canal toward the end of the 19th century. In the foreground is one of the dredgers constantly in use to keep sufficient depth of water beneath the keels of the larger ships. The steamer retains the masts and yards of the sailing ship era

were linked by river systems, and if they were not, to pioneer a route across the Rockies. The expedition left St Louis, probed up the Mississippi, made the first exploration of the Missouri (discovered by Marquette and Joliet) from its headwaters to its confluence with the Mississippi, struck west across the Rocky Mountains, then followed the Snake and Columbia Rivers to the Pacific.

Lewis, Oscar (born 1914) American anthropologist who is famous for his first-hand accounts of the sociology of poverty, based on conversations with the poor.

Lewis, Percy Wyndham (1884-1957) American-born English painter, novelist and critic, who was a founder of Vorticism, a cultural movement that believed in hard, clear images and sharply defined patterns. His own writing is vigorous, as in the ironic novel *The Apes of God* (1930), an attack on cultural life in the 1920s. His major work, a trilogy, *The Human Age* (1928-55), depicts humanity outside heaven, awaiting the final examination.

Lewis, Sinclair (1885-1951) American novelist, who wrote satirical novels about the banality and complacency of small-town life. His first novel, *Main Street* (1920), was a great success. *Babbitt* (1922) attacked the stupidities of the city businessman, and *Elmer Gantry* (1927) exposed the world of religious hucksters. He was the first American author to win a Nobel Prize (1930).

Leyden, Lucas van (1494-1533) Netherlandish graphic artist who is best known for his numerous wood and copper-plate engravings, of which the first were produced when he was only 13. Many of his prints, which are mainly of religious subjects, are influenced by DÜRER, but his larger engravings are original and characterized by exceptionally precise draughtsmanship.

Lhote, Henri (born 1903) French archaeologist whose excavations shed dramatic light on the prehistory of the Sahara Desert. Encouraged by explorers' finds of Saharan rock pictures, he discovered, in 1956, a wealth of rock paintings and engravings, depicting giant human shapes, herdsmen, charioteers, hunting scenes and wild animals in the Tibesti Mountains, 900 miles southeast of Algiers. Dating from before 3500 BC to the time of Christ, they establish the former fertility of what is now an immense desert.

Libby, Willard Frank (born 1908) American chemist whose method of radio-carbon dating enables archaeologists to assess the age of plant and animal remains up to 70,000 years old. In 1947, he discovered it is possible to determine the age of these remains by measuring the amount of 'decay' that has taken place in the carbon-14 – a radioactive form of carbon atom present in all organic matter. A scientist can, therefore, measure the radioactive emissions of a processed organic specimen with a Geiger counter, and determine its approximate age. This procedure has proved invaluable for dating archaeological remains, most famously in the case of the Dead Sea Scrolls, for which work Libby was awarded the Nobel Prize for Chemistry (1960).

Li Ch'eng (10th cent.) Chinese landscape painter of the late Five Dynasties period, whose desolate snow and mountain scenes were forerunners of the 'Monumental' style of the Sung period.

Li-chi (born 1896) Chinese archaeologist, whose excavations in Honan province revealed the birthplace of Chinese civilization. At Anyang, between 1928 and 1937, he found richly furnished tombs, and the palaces of rulers who had flourished c. 1400-1100 BC. Inscriptions on bones, geometrically shaped bronze vessels, earthenware similar to porcelain, and silk articles, prove the existence of China's early Shang dynasty.

Lichtenstein, Roy (born 1923) American Pop artist who makes use of the cartoon and comic strip to which he gives new and critical emphasis through subtle alterations of perspective and context.

Lie, Jonas (1833-1908) Norwegian naturalistic novelist, whose studies of Norwegian middle-class life have earned him the title of 'the poet of the home'. *The Pilot and his Wife* (1874) and *The Commodore's Daughters* (1886) were notable examples of his 'middle-class interiors'. Lie's most outspoken social novel was *One of Life's Slaves* (1883).

Lie, Marius Sophus (1842-99) Norwegian mathematician, who carried out work on differential equations, developing new methods using his theory of continuous transformation groups. He also worked on algebraic invariants.

Lie, Trygve Halvdan (1896-1968) Norwegian, the first Secretary-General of the United Nations (1946-53), who established the executive, rather than the administrative role for himself and his successors in office. As Foreign Minister of the exiled Norwegian government (1941-6), he was instrumental in saving the Norwegian fleet for the Allies. His most important achievement at the UN was to establish the guide-lines and the authority of the Secretary-General's position from 1946-53. During a period of Soviet boycott of the UN, it was Lie who recommended, in 1950, that a UN force should be sent to support South Korea, with the result that Russia began to recognize the significance of the UN organization.

Lieber, Francis (1800-72) American political philosopher, born in Germany, who codified the laws of war. His code of military regulations for the conduct of federal troops in the Civil War, *Instructions for the Government of the Armies of the United States in the Field* (1863), became the basis of the 1907 Hague Convention, and thus a part of international law.

Liebknecht, Karl (1871-1919) German social democratic revolutionary, who was murdered with Rosa LUXEMBURG. As a member of the Reichstag from 1912-16, he was an

Apostle of Pop art, Roy Lichtenstein in front of one of his works, with its giant strip-cartoon theme

outspoken opponent of militarism, and was imprisoned for two years during the First World War. After the armistice, he and Rosa Luxemburg started what was known as the Spartacist Revolution in January 1919. Both were arrested and murdered.

Lilburne, John (c. 1615-57) English republican agitator and champion of democratic rights. He was whipped, pilloried and imprisoned (1637-40) for preaching and publishing pamphlets against CHARLES I's autocratic rule, and fought Charles's Royalists as a lieutenant-colonel in the Parliamentarian army. He resigned (1645) to help lead the Levellers, a radical movement so-called because (according to their critics) they sought to 'level' men's estates. Opposing CROMWELL's government as being too aristocratic, Lilburne urged democracy based on manhood suffrage, and law reform. He was repeatedly imprisoned and once banished.

Lilienthal, Otto (1848-96) German pioneer of heavier-than-air flight. From 1881 Lilienthal made more than a thousand flights in gliders of his own design. He showed the importance of having a curved aerofoil wing shape and of rising air currents for soaring. Lilienthal experimented with a biplane (1895) and with a small motor to flap the wings (1896).

Lilley, William (1602-81) English astrologer, author and apologist for the Parliamentary cause, notorious for his prophesies of the Plague and the Great Fire of London (1665-6). Lilley's *Christian Astrology* (1647) greatly influenced those active in the 19th-century astrological revival.

Lincoln, Abraham (1809-65) American President who led the Union (North) to victory over the Confederate states in the Civil War (1861-5). Born into a poor, illiterate family, he began working life as a storekeeper and postmaster in Illinois while studying law. Called to the Bar in 1836, he soon made his name. He ran for the state legislature and served four terms and was Representative for Illinois in Congress (1847-9). He attained national fame in 1854 when he attacked the Kansas-Nebraska Act because it denied Congress the right to interfere in the slavery dispute in the new states. He joined the Republican Party and ran for the Senate against Douglas in 1858, losing the election but gaining enormously in stature during seven great debates with Douglas, in which he declared his anti-slavery position although without adopting extreme Abolitionism. He won the Republican nomination as presidential candidate in 1860

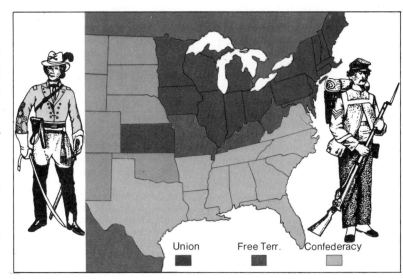

Union   Free Terr.   Confederacy

Lincoln's election in 1860 split the young republic into two camps and brought a fratricidal war between North and South

and then the election, as a result of splits in the Democratic Party. His known position on slavery led to the immediate secession of seven slavery states, including South Carolina where, against his Cabinet's advice, Lincoln insisted on maintaining and provisioning the garrison of Fort Sumter, thus precipitating the Civil War. In his words, the war was '. . . to save the Union, and not to save or destroy slavery', but he would not countenance punitive treatment of the South, calling for a conciliation 'with malice towards none, with charity for all'. He was murdered by an actor, John Wilkes BOOTH at Ford's Theatre on 14 April 1865. A careful conservative, Lincoln's integrity was his strength as it is his monument, and his oratory was among the noblest in the English language.

Lindbergh, Charles (born 1902) American aviator, the first to fly the Atlantic solo (May 1927), eight years after the first non-stop crossing by ALCOCK and Brown. The kidnap and murder of his two-year-old son in 1932 was one of the most celebrated crimes of the decade and led directly to new, anti-kidnapping legislation.

Linde, Carl von (1842-1934) German engineer who invented the first continuous process for liquefying gases. Using the JOULE-THOMSON effect, in which an expanding gas cools because of the attraction between its molecules, Linde was able to produce liquid air, nitrogen and oxygen in commercial quantities.

Lindemann, Ferdinand von (1852-1939) German mathematician, who proved that π is a transcendental number – that is, not the root of any equation with rational coefficients. This shows that the ancient problem of squaring the circle with a compass and ruler cannot be solved.

Lindsay, Vachel (1879-1931) American poet, who set out to be a folk minstrel of new America, reconciling 'culture and manliness' and 'trading rhymes for bread'. His 'General William Booth Enters into Heaven' (1913) and 'The Congo' (1914) are typical of the chanting verse he called 'the higher vaudeville'.

Ling, Per (1776-1839) Swedish educationalist, poet and playwright, also known as the originator of the Swedish system of gymnastic exercises. These stressed fixed postural positions as a basis of physical development, and were popular as a remedy for muscular and postural defects.

Linnaeus, Carolus (1707-78) Swedish botanist who devised the classification of plants and animals that is the basis of modern taxonomy (classification and systematics). Linnaeus's classification, based mainly upon external features of resemblance, used the now universal system of binomials, in which all living things are given two names: one for the genus, and one for the species. Linnaeus did not believe in evolution and admitted of no new additions or extinctions since the Creation. Despite this limitation, his numerous publications provided descriptive biology with a more precise framework than ever before.

Lin Piao (1908-71) Chinese Communist soldier-politician, who died in a mysterious air crash after his implication in a plot to oust Chairman MAO. With CHOU EN-LAI, Lin fought against the Kuomintang (Chinese Nationalist Party) of CHIANG KAI-SHEK during the civil war of the 1930s and was with Mao Tse-tung in the Long March from Kiangsi to Shensi (1934-5). After the end of the Second World War he played a major role in defeating Chiang Kai-shek in the renewed civil war (1946-8) and later commanded the Chinese 'volunteers' in the Korean War (1950-3). He was made Deputy Premier in 1954. In the following year he was admitted to the Politburo and awarded the rank of marshal. As Minister of Defence (1959) he re-established discipline in the Red Army through a programme of political indoctrination in which the *Quotations from Chairman Mao* was introduced as an army handbook. In 1965, his publication *Long Live the Victory of the People's War* declared that revolutionary war in the underdeveloped countries would lead to the encirclement of the US and western Europe. The height of Lin's power was probably reached at the ninth party congress in 1969 when he was designated as Mao's successor. However, he clashed with Mao over foreign policy and domestic economic programmes. The fourth five-year economic plan inaugurated in September 1970 was opposed by Lin and other military leaders because they considered it would divert finance from military and defence needs. It was later stated by foreign correspondents (and confirmed by the Chinese hierarchy) that Lin had died in an air crash over Mongolia whilst attempting to escape after the detection of a plot to remove Mao.

Liouville, Joseph (1809-82) French mathematician, who discovered transcendental numbers. His boundary value methods for solving differential equations are vital in mathematical physics, and in differential geometry he introduced the idea of geodesics (curves of least distance).

Lipchitz, Jacques (1891-1973) Lithuanian-born sculptor whose early work was influenced by Cubism. Shedding all exterior influences by 1925, he sought a lighter sculptural form and introducing emotional values, as in *The Couple* (1928-30). Later he became involved in the surrealists' world of the subconscious (*Figure*, 1926-30). In 1941 he went to America, where he developed a mature style in which he dwells on the mysteries of regeneration (*Blossoming*, 1941-2).

Li Po (701-62) Greatest (with TU FU) of Chinese poets. Sometime court poet to Hsuang TSUNG, he became involved in a revolt and was banished, only to be pardoned before he reached his place of exile. Li Po was romantic and irresponsible, and had a zest for life that is reflected in his poetry. His verse followed no rules – his poems were of all lengths, covering every

subject, from moving descriptions of the countryside to bacchic celebrations. Above all, his language was plain, simple and vigorous. It is said he was drowned while drunkenly attempting to embrace the moon's reflection.

Lippi, Fra Filippo (c. 1406-69) Florentine painter and monk, best known for his completion of MASACCIO's Brancacci Chapel frescoes. He also painted numerous altarpieces and fresco cycles at Prato Cathedral.

Lippmann, Walter (born 1889) American journalist noted for his commentaries on current political and economic affairs. He co-founded the journal *New Republic*, which supported Woodrow WILSON's liberalism, became assistant to the Secretary of War (1917) and prepared data for the Paris Peace Conference (1918-19). On the editorial staff of the *New York World* until 1931, he then became a special writer for the *New York Herald Tribune*. His articles have an international readership and display his shrewd grasp of world political trends.

Li Shih Min see T'AI TSUNG

Lissitzky, Eliezer (1890-1941) Russian sculptor of the Constructivist school. His importance lies in his ability to communicate with other artists influencing the De Stijl movement, Bauhaus teachers and generations of artists through his writings and lectures. In 1919, after studying engineering in Germany, Lissitzky returned to Russia, where he painted a number of Constructivist compositions (e.g. *Proun*, 1919). In 1921, he was appointed Professor at Moscow Art School, but was forced to leave the country in 1923 as a result of the Soviet government's disapproval of modern art. Some years later he returned to Russia, where he died.

Lister, Lord Joseph (1827-1912) English surgeon and pioneer of antiseptic surgery after hearing of

PASTEUR's work on putrefaction and of the disinfectant power of carbolic acid. His success was both immediate and dramatic and alerted surgeons to the importance of working in conditions as germ-free as possible. Lister's antisepsis was replaced by asepsis, which included the sterile instruments, filtered air and sterilized cap, gown and gloves of the modern operating theatre.

Lister, Martin (c. 1638-1712) British zoologist and geologist, who first put forward the idea of drawing up a geological map (1683). He was the first British conchologist.

Liszt, Franz (1811-86) Hungarian composer and pianist of humble origins who is best known for his *Hungarian Rhapsodies*, but who also invented the tone poem. As an 11-year-old vituoso pianist, Liszt was acclaimed by BEETHOVEN and, during his youth, was lionized throughout Europe, his flamboyant personality fascinating audiences. Liszt never married, but had a family by the Countess d'Agoult, one of his daughters being Cosima (wife to BÜLOW, then to WAGNER). The unstinting generosity he showed to fellow artists became a legend. In 1865 Liszt took minor orders as an abbé, but he was never able to settle and in his later years periods of hard work were punctuated by restless travelling. His tone poems include *Mazeppa* (1851, based on BYRON and HUGO) and *Hamlet* (1858); his symphonies, the *Dante Symphony* (1855-6) and the *Faust Symphony* (1857).

Littleton, Sir Thomas (c. 1407-81) English judge whose book on *Tenures* (1481-2), written in Norman French, was the first printed treatise on English law.

Littré, Emile (1801-81) French lexicographer and political philosopher who compiled, virtually alone,

With his Bible and bearers Chuma and Susi, Livingstone took Christianity deep into tropical Africa—and died there

Chuma & Susi

a *Dictionary of the French Language* (1863-72), in which he attempted to give a full historical account of French as a literary language. Littré popularized the views of his friend COMTE in numerous philosophical works, but expressed his own divergent ideas on positivism after Comte's death (1858) in *Notes of Positivist Philosophy* (1859) and *Auguste Comte and Positivist Philosophy* (1863).

Litvinov, Maxim (1876-1951) Soviet statesman, who initiated the policy of co-existence of Communism and capitalism. Having lived and married in London while exiled as a revolutionary, Litvinov became Soviet Russia's first representative in Britain during the Revolution (1917-18). From 1926 onwards, he controlled Soviet foreign policy, and was officially appointed Foreign Commissar in 1930, his policy being one of conciliation of the Western powers, strong support for the League of Nations (1934-8) and resistance to the Nazis. He was dismissed when STALIN decided to appease HITLER in May 1939, but during the Second World War, he served as Soviet Ambassador in Washington from 1941 to 1943 and was Deputy Commissar for Foreign Affairs from 1943 to 1946.

Livermore, Mary Ashton (1820-1905) American reformer and pioneer of women's suffrage. She was active in sanitary relief work during the American Civil War (1861-5) both in the field and in the northern cities, and after 1865 devoted herself to temperance reform and the cause of women's suffrage. She became a distinguished public speaker, lecturing extensively on women's suffrage.

Liverpool, Robert Banks Jenkinson, Second Earl of (1770-1828) British Prime Minister in succession to the assassinated PERCEVAL (1812). Lord Liverpool remained in office until 1827, a period as prime minister exceeded only by WALPOLE and PITT. Although premier at the time of NAPOLEON's defeat, the high taxation which followed the war did not endear him to his countrymen, and he incurred odium due to his opposition to parliamentary reform and Catholic emancipation. Britain's foreign policy during his tenure of office was capably and successfully handled by CASTLEREAGH and CANNING.

Livingstone, David (1813-73) Scottish missionary in central Africa who explored the course of the Zambesi and the sources of the Nile. He spent some 30 years mapping 30,000 square miles of Africa south of the Equator, and his published books and journals did much to open equatorial heartlands to European missionaries and

explorers, and to raise opinion against slave-trading. From 1844 on, Livingstone made many journeys, crossing the Kalahari Desert, discovering the Victoria Falls and the Zambesi. In 1858, in charge of a government expedition for exploring eastern and central Africa, Livingstone explored the Zambesi River system, and discovered Lake Nyasa. He made a last expedition to Africa, for the Royal Geographical Society, to explore the watershed between Lakes Nyasa and Tanganyika, and the sources of the Nile. He pushed from Lake Nyasa to Lake Tanganyika over unexplored country, discovered Lakes Mweru and Bangweulu, and saw the Lualaba, which he believed to be the head river of the Nile. He returned, ill, to Ujiji on Lake Tanganyika, where he was found by Henry STANLEY, with whom he later explored the northern part of Lake Tanganyika. After Stanley left, Livingstone made another search for the source of the Nile, but died during the trip.

Livy (59 BC-AD 17) Roman historian whose monumental *History from the Founding of the City* filled 142 books, 35 of which survive, covering the years down to 293 BC and from 218 to 187. Drawing on official annals and on the work of previous writers, especially POLYBIUS, Livy traced, with patriotic zeal which sometimes confused legend with fact, the rise of the Romans to power in Italy, their conquest of HANNIBAL's Carthage and their mastery of the Eastern Mediterranean. His history is a valuable record of the rise of one of the world's great civilizations.

Li Yüan (565-635) Chinese emperor known as Kao Tsu (High Progenitor), who founded the T'ang dynasty (618-907). He began as a government official under the Sui régime, skilled in handling peasant risings and Turkish barbarian incursions into Shansi. In 617, urged on by an ambitious son, he himself rebelled, with Turkish help, and seized the key Chinese city of Ch'ang-an. Under Li Yüan and his dynamic son Li Shihmin – called T'AI TSUNG (Grand Ancestor) – the T'ang dynasty began to rank with Liu Pang's former Han dynasty as a golden era in the history of Chinese culture.

Llewelyn ab Gruffydd (13th cent.) Prince of North Wales (from 1246) and champion of Welsh independence. He was forced at first into northwest Wales by Henry III, but by 1257 had regained much lost territory, securing in 1258 the allegiance of other Welsh princes and proclaiming himself Prince of Wales. Llewelyn was able to master all Wales while Henry's forces were engaged in

the Barons' War, and was recognized as its overlord by the Treaty of Shrewsbury (1265). When Llewelyn refused to recognize EDWARD I's overlordship (1276), Edward attacked and defeated him. Llewelyn was killed in a skirmish when he revolted again, and his death ended Welsh independence.

Llewelyn ab Iorwerth (1173-1240) Welsh prince of Gwynedd (North Wales) called Llewelyn the Great. He was born in exile but returned to defeat his uncle David I and claim his throne. He married the illegitimate daughter of England's king JOHN and for a time was aided by him in wars against South Wales, but in 1211 John seized all his lands. Llewelyn regained them the following year and took Shrewsbury (1215), forcing John's recognition of his rights in Magna Carta. The later years of Llewelyn's reign were comparatively peaceful.

Lloyd, Edward (17th-18th cent.) English coffee house owner, whose premises in London became the centre for marine insurance. The business begun in his shop has expanded into a company of underwriters with an international organization and a reputation for financial security.

Lloyd George, David, First Earl of Dwyfor (1863-1945) British statesman and Prime Minister. After practising as a solicitor, he was elected Liberal MP for Caernarvon (1890), representing it until his death. He first held office in 1905 as President of the Board of Trade, and became, in 1908, Chancellor of the Exchequer, in which year he put through the Old Age Pensions Act. The National Health Insurance Act followed three years later. As Chancellor (from

Lloyd George the 'Welsh wizard', right, with US President Woodrow Wilson

1908-15) his budget of 1909, which provided for super-tax and land value duties, was rejected by the Lords. The ensuing animosity between the Liberal government and the Upper House led to the Parliament Act of 1911, which curtailed the powers of the latter. As Minister for Munitions in 1915, he combined with the Conservatives in the coalition war cabinet, overthrew ASQUITH and succeeded him as Prime Minister (1916) retaining the office until 1922. Both his war leadership and his role at the Paris Peace Conference (1919) were decisive, and his government came to terms with the Irish, led by Michael COLLINS, in creating the Irish Free State. But eventually his coalition government fell, the Conservative element becoming alarmed at his aggressive attitude towards KEMAL over the Turkish threat (more apparent than real) to the Allied occupation force covering Istanbul. Out of office, Lloyd George became isolated, rejected by both Liberals and Tories. The 'Welsh Wizard' as he was known, never again held office.

Llull, Ramon (c. 1235-1315) Catalan writer, philosopher and lay missionary, the creator of literary Catalan who wrote 300 works, including novels, lyrics and the mystical prose poem *Book of the Lover and the Beloved*, in Catalan, Arabic and Latin. His encyclopedia of medieval thought, *Book of Contemplation* (1272), discussed, for the first time in Romance language, theology, philosophy, moral and scientific subjects.

Lobachevsky, Nikolai Ivanovich (1793-1856) Russian mathematician, and pioneer in the development of non-Euclidean geometry. Lobachevsky was not alone in this field, but was the first to publish his views (1829).

Lobb, William (1809-63) British gardener and plant collector, who introduced into Europe many plants from Chile and California, including the monkey-puzzle and wellingtonia trees and gloxinia.

Lobengula (1833-94) Matabele king, who led his tribe in the Matabele War. In 1888, he concluded a treaty with Britain, accepting her protection, and later, in the same year, ceded to RHODES exclusive mining rights in Matabeleland and Mashonaland, which enabled Rhodes's British South Africa Company to colonize and develop the region. Lobengula proved antagonistic to European penetration of his country on this scale and in 1893 led his tribe to war. He was driven from his capital, Bulawayo, and defeated by the forces of Rhodes's Company. He died in hiding.

Locke, John (1632-1704) English philosopher whose theory of knowledge greatly influenced the development of the British empiricist tradition. In *Essay Concerning Human Understanding* (1690), he discounted philosophical speculation as a source of knowledge, stating that this must proceed from experience, as in scientific method. The philosopher's task was to examine the scope and nature of understanding. Above all a philosopher of common sense, Locke argued against absolutism in politics, his covert target being the Stuart monarchy, but his insistence on tolerance excluded Catholicism. He distrusted religious and political fanaticism (or enthusiasm, as it was called), seeing political power as sanctioned by social contract, a view that later influenced ROUSSEAU.

Lockhart, John (1794-1854) Scottish essayist, editor and biographer, who was an important contributor to *Blackwood's Magazine* and one of the early admirers of WORDSWORTH and COLERIDGE. He edited (1825-53) the *Quarterly Review* and wrote a famous biography of his father-in-law, *Life of Scott* (1837-8).

Lockyer, Sir Joseph Norman (1836-1920) British astronomer who discovered the element helium. Lockyer was a pioneer of the study of the Sun's spectrum. In 1868 he developed a technique for examining prominences at the edge of the Sun, and attributed a portion of the spectrum to a new element which he named helium, 40 years before helium was discovered on Earth.

Loeb, Jacques (1859-1924) American biologist of German origin who performed experimental work on the chemical processes of living organisms and showed that both plants and simple animals respond in a similar fashion to such stimuli as light and gravity.

Loewi, Otto (1873-1961) German physician who with Sir Henry DALE first proved that chemicals are involved in the transmission of nerve impulses at the nerve-muscle junctions. For this they shared a Nobel Prize in 1936.

Loisy, Alfred Firmin (1857-1940) French theologian, one of the foremost biblical scholars of his time. His application of modern historical criticism to the Gospels, in such works as *L'Evangile et l'Eglise* (1902), led to his condemnation (by Pius X in the papal encyclical *Pascendi Gregis*, 1907) as a modernist. As a result of the encyclical, Loisy was excommunicated from the Roman Catholic Church.

Lombroso, Cesare (1836-1909) Italian criminologist, who combined the evolutionary ideas of DARWIN with the pseudo-science of phrenology. He believed that criminals are distinguished from non-criminals by certain peculiarities; that criminals are biological throwbacks to earlier stages of evolution or are degenerates who have ceased to evolve progressively. Although his theories are now discredited, his approach encouraged the more humane treatment of criminals by presenting them as 'patients'.

Lomonosov, Mikhail (1711-65) Russian poet, grammarian, and scientist, called the founder of Russian literature because he reformed the Russian language to produce a workable literary language. In his *Russian Grammar* and *Rhetoric*, he worked out a compromise between Church Slavonic, with its complicated syntax, and contemporary spoken Russian. Throughout his career he wrote verse, which influenced later Russian poetry. Lomonosov was appointed Professor of Chemistry at St Petersburg, and became a secretary of state, in 1764.

London, Jack (1876-1916) American short-story writer and novelist, best known for vivid adventure stories of the wilderness. In 1897 he joined the Klondike gold-rush, the scene for his first book of stories, *Son of the Wolf* (1900). His other works include adventures such as *The Call of the Wild* (1903) and *White Fang* (1906), and also *The Iron Heel* (1907), a prophetic novel of life in a totalitarian state. Fame and wealth led to alcoholism, despair and death.

Long, Crawford (1815-78) American surgeon, who was the first doctor to use ether as an anaesthetic.

Long, Huey Pierce (1893-1935) American politician and lawyer whose demagoguery and 'police state' governorship of Louisiana contrasted with a populist social programme of public works, free hospitalization and free school books. A thorn in the flesh of the first ROOSEVELT administration, he was assassinated by the son of a political opponent at Baton Rouge, Louisiana.

Longden, John (born 1907) British-born American who became the world's most successful jockey. Between 1927 and 1966, he won 6032 out of more than 30,000 races, beating the previous record set by Gordon RICHARDS.

Longfellow, Henry Wadsworth (1807-82) American poet and scholar, best known for 'Hiawatha' (1855), a long poem of American Indian life. Longfellow was a prolific poet, and wrote many volumes of Romantic verse, as well as essays, philosophical discourses and translations. He was Professor of Modern Languages at Harvard University, and in 1842 he visited London as the guest of DICKENS.

Longinus (1st cent. AD) Greek author to whom the work *On the Sublime* is ascribed. It analyses the sublime in literature, which is traced by Longinus to five sources. The author was a discerning critic, at times refreshingly outspoken, and gifted at expressing and transmitting his own enthusiasm.

Loon, Hendrik van (1882-1944) Dutch-born American author of popular educational books, whose *The Story of Mankind* (1921) ranks with H. G. WELLS's *Outline of History* (1920) as one of the century's most popular historical digests.

Loos, Adolf (1870-1933) Austrian architect of outstanding ability in the early years of 20th-century architecture. His American Bar in Vienna employed rich materials, but he stringently refused to employ any applied decoration. His Steiner House has a façade that appears almost bleak. In 1908 he published a lecture entitled *Ornament and Crime*. His appeal to the younger generation lay in his reduction of the decorative forms of a building to a minimum so that structure and form could clearly be seen to be related.

Lopez de Ayala, Pedro (1332-1407) Spanish statesman, poet and historian, whose chronicles of the kings ruling Castile from 1350 to 1396 are the liveliest and psychologically the most perceptive histories written in medieval Castile. His translations of LIVY, BOETHIUS and BOCCACCIO make him the first Castilian humanist, but his translations of St Gregory are equally important and strongly influence his verse, notably the *Palace Poetry*, which discussed the major religious, moral and political problems of his day.

Lorca, Frederico Garcia (1898-1936) Spanish poet and dramatist, best known for his poetic works *Gypsy Songs* (1928 and 1935), based on the gypsies of Andalusia, and for his poignant collection of verse *Poet in New York* (1929), on the theme of his vision of death in modern life. *Blood Wedding* (1933) and *Yerma* (1934), both gypsy plays, and *The House of Bernarda Alba* (1936), his last play, are the most outstanding of his dramatic works. At the height of his career, he was shot by Nationalist partisans in the Spanish Civil War and buried in an unmarked grave.

Lorentz, Hendrick Antoon (1853-1928) Dutch physicist whose theories on the behaviour of swiftly moving electrons anticipated much of EINSTEIN's theory of special relativity. Lorentz was responsible for much of the modern electron theory of the interaction between matter and electromagnetic waves. In this field his work on the effect of magnetism on spectral lines won him the Nobel Prize in 1902. One persistent difficulty of the electron theory was the experiment of MICHELSON and MORLEY, which had shown that motion through the ether was undetectable. Lorentz adapted a suggestion of FITZGERALD that fast-moving bodies might contract slightly in their direction of motion and developed it in 1903 into the general 'Lorentz transformation', which describes the behaviour of bodies in relativity theory.

Lorenz, Konrad (born 1903) Austrian psychologist. His most arresting experiments, demonstrating the process of memory imprinting in animals, show that some young creatures, deprived at birth of normal mother figures, will adopt whatever they see first (even a stone decoy) as a parent figure, and come to see themselves as members of the substitute parent's species for the rest of their lives, even seeking mates from within that species in preference to their own. He was awarded a Nobel Prize in 1973 for his work on animal behaviour.

Lorenzetti, Ambrogio (c.1300-c.1348) Sienese artist, whose most famous works are the allegorical frescoes of *Good and Bad Government* in the Palazzo Pubblico, Siena (1338-40). They depict good government in the town and country and show Siena and its environs in delightful detail. They were the first Italian paintings since Roman times in which landscape formed an integral part of the theme.

Lorenzo, Monaco (c. 1370-c. 1422) Sienese manuscript illuminator and painter of altarpieces, who was also a monk at the monastery of Sta Maria Degli Angli in Florence. His larger works, colourful and decorative, owe much to his illuminatory talents.

Lorraine, Charles de see GUISE

Lorraine, François de see GUISE

Losey, Joseph (born 1909) American film director who has worked in Britain since 1952. For a time he worked on small productions, turning banal science fiction tales such as *The Damned* (1962) into superb cinema. Critical success came with *The Servant* (1963), followed by *Accident*

(1967), since which he has become generally recognized as one of the cinema's great stylists.

Loti, Pierre (1850-1923) French author, whose romantic novels and travel books capture the atmosphere of faraway lands, especially the Middle and Far Eastern countries which he visited as an officer in the French navy. Among his best-known books are *My Brother Yves* (1883), *Iceland Fisherman* (1886), *Madame Chrysanthème* (1887) and *Disenchanted* (1906).

Lotto, Lorenzo (c. 1480-1556) Italian painter of religious subjects, frescoes, altarpieces and portraits. His paintings reflect a departure from the mainstream of Venetian art. He was, nevertheless, inevitably influenced by TITIAN, as in the Carmine altarpiece *St Nicholas of Bari* (1529), though he retained his own fluidity of style and, in his use of colour, broke away from Titian's low golden tones to a striking boldness.

Loubet, Emile (1828-1929) French statesman and successor to Faure as president of the Third Republic (1899-1906). His short administration was not uneventful, being chiefly remembered for the DREYFUS Affair. The resulting bitterness engendered by the scandal lingered on, and resulted in the separation of Church and State in 1905.

Loudon, John (1783-1843) Scottish garden designer, architect and horticultural writer who created the suburban garden style and wrote *The Encyclopedia of Gardening* (1822).

Louis VI 'The Fat' (1081-1137) Warrior king of France (1108-37), who fought for 24 years, campaigning to subdue turbulent barons, in wars against HENRY I of England and the Emperor HENRY V, and to gain control of Flanders. His military prowess made him a national hero; by ousting from power self-seeking feudal nobles, notably the Garlande family, he strengthened the central government and opened major government posts to his loyal career men.

Louis IX (1214-70) Crusader king of France (1226-70). Famed for chivalry, piety and justice, he arbitrated among Europe's discordant rulers, and championed Christendom in crusades against Egypt (1248-54), during which he was held captive in Syria for four years, and against Tunis (1270), where he died from plague. Before crusading, Louis suppressed the only rebellion of his reign (1242) by defeating the nobles and Henry III of England, who assisted them. After the Egyptian crusade he maintained peace at home, enabling French trade and culture to blossom, especially in Paris, which was made a hub of Christian philosophy.

Louis XI (1423-83) King of France (1463-83), an absolute monarch who strengthened the crown by restoring centralized royal power and ruling by decree. Louis overcame the League of Public Weal (an alliance of nobles against him) by arms, treaties, intrigue, and the timely deaths of some of its most dangerous members. He defeated in battle and killed his principal rival, CHARLES THE BOLD, so gaining Burgundy. He also acquired Anjou, Var, Maine, and Provence when the powerful Anjou family became extinct. Wily, avaricious and superstitious Louis was, none the less, one of the ablest of French kings.

Louis XIV (1638-1715) King of France for 72 years, longest-reigning European monarch, an ambitious and despotic ruler who brought immense splendour to the throne and France, but at a high price. He inherited a state strengthened and centralized by RICHELIEU and MAZARIN, and, from 1661, ran it himself through able ministers such as COLBERT. Reputedly declaring 'l'état c'est moi' ('I am the state'), Louis wielded absolute power. To assure religious and political conformity, Louis, a Catholic, persecuted Huguenots and banned 'progressive' books (by DESCARTES and others). With all the powerful nobles under his aegis at Versailles, Europe's showpiece of Baroque art and architecture, Louis was able to avoid any possible threats. As patron of RACINE, MOLIÈRE, LE BRUN and others, Louis helped to raise French arts to new heights. His ambition to make France militarily supreme over the Hapsburg domains of Spain and the Empire involved France in four major wars. His armies were brilliantly directed by LOUVOIS, TURENNE and VAUBAN, but defeats by MARLBOROUGH and Prince Eugène at Blenheim, Oudenarde and Malplaquet eclipsed France's former gains, prestige and wealth.

Louis XV (1710-74) King of France (1715-74), whose chaotic and capricious reign roused in its later stages a popular hatred which culminated in the French Revolution. After the regency of the Duke of Orleans, the ministry of the incapable Duke of Bourbon, and the death of Fleury, Louis managed the administration himself. A pleasure-loving man of little ability, he let court favourites and mistresses (notably the Comtesse DU BARRY and the Marquise DE POMPADOUR) influence the administration and rob the treasury. As a result of the Seven Years' War (1756-63) he lost Canada and India, and with them

the prestige which had made France supreme in Europe.

Louis XVI (1754-93) King of France (1774-92) who tried to redress the social injustices that had made the monarchy hated, and which abroad had aided the republican American colonists against Britain. Louis came to be influenced by his extravagant queen, MARIE ANTOINETTE, and the aristocracy, who blocked reforms intended to end widespread poverty in France. The ensuing social unrest and financial difficulties forced Louis to call the States General (1789), its first summons for 175 years, but demands by the commoners led directly to the French Revolution in 1789. The king was seized and guillotined.

Louis XVIII (1755-1824) Bourbon king of France, and brother of LOUIS XVI, who ascended the throne after the defeat of NAPOLEON. He escaped from France in 1791, going first to Brunswick and then to England, where he remained until Napoleon's defeat in 1814. At a meeting in Ghent in 1814 he conceded to TALLEYRAND a guarantee for the principal reforms accomplished by the Revolution, in return for the throne. He fled to Ghent following Napoleon's escape from Elba but returned to France after Waterloo. As king, he tried to enforce his pledge, but was unable to stand up to a reactionary parliament and the ultra-royalist influence of his brother (and successor) CHARLES X.

Louis II de Bourbon, Prince de Condé (1621-86) French general, called 'le Grand Condé' for his many victories. When only 21 he defeated Spanish troops at Rocroi (1643), France's greatest victory for a century. Campaigning deep into Germany (1643-66), often with TURENNE, he won many battles against the empire, including those at Dunkirk (1646) and Lens (1648). Opposing MAZARIN's régime, he sided with Spain against France (1651), continuing his victories until defeated by an Anglo-French army at Dunkirk (1658). The following year a Franco-Spanish peace treaty allowed him to return home to Chantilly, which he made a centre of culture.

Louis II the German (c. 804-76) King of the East Franks (843-76), regarded as the founder of Germany. He received Bavaria and nearby lands from his father, the Emperor Louis I the Pious, as his share of the empire won by his grandfather CHARLEMAGNE. On the death of their father, Louis and his brother, Charles II the Bald, defeated a third brother, who had now succeeded as the Emperor Lothair I, at Fontenoy (841), and by the Treaty of Verdun (843) Louis

became king of almost all the Carolingian lands east of the Rhine, adding a political identity to its Teutonic cultural unity.

Louis II (1506-26) King of Hungary and (as Louis I) of Bohemia (1516-26), whose death effectively ended the independence of the two kingdoms. Louis was dominated by his nobles whose factions weakened his kingdom and strengthened its powerful Hapsburg rivals. He failed to stem the Turkish advance on Hungary and died in the disastrous Battle of Mohács.

Louis, Joe (born 1914) American heavyweight boxer who became the longest-reigning world champion of any division (1937-49).

Louvois, Marquis de (1641-91) French war minister (from 1666) who, with TURENNE and VAUBAN, built up French military might for LOUIS XIV. Louvois reorganized and modernized the French army, improved soldiering conditions and planned a number of major victories achieved by the armies of Louis XIV between 1672 and 1678.

Lovecraft, Howard Phillips (1890-1937) American author of much supernatural fiction, including the *Haunter in the Dark* and *The Case of Charles Dexter Ward*, dealing with 'the cult of Cthulu', the supposed secret worship of the 'Elder Gods'. Lovecraft's theories are now part of the ideology of the San Francisco-based Church of Satan.

Lovelace, Richard (1618-c. 1657) English courtier and lyric poet, who, with Suckling, is the best-known Cavalier poet. A follower of CHARLES I, Lovelace was imprisoned and impoverished in the Civil Wars, and wrote many of his polished, slightly cynical lyrics in prison. In 1649 he published *Lucasta*, which contains his best poems.

Loveless, George (1797-1874) English farm-labourer and leader of the 'Tolpuddle Martyrs'. In 1834 Loveless and five other farm labourers of Tolpuddle, Dorset, formed a trade union to better the pay and conditions of farm workers. All five were prosecuted under an Act against administering oaths that was never intended for such use, and were convicted by a jury of farmer employers. They were condemned to seven years' transportation to New South Wales. Public indignation forced a bitterly anti-trade union Whig government to pardon and release them in 1836. Loveless returned to England but with four of his fellow 'martyrs' later emigrated to Canada.

Lovell, Sir Bernard (born 1913) English astronomer, originator and Director of the Jodrell Bank Experimental Station. Its 250-ft diameter radio telescope was completed in 1957, and remained the world's largest fully steerable radio 'dish' until 1971. Although famous for tracking lunar and space probes, the Jodrell Bank radio telescope is mostly used for basic researches into the nature of the Universe.

Low, Sir David (1891-1963) New Zealand-born political cartoonist and caricaturist, whose cartoons in the *London Evening Standard*, which appeared from the 1920s until the 1950s, were distinguished not only by their draughtsmanship but by a savage and ingenious wit.

David Low, by himself. He claimed his subjects grew to look like his cartoons

Lowell, Amy (1874-1925) American poet, one of the leaders of the 'imagist' movement, which Ezra POUND, a former moving spirit, retitled 'the Amygists'. She wrote some neat, concentrated verse in *Sword Blades and Poppy Seed* (1914), then became more expansive in a vast, ornate biography, *John Keats* (1925).

Lowell, James (1819-91) American poet, critic, editor and diplomat, whose writings increased the reputation of American literature amongst the European literary establishment. Lowell attempted to found a literary magazine, *The Pioneer*, but achieved little success. He wrote romantic poetry and literary criticism, such as *The Vision of Sir Launfal* (1848) and *A Fable for Critics* (1848), and gained a reputation as a satirist after the publication of the *Biglow Papers* (1848), social and political lampoons. In 1855 he became Professor of Modern Languages at Harvard and was the first editor of the *Atlantic Monthly*, and, from 1864, of the *North American Review*. In 1877 he was appointed United States Ambassador to Madrid, and in 1880 took up a similar appointment in London.

Lowell, Percival (1855-1916) American astronomer, who instituted the search for the planet Pluto. Lowell set up his own observatory at Flagstaff, Arizona, where he installed a 24-inch refractor to observe the planet Mars. With this instrument he charted numerous 'canals' which he thought existed on the surface of Mars, and expounded his theory of Martian habitation in *Mars and its Canals* (1906). Lowell spent a decade computing the position of the 'Planet X' he believed must lie beyond Neptune. His final figures were published in 1915, but he died 14 years before Clyde TOMBAUGH discovered Pluto.

Lowell, Robert (born 1917) American poet whose moral message derives from his intense Christianity and pacifism and is expressed in symbolic and dramatically effective language.

Lowry, Malcolm (1909-57) English writer, who drew from his experience in foreign lands and his own struggle with drink the powerful material of his novel *Under the Volcano* (1947). The stories in *Hear Us, O Lord from Heaven Thy Dwelling Place* (1961) were published posthumously.

Lowry, Thomas (1874-1936) English chemist remembered for his experiments on optical activity. Jean Biot and Louis PASTEUR had established that the polarization of light passing through what they called 'optically active' substances depended on their chemical structures. In the early 1900s, Lowry confirmed that optical activity depended on the wavelength of the light.

Loyala, Saint Ignatius (c. 1495-1556) Basque founder of the Order of Jesuits. A soldier who underwent conversion after being wounded. He attracted a large following and established his militant missionary Order in 1534.

Lubbe, Marinus van der (1910-34) Dutchman who was accused of setting fire to the Reichstag. Six days before the election of 1933, the Reichstag in Berlin was burnt down. The Nazis immediately accused the Communists of causing the fire, and a case was fabricated against van der Lubbe, who was of low intelligence. At his trial, Georgi Dimitrov, later Premier of Bulgaria, accused GOERING of starting the fire for the political purpose of providing an excuse to persecute left-wing groups. Although the evidence against van der Lubbe was inconclusive, he was executed immediately after the trial. HITLER later used the fire as a pretext for disqualifying the 81 Communist Deputies in the Reichstag.

Luce, Henry (1898-1967) American founder of the international best-selling magazines, *Time*, *Fortune* and *Life*. In 1923, Luce co-founded *Time*, a weekly news magazine which built a three million circulation by idiosyncratically written, brightly presented news and comment. Luce's later successes included the luxury monthly business magazine *Fortune* (1930) and the pictorial weekly magazine *Life* (1936), which developed world-wide sales of over seven millions. By the mid-1950s, Luce's Time-Life Inc. had become one of the biggest and richest of all private publishing concerns.

Luciano, Charles 'Lucky' (1897-1962) American racketeer who controlled New York prostitution, narcotics and 'numbers' during the 1920s and 1930s. Luciano was deported to his native Sicily in 1946, and died there, of natural causes.

Lucius Tarquinius Superbus (ruled 534-510 BC) Last of Rome's seven legendary kings, whose despotic rule ended with his being driven into exile and Rome becoming a republic.

Lucretius (c. 96-55 BC) Roman poet, author of the didactic poem 'On the Nature of Things', which gave a full account of the doctrines of EPICURUS and his school.

Ludendorff, Erich (1865-1937) German general, who, jointly with HINDENBURG, was the 'hero' of Tannenberg. In 1914, when he was a major-general, he was sent as Hindenburg's Chief-of-Staff to stop the Russian advance in Prussia. He was a soldier of no particular merit, but, like Hindenburg, received the credit for General Hoffman's handling of the battle, to which he contributed competent staff work. German success was exaggerated by Russian generals and ill-equipped Russian armies. In 1918, seeing defeat in sight, he fled to Sweden in disguise. Later, he became a Nazi

Ludwig, Karl (1816-95) German physiologist, who, in 1856, performed the first organ perfusion (the passing of blood through an organ severed from its parent body). He also invented a blood-velocity meter and a pump to separate gases from the blood.

Lu Hsun (1881-1936) Chinese author of politically significant prose works. His opposition to the established order in such books as *The True Story of Ah Q* (1921) led to the Communist Party's adoption of his works as outstanding examples of socialist realism. He translated GOGOL.

Lukács, György (1885-1971) Hungarian philosopher and literary critic, who was an outstanding figure in the history of Marxist thought. His most famous work was *History and Class Consciousness* (1923), which, under pressure from the Comintern, he renounced, but then republished 45 years later. His aesthetic theory is best expressed in *The Specific Nature of the Aesthetic* (1963). The finest exponent of Marxist literary criticism, he had an encyclopaedic knowledge of world literature, relating it to its historical and social context. Lukács never accepted the political dogmas of Soviet Communism, and frequently conflicted with the authorities during the 1940s and 1950s. He was Commissar for Culture in Béla KUN's Communist government (1919) and was appointed Minister for Culture in the government of Imre NAGY after the Hungarian revolt of 1956. Expelled to Rumania, he was allowed to return to Hungary in 1957 and was readmitted to the Communist Party ten years later.

Luke (1st cent. AD) Turkish-born Christian saint, apostle and evangelist, author of the third Gospel of the New Testament and of Acts of the Apostles, which together constitute the earliest history of the Christian Church. The most literary of the New Testament writers, his Gospel is the last of the three Synoptic Gospels and the only one to give an account of the Ascension. Based on eye-witness accounts and documents, it is thought to have been written in the last two decades of the 1st century. By tradition a physician, Luke is the patron saint of doctors and artists. He accompanied PAUL on his second missionary journey.

Lully, Jean-Baptiste (1632-87) French composer at the court of LOUIS XIV. Lully, an innovatory composer, collaborated with MOLIÈRE in writing incidental music to *Le Bourgeois Gentilhomme*, among other plays. By 1684 he had secured a total monopoly of French opera. He also wrote church music and pastorals.

Lumière, Auguste Marie Louis (1862-1954) Frenchman who, with his brother Louis Jean (1864-1948), pioneered the cinema as a form of entertainment. They developed a satisfactory camera and projector and were the first to make and show films to the general public. Inspired by EDISON's kinetoscope and the hand-painted productions (forerunners of animated films) of Paris's *Theatre Optique*, they devised a claw mechanism to pull the film a fixed distance past the projector (and camera) lens while the light was cut off by a shutter. Their choice of 16 frames (pictures) per second remained the standard filming and projection rate through all the years of silent films.

Lunacharsky, Anatoli (1875-1933) Russian dramatist, who devised the theory of Socialist Realism, attempting to bring the theatrical experience closer to everyday existence. Appointed Commissar for Education by the Bolshevik government in 1917, he evolved his theory to promote a theatre at the service of the Communist revolutionary ideal. He also attempted to foster all that was good in pre-Revolutionary dramatic traditions.

Lushington, Stephen (1782-1873) English Judge of the Consistory Court of London (1828-58) and of the Admiralty Court (1838-67) and expert in civil law. In his time there were added to the old Admiralty jurisdiction (principally concerning collisions between ships) new powers over the probate of wills and matrimonial matters, previously vested in the ecclesiastical courts.

Luther, Martin (1483-1546) German reformer, theologian and writer whose lifelong struggle against established Church doctrine permanently changed the face of Christianity. A monk and professor, Luther's insights emerged at a time of decadence in the Church, with indulgences peddled to raise papal income. His nailing of the 95 Theses to the door of Castle Church in Wittenburg (1517) precipitated the schism with the Church that led to his condemnation by the pope three years later. By this time Luther's religious reforms had won widespread public support, an approval that could even weather his unpopular stand during the Peasants' Revolt and his doctrinal break with ERASMUS. His many achievements include translating the Bible from the original tongues into contemporary German, and composing forceful tracts, hymns and catechisms. Also, Luther's various commentaries on books of the Bible place him highly among biblical scholars.

Luthuli, Albert John (1898-1967) South African nationalist leader and Zulu chieftain whose non-violent methods to oppose racism in his country won him the Nobel Peace Prize (1960). Having held various offices in Church and Mission movements, in 1952 he was elected Natal leader of the African National Congress and as such took part in a passive resistance campaign as a result of which the South African government deprived him of his chieftainship. In 1956 he was charged with treason, but the charges were withdrawn for lack of evidence. In 1959 he was banished to his farm under the Riotous Assembly Act. Following the police massacre of passively demonstrating Africans at Sharpeville (1960), Luthuli challenged the government's persecution of blacks by publicly burning the pass which all people of his race have to carry. He was fined, then arrested, but released after the African National Congress had been banned by the government.

Lutoslawski, Witold (born 1913) Polish composer who is among the leading progressives in Eastern European music. Lutoslawski moved from a style that synthesized Poland's folk music to an experimental one. Some of his work, including his *Funeral Music* for strings, has won international praise.

Lutyens, Sir Edwin Landseer (1869-1944) English architect well known for his designs of large-scale buildings, notably the splendid and formally designed Viceroy's House at New Delhi, India. His feeling for the dramatic is illustrated by Lindisfarne Castle on the exposed island in the North Sea off England, and his more informal style by the country houses at Tigbourne Court and Godalming. His architecture, which varied in style from gentle arts and crafts to Neo-classicism, was usually vigorous and sympathetic to its setting, although often at variance with the ideas of his more advanced contemporaries.

Luxemburg, Rosa (1870-1919) German socialist revolutionary and joint founder, with LIEBNECHT, of the Spartacus League. She took part in the Russian Revolution of 1905 and during the First World War was imprisoned, afterwards becoming one of Europe's leading militant revolutionaries. She was seized by a group of German officers in 1919 and was murdered while awaiting trial.

Lyautey, Louis Hubert (1854-1934) French soldier and France's greatest colonial administrator. After serving in Algeria, Madagascar and Indo-China Lyautey became Resident-General (1912-25) of the French Protectorate of Morocco. Although he was a devout Catholic, he respected Islam, and by his enlightened policy and generous and liberal understanding, helped encourage the assimilation of North Africa into metropolitan France, as a desirable alternative to French domination of the Protectorate.

Lyell, Sir Charles (1797-1875) British geologist, whose most famous work is his book *Principles of Geology*. His field work was mainly with the younger rocks, to which he gave the names (now universally accepted, with some additions and modifications), Eocene, Miocene and Pliocene to mark their geological ages. Lyell's *Principles of Geology* publicized HUTTON's theories of Uniformitarianism and Vulcanism. He was a friend of Charles DARWIN and one of the first converts to the new ideas on evolution.

Lyly, John (c. 1554-1606) English writer whose two prose books *Euphues* (1578) and *Euphues and his England*

(1580), established an ornate, lofty and sonorous English prose. Lyly's plays were comedies written in prose, a theatrical innovation.

Lyon, Mary Mason (1797-1849) American pioneer in female higher education whose Mount Holyoke female seminary gave the best available education to students of modest means.

Lysenko, Trofim (born 1898) Russian plant physiologist, who put for-

ward the view that certain strains of wheat could pass on resistance to climatic conditions. This revival of LAMARCK's 'heredity of acquired characteristics' fitted in with the ideological requirements of the official Soviet dialectical materialism, but was soon discredited and quietly dropped. Lysenko's book *Agrobiology* won the Stalin Prize 1949.

Lysias (c. 456-c. 380 BC) Greek orator, recognized as a master of pure Attic Greek. His main activity was

The cave in use
This cave is modelled upon European examples of about 25,000 years ago, the time when cave paintings appear to have become widespread

A bone cave *above and below*
Since Charles Lyell's discovery in 1833 of flint implements buried in very old geological strata, almost all our knowledge of early man has come from digging. From about 100,000 years ago caves provided man with a ready-made refuge; many of these caves still exist. Although often buried under later strata, and changed by subsequent developments, it is still possible with experience to read the message contained within them

Cave art Most of the best-preserved cave paintings are found in almost inaccessible places. They usually show hunting scenes, and their power, colour and dynamic energy can be startling

Petrification Here, a large fall of rock from the cave roof preceded the gradual growth of pendulous stalactites and upright stalagmites, caused by the slow seepage through the limestone roof of water containing dissolved minerals

River level In general, the lowest geological sediments are the oldest, but this is not always the case. In this hypothetical cave the earliest of all the deposits is a river terrace A above the cave on the hillside, indicating that the whole cave was originally submerged. At about this period insoluble limestone residue was settling on the cave floor at B. As the river cut its valley its level fell to C, leaving silt bed D. Continued deepening of the valley brought the river to its present level, leaving the cave dry and eroding the thick layer of silt at the mouth of the cave

The bear cult Carefully prepared arrangements of animal bone fragments, such as in this store compartment filled with bear skulls, are evidence of early man's hunting superstitions. Men could hardly have chosen a more dangerous opponent

A rock fall A massive collapse of the cave roof left a gaping open shaft which became gradually filled in with new layers of flowstone, earth and rock debris, and sediment

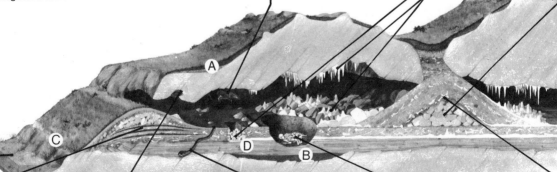

An obstructed mouth Early man sheltering in the cave mouth lit fires whose ashes gradually accumulated in three main layers. Later the cave was abandoned by man and the mouth became blocked by rock debris

A burrow in the cave Here a small animal burrowed into the cave floor, throwing up fossil bones—to die when it reached the end of its burrow

A buzzard's nest Just inside the lip of the cave mouth a bird of prey built its nest. Small rodent bones lie scattered beneath it

Human burial Early men buried their own kind in many different ways. This skeleton shows evidence of careful burial in a sleeping posture

Animal remains The cave is littered to a depth of more than a foot (0.3 m) with the debris of carnivores and the remains of animals which fell in through the hole above

writing speeches for clients to deliver in the law-courts and most of the surviving speeches are of this kind. Of particular historical interest is the speech *Against Eratosthenes*, an indictment of one of the 30 tyrants accused by Lysias of murdering his brother Polemarchus. Eloquently written, it clearly depicts the reign of terror they established over Athens.

Lysippus (4th cent. BC) Greek sculptor who was prolific in producing bronze statues of athletes and gods. His mastery of the techniques of bronze casting enabled him to produce a new system of proportion for the human body, giving a much more slender and supple effect, and to give a freer interpretation of the form.

M

MacArthur, Douglas (1880-1964) American general, Supreme Commander of occupation forces in Japan after the Second World War. As commanding general of the American armed forces in the Far East in 1941, he was forced to evacuate the Philippines when YAMASHITA captured Bataan and Corregidor in 1942. His use of combined operations and his development of the 'leap-frogging' strategy led eventually to the recapture from the Japanese of many Pacific islands by 1945. After the atomic bomb attacks on Hiroshima and Nagasaki, and the Japanese surrender, MacArthur became supreme commander of the occupation

General MacArthur, colourful leader of the American Army during the Second World War, gets the hero's ticker-tape welcome in New York

forces in Japan, where for six years he exercised almost unlimited authority, demilitarizing the country and introducing sweeping reforms, among them HIROHITO's renunciation of the Mikado's traditional divinity, and a new constitution. From Japan, MacArthur directed the United Nations forces at the outbreak of the war in Korea (1950-51), and with the entry of Communist Chinese troops in North Korea, demanded forces with which to attack Chinese territory. They were refused by President TRUMAN; MacArthur appealed directly to the American people, and was dismissed by the President to emphasize the limited purpose of US involvement in Korea in support of United Nations action. In 1952, he failed in an attempt to be nominated for the presidency.

Macaulay, Baron Thomas (1800-59) British historian and statesman, who wrote a popular history of England, his (unfinished) *History of England from the Accession of James II* (1848-61), which examined the significance of the English Revolution. At one time Secretary of War, Macaulay contributed frequently to the *Edinburgh Review* and was author of the popular *Lays of Ancient Rome*. A scholar of extensive memory and mastery of detail, his critical writings often included savage reviews of the work of others. In practical politics, he contributed towards the structure of the Civil Service.

Macbeth (11th cent.) King of Scotland (1040-57) and hero of SHAKESPEARE's play *Macbeth*. Hereditary ruler of Moray and Ross, Macbeth murdered (1040) Duncan, King of Scotland, and seized the throne. Backed by northern Scotland, he

Rob Roy Macgregor, whose deeds were both factual and fanciful

fought off southern Scottish efforts to unseat him until he was killed by Duncan's son Malcolm, who then became King Malcolm III.

MacDiarmid, Hugh (born 1892) Pen-name of Christopher Grieve, the Scottish poet, a leader of the 20th-century revival of Scottish poetry. MacDiarmid encouraged Scots poets to use 'Lallans', a language which includes English, Scottish dialect and the literary tongue of medieval poets.

Macdonald, Flora (1722-90) Scottish Jacobite supporter who helped Prince Charles Edward STUART to escape from the Hebridean island of Benbecula, where he had taken refuge after his defeat at Culloden (1746). Betrayed later by a talkative boatman, Flora was imprisoned in London until 1747.

MacDonald, James Ramsay (1866-1937) First Labour Party Prime Minister of Britain. He became an MP in 1906 and Leader of the Independent Labour Party (1911-14), but his pacifism resulted in political eclipse during the First World War. In 1922, he made a comeback as MP for Aberavon and was elected Leader of the Labour Party chiefly by the Scottish element. In 1924 the General Election gave no Party a clear majority, but the Labour Party accepted the chance to form a minority government and MacDonald became Prime Minister and Foreign Secretary. In the General Election nine months later (November 1924) right-wing sections of the press exploited the 'ZINOVIEV letter', contrived to suggest that the Labour Party was taking orders from the Russian Bolsheviks and the Labour Party was defeated. In 1929, it was returned to

power and MacDonald again became Prime Minister. Within two years, financial crisis led to the formation of a Conservative-dominated coalition government. MacDonald was reluctant to abandon his position and continued as Prime Minister until 1935.

MacDougal, William (1871-1938) British psychologist who described individual psychology in physiological terms. He studied nervous activity connected with attention, and showed, amongst other things, that mental activity is based on a hierarchy of nerve circuits.

Macgregor, Robert (1671-1734) Scottish Highland clan chief known as Rob Roy (Red Robert) because of his red beard, and subject of Sir Walter SCOTT's novel *Rob Roy*. Outlawed for debts incurred in cattle dealing, he fled to the hills and lived by robbing his creditor the Duke of Montrose, and by forcing farmers to pay him money. Popular legend idealized Rob Roy's crimes as robbing the rich to pay the poor.

Mach, Ernest (1838-1916) Austrian physicist and philosopher of science. In physics, the ratio of an object's speed to the local speed of sound is called the *Mach number*, after his name. His philosophic outlook was phenomenalist, and his critique of absolute space helped to clear the ground for the relativity theories of EINSTEIN.

Mácha, Karel Hynek (1810-36) Czech Romantic poet, whose outstanding work, *May* (1836), is a Byronic epic written with a powerful yet immensely personal lyricism inspired by the revolt of the individual against society. He also wrote romantic tales and sketches and some vivid autobiographical stories.

Machado, Antonio (1875-1939) Spanish poet, whose earliest work, *Solitudes* (1903), shows modernist characteristics. His best work, *Castilian Fields* (1912) is more austere, simple and melancholy, dealing with the landscape of Old Castile, where he was a school master, and with the problem of Spanish decadence, as seen by a reverently agnostic radical intellectual. In the Civil War, he expressed more left-wing views, partly through prose works which he attributed to the authorship of imaginary poets.

Machen, Arthur (1863-1947) Welsh writer of macabre tales, who continued the tradition of the Gothic novelists and Edgar Allan POE into the 20th century. Among his chief works are *Hieroglyphics* (1902), *The Hill of Dreams* (1907) and *The Shining Pyramid* (1924).

Machiavelli, Niccolo (1469-1527) Italian writer and political theorist, whose name has become synonymous with political despotism. A professional diplomat, he expressed in *The Prince* (1513) concepts of statecraft whereby the welfare of the state is the aim to which all rulers should strive, whatever the moral consequences of their actions.

Macintosh, Charles (1766-1843) Scottish chemist. Macintosh's most important invention (1823) resulted from experiments on the possible uses of naptha, a coal tar distillation product and a process for waterproofing fabric with a film of rubber. Two pieces of coated cloth were then bonded together to form an impermeable compound fabric. Macintosh commenced manufacture in Glasgow, and later in Manchester, where after 1834 he was partnered by HANCOCK. By 1836 waterproof coats were being called after him.

Mackenzie, Sir Alexander (c. 1755-1820) Scottish-born Canadian explorer, thought to have been the first person to cross the full breadth of North America. After several years in the fur trade Mackenzie embarked on his first voyage (1789). Travelling up to the Great Slave Lake, he continued north along the river now named after him for nearly 1000 miles, finally reaching the Arctic Ocean. Three years later, Mackenzie set out with a party of English, French, and Indian settlers in hopes of finding the Pacific. The expedition headed west along the Peace River and travelled some 500 miles to its source. Despite an accident in which they lost most of their provisions, Mackenzie's party managed to traverse the rugged Coast Range and ride down the Bella Coola River. In July 1793 Mackenzie reached the Pacific coast near Cape Menzies.

Mackenzie, Sir Compton (1883-1972) Scottish author, who, amongst numerous works, produced *Sinister Street* (1913-14), a long detailed study of a student's development into maturity. He came to notice with *Carnival* (1912), a story of theatrical life. Of his later works, the best known are the farcical novels *The Monarch of the Glen* (1941) and *Whisky Galore* (1947).

Mackenzie, Sir Morell (1837-92) British physician, and one of the founders of the science of laryngology. His two-volume *Diseases of the Throat* (1880-4) is one of the first systematic texts on the subject.

Mackinder, Sir Halford John (1861-1947) British political geographer who stressed the geopolitical implications of controlling the interiors of continents. In his paper *The Geographical Pivot of History* (1904), he drew attention to the huge historical differences between the land-locked Eurasian interior and its fringing coasts. Developing this idea, he saw the Afro-Asian landmass as a 'World Island' surrounded by islets (the 'lesser' continents). By declaring that the key to world power was control of the Eurasian interior (notably the so-called heartland area of Germany, Poland, and Russia), Mackinder unwittingly provided arguments in favour of HAUSHOFER's attempt to justify Nazi aggression which culminated in the Second World War. Mackinder later helped found the School of Geography at Oxford University.

Mackintosh, Charles Rennie (1868-1928) Scottish architect who established a style of architectural Art Nouveau that was restrained and individual. Mackintosh's major works are in Glasgow, and of these his Glasgow School of Art is the most important. The houses he designed reveal a controlled rhythm, but at the same time show a debt to traditional Scottish baronial architecture.

Mackmurdo, Arthur Heygate (1851-1942) Scottish Art Nouveau designer, outstanding for the flourishing linear rhythms of his work in graphics, furniture design and architecture, who knew and was influenced by RUSKIN and MORRIS. His own group of artist-designers, The Century Guild, produced a periodical named *The Hobby Horse*.

Maclaurin, Colin (1698-1746) Scottish mathematician, the foremost British mathematician of his day, who was the first to give a proper account of the method for distinguishing minima and maxima. Most of his writings concerned geometry and calculus.

Maclean, Donald (born 1913) English spy for the Russians, who in 1951 fled to the Soviet Union with Guy BURGESS after being secretly warned by Kim PHILBY that the Foreign Office was investigating him

MacLeish, Archibald (born 1892) American poet and playwright whose verse studies American tradition and society. His early work was influenced by POUND and ELIOT, but in *New Found Land* (1930) he discovered a more individual voice. From *Conquistador* (1932) to *The Irresponsibles* (1940) his work preached the values of American democracy.

The Magellan Strait shown on a map drawn after the Portuguese captain first made a passage through it—but before Drake proved there was open sea to the south of Tierra del Fuego

Magritte's spectral forms hover mistily over some deserted coastline

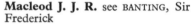

MacLennan, Hugh (born 1907) Canadian novelist, best known for *Two Solitudes* (1945), a novel which conveys the effects of the differing French and English traditions in Canada. His other volumes include *Barometer Rising* (1941) and *The Watch that Ends the Night* (1959) and *Return of the Sphinx* (1967).

Macleod J. J. R. see BANTING, Sir Frederick

MacMahon, Patrice (1808-93) French soldier, of Irish descent, who became President of France, having made his name in the Crimean War by commanding the forces which captured the Malakoff Fort in 1855 and by defeating the Austrians at Magenta (1859) in the Franco-Piedmontese war against Austria. He was appointed Governor-General of Algeria in 1864. He returned to France in 1870 and fought in the Franco-Prussian war, but was beaten and captured by the Prussians. On his release he commanded the troops which suppressed the Commune (1871), and was rewarded by being elected President of the Third Republic (1873) by a royalist Assembly. He tried to use his position to restore the monarchy, but failed despite election rigging, and in 1879 he resigned. He was made Duke of Magenta in 1850.

Macmillan, Harold (born 1894) British Conservative politician, who became Prime Minister when Anthony EDEN resigned following the Suez crisis (1956). In turn Minister of Housing, Minister of Defence and Foreign Secretary during the early

1950s, Macmillan was Chancellor of the Exchequer at the time of Eden's resignation. He worked hard to repair Anglo-US relations strained by the Suez crisis, but the closer links he established, culminating in the Nassau agreement (by which Britain gained Polaris equipment), antagonized DE GAULLE and the French. British attempts to join the Common Market were prejudiced, then vetoed by De Gaulle. Macmillan resigned in 1963 to be succeeded by DOUGLAS-HOME.

Macmillan, Kirkpatrick (1810-78) Scotsman, who in 1839 built the first ridable bicycle. Earlier machines had to be propelled by the rider with his feet and were not fitted with a brake. Macmillan effectively added a pedal system and brakes to this type of frame.

MacMurrough, Dermot (c. 1110-71) Irish King of Leinster (1126-71). In his attempts to overthrow Rory O'Connor, Last High King of Ireland (1166-75), he sailed to England for help, and gained HENRY II's permission to recruit Norman-English troops. Led by 'Strongbow' (Richard de Clare), these troops started to conquer the land for themselves, and began the Anglo-Norman occupation of Ireland.

MacNeice, Louis (1907-63) Irish poet, who was noted for the wry irony of his comments on 20th-century society. Though connected in the 1930s with AUDEN and SPENDER, his verse was less political than theirs. In his several volumes of verse, the most memorable poems are the sombre ones about the tragedy and sadness of modern life. MacNeice was also known as a broadcaster.

Macpherson, James (1736-96) Scottish poet, who wrote two popular epic poems that he presented as the work of a Gaelic writer called Ossian. *The Ossian Poems* (1762-3) were in fact his own reconstructions loosely based on certain Gaelic themes. Dr JOHNSON, among others, doubted their authenticity.

Macready, William (1793-1873) British actor-manager who was KEAN's greatest rival and was especially successful in Shakespearean tragedy. He did much to raise the standards both of plays and acting.

Maderna, Carlo (1556-1629) Italian architect whose most important commission was the remodelling of the Basilica of St Peter's, Rome, by adding a nave and façade to the Greek cross building. This and his other work greatly influenced the next generation of Roman architects.

Madero, Francisco Idalecio (1873-1913) Mexican politician and leader of the revolution against DIAZ. While opposition candidate in the presidential elections of 1910, he accused Diaz of irregularities in government, was arrested but escaped to the USA, where he issued a call for the Mexicans to revolt. He returned to Mexico during ZAPATA's revolution and, on the resignation of Diaz in 1911, became Provisional President, having won popular support through his liberal proclamations. He was elected President in November 1911 by a large majority, but found his proposed land reforms impeded by the old Diaz congress. To counter this obstruction, he appointed members of his family to various government posts. In 1913, while Zapata was still waging war in the south, a revolution broke out in Mexico City. The army deserted Madero and he was overthrown.

Madison, James (1751-1836) Fourth American President (1809-17), who was chiefly responsible with JEFFERSON for drafting the terms of the US Constitution. A Virginian, he represented the state in the Continental Congress (1780-3) and the Constitutional Convention (1787). He was Jefferson's Secretary of State (1801-9) in which office he was involved in the Louisiana Purchase (1803) and the rights of neutral states during the Napoleonic wars. He succeeded Jefferson as President. In 1812 he was re-elected, but his second term of office was marred by the Anglo-American war (1812-14), during which his leadership proved ineffective.

Maeterlinck, Maurice (1862-1949) Belgian poet-dramatist, whose play *The Blue Bird* was first staged by STANISLAVSKY at the Moscow Art Theatre. Despite its fairy-tale whimsical style it has been widely acclaimed. His other famous work, *The Life of the Bee*, is a fascinating exercise in natural history.

Magee, Carl C. (1873-1946) American inventor of the coin operated parking meter, which he patented in 1935.

Magellan, Ferdinand (c. 1480-1521) Portuguese explorer who led – for Spain – the first expedition to circumnavigate the earth, but was killed before completion of the voyage. Magellan won the backing of CHARLES V of Spain to seek a western route to the Spice Islands (The Moluccas) and set out from Spain in September 1519 with five small vessels – *Trinidad* (his flagship), *San Antonio*, *Concepción*, *Vittoria* and *Santiago*. Four ships reached the channel, now called the Magellan Strait, in October, but during the tortuous passage through it, the *San Antonio* deserted and returned to Spain. *Trinidad*, *Concepción* and *Vittoria* reached the ocean, which Magellan named the Pacific, in late November and began the long north-westerly crossing. After 98 days they discovered Samar in the Philippines, and shortly afterwards went on to Cebu, where Magellan joined in a local dispute. He and several leaders of the fleet were killed. The survivors escaped with two ships to the Spice Islands. Only the *Vittoria*, commanded by Sebastian del CANO, completed the circumnavigation of the globe.

Magnasco, Alessandro (1677-1749) Genoese painter of macabre and phantasmagoric subjects. His highly individual manner – flickering light in the manner of CARAVAGGIO, attenuated figures, and nervous brushwork – influenced GUARDI and the Riccis. His interiors and melodramatic landscapes often include funerals, torturings, emaciated hermits, bandits and penitent monks.

Magnus II, Eriksson (1316-74) King of Sweden (1319-65) who became Magnus VII of Norway (1319-43), and who ruled the first union of the two kingdoms.

Magritte, René (1898-1967) Belgian Surrealist painter, whose art is unlike that of other pioneers of the movement. He did not rely on automatic or unconscious techniques, but on the unexpected juxtaposition of recognizable images, painted with careful precision but placed in unlikely situations. By these means, and by contrasts of scale, he called attention to unrealized poetic aspects of such images, he himself regarding his painting as an instrument of knowledge.

Mahan, Alfred (1840-1914) American admiral and naval historian, whose views contributed to the build-up of navies that preceded the First World War. He argued the case for gaining military and commercial mastery of the oceans in *The Influence of Sea Power Upon History, 1660-1783* (1890).

Mahavira (c. 6th cent. BC) Indian founder of Jainism, an offshoot of Hinduism. Jainism, fundamentally atheistic, rejects the authority of the *Vedas* and modifies the Hindu doctrine of transmigration by asserting that saintliness will achieve immortality immediately after death. The ethical code is high, based on the need to show kindness to all forms of life. The teaching is set out in the

Cave painting, Lascaux, France *c*.15,000-10,000 BC

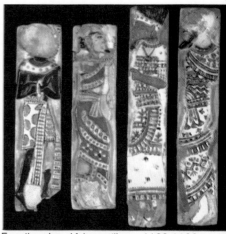

Egyptian glazed faience tiles *c*.1198-1166 BC

Romanesque fresco by Giotto *c*.1296-1304

Late Gothic triptych: 1428

Adoration of the Magi by Botticelli

Rape of the Daughters of Leucippus by Rubens *c*.1615

Across countless centuries, Man has celebrated the world around him, his gods and his beliefs, in his art. Some of these pictures—the early examples— are by anonymous craftsmen; others were painted by masters whose names have come down the centuries with their works —and who are mentioned in *Who Did What*. The talents of the long-vanished cave- man and those of modern painters such as Cézanne and Picasso have a tangible link—a concern with the immediate facts of life, the animals with whom prehistoric man lived in harmony, the tablecloth and fruit which inspired Cézanne. Between them lie the arts of old Egypt, of Byzantium and Rome, of the giants of the Renaissance, eras in which inspiration was drawn from religion and its deities and the god-like representation of rulers

The Fifer by Manet 1866

Pompeiian wall painting c.AD 65-70

Byzantine mosaic: The *Baptism of Christ* 5th cent.

c.1477

David with Goliath's Head by Caravaggio c.1606

John the Baptist by Leonardo da Vinci c.1506

Pigeon with Baby Peas by Picasso 1912

Apples and Oranges by Cézanne c.1895-1900

Augas, sacred books finally compiled in the 5th century AD. Jains believe that Mahavira is the last of 24 saints or prophets who, after achieving enlightened perfection, preached the faith to the world.

Mahler, Gustav (1860-1911) Austrian composer, the last major symphonist in the 19th-century tradition and one of the key figures in the development of 20th-century music. Mahler studied under BRUCKNER, and became one of the leading conductors of his day (chief conductor of the Vienna State Opera, 1897). He saw

Mahler was a bridge between 19th and 20th century music

this work as a means to an end which would enable him to devote time to composition. His outstanding orchestral song cycles include *Songs of a Wayfarer* (1883), and *Songs on the Death of Children* (1902), and in them, as in his nine symphonies, he extended his personal vision and sense of harmony to their limits. By the time he wrote his last major

works he was seriously ill, and eloquently communicated his sense of approaching death in his Ninth Symphony, and the song cycle *The Song of the Earth* (1911). In his vast Eighth Symphony, *The Symphony of a Thousand* (1910), Mahler wrote the first completely choral symphony.

Mailer, Norman (born 1923) American novelist whose energetic, self-centred fiction is complemented by his notorious public escapades. His most acclaimed work, *The Naked and the Dead* (1948), scrutinizes American society within the framework of a war novel, while his later writing, most notably *The Armies of the Night* (1968), is semi-journalistic in style.

Maillol, Aristide (1861-1944) French sculptor who began life as a tapestry designer and painter and took to sculpture only at the age of 40. His work was almost exclusively concerned with the female nude and after his visit to Greece in 1908 his work lost its early Romantic flavour, reminiscent of RODIN, and became more restrained in its air of classical sensitivity. Maillol's figures, apparently quietly posed but with a restrained power, have a simplicity which helps forge the link between the emotive, Romantic ideal of Rodin and the fully three-dimensional forms of modern sculpture.

Maiman, Theodore Harold (born 1927) American physicist who, in 1960, was the first to generate a laser beam, an intense, narrow beam of light. Current applications of lasers include high-speed cutting of materials, precision measurement and delicate welding (including re-attachment of the retina in the human eye) and as a guidance system for missiles.

Maimonides (1135-1204) Spanish-born Jewish religious writer and philosopher, known also as 'Rambam', author of *Mishne* (1180), a famous exposition of Jewish law. His *Guide of the Perplexed* (1190), a study of the Jewish religion in which he adopted methods of Aristotelian philosophy, had a profound influence upon Jews and Christians and was highly controversial for 200 years. He also wrote on logic, mathematics and medicine.

Maine, Sir Henry (1822-88) English jurist and historian who pioneered the study of comparative law. In his book, *Ancient Law* (1861), he explained legal ideas and their development by tracing changes in Roman, Indian and East and West European legal systems. It established the historical study of comparative jurisprudence, shaped politi-

cal theory and influenced anthropology by posing new theories on the nature of primitive law. Maine was responsible for the codification of Indian law (1863-9), and became the first Professor of Comparative Jurisprudence at Oxford (1869).

Maisonneuve, Sieur de (1612-76) French founder of Montreal, where, with a party of 50 settlers, he established a mission station in 1641.

Makarios III, Archbishop (born 1913) Ethnarch of the Orthodox Church in Cyprus and President of Cyprus. As Archbishop of Cyprus from 1950, he became deeply involved in politics as leader of the *Enosis* (Union with Greece) movement. The ambiguity of his attitude to the violent tactics of the *Enosis* militants appeared to implicate him in the terrorists' campaign, and he was deported in 1956 to the Seychelles Islands by the British Governor of Cyprus. After the settlement which followed the terrorism and civil strife of the years 1955-9, he was released and on his return to the Island, was elected provisional President of the Republic of Cyprus, having concurred in the settlement conditions, which excluded *Enosis*. He has survived several attempts to assassinate him by supporters of the *Enosis* movement.

Malamud, Bernard (born 1914) American novelist whose fiction principally deals with love, suffering, and the Jewish experience. Malamud's scope is wide, ranging from *The Natural* (1952), a mythopoetic blend of baseball lore and the Grail legend, to *The Fixer* (1966), a story of Jewish tribulations in Tsarist Russia.

Malan, Daniel François (1874-1959) Afrikaaner nationalist and prime mover of South Africa's apartheid policy. He began his career as a minister of the Dutch Reformed Church and retained a Calvinistic, crusading spirit in politics as leader of the extreme Nationalist opposition to SMUTS and HERTZOG. He was opposed to South Africa's participation in the Second World War, and in 1942 proposed that the country should withdraw from the war and separate from the British crown. His premiership (1948-54) saw the inception of republicanism and apartheid as official government policy, the Group Areas Act being the first of many aimed at dividing the country into white, black and coloured districts.

Malebranche, Nicolas (1638-1715) French philosopher whose theory of occasionalism held that God implants in the mind an appropriate idea to correspond with material events when they occur. Malebranche was a follower of DESCARTES, and was especially concerned to solve the Cartesian problem of how minds and bodies interact with one another.

Malenkov, Georgi (born 1902) Soviet soldier and politician, the only Chairman of the USSR Council of Ministers (Prime Minister) to resign voluntarily. He was a member of STALIN's War Cabinet in the Second World War and succeeded him as Chairman when Stalin died (1953). He resigned less than two years later, pleading insufficient experience and admitting responsibility for the failure of Soviet agricultural policy. He was succeeded by BULGANIN. In July 1957, he was accused with MOLOTOV and Kaganovitch of setting up an 'anti-party' group and was dismissed from the government, the party Praesidium and the Central Committee. He was demoted to the management of a hydroelectric plant in Kazakhstan until his retirement in 1963.

Malinowski, Bronislaw (1884-1942) Austrian-born social anthropologist, who revolutionized social anthropology by living for extended periods with the societies he studied, thus providing a method of research which freed the discipline from its early reliance on travellers' tales. Malinowski aimed at establishing 'a science of culture', and the four years he spent in New Guinea and the Trobriand Islands provided him with the material for thorough analysis of his assumption that a culture is an integrated whole.

Mallarmé, Stéphane (1842-98) French poet, disciple of BAUDELAIRE, and originator of the Symbolist movement, to whose members poetry was a means of reaching beyond the everyday world to a higher reality – 'To paint, not the thing, but the effect which it produces', to suggest with words the very essence of things, was a task to which he devoted his life. Mallarmé is best known for the poem L'Après-midi d'un faune (set to music by DEBUSSY), the verse drama Hérodiade and his most ambitious work, Un Coup de dés, in which he experimented with typography and the possibility of random sentence and word order on the page. After 1884, the famous Tuesday gatherings at Mallarmé's Paris apartment were frequented by many of the leading writers of the day.

Malory, Sir Thomas (15th cent.) English author who wrote Le Morte D'Arthur (1470), a prose adaptation of the French Arthurian romances. The book deals with the rise and fall of the Round Table, Arthur's court, and the search for the Holy Grail, the vessel supposed to have been used by CHRIST at the Last Supper.

Malpighi, Marcello (1628-94) Italian physiologist and microscopist who showed how blood reaches the tissues through tiny vessels (capillaries) that are too small to be seen with the naked eye. HARVEY had inferred that there must be capillaries, but had never seen them; Malpighi – the first man to use the microscope to study the fine structure of plant and animal tissues – was able to pinpoint and explain the network of tiny veins he could see on the lung surface. He extended the use of the microscope into many fields, including the study of gland cells and of the brain, and also ventured into the field of embryology.

Malraux, Andre (born 1901) French novelist, critic and politician. His novels of action reflect his dangerous way of life: as a Communist during the Chinese revolution in The Conquerors (1928); Man's Estate (1933), set in Shanghai, 1927; as an anti-Fascist and pilot in the Republican air force during the Spanish Civil War, Days of Hope (1938) and as a French Resistance fighter during the Second World War, Les Noyers de l'Altenburg (1948). After the war, he became an art critic and wrote the monumental Psychologie de l'Art (1947-50). Later, during the Fifth Republic, Malraux was appointed France's Minister for Cultural Affairs.

Malthus, Thomas Robert (1766-1834) English economist and demographer whose pessimistic An Essay on the Principle of Population (1798) argued that population increases geometrically to absorb resources which increase arithmetically, so that the masses remain at subsistence level. Numbers were checked by natural disasters, or by such deliberate acts as birth control, abortion and infanticide. As an explanation of poverty, the theory was appealing, but with increases in the standard of living and the failure of the 'checks', Malthus introduced a 'moral restraint', entailing late marriages and sexual abstinence. His theory discounted the ability of men to develop new resources for the more affluent societies, but its relevance to under-developed areas and his pioneering of demographic studies remain lasting legacies.

Mamum, al- (786-833) Arab caliph of Baghdad (813-33) and patron of the study of arts and sciences. A son of HARUN-AL-RASHID, Mamum built observatories at Baghdad and Damascus and had astronomical measurements accurately made and recorded. He founded study centres for the translation of literary, philosophical and scientific works into Arabic from Greek, Persian, Sanskrit and Syriac, and thus helped to revive the largely forgotten learning of men of genius, including EUCLID, ARCHIMEDES and ARISTOTLE.

Manby, George William (1765-1854) English army officer, who, in 1813, invented the first portable fire extinguisher after witnessing the inability of firemen to fight a fire on an upper floor of an Edinburgh building.

Manco Capac (11th cent.) Traditional founder of the Inca Dynasty of Peru, who led the Incas to Cuzco and there made them a ruling caste among the other tribes.

Mandelshtam, Osip (1891-1938) Russian poet who achieved fame with The Stone (1913) and Tristia (1922), two works steeped in Russian history. Mandelshtam rebelled against the vagueness of the Symbolist poets and joined Akhmatova's 'Acmeists'. His evocative, descriptive poetry is ranked among the finest of 20th-century Russian verse. Politically suspect, he was twice arrested and died in Siberia, travelling to a concentration camp.

Manes (c. 216-276) Persian sage and founder of Manichaeism, a complicated system of knowledge based on the conflict between the dual principles of light (goodness) and darkness (evil). The faithful are divided into two classes: the Perfect, who lead strict, ascetic lives and the Hearers, who are less severely disciplined. Manes's combination of philosophy and morality had a wide and long-lasting influence and spread to both East and West, where its ideas possibly coloured those of several Christian heretical sects, notably the Albigenses.

Manet, Edouard (1832-83) French Impressionist painter, whose Déjeuner sur l'Herbe (1863) and Olympia (1865) scandalized the official art world by their alleged indecency and their repudiation of the academic history-painting that was then fashionable. He was an artistic rebel and his early works are characterized by broad, fluid brushwork and a direct, rational treatment of his subject in which tonal contrasts are emphasized. After 1870, he painted in lighter, softer colours, bringing him closer to the Impressionists, though he refused to exhibit with them and still hankered for the official recognition of the academic salons. His compositional gifts and feeling for colour were of the highest order and are apparent in such paintings as The Balcony (1869) and The Bar at the Folies Bergères (1882).

Mann, Heinrich (1871-1950) German novelist, brother of Thomas MANN and author of *Professor Unrat* (1905), a story of the moral degradation of an apparently respectable schoolmaster, which was filmed as *The Blue Angel* (1932). *Man of Straw* (1947), was a satirical description of German society before the First World War.

Mann, Thomas (1875-1955) German novelist, author of *The Magic Mountain* (1927), an ironical analysis of contemporary civilization. *Buddenbrooks* (1901), his first important novel, and *Death in Venice* (1911) a novella, both introduce the themes with which he was concerned in many of his writings: the conflict between art and life, and the depiction of early 20th-century German society. In 1933 Mann left Germany and later settled in the United States where he became naturalized. *Doctor Faustus* (1947), the story of the life and downfall of a demonic composer, written in exile, reflects his feelings about Nazi Germany. *The Confessions of Felix Krull, Confidence Man* (1954), is a novel of Mann's old age and one of Germany's great comic novels. Its underlying theme is the author's fear that his own search for art might turn out to be a confidence trick. Mann was awarded the Nobel Prize for Literature in 1949.

Mannerheim, Baron Carl Gustaf Emil von (1867-1951) Finnish soldier-statesman of Swedish descent, who secured Finland's independence from Russia. Whilst Finland was a Russian Province he served in the Russian Imperial army, and in the Russo-Japanese war (1904-5). In 1918 he recaptured Helsinki from the Bolsheviks, who had seized it, and as Chief of State of an independent Finnish government (1919-20), commanded a Finnish army against the Russians, obtaining recognition of his country's sovereign status by the Soviet government. He was made a Marshal and President of the Defence Council. He returned to active service when the USSR invaded Finland in 1939. Following his country's defeat, he sought an alliance with Nazi Germany and took Finland into the war against the USSR in 1941.

Mannheim, Karl (1893-1947) German sociologist who pioneered the sociology of knowledge by studying the relationship between the ways people live and the intellectual life of their society, and highlighted in *Ideology and Utopia* (1940) the major problem of the age – the finding of a workable solution to social life between the extremes of a planless democracy and the totalitarian society.

Mannheim took as an established fact that society is organized into various classes, and argued from this that the individual was bound to have a different perspective of knowledge according to his class.

Mansart, François (1598-1666) French architect whose masterpiece is Maisons Lafitte, a country house outside Paris, part of which was demolished as soon as it was built because of Mansart's insistence on perfection. His un-theatrical, elegant style epitomizes the ideals of the rich bourgeoisie, for whom he mostly worked, in contrast to the flamboyant style favoured by the Court.

Mansart, Jules Hardouin (1646-1708) French architect, grand nephew to François MANSART, whose best-remembered work is probably the Galerie des Glaces, Versailles, which he built in collaboration with Lebrun; it is a masterpiece totally in sympathy with his role as court architect to LOUIS XIV, and it was at Versailles that much of his work was executed.

Mansfield, Katherine (1888-1923) Pen-name of Katherine Middleton Murry, New Zealand short-story writer, whose delicate, impressionistic stories, in the manner of CHEKHOV, describe emotions and sensations rather than narrate events. Among her principal stories were *Bliss* (1920), *The Garden Party* (1922), *The Dove's Nest* (1923) and *Something Childish* (1924). She died of tuberculosis.

Mansfield, William, 1st Earl of (1705-93) A Scot by birth who became one of England's greatest Chief Justices and is regarded as the father of Anglo-American commercial law. He became Attorney-General (1754) and Chief Justice of the Court of King's Bench (1756). He was deeply interested in commerce and, realizing that English law was not then equal to the problems arising from England's rapidly expanding trade, he developed the law relating to shipping, commercial cases and insurance by decided cases.

Mansur, al- (c. 712-75) Arab caliph who firmly established the Abbasside dynasty founded by his brother Abu-al-ABBAS. Making Baghdad his capital, he consolidated Iraq as the core of Abbasside power.

Mansur Ustad (16th-17th cents.) Court painter to JAHANGIR, Mogul Emperor of India. His earliest work appeared in manuscripts of the previous reign, but his particular talent for sympathetic and accomplished depictions of wild life caused him to specialize in this field for his nature-loving patron. It is thought that his

flower paintings, influenced by imported European herbals, were the inspiration for the type of decoration found on the Taj Mahal.

Mantegna, Andrea (c. 1431-1506) Italian Renaissance artist, whose paintings are noted for their illusions of realistic depth. This is seen in his *Scenes from the Life of Saint James* in the Eremitani Church, Padua, only part of which survived the Second World War. Mantegna left Padua in 1460 to become Court Painter to the Gonzagas at Mantua, for whom he decorated the Camera degli Sposi (1474).

Manutius, Aldus (1450-1515) Italian author and printer, who was the first to design and use italic type. The new italic first appeared on an illustration of *Letters of St Catherine of Siena* (1500), and the first italic book, the works of VIRGIL, appeared in 1501. He was a tutor to the princes of Carpi, and from them received money with which to establish his press in Venice, in 1490.

Manzoni, Alessandro Francesco (1785-1873) Italian novelist and poet, the leading figure in the Italian romantic school. He wrote the famous novel, *The Betrothed* (1825-7), in which irony, strong characterization and psychological penetration feature in a story of two star-crossed lovers in 17th-century Milan, which is not without reference to 19th-century Italy. The form of language used was to be fundamental to the emergence of a uniform, modern Italian.

Mao Tse-Tung (born 1893) Chairman of the Central Committee, Chinese Communist Party (CCP). He fought in the 1911 Revolution and after 1918, as a Marxist, he was responsible for co-ordinating policy during the period of CCP alliance with SUN YAT-SEN'S *Kuomintang* (Nationalist) party. In forming the first Chinese Peasants' Union he pursued an independent line after 1925, but his prestige in the party grew when, after the Communist wing of the *Kuomintang* broke away from the parent movement led by CHIANG KAI-SHEK, he set up the first Chinese Soviet in Kiangsi (1930). Following Communist reversals in the struggle against the *Kuomintang* (1927–37) Mao led the Long March (1934–5) to the Shensi/Yenan border, where he organized a peasant army, harrassed the nationalists and, after 1937, the Japanese. When the *Kuomintang* were finally defeated in the Civil War (1946–9) Mao became Chairman of the People's Republic of China (1949–59), a post he was forced to relinquish to Liu Shao-Ch'i after a protracted power struggle, while retaining his prestige as Chairman of the CCP. His leadership since 1949 has been marked by the growth of a personality cult centred around him, and by ideological differences with the USSR.

Marat, Jean Paul (1743-93) French revolutionary leader. He assimilated his radical politics from WILKES in England, practised medicine in Paris but in 1789, abandoned it for revolutionary journalism, calling for a dictatorship of the people in his newspaper *L'Ami du peuple*. In September 1792, as a member of the Vigilance Committee, he was responsible for the massacre of aristocrats and other suspected enemies of the Revolution imprisoned in Paris. He attached himself to the Jacobins and, with ROBESPIERRE and DANTON, attacked the more moderate Girondin party who were in a majority in the Convention in 1792 and the early part of 1793. He was assassinated, in his bath, by a young aristocrat of royalist sympathies, Charlotte CORDAY.

Marbut, Curtis Fletcher (1863-1935) American soil scientist whose classification of soils won world-wide recognition in 1927. As chief of the United States Soil Survey, he helped to develop detailed studies of soils in local areas, classified as 'soil series' and subdivided according to textural differences into 'soil types'. Marbut combined these detailed studies with GLINKA's Russian classification of major world soil groups to produce a new combined reclassification which applied equally to vast tracts of land and to a single field.

Marchand, Jean Baptiste (1863-1934) French soldier-explorer, central figure of the 'Fashoda incident' (September-November 1898). In 1897-8, he led an expedition in an 18-month march from Brazzaville in the Congo to the Sudan and occupied the small town of Fashoda, on the Upper Nile (July 1898). KITCHENER, following his victory at Omdurman, proceeded up the Nile, met Marchand and refused to recognize French claims to the region by right of prior occupation. The confrontation produced a crisis in Anglo-French relations at a time when various European powers were intent on enlarging or acquiring African territory. France subsequently withdrew her claims, due to lack of support from her principal ally, Russia, and to preoccupation with the DREYFUS case. The humiliation was partly eased by the Anglo-French entente of 1904.

Marconi, Guglielmo (1874-1937) Italian inventor who developed commercial wireless telegraphy. He began radio experiments in 1894 and within four years, the first commercial wireless message and also the first news transmissions were made when the results of the Kingstown (now Dun Laoghaire) Regatta were transmitted to a Dublin newspaper. He carried out the first international (England-France) (1899) and intercontinental (Poldhee, Cornwall, to Newfoundland, 1901) transmissions. Marconi's invention, together with the development of radio valves, saw the birth of modern radio. In 1909, Marconi shared the Nobel Prize in Physics and in later years experimented with shortwaves for military applications and long-distance wireless communication.

Marcuse, Herbert (born 1898) American sociological writer who is best known for his critique of modern western society in *One Dimensional Man* (1965). He claims that the so-called 'free' institutions and 'democratic' processes are used to limit freedom and disguise exploitation. Within this totalitarianism, only those 'outside the productive process', minorities such as students, unemployed and coloured people, have the revolutionary energy to change society.

Marey, Etienne-Jules (1830-1904) French physiologist, and inventor of the ciné camera, which used a ribbon of light-sensitive paper moving intermittently behind the camera lens. In 1888, Marey showed his first scientific films to the Académie des Sciences. It was the beginning of cinematography. He was also the first to use high-speed (1890) and time-lapse techniques respectively to slow down and speed up motion.

Margaret of Denmark (1353-1412) Danish-born queen, who, for a time, united all Scandinavia. The deaths of her father (WALDEMAR IV of Denmark, 1376) and husband (HAAKON VI of Norway, 1380) made Olaf, her son, the nominal King of Denmark, then of Norway. But it was Margaret who actually ruled, as regent, until Olaf died, then as undisputed queen. She became Queen of Sweden (1389) on the invitation of the Swedish nobles, whose king, Albert of Mecklenburg, she had helped to depose. The Union of Kalmar (1397) officially united the three kingdoms and made Margaret's grand-nephew, Eric of Pomerania, nominally their king while Margaret retained effective control. The union did not prosper, and collapsed by the 1430s.

Maria Theresa (1717-80) Archduchess of Austria, Queen of Hungary and Bohemia (1717-80) and, for 40 years, effective ruler of the Holy Roman Empire. She was made heir to the Empire by the Pragmatic Sanction of her father, the Emperor CHARLES VI, the last male Hapsburg heir. When, on his death (1740), Bavaria, France, Prussia and Spain tried to parcel her lands in the War of the Austrian Succession (1740-8), Maria Theresa rallied Hungary to her aid. She lost Silesia to Prussia, and later saw Austria humbled by the Seven Years' War (1756-63), but, with Prussia and Russia, she gained part of Poland (1772).

Marie Antoinette (1755-93) Queen of France (1774-92), daughter of MARIA THERESA, whose marriage to the Dauphin (afterwards LOUIS XVI) in 1770 was a pledge for the new Franco-Austrian alliance. Her political influence before 1789 has been much exaggerated, but her youthful irresponsibility and extravagance cost her popularity. Between 1789 and 1792 her influence was considerable and she was rightly identified with court resistance to the Revolution. Her support for foreign intervention in France helped to cause the downfall of the monarchy (September 1792) and her own execution.

Marini, Marino (1901-66) Italian sculptor, best known for his bronze figures of horses and nude riders, e.g. *Horse and Rider* (1949-50).

Marino, Gianbattista (1569-1625) Italian poet, whose virtuosity and

Marconi, in a 'Spy' cartoon. His experiments with radio were fundamental to the rapid expansion of radio telegraphy in the 20th century

stylistic innovation led to a movement in 17th-century Italian literature called 'Marinismo' after him.

Marivaux, Pierre de (1688-1763) French playwright and novelist, wrote a series of extremely successful comedies. His best plays owed much to the Italian tradition and included *The Game of Love and Chance* (1730) and *The School for Mothers* (1732). Marivaux also embarked upon two novels, *Marianne* (1731-41) and *The Poor Peasant* (1735-6), though both remained unfinished. He was an independent writer who firmly refused to imitate or idolize the great writers of antiquity, and defended the 'Moderns' in their quarrel with the 'Ancients'.

Mark, St (1st cent. AD) Cyprus-born Christian, apostle and evangelist, author of the second Gospel of the New Testament. The first of the three Synoptic Gospels to be written, it provided much of the material for those of MATTHEW and LUKE. The Egyptian Church claims Mark as its founder. His gospel presents an accurate picture of the life and ministry of CHRIST, told for the first time as a continuous narrative, so that Mark can be said to have created the gospel form. Its core is the Passion of Christ. A Jewish convert, Mark accompanied PAUL and Barnabas on their first missionary journey.

Markova, Dame Alicia (born 1910) English ballerina, inspired by PAVLOVA, who danced with DIAGHILEV's company. Her superbly delicate interpretation of romantic roles such as Giselle recalled the style of TAGLIONI and helped to kill the belief that Britain had no ballerinas of any significance.

Marlborough, 1st Duke of see CHURCHILL, John

Marlowe, Christopher (1564-93) English dramatist, who wrote *Edward II* and *The Jew of Malta* and who first successfully used blank verse in English. In all his writings he was concerned with the problem of power and its effects. His first success – and possibly his first play – was an historical spectacle, *Tamburlaine the Great* (1587), a masterpiece of rhetorical poetry. The *Tragical History of Dr Faustus* is the first treatment in English and in verse of what was to become an archetypal theme of European drama. *Edward II*, a subtle study of power and homosexual love, is the first historical play of its kind in English theatre. *The Jew of Malta* is melodrama informed with cruel comedy. As a poet, Marlowe is best represented by his lyric 'The Passionate Shepherd' and by the unfinished

'Hero and Leander'. It is believed that he acted as a spy for Queen ELIZABETH. He was murdered in a tavern brawl at the age of 29.

Marot, Clément (c. 1495-1544) French poet, in the personal employ of FRANCIS I, introducer of the elegy, epigram, eclogue and epithalamium into French poetry. His easy, elegant, witty writing – particularly the epistles, madrigals and other short pieces in which he excelled – and his imitations of classical writers such as VIRGIL, OVID and PETRARCH – substantially influenced the course of French poetry, leading it towards the Renaissance ideal.

Marryat, Frederick (1792-1848) English author of seafaring novels based on his own experiences in the Royal Navy. *Peter Simple* (1834) and *Mr Midshipman Easy* (1836) are adventures with strong characters, full of nautical detail and were praised by Joseph CONRAD.

Marshall, Alfred (1842-1924) British economist of considerable influence who defined economics as 'the study of man in the ordinary business of life'. Marshall developed, in his *Principals of Economics*, a partial equilibrium analysis to demonstrate the importance of time in determining price, value and demand, and thus related the classical cost of production theory to that of JEVONS's marginal utility. Marshall was reluctant to commit his ideas to print and it was often upwards of 20 years before they were exposed to the public. At Cambridge he succeeded in establishing economics as a discipline in its own right.

Marshall, David Saul (born 1908) Singapore politician, founder of the Labour Front Party and chief minister (1955-6). He resigned after talks broke down in London concerning the island's internal security.

Marshall, George Catlett (1880-1959) Director of the American war effort, who originated the Marshall Aid Plan. He was appointed Chief of Staff in 1939, and was responsible for the direction of American strategy throughout the Second World War and for US co-operation with the Allied armies. As TRUMAN's Secretary of State (1947-9), he evolved the Marshall Plan by which American money played a huge part in the post-war reconstruction of Europe. He was awarded the Nobel Peace Prize in 1953.

Marshall, Sir John Hubert (1876-1958) British archaeologist, who directed the excavations in India, at Mohenjo-Daro and Harappa (1921-

2), revealing the existence of the Indus Valley Civilization, which flourished from 2500 to 1500 BC.

Marshall, John (1755-1835) US judge, Secretary of State (1800) and Chief Justice from 1801. His decisions in a number of cases have since become standard authority on constitutional law.

Marshall, Thurgood (born 1908) American judge. Himself a negro, he was chief counsel for the National Association for the Advancement of Coloured People (1938-61), when his argument against racial segregation in schools in the historic *Brown v Board of Education of Topeka* case led to Earl WARREN's Supreme Court ruling of 1954 that racial segregation in public schools was unconstitutional. He was the first negro to be appointed to the Supreme Court (1967).

Martel, Charles see CHARLES MARTEL

Marti, José (1853-95) Cuban national hero, revolutionary and poet, who led the struggle for independence from Spain, and was killed in the rising. His poetry is patriotic or lyric, his style modernistic and exotic, as in *Little Ishmael* (1882) and *Free Verse* (1913). His prose works, written in New York, revolutionized and enlivened Spanish prose style.

Martial (1st cent.) Spanish-born Roman epigrammatist, author of books of mottoes, *Xenia* and *Apophoreta*, and of 12 books of epigrams. His work is marked by his intense interest in his fellow human beings, which he expresses with keen observation and cutting realism. Many of his epigrams, usually in elegiac couplets, in imitation of CATULLUS and OVID, mirror the life of his day. A satirist at heart, with strains of obsequiousness and gross obscenity, Martial was nevertheless a writer of great versatility.

Martin, Archer John Porter (born 1910) English biochemist, who, with Richard Laurence Millington Synge, in 1944 developed paper chromatography. Their discovery showed how complex mixtures such as protein molecules could be separated into their constituents (amino acids), which had been impractical by ordinary chemical methods. Martin and Synge jointly received the 1952 Nobel Prize for Chemistry for their invention of a technique which has made possible important biochemical discoveries.

Martin, Frank (born 1890) Swiss composer whose works include the *Petite Symphonie Concertante* (1945) for harpsichord, harp, piano and double string orchestra, and the oratorio *Golgotha* (1948). In his music he used a modified form of note-row technique by incorporating it into a conventional harmonic setting.

Martin du Gard, Roger (1881-1958) French novelist and dramatist. Du Gard's 11-volume work, *Les Thibault* (1922-40), is generally regarded as one of the outstanding family chronicles of this century, mirroring French society before the First World War.

Martin of Tours (c. 315-c. 397) French prelate and missionary saint who founded the first monastery in Gaul. He became Bishop of Tours in 372.

Martini, Simone (c. 1284-1344) Sienese painter who was, after GIOTTO, the most important Italian painter of his time. His early work is in DUCCIO's manner, but he became increasingly attracted to the courtly style of French Gothic art. His works are characterized by graceful, curvilinear outlines and a lyrical mood. He spent his later years at Avignon, where he is supposed to have painted a portrait of PETRARCH's 'platonic love', Laura.

Martinson, Harry (born 1904) Swedish poet, novelist and dramatist whose deep interest in science and technology expresses a growing alienation from modern industrial society. Typical of his work is 'The Songs of Aniara' (1956), a narrative poem about a space-ship which is diverted from its pre-planned route into an irreversible journey into the void. An orphan and an inveterate wanderer, Martinson draws from his own unusual and poignant experiences, which he explores and recreates both objectively and subjectively. The first of a number of self-educated writers from a proletarian background, Martinson was elected a member of the Swedish Academy in 1949.

Martinu, Bohuslav (1890-1959) Prolific Czechoslovak composer who began his professional life as a violinist. The style he adopted was Neoclassical, as shown by his *Concerto Grosso* (1938), and he did not attempt a symphony until he lived in America during the Second World War. The six symphonies that he wrote between 1942 and 1953 were among his best work, but the standard of his output was uneven.

Marvell, Andrew (1621-78) English poet and politician who is best remembered for his early verse 'To his Coy Mistress' and 'The Garden', which show the influence of DONNE. In 1657, Marvell became assistant to MILTON at the Latin Secretaryship to the Council of the Commonwealth and was later MP for Hull. He wrote several poems in praise of CROMWELL and, later, powerful satires, such as the *Last Instructions to a Painter* (1667), on CHARLES II's policies.

Marx, 'Groucho' (born 1890) American vaudeville comedian and humourist, who, with his brothers Harpo and Chico, formed one of the most famous theatre and cinema comedy acts. The team, which originally included two other brothers, Zeppo and Gummo, achieved a huge success with a fast, wild and disruptive approach to comedy, and no institution was safe from their attacks.

Marx, Karl (1818-83) German philosopher and theorist of socialism, author of the revolutionary pamphlet *The Communist Manifesto* (1848), which he wrote with ENGELS shortly before the revolutions of 1848, and of *Das Kapital* (1867). The official doctrine of the Soviet Union is based on his ideas. Marx's theory, much influenced by Hegelian philosophy, turns the latter upside down and makes matter rather than spirit the primary stuff of the world. His social and political influence on the 20th century has been immense.

Mary I, Tudor (1516-58) Queen of England and Ireland (1553-8). The daughter of HENRY VIII and CATHERINE OF ARAGON, she was nicknamed 'Bloody Mary' for the brutality of the attempts to crush Protestantism during her reign. She succeeded her half-brother, Edward VI, after Lady Jane GREY's brief reign. Having reversed Edward's Protestant reforms, she married the Catholic PHILIP II of Spain and began a purge of those opposed to Catholicism, in which some 300 'heretics' were killed, including such leading churchmen as Thomas CRANMER, Hugh LATIMER and Nicholas RIDLEY. During Mary's reign, France seized Calais, England's last enclave on the mainland of Europe.

Mary Stuart, Queen of Scots (1542-87) Successor to her father JAMES V as ruler of Scotland (1542-67), Queen of France (1559-60) as wife of Francis II, and next in line to the English throne after ELIZABETH I. Mary was brought up in France and widowed at 18. She returned to govern Scotland, which had become mainly Protestant, in 1661, and, as a convinced Catholic, tried to end Protestant persecution of those of her faith. She thus made powerful enemies, including Elizabeth I, John KNOX, and leading Scottish nobles. She married the Catholic Lord Darnley, but refused to secure the throne to him in his own right on the advice of her secretary, Rizzio. Darnley murdered Rizzio, and was himself murdered, almost certainly by the 4th Earl of Bothwell, whom Mary then married. The marriage provoked revolt among the nobles and Mary was imprisoned and forced to abdicate (1567) in favour of her (and Darnley's) son James VI, later JAMES I of England. She escaped to England, where Elizabeth had her imprisoned for 18 years, and finally beheaded.

Four of the Marx brothers—Groucho, Chico, Harpo and Zeppo—in one of their early Hollywood classics

Masaccio (1401-28) Florentine painter, who inherited and developed GIOTTO's realism and narrative power. Among his works is the fresco of the Trinity in Sta Maria Novella, Florence (1425-8), a work of monumental grandeur, revealing an unprecedented ability to use perspective for illusionistic effect. His best-known frescoes, such as *The Tribute Money*, are in the Brancacci Chapel of Sta Maria del Carmine, Florence (*c.* 1425-8), and contain figures of heroic proportions, whose dramatic gestures are in strong contrast to the more decorative style of painting then current in Florence. MICHELANGELO's early work reflects his study of these paintings.

Masaoka Shiki (1867-1902) Japanese poet, who was leader of the 19th-century revival in the writing of the two traditional forms of Japanese verse, the 17-syllable *haiku* and the 31-syllable *tanka*. As well as being a poet of considerable merit, he was also an influential critic, advocating naturalism in poetry and a return to the simple style and spirit of the earliest periods.

Masaryk, Jan see MASARYK, Tomáš

Masaryk, Tomáš (1850-1937) Czechoslovak philosopher-statesman who created Czechoslovakia as a sovereign state. Masaryk, a professor of philosophy, sat in the Austrian parliament representing the Young Czech Party (1891-3) and the Czech Realist Party (1907-14), but he never thought of himself as representing only the Czechs; he was respected by Croats, Serbs and Slovenes as well. He fled to London at the outbreak of the First World War to preside over the Czech National Council, working to persuade Allied politicians and journalists to aid in the establishing of a Czechoslovak nation state. He went to Russia in 1917 to organize the Czech prisoners of war into a fighting Legion, and thence by way of Siberia to the US. There he won support for his cause from President WILSON when he received recognition in September 1918 as an Allied chief-of-state. He returned to Europe as President-elect and was in office until 1935, when he resigned for health reasons. His son Jan Masaryk, Czech Foreign Secretary when the Communists seized power in 1948, died in mysterious circumstances after a fall from a window.

Masefield, John (1878-1967) English poet and novelist, notable for fluent, narrative verse and vigorous prose, who became Poet Laureate in 1930. He is best known for his verse on the sea and the English countryside, although 'The Everlasting Mercy' (1911) shows an intimate knowledge of the harsh side of country life.

Maskelyne, Nevil (1732-1811) English astronomer, whose observations revolutionized navigation. A journey in 1761 to St Helena, where he was sent to observe the transit of Venus, aroused his interest in navigation. On the voyages out and back he used lunar distances to calculate longitude at sea, and on his return published *The British Mariner's Guide* (1763).

Mason, Charles (1730-87) English astronomer who, with the surveyor Jeremiah Dixon (1733-79), was engaged by the proprietors of Maryland and Pennsylvania to survey the boundary line between the two states, which was in dispute. The line, which became known as the Mason-Dixon line, was drawn along latitude 39°43'3"N and marked by milestones. It later came to represent a division between the slave states and free states of the US, and remains an arbitrary line dividing north from south.

Massenet, Jules Emile Frédéric (1842-1912) French composer of 25 operas, including *Manon* (1884) and *Thaïs* (1894). A number of his orchestral compositions are still performed and his *Don Quichote* (1910) was popularized by CHALIAPIN's singing of the title role. He also composed overtures, a piano concerto, incidental music to plays and many songs.

Massine, Léonide (born 1894) Russian dancer and choreographic innovator. In 1914 he replaced NIJINSKY as DIAGHILEV's leading male dancer, and by the following year had become Diaghilev's best choreographer after FOKINE, creating dramatic ballets, including *The Magic Toyshop* and *The Three-Cornered Hat*, on subjects as diverse as Cubism and Russian folklore. After 1926 he worked for leading companies throughout the world, proving both a meticulous planner and a bold pioneer.

Masson, André (born 1896) French Surrealist painter, who was a pioneer of their 'automatic' way of painting, i.e. the process of letting the subconscious take over. After painting in a Cubist style, Masson came into contact with BRETON and the Surrealist group in 1924, and was associated with them for several years.

Massys, Quentin (c. 1464-1530) Flemish painter who was one of the first northern artists to visit Italy. The architectural details in his work are classical and his figures often recall those of LEONARDO. He produced religious pictures (the landscape backgrounds of which were sometimes possibly painted by PATENIER), portraits (which influenced HOLBEIN) and genre studies on popular themes.

Masters, Edgar Lee (1868-1950) American poet, who, like SANDBURG, spoke with the new, distinctive voice of the American mid-West. His major work is the *Spoon River Anthology* (1915).

Mata Hari (1876-1917) Dutch courtesan and double agent shot by

Finney   Puskas   Didi   Charlton   Di Stefano   Eusebio   James
England   Hungary   Brazil   England   Argentina   Portugal   Scotlan

Successful courtesan, unsuccessful spy, Mata Hari was shot by a firing squad

the French as a spy in the First World War. Born Gertrud Zelle, she was the wife of a Dutch colonial officer named MacLeod, with whom she lived in Java until 1901. She deserted him and travelled to Europe, calling herself Mata Hari and claiming to be a former temple dancer of Javanese birth. She became a well-known demi-mondaine in Paris, distributing her favours freely while in the pay of both French and German intelligence services.

Mather, Cotton (1663-1728) American author and Puritan minister. Mather wrote numerous books on diabolical possession and witchcraft and did much to create the hysterical atmosphere which led to the Salem witchcraft persecution of 1692, in which many innocent people unjustly perished.

Mathers, Samuel (1854-1918) British translator of the magical textbooks *Key of Solomon* (1885) and *Abremelin* (1898), who, in 1888, founded and was chief of the Golden Dawn, a mystical secret society.

Yashin
USSR

Pele
Brazil

Matisse, Henri (1869-1954) French artist, who asserted that colour in art should parallel light in nature. His use of complementary colours, working together in harmony, anticipated the work of the Futurists. Matisse began by studying and copying the works of the old masters and the Impressionists in the Louvre. He soon progressed from the obvious influence of BONNARD and VUILLARD, as seen in the painting *Dinner Table* (1897), and continued logically to the study of Neo-Impressionism and the works of GAUGUIN and CÉZANNE, after which he developed his own theories on the function of light and colour. In 1906, Matisse exhibited his first masterpiece, the large figurative work *Joy of Life*, and it was from this point on that colour took a leading place in his art. Matisse was regarded as the leader of the 'Fauves', an informal group of painters whose common technique of distortion and bright colour caused their work to be hung together, first in 1905.

Matsuo Bashoh (1644-94) The most popular of all Japanese poets, Bashoh is notable for having brought the art of *haiku* writing to near perfection. Strongly influenced by Zen Buddhism, he rejuvenated the *haiku*, turning it into a medium capable of

expressing profound thoughts and feelings, though he retained a lightness of style. From about 1680, he began to live as a recluse and to travel, at which time he began his great creative period, which produced his best-known work, *The Narrow Road of Oku*, in which the *haiku* are set in a prose narration.

Matteotti, Giacomo (1885-1924) Italian socialist deputy whose denunciation of Fascist atrocities led to his murder. Matteotti, revolted by MUSSOLINI's brutality towards his opponents, denounced Fascism in a book entitled *The Fascisti Exposed* and organized the opposition United Socialist Party. His murder (June 1924) led to widespread criticism of Mussolini's régime both abroad and in Italy, where a parliamentary crisis ensued when many non-Fascist members refused to attend the sessions. This weakened the Fascists for a time, but eventually their secession served to consolidate Mussolini's position.

Matthew, St (1st cent. AD) Palestine-born Christian apostle and evangelist, author of the first Gospel of the New Testament. Based partly on the Gospel According to St Mark, it is the second of the three Synoptic Gospels and stresses the message and teachings of CHRIST. Presented in the form of ecclesiastical instructions, it has become the manual of conduct and discipline for the Church. Matthew was born Levi, a tax-collector for Herod the Tetrarch. He is thought to have been martyred 15 years after Christ was crucified.

Matthews, Sir Stanley (born 1915) English footballer, who made 56 international appearances. He played at club level till over 50 and is the only footballer to have been knighted for his services as a player.

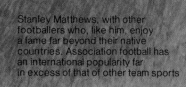

Stanley Matthews, with other footballers who, like him, enjoy a fame far beyond their native countries. Association football has an international popularity far in excess of that of other team sports

Matthias Corvinus (1440-90) King of Hungary (1458-90), which he made the most powerful country in central Europe. A statesman, soldier and scholar, Matthias used lesser nobles to break the power of dissident rebellious lords, reformed laws, enriched the treasury by taxation and built a large standing army, the envy of Europe. It enabled him to repel his rival, the Emperor FREDERICK III, and to take Bohemia, Lusatia, Moravia, Silesia and Lower Austria.

Maudslay, Henry (1771-1831) English engineer, who after working with BRAMAH (1789-97) set up his own firm specializing in engines, which prospered throughout the 19th century. In 1807, he patented a table engine (a compact power unit for industrial purposes, which became used extensively), and was also a leading builder of marine engines. Maudsley introduced important improvements in engineering practice, including the production of accurate plane surfaces, the use of a lathe slide rest, a practical screw-cutting lathe for the production of accurate screws and a minutely accurate bench micrometer.

Maugham, Somerset (1874-1965) English author of anti-romantic novels, short stories and plays, whose chief works include *Of Human Bondage* (1915) and *Cakes and Ale* (1930), a sardonic study of a literary man. His plays, the best known being *East of Suez* (1923), are still popular.

Maupassant, Guy de (1850-93) French novelist and author of some of the world's best-known short stories, notably *Boule de Suif* (1880) which made him immediately famous. Having learned his craft under FLAUBERT's guidance, Maupassant produced more than 300 *contes*, many of which (e.g. *Miss Harriet*) were masterpieces of their kind. He also wrote six novels, notably *Une Vie* (1883), *Bel-Ami* (1885) and *Pierre et Jean* (1888). His realistic and ironic tales, often set in his native Normandy, are told with great economy of style. As his health deteriorated, he developed an obsession with the macabre and the supernatural and later stories, like *Le Horla*, reflect these strange hallucinations. Disease and insanity ended his career.

Maupertius, Pierre de (1698-1759) French mathematician and astronomer, who is best known for his 'principle of least action', and for proving (1736) NEWTON's contention that the Earth is a sphere flattened at the poles. While at the Academy of Sciences in Berlin (1741-53), he developed his theory that all natural processes go on in such a way that a certain dynamic function called 'action' is a minimum.

Mauriac, François Charles (1885-1970) French Catholic novelist and author of poems, plays, biographies and literary criticism. His major novels, such as *A Kiss for the Leper* (1922), *Génétrix* (1923), *Thérèse Desqueyroux* (1927) and *The Knot of Vipers* (1932), are concerned with religious themes, particularly the problems of grace and redemption. These tense psychological dramas, smouldering behind the respectable façade of his native Bordeaux, established Mauriac as one of the masters of modern French prose. He was awarded a Nobel Prize in 1952.

Maurice of Nassau (1567-1625) Prince of Orange, who, after the assassination of his father, WILLIAM THE SILENT, successfully consolidated the position of the United Provinces. As Captain-General of the Dutch forces, he first checked Parma's advance, then (1590-1606) regained earlier losses. Maurice was one of the great military innovators of the age, adopting scientific methods of siege warfare, founding a school of engineers at Leyden, introducing battalion of 550 men, and ensuring regular payment of troops. Though he did not favour an attack on the southern provinces, he only reluctantly accepted the Truce of 1609 with Spain. With the merchants of Amsterdam, Maurice shared an interest in Dutch expeditions to Brazil and the Far East.

Maurois, André (1885-1967) French biographer, novelist, essayist and critic, renowned for his studies of the English, including biographies of SHELLEY (*Ariel*, 1923), DISRAELI (1927) and Lord BYRON (1930). His ironical novels, *Les Silences de Colonel Bramble* (1918) and *Les Discours du Docteur O'Grady* (1922), amiable burlesques of the English character, were inspired by his experiences as an interpreter with the British Army during the First World War. His numerous publications include historical works on England (1937) and the United States (1947).

Maurras, Charles (1868-1952) French writer and political philosopher. An admirer of classical antiquity and of the old order, he founded the extreme nationalist, anti-semitic group 'Action Française', whose main aim was to restore the hereditary monarchy in France. His ideas were best expressed in his *Dictionnaire politique et critique* (1932-4). Maurras was a controversial figure and a major influence on reactionary opinion in the first half of the 20th century. His support of the Vichy government led to expulsion from the Academy and imprisonment in 1945, though he was released on health grounds shortly before his death.

Maury, Matthew Fontaine (1806-73) American naval officer and hydrographer whose oceanographic research received wide recognition. Disabled after an accident, Maury was placed in charge of the charts and instruments section which evolved into the United States Naval Observatory. He is well known for his comprehensive data on winds and currents, his charts of the floor of the Atlantic and for his publication *The Physical Geography of the Sea* (1855), the first textbook of modern oceanography.

Mauss, Marcel (1872-1950) French sociologist and follower of DURKHEIM, who studied change in social groups. By his research into changing living patterns among Eskimos, he showed that any one alteration cannot be isolated, but affects every aspect of life. In *The Gift* (1898) he revealed how seemingly unimportant elements of social life have an important function in preserving the bonds which unite individuals or groups, and therefore preserve the unity of the society as a whole.

Mavor, Osborne Henry see BRIDIE, James

Maxim, Sir Hiram Stevens (1840-1916) American-born engineer, whose most famous of many inventions, after he went to England (1881), was the first fully automatic machine gun (1883). This was an advance over GATLING's gun in that it used each bullet's recoil energy to eject the spent cartridge, insert the next round and fire it. The Maxim/Vickers gun was adopted by the British Army in 1889 and later used by every major power.

Maximilian (1832-67) Archduke of Austria and Emperor of Mexico. The younger brother of Emperor Francis Joseph, he was Governor of the Hapsburg imperial province of Lombardy-Venetia, which was 'liberated' by French and Piedmontese armies (1859). In 1863, NAPOLEON III, who was seeking to establish a 'Catholic Empire' under his domination, induced Maximilian to accept the crown of Mexico. Maximilian and his wife, Carlota, took their role seriously and adopted the last prince of the line of Montezuma as their heir, but when United States pressure forced Napoleon to withdraw his armies (1867), Maximilian was left at the mercy of the Mexican Republican forces under JUAREZ. Carlota went to Europe to beg for help, but was unsuccessful. Meanwhile Juarez's forces captured Maximilian, who was shot (June 1867).

Maximilian I (1459-1519) King of Germany (1486-1519) and Holy Roman Emperor (1493-1519), who began the growth of the dynastic empire of the Hapsburgs. His son Philip became PHILIP I of Spain, whose sons, CHARLES V and FERDINAND I, were the Holy Roman Emperors under whom the Hapsburg family reached its peak of imperial power. Maximilian gave little attention to governing his lands, except to raise money, and devoted himself to unrealistic plans and warfare for personal aggrandizement, which won him the title 'the Last of the Knights'.

Maximowicz, Carl Johan (1827-91) Russian botanist who travelled widely in China and collected, classified and described thousands of previously-unknown plant species, several of which now bear his name.

Maxwell, James Clerk (1831-79) Scottish scientist and leading 19th-century theoretical physicist who worked out the complete electromagnetic theory of light based upon the ideas of FARADAY. His *Treatise on Electricity and Magnetism* (1873) is a landmark in the history of science. Like Faraday, Maxwell was opposed to the idea of action at a distance and adopted the notion of an all-pervading ether (originally introduced by HUYGENS in his wave theory of light) as the carrier of electromagnetic waves. Noticing that the speed of electric current in wires is roughly the same as that of light in empty space, he suggested that light is an electromagnetic vibration, a result later confirmed experimentally by HERTZ. The ether doctrine led to difficulties and became suspect after the work of MICHELSON and MORLEY, who failed to detect an effect predicted by the theory. Maxwell contributed also to other fields: colour sensation, Saturn's rings and, arising from this, the kinetic theory of gases.

May, Phil (1864-1903) English humorous artist, who evolved an original and economical technique that had considerable influence on the de-development of British comic art. After working for some time in London, he spent three years on the *Sydney Bulletin* in Australia. After his return to England, he worked for the *Daily Graphic*, drawing theatrical celebrities, and in 1895 joined the staff of *Punch*.

Mayakovsky, Vladimir (1893-1930) Russian dramatist and poet, the first notable Soviet Communist playwright. *Mystery-Bouffe*, the first post-Revolutionary play, produced in Moscow in 1918, is a high-spirited drama about Communism spreading all over the world. *The Bed Bug* (1929) is a satire showing a bourgeois and a bed bug as anachronisms in a Communist world. *The Bath House* (1930) satirizes the persistence of bourgeois behaviour in Soviet society.

Maybach, Wilhelm (1847-1929) German engineer, who associated with DAIMLER in the manufacture of high-speed internal combustion engines. Maybach was associated with the early development of motorcycles and four-wheeled cars and was responsible for several important technical innovations, notably the float-feed carburettor (1893). Maybach designed the first Mercedes car (1901). In 1907, he left the Company to set up a factory to manufacture engines for ZEPPELIN's airships.

Mayhew, Henry (1812-87) English journalist, noted for his exposure of London's conditions in the 1840s. Articled as a lawyer, he soon abandoned law for literature, publishing two weekly journals, *Figaro in London* (1831-9) and *The Thief* (1832). He also wrote farces and comedies, and in 1841 became a co-founder and editor of *Punch*. His principal work, assisted by John Binney, was *London Labour and the London Poor* (1851), a series of anecdotal, statistical articles based on first-hand interviews with London's petty tradesmen, originally appearing in the *Morning Chronicle*. The articles were stopped after 15 months through litigation by a powerful tailoring firm and Mayhew continued to publish the work himself, completing it in 1862. The survey, although a valuable sociological document, failed to produce immediate improvement in social conditions.

Mayo, William James (1861-1939) American surgeon who, with his brother Charles MAYO (1865-1939) and his father William MAYO (1819-1911), both of them also surgeons, founded the Mayo Clinic at St Mary's Hospital, Rochester, Minnesota. William Mayo was a gastric surgeon specializing in cancer and gallstones, while his brother performed many operations for goitre.

Mazarin, Jules (1602-61) Italian-born French cardinal and statesman, one of the ministers who made LOUIS XIV all-powerful, and France a major European power. After several years as a papal diplomat, Mazarin entered the service of RICHELIEU, became a naturalized French citizen in 1639, a cardinal in 1641 and succeeded Richelieu as chief minister of France in 1642. His prime interest was foreign affairs, in which he continued Riche-

lieu's policies, persisting successfully with the 30 Years' War. He sought to humiliate the Hapsburgs in Austria and Spain and made counterbalancing alliances with their enemies. Exiled for a time as a result of his domestic policies, Mazarin recovered his position and thereafter curbed the nobles' surviving feudal rights, continued to destroy their castles, and built the crown into the undisputed ruling instrument of France, albeit under ministerial domination.

Mazepa, Ivan Stepanovich (1644-1709) Cossack leader who intrigued for Ukrainian independence. Reputedly his affair with a Polish noblewoman led her husband to tie him naked to a wild horse which galloped to its Ukrainian homeland, where Cossacks freed Mazepa. He became their leader, and, siding with pro-Turkish, then pro-Muscovite Cossacks, finally joined CHARLES XII of Sweden against PETER I of Russia upon Charles's promise of Ukrainian independence. Peter defeated them at Poltava in 1709.

Mazzini, Giuseppe (1805-72) Italian patriot and revolutionary. In his twenties, he joined the Carbonari, a political secret society formed in 1815 to unite Italy as a republic. In 1831 he formed the 'Young Italy' movement and, becoming the apostle of international brotherhood, expanded it into a 'Young Europe' movement. In the revolutionary atmosphere of 1848, Mazzini's forces liberated Milan and set up a Roman republic, whose military force was commanded by GARIBALDI. As a fervent republican, Mazzini did not approve of the Kingdom of Italy created by CAVOUR and Garibaldi under the Piedmontese crown, and spent his later years in exile, though he visited Italy secretly from time to time.

Mazzola, Francesco see PARMIGIANINO

Mboya, Thomas Joseph (1930-69) Kenyan politician and pan-African leader assassinated as a result of tribal friction. He was appointed Minister of Labour in 1962 and Minister of justice in 1963, when Kenya achieved self-government and was responsible for the introduction of the country's new constitution. After full independence was obtained in 1964, Mboya was appointed Minister of Economic Planning and Development. He played a considerable part both in the formation of the East African Community and in associating it with the European Economic Community. He typified the young, forceful, professional politician who has emerged in the course of Africa's recent development.

McAdam, John Loudon (1756-1836) Scottish inventor who gave his name to the surfacing of roads with granite or other durable stone, broken small enough to make a hard, smooth, water-resistant surface suitable for traffic. By the end of the 19th century, most of Europe's main roads were built according to his methods, while the word 'macadamize' is still used to describe aspects of road construction. McAdam, who spent several of his early years in the US was appointed Surveyor-General of London Metropolitan roads in 1827.

McCarthy, Joseph (1909-57) American senator who, from 1950-4, acquired world-wide notoriety by promoting anti-Communist 'witch-hunts'. In public sessions of Senate sub-committees he made accusations which were frequently quite without substance. He was protected from retaliatory legal action, however, by claiming Congressional privilege. His conduct eventually became so scandalous, he even began making personal attacks on Presidents EISEN-HOWER and TRUMAN and involved the ruin of so many careers, that in 1954 the Democrat-controlled Senate, by a two-thirds majority, passed a vote of censure on him for bringing their House into dishonour and disrepute.

McCormack, John (1884-1948) Irish tenor whose 'golden voice' brought him great success and made him a popular legend. Like CARUSO, he lives on through the gramophone. He became an American citizen in 1917 and was raised to the papal peerage 11 years later.

McCormick, Cyrus Hall (1809-1884) American agricultural engineer who patented a harvester (1833) after others had been only moderately successful. The commercial exploitation of McCormick's machines was caused by labour shortages during the American Civil War and the resulting need for mechanization. By product improvement and better marketing than his rivals, McCormick's firm emerged as the principal American manufacturer.

McCullers, Carson (1917-67) American novelist, who presents a world of violence, pain and grief, many of its inhabitants isolated, outcast and suffering from physical or psychological disability. *The Heart is a Lonely Hunter* (1940) explores the situation of a lonely deaf-mute; *Member of the Wedding* (1946) portrays the emotional problems of a maturing adolescent; *The Ballad of the Sad Café* (1951), a collection of stories, provides an introduction to her fictional world, based on a reality of ugliness and conflict.

McGovern, George Stanley (born 1922) American politician, Democratic candidate for President in the 1972 elections. He lost to Richard NIXON by a landslide, gathering barely 40 per cent of the vote.

McGregor, William (1847-1911) British founder of the Association Football League. In 1888, his proposal that leading football clubs should combine to form a league and play one another in a sequence of home and away matches in an annual championship was accepted. By the addition of more clubs and the formation of first, second and third league divisions, the Football League became the biggest and most influential of all such bodies.

McKinley, William (1843-1901) American President, assassinated during his second term of office, who expanded US territory by annexing Havana, the Philippines, Puerto Rico and Guam following the Spanish-American War of 1898. He began his career as a lawyer and in the Civil War served in the Union Army. As a Republican Congressman, he advocated a high tariff policy and was elected President in 1896 as a result of a campaign managed for him by major business interests. In office, he raised US tariffs to the highest level. He was hustled into the Spanish-American war by a popular campaign (a mixture of expansionism and a real resentment of Spanish repression in Cuba). Public indignation reached its peak with the sinking of the US battleship *Maine* in Havana harbour (February 1898). In 1900, he was elected President for a second term but was assassinated by an anarchist a year later.

McMillan, Edwin Mattison (born 1907) American physicist who discovered the first transuranium elements (1940). During his study of the nuclear fission of uranium he detected the presence of a radioactive element heavier than uranium. Mc-Millan called it neptunium, and later he discovered another, heavier element, which he named plutonium.

McNamara, Robert Strange (born 1916) American Secretary of Defence during the escalation of the Vietnam war. The first man outside the Ford family to become president of the Ford Motor Company, he was appointed Secretary of Defence by KENNEDY in 1961, a post he retained for seven years. McNamara subjected the Pentagon to increased cost-effectiveness, streamlined its administration and brought a semblance of unity to the various defence arms. He resigned in 1968 to become President of the World Bank.

Mead, Margaret (born 1901) American anthropologist, who specializes in studying the relationship between personality and culture. Her first field-work resulted in *Coming of Age in Samoa* (1928), which showed that young Samoans, reared in a different family structure, do not suffer the adolescent disturbances which Western civilization regards as 'natural'. Later work in New Guinea and Bali increased her interest in the effect of child-rearing practices on adolescent and sexual behaviour, and in *Sex and Temperament in Three Primitive Societies* (1935) significant differences in these contrasted societies are shown to correlate with differences in temperament.

Medawar, Sir Peter (born 1915) Brazilian-born British scientist who was a leading researcher into immunological tolerance and tissue rejection in skin grafting, and organ transplants. He shared a Nobel Prize with BURNET in 1960.

Medici, Catherine de (1519-89) Queen of France from 1547 and its virtual ruler from 1560-74, who, to keep her family in power, provoked continual religious wars and was responsible for the St Bartholomew's Day Massacre of Huguenots (1572). She played no part in politics until her husband, HENRY II, died. During the reigns of her three sons, Francis II (1559), Charles IX (1560-74) and Henry III (1574-89), she favoured Catholics and Protestants in turn to prevent the leading families of either faction presenting a threat to royal power.

Medici, Cosimo de (1389-1464) Florentine banker, Renaissance patron, and founder of a dynasty which ruled Tuscany until 1737. Cosimo seized power in 1434 and was virtual ruler of the State for 30 years, though he retained republican forms of government and was content to be called 'pater patriae'. He helped to make Florence the leader of Renaissance Italy in the arts and learning and was patron of men like ALBERTI, BRUNELLESCHI, GHIBERTI and DONA-TELLO. He sponsored the first public library in Florence, founded the Platonic Academy for the encouragement of Greek studies, and collected codices and books. The source of Cosimo's great wealth was the Medici bank, which handled papal financial business.

Medici, Lorenzo de (1449-92) Virtual dictator of Florence, known as 'The Magnificent', he wielded absolute, tyrannical power through a puppet council. Planning to unite Rome and Florence, Lorenzo schooled the future Medici popes, Leo X and CLEMENT VII, and kept peace among rival Italian states by clever diplomacy. Under Lorenzo, Florentines of all classes shared in a prosperity, based on a progressive approach to trade and industry, unrivalled in western Europe. Lorenzo also financed Renaissance Italian arts and was himself a talented poet.

Meegeren, Hans van (1889-1947) Dutch art forger who received approximately £750,000 for his forgeries. He was obliged to confess in order to clear himself of a charge of collaborating with the Nazis arising out of the sale of one of his paintings to Field-Marshal GOERING. Sentenced to 12 months' imprisonment, he died before serving the sentence.

Megasthenes (4th cent. BC) Greek statesman, geographer and historian, who explored farther inland in India than ALEXANDER and gave the Greek world new insight into Indian civilization.

Mège-Mouriès, Hippolyte (1817-80) French chemist and inventor who developed an economic method for the production of an acceptable substitute for butter. It became known as margarine on account of its pearly texture (from the Latin, 'margita', a pearl). Margarine was soon manufactured widely, although it was banned for a long time by large scale butter producers. Later manufacturers substituted cheaper vegetable oils for the costly animal fats.

Mehemet Ali (1769-1849) Founder of the dynasty which ruled Egypt from 1841-1952. An Albanian, he became a soldier for the Ottoman Empire fighting against the French in Egypt in 1799. In 1805, he was made Governor of Egypt by the Turks, and then given independent authority. For helping Turkey in the Greek War of Independence (1824-7), he was made governor of Crete, but his ambitions were still not satisfied and in 1832 he attacked the Turkish Empire, and annexed Syria and Adana. Following the war of 1839-41 he was forced by the major European powers, and Britain in particular, to abandon these territories but was compensated by recognition as hereditary ruler of Egypt. A council of regency governed Egypt during the last two years of his life when he became mentally deranged.

Meikle, Andrew (1719-1811) Scottish agricultural engineer and developer, in 1786, of the first successful threshing machine, embodying the basic principle of the modern thresher, by which the grain was removed by rubbing the corn between a rotating drum and a concave metal sheet.

Meillet, Paul (1866-1936) French linguistics scholar who corrected and amplified BRUGMAN's work on Indo-European and comparative philology. His belief, following DE SAUSSURE, in language as a system influenced 20th-century structuralists.

Meinong, Alexius (1853-1920) Austrian philosopher whose 'objective' philosophy influenced MOORE and RUSSELL, although it was rejected by the latter. In 1894, he established the first Austrian laboratory for experimental psychology.

Meir, Golda (born 1898) Russian-born Prime Minister of Israel. Having grown up in America, she settled in Palestine in 1921, and increasingly devoted herself to the Jewish community there, becoming a founder member of the Mapai (Labour) Party, and later playing a prominent part in the struggle to establish a Jewish state. Having been Minister of Labour for seven years (1949-56) and Foreign Minister for ten (1956-66), she became Prime Minister in 1969, on the death of ESHKOL. She is considered something of a matriarchal disciplinarian and BEN GURION once spoke of her as 'the only man in my cabinet'.

Meitner, Lise (1878-1968) Austro-Swedish physicist who worked closely with Otto HAHN in the discovery of nuclear fission. In the 1930s, Hahn and Meitner studied the effect of bombarding uranium with neutrons and established that uranium nuclei were splitting up into the nuclei of lighter elements.

Melanchthon, Philipp (1497-1560) German theologian who helped LUTHER with the Greek Bible texts and who was mainly responsible for drafting the *Augsburg Confession*, a reasoned, definitive statement of the Lutheran position.

Melbourne, William Lamb, 2nd Viscount (1779-1848) English statesman and mentor of Queen VICTORIA during her early years on the throne. At first a Whig MP, he lost his seat (1812) because of his support for Catholic emancipation. He became a follower of CANNING and served under him as Secretary for Ireland (1827), a post which he continued to hold under Goderich and WELLINGTON. His loyalty to Canningite principles forced him to resign in 1828 and, after refusing overtures to rejoin the Wellington ministry, he reverted to the Whigs and took office as Home Secretary under GREY in 1830. He incurred severe criticism for his uncompromizing attitude towards agricultural unrest in southern England and was Prime

Minister for a brief period in 1834 during the episode of the Tolpuddle martyrs. He was again Prime Minister from 1835-41, during which time he became the close and trusted adviser of Victoria after her accession in 1837, and was virtually her private secretary until her marriage to the Prince Consort in 1840.

Melville, Herman (1819-91) American poet and novelist, who wrote the huge symbolic novel *Moby Dick* (1851). In seas and ships, far from the parochial subjects of American writing to this date, Melville discovered a metaphor for the strangeness and intractability of life. He spent his early years on whalers and warships and used the experience to write, producing seven works in six years. *Billy Budd* was later used by BRITTEN as the subject of an opera.

Memling, Hans (c. 1430-94) German-born painter who is one of the best-known artists of the early Netherlandish school. His religious paintings are notable for their atmosphere of calm devotion and the precise reproduction of precious materials, though they add little to the inspiration taken from his master, Rogier van der WEYDEN.

Menander (c. 342-291 BC) Greek dramatist, the outstanding writer in the New Comedy form, whose works formed the basis of the Roman comedies of PLAUTUS and TERENCE and stand as forerunners of all European comedy. Recent discoveries have produced one almost complete play, the *Dyscolus*, and large parts of three others, *Samia*, *Aspis* and *Sicyonius*. Considerable sections also survive of *Epitrepontes* and *Perikeiromene*, which were reconstructed by Sir Gilbert Murray.

Mencken, Henry Louis (1880-1956) American editor and satirist whose caustic wit made him a national figure. Editor and writer for four Baltimore newspapers, Mencken was known for his investigations of American linguistics. In *Prejudices* (1919-27) he coined characteristic maxims like, 'It is a sin to believe evil of others, but it is seldom a mistake.'

Mendel, Gregor (1822-84) Austrian monk of the Augustinian order, who discovered the fundamental principle of heredity which initiated the rise of modern genetics. By crossing certain varieties of garden peas he recognized that various characteristics depend on certain basic units (now called genes) that exist in either dominant or recessive form.

Mendele, Mocher (c. 1835-1917) Russian-born Jewish writer, whose novel *The Travels and Adventures of Benjamin the Third* (1875) is considered his best work. *Fishke the Lame* (1869) is perhaps the best known of his many satirical stories, and was the first to be written in colloquial Yiddish. His pen-name means Mendele the Bookseller; he assumed the role of a wandering disseminator of knowledge and culture, visiting and linking Jewish communities in Russia and Poland.

Mendeleyev, Dmitri (1834-1907) Russian chemist who devised the periodic table of chemical elements. By arranging the elements in order of increasing atomic weight, he was able to explain certain chemical similarities and to predict the properties of hitherto unknown elements from the gaps in the table. The table also suggested errors in some of the accepted values of atomic weights, and this too was confirmed by experiments. The periodic law put the whole of chemistry on a new rational basis.

Mendelsohn, Erich (1887-1953) German architect. An exponent of Expressionist architecture, Mendelsohn developed a sculptural feeling for fluid forms in such early works as the Einstein Tower at Neubabelsberg near Berlin of 1919-21. He later rejected this sculptural plasticity to produce buildings in a more direct line of descent from the industrialist architects BEHRENS and Poelzig. In the 1930s he settled in England but later moved on to work in Israel and the United States of America.

Mendelssohn Bartholdy, Felix (1809-47) German Romantic classical composer. A musical child prodigy, Mendelssohn was 17 when he wrote his *Midsummer Night's Dream* overture (the rest of the incidental music, which includes the 'Wedding March', was written later). During his relatively short creative life, he also composed the *Hebrides* overture and the *Scottish Symphony*, the *Italian Symphony* and the oratorio *Elijah*, first performed in Birmingham, England (1846), and for long a favourite with choral societies. The qualities of 'prettiness' in Mendelssohn's music led to his fashionable devaluation in the 20th century, but in pure musical terms his *String Quartet in F Minor* is probably the only one from the 19th century to rank with BEETHOVEN'S quartets. Mendelssohn was also a notable conductor and head of the Leipzig Conservatory. We are in his debt for the rediscovery of the music of J. S. BACH after nearly a century of neglect.

Mendoza, Pedro de (c. 1487-1537) Spanish soldier and explorer who founded Buenos Aires (1536), which

later had to be abandoned because of disease, starvation and Indian attacks. He also founded Asunción, in Paraguay.

Menelaus (1st. cent. AD) Greek mathematician, who applied EUCLID's theories to spherical trigonometry.

Menendez de Aviles, Pedro (1519-74) Spanish navigator and colonist who ousted the French from Florida and established Spanish power there.

Menéndez Pidal, Ramón (1869-1968) Spanish philologist, scholar, critic and humanist, who is considered the leading modern interpreter of the Spanish spirit. His many works, on a variety of subjects, have revealed to the modern world much about medieval Spanish literature.

Menendez y Pelayo, Marcelino (1856-1912) Spanish historian and literary critic, who established the foundations for all later research into Spanish literature. Immensely learned, steeped in the tradition of Classical and western European literature, deeply religious and patriotic, his ideas were propounded in works such as *History of Aesthetic Ideas in Spain* (1883-91) and *Origins of the Novel* (1905-10).

Menotti, Gian-Carlo (born 1911) American operatic composer and librettist of *The Medium* (1946), *The Telephone* (1947), *The Consul* (1950) and (for television) *Amahl and the Night Visitors* (1951). *The Consul* in particular, a contemporary fable of bureaucracy and totalitarianism, has caught the public imagination.

Menzies, Sir Robert (born 1894) Prime Minister of Australia for 19 years in all. He entered the Victorian parliament in 1928. He was Prime Minister during the early years of the Second World War and also held the portfolios for trade and customs, treasury, munitions, co-ordination and defence. From 1943-9 he was the leader of the opposition and from 1949-66 again Prime Minister, until he retired from active politics. During the Suez crisis of 1956 he led the mission of negotiation to NASSER.

Mercator, Gerhardus (1512-94) Flemish cartographer who developed the first modern type of map projection. He worked as cartographer to the Emperor CHARLES V and as cosmographer to the Duke of Jülich and Cleves (from 1559). In 1569 he produced the first nautical chart to use the Mercator projection (of which he was not the inventor). By showing lines of longitude (meridians) and latitude (parallels) as parallel lines intersecting at right angles, the pro-

jection allows seamen to draw a compass course on the chart as a straight line, and meteorologists to show true wind directions. The projection's main disadvantage is its magnification of polar areas. Mercator also popularized the name *atlas* for a bound collection of maps, by prefacing such a collection with an illustration of the Titan Atlas supporting a globe.

Merckx, Eddy (born 1945) Belgian racing cyclist, the most famous prizewinner of his generation. Merckx won the Tour de France, perhaps the most gruelling of all cycling events, four times in four years (1969-72).

Meredith, George (1828-1909) English novelist and poet, a detached observer, who wrote with elegance and irony on human conflicts. His early *Shaving of Shagpat* (1856) was a fantasy in the manner of PEACOCK, his father-in-law. His later novels, leading up to *The Egoist* (1879), deal with social and moral conflicts set in ordinary surroundings. His poetry complements his fiction: *Modern Love* (1862), based on his first marriage, takes a bleak view of human relations. He did much work for magazines, and was a friend of SWINBURNE and ROSSETTI.

Mergenthaler, Ottmar (1854-99) German-born American inventor of the first Linotype setting machine. In 1884 he patented his machine for setting solid lines of type, now used by many newspapers. The next year the machine was improved by a device which automatically justified the type – that is, it ranged to a regular margin at both ends of the lines.

Mérimée, Prosper (1803-70) French author, and master of the novella, or long short-story; also a novelist, dramatist, essayist, historian

Gerhardus Mercator
first of the modern mapmakers

and archaeologist. He is now remembered chiefly as the author of *Carmen* (1845), the source of BIZET's opera, and other fine stories, including *Mattéo Falcone* and *La Vénus d'Ille*. Objectivity, realism, exotic themes, an ironic humour and a terse style are characteristic of his writing. His translations from the works of PUSHKIN, GOGOL and TURGENEV first introduced Russian literature to France.

Mersenne, Marin (1588-1648) French mathematician, theologian and friend of DESCARTES, who researched various physical and mathematical topics. He is known for his investigation of a class of numbers now called after him.

Mesmer, Franz (1734-1815) Austrian physician who claimed to be able to heal the sick by 'animal magnetism', later known as *mesmerism*. At his public demonstrations, many patients fell into hypnotic trances and convulsions. In 1784, a commission of scientists denounced Mesmer as a charlatan, and mesmerism fell into disrepute until its respectability as a form of treatment for nervous disorders was established by the English physician, James Braid.

Messerschmitt, Willi (born 1898) German aircraft designer and industrialist, who produced many Luftwaffe aircraft (including the Me 262, the first jet aircraft to enter military service) during the Second World War. In the 1950s he helped revive the Lufthansa airline.

Messiaen, Olivier (born 1908) French composer and organist and a strongly individual voice in modern French music. Organist at the Church of La Trinité, Paris, since 1931, Messiaen's Catholicism has made his music sacred in the broadest sense, incorporating elements such as Hindu rhythm and birdsong to make a mystic's vision of creation. His works include the seven *Visions of the Amen* (1943) for two pianos, and the *Turangalila Symphony* (1948), with its vast orchestra and scoring for exotic percussion. He ranks with WEBERN as an influence on such younger European composers as BOULEZ and STOCKHAUSEN.

Messier, Charles-Joseph (1730-1817) French astronomer, who discovered 21 comets and gave his name to the 'Messier numbers' by which nebulae are identified. Nicknamed the 'comet ferret' by LOUIS XV, he observed the return of HALLEY's Comet in 1758. In 1771 he published his first catalogue of nebulae to aid his search for comets, giving them the numbers by which many are still known today.

Metastasio, Pietro Antonio Bonaventura Trapassi (1698-1782) Italian poet and dramatist, author of numerous melodramas, whose popularity stimulated the development of Italian opera.

Metcalf, John (1717-1810) Pioneer English road-builder, known as 'Blind Jack', due to his loss of sight at the age of six, after an attack of smallpox. He could tell the quality of a road-surface better than any sighted person, and the 180 miles of road he built between 1767 and 1792 were renowned for their permanence. He was also a stagecoach operator, fish merchant, musician and a keen huntsman.

Metsu, Gabriel (c. 1630-67) Dutch painter of genre scenes and interiors whose early religious work was influenced by STEEN and REMBRANDT. His lively depiction of outdoor scenes of the market-place and the tavern and his ability to capture an expression reflects the work of his contemporary Frans HALS.

Metternich, Klemens (1773-1859) Austrian statesman, who presided over the Congress of Vienna and gave his name to the diplomatic system which controlled inter-European relations for 30 years. He became Austria's Foreign Minister in 1809 and Chancellor in 1821, positions which he held until driven into exile in the European revolutions of 1848. His aim was to maintain aristocratic government in Europe, to keep the rising radical middle-class from acquiring political power, and to keep the peace by adjusting differences at periodical congresses of the powers.

Meung, Jean de (c. 1240-c. 1305) French medieval poet and scholar, who continued, after an interval of a generation or more, Guillaume de Lorris's poem 'Roman de la Rose'. The simplicity of the original allegory contrasts starkly with the welter of erudition added by de Meung.

Meyer, Conrad Ferdinand (1825-98) Swiss-German writer who devoted himself primarily to writing stories on historical themes. His novel *Jürg Jenatsch* (1876) was set in the Swiss Canton of Graubünden and described the repercussions there of the incipient 30 Years' War. His shorter works include *The Saint* (1880) and *The Tempting of Pescara* (1887). Meyer was not an objective story-teller, but used historical settings to express his own views and feelings while remaining withdrawn from the reader.

Meyer, Viktor (1848-97) German chemist who devised a method of measuring the density (mass per unit volume) of gases and vapours. His method is still widely used.

Meyerbeer, Giacomo (1791-1864) German operatic composer, son of Herz Beer, a banker, whose works include *Robert the Devil* (1831) and *The Huguenots* (1836). Most of Meyerbeer's working life was spent in Paris, where he enjoyed considerable public success.

Meyerhold, Vsevolod (1874-c. 1940) Russian actor-director, who was the first great experimentalist of early Soviet theatre. He was a member of the Moscow Art Theatre (1898), toured Russia with his own Society of the New Drama, ran STANISLAVSKY's experimental theatre studio, introduced Gordon CRAIG's ideas to Russia while directing Vera Komisarjevskaya's company and directed at the Imperial Theatre. After the Revolution, he staged some *avant-garde* productions, notably of MAYAKOVSKY's works. The Stalinist imposition of Socialist Realism brought his work to an end and it is presumed that he died in a labour camp.

Michael (1596-1645) First Romanov Tsar of Russia (1613-45). He was dominated for years by his patriot father Patriarch Philaret, who continued GODUNOV's measures to end national chaos by stopping tax-paying peasants leaving the land to become nomadic robbers, and introducing proportional taxation for formerly privileged classes. During Michael's reign, Russian trans-Siberian frontiersmen reached the Pacific Ocean.

Michael VIII Palaeologus (1234-82) Byzantine Emperor (1261-82) who restored Greek rule to Constantinople and founded the last Byzantine dynasty (1261-1453).

Michelangelo, Buonarroti (1475-1564) Italian painter, architect, sculptor and poet and one of the most important figures of the Renaissance. His most famous work is the ceiling of the Sistine Chapel in the Vatican (1508-12), consisting mainly of a series of scenes from the Act of Creation to the Drunkenness of Noah, divided by painted architecture and flanked by nude youths with, below, prophets and sybils. Together with RAPHAEL's tapestry designs for the Sistine Chapel the ceiling's exaltation of the beauty of the human figure in motion has probably had more influence than any other work of art. In 1536 Michelangelo began his epic *Last Judgement* on the altar wall of the Sistine Chapel and later he painted the *Conversion of Saul* and the *Crucifixion of Peter* in the adjoining Capella Paolina (1542-50). His sculpture includes the *Fight between the Lapiths and Centaurs*, *Bacchus* (1496), *Pieta* (1498) and the famous *David* (1504).

Michelson, Albert Abraham (1852-1931) American physicist, of German extraction, who is mainly remembered for his work on the velocity of light. Using his interferometer (invented in 1881), he and Edward W. Morley showed in 1887 that the speed of light in a vacuum is the same in all inertial reference systems (co-ordinate systems moving at constant velocity relative to each other). It had been held since the days of HUYGENS that light travels through a stationary substance filling the whole of space (the so-called *ether*), but Michelson and Morley's experiments proved that there was no such thing. This led directly to the development of the special relativity theory by LORENTZ and EINSTEIN. In 1907 Michelson became the first American to be awarded a Nobel Prize for Physics.

Michelin, André (1853-1931) French industrialist, who, with his brother Edouard, was the first to manufacture rubber tyres for motor cars (1895).

Michelozzo Di Bartolommeo (1396-1472) Italian sculptor and architect, who was a contemporary and acquaintance of many early Renaissance artists in Florence, and who worked as a sculptor under both GHIBERTI and DONATELLO. He built an imposing and massive palace for the Medici in Florence (Palazzo Medici Riccardi) which influenced the style of many Italian Renaissance palaces. His ecclesiastical architecture shows great inventiveness and sensitivity and a devout respect for the classical past.

Mickiewicz, Adam (1798-1855) Poland's foremost poet and the founder of Polish Romanticism. His 'Thaddeus' (1834), an epic poem inspired by his childhood memories of Lithuania and NAPOLEON's Russian campaign, is one of the masterpieces of Slavonic literature. His earlier 'Poems' (1822-3) became the Polish Romantic movement's manifesto. Mickiewicz was deported to Russia in 1823, and later lived as an exile in Paris where he wrote *Forefather's Eve* (1832), a romantic drama which includes some criticisms of Russian life.

Middleton Murry, Katherine see MANSFIELD, Katherine

Mies, van der Rohe, Ludwig (1886-1969) German architect and designer of skyscrapers who, like LE CORBUSIER, studied under BEHRENS

and subsequently became one of the most influential pioneers of modern 20th-century architecture. The glass-walled skyscrapers he designed after the First World War were the fore-runners of buildings that have now become a predominant feature of city life, and preoccupied him in later

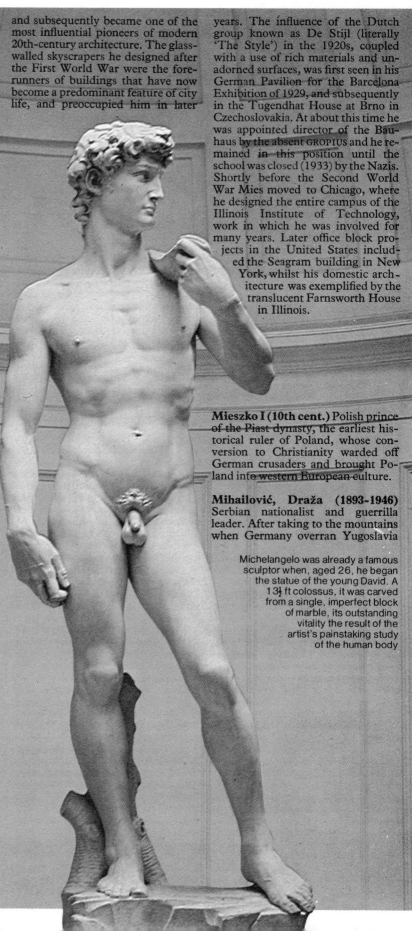

Michelangelo was already a famous sculptor when, aged 26, he began the statue of the young David. A 13½ ft colossus, it was carved from a single, imperfect block of marble, its outstanding vitality the result of the artist's painstaking study of the human body

years. The influence of the Dutch group known as De Stijl (literally 'The Style') in the 1920s, coupled with a use of rich materials and unadorned surfaces, was first seen in his German Pavilion for the Barcelona Exhibition of 1929, and subsequently in the Tugendhat House at Brno in Czechoslovakia. At about this time he was appointed director of the Bauhaus by the absent GROPIUS and he remained in this position until the school was closed (1933) by the Nazis. Shortly before the Second World War Mies moved to Chicago, where he designed the entire campus of the Illinois Institute of Technology, work in which he was involved for many years. Later office block projects in the United States included the Seagram building in New York, whilst his domestic architecture was exemplified by the translucent Farnsworth House in Illinois.

Mieszko I (10th cent.) Polish prince of the Piast dynasty, the earliest historical ruler of Poland, whose conversion to Christianity warded off German crusaders and brought Poland into western European culture.

Mihailović, Draža (1893-1946) Serbian nationalist and guerrilla leader. After taking to the mountains when Germany overran Yugoslavia in 1941, he formed the Chetniks (guerilla bands which inflicted heavy losses on the Germans), supported by Allied money and equipment. His Serbian nationalism led him to clash with TITO and the Communist partisans, however, and in 1944 Allied support for him was withdrawn, after he had allied himself with Germany and Italy to fight the Communists. He was captured in March 1946 and, despite Western protests, shot as a collaborator under Tito's orders.

Mikoyan, Anastas Ivanovich (born 1895) Russian politician and one of the few veteran Bolsheviks to survive the STALIN era and become President of the USSR. He was educated at the American Ecclesiastical Seminary, Tiflis, joined the Communist Party in 1915, and fought in the Revolution and Civil War (1917-20). By 1922 he was a member of the Communist Party Central Committee, and thereafter he held a series of increasingly important government posts, culminating in 1964 with the presidency of the Praesidium of the Supreme Soviet (1964-5). Mikoyan was regarded as one of the most efficient members of the Soviet government, and successfully obtained military and other supplies from Russia's allies during the Second World War.

Milhaud, Darius (born 1892) French composer who has synthesized the folk-music of his native Provence with that of Brazil. Milhaud, despite years of illness, is among the most prolific modern composers. His ballet *La Création du Monde* (1923) was the first work to make genuine creative use of jazz in a symphonic score. He has collaborated with CLAUDEL on operas such as *Christopher Columbus* (1930). He was for a time a member of 'Les Six'.

Mill, John Stuart (1806-73) British philosopher and economist, author of *Principles of Political Economy* (1848), one of the most important 19th-century economic texts. A liberal and originally a disciple of BENTHAM, he pursued the Utilitarian doctrine of 'greatest happiness' as an end to be achieved through legislation.

Millais, Sir John (1829-96) English painter, who co-founded with HUNT and ROSSETTI the Pre-Raphaelite Brotherhood (1848). He was a child prodigy, and his early Pre-Raphaelite pictures, e.g. *Christ in the House of His Parents* (1850), combine technical virtuosity with edifying subject matter. Later works, however, pandered increasingly to the Victorian taste for sentiment which, though held in check in *The Blind Girl* (1856) by his pictorial flair, is clearly apparent in

portraits of children, one of which, *Bubbles* (1886), achieved fame as a soap advertisement.

Millay, Edna St Vincent (1892-1950) American poet, who was popular in the 1920s. Her mastery of the sonnet form can be seen in 'The Harp Weaver and Other Poems' (1923) and 'Collected Sonnets' (1941).

Miller, Arthur (born 1915) American dramatist, author of *Death of a Salesman* (1948). His first success was *All My Sons* (1947), a denunciation of war-profiteering. *The Crucible* (1953), ostensibly about 17th-century witch-hunting in Salem, exposed the American Senator MCCARTHY's anti-Communist 'witch-hunt' of the 1950s. In *A View from the Bridge* (1955) his characters are forced to face the truth about themselves, a theme developed in Miller's later plays.

Miller, Henry (born 1891) American writer of energetic, Rabelaisian novels such as *Tropic of Cancer* (1934). Like much of Miller's fiction, *Cancer* is written in the first person, a semi-autobiographical novel based upon his life in Paris as a struggling artist. A prolific writer, Miller's notoriety arises from his uninhibited use of sexual anecdotes in his novels; his use of obscene words was revolutionary in the 1930s. *Tropic of Capricorn* (1939) is a complementary volume about his early life, thoughts and adventures in New York. Between 1945 and 1960 he produced an ambitious trilogy *The Rosy Crucifixion* (*Sexus* (1945), *Plexus* (1949) and *Nexus* (1960)). *Order and Chaos Chez Hans Reichel* (1966) is a collection of reminiscences of his personal friends.

Miller, Philip (1691-1771) British gardener and father of horticultural journalism. He compiled the *Gardener's Dictionary* (1731), and was for many years the curator of Chelsea Physic Garden. He was among the first horticultural writers to use the LINNAEAN system of plant nomenclature, which is still in use today.

Miller, Stanley (born 1930) American biochemist who first synthesized amino acids, a basic constituent of living matter, in the laboratory. He used his discovery to demonstrate that the atmosphere and oceans of Earth before life evolved were very different in composition from today.

Miller, William (1782-1849) American sectarian leader, founder of the Adventists, who believed in CHRIST's imminent return to Earth.

Millikan, Robert Andrews (1868-1953) American physicist who deter-

mined the charge on the electron. In the early 1900s, he studied the effect of an electric field on charged droplets of oil falling freely under gravity. By 1912, he had discovered that the charge on the droplets was always a whole multiple of a certain basic quantity of charge; this, he realized, was the charge on an individual electron.

Mills, C. Wright (1916-62) American sociologist who helped to initiate a neo-Marxist approach to sociology, stressing the political commitment of the sociologist. In *The Power Elite* (1957) he argued that the United States is governed by a commercio-military power élite which makes all the most important decisions affecting life in America.

Mills, Sir William (1856-1932) English engineer who in 1915 developed, and started to manufacture, the Mills bomb. The most successful grenade used in the First World War (over 75 million were produced), it was the forerunner of later grenades.

Milne, Alan Alexander (1882-1956) English essayist and children's writer, who created the world of Pooh Bear in *Winnie-the-Pooh* (1926) and *The House at Pooh Corner* (1928), tales about his son's toy animals, which became nursery classics. He also wrote verses for children and adapted Kenneth GRAHAME's *Wind in the Willows* as *Toad of Toad Hall* (1930), a play even more popular than his successful *Mr Pim Passes By* (1919).

Milton, John (1608-74) English poet who, in his writing, was a learned artist who united the classical inheritance of the Renaissance with his own Christian faith. His genius appeared early: the ode 'On the Morning of Christ's Nativity' (1629) is lyrical and rich in language. As contemporary conflicts of religion and politics grew more serious, Milton's poems became more sombre; the light delicacy of 'L'Allegro' and 'Il Penseroso' (1632) turned into the gravity of 'Lycidas' (1637). In his later years he wrote *Paradise Lost* (1667), a Christian epic to justify God's ways to man, and *Paradise Regained* and *Samson Agonistes* (1671), showing the triumph of faith over pain and trial, all written with a consummate control of rhythm, in a rich and lofty language. He was also a writer of voluminous prose, and often, as in *Areopagitica* (1644), in defence of freedom of the press, he achieved a grand, powerful rhetoric. During the Commonwealth, he was Cromwell's Latin secretary, but at the Restoration he retired, blind and in disgrace, and wrote his greatest poems.

Mindszenty, Cardinal Josef (born 1892) Roman Catholic Primate of Hungary, and twice a political prisoner. Arrested after the First World War by the brief Communist régime of Béla KUN, he was a popular figure and a conservative, opposing land reform because of its effects on religious education. He was charged with treason in 1948 by the Communist government in Budapest and at his trial in 1949, pleaded guilty in circumstances that recalled STALIN's purges in the 1930s. He was sentenced to life imprisonment, but was released in 1955 on condition that he did not leave Hungary. In 1956 he obtained asylum in the American Legation in Budapest, where he remained for 15 years. In 1971, he left Hungary after persuasion by the Vatican and now lives in a seminary in Vienna.

Minot, George see MURPHY, William

Minuit, Peter (c. 1580-1638) Dutch colonist who bought Manhattan Island from local American Indians and founded the Dutch colonial capital, New Amsterdam (now New York City).

Mirabeau, Honore Gabriel Riqueti, Comte de (1749-91) French politician and orator, a powerful force in the National Assembly during the first two years of the French Revolution when he fought for the establishment of a constitutional monarchy based on the English pattern. He constantly urged that the monarchy should accept a new role at the head of the revolutionary movement, the expression of popular sentiment (rather than the interests of the *ancien regime*), while retaining real powers. Mistrusted, by LOUIS XVI and his queen MARIE ANTOINETTE, for his revolutionary convictions, and by his colleagues in the National Assembly for his ambitions and abilities, he failed to achieve his vision, but succeeded in influencing the constitution before his death.

Miró, Joán (born 1893) Spanish Surrealist artist, who evolved a highly personal style involving ameobic shapes in pure bright colours, often with punning and quizzical titles. He went to Paris in 1919 and from 1923 was one of the foremost Surrealists, developing a style all of his own.

Mir Sayyid 'Ali (16th cent.) Persian court painter. In 1567, he was placed in charge of Hindu and Muslim painters working on the illustrations of a large manuscript of the *Romance of Hamza*.

Mishima Yukio (1925-1970) Japanese novelist. Mishima published his first work at 19 and by 1946 was a protégé of KAWABATA Yasunari. His work covers a variety of themes, often displaying an obsession with the physical, written in an elaborate style with a penchant for the psychological. His best works include *Temple of the Golden Pavilion*, *Confessions of a Mask* and the posthumously published *The Sea of Fertility*. Despair over the decay of traditional Japanese values led to his ritual *seppuku* (harakiri) suicide in 1970.

Mistral, Frédéric (1830-1914) Provençal poet, who shared the Nobel Prize for Literature in 1904. His *Lou Tresor dou Félibrige* (1879-86), a vast dictionary of Provençal grammar, words and proverbs, and his epic romances, notably *Song of the Rhône* (1897), led to a renaissance of the Provençal language.

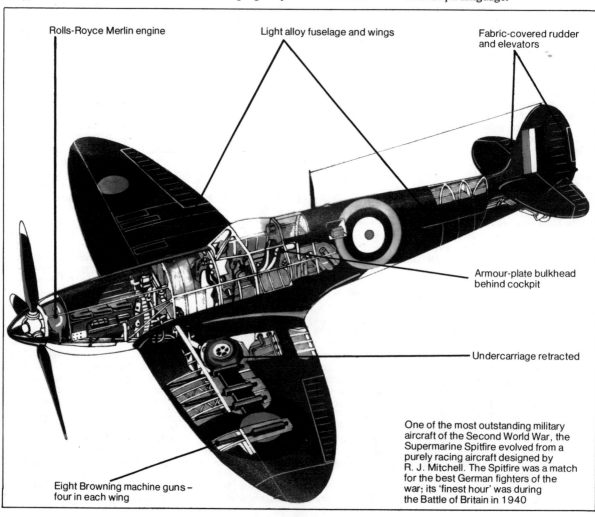

Rolls-Royce Merlin engine

Light alloy fuselage and wings

Fabric-covered rudder and elevators

Armour-plate bulkhead behind cockpit

Undercarriage retracted

Eight Browning machine guns – four in each wing

One of the most outstanding military aircraft of the Second World War, the Supermarine Spitfire evolved from a purely racing aircraft designed by R. J. Mitchell. The Spitfire was a match for the best German fighters of the war; its 'finest hour' was during the Battle of Britain in 1940

Mistral, Gabriela (1889-1957) Chilean poet, who was the first Spanish-American writer to be awarded a Nobel Prize for Literature (1945). She was internationally recognized as a teacher, and collaborated in Mexico's educational reform programme in 1922. She was successively Chilean Consul and Cultural Attaché in Mexico, Brazil and the United States.

Mitchell, John Newton (born 1913) Former US Attorney-General in the NIXON Administration, indicted (with former Secretary of Commerce Maurice Stans) in 1973 on charges connected with fund-raising for Nixon's 1972 Presidential Campaign. The last US cabinet official to be involved in a criminal case of such dimensions was Albert B. Fall, Secretary of the Interior under Warren HARDING, who was gaoled for bribery offences in what became known as the 'Teapot Dome' scandal. Mitchell, a confidant of President Nixon, served in the US Navy in the Second World War, at one time commanding the torpedo boat squadron which included John KENNEDY's PT-109.

Mitchell, Reginald Joseph (1895-1937) English aircraft designer, who joined Supermarine Aviation in 1916 and four years later became their chief designer. He designed a wide range of aircraft from large flying-boats to a brilliant series of small racing seaplanes, which won the Schneider Trophy on several occasions between 1922-31. From the latter evolved his last and most famous aircraft, the Spitfire. It first flew in March 1936, and was operational in June 1938. Over 22,000 Spitfires were built, serving in many capacities during the Second World War, but they are remembered particularly for their contributions to the victory of the Allies in the Battle of Britain (1940) and the defence of Malta (1942).

Mitchell, Silas (1829-1914) Pioneer American neurologist who gave his name to a form of treatment for some nervous diseases which involved complete rest and isolation. He produced a widely read treatise on *Fat and Blood*, and was also a poet and novelist.

Mithridates VI (c. 132-63 BC) King of Pontus (c. 121-63 BC), and formidable rival to Rome's power in Asia Minor, who fought three wars against the Romans and massacred some 80,000 Roman citizens. In the first war (88-84 BC) he was defeated by SULLA; in the second (83-81 BC) he drove out the Roman invaders; and in the third (74-64 BC) he was defeated by POMPEY, fled to the Crimea, and committed suicide.

Mittelholzer, Edgar (1909-65) West Indian poet and novelist whose work captures the mixed racial and cultural traditions of the West Indies. His books include *A Morning at the Office* (1950) and the Guianese colonial trilogy, *Children of Kaywana* (1952), *The Harrowing of Hubertus* (1954) and *Kaywana Blood* (1958).

Moawiyah I see MUAWIYAH I

Möbius, August Ferdinand (1790-1868) German mathematician and astronomer, whose name is associated with the Möbius strip. A long strip of paper is given a single twist and then joined together end to end. The resulting shape has only one edge, for its boundary consists of a single continuous closed curve enclosing a single surface.

Modigliani, Amedeo (1884-1920) Italian painter and creator of a highly personal portrait idiom in which the sitters and their features were attenuated, yet retained a remarkable degree of individuality. After training in Italy Modigliani went to Paris in 1906, where for some years he worked as a sculptor, influenced by BRANCUSI and the vogue for African art. He returned to painting (1914), producing his finest art in these years.

Mohammed (570-632) Arab prophet and founder of Islam, the world religion which now commands the allegiance of 450-500 million people. Born at Mecca, Islam's holy city, he was a rich merchant who spent years in meditation before rejecting the polytheistic beliefs of his contemporaries. Claiming inspiration from messages sent by God through the angel Gabriel, he preached belief in one God whose judgement damns the faithless and sends his Muslims ('Submissive Ones') to paradise. The simple appeal of Mohammed's message, embodied in the *Koran*, won acceptance and welded the warring tribes of Arabia into a united fighting machine. Mohammed himself acted as his empire's lawmaker, commander-in-chief, and judge; he did not set up any governmental administration, but left the conquered or converted peoples to manage their own affairs. The chief of the reforms he attempted were the abolition of infanticide, the granting of property rights to women, and – most important for the unity of his empire – the ending of the blood feud which held a whole tribe responsible for a murder and had led to much tribal warfare. Under Mohammed's successors the empire reached from Spain to India, but its civilizing religious role lasted far longer than its political unity, which collapsed after the reign of HARUN-AL-RASHID.

Mohammed II (1430-81) Sultan of Turkey (1451-81), called 'the Conqueror', who dealt the shrunken Byzantine empire its death blow by seizing Constantinople and Trebizond. After four months of attack (1453), Mohammed's troops swarmed through the Romanos Gate, and killed CONSTANTINE XI PALAEOLOGUS, the last Byzantine emperor, during three days of frenzied pillaging. Thereafter Constantinople became the Ottoman capital (as Istanbul). Mohammed II ended the last surviving Greek state in Asia Minor (1461), took all Serbia except for Belgrade, and conquered Bosnia, Herzegovina, Albania, Greece and the Crimea. He captured and for a time held Otranto in southern Italy.

Mohammed Ahmed of Dongola (c. 1843-85) Sudanese 'Mahdi' (Muslim Messiah), who by his militant preaching roused the Sudan to revolt against Egypt. During an armed rising in 1885, the Mahdi's dervishes – fanatical warriors – besieged and captured Khartoum and killed General GORDON. At the time of the Mahdi's death, his followers held the whole of the Sudan except the Red Sea ports, and continued to do so for 13 years, until their leader, the Khalifa Abdullah el Taashi, was defeated by KITCHENER at Omdurman (1898).

Molière, Jean-Baptiste Poquelin (1622-73) French dramatist, the greatest writer of comedies in the French language. Among his earliest were *L'Etourdi* (1655) and *Le Dépit Amoureux* (1656), but his first great success was *Les Précieuses Ridicules* 1659), a farce satirizing the pretentious 'blue-stockings' who haunted the literary salons of the day. He later returned to the subject of women's education in two of his greatest comedies, *L'Ecole des Femmes* (1662) and *Les Femmes Savantes* (1672). Meanwhile, though his success earned him a royal pension, he also became a target for violent abuse by rivals or irate victims of his satire. His most famous and controversial play *Tartuffe*, ostensibly an attack on hypocrisy, unleashed the wrath of powerful religious interests and was twice banned before the modern, amended version was accepted in 1669. Molière had further offended the sensibilities of the devout with his *Dom Juan* (1665). As well as the hypocrite Tartuffe, other great creations of Molière's comic genius include Alceste (*Le Misanthrope*, 1666), Arpagon (*L'Avare*, 1668), M. Jourdain (*Le Bourgeois Gentilhomme*, 1670) and Argan (*Le Malade Imaginaire*, 1673). Ironically, it was during a performance of this latter play, while acting the title role, that Molière collapsed and died in February 1673.

Molnár, Ferenc (1878-1952) Hungarian dramatist, who wrote *The Guardsman,* a play which was made famous by the celebrated husband-and-wife acting partnership of Alfred Lunt and Lynn Fontanne, who played the leading parts on both stage and screen. Molnár's only other work of international standing is *Liliom* (1909), which was the basis of the musical, *Carousel* (1945).

Molotov, Vyacheslav Mikhailovich (born 1890) Russian politician and veteran Bolshevik, who survived the STALIN era and remained in office until KHRUSCHEV's denunciation of Stalin. He was imprisoned six times and twice exiled as a Communist agitator, and was co-founder of *Pravda* (1912), with Stalin, whose second secretary he became in 1921. As Prime Minister from 1930-41 he was responsible for the two Five-Year Plans for expanding commerce and industry. When Stalin decided to conclude a peace pact with HITLER in 1939, Molotov replaced LITVINOV as Foreign Minister in order to implement it, and held the office until 1949, and again from 1953-6. He was notorious in the West for his inflexible attitude towards every attempt to reduce international tension. Following Khruschev's denunciation of Stalin's crimes, Molotov, with MALENKOV and Kaganovich, was expelled from the Central Committee and the Praesidium, and was sent as Ambassador to the Mongolian Peoples' Republic. He became USSR representative at the International Atomic Agency in 1960.

Moltke, Helmuth von (1800-91) Prussian Field-Marshal, creator and first chief of the German General Staff. He was commissioned into the Prussian army at 22 and retired from it 66 years later, having served without a break, except for a period of secondment to the Turkish army (1835-9). As Chief of the Prussian General Staff in 1857, he assisted BISMARCK to reorganize the Prussian army, and planned the campaigns against Denmark (1864), Austria (1866) and France (1870). With the establishment of the German Empire 1871, he was able to bring into existence the German General Staff, of which he remained Chief for 18 years.

Monck, George, 1st Duke of Albemarle (1608-70) English general and naval commander who helped to restore the monarchy after CROMWELL's Commonwealth. He changed sides in the Civil War after supporting the king, and as a Parliamentarian fought the Dutch (1653) and became ruler of Scotland after it had been conquered (1650-1). When Cromwell died (1658), Monck changed sides again and ended the anti-royalist Rump Parliament by restoring the members expelled by PRIDE in 1648. In 1660 the enlarged Parliament invited the banished Prince Charles to return as King CHARLES II. Charles made Monck Duke of Albermarle for his smoothing of the Restoration negotiations and for preventing bloodshed.

Mondrian, Piet (1872-1944) Dutch pioneer of geometric abstract painting. In 1911 he went to Paris, where he became influenced by Cubism. Later, in Holland, he developed a theory of abstract painting, based on a co-ordinated system of horizontals and verticals, and in 1917 founded the De Stijl group with Theo van DOESBURG. Fundamental to this was the theory of Neo-Plasticism – the use of pure abstraction to denaturalize art by eliminating representation, and suggesting three-dimensional space simply by curves and lines. His last works, the *Boogie-Woogies,* show a renewed and complex dynamism, inspired by the ambience of New York.

Monet, Claude (1840-1926) French Impressionist painter, who was at first naturalist in outlook, but showed a special sensitivity to effects of light resulting from the practice of painting out of doors. His *Impression: Sunrise,* shown at the first Impressionist exhibition (1874), gave the movement its name. Monet's work is closest to that of PISSARRO and SISLEY, but he pursued Impressionist ideas further than they, notably in several series of paintings of the same subject under different conditions, e.g. *Rouen Cathedral* (1892-4). Gradually an increasingly lyrical note entered his works, as is seen in the late paintings of *Water-lilies.*

Monge, Gaspard (1746-1818) French mathematician who invented descriptive geometry. At first the method was a military secret, but later it was published and became adopted by most engineers in Europe.

Monier, Joseph (1823-1906) French inventor of reinforced concrete (1849).

Moniz, Antonio (1874-1955) Portuguese physician, who, with Walter Hess, invented cerebral angiography, a technique by which radio-opaque dyes injected into the bloodstream reveal brain tumours and other lesions. Moniz also pioneered the technique of human frontal lobotomy.

Monmouth, James Scott, Duke of (1649-85) Pretender to the English throne and illegitimate son of CHARLES II. Charles made him Duke of Buccleuch and Captain-General of his forces after MONCK's death. As a popular public figure and a Protestant, Monmouth was drawn into the Rye House Plot (1683), in which radical Whigs planned to make him king by killing Charles II and his pro-Catholic heir, James. The plot failed and Monmouth fled abroad, but in 1685 he invaded Dorset to depose James, now King JAMES II. Monmouth lost the Battle of Sedgemoor and was captured and executed. His followers were punished savagely by Judge JEFFREYS.

Monroe, James (1758-1831) Fifth President of the US, who was JEFFERSON's envoy extraordinary in 1803, when he negotiated the Louisiana Purchase from France, but failed to acquire the Floridas from Spain. In 1816 he was elected President of the US and was re-elected almost unanimously four years later. The Floridas were eventually purchased in 1819, and the Missouri Compromise (1820) peacefully settled the first slavery conflict under the constitution. Monroe will always be associated with the Doctrine bearing his name, which rejected European interference in the affairs of North and South America, and remained the basis of American foreign policy for over a century.

Monroe, Marilyn (1926-62) American film star, one of Hollywood's most famous 'sex goddesses', and also a fine screen actress. She showed a great talent for comedy, as in *The Seven-Year Itch* (1955) and *Some Like It Hot* (1959). In her last film, *The Misfits* (1961), written by Arthur MILLER, she also began to show her dramatic prowess.

Montagu, Charles, 1st Earl of Halifax (1661-1715) English wit,

Marilyn Monroe, whose short life symbolized the glamour and tragedy of stardom

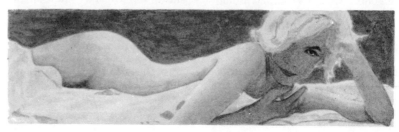

poet, patron of literature, Whig politician and financial genius who, as a Lord of the Treasury (1692), devised ways of raising money for WILLIAM III's war with France. He started the National Debt (1693) by borrowing £1 million by life annuities, and formed the Bank of England (1694), originally as a merchant company which lent money to the government for interest and for privileges, including permission to issue banknotes.

Montaigne, Michel Eyquen de (1533-92) French moralist and creator of the essay, a word invented by him for his written reflections, the first volumes of which were published in 1580. The *Essais*, which provide an intriguing and penetrating self-portrait of the author, are remarkable for their sincerity, lucidity, tolerance and wisdom. Written in a languorous, familiar and racy style, they had an important influence on both French and English literature.

Montanus SEE TERTULLIAN

Montcalm de Saint-Véran, Marquis de (1712-59) French lieutenant-general, commander of the French troops in Canada in the Seven Years' War (1756-63). After three years of staving off British attacks on Canada, Montcalm was killed when Quebec fell to James WOLFE.

Montesquieu, Charles de Secondat, Baron de (1689-1755) French political philosopher, author of *Lettres Persanes* (1721), a witty satire on Parisian society, ostensibly seen through the eyes of two Persian visitors, attacking contemporary religious and political abuses. Montesquieu also published two other important works, most notable of which is his famous historical essay, *De l'Esprit des Lois* (1748), which influenced political thought in both Europe and America.

Montessori, Maria (1870-1952) Italian educator who advocated 'free discipline', with children moving naturally about their tasks, and the provision of simple but stimulating teaching apparatus. She was the first woman medical graduate of Rome University, where she lectured (1900-7). Following the ideas of E. Seguin, she taught backward children to read and write – *The Montessori Method* (1912) describes how she applied similar methods to normal slum children from three to six years of age and *The Advanced Montessori Method* (1917) developed the material for six to ten year olds.

Monteverdi, Claudio (1567-1643) Italian composer of the late Renais-

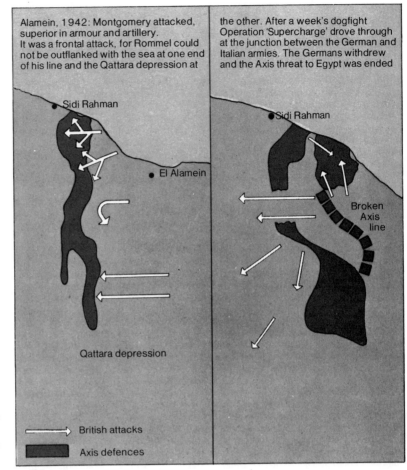

Alamein, 1942: Montgomery attacked, superior in armour and artillery.
It was a frontal attack, for Rommel could not be outflanked with the sea at one end of his line and the Qattara depression at the other. After a week's dogfight Operation 'Supercharge' drove through at the junction between the German and Italian armies. The Germans withdrew and the Axis threat to Egypt was ended

Sidi Rahman

El Alamein

Qattara depression

Sidi Rahman

Broken Axis line

→ British attacks

■ Axis defences

sance. He wrote *Orpheus* (1607), one of the finest early operas, and the *Vespers* (1610), settings of the vesper psalms and motets, which were probably published as a collection to show a potential employer the range of which he was capable, and were never intended for performance as a unity. His madrigals (more than 250) show a strong sense of dramatic colour, as do his specifically religious works. Of Monteverdi's operas that survive, *The Coronation of Poppaea* (1642), on the theme of NERO's rejection of his wife for his mistress, is probably his masterpiece. Monteverdi took the post of *maestro di cappella* at St Mark's, Venice, in 1613 and remained there until the end of his life. He became a priest in 1632.

Montezuma II (c. 1480-1520) Aztec emperor (1502-20) of Mexico at the time of the Spanish conquest. He ruled some five million people from Tenochtitlán (Mexico City), enlarging an empire that already stretched from the Pacific to the Atlantic. Unfavourable omens convinced Montezuma of impending punishment by the god Quetzalcoatl and made him try to propitiate CORTÉS, the Spanish conquistador, who imprisoned him. Montezuma was killed by his own subjects when Cortés brought him

out to tell them to end their uprising against the Spaniards.

Montfort, Simon de (c. 1208-65) English statesman, 6th Earl of Leicester, who led a rebellion of barons against the autocratic rule of Henry III. His alliance of barons, knights, clergy and burgesses won the Barons' War (1263-5) and made de Montfort virtual ruler. His Parliament (1265) included (with the barons) middle-class knights and burgesses to represent shires and boroughs. De Montfort was killed at the Battle of Evesham.

Montgolfier, Joseph Michel (1740-1810) and **Jacques Etienne (1745-99)** French pioneer balloonists, who in 1782 carried out their initial experiments with a model hot air balloon and gave their first public demonstration in June 1783.

Montgomery, Sir Bernard Law, First Viscount of Alamein (born 1887) British Field-Marshal who, as Commander of British Forces in North Africa during the Second World War, defeated the legendary ROMMEL at El Alamein (October 1942) and ousted Axis forces from the continent. His success lay in careful planning, refusing to commit his forces to any action until he had sufficient supplies of men and material. He had an unusual ability to inspire men with his own confidence and to this end made a cult of his own personality. After the invasion of Normandy in 1944, his strategy of drawing the main weight of the German counter-offensive on to the British flank played a major part in the Americans' rapid advance, and he put forward a plan for a thrust to the Rhine, which might well have shortened the war, but EISENHOWER opted for a safer advance on a broad front. Montgomery's handling of the Allied armies in the Ardennes resulted in the failure of Germany's final offensive under von Rundstedt, from whom Montgomery later accepted the capitulation of the German army. He commanded the British-occupied zone of Germany (1945-6) and was Deputy Supreme Allied Commander, NATO (1951-8).

Montherlant, Henri de (1896-1972) French novelist, essayist and dramatist. His reputation as a novelist chiefly rests upon *The Bachelors* (1934), an ironic portrait of three degenerate noblemen, and *The Young Girls* (1936-9). This was a series of satirical volumes consisting largely of an imaginary correspondence between a lecherous writer and a group of female admirers. Montherlant later won fame as a dramatist with plays such as *The Dead Queen* (1942), *Malatesta* (1946), *The Master of Santiago* (1948) and *Broceliande* (1956).

Monticelli, Adolphe (1824-86) French painter of sumptuous, richly-coloured still-lifes and flower pieces, circus scenes, and *fêtes galantes*. He was much admired by van GOGH, who was stimulated by his use of *impasto* (paint thickly applied) and his emotional use of colour. Evidence of his popularity is shown by the existence of numerous forgeries of his work.

Montini, Giovanni Batista see PAUL VI

Montrose, James Graham, 1st Marquis of (1612-50) Leading Scottish royalist during the English Civil War. Deserting the Presbyterian cause, he fought for CHARLES I, winning the battles of Tippermuir, Inverlochy and Kilsyth, and seizing Aberdeen and Dundee to gain royalist supremacy in Scotland. He was defeated at Philiphaugh (1645) and fled abroad. Montrose returned to Scotland in 1650 and tried unsuccessfully to raise the clans for Prince Charles, the future CHARLES II, but was seized and executed.

Moore, George (1852-1933) Irish novelist, who wrote naturalistic fiction and chronicles of his time. His best-known novels are *Esther Waters* (1894), and *The Brook Kerith* (1916), about CHRIST. His memoirs, such as the trilogy *Hail and Farewell* (1911-14) and *Conversations in Ebury Street* (1924), are a personal guide to the literary life of Dublin and London.

Moore, George E. (1873-1958) English philosopher who, with RUSSELL, led the revolt against Idealist philosophy. His approach to analysis greatly influenced WITTGENSTEIN and analytic philosophy at Oxford in the 1950s.

Moore, Marianne (born 1887) American poet and Pulitzer prize winner who tries to visualize 'insects, lower animals, or human beings – to wonder if they are happy and what will become of them'. The results are short, odd, colourful poems. A friend of POUND, she edited *The Dial* in New York from 1925 to 1929. Her *Collected Poems* were published in 1951.

Moore, Thomas (1779-1852) Irish song-writer and lyric poet whose *Irish Melodies* (1807-34) contain his most tuneful lyrics. In his day he was known for ephemeral political satire on behalf of the Whigs.

Moraes, Dom (born 1938) Indian poet whose work brought him fame at an early age. With his first poems, *A Beginning* (1957), he became the first non-English poet to win the Hawthornden Prize. Later volumes include *John Nobody* (1965). His work is primarily concerned with racial and social issues.

Moravia, Alberto (born 1907) Italian novelist, whose work analyses contemporary Roman society and explores the twin themes of social alienation and loveless sexuality, as in *The Woman of Rome* (1947), a sympathetic portrayal of a prostitute. In his later works Moravia portrays working-class life, which to him is a world of boredom, indifference to cruelty, and promiscuity.

More, Sir Thomas (1478-1535) English lawyer, politician, scholar and author, who became Lord Chancellor to HENRY VIII. His best-known literary work is *Utopia* (1516), which concerns a land with an ideal form of government. More had an international reputation as a humanist scholar and was on close terms with COLET, Lily and ERASMUS. He was executed for his refusal to deny papal authority and to acquiesce in the divorce of CATHARINE of Aragon.

Moreau, Gustave (1826-98) French Symbolist painter, the teacher of MATISSE and ROUALT. With paintings such as *Salome before Herod* (1870), Moreau both anticipated and exemplified that aspect of French Symbolism known as 'decadent', which emphasizes the morbid side of sexuality and death. The combination of Moreau's mysterious subject-matter and the enamel-like luminosity of his colours produces a bizarre effect.

Morgagni, Giovanni (1682-1771) Italian physician, founder of the science of pathology. One of the first doctors to look beyond the symptoms of disease to the inner causes and mechanisms that produce it. His *On the Sites and Causes of Diseases* (1761), contains accounts of the causes and courses of such ailments as consolidation of the lung, cirrhosis of the liver, aneurysm and disease of the heart valves.

Morgan, Sir Henry (c. 1635-88) Welsh buccaneer who became Lieutenant-Governor of Jamaica. Taken to Jamaica as a boy, he became leader of the English, French and Dutch buccaneers who terrorized Spanish Central America, sailing as a privateer against Spanish ships in time of war. His capture of Panama City in 1671 breached an Anglo-Spanish treaty of 1670 and he was tried, but CHARLES II forgave and knighted him. Morgan became Lieutenant-Governor of Jamaica in 1674 – with the task of ending buccaneering.

Morgan, John (1735-89) American physician, who pioneered medical education in America. He founded the school of medicine at the University of Pennsylvania.

Morgan, John Pierpont (1837-1913) American industrialist who built up one of the world's most powerful banking houses, specializing in the provision of financial services which made possible the formation of large industrial corporations, including US Steel, General Electric and International Harvester.

Morgan, Lewis (1818-81) American ethnologist and lawyer, who defended the land rights of an Iroquois tribe. In 1871, he published *Systems of Consanguinity and Affinity of the Human Family*, a detailed study of kinship terminology, based mainly on his own visits to other tribes. His work *Ancient Society* (1877), in which he divided human history into three stages – savagery, barbarism and civilization – led to the recognition of different kinship systems, and to the study of small and simple societies in which the forms of organization are largely centred around kinship.

Morgan, Thomas (1866-1945) American biologist whose work in genetics has vastly improved our understanding of the laws and mechanisms of heredity, with far-reaching consequences in medicine, animal and plant husbandry. Morgan's experiments with the fruit flies pinpointed the location of genes in the chromosomes of the cell nucleus and proved the theory of hereditary transmission. All subsequent research in genetics has been based on his pioneer work. He was awarded the Nobel Prize for Medicine in 1933.

Móricz, Zsigmond (1879-1942) Hungarian novelist, playwright and journalist. His novels and short stories chronicle the debilitating narrowness of Hungarian village and provincial life.

Mörike, Eduard (1804-75) German novelist and lyric poet. His slender output of poetry, which at first passed unnoticed, was collected in *Poems* (1838), which includes 'Peri-grina', 'The abandoned servant girl', and 'Agnes', lyrical works pervaded by a nostalgia for the lost happiness of youth. Mörike's educational novel, *Artist Nolten* (1832), describes the life of an artist who commits suicide and is regarded as a landmark in German Romantic fiction.

Morison, Stanley (1889-1967) English bibliographer and typographer who greatly influenced newspaper and book design. In 1923 he became typographical adviser to the Monotype Corporation and held similar positions at the Cambridge University Press and *The Times*, where he designed the Times Roman type face. He wrote the official history of *The Times* in addition to many books on typography.

Morley, Thomas (c. 1557-1603) English composer who introduced the ballet (a dance and refrain) into the English madrigal. Besides being a leading Elizabethan madrigalist, he

Design by Stanley Morison, whose typeface for *The Times* newspaper, Times Roman, is popular also for books

also composed church, lute, viol and virginal music. Morley wrote a textbook, *A Plain and Easy Introduction to Practical Music* (1597), which was used for two centuries, and composed songs for SHAKESPEARE, including 'It was a Lover and His Lass' in *As You Like It*.

Morris, William (1834-96) English poet, painter, printer and designer, one of the leaders of the Pre-Raphaelite Brotherhood, who had a strong, enduring influence on English visual taste. Inspired by RUSKIN he applied himself to providing a worthy and beautiful setting to life, and with BURNE-JONES, ROSSETTI and Madox BROWN, formed a company of craftsmen and interior designers. Morris began writing poetry in the early days of the 'Brotherhood' at Oxford and in 1858 he published *The Defence of Guenevere*, which an-

nounced a new Romantic age in a rich, archaic style. As much a convinced socialist as a herald of the Gothic revival, his ideals found literary expression in political romances such as *News from Nowhere* (1891), which reveals his horror of the effects of capitalism and industrialization.

Morse, Samuel Finley Breese (1791-1872) American artist of distinction, who at the age of 40 became interested in electrical telegraphy, but was just beaten into second place for its invention by COOKE and WHEATSTONE, working independently in Britain. He introduced the use of electromagnetic relays to extend the range of transmission and also the now famous code of dots and dashes. In 1843, Congress was persuaded to finance him to set up the first experimental telegraph in the US, from Washington to Baltimore, completed in June 1844. A whole network was installed during the next decade by several competing companies, which eventually amalgamated into Western Union (1856).

Morton, William Thomas Green (1819-68) American dentist who recognized the possible application of ether in surgery and patented the process in collaboration with Charles Jackson. In 1846, he successfully demonstrated that ether could create general anaesthesia during a major operation in the Massachusetts General Hospital, thus establishing the procedure as an integral part of surgery.

Moses (late 13th cent. BC) Hebrew lawgiver whose precepts underlie Judaism and Christianity. According to the Book of Exodus in the Bible, Moses was born among Hebrew tribes enslaved in Egypt (possibly by

After more than a century, Morse's code remains in widespread use. Left, an early print-out machine for Morse code

A .—	J .———	S ...
B —...	K —.—	T — *(3 units)*
C —.—.	L .—..	U ..—
D —..	M ——	V ...—
E . *(1 unit)*	N —.	W .——
F ..—.	O ———	X —..—
G ——.	P .——.	Y —.——
H	Q ——.—	Z ——..
I ..	R .—.	

1 .————	5	9 ————.
2 ..———	6 —....	0 —————
3 ...——	7 ——...	
4 ....—	8 ———..	

Period .—.—.—	Query ..——..	Fraction bar —..—.
Comma ——..——	Apostrophe .————.	Parentheses —.——.—
Colon ———...	Hyphen —....—	Quote marks .—..—.

A REMINDER
to *Prime Ministers, Tyrants, Red Revolutionaries, Big Men, Treaty-Makers, Hotheads, Journalists, Ex-Conchies, Nationalists, &c., &c.*

Submitted with Best Wishes for Christmas and for the Peace of the World by
MABEL & STANLEY MORISON
No. 11 Hollyberry Lane, Hampstead, N.W. 5

RAMSES II), led their escape through the Sinai Desert towards Canaan, and at Mount Sinai delivered to the young Israelite nation its moral and religious basis, the Ten Commandments. The strict Mosaic law was eventually reinterpreted by JESUS.

Mosley, Sir Oswald Ernald (born 1896) Founder and leader of British fascism. Successively a Tory, Independent and Labour MP in the 1920s, he became a minister in the Labour Government of 1929, but resigned in 1930, complaining of the government's 'spineless apathy' in failing to combat unemployment. He founded the British Union of Fascists in 1932, which became so anti-Semitic, violent and pro-German that an Act of Parliament was passed in 1936 to suppress its para-military organizations. From 1940-3 Mosley was imprisoned under the Defence Regulations. His political life was a tragedy; in the 1920s he was regarded as one of the ablest men in Parliament and possibly a future Labour or Conservative Prime Minister. He had a brilliant mind and his economic policies were both daring and original, but his rabid anti-Semitism and Fascist sympathies eventually rendered him impotent as a political force.

Mossadegh, Mohammed (1881-1967) Persian politician, who nationalized British oil interests in Persia. While Prime Minister of Persia from 1951-3, he introduced the Oil Nationalization Act in 1951, which expropriated the assets of the Anglo-Iranian Oil Company (though production was eventually taken over in 1954 by a consortium 40 per cent owned by British Petroleum). His aim was to overthrow the Shah, but he himself was ousted by a royalist uprising in 1953, and imprisoned. Mossadegh sometimes wept copiously in public and often appeared carried on a bed.

Mössbauer, Rudolph Ludwig (born 1929) German physicist who showed that atoms emitting gamma-rays can sometimes do so without recoiling. Under certain conditions, atoms give out gamma-rays and recoil as they do so in the same way as a gun when it is fired. In the late 1950s, Mössbauer found that if the source of the gamma-rays is a crystalline solid, some atoms emit rays without recoiling, the recoil being taken up by the whole crystal. He explained this effect (now known as the Mössbauer effect) by showing that the overall crystal structure could take the part of the individual atom and, being far more massive, not recoil at all. Among other things the Mössbauer effect has enabled the gravita-

tional red shift of light predicted by EINSTEIN's general theory of relativity to be measured in the laboratory.

Motherwell, Robert (born 1915) American Abstract Expressionist painter, who knew Surrealist painters, such as DE KOONING and POLLOCK, in New York, and under their influence moved towards an automatic way of painting that led to Abstract Expressionism. He has written extensively on art, particularly on Dadaism and the Surrealists.

Mountbatten, Louis, First Earl Mountbatten of Burma (born 1900) British naval officer and uncle of the Duke of Edinburgh, who during the Second World War was Supreme Allied Commander in South-East Asia (1943-6), and afterwards, the last Viceroy of India. A specialist in combined operations, he was responsible for the British plans for the Allied landings in North Africa in 1942, before his appointment in South-East Asia. With an army of Indian, British, Gurkha, American and Chinese troops, he drove back the Japanese and recaptured Burma. His plans for the reconquest of Malaya were forestalled by the surrender of the Japanese in South-East Asia in 1945. In 1947 he was appointed to succeed WAVELL as Viceroy of India and within five months had performed the difficult task of transferring power to India and Pakistan. Although there was animosity between the two countries, he not only retained the friendship of both, but was asked by India to become its first Governor-General (1947-8). Despite an atmosphere disturbed by the threat of violence, he was able to hand over responsibility to JINNAH and NEHRU in circumstances of comparative peace.

Mozart, Wolfgang Amadeus (1756-91) Austrian composer whose talents emerged at an early age. When he was six, he was a harpsichord prodigy and by 12 he had written his first opera – and had it produced. The promise which was to make him unequalled in terms of musical imagination and achievement was to be fulfilled in the course of his short creative life, but his maturity was marked by personal troubles, fickle audiences, unreliable patrons and periods of extreme poverty. Mozart wrote about 40 symphonies, important among them No. 31 (The *Paris*), No. 36 (The *Linz*), No. 38 (The *Prague*) and No. 41 (The *Jupiter*). The classical, three-movement concerto was, however, Mozart's own creation: his 21 piano concertos are the form's first and most splendidly varied monuments. He also brought operatic art to one of its highest

points, first in his collaborations with Lorenzo da Ponte as librettist (*The Marriage of Figaro*, 1786, based on BEAUMARCHAIS), *Don Giovanni* (1787) and *Cosi fan Tutti* (1790), then in his humanistic masterpiece with its Masonic symbolism, *Die Zauberflöte* (*The Magic Flute*, 1791). Mozart made a distinguished contribution to chamber music with his 24 string quartets, violin sonatas and other works. His final masterpiece, a setting of the Requiem, was unfinished when he died from typhus. Mozart was buried in Vienna in an unmarked, pauper's grave.

Muawiyah I (602-80) Arab caliph (661-80) who made the caliphate hereditary and organized the Arab empire founded by ABU-BAKR. Muawiyah became a follower of Mohammed about 630 and, as one of Abu-Bakr's generals, conquered Syria and Egypt. He was elected caliph after the death of Ali, and founded the Omayyad dynasty (661-750). Muawiyah campaigned against the Greeks, threatened Constantinople, and extended the empire to the Indus.

Mudie, Charles Edward (1816-90) English lending library proprietor who greatly influenced Victorian literary taste. Mudie's Lending Library, founded in 1842, made easily available the three-volume novels of the time. He banned books he thought likely to offend Victorian sensibilities (e.g. MEREDITH's *Ordeal of Richard Feverel*), while his approval made best-sellers of melodramas, including Mrs Henry Wood's *East Lynne* and the novels of Marie Corelli.

Muhammad Zaman (17th cent.) Persian artist, who revolutionized painting during the Safavid period by introducing European techniques.

Muhammadi of Herat (16th cent.) Persian court painter to Prince Ibrahim. His work marked a new movement in Persian miniature painting of the 1570s towards a more naturalistic depiction of figures in their pastoral environment. He also made a number of single figure studies, a trend which became fashionable during the following century.

Muhlenberg, Henry Melchior (1711-87) German-born clergyman who emigrated to Pennsylvania in 1742 and founded several Lutheran churches. He is recognized as the founder of Lutheranism in the US. His three clergyman sons played a part in American political life during the War of Independence.

Muir, Edwin (1887-1959) Scottish poet, much of whose work is in the form of symbolic tales of visions and mystical events. His books include *Chorus of the Newly Dead* (1926), *The Narrow Place* (1943) and *Collected Poems* (1952). He also wrote three novels, literary criticism and an autobiography (1954). With his wife Willa, he made important translations from German literature, notably the works of KAFKA and BROCH.

Mulcaster, Richard (c. 1530-1611) English educator who was far ahead of his time in his belief that pupils should be taught, by the use of familiar language, according to their abilities.

Müller, Paul (1899-1965) Swiss chemist who first prepared DDT. He searched for a new pesticide which, unlike those in use at the time, would be deadly for insects only, centring his work around complex chlorinated hydrocarbons. In 1939 he found what he was looking for. Its chemical name, dichlorodiphenyltrichloroethane, was abbreviated to DDT. Within a few years it was used throughout the world, especially against mosquitoes.

Müller, Johannes (1801-58) German physiologist who clarified the nature of sensory nerves. He showed that the type of response that follows stimulation of a sensory nerve depends not on the type of stimulation (heat, dampness, etc.), but on the type of sensory nerve. The optic nerve, for example, however it is stimulated, will record a flash of light.

Multatuli see DOUWES DEKKER, Eduard

Mumford, Lewis (born 1895) American writer and social critic. His central ideas on city living and the machine age are discussed in works including *The Culture of Cities* (1938) and *Art and Technics* (1952). *City in History* (1961) was a study of urban dwelling, the technology of which was examined in *The Myth of the Machine* (1967). His advice on planning has been widely sought in the US and elsewhere.

Munch, Edvard (1863-1944) Norwegian painter who was preoccupied with the Symbolist themes of love and death. In Paris in the early 1890s he was influenced by GAUGUIN's style, its synthetic approach to form and colour being developed by Munch as a means of expressing his own neurotic vision. He lived in Germany from 1892 to 1908, and strongly influenced the German Expressionist movement, especially through his mastery of woodcut and lithography.

Münzer, Thomas (c. 1489-1525) German religious enthusiast and Anabaptist. Denouncing LUTHER's form of Protestantism, he mobilized discontented peasants in Thuringia during the Peasants' War (1524-5), ousted Mülhausen's civic government, and founded a Socialist theocracy. His war on the nobility soon ended in capture and he was executed by PHILIP OF HESSE.

Murad I (1319-89) Sultan of Turkey (1359-89) who extended the Ottoman Empire into southeastern Europe. He took Adrianople (1365) and made it his capital, conquered eastern Thrace and much of Bulgaria by 1372, raided Albania and Greece (1371) and captured Sofia (1385). He withstood repeated attacks by Christian armies from Venice, Hungary, the Byzantine Empire and elsewhere, but at Kossovo (1389), where his troops defeated a Balkan army 100,000 strong, he was killed.

Murad III (1546-95) Sultan of Turkey (1574-95), whose reign marked the beginning of the decline of the Ottoman Empire. Corruption in government and the army was rife as Murad sold offices and advanced his harem favourites. His armies conquered parts of the Crimea, Persia and Georgia, but their successes did not halt the decline at home.

Murasaki-Shikibu (c. 978-c. 1016) Japanese female novelist and diarist, author of what is generally recognized as the masterpiece of Japanese literature, *The Tale of Genji*, relating his adventures with women, by an allusive rather than erotic approach. Although this work contains many poems, it differs markedly from earlier works, such as ARIWARA NO NARIHIRA's *The Tales of Ise*, in that it is a work of subtlety and depth in which prose and verse are equal.

Murchison, Sir Roderick (1792-1871) Scottish geologist, whose work on the rocks underlying the old red sandstone in South Wales led to the definition of the strata known as the Silurian System. He had earlier worked with LYELL on the Auvergne volcanics and with SEDGWICK on the structure of the Alps, and later collaborated again with Sedgwick on a study of the rocks that were to become known as the Devonian System.

Murdock, William (1754-1839) Scottish steam engineer, who invented a coal-gas process. From 1779 while working for BOULTON and WATT in Cornwall he carried out numerous investigations, including the destructive distillation of wood, peat and coal, and (1799) developed methods for storing and purifying gas.

Murillo, Bartolomé (1617-82) Spanish painter of religious and genre subjects, best known for the sentimental charm of his pictures of the Virgin Mary and of beggar boys clad in picturesque rags.

Murphy, William (born 1892) American doctor who with Minot and Whipple discovered in 1926 that patients with pernicious anaemia could be treated with raw liver. Since then the active substance has been isolated from raw liver and is now given by injection. The three men shared a Nobel Prize in 1934.

Murray, Sir James (1837-1915) Scottish editor of the Oxford *New English Dictionary* (1884-1928). This monumental scholarly work listed all words current from the 12th century onward, giving for each its etymology, current pronunciation and a range of meanings, fully illustrated by quotations. Murray was appointed by the Philological Society, on whose material, including two million quotations collected from 1857, the dictionary was based.

Murray II, John (1778-1843) Scottish Victorian publisher, notably of BYRON. He founded the Tory *Quarterly Review* (1809), to which SOUTHEY, HAZLITT and Walter SCOTT contributed.

Murray, Margaret (1863-1963) English Egyptologist, anthropologist and author who won fame with her idea that medieval witchcraft represented a survival of Stone Age religion. Her publications included the *Witch Cult in Western Europe* (1921) and the *Divine King in England* (1954).

Murray, William see MANSFIELD, First Earl of

Murrow, Edward (1908-65) American war correspondent, whose vivid descriptions of the Battle of Britain and the 'Blitz' were broadcast from London during the Second World War. He joined The Columbia Broadcasting System in 1935, became its European director and, from 1939 to 1945, war correspondent. After the war he became CBS Vice-President and then news analyst. Murrow also produced many programmes for television, including the popular *See It Now*. From 1961 he was Director of the US Information Agency.

Musa, Gongo see GONGO MUSA

Musil, Robert (1880-1942) Austrian novelist, author of the outstanding novel *The Man Without Qualities* (1953-60).

Musschenbroek, Pieter van (1692-1761) Dutch physicist who in 1745 developed a device which could store and then release electricity from an electrostatic machine. It became known later as a Leyden jar, and was the first electric condenser (now called a capacitor).

Musset, Alfred de (1810-57) French Romantic poet, dramatist and novelist. Several of Musset's best-known works were inspired by his stormy liaison with novelist George SAND, including the novel *La Confession d'un enfant du siècle* (1836) and particularly the lyrics known collectively as *Les Nuits* (1835-7). Musset also achieved success as a playwright with such works as *Fantasio* (1833), *Lorenzaccio* and *On ne badine pas avec l'amour* (1834).

Mussolini, Benito (1883-1945) Italian dictator, known as 'Il Duce', whose schemes for Italian aggrandisement led Italy to war in partnership with HITLER's Germany, and, ultimately, to his death at the hands of Italian partisans in 1945. A one-time Socialist, Mussolini organized 'fasci' or groups, of working men to agitate for social revolutionary change after the First World War. By 1921 these had merged into a Fascist party – violently nationalist and anti-Communist – and the following year Mussolini led his 'March on Rome' and was invited by King Victor Emmanuel III to form a government. Mussolini assumed dictatorial powers and opponents were summarily dealt with. An aggressive foreign policy was backed by all-out militarism. When Italy invaded Abyssinia (1935), the hostility of the western democracies enabled CIANO, the Italian Foreign Minister, to bring together his master, Mussolini, and Hitler, in the 'Rome-Berlin Axis'. With support from Germany, Mussolini annexed Albania (1939), and as soon as Germany had defeated France, he entered the war in the summer of 1940. But the Italian armies were defeated in Greece, Libya and East Africa and Mussolini had repeatedly to be helped by Hitler, on whom he became completely dependent. In 1943, he was forced to resign, and was imprisoned. He was rescued by a German parachute commando (September 1943) and set up as puppet ruler of a Fascist Republic in northern Italy, under German control. When the Allies forced the Germans out of Italy, Mussolini fled to the Swiss frontier with his mistress Clara Petacci but they were caught by Italian partisans and shot.

Mussorgsky, Modest Petrovich (1839-81) Russian composer. Mussorgsky served in the army and civil

Mussolini, the pocket caesar, at his peak, with newspapers announcing his downfall

service before becoming a composer whose style developed a daring, original use of harmony. He is probably best known for *Pictures from an Exhibition* for piano, and *Night on the Bare Mountain* which RIMSKY-KORSAKOV edited, but which is far more striking in Mussorgsky's rarely heard original. Rimsky-Korsakov also edited Mussorgsky's chief work, the opera *Boris Godunov*, though SHOSTAKOVICH's edition is far closer to Mussorgsky's intention. This work was hindered by drink and he died from alcoholism.

Mutanabbi, al- (915-65) Leading Arab poet, who modified the *qasida*, the traditional verse form.

Mutsuhito (1852-1912) Emperor of Japan from 1867, known during his reign as 'Meiji', who broke the seven centuries' rule of the Shoguns (Feudal Lords) and initiated the Westernization of Japan. He and his Prime Minister, ITO, put an end to feudalism and Japan's isolation and set up a Western-style parliamentary and bureaucratic government. An army and a navy, were raised and trained (the one on German lines, the other on British), and by aggressive expansion in Korea and Manchuria and victories against China (1894-5), and Russia (1904-5), established Japan as a world power.

Muybridge, Eadweard (1830-1904) English-born photographer, who in 1852 emigrated to the United States and became a pioneer of motion photography. Following an argument about the gait of a horse, he demonstrated photographically that there was an instant when the horse had all four feet off the ground. In his major work on human and animal locomotion, carried out principally after 1878, Muybridge required his objects to move in front of a series of up to 30 cameras, a foot apart, facing a white wall. Their electromagnetic shutters were set off independently, either by clockwork, or by trip wires broken by the subject's movement.

Myers, Frederic (1843-1901) English scholar and pioneer of psychical research in Britain, and co-author with Edmund Guerney of *Phantasms of the Living* (1886).

Myron (5th cent. BC) Athenian sculptor of the Classical period, whose *Discus-thrower* (*c.* 440 BC) is one of the most famous pieces of all time. Originally cast in bronze, stone copies, probably Roman, are all that remain. Designed round a half-circle crossed by an S-curve, it is a convincing symbol of rapid motion, as well as a revolutionary concept for sculpture in the round.

Fridtjof Nansen aboard the *Fram*

N

Nabokov, Vladimir (born 1899)
Russian-born American novelist,
poet and lepidopterist whose highly
stylized fictions abound in artifice,
self-parody and urbane humour.
Nabokov's formal exuberance is
epitomized by *Pale Fire* (1962), a
curious hybrid novel in the form of a
poem and its eccentric commentary.
Even *Lolita* (1955) and *Ada* (1969),
which explicitly treat deviant sexuality, are saturated with erudite word
games and elaborate literary jokes.
Nabokov considers his greatest
achievement to be the discovery of a
species of butterfly, which now bears
his name.

Nader, Ralph (born 1934) American lawyer and 'consumer advocate'
whose pressure on the US automobile
industry and public opinion brought
national legislation enforcing the
adoption of a number of safety
features in motor vehicles. Nader later
turned his attention to other issues
such as pollution, health hazards in
industry and food packaging.

Nadir Shah (1688-1747) Turkish-
born Shah of Persia (1736-47). A successful commander, he helped Shah
Tahmasp II to repel Afghan, Turkish
and Russian invaders (1726-31), then
deposed him to become Shah by
popular acclaim. He restored Persia's
rule over northern India and seized
Delhi (1739), taking back to Persia
Mogul treasures, including the Koh-
i-noor diamond and the Peacock
Throne. His own bodyguard assassinated him.

Nagy, Imre (1895-1958) Leader of
the Hungarian revolt against the
Soviet Union in 1956. As Prime
Minister (1953-5) Nagy instituted
a measure of political and economic
freedom, but was ousted by Rakosi,
the most powerful and most hated
man in Hungary. KHRUSCHEV forced
Rakosi out in 1956, and Nagy became
Premier once again, promising the
withdrawal of Russian troops and
free elections. For the first time a
Communist leader tried to govern
within the framework of a multi-
party administration, but his efforts
were foiled by the spread of the
anti-Soviet revolt. Eventually, Nagy
renounced the Warsaw Pact, declared Hungary's neutrality, and appealed to the United Nations for
protection. Russian tanks suppressed
the revolt early in November; Nagy
was replaced and later betrayed by
KADAR, a member of his government.

Nainsukh (18th cent.) Indian painter whose naturalistic and graceful
style revolutionized miniature painting in the Punjab hill states.

**Naipaul, Vidiadhar Surajprasad
(born 1932)** Trinidad-born Indian
novelist. His novels *The Mystic
Masseur* (1957), *Miguel Street* (1959)
and *A House for Mr Biswas* (1961)
are rich comedies of Hindu life in the
West Indies. *An Area of Darkness*
(1964) is a sombre and powerful
book about India.

Nanak (1469-1538) Indian teacher
and founder of Sikhism, a religion
combining Islamic and Hindu beliefs
advocating universal religious toleration and the worship of a single God.
A 'sikh' or disciple of the religious
teacher Kabir (c. 1450-1518), who
held similar ideas, Nanak spread the
new teaching all over India and the
Middle East. Later, gurus (teachers)
established a sikh centre at Amritsar
and compiled the *Adi Granth*, the
sacred writings. In the 17th century
persecution forced the sikhs to become a militant community with
special rites and customs, including
long hair and the addition of the word
singh (lion) to their own names.

Nansen, Fridtjof (1861-1930) Norwegian explorer, zoologist, artist and
statesman, who was the first man to
cross Greenland (from east to west),
and who tried to reach the North
Pole by drifting with the ice. Off
Novaya Zemlya, Nansen deliberately

let the pack-ice freeze round his specially-built vessel *Fram* and, using ocean currents, drifted with the ice to 85° 55′ N before abandoning it (1895). Taking to skis and dog-sleds, he reached 86° 14′ N, a record northerly latitude. Nansen became a leading Norwegian statesman, and won the Nobel Peace Prize (1922), after organizing food supplies for famine-stricken Russia and the repatriation of First World War prisoners.

Napoleon I, Bonaparte (1769-1821) French emperor and military leader of genius. Corsican-born, he became an artillery officer and achieved promotion rapidly, establishing his reputation in the Revolutionary wars in northern Italy. His marriage in 1796 to Josephine de Beauharnais

helped him to political powers. In 1799 he returned from an unsuccessful campaign in Egypt to overthrow the Directory and was appointed First Consul. In 1802 he became Consul for life and was virtual dictator of France; in 1804 he crowned himself Emperor. In a series of brilliant campaigns he defeated Austria (Austerlitz, 1805) and Prussia (Jena and Auerstadt, 1806), but in the Peninsula War (1809-14) WELLINGTON's strategy drained his strength and the Continental System (1806), which entailed a commercial blockade of Britain, became unpopular with its participants, whose trade also suffered. In another campaign against Austria, Napoleon routed her army at Wagram (July 1809), and dictated peace terms in Vienna. He invaded

Russia in 1812, won the battle of Borodino and reached Moscow, but was forced to retreat from the burning city which the Muscovites had deliberately fired to deny the French shelter and supplies. His Grand Army was virtually destroyed by the harsh winter during the subsequent retreat, and by Russian 'guerilla' and scorched-earth tactics. As a result of French defeats in the War of the Fourth Coalition (1813-14) the allies entered Paris at the end of March 1814. Napoleon abdicated and was granted the principality of Elba. He escaped from Elba in February 1815 and returned to France where he resumed power for the period known as the Hundred Days (March–June 1815), which ended in his defeat at Waterloo (18 June 1815) and imprisonment on St Helena, where he died.

Napoleon III (1808-73) Emperor of the French from 1852-70 and creator of the Second Empire. He was the son of Louis Bonaparte (the brother of NAPOLEON I) and of Hortense Beauharnais, Napoleon's step-daughter. He was probably a member of the Carbonari secret society and led two unsuccessful risings against LOUIS-PHILIPPE's 'July Monarchy', following the second of which (1840) he was caught and imprisoned. He escaped to England and on the death of the Duke of Reichstadt (1832), the only son of Napoleon I, he became head of the Napoleonic dynasty. His family connection facilitated his election as President of the Second French Republic (1848). After a referendum in 1851 he seized dictatorial powers and in 1852 the imperial title. His successes (the Crimean War, and the subsequent Congress of Paris, 1856) gave him an international reputation, and from 1856-66 he dominated Europe. He helped Piedmont in her campaign for a united Italy, but deserted his ally (1859) when it suited him. An abortive attempt (1863-7) to set up a puppet Mexican Empire under MAXIMILIAN's rule weakened his position. He was no match for BISMARCK, who isolated him diplomatically and then provoked the Franco-Prussian War (1870) during which Napoleon was captured at Sedan after a crushing defeat. Imprisonment in Germany was followed by exile in England, where he died.

Narayan, Rasipuram Krishnaswami (born 1907) Indian novelist, who writes ironic, humorous fiction about the middle-classes in southern India.

Nares, Sir George Strong (1831-1915) Scottish captain of maritime exploration vessels in the latter half of

Learning his lesson from ships destroyed by the crushing power of the northern ice, Nansen designed his *Fram* to survive by riding up above the pressure of the floes. It succeeded—to make an historic journey.

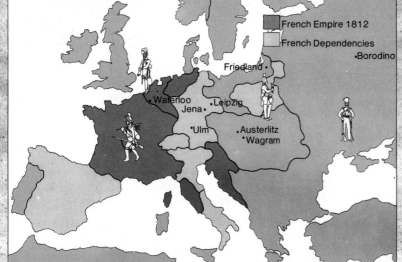

Europe, in 1812, at the watershed of Napoleonic power. Dominated by France and the territories under its control, Europe lived for three years in the shadow of the 'little corporal' before defeat at Waterloo ended for him in exile.

French Empire 1812

French Dependencies

•Borodino
Friedland •
•Waterloo
Jena • •Leipzig
•Ulm
•Austerlitz
•Wagram

the 19th century. Nares commanded HMS *Challenger* on its voyages to the Antarctic, Australia and South America.

Nash, John (1752-1835) English architect who developed the Regency style and also designed the fine town planning scheme for London which included Regent Street and its Quadrant. Many buildings in London bear witness to his architectural gifts, notably All Souls' Church, Langham Place, Carlton House Terrace, and the villas which he included in his plans for Regent's Park. Trained under a London architect, he began his career with the landscape gardener REPTON and was always ready to adapt his style to the wishes of his patron. The Brighton Pavilion, which Nash remodelled for the Prince Regent (later George IV), is externally Indian in style and internally mainly Chinese and Gothic.

Nash, Ogden (born 1902) American humorous poet, who takes many of the faults of bad verse – rambling, uncontrolled lines, irrelevant digressions, puns, ridiculous rhymes – and combines them into witty, satirical or fantastic works.

Nasier, Alcofribas see RABELAIS, François

Nasmyth, James (1808-90) Scottish engineer, who invented the steam hammer (1839), which increased the size of forging possible without loss of precision. It was designed to help in the forging of the giant paddle-wheel shaft of BRUNEL's ship the *Great Eastern*, but was never made because the ship was changed to screw propulsion. Nasmyth invented many other new appliances, including a planing machine and a steam piledriver, which, with other machine tools and machines (including steam locomotives after 1839), were made at his foundry at Patricroft.

Naso, Publius Ovidius see OVID

Nasser, Gamal Abdul (1918-70) Egyptian soldier-politician, creator (1958) and civilian dictator of the

United Arab Republic. His nationalization of the Suez Canal led to the Israeli-Franco-British attack on the Canal Zone in 1956. In 1952, his secret Free Officers Movement, with General Mohammed Neguib as its figurehead, seized power, forcing King FAROUK to abdicate, making Neguib Prime Minister and President, with Nasser as his deputy. In April 1954, he accused Neguib of absolutist ambitions and assumed the Premiership and presidential powers in November of the same year when Neguib was deposed. Two years later (June 1956) Nasser was officially elected President of Egypt. Nasser's achievements included a number of important social reforms and the building of the Aswan High Dam, with Soviet aid (1964). Nasser was ousted in the Six-Day war of

The orient in an English seaside town. Nash's Brighton Pavilion was externally Indian, Chinese and Gothic inside

1967, when Israel simultaneously defeated Egyptian, Jordanian and Syrian armies and extended her frontiers.

Nast, Thomas (1840-1902) German-born American political cartoonist, whose drawings in *Harper's Weekly* injected a new and vitriolic element into American political comment. Nast created the 'Tammany Tiger' (symbol of the corrupt Tammany Organization under 'Boss' Tweed), the 'Democratic Donkey' and the 'Republican Elephant'. His cartoons are said to have been the means of destroying Horace GREELEY's political career and hastening his death. In 1902 Nast was appointed US Consul to Ecuador, where he died.

Natsume Soseki (1867-1916) Japanese novelist and literary critic who studied English literature, an influence reflected in his subsequent writings, which began in 1905 with *I am a Cat*. In 1908, he began writing professionally for the *Asahi* newspaper which published his novels, including the outstanding *Sonny, Grass for a Pillow* and *Light and Darkness*, in serial form.

Nattier, Jean (1685-1766) French painter, famous for his portraits of

Traditional teaching—the educational force-feeding of children—was anathema to Scotsman Alexander Neill

the ladies at the court of Louis XV. His idealized female images, with oval heads, and doe-eyed expressions, are inclined to become repetitive. Unlike LA TOUR, he did not indicate his sitters' personalities but relied on flattery, approximating their attributes to Venus, the goddess of love, various other deities.

Nearchus (4th cent. BC) Macedonian admiral who supported ALEXANDER THE GREAT's attempts to explore the area in and around the north Indian Ocean and Persian Gulf. He commanded a data-collecting fleet, which sailed from the mouth of the Indus to the head of the Persian Gulf.

Nebuchadnezzar II (6th cent. BC) Chaldean King of Babylon who restored its ancient cities, perfecting the city of Babylon and its glories, the 'Hanging Gardens' and the immense ziggurat (stepped pyramid) to the god Marduk – the 'Tower of Babel'. Nebuchadnezzar defeated NECHO of Egypt, drove the Egyptians out of Asia, annexed Syria, and crushed Judaea, capturing many Jews as prisoners.

Needham, John (1713-81) English Catholic priest and scientist who held that all life, including animal life, arises from vegetation. This view ('spontaneous generation') was disproved when WEISSMANN developed his theory of germ plasm.

Nehru, Jawalharlal (1889-1964) Indian statesman, who became the first Prime Minister of India following her independence. Nehru joined GANDHI's non-violent Nationalist Movement (1919) and was repeatedly imprisoned (1921-34) by the British for his political activities. He became

general secretary of the Indian National Congress and its President (1929-30; 1936-7). He supported the British against the Axis powers in the Second World War but rejected the offer of dominion status made by the CRIPPS mission (1942). After independence (1947) he co-operated with the last viceroy, MOUNTBATTEN, in the partitioning of the sub-continent into India and Pakistan, and in the transfer of political power. As Prime Minister of India from 1947 until his death, he was a world leader of great moral stature, steadily advocating the settlement of international disputes without force, and holding a neutral position between the mutually hostile Western capitalist and Eastern Communist blocs. He committed India to industrialization and instigated the reorganization of the states on a linguistic basis.

Neill, Alexander Sutherland (1883-1973) Scottish educational reformer who, from 1924, was headmaster of Summerhill School in England. Neill challenged the practices of traditional schooling, including compulsory lessons and the authoritarian role of the teacher. He maintained that in a free atmosphere a child is more likely to develop into a well-balanced individual with a genuine feeling of responsibility for others.

Nekrasov, Nikolai Alekseyevich (1821-77) Russian poet and friend of DOSTOEVSKY and TURGENEV, with whom he collaborated on various literary periodicals, notably *Sovremennik*.

Nelson, Horatio, Viscount Nelson (1758-1805) British admiral whose victory at the Battle of Trafalgar (1805) destroyed Franco-Spanish naval power during the Napoleonic wars. Nelson was a supreme exponent of superior fire power to annihilate the enemy. His battle plans, which left much to the initiative of his captains, depended on careful timing and surprise, the objective being to break up the opposing fleet and 'bring about a pell-mell battle'. Nelson lost the sight of his right eye in action off Corsica (1794). He was appointed commodore in 1796, Rear Admiral in 1797 and lost his right arm at Santa Cruz later that year. In 1798 he virtually annihilated a fleet of French ships near the mouth of the Nile. In 1801, he was promoted to Vice-Admiral and, in the Baltic, as second-in-command to Sir Hyde Parker, he led a crippling attack on the Danish fleet anchored off Copenhagen (2 April 1801). Following the engagement he was created a Viscount. In 1803 he was given command of the Mediterranean fleet. During the Battle of Trafalgar, 18 out of 33 enemy ships were taken or destroyed, but Nelson's fleet remained intact. Nelson himself was mortally wounded on board his flagship, *Victory*, shortly after the start of the action.

Naval history's most famous signal, right, 'England expects . . .' flown as the British fleet engaged the fleets of France and Spain at Trafalgar in 1805. Below, the death of Nelson, shot by a French marksman during the early moments of his greatest victory

Nemcová, Božena (1820-82) The first Czech woman writer to become well known, who wrote the poetic, *Granny* (1855), describing a year in the life of a village community. She also wrote patriotic poems, as well as fairy and folk-tales.

Nemirovich-Danchenko, Vladimir Ivanovich (1859-1943) Co-founder (with STANISLAVSKY) and director of the Moscow Art Theatre who began his career by writing several novels and light comedies. In 1891 he was made director of the Moscow Philharmonic Society's Drama Course, and introduced reforms which gave the Russian theatre a less rigid style. After the Revolution he founded the Moscow Musical Studio where he applied his ideas to the development of a new style for opera and operetta.

Nenni, Pietro (born 1891) Italian politician, who united and led the Italian Socialist parties. He was one of the Socialists imprisoned with MUSSOLINI (1911) for rioting in protest against the war with Turkey. He became a left-wing journalist and, when Mussolini later suppressed his newspaper, *Avanti* (1926), was forced to take refuge in France. He was deported to Italy in 1942 and imprisoned. After the war, he became successively Deputy Premier and Foreign Minister, and was leader of the left-wing Socialists when the right wing split away from the party. As Deputy Premier again from 1963 to 1968 he reunited the Italian Socialist Party, and was elected its leader in 1966.

Nernst, Walter Hermann (1864-1941) German chemist who formulated the third law of thermodynamics (1906) and for which, with other contributions to physical chemistry, he was awarded the Nobel Prize in 1920. The law states that at the absolute zero of temperature ($-273\cdot12°C$), specific heats themselves become zero. As a result, it became possible to calculate the actual values of constants that characterize chemical reactions.

Nero (AD 37-68) Roman emperor whose excesses earned him widespread hatred. Although his reign saw a number of military successes in Asia Minor, Judaea and Britain, and the formation of a Black Sea fleet, Nero preferred sport, profligacy and the arts to the tasks of government. Opponents, real and imagined, were murdered, and many of Rome's Christians were massacred as scapegoats for a fire which destroyed most of the city in AD 64. The loathing in which Nero was held, and the huge taxes levied to rebuild Rome, culminated in provincial riots, and the Senate passed the death sentence on the emperor, who subsequently committed suicide.

Neruda, Jan (1834-91) Czech radical author and critic, whose poetry ranged from the limpid lyrics of *Simple Themes* (1883) to the nationalistic visions of *Good Friday Songs* (1896). His hatred of the upper classes gave his short stories a biting realism, notably *Tales of the Little Quarter* (1878), a powerful collection of stories about the inhabitants of Prague's old quarter. After 1862, he was the drama and literary critic of the leading Prague newspaper *Národnilisty*.

Neruda, Pablo (1904-73) Penname of Neftali Richardo Reyes Basualto, Chilean poet and diplomat, author of the *Canto General* (1950), *Cantos Ceremoniales* (1962) and *Soledades*. He was awarded the Nobel Prize for Literature (1971).

Nerval, Gérard de (1808-55) French poet whose hallucinatory writings, notably *Les Chimères*, a volume of sonnets, anticipate the Symbolists and Surrealists. Nerval's works also include an account of his travels in the Near East, *Voyages en Orient* (1843-51) and a translation of *Faust*, on which BERLIOZ based his *Damnation of Faust*.

Nervi, Pier Luigi (born 1891) Italian architect who has explored the handling of the structural and engineering possibilities of concrete. A major early work was the sports stadium at Florence, and he also designed exhibition halls and hangars. Later buildings which relied on Nervi's structural knowledge are the Unesco Building in Paris, and the soaring Pirelli Building in Milan.

Nestorius (5th cent. AD) Syrian Christian and Patriarch of Constantinople from 428 to 431. He is the author of the heresy that Mary, being human, should not be called the Mother of God. This view was condemned at the Council of Ephesus (431).

Neumann, Johann Balthasar (1687-1753) German architect and exponent of Rococo grandeur and spatial complexity. His most impressive work was in the Bishop's Residence at Wurzburg, where he redesigned the staircase. His masterpiece, the pilgrimage church of Vierzehnheiligen (1743-72), gives the finest expression to the light and vivacious complexities of Rococo architecture.

Neville, Richard, Earl of Warwick (1428-71) English nobleman

Dedicated and practical nationalists, Jan Neruda and his circle aimed to create a new Czechoslovak literature

called 'Warwick the Kingmaker'. During the Wars of the Roses, Neville first supported Richard, Duke of York against the Lancastrian Henry VI. After capturing Henry at Northampton (1460), Neville kept him as puppet king, but was himself the effective ruler. When Richard was killed at Wakefield (1460) and the Lancastrians recaptured Henry, Neville recognized Richard's son as King EDWARD IV (1461) after helping him to win the battle of Towton. Failing to manipulate Edward, he drove him away (1470) and reinstated Henry VI, by then in Yorkist hands. Edward IV returned with an army, and Neville was defeated and killed at Barnet.

Nevski, Alexander see ALEXANDER NEVSKI

Newcomb, Simon (1835-1909) Canadian astronomer, who made exhaustive researches into the movements of the Moon, the planets and the velocity of light.

Newcomen, Thomas (1663-1729) English metal worker and toolsmith, who in 1712 erected the first practical working steam engine, which played a vital role in the Industrial Revolution.

Newlands, John Alexander (1838-98) English chemist who classified the elements by arranging them in order of increasing atomic weights. He noticed that elements with similar chemical properties recurred at every eight places along the list. He called his discovery the law of octaves, referring to the tonic scale in music.

Newman, John Henry (1801-90) English theologian and a key figure in KEBLE's Oxford Movement. In 1833, while vicar of St Mary's, Oxford, Newman began producing *Tracts for the Times*, the mouth-piece of the movement. In 1841, the controversy over *Tract XC*, which argued that the 39 Articles were compatible with Roman Catholic doctrine, caused Newman to reconsider his religious position. He entered the Roman Catholic Church in 1845, and after ordination founded congregations of the Oratory in Birmingham and London. For many years he was unpopular with both Catholics and Protestants, but his *Apologia pro Vita Sua* (1864), a vindication of his spiritual quest, largely restored his reputation as an outstanding religious figure. He was made a Cardinal in 1879.

Newton, Sir Isaac (1642-1727) English mathematician and physicist, one of the greatest natural philosophers of all time, and perhaps best known for his laws of motion and gravity. In 1665-6, he discovered the binomial theorem, the basic idea of his method of fluxions (what is now called differential calculus), inverse fluxions (integral calculus), and the first ideas concerning universal gravitation. By that time, Newton had also begun his investigations on light and optics. He used a prism to split sunlight into a spectrum, so proving that white light is made up of a mixture of rays of different colours, each of which has its own refractive index. In 1668 he invented the reflecting telescope, and further investigation led him to propound a sophisticated form of corpuscular theory, which regards light as a stream of tiny particles travelling in straight lines. The theory was criticized by HOOKE, who had adopted the wave theory of HUYGENS. A century later the work of YOUNG and FRESNEL overcame Newton's objections to the wave theory, and the latter held undisputed sway until the quantum theories of the present century, which are curiously reminiscent of some of Newton's ideas. In 1684, Newton presented his theory of gravitation based on the inverse square law, which states that the gravitational force of attraction between two objects is proportional to the product of their masses and inversely proportional to the square of the distance between them. This enabled him to give a full account of the motions of heavenly bodies. In 1687 he published his masterpiece, the monumental *Philosophiae Naturalis Principia Mathematica*, one of the greatest achievements of the human mind. In the grand manner of EUCLID, the *Principia* starts with certain definitions and the famous three laws of motion: force-free motion is uniform (GALILEO's inertia principle);

that accelerated motion is proportional to the impressed force; and for every action there is an equal and opposite reaction. From these, together with the inverse square law of universal gravitation, the whole science of matter in motion is derived. In particular, the new astronomical findings of COPERNICUS and KEPLER could be derived as special consequences of the laws. The approach of *Principia* has dominated science ever since, and there was no significant advance in gravitational theory until the general relativity theory of EINSTEIN in 1915.

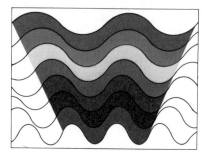

The wave-motion of light, above, shows how, in the visible range, red has the longest wavelength while violet has the shortest. Newton, best known for his laws of motion and gravity, was the first to notice that when light was passed through a prism it was split up into the colours of the rainbow, as in the uppermost of the three illustrations below; the second illustration shows that when the light of one particular wavelength passes through a hole in a screen, then through a second prism, there is no further splitting of the light, i.e. the colours of the spectrum are fundamental. The third illustration shows how, by introducing a second prism, upside-down in relation to the first, Newton was able to recombine the colours of the spectrum into the original beam of light

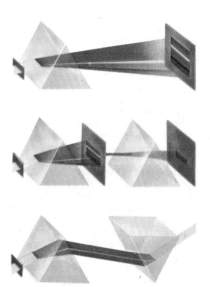

Newton, John (1725-1807) English evangelical clergyman and author of the *Olney Hymns* (1779). Written with his friend, the poet William COWPER, they became known all over the English-speaking world. Newton's Calvinist views influenced many who took part in the Evangelical revival in the Church of England, which, like Methodism, was a reaction against an apathetic and worldly clergy.

Ney, Michel (1769-1815) French soldier in the Revolutionary and Napoleonic armies, 'the bravest of the brave', according to NAPOLEON. He first distinguished himself at the battle of Ulm (1805), and at Borodino (1812) he showed such dash and courage that Napoleon made him Prince of the Moskowa. After Napoleon's abdication, he retained his rank under LOUIS XVIII. When sent to arrest Napoleon after his return from Elba, Ney defected to his side, and fought for him at Waterloo where he commanded the Old Guard. Despite Louis XVIII's efforts to save him, he was tried and condemned for treason by the Chamber of Peers, and shot.

Nicholas I (1796-1855) Tsar of Russia (1825-55), and a reactionary successor to his brother ALEXANDER I. At the outset of his reign he suppressed the 'Decembrist Conspiracy' (1825) of army officers and nobles seeking a liberalization of government, crushed the Polish nationalist revolt (1830-1) and intervened to help Austria crush the Hungarian Revolution (1848-9). His proposals to partition the Ottoman Empire led Turkey to declare war on Russia (1853). This was one of the causes of the Crimean War, since Britain and France both decided to give Turkey active support. Alexander died as the war was drawing to a close.

Nicholas II (1868-1918) Last Tsar of Russia (1894-1917). Having been inculcated with reactionary ideas by his tutor, POBEDONSTEV, he was intellectually ill-suited and unprepared to rule over the disturbed state of Russia to which he succeeded on the death of his father, Alexander III. Strikes, agrarian unrest, the humiliation of Russian defeat in her war with Japan (1904-5) and revolutionary propaganda, compelled him to moderate autocratic rule and call the first Russian parliament (Duma) in 1905. In addition a threat to the stability of government was presented by the influence of RASPUTIN over his wife and his heir Alexis. In 1917, after Russian defeats in the First World War, during which Nicholas had assumed personal command of the army (1915), his increasingly precarious situation com-

pelled him to abdicate. The Imperial family was kept under house arrest until the Bolsheviks seized power in November 1917, when they were sent to Ekaterinburg (now Sverdlovsk), where they were murdered in the following year (July 1918).

Nicholas of Verdun (late 12th-early 13th cent.) Lorraine-born enameller, goldsmith, sculptor and master of the Maas school. His most developed work is the *Shrine of the Three Kings* in Cologne Cathedral (*c.* 1190-1200), and his importance lies in his being the last of the great Romanesque designers, in whose work can be seen the beginnings of the movement towards the greater naturalism of the Gothic period.

Nicholson, Ben (born 1894) British painter, and an important pioneer of abstraction, whose work is much influenced by that of MONDRIAN.

Nicholson, Sir Francis (1655-1728) English administrator in the American colonies, Governor of Maryland (1694-8), Virginia (1698-1705) and South Carolina (1720-5). His capture of Port Royal in 1710 marked the final overthrow of the French in Nova Scotia.

Nielsen, Carl August (1865-1931) Danish composer whose musical career began when he was a boy bugler in the army. Later he became a notable operatic conductor in Copenhagen and turned to composition. His works include an opera, *Masquerade* (1906); a flute, a clarinet and a violin concerto; and the six symphonies by which he is probably best known outside Denmark.

Niemöller, Martin (born 1892) German pastor, who was imprisoned for his opposition to HITLER. A U-boat commander in the First World War, he refused to co-operate with the Nazis on Hitler's accession to power, and preached openly against the excesses and inhumanity of the Nazi régime. He was imprisoned from 1937-45 in the concentration camps of Sachsenhausen and Dachau. Niemöller was strongly opposed to Germany's rearmament and was, from 1961 to 1968, President of the World Council of Churches.

Niepce, Joseph Nicéphone (1765-1833) French inventor and producer of the first permanent camera photograph, using a pewter plate coated with light-sensitive asphalt. Niepce was also the inventor of photo-etching, which together with photography, he called heliography. DAGUERRE was working concurrently on similar projects and, in 1829, they formed a partnership to perfect the

process, but Niepce died four years before its completion.

Nietzsche, Friedrich (1844-1900) German philosopher and poet, author of *Thus Spake Zarathustra* (1880), the first comprehensive statement of his mature thought, whose central doctrine saw the will for power as the driving force of all human endeavour. His writings include *The Will to Power* (1888) and *The Genealogy of Morals* (1886). His influence on Existentialism, theology, psychiatry and literature has been significant.

Nightingale, Florence (1820-1910) English founder of nursing as a profession, and pioneer of hospital reform. Despite strong opposition from her family she became a nurse, and in 1854, during the Crimean War, took a party of nurses to Scutari. After the Battle of Inkerman she cared for 10,000 wounded British soldiers and found that more deaths were caused by disease and insanitary conditions than by wounds. Her fight to improve conditions and her gift for administration helped to win public support for her views. She returned to England in 1856 and with a testimonial fund of £50,000, she founded nursing colleges inside London hospitals. Her system of nursing was adopted and developed all over the world.

Nijinsky, Vaslav (1890-1950) Russian dancer and choreographer who helped to revitalize ballet outside Russia. Before he appeared in DIAGHILEV's Ballets Russes in 1909, male dancing in western Europe had become emasculated. Nijinsky brought to the West the new Russian school of male dancing as developed by PETIPA. Insanity ended his meteoric career abruptly in 1917.

Nimitz, Chester William (1885-1966) American admiral, who defeated the Japanese in the Pacific during the Second World War. As

Friedrich Nietzsche, 19th-century influence on 20th-century thought

Commander-in-Chief of the Pacific Fleet from 1941 to 1945, he based his plans on the use of fast aircraft carriers and massive air strikes supported by submarine campaigns. He recaptured the Solomon and Gilbert Islands in 1943, and the Marianas and Marshalls in 1944.

Ni Tsan (1301-74) Chinese painter, calligrapher and scholar, one of 'The Four Great Masters of the Yüan Dynasty' who, refusing to serve their Mongol rulers, formed a select group of their own, concentrating almost exclusively on landscapes and the abstract qualities of the calligraphic brushstroke. Ni Tsan, the most original of the four, eventually became a wandering Taoist recluse. His austere, refined and simple style, and his technique of peculiar, sharp-angled brush strokes, were much imitated later.

Nitze, Max (1848-1906) German urologist, who invented the cystoscope and so laid the basis of modern genito-urinary surgery.

Nixon, Richard Milhous (born 1913) Thirty-seventh President of the US. He first became known through his part in the case that led to the indictment of HISS in 1948 for perjury. He was EISENHOWER's Vice-President (1953-61), but was beaten by John KENNEDY in the presidential election of 1960. Nixon did not abandon politics, however, and in 1969 became President after one of the closest elections of the century. His withdrawal of American forces from Vietnam and limitation of US commitments to oppose external aggression (while providing economic aid to encourage Far Eastern countries to become more self-sufficient) were positive achievements. The Watergate 'bugging' scandal and the indictment of some of his closest associates within months of his inauguration for a second term caused his administration to come under heavy attack and the spectre of impeachment to be conjured up.

Nizam-al-Mulk, Hassan ibn-Ali (1018-92) Persian vizier, and administrator (under sultans ALP ARSLAN and Malik Shah) who based the economy on land, not money. To end unrest and restore prosperity, he gave the unruly Turkish troops both land and its revenues, thus encouraging them to farm in return for specified numbers of armed men. He was a patron of scholarship, founded universities, mosques, hospitals and observatories, and ordered the revision of the calendar by OMAR KHAYYAM.

Nkrumah, Kwame (1909-72) Ghanaian nationalist politician, and first President of the Republic of Ghana. In 1949 he founded the Convention People's Party to work against the new Gold Coast constitution, which he saw as an impediment to full independence. He was arrested for political agitation and imprisoned, but was released in 1951, when his party won the general election. He became Prime Minister of the Gold Coast in 1952 and of Ghana in 1957, and President of the Republic in 1960. Personal extravagance, reckless public spending and his authoritarian behaviour led to his deposition while he was visiting MAO TSE-TUNG in Peking in 1966. Being unable to return to Ghana, he flew to Guinea, where President Sekou-Touré made him joint head of state. He died at Conavry, Guinea.

Nobel, Alfred (1833-96) Swedish explosives manufacturer, discoverer of dynamite (1867) and cordite, philanthropist and endower of Nobel Prizes. In 1886, he showed that high explosive nitroglycerine could be made safer to handle by absorbing it into an inert clay, and the result, dynamite, was the basis of his fortune. In 1875 he invented blasting gelatine and, in 1888, cordite. He also experimented with armour plate, artificial rubber and nearly 100 other patented items. The Nobel Prizes, the first of which was presented in 1901, are awarded annually for outstanding contributions to physics, chemistry, physiology and medicine, literature and peace.

Nobunaga (1534-82) Japanese general, who began the country's political unification. He seized the capital, Kyoto (1568), and became acting shogun (1568-82) in control of the central government. Helped by General Hideyoshi, he destroyed the power of the feudal lords and Buddhist monasteries, burning 3000 monasteries and massacring thousands of priests.

Nolan, Sidney (born 1917) Influential Australian artist, whose work is characterized by oddly-juxtaposed images set in boldly-painted landscapes of the Australian hinterland.

Nono, Luigi (born 1924) Italian composer whose opera *Intolleranza*, about a refugee who endures the oppressions of the 20th century, was dedicated to SCHOENBERG.

Nordenskjöld, Nils Adolf Eric (1832-1901) Swedish mineralogist and polar explorer who found the North East Passage (1878-9). Successful early expeditions to the Arctic inspired him to try to find the long-sought North East sea passage from Europe to eastern Asia. He sailed in the steamship *Vega* from Tromsö and neared the Bering Strait before being frozen in for the winter. He continued the voyage successfully when the ice broke up the following spring.

Norris, Frank (1870-1902) American novelist, who was one of the pioneers of naturalism in American fiction. *McTeague* (1899) shows the influence of ZOLA, mixing romance and realism. *The Octopus* (1901) and *The Pit* (1903), parts of an uncompleted trilogy on the subject of wheat, are strong indictments of the business forces that oppress the farmer. Despite Zola's influence, Norris represented the older American tradition of romantic protest.

North, Frederick, 2nd Earl of Guilford (1732-92) British Prime Minister (1770-82), better known by his courtesy title of Lord North, who,

The music masters—Bach, Haydn, Mozart, Beethoven and others whose stories appear in *Who Did What*—were circumscribed, or given greater scope, by the musical instruments at their disposal. On this page are shown instruments which, through the ages and in many countries, have provided music for solo performance, or as accompaniments to the human voice, or as units of an orchestra

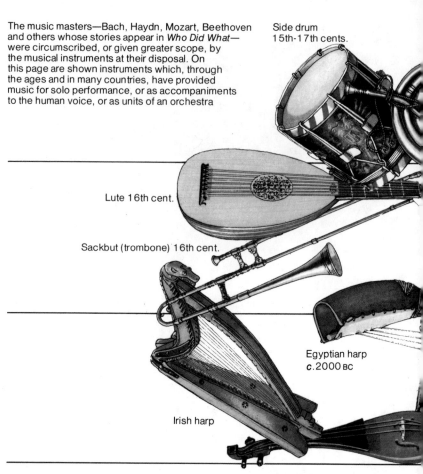

Side drum
15th-17th cents.

Lute 16th cent.

Sackbut (trombone) 16th cent.

Egyptian harp
c.2000 BC

Irish harp

Rebec to 18th cent.

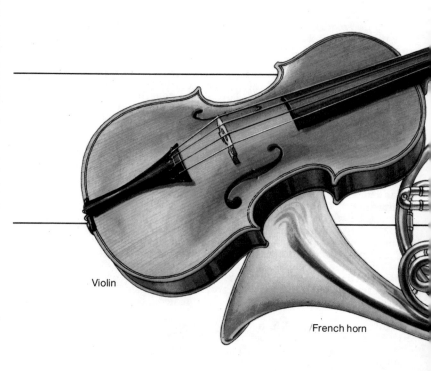

Violin

French horn

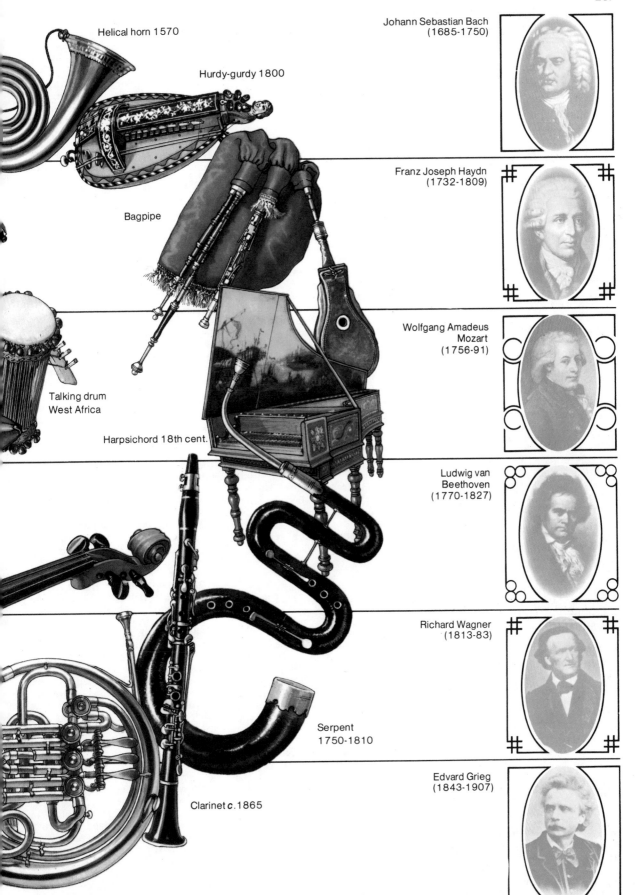

Helical horn 1570

Hurdy-gurdy 1800

Bagpipe

Talking drum
West Africa

Harpsichord 18th cent.

Serpent
1750-1810

Clarinet *c*.1865

Johann Sebastian Bach
(1685-1750)

Franz Joseph Haydn
(1732-1809)

Wolfgang Amadeus
Mozart
(1756-91)

Ludwig van
Beethoven
(1770-1827)

Richard Wagner
(1813-83)

Edvard Grieg
(1843-1907)

as GEORGE III's prime minister, condoned the colonial policy which provoked the American War of Independence. He promised to levy no fresh taxes on the disgruntled American colonists, but to maintain the principle of Britain's right to tax tea, provoking the Boston Tea Party, which precipitated America's struggle for independence (1775-83).

Northcliffe, Alfred Harmsworth, 1st Viscount (1865-1922) English newspaper magnate, pioneer of popular modern journalism. The 1870 Education Act encouraged him to aim at a new reading public, and in 1894, with his brother Harold (later Lord Rothermere), he bought the failing *London Evening News*. In 1896, he launched the *Dail Mail*. The secret of Northcliffe's success was that he published human interest stories and allowed his readers to see 'their own opinions and prejudices echoed in a newspaper'. By 1929 the *Mail*'s circulation was the largest in the world.

Nostradamus (1503-66) French astrologer, physician and prophet, Nostradamus was famous in his own lifetime for his alleged success in the treatment of plague and as the occult consultant of Catherine de MEDICI.

Nottingham, Heneage, 1st Earl of (1621-82) English judge who from his work in the Court of Chancery is traditionally called 'the father of modern equity'. This system of law, based on principles of justice, had since the late Middle Ages flourished in the Courts of Chancery, for which the Chancellor had special responsibility, but lacked system and organization. Nottingham maintained that cases should not be decided at the whim of a Chancellor, and his great contribution to this branch of the law was to determine and establish the principles upon which the Court would be able to act.

Novalis (1772-1801) German poet, novelist and theorist of the Romantic movement, who, with TIECK and the brothers SCHLEGEL, outlined the new literary theory in the journal *The Athenaeum*. His belief in the fusion of art, music and life into one experience is expressed in his unfinished novels, *The Novices of Sais* and *Heinrich von Ofterdingen*.

Nuffield, Lord (1877-1963) English industrialist who, as Henry FORD had done in America, popularized cheap motoring in Britain. He combined notable inventive powers with successful production methods and made a fortune, which he later devoted to philanthropy. As William Morris, he worked for 20 years in vehicle workshops before concentrating on cars,

founding the Morris Motors Company in 1919. The firm expanded steadily and merged with Austin (1952) to form the giant British Motor Corporation (now British Leyland).

Nureyev, Rudolf (born 1939) Russian-born dancer. In 1961 as a rising star of the Kirov Ballet he defected to the West during a visit to Paris. His partnership with Margot FONTEYN, especially in performances with the Royal Ballet and the Australian Ballet, have become legendary.

Nurhachi (1559-1626) Jürched tribal leader, the virtual founder of China's last imperial dynasty, the Ching or Manchu (1644-1912). As the Ming dynasty declined, Nurhachi built up Jürched power north of China proper. He united Jürched tribes, organized troops and adopted Chinese techniques to strengthen government. In 1616 he proclaimed himself Emperor, then openly attacked China. He took the Liao Basin east of Peking (1621) and ruled from Mukden (1625). His successors became undisputed rulers of all China.

Nyerere, Julius (born 1922) Tanzanian nationalist leader who became the first Prime Minister and later President, of his country. He began his career as a schoolteacher but in 1955 decided to devote himself to nationalist politics, becoming leader of the Tanganyika African National Union, and Premier when the Union won the 1961 elections. In 1962, when Tanganyika and Zanzibar jointly attained independence as Tanzania, he was elected President.

O

Oates, Titus (1649-1705) English Protestant priest, who revealed the mythical Popish Plot (1678). Using knowledge gathered during spurious studies for the Catholic priesthood, Oates, with Israel Tonge, a fanatical anti-Jesuit, concocted a Jesuit plot to kill CHARLES II, place the Duke of York on the throne, burn London and massacre Protestants. When revealed, the plot terrified England and resulted in the execution of 35 probably blameless citizens. Oates was awarded a pension, but later, his perjury having been proved, he was severely flogged, successfully sued by the Duke of York for £100,000 and imprisoned.

Oberth, Hermann Julius (born 1894) German rocket pioneer who, as early as 1923, foresaw the practicality of manned space-flight and, in

1929, described designs of suitable vehicles powered by liquid-fuelled motors and other forms of propulsion, which subsequently were developed. His research, which attracted the support of the army and eventually led to the formation of the Peenemünde research establishment in Germany and the development of the V2 missile.

Obregon, Alvaro (1880-1928) Revolutionary and President of Mexico. In 1912 he joined MADERO in the struggle against DIAZ, and supported Carranza in the counter-revolution following Madero's death, defeating Huerta (1913-14), ZAPATA and VILLA in 1915. He was a man of liberal ideals and forced Carranza to agree to the restoration of land to the Indians, and later, when Carranza attempted to violate the constitution, Obregon raised a revolt which resulted in his becoming President in 1920. His administration (1920-4) was notable for its land, educational and financial reforms and the establishment of friendly relations with the USA. In 1928, Obregon was again elected President, but was assassinated before he could take office.

O'Casey, Sean (1880-1964) Irish dramatist, who wrote *Juno and the Paycock* (1924). He specialized in tragi-comedies of Dublin slum life, such as *The Shadow of a Gunman* (1922), his first play. The Abbey Theatre, which had staged his other plays, turned down *The Silver Tassie* (1928), in which he shifted to Symbolism. O'Casey thereupon moved to England and for a time refused to allow his work to be performed in Ireland. The best known of his other plays are *The Plough and the Stars* (1926), about the 1916 Easter Rising, *Purple Dust* (1940) and *Red Roses for Me* (1943).

Ochs, Adolph Simon (1858-1935) American newspaper publisher who injected fresh integrity into American journalism. Buying the *New York Times* in 1896, he boosted its 9000 circulation to 466,000 before his death, publishing 'All the News That's Fit to Print' (which remains the paper's slogan), and so strengthening the high moral standards set by its first editor, Henry Jarvis Raymond (1820-69).

O'Connor, Feargus (1794-1855) Irish barrister and Chartist leader. He was elected MP for Nottingham in 1847, and organized the 1848 Chartist demonstration. Later, he presented the Chartists' petition to parliament. O'Connor died insane.

O'Connor, Frank (1903-66) Pen-name of Michael O'Donovan, Irish short-story writer, who won fame with *Guests of the Nation* (1931), tales of the Irish Revolution, arising out of the Civil War, and a spell of imprisonment in 1923.

Octavius see AUGUSTUS

Oda Nobunaga see NOBUNAGA

Odoacer (c. 433-93) German barbarian ruler who formally ended the Roman Empire in the West when he deposed Romulus Augustulus in 476. He was accepted as King of Italy by the eastern emperor, ZENO, and by the Roman Senate, but was killed when the Ostrogoths under THEODORIC invaded Italy.

Odoric (1286-1331) Italian Franciscan friar who spent 14 years travelling through Persia, India, southern Asia and China. He left Constantinople in 1316, passing through Tabriz to Bagdad, and on to India, visiting Malabar, Madras and Ceylon. After reaching Sumatra, Java and Borneo he travelled to Canton, visited northern China and spent three years in Peking.

Oersted, Hans Christian (1777-1851) Danish physicist who discovered the magnetic effect produced by an electric current (1819) after noticing that a compass needle close to a wire carrying a current swung about wildly and eventually settled at right-angles to the wire. He realized that there must be a magnetic field around the wire produced by the current. His momentous discovery was the starting point for FARADAY, AMPÈRE and other scientists.

Oertel, Abraham see ORTELIUS

Offa (8th cent.) King of Mercia, an English kingdom, who was the first Anglo-Saxon king to acquire a European reputation. He dominated all the kingdoms south of the River Humber and, to protect his boundary with Wales, built an immense earthwork and ditch, which still survives and is known as Offa's Dyke.

Offenbach, Jacques (1819-80) French composer of the highly successful operettas *La Belle Hélène* (1864) and *Orpheus in the Underworld* (1858), and of the opera *Tales of Hoffman* (1881), based on the works of Eta Hoffman. With their light satire and catchy tunes, Offenbach's operettas (he wrote more than 90) are important in the history of the genre.

O'Flaherty, Liam (born 1897) Irish author whose work attempts a blend of realism, drama and mysticism. His novel *The Informer* (1926) is a powerful, brutal tale of the Irish

Civil War. Among his other works on Ireland, which he left in 1922, are *The Puritan* (1931) and *Famine* (1937).

Ogadai (1185-1241) Mongol Great Khan, who enlarged the empire built by his father, GENGHIS KHAN. Although he inherited only Outer Mongolia, he was elected supreme Mongol leader. From his capital he supervised the suppression of revolts in northern China, Korea and central Asia, the administration of Persia, and the Mongol advance through Russia, Poland and Hungary.

Ogethorple, James (1696-1785) British general and philanthropist, founder of the American state of Georgia (1733). After acquiring a 21-year charter he arrived with 120 settlers to found a colony as a refuge for unemployed debtors and persecuted Protestants from Europe. Having fought off Spanish attacks, in 1752 he made over Georgia, whose population by then totalled about 4000 colonists, to the British Crown.

Ohm, Georg Simon (1789-1854) German physicist who discovered the law describing the flow of electric current through a conductor. In the 1820s, after painstaking experiments, he found that the current flowing through a wire depends both on its length and thickness. From this he was able to define what is now called electrical resistance. By 1827 he had formulated Ohm's law, which underlies the study of current electricity. It states that the current flowing through a conductor is proportional to the voltage across it and inversely proportional to its resistance.

Oistrakh, David (born 1908) Leading Russian violin virtuoso and the first Russian musician to travel abroad and make a name in the West after the Second World War. PROKOFIEV, among other composers, wrote works especially for him. Oistrakh's son, Igor, is also a virtuoso violinist.

Okyo Maruyama (1733-95) Japanese painter, founder of the Shijo (Realist) School of painting. A farmer's son, he trained in the Kano tradition but later took an interest in western art. In about 1760 he was commissioned by a Kyoto dealer to make copies of some western prints which were appearing in Japan. His bold, decorative painting combines superficial western perspective with Chinese-derived landscape.

Olaf I, Tryggvesson (969-1000) King of Norway, who converted his country to Christianity. Olaf was converted while leading raids on the

coasts of Britain and France, and employed English priests to evangelize Norway. He was eventually defeated at sea by the combined fleets of Denmark and Sweden and drowned himself.

Olbers, Heinrich (1758-1840) German astronomer, a doctor by profession, who discovered five comets (one is now called Olbers's Comet), and the minor planets Pallas and Vesta.

Olcott, Henry see BLAVATSKY, Helena

'Old Crome' see CROME, John

Oldenburg, Claes (born 1929) American Pop artist, inventor of soft sculpture, and, partly, of so-called happenings.

Oleg (10th cent.) Varangian (Russo-Scandinavian) leader, who consolidated the state which forms the nucleus of modern Russia. From Novgorod he captured Smolensk and Kiev, and made Kiev the capital of a Kievan-Novgorod state. He forced the Byzantine emperor Leo VI to agree to a commercial treaty, which greatly increased Russian wealth.

Olivier, Laurence, Lord (born 1907) English actor, director and theatre manager, one of the outstanding creative influences on British acting. He was director of the National Theatre from 1962-1973.

O'Malley, King (1858-1953) Canadian-born politician in the first federal Australian government. During the 1880s he migrated to Australia and settled in Adelaide. In 1901 he was elected to the first House of Representatives as an independent. He proposed the establishment of a National Bank, and, later, as the Minister for Home Affairs, secured land and drew up plans for the nation's capital city, Canberra.

Omar Khayyám (c. 1050-c. 1120) Persian astronomer and poet, known chiefly in Europe through the translation of his *Rubáiyát* by Edward FITZGERALD. He also undertook important astronomical research and supervised a calendar reform for the sultan Malik-Shah. He was one of the great mathematicians of the period.

O'Neill, Eugene (1888-1953) American dramatist whose plays, initially controversial for their use of drab, common language, combined a realism and expressionism which soon established him as a leading dramatist. He was awarded the Pulitzer Prize for his play *Beyond the*

Horizon (1920), which was followed by the successful *The Emperor Jones* (1920); *All God's Chillun got Wings* (1924) which introduced the negro-white relationship; *Desire Under the Elms* (1924); *Strange Interlude* (1928) an experimental nine-act play using long asides; the trilogy *Mourning Becomes Electra* (1931) in which O'Neill recounts the Greek legend in American terms, and the comedy *Ah Wilderness* (1933). *The Iceman Cometh* was produced after 12 years silence from O'Neill. His autobiographical *A Long Day's Journey into Night* was not produced until after his death, in 1955.

O'Neill, Hugh, 2nd Earl of Tyrone (c. 1540-1616) Leader of the northern Irish in their resistance to English power in Ireland. After serving with the English, he rebelled and defeated an English force at Yellow Ford on the Blackwater River, but, even with Spanish aid, lost the crucial Battle of Kinsale (1601). He submitted to the English Crown, but later fled to Europe. JAMES I redistributed his lands in Ulster mainly among Protestant Scots and English.

Oparin, Alexander (born 1894) Russian biologist, whose theory on the origin of life states that the original amino acids, from which cells were formed, arose through physico-chemical action of the atmosphere on the fluid mixtures covering vast parts of the globe.

Oppenheimer, Sir Ernest (1880-1957) German-born South African mining magnate and philanthropist. In the space of 40 years, his Anglo-American Corporation of South Africa, founded in 1917, came to control 95 per cent of the world's diamond supply. He was a close friend of SMUTS and raised the Kimberley Regiment in the First World War. His benefactions include university chairs and slum-clearance schemes in Johannesburg.

Oppenheimer, Robert (1904-67) American physicist in charge of the development of the first atomic bomb. In the early 1950s, as McCarthyism raged through the United States, Oppenheimer's political motives were brought into doubt and he was declared a 'security risk'.

Orellana, Francisco de (1500-49) Spanish soldier and explorer, first to navigate the Amazon from its upper reaches to the sea. He was with Gonzalo PIZARRO's east-bound expedition from Quito, which followed the Napo River to the Amazon (1540-1). Orellana then navigated the Amazon to its outlet, hoping to establish a claim to colonize new territory on his own ac-count. He returned to Spain and obtained the necessary authority for conquest, but had little success, and died soon afterwards.

Orff, Carl (born 1895) German composer whose best-known work is *Carmina Burana* (1936), a 'cantata' designed to be performed on the stage. Consisting of settings of hedonistic medieval Latin poems celebrating spring, drink and love, it shows all the characteristics of his style: constantly reiterated rhythms hammered out by a large orchestra with strong percussive support and, by consciously avoiding counterpoint, re-creating some of the energy of medieval music.

Orsini, Felice (1819-58) Italian nationalist and revolutionary who in 1858 led a conspiracy to assassinate NAPOLEON III, for which crime he was arrested and guillotined. A member of an old and noble Italian family, Orsini had agitated in support of Italian independence since his youth.

Ortega y Gasset, José (1883-1955) Spanish philosopher, writer and statesman, whose most influential works are his analyses of Spain and Europe in the 1920s: *Invertebrate Spain* (1921), *The Revolt of the Masses* (1929-30) and *The Modern Theme* (1923). A humanist, he believed in the value of individualism: 'I am I and my circumstance.'

Ortelius (1527-98) Flemish cartographer and antiquarian who produced the first known modern atlas. An engraver turned antiquarian, he began map-making after 1560 under MERCATOR's influence. In 1570 he produced *Theatre of the Lands of the Globe* – the earliest known modern collection of maps to be bound together in one volume. It comprised 53 plates totalling 70 maps produced in a standard form from the best sources available.

Orwell, George (1903-50) Pen-name of Eric Blair, English journalist, critic and novelist, who wrote *Animal Farm* (1945) and *Nineteen Eighty-four* (1949), powerful political fables pointing out the dangers of bureaucratic, totalitarian government. Born in India, he left a bitter criticism of Imperial England in *Burmese Days* (1934). After a period of wandering, recalled in *Down and Out in Paris and London* (1933), he lived by writing. *Keep the Aspidistra Flying* (1936) was a document of the depression in England. In essays, from *Inside the Whale* (1940) to *England Your England* (1953), he examined the institutions and social structure of England.

Osborne, John (born 1929) English dramatist and actor, whose play *Look Back in Anger* (1956) began a revival in English drama, and introduced the term 'angry young man', personified by the leading character, Jimmy Porter. *The Entertainer* (1957), in which Laurence OLIVIER created the part of Archie Rice, was another success, and established Osborne as a leading exponent of British social drama. The musical *The World of Paul Slickey* (1959), which was a failure, was followed by the widely acclaimed *Luther* (1961). Other plays include *Inadmissible Evidence* (1964), *A Patriot for Me* (1965), *Hotel in Amsterdam* (1968) and *A Sense of Detachment* (1973).

Osei Tuti (17th-18th cent.) Founder of the Ashanti Union of Akan clans (*c.* 1695), which produced a powerful African Empire, including most of modern Ghana, in the 18th and 19th centuries. Osei welded the fighting forces of the clans into a single army, which established his supremacy over the previously dominant neighbouring state of Denkyira.

Osman I (1259-1326) Turkish founder of the Ottoman Dynasty (*c.* 1300-1922), members of which established the Ottoman Empire, based on Asia Minor.

Ossietzky, Carl von (1889-1938) German pacifist, who was victimized by HITLER. He became a pacifist early in life and in 1931 was imprisoned for 18 months for publishing details of infringements of the Versailles Treaty that had been planned by SEECKT. Later, he was sent to a concentration camp (1933-6) as an enemy of the state. In 1935, he was awarded the Nobel Peace Prize, but Hitler declared the award to be a challenge to his rule and decreed that no German was in future to accept such prizes.

Ostrovsky, Alexander (1823-86) Dramatist, the leading realistic playwright of his period. Most of his 80 or so plays were staged at the Maly Theatre in Moscow. *The Bankrupt* (1848), which depicts the higher Russian bourgeoisie as dishonest, was banned, but achieved fame by being circulated in manuscript form. His first successful play was *Poverty is No Disgrace* (1854). *The Snow Maiden* (1873) was used by RIMSKY-KORSAKOV for his opera of that name. *The Storm* (1860), his most famous play, is a picture of Russian provincial life.

Ostwald, Wilhelm Friedrich (1853-1932) Russian-German chemist who established the nature of catalysis. After studying Josiah GIBBS's work on chemical thermodynamics, Ostwald suggested that catalysts are substances which can increase or decrease the rate of a chemical reaction without themselves taking part in it – a view which, in a modified form, is still held today.

Oswald, Lee Harvey (1940-63)
American assassin of US President, John F. KENNEDY, on 22 Nov. 1963.

Otis, Elisha Graves (1811-61)
American inventor of a safety device for mechanical lifts (1852), which made very tall buildings practicable. His first steam-powered, passenger lift was installed in the five-storey New York store of E. G. Haughwort and Co. in 1857. The first electrically operated elevators date from 1889.

Otis, James (1725-83)
American lawyer, who urged Massachusetts colonists to resist the British government. He resigned his position as Advocate-General to protest against the government's enforcement of lapsed customs laws, which allowed officials to search any house thought to hold smuggled goods.

Otto, Nicholaus August (1832-91)
German inventor, in 1876, of the four-stroke internal combustion engine. In the following decade 30,000 of his engines were sold, the forerunners of modern automobile and aeroplane power plants.

Ottokar II 'The Great' (c. 1230-78)
King of Bohemia (1253-78), who made Bohemia the leading Germanic nation. He was the ruler of Moravia and Austria, which had been vastly enriched by the discovery of silver mines, and enlarged by his seizure of Styria and inheritance of Carinthia and Carniola. To counterbalance Bohemia's power, the other German princes elected Rudolf of Hapsburg as emperor (1273). Ottokar, however, refused to recognize Rudolf. War ensued and he was compelled to cede all his lands except Bohemia and Moravia.

Otway, Thomas (1652-85)
British dramatist, who wrote *Venice Preserved* (1682), one of the best post-Jacobean tragedies. His other plays are no longer remembered, although he had a success with his first, *Alcibiades* (1675), and with *The Orphan* (1680). Otway translated and adapted plays by RACINE and MOLIÈRE for the English stage.

Oughtred, William (1575-1660)
English mathematician who invented the slide rule. He also introduced the terms sine, cosine and tangent for the common trigonometrical ratios.

Ould, Sir Fielding (1710-89)
Irish gynaecologist, who pioneered or

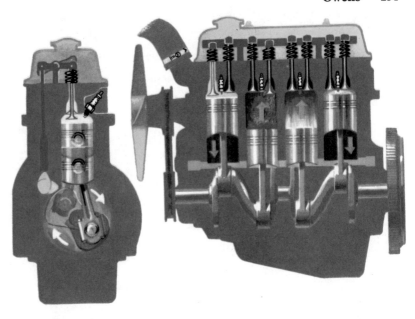

Now the commonest form of motive power for transport, the four-stroke internal combustion engine. The first of its kind was made by Otto in 1876

popularized many practices that later became standard in midwifery.

Ovid (c. 43 BC-c. AD 17)
Roman poet and story teller, author of *Metamorphoses*, a collection of stories written in 15 books of hexameter verse, which have entertained and inspired artists and poets since the Middle Ages. His other works include the short, erotic elegies *Amores* (16 BC); the contrived elegiac letters of the *Heroides* and *Ars Amatoria* (c. 1 BC); a cynical elegiac poem in three books dealing with the *demi-monde* and presenting Love as a science, in mockery of contemporary textbooks. The disapproval caused by the work's 'immorality' was a probable cause of Ovid's banishment by AUGUSTUS in AD 8 to Tomis on the Black Sea, where he lived out his life writing verse.

Owen, Sir Richard (1804-92)
British biologist, who was a pioneer in vertebrate palaeontology and in concise descriptive nomenclature. His prolific publications, including *Odontography* (1840-5), an exhaustive study of teeth, and *History of the British Fossil, Mammals and Birds* (1846), were important contributions to comparative anatomy and palaeontology.

Owen, Robert (1771-1858)
Welsh industrialist, who pioneered practical, cooperative socialism. After being a draper's apprentice at Stamford he borrowed capital to start his own textile workshop in Manchester. In 1800, as a result of his marriage to the daughter of David Dale, he became manager and a partner in his father-in-law's textile mills at New Lanark. New Lanark became the centre not only of his business interests but also of his educational,

philanthropic and propagandist activities in which he was supported by the Quaker philanthropist William Allen and the philosopher Jeremy BENTHAM. Contrary to common industrial practice, he improved the working and moral conditions of his employees.

Owen, Wilfred (1893-1918)
Welsh poet, killed in action shortly before the end of the First World War, whose *Poems* (1920) portrayed, without nationalistic bias, the human suffering of war.

Owens, Jesse (born 1913)
American athlete, who is famous for his performances in the 1936 Berlin

Jesse Owens, the US negro athlete whose achievements at the 1936 Berlin Olympics were an affront to Hitler and his beliefs in Aryan supremacy

Olympic Games. Owens refuted HITLER's theory of Aryan supremacy by breaking two Olympic records, equalling a third and helping smash the world record for the 400 yards relay. He became one of seven American negro athletes to win gold medals in the Games.

P

Paasikivi, Juho Kusti (1870-1956) Prime Minister and President of Finland. As Finland's negotiator with the Soviet Union between the two World Wars, his task was a difficult one, for, although he believed in Finland's independence, he had to face the reality of living with a powerful and predatory neighbour. He represented Finland in the Finnish–Soviet negotiations which sought to avoid war in 1939, and conducted the Armistice negotiations after the war with Russia, which followed. He was Prime Minister from 1944 to 1946, during which time Finland declared war on Germany, and in 1946 was elected President in succession to MANNERHEIM, a position he held for ten years.

Paccard, Michel Gabriel (1757-1827) French doctor who, with Jacques BALMAT, was the first to climb Mont Blanc, Europe's highest peak (15,771 feet), winning the prize offered by de SAUSSURE.

Paderewski, Ignacy Jan (1860-1941) Polish virtuoso of the piano who became his country's first Prime Minister (1919-20). Internationally famous for his romantic approach, among his best-known works are his *Polish Fantasia* for piano, and the opera *Manon*.

Paganini, Niccolò (1782-1840) Leading Italian violin virtuoso of the Romantic era whose technique was such that its brilliance led to an extensive folklore about his having made a pact with the Devil. As a consequence, for five years following his death, the Church denied him burial in consecrated ground.

Paine, Thomas (1737-1809) English social and political reformer and author of *The Rights of Man*. Paine was an excise officer, but was dismissed for attempting to improve the salaries of his profession and emigrated to Pennsylvania (1774), where he wrote the pamphlet *Common Sense* (1776), in which he demanded independence for the American colonies. He fought in the War of Independence and was Secretary to the Foreign Affairs committee of the Continental Congress (1777-9). He returned to England in 1787 and published *The Rights of Man* (as a riposte to BURKE's attack on the French Revolution) which advocated the overthrow of the British monarchy and the introduction of a republican form of government. He was tried for treason *in absentia* and outlawed and fled to France. Later, he became a member of the Convention and identified himself with the Girondins, but after their fall in June 1793, he was imprisoned until the demise of ROBESPIERRE and the Jacobins (1794). In 1802 he returned to the US but found radicalism so unpopular there that he was treated as an outcast.

Palamas, Kostis (1859-1943) Greek poet, who played an important part in the evolution of modern Greek literature. His best-known works are the verse collections *The Grave* (1898), *Life Immovable* (1904) and the lyrical epic *The 12 Lays of the Gypsy* (1907). He was a central figure in the movement of the 1880s which condemned Romanticism, advocating a return to the use of everyday language in literature and to the life of the ordinary people as inspiration.

Palestrina, Giovanni Pierluigi da (c. 1525-94) Italian composer, regarded as one of the most important composers of sacred music. He was technically conservative, consolidating the work of precursors like DE PRES, imposing strict rules and creating absolute standards. The many masses that he composed as choirmaster at the Julian Chapel in St Peter's Rome, are claimed ecclesiastically to be supreme examples of a liturgical style. When he died, 'Prince of Music' was inscribed on his coffin.

Palladio, Andrea (1508-80) Italian architect of the late Renaissance. Through his theoretical writings he exerted a great influence in England, Germany and Scandinavia, where a vigorous and restrained style known as Palladianism or Neo-Palladianism developed in the 18th century. His intense interest in Roman antiquity was stimulated by reading the Roman architectural scholar Vitruvius and by studying antique buildings in Rome. Most of his own work, which is in Venice and Vicenza, reveals that he was an architect of originality who could employ classical motifs to new effect. His Villa Rotunda at Vicenza has four porticos arranged symmetrically around a central hall, and other buildings by him include the churches of Il Redentore and San Giorgio Maggiore in Venice.

Emmeline Pankhurst's militant Women's Social and Political Union of 1903 fought press indifference to Women's Lib— but by 1910, over 500 women, Mrs. Pankhurst and her daughters included, had suffered imprisonment and forced feeding

Palmer, Arnold (born 1929) American golfer, who won the US Masters' Tournament on four occasions (1958, 1960, 1962 and 1964), and during his career has won the US Open and Amateur titles.

Palmer, Samuel (1805-81) English landscape artist, who was influenced by BLAKE in using his art to express a mystical relationship with nature. The originality of his style has the effect of focusing attention on individual objects so that their symbolic significance becomes clear to the observer.

Palmerston, Henry John Temple, 3rd Viscount (1784-1865) British statesman, notable for his vigorous and aggressive assertion of British foreign policy. He was cabinet minister for 38 of his 58 years in parliament, and Foreign Secretary almost continuously from 1830 to 1841, under GREY, and again from 1846 to 1851 under RUSSELL. As a champion of the independence of small states, he was largely responsible for the independence of Belgium in 1831, but by 1846 he had developed the high-handed imperialistic diplomacy for which he became famous – a mixture of bluff and belligerency which was the despair of both Queen VICTORIA and his colleagues, but which endeared him to the British people. The mismanagement of the Crimean War led to his becoming Prime Minister in 1855 and, partly as a result of his appointment, the war was soon brought to an end.

Pan Ch'ao (c. 31-102) General, who, by conquering huge tracts of central Asia, helped China's later Han emperors to rival their Roman counterparts in imperial power, and to regain lands lost since Liu-Pang's former Han dynasty passed its peak. At one time during his leadership only Parthia (now Khorasan) lay between the Chinese and Roman armies.

Pandit, Viljaya Lakshmi (born 1900) Indian politician, the first woman President of the United Nations Assembly (1953-4) and the first to become her country's ambassador to a major power.

Pankhurst, Emmeline (1858-1928) English suffragette, whose militant actions helped to secure the franchise for women in Britain. She and her followers broke windows, chained themselves to railings in public places and even resorted to arson. After being arrested on several occasions, Mrs Pankhurst was sentenced to three years' imprisonment in 1913, though she served only one year of her sentence, during which she went on hunger strike. In the First World War, she persuaded women to do war work, which helped to reconcile masculine opinion to her cause and in 1918, women over the age of 30 received the vote. In 1928, the franchise was extended to those between the ages of 21 and 31.

Papin, Denis (1647-c. 1712) French mathematician and physicist. Having worked as assistant to HUYGENS, he went to England (1675) to work for BOYLE. In 1679, he showed that the boiling point of water depends on atmospheric pressure, and built the world's first pressure cooker and the steam safety valve to make the device safe.

Pappus (4th cent.) Greek geometer in Alexandria, whose *Collection*, now partly lost, is a comprehensive treatise on the whole of Greek mathematics and includes some results of his own. Parts of his other works also survive.

Paracelsus (c. 1493-1541) Swiss alchemist and doctor, sometimes called the Father of Chemistry. Paracelsus ridiculed the classical theory of the four humours which dominated medieval medicine. After extensive study in the mines of the Tyrol he initiated the use of minerals such as arsenic, lead, mercury and iron, as well as tinctures and alcoholic extracts, into the chemical treatment of disease.

Paré, Ambroise (c. 1510-90) French surgeon, a pioneer of modern surgery. Haemorrhage was the greatest 16th-century surgical problem which Paré solved by using ligatures and simple dressings rather than boiling oil, as was the common practice.

Pareto, Vilfredo (1848-1923) Italian economist and sociologist, whose ideas on systematic sociology and analysis of social and political change have had a powerful influence on sociological theory. One of the main elements in his system of sociology was the concept of 'residues', or underlying qualities of social action. Pareto was also one of the most influential economic theorists of his time and helped to establish economics as a recognized science.

Park, Mungo (1771-1806) Scottish surgeon and explorer in West Africa, Seeking a rumoured giant river, he travelled up the Gambia, crossed the upper Senegal Basin, and discovered the Niger at Segou (1795-6). Surviving fever, robbery and imprisonment, he returned to England, where his *Travels in the Interior of Africa* (1799) revolutionized knowledge of West African tribes. Park drowned in the Bussa Rapids after a 1000-mile voyage down the Niger in an attempt to trace its mouth.

Parker, Dorothy Rothschild (1893-1967) American writer and humorist who achieved literary notoriety for her acerbic poems and commentary. She once described a prominent actress as 'running the whole gamut of emotion from A to B'. Parker eventually committed suicide.

Parkinson, James (1755-1824) English physician noted for his work on '*paralysis agitans*' (Parkinson's disease).

Parkman, Francis (1823-93) American historian, whose geographical travels were the basis of most of his work. He wrote on the activities of missionaries, explorers and soldiers in opening up the United States and gave to his work a literary and imaginative flavour which enhanced his historical skill.

Parler, Peter (1330-99) German architect who designed Prague Cathedral, with its fantastic system of interlacing rib-vaults, in a style similar to that developed earlier in the west of England. Parler came from a famous family of southern German master-masons: his father, Heinrich, probably designed the chancel of Schwäbish-Gmünd, a hall church in the late Gothic style.

Parmigianino, Il (1503-40) Italian painter and etcher, whose frescoes in the Cathedral (1522) and S Giovanni Evangelista (1522-3) at Parma show the influence of CORREGGIO. Parmigianino's obsession with distorted forms is found in both the bizarre and highly artificial elongation of limbs in his Madonnas and in the early *Self-Portrait*, painted with the aid of a convex mirror.

Parnell, Charles Stewart (1846-91) Irish Home Rule leader. An Anglo-Irish Protestant, he became an MP in 1875. As leader of the Home Rule movement from 1880 he tried to further the cause by his skill as an orator, by his parliamentary tactics of disrupting House of Commons business, and by advocating protests among Irish peasants, such as the boycotting of landlords. He was arrested and imprisoned for incitement to riot (1881), but was released when GLADSTONE realized that only Parnell could pacify the Irish. Parnell supported Gladstone's Home Rule Bill of 1886 and he remained a potent influence in English and Irish politics until 1890, when he was discredited by a divorce action.

Parr, Catharine see HENRY VIII

Parry, Sir William Edward (1790-1855) British naval officer and Arctic explorer who made one of the earliest attempts to reach the North Pole. He made four unsuccessful voyages (1818, under John Ross; 1820; 1821; 1824) in search of the North West Passage from Europe to eastern Asia. In his bid to reach the North Pole (1827), he used sledge-boats over the ice from Spitzbergen to a point 82° 45′ N, for 50 years the most northerly latitude reached.

Parsons, Sir Charles Algernon (1854-1931) English developer of the steam turbine, to power generators. His first engine (1884) developed 10 h.p. at 18,000 r.p.m., and by 1900, he was building 1000 kW machines. In 1896, he built *Turbinia*, the first turbine-propelled launch, which reached the unprecedented speed of 34½ knots and created a sensation at the Spithead naval review, marking Queen VICTORIA's jubilee (1897).

Parsons, Talcott (born 1902) Influential American sociological theorist who stimulated an interest in classical European social theory in the United States.

Pascal, Blaise (1623-62) French philosopher, scientist, mathematician and writer whose major literary works include *Lettres Provinciales* (1656-7) and *Les Pensées* (1670). In his comparatively short life, Pascal invented a calculating machine, shared with FERMAT the discovery of the theory of mathematical probability, founded the science of hydrodynamics, wrote treatises on conic sections and experimented with atmospheric pressures. In 1654, Pascal underwent a profound spiritual crisis which led him to concentrate on religious matters, rather than the physical universe. The *Lettres Provinciales* are brilliant anti-Jesuit satires in defence of Antoine ARNAULD, while the unfinished apologia for Christianity, *Les Pensées*, published posthumously and based on notes from his manuscript, is one of his most important works.

Pascoli, Giovanni (1855-1912) Italian pastoral poet whose early compositions, such as *Myricae* (1891), portray the world of nature and particularly the country life of his native Romagna. They are characterized by a considerable attention to detail and by a sense of melancholy and an awareness of death. His later *Poemi Conviviali* (1904) and *Hymns and Odes* (1906) dwell more on social and moral themes.

Pasternak, Boris (1890-1960) Russian novelist and poet, who wrote *Doctor Zhivago* (1957), a vast novel which analyses the role of the intelligentsia in Russia before, during and after the Revolution, and evoking the beauty of the Russian countryside. Because the book rejected Marxism in favour of the individual it had to be smuggled out of Russia and was published in Milan. Pasternak was awarded a Nobel Prize for Literature (1958), but the Soviet authorities forced him to decline it. Eventually the Communist demand for 'socialist realism' stifled his poetic talents and he turned to the translation of foreign literature.

Pasteur, Louis (1822-95) French chemist, whose work, with that of Robert KOCH, led to a general acceptance of the theory that disease is caused by living organisms. He laid the groundwork for modern vaccine therapy and developed a vaccine against rabies. Pasteur's involvement with disease-causing organisms began in 1854, when he was able to prove that fermentation in sugar-beet was caused by minute living organisms. Twenty years later he was inspired by the work of Koch to study anthrax, which was at that time killing a large number of French sheep, and cholera in chickens. In the course of this work, he happened to inoculate some chickens with a culture of chicken cholera that was several weeks old, hoping that they would get the disease. But they survived, and proved immune to all subsequent inoculations of the same virus. What Pasteur had done – unknowingly – was to attenuate the virus (weaken it to such a degree that the body's natural defences could deal with it and so gain immunity). This attenuation technique is still the basis of many modern vaccines. Pasteur demonstrated its value in 1881 when, before a large crowd of doctors and journalists, he injected 48 sheep with a virulent form of anthrax, 24 of them having been vaccinated previously with an attenuated anthrax culture. These 24 were the only ones to survive.

Paston (15th-16th cents.) Name of an established family of Norfolk, England, whose collected letters and documents (*The Paston Letters*) describe social, economic and political events in the troubled years from 1422 to 1509. The letters, many of them from Margaret in Norfolk to her husband Sir John Paston, a London lawyer, show in particular the anarchy of HENRY VI's reign, public events, manners and dealings with the law.

Patenier, Joachim (c. 1485-1524) Dutch artist and perhaps the most important landscape painter before BRUEGEL. His pictures, which invariably include tiny biblical figures such as St Jerome or the Holy Family on their flight to Egypt, are notable for their fantastic rocky outcrops and vast panoramic views. Although basically imaginary, they reveal some naturalistic observation, particularly in the atmospheric blues of distances.

Pater, Walter (1839-94) English critic and prose writer, whose criticism and style greatly influenced 19th-century ideas on aesthetics. He became famous with *Studies in the History of the Renaissance* (1873) and *Marius the Epicurean* (1885).

Pasteur, in his *Etudes sur le vin*, recorded the effect of time and oxygen on wine. Red wine A without air retains its colour; with air it fades, B; white wine without air C does not change; with air it turns brown, D.

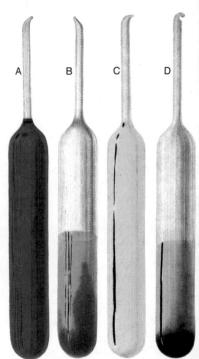

A B C D

Paterson, William (1658-1719) English financier who founded the Bank of England. In 1694, WILLIAM III approved his plan for a national bank formed as a joint-stock organization by merchants who raised £1,200,000 from shareholders and lent it to the king at 8 per cent interest. William granted the Bank a royal charter allowing it to issue bank notes to the value of the royal loan. Paterson thus founded what is now the United Kingdom's wholly government-owned central bank.

Patmore, Coventry (1823-96) English critic and poet, whose principal works were *The Angel in the House* (1854-62), a series of long poems celebrating marriage, and *The Unknown Eros* (1877), poems on religious themes written after Patmore's conversion to Catholicism.

Paton, Alan (born 1903) South African novelist, whose books are strong and moving protests against apartheid and the treatment of Africans in his country. From his experience of politics and native life, Paton wrote the lyrical *Cry, the Beloved Country* (1948), an examination of racial relations.

Patrick (c. 389-c. 461) Romano-British saint and evangelizer of the Irish. He set up an organized church in Ireland with his episcopal see at Armagh and encouraged monastic foundations.

Patterson, Joseph (1879-1944) American journalist and publisher of the New York *Daily News*, America's first successful tabloid newspaper. Patterson joined the Chicago *Tribune* in 1901, became its co-editor in 1914 and was a war correspondent in Germany, Belgium and France.

Patton, George Smith (1885-1945) American general, known as 'Blood and Guts'. In the First World War, he commanded an armoured brigade on the Western Front and in the Second World War led the first American troops to fight in North Africa (1942-3). He commanded the 7th Army in the Sicilian campaign (1943) and the US 3rd Army in 1944, leading it in a sweep to Paris and beyond.

Paul (1st cent. AD) Apostle to the gentiles. Born a Jew and a Roman citizen at Tarsus (Asia Minor), into a Pharisaic family, Paul may have trained as a rabbi. His conversion to Christianity shaped the remainder of his life, driving him to preach the Gospel throughout an extensive part of gentile territory to the north of the Mediterranean until his death, which, according to tradition, was by be-heading in Rome during NERO's persecution in AD 64. Paul's letters form a substantial part of the New Testament, showing him to be a vigorous man and a thinker whose statement of the Christian faith provided a framework for traditional Christian theology. In spite of severe difficulties, described by some as malaria, epilepsy or glaucoma, Paul played an important part in the growth of the Early Church, and dominated much of its later development.

Paul VI (Giovanni Batista Montini) (born 1897) 264th Pope who, despite world-wide anxiety over the 'population explosion' reaffirmed, in his encyclical *Humanae Vitae* (1968), the Roman Catholic Church's prohibition of artificial methods of birth control. He was elected Pope in 1963. He has reformed the curia by reducing the number of its departments and restricting major appointments to a period of five years instead of for life, all such appointments terminating with the death of the reigning Pope. He has inaugurated in the Curia a Foreign Affairs Department (the Council for Public Affairs of the Church) and has authorized Mass to be said in the vernacular.

Pauli, Wolfgang (1900-58) Austrian physicist who discovered the exclusion principle in 1925, for which he was awarded a Nobel Prize 20 years later. The Pauli exclusion principle states that no two electrons in an atom can occupy the same quantum state at the same time. In 1931 he was the first to suggest the existence of the neutrino, a particle without charge or mass.

Pauling, Linus Carl (born 1901) American chemist and resolute opponent of nuclear weapons and the only person (other than Marie CURIE) to receive two Nobel Prizes, one for Chemistry (1954) and one for Peace (1962). He applied quantum mechanics (an approach established by Erwin SCHRÖDINGER and Paul DIRAC) to the problem of how atoms and molecules enter into chemical combination with each other and (1939) he produced a full account of chemical bonding.

Paustovsky, Konstantin (1892-1968) Russian short-story writer and novelist. His major work is the autobiographical trilogy *Story of a Life* (1946-64) which covers a span of more than 30 years. Some of his works have been filmed.

Pavese, Cesare (1908-50) Italian novelist, critic and poet, author of *The Comrade* (1947) and *The Moon and the Bonfire* (1950). Pavese's novels mingle realism and symbolism with a strong sexual undercurrent highlighting his pessimistic view of the futility of a moral code, and even of life itself.

Pavlov, Ivan (1849-1936) Russian physiologist and father of behaviourist psychology. His great contribution to psychological knowledge is his theory of the 'conditioned reflex', which he took to be the basic model of mental activity. His many laboratory experiments to establish this theory included those in which the sound of a bell could be made to produce exactly the same effect on a dog as the sight and smell of food which, for instance, evokes the response of salivation. Pavlov showed that if a bell was rung when the food was presented, in time the sound alone caused salivation. The animals had thus been 'conditioned' to respond.

Pavlova, Anna (1881-1931) Russian ballerina and the first popularizer of ballet on a world-wide scale. She performed in Russia, then in 1909 became DIAGHILEV's first ballerina, gaining fame as creator of the leading roles in *The Dying Swan* and *Les Sylphides*.

Paxton, Sir Joseph (1801-65) English designer of the Crystal Palace for the Great Exhibition held in London in 1851. This enormous building made of glass, wood and iron included full-grown trees among its arcades and was a development of Paxton's previous designs for giant glasshouses at Chatsworth, Derbyshire. His use of prefabricated methods of erection on a large scale was unprecedented.

Peacock, Thomas Love (1785-1866) English critic, poet and novelist who wrote satirically of the literary, political and social fashions of the day. The satires *Headlong Hall* (1816), *Nightmare Abbey* (1818) and *Crotchet Castle* (1831) are comprised mainly of conversations at house-parties. He was a close friend of SHELLEY, 'Mr Scythrop' in *Nightmare Abbey*.

Pearson, Lester Bowles (1897-1972) Canadian Liberal statesman. As Foreign Minister from 1948 to 1957, he was Canada's spokesman at the United Nations, and was President of the General Assembly from 1952 to 1953. Russian opposition prevented his election as Secretary-General. His efforts to create a UN Emergency Force during the Suez crisis of 1956 won him the Nobel Peace Prize in 1957. He was Prime Minister of Canada from 1963 to 1968.

Peary, Robert Edwin (1856-1920) American Arctic explorer, credited with being the first man to reach the North Pole. After a four-year reconnaissance, Peary tried in 1905 to reach the Pole, and got to within 200 miles of it before harsh weather forced him back. His second attempt (1908-9) proved successful and Peary finally reached the North Pole on 6 April 1909, with Matthew Henson (a negro servant) and four eskimoes. The United States Congress confirmed Peary's claim to have been first to the Pole, discrediting Frederick COOK's counter-claim to have reached it a year earlier.

Pedersen, Knut see HAMSUN, Knut

Pedrarias Davila (c. 1440-1531) Spanish soldier and colonial administrator, who founded Panama City. He succeeded BALBOA, whom he later executed, as Governor of Darien Colony, now Panama. Panama City, which he founded on the site of a native fishing village, became the springboard from which ALMAGRO and PIZARRO set out for Peru.

Peel, Sir Robert (1788-1850) English statesman, Prime Minister and founder of the Metropolitan Police force, known after him as 'Peelers'. In his ministry of 1841-6 the government, though committed to retain the Corn Laws, introduced a series of free trade budgets, passed measures to increase financial stability (Bank Charter Act 1844) and revised income tax (1842). As a result of the crisis caused by the Irish potato failure (1845-6), the pressure of the Anti-Corn Law League, and, perhaps, his own conviction of the inevitability of repeal, the Corn Laws were abolished. The consequent split in the Conservative party kept it out of effective office for a generation.

Péguy, Charles (1873-1914) French poet and socialist publisher, who founded the influential journal *Cahiers de la Quinzaine* (1900). Catholic and patriot, he sought to reconcile often contradictory views.

Peirce, Charles (1839-1914) American scientist and philosopher, who believed that in order to discover meaning, we should observe what people do with concepts. This pragmatic maxim was later expanded into a criterion of truth by William JAMES.

Pele (born 1940) Brazilian association footballer who played his first international for Brazil in 1957. In 1969, during his 909th match, he became the world's first player to score 1000 goals in football.

Pellegrini, Carlo see APE

Penn, William (c. 1644-1718) English Quaker, founder of the state of Pennsylvania. Despite the later disputes that divided the colony, Penn's vision of a tolerant and humane society helped to mould American constitutional history, and his religious devotion softened hostility to Quakers in England. A life-long champion of religious toleration, Penn was persecuted for his writing and preaching, and despairing of achieving toleration in England, successfully negotiated for the new colony of Pennsylvania in 1682, seeing it as a haven in which persecuted Quakers could freely practise their religion and maintain friendly relations with their Indian neighbours.

Pepys, Samuel (1633-1703) English civil servant, who is famous for the *Diary* which he kept between 1660 and 1669. It is a vivid record of public and private London life, the court of CHARLES II and the administration of the Royal Navy.

Perceval, Spencer (1762-1812) The only British Prime Minister to have been assassinated. He was

Samuel Pepys, remembered for his diary, played a large part in the modernization of the Royal Navy

Chancellor of the Exchequer under Portland (1807), and succeeded him as Prime Minister in 1809. Three years later he was shot in the lobby of the House of Commons. His assassin, John Bellingham, was not a political opponent, but a bankrupt with a personal grievance against the government.

Percy, Sir Henry (1364-1403) English knight, known as Harry Hotspur for his fiery fighting qualities, who helped to place HENRY IV on the throne in 1399. After quarrelling with Henry, he rose in rebellion, supported by the Welshman, Owen Glyndower, but was killed at Shrewsbury.

Perelman, Sidney Joseph (born 1904) American humorist who was for a time scriptwriter for the MARX Brothers. His stories, many of them written for the *New Yorker*, appear in several collections. Their humour is based on verbal fantasy, arising out of the ironies in everyday situations.

'Peelers' past and present. London's Metropolitan Police owed their existence and, for many years, their nickname, to Sir Robert Peel, the Victorian statesman

The status of Athens as the birthplace of democracy and as one of the glories of western culture owes much to Pericles, who dominated its affairs for nearly 30 years. He was instrumental in building the Parthenon, which still looks over Athens

Perez Galdos, Benito (1843-1920) Spanish novelist who has been compared, in scope, quantity and quality of work, with BALZAC, DICKENS and TOLSTOY. Beginning with *The Golden Fountain* (1870), he produced a cycle of 46 historical novels covering events in Spain between 1805 and 1875. This was followed by 30 volumes of novels dealing with contemporary Spanish life, including his most famous work, *Fortunata and Jacinta* (1886-7), a four-volume novel whose range and depth of characterization have been compared with *War and Peace*. Though concentrating on Madrid, and on the middle-classes, his attitudes developed and matured from a youthful, dogmatic belief in material progress to a more tolerant and sympathetic interest in all human experience.

Pergolesi, Giovanni Battista (1710-36) Italian composer who, before his early death from tuberculosis, evolved a style of exceptional charm. After his death, opportunist music publishers put out minor works under his name to exploit his popularity, hence correct attribution of his works has always been a problem: it is uncertain whether the songs STRAVINSKY used as the basis for his ballet *Pulcinella* were in fact by Pergolesi. Authenticated works, however, include several operas and a Stabat Mater.

Pericles (c. 495-429 BC) Athenian statesman, who was the dominant figure in Athens at the height of its fame and made it the intellectual centre of Greece. Pericles, who was *strategus* (general-in-command) for nearly 30 years, introduced payment for public government and jury service, and by opening government posts to all citizens, irrespective of social status, ended the privileges attached to noble birth. He made Athens artistically supreme by inviting men of genius from abroad, initiating the building of the Parthenon and other beautiful edifices, befriending the philosophers SOPHOCLES and ANAXAGORAS, and the sculptor PHIDIAS. At first he sought expansion by aggressive means and fought imperialist wars in Egypt, Boeotia and the Aegean Islands, but after the collapse of an Athenian army in Boeotia (447 BC), he changed his policy and began to consolidate the empire, while maintaining the naval supremacy by which Athens had attained its unprecedented commercial prosperity. Pericles died of plague whilst leading Athens in the unsuccessful Peloponnesian War against Sparta.

Perkins, Jacob (1766-1849) Versatile American inventor who designed, among other things, a machine to cut and put heads on nails (1790), a process and equipment for printing bank notes and stamps (1819), an improved high-pressure steam boiler (1823-36) and an experimental refrigerator (1834). He established a factory in England for security printing, which printed the first penny postage stamps (1840).

Perkin, Sir William Henry (1838-1907) British chemist who discovered mauveine, the first artificial dye, and with it established the aniline dye industry.

Perón, Juan Domingo (born 1895) Argentinian dictator, who was a member of the right-wing group of army officers who seized power in 1943. He achieved wide popularity through a programme of social reforms, and was elected President in 1946. In suppressing all opposition and trying rapidly to industrialize his country, he relied for popular support to a great extent on the personality cult of his wife, Eva, through his control of various newspapers and her much-publicized interest in social welfare. After her death (1952), however, Perón's popularity declined, and his alienation of the Church and the army led to his deposition and exile in 1955. He maintained his interest in Argentinian affairs from abroad, and in 1973 after a second general election, once more assumed the presidency, assisted by his new wife, Isabella.

Pérrault, Charles (1628-1703) French poet and writer of fairy tales, including *Tom Thumb*, *Red Riding Hood*, *Cinderella* and *Blue Beard*. He also wrote *Parallèles des Anciens et des Modernes* (1688-97) in which he pleaded the cause of the 'moderns' against BOILEAU.

Perrault, Claude (c. 1613-88) French architect, doctor and sculptor, who was probably largely responsible for the imposing east front of the Louvre, with its colonnade of coupled Corinthian columns. BERNINI had submitted designs for this project and LEVAU and LEBRUN were also on the design committee.

Perret, Auguste (1874-1954) French architect and early user of reinforced concrete in architecture, to whom LE CORBUSIER was once apprenticed. His early flats in the rue Franklin, Paris, were faced with Art Nouveau ceramic panels of leaves and berries, but three years later, on his Ponthieu Garage, Paris, he left the concrete structure clearly exposed.

Pershing, John Joseph (1860-1948) Commander-in-Chief of the American forces in France in the First World War. After distinguishing himself in the Spanish-American war (1898), he was sent to the Philippines, where he succeeded in pacifying the fanatical Moros of Mindanao (1913), for which Theodore ROOSEVELT promoted him from captain to brigadier general. He was appointed Commander-in-Chief of the American Expeditionary Force to France in 1917.

Perugino, Pietro (c. 1445-1523) Italian artist of the Umbrian school, best known for his religious paintings and particularly significant because he was the master of RAPHAEL from c. 1500-4. Perugino's earliest surviving work is a picture of St Sebastian, which is the sole remnant of a series of frescoes that he painted in the church at Cerqueto. This painting synthesizes the highest qualities of Perugino's art and anticipates those of the High Renaissance – simplicity of composition and an uncluttered, lucid style. At the turn of the century the Perugian Guild of Bankers commissioned him to paint a cycle of frescoes in their Salo del Cambio, and it is likely that this was the period during which the young Raphael learned the basics of fresco technique. His many altarpieces are characterized by harmonious, symmetrical designs and a certain sentimentality of treatment.

Peruzzi, Baldassare (1481-1536) Italian High Renaissance architect, whose most famous building is the Villa Farnesina, Rome, which he designed and which RAPHAEL decorated. His style is often characterized by an almost flippant grace and an apparently facile quality.

Pestalozzi, Johann Heinrich (1746-1827) Swiss educator and social reformer who emphasized a reality-based education. Pestalozzi stressed the importance of the mother's role and saw moral education as giving unity to the various aspects of learning. He presented his reforming ideas in a series of writings, including the novel *Leonard and Gertrude* (1781-7), and developed the theme in *How Gertrude Teaches Her Children* (1801). He also attempted to put his ideas into practice by founding a home which attempted to combine vocational training with an elementary education (1774-80) for poor children. He looked after homeless children after the massacre of Stans (1798-9) and established boarding schools at Burgdorf (1800-4) and Yverdon (1805-25), which also trained teachers.

Pétain, Henri Philippe (1856-1951) Marshal of France, a hero of his country in the First World War and who died, serving a life sentence for treason, after the Second. Pétain distinguished himself in the First World War by his courageous defence of Verdun in 1916 and the following year he was appointed Commander, French Army. He was later replaced by FOCH. He was ambassador to Spain in 1939 and in 1940, when the French defences collapsed, succeeded Reynaud as Prime Minister, almost immediately signing an armistice with Germany (June). At the head of the Vichy government in unoccupied France, Pétain applied a reactionary and pro-clerical policy, but when the Germans occupied the whole of France (November 1942), he became their puppet. He was abducted to Germany by the retreating Nazis in 1944, but was arrested by the French after the war and tried for high treason. He was condemned to death, but DE GAULLE commuted the sentence to one of life imprisonment, and Pétain died in prison.

Peter I 'The Great' (1672-1725) Tsar of Russia (1682-1725), who brought Russia into Europe and transformed it from a backward country into a modern state. Peter was determined to give Russia outlets to the sea and made the study of naval and military technology the basis for a policy of forceful expansion. He made incognito visits to Austria, England, Germany and the Netherlands (1696-7), and was impressed by the West's material progress. His observations while abroad helped him to modernize the Russian army and to found a navy on Western lines. His return to Russia was precipitated by a rebellion (1698), which he suppressed. Peter then embarked on a long war (1699-1721) against Sweden, and despite a crushing defeat at Narva (1700), recovered and won the decisive battle of Poltava (1709) against CHARLES XII. Eventually, under the Treaty of Nystadt (1721), Russia acquired certain Baltic territories, which included Estonia and Livonia. By thus establishing Russia as northern Europe's leading military power, and by making his newly founded capital of St Petersburg a safe Russian outlet onto the Baltic, Peter assured the country's future as a leading European state.

Peter the Hermit (c. 1050-c. 1115) French monk, who recruited troops for the First Crusade (1095). He crossed Europe by mule, brandishing a crucifix, to publicize Pope Urban II's call for a crusade to seize Muslim-held Jerusalem. He attracted 7000 ill-disciplined followers, who were joined by another 5000 under Walter the Penniless. They eventually reached Asia Minor, but there were

defeated by the Turks. Peter survived and later joined Godfrey of Bouillon (1097) in the capture of Jerusalem.

Peter, St (1st cent.) Galilaean fisherman who became a leader of JESUS's disciples, their spokesman and their representative. His character is the most clearly delineated of the apostles', and his human, impetuous love of and devotion to Jesus have inspired Christians in all ages. Although little is known of his activity after Jesus's death, it is known that Peter held a leading position in the Early Church, clashed with St PAUL about the importance of the Jewish Torah (Law) for Christians, and that he appears to have travelled to Rome where, according to tradition, he was crucified upside down, possibly during NERO's persecution in AD 64. Later tradition made him the Bishop of Rome, where the Church of St Peter is said to stand upon the site of his crucifixion.

Petipa, Marius (1819-1910) French choreographer and ballet master of the Imperial Russian Ballet and architect of the Bolshoi and Kirov Ballets.

Peto, Sir Samuel (1808-89) English civil engineer, politician and contractor whose skill at organizing large bodies of 'navigators' (itinerant labourers and skilled men, later known as 'navvies') won him many canal- and railway-building contracts in England, France, Algiers, Australia, Norway and Russia.

Petöfi, Sándor (1823-49) Hungarian lyric poet, whose main works were love poems, characterized by a sense of impending doom that weighs heavily on present happiness, and revolutionary lyrics.

Petrarch (1304-74) Italian scholar and humanist, who was one of the great forerunners of the Italian Renaissance. His love poems to the unknown Laura have inspired imitators down the ages and rank among the greatest of all European love poems.

Petronius Arbiter, Gaius (1st cent.) Roman writer, author of the *Satyricon*, a picaresque novel, part verse and part prose, and extant only in fragments, but unique in Latin literature. Witty and obscene, it recounts the adventures of three disreputable young freedmen in the low haunts of Campania and Magna Graecia, and paints an unforgettable picture of the *nouveau-riche* Trimalchio, a dinner at whose house forms the subject-matter of the longest surviving part. The novel is our chief source book for 'Vulgar Latin'.

Pevsner, Antoine (1886-1962) Russian abstract sculptor and Constructivist. His abstractions were based on the pure scientific and geometric theories of aesthetics, the creation of forms being related to mathematics and physics. Pevsner worked on surfaces that enclosed, covered and separated space, as in his *Peace Column*, an abstract sculpture in bronze. With his brother, Naum GABO, he wrote (1920) the Realist Manifesto, in which were presented the fundamental concepts of Constructivism.

Pheidippides (5th cent. BC) Athenian long-distance runner who ran 140 miles in 48 hours to seek Spartan aid against Persian invaders who had landed at Marathon, and then reputedly returned to take part in the battle. This story inspired the idea of a long-distance race (from Marathon to Athens) in the first Olympiad of modern times (1896).

Philby, Harold Adrian Russell 'Kim' (born 1911) English master spy for the Russians. Recruited by them in 1933, he became a member of the British Secret Intelligence Service, and in 1944, set up the British anti-Russian counter-intelligence system, which he ran until 1946. From 1949-51 he worked closely with the American CIA in Washington and thus was able to inform Russia of almost all the West's counter-espionage operations – and to protect other Soviet agents, such as Burgess and MACLEAN, whose defection and escape he assisted in 1951. It was at this time that he came under suspicion, and was asked to leave the Foreign Service. In 1955, following a Foreign Office investigation, his reputation was rehabilitated. In 1963, however, he admitted that the allegations that had been made against him were true, and fled to Russia, where he was granted Soviet citizenship.

Philip I (1052-1108) King of France (1060-1108). Though overshadowed by vassals like WILLIAM I, he began the task of re-establishing royal authority over the royal domains.

Philip II (1165-1223) King of France (1180-1223), also called Philip Augustus, a member of the Capetian dynasty who took the Angevin Empire from the kings of England. He joined RICHARD I in leading the Third Crusade, but quarrelled with him, fell ill and returned home (1191). He then conspired with Richard's brother JOHN to seize control of England's French possessions – all western France, except for some parts of Normandy, which Philip had won back (1187-9) from Richard's father HENRY II. Richard, returning to Normandy in 1194, defeated Philip at Freteval, but Philip continued to fight (1194-9), and by 1208, after John had succeeded Richard as King of England, had taken back Normandy, Maine, Touraine, Anjou, Poitou and Brittany. Philip then defeated an alliance of rebellious feudal lords, John, the Holy Roman Emperor, and several princes of Germany at the Battle of Bouvines and thus secured his expanded kingdom.

Philip II (1527-98) King of Spain (1556-98), whose policies permanently weakened the state that had been made powerful by FERDINAND V and Isabella I. He was the only legitimate son of the Emperor CHARLES V, and was ruler not only of Spain, but of its colonies in the New World, as well as Italy, Naples and Sicily, Milan and the Burgundian provinces of the Netherlands and Franche-Comté. Fanatically set upon championing Roman Catholicism and bolstering the power of the Spanish Hapsburgs in Europe, Philip grappled unprofitably with France (1556-9 and 1589-98); and provoked WILLIAM THE SILENT's struggle for Dutch independence, which began in 1567. After the death of England's queen, MARY I, the second of his four wives, he fought England, led by ELIZABETH I, losing the Spanish Armada (1588). With it went control of the seas, which had given Spain its immense empire in America. Though Philip successfully claimed Portugal (1580), Spain's economic decline was caused by his costly wars and inefficient government.

Philip IV 'The Fair' (1268-1314) King of France (1285-1314), who strengthened the monarchy by ending the feudal privileges of the Church. Philip's demands for taxes from the clergy caused a long dispute with Pope Boniface VIII, but Philip dominated Boniface's French successor, Clement V (who moved the Papal court to France in 1305), and founded Gallicanism (independence of the French Church). To find money for wars with England and Flanders, Philip raised levies, robbed and expelled the Jews, suppressed and despoiled the rich Order of Knights Templars, and called the first States General (1302), which he used as a means of exacting taxes from the nation.

Philip V (1683-1746) King of Spain (1700-46), first of the Spanish Bourbon dynasty (1700-1931), whose accession started a major European war. He was the grandson of LOUIS XIV of France, who contrived Philip's inheritance of the vast Spanish empire from the childless Charles II, the last Spanish Hapsburg ruler. By

seemingly uniting Spain with France, Philip's accession altered the European balance of power, and provoked the War of the Spanish Succession (1701-14), which left Philip in power, but caused Spain's permanent separation from France.

Philip VI (1293-1350) King of France (1328-50), and first of the Valois dynasty (1328-1589), whose disputes with EDWARD III of England led to the 100 Years' War (1337-1453), waged by Edward to retain his lands in France and by Philip to rid France of English occupation. The war, begun by a revolt in Flanders, brought immediate disasters to Philip, with an English victory at sea off Sluys (1340), and on land at Crécy (1346).

Philippe de Comines see COMMYNES, Philippe de

Philip of Hesse (1504-67) Landgrave of Hesse (1509-67), known as 'the Magnanimous' whose activity during the Reformation decisively influenced the course of German history. After embracing Lutheranism (1524), Philip formed an alliance with Saxony which became the axis of German Protestantism. The Saxon-Hesse alliance was extended to a Protestant League (1526) and to the Schmalkaldic League (1531) to resist the Emperor CHARLES V, but, after Philip had made a bigamous marriage, widespread personal hostility forced him to submit to the emperor. Further conflict between the two caused Charles to imprison Philip in 1547. Released in 1552, he continued in vain to form a strong league of Protestant states.

Philip, Arthur (1738-1814) English naval commander, who established a penal colony (1788) in Australia at Sydney (named after the British Home Secretary of the time), and became first Governor of New South Wales.

Piaget, Jean (born 1896) Swiss psychologist, one of the foremost researchers into the thought processes of children, whose studies on child psychology have had a vital influence on modern education policy. Piaget sees perception in the child as unstable, distorted and fraught with illusion, and the process of learning, or growing up, as a gradual advance towards an orderly organization of experience, which helps the child to adapt more comfortably to its environment.

Picard, Jean (1620-82) French astronomer who first accurately measured a degree of longitude. Working under Jean Dominique CASSINI, in 1669-70, he made the first

precise measurement of an arc of the meridian when he measured a degree of longitude between Amiens and Mahoisine, north of Paris. Superseding medieval estimates of the degree, Picard's achievement – together with the triangulation surveying technique developed by Gemma Frisius – made possible the accurate mapping of the entire world.

Picasso, Pablo (1881-1973) Spanish-born artist, who was perhaps the greatest and certainly the best known of modern painters. As a boy in Spain, he possessed a remarkable technical virtuosity, and the stylistic innovations he subsequently developed must be seen in the context of this early mastery of traditional artistic means. He went to Paris in 1900, settling there in 1904. This was his 'Blue Period', so called because of the predominant colour of his canvases, which were a personal expression of the social and psychological concerns of the Symbolist movement (e.g. *La Vie*, 1903). This phase of his development was succeeded by the 'Pink Period', during which he painted the *Family of Acrobats* (1905). Then in 1907, with the large, figurative composition, *Les Demoiselles d'Avignon*, Picasso abruptly banished sentiment from his work and, with the support of BRAQUE, embarked on a series of formal researches, inspired by CEZANNE and by African carvings. The result was Cubism, the most influential and far-reaching of all modern art movements. Picasso's individuality is evident in all but the more 'scientific' of his Cubist paintings, and from about 1915 he reintroduced a style of figurative Classicism into his work

A Spaniard who turned his back on Spain, disliking its régime, Picasso ranks with the giants of art

concurrent with the development of 'analytical' Cubism. In 1917 he made his first stage designs (*Parade*, in collaboration with DIAGHILEV, SATIE and COCTEAU). His later paintings (e.g. *Three Dancers*, 1925, and *Guernica*, 1937, painted in protest against FRANCO's bombing of that town during the Spanish Civil War) still owe much to Cubism, rendered highly expressive, especially in the handling of the human figure, and showing something of the humanitarian motivation of his earliest work.

Piccard, Auguste (1884-1962) Swiss physicist, balloonist and deep-sea explorer. In a balloon, he reached a world record altitude of 53,153 feet in 1932 and, in a deep-sea research vessel called a bathyscaphe, he descended 10,000 feet into the Tyrrhenian Sea in 1953.

Piccard, Jacques (born 1922) Swiss oceanographic engineer who (with Don Walsh of the United States Navy) first reached the lowest-known point of the Earth's crust, 35,800 feet down, in an attempt to reach the bottom of the Challenger Deep in the Pacific's Mariana Trench.

Pickering, Edward Charles (1846-1919) American astronomer who invented the meridian photometer, a device for finding the magnitude of a star by comparison with a star of known brightness. He was responsible for the publication of a giant catalogue of the spectra of all the stars of the northern hemisphere.

Pierce, Franklin (1804-69) Fourteenth President of the US (1853-57), whose domestic policies caused a resumption of the conflict which led to the Civil War. In 1852, after a period of retirement from politics, he was adopted as a compromise Democratic candidate. He encouraged the building of trans-continental railroads and extended US territory by the Gadsden Land Purchase from Mexico (1853). His main achievement in foreign affairs was the opening of Japan to American trade through the expedition of Commodore Perry in 1853. He is now chiefly remembered for his approval of the Kansas-Nebraska Act, which opened up those territories for settlement, leaving the question of slavery to be resolved locally. Contrary to his inaugural promise to bury the slavery controversy, the Kansas-Nebraska Act served to raise the issue again, and his Southern sympathies alienated much Northern opinion, so that under his successor, BUCHANAN, the spectre of civil war reappeared.

Piero della Francesca (c. 1420-92) Italian artist who synthesized the Florentine interest in form with the

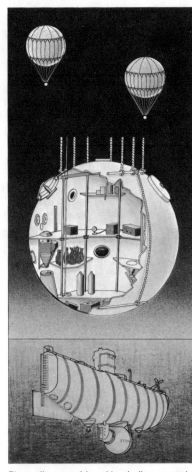

Piccard's record-breaking balloon cupola and undersea bathyscaphe

Venetian painters' study of light and atmosphere. The scientific precision of his compositions and his eye for harmonic proportion are evident even in what is probably his earliest known work, the *Baptism of Christ*, whose pale colours, combined with the calm grandeur of the figures, lend the air of timelessness for which he is celebrated. The fresco cycle *Legend of the True Cross* (1452-c. 1459) in the choir of St Francesco at Arezzo, though virtually unknown until the 19th century, is generally considered to be Piero's greatest achievement.

Pietro da Cortona (1596-1669) Florentine architect and painter, who is particularly known for his frescoes, the most famous of which is the *Allegory of Divine Providence and Barberini Power* in the Barberini Palace, Rome.

Pilon, Germain (c. 1535-90) French sculptor, whose best-known work is the group of the Three Graces carved for the monument for the Heart of Henry II (1560-3) at St Denis (now in the Louvre). The graceful Mannerist elegance of his work becomes more fluid and realistic in the treatment of the *Tomb of*

Henry II and Catherine de Medici (1563-70), and in his later work, during the 1580s, the fluidity of style formed a stylistic stepping-stone from a Mannerist towards a more Baroque feel.

Pilsudski, Józef (1867-1935) Polish soldier, who became dictator of Poland. A student revolutionary, in 1887 he was sent to Siberia accused of being a socialist agitator and involved in a conspiracy to assassinate ALEXANDER III. In 1894, he became editor of the Polish nationalist and socialist 'underground' newspaper *Robotnik* (*The Workman*). In the First World War, he recruited 10,000 Poles to fight for the Central Powers against Russia, but resigned his command because of German and Austrian interference in Polish affairs.

Pindar (518-c. 438 BC) The most famous lyric poet of Ancient Greece. Pindar wrote all kinds of choral lyric, but the poems which survive complete are all *epicinians*, odes written to celebrate a victory in one of the great athletic festivals. His works supported moral conclusions about human virtue and the laws of the gods.

Pinero, Sir Arthur Wing (1855-1934) British dramatist, who wrote *The Second Mrs Tanqueray*. He began as an actor and first wrote some unsuccessful farces. His earliest success was *The Magistrate* (1885), which was followed by more farces. *The Second Mrs Tanqueray* (1893), *Trelawney of the Wells* (1895) and *The Gay Lord Quex* (1899) are the best known of his straight social dramas.

Pinkerton, Allan (1819-84) Scottish-born founder of one of the first and best known of the American detective agencies, the Pinkerton National Detective Agency. It was established in Chicago in 1850.

The West's great thief-taker, Allan Pinkerton, centre, with two agents

Buffalo Bill

Sitting Bull

Calamity Jane

General Custer

Geronimo

Legend and fact are inextricably mixed in the history of America's west. Heroes and villains came and went but have survived in a unique mythology, thanks to the movies. History is now reinstating many of the traditional 'baddies'– such as the Indians– in an heroic role, while taking a cooler look at some of the old heroes and the facts of America's unique folklore

Billy the Kid

THE KID.
REWARD.

I will... reward to any person or persons who will... capture William Bonny, alias The Kid, and deliver him to any sheriff of New Mexico. Satisfactory proofs of identity will be required.

LEW. WALLACE,
Governor of New Mexico.

Pinter, Harold (born 1930) British dramatist and actor, and leading exponent of the Theatre of the Absurd. *The Birthday Party* (1957), though a commercial failure, had a critical success on the stage and subsequently on television. His first success was *The Caretaker*. He wrote a number of short plays for radio and television which were later staged. He returned to full-length plays with *The Homecoming* (1965), and has also written film scripts.

Pintoricchio, Bernardino (c. 1454-1513) Italian painter of large, multi-figured frescoes, whose work developed under the influence of PERUGINO, with whom he worked as an assistant on some of the frescoes in the Sistine Chapel. The fresco cycles (1492-5) in the Borgia apartments of the Vatican and the ten scenes from the life of Pius II in the Cathedral Library at Siena (1503-9), are generally considered to be his most important works.

Pinzón, Vicente Yañez (c. 1460-c. 1524) Spanish navigator who shared in COLUMBUS's first Atlantic crossing and explored in South America. He helped to prepare Columbus's expedition and captained the *Niña* on the 1492-3 voyage. Later Pinzón led his own expedition (1500) across the Atlantic to Cape St Roque, the eastern extremity of Brazil.

Pirandello, Luigi (1867-1936) Italian dramatist, who wrote *Six Characters in Search of an Author* (1921). His work has affinities with the Theatre of the Absurd. He was at one time a short-story writer and later wrote one-act plays. In 1916 came his first full-length play *Think of it, Giacomino* and *Right You Are if You Think You Are*. Apart from the world-famous *Six Characters*, his best-known plays are *Beast and Virtue, Man, Each in His Own Way, As You Desire Me* and *Henry IV*.

Pisano, Nicola (c. 1225-c. 1278) Italian sculptor and architect, regarded as the last of the medieval classicists. In his first important work, the Baptistry pulpit at Pisa (1260), and in the pulpit at Siena Cathedral (1265-8) – a development of the earlier work – the classical influence is strong, in both the architectural structure and the sculptured parts.

Pisistratus (6th cent. BC) Athenian dictator and statesman, who enriched Athens at the nobles' expense. He seized power in 546 BC and to support the landless peasants, mostly neglected by SOLON's reforms, he gave them fields confiscated from the nobles' estates. Further to sap the nobles' power, he fostered trade and industry by transforming Athens into an international city.

Pissarro, Camille (1830-1903) French Impressionist painter, whose early works were much influenced by COROT and COURBET, but by 1869 had acquired a definitive Impressionist style. His best works were done during the ensuing decade. Pissarro's example was crucial in encouraging CEZANNE to abandon his early Romanticism. GAUGUIN too was much indebted to him, and he had the reputation of being both brilliant and sympathetic. His letters provide an anecdotal history of French painting in the second half of the 19th century.

Pitman, Sir Isaac (1813-97) English publisher, and inventor of a short-hand system of writing. The company he founded still publishes books on short-hand and commercial subjects.

Pitt, William, Earl of Chatham (1708-78) British statesman, known as 'Pitt the Elder', to distinguish him from his equally famous son, William PITT the Younger. He was called into the government to help to defeat France, Britain's greatest rival, in the Seven Years' War (1756-63). Pitt became Secretary of State (1756), and masterminded the intercontinental land and sea war. French forces in Canada and India were attacked, her communications were hamstrung by sea blockades and FREDERICK II of Prussia's continental armies were subsidized. GEORGE III, on his accession (1760), was determined to end the war, and faced with his opposition, the Cabinet refused to declare war on Spain, as Pitt wished to do, and he resigned (1761). George III's policy ended the war in 1763, but Pitt's strategy had brought the British Empire towards its zenith by assuring Britain's hold on North America and India, and annexing territories in Africa and the West Indies.

Pitt, William (1759-1806) British statesman and Prime Minister (1783-1801, 1804-6), called 'the Younger Pitt', son of William PITT the Elder. At the age of 23 he became Chancellor of the Exchequer (1782), and then, at 24, Britain's youngest Prime Minister. He increased the power of the cabinet and incidentally that of the prime minister within it. Finance was his first concern, and to reduce and fund the National Debt he floated loans, increased the tax on windows in private houses, introduced many new taxes, and organized a sinking fund. To revitalize the economy he tried to establish free trade and made a commercial treaty with France. His India Act (1784) transferred political control of the country, previously vested in the East India Company, to the crown. By formally uniting Ireland with Great Britain (1801) he established the United Kingdom. His years of office were marked by the rise of French power. After the young French republic had declared war (1793), Pitt organized and subsidized three European coalitions against France (1793, 1799, 1805). The cost of these operations undermined his financial position and forced him to raise loans, increase general taxation, impose duties on legacies and introduce income tax. He died at the height of Napoleon's successes.

Pius IX (1792-1878) The longest reigning Pope (1846-78) who promulgated the dogmas of the Immaculate Conception (1854) and Papal Infallibility (1870). While a cardinal, he professed liberal sentiments and inspired Italian patriots, but after being elected Pope in 1846, he became progressively reactionary and during the insurrections of 1848 in Rome fled to Gaeta in the kingdom of Naples. He returned to Rome under French military protection, established the Roman Catholic hierarchy in Britain (1850) and Holland (1853), attacked all forms of social progress, and sought by new dogmas to enhance his religious authority in compensation for his loss of secular power. From the day in 1870 when Italian troops entered Rome, he regarded himself as a prisoner in the Vatican.

Pius X see LOISY, Alfred Firmin

Pius XI (1857-1939) Pope who opposed both Fascism and Communism during the inter-war years. He publicly declared himself against Communism and in 1937 supported FRANCO because of the anti-clericalism of AZAÑA. He concluded the Lateran Treaties with MUSSOLINI in 1929, which restored the temporal power of the papacy in the Vatican City, and reached a concordat with the government which defined the position of the Church in the Fascist state. He also agreed a concordat with HITLER in 1933, but friction continued between the Church in both Italy and Germany, and conflict was inevitable.

Pius XII (1876-1958) Pope during the Second World War, whose ambivalent attitude to the Fascist and Nazi dictatorships proved controversial. After being elected Pope (1939) he refused to condemn the seizure of Czechoslovakia, to support ROOSEVELT's appeal to HITLER to urge MUSSOLINI to desist from aggression, or to condemn the invasion and occupation of Poland. Above all, while expressing sympathy for Belgium, Holland and France when they were invaded, he refused to rebuke Germany. At no time did he condemn the Nazis' extermination of the Jews. After the war, Pius XII was influential in social and economic policies of the United Nations, and called for disarmament.

Pizarro, Francisco (c. 1470-1541) Spanish conqueror of the Inca empire, who took part in ALMAGRO's expeditions (1524-5, 1526-7) which discovered the Peruvian civilization of the Incas. Pizarro obtained permission to conquer and govern Peru south of the Gulf of Guayaquil, and although heavily outnumbered by Inca warriors, Pizarro cowed them by killing their chief, ATAHUALPA (1533). He acquired great wealth in Peru and founded Lima, but fought with and killed Almagro (1538), whose followers killed Pizarro in revenge.

Planck, Max Karl Ernst Ludwig (1858-1947) German physicist, who was awarded the 1918 Nobel Prize in Physics for his discovery of the quantum theory of radiation. Planck's famous hypothesis is that energy from an oscillating particle is emitted not continuously but in discrete quanta (or 'packets' of energy). The energy for any given frequency of oscillation is h times that frequency, where h is a universal constant, later called Planck's constant. The full significance of this new idea lay in its development by others into modern quantum theory.

Plantin, Christophe (1514-89) French printer and typographer, whose work was characterized by its single clarity of design. A bookbinder and bookseller, he took up typography in 1555 and his books became famous for their copperplate engravings for illustrations. His most notable work was the Antwerp Polyglot Bible, an eight-volume work which attempted to standardize the texts of the Old and New Testaments. Plantin became one of Europe's outstanding printers, and a Plantin typeface is used for the main text of Who Did What.

Plath, Sylvia (1932-63) American poet and wife of Ted HUGHES, who, through her work, struggled with the human difficulties and torments which finally overcame her, and she committed suicide. Her best-known work is Ariel (1965).

Plato (c. 427-347 BC) Greek philosopher in whom the great pre-Socratic trains of Greek philosophy meet: the mathematically inspired doctrines of PYTHAGORAS and his followers; the logic of PARMENIDES and the Eleaticism of ZENO and the theories of HERACLITUS. Plato never composed a systematic treatise of his views, believing such a treatise to be inimical to philosophy, which should be disinterested enquiry arising from the general critical examination of all knowledge. There are two phases in his work. The earlier, Socratic, stage is marked by the Pythagorean theory of Ideas or Forms. The later, Platonic, stage avoided this split between the real and the ideal, and also gave much direct advice on social matters. Throughout this development ran a theory of ethics equating the ultimate good with perfect knowledge. The Republic, Plato's best known work, is a discussion on the nature of justice, the citizen and the state, touching on a vast range of issues in philosophy, ethics and social sciences. Among the other dialogues, the Apology describes the trial of his friend SOCRATES, who was executed in 399 BC; the Phaedo records Socrates's last hours, spent in discussion with friends about immortality; the Sophist showed a beginning of Plato's own logical theories; the Timaeus presented a mathematical theory of the world and the Laws offered advice on practical, legal and other social problems.

Plautus (late 3rd-2nd cent. BC) Roman dramatist, highly successful in freely adapting the Greek New Comedy of Manners for Roman audiences. Unworried about realism or authenticity, he exaggerated Greek conventions and introduced Roman elements for comic effect, exploiting situations of mistaken identity or deception with great skill. Of 20 surviving plays, the Menaechmi was used by SHAKESPEARE for his Comedy of Errors and several, notably the Captives, Truculentus and Bacchides, are occasionally revived.

Plekhanov, Georgi Valentinovich (1857-1918) Russian Marxist revolutionary, theorist and mentor of LENIN. He joined the populist revolutionary movement while still a student, and as a result was forced to spend 40 years in exile, mostly in Geneva, where he developed MARX's philosophy and played a large part in forming Lenin's early ideas. He was the founder (1900), with Lenin, and co-editor of Iskra (The Spark). After the Menshevik-Bolshevik split of 1903, he moved towards the Mensheviks, and during the First World War, advocated opposition to the Bolsheviks.

Plimsoll, Samuel (1824-98) English politician and social reformer, best remembered for his strenuous campaign to prevent shipowners from sailing undermanned, unsafe and overinsured ships. Eventually the Parliamentary Bill of 1876 gave powers of government inspection and obliged all ships to carry a mark (the Plimsoll mark) showing the waterline at maximum loading. In 1890, his publication, Cattle-Ships, exposed the danger and cruelty of the sea trade in cattle.

Pliny the Elder (23-79) Roman writer and author of the 37-volume Historia Naturalis, usually known as Pliny's Natural History. The most comprehensive extant work of the period, it deals with his views on cosmology, philosophy, mineralogy and the living world.

Pliny the Younger (62-113) Roman orator and writer, nephew of PLINY THE ELDER. His books of letters, polished for publication, constitute a social history, with varied pictures of cultural life under the emperor TRAJAN. An outstanding example of his descriptive style is the account of Vesuvius' eruption (AD 79), in which his uncle died. Book 10, an exchange of letters with Trajan, is of great historical interest and includes Pliny's well-known report from Bithynia of the treatment of the Christians.

Plomer, William (born 1903) South African poet and novelist whose work gives a clear and sensitive view of the ironies and divisions of life in South Africa. In 1926 he was co-editor, with Roy CAMPBELL, of the literary magazine Voorslag (Whiplash). His angry novel about South Africa, Turbott Wolfe (1926), upset many settled notions on that country. Amongst his other works is a penetrating biography of Cecil RHODES.

Plotinus (c. 205-270) Greek philosopher, probably of Egyptian origin, and the foremost of Neo-Platonists, who saw the ultimate source of everything as the One or the Good; in contact with it, but on a lower level, is Nous or Mind, below which is the Soul. This three-fold division has influenced the Christian theology of the Trinity.

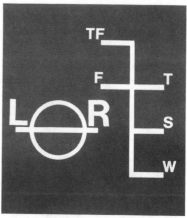

The Plimsoll line on ships grew from a concern for the safety of mariners

Plunkett, Roy Joseph (born 1910) American chemist, who in 1938 synthesized the plastic, polytetrafluoroethylene (PTFE or Teflon), whose remarkable properties include excellent electrical insulation, stability over a wide temperature range, resistance to attack by most corrosive agents and an extremely low coefficient of friction. Teflon was marketed commercially by Plunkett's company in the 1950s, and has found innumerable industrial applications, as well as providing the essential coating in domestic non-stick hardware.

Plutarch (c. AD 46-c. 120) Greek biographer whose 46 *Parallel Lives of Illustrious Greeks and Romans* remain some of the best records of eminent men of the classical world, despite some factual inaccuracy. Pairing Greek soldiers, statesmen, lawmakers, etc., with Roman counterparts, Plutarch drew' comparisons between ALEXANDER THE GREAT and CAESAR, incorporating legends which Arrian (2nd century AD) omitted from his more strictly factual account.

Pobedonostsev, Konstantin Petrovich (1827-1907) Russian university professor, who was tutor to Tsars ALEXANDER III and NICHOLAS II. He believed that democratic parliamentary institutions were pernicious, and autocracy the only valid form of government – that minority nationalities in the empire should be subjugated, and that complete religious orthodoxy was the only way to salvation.

Pocahontas (c. 1595-1617) American Indian princess who saved the life of John SMITH, a Virginian colonist, by shielding his head from the blows of the warriors of Chief Powhatan, Pocahontas's father. Captured by the settlers, Pocahontas was converted to Christianity, married John Smith and voyaged to England where she died of smallpox.

Poe, Edgar Allan (1809-49) American writer of mystery stories and supernatural tales, among which was the first modern detective thriller, *The Murders in the Rue Morgue*. The outcome of his horrific tales (e.g. *The Fall of the House of Usher* and *The Pit and the Pendulum*, both of which have been filmed), many of which were written under the influence of opium, swings between death and insanity. His poem, 'The Raven' (1845), later published in book form, consolidated his success.

Poincaré, Raymond (1860-1934) French politician and President of France during the First World War, whose chauvinism in the post-war years provoked Germany's nationalist

resurgence. He was Prime Minister of a right-wing government in 1912, and President, 1913-20. As Prime Minister again (1922-4), his patriotism blinded him to the consequences of such policies as re-occupation of the Ruhr (1923) when Germany defaulted on her payments of reparations. His government of National Union (1926-9) made large cuts in public expenditure and stabilized the franc, but at the expense of living standards in France.

Polk, James Knox (1795-1849) Eleventh President of the United States who initiated the war with Mexico (1846-8). Though responsible, with his Secretary of State, BUCHANAN, for the settlement of the Oregon boundary dispute with England (1846) and the establishment of the independent treasury system, the main event of his term of office was the Mexican War. Polk exploited settlers' grievances and frontier disputes with Mexico which had resulted in annexation of Texas (1845). When war broke out, Mexico City was captured (1846) and by the treaty of Guadeloupe Hidalgo (1848), Mexico renounced her claims to Texas and ceded California and New Mexico to the US.

Pollaiuolo, Antonio (c. 1432-98) Italian sculptor who was the first artist known to have studied anatomy by means of dissection (anticipating LEONARDO by some years), and the detailed analysis of the human anatomy under conditions of active strain. This knowledge is displayed in the painting of the *Martyrdom of St Sebastian* (c. 1475), and in the bronze *Hercules and Antaeus* (early 1470s). The two largest works which display Antonio's best compositional ability, as well as his mastery of the form of the human body, are the tombs of Pope Sixtus IV (1493) and of Pope Innocent VIII (c. 1495), the first-known tomb to display a sepulchral effigy in the form of a living man.

Pollock, Jackson (1912-56) American painter and pioneer of Abstract Expressionism. After painting in a style influenced by American Realism and the city-scapes of Joseph Stella, he absorbed the Surrealism of MIRÓ and of Gorky, both of whom allowed the subconscious to play an important role in their painting. Pollock went further, dripping pigment over large areas of canvas to form a complex web of lines and areas of colour. This process became known as 'action painting'.

Polo, Marco (c. 1254-c. 1324) Venetian merchant whose travels in Asia were probably the most extensive of medieval times. He accompanied his

father Nicolo and uncle Maffeo on their second trading trek to China, reaching Peking in 1275 after travelling via Palestine, Persia, the Pamirs and the Gobi Desert. In Peking, Marco Polo entered the service of KUBLAI KHAN, who employed him on various missions in the Mongol Empire – including visits to Shansi, Shensi, Szechuan, Yunnan, the Tibetan borders and northern Burma. Kublai would not hear of the Polos returning home until, in 1292, they were allowed to take a new Mongol wife to Kublai's widowed grandnephew, the Khan of Persia. They travelled, with many delays, via Sumatra, India, Persia, Trebizond and Constantinople, eventually reaching Venice in 1295. Marco's account of his travels, *The Book of Marco Polo*, told Europeans for the first time of Oriental marvels, including asbestos, burning coal, paper money and block-printing, and gave a first glimpse of China's immense wealth, size and powerful neighbours.

Polybius (c. 200-c. 120 BC) Greek historian who described in 40 books the rise of the Romans to the domination of the Mediterranean. The first five books survive complete, together with considerable excerpts of the rest, which were widely used by LIVY.

Polykleitos (5th cent. BC) Greek sculptor whose *Doryphoros* (c. 450) illustrates his dogma that ideal beauty can be achieved by mathematics, especially in the proportion of one part of the body to another. Although famed for his bronze sculptures, the colossal statue of *Hera*, which stood in the temple near Mycenae, was probably made of ivory and gold.

Pompadour, Marquise de (1721-64) Renowned French beauty and mistress of LOUIS XV. As Jeanne Antoinette Poisson she deserted her husband to become the King's mistress, then Duchesse de Pompadour. She dominated the weak-willed Louis but had less influence on domestic and foreign policies than was once thought.

Pompey the Great (106-48 BC) Roman general and statesman, who became master of the East, and was an opponent of Julius CAESAR. He served as consul (70 BC), then, having swept the eastern Mediterranean clear of pirates (67-63 BC), assumed control of southwest Asia after defeating MITHRIDATES of Pontus (66 BC). He then seized Palestine and Syria, and penetrated as far as the Caspian and the Euphrates. With Crassus and Caesar he formed the first triumvirate (60 BC). He supported the aristocratic senate against Caesar, the popular leader, and was his last obstacle to the dictatorship. But he himself was defeated at Pharsalus (48 BC) and murdered in Egypt.

Pompidou, Georges (born 1911) French politician, who became President of France after DE GAULLE's defeat in the referendum of 1969. Pompidou fought in the Resistance movement during the Second World War and afterwards served in various government agencies. He was Prime Minister from 1962 to 1963 and, after that year's election, from 1963 to 1968, when he was dismissed by De Gaulle following the student riots and industrial unrest of that year. On De Gaulle's retirement, he stood for President and was elected at the second ballot with 58 per cent of the votes.

Ponce de León, Juan (1460-1521) Spanish explorer and apparent discoverer of Florida. Travelling with COLUMBUS, he arrived in America in 1493, and later conquered Puerto Rico (1509), where he became Governor. Under royal orders from Spain, Ponce de León once more set sail, in 1513, in a continuing search for new lands and for the legendary 'Fountain of Youth', which was said to be located on the island of Bimini. On East Sunday (in Spanish *Pascua Florida*) of that year, Ponce de León discovered the mainland and landed at a site near present-day St Augustine. He continued explorations around the peninsula and ultimately abandoned the search for the 'Fountain of Youth'.

Pontiac (c. 1720-69) American Ottawa India chief who mobilized Indian tribes against the British in North America. In 1762 (with promises of French help) he united almost all Indian tribes from the

One of history's most famous beauties, Antoinette, Marquise de Pompadour

Mississippi Valley to Lake Superior in the most ambitious of all Red Indian alliances. Indians seized every important fort with the exception of Pittsburgh and Detroit in a plan to slaughter all British colonists.

Pontoppidan, Henrik (1857-1943) Danish author whose novels *The Promised Land* (1891-5), *Lucky Peter* (1898-1904) and *The Kingdom of the Dead* (1912-16) comment on social injustice and the effect of environment on the individual. They are considered outstanding in Danish literature for their penetrating psychological studies of character and their vivid descriptions. He was considerably influenced by BRANDES.

Pope, Alexander (1688-1744) English poet, who was one of the foremost literary figures of the 18th century. He polished the heroic couplet, a specific metrical verse form, to an unrivalled perfection, and made it ideal for his varied subjects. His satires, 'The Rape of the Lock' (1712), a mock-heroic attack on London's fashionable society, and the 'Dunciad' (1728), a diatribe against dullness and pedantry, are outstanding for their pithy, telling criticism and their descriptions of city life. In his moral and philosophic poems – the verse 'Epistles', the *Moral Essays*, and the *Essay on Man* – the exposition is brilliant, but the thought conventional. Pope first gained public acclaim for his free translations of HOMER's *Iliad* and *Odyssey*, and became a leading member of the literary world of ADDISON, SWIFT and GAY.

Popper, Sir Karl Raimund (born 1902) Austrian-born British philosopher who regards falsifiability as the mark of a scientific statement (i.e. that hypotheses stem from imaginative theories). Popper stresses the role of bold hypotheses which are scientific because open to falsification. His social philosophy favours a problem-solving approach to social policy, rather than the setting up or maintenance of total systems.

Porta, Giacomo della (1541-1604) Italian architect who designed the magnificent dome of the Basilica of St Peter's, and façade of the Gesù, Rome.

Portalis, Jean (1746-1807) French jurist largely responsible for drafting the Code Napoléon. He based the Code Civil (a collection of French civil as opposed to criminal laws) on Roman law as re-taught by IRNERIUS, and personally drafted major sections of the code, including those on succession and marriage. All citizens were made equal before the law, primogeniture and social privilege were

Characters from Beatrix Potter's famous children's stories

abolished and secular bodies were freed from Church control.

Porter, Katherine Anne (born 1890) American author, who often uses southern states and Mexico as a setting. She writes carefully constructed, atmospheric stories, as in *Pale Horse, Pale Rider* (1939).

Potter, Beatrix (1866-1943) English writer of children's stories. Many of her popular tales concern Peter Rabbit and other shrewd, humorous, unsentimental animals. Her delicate illustrations match her stories.

Potter, Stephen (1900-70) English humorous writer, who in 1947 published *Gamesmanship*, and followed it with *Lifemanship* (1950), *One-Upmanship* (1952) and others, which taught the art of getting ahead by exploiting English manners and social traditions.

Poulenc, François (1899-1963) French composer and piano accompanist. Poulenc's works include the ballet *Les Biches* (1924).

Poulsen, Valdemar (1869-1942) Danish inventor of the 'telegraphone', which he patented in 1898, which stored sound messages on movable magnetic steel wire. Although the forerunner of the modern tape recorder, it only became practical after the availability of electronic amplifiers.

Pound, Ezra (1885-1973) American poet, and one of the most influential critics and controversial writers of the century. Apart from his own writing, his principal importance was his encouragement to and battles for T. S. ELIOT and James JOYCE. He was a leading member of the Imagist and Vorticist movements, and the poems in *A Lume Spento* (1908), *Personae* (1909) and *Umbra* (1920), with their rhythms of the human voice and sharp, brilliant images, helped to continue the metric revolution begun by WHITMAN. *Hugh Selwyn Mauberley* (1920) asks poets to abandon 19th-century aesthetic pastures. Throughout his life he worked on *The Cantos* (even when declared insane and incarcerated in hospital for a time), intended as a huge, poetic, human comedy in 100 sections, reviewing world history, thought and economics.

Poussin, Nicolas (1594-1665) French artist and leading exponent of 17th-century pictorial Classicism, most of whose working life was spent in Rome. Poussin's early work was experimental and consequently crude (e.g. the series of drawings illustrating the *Metamorphoses* of OVID). For a time he followed the style of the Italian masters of the Baroque (notably DOMENICHINO), a period culminating in his large altarpiece for St Peter's, Rome, the *Martyrdom of St Erasmus* (1629). Later, under the influence of TITIAN, his work became more romantic and lyrical and by 1640, when he was summoned to Paris by LOUIS XIV and Cardinal RICHELIEU to decorate the long gallery of the Louvre, his style was modified to a more serene, geometrical design. Two years later Poussin returned to Rome where the mathematical composition of his later work and the classical themes illustrating the victory of virtue over vice, reason over passion, paralleled the religious dramas of CORNEILLE.

Powell, Anthony (born 1905) English novelist noted for delicate, satiric social comedies about the English middle-classes. His earlier books, such as *Venusberg* (1932) and *From a View to a Death* (1933), were wittily comical. Since 1951 he has been publishing a more ambitious sequence of novels under the title *The Music of Time*.

Powell, Enoch (born 1912) British Conservative politician, and a frequent speaker on racial and economic issues. A noted classical scholar (at one time Professor of Greek at Sydney University, Australia), he became Minister of Housing and Local Government (1955-7), Financial Secretary (1957-8) and Minister of Health (1960-3), but refused to serve in the DOUGLAS-HOME government. After unsuccessfully contesting the leadership of the Conservative party, he was dismissed by HEATH from the shadow cabinet in 1968. From the back benches, he has taken independent lines in stressing his belief in unfettered free market economy and in government control of immigration.

Powers, Francis Gary (born 1929) American pilot whose U-2 spy plane was shot down over the Soviet Union in May 1960. The resulting international uproar intensified Cold War hostility and caused the cancellation of the scheduled Summit Conference between EISENHOWER and KHRUSCHEV. In 1962, Powers was exchanged with the Russian spy Rudolf ABEL.

Powys, John Cowper (1872-1963) English novelist and writer of many popular books about the English west country of his upbringing, who spent most of his life travelling and lecturing in America. His novels include *Wolf Solent* (1929), *A Glastonbury Romance* (1932) and *Maiden Castle* (1936).

Praetorius, Michael (1571-1621) German composer, theorist and musical historian whose *Musical Treatise* (1615-20) is one of the main sources of modern knowledge of the origins of 17th-century music. His own compositions were many and include the *Muses of Zion* (1605-10), a collection of Lutheran chorales for the Church year.

Prandtauer, Jakob (1660-1726) Austrian architect and designer of the Baroque monastery and church of Melk, whose pinnacled towers, bulbous spires and great dome tower over the River Danube. Less ambitious buildings designed by Prandtauer include the church at Sonntaberg and part of St Florian.

Prasad, Rajendra (1884-1963) Indian nationalist leader and first President of the Republic of India. He was a follower of GANDHI, from 1920, and was several times imprisoned for civil disobedience. He became President of the Constituent Assembly in 1946 and in 1950 was elected first

Enoch Powell, maverick Tory politician and outspoken opponent of British domestic immigration policy

President of the Republic, an office he held for 12 years.

Pratt, Edwin John (1883-1964) Canadian poet whose work was inspired by the scenery of his land, and by man's struggles to conquer the huge terrain. Among his later work was *Towards the Last Spike* (1952), 'a verse panorama of the struggle to build the First Canadian Transcontinental Railway'.

Praxiteles (4th cent. BC) Greek sculptor who excelled in the portrayal of women, his most famous statue being the *Aphrodite of Knidos*, depicted naked, a revolutionary innovation at that time. With Kephisodotus, of whom he was a disciple and, possibly, son, he reacted against the Attic sculptors' excessive refinement, developing a new classical style, at once softer and more sensitive, yet not lacking in strength. Praxiteles's work is characterized by flowing, smooth surfaces, contrasting textures of drapery and hair, and a subtle balance of light and shadow. His technique and choice of subjects influenced the sculpture of the Hellenistic Age, and thus that of the Renaissance.

Praed, Winthrop Mackworth (1802-39) English lawyer, Conservative politician and poet, whose social connections coupled with a caustic wit enabled him to excel at *vers de société*. He is also remembered for his satirical verse tales.

Prescott, William (1796-1859) American historian whose descriptions of the Spanish conquests of Peru and Mexico in *The History of the Conquest of Mexico* (1843) and *The History of the Conquest of Peru* (1847) vividly retold the adventures of CORTÉS and PIZARRO.

Prévost, l'Abbé (1697-1763) Pen-name of Antoine Prévost d'Exiles, French novelist, journalist and historian and author of *Manon Lescaut* (1731), the story of an infatuated aristocrat's passion for a *demi-mondaine* and his consequent degradation. The economy of its narrative contrasted sharply with the effusions of other contemporary romances and achieved instant popularity. In the force of its emotion, it foreshadowed ROUSSEAU and the Romantic movement.

Pride, Thomas (17th cent.) Parliamentary colonel in the English Civil War. He is remembered because of 'Pride's Purge', in which, while executing the army council's orders, he expelled or arrested some 140 Presbyterian members of parliament, the remainder, some 60 members in all, being known as the Rump Parliament. This parliament, reversing an earlier decision, ended talks with CHARLES I, who was being held prisoner, and ordered his trial, at which Pride was one of the judges. He was also among those who signed the king's death warrant.

Priestley, John Boynton (born 1894) English author who is one of the most fertile and popular chroniclers of English life in the first half of this century. His well-known *The Good Companions* (1929) relates the adventures of a touring concert party, in a rambling book full of humour and rich characterization. Since then he has written many more novels, plays and a host of miscellaneous works.

Princip, Gavrilo (c. 1893-1918) Serbian nationalist and revolutionary, who precipitated the First World War by assassinating Archduke Franz Ferdinand at Sarajevo on 28 June, 1914.

Prior, Matthew (1664-1721) English diplomat and poet, author of elegant wordly poems taking a shrewd and ironic view of love. He had a distinguished diplomatic career and prepared the Treaty of Utrecht (1713). Though he wrote long poems, such as 'Alma' and 'Solomon' (1718), Prior's reputation rests on the realistic wisdom, wit and technical experiments of short poems like 'The English Padlock.'

Procopius (before 500-c. 565) Byzantine historian and secretary to the general BELISARIUS from 527. Procopius wrote two conflicting histories of JUSTINIAN's reign. His official *Histories*, in eight books, cover the wars of the years 527-554 and deal with the campaigns in the East and West. In addition he wrote an approved account of Emperor Justinian's building activity down to 560. He also wrote an unpublished interpretation – the *Secret History*, a virulent and often tendentious attack on government policies.

Prokofiev, Sergei (1891-1953) Russian composer, and a leading innovator in 20th-century music. Prokofiev made his name early as a pianist and as an *enfant terrible* among composers. His style was at first marked by energetic and audacious rhythm and a melodic gift that could turn to satire. In 1918 he went to work in Europe, but in 1934 returned to the USSR. Prokofiev's works include *Peter and the Wolf*, the children's musical tale for narrator and orchestra (1936); seven symphonies (No. 1 being the *Classical*); concertos, chamber music and ballet music, including a version of *Romeo and Juliet*. He also wrote the scores for EISENSTEIN's films *Alexander Nevsky* (music that

later became a patriotic cantata) and *Ivan the Terrible*.

Propertius, Sextus (c. 50-c. 15 BC) Roman poet whose four books of *Elegies* are extant, ranging in subject matter from the ecstasy of love to the fading of passion and the violence of renunciation, with its attendant melancholy and cynicism. His later work on national themes with mythological allusions, though lacking the earlier freshness of feeling, has an increased strength.

Protagoras (5th cent. BC) The first and most important of the Greek itinerant teachers called Sophists. An agnostic, he held that all knowledge is relative, based on opinion or the nature of sense perception (what is warm for one may be cold for another). This view was extended in his dictum 'a man is the measure of all things'.

Proudhon, Pierre (1809-65) French political theorist, who gave the answer 'property is theft' to the question posed by his famous essay entitled *What is Property?* (1840). He described ownership of capital as the right of *aubaine* – of exploiting the labour of others without just reward – and advocated that the ideal state should be brought about by the gradual abolition of the right of *aubaine* by progressive reductions in interest and rent. Unlike SAINT-SIMON and his followers, he mistrusted state intervention, and aimed to foster the development of the individual through associations.

Proust, Marcel (1871-1922) French author of the celebrated novel sequence *Remembrance of Things Past* (1913-17). A complex work with over 200 characters, it follows the life-span of its narrator-hero in an attempt to recapture, through art, the living past and to arrest, even if only for a moment, the passage of time. Proust's subtle exploration of the subconscious, in which a mere taste or aroma enables him to recall past experiences, makes *Remembrance of Things Past* an original work of a very high order. It has had a profound influence on the development of the modern novel.

Prout, William (1785-1850) English chemist who suggested that all atoms are made up of various numbers of hydrogen atoms. He made this proposition in 1815 after pointing out that the atomic weights of the known elements were all whole multiples of the atomic weight of hydrogen. More accurate analysis, however, showed chlorine to have a non-integral weight, and for this reason Prout's hypothesis was dismissed, only to be

revived in a more sophisticated form in the 20th century.

Prudentius (348-c. 410) Christian Latin poet, author of a collection of hymns, the *Cathemerinon*, allegories, didactic poems and a martyrology. A highly gifted, though at times abstruse, poet, he showed great skill in a wide range of metres and brought a new religious spirit to the old classical forms.

Przewalski, Nikolai Mikhailovich (1839-88) Russian explorer and naturalist who made four expeditions into Central Asia and discovered the Bactrian camel and the last of the wild horses, now called Przewalski's Horse.

Ptolemy I (c. 367-283 BC) Macedonian general and founder of Egypt's Ptolemaic dynasty (which persisted until CLEOPATRA's death in 30 BC). He was one of ALEXANDER THE GREAT's generals, and after the king's death fought for lands in his recently won empire. Ptolemy seized Egypt, which he ruled (323-285 BC) first as satrap (governor), then (from 305 BC) as self-styled king. He was continually compelled to ward off attacks by Alexander's other generals, including Antigonus, who presented the greatest threat. Ptolemy built the library and museum at Alexandria and made the city the cultural capital of the Hellenistic world.

Ptolemy, Claudius (2nd cent. AD) Greek astronomer, mathematician and geographer, whose work was the basis for the study of astronomy until the Renaissance, a span of over 1200 years. Ptolemy's astronomy is contained in a work known as the *Almagest*, which dealt in detail with the motion and distance of the Sun and the Moon, their eclipses, planetary conjunctions and oppositions. Ptolemy believed in a system of solid, concentric crystalline spheres to which the planets and the fixed stars were attached. Encircling them all was the *primum mobile* ('the prime mover'), providing the energy for the motion of the Universe. Ptolemy's opinions became dogmatic articles of faith of the Christian Church, but the growing number of observations caused his system to become too elaborate. Doubts about its validity grew, until COPERNICUS was forced to conclude that it was wrong. So intense was religious feeling on the nature of the universe that GALILEO was tried for heresy for upholding the views of Copernicus.

Puccini, Giacomo (1858-1924) Italian composer whose *La Bohème* (1896), *Tosca* (1900) and *Madame Butterfly* (1904) are cornerstones of the operatic repertoire. His gift for a free-flowing melody that underlined drama and characterization made him one of the most successful composers in the genre. The harmonies he used were modern enough not to demand too much of audiences and they responded accordingly. Puccini also wrote *The Girl of the Golden West* (1910) and the unfinished *Turandot* begun in the year of his death.

Pugachev, Emelyan Ivanovich (c. 1726-75) Russian Cossack soldier and leader of a revolt against CATHERINE II. As a self-styled Tsar, 'Peter III', he promised to introduce urgently needed reforms, and so became a focus for peasant and Cossack discontent which erupted into a revolt (1773) that swept Russia from the Volga to the Urals. Though at first successful, Pugachev was defeated in 1774 and 10,000 rebels were killed or captured. He himself was taken in an iron cage to Moscow and there executed.

Pugin, Augustus Welby North-more (1812-52) English architect, who was one of the chief exponents of Victorian Gothic and (with BARRY) architect of the Palace of Westminster (Houses of Parliament). Pugin's architecture contained strong religious overtones and his famous book *Contrasts in Architecture* promoted his vision of what he termed the Christian architectural style and the ideals of the Gothic age. His numerous buildings include the Roman Catholic cathedral, Birmingham, St George's Cathedral, Southwark and St Augustine's, Ramsgate.

Pulci, Luigi (1432-84) Author of the first important Italian revival of the Carolingian epic, the *Morgante Maggiore*, in which, in 28 cantos, he recounts the mock-chivalric adventures of two giants, Morgante and Margutte.

Pulitzer, Joseph (1847-1911) Hungarian-born American newspaperman who pioneered sensational journalism and founded the Pulitzer Prizes. A journalist turned Democrat politician, he bought the *New York World* (1883) and made it the nation's biggest daily by crusading powerfully for oppressed workers and against alleged big business and government corruption, using the 'yellow-press' techniques which HEARST copied successfully. Part of Pulitzer's $2 million bequest to found Columbia University's school of journalism finances the annual Pulitzer cash prizes in American journalism, literature and music.

Pullman, George Mortimer (1831-97) American industrialist.

Railway sleeping cars were first operated in the United States in 1837. Pullman started work on an improved version in 1855 and the first Pullman car appeared 10 years later. In 1867 he organized the Pullman Palace Car Company to build cars and operate them under contract for the railways. He also devised dining cars (1868), and coaches with end-vestibules (1887).

Purcell, Henry (1659-95) English composer who is probably the most illustrious figure in his country's music. As a composer he absorbed the new French and Italian styles favoured at the Restoration court of CHARLES II but made of them something totally individual. He wrote many songs of great melodic beauty, as well as trio sonatas and fantasies for string groups, anthems and other church music. He composed a great deal of music for the stage, including one true opera, *Dido and Aeneas* (c. 1689). Some of Purcell's finest music was written for DRYDEN's extravagant stage spectacle, *King Arthur* (1691), while *The Fairy Queen* (1692) was an adaptation of SHAKESPEARE's *A Midsummer Night's Dream*. Purcell's untimely death at the age of 36 cast a shadow over the native English tradition and left a vacuum for HANDEL to exploit a few decades later. Purcell has, however, had a profound influence over such 20th-century composers, as HOLST, BRITTEN and TIPPETT.

Purkinje, Johannes (1787-1869) Czech physiologist, who was one of the pioneers of histology – the study of the fine structure of tissues – and the first to use the term protoplasm (first-formed material) in a scientific sense.

Pushkin, Aleksandr Sergeyevich (1799-1837) Russian poet and writer. The Byronic verse-novel *Eugene Onegin* (1833), and *Boris Godunov* (1831) an historical tragic drama, provided libretti for operas by TCHAIKOVSKY and MUSSORGSKY respectively, and are considered his finest works. Pushkin was a prodigious writer; besides his verse-tales and dramas he was a master of the short story, of which *The Queen of Spades* (1834) is one of the most famous. *The Bronze Horseman*, unpublished in his lifetime, is among the best known of his epic poems and the folk poem *The Golden Cockerel* (1835) was the basis of an opera by RIMSKY-KORSAKOV. Pushkin's narrative style had a profound influence on the formal and artificial Russian literary language of his time.

Putnam, George (1814-72) American publisher, noted for his campaign,

begun in 1837, for international copyright agreements. He moved to London in 1841 and opened a bookshop that specialized in American books. He returned to New York and in 1866 founded the publishing company of G. P. Putnam and Son.

Puvis de Chavannes, Pierre (1824-98) French mural painter, one of the few artists respected by both the academic and *avant-garde* factions in contemporary French art, belonging to no school or movement, yet strongly influencing the symbolism of GAUGUIN and the Nabis (a group which included BONNARD and VUILLARD). He painted mural decorations for public buildings all over France, among them being the *Ste Geneviève* cycle in the Panthéon, Paris. He also painted a sequence of murals for the Public Library at Boston, Massachusetts.

Pu-yi, Henry (1906-67) Last emperor of China (1908-12) and puppet emperor of Manchukuo (1934-45). He ascended the throne, his father becoming regent, in 1908, and was the last emperor of the Manchu dynasty of China under the name Hsüan T'ung. After the revolution of 1911-12 he abdicated. In 1924 (having taken the name Henry Pu-yi) he was driven from Peking, and lived under Japanese protection at Tientsin until 1932, when the Japanese appointed him head of the puppet state of Manchukuo (Manchuria), and enthroned him as the Emperor K'ang Te in 1934. He was captured by the Russians in 1945 and in 1949 handed over to MAO TSE-TUNG by whom he was set free in 1959. He became a member of the Chinese parliament in 1964.

Pym, John (1584-1643) English statesman, and leader of parliamentary opposition to JAMES I and CHARLES I. In the Short (1640) and Long (1640-60), Parliaments, Pym opposed 'papistry', monopolies and absolute royal power. He was foremost in attempts to impeach the royal favourites Buckingham, STRAFFORD and LAUD. Charles's attempt to arrest Pym hastened the Civil War, during which Pym brought about the acceptance of an excise tax and the alliance with Scotland, and promoted the Grand Remonstrance (1641), a list of grievances against the king.

Pyrrhus (c. 318-272 BC) King of Epirus in northwestern Greece, whose name is associated with the phrase 'Pyrrhic victory'. In combat with the Romans at Heraclea (280 BC) and at Asculum (279 BC) he won, but at the cost of such enormous losses that he is said to have remarked: 'Another such victory and I shall be ruined.' He also waged war against the Carthaginians in Sicily and was defeated by the Romans at Beneventum (275 BC). He died in a skirmish at Argos.

Pythagoras (c. 582-500 BC) Greek philosopher, founder of the Pythagorean school of thought, which became a way of life for its followers. To Pythagoras, 'all things are numbers' and his mathematical work was important, reflected also in his studies of music, architecture and astronomy.

Pytheas (4th cent. BC) Greek navigator and geographer who coasted Europe's Atlantic seaboard. He sailed west from Marseille (c. 325 BC), passed through the Strait of Gibraltar, and explored the coasts of Portugal, Spain, France and Britain, and reached 'Thule' – perhaps the Orkneys or Norway. His account of the voyage included the first Greek description of sea ice and the first correct explanation of ocean tides, and stated – accurately – that the Pole Star is not directly over the North Pole. Only fragments of his work survive.

Q

Queensberry, John, 9th Marquess of (1844-1900) British boxing administrator who gave his name (1867) to the rules under which the sport is conducted.

Quental, Antero de (1842-92) Portuguese left-wing intellectual poet and literary revolutionary, author of the melancholy *Sonnets* (1886), considered to be among the world's greatest sonnets. He was the leader of a group of writers who called themselves the 'Generation of 1870', whose aim was to reverse what they considered to be Portugal's intellectual decline.

Quercia, Jacopo della (1374-1438) Sienese sculptor to whom the tomb of Ilaria del Carretto (c. 1406) is attributed as his earliest known work. He participated in the competition for the Baptistry doors of San Giovanni in Florence, which was won by GHIBERTI (1401) and then from 1417-31, worked with Ghiberti and DONATELLO on reliefs for the doors of the Baptistry at Siena. Quercia's final great work was for the portals of St Petronio, Bologna, a series of reliefs of scenes from Genesis and the Nativity.

Quesada, Gonzalo Jimenez de (c. 1500-c. 1579) Spanish conquistador in South America, the most prominent of those who conquered new Granada (roughly equivalent to modern Colombia). About 20 years later, he crossed the Andes and reached the upper Orinoco.

Quételet, Adolphe (1796-1874) Belgian mathematician and scientist, who pioneered the use of statistics in the service of government and first presented the statistical concept of the 'average man' in *On Man* (1835).

Quevado y Villegas, Francisco Gomez de (1580-1645) Spanish writer, one of Spain's leading prose authors, who created the Baroque style known as *conceptismo*, which involves a highly intricate use of the language.

Quincey, Thomas de (1785-1859) English author and critic, best known for his autobiographical *Confessions of an English Opium Eater*. After an unsteady progress by way of prostitutes, opium and Oxford, he went to the Lake District, the land of his romantic heroes, and lived by writing criticisms and essays. His critical essays were daring, typified by *On Murder Considered as One of the Fine Arts*.

Quine, Willard van Orman (born 1908) American philosopher and logician. Quine regards all statements as revisable, though in practice, we revise some (e.g. historical ones) more readily than others (e.g. mathematical ones). His works include the standard text *From a Logical Point of View* (1953).

Quintero, José (born 1924) American theatrical director who founded the off-Broadway Circle-in-the-Square theatre in New York. In directing, he is guided solely by respect for the author's text, which he follows to the letter. He has been particularly successful with *Long Day's Journey into Night* and *The Iceman Cometh*, both by Eugene O'NEILL.

Quintilian (c. 35-c. 100) Spanish-born Roman rhetorician and author of *Institutio oratoria* (c. 95), an account of an orator's education, the most complete in classical literature, including, in Book 10, a collection of famous critiques of Greek and Roman writers.

Quisling, Vidkun (1887-1945) Norwegian politician and Nazi collaborator. While Norway's Defence Minister (1931-3), he secretly recruited a Norwegian Nazi Party with German assistance, and on the outbreak of war went to Berlin to confer with HITLER about a Nazi takeover in Norway. After Germany occupied Norway in April 1940, Quisling became head of a puppet government (Feb. 1942-

May 1945) and was in power until the country's liberation in the spring of 1945. He was tried for high treason and executed after the Allied victory in 1945.

R

Rabelais, François (c. 1494-c. 1553) French physician and humanist who became a monk and then a lay priest, and whose name added a new epithet, 'Rabelaisian' to describe a vigorous, bawdy satire, to the languages of the western world. In his satirical tales *Pantagruel* (1532) and *Gargantua* (1534), Rabelais attacked contemporary society with scatalogical humour, and in a fantastic florid style mocked pious theories on education, politics and religion. The narrative is vigorous, coarse and picturesque, reflecting the author's erudition, though anticipating MOLIÈRE in his derision of pedants and fanatics.

Rachel (1820-58) French actress, who was considered the greatest tragedienne of her time. Her most famous roles were RACINE's Phèdre in the play of that name, Hermione in his *Andromaque*, and Roxane in *Bajazet*.

Rachmaninov, Sergei (1873-1943) Russian musician and the country's last important Romantic composer. Rachmaninov is said to have been the most impressive virtuoso pianist since LISZT, cultivating an often melancholy emotionalism which placed the second of his three piano concertos among the most popular works in the concert repertoire. Among his best-known works are the tone poem *The Isle of the Dead* (1907), his first symphony and *Rhapsody on a Theme of Paganini* (1934). He died in America, having lived outside Russia since the Revolution.

Racine, Jean (1639-99) French poet and dramatist, the most accomplished writer of tragic verse in the French language. Unlike the superheroes of his ageing rival, CORNEILLE, Racine's protagonists have a terrifying reality. He had a unique talent for investing simple words with intense power and significance. *La Thébaïde* (1664), his first play and *Alexandre le Grande* (1665) were both put on by MOLIÈRE with some success. Following a quarrel with Molière, Racine's plays were staged by other companies. His first notable success, *Andromache* (1667), was one of his finest tragedies, followed by his only comedy, *Les Plaideurs* (1688). In the next ten years, he wrote six great tragedies: *Britannicus* (1669); *Bérénice* (1670) – regarded as the purest expression of the classical ideal, because of the simplicity of its plot; *Bajazet* (1672); *Mithridate* (1673); *Iphigénie* (1674) and *Phèdre* (1677). Thereafter, embittered by critics and rivals, he renounced the theatre and wrote no more plays until 1689, when, at Madame de Maintenon's request, he wrote two plays on biblical subjects, *Esther* (1689) and *Athalie* (1691, considered one of his finest plays).

Radetzky, Joseph (1766-1858) Austrian soldier who defeated the Piedmontese in the battles of Custozza (1848) and Novara (1849) and recovered Venice for Austria (1849). He fought for Austria against the French throughout the Napoleonic Wars and, after Wagram (1809), was appointed Austrian Chief-of-Staff. He became Governor-General of Lombardy-Venetia in 1849.

Raffles, Sir Thomas Stamford (1781-1826) British founder of Singapore. While working for the East India Company, he persuaded Lord Minto to attempt the capture of Java. This having been accomplished (1811), Raffles was appointed its Lieutenant-Governor (1811-16) and set about reforming its administration. While Governor of Benkuilen in Sumatra (1818-23), he founded an unauthorized settlement in Singapore (1819). After being recalled to England in 1824, for disregarding government orders and taking independent steps to check the slave trade, he founded and became the first President of the London Zoological Society.

Rahman, Tunku Abdul (born 1903) Malaysian prince and politician, who became the first Malaysian Prime Minister when his country achieved its independence. Rahman, whose father was Sultan of Kedah, was elected leader of the United Malays National Organization and of the Alliance Party in 1951, became Chief Minister in 1955 and Prime Minister two years later.

Raikes, Robert (1735-1811) British publisher, the founder of Sunday schools, in which pupils were taught reading and the catechism. Raikes's imaginative solution to the problem of rowdy behaviour by working-class children on Sundays was opposed both by diehards who disapproved of any popular education and by strict Sabbatarians. Others, however, took up his ideas with enthusiasm, and by his death Sunday schools had been set up in many parts of England.

Raleigh, Sir Walter (c. 1552-1618) English Elizabethan adventurer. After taking part in piratical expeditions against the Spaniards (1578), and overcoming rebels in Ireland (1580) he became ELIZABETH I's favourite. With her support he sent settlers to colonize North Carolina (1585), but in this, and in a later attempt to colonize Virginia, he was unsuccessful. In 1588, he was displaced as the Queen's favourite by the 2nd Earl of ESSEX. Later (1590), he was accused of atheism, then discredited for seducing one of the Queen's maids (1592). In 1595 he led an unsuccessful expedition to South America to look for gold. His exploits against Spain, at Cadiz (1596) and the Azores (1597), and against the rebellious Essex (1601), reinstated him in Elizabeth's favour, but when JAMES I came to the throne Raleigh was accused of complicity in plots against the Crown and sentenced to death. He was, however, only imprisoned (1603-16) and while in gaol wrote a *History of the World*.

Ramakrishna Sri (1834-86) Indian Hindu religious teacher whose ideas, based on the ancient *Vedic* scriptures, form the basis of the Ramakrishna mission. Its impact has been considerable, not only in India but also in the West. He stressed the essential unity of religions, seeing them as different paths to the realization of the divine.

Raman, Sir Chandrasekhara Venkata (1888-1970) Indian physicist who showed that light scattered from molecules can be used to determine details of molecular structure.

Ramazzini, Bernardino (1633-1714) Italian physician, who was one of the first doctors to understand that many diseases had their origins in industrial conditions. Among the diseases he traced to specific industries are lung diseases (in stone masons), eye diseases (among gilders and blacksmiths) and lead poisoning (among paintmakers and printers). He also traced an epidemic of spastic paraplegia to the use of flour contaminated by bean meal.

Rambert, Dame Marie (born 1888) Polish-born dancer and, with de VALOIS, co-founder of modern British ballet. Influenced by Isadora DUNCAN and Jacques Dalcroze, in 1912 she helped DIAGHILEV and NIJINSKY to create a ballet to STRAVINSKY's complex rhythms for the *Rite of Spring*. In 1920, she founded the Rambert Ballet School in London on CECCHETTI's principles, establishing her Ballet Club (known later as the Ballet Rambert) company in 1930.

Rameau, Jean Philippe (1683-1764) French composer and organist who wrote the *Treatise on Harmony* (1722), the first real attempt to categorize harmony as expression, which remains a cornerstone of musical theory. When Rameau emerged at the relatively late age of 50 as a composer, he put his theories into vivid practice, particularly in the 24 operas and ballets which led to his appointment to the court of LOUIS XV.

Ramón Berenguer IV (12th cent.) Count of Barcelona (1131-62) who united northeastern Spain. In 1137 he was betrothed to Petronilla, the infant Queen of Aragon and combined her kingdom with his own Catalonian state, centred on Barcelona. Their son, Alfonso II of Aragon (reigned 1162-96), thus formally acquired a unified kingdom in northeastern Spain which – under powerful successors, including FERDINAND V of Castile – played an influential part in European history.

Ramsay, Sir William (1852-1916) Scottish chemist who discovered the so-called inert gases. With Lord RAYLEIGH, he removed from air various known gases, such as nitrogen, oxygen and carbon dioxide, leaving a gas which was chemically inert. He called it argon, from the Greek word for inactive, and found that it makes up about 1 per cent of air (1894). Later Ramsay, with his co-worker Travers, discovered small quantities of three other inert gas elements in air. They were krypton (hidden), neon (new) and xenon (stranger).

Ramses II (13th cent. BC) Egyptian pharaoh, whose buildings included the famous temples cut in the rockface at Abu Simbel. Four statues, each 67 feet high, of the seated pharaoh guarded the great temple, which had 14 chambers, penetrating 200 feet into the cliff beside the Nile. He is thought to have been the pharaoh whose oppression of Hebrew slaves in Egypt caused MOSES to lead the Israelites out of Egypt into Canaan.

Sir C. V. Raman holding a model of the atomic structure of a diamond

Rank, Otto (1884-1939) Austrian psychologist, who believed that the trauma of birth was the root cause of many psychological difficulties in adult life. He also analysed artistic creativity in psychoanalytical terms.

Ranke, Leopold von (1795-1886) German historian, author of the three-volume *Ecclesiastical and Political History of the Popes during the 16th and 17th Centuries* (1834-7). In his philosophical approach Ranke dismissed tradition and legend and urged objectivity and critical appraisal of sources, stressing the importance to the study of modern history of eye-witness accounts and of closely sifted archives.

Rapacki, Adam (born 1909) Polish politician, who devised the Rapacki Plan, in October 1957, for the establishment of a nuclear-free zone in the countries of Central Europe (Poland, Czechoslovakia and East and West Germany). Though this would have meant the military loss of her satellites, Russia accepted the plan, but America rejected it, on the grounds that it would have necessitated West Germany's withdrawal from NATO.

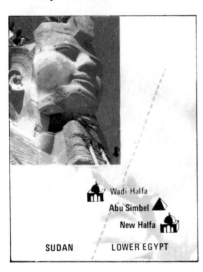

Abu Simbel, the 3200-year-old temple of Ramses II beside the Nile

Raphael (1483-1520) Italian artist whose work most typifies the classical phase of the High Renaissance. After studying under PERUGINO, Raphael went to Florence, where both his portraits and his pictures of the Madonna and Child reflected the influence of LEONARDO's experiments in compositional arrangement. In 1508 he went to Rome, where he began work on the decoration of some of the papal apartments (The Stanze) planned by Julius II. The first of these, the Stanza della Segnatura, is the best known and contains the famous *School of Athens* fresco – a

representation of philosophy which became the archetype for compositions based on the classical ideals of balance and order. The Madonnas of these years, e.g. the *Sistine Madonna*, also exhibit the idealized forms and calm dignity towards which Raphael's art was moving. Raphael made a close study of the work of MICHELANGELO, whose influence can be seen in the more dramatic style of the later Stanze, which were completed after the unveiling of the Sistine Chapel ceiling in 1512.

Rashid al-Din (c. 1247-1318) Arabic scholar-statesman in Persia, one of the foremost patrons of Persian art and learning, who compiled the major work *History of the Mongols of Persia*. Numerous scholars, artists and scribes came from all over Asia to work in the university suburb which he built outside Tabriz. It was in his book studio that the first known Persian manuscripts were produced, illustrated in a strong original style which blended Chinese and Mesopotamian influences.

Rasp, Charles (1846-1907) German-born mining prospector in Australia. In the west of New South Wales Rasp discovered outcrops of minerals, which later were found to be huge deposits of silver, lead and zinc. He staked the first claim at Broken Hill, and with six others, established the Broken Hill Mining Company which has become one of the largest concerns of its kind in the world.

Rasputin, Grigori (c. 1871-1916) Russian monk and mystic who exerted influence over Russian politics and the Court (*c*. 1911-16). His influence was based on his personal magnetism and alleged power as a healer after he had alleviated the sufferings of the haemophilic Tsarevitch, Alexei. But his drunkenness, sexual excesses and nepotism in securing the appointment of his colleagues to high office in Army, Church and State, combined with the belief that in the First World War he was a German agent, led a group of noblemen headed by Prince Yusupov, to assassinate him.

Rathenau, Walther (1867-1922) German industrialist and statesman, who devised a system of 'war-socialism' which contributed to German economic survival in the First World War. Rathenau was an engineer and economist, and head of the largest electrical combine in Europe. Under him the German Ministry of War controlled all means of production and the deployment of labour. After Germany's defeat in 1918, Rathenau founded the Democratic Party and in 1921 he became Minister of Reconstruction, and of Foreign Affairs in

1922. His internationalism, socialist sympathies and diplomatic successes, such as his financial settlements with the US and France and the Treaty of Rapallo with Russia (1922), were bitterly resented by extreme right-wing anti-Semites, by one of whom he was murdered in June 1922.

Rattigan, Sir Terence (born 1911) British dramatist, whose widely popular successes include *French Without Tears* (1936), *The Winslow Boy* (1946), *The Deep Blue Sea* (1952) and *Ross* (1960).

Ratzel, Friedrich (1844-1904) German geographer who helped to found the study of human ecology. In *Anthropogeographie* (1882-1912) he related human cultures to natural geographical conditions, taking into account local historical and economic variations, and so (with VIDAL DE LA BLACHE) helping to pioneer the subject loosely called human geography. In the 1920s, Ratzel's 'anthropogeography' was linked with C. H. Cooley's 'territorial demography' and Emile DURKHEIM's 'social morphology' to form the newly named study of human ecology. It was developed at Chicago University by Robert Ezra Park to probe the adaptive processes by which human societies adjust to their natural and man-modified environments.

Rasputin ('the debauchee') survived a dose of cyanide before being shot dead

Rauschenberg, Robert (born 1925) American Pop artist, whose use of photomontage and commonplace objects had a powerful effect on the Pop movement.

Ravel, Maurice (1875-1937) French composer and a master of orchestration. He was also highly successful in exploiting harmonic colour in the piano, as in *Le Tombeau*

de Couperin (1917). Ravel's works include *The Pavan for a Dead Infanta*, *Bolero*, the suite *Mother Goose* and the ballet *Daphnis and Chloë*. He also wrote the fantasy opera, *L'Enfant et les Sortilèges*, to a libretto by COLETTE, and orchestrated MUSSORGSKY's *Pictures from an Exhibition*.

Rayleigh, John, 3rd Baron (1842-1919) English physicist who opened the way to the discovery of argon, the first of the inert gases. In the 1880s Rayleigh tested William PROUT's already discredited hypothesis that atomic weights are always whole multiples of the atomic weight of hydrogen. He measured the densities of gases and calculated atomic weights from them. In the course of his work he found that nitrogen obtained from a chemical compound was always slightly denser than nitrogen obtained from the air. He threw the problem open to the scientific world, and in 1894 William RAMSAY discovered that the nitrogen from air was 'diluted' by small traces of another gas which he and Rayleigh jointly named argon.

Read, Sir Herbert (1893-1968) English scholar, poet and critic, an influential writer on culture and aesthetics. He fought in the First World War and wrote of the experience in 'Songs of Chaos' (1915) and 'Naked Warriors' (1919). His criticism of painting, literature and politics, contained in many books from *Reason and Romanticism* (1926) to *Poetry and Experience* (1966), is a modern version of Romanticism which believes in an underlying cultural order that resists the imposition of rational forms.

Réaumur, René (1683-1757) French naturalist and physicist. He invented a thermometer, using alcohol and water, in which 0° marks the freezing point and 80° the boiling point of water, which is sometimes used for medical and domestic purposes; wrote a comprehensive six-volume work on insects; proved that digestion in animals was a chemical process; invented the opaque white glass known as Réaumur porcelain; and a method of tinning steel. His many other scientific achievements include researches into auriferous rivers and turquoise mines; the chemical differences between iron and steel; the regeneration of lost parts in crustaceans; and the artificial incubation of eggs.

Redon, Odilon (1840-1916) French Symbolist artist, who allowed his fantasy to draw visionary material from minutely observed phenomena.

Reed, Walter (1851-1902) American army surgeon, whose work led to

the eradication of yellow fever in parts of Central America.

Régnier, Mathurin (1573-1613) French satirical poet whose lively and uncompromizing pen-portraits of 'types' – the poet, the physician, the adventurer – were based on Latin models and anticipated those of MOLIÈRE.

Reimarus, Hermann (1694-1768) German philosopher and scholar who put forward the view that natural religion, being accessible to reason, was the only one that could ever become universal.

Reinhardt, Max (1873-1943) Austrian theatrical and film director, and manager, famous for his spectacular production *The Miracle* (1911). He made use of Gordon CRAIG's theories and was remarkable for his management of enormous casts. He had a triumphant American tour with his own company (1927-8) and directed plays in Britain and America.

Reith, John Charles Walsham, 1st Baron (1889-1971) First Director-General of the British Broadcasting Corporation.

Remarque, Erich (1898-1970) German novelist, author of the war novel, later filmed, *All Quiet on the Western Front* (1929).

Rembrandt van Ryn (1606-69) Outstanding Dutch painter, renowned for his penetrating portraits. His success in this genre began with *Anatomy Lesson of Dr Tulp* (1632), and reached its zenith with the celebrated *Night Watch* (1642). Rembrandt's best-known portraits, however, are those of individuals, and his later studies in particular demonstrate his considerable ability to probe his sitters' characters. Rembrandt was deeply religious and his fondness for biblical subjects was unusual, since there was little demand for such works and it seems likely that he often painted them without being commissioned. His marriage to Saskia van Vylenborch (who died in 1642) brought him a considerable dowry, which, with his success as a portrait painter, made him comparatively wealthy. An extravagant style of living, in particular his passion for collecting works of art, eventually created financial difficulties from which he never recovered. He was, however, assured of a steady income through the sale of his etchings, which during his lifetime were much more widely known and praised than were his paintings. The subsequent popularity of etching among artists was a direct result of Rembrandt's work, and his prints (there are about 300

different subjects) were enormously influential. Far less well known in his day were Rembrandt's drawings (nearly 2000 survive) which cover a wide range of subjects: religion, history, mythology, landscape, genre and the nude. Popular interest in Rembrandt owes much to the numerous paintings and drawings of his family (Saskia and her son Titus, and Hendrickje Stoffels, Rembrandt's mistress in his later years) but above all to the self-portraits executed at various stages of his life.

Remizov, Aleksei Mikhailovich (1877-1957) Russian moralist and author of short stories, whose obsession with neologisms, syntax and speech-rhythms revolutionized the writing of Russian prose. He wrote fantasies, fairy-tales and humorous Symbolist novels, such as *The Pond* and *The Clock*. Many of his stories were inspired by dreams.

Renan, Joseph Ernest (1823-92) French scholar and historian of Christianity, chiefly remembered for his controversial and subjective biblical interpretation, *History of the Origins of Christianity* (1863-83).

Reni, Guido (1575-1642) Italian painter who is remembered mostly for the intense pathos of his depictions of JESUS CHRIST as the Man of Sorrows, and for the bright and rhythmic *Aurora* fresco on the ceiling of the Palazza Rospigliosi, Rome (1613). The latter shows his debt to the graceful, idealizing art of RAPHAEL and, in its design and individual quotations, to antique sculpture.

Rennie, John (1761-1821) Scottish civil engineer, bridge builder and canal architect, who built the original Waterloo Bridge over the Thames (1810-17), Southwark Bridge (1815-19), London Bridge (completed by his son, John in 1831) and many others. His canals include the Kennet and Avon, the Great Western and the Lancaster. Rennie also carried out major drainage improvements of East Anglian fens (1800), of harbours in Great Britain and abroad and several of naval dockyards. In 1804, he adopted a WATT steam engine to work the first powered bucket dredger at Hull. At Plymouth in 1811, he commenced the construction of the first breakwater on the English side of the English Channel.

Renoir, Jean (born 1894) French film director and writer, son of artist Auguste RENOIR, with whom he shared the same feeling for light and landscape and a love of nubile women, as expressed in the film classics *La Règle du Jeu* (1939) and *Le Déjeuner sur l'Herbe* (1959).

Greatest of portraitists, Rembrandt painted many pictures of himself

Renoir, Pierre Auguste (1841-1919) French Impressionist painter, who developed an early admiration for the work of BOUCHER and FRAGONARD, which is reflected by his emphasis on the female nude. In 1862 he met MONET and SISLEY and through working with them, developed an impressionistic sensitivity to nuances of colour and light (e.g. *The Swing*, 1876). But Renoir was always more concerned with the human figure than any other Impressionist, except DEGAS. He designed fine sculptures, which were executed by an assistant.

Respighi, Ottorino (1879-1936) Italian composer who wrote the vivid orchestral tone poems *The Fountains of Rome* (1917) and *The Pines of Rome* (1924). In the cause of realism, the score of the latter includes a gramophone recording of a nightingale. Respighi studied with RIMSKY-KORSAKOV, and he also conducted, taught and edited early Italian music.

Retz, Gilles de (c. 1404-40) French feudal lord, distinguished soldier, and one time friend of JOAN OF ARC, who is supposed by many to be the original 'Bluebeard'. De Retz engaged in Satanic practices in the course of which he ritually murdered numerous children. He was eventually burnt at the stake.

Retz, Jean François Paul de Gondi, Cardinal de (1614-79) French ecclesiastic and politician. His *Mémoires* (first published in 1717) give a vivid firsthand account of the violent episodes of the Fronde (the two popular revolts against monarchial absolutism in 1648 and 1651-2), in which Retz played a leading role, revealing the men and events of the period.

Reuter, Paul Julius von (1816-99) German founder of one of the world's biggest news agencies. In Göttingen, he met GAUSS, then experimenting with telegraphy, and evolved the idea of a telegraphic news service. He moved to London (1851) and set up a continental cable service of stock market prices, which was later extended to general news. In 1858 *The Times* used a Reuter's report of a speech by NAPOLEON III, and the service became extensively used. As international cables were laid, Reuter's news became world-wide.

Reuther, Walter Philip (1907-70) American labour leader. An employee of the Ford Motor Co. in his twenties, he was dismissed for trying to organize a union among fellow workers. His efforts led, by 1941, to the recognition by Ford's of the Union of Automobile Workers. Reuther later became Vice-President of the combined American Federation of Labour and the Congress of Industrial Organizations, and as such was one of the most powerful men in American industry, though he continued to oppose Communist infiltration of the unions. He was killed in an aeroplane crash.

Revere, Paul (1735-1818) American patriot, who rode from Boston to Lexington in two hours to warn the revolutionary leaders Adams and Hancock that British troops were about to arrest them and seize gunpowder hidden by dissident colonists. This enabled the leaders to escape and the colonists to prepare for the battles of Lexington and Concord, the first of the War of Independence, which were fought the next day (19 April 1775). Revere was immortalized in LONGFELLOW's poem *The Midnight Ride of Paul Revere*.

Reynolds, Sir Joshua (1723-92) English painter, who is one of the most important figures in British art, both for his painting and his theories. Through his painting (he was, with GAINSBOROUGH, one of the outstanding portrait painters of his day) and his ideology, propounded in discourses delivered at the Royal Academy in his capacity as its first President, Reynolds influenced taste and the practice of contemporary artists and those of subsequent generations. The foundation of the Academy (1768) and the intellectual basis on which Reynolds tried to establish a school of British painting to equal those of Italy and France, did much to improve the status of artists in England.

Rhazes (850-923 AD) Persian physician and alchemist, who wrote the first accurate medical descriptions distinguishing between smallpox and measles.

Rhee, Syngman (1875-1965) Founder and virtual creator of South Korea. After trying unsuccessfully to bring the case of Japanese-ruled Korea to the attention of the Versailles Peace Conference, he became the head of a Korean Provisional Government in exile in 1919, and returned to Korea after the Japanese defeat in 1945. In 1948 he was elected President of South Korea, and thereafter became increasingly antagonistic to the Communist régime in the North. He was elected President for a second term in 1952. His opposition to the truce at the end of the Korean War in 1953, politically embarrassed the US but in 1956 and 1960 he was again elected President. He became increasingly authoritarian, frequently introducing martial law and resorting to intimidation. Popular indignation forced him to resign in 1960, and thereafter he lived in Hawaii.

Rhine, Joseph (born 1895) American pioneer of the study of parapsychology. He has investigated paranormal human abilities – telepathy, clairvoyance and precognition (collectively called extra-sensory perception) and psychokinesis (the movement of physical objects by the mind alone).

Rhodes, Cecil John (1853-1902) British businessman, colonial statesman and leading protagonist of imperialism in South Africa. The founder of Rhodesia. He went to Cape Colony in 1870 and quickly made a fortune from diamond mining in the Orange Free State. He used his control of the De Beers Diamond Company and his interests in the Transvaal gold mines to further his vision of British imperialism in Africa. In 1887, he founded the British South Africa Co., which received a royal charter two years later, to colonize the country north of the Transvaal, later known as Rhodesia. He entered politics and by 1890 had become Premier of Cape Colony. In 1896, he was forced to resign, because of his implication in the JAMESON Raid.

Ribbentrop, Joachim von (1893-1946) Nazi diplomat. A sometime wine salesman, he joined the Nazi Party in the 1920s, and his many foreign contacts formed during his commercial travels were useful to HITLER, who in 1936 sent him as Ambassador to Britain. He was made much of by Nazi sympathizers, though his insolence gave offence to many. In 1938 he was appointed Foreign Minister and was responsible, a year later, for the Nazi-Soviet Pact, which gave Hitler a free hand to wage war on western Europe. He was tried as a war criminal at Nuremburg in 1946 and subsequently hanged.

Ribera, Jusepe de (1588-1652) Spanish painter, whose paintings, which are frequently of the brutal martyrdoms or passion scenes typical of the period of the Counter-Reformation, combine a realism in the depiction of surface details with a slightly less harsh version of CARAVAGGIO's contrasts of light and shade.

Ricci, Curbastro Gregorio (1853-1925) Italian mathematician, who was the principal discoverer of the absolute differential calculus, a systematic account of tensor analysis originating from differential geometry. This work was further developed by his pupil LEVI-CIVITA.

Ricci, Matteo (1552-1610) Italian Jesuit missionary, the first of many Jesuits (notably Schall, Verbiest, Fontaney and Regis), who were tolerated in China for having advanced Chinese science. Earlier missions had failed, but Ricci excited Chinese curiosity with clocks, globes, engravings and his knowledge of mathematics and map projection. Eventually he was allowed to establish a mission in Peking, where he aroused interest in his religious doctrines and his prolific publications in Chinese.

Rice, Hamilton (1875-1956) American explorer in South America, where he made five expeditions (1907-25) to explore tributaries of the Amazon and the Orinoco, including the rivers Negro, Uaupés, Icana, Inirida and Casiquiare. He used aircraft and radio (1919-20) as aids in his travels.

Richard I Coeur de Lion (1157-99) King of England (1189-99), who spent less than a year of his reign in England, the rest in crusading and defending his French possessions, Normandy and Anjou. After joining PHILIP II of France in the Third Crusade (1189-92), he sent 8000 troops to Palestine, seized Cyprus and Acre, and fought off SALADIN before dissension forced him to return home. On the way back he was seized by Leopold of Austria (1192), but regained freedom by payment of a huge ransom raised by taxation.

Richard III (1452-85) Last Yorkist king of England (1483-5) and one of the most controversial of English rulers. Tudor propaganda depicted him as a villain, a view adhered to by SHAKESPEARE in *Richard III*, based on a suspicion of his having murdered the Princes in the Tower. Loyal to his brother EDWARD IV while he lived,

Richard became regent for his young nephew Edward V in 1483, and quickly seized and executed possible opponents, especially supporters of the Queen Mother, Elizabeth Woodville. Following the liquidation of the Queen's friends, Richard seized the throne and imprisoned Edward V and his brother in the Tower, where they died in October 1483, perhaps by the King's order. Growing belief that Richard was the murderer caused his support to dwindle and helped to bring about his defeat and death at the hands of Henry Tudor (later HENRY VII) at Bosworth Field.

Richards, Sir Gordon (born 1904) English jockey, the first jockey to be knighted. He was champion jockey for 26 of his 34 active racing years, winning 4870 of his 21,834 races.

Richards, Theodore William (1868-1928) American chemist remembered for his accurate determinations of atomic weights.

Richardson, Dorothy (1873-1957) English novelist, who was one of the earliest writers to attempt literally to depict the complex streams of associations which make up consciousness. Between 1915 and 1938 she wrote a connected series of 12 novels, under the general title of *Pilgrimage*, giving the thoughts and impressions of Miriam Henderson, her interior monologue.

Richardson, Henry Hobson (1838-86) American architect whose commercial architecture was noted for its massive quality and testified to his interest in Romanesque architecture. The heavy but vigorous rustication (masonry cut in huge, deeply-pointed blocks) that he often employed added to the taut but cliff-like surfaces of his façades.

Richardson, Lewis Fry (1881-1953) British mathematician who applied his subject to weather forecasting. Between 1913 and 1922, he tried to evolve a scientific system of weather prediction based on calculations applying the laws of heat and motion to meteorological data.

Richardson, Samuel (1689-1761) English novelist, who, together with DEFOE, was an important influence in the development of the novel in the first half of the 18th century. A commission to write a model letterbook gave Richardson, a printer, the form and idea of *Pamela* (1740). He followed this with *Clarissa Harlowe* (1747-8) and *Sir Charles Grandison* (1754). For the first time he made affairs of the heart, not adventure, the subject of fiction. At his best, in *Clarissa Harlowe*, he is a fine epistol-

ary novelist with a sure understanding of women's motives and psychology. He had a considerable influence on DIDEROT and ROUSSEAU.

Richelieu, Duc de (1585-1642) French cardinal (1622) and statesman, who, for the greater part of Louis XIII's reign, controlled France and made royal authority absolute. From the time he became Chief Minister (1624) until his death, Richelieu dominated Louis and made the royal authority (and thereby his own) supreme, countering threats – at home – from the feudal nobles and the Huguenots, and – abroad – from the Hapsburgs of Spain and the Holy Roman Empire. Although he executed nobles who were plotting his overthrow, he showed mercy to the disarmed Huguenots and permitted them freedom of worship. To make France supreme in Europe over its Hapsburg rivals (Spain and Austria) he increased the country's influence at their expense by making alliances with German states and Sweden, capturing Rousillon from Spain, and Turin from the emperor. France was stronger than it had ever been.

Richter, Hans (1843-1916) German conductor who became the leading interpreter of WAGNER and, in Britain, a champion of ELGAR while resident conductor of the Hallé Orchestra.

Richter, Johann Paul (1763-1825) German writer (pseudonym Jean Paul) author of *The Invisible Lodge* (1793), *Hesperus* (1795), and *Titan* (1800-3), a series of humorous novels which deal with the problems of achieving a balanced personality and the conflict between the real and the ideal.

Rickenbacker, Eddie (1890-1973) American air ace and corporation president. Entering the First World War as a chauffeur to General PERSHING, Rickenbacker transferred to the Air Service where he became the top American fighter pilot, downing 26 German aircraft.

Rickover, Hyman George (born 1900) Polish-born American admiral, who directed the US project for nuclear-powered submarines that could remain submerged for several months. The first, USS *Nautilus*, was launched in 1955. Rickover was subsequently responsible for the development of the Polaris intercontinental missile, which could be launched from a submerged nuclear submarine.

Ridley, Nicholas (c. 1500-55) English Protestant reformer and martyr. As Bishop of Rochester (1547), and then of London (1549), he helped

CRANMER to compile the first Book of Common Prayer and the 139 Articles of the English Protestant Church. He denounced MARY and ELIZABETH (the later queens) as illegitimate, regarding them as a danger to Protestantism, and supported Lady Jane GREY's accession. When Mary I became queen, Ridley, Cranmer and LATIMER were condemned as heretics. Ridley and Latimer were burnt at the stake.

Riebeeck, Jan van (1634-77) Dutch naval surgeon and colonist, founder of Cape Town (1652). As part of the Dutch East India Company's plan for a victualling station for ships on the long voyage between the Dutch Republic and the East Indies, he built the fort which later became Cape Town.

Riefenstahl, Leni (born 1902) German actress who went on to direct the brilliant pre-war Nazi propaganda films, notably *Triumph of the Will* (1936), recording the Nuremburg rallies of 1934, and *Olympia* (1938), documenting the 1936 Olympic Games.

Riemann, Georg (1826-66) German mathematician, who was the first to formulate a general theory of multi-dimensional geometry, of which Euclidean and non-Euclidean geometries are special cases. This led directly to the later work of RICCI and LEVI-CIVITA, and to the mathematical side of the general relativity theory of EINSTEIN.

Rienzi, Cola di (1313-54) Italian notary, leader of a popular revolution which overthrew the patrician rulers of Rome (1347). Within months he alienated the masses by levying heavy taxes, and angered the pope and the Holy Roman Emperor by calling a

Cardinal Richelieu, the 'Red Eminence' of France whose life's aim was to destroy the power of the Hapsburgs

national parliament and proposing to revive the Roman Empire. Increasing unrest caused him to abdicate and flee. Later, he returned and regained his position as tribune (1354), but was murdered during a riot.

Rilke, Rainer Maria (1875-1926) Austrian poet, widely regarded as his country's leading poet. He is the author of a number of works which typify the moods and sentiments of the *fin-de-siecle* period, including the religious cycle, *Das Stundenbuch* (1905).

Rimbaud, Arthur (1854-91) French poet whose work had a significant influence on the development of modern poetry. He was a precocious genius and by the age of 20 had already completed his main works, *Le Bateau ivre*, *Les Illuminations* and *Une Saison en Enfer*. Ever a rebel, scornful of tradition, defiantly seeking freedom (both personal and literary), Rimbaud believed that the poet must intensify his perception by submitting himself to all kinds of experience (what he called the 'dérèglement de tous les sens') and then, without conscious control, to transmit what he perceives, a theory anticipating the work of the Surrealists.

Rimsky-Korsakov, Nikolai (1844-1908) Russian musician and leading composer of the Nationalist school. Rimsky-Korsakov was a naval officer before making music his career and he wrote the earliest Russian symphonic poem (*Sadko*, 1867, later an opera) while on duty. In 1871 he was made a Professor at the St Petersburg Conservatory. He became a notable teacher and STRAVINSKY was among his later pupils. Rimsky-Korsakov's compositions were distinguished by rich orchestration. They include the *Spanish Caprice* (1887) and the suite *Scheherazade* (1888). His best-known opera is *The Golden Cockerel*, which was not performed until after his death.

Rippon, Geoffrey (born 1924) English politician who negotiated Britain's entry into the European Economic Community (Common Market) in January 1972. Later that year, Rippon was appointed Secretary of State for the Environment in the government of Edward HEATH.

Ritter, Karl (1779-1859) German founder (with HUMBOLDT) of scientific geography. He treated geography as the physiology and comparative anatomy of the Earth's surface. He rejected the old descriptive catalogue approach, and helped to give the subject system and shape by drawing attention to similarities and differences on the Earth's surface and

pointing out the interconnections between its often seemingly unrelated phenomena.

Rivera, Miguel Primo de (1870-1930) Spanish general, who became dictator of Spain. When, in 1921, defeats in the Riff War in Morocco, Catalan nationalist agitation and the rapid growth of the Anarchist movement alarmed the Spanish establishment, de Rivera, with the connivance of King Alfonso XIII, seized power and dissolved parliament (1923) establishing a military directorate (1923) followed by civil dictatorship. It lasted until late 1925, when a semblance of parliamentary rule, with de Rivera as Prime Minister, was restored. He was eventually forced out of office by the king and army officers, because of growing social, industrial and intellectual unrest. He died in exile in Paris.

Rivers, William (1864-1922) English anthropologist and psychologist whose study of a southern Indian people *The Todas* (1906) and his *History of Melanesian Society* (1914) are the first precisely documented field studies of kinship.

Robbe-Grillet, Alain (born 1922) French novelist and leading exponent of the 'new novel', in which, by the use of film techniques such as flashback, he rejects the time scale, plot and characterization of the conventional novel. His works include *Les Gommes* (1953), *La Jalousie* (1957), *Le Voyeur* (1957) and screenplays such as *L'Année Dernière à Marienbad* and *L'Immortelle*.

Robbia, Luca della (c. 1400-82) Florentine sculptor, whose first major work was the *Cantoria* for the cathedral in Florence (1431-8). Early in his career, he discovered a means of applying vitrified lead glazes to terracotta, and made a number of small half-length works of Virgins and Madonnas, being the first artist to exploit the sentimental in the motherhood theme. He built up a large family business, which was carried on by his nephew, Andrea.

Robbins, Jerome (born 1918) American dancer and choreographer of some of the most popular and influential modern dance dramas and musicals, including *West Side Story*. Since 1949, he has been an associate artistic director of the New York City Ballet and has created several masterpieces which have been remounted for other companies, including a version of *L'Après-midi d'un faune* (quite different from NIJINSKY's original) and *Dances at a Gathering*, to piano pieces originally written by CHOPIN.

Robert I 'The Bruce' (1274-1329)
King of Scotland (1306-29), chief architect of Scotland's independence. He filled the gap in Scottish leadership left by Edward I's capture of BALIOL and WALLACE, and, though of Norman descent, claimed the Scottish throne and rallied the Scots against England. He was defeated by Edward I at Methven (1306), and fled to Ireland, but returned on Edward's death (1307). Gradually he won control of Scotland and in 1314 defeated Edward II's army at Bannockburn. Subsequent attacks on Scotland were warded off and in 1328 the Treaty of Northampton put an end to the fighting and affirmed Edward III's recognition of Scotland's independence.

Robert Guiscard see GUISCARD, Robert

Robert, Hubert (1733-1808) French landscape painter who, like his friends PANINI and PIRANESE, was much affected by the grandeur of ancient Rome and stimulated by recent excavations in Herculaneum and Pompeii.

Roberts, Richard (1789-1864) Welsh inventor who worked with MAUDSLAY until 1814, then alone in Manchester, where he devised a machine for planing metal (1817), a screw-cutting lathe (1817), numerous weaving improvements, including a self-acting mule (1825), improvements to steam locomotives and carriages, a machine for punching holes of any angle or shape in boiler and bridge plates (1848), an electromagnet (1854) and numerous steamship improvements.

Robertson, William (1721-93) British historian whose *History of America* (1777), was the first detailed and popular account of events in Spanish America since COLUMBUS.

Robeson, Paul (born 1898) American negro actor and singer, famous for his performances of *Othello* and his singing of negro spirituals.

Robespierre, Maximilien de (1758-94) French Revolutionary leader. A lawyer from Arras, he was elected to the Estates General in 1789 and acquired a reputation for radicalism in the Constituent Assembly (1789-91). He was one of the founders of the Society of Friends of the Constitution (Jacobins), the most radical of the main revolutionary groups. Robespierre dominated the Committee of Public Safety (formed in the spring of 1793 after the failure of the war policy of the Girondins) and by April 1794 had overthrown his rivals, the Girondin Party, DAN-TON and Hébert. With his followers, he established a dictatorship from April until July 1794. Believing himself the incarnation of the people's will, he decreed the confiscation of the property of enemies of the Revolution and its distribution to the poor. Arbitrary power of arrest, condemnation and execution were given to the Revolutionary Tribunal, which Robespierre controlled, and the 'Cult of the Supreme Being' was introduced as a state religion to replace Roman Catholicism. The measures led to a *coup d'état* by more moderate revolutionaries and Robespierre was arrested and guillotined.

Robinson, Edwin Arlington (1869-1935) American poet, outstanding and prolific, who won the Pulitzer Prize three times. 'The Children of the Night' (1897) showed his typical ironic melancholy; verse novels, like *Captain Craig* (1902), brought him fame.

Robinson, James Harvey (1863-1936) American historian concerned with the role of cultural history, who examined man's intellectual, artistic, social and scientific progress in books such as *The New History* (1911).

Robinson, William (1839-1931) British gardener, journalist and writer of Irish descent. He, more than any other (apart from Gertrude JEKYLL, with whom he collaborated on occasions), facilitated the transition of garden design from a period of high Victorian taste to its 20th-century position, emphasizing the use of shrubs and herbaceous plants in naturalistic plantings, carefully blending colour and form.

Rob Roy see MACGREGOR, Robert

Rochester, John Wilmot, 2nd Earl of (1647-80) English courtier and poet, whose verse is often savage and despairing, expressing an aristocrat's disgust at a changing social order. In *A Satire against Mankind* (1675) he showed a determined antirationalism and distrust of the brand of optimism offered by the Royal Society.

Rockefeller, John (1839-1937) American founder of Standard Oil, one of the world's largest petroleum companies, and of a dynasty of successful business men, administrators and public servants. After amassing a huge fortune, he engaged in planned philanthropy for the benefit of educational, cultural and medical institutions. Rockefeller began oil refining in 1863, and subsequently founded Standard Oil, which, by 1882, had a near-monopoly of the business in the US. Its dominance brought about anti-trust legislation which left Standard Oil of New Jersey the largest surviving unit. In all, he and his son John D. Rockefeller Jun. gave away $930 million in benefactions.

Rockwell, George Lincoln (1918-67) Founder and leader of the American Nazi Party. He formed the Union of Free Enterprise National Socialists in 1959, after having organized a number of short-lived right-wing bodies throughout the 1950s; he later changed its name to the American Nazi Party. The organization subsequently underwent another change of name, becoming the National Socialist White People's Party, its efforts then being directed against negroes rather than Jews. Rockwell was shot dead by an ex-member of his party in 1967.

Rodney, George Brydges 1st Baron (1719-92) English admiral in the American theatre of action in the Seven Years' War (1756-63). As Commander-in-Chief of the Leeward Islands, he subdued (1762) the French-held islands of Grenada, Martinique, St Lucia and St Vincent, and thus strengthened Great Britain's bargaining position at the time of the Treaty of Paris in 1763. He achieved several victories later in actions against Spanish and French fleets, and Dutch trading settlements in the West Indies, especially at the battle of the Saints (1782), which ended a French threat to the West Indies.

Rodo, José Enrique (1872-1917) Uruguayan author, whose famous essay, *Ariel* (1900), urged Latin American intellectuals to resist the dominant materialism of the US.

Rockefeller, his name a synonym for limitless wealth, founded one of the world's largest oil combines in the 19th century

Rodrigo Díaz de Vivar see CID, El

Rodriguez de Fonseca, Juan (1451-1524) Spanish prelate, who founded (1511) and supervised the Council of the Indies (Spanish America), which controlled Spain's huge colonial empire. He organized its division into viceroyalties and sub-division into so-called kingdoms, each under a governor advised by a tribunal. This system was preserved until the early 1800s. Rodriguez persistently opposed COLUMBUS and sent BOBADILLA to displace him as Viceroy of the Indies.

Roethke, Theodore (1908-63) American poet, who wrote of the links between the unconscious and nature. His books include *Open House* (1941), *The Lost Son* (1948), *Praise to the End* (1951) and *The Waking* (1953).

Roger II (1095-1154) Norman King (1130-54) of Sicily and one of medieval Europe's most powerful and cultured monarchs. He united and enforced order in Sicily and southern Italy, which had been captured by his father Roger I and uncle Robert GUISCARD, then built up a strong fleet, which seized parts of the coasts of Tunis and Tripoli (1135-53). In 1147 he invaded Greece and threatened Constantinople (1149). Meanwhile, he had organized a strong centralized government.

Rojas, Fernando de (c. 1475-1541) Spanish lawyer and author of most of the *Trajicomedy of Calisto and Melibea*.

Rolfe, Frederick William (1860-1913) Eccentric English writer, obsessed with the Roman Catholic Church, who, under the name of Baron Corvo, wrote *Hadrian the Seventh* (1904), a novel about his frustrated priestly ambition.

Rolfe, John (1585-1622) English colonist of Virginia, who devised a method of curing tobacco, which became the cornerstone of the colony's trade.

Rolland, Romain (1866-1944) French novelist, musicologist and winner of the Nobel Prize for Literature in 1916. His 10-volume novel *Jean Christophe* (1904-12), the story of a composer, exemplifies Rolland's belief in the fusion of races and the sinking of cultural differences. He also wrote several biographies, notably of BEETHOVEN (1903), MICHELANGELO (1905) and TOLSTOY (1911). Rolland's pamphlet, *Au-dessus de la mêlée* (1914), established him as the voice of the pacifist intellectuals and because of his forthright views, he

Elegant design and superlative engineering hallmarked the cars of C. S. Rolls and Frederick Royce

was obliged to take refuge in Switzerland.

Rollo (c. 860-933) Norse chieftain, who led the Viking conquerors of northwestern France and became the first Duke of Normandy.

Rolls, Charles (1877-1910) English co-founder, with Frederick Royce (1863-1933), of the car and aero-engine firm that bears their name. Royce was a superb engineer; Rolls knew the market and its needs. The first Rolls-Royce motor car, the Silver Ghost, was in production from 1906 to 1925. The firm's aero-engine division pioneered many developments, including giant jet engines and the use of carbon fibres.

Romains, Jules (born 1885) French dramatist, novelist and poet, originator of the 'Unanimist' poetic movement, named after his book of poems *La vie unanime* (1908). He is also the author of the popular farce *Knock ou le triomphe de la médecine* (1923) and is perhaps chiefly remembered for his vast saga *Les Hommes de bonne volonté* (27 vols., 1932-47), a survey of French society.

Romero, Francisco (18th cent.) Spanish bullfighter and the first great professional of the sport. Fighting in Spain's oldest bullring at Ronda in Andalusia, he became famous as one of the *espades*, actual killers of bulls.

Romilly, Sir Samuel (1757-1818) English lawyer who devoted himself to the reform of English criminal law. From 1807, as an MP, he worked to end the death penalty for trivial offences, successfully achieving the repeal of provisions imposing capital punishment for theft from the person (1808) and for soldiers caught begging without permits. During his lifetime much of his reformist legislation met with bitter opposition, but Romilly's humanitarian writings became the basis for major reforms later in the century.

Rommel, Erwin Eugen Johannes (1891-1944) German general, later Field-Marshal, Commander of the Afrika Korps during the Second World War. During the invasion of France in 1940, he showed skill and resource as the head of a Panzer division. He was appointed, by HITLER, commander to the Afrika Korps in Libya, where his bold, unorthodox

The 'Desert Fox', Field-Marshal Erwin Rommel's skill at handling armour made him into a legend among his opponents, the British 8th Army

leadership won him the name of 'the Desert Fox'. After inflicting a number of major reverses on the British 8th Army, he was defeated at El Alamein (November 1942) by MONTGOMERY, and driven back to Tunisia. In 1944, he became commander of the anti-invasion forces in France. Following his complicity in the plot of 20 July 1944 to assassinate Hitler, he was given the choice of being court martialled and shot, or of committing suicide. Though there is some doubt about the means of his death, it is generally assumed that he died by his own hand.

Romney, George (1734-1802) Fashionable English portrait painter. Not as skilled as either GAINSBOROUGH or REYNOLDS, his infatuation for Lady Hamilton resulted in the well-known pictures of her, *déshabillée*, in mythological poses. He projected many vast historical pictures, which never developed further than drawings.

Ronsard, Pierre de (1524-85) French Renaissance poet, regarded as the father of French lyric verse. His devotion to the Latin and Greek poets is reflected in all his work, including the *Odes* (1550), *Amours* (1552), *Hymnes* (1555) and *Sonnets pour Hélène* (1578). One of the poet's favourite themes is that beauty and joy are ephemeral and time's ravages cruel. Ronsard's principal importance was as an innovator, experimenting with verse forms, diversifying his style and leading the *Pléiade* poets, such as DU BELLAY, in their attempt to rejuvenate French poetry.

Röntgen, Wilhelm Conrad (1845-1923) German physicist who was awarded the first Nobel Prize for Physics in 1901 for his discovery of X-rays six years before. X-rays have been of vital practical importance, first in medicine (both to photograph bones and other body tissues and to irradiate and so treat tumours), and then in engineering for the testing of metals. They also have a great role in science itself: X-rays can be used to determine crystal structures and, since every element has a characteristic X-ray spectrum, they can be employed to analyse complex mixtures of elements.

Rooke, Sir George (1650-1708) British admiral who captured Gibraltar (1704). His victory gave Britain control of the Strait of Gibraltar and prevented France's Mediterranean and Atlantic fleets from joining forces. British possession of Gibraltar dates from this time.

Roosevelt, Franklin Delano (1882-1945) American President (1933-45) who served an unprecedented third term and was elected for a fourth shortly before his death. America's leader in the years leading to the Second World War, during most of which he was a victim of polio, which he contracted in 1921, and which crippled him. In 1928, he was elected Governor of New York State and, as the Democratic presidential candidate in 1932, was returned with a majority of 12 million votes. As President, he inaugurated the 'New Deal' programme of government intervention in industry and business, to overcome the great depression, including public works on a vast scale, farm subsidies, and legislation to liberalize and control relations between capital and labour. In 1933 he recognized and exchanged diplomatic missions with the USSR and thus ended US isolationism. From 1941 he found, in the Lease-Lend Act, means to give massive support to Britain against the Nazis in the Second World War, while officially maintaining US neutrality. After the Japanese attack on Pearl Harbor (December 1941) had forced the US into the war, Roosevelt began that close co-operation with CHURCHILL, signified by periodic personal meetings, which gave cohesion to the operations of the British and American forces. He was elected President for a third term in 1940 and for a fourth in 1944.

Roosevelt, Theodore (1858-1919 Twenty-sixth President of the United States. He became a national hero as the leader of 'Roosevelt's Rough Riders' in the Spanish-American War of 1898, and President on MCKINLEY's assassination in 1901. In 1905 he was elected for a second term. He campaigned against big business and began to enforce the anti-trust laws, though his supporters were disappointed that he did not do more. In foreign affairs his 'dollar diplomacy' claimed the right of the US, through its commercial interests, to intervene in Latin America, and though his mediation after the Russo-Japanese war (1904-5) won him the Nobel Peace Prize, his militaristic and threatening foreign policy betrayed his essentially pugnacious, jingoistic conception of America's role in the world. This was demonstrated when he fomented rebellion in Colombia in 1903 to facilitate the building of the Panama Canal.

Rosenberg, Julius (1917-53) and **Ethel (1916-53)** American spies for the Soviet intelligence service. They were members of a transatlantic spy ring which also involved FUCHS, and obtained atomic secrets through Ethel's brother, David Greenglass, a worker at the Los Alamos nuclear research station. At their trial Greenglass gave evidence for the prosecution, and they were convicted and sentenced to death, two of the very few spies to be executed in peacetime.

Rosenfeld, Lev Borisovich see KAMENEV, Lev Borisovich

Rosenstein, Nils von (1706-73) Swedish physician, who founded the science of pediatrics (the medical care of infants and children). Although it had several medieval forerunners, his *The Diseases of Children and Their Remedies* (1765) was the first systematic modern treatise of its kind.

Ross, Harold Wallace (1892-1951) American journalist who founded the *New Yorker* magazine. In 1925 he

Cartoon by Thomas Rowlandson. He began as a portrait painter, but found his true métier as a caricaturist

started the magazine, in which he recorded the New York scene in satire and parody, featuring cartoons, social reporting, biographical profiles and short stories. Ross's tireless quest for purveyors of witty and intelligent journalism helped to make famous such writers as Alexander WOOLL-COTT and James THURBER.

Ross, Sir James Clark (1800-62) Scottish polar explorer who penetrated the Antarctic more deeply than any man before him, and located the North Magnetic Pole (1831). Later (1839-43) he led the ships *Erebus* and *Terror* in the first thrust through Antarctic pack-ice and reached 78° 9′S, which remained for 60 years the most southerly latitude reached. Ross discovered Victoria Land, the Admiralty and Prince Albert ranges, the Ross Sea, Ross Ice Shelf and Ross Island.

Rosse, William Parsons, 3rd Earl of (1800-67) British astronomer, who enormously enlarged the range of telescopes. He developed his own 'speculum metal' for telescope reflecting mirrors, which would take the high polish necessary, and in 1845, at Birr Castle, Ireland, succeeded in casting a giant 72-inch mirror – easily the largest made at that date.

Rossellino, Bernardo (1409-64) Florentine sculptor and architect, best known for his tomb for Leonardo Bruno (1444-50), which was a prototype Renaissance tomb. Other works by Rossellino include a delicate terracotta *Annunciation* for the Cathedral at Pienza, which, as an architect, he designed, and a relief, the *Madonna della Misericordia*, for the façade of the church at Arezzo.

Rossetti, Christina (1830-94) English poet, who expressed a deep religious faith in simple, tender lyrics. The sister of Dante Gabriel ROSSETTI, her poetry shared with his a mysticism and a sense of colour. After *Goblin Market* (1862), the first Pre-Raphaelite literary success, her work grew more religious as seen in *New Poems* (1896), published posthumously.

Rossetti, Dante Gabriel (1828-82) English painter and poet who, with Holman HUNT and MILLAIS, was a founder-member of the Pre-Raphaelite Brotherhood. His first important picture, *The Girlhood of Mary Virgin* (1849), is comparable to their early works, exhibiting the same slightly gauche realism. His painting *Found* (1854) exemplifies the 'modern moral subject' with which the Pre-Raphaelites were preoccupied – in this case the 'fallen woman'. Rossetti was a

poet of some standing, as was his sister, Christina.

Rosso, Medardo (1858-1928) Italian sculptor, who tried to relate his figures closely to their surroundings, an aspect of his work which interested the Futurists, especially BOCCIONI. Rosso worked in wax and plaster, always aware of the immediate sensations of light and movement. His aims were related to those of Impressionism, catching the quality of movement and of elusive shapes.

Rostand, Edmond (1868-1918) French verse dramatist, who wrote in a Romantic style, as in *Cyrano de Bergerac* (1898). This, his third play, was based on the life of that romantic dramatist (1620-55), who was said to have had an unusually long nose. Rostand's only other work of lasting fame is *L'Aiglon*, in which Sarah BERNHARDT created (1910) the role of NAPOLEON's son.

Rostropovich, Mtislav Leopoldovitch (born 1927) Russian cellist. As a young man, Rostropovich befriended PROKOFIEV and completed this composer's posthumous *Cello Concerto*. BRITTEN has also written for him. Rostropovich's wife is the distinguished Russian soprano, Galina Vishnevskaya.

Rothermere, Harold, 1st Viscount (1868-1940) English newspaper magnate, who was the financial backbone of the publishing empire of his brother, Lord NORTHCLIFFE.

Rothko, Mark (1903-70) Russian-born American Expressionist painter of large abstracts dominated by horizontal bands of colour.

Rothschild, Meyer (1743-1812) German banker and founder of a dynasty of financiers and bankers who played a part in shaping European history. Backing the new French and German education systems, financing industry and financing or refusing to finance wars, the Rothschild bankers became wealthy enough to exercise an influence on international events. In London, they helped to introduce full political rights for practising Jews when Lionel Rothschild (1808-79) became the first Jewish member of the House of Commons in 1859 and his son, Sir Nathan Meyer, 1st Baron Rothschild (1840-1915), the first Jewish peer to sit in the House of Lords.

Rouault, Georges (1871-1958) French Expressionist painter of the school of Paris, whose colour was intense and jewel-like, with heavily outlined areas, reflecting the influence of his stained-glass work. After

an apprenticeship to a stained-glass maker, he met MATISSE and MOREAU, and from 1905 was associated with the Fauve painters led by Matisse.

Roubiliac, Louis François (c. 1705-1762) French-born sculptor, who settled in England, whose masterpiece is the statue, *Newton*, which set a new example of careful symmetry, combined with the romantic, in English sepulchral monuments.

Rousseau, Henri (1844-1910) French 'primitive' painter, who, untutored and with naïve directness, concentrated on painting after retiring from his job as a customs officer (hence his nickname, Le Douanier). He painted Parisian landscapes, family scenes and portraits, but he is best known for a number of brightly coloured fantastic or allegorical canvases (e.g. *War*, *The Snake Charmer*, *The Dream*). These impressive pictures of visionary subjects are painted in a would-be realistic, supremely self-confident, though childlike manner and show why both PICASSO and Delaunay were among Rousseau's admirers.

Rousseau, Jean-Jacques (1712-78) French writer and philosopher born in Geneva, whose works have profoundly influenced European literary and political thought. In his first major essay *Discours sur les Arts et les Sciences* (1750), Rousseau advanced his theory of the 'noble savage' whose innate goodness is corrupted by civilization. His *Discours sur l'origine de l'inégalité parmi les hommes* (1755) is another eloquent attack on structured society. It was with the publication of his novel, *La Nouvelle Héloïse* (1761), that Rousseau emerged as the prophet of the French Romantic movement. In his next work, *Emile* (1762), Rousseau expounded his views on education, some of which have left their mark on today's schools. In 1762, Rousseau also published *Du Contrat social*, his greatest work of polemical philosophy, in which he argued that power is vested not in princes, but in the common people, and that government must be by general consent. Rousseau's bold investigation of the paradox of human society – man is born free, but everywhere is in chains – placed his own freedom in jeopardy.

Rowlandson, Thomas (1756-1827) English water-colour painter and caricaturist, whose work, which is characterized by a virility of line that contrasts with the delicacy of the colouring, provides a valuable record of the manners and appearances of the Georgian era.

Royce, Josiah (1855-1916) American metaphysician who combined idealism with an American tradition of pragmatism. Royce's fundamental preoccupation was with the problem of how thought is related to reality – a problem which he approached within an idealist framework, but which could for him be reduced to the question: How can a thing be the object of a thought when it in some sense exists independently?

Rozov, Victor (born 1913) Russian dramatist, who has been extremely popular in the Soviet Union since the Second World War. His plays are concerned with the conflict between the old and the young generations and the problems of young people in Soviet society. *In Search of Happiness* has been performed on British television and another example of his work seen in the West was the film *The Cranes are Flying* (1957).

Baseball, North America's fast and exciting national game is played between two nine-man teams around the 'diamond' enclosing the infield. The diagram below shows how the players are dispersed around the field. In the centre of the diamond is the pitcher, 1; the batter and the catcher are at 2; 1st base 3; 2nd and 3rd bases, 4 and 5; 1st and 2nd baseman, 6 and 7; short stop 8; 3rd baseman 9; right, centre and left fielders, 10, 11 and 12; infield 13; outfield 14

Rubens, Sir Peter Paul (1577-1640) Flemish painter, immensely popular throughout Europe, who sustained a prodigious and varied output. He began his career in Italy, where he travelled extensively as court painter to the Duke of Mantua. In 1608 he returned to Antwerp to become court painter to the Spanish Governors of the Netherlands. His first major works on his return were the *Elevation of the Cross* (1610) and *Descent from the Cross* (1611-14) for Antwerp Cathedral, which exhibit the combination of Flemish realism and dynamic movement characteristic of his early style. Rubens was much in demand as a painter of portraits, altarpieces and, from about 1620, decorative schemes for churches and palaces. So large a number of commissions necessitated his establishing a workshop in which his sketches could be worked up by assistants. His output was vast: in addition to projects such as the *Medici* cycle painted for the Palais de Luxembourg in Paris and the ceiling of the Banqueting House in Whitehall, London, he produced hunting scenes, mythological and historical subjects, designs for triumphal processions and huge panoramic landscapes. The sensuous colour and rich textures of paintings such as the *Garden of Love* (*c*. 1632-4) reveal the influence of TITIAN upon his later works.

Portraits, landscapes, allegories were all part of Ruben's tremendous output

Rubinstein, Anton (1829-94) Russian pianist who founded the Conservatory of Music in St Petersburg and was the only serious rival to LISZT.

Rudolf I of Hapsburg (1218-91) First (uncrowned) Hapsburg Holy Roman Emperor (1237-91). In the turmoil after the death of Conrad IV, the last Hohenstaufen Holy Roman Emperor (also uncrowned), Rudolf became southwestern Germany's most powerful prince. He was elected King of Germany (1273) and recognized as Emperor by Pope Gregory X, in return for a promise to end imperial aggression in Italy and to

lead a new crusade. By defeating and killing his only major rival, OTTOKAR II of Bohemia, Rudolf assured that future Hapsburgs would be kings of Germany, Spain, Hungary and Bohemia, archdukes of Austria, and Holy Roman Emperors.

Ruisdael, Jacob van (c. 1628-82) Dutch landscape painter, whose work, after a relatively realistic and topographically exact early period, became increasingly romantic in content and was for this reason an important influence on early 19th-century landscape painting.

Ruiz, Juan (early 14th cent.) Spanish writer known as 'Archpriest of Hita' and author of the *Book of Good Love* (1330), one of the outstanding Spanish poems, comparable with CHAUCER's *Canterbury Tales*.

Rumford, Sir Benjamin Thompson (1753-1814) American-British physicist who was the first to regard heat as a form of energy. In the 1790s, while supervising the boring of cannon barrels, he noticed that the heat generated by the drill was too great to be explained by Antoine LAVOISIER's idea that objects contain a fixed quantity of 'caloric', all or part of which can be converted into heat. Rumford suggested that as the drill bit into the metal its mechanical energy was being converted into heat.

Rumi (1207-73) Persian poet and mystic, who founded the Mevlevi Order of Dervishes, known as the Dancing Dervishes. In 1244 Rumi met the wandering dervish, Shams al-Din of Tabriz, an event which transformed Rumi's life, causing him to give up orthodox Islam to join the Dervishes.

Runcorn, Stanley (born 1922) British geophysicist, whose studies of palaeomagnetism (the north-south alignment of magnetized particles when the particles are 'frozen' into the rocks as they solidify) have enabled him to reconstruct the original positions of these rocks and to build up a picture of the positions of the continents as they were before they 'drifted' to their present positions.

Runyon, Damon (1884-1946) American sports writer and journalist, who wrote short stories about the colourful extroverts of American life, particularly lively portraits of the underworld – gamblers, petty criminals and hucksters, usually hiding hearts of gold under ferocious exteriors.

Rupert, Prince (1619-82) German count, nephew of CHARLES I and royalist cavalry commander in the English Civil War, during which he became known as 'the Mad Cavalier', leading brave but undisciplined cavalry charges against parliamentarian troops. He fought at the battles of Edgehill, Marston Moor and Naseby, and in 1644 became royalist Commander-in-Chief. Subsequently he led a royalist fleet (defeated by BLAKE in 1650), then fought as a pirate. After the Restoration he served CHARLES II with distinction as an admiral in the second Dutch War (1664-7). He was a keen amateur scientist and developed a process of mezzotint engraving, improved gunpowder, invented a zinc-copper alloy and found a new way of boring cannon.

Rusk, David Dean (born 1909) American statesman, and an expert in Far Eastern affairs. He joined the US army in the Second World War and became Chief-of-Staff in the Far Eastern war zone. He was appointed State Department administrator in the International Security Division in 1946, and Director of the Office of UN Affairs, 1947-9. Rusk was Assistant Secretary of State with special responsibility for Far Eastern affairs from 1950-2 and Secretary of State from 1961 to 1968 under KENNEDY and JOHNSON.

Ruska, Ernst August Friedrich (born 1906) German electrical engineer who in 1931, with Max Knoll, demonstrated the first electron microscope. With a later version, Ruska obtained magnifications of up to 12,000, which considerably exceeded the resolution of the optical microscope.

Ruskin, John (1819-1900) English art critic, historian and theorist, whose writings on aesthetics and ornate prose style, greatly influenced many late-Victorian writers. In his writing, he endeavours to make beauty applicable to all walks of life, and wrote on diverse subjects such as painting and economics, literature and war. 'Food can only be got out of the ground, and happiness out of honesty' was one of Ruskin's ethical slogans.

Russell, Bertrand (1872-1970) English philosopher, mathematician, social reformer and winner of the Nobel Prize for Literature in 1950.

Russell, Henry Norris (1877-1957) American astronomer who produced the diagram relating a star's luminosity and temperature. In 1913 Russell suggested that the relationship between a star's luminosity and temperature (discovered by HERTZSPRUNG) is best shown diagrammatically, and the resultant plot became known as the Hertzsprung-Russell diagram.

Russell, John 1st Earl (1792-1878) British Prime Minister, and sponsor of Parliamentary reform. In 1831 GREY entrusted to Russell the drafting and introduction of the first Reform Bill which was passed in 1832. As Home Secretary from 1835 to 1839 under MELBOURNE, Russell introduced the Municipal Reform Bill of 1835 and reduced the number of capital crimes. He supported the repeal of the Corn Laws and succeeded PEEL as Prime Minister in 1846. His Premiership (1846-52) was notable for the dominance of his foreign secretary PALMERSTON, the application of both coercion and relief to Ireland and commitment to free trade by the government. Palmerston's felicitations to NAPOLEON III on his coup in 1851, sent without Cabinet consultation, caused Russell to dismiss him from the post of Foreign Secretary. Palmerston in retaliation brought Russell's ministry down the following year. On Palmerston's death in 1865, Russell became Premier again, but his proposal of a new Reform Bill in 1866 split his Party and led to his resignation.

Russell, Sir William Howard (1821-1907) Irish-born journalist, who was the first fully-accredited war correspondent. His exposure in *The Times* of the mismanagement of the Crimean War in 1854-6, helped to bring down the Aberdeen ministry, and led to public demands for the reform of military medical services and a complete overhaul of the army.

Ruth, 'Babe' (1895-1948) American baseball player. In his career (1914-35), mainly with the Boston Red Sox and New York Yankees, he hit a big-league record of 714 regular season home runs.

Rutherford, Ernest, Lord (1871-1937) New Zealand physicist, and founder of modern atomic theory. In 1910 he produced his theory of the scattering of alpha particles (helium nuclei) by atoms, which led him to picture the atom as consisting of a positively charged central nucleus surrounded by orbiting planetary electrons. It was to this model (the Rutherford atom) that BOHR in 1912 applied quantum notions and thus took the vital step towards modern quantum mechanics. Rutherford undertook a systematic study of radioactive substances and their disintegrations. This led to the idea that a substance can be made artificially radioactive by bombardment with fast alpha particles, so causing atomic disintegrations. In the early 1920s he was the first to split the atom.

Ruyter, Michel de (1607-76) Dutch admiral who, with van Tromp, made the Dutch Republic a major sea power. He fought against Spanish, English, Swedish, French and Sicilian fleets, but it was in the three Anglo-Dutch wars that he achieved his greatest success. In the first (1652-3), he helped van Tromp to out-manoeuvre the English; in the second (1665-7), as van Tromp's successor, he defeated MONCK's fleet off Dunkirk and made a daring raid on English shipping in the Medway; in the third (1672-4) he fought four indecisive battles, often against heavy odds, but prevented an Anglo-French invasion of the United Provinces.

Rydberg, Abraham Viktor (1828-95) Swedish poet, novelist and philosopher, author of *The Bible's Doctrine Concerning Christ* (1862), a treatise which challenges CHRIST's divinity. His humanistic faith in man is also to be seen in his idealistic verse, collected in the two-volume *Poems* (1882 and 1891).

S

Sá, Mem de (c. 1500-72) Portuguese Governor-General of Brazil (1556-72) and founder (with his nephew ESTACIO DE SA) of Rio de Janeiro.

Sacco, Nicola (1891-1927) American anarchist who was tried for murder with Bartolomeo Vanzetti. They were arrested for murder in the course of a robbery of S16,000 in May 1920 and convicted in July 1921, but the trial aroused bitter controversy because it was believed to have been prejudiced by the extreme left-wing views of the accused. Several unsuccessful attempts were made to secure a re-trial, but death sentences were passed in April 1927. Protests followed from all over the world, but an investigating committee found no reason to order a re-trial and the two men were executed.

Sachs, Julius von (1832-97) German botanist whose researches into the microchemistry of plants and especially into the mechanics of photosynthesis (the formation of organic compounds in the presence of sunlight) showed that chlorophyll acts as a catalyst in the presence of light, enabling a plant to build up more complex compounds (such as sugars) from carbon dioxide and water.

Sackville-West, the Hon. Victoria (1892-1962) British poet, novelist and horticulturist, whose garden, at Sissinghurst, Kent, upon which she worked with her husband, Harold Nicholson, figures in her poem 'The Garden' (1946).

Sadat, Anwar (born 1918) President of Egypt since September 1970, member of the original Egyptian junta, which in 1952 seized power from FAROUK and close friend and confidant of NASSER. Given important posts in the government and bureaucracy of Egypt from 1952 on, he was appointed vice-President of Egypt in 1969, and upon Nasser's death assumed power by succession. He was responsible for expelling Soviet technicians and military personnel (July 1972) and for affecting the Egyptian-Syrian alliance which culminated in the October 1973 war with Israel.

Sade, Donatien Alphonse François, Marquis de (1740-1814) French writer, notorious for his tales of sexual perversion and cruelty, from whom the term 'sadism' is derived. His erotic novels include *Justine* (1791), *La Philosophie dans le boudoir* (1795) and *Juliette* (1798), many of them written in prison. Much in his work anticipated the writings of FREUD.

Sadi (c. 1184-c.1292) Persian moralist and poet, whose most popular work is *The Rose Garden*, a mixture of anecdote and verse. His other famous work is *The Orchard*, a long, moralizing poem. He is also important as a writer of *ghazals* or lyrical poems.

Sagan, Françoise (born 1935) French novelist and playwright. Her novels, *Bonjour Tristesse* (1954), *Un certain sourire* (1956), *Aimez-vous Brahms?* (1959) and *Dans un mois, dans un an* (1957) are written in a spare, simple, dispassionate style, depicting a world of boredom, transient love-affairs and ephemeral happiness. Several of her popular tales have been filmed.

Saint-Denis, Michel de (born 1897) French actor, producer and Director of the famous Compagnie des Quinze whose plays, performed with naturalistic settings, were well received in Paris and London.

Saint-Exupéry, Antoine de (1900-44) French novelist, pilot and journalist, author of *Night Flight* (1931), *Wind, Sand and Stars* (1939), *Flight to Arras* (1942) and other stories recounting the courage, idealism and experiences of the pioneers of aviation.

Saint-Saëns, Charles Camille (1835-1921) French composer of *Danse Macabre* (1874) and *Carnival of Animals* (1886) among other works.

Saint-Simon, Claude, Comte de (1760-1825) French socialist thinker, who advocated a type of meritocracy in which everyone is employed by the state according to his capacity and rewarded according to his contribution. In *New Christianity* (1825) he argued that society should strive to alleviate the lot of the poor, and should organize itself with that end in view.

Saint-Simon, Louis de Rouvroy, Duc de (1675-1755) French author and nobleman, whose outstanding *Mémoires* (written between 1728 and 1750, but published 1829-30) portray the French court during the last years of LOUIS XIV's reign. Saint-Simon's prejudiced and malicious eye makes them historically unreliable, but they are keenly observed pen-portraits of Louis's outwardly decorous court.

Sainte-Beuve, Charles-Augustin (1804-69) French poet, dramatist and critic who, after publishing several volumes of poems, devoted the rest of his career to literary criticism. His preliminary approach was biographical and his ability to dissect the life and character of a writer, combined with his shrewd, unerring aesthetic judgement, caused him to be acclaimed as one of the great masters of literary criticism.

Saki (1870-1916) Pen-name of Hector Hugh Munro, English short-story writer best known for sardonic, humorous tales of languid young wastrels doing the rounds of the high, fashionable life. Collections of his stories include *Reginald* (1904), *The Chronicles of Clovis* (1911) and *Beasts and Super-Beasts* (1914).

Saklatvala, Shapurji (1874-1936) The first Indian and the first Communist to become a British MP. He belonged to the Tata family, which founded the Tata iron and steel works in Bengal, and was MP for a London constituency from 1922 to 1923 and again from 1924 to 1929.

Salacrou, Armand (born 1899) French dramatist whose plays combine elements of tragedy, comedy and farce. His best-known works include *L'Inconnue d'Arras* (1935), *Un Homme comme les autres* (1936), *La Terre est ronde* (1938) and *L'Archipel Lenoir* (1948).

Saladin (1138-93) Muslim general, who put an end to the supremacy of Christian crusaders in Palestine. He was of Armenian Kurdish origin, and became vizier, then (1174) first Ayyubid sultan of Egypt. After resolving a Muslim religious schism, he organized the recapture of Syria and most of Palestine from the Christians, recovered all the kingdom of Jerusalem (founded by Godfrey of Bouillon and BALDWIN I) except Tyre, and forced RICHARD I to a stalemate in the Third Crusade (1189-92). The Christians admired him for his generous treatment of prisoners, allowing Christian pilgrims free access to Jerusalem and encouraging east-west trade.

Salazar, Antonio de Oliveira (1889-1970) Portuguese politician, who was for 36 years Prime Minister of Portugal. Following seizure of power by a military junta (1926), after a period of social, political and economic chaos, he was asked to serve as Minister of Finance. He agreed to do so, but resigned within a week because he was not guaranteed freedom of action. He reassumed the post in 1928, reorganized and stabilized the national finances, and in 1932 accepted the Premiership offered to him by President Carmona. His 'New State' and its authoritarian constitution was approved in 1933 by a national plebiscite. In the Second World War Portugal proclaimed a doctrine of neutrality, but, in 1943, an agreement was signed with Britain to give her naval facilities in the Azores to protect British shipping in the Atlantic. In 1965, Salazar announced the determination of Portugal to defend her colonial possessions despite the ambitions of African states to subvert or overthrow her rule over them.

Salinger, Jerome David (born 1919) American novelist, whose *Catcher in the Rye* (1951), the story of a teenager's weekend in 'phoney' New York, appealed to the youth of post-war America. After *Nine Stories* (1953), Salinger's novels and stories of the 1950s and 1960s have formed a continuous saga about the Glass family, the unusual, talented children of a couple who formed a Jewish-Irish stage act. *Franny and Zooey* (1961) and *Raise High the Roof-beam, Carpenters and Seymour* (1963) contain the bulk of the saga, in which Salinger writes of family relations in a middle-class home, and of childhood innocence perverted by the adult world.

Salisbury, Robert Arthur Talbot Gascoyne-Cecil, 3rd Marquess of (1830-1903) British statesman and Prime Minister. He succeeded to the leadership of the Conservative Party on the death of DISRAELI in 1881, and was three times Prime Minister; for all but a short period he was simultaneously Foreign Secretary. He was suspicious of democracy and opposed Parliamentary reform and Irish Home rule, and his later administrations were markedly imperialist in character. Though his influence in South Africa was weakened by the second Boer War (1899-1902), his handling of the Fashoda incident of 1898-9 ensured British domination of the Sudan and the Nile valley.

Salk, Jonas Edward (born 1914) American microbiologist, who developed a vaccine against poliomyelitis, which, in 1952, he successfully tested on children. By 1954 the vaccine was being produced in quantity. Subsequently, an alternative vaccine was developed which could be taken orally, and together the vaccines have considerably diminished the incidence of poliomyelitis.

Sallust (c. 86-34 BC) Roman historian who studied military strategy under Julius CAESAR and became proconsul in Numidia. He was an accurate historian whose *Conspiracy of Catalina* and *Jugurthine War* were critical examinations of the complex political situation in contemporary Rome.

Salza, Hermann von (c. 1170-1239) Grand Master of the German military order of the Teutonic Knights (1210-39), which became a powerful force for conquest and conversion of pagans to Christianity in northeast and eastern Europe. He sent the Knights into Hungary, Prussia and Poland and acquired considerable land for the order.

Sanchez, Florencio (1874-1910) Leading Uruguayan dramatist whose best-known play is *My Son the Doctor* (1903). As in all his work, the theme concerns the problems of reconciliation between rural traditions and urban society, and the relations between the old and the young generations.

Sancho III (970-1035) King of Navarre (1000-35), known as 'Sancho the Great', self-styled 'King of Spain'. From his small Basque kingdom at the western edge of the Pyrenees, he extended his rule across northern Spain, seizing rival Christian states in the process. Under his grandson, ALFONSO VI of Castile, Sancho's ideal of a Christianized Spain was fulfilled.

Sand, George (1804-76) French novelist and feminist whose early works were unashamedly romantic and sentimental – *Indiana* (1831), *Valentine* (1832), *Lelia* (1833). Later she turned her attention from love and marriage to problems of social justice, in works such as *Consuelo* (1843) and *Le Meunier d'Angibault* (1845). Sand also wrote a number of pastoral novels and her notorious liaisons with Alfred du MUSSET and CHOPIN inspired her other writings, *Elle et lui*, *Un hiver à Majorque*.

Lord Salisbury, Prime Minister and one of a family at the heart of British politics for 300 years

Sandburg, Carl (1878-1967) American poet, who wrote of rural and urban life in the Middle West, giving a radically different view of America to that presented by the dominant New England tradition. His *Chicago Poems* (1916) celebrated the diversity and energy of the city. His *Abraham Lincoln – The War Years* won the Pulitzer Prize (1939).

Sangallo, Antonio da (1483-1546) Italian architect, who played a significant part in the High Renaissance in Rome. He was a member of an important family of Florentine artists (one uncle, Antonio (1455-1534), designed S Biagio, Montepulciano, while another uncle, Giuliano (1445-1516), was a follower of BRUNELLESCHI). The younger Antonio's best-known work is the Palazzo Farnese, the most monumental of the Renaissance palaces in Rome.

Sán Martín, José de (1778-1850) Argentinian revolutionary who liberated Chile and Peru from Spanish rule. After helping the newly-formed Argentinian government in its War of Independence (1812-13), he was given command of the revolutionary armies operating against Spanish rule in Peru in 1814. Considering it most feasible to strike at Peru through Chile, he made an astonishing march over the Andes and defeated the Spanish army at Chacabuco, in February 1817. With the help of the former British admiral, Lord COCHRANE, he afterwards formed a fleet and reorganized his army, sailing for Peru in August 1820. After six months of fruitless negotiation with the Spaniards, he entered Lima in July 1821 and accepted the title of Protector. In

1822, the rivalry of BOLÍVAR and local suspicion of Sán Martín's intentions led him to resign his command and leave for Europe, where he died in poverty in 1850.

Sannazaro, Jacopo (c. 1458-1530) Italian poet, who established the pastoral romance as a literary form. His *Arcadia* (1504), set the pattern for the genre in the 16th and 17th centuries.

Sansovino, Andrea (c. 1460-1529) Italian sculptor and architect whose *Virgin and Child* (1503-4) reveals a deep understanding of classical sculpture and a break from the artistic conceptions of the late 14th century.

Sansovino, Jacopo Tatti (1486-1570) Florentine sculptor who took the name of his master Andrea SANSOVINO. Early in the 16th century he joined BRAMANTE in Rome until its sack, and then in 1527 fled to Venice. Sansovino was responsible for several buildings in Venice, notably the Library of St Mark, the pediment of which is surmounted by many of his statues. The Scala de' Giganti contains his largest and best works, *Mars* and *Neptune*.

Santa Anna, Antonio Lopez de (1795-1876) Mexican soldier, politician and revolutionary, five times President of Mexico. Before he became President for the first time in 1833, Santa Anna led revolutions which deposed three presidents. Once in office, his harsh rule led to a revolt in Texas, where he was defeated and captured (1836). He was President briefly in 1839, and was either President himself or controlled the President from 1841 to 1847. After being appointed President for the fifth and final time in 1853 after an army revolt, he became a dictator, subordinating all branches of government to his will, but eventually, in 1855 he was exiled.

Santos-Dumont, Alberto (1873-1932) Brazilian aeronautical engineer who pioneered dirigible and aeroplane design. In 1901, Santos-Dumont won several prizes for piloting an airship from St Cloud to the Eiffel Tower and back.

Sapir, Edward (1884-1939) American anthropologist and linguistics scholar, whose intensive studies of American-Indian tribes showed that their 75 recognized languages belong to six main families.

Sappho (c. 7th cent. BC) Poet of Ancient Greece, a few of whose poems survive. She was the dominating figure in a group of girls bound by her forceful personality and their shared emotional sensibilities and devotion to poetry.

Saragat, Giuseppe (born 1898) Italian politician and journalist, the first socialist to become President of Italy. During MUSSOLINI's régime, he lived in exile, but returned to Italy in 1943 and in the following year became a minister in Bonomi's government. He was Ambassador to France 1946-7. Co-operation between the Socialist Party's leader, NENNI, and the Italian Communist Party under TOGLIATTI, caused Saragat to break with his leader and set up the Social Democratic Party which he led thereafter. He was Minister of Foreign Affairs (1963-4) and President from 1964-71.

Sardou, Victorien (1831-1908) French dramatist, who wrote plays for Sarah BERNHARDT, including *Dora* (1877), *Fedora* (1882), *La Tosca* (1887) (which became the basis for PUCCINI's opera), *Theodora*, *Cléopatre* (1890) and *La Sorcière* (1903). He also wrote some successful comedies and the famous historical drama *Madame Sans — Gêne* (1893). SHAW dismissed his work as 'Sardoodledom'.

Sargent, Charles Sprague (1844-1927) American botanist who was the first director of the Arnold Arboretum, Boston, Mass., where he built up a fine tree collection based upon his own travels within North America and those of professionals employed by him to collect specimens from the Far East. The cherry, *Prunus Sargentii*, commemorates him.

Sargent, John Singer (1856-1925) American portrait painter, who worked mostly in London. He was both fashionable and successful.

Sargeson, Frank (born 1903) New Zealand novelist, whose fiction is based on the local qualities of New Zealand life. The novels *I Saw in My Dream* (1949) and *I, for One* (1954) develop Sargeson's criticism of bourgeois values.

Sartre, Jean-Paul (born 1905) French philosopher, novelist and dramatist, leader of the Existentialist movement, who maintained that the existence of man had no predetermined purpose or 'essence', that man must assume responsibility for his own destiny and so create a meaning for his existence. Sartre's theories were first propounded in the semi-autobiographical novel *La Nausée* (1938). He also published a collection of stories, *Le Mur* (1939), and a further sequence of novels under the general title *Les Chemins de la Liberté* (1945-9). He is the author of a number of philosophical essays, including *L'Etre et le Néant* (1943) and *L'Existence est un Humanisme* (1947). Sartre is also a very talented dramatist, and

as well as diffusing his theories, plays such as *Les Mouches* (1942), *Huis Clos* (1944), *La Putain respectueuse* (1946) and *Le Diable et le Bon Dieu* (1951) testify to the author's theatrical skill.

Sassetta, (c. 1400-1450) Sienese artist, who produced religious paintings in a Gothic style imbued with a mystic quality. A fine example of his work was the altarpiece for S Francesco, Sansepolcro (1437-44, now dismantled). Sassetta was the pseudonym of Stefano di Giovanni.

Sassoon, Siegfried (1886-1967) English poet and memoir writer, whose *Counterattack* (1918) is a bitter, satirical attack on those who prolonged the horrors of the First World War. The reminiscent *Memoirs of a Fox-hunting Man* (1928) and *Memoirs of an Infantry Officer* (1930) are accounts of social change, of the passing of a settled and privileged world into the realities of war.

Satie, Erik (1866-1925) French composer of piano pieces and one of music's eccentric prophets. As an integral part of the French *avant-garde* at the turn of the century, Satie sought to deflate both post-Wagnerian romanticism and the French musical establishment and wrote the score for COCTEAU's ballet *Parade* (1917).

Saul (11th-10th cent. BC) First king of Israel. The Israelites, threatened by the Philistines' iron weapons (their own were still of bronze), abandoned their system of government by separate tribal leaders, became united, and elected Saul as their sole leader after he had raised the seige of Jabesh.

Saussure, Horace Benedict de (1740-90) Swiss scientist, noted for his Alpine studies, who introduced the general use of the word 'geology'. He made major contributions to a wide range of studies, including botany, geology and meteorology, and devised a number of new scientific instruments.

Savonarola, Girolamo (1452-98) Italian Dominican friar and orator, who advocated the reform of the Roman Catholic Church. He was prior of St Mark's, Florence, from 1491, and in fiery sermons he condemned corruption in Church and State, claimed prophetic inspiration, and predicted that divine punishment would be visited on Italy and its immoral pope, Alexander VI. Savonarola became the leader of Florence's democratic faction, and after the death of Lorenzo de Medici, seized control of Florence from his successor, Pietro (1494), and tried to establish a Christian state based on the renunciation of worldly enjoyments. As a result, Alexander excommunicated him in 1497. Eventually he was captured by the aristocratic faction, tortured, tried for sedition and heresy, and then executed.

Sax, Adolphe (1814-94) Belgian instrument maker who invented the saxophone family of hybrid instruments, and also their brass cousins, the saxhorns.

Saxton, Christopher (c. 1542-c. 1606) English cartographer who made and recorded the earliest topographical survey of Britain.

Say, Jean Baptiste (1767-1832) French economist and businessman who stated by his 'law of markets' that supply creates its own demand. Say regarded slumps as temporary imbalances between production and consumption. He also distinguished the functions of the creative entrepreneur from those of the capitalist.

Scanderbeg (c. 1403-68) National hero of Albania, leader of an unsuccessful fight for Albania's independence from the Ottoman Turks. He acted as a provincial governor for the Turks, but an Albanian revolt (1443) inspired him to become a Christian and try to unite the Albanian clans against the Turks. After some successes he was deserted by his Christian allies and defeated.

Scarlatti, Alessandro (1659-1725) Italian musician, whose works were a major influence on the development of opera. He is credited with the invention of the *aria da capo*.

Scarlatti, Domenico (1685-1757) Italian harpsichord virtuoso and composer who wrote approximately 600 one-movement harpsichord sonatas containing some of the richest music in the instrument's repertoire, at the same time contributing to the basis of future keyboard composition and the concept of the sonata form.

Schacht, Hjalmar Horace Greely (1877-1970) German economics minister, whose policies financed Germany's rearmament under HITLER. Appointed Germany's Minister of Economics in 1934, he restored the German economy by a policy including expropriation of Jewish property, and forcing smaller countries into credit deals that were advantageous to Germany. He was dismissed by Hitler in 1939, because his policies were 'too orthodox', and later his increasing disapproval of the excesses of the Nazi régime led to his imprisonment after the failure of STAUFFENBERG's plot.

Scharnhorst, Gerhard Johann von (1755-1813) Prussian soldier, who remodelled the Prussian army. He fought in the 1806-7 campaign against NAPOLEON, during the War of the Third Coalition, and following the peace of Tilsit was given the task of organizing and training the small Prussian army. He improved the standing of the private soldier and officers' treatment of other ranks, introduced short-service enlistment and so recruited large numbers of men, and modernized drill and manoeuvres.

Schaudinn, Fritz (1871-1906) German zoologist who discovered *Spirochaeta pallida*, the organism responsible for syphilis. He also showed that tropical dysentery is caused by an amoeba-like organism (*Entamoeba histolytica*).

Scheele, Karl Wilhelm (1742-86) Swedish chemist who discovered oxygen (1771) and chlorine. Unfortunately for Scheele, his discovery was not published until 1777, by which time Joseph PRIESTLEY had also prepared the gas, later to be called oxygen, and is generally credited with the discovery. In 1774, the same year in which Priestley was experimenting with oxygen, Scheele discovered chlorine.

Schiaparelli, Giovanni Virginio (1835-1910) Italian astronomer renowned as an expert planetary observer, who discovered the association between comets and meteors.

Schinkel, Karl Friedrich (1781-1841) German architect whose public buildings in Prussia, while severely Grecian in style, are original. Many of Schinkel's works are in Berlin and include the New Guard House, The Theatre, the Old Museum and also the Werdersche Kirche, which is in the Gothic style.

Schlegel, August Wilhelm (1767-1845) German poet, critic and scholar who, with NOVALIS, TIECK, Schelling and his brother Friedrich, laid the foundations of German Romanticism with *A Course of Lectures on Dramatic Art and Literature* (1809). He is chiefly known today for his translations with Tieck of SHAKESPEARE's plays, which are still in use.

Schleirmacher, Friedrich Daniel Ernst (1768-1834) Influential German Protestant theologian and philosopher, who saw religion as the expression of a dependence on something beyond the everyday world, independent of morality or knowledge. He led the movement which led to the union of the Prussian Lutheran and Reform Churches.

Schlick, Moritz (1882-1936) German logical positivist philosopher who held that the communicable element in experience was structure rather than content. His ethics were broadly utilitarian and he held that moral concepts were reducible to emotional attitudes.

Schliemann, Heinrich (1822-90) German archaeologist whose spectacular excavations at Mycenae and Troy, begun in 1870, dramatically confirmed HOMER's account of life in Mycenean times and helped to inspire Sir Arthur EVANS's discoveries in Crete.

Schnitzler, Arthur (1862-1931) Austrian dramatist, whose *Reiger* (1902) became internationally famous as a film, *La Ronde*. All his dramas combine an easy elegance of manner with tough cynicism. Of his other plays, two are worth noting: *Anatol* (1893), a study of the life of a man of fashion, and *Liebelei* (1895), which concerns a poor girl's hopeless love for a cold-hearted aristocrat.

Schoenberg, Arnold (1874-1951) Austrian composer who evolved the 'note-row', the most radical innovation in 20th-century music. Schoenberg won the early support of Richard STRAUSS and MAHLER as an exponent of 'post-Romantic music' – breaking new ground, while still influenced by WAGNER. By 1908 he had moved towards atonality, his song-cycle *Pierrot Lunaire* (1912) on 21 poems by GIRAUD being generally acknowledged as a cornerstone of modern music. By the early 1920s he was writing in his 12-note style – a method for imposing order on the anarchy of atonalism which he used thereafter with variable consistency. Schoenberg's other works include the impressive, though unfinished, opera *Moses and Aaron* (1957) and the moving cantata *A Survivor from Warsaw* (1947) on the Nazi persecution of the Jews, as well as concertos and many chamber works. Having been declared a 'degenerate' composer, Schoenberg was driven out of Nazi Germany and emigrated to America, where he took citizenship.

Schönbein, Christian (1799-1868) German chemist who invented gun cotton (cellulose nitrate, a powerful but unpredictable explosive). Gun cotton was used in fire-arms until banned as being too dangerous. Schönbein also made a bowl from the same material, an early form of plastic.

Schopenhauer, Arthur (1788-1860) German philosopher, the founder of the modern system of thought known as pessimism. An invective critic of all branches of philosophy since SOCRATES, his major contribution to philosophy was his study of the will, as expounded in *The World as Will and Idea* (1819).

Schreiner, Olive (1855-1920)
South African novelist, who won literary fame with *The Story of an African Farm* (1883), a study of Boer life, which preached the emancipation of women.

Schrödinger, Erwin (1887-1961)
Austrian physicist who shared the 1933 Nobel Prize for Physics with DIRAC for his development of wave mechanics. This is one of the versions of modern quantum theory, based on earlier suggestions of DE BROGLIE.

Schubert, Franz Peter (1797-1828) Austrian composer who displayed a profound melodic gift and did more than any other composer to establish the German *lieder* ('songs') tradition. Schubert showed an early maturity, his first acknowledged masterpiece being a song he wrote at the age of 17. Before his early death from typhus at 31, he had written over 600 songs which explored the medium's possibilities from light lyrics to the major song-cycle of 24 poems on unrequited love, *The Winter Journey* (1827). His enormous output also included 15 string quartets, including that in D minor nicknamed *Death and the Maiden*; 21 piano sonatas and the quintet known as *The Trout*. The apparently fluent ease with which he composed in no way detracts from his standing, for as BRAHMS said, 'There is not a song of Schubert's from which one cannot learn something.' Schubert's works are now often referred to by their Deutsch (or 'D') numbers, named after the Austrian musicologist Otto Erich Deutsch, who compiled the complete catalogue (1951).

Schumacher, Kurt Ernst Karl (1895-1952) German politician, an opponent both of HITLER and German participation in NATO. As a Reichstag deputy from 1930 to 1933, he was an outspoken critic of Hitler, and over a period of 10 years, was imprisoned in various concentration camps. After the war, he became Chairman of the reconstituted Social Democratic Party, which under his leadership adopted a policy of strenuous opposition to German's rearmament and to membership of NATO and the European Defence Community.

Schuman, Robert (1886-1963) Premier of France (1947-8), Foreign Minister (1948-52) and originator of the Schuman Plan (1950). This defined a policy for pooling West European coal and steel resources, and eventually took shape as the European Coal and Steel Community. From this, all subsequent progress towards European integration, including the European Economic Community, has developed. Schuman's plan was to remove national barriers to the flow of raw materials for steel products, to eliminate cartels and monopolies and to reduce the commanding power of specific national areas like the Ruhr.

Schumann, Robert (1810-56)
Composer, among the leaders of Romanticism in German music. A contemporary of CHOPIN and MENDELSSOHN, Schumann set out to become a piano virtuoso, but after injuring his hand turned to composition. Among his best-known piano pieces are *Papillons* (1829-31), *Carnival* (1834-5) and *Scenes from Childhood* (1838); his contributions to the concert repertoire include a piano concerto, a cello concerto and four symphonies (the Third sub-titled *The Rhenish*), and he also wrote three string quartets. His wife, Clara Schumann, was a fine pianist and a composer of songs and piano pieces. In 1854, Schumann's mind gave way and he tried to drown himself in the Rhine. His last two years were spent in an asylum. Clara devoted the rest of her life to performing and promoting her late husband's music.

Schuschnigg, Kurt von (born 1897) Austrian Chancellor (1934-8) during one of the most tense periods in Austrian history. Nazi efforts to prevent Austria gaining independence was growing both within and outside the state, and in February 1938 Schuschnigg was forced to accept SEYSS-INQUART, the Nazi's agent, as Minister of the Interior. With Nazi-inspired unrest increasing, Schuschnigg announced in March 1938 his intention of holding a plebiscite on the question of Austrian independence. On 11 March HITLER assembled troops on the border, the invasion of Austria began, and the next day Schuschnigg was imprisoned. Seyss-Inquart, who replaced him, proclaimed the *Anschluss* – the annexation of Austria by Germany. Schuschnigg was released by American troops in 1945, and from 1948-68 he was Professor of Political Science at St Louis University, USA.

Schütz, Heinrich (1585-1672) German composer who wrote *Daphne*, the first German opera (the music is now lost), and the earliest German oratorios, including *The Seven Last Words from the Cross*. Schütz studied with GABRIELI in Venice and his music represents a synthesis of the High Renaissance Italian and the German styles of composition. His church music anticipates the Baroque style of the 18th century and the music of J. S. BACH. From 1615 until his death, Schütz was Kapellmeister at Dresden.

Schwann, Theodor (1810-82) German physiologist who was one of the founders of the cell theory of biology according to which all living organisms are made up of cells.

Schweitzer, Albert (1875-1965) German Lutheran theologian, philosopher, musician and missionary doctor at Lambarene in French Equatorial Africa, where he built his own hospital and gave free treatment to the native population. He was awarded a Nobel Peace Prize in 1954.

Schwitters, Kurt (1887-1948) German painter, now recognized as a leading pioneer of a major development in 20th-century art – the move away from traditional materials.

Scipio, Publius Cornelius (237-183 BC) Roman general, whose defeat of Carthage in the Second Punic War gave Rome mastery of the western Mediterranean. After reversing earlier Roman setbacks in Spain, he drove the Carthaginians out of Spain (206 BC). He invaded Carthaginian North Africa and forced HANNIBAL to abandon the invasion of Italy and defend his homeland. At the decisive battle of Zama (202 BC), which he won, Scipio abandoned the deep Roman battle phalanx and adopted Hannibal's formation of a front line concealing mobile groups.

Scopas of Paros (4th cent. BC) Greek sculptor, who assisted in the reconstruction of the Temple of Athena at Teges and in the Mausoleum of Helicarnassus (*c.* 350 BC) with Bryaxis, Leochares and Timotheus. The remains of several works from this period can be attributed to Scopas on stylistic grounds, including part of the freize from the Mausoleum depicting the Battle of the Greeks and Amazons, a marble statue of Meleager.

Scott, Charles Prestwich (1846-1932) English editor, who transformed the *Manchester Guardian* into a national paper of world-wide reputation.

Scott, Sir George Gilbert (1811-78) English architect who led the English Gothic revival. Scott produced a great number of dramatic and inspired buildings – notably the red-brick Venetian-Gothic hotel for St Pancras Station, London, and the richly ornamented Albert Memorial, Kensington. He was also an active

A parable inspired Albert Schweitzer to devote his life to helping the sick

restorer of Gothic buildings and was associated with the restoration of Westminster Abbey.

Scott, Robert Falcon (1868-1912)
English Antarctic explorer, leader of an ill-fated expedition to the South Pole. A naval officer, Scott had led an Antarctic expedition (1900-4) in the specially-built ship *Discovery*. He organized his own Antarctic expedition in the *Terra Nova* (1911), and, with Edward Wilson, Edgar Evans, Lawrence Oates and H. R. Bowers, set out on the expedition's final stage, intending to become the first man to reach the South Pole. Taking only one sledge of supplies, they trekked 950 miles in two and a half months to meet bitter disappointment when, on 18 Jan. 1912, they reached the South Pole and found AMUNDSEN's flag already there. Suffering from scurvy, frostbite and hunger and hampered by soft snow and unseasonable blizzards, Scott's party embarked on a grim two-month return journey that ended when the survivors Scott, Wilson and Bowers died, blizzard-bound, in their tent.

Scott, Sir Walter (1771-1832)
Scottish Romantic poet and novelist, who, in such works as *Ivanhoe* (1819) and *Kenilworth* (1821), created a strong tradition of the historical novel. Scott was pre-eminent as a story teller. In *Waverley* (1814), *Old Mortality* (1816), *Rob Roy* (1817) and others, he created vivid stories set in detailed Scottish landscapes. His wide range of literary activities, which included contributions to the *Edinburgh Review* and the first number of the *Quarterly Review*, began with translations of German Romantic works and developed through his own collections of Scottish folk-songs and ballads. His first major original

work was a verse romance, *The Lay of the Last Minstrel* (1805). Scott was imbued with the traditions of an enlightened aristocracy, and bought an estate at Abbotsford. Extensive borrowing and poor business partners led to financial ruin and Scott spent his last years working prodigiously and successfully to pay off the £130,000 he owed.

Scriabin, Alexander (1872-1915)
Russian composer and pianist. He is known today chiefly for two of his orchestral works: the sensuous *Poem of Ecstasy* (1908) and *Prometheus* (*Poem of Fire*) (1911). Scriabin evolved the 'mystic chord' of ascending fourths to express his personal mystical and occult beliefs.

Ivanhoe, most famous of Scott's novels, was a colourful tale of knight-errantry, tourneys and jousts

Scribner, Charles (1821-71)
American publisher who in 1846 founded the company of Baker and Scribner, with Isaac D. Baker, and incorporated his own company, Charles Scribner's Sons, in 1878. He published theological and philosophical works, founded the periodical *Scribner's Monthly* (later *Scribner's Magazine*) in 1870, and the company has published, among other authors, Henry JAMES, Theodore ROOSEVELT, Robert Louis STEVENSON and John GALSWORTHY.

Scripps, Edward (1854-1926)
American journalist who founded the first United States newspaper chain. His *Cleveland Penny Post* (founded 1878) became the first of 34 newspapers which he bought or founded in 15 states. All were popular, prolabour newspapers in medium-size cities.

Scudéry, Madeleine de (Sapho) (1607-1701) French Romantic novelist, author of *Artamène ou le Grand Cyrus* (1649-60) and *Clélie, histoire romaine* (1654-61). These diffuse, sentimental tales of ardent love and selfless devotion enjoyed great popularity.

Searle, Ronald (born 1920) English humorous artist and illustrator, who created the St Trinians' series of diabolical schoolgirls. He is a prolific artist and in addition to many drawings for the press has produced book illustrations, advertisements and film credit titles.

Sears, Richard Warren (1863-1914) American businessman and pioneer of mail-order shopping. For many turn-of-the-century American settlers, the Sears catalogue was the only bridge to the tools, fashions, machines and medicines of the industrial East. Sears, Roebuck & Co. moved to Chicago in 1893 and rapidly became the world's largest mail-order store.

Sedgwick, Adam (1785-1873)
British geologist, who unravelled the strata of succession of Cambrian rocks in Wales. He was the first man to recognize the outstanding ability of the young Charles DARWIN.

Sefiris, George (1900-71) Greek poet, translator, literary critic and diplomat whose symbolic work is seen at its best in the two collections *Turning Point* (1931) and *The Cistern* (1932).

Segovia, Andres (born 1893)
Spanish guitarist responsible for the revival of the classical guitar in this century. FALLA and other composers have written for him and such soloists

as Julian Bream and John Williams have followed his example.

Sei Shohnagon (11th cent.) Japanese lady-in-waiting at the court of the Empress Sadako, who recorded her experiences and comments on court life and courtiers in the brilliantly malicious and witty diary, *Pillow Book*.

Sekou-Touré, Ahmed (born 1922) African nationalist and Marxist politician, who became first President of the Republic of Guinea when independence was declared in 1958. He has been re-elected President at every election since.

Selden, John (1584-1654) English law historian. He had a deep understanding of many legal systems, including the Jewish, Roman and English. His *History of Tithes* (1618) angered the Church by its denial that this form of clerical taxation was divinely ordained.

Seleucus I (c. 358-280 BC) Macedonian founder of the Seleucid dynasty of southwestern Asia (312 BC-65 BC). He was one of ALEXANDER THE GREAT's generals and fought for the dead king's newly-won empire, eventually emerging as its ruler except for northwest India – which he sold to CHANDRAGUPTA for 500 elephants – and Egypt, which was captured by PTOLEMY I, whose son Ptolemy Ceraunus murdered Seleucus.

Selfridge, Harry Gordon (c. 1857-1947) American-born merchant and businessman who introduced the large department store to Britain. After a successful career with Marshall FIELD & Co. of Chicago, Selfridge took his innovative marketing ideas to London and established (1909) the famous Oxford Street store that bears his name.

Selim I (1467-1520) Sultan of Turkey (1512-20), who almost doubled the extent of the Ottoman Empire founded by Osman I and Orkham. Embarking on ruthless and bloodthirsty campaigns, he invaded Persia (1514), seized Azerbaijan and Kurdistan, and then defeated Mameluke forces (1516-17), adding Syria and Egypt to the empire, which reached its apogee under his son SULEIMAN I.

Semënov, Nikolai Nikolaevich (born 1896) Russian chemist who established the importance of chemical chain reactions. Semenov showed that even the simplest chemical reactions rely on a chain of reactions between individual atoms.

Semple, Ellen Churchill (1863-1912) American geographer, instrumental in establishing the reputation of the Graduate School of Geography at Clark University. Regarded as one of the chief exponents of theories of 'Geographical Determinism' (a school strongly influenced by Darwinism), her studies and books sought to explain human behaviour, character, even religion as determined by the influence of location, climate and national resources.

Seneca, Lucius (c. 54 BC-c. AD 39) Roman rhetorician, father of Seneca the Younger. A connoisseur of the art of rhetoric, Seneca drew up an anthology of rhetorical practice for his three sons: extracts from famous rhetoricians with his own pithy observations. In this work is found all that is known of Roman rhetoric in the reigns of AUGUSTUS and TIBERIUS.

Senefelder, Alois (1771-1834) Austro-Czech inventor of lithography, in which the subject matter to be printed remains effectively on the plate surface. This technique relies on the incompatibility of water and grease, so that ink from a grease base is deposited on the grease-treated printing regions and is rejected by the damp non-printing areas.

Sennacherib (705-681 BC) King of the Assyrian Empire, who waged war against the Babylonian Empire and razed its capital, Babylon, in 689 BC. Sennacherib used armies of enslaved captives to build a palace for himself at Nineveh.

Senoa, August (1838-81) Croatian poet, novelist and critic, who combines individual drama with realistic detail and social-reformative themes. In the *Jeweller's Daughter* the story is set against a realistic background of social conflict.

Sequoya (c. 1770-1843) American Indian who invented a writing system. Completed in 1821, it became a basis for Cherokee literacy, making possible the first American Indian press in North America. Sequoya's cultural achievements are commemorated in the names of the Sequoia tree and Sequoia National Park.

Serlio, Sebastiano (1475-1554) Italian architect best known for his practical and widely read handbook *L'Architettura*, which, among other things, defined the five orders of the classical column, with base and capital. Serlio worked first in Rome under PERUZZI, then in Venice and finally in France.

Serrão, Francisco (c. 1480-c. 1519) Portuguese adventurer who was shipwrecked in the East Indies and became the first European to settle there. His enthusiastic letters about the islands partly inspired the voyage of his friend MAGELLAN.

Service, Robert (1874-1958) English-born Canadian poet, who was well known for his vigorous ballads of deeds of Canadian frontiersmen, prospectors and wanderers. The Klondike gold rush provided the material for *Songs of a Sourdough* (1907) and the novel *Trail of '98* (1910).

Sesshu Ota (1419-1506) Japanese Zen priest generally considered to be Japan's greatest landscape painter. His Indian ink landscapes of China are more powerful and convincing than those of his contemporaries, partly due to his first-hand knowledge of the scenery gained during a visit to China (1468-9).

Sessions, Roger (born 1896) American composer and symphonist who studied with BLOCH. His five symphonies are complex, dense constructions, based on tonality but 'modern' in effect. Other works by Sessions include a violin concerto, string quartets and piano sonatas.

Seurat, Georges (1859-91) French artist famous for his 'pointillist' technique – that of using minute touches of pure colour to put the Impressionists' instinctive response to light on to a scientific basis. Seurat developed his unique style through studying various scientific and art-theoretical texts. It is to be seen at its most effective in his *Sunday Afternoon at the Island of the Grande Jatte* (1886) and in the coastal landscapes painted around Le Havre.

Sévigné, Marie de Rabutin-Chantal, Marquise de (1626-96) French socialite and friend of LOUIS XIV, whose *Lettres*, written mainly to her daughter, Comtesse de Grignan,

Two examples of Serlio's work can be seen today. One is at Fontainebleu

were published posthumously from 1725 onwards. Invaluable as socio-historical documents, recounting the news and gossip of the day, the letters are written in a warm, spontaneous style, witty and yet full of compassion.

Seyss-Inquart, Artur von (1892-1946) HITLER's agent in Austria, who helped to bring about the merging of Austria with Germany – the *Anschluss*. Seyss-Inquart was a member of the Austrian Nazi Party, and Hitler forced SCHUSCHNIGG, the Austrian Chancellor, to accept him as Minister of the Interior in 1938. By informing Hitler of all Schuschnigg's moves, Seyss-Inquart was instrumental in preparing the way for the *Anschluss* in March 1938. He was, successively, Governor of Austria and Deputy Governor of Poland and, later, German High Commissioner of the Occupied Netherlands (1940-5), where he was responsible for the deaths of hundreds of Jews and Resistance workers. He was hanged as a war criminal in October 1946.

Sforza, Francesco (1401-66) Italian *condottiere* (leader of mercenaries), whose powerful family ruled Milan in the 15th and 16th centuries. His rule began a period of 50 years' unparalleled peace and prosperity in Milan.

Shackleton, Sir Ernest Henry (1874-1922) English explorer, the first to attempt to cross Antarctica. After serving with SCOTT's *Discovery* expedition (1901-4), Shackleton led the *Nimrod* expedition (1907-9), which reached a point 97 miles from the South Pole. His attempt to cross Antarctica (1914-17) failed when his ship *Endurance* was crushed by ice, but he escaped, travelling 800 miles in an open boat with five companions, and eventually rescued the remainder of the crew.

Shadwell, Thomas (c. 1642-92) English dramatist whose first success was the comedy *The Sullen Lovers* (1688). He succeeded DRYDEN, with whom he was involved in a protracted politico-literary quarrel, as Poet Laureate.

Shafi, Mohammed ibn Idris al-(727-820) Arab thinker and founder of the Shafite one of four Islamic schools of law which evolved in the 8th century. Each took a slightly different view of the *Shari'a*, the sacred law.

Shaftesbury, Anthony Ashley Cooper, 7th Earl of (1801-85) English philanthropist who, as an MP, sponsored a series of factory acts to improve working conditions in 19th-century Britain.

Shakespeare, William (1564-1616) English dramatist and poet, who created the finest plays and the richest poetic and dramatic language in English literature. His plays fall into three categories: histories, comedies and tragedies. The histories form two distinct cycles, although not written consecutively. The first, the three parts of *Henry VI* and *Richard III* (1589-93), contains some of Shakespeare's earlier work and traces a sequence through the events of the War of the Roses, establishing the Tudor view of Henry Tudor's claim to the throne. The second is based upon the life of HENRY V, from his youth, in the two parts of *Henry IV* (1597-8) to his victories in France in *Henry V* (1599). The early comedies are satirical and farcical, full of verbal humour, and their central theme is the trials and joys of love, which is pursued more subtly, with greater depth of character, in such later plays as *Twelfth Night* (*c.* 1600) and *As You Like It* (*c.* 1600). The major tragedies, *Hamlet* (*c.* 1600), *Othello* (*c.* 1604), *King Lear* (*c.* 1605), *Macbeth* (*c.* 1605) and *Antony and Cleopatra* (1607) are unequalled in western literature. Their heroes are strongly individual, separate from the common run of men, with ambitions and hopes, incompatible with the circumstances around them, which end in grief. *Antony and Cleopatra* also forms part of the group of Roman plays, with *Julius Caesar* (*c.* 1599) and *Coriolanus* (*c.* 1609). Shakespeare's final plays were written for the aristocratic audience of the Blackfriars theatre, more sophisticated than the general public of the Globe. His poems include the long narratives 'Venus and Adonis' (1593) and the 'Rape of Lucrece' (1594) and the well-known sequence of sonnets. Shakespeare was a successful and immensely

'A Midsommer night's dreame as it hath been sundry times publickly acted'

popular dramatist and actor in his own lifetime.

Shankara (c. 788-820) Indian philosopher and founder of the Advaita Vedanta school of philosophy, which still exercises the most profound influence on Hindu thought. The chief exponent of orthodox Hindu teaching, Shankara wrote profound and subtle commentaries on the *Upanishads*, the *Bhagavad Gita* and the *Brahma Sutra*.

Shapley, Harlow (1885-1972) American astronomer, who determined the size of the Galaxy and the Sun's position in it, and did much to popularize astronomy.

Sharp, Cecil James (1859-1924) British musician who saved the English folk-music tradition from oblivion. His life's work was the collection of over 5000 songs of the English aural tradition and he made field trips to the Appalachian Mountains in America (1916-18) to collect the English songs preserved among settlers' descendants in isolated valleys. Sharp founded the English Folk Dance Society in 1911.

Shastri, Shri Lal Bahadur (1904-66) Indian statesman and Prime Minister. Influenced as a young man by GHANDI, his civil disobedience and militancy cost him a total of nine years' imprisonment. He was a leading member of the United Provinces (later Uttar Pradesh) Assembly from 1937, and succeeded NEHRU as General Secretary of the Indian National Congress. He became Minister of Transport and Railways in 1952, resigning in 1956 following a railway accident for which he felt compelled to take responsibility. He returned to his Ministry a year later, was Minister of Commerce and Industry in 1958, of Home Affairs in 1961, and Prime Minister from 1964 until his death.

A Midsommer nights dreame.

As it hath beene sundry times publikely acted, by the Right Honourable, the Lord Chamberlaine his seruants.

Written by William Shakespeare.

Printed by Iames Roberts, 1600.

George Bernard Shaw, with members of the cast of one of his plays. A lifelong socialist, Shaw used his work to express his views on the society around him

Shaw, George Bernard (1856-1950) Irish dramatist, journalist and novelist, who was one of the leaders of a realist movement in the English theatre of the early 20th century. Throughout his career Shaw used his work to propound his views on society. In his lesser plays the dramatic quality suffers from over-insistent ideology. His first works, novels, were unsuccessful, but he achieved some renown as a drama and music critic, advocating the works of MARX, WAGNER and IBSEN, and as a socialist orator. His first play, *Widowers' Houses* (1892), on the state of slum dwellings, had only two performances, being thought too radical for the commercial theatre, but such later works as *Arms and the Man* (1894), *Candida* (1895) and *The Devil's Disciple* (1900) gained popularity. In *Man and Superman* (1903), a well-written comedy, Shaw put forward his theory of a Life Force as the energetic impulse of man's progress. His greatest success was *Pygmalion* (1913) from which was made the musical and film *My Fair Lady*. *St Joan* (1923) is also frequently revived. *Heartbreak House*, written in the manner of CHEKHOV, is one of Shaw's most accomplished works.

Shaw, Percy (born 1890) British inventor (1934) of cat's-eyes, reflectors marking lane divisions on roads. They became established during the blackout of the Second World War, as they were the only markers which reflected light in the direction from which it came.

Shaw, Richard Norman (1831-1912) English architect who designed New Scotland Yard, London. He raised the standard of taste in Victorian architecture by abandoning the over-ornamented style of many architects, and adopting simpler lines.

Shays, Daniel (c. 1747-1825) American soldier. In the depression following the American War of Independence, he led impoverished farmers protesting against their threatened imprisonment for debt. At Springfield, Massachusetts, they clashed with the state militia (1786). These clashes, known as Shays' Rebellion, persisted until his defeat (1787).

Sheldon, William (born 1899) American psychologist who specializes in the study of the relationship between bodily constitution and psychological case history. His work refers especially to incidences of mental illness, delinquency and high achievement.

Shelley, Mary Wollstonecraft (1797-1851) English novelist, wife of Percy Bysshe SHELLEY, who wrote, on BYRON's suggestion, *Frankenstein* (1818), a horror story which combined a Gothic atmosphere with plausible logic.

Shelley, Percy Bysshe (1792-1822) 'Poets are the unacknowledged legislators of the world,' claimed Shelley, the wildest, most ardent and most unconventional of the younger generation of English Romantic poets. After a revolutionary career at Oxford, he eloped with Mary Godwin and travelled abroad with BYRON. His longer poems, such as 'Prometheus Unbound' (1820), 'Epipsychidion' (1821) and 'Adonais' (1821), rely on grandiose symbolism for their visionary quality and unearthly atmosphere. Like Byron and KEATS, he died abroad, drowned in a storm at Spezzia.

Sheridan, Richard Brinsley (1751-1816) Anglo-Irish dramatist and theatre manager, whose career began with three simultaneous successes in 1775: *The Rivals*, *St Patrick's Day*, and a musical play, *The Duenna*. Among his other plays were *The School for Scandal* (1777), *The Critic* (1779) and *Pizarro* (1799). He became the Manager of Drury Lane Theatre (1776), rebuilt it (1794) and was financially ruined when it was burnt down (1809). After entering politics as a Whig MP (1780), he held office and took a prominent part in the impeachment of Warren HASTINGS.

Sherman, William Tecumseh (1820-91) US Civil War Unionist general. His famous offensive march through Confederate territory to the coast (Georgia campaign, 1864) left a trail of devastation and bitterness. He was Commander-in-Chief of the US army from 1869 to 1884, when he retired.

Sherrington, Sir Charles (1861-1952) English neurologist who worked out the body's motor-nerve system, introduced the concept of the synapse (a gap between connecting nerve cells across which chemicals can pass) and mapped the parts of the brain, relating them to function. He was awarded a Nobel Prize in 1932.

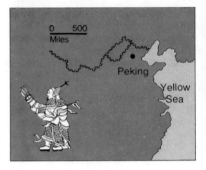

Largely intact after 2000 years, the Great Wall of China weaves inland for 1500 miles from the Gulf of Chihli

Shih Huang Ti (259-210 BC) First Chinese emperor (221-210 BC), who, as King of China, conquered the independent states in China and unified the country. He standardized Chinese writing and began the Great Wall, constructed to keep out barbarians. In 212, he decreed the burning of all historical documents.

Shivaji (1627-80) Mahratta leader and national hero, who gave the Mahrattas of India a sense of unity and purpose they had never before possessed. After several military operations against the Moguls (1659-70), he declared himself independent in 1674. He owed his military successes to a skilled infantry and cavalry, which enabled him to lay the foundations of a compact kingdom in western India, expanding to an empire in the 18th century. He organized a sound administration for the kingdom and tried to establish an equitable land system.

Shockley, William (born 1910) American physicist who, with Bardeen and Brattain, developed the transistor. 'Solid-state' devices – in which junctions involving materials called semiconductors act like electronic valves – had been used since the 1930s for rectification (the changing of alternating into direct current).

Sholem, Aleichem (1859-1916) Russian-born Yiddish writer, who founded and edited the first Yiddish literary annual, *Di Yiddishe Folksbibliothek* (1888). Apart from his wryly humorous stories and novels, he also wrote comedies, essays and an autobiography.

Sholes, Christopher Lathan (1819-90) American inventor who, with Carlos Glidden and Samuel W. Soule, made the first prototype of the modern typewriter (1867). Encouraged by two businessmen, James Densmore and George Washington Newton Yost, Sholes eventually (1873) constructed a machine capable of rapid fingering, by the separation of the most commonly used letters as far as possible to prevent jamming. Densmore and Yost bought Sholes's patents and in 1873 persuaded the Remington Fire Arms Company to manufacture the machine. It was first marketed in 1876 and eventually, after a few years, proved a commercial success.

Sholokov, Mikhail Aleksandrovich (born 1905) Russian novelist, author of *And Quiet Flows the Don* (1934), the story of a man torn by love for two women and by his conflicting loyalties to the Cossacks and the Bolsheviks. The book describes the problems and bitterness engendered by the Revolution for those who lived through it. In 1940 he produced a sequel, *The Don Flows Home to the Sea*. While his earlier works were notable for their objectivity, Sholokov's later writings are less impartial. Between 1932 and 1960 he produced *Virgin Soil Upturned* and a second part, *Harvest on the Don*, about the collectivization campaign in the Don region. He was awarded the Stalin Prize (1941) and the Nobel Prize for Literature in 1965.

Shostakovich, Dmitri (born 1906) Russian symphonist who is the leading composer of the USSR. He has written 15 symphonies ranging from the First, an exuberant work of his student days, to the patriotic Seventh, which celebrates the Siege of Leningrad in the Second World War, and the darker, more introspective Tenth. Shostakovich has periodically encountered official disapproval. In 1936, his opera *The Lady Macbeth of Mtsensk*, was denounced and withdrawn after it had angered STALIN. But Shostakovich, while admitting to certain 'errors', has remained larger than the vagaries of bureaucracy and has avoided compromising his status as a major artist.

Shotoku (574-622) Japanese crown prince, statesman, soldier and scholar, who controlled the government in the reign of Japan's first formally acknowledged empress, Suiko (ruled 593-628). Through Shotoku's support, Buddhism became firmly established and he founded huge Buddhist monasteries.

Shovell, Sir Cloudesley (1650-1707) English admiral, who distinguished himself against France in the battle of La Hogue and against Spain in the capture of Gibraltar (1704) and Barcelona (1705). After 43 years of success and promotion, he died when his fleet struck the rocks off the Scilly Isles, and his flagship *Association* sank with 800 hands aboard.

Shubbiluliu (c. 1380-1346 BC) Hittite ruler, who restored the Hittite Empire, substantially extended it by wars, treaties of alliance and marriages, and made it for a short time the leading military and political power in the Near East.

Sibelius, Jean (1865-1957) Finland's leading composer and one of the master symphonists of the 20th century. Sibelius's earliest works were orchestral tone poems based on events in the lives of the heroes of the Finnish national epic, the *Kalavala*. Among these are *En Saga*, *The Swan of Tuonela* and *Finlandia*. At 32, Sibelius was granted a government annuity, enabling him to give himself entirely to composition. He wrote seven symphonies, the first in 1899 and the last in 1925. The first two showed a strong TCHAIKOVSKY influence, but thereafter the cycle developed a progressive economy of expression. In 1926 Sibelius published his last major work, the tone poem *Tapiola*, a vision of the forces of nature in the dark northern winter. Its austere appeal is not a universal taste. 'Others can provide the cocktails,' said Sibelius, 'I serve only plain water.'

Sickert, Walter (1860-1942) German-born English artist, whose style was basically Impressionistic, but which showed a marked concern for intimate subject matter that at times approached voyeurism. He studied with both WHISTLER and DEGAS and spent much time abroad, painting in Venice and Dieppe. Later he helped to form the Camden Town Group.

Siddons, Sarah (1755-1831) English actress, the greatest tragedienne of her time, whose roles included Belvidera in *Venice Preserved*, by Thomas OTWAY, Isabella in *The Fatal Marriage*, and Lady Macbeth.

Sidgwick, Nevil (1873-1952) English chemist who developed the electronic theory of chemical bonding. Using Nils BOHR's idea of atomic structure, Sidgwick showed that the explanation of chemical bonding (in terms of interactions between electrons) applies also to inorganic chemistry, not merely organic chemistry as had been thought until that time.

Sidney, Sir Philip (1554-86) Aristocratic English soldier, courtier, diplomat and poet whose *Astrophel and Stella* (1580-4) was the first of the Elizabethan sonnet sequences. The prose *Arcadia* (1580-3), a chivalric romance, developed an English literary style, and his *Defence of Poesie* (c. 1580) was the most lucid, coherent critical essay of the age, written as a reply to an abusive Puritan pamphlet.

Siemens, Sir Charles William (Karl Wilhelm) (1823-83) who was a member of the famous German inventive family and came to England in 1843. He is best known for an open-hearth steel-making process, utilizing his regenerative principle for the conservation of waste heat, which improved, and eventually replaced, the BESSEMER process. Other notable achievements were his design of the ship *Faraday*, which laid the transatlantic telegraph cable of 1874, and his installation of an early electric tramway at Portrush, Northern Ireland (1883).

Siemens, Ernst Werner von (1816-92) German inventor, who in 1847, with J. G. Halske, founded the firm of Siemens and Halske, which became one of the world's main electrical equipment manufacturers, associated with extensive telegraphic systems in Germany and Russia and with electric traction.

Sienkiewicz, Henryk (1846-1916) Polish novelist, author of *Quo Vadis?* (1896), a story of the Christian persecutions in NERO's Rome. It has been filmed several times (the earliest version was in 1912).

Sieyès, Emmanual Joseph (1748-1836) French Revolutionary leader and publicist, known as Abbé Sieyès. Though educated for the priesthood, Sieyès's clerical career was a mere formality, but he was moved by compassion for the poor to study social conditions and gave a clear shape to the aspirations of reformers in two pamphlets: *Essay on Privileges* (1788) and *What is the Third Estate?* (1789). During the Terror (1794) he withdrew from public life, but returned to politics as a member of the Directory in 1799, drafted the Constitution of the Consulate and helped NAPOLEON to seize power. In 1814, he took refuge in Belgium and did not return until 1830.

Sigismund II Augustus (1520-72) Last of the Jagiellon kings of Poland, at whose death Poland became in effect a republic with a puppet king. During Sigismund's reign, the forces of radicalism grew, and though he struggled against them, the nobles gained political control. Sigismund died childless, whereupon the gentry put into practice an elective monarchy, which made the king merely the titular head of state. Sigismund achieved the Union of Lublin (1569), uniting Lithuania with Poland.

Signac, Paul (1863-1935) French Neo-Impressionist painter and gifted follower of SEURAT.

Signorelli, Luca (c. 1445-1523) Italian artist, and pupil of PIERO DELLA FRANCESCA, whose monumental treatment of the human form is seen in his fresco cycle illustrating the *End of the World* and the *Last Judgement* in Orvieto Cathedral (1499-1500). This shows the use of the nude figure for dramatic purposes, which was taken up by MICHELANGELO in his *Last Judgement* painted on the wall of the Sistine Chapel.

Sikorski, Wladyslaw (1881-1943) Polish general and Prime Minister-in-exile during the Second World War. He retired to Paris (1928) after PILSUDSKI's *coup d'état* of 1926, and was appointed Prime Minister-in-exile (first in France, then England) when Poland fell in 1939. Realizing that the friendship with the Soviet Union was necessary for Poland's survival, he concluded an agreement with Russia in 1941, annulling the 1939 Russo-German partition of Poland and providing for the release of Polish prisoners and the formation of a Polish army in Russia. He was killed in a plane crash at Gibraltar in July 1943.

Sikorsky, Igor Ivanovich (born 1889) Russian-born American aeronautical engineer who in 1913 built and flew the world's first multi-engined aeroplane. His many aircraft companies were merged to form United Aircraft Manufacturing Corporation for which he developed flying boats and other aircraft. Sikorsky built (1909) the first, although unsuccessful, helicopter and 30 years later, returning to this type of aircraft, developed the single-seat Sikorsky VS-300, which was the prototype of the modern machines.

Simenon, Georges (born 1903) Belgian-born French author of several hundred detective stories featuring Inspector Maigret of the Sûreté, novels which raised the detective story to a minor art-form. His autobiography, *Pedigree*, appeared in 1948.

Simeon (10th cent.) Bulgarian king, formerly a monk, under whom Bulgaria reached the peak of its power. Hoping to become Byzantine emperor, Simeon fought Byzantine armies five times (894-923), and

though he did not achieve his aim, his capital, Preslav, rivalled Constantinople as a centre of culture.

Simnel, Georg (1858-1918) German sociologist and philosopher to whom society was not merely a collection of individuals but comprised both the individuals and their relationships with each other.

Simon, Sir John (1816-1904) English physician, who in 1848 became London's first Medical Officer of Health. He instituted routine inspections of public and commercial premises, campaigned for the improvement of water supplies and sewage systems and began a system of quarantine and isolation for infections. He was also an advocate of compulsory immunization.

Simon, Theodore (1873-1961) French psychologist who with BINET devised a scale for intelligence quotients (IQs).

Simonides of Ceos (c. 556-468 BC) Greek lyric poet. The best known of his few surviving works are an early poem on the nature of virtue, splendid commemorative hymns and moving short elegiac epitaphs written after the victory over the Persians in 480-479 BC.

An early multi-engined plane built by Sikorsky, greatest of helicopter designers

Sinclair, Upton Beal (1878-1968) American social reformer and novelist, who was a prolific, popular author of books exposing the limitations of capitalist society. A visit to the Chicago stockyards resulted in *The Jungle* (1906), a best-seller which caused great hostility amongst the meat-packers whom it described. Similar exposure to abuse followed in *King Coal* (1917), *Oil* (1927) and *The Flivver King* (1937).

Singer, Isaac Merrit (1811-75) American inventor and manufacturer of the sewing machine, which, from the middle of the 19th century, revolutionized the manufacture of clothing and soft furnishings.

Sinyavsky, Andrei Donatovich (born 1925) Russian novelist and

critic who, with Yuli Daniel, was sentenced to seven years' hard labour in 1965 for publishing 'works critical of the Soviet Union'.

Sisley, Alfred (1839-99) French Impressionist painter of English descent. Confining himself almost exclusively to landscape painting, his work did not develop beyond Impressionism, as did MONET's and CÉZANNE's. Throughout his life, despite unrelieved poverty, he concentrated on sensitive and luminous interpretations of modest scenes, at different seasons. He was initially influenced by COROT and by the paintings of TURNER and CONSTABLE, which he had seen on visits to London.

Sitting Bull (1831-90) American Indian chief of the Hunkpapa Sioux. His prestige was at its height when he defeated the Seventh Cavalry under CUSTER at the battle of the Little Big Horn. During the Ghost Dance scare of 1890, he was killed resisting arrest.

Sitwell, Dame Edith (1887-1964) English poet, who possessed brilliant powers of language and a humane sensibility. In 1916 she attracted attention by editing *Wheels*, an anthology of modern verse opposed to the ideals of the Georgian poets of Munro's anthologies.

Sitwell, Sir Osbert (1892-1969) English author, who wrote of himself, 'I belonged by birth, education, nature, outlook and period to the pre-war era, a proud citizen of the great free world of 1914.' His achievement in prose and verse has been a skilful re-creation of the temper and colour of those times. His best-known novel, *Before the Bombardment* (1926), is a realization of Edwardian society. He has also written five volumes of vivid autobiography, and many books of verse.

Sitwell, Sir Sacheverell (born 1897) English writer, best known for reflections on European Baroque art. His poetry, showing an affinity with the work of his sister Edith SITWELL, but more traditional, draws its inspiration from the arts.

Skinner, Burrhus (born 1904) American experimental psychologist, and inventor of the Skinner Box for animal experiments. A lever, when depressed, opens a door and frees the animal, or drops a food pellet into the cage as a reward. Using this technique of conditioned learning reinforced by reward, Skinner was able to train animals to perform elaborate acts. He has since explored ways of teaching the basic skills of spelling, arithmetic, etc., to children, with the aid of specially-designed machines.

Slaveikov, Petko (1827-95) Bulgarian poet, who, by demonstrating the language's potential as a literary medium, laid the foundations of Bulgarian literature.

Sloane, Sir Hans (1660-1753) English physician and naturalist whose collections formed the basis of the British Museum. In 1727 he became George II's first physician, and succeeded NEWTON as President of the Royal Society. He built up and catalogued a large botanical collection, bought William Courten's unique collection of curiosities, acquired a major library, and then bequeathed his thousands of manuscripts, books and natural history specimens to the nation. The collection (with others) went on public view in London and became the nucleus of the British Museum (1759).

Slocum, Joshua (1844-1909) American sailor who completed a solo circumnavigation of the world. He left Newport, Rhode Island, in 1895 in the sloop *Spray* and returned in 1898, after circling the world in three years and two months. In November 1909, he set out once more, but was never heard of again.

Sluter, Claus (late 14th-early 15th cent.) Dutch sculptor whose importance lies in the fact that he freed sculpture from its secondary place as a part of architecture in northern Europe and in so doing, he anticipated DONATELLO and paved the way for artists from Van EYCK on. His best-known work, the *Well of Moses* (1395-1403), was carved for PHILIP THE BOLD of Normandy, at whose court he worked.

Smetana, Bedřich (1824-84) Czech composer who founded his country's musical style. He also made a name as a conductor and pianist and received encouragement from LISZT. Associated with the unsuccessful 1848 revolt against Austria-Hungary, Smetana used folk-music to evoke national feelings. *The Bartered Bride* (1886) has always been his best-known opera abroad. In 1874, while he was writing his set of six tone poems *My Country*, he went deaf and shortly afterwards his career was ended by a nervous breakdown.

Smirke, Sir Robert (1781-1867) English architect, who designed the British Museum, London, perhaps the most important of his buildings and the best example of the Greek Revival in Britain.

Smith, Adam (1723-90) British economist whose five-volume *The Wealth of Nations* (1776) laid the foundations of the classical school of economics. This work describes labour, discusses capital and the industrial development of European countries, argues for free trade and deals with the expenses of national administration. It had a profound influence on government institutions of the time.

Smith, David (1906-65) American sculptor, who experimented with constructed sculpture after seeing reproductions of PICASSO's work in welded steel.

Smith, George (1840-76) English Assyriologist whose flair for deciphering cuneiform (wedge-shaped) scripts led to discoveries which revealed the basis of many ancient Hebrew tales. In 1872 he deciphered an almost complete Assyrian account of the Flood, which closely matched that in the Bible. His discovery of other parallels with The Book of Genesis were reinforced by WOOLLEY in 1928.

Smith, Sir Grafton Elliot (1871-1937) Australian anatomist and anthropologist who supported the diffusionist view that human customs and practices originate in one area of the world. They spread as a result of contacts between people and this interaction, according to Smith, explains almost all cultural similarities throughout the world.

Smith, Ian Douglas (born 1919) Rhodesian politician, who withdrew Rhodesia from the Commonwealth and declared 'UDI' (Unilateral Declaration of Independence) in 1965. As Deputy Prime Minister to Winston Field (1962-4), Smith's opposition to majority rule and policy of permanent white supremacy appealed more to the white Rhodesians than Field's more liberal policy, and in 1964, he succeeded him. An election in 1965 gave him an overwhelming (white) mandate for his policies. The British government's requirement that the black majority should be given a fair share of political power before the granting of independence led him to declare independence unilaterally in November 1965, and, following Britain's refusal to bring him to reverse his action by force (as urged by Zambia and other African states), he declared Rhodesia a republic with a policy of apartheid on the South African model.

Smith, Jedediah (1798-1831) American explorer, the first to make the central overland crossing of the US to the Pacific and open up the American West. Seeking fur-trade routes to the Pacific, he went by way of the Great Salt Lake and the Colorado River to San Diego (1826). He became the first to cross the Sierra Nevada and travel west to east across the Great Basin (1827) and (1827-8) made the first land exploration of Oregon and Washington. He was killed by Comanche Indians before his maps of the west were published.

Smith, John (1580-1631) English soldier and colonist, a leader of England's first permanent American colony. As one of 104 male settlers who founded Jamestown, Virginia, in 1607, he took command of the few who survived the first winter of starvation and disease, traded with Indians for maize, and organized defences against Indian attack. He explored Chesapeake Bay, the Potomac, the Rappahannock and the Chickahominy where, he claimed, POCAHONTAS saved his life. He published several works on Virginia and New England.

Smith, Joseph (1805-44) American religious leader, founder of the Church of Jesus Christ of Latter-Day Saints, generally known as Mormons. The name comes from the *Book of Mormon*, which was discovered by Smith written in Reformed Egyptian on golden plates. Smith's message, that God was coming to gather his Saints together in a New Jerusalem, gained many followers in spite of ridicule and even violence. Smith was later murdered by a mob in Illinois.

Smith, Sir Matthew (1879-1959) British painter, who studied with MATISSE, whose influence appears in Smith's characteristic nudes, landscapes and still-lifes.

Smith, Sydney (1771-1845) English writer, co-founder, with Francis Jeffrey and Henry BROUGHAM, of the Whig quarterly, *The Edinburgh Review*.

Smith, Theobold (1859-1934) American pathologist whose work on the cattle disease known as Texas fever showed conclusively that it was transmitted by a cattle tick – the first proven connection between insects and disease.

Smith, William (1769-1839) British surveyor and geologist, known as the father of English geology. His examination of the rock strata of England during the course of his work as a surveyor led him to the conclusion that each layer contains its own characteristic assemblage of fossils and that this could be used to determine the sequence and succession.

Smith, William Henry (1825-91) English founder of a bookselling chain. He developed his father's shop in the Strand, London, negotiated with the growing railway companies for rights to open station bookstalls and soon became Britain's biggest bookseller/newsagent. In 1868 he entered Parliament and had a distinguished ministerial career.

Smollett, Tobias (1721-71) Scottish novelist, who wrote in the picaresque tradition, filling his novels with incidents drawn from his own experience, especially as a ship's surgeon. His best-known novels are *Roderick Random* (1748), *Peregrine Pickle* (1751) and *Humphry Clinker* (1771), in which his blunt, vigorous style of writing is best suited to satire and caricature. Smollett wrote many miscellaneous works, including a critically respected *Complete History of England* (1757-61).

Smuts, Jan Christiaan (1870-1950) Afrikaner soldier-statesman who fought against the British in the South African War (1899-1902) and went on to become an elder statesman of the British Empire. Colonial Secretary in BOTHA's government, Smuts went to war again, on the side of his old enemies, when the First World War broke out and he defeated the German forces in South West Africa. He became a member of the Imperial War Cabinet in 1917 and, after the war, helped to draft the League of Nations Covenant. Between the wars, he was twice Prime Minister of South Africa and founded the anti-republican, anti-racialist United Party in 1934. A close colleague of CHURCHILL during the Second World War, he had a hand in the founding of the United Nations Organization.

Smyth, John (c. 1554-1612) British clergyman, generally claimed as the founder of the English Baptists, whose members (adult penitents and believers) had to be baptized into their new faith by their leader. Smyth led his party of exiled separatists to Amsterdam in 1608. His views constantly fluctuated and caused great dissension among the English separatists, most of whom eventually repudiated him.

Snoilsky, Count Carl (1841-1903) Aristocratic Swedish poet, who tried vainly to reach the heart of common men with his urbane, polished lyrics. He pursued a traditional diplomatic career, but expressed his frustration and bitterness in *Sonnets* (1871). After a divorce he went abroad and later wrote *Swedish Pictures* (1886), a collection of historical themes which he hoped would strike a patriotic and democratic note by creating a poetic world for the Swedish people.

Snorri, Sturluson (1179-1241) Icelandic poet, story-teller and historian, who was the most important literary figure in medieval Scandinavia. His major work, the *Edda* (c. 1223), a textbook for poets, includes his own poetry and his re-telling of the ancient myths, masterpieces of grace and irony. Snorri is thought also to have been the author of the *Egils Saga*. His other works include *The Orb of the World* (c. 1223-35), a history of the Norwegian kings down to 1177, and *The Olaf Saga.*

Snow, John (1813-58) English physician, who put forward the idea that some diseases could be carried by water.

Snowden, Philip, 1st Viscount (1864-1937) British Labour Chancellor of the Exchequer, whose policies aggravated the effects of the depression. He was an orthodox economist, and, as Chancellor of the Exchequer in 1924 and from 1929 to 1931, he advocated deflation of the economy, free trade, and adherence to the gold standard – policies which worsened unemployment and intensified the effects of the depression. His hostility to protection led to his resignation from the government in 1932.

Soane, Sir John (1753-1837) English architect whose style was influenced by Roman and Byzantine architecture. In his own house in Lincoln's Inn Fields, London (now a museum), the intimate scale and purpose of the building permitted an unusual use of mirrors and alcoves.

Socrates (c. 470-399 BC) Greek philosopher and inventor of a new method of study in terms of proposition and argument, a procedure of hypothesis and deduction which now lies at the heart of scientific method. Socrates was inspired by a divine mission to teach men their own ignorance, but the method of question and answer, by which he deflated the self-opinionated and taught those who followed him to question established assumptions, made him many enemies. He was eventually condemned to death and given hemlock to drink.

Soddy, Frederick (1877-1956) English chemist who, while studying the radioactive decay of uranium (1913), suggested that various forms of a single element can exist, differing from each other only in atomic weight. He noticed that large numbers of apparently new elements were being formed and suggested that these were merely different forms, or isotopes, of known elements.

Solís, Juan Diaz de (c. 1470-1516) Spanish navigator who, seeking a westward route to India, followed the South American coast south and discovered the Plate estuary.

Solomon (c. 973-c. 933 BC) King of Israel, under whom it reached the height of its fame. He made allies of Tyre and Egypt and was thus free to trade profitably in the Mediterranean and southeastern Asia. He built fortified cities, sumptuous palaces, and a temple at Jerusalem. The taxes and forced labour exacted for his lavish court, harem and buildings caused discontent, which after his death split the kingdom into Israel and Judah. Solomon is credited with having written the Song of Solomon, Proverbs and Ecclesiastes.

Solomos, Dionysios (1798-1857) The first significant poet of modern Greece, whose *Hymn to Liberty* (1823) established him as a national poet. Its first few stanzas were adopted as the Greek national anthem. He was the first writer to link Greek literature with that of modern Europe and his simple language had a great influence on later Greek poets.

Solon (c. 638-c. 558 BC) Athenian lawgiver, who was elected to the office of Archon in 594 BC, especially to reconcile the existing differences between the aristocratic, mercantile and popular factions. His proposals were embodied in a code, containing constitutional, economic and general reforms: his constitution provided for a limited oligarchy based on citizenship classes and a deliberative council. His main economic ordinance reduced the burden of debt on poor persons.

Solzhenitsyn, Aleksandr Isayevich (born 1918) Russian author and poet of international reputation and outspoken critic of academic oppression in the USSR. His most famous work *A Day in the Life of Ivan Denisovich* (1962), an account of life in a labour camp during the STALIN era caused a sensation in the Soviet Union when it was published at the height of KHRUSCHEV's de-Stalinization campaign. Like *First Circle, Ivan Denisovich* was based on his own experiences of prison camps. *Cancer Ward* (1968) recalls his experiences while undergoing treatment for a stomach cancer while in exile in Kazakhstan. *August 1914* (1971), a later novel about the events leading up to the fatal battle of Tannenberg in East Prussia, is an epic work in the tradition of TOLSTOY's *War and Peace.* In 1970, Solzhenitsyn was awarded a Nobel Prize for Literature, but was refused permission to accept it by the Soviet authorities. With the publication in the West of *The Gulag Archipelago*, he was expelled from Russia in 1974.

Somers, Sir George (1554-1610) English admiral, who claimed Bermuda for JAMES I when his ship *Sea Venture* was wrecked off the Bermuda Islands (1609) on the way to Virginia with settlers. Somers took the castaways on to Jamestown, Virginia (1610), though two stayed at Bermuda and founded an English settlement. Somers went back to Bermuda for supplies and while he was there he died.

Sophocles (496-406 BC) Greek dramatist, who was one of the three great tragic poets of the period. In form, his work lies somewhere between the traditional ritual drama of AESCHYLUS and the modern, almost psychological approach of EURIPIDES. Sophocles was used as a model by ARISTOTLE, who criticized Euripides as 'decadent' in his *Poetics*. In a sense, the concept of the three Unities of time, place and action, for centuries fundamental to European theatre, is derived from Sophoclean drama. Of the some 100 plays which he wrote, only seven tragedies survive: *Ajax, Antigone, Trachiniae, Oedipus Rex, Electra, Philoctetes, Oedipus at Colonnus* and some fragments (450-406 BC). A master of plot construction and the use of dramatic irony, Sophocles used three characters as well as the chorus, and, using the traditional myths as his subjects, dealt in personalities, relationships and man's predicament confronted by fate. Such was his power of language that his works are as effective in production today as they were 2400 years ago.

Sorel, Albert (1842-1906) French diplomat and foremost historian of the French Revolution, the author of *Europe and the French Revolution* (1885-1904).

Sorel, Georges (1847-1922) French journalist and social philosopher whose doctrine of violence, as expounded in *Reflections on Violence* (1908), is often misrepresented as one of the inspirations of Communism and Fascism. Since evolution toward socialism seemed to him impossible, Sorel advocated direct action, by means of a general strike organized by revolutionary syndicates.

Sorge, Richard (1895-1944) Japan-based German national who spied for the Soviet Union during the Second World War. Among his major espionage coups was advance knowledge of the Pearl Harbour attack. Sorge was eventually caught and hanged, betrayed by his mistress.

Sotatsu Tawaraya (1576-1643) Japanese painter and calligrapher, whose original treatment of traditional, mythological and narrative subjects started a new vogue in contrast with the Chinese-derived art of the KANO family.

Soto, Hernando de (c. 1500-42) Spanish explorer, one of the first to travel extensively in southern North America. He travelled widely in Panama, Guatemala, Yucatan and Peru, then (1539), inspired by rumours of treasure in Florida, obtained Emperor CHARLES V's commission to colonize it. He explored north to the Appalachians and west to the Arkansas River, discovered and crossed the Mississippi, surviving many attacks by hostile Indians.

Soufflot, Jacques Germain (1713-80) French architect of the Pantheon, Paris, which, although classical in style and very severe in feeling avoids the monumental heaviness of ancient Roman architecture and has the lightness of the Gothic buildings admired by Soufflot.

Sousa, John Philip (1854-1932) American bandmaster who became the acknowledged king of the American march. Sousa's intention was to write music 'for the feet instead of the head', and which would moreover make 'a man with a wooden leg step out'. In 'The Stars and Stripes Forever', 'Washington Post', 'Liberty Bell' and 'El Capitan' among many others he succeeded magnificently. In 1892, he founded the internationally famous Sousa's Band, responsible for the later high standards of American band performance. The Sousaphone, a kind of large tuba, was made for his band.

Sousa, Martim Affonso de (c. 1500-64) Portuguese admiral, who led the colonization of Brazil and founded its first Portuguese colony, at Sao Vicente (1532).

Southey, Robert (1774-1843) English author, whose poems, particularly 'Thalaba' (1801), in irregular, unrhymed form, were among the early documents of the Romantic movement. Today he is remembered for short poems like 'Bishop Hatto' and 'The Inchcape Rock'. Southey wrote a mass of miscellaneous work, the most successful of which was a *Life of Nelson* (1813). He was a friend of WORDSWORTH and brother-in-law of COLERIDGE.

Spallanzani, Lazzaro (1729-99) Italian biologist, who solved the theory of spontaneous generation. He showed that if water is boiled for long enough, no micro-organisms appear in it and deduced that if any did appear they would have to have hatched from eggs or spores already present either in the water or the air of the vessel in which the water had been boiled.

Spartacus (1st cent. BC) Thracian leader of a slave revolt which terrorized Roman Italy for two years. Two Roman armies were defeated and Rome threatened before Crassus defeated the slaves and killed Spartacus.

Spearman, Charles (1863-1945) British psychologist who believed that general ability alone could account for the wide variety of human achievement. Thus, he was at variance with GALTON's earlier idea that intellectual processes depend to some extent on general ability, but also on 'special abilities'. Spearman's arguments with his many critics sparked off valuable research into both theories.

Spencer, Herbert (1820-1903) English philosopher whose *System of Synthetic Philosophy* (1860-93) surveyed the social and biological sciences with an underlying philosophic notion of evolution. Life was regarded by Spencer as a continuous process of adaptation and ethics, following his evolutionary principle.

Spencer, Sir Stanley (1891-1959) British painter of religious pictures which caused much controversy because of their earthy and recognizable settings.

Spender, Stephen (born 1909) English poet, who, with AUDEN and others, made the state of society in the 1930s the starting point for their verse. Educated at Oxford, he travelled in Germany, and worked for the Republicans in the Spanish Civil War.

Spener, Phillip (1635-1705) German Protestant theologian, founder of Pietism, a religious reform movement within the German Lutheran Church, which aimed at inspiring a more personal and intimate form of devotion.

Spengler, Oswald (1880-1936) German philosopher and historian, whose pessimistic views on the decline of Western Civilization were published in the Germany of the Nazi era. His great study *The Decline of the West* was published between 1918 and 1922.

Spenser, Edmund (c. 1552-99) English poet, in whose work is a rich blend of the principal elements of 16th-century English poetry. Spenser was a humanist and a classicist, learned and philosophical, and wrote in the forms the Renaissance had established – the pastoral of the 'Shepherd's Calendar' (1579) in honour of Philip Sidney, the satire of 'Mother Hubbard's Tale' (1590), the sonnet-sequence *Amoretti* (1595) and the lyrical ode 'Epithalamion' (1595). But he drew from the strength of the old world also and, in the *Faerie Queene* (1590-6), joined the medieval allegory to the new romantic epic, forming a map of Christian virtue, an allegory of the State of England and a gallery of striking images.

Sperry, Elmer Ambrose (1860-1930) Prolific American inventor who is best known for the application of the gyroscope, whose properties he started to investigate in 1896. Although the invention of the gyrocompass is credited to the German, Anschutz-Kaempfe (1908), the Sperry model was used in the USS *Delaware* in 1910. He introduced gyroscopic stabilizers for ships in 1931. Sperry also worked in electrochemistry, devising methods for making caustic soda from salt and recovering tin from scrap food cans. He also invented (1918) the high-intensity arc-searchlight, now standard for military and display uses.

Spitz, Mark (born 1950) American swimmer, who won four individual gold medals in the 1972 Olympic Games at Munich.

Spode, Josiah II (1754-1827) English potter. Spode perfected the standard hybrid bone china body and was able to popularize this type of translucent china, as it met the prevailing preference for Orient-inspired porcelain. He was the foremost potter of the day, gaining a royal appointment in 1806.

Springer, Axel (born 1912) German publisher, who is one of Europe's most powerful Press magnates. His group includes a large proportion of West Germany's newspapers, including *Die Welt*, *Bild Zeitung*, *Hamburger Abendblatt*, *Berliner Zeitung* and *Berliner Morgenpost*. Springer is also the major shareholder in the Ullstein publishing house. A conservative who favours German reunification and reconciliation with the Jews, his attitudes are often attacked by German left-wing and student movements.

Ssu-ma Ch'ien (145-c. 87 BC) China's first great historian, whose vast *Historical Records* spanned some 2000 years of Chinese history from its recorded beginnings, and provided a key source for western histories of China. It included chronological tables of major events and essays on aspects of government and developments in astronomy, economics and music. It established standards of historical scholarship unmatched in the western world until recent centuries and founded a chronology and literary pattern followed in subsequent dynastic histories.

Staël, Madame de (1766-1817) French writer and literary critic whose works, particularly *De l'Allemagne* (1810) had a marked influence on the development of the Romantic movement in France. In an earlier book, *De la littérature considérée dans ses rapports avec les instituitions sociales* (1800), Madame de Staël had already revealed her cosmopolitan outlook and her theories about the distinct cultures of North and South. She also wrote two sentimental novels, *Delphine* (1802) and *Corinne* (1807), the first works to introduce the idea of the liberated woman to French fiction, anticipating the work of George SAND.

Staël, Nicolas de (1914-55) Russian-born painter, one of the first European artists to rival the American Abstract Expressionists in their own sphere.

Stagnelius, Erik Johan (1793-1823) Swedish Romantic poet, whose exotic lyrics combine erotic and religious themes. A repulsive appearance caused him to be sexually frustrated, involved him in religious crises, and

A Spode plate. The willow pattern depicted upon it remains one of the most popular designs of all for tableware

drove him to drink and opium. In 1821 he published numerous strange, devout lyrics and in 1822 two dramas, *The Martyrs* and *The Bacchantes*. After his death, his remaining manuscripts, published as *Collected Works* (1824-6), revealed the strange fantasies of his erotic yearnings.

Stahl, Georg Ernst (1660-1734) German chemist who elaborated the phlogiston theory of combustion. This theory had already been suggested by BECHER, based on work of the 7th-century Arabian alchemist JABIR.

Stalin, Joseph (1879-1953) (real name J. Vissarionovich Dzugashvili) Russian politician who, after LENIN's death (1924) became dictator of the USSR. A member of the Social Democratic Party from 1899, after 1904, he was repeatedly exiled to Siberia for political crimes and in 1913 was imprisoned up to the 1917 February Revolution. Siding with the Bolsheviks after the party split (1903) he worked closely with Lenin, took part in the October Revolution, and became Secretary of the Central Committee of the Communist Party (1922-41). After 1924, Stalin systematically eliminated his rivals, including Trotsky, and won control over the Comintern. In the 1930s he ordered purges of the Party and Army and in 1939 he made a non-aggression pact with HITLER, but took charge of his armies after the German invasion (1941). From 1945

he extended the USSR frontiers to the surrounding satellite countries in a climate of deteriorating relations with the West. He died in uncertain circumstances, reportedly on the verge of another purge and a change in foreign policy.

Stambolisky, Alexander (1879-1923) Bulgarian politician, champion and leader of the only peasants' government of modern times. A student of agriculture in Germany in the 1890s, he returned to Bulgaria and began to work and agitate for a peasant government. A brilliant orator and a demagogue, Stambolisky was able to rally the peasant masses to his cause and, although he was imprisoned for trying to prevent Bulgaria's entry into the First World War, he was able upon his release to bring about King Ferdinand's abdication (1919) and to become Prime Minister from 1919 to 1923. He freed the peasants of taxation, while increasing taxes on the middle-classes and the urban working-class. He tried to co-operate with Yugoslavia in suppressing the Internal Macedonian Revolutionary Organization, and subsequently was murdered by right-wing Macedonian terrorists.

Stamp, Sir Laurence Dudley (1898-1966) Leading British geographer most widely known for his influence on the study of land utilization. His work directly influenced British governments in their wartime and post-war policies in the planned use of national resources. From 1942-55 he was Chief Advisor in Rival Land Use to the British Government.

Stanislas II, Augustus (1732-98) Last king to rule Poland as an independent state. While representing Poland in Russia, he became a favourite of CATHERINE II, who engineered his election to the Polish throne (largely at Russia's mercy since AUGUSTUS II's reign). Prusso-Russian interference in Polish religious affairs grew and provoked the anti-Russian Confederation of Bar (1768). In the civil war and invasions that followed, Stanislas lost a third of Poland to Catherine, FREDERICK II of Prussia, and MARIA THERESA of Austria (1772). Subsequent partitions (1793, 1795) erased Poland from the map of Europe until 1919.

Stanislavsky, Konstantin Sergeyevich (1865-1938) Russian actor, director, drama teacher and one of the most important theorists of the modern theatre.

Stanley, Sir Henry Morton (1841-1904) Welsh-born American journalist and explorer who traced the source of the Nile and found the lost explorer, David LIVINGSTONE. Already an experienced war correspondent, Stanley was sent by the New York *Tribune* newspaper to Africa to find Livingstone, and found him at Lake Tanganyika (1871). Stanley continued as an explorer, leading an expedition (1874-7) which traced the Nile's source, circumnavigated Lakes Victoria and Tanganyika and traced the whole course of the River Congo. He spearheaded colonization of the Congo regions for Leopold II of Belgium, and (1887-90) traced Lake Albert's source to Lake Edward and identified the Ruwenzori Range as the fabled Mountains of the Moon.

Stanley, Wendell (1904-71) American biochemist who first prepared a crystalline virus, a Nobel Prize winner (1946). Stanley's discovery that a virus is essentially a protein molecule was important, for it placed viruses on the borderline between living matter (viruses are capable of reproducing themselves) and non-living matter (they resemble enzymes in molecular structure).

Stanley, William (1858-1916) American electrical engineer who in 1885, working with WESTINGHOUSE, perfected a practical transformer for large electricity supply networks. This enabled them to carry out the first practical demonstration of an alternating current system at Great Barrington, Massachusetts, in March 1886. He also devised two-phase electric motors and generators, as well as a consumption meter in which the moving parts were suspended magnetically to avoid friction.

Starling, Ernest (1866-1927) English physiologist who discovered the laws that govern the activity of the heart and the mechanism by which lymph and other bodily fluids are secreted. He also identified a number of digestive hormones, coining the term hormone to describe these and other secretions.

Stauffenberg, Count Claus Schenk, von (1907-44) German staff officer, leader of the abortive plot against HITLER in 1944. Revolted by the Jewish pogroms of 1938 and the brutality of the SS (Sturm Schutz) on the Russian front, he was chosen by his fellow conspirators to plan and carry out the assassination of Hitler and the seizure of power from the Nazis. The deployment of troops and disarming of the SS was planned to the last detail, and on 20 July 1944, Stauffenberg attended a conference at the Wolfsschanze, Hitler's headquarters in Rastenburg. There he planted a bomb hidden in his briefcase and made good his escape. Hitler survived the explosion, and the conspirators were rounded up. Stauffenberg and about 150 alleged conspirators were executed. Some 20 others, including ROMMEL, committed suicide.

Stavisky, Serge (1886-1934) French speculator and bond-forger. His suicide, following accusations of forgery, led to revelations that deputies, ministers and important civil servants in France had protected him and had shared in the spoils of his crimes. A political crisis followed, resulting in serious rioting by the right and left-wing extremists, and eventually, the fall of two governments, those of Chautemps (January 1934) and DALADIER (February 1934).

Steele, Sir Richard (1672-1729) Dublin-born playwright and essayist, whose achievement was to shape and to launch the popular literary periodical of instruction and amusement. He founded the *Tatler* in 1709, and later collaborated on the *Spectator* (1711-12) and *Guardian* (1713). Steele was more bound up in political warfare than his friend ADDISON, and his periodicals became more ardently Whig as time went on.

Steen, Jan (1626-79) Dutch painter of portraits and biblical scenes, who is best known for his pictures of 17th-century Dutch life and customs, such as the *Eve of St Nicholas* (c. 1660). These paintings are full of sharply observed detail and humorous incident. Some of Steen's mildly satirical genre scenes are based on popular proverbs.

Stein, Sir Aurel (1862-1943) Hungarian-born archaeologist who specialized in explorations of the Far East. Stein's greatest discovery came in 1907, when he discovered the western-most section of the Great Wall of China, where he collected thousands of ancient manuscripts.

Stein, Gertrude (1874-1946) American experimental novelist who studied psychology with William JAMES, and went to live in Paris in 1903. Interested in language and psychology, spurred on by the example of modern painters like PICASSO, she began her experiments in *Three Lives* (1909); other attempts were *The Making of Americans* (1925) and *The Autobiography of Alice B. Toklas* (1933), her own career told as the life of her secretary. Her deliberately prosaic, repetitive writings are obsessed with technique.

Steinbeck, John (1902-68) American novelist, whose fiction combined picaresque description with reforming zeal. His romanticism was expressed in books like *Cup of Gold* (1929), *Tortilla Flat* (1935) and *Cannery Row* (1944). The radical, reforming theme appeared in *In Dubious Battle* (1936), *Of Mice and Men* (1937) and *The Grapes of Wrath* (1939), the latter a sombre story of the migration of sharecroppers from eroded farms in the Mid-West to California.

Steiner, Rudolph (1861-1925) Influential Austrian educationalist. His methods, such as eurhythmy (movement to music), have had considerable impact in Europe and the US, and today there are many 'Steiner schools', noted for their success in educating the handicapped.

Stendhal (1783-1842) Pen-name of Henri Beyle, French author of *Le Rouge et le Noir* (1831) and *La Chartreuse de Parme* (1839), psychologically penetrating novels describing the alienation of a central character from his environment. An army officer, he participated in NAPOLEON's disastrous 1812 campaign and after the 1830 Revolution he spent his time writing and in dilettante pursuits in Europe.

Stensen, Niels (1638-87) Danish anatomist who discovered that the heart was chiefly composed of muscle fibres, and identified the secretory duct of the parotid gland which bears his name.

Stephen I (c. 977-1038) King of Hungary (997-1038), statesman and saint, first of the dynasty founded by ARPAD. After embracing Roman Christianity, he devoted himself to defeating Hungarian chiefs who clung to paganism or Eastern Orthodoxy. He introduced Roman churchmen into Hungary and, with specially appointed nobles, they ran the land through a royal council answerable to the king. Stephen strengthened the national economy by encouraging agriculture and commerce, and organized a standing army and a system of frontier defences which helped him to withstand German and other invasions. He became the patron saint of Hungary.

Stephen Báthory (1533-86) King of Poland (1575-86), which he made supreme in eastern Europe. A powerful monarch and a gifted soldier, he routed the forces of IVAN IV at Wenden in 1578, and in 1582 forced the Tsar to cede all non-Swedish Livonia. Stephen Báthory dreamed of uniting Poland with Hungary and Muscovy in a great eastern empire at the expense of Turkey. He was a cultured man and, though a strong Roman Catholic, was tolerant of other faiths.

Stephen Dushan (c. 1308-55) King of Serbia (1335-55), who created a Serbian Empire (wresting Albania, Epirus, Macedonia and Thessaly from the crumbling Byzantine Empire) in order to forestall the Ottoman Turks, who were pushing westward from Asia Minor.

Stephen Nemanya (1114-1200) Serbian tribal chief, who founded the first Serb kingdom and its Nemanyich dynasty (1190-1371). He became Grand Zuphan (politico-military chief) of Rashka, one of several petty Serbian states, and succeeded in uniting all the others, except Bosnia, under his supreme leadership.

Stephen, Sir James (1829-94) English judge, whose codification of the English criminal law had great influence on the drafting of legislation in the British Empire and Commonwealth. In 1863 he wrote the first account of English criminal law since BLACKSTONE and followed MACAULAY and MAINE in codifying Indian law.

Stephens, James (1882-1950) Irish poet and novelist, who recreated in his writing the heroic age of Irish myth and legend. A. E. assisted him to publish his first volume, *Insurrections* (1909), which was followed by *The Charwoman's Daughter* (1912), a novel of working-class Dublin, and *The Crock of Gold* (1912), a famous fairy tale. In many of his poems old Gaelic material is revivified by the freshness and the humour of the author's invention.

Stephens, John Lloyd (1805-52) American civil servant and amateur archaeologist, who visited and popularized the massive stone pyramid-temples of the Maya civilization (AD 300-900) in the Honduras jungle, and laid the foundations of Central American archaeology.

Stephenson, George (1781-1848) English engineer and builder of the famous *Rocket*, who became the leading figure of the new Railway Age of the early 19th century. He was appointed engineer for the construction of the Stockton and Darlington Railway (1821), which was opened four years later. In 1829, his *Rocket* (built mainly by his son Robert STEPHENSON) won the famous Rainhill trials, to choose a locomotive for the new Liverpool-Manchester Railway, for which he became engineer. It was the first line to carry passengers by steam haulage, ushering in the Railway Age.

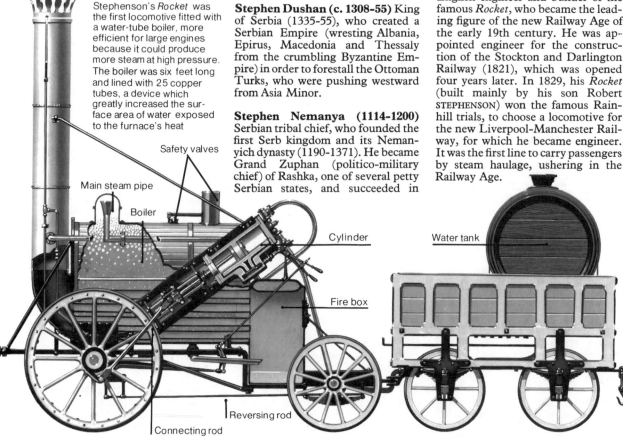

Stephenson's *Rocket* was the first locomotive fitted with a water-tube boiler, more efficient for large engines because it could produce more steam at high pressure. The boiler was six feet long and lined with 25 copper tubes, a device which greatly increased the surface area of water exposed to the furnace's heat

Safety valves

Main steam pipe

Boiler

Cylinder

Water tank

Fire box

Reversing rod

Connecting rod

The works of Sterne were eccentric, sentimental—and sometimes indecent

Stephenson, Robert (1803-59) English mechanical and civil engineer who, in partnership with his father George STEPHENSON, was a pioneer of the Railway Age. In 1827 he joined his father's firm as manager, and in 1829 was largely responsible for the design of the successful *Rocket*, the first locomotive with a multi-tubular boiler of the modern type, and later made other significant innovations in engine design. Robert Stephenson was appointed chief engineer for the London-Birmingham Railway (1831) and after surmounting considerable problems, the 112-mile-long line was opened in 1838. Robert Stephenson also designed bridges, notably the Britannia railway bridge over the Menai Straits.

Sterne, Laurence (1713-68) English novelist, whose *Life and Opinions of Tristram Shandy* (1760-7) was the most original and eccentric novel of the 18th century. It is a brilliant, wayward improvisation round the comic figures of Walter Shandy, Uncle Toby, Corporal Trim and Parson Yorick, and extended the range of the novel with a much more subjective organization of material. He also wrote *A Sentimental Journey Through France and Italy* (1768).

Stesichorus (c. 640-550 BC) Greek choral lyric poet of whose work only few fragments survive. Stesichorus boldly reshaped legends, adapting Sicilian folklore in an original and creative manner, and had a great reputation in antiquity for the grandeur of his epics and for bringing the choral ode to a height of pan-Hellenic importance.

Stevens, Alfred (1817-75) English sculptor, who at first worked with the celebrated Danish sculptor THOR-WALDSEN in Rome. From 1845-7, Stevens was appointed to the Board of Trade School of Design to teach drawing and modelling, where he had considerable influence on a generation of young artists.

Stevens, John (1749-1838) American lawyer, inventor and US transportation pioneer, who in order to protect his invention of a multi-tubular boiler for marine engines (1788), secured America's first patent legislation. Stevens later developed high pressure steam engines and boilers and in 1808, launched the *Phoenix*, the world's first sea-going steamboat, only a few days after FULTON's *Clermont*. Stevens then became interested in railways and was granted the first US charter for a railway between the Delaware and Raritan rivers (1815), founded the Cambed and Ambroy Railway Company (1830) and constructed and operated the first railway across New Jersey (1832).

Stevens, Wallace (1879-1955) American poet whose verse is technically accomplished and intimate poetry, unconcerned with public attitudes, rich with imagery, and often drawn from music and painting. 'Harmonium' was published in 1923, but he wrote little until he was over 50. His works include *Ideas of Order* (1935), *Notes Toward a Supreme Fiction* (1942) and *Collected Poems* (1954).

Stevenson, Adlai Ewing (1900-65) Democratic presidential candidate and champion of American liberalism, who was instrumental in the establishment of the United Nations. He was elected Governor of Illinois (1948) by a record majority and ran the State with remarkable efficiency and honesty. He was twice beaten by EISENHOWER in the presidential campaigns of 1952 and 1956. KENNEDY appointed him US Ambassador to the United Nations in 1960, a post he fulfilled with wit and humanity for over four years (1961-5).

Stevenson, Robert Louis (1850-94) Scottish author, whose individual prose style and rich invention created such novels as *Treasure Island* (1883) and many essays, fantasies, travel-books, children's tales and adventurous romances. Among them were, *An Inland Voyage* (1878), *Virginibus Puerisque* (1881) and *The New Arabian Nights* (1882). He wrote romances, usually on Scottish themes, such as *Kidnapped* (1886) and the unfinished *Weir of Hermiston* (1896); a tale of the macabre and the fantastic in *Dr Jekyll and Mr Hyde* (1886); and vivid and interesting letters. Of his poetry, *A Child's Garden of Verses* (1885) is the best known. In 1888 he left with his family for the South Seas, and died in Samoa.

Stevin, Simon (1548-1620) Dutch mathematician, civil and military engineer, who discovered the triangle of forces, a basic theorem in statics (the study of objects in equilibrium).

Stewart, Balfour (1828-87) British physicist, who suggested that the daily changes in the Earth's magnetic field might be due to horizontal electric disturbances in the atmosphere. This was later proved to be the case.

Stifter, Adalbert (1805-68) Austrian writer, author of novels and novellas that are characterized by subtlety and an air of intrigue. In stately, liturgical prose, piling detail upon detail, His technique is generally considered to be at its height in the novels *The Indian Summer* (1857) and *Witiko* (1867), and in the collection of novellas entitled *Bright Stones* (1853).

Stockhausen, Karlheinz (born 1928) German composer and a leader of the *avant-garde* in European music. Stockhausen began with serialism and moved on to become an advocate of electronic music in the 1950s.

Stoker, Bram (1847-1912) Irish novelist, who wrote *Dracula* (1897). The story of the vampire, Count Dracula, was supposedly taken from Transylvanian legend, retold by Stoker with narrative skill. He was for many years touring manager and secretary to Sir Henry IRVING.

Stokes, William (1804-78) Irish doctor, who was a pioneer of the systematic study of heart and lung disease. He ridiculed purging and bleeding as cures for disease, helped to introduce LAENNEC's stethoscope into Ireland and gave the first accurate account of aortic aneurysm (abnormal enlargement of the aorta).

The childhood home of Robert Louis Stevenson in Edinburgh. His grave is in Samoa, where he spent his last years

Stokowski, Leopold (born 1887)
English-born American conductor who made the Philadelphia Symphony Orchestra one of the world's best. Stokowski was an organist in London before he went to America.

Stone, Nicholas (1586-1647) English sculptor and mason who went, as a foundryman to Holland, returned to England and built up an unrivalled practice as a tomb-maker, his early work showing him to be the most accomplished contemporary English sculptor. Stone's *Monument to Francis Holles* (1622) introduced a motif new to England: a figure in Roman armour.

Storm, Theodor (1817-88) German novelist and lyric poet. The preoccupation with love, solitude and death in his collection of lyrics *Deep Shadows* (1865), was inspired by the loss of his wife. In the earliest of his many long short-stories, notably *Immensee* (1849) and *Renate* (1878), he develops the themes of solitude and the difficulties of communication.

Stowe, Harriet Beecher (1811-96) American novelist who wrote *Uncle Tom's Cabin* (1852). The novel is not only an anti-slavery tract, but also an analysis of many aspects of racialism.

Strachey, Lytton (1880-1932) English biographer and critic, who helped to debunk the grandeur of Victorian life and art. He put into practice his principles of biography which were to attack 'in unexpected places', and to send a 'revealing searchlight into obscure recesses'. *Eminent Victorians* (1918), *Queen Victoria* (1921) and *Elizabeth and Essex* (1928) were the results of this technique, which he called psychography. Strachey was a member of the Bloomsbury Group of writers and artists, which included Virginia WOOLF.

Stradivari, Antonio (c. 1645-1737) Italian instrument maker who brought the craft of violin making to its peak about 1700. The Stradivaris, Antonio and his sons, Francesco and Omobono, were the best known of three families of string-instrument makers at Cremona (with Amatis and the Guarneris).

Strafford, Sir Thomas Wentworth, 1st Earl of (1593-1641) English statesman, a moderate supporter of CHARLES I, who favoured the royal prerogative, but was opposed to arbitrary taxation and imprisonment. As Lord Deputy of Ireland (1633-9), he enforced his 'thorough' policy of coercing the unwilling Irish to accept English laws and increasing Protestant immigration in order to counter

Catholic dissidents. In 1640 Charles I made him his chief adviser and an earl. He was impeached by Parliament, at the instigation of PYM, for abuse of fundamental English law, and was executed.

Strauss, Johann II (1825-99) The most famous member of the Viennese family of Austrian waltz composers. He wrote 'The Blue Danube' and 'Tales from the Vienna Woods', the operetta *Die Fledermaus* (1874), and more than 400 waltzes.

Strauss, Richard (1864-1949) German composer who brought the symphonic poem to its highest point of sophistication. From his earliest tone poem, *Don Juan* (1888), Strauss showed an egocentric but audacious expressiveness. The tone poems *Till Eulenspiegel* (1895), *Thus Spake Zarathustra* (1896) and *Don Quixote* (1897) followed, as did his musical 'autobiography' *A Hero's Life* (1898). Strauss's 'modernism' sometimes scandalized his contemporaries, notably in his opera *Salome* (1905), based on WILDE's play. His other operas, *Elektra* (1909), *Der Rosenkavalier* (1911) and *Ariadne on Naxos* (1912-16), with librettos by HOFMANNSTHAL, are classics of the modern repertoire. The *Metamorphoses* (1945) for 23 solo strings is a work of his old age.

Stravinsky, Igor (1882-1971) Russian-born American composer who studied with RIMSKY-KORSAKOV, and soon attracted the attention of the impressario DIAGHILEV. The first full score he wrote for Diaghilev's Ballets-Russes in Paris was *The Firebird* (1910), which made his name. *Petrushka* (1911) followed, and *The Rite of Spring* (1913), which provoked a riot at its first performance, but which has remained a cornerstone of modern music. For the rest of his creative life Stravinsky remained a step ahead of both public and critics. He adopted Neo-classicism in the 1920s, giving it hard, monumental outlines and rhythmic subtlety, as in *Oedipus Rex* (an opera-oratorio with text by COCTEAU) or the *Symphony of Psalms* (1930). In 1939 he left for America where he became a naturalized citizen. He had already used ragtime in, for example, his astringent chamber opera, *The Soldier's Tale* (1918), and now he absorbed jazz influences, writing his *Ebony Concerto* for Woody Herman's band. In 1951, he completed the entertaining Hogarthian opera *The Rake's Progress* (with text by W. H. AUDEN).

Streicher, Julius (1885-1946) German journalist and politician, founder of the violently anti-Semitic German Socialist Party. He was at first an enemy and rival of HITLER, but later

joined forces with him, and took part in the Munich *putsch* of 1923. In 1924, Streicher launched the anti-Jewish weekly *Der Stürmer* which, with the *Volkischer Beobachter* (edited by Alfred Rosenberg) became one of the main propaganda vehicles of the Nazi Party. He was appointed *gauleiter* (provincial political officer) of Franconia by Hitler in 1933. He was executed as a war criminal.

Stresemann, Gustav (1878-1929) German statesman, who restored Germany's status in the League of Nations after the First World War. As a nationalist, convinced that Germany had a mission to dominate Europe, he believed that she must first regain the confidence of the other powers. As Chancellor (1923) and Foreign Minister (1923-9), he attempted to carry out the terms of the Treaty of Versailles. He secured the signing of the Locarno Treaties (1925), securing Germany's admission to the League of Nations as a major power (1926), negotiated a reduction in the amount of reparation payable by Germany, and persuaded the Allies to evacuate the Rhineland (Britain in 1926, France in 1930). He was awarded the Nobel Peace Prize in 1926.

Strindberg, August (1849-1912) Swedish dramatist who, with IBSEN, was a leading exponent of uncompromising realism. His plays were an innovation in their exposure of the battle between the sexes, notably in *The Father* (1887) and *Miss Julie* (1888). He wrote more than 50 plays, including a huge symbolic work, *To*

The Rite of Spring ballet, for which Stravinsky composed the score, caused an uproar when it was staged in Paris in 1913

Damascus (1898), dramas of Swedish history, and others charged with symbolism and mysticism, such as *Advent* (1898) and *Dance of Death* (1901). He helped to found the tiny Intima Teatern in Stockholm (1907), for which, in the same year, he wrote *The Storm* and *The Burnt Lot.*

Struensee, Count Johann von (1737-72) German-born Danish political philosopher and statesman, who became physician to and then dominated the degenerated Christian VII. He was a supporter of the *encyclopédistes*, who included VOLTAIRE and MONTESQUIEU, and devised his reforms in accordance with the enlightened policies that they advocated. In ten months (1771-2) Struensee issued 1069 orders, which drastically reformed the Danish law and administration. He was overthrown during a palace revolution, tortured and beheaded.

Struve, Friedrich Georg Wilhelm (1793-1864) German astronomer, who made detailed observations of double stars.

Strzelecki, Sir Paul Edmund de (1797-1845) Polish explorer and geologist. After much travelling through the Americas and the Pacific, he arrived at Sydney Cove in April 1839. His explorations took him all over eastern Australia and on one expedition he discovered, climbed and named Mount Kosciusko.

Stuart, Charles Edward (1720-88) English prince, known as 'Bonnie Prince Charlie' or the 'Young Pretender'. He led the second Jacobite rebellion to oust the Hanoverian GEORGE II and re-establish Stuart rule in Scotland and England under Charles's father, James Edward Stuart (the 'Old Pretender'), son of James II. Charles landed in western Scotland from France (1745) and by sheer dash and charm rallied many highland clansmen, who, in under four months, seized Edinburgh, defeated a British army at Prestonpans and invaded England as far south as Derby before forcing their leader reluctantly to withdraw to Scotland. The Duke of CUMBERLAND's army shattered Charles's now ragged Jacobite force at Culloden (1746) and Charles became a fugitive. With the help of loyal supporters (notably Flora MACDONALD), he escaped to France, and lived out the remainder of his life in drunkenness and debauchery.

Stuart, John McDovall (1815-66) Scottish-born Australian explorer who was the first to discover an all-season north-south route across the Australian interior.

Stubbs, George (1724-1806) Superlative English animal painter, whose detailed observation and sense of pictorial balance distinguish him from traditional sporting painters such as Seymour and Marshall and sometimes anticipate a Neo-classical interest in surface pattern and form. His opinion that nature, not art, was his tutor was endorsed by a visit to Italy, and demonstrated by his publication, after many years of detailed study, of *The Anatomy of The Horse* (1766). *Gimcrack on Newmarket Heath* and *The Grosvenor Hunt* are examples of the type of picture that won him fame among the landed gentry and aristocracy.

Sturgeon, William (1783-1850) English physicist, who devised the first electromagnet. His invention, made in 1823, consisted of a coil of insulated wire wound round a bar of soft iron; when a current flowed in the coil, the bar became a temporary magnet and could lift nine times its own weight. In 1836, he devised the moving-coil galvanometer, a current-detecting device, based on the same principle.

Sturm, Johannes (1507-89) German educator and founder of a Latin *gymnasium*, later Strasbourg University (1621), which became the model for Protestant and Jesuit grammar schools.

Sturt, Charles (1795-1869) British Army officer who explored the barren heartlands of the Australian continent. In 1828, he was appointed leader of an expedition into the interior drylands and discovered the Darling River. A year later he commanded a second expedition, which floated down the Murrumbidgee River in a whaling boat, and followed the course of the Murray River. His most ambitious expedition, in 1844, took him to the unexplored interior of the continent, north of Lake Eyre.

Stuyvesant, Peter (1592-1672) Dutch colonial governor in America, who surrendered New Amsterdam (now New York City) to an English invasion fleet in 1664.

Sudermann, Hermann (1857-1928) Germany's leading dramatist of the 1890s. His first success was *Honour* (1889), an exposition of contemporary German class divisions. His other plays included *Magda* (1893), *Battle of the Butterflies* (1895) and *Morituri*, a cycle of three one-act plays (1896).

Suetonius Tranquillus, Gaius (c. 69-c. 140) Roman biographer and author of *Lives of the 12 Caesars*, his greatest extant work. Of historical interest because of their great and varied detail, these books cover the period from the end of Julius CAESAR's rule to that of Emperor DOMITIAN.

Suger, Abbot (c. 1081-1150) French cleric who, by drawing together architects of different regions in France, and by his own stringent and original ideas of what a building should be like, inaugurated the Gothic style in the Ile de France.

Suharto (born 1921) President of Indonesia who seized office by a military coup, overthrowing SUKARNO. He succeeded as Indonesia's army commander after his predecessor was murdered in an abortive coup by the Communists in 1965, and deposed Sukarno in 1967. Suharto has pursued a fiercely anti-Communist policy ever since.

Sukarno, Ahmed (c. 1901-70) Indonesian Nationalist leader, and dictator of his country from 1949 until deposed in 1967. He first led an unsuccessful revolt against Dutch colonial government in 1926. He was arrested three times, imprisoned and once exiled to Sumatra (1940). When the Japanese drove the Dutch out of Indonesia in the Second World War, they appointed Sukarno President of the Java Central Council, and when the Japanese in turn were forced to withdraw in 1945, Sukarno declared Indonesia a republic and embarked on a four-year war with the Dutch and officially became President in 1949 when the Dutch formally ceded Indonesia. His aggressive attitude to Malaysia and his leftist leanings culminated in his implication in a Communist plot (1965) to seize power, and he was deposed in 1967 by General SUHARTO and a group of army officers. He was kept under house-arrest until his death.

Suleiman I 'The Magnificent' (c. 1496-1566) Sultan of Turkey, whose reign brought the Ottoman Empire to its peak. His troops thrust westwards into Europe (1521), took Belgrade, and – after killing Hungary's LOUIS II at Mohacs (1526) – seized much of Hungary, which Suleiman ruled through John Zapolya. To retain Hungary against the claims of Ferdinand of Austria (later Emperor FERDINAND I), the Turks made several attacks on Austria which terrorized all central Europe. Possession of Hungary remained in dispute until, and after, Suleiman's death. In Asia, Suleiman ended Persian threats by seizing Georgia and Baghdad (1534). Helped by corsairs headed by Barbarossa II, he established a formidable fleet, which swept the Mediterranean Sea.

Sulla, Lucius Cornelius (138-78 BC) Roman consul, general and dictator, who reformed Roman law. Using Roman troops for the first time to suppress political rivals, he defeated Marius to become dictator (82-79 BC). His 'Cornelian laws' restored government machinery which had been crippled by wars, and rebuilt the Senate's strength at the people's expense. Antagonism to Sulla's patrician rule triggered the revolt of SPARTACUS and brought forth new, popular leaders.

Sullivan, Sir Arthur (1842-1900) British composer who collaborated with W. S. GILBERT to write the 'Savoy' operas, which have become one of Britain's national institutions.

Sullivan, John L. (1858-1918) American boxer recognized in 1882 as the first professional world heavyweight champion. He held the title until beaten by James J. Corbett in the first world heavyweight title fight fought under QUEENSBERRY rules, in 1892.

Sullivan, Louis Henri (1856-1924) American architect, who led the so-called Chicago school of architects which, in the late 19th century, devised the massive commercial palaces of Chicago, the forerunners of skyscraper office blocks. Although he designed on an enormous scale, Sullivan's attention to decorative detail did not suffer and he retained his intense interest in the relationship of form and function. The degree of elaboration in his decoration of interiors such as in the Chicago Auditorium, was often comparable with European Art Nouveau. He was known as the 'father of modernism' and greatly influenced Lloyd WRIGHT.

Sully, Duc de (1560-1641) French statesman, convinced Protestant and a friend of the Calvinist, Henry of Navarre (later HENRY IV). He fought for Henry in the religious civil wars and when Henry became king was appointed his finance minister (1597-1611). Sully revived France's economy and strengthened national defences, and kept internal peace by quelling religious disturbances regardless of the insurgents' faith. When Henry was assassinated, Sully was ousted.

Sundback, Gideon (1880-1954) Swedish-born American inventor. Although a zip fastener was invented, and patented, by Whitcomb L. Judson (1891), Sundback, after several years' work, developed the first dependable commercial zip fastener (1913), with all the essentials of its modern counterpart and also efficient machines for its manufacture.

Sun Yat-sen (1866-1925) Chinese revolutionary, who founded the Chinese Nationalist Party (Kuomintang, 1912) on the 'Three Principles' of nationalism, democracy and socialism. After revolt against the Manchu broke out in Hankow (1911), a revolutionary assembly at Nanking elected him Provisional President of the United Provinces of China. Meanwhile, the national assembly in Peking had appointed the northern general Yüan Shih-k'ai as Prime Minister (and later President). For the sake of national unity, Sun gave way to Yüan (1912), who from 1913-16 used his presidency to become virtual dictator. Sun opposed this régime, but was defeated and exiled. In 1921, he returned to power as Provisional President of the South China Republic. He was deposed by the war lords, but after being restored to power at Canton in 1923, accepted Russian help to broaden the Kuomintang to admit Communists.

Surrey, Henry Howard, Earl of (c. 1517-47) English poet who, together with Sir Thomas WYATT, adapted Italian Renaissance verse forms, especially the sonnet, to English. His translation of part of the *Aeneid* also introduced blank verse into England.

Surtees, Robert (1803-64) English humorist, whose comic novels about Mr Jorrocks, the hunting grocer, are often an astute observation of English social life and manners. Surtees founded *The New Sporting Magazine* (1831), in which Mr Jorrocks first appeared. These sketches were later published as *Jorrocks's Jaunts and Jollities* (1838).

Sutherland, Graham (born 1903) British artist, who took up painting after being a railway engineer. His

Sutherland's work draws heavily on the forms of nature

earliest works were landscapes and his painting has an organic feeling of growth, often based on natural forms such as roots, trees and birds. In the 1950s he began to paint portraits and turned also to religious painting. His best-known works in this vein are the *Crucifixion* for St Matthew's, Northampton, and the design for the tapestry in Coventry Cathedral.

Swammerdam, Jan (1637-80) Dutch entomologist whose careful microscope studies of insect anatomy produced the first detailed descriptions of metamorphosis (change of form) in insects and of the structure of their mouth parts and compound eyes.

Swan, Sir Joseph Wilson (1828-1914) English physicist and chemist who invented several important devices and processes. For many years from 1848 he experimented (like many European and American inventors) with the production of a long-lasting electric filament lamp. In 1878, after being joined by high-vacuum specialist, Charles H. Stearn, he produced a successful lamp. EDISON achieved a similar breakthrough at the same time, and just beat Swan to an English patent. The two joined to form the company of Ediswan (1883). Swan's subsequent system for making lamp filaments from nitrocellulose (1883) was adopted by CHARDONNET for making artificial silk (rayon).

Swedenborg, Emmanuel (1688-1772) Swedish scientist, philosopher and religious writer whose teaching inspired the Swedenborgian sect and led to the setting up of the Jerusalem Church after his death.

Sweelinck, Jan Pieterszoon (1562-1621) Dutch organist and composer who first fully developed fugal writing in organ composition as well as independent pedal playing, in this he was a considerable influence on the northern European tradition and helped to prepare the way for J. S. BACH.

Sweyn I (11th cent.) King of Denmark, known as Sweyn Forkbeard, who made Denmark's authority felt in Norway, Sweden and northern Germany through his raids and battles. He also sent or led annual raids to ravage England (1002-13) and collect tribute payments (Danegeld). In 1013 Sweyn became the acknowledged King of England.

Sweyn II (11th cent.) King of Denmark, also known as Sweyn Estrithson, who founded the Estrith dynasty (1047-1375). He fought off Norway's Magnus I and HAROLD III HAAR-

DRAADE, who claimed Denmark as part of the Norwegian kingdom and twice tried to invade England (1069, 1075), to whose throne he laid claim (he was the last Danish king to do so) but was repulsed by WILLIAM I.

Swift, Jonathan (1667-1745) Irish-born satirist, essayist, novelist and poet, the most powerful prose writer of the 18th century, who wrote *Gulliver's Travels* (1727). He became secretary to Sir William Temple, then sought a career, unsuccessfully, in the Church. He wrote many political pamphlets, and was the editor (1710-11) of the Tory *Examiner*. He formed a close association with such writers as POPE, ARBUTHNOT and GAY. Eventually, Swift returned to Ireland as Dean of St Patrick's Cathedral, Dublin, and continued to write savagely satirical pamphlets on the English administration of Ireland, in such works as *The Drapier Letters* (1724) and *A Modest Proposal* (1729).

Swinburne, Algernon Charles (1837-1909) English poet, a master of mellifluous verse with which he attempted to attack Victorian conventional morality. He was educated at Oxford, where he met ROSSETTI and the Pre-Raphaelites. Swinburne was excitable, passionate and loved to shock; the *Poems and Ballads* (1866, 1878, 1889) did shock, though their sensuality was mainly affectation.

Swinton, Sir Ernest Dunlop (1868-1951) British soldier who played a leading role in the invention of the military tank. The first major tank attack was at Cambrai (November 1917), when four hundred tanks, on a six-mile front, advanced before the infantry. A new tactical weapon had arrived.

Sydenham, Thomas (1624-89) English doctor and sometime Captain of Horse in CROMWELL's army, who was the first person to recognize hysteria as a disease. A follower of LOCKE and the empiricists, throughout his career Sydenham stressed the importance of accurate clinical observation rather than chemical theorizing, and his *Of the whole course in illnesses and almost all ways of curing them* (1692 posthumously) was widely used until the early 19th century.

Sylvester, James Joseph (1814-97) English lawyer and mathematician, who, with CAYLEY, invented the theory of algebraic forms. He also founded the *American Journal of Mathematics*.

Symington, William (1763-1831) Scottish engineer who installed a direct action (i.e. without a beam) steam engine into a paddle boat (1788). Although this was the first practical steamship, it aroused no commercial interest. Later, in 1801, Symington was commissioned by Lord Dundas, Governor of the Forth and Clyde Canal Company, to build a larger boat, the *Charlotte Dundas*, which worked for a time until abandoned because its wash damaged the canal banks.

Synge, John Millington (1871-1909) Irish dramatist, who wrote *The Playboy of the Western World* (1907), one of the masterpieces of the Irish theatre. When it was first staged at Dublin's Abbey Theatre (1907) it caused a riot. Synge wrote only six plays, but all are remarkable for their poetic interpretation of the Irish character and vernacular speech. *The Well of the Saints* (1905) and *The Tinker's Wedding* (1907) are rich with the flavour of folk-speech. He left an unfinished poetic drama, *Deirdre of the Sorrows*. Synge was director of the Abbey Theatre from 1904.

T

Tabari, al- (838-923) Arab historian, who is mainly notable for his vast history of the world, the *Annals*, from the Creation to the beginning of the 10th century, the major source book for early Arabic history. Al-Tabari was also author of one of the principal commentaries on the *Koran*.

Tacitus, Cornelius (c. 55-c. 120) Roman historian, a successful orator and politician who described the early Roman Empire after AUGUSTUS. His *Histories*, published before 110, covering the years from NERO's death (68) to DOMITIAN's (96), and his later *Annals*, covering 14-69, survive in part, revealing an essentially honest and careful writer, unable to conceal his distaste of the Imperial system.

Taglioni, Maria (1804-84) Italian ballerina whose dancing particularly in *La Sylphide* largely created the immense 19th-century vogue for romantic ballet.

Tagore, Sir Rabindranath (1861-1941) Indian poet, playwright and novelist. A religious and lyrical writer, Tagore revealed to the West something of the dignity, complexity and beauty of Indian culture. His life was devoted to literature, and the political and social service of his people. Although he wrote in Bengali, he translated several of his own works into English, the best known being *Gitanjali* (1912), which earned him the Nobel Prize for Literature in 1913.

Taine, Hippolyte (1828-93) French historian, philosopher and critic whose theories are expounded in the Introduction to *History of English Literature* (1863) and in *On Intelligence* (1870). In accordance with his concept of criticism as a strictly objective, scientific process, Taine emphasizes the importance of physical, psychological and environmental factors in the study of art, literature and history, with his formula of 'la race, le milieu et le moment'.

T'ai Tsung (597-649) Principal founder of the T'ang dynasty in China, whose reign (627-49) marked the zenith of Chinese and T'ang power. After a period of chaos (618-23) T'ai Tsung reunited all China, overthrew the northern Turks in Mongolia and occupied Sinkiang. Internally he reformed the administration, established an efficient bureaucracy, and tried to prevent the formation of large estates. He endeavoured to be a model Confucian ruler, open to advice and criticism. Under his patronage there began the development of arts and literature for which the T'ang dynasty is famous.

Takanobu, Fujiwara (1142-1205) Japanese poet and portrait painter. His work represents the general tendency of the period towards secular realism, in a series of portraits which are bold and simplified in design and colour, differing considerably from earlier religious examples. In 1173, his portraits completing a processional mural painting by another artist were reported to be so realistic that shocked court officials hid them from view.

Talbot, William Henry Fox (1800-77) English inventor who, in 1834, retired from political life and started to experiment with photography. Talbot published the first book illustrated with photographs, *The Pencil of Nature* (1844-6), pioneered flash photography of moving objects (1851), and invented photoglyphy (1852). He was also a distinguished mathematician, and decipherer of Assyrian cuneiform inscriptions.

Talleyrand-Périgord, Charles Maurice de (1754-1838) French statesman, who negotiated NAPOLEON's deposition and the restoration of the Bourbons. As Bishop of Autun, he sat in the States General of 1789, where he sided with the revolutionary party. However, he was never an extremist, and fled to the US after the execution of LOUIS XVI. Talleyrand returned during the Directory and became Foreign Minister (1797-9). He helped Napoleon seize power in 1799 and served him until 1807.

Believing that Napoleon's policies would prove ruinous to France, he engaged in a secret correspondence with the Allies, notably ALEXANDER I of Russia, with whom, following the fall of Paris (1814), he negotiated the terms of Napoleon's overthrow. At a meeting with LOUIS XVIII, he secured a guarantee (the Charter of Ghent) of the main reforms accomplished by the Revolution as the price of the Bourbon restoration. At the Congress of Vienna (1814-15), he represented France and induced the Allies to deal with her not as a beaten enemy but as an equal. He helped LOUIS-PHILIPPE to attain the throne in 1830, serving him as ambassador in London until 1834. An opportunist rather than a sincere churchman, Talleyrand had resigned his episcopal see in 1791, but he requested and received the last sacraments as a bishop in return for having achieved a reconciliation between Church and State in France.

Tallis, Thomas (c. 1505-85) English composer of church music who wrote the Anglican hymn tune, 'Tallis's Canon' and the tune used by VAUGHAN WILLIAMS for his *Fantasia on a Theme of Thomas Tallis*. Tallis, whose career spanned the Reformation in England, could catch the beauty and dignity of words whether he was writing to English or to Latin texts.

Tamerlane (c. 1336-1405) Mongol Turkish warrior, and creator of the last great Mongol Empire. Conquering Turkestan and setting up his capital at Samarkand, he set out to restore the Mongol Empire founded by his indirect ancestor GENGHIS KHAN. His troops swept across central Asia and seized Persia, Mesopotamia and southern Russia (1380-95), and invaded northern India, sacking Delhi (1398-9). Tamerlane razed Aleppo in Syria and crushed Ottoman troops in Turkey (1401-2), before heading east to China, but died from fever on the way. His empire disintegrated, ending Mongol power in central Asia.

Tancred (12th cent.) Last of the Norman kings of Sicily (1190-4) and illegitimate son of ROGER II's eldest son, he fended off the German emperor Henry VI, who claimed Sicily and Naples through his marriage to Roger II's daughter Constance.

Taney, Roger Brooke (1777-1864) American jurist who helped to create the climate in which the Civil War began. Succeeding John Marshall as Chief Justice of the Supreme Court, he extended federal authority over corporations and held that the federal government had exclusive authority over foreign relations. Taney clashed with STORY by defending states' rights, except where they interfered with the exertion of federal power. In the *Dred Scott Decision* (1857) he denied that Congress had power to end slavery in individual states, thus exacerbating the hatred between North and South which helped to precipitate the South's secession.

T'ang Hsien-tsu (1550-1617) Chinese dramatist and poet, leading exponent of *Ch'uan ch'i*, or Southern drama. Drama in South China had for centuries been little more than strings of popular songs, but *Ch'uan ch'i* was more dramatic and brought it new serious artistic standards. T'ang's work in the new medium was outstanding and helped to establish the popularity of the form. His four plays, *Dreams of Yu Ming Hall*, the most celebrated of which is *The Peony Pavilion*, remain classics.

Tao Chi (1641-c. 1717) Chinese painter of the Ch'ing dynasty. A Buddhist monk, descended from one of the Ming emperors, he rebelled against the contemporary fashion of drawing on past artists for ideas, and, in his own words, adopted 'the method which consists of not following any method'.

T'ao Ch'ien (365-427) Chinese recluse poet whose poem 'Home Again' is generally regarded as his masterpiece. T'ao Ch'ien began life as a minor official, but retired at 40 to support himself by farming. He remained poor, but it was this period which produced his finest poetry, extolling the virtues of the simple life in a complementary style which made him remarkable among contemporary Chinese poets.

Tariq ibn-Ziyad (7th-8th cent.) Berber general who began the Muslim invasion of Spain (711). He crossed the Strait of Gibraltar from Morocco with 7000 troops, captured the Rock and, strengthened by reinforcements, crushed Visigothic resistance in Spain by defeating King Roderick near the coast. Thrusting inland he took Cordoba, Toledo and other areas, beginning Spain's eight centuries of Muslim rule, which lasted until Boabdil's expulsion. The name Gibraltar is a corruption of the Arabic *jabal Tariq*, 'mount Tariq'.

Tartaglia, Niccola Fontana (c. 1500-57) Italian mathematician, who was one of the discoverers of the solution to cubic equations. The results were later published by CARDANO in a breach of confidence, and the angry dispute which followed led to Tartaglia's dismissal from his public lectureship at Brescia.

Tartini, Giuseppe (1692-1770) Italian violinist who developed a legendary skill and founded the 'School of Nations' in Padua for violinists. He was also a renowned theoretician who made innovations in violin structure as well as acoustic discoveries.

Tasman, Abel Janszoon (1603-59) Dutch navigator who discovered large parts of Australasia. Sailing from Mauritius, Tasman discovered 'Van Dieman's Land' (Tasmania) and New Zealand (1642), whose west coast he followed northward before striking northeast to Tonga and then turning west to discover the Fijis (1643). By encircling Australia (without seeing it), Tasman proved it was not part of the rumoured giant continent 'Terra Australis'. Tasman's second voyage (1644) explored the north and west coast of Australia.

Tasso, Torquato (1544-95) Italian poet, author of *Jerusalem Delivered* (1581-4), an epic poem on the First Crusade, which elucidated the anxiety that was to overshadow Tasso's life and undermine all his subsequent work: the conflict between his lyric sensuality and his deeply held religious and moral beliefs. Unhappy about the pagan lyricism of what was essentially a religious work, he submitted the work to the Inquisition for judgement. Continuous revisions eventually transformed it into the cold, stilted *Conquest of Jerusalem* (1593). In 1573, he published the influential pastoral drama *Aminta*. The only significant work of his later years was *Re Torrismondo*, a tragedy of incest and betrayal.

Tata, Sir Dorabji Jamsetji (1859-1932) Indian industrialist and philanthropist, who laid the foundations of India's iron and steel industry. After discovering (with SAKLATVALA) a hill of almost solid iron ore in Orissa in 1903, he founded the Tata iron and steel empire, which, with cotton mills established by his father, formed the cornerstone of modern India's economic development. He also provided Bombay with power from hydro-electric installations in the Western Ghats and followed his father's example in encouraging scientific education.

Tauchnitz, Christian Bernard (1816-95) German publisher, who founded (1841) the *Collection of British Authors* (later *British and American*), one of the first series of pocket-books in Europe.

Tauler, Johann (c. 1300-61) German Dominican monk and preacher, one of the great Christian mystics of the Middle Ages. His teachings stress practical rather than speculative theology, emphasizing the immanence of God and the need to abandon oneself to His will. He gained great fame as a preacher in his adopted town of Basle.

Taylor, Alan John Percivale (born 1906) English historian whose prolific output has established him as one of the most widely known scholars of his generation. He has written principally on the 19th and 20th centuries and contributed major analyses in *The Course of German History* (1945) and *The Origins of the Second World War* (1961).

Taylor, Zachary (1784-1850) American general who distinguished himself in the Mexican War and became the twelfth President of the US. Taylor was elected President in 1848 and soon had to face the slavery problem. He favoured the admission of California and New Mexico to the Union as an anti-slave state, but the Southern leaders violently opposed this and threatened to withdraw their support for Taylor. His contempt for the Compromise of 1850 (legislation designed to solve the dilemma of the slavery question) was undisguised, but before the measure could be passed by Congress, Taylor died.

Tchaikovsky, Pëtr Ilyich (1840-93) Russian composer. Tchaikovsky left government service at the age of 23 to study music. He reacted sharply against the Russian nationalist school of composers, and, in forming his style, looked towards western Europe. In 1877 his one attempt at marriage broke up after a few weeks. Later his work was made possible by the patronage of a wealthy widow, Nadezhda von Meck, who made him an allowance, on condition that they should never meet, although they carried on a copious correspondence. Tchaikovsky's best-known works are the fantasy overture *Romeo and Juliet* (1869-70), the concert overture *1812* (1882), which contains optional cannon in the scoring; the ballets *The Sleeping Beauty* (1890), *The Nutcracker* (1892) and *Swan Lake* (1877); the *Piano Concerto No. 1* (1875); the *Violin Concerto* (1878) and the Fourth, Fifth and Sixth (*Pathétique*) Symphonies. He also wrote two major operas – *Eugene Onegin* (1879) and *The Queen of Spades* (1890), both based on PUSHKIN. Tchaikovsky died of cholera.

Tchernichowski, Shaul (1875-1943) Russian-born Hebrew lyric poet, who was the first Hebrew writer to reflect strongly the influence of the non-Jewish environment. He translated HOMER's *Iliad* and *Odyssey* into Hebrew.

Indian fighter and victor over Mexico's Santa Anna, Zachary Taylor was US President for only 16 months

Teach, Edward (17th-18th cent.) English pirate, known as 'Blackbeard', notorious for his depredations along the Virginia and North Carolina coast and in the Caribbean Sea, where he blockaded ports and plundered ships. In 1718, the Governor of Virginia sent two sloops against him, and after a fierce battle he was killed, his head being taken to Virginia as a trophy.

Tegner, Esaias (1782-1846) Swedish Romantic poet, who achieved fame in 1811 with *Sweden*, a long narrative poem inspired by Sweden's humiliating fate after the Finno-Prussian War. His *Frithiofs Saga* (1825), the most popular Swedish Romantic cycle, won the praises of GOETHE and was translated by LONGFELLOW.

Teisserenc de Bort, Léon Philippe (1855-1913) French meteorologist who discovered the stratosphere. Working at first for the French Central Bureau of Meteorology and then

The music of Tchaikovsky—best known if by no means the greatest Russian composer—has an evergreen popularity

privately (from 1896), he explored the upper atmosphere with free balloons containing recoverable instruments for measuring atmospheric temperature and pressure. By 1902, with the German, Assmann, he had found that above a certain level (ranging from five to ten miles) the atmospheric temperature stops falling with increasing altitude and remains constant, or even rises.

Telford, Thomas (1757-1834) Scottish civil engineer, who became a leading bridge, road and canal builder of the Industrial Revolution. His first major commission was the planning of the Ellesmere Canal, in Shropshire, which he began in 1793. In 1801, he received a government commission to report on the highway needs of Scotland, as a result of which he went on to build more than 900 miles of road, 1200 bridges and improve many Scottish harbours. Telford also built roads in England and Wales and his influence as a road maker was second only to that of MCADAM. His other works included the Caledonian Canal (from 1804), the Menai suspension (road) bridge, linking Anglesey with the mainland (1819-26), and the Gotha Canal in Sweden.

Teller, Edward (born 1908) Hungarian-American physicist largely responsible for the development of the hydrogen bomb. After working on the atomic bomb project at Los Alamos, New Mexico, in the 1940s, he became an enthusiastic proponent of a new and more powerful weapon, the hydrogen bomb.

Tenniel, Sir John (1820-1914) English humorous artist, the original illustrator of *Alice's Adventures in Wonderland* and *Alice Through the Looking Glass*. His illustrations also include those for the well-known Happy Family playing cards (1851). The leading political cartoonist of the Victorian era, he worked regularly for *Punch* as its chief cartoonist. His technique was laboured and his drawings were rigid, but they were redeemed by the originality of his ideas and the sharp, satirical likenesses to well-known people.

Tennyson, Alfred, Lord (1809-92) English poet, immensely popular in his lifetime, whose main achievement was his mastery of the rhythmic qualities of the English language. His subjects were mainly legendary and historical, although a principal theme in his work is the heroism of ordinary people faced with difficulties. Tennyson slowly won recognition, till in 1850, he published the famous elegiac lyrics *In Memoriam*, and became Poet Laureate.

Tenzing, Norgay (born 1914)
Nepalese mountaineer who (with
Edmund HILLARY) became the first
to climb Everest, the world's highest
mountain.

Terborch, Gerard (1617-81) Dutch
painter, best known for his elegant
and harmoniously coloured genre
scenes. These, like those of METSU,
are usually confined to the domestic
activities of the prosperous middle-
classes.

**Terbrugghen, Hendrick (1588-
1629)** Dutch artist and member of a
group of Utrecht painters, who were
influenced by CARAVAGGIO's pictorial
innovations. After a visit to Italy,
Terbrugghen adopted Caravaggio's
sharp tonal contrasts and everyday
realism, though he used them with
less dramatic force.

Terence (c. 190-159 BC) Roman
dramatist, originally a slave from
Africa, who adapted Greek New
Comedy for Roman audiences. Of
his six surviving Comedies of Manners, four are based on MENANDER,
the other two on his admirer and
imitator Apollodorus. Though more
faithful to his Greek originals than
PLAUTUS, Terence made changes to
increase realism, adding characters,
clarifying obscurities in the Greek
settings and in one case taking a
scene from a second play.

Teresa of Avila (1515-82) Spanish
mystic and an important reformer of
the Carmelite order. Her *Life* (1562-
65) describes her early mystical experiences and visions and her spiritual growth. Written in unadorned
prose, it is a remarkably intimate, self-
analytical document. Among her
other writings are *Way to Perfection*
(1565) a spiritual guide for the Avila
nuns – and *The Mansions* (1588),
which describes the seven stages of
union with God in terms of seven
dwellings. She was canonized in
1622.

Terman, Lewis (1877-1956) American psychologist who with BINET produced the first intelligence test to be
put to general use. He also devised
the term intelligence quotient (IQ)
to describe the score achieved in a
test adjusted for age so that the average person will score 100.

Terry, Dame Ellen (1847-1928)
English actress, the most famous of
her day and memorable as IRVING's
leading lady.

Tertullian (c. 160-c. 230) Carthage-
born Roman ecclesiastical writer, one
of the Fathers of the Church. A
Christian convert, he became the
chief defender of the faith and one of

the greatest early Christian writers of
the West.

Tesla, Nikola (1857-1943) Austro-
Hungarian electrical engineer, who
emigrated to the United States in
1884. There, working successively
with EDISON, the Westinghouse Company and in his own laboratory, Tesla
made a number of significant contributions, which made alternating-
current practical. These included the
development of one of the earliest AC
motors and generators, AC transmission systems and high-frequency
AC devices.

Tetzel, Johann (c. 1465-1519) German Dominican monk who, by selling indulgences (particularly by tout-
ing for money to help build St Peter's
in Rome) and by promising that cash
gifts alone would secure indulgences
for the dead, provoked LUTHER to
publish his 95 theses against indulgences, an immediate cause of the
Reformation.

**Thackeray, William Makepeace
(1811-63)** English novelist, who
wrote *Vanity Fair* (1847-8), one of
the outstanding satirical novels of the
19th century. Thackeray was at first
divided between literature and painting, but, pressed for money, took up
journalism for a living. His early work
– essays, stories, travel-pieces –
passed without notice; in 1847 he
made his mark with *The Book of
Snobs* and *Vanity Fair*, and gained
success as a novelist, editor and lecturer. From his lectures he published
*The English Humorists of the 18th
Century* (1853) and *The Four Georges:
Sketches of Manners, Morals, Court
and Town Life* (1860). His novels in-

Ellen Terry first appeared on the stage
at the age of nine

clude *Pendennis* (1848-50), *Esmond*
(1852) and *The Newcomes* (1853-5).
Influenced by FIELDING, he had the
ability to recreate society, in satirical
portraits of enduring vitality.

Thant, U (born 1909) Burmese
educationalist and second Secretary-
General of the United Nations Organization. U Thant became Burma's
permanent UN representative in
1957 and two years later he was
elected Vice-President of the UN
General Assembly, becoming Secretary-General following Dag HAM-
MARSKJOLD's death in 1961. He was
re-elected for a further five years in
1966.

**Thayer, Alexander Wheelock
(1817-97)** American writer who made
it his life's work to write the standard
biography of BEETHOVEN. To achieve
this he lived many years on slender
means in Austria and Germany, ex-
haustively researching every detail of
Beethoven's life.

Themistocles (c. 527-c. 460 BC)
Greek statesman who saved Athens
(and Greece) from conquest by the
Persians. Following the Greek victory at Marathon (490 BC), Themistocles believed that a powerful navy
was essential if Athens was to survive
a further Persian onslaught, and increased the Athenian navy from 120
to 300 triremes. The land defences of
Greece were the joint responsibility
of the Athenians and Spartans. When
XERXES of Persia attacked Greece in
480 BC he was defeated in the naval
battles of Artemisium and Salamis
and forced to retreat. Themistocles,
however, distrusted his Spartan allies
and wished to break with them; but
the Athenians refused to follow him
in opposing Persia and Sparta simultaneously. Losing most of his power
c. 479 BC, Themistocles was ostracized six years later and went into
exile.

Theocritus (c. 310-250 BC) Greek
poet, originator of the pastoral idyll,
who influenced VIRGIL's *Eclogues*
with a group of poems which portray
the timeless and romantic quality of
country life in Sicily, with some fine
descriptions and vivid dramatic
scenes. In other poems the subject is
town life; others are short epics with
mythological themes.

Theodore I Lascaris (c. 1175-1222)
First emperor of Nicaea (1208-22).
He was son-in-law of the Byzantine
emperor Alexius III and helped
Alexius V's defence of Constantinople
against the Fourth Crusade. When
the Byzantine Empire temporarily
came to an end with the fall of Constantinople (1204), Theodore founded
a Byzantine succession state based on

Nicaea, southeast of Constantinople. He fought against crusaders, Seljuk Turks and the emperors of Trebizond, to bring most of northwest Anatolia under his rule.

Theodoric the Great (c. 454-526) King of the Ostrogoths (474-526) and ruler of Italy (493-526). Commissioned by the Byzantine emperor Zeno (who sought to divide the barbarians), Theodoric attacked Italy (488-93) and killed the Herulian leader ODOACER, who had deposed the last western Roman emperor. Theodoric then ruled Italy from Ravenna and brought prosperity to the kingdom. At the end of his reign, after 30 years of peace and tolerance, Theodoric, an Arian, took savage reprisals against orthodox Roman Catholics because of Emperor JUSTINIAN's persecution of Arians. After Theodoric's death, BELISARIUS drove the Ostrogoths from Italy.

Theopanes (c. 752-818) Byzantine historian and theologian. His *Chronical*, an historical narrative covering the years 284-813, preserved the evidence of authorities now lost and presents a very readable account of the Byzantine dark ages.

Theophrastus (c. 372-287 BC) Greek botanist, often called the founder of scientific botany. He described over 500 species and attempted a systematic classification.

Thesiger, Wilfred Patrick (born 1910) British explorer who (1945-50) made the most detailed exploration ever of southern Arabia and its mysterious 'empty quarter'. He had earlier explored in Africa, Abyssinia and the Sudan.

Thiers, Louis Adolphe (1797-1877) French statesman and President of France, who negotiated the treaty that ended the Franco-Prussian War and who suppressed the Paris Commune (1871). After helping LOUIS-PHILIPPE to ascend to the French throne (1830), he became his Minister of the Interior, making himself notorious by the severity with which he suppressed working-class disturbances in Lyons and Paris. Following the Bonapartist *coup d'état* of 1851, he was exiled to the provinces. He became a deputy again in 1863, but was an opponent of NAPOLEON III's policies. After France's defeat in the Franco-Prussian War, (1870) Thiers became head of the provisional government. He came to terms with BISMARCK, and in less than three years managed to raise the whole of the indemnity demanded by him through government loans, thus securing the Germans' evacuation of France. He put down the Commune

by using provincial troops against Paris in May 1871 and was President of the Third Republic from that year until 1873.

Thomas à Kempis (1380-1471) German ecclesiastic and writer thought to be the author of *The Imitation of Christ*, the most widely read handbook of Christian devotion ever written. In simple terms it instructs the Christian on how to seek spiritual perfection by taking CHRIST as a model. Its direct call to religious devotion has appealed to Christians ever since it was first published and no book, except the Bible, has been so often reprinted in the Western World.

Thomas, Brandon (1857-1914) English dramatist, actor and theatre manager, who wrote the ever-popular farce *Charley's Aunt* (1892).

Thomas, Dylan (1914-53) Welsh poet, whose early verse, packed with imagery and revelling in language, formed a striking contrast with the poetry of the late 1930s. The verse of *Eighteen Poems* (1934) and *Twenty-five Poems* (1936) was a celebration of the processes of life; in his mature work, *Deaths and Entrances* (1946) and *Collected Poems* (1952), elegies and memories become part of a ritual that assures man of his triumph over death. He wrote *Under Milk Wood* (1954), a brilliant verse play for radio, the semi-autobiographical prose of *Portrait of the Artist as a Young Dog* (1940) and an unfinished novel, *Adventures in the Skin Trade* (1955).

Thomas, Edward (1878-1917) English poet, influenced by Robert FROST, who wrote of rural life and scenes, a peaceful world contrasting with the battlefield of Arras, where he died. His collected poems were published in 1920.

Thomas, Theodore (1835-1905) German-born American conductor who founded the Chicago Symphony Orchestra (1891). Thomas did much to popularize classical music in the United States.

Thompson, David (1770-1857) English explorer and fur-trader who made the first reliable maps of western Canada, while working for a British fur-trading concern in western North America. Thompson mapped more than a million square miles of Canada between Lake Superior and the Pacific, tracing lakes and rivers, including the Columbia, Mississippi and Saskatchewan. His trading post in Idaho was the first building in that state (1809) and he built Spokane House (1810), the first permanent building in Washington State. Thompson supervised the

British survey establishing the boundary between Canada and the United States (1816-26).

Thompson, Edward Herbert (1860-1935) American explorer-archaeologist who excavated the sacred Maya city of Chichén Itzá in Yucatán, with its famous well containing relics of human sacrifice.

Thompson, Francis (1859-1907) English poet of ecstatic, mystical verse, whose work is strongly influenced by CRASHAW, whom Thompson greatly admired. *Poems* was published in 1893 and 1897, the former volume containing 'The Hound of Heaven', a complex ode of faith and struggle.

Thomsen, Christian (1788-1865) Danish archaeologist, who first gave shape to prehistory by dividing it into three ages. As first curator (1816-65) of the world's first ethnographical museum (in Copenhagen), he arranged the museum's prehistoric antiquities according to their composition – of stone, bronze, or iron. He believed that the huge span of prehistory could be divided into three successive technological periods: a Stone Age, a Bronze Age and an Iron Age. The first clear statement of his classification appeared in 1836.

Thomson, Sir Charles Wyville (1830-82) Scottish professor and naturalist whose pioneering marine voyages, most notably that of the *Challenger*, provided a wealth of oceanographic knowledge.

Thomson, Elihu (1853-1937) English-born American electrical engineer, who invented and improved numerous electrical devices and systems and held over 700 patents. In 1882, together with Edward J. Houston, he formed the Thomson-Houston Electric Company, which 10 years later merged with the Edison General Electric Company to form the General Electric Company, the world's largest manufacturer of electrical equipment.

Thomson, James (1700-48) Scottish poet who tried new subjects and other verse forms when POPE's town themes and heroic couplets were dominant. *The Seasons* (1726-30), four poems in blank verse on the changing year, shows a sympathetic feeling for nature and a keen observation of the countryside. He also wrote 'Rule Britannia'.

Thomson, Sir Joseph John (1856-1940) English physicist who discovered the electron. Measuring the deflection of cathode-rays by magnetic fields, he derived the ratio of mass to charge for cathode-ray particles, about 1000 times smaller than the smallest known values for ions in solution. In this way, he discovered the first sub-atomic particle and called it *electron*. His later discovery that electromagnetic deflection of positive rays (consisting of ionized atoms) depends on their atomic weights led to the development of the mass spectrograph by Aston and others. For his work on the conduction of electricity through gases Thomson was awarded the 1906 Nobel Prize for Physics.

Thomson, Robert William (1822-73) Scottish engineer who, in 1845, patented the pneumatic tyre, an air-filled rubber inner tube within a non-expandable outer cover. He intended these for carriages, and an early set travelled 1000 miles on an English brougham. Nearly 50 years later, the tyres were revived by Dunlop for bicycles.

Thomson, Roy, 1st Baron of Fleet (born 1894) Canadian newspaper proprietor and owner of one of the world's largest publishing empires. He moved to Britain (1953) and acquired control of *The Scotsman* and Scottish Television. In 1959 he bought Kemsley Newspapers Ltd (including *The Sunday Times*), and in 1967 took over *The Times*. He also owns hundreds of newspapers and magazines all over the world, five book publishing firms and a travel agency.

Thoreau, Henry (1817-62) American writer, best known for *Walden, or Life in the Woods* (1854), an original blend of biography and reflection. In 1845 he retired to a hut near Walden Pond, Massachusetts, and out of his seclusion came *Walden*, an individual combination of social criticism, appreciation of nature and practical husbandry.

Thorndike, Dame Sybil (born 1882) English actress, among the most accomplished of her time, and famous for her portrayal of SHAW's *Saint Joan*.

Thornton, William (1759-1828) English born American architect who designed the Capitol building in Washington (1793). In 1814 the Capitol was burned by British troops, but was rebuilt according to original designs for the exterior.

Thorwaldsen, Bertel (1768-1844) Internationally famous Danish sculptor who worked mostly in Rome and became a leader of the Neo-classic movement. An antiquarian as well as an artist, he was involved in reconstruction and restoration of classical works. The *Lion of Lucerne* was the

first of Thorwaldsen's many public monuments.

Thucydides (c. 471-c. 400 BC) Greek writer, considered to be the first truly critical historian. His *History* is a detailed account, based on painstaking research, of the Peloponnesian War between Athens and Sparta (431-404), breaking off unfinished in 411, to be continued by XENOPHON in his *Hellenica*. Thucydides discussed the causes of the war, explained its strategy, and, by contrasting the mercurial Athenians with the stolid Spartans and analysing the roles of such men as PERICLES and ALCIBIADES, sought to explain the defeat of Athens.

Thurber, James Grover (1894-1961) American humorous artist and author. His work is immediately recognisable by its peculiarly nebulous style. He specialized in what he defined as 'the war between men and women', in dogs and in Surrealist situations. His first drawings, which appeared in *The New Yorker* in 1930, were unlike those of anyone else, being little more than incompetent doodles.

Thutmosis III (15th cent. BC) Egyptian pharaoh, who led 20,000 troops and a fleet of warships (the world's first) to seize Palestine, Phoenicia and Syria, and subdue the Aegean islands, thus bringing Egypt's empire to its largest extent. Besides being an efficient administrator, Thutmosis built many temples and obelisks (including the 'Cleopatra's Needles', now in London and New York).

Tiberius (42 BC-AD 37) Second Roman emperor (AD 14-37), stepson of AUGUSTUS, whose policies he continued, in particular the maintenance, but not the extension, of the existing imperial frontiers. A competent soldier and administrator. Tiberius brought peace to the empire and prosperity to the provinces, but he alienated the Senate and the people of Rome by his aloof manner. After an attempt by Sejanus to seize power (AD 29), Tiberius retired to Capri.

Ticknor, William (1810-64) American publisher who helped to end piracy in international publishing. He paid British writers – including TENNYSON and BROWNING – for American rights in their works, and his firm (which published HAWTHORNE, LONGFELLOW and THOREAU) also produced the influential *Atlantic Monthly* and *North American Review*.

Tieck, Ludwig (1772-1853) German poet, novelist and dramatist who was one of the founders of the Ger-

man Romantic movement. A versatile and energetic author, he wrote many romantic *Marchen* (tales) like *Blond Eckbert* (1797), an ironic, satirical tale of the supernatural, and novels such as *The Wanderings of Franz Sternbalds*. He translated *Don Quixote* (1799-1804) and helped SCHLEGEL with his translations of SHAKESPEARE.

Tiepolo, Giovanni Battista (1696-1770) Venetian Rococo artist, primarily famous for his frescoes, depicting airy historical and mythological visions, as in the Palazzo Labia. He achieved his first success in Wurzburg (1750-3), where he decorated the Grand Staircase and Kaisersaal in the Residenz. After returning to Italy, he decorated the Palazzo Valmarana at Vicenza, and in 1769 moved to Madrid, where he decorated the Royal Palace at the invitation of Charles III.

Tintoretto, Jacopo (1518-94) Venetian painter, whose work consists mainly of religious subjects. He claimed to have studied under TITIAN and is reported to have said that he wished to paint like his master and design like MICHELANGELO. His paintings, however, are highly individual: their most characteristic features are elongated figures – sometimes seen in exaggerated foreshortening – in agitated movement, sudden transitions from shadow to flickering light, and diagonally orientated compositions. His first important work, *St Mark Rescuing a Slave* (1548), his largest, the *Paradise* for the Doges' Palace and his decorations for the Scuola di S Rocco in Venice (1576-88) are generally thought to be among his best works.

Tippett, Sir Michael Kemp (born 1905) British composer whose works combine the influences of Elizabethan counterpoint and modernity, most particularly that of HINDEMITH and STRAVINSKY. Tippett has also used negro spirituals, as in his wartime oratorio, *A Child of Our Time*, and jazz, as in some of the songs in his opera *The Knot Garden*. His other works include the *Concerto for Double String Orchestra*, three symphonies and the opera *The Midsummer Marriage*.

Tirpitz, Alfred von (1849-1930) German admiral, who created the high seas fleet that waged unrestricted submarine warfare in the First World War. He began his career as a midshipman in the Prussian navy (1865), became a torpedo specialist, and embodied his ideas and reasons for a powerful German navy in a memorandum which, under Kaiser WILLIAM II's influence, was acted on in 1894. He was Secretary of State for the Imperial German navy (1897-1916) and his introduction of submarine blockades and warfare were instrumental in bringing the US into the First World War. He fled to Switzerland after the war, but returned in 1924 and became a member of the Reichstag.

Tirso de Molina (c. 1584-1648) Spanish dramatist and disciple of LOPE DE VEGA, whose play *The Rogue of Seville* was the first dramatization of the Don Juan story, one of the archetypal themes of European literature. A priest turned playwright, he wrote more than 400 plays, of which 86 survive.

Tisza, Kálmán (1830-1902) Hungarian politician, who ensured Hungary's continued adherence to the Hapsburgs despite her autonomy within the Austro-Hungarian Empire following the *Ausgleich* of 1867. He founded the Hungarian Liberal Party (1875) and was Prime Minister of a government that had an overwhelming majority until 1890. His son, Istvan (1861-1918), Prime Minister from 1903-5 and 1913-17, followed his father's pro-Hapsburg policy and was assassinated when the nationalists secured Hungary's independence after the First World War.

Titian (c. 1487-1576) The greatest of the Venetian painters. He was probably a pupil of the brothers Gentile and Giovanni BELLINI, but the most important early influence on his work was the rich colour and poetic mood of GIORGIONE's painting. After the deaths of Giorgione and Giovanni Bellini (whom he succeeded as Painter to the Republic), Titian dominated Venetian painting. His first major work was the *Assumption* in the Friari Church, Venice (1518), which shows the influence of RAPHAEL's formal values, but places a typically Venetian emphasis on colour. Besides religious pictures Titian painted a number of mythologies (e.g. *The Bacchanal*), which were inspired by the writings of classical authors and which show the more sensuous aspect of his work. He also excelled in portraiture: the *Man with a Glove* (*c.* 1520) is typical of the elegance and, at the same time, grasp of character which he brought to the aristocratic portrait. In 1533 Titian was made court painter to the Emperor CHARLES V, of whom he painted a number of portraits, notably an equestrian picture at the Battle of Muhlberg (1548), which was emulated by later painters.

Tito, Marshal (born 1892) Founder and President of Communist Yugoslavia. Croatian born, Tito served with the Bolsheviks during the Russian Civil War and on his return to Yugoslavia in 1920 became a trade union organizer and political agitator for the illegal Communist Party and was arrested and sent to prison for six years. When Germany invaded Yugoslavia in the Second World War, Tito organized the National Liberation Front to resist their advance. His partisans were more effective in fighting the Germans than the royalist resistance movement of General MIHAILOVICH, and Tito became recognized as the country's leader. In 1945, he was elected Prime Minister and Minister of Defence, and in 1953 became President of the Republic and Supreme Commander of the Armed Forces. Tito has applied Marxist principles to industry, trade and the management of living accommodation, but has left the peasants in possession of their land. Under his rule, Yugoslav Communism is less oppressive and more democratic than the orthodox Soviet form which he has steadfastly refused to adopt.

Titus (c. AD 39-81) Roman emperor (79-81). Co-ruler with his father VESPASIAN after capturing Jerusalem (70) and sole emperor from 79, Titus showed unusual tolerance to political opponents by ending treason trials and expelling informers. In 79 he gave material aid to Pompeii when it was devastated by volcanic eruption, and to Rome when it was damaged by fire. During his reign the empire was at peace, except in Britain, where AGRICOLA conquered as far north as the Tay.

Tobey, Mark (born 1890) American painter, whose characteristic 'white writing' or calligraphic style had considerable influence on the Abstract Expressionists.

Tocqueville, Alexis, Comte de (1805-59) French historian, particularly known for his study, *Democracy in America* (1835-40), an impressive analysis of a new civilization's governmental machine whose democratic principles were set before

Titian: a self portrait. Greatest of Venetian painters, he lived into his 90s

the French people for the first time. His other great work is *The Ancient régime and the Revolution* (1856), in which he sought to demonstrate that, far from being a rupture with the past, the 1789 Revolution was a logical development from the old order.

Todd, Garfield (born 1908) Rhodesian Prime Minister (1953-8) who proposed educational, electoral and wage reforms for the indigenous African population. His continued advocacy of black advancement incurred the wrath of Ian SMITH's government, which twice imprisoned Todd and his daughter, Judith.

Togliatti, Palmiro (1893-1964) Italian Communist leader of the largest Communist Party beyond the Societ bloc and advocate of comparative independence and freedom within the Communist movement. After leaving Fascist Italy and fighting in the Spanish Civil War, he returned to Italy in 1944 and, amid general surprise, persuaded the Left to enter BADOGLIO's all-Party interim government. For 20 years he showed himself to be an unusual Communist by his advocacy of conciliation towards the Vatican. He also proposed democratic methods as a means of achieving power, holding that other Communist parties, while following basic Marxist philosophy, should adapt Communist doctrine to suit local circumstances and not adhere rigidly to the Moscow line.

Tojo, Hideki (1885-1948) Japanese Prime Minister at the time of the attack on Pearl Harbour. While still a professional soldier, he was Minister of War from 1940 to 1941, and was responsible for much of the planning which resulted in the Japanese surprise attack on Pearl Harbour (December 1941). Tojo resigned in 1944 after the disaster at Imphal, in the Burma campaign (1944) and was arrested as a war criminal one year later. After a defence of his actions, and acceptance of full responsibility for them, he was found guilty and executed in 1948.

Toledo, Francisco Alvarez de (c. 1515-84) Spanish Viceroy of Peru (1569-81), where he introduced the Inquisition, and beheaded the last male-line Inca chief, Tupac Amaru.

Tolkien, John Ronald Reuel (1892-1973) English novelist and philologist, who created an immensely popular, mythological world in *The Hobbit* (1937) relating the adventures of Bilbo Baggins and the dwarfs on their journey to recover treasure from Smaug the dragon, and its more complex three-book sequel *The Lord of the Rings* (1954-5).

Toller, Ernst (1893-1939) German-Jewish dramatist and poet whose most successful plays were written in prison, where he spent five years for his part in the Munich uprising of 1919. *Masses and Man* (1921), the story of a woman revolutionary executed by her own followers, posed the question of whether murder in the cause of progress is tolerable. On his release from prison, he produced *The German Hangman* (1923) about a soldier made impotent by a war wound. In 1932 he emigrated to the United States, where his work was little known, and produced the autobiographical *I Was a German* (1933). Toller committed suicide in New York just before the outbreak of the Second World War.

Tolman, Edward (1886-1959) American psychologist who sees all behaviour as 'molar', or 'purposive', i.e. directed by perceptions and ideas towards specific goals. Although the goals in question may not all be known to the conscious mind, behaviour, according to Tolman, is never random, the conscious and unconscious motives combining to direct each and every action or physical movement.

Tolstoy, Alexsei Nikolaevich (1882-1945) Russian novelist, poet and dramatist, author of *The Road to Calvary* (1919-41), describing his experiences in the White Army after the Revolution of 1917.

Tolstoy, Count Leo Nikolaevich (1828-1910) Russian novelist, short-story writer, dramatist and philosopher, whose greatest novels, *War and Peace* (1863-9) and *Anna Karenina* (1873-7) have become world famous. *War and Peace* is a panorama of life at every level of Russian society during the Napoleonic Wars. The longest of 19th-century novels, with over 500 characters, it is an epic in which historical, social, ethical and religious issues are explored on a scale never before attempted in fiction. *Anna Karenina* is a psychological novel in which motivation and its moral impact are analysed through the story of a morally tortured woman. Two plots and two contrasting love affairs present a dialogue on the search for faith and the meaning of life, the prevailing theme of this work, one of the world's greatest tragic novels. That he was also a powerful dramatist is evident from the tragedy *The Power of Darkness* (1886) and the satire *The Fruits of Enlightenment* (1890).

Tombaugh, Clyde William (born 1906) American astronomer, who discovered the planet Pluto. While still a student with a keen interest in astronomy, he was appointed to the Lowel Observatory in 1929 to make routine examination of photographs taken in the search for the new planet predicted by Percival LOWELL. He discovered the ninth planet of the solar system, later named Pluto, in 1930.

Tomkins, Thomas (1572-1656) English organist and composer of church music, madrigals and instrumental works. A pupil of BYRD, he was organist of Worcester Cathedral, and of the Chapel Royal (1621). In 1626 he composed the music for CHARLES I's coronation.

Tomlinson, Henry Major (1873-1958) English essayist and novelist best known for his travel stories such as *Tidemarks* (1924), describing a trip to the East Indies.

Tone, Theobald Wolfe (1763-98) Irish nationalist, who with French aid fermented revolution against British rule in Ireland. He was much influenced by the principles of the French Revolution, and in 1796 persuaded the French Directory to undertake an expedition against Ireland which proved abortive. While participating in a further raid during the Irish rebellion of 1798, he was captured by the British and committed suicide while in prison.

Tonson, Jacob (c. 1656-1736) English publisher, who gave impetus to English literature as the publisher and friend of DRYDEN, POPE, ADDISON and Steele. With Dryden, Tonson compiled and published *Miscellany* (1684-1708), the definitive collection of Augustan poets. He also published Dryden's translation of VIRGIL, Nicholas Rowe's edition of SHAKESPEARE, and reprinted MILTON's *Paradise Lost*, in 1688.

Torelli, Giacomo (1608-78) Italian stage designer, the greatest creative artist of the Baroque theatre and the inventor of 'wings' – narrow, obscuring flats at the side of the stage. He designed sets for the Venice Teatro Novissimo (1641-5) and, in Paris (1645-61), revitalized MOLIÈRE's theatrical mechanics at the Petit-Bourbon. His inventions and innovations made spectacular staging possible and were adopted all over Europe.

Torquemada, Tomás de (c. 1420-98) Spanish Dominican monk who organized the Spanish Inquisition. Gaining influence under ISABELLA I and FERDINAND V, and praised by popes Sixtus IV and ALEXANDER VI, he determined ruthlessly to remove Jews and Muslims as supposed obstacles to Spain's national security and the Roman Catholic religion. Spain's first Inquisitor-General (1483), he established the Inquisition's powers to try people accused of heresy, apostasy, bigamy, witchcraft, usury, etc.; authorized the use of torture to extract confessions and regularized tribunals and their procedure.

Torres, Luis Vaez de (17th cent.) Spanish explorer and navigator. In 1605 he commanded one of three ships under the leadership of de QUIRÓS, to search for Terra Australis Incognita. After they had all reached the New Hebrides, he sailed alone on a voyage which took him through the strait between Australia and New Guinea which now bears his name. He is believed to have died at Manila in the Philippines (c. 1613).

Torricelli, Evangelista (1608-47) Italian physicist and mathematician – who invented the barometer. He made the fundamental discovery that a suction pump cannot lift a greater column of water than can be supported by atmospheric pressure (about 33 ft at sea level). Applying this principle to a glass tube filled with mercury, Torricelli invented the barometer, in which the height of the mercury column is a measure of the atmospheric pressure.

Toscanini, Arturo (1867-1957) Italian musician who became the most widely known conductor of his generation. He began his career as a cellist, but in 1898 became chief conductor at La Scala, Milan, where he was responsible for first performances of operas by VERDI and PUCCINI, among others. In 1928, disturbed by the rise of Fascism, he left Italy to take over the New York Philharmonic Orchestra. Toscanini was a prodigious musician, offsetting poor eyesight by a formidable memory – he never conducted with a score.

Toulouse-Lautrec, Henri de (1864-1901) French artist, whose work was much influenced by that of DEGAS. He was a master of the poster and coloured lithograph, and his ability to make a design both decorative and significant is also evident in his oil paintings. His style is charac-

Tolstoy, Russian nobleman and author of some of the world's greatest novels

terized by a combination of plunging perspectives and flat colouring, emphasizing the picture surface. By his choice of subject, the actresses and artistes of the Montmartre cafés and dance-halls which he frequented – Toulouse-Lautrec dispassionately records the life of the Parisian *demi-monde.*

Tovey, Sir Donald Francis (1875-1940) English pianist and musicologist who did more than anyone to popularize the classical repertoire in Britain during the early 20th century. His concert notes are considered to be among the finest written.

Toynbee, Arnold Joseph (born 1889) English historian, who wrote world history based on a broad theory of succeeding civilizations rather than concentrating on nations or periods of rule. While Professor of International History at London University (1925-55), he began his *Study of History* (1934-61), which identified 26 civilizations in world history, and traced their growth (which Toynbee attributed to small but energetic social groups responding to environmental challenge) and fall (blamed by him on lack of leadership in meeting further challenges).

Tradescant, John (17th cent.) English gardener and plant collector who introduced plants (e.g. lilac and acacia) from many parts of the world, including Russia, Africa and North America, and formed the natural history collection completed by his son, John TRADESCANT the Younger, which became the nucleus of the Ashmolean collection, Oxford.

A lithograph by Henri de Toulouse-Lautrec. The crippled son of a great French family, he was a shrewd observer of the life around him in Paris

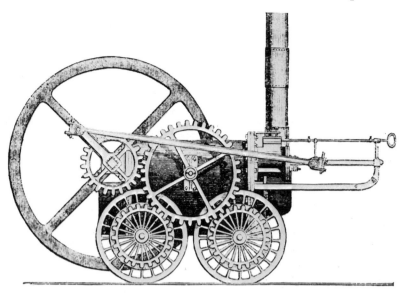

Locomotive built by Cornishman Richard Trevithick at his works near Merthyr Tydfil, Wales, in 1803. At work many years before the greatest locomotive engineers of the 19th century, Trevithick built road as well as rail vehicles

Traherne, Thomas (c. 1637-74) English mystical poet and prose writer whose work is a plea for a return to a primal state of goodness and simplicity. His poetry is both exalted and stark; the prose *Centuries of Meditations* are illuminating meditations on devotion.

Trajan (c. 53-117) Spanish-born Roman emperor (98-117). He enlarged the empire by seizing Armenia, created new provinces in Dacia, Assyria, and Mesopotamia and linked Rome's northern frontiers from Britain to the Black Sea by a string of garrisons.

Travers, Ben (born 1886) British dramatist, famous in the 1920s and 1930s for farces, such as *A Cuckoo in the Nest, Rookery Nook* and *Thark,* all of which were box-office successes.

Tree, Sir Herbert Beerbohm (1853-1917) British actor-manager, who created the role of Svengali in DU MAURIER's *Trilby.* He made his debut in 1878 and went into management in 1887. His productions, mostly at the Haymarket Theatre, began with *Hamlet,* in which he played the lead.

Tresaguet, Pierre (1716-96) French civil engineer, who introduced and improved cheaper road construction methods. He also realized and demonstrated the importance of regular maintenance.

Trevelyan, George (1876-1962) British historian, whose scholarly yet popular books on English history (*History of England* (1926) and *English Social History* (1942)) contributed to the growth of the subject as a university discipline, stressing social and topographical importance, as well as politics and economics.

Treviranus, Gottfried (1776-1837) German naturalist and physician, who first used the term 'biology' for the study of living organisms.

Trevithick, Richard (1771-1833) English engineer and pioneer of the steam railway locomotive. To improve the efficiency of the steam engine to cope with the increasing depth of the mines, he developed a model that used higher pressures than those of WATT, which he, and his cousin Andrew Vivian, patented in 1802 for stationary and locomotive use. During the next few years he erected nearly 50 stationary engines in Cornwall and Wales for mills, ironworks and mines. Trevithick built his first steam carriage in 1801, and another in London two years later, but neither public opinion nor road surfaces were yet favourable. He then constructed a steam locomotive at the Pen-y-Darran ironworks, near Merthyr Tydfil, Wales, which in 1804, 10 years before that of George STEPHENSON, successfully hauled five wagons, containing 10 tons of iron and 70 men, though the track, however, proved to be inadequate. Nevertheless, Trevithick had demonstrated an important principle that the friction between smooth rails and wheels would be sufficient to permit traction.

Trollope Anthony (1815-82) English novelist, author of the 'Barsetshire' novels which create in the most faithful detail the middle-class life of an English count. *The Warden* (1855) was the first Barsetshire novel, succeeded by five others, of which the best known are *Barchester Towers* (1857) and *The Last Chronicle of Barset* (1867). Equally interesting are the Pallister series, six novels on property and politics, and the famous *Autobiography* (1883).

Tromp, Maarten Harpertszoon (1597-1653) Dutch admiral who, with de RUYTER, helped to establish the young Dutch Republic as a major sea power. He won important victories against Spanish (1639), Spanish-Portuguese (1639) and English (1652) fleets. He was killed fighting English ships led by MONCK.

Trotsky, Lev Davidovich (1879-1940) Russian revolutionary, one of the founders of the USSR and organizer of the Red Army. A Ukrainian Jew, he was exiled to Siberia (1898) because of his revolutionary activities. In 1902, he escaped and came to London, where he worked with LENIN, PLEKHANOV and other Russian Social Democrats, but he later found his allegiance divided between Lenin and the Bolsheviks, and the Mensheviks, whose differences he tried to reconcile. He was in America when, in 1917, he received news of the March Revolution. He returned to Petrograd (later Leningrad), where he became chairman of the Petrograd Soviet. As first Soviet Commissar for Foreign Affairs (1917-18), his diplomacy and oratory gave Bolshevik Russia a breathing space by delaying the signature of the Treaty of Brest-Litovsk with Germany (signed 3 Mar. 1918). At the outbreak of the Civil War, he was made Commissar for War. He established the Red Army, and was chiefly responsible for

As People's Commissar for War in 1918, Trotsky created and trained the Red Army from a disorganized volunteer force which he inspired to victory in the Civil War through his powers of oratory

its victories over the 'white' reactionary armies, supported by Britain, the US and Japan. Trotsky was an internationalist, who believed in 'permanent world revolution' rather than in stable, nationalist, revolution. After the death of Lenin (1924), he was manoeuvred out of office by STALIN and ZINOVIEV, and after being expelled from the Communist Party, was exiled (1929) and found asylum in Mexico, where he wrote *The Revolution Betrayed* (1937), one of the best accounts of the Revolution and its aftermath. Condemned to death *in absentio* in 1937, Trotsky was assassinated in Mexico City by an agent of Stalin. Since his death, Trotsky's writings have inspired the formation of a number of left-wing groups.

Truman, Harry S. (1884-1972) Thirty-third US President who assumed office on the death of ROOSEVELT (1945). His was the awesome task of authorizing the use of the atomic bomb against Japan (Hiroshima and Nagasaki, 6 and 9 Aug. 1945), thus ending the Second World War. In 1947, he proclaimed the 'Truman Doctrine' of assistance to countries threatened by Communist expansion in the immediate post-war years. Some $400,000,000 was allocated to preserve Greece and Turkey. In 1948, he sanctioned the MARSHALL Plan to aid post-war European recovery, an offer which extended to Eastern Europe as well as to the West. Under his 'Four Point' programme of 1949, US economic, scientific and technical aid was given to underdeveloped countries. In 1948, he was re-elected against DEWEY in a result which confounded all predictions. At the start of his second term, his first major policy initiative was the formation of NATO in 1949. In the following year he authorized US intervention in Korea and nominated MACARTHUR as Commander-in-Chief of UN forces.

Trumbull, Jonathan (1710-85) American statesman and patriot, deputy governor of Connecticut (1766-9).

Ts'ao Hsueh-ch'in (c. 1719-63) Chinese novelist who wrote one of the most famous works of Chinese literature, *The Dream of the Red Chamber*. This tragic novel, which follows the declining fortunes of a once-great family, draws greatly on Ts'ao's own life, but the great strength of the work is its background of Buddhist philosophy which gives the story depth and greater meaning. The whole novel consists of 120 chapters, only 80 of which were written by Ts'ao before his death. The work was concluded by Kao E.

Tshombe, Moise (1919-69) Congolese politician and leader of the break-away province of Katanga. He was deposed by General Mobutu in 1965 and another period of exile followed. In 1967, his plane was hijacked and he was kidnapped and flown to Algiers, where he died of heart failure in prison.

Tu Fu (712-70) With LI PO, Tu Fu is widely recognized as the greatest of Chinese poets, though his life and poetry form a complete contrast to those of the older poet, whom Tu Fu met and admired. His hard, disappointing life, in a time of national chaos and disorder, generated his moving, evocative and often tragic verse, which has an emotional range and depth unmatched in Chinese poetry.

Tull, Jethro (1674-1741) English agriculturist, whose inventions rapidly advanced the mechanization of agriculture. He introduced the seed drill (which sowed three parallel rows of seeds simultaneously) and a horse-drawn hoe which destroyed weeds mechanically.

Tulsi Das (1532-1623) Indian poet, who flourished during the reign of AKBAR. Dedicated to the worship of Rama, his works, notably the epic *Ramcharit-manas*, are in dialect.

Tung Ch'i-ch'ang (1555-1636) Chinese statesman, calligrapher, painter, collector and art critic of the Ming period.

Turenne, Vicomte de (1611-75) French marshal who, with LOUVOIS and VAUBAN, carried out LOUIS XIV's plan to make France militarily supreme in Europe. Born in Holland, a grandson of WILLIAM THE SILENT, Turenne first fought in the Dutch War of Independence (1625-30). He left Holland to join the French army and made a reputation in successful

Samuel Clemens took his pen-name 'Mark Twain' from the cry of the leadman sounding the shallows from the bow of a Mississippi steamer

campaigns during the Thirty Years' War. Between 1667 and 1675 he commanded the French armies in aggressive wars in the Spanish Netherlands, the Palatinate and Alsace, with a skill which won NAPOLEON's admiration.

Turgenev, Ivan (1818-83) One of Russia's foremost novelists, author of *Fathers and Sons* (1862) and other novels and stories which depict the life of country districts in pre-Revolutionary Russia. Turgenev, who was a friend of FLAUBERT and ZOLA and much admired by Henry JAMES, was the first Russian writer to acquire a European reputation.

Turner, Joseph Mallord William (1775-1851) English landscape painter and watercolourist, outstanding for his use of brilliant colours and delicate, luminous impressions.

Turpin, Dick (1706-39) Notorious British highwayman who was finally captured in York, charged with horse stealing and executed.

Tutuola, Amos (born 1920) Nigerian novelist, author of *The Palm-Wine Drinkard* (1952) and *Feather Woman of the Jungle* (1962), narrative fantasy tales of ghosts and magic.

Twain, Mark (1835-1910) Pen-name of Samuel Clemens, American author, who brought the colloquial, earthy voice of the frontier West into American literature. From his time as a steamboat pilot on the Mississippi came the background for his best books, *Tom Sawyer* (1876), *Life on the Mississippi* (1883) and *Huckleberry Finn* (1884).

Tyler, John (1790-1862) Tenth President of the US who was rejected by his Party. He was elected Vice-President to William HARRISON in 1840 in order to carry the South for the Whigs, and became President when Harrison died (1841). Immediately, he found himself in opposition to the rest of his Party. In September 1841, his veto of two Bills to re-establish the national bank was rejected through the efforts of Andrew JACKSON, and all but one of his cabinet resigned. His veto of two protective Bills in 1842 led to his public repudiation by his Party. Denied the support of both Whigs and Democrats, even the annexation of Texas (1845) could do little to bring lustre to his Presidency.

Tyler, Wat (14th cent.) English tiler, leader of the Peasants' Revolt. In 1381 Tyler and Jack Straw led thousands of Kentish and Essex peasants, angered by the forced labour and heavy taxes following the Black Death, to London, where they were joined by others. In the rioting which followed several people were killed and buildings burned. When Richard II agreed to end serfdom and repressive labour laws, Tyler increased his demands and was killed by the Lord Mayor of London. Troops crushed the rebellion, and Richard revoked his agreements.

Tylor, Sir Edward (1832-1917) British anthropologist and pioneer of the study of cultures by systematic comparison, whose main work *Primitive Culture* (1871) is devoted to comparative studies in 'animism', or the belief in spiritual things. His discovery of the parallels of primitive customs to modern culture helped to foster a less-prejudiced attitude towards non-literate peoples.

Tyndale, William (c. 1492-1536) English priest, translator of much of the Bible from Greek into English. He suffered ecclesiastical persecution for unorthodoxy and fled to Germany, printing his New Testament at Cologne and Worms. Tyndale's Bible translations became a basis for the Authorized Version of JAMES I and greatly influenced English prose. His Reformation teachings, which were influenced by LUTHER and ZWINGLI, helped to shape English Puritan theology. Tyndale, betrayed in Antwerp by a supposed friend, was strangled and burned there for heresy.

Tyutchev, Fëdor (1803-73) Russian lyric poet, who spent most of his adult life out of Russia as a member of the Russian diplomatic corps. Although influenced by the European Romantics, particularly HEINE and Schelling, he never severed his ties with his native land and some of his verse is intensely Slavophile in spirit.

Tz'u Hsi (1834-1908) Dowager empress, who ruled China for 50 years. A Manchu, Tz'u Hsi, whose real name was Yehonala, began her career as a concubine of the emperor Hsien Feng (1851-61). She administered her reactionary policies with considerable statesmanship, but her extreme anti-European sentiments led her to encourage the xenophobic Boxer Rebellion against foreigners (1900) and led to foreign domination of her country.

U

Uccello, Paolo (1396 7-1475) Florentine painter, renowned for his experiments in perspective. In an early fresco, the equestrian monument to Sir John Hawkwood in Florence Cathedral (1436), he attempted to create the illusion of a real statue seen from below. His most famous work is the *Deluge* fresco in Sta Maria Novella (c. 1445), which shows the influence of ALBERTI's treatise on perspective. The combination in Uccello's work of the decorative aspects of Gothic art – brilliant colour and the use of gold – with the new science of perspective is evident in the three *Battles* (1454-7) commissioned by the MEDICI family.

Uhland, Johann (1787-1862) German Romantic poet and famous ballad writer. His 'Little Roland', 'The Good Companion', 'The Innkeeper's Daughter' and 'The Bard's Curse' are among the most popular in the German language.

Ulanova, Galina (born 1910) Russian ballerina whose artistry helped to show the Western world the standards of classical ballet maintained by Soviet Russia since the Bolshevik Revolution.

Ulbricht, Walter (1893-1973) East German politician, at whose instigation the Berlin Wall was erected. During the Second World War, he was political adviser to Marshal ZHUKOV in Russia, and returned to Germany in 1945 to head the Socialist Unity Party, a forced merger of the Social Democratic and Communist Parties. A Stalinist to the core, with no noticeable German nationalist feeling, his policy was one of consistent sovietization of industry and agriculture. In 1953, some of his colleagues rose against him, including the secret police chief, Zaisser, but Ulbricht suppressed ruthlessly this attempt to unseat him. He survived

'A painter of walls', Utrillo took for his subjects the streets and buildings (Sacré Coeur, above) of Paris

KHRUSCHEV's denunciation of STALIN in 1956 and continued building the Berlin Wall in 1961 in an effort to halt the loss of a quarter of a million refugees to the West each year.

Ulpian (c. 170-228) Roman jurist whose works, with those of GAIUS and others, deeply influenced Roman law. Ulpian's writings included a comprehensive restatement of civil and edictal law, and accounted for one-third of the *Digest* later compiled by JUSTINIAN.

Unamuno, Miguel de (1864-1936) Spanish philosopher, poet, essayist and novelist, whose thought is consistently anti-rationalist but obsessed with the problems of immortality and free will. In *The Tragic Sense of Life* (1913) he argues that one should struggle to believe in God and immortality, even though it is irrational and even mistaken to do so. In novels such as *Mist* (1914) and plays like *Brother John* (1934), Unamuno studied the free will of his literary creations as a parallel to that of real men.

U Nu (born 1907) Burmese politician, and Burma's first Prime Minister after its independence. At one time imprisoned by the British as a nationalist agitator, he was released by Japanese occupation forces and made Foreign Minister (1943-44) of the puppet Burmese government. He remained in office when the Japanese withdrew, and became Speaker of the Constituent Assembly in 1947 and Prime Minister (1948-56, 1957-8 and 1960-2). He was ousted after his last period of office by an army coup, which abolished parliament and suspended the constitution. In custody from 1962-6, U Nu left Burma in 1969 to organize opposition to the military régime. He returned to Burma in 1970 to campaign

against the government of General Ne Win.

Urey, Harold Clayton (born 1893) American chemist who discovered deuterium (heavy hydrogen). In 1931, he joined the growing number of scientists searching for an isotope of hydrogen (a form distinguished from ordinary hydrogen by its higher atomic weight). Using an ingenious evaporation technique, Urey isolated a small quantity of deuterium from several litres of liquid hydrogen.

Urfé, Honoré d' (1568-1625) French author of the four-volume romance *L'Astrée* (1607-27), a pastoral novel telling of the love of the loyal Celadon and the shepherdess Astrée. This idealized tale of chivalry and youthful innocence is regarded as the first French novel.

Utamaro Kitagawa (c. 1754-1806) Japanese print artist, among the first to be known in the West, whose work was shown at the 1889 Paris Exhibition. His subjects included female beauties, actors and deities, but it was his use of large areas of flat pattern and the creation of form without outline which were adapted by the Post-Impressionists. He was also a skilful painter of natural history subjects. In 1805 he was imprisoned for a print considered libellous and died soon after.

Utrillo, Maurice (1883-1955) French landscape painter whose early work resembles that of PISSARRO. His scenes of Paris, and Montmartre in particular, which have enjoyed world-wide popularity in reproduction, were mostly personal adaptations of Impressionism, though from 1910 onwards, some of his work showed a Cubist influence.

Utzon, Jørn (born 1918) Danish architect, former furniture and glassware designer, who designed Sydney's fantastical Opera House (1957-73). In 1966 he resigned after conflict over rising costs, but was awarded the Australian Institute of Architects' gold medal for 1973.

The Sydney Opera House, opened for the first time in 1973

V

Vaca, Alvar Nuñez Cabeza de (1490-1557) Spanish explorer in the New World. He joined an expedition from Spain (1527) which was wrecked in the Gulf of Mexico. Vaca reached the coast of Texas and, after being held prisoner by Indians for six years, escaped (1536) and, with three companions, made his way through northern Mexico to Mexico City. In 1542 he led a party of about 150 Spanish colonists from the south Brazilian coast to Asunción, 600 miles inland.

Vaclav see WENCESLAUS

Vaillant, George Clapp (1901-45) American archaeologist and prehistorian, who described the growth of the Aztec civilization in his book *The Aztecs of Mexico* (1944), which became a classic account of Mexico before its discovery by COLUMBUS. His excavations on the western shores of Lake Texcoco in Mexico helped to trace the sequence of cultures (including Olmec, Teotihuacan, Toltec) which had culminated in the foundation, in 1325, of the Aztec Empire.

Vakhtangov, Yevgeny (1882-1922) Russian theatrical director and originator of the Expressionist non-realistic production. He became head of STANISLAVSKY's Moscow Art Theatre acting studio, which was later combined with Vakhtangov's Mansurov Studio to form the Third Studio.

Valdivia, Pedro de (c. 1510-59) Spanish soldier who, after the conquest of Peru in 1540, led the settlement of the entire coastal lowlands of Chile, from the frontier of Peru to the Strait of Magellan.

Valentino, Rudolph (1895-1926) Italian romantic screen actor whose success became assured after making *The Four Horsemen of the Apocalypse* in 1921. After starring in *The Sheik*, made in the same year, for five years, Valentino was the object of unsurpassed female adulation and when he died, his funeral was an event of national importance.

Valéry, Paul Ambroise (1871-1945) French poet, critic and essayist. After experimenting with some Symbolist verse, which had echoes of MALLARMÉ, Valéry wrote two prose works, but he is chiefly remembered for the profound and subtle Symbolist poems composed in the years of his maturity – 'La Jeune Parque' (1917), 'Le Cimetière marin' (in the collection *Charmes*, 1922).

Vanbrugh's Blenheim Palace, built for Marlborough, and birthplace of Winston Churchill

Vanbrugh, Sir John (1664-1726)

English architectural genius of the English Baroque, whose extravagant, witty and theatrical style suited the tastes of the English aristocracy, both in his dramatic works and in his architecture. After a career as soldier and playwright he was asked by the young Earl of Carlisle to design Castle Howard, a grandiose pseudo-castle set behind a series of sham fortifications. It brought him meteoric success and led to his appointment as Comptroller of the Office of Works (where he worked with WREN). It led also to his greatest architectural commission, to design Blenheim Palace, which was to be presented to MARLBOROUGH by a grateful nation after the Battle of Blenheim.

Van Buren, Martin (1782-1862)

Eighth President of the US. His most important measure was to establish the Treasury as an independent organization unconnected with private banks, though this lost him much support in his own Party, the Democrats, as did his later opposition (1844) to the admission of Texas to the Union as a slave state. He was JACKSON's Secretary of State from 1829-31 and Vice-President from 1833-37. Although he had previously opposed the admission of Missouri as a slave state and advocated negro suffrage, he was elected President in 1837, mainly because of Jackson's support and influence.

Vance, Alfred Glenville (1838-88)

English comic singer and pantomimist, known as 'the Great Vance'.

Vancouver, George (c. 1758-98)

English explorer and navigator who sailed with Captain COOK on his second and third voyages. With two ships under his own command, Vancouver left Falmouth in 1791 to explore the west coast of America between latitudes 60° N and 30° N, to search for a western entrance to the North West Passage, as well as to negotiate the settlement of a dispute with the Spanish, who had seized a British outpost at Nootka Sound. He completed three seasons of work, charting the Strait of Juan de Fuca, the Puget Sound and the entire coastline to Cooks Inlet.

Van de Graaff, Robert Jemison (1901-67)

American physicist who developed the high-voltage, nuclear accelerator named after him. This device, in which electric charge is

Valle-Inclán, Ramón María del (1866-1936)

Spanish novelist, poet and author of *Esperpentos* – plays which anticipate today's Theatre of the Absurd by using gross exaggeration to caricature society, as in *Mr Trifle's Horns* (1921), which satirizes army officers. Other works, such as *Sonatas* (1902-5), romanticize the lush decadence of rural society in northern Spain; *Romance de Lobos* (1915) is a series of essays on 19th-century Spain.

Vallejo, César (1892-1938)

Peruvian poet and one of Latin America's outstanding literary figures. The Spanish Civil War inspired the poems of *España aparta di mí este cáliz*, whose main theme is death and the anguish at his inability to share the fate of his fellow men who died for their political convictions. It was published posthumously.

Valois, Dame Ninette de (born 1898)

Irish born ballerina, teacher, and, with Marie RAMBERT, co-founder of modern British ballet. A soloist for DIAGHILEV, she founded what is now the Royal Ballet and choreographed vivid dances for ballets inspired by English literature, music and painting, such as *Job*, *The Rake's Progress* and *Checkmate*. She helped create a distinctive English style of ballet.

RUDOLPH VALENTINO in "THE SON OF THE SHEIK"
A SEQUEL TO "THE SHEIK"
With VILMA BANKY

UNITED ARTISTS PICTURE

Slumbrous-eyed Romeo of the (Hollywood) desert, Rudolph Valentino

carried to a hollow terminal by a continuously moving belt, was first tried out in 1931. Generators based on developments of the same basic principle are in current use in nuclear physics laboratories all over the world.

Vanderbilt, Cornelius (1794-1877) American shipping and railroad magnate, founder of the Vanderbilt fortune. By 1861, he had accumulated at least $20 million, after an enterprising career in shipping and freight. He then entered the railroad business, while continuing to exploit the nation's need for shipping and carriers during the Civil War. His methods of acquiring control of railroads resulted in a number of Congressional and other public investigations into his operations. He died worth more than $100 million.

Van der Waals, Johannes Diderik (1837-1923) Dutch physicist who formulated an equation describing the behaviour of real (as distinct from 'ideal') gases. The equation was used by KAMERLINGH ONNES in his technique for liquefying helium, and is today still used as a basis for the study of gases.

Vanzetti, Bartolomeo see SACCO, Nicola

Varen, Bernhard see VARENIUS, Bernardus

Varenius, Bernhardus (1622-c. 1650) German geographer who was one of the first scholars to see geography as a whole. His book *Universal Geography* (1650) was a systematic study on an unprecedented scale, dividing the subject into 'general geography' (an ordered consideration of the whole earth) and 'special geography' (dealing in depth with separate topographical regions, and so foreshadowing modern regional geographies). Translated into English, this work remained influential until HUMBOLDT and RITTER put geography on a more scientific footing.

Varèse, Edgar (1885-1965) French-born American composer, who pioneered the *avant-garde* concept of music as pure sound. A former pupil of D'INDY and ROUSSEL, Varèse left Europe for America in 1916, later disowning all the music he had written before that date. Typical examples of the work of his American period are *Ionisation* (1931), a complex work for 13 percussion players and two sirens, and *Density 21.5* (1936). Varèse almost abandoned composition between the late 1930s and the 1950s, when he re-emerged with some experiments in taped electronic music. He was founder and president (1921-7) of the International Composers Guild.

Vargas, Getulio Dornelles (1883-1954) Brazilian dictator, later democratically elected President. He became Provisional President by a *coup d'état* in 1930, and four years later was elected permanent President under a new constitution. He wielded dictatorial powers, and, after 1937, governed by decree, banning all political parties, censoring the Press, and embarking on a large nationalization, social and economic programme. He was strongly opposed to both Fascism and Communism and during the Second World War, he supported the Allies. In 1945, the army forced him to resign, but he was elected President again in 1950. Brazil's financial instability, rising prices, and a political crisis led to his resignation and suicide in 1954.

Varro, Marcus Terentius (116-27 BC) Roman man of letters whose *Disciplinarum libri IX*, advocating the study of seven liberal arts (grammar, dialectic, rhetoric, geometry, arithmetic, music and astonomy) influenced medieval education.

Varthema, Lodovico di (15th-16th cents.) Italian traveller and writer who became a soldier for the Mamelukes at Damascus (1503) and made pilgrimages from there to Mecca and elsewhere before sailing round Arabia to India, and travelling in the Malay Peninsula and Indonesia. Varthema then fought for the Portuguese in India before sailing back to Lisbon via Mozambique and the Cape of Good Hope. He wrote an accurate and detailed account of the people and places he saw.

Vasari, Giorgio (1511-74) Italian Mannerist painter, and author of a celebrated history of art, *Lives of the Painters* (1550-68). The book consists of a series of biographies, beginning with that of CIMABUE and ending with those of LEONARDO da Vinci, RAPHAEL, and MICHELANGELO. Although not altogether reliable, it is a useful firsthand account of the artists' personalities and techniques.

Vattel, Emerich de (1714-67) Swiss jurist whose support for neutrality, expressed in *The Right of Peoples*, influenced the development of international law, especially in the United States where the federal judges gave his statements the force of legal precedent.

Vauban, Marquis de (1633-1707) French military engineer (the first to be appointed a Marshal of France) for LOUIS XIV. Developing fortifications on lines begun by MACHIAVELLI and LEONARDO da Vinci, he turned city walls into artillery platforms, devised defences in depth, and angled walls mathematically to cover all lines of fire. He also conducted attacks on many fortified towns, developing new artillery and mining techniques. He lost favour when the War of the Spanish Succession (1702-14) proved his forts far from impregnable.

Vaughan, Henry (c. 1621-95) Welsh metaphysical poet and physician, who, in *Silex Scintillans* (1650-5), combined the simple vocabulary of HERBERT with an imaginative mystical vision.

Vaughan Williams, Ralph (1872-1958) British composer whose roots ran deep in British folk-music and hymnody. The son of a country rector, he was a lifelong agnostic, yet edited the *English Hymnal* (1906), in which he included some of his own tunes. A notable collector of folk song, he studied with RAVEL and worked closely with HOLST, the other leading English composer of his generation. Vaughan Williams's first three symphonies (*The Sea*, *The London* and *The Pastoral*), together with such works as the *Fantasia on a Theme of Thomas Tallis*, the rhapsody for violin and orchestra, *The Lark Ascending* and the ballad opera *Hugh the Drover*, established him as a highly distinctive voice. In 1935, he wrote his violent and dissonant Fourth Symphony. In 1943 the Fifth Symphony projected an image of serenity in time of war, and in 1948, the Sixth Symphony seemed prophetic of desolation in the atomic age.

Vavilov, Nikolai Ivanovich (1887-1943) Russian geneticist who probed the geographical origins of cultivated plants. From 1917, he travelled abroad to trace the wild ancestors of modern cultivated food plants and virtually proved that the grain plants basic to Western civilization were first cultivated within a broad east-west belt, known as 'the fertile crescent', between Turkey and West Pakistan. But his inability to produce a new wheat variety within a two-year period stipulated by STALIN, caused his imprisonment (1940-2) and later replacement by LYSENKO. He died in Siberia.

Vazov, Ivan (1850-1921) Bulgaria's foremost poet and novelist, who wrote 'The Banner and the Rebec' (1876), the national poem of the 1876 uprising, and a novel on the same theme, *Under the Yoke* (1894). With Velichko, he edited the first anthology of Bulgarian literature.

Veblen, Oswald (1880-1960) American mathematician, who made advances in the field of topology and contributed to developments in differential geometry.

Vega, Lope de (1562-1635) The first major Spanish dramatist who ranks amongst the most prolific playwrights of all time, having written approximately 2000 plays, of which some 500 survive. He established the distinctive type of Spanish play which was to prevail for almost a century, the new three act *comedia*, an essentially popular poetic drama containing a mixture of comedy and tragedy and often centring on the theme of honour. One of his most successful historical plays, *The Sheep Well* (1614) anticipates Expressionist drama with its lively presentation of mob violence. Lope de Vega also wrote high tragedy, such as *Punishment without Vengeance* as well as novels, pastoral romances, history and poetry. He defended his new style *Comedia* in *The New Art of Writing Plays in this Age* (1609). Although ultimately limited in his range of situation and intrigue, his plays reveal his great lyrical ability and a supreme sense of stagecraft.

Veitch, John Gould (1839-70) British nurseryman, who introduced many new species to British and American horticulture. He travelled widely in the Far East, sending home plants and seeds, introducing the Japanese larch, the Virginia creeper, and Japanese primulas. His son J. H. Veitch did much to popularize Japanese flowering cherries.

Velasquez, Diego (1599-1660) Spanish painter, who worked almost exclusively on portraits. His early work consists of naturalistic still-lifes with kitchen themes (*bodegones*), in which the objects portrayed are lit by strong light; he also painted some devotional pictures. In 1623 he was

Detail from *Prince Baltazar Carlos* by Velasquez, court painter to Philip IV of Spain, for nearly 40 years

appointed court painter to the Spanish royal family and began work on portraits, many of which were of King PHILIP and his heir, Don Balthasar Carlos, both equestrian and full-length portraits against a plain background. During RUBENS's visit to Madrid in 1628, he obtained permission for Velasquez to visit Italy, an enterprise that resulted in his more fully appreciating Venetian painting. During a later visit to Italy (1648-51), Velasquez painted the portrait of *Pope Innocent X*, and the famous nude, the *Rokeby Venus*. His best-known work after 1651 is *Las Meninas*, a portrait of the Infanta Margareta Teresa with her ladies-in-waiting and dwarfs, in which he included himself painting the scene. Velasquez's late portraits are painted with a detachment that reveals his interest in the properties of light rather than his sitters' characters.

Velde, Willem van de, the Younger (1633-1707) Dutch marine painter. His father, Willem the Elder, was also a marine artist, and the son may initially have coloured some of his studies of naval engagements. His own battle scenes and marine views are much more competent and influenced English seascape painters.

Venizelos, Eleutherios (1864-1936) Cretan-born Greek statesman. As Prime Minister (1910-15) he took Greece into the first Balkan War against Turkey, alongside Bulgaria, Serbia and Montenegro and by the Treaty of Bucharest (1913), most of Macedonia was acquired for Greece. During the First World War, Venizelos set up a provisional government at Salonika, forced the abdication of the pro-German king Constantine and in 1917 took Greece into the war against Germany and her Allies. He was again in office for a short term in 1924, from 1928-32 and again briefly in 1933. In 1935, he provoked a civil war in his efforts to seize power again, but was defeated and fled to Paris, where he died.

Verdi, Giuseppe (1813-1901) Italian composer, the son of an innkeeper, who brought to his country's opera the new status of music drama. Verdi's tenth opera, *Rigoletto* (1851), was the first to demonstrate fully his gift for dramatic action and characterization in music. *Il Trovatore* and *La Traviata* followed, with other works that provide opera singers with real opportunities both to sing and act. In 1871, Verdi wrote *Aïda* for the opening of the Suez Canal. In 1874 he composed his *Requiem* and proposed to write no more operas, but collaboration with the poet Boito as librettist led to his masterpieces, *Otello* (1887) and *Falstaff* (1893).

Vérendrye, Sieur de la (1685-1749) French-Canadian explorer who, with his three sons, explored the vast unknown wild country to the west of Lake Superior, discovering Rainy Lake, Lake of the Woods and Lake Winnipeg. During later travels he apparently visited the Upper Missouri River drainage, including the Black Hills of Dakota.

Verga, Giovanni (1840-1922) Sicilian novelist, dramatist and short-story writer, perhaps the greatest writer of fiction in Italy since MANZONI. He abandoned the style of his early sensual novels, and turned to writing about the peasants of southern Sicily. It is for the two novels of his planned realist series, *The Vanquished*, that he is most celebrated. *The House by the Medlar Tree* (1881) and *Mastro Don Gesualdo* (1889) both set out to show how underprivileged classes suffer in the wake of the progress of society. Some of his works were translated into English by D. H. LAWRENCE.

Verhaeren, Emile (1855-1916) Belgian poet, whose *Toute la Flandre* (1911) blends symbolism and nationalism, and has affinities with the work of WHITMAN. His earlier volumes include a Symbolist 'trilogy of suffering' and a trilogy of the brotherhood of man.

Verlaine, Paul (1844-96) French poet who was influenced at first by the Parnassian poets and later became a leader of the early Symbolists. His finest pieces are renowned for their musical quality, exquisite harmonies and suggestive power. His aesthetics are summarized in *L'art poétique* (1884) and *De la musique avant toute chose*. His wild and dissolute existence, in the course of which he fled to England and Belgium, suffering two years in gaol for wounding his friend RIMBAUD, inevitably left its mark on his work. His main collections of verse were *Poèmes saturniens* (1866), in which the Parnassian influence is apparent, *Fêtes galantes* (1869), inspired by WATTEAU's paintings and *Sagesse* (1881) reflecting a new religious inspiration after conversion to Catholicism in prison.

Vermeer, Jan (1632-75) Dutch artist, whose few surviving pictures (about 40) have earned for him the foremost place among Dutch interior painters. His most typical paintings are of interiors with one or two figures, usually women, engaged in domestic activities, such as reading letters or making music. The difference, however, between these pictures and works by other Dutch interior painters such as METSU or de HOOCH, is that Vermeer was less concerned with anecdote or incident. His compositions (e.g. *The Lady Standing at the Virginals*, c. 1660), are studies in the play of light on differently textured surfaces and, above all, the arrangement of interlocking shapes, particularly rectangles, into relationships that form a two-dimensional design and create spatial depth. These paintings are, however, far from being mere geometrical exercises. They have a quality of calm and timelessness which is conveyed by Vermeer's exploitation of the qualities of light and the way it transforms the objects on which it falls. In recent times his influence is to be found in abstract geometricism of painters such as MONDRIAN.

Verne, Jules (1828-1905) French author of extremely popular science fiction stories which were strangely prophetic. His best-known works include *Journey to the Centre of the Earth* (1864), *Twenty Thousand Leagues under the Sea* (1870) and *Round the World in 80 Days* (1873).

Verner, Karl (1846-96) Danish linguistics scholar noted for his modification of GRIMM's law (known as Verner's law), by which some of the apparent exceptions and irregularities were explained. Verner showed that some of the sound changes were affected by the position of accents in the original Indo-European words.

Veronese, Paolo (c. 1528-88) Venetian painter of large, multi-figured and sensually-brilliant biblical, historical and allegorical compositions. In contrast to his contemporary, TINTORETTO, his works are balanced and orderly, but lacking in dramatic content: *Feast in the House of Levi* (1573) is typical of the way in which his themes frequently become lost in sumptuous pageantry. He was at his best in purely decorative work (e.g. the frescoes for the Villa Maser, near Vicenza, c. 1560).

Verrazano, Giovanni da (c. 1485-1528) Italian navigator who, in the service of France (1524), explored the east coast of North America from Cape Fear north to Newfoundland.

Verwey, Albert (1865-1937) Dutch lyric poet, critic and translator, who published many volumes of contemplative verse, notably the lyrical *Persephone* (1885), inspired by the early death of his parents. He wrote three poetic dramas, a number of scholarly works on Dutch writers, and many essays. He also translated DANTE's *Divine Comedy* into Dutch.

Verwoerd, Hendrik Freusch (1910-66) Founder of the South African Republic and apostle of apartheid. Although he did much to improve housing in South African cities, he was chiefly responsible for extending apartheid legislation as Minister of Native Affairs (1950-58) under MALAN and Strijdom. This policy was further intensified when he became Prime Minister in 1958. With the Commonwealth's growing opposition to South Africa's internal policies, he declared the country a republic in 1961, a situation of which he had long been in favour, and declined to seek readmission to the Commonwealth. He was assassinated in 1966.

Vesalius, Andrea (1514-64) Belgian physician and anatomist. Vesalius broke with tradition by dissecting human corpses and by recording only what he saw instead of what the textbooks said he should see. His anatomical discoveries became the talk of Europe and students flocked to hear him. He summarized his work in *On the Fabric of the Human Body* (1543), which contradicts GALEN. Apart from his pioneer anatomical work, Vesalius is also important for being the first person to challenge ARISTOTLE's doctrine that thought and personality are in the heart; he favoured the view that they were in the nervous system, especially the brain.

Vespasian (AD 9-79) Roman emperor (69-79) and soldier whose successes in Britain, Germany and Judaea, won the support of the army, which proclaimed him emperor and defeated the armies of the rival leader Otho and the emperor Vitellius. Vespasian reorganized the Senate, the tax system, the army and the administration of the eastern provinces. He banished dissident philosophers and put down revolts, notably in Palestine. His troops thrust into Germany, and, under AGRICOLA, into Wales and Scotland.

Vespucci, Amerigo (1454-1512) Florentine explorer whose unreliable accounts of his travels show that unlike COLUMBUS, he realized that the lands west of the Atlantic were a 'New World' and not part of Asia, and whose name was therefore given by European geographers to those lands. Vespucci made early voyages to the New World, but his claim to have discovered mainland America has long been discredited. He sailed to northern South America (1499) and (1501-2) sailed down the eastern South American coast, probably to a little beyond the Rio Grande region of Brazil (32° S), but later claimed to have reached Antarctic latitudes.

Vestris, Madame (1743-1804) French tragedienne, who created the role of Irène for VOLTAIRE (1778) and was famous for her death-scene in *Gabrielle de Vergi*.

Vianney, Jean-Baptist (1786-1859) French Roman Catholic priest whose preaching power and insight as a confessor were so remarkable that Ars-en-Dombes, the remote and neglected parish to which he was appointed as curé in 1818, became a place of pilgrimage for thousands of penitents from all over the world. He was canonized in 1925.

Viaud, Louis Marie Julian see LOTI, Pierre

Vico, Giambattista (1668-1744) Italian philosopher, whose sociological account of man, in terms of human cultural history, broke new ground. Vico's theory of knowledge reversed the current rationalist or empiricist theories, since he held that history, being of our own making, is the field in which our knowledge is most vivid and sound, whereas the abstractions of mathematics and science are less well known to us, and can be clearly understood only by their maker, God. His view of history as being a series of cyclic developments greatly influenced later sociopolitical thought.

Victor Emmanuel II (1820-78) King of Sardinia-Piedmont, who became, in 1861, the first effective constitutional monarch of the kingdom of Italy. He took part in the Piedmont-Sardinia war against Austria 1848-9 and after accession, as king of Sardinia-Piedmont, in co-operation with CAVOUR, prepared his country to take the lead in the struggle for Italian unity. To this end, he entered the Crimean War (1854-6) to gain recognition by major powers, and allied with France against Austria (1858-9) to liberate Lombardy. After the union of the northern duchies with Piedmont (1860) and the campaigns of GARIBALDI in Sicily, Victor Emmanuel became king of Italy. He took part in the Austro-Prussian war of 1866 and gained Venentia.

Victoria (1819-1901) Queen of Great Britain and Ireland from 1837, and Empress of India (1877), who gave her name to Britain's period of imperial greatness and to the architecture, art and literature of her time. She married (1840) her first cousin, ALBERT of Saxe-Coburg-Gotha, who assumed the title Prince Consort and whose influence on her was paramount. Victoria, though accepting her constitutional role in theory, was too wilful and too strong in her prejudices to refrain from interference with her ministers' policies, hampering

PALMERSTON and GLADSTONE, and favouring MELBOURNE, PEEL and DISRAELI. After Albert's death (1861), she went into seclusion and consequently lost much of her popularity with the public. Under Disraeli's influence she eventually re-entered public life, however, and in her later years was venerated as a matriarch.

Vidal de la Blache, Paul (1845-1918) French geographer who founded the study of the human geography of small areas. Stressing the interaction between man and his natural environment, he inspired a universal geography consisting of a multi-volume study of continents, nations and regions.

Vieira, António (1608-97) Portuguese preacher, missionary and prose-writer. Crisp, incisive, often spiked with humour, the clear, vigorous prose of his letters and sermons is unequalled in Portuguese literature.

Viète, Francois (1540-1603) French lawyer and one of the most important mathematicians of the 16th century, whose first work on mathematics was published during 1579. He wrote mainly about algebra (using letters to represent numbers), geometry and the calendar.

Contrasting prosperity and poverty, imperial pomp and British power, marked the long reign of Victoria

Vignola, Giacomo da (1507-73) Italian architect, who worked mostly in Rome and introduced the oval plan into church design, that was to become popular with architects of the Baroque. He designed the *Gesù*, Rome (which had a centralized plan with a dome, and a long nave necessary for processions). His palaces (Palazzo Farnese and Villa di Papa Giulio, Rome), have the rather brittle elegance of the Mannerist style.

Vigny, Alfred de (1797-1863) French Romantic poet, novelist and playwright. In *Poèmes Antiques et modernes* (1826), he affirmed the idea of the inevitable anguish and solitude to which great men are condemned (e.g. in the poem 'Moïse'). This notion, together with the conflict of the poet and society (as in the novel *Stello*, 1832 and in his best play, *Chatterton* 1835), formed one of the dominant themes of his work. Some of Vigny's finest verse is contained in *Les Destinées* (published posthumously, 1864) a collection of poems ranging in mood from stoic resignation to despair and including the pinnacle of his achievement, 'La Maison du Berger'.

Villa-Lobos, Heitor (1887-1959) Brazilian, the first Latin American composer to win international standing. Villa-Lobos was a prolific composer writing in a style that drew its influences from Brazilian national folk music (Indian, Portuguese and African) with polytonality and Neoclassicism. He wrote 12 symphonies, five piano concertos and a number of songs, as well as guitar and chamber music. Among his best-known works are the series of lyrical and evocative *Bachainas Brasileiras* for various combinations of instruments, which sought to introduce the spirit of BACH into a Brazilian idiom. For some years Villa-Lobos was his country's Director of Music in Education.

Villa, Pancho (1877-1923) Mexican bandit and revolutionary general. Sometime cattle stealer and bandit, he joined the revolutionary force against President DIAZ in 1910, and continued his bandit-rebel activities in the north, where he became a virtual dictator during the period of ensuing political and social turmoil. In 1920, he made peace with the government, and retired to a ranch where he lived until he was murdered in 1923.

Vincent de Paul (c. 1581-1660) French founder of the Congregation of the Mission (The Lazarists, dedicated to the service of the poor) and co-founder of the Sisters of Charity. Though short-tempered, Vincent de Paul was sensitive and kind, and his

natural goodness is shown in his order to his missionaries that Protestants were to be treated with brotherly love and respect. He was canonized in 1737.

Viollet-Le-Duc, Eugène-Emmanuel (1814-79) French architect well known for his largely sympathetic restoration of medieval churches and castles, such as Notre Dame, Paris, and the Château de Pierrefonds, and for his personal re-assessment of Gothic structure in terms of modern materials, such as iron. His surviving original work includes the church of St Denys-de-l'Estrée, Paris.

Virchow, Rudolph (1821-1902) German pathologist who was the first man to recognize the importance of the living cell in disease. The existence of living cells had long been known, but it was Virchow who realized that the cell and the processes within it lay at the very heart of all disease. He also asserted that poverty was a root cause of typhoid and dedicated his life to establishing the German public health service.

Virgil (70-19 BC) Roman poet, author of the *Aeneid*, an epic poem telling of the wanderings of Aeneas and his fellow-survivors of the sack of Troy, until they settled in Italy as the ancestors of Rome. Virgil's intention was to celebrate the grandeur of Rome and its sense of destiny under AUGUSTUS. Earlier Virgil wrote the *Eclogues* (45-37 BC), based on THEOCRITUS's *Idylls*, with the addition of an element of Italian realism, and the *Georgics* (36-29 BC), a four-volume agricultural treatise, full of careful observation of animals and nature and written with typical Virgilian pathos and love.

Visconti, Gian Galeazzo (1351-1402) Duke of Milan (1378-1402), the most powerful member of the family that ruled Milan and much of northern Italy in the 14th and 15th centuries. He sought to rule all Italy, and by conquest, intrigue, and purchase took most of the north and centre of the country. He died of plague while attacking Florence.

Vitruvius Pollio, Marcus (1st cent. BC) Roman architect, whose *De Architectura* (though without the author's plans) is the only surviving work from antiquity on architecture and engineering. It had an enormous influence on European architects from the 12th century onwards. ALBERTI based his designs and his writings on it and it was subsequently published as a printed book first in 1486, then, with commentary and illustrations, in 1511.

Vittoria, Tomás Luis de (c. 1549-1611) Spanish composer of unaccompanied church music. Vittoria worked for long in Rome and was a friend (and possibly a pupil) of PALESTRINA, on whom he based his contrapuntal style.

Vivaldi, Antonio (c. 1676-1741) Italian composer and violinist who wrote *The Four Seasons*, a set of four 'concerto grossi' which vividly evoke the passing seasons. Vivaldi was a priest in charge of music at a girls' conservatory in Venice. He wrote over 400 concertos, mostly for strings, which had a considerable influence on J. S. BACH. Vivaldi's music was popular in his own day, but was largely forgotten until the present century rediscovered its charm and originality.

Vivar, Rodrigo Diaz de see CID, El

Vives, Juan Luis (1492-1540) Spanish-born scholar who propounded many ideas about education and psychology which are remarkably modern in their outlook. He attempted to analyse the differences between mental abilities and recognized that instruction in schools should bear these differences in mind. He also stressed the importance of the senses and value of first-hand experience.

Vladimir I (c. 956-1015) Ukrainian-Scandinavian saint. Prince of Kiev, he was responsible for making Russia Christian. A brutal and drunken Viking until his conversion and marriage to Anne, sister of the Byzantine emperor BASIL II, either his baptism or his wife civilized him. He set about imposing Christianity on his subjects through Greek missionaries, and sometimes by force, but always setting an example of mildness and charity.

Vlaminck, Maurice (1876-1958) French painter, who, with DERAIN and MATISSE, was a leading exponent of Fauvist painting between 1905 and 1907. The main source for his violent brushwork and shrill colour was the work of van GOGH, which he discovered in 1901. His most characteristic work, consisting chiefly of landscapes, was done in these early years; and it is the expression of a rumbustious personality opposed to tradition.

Vogelweide, Walther von der (c. 1170-c. 1230) Germany's greatest medieval lyric poet and author of many love poems, notably the famous 'Under the Lime Tree'. The moral and political poems of his *Sayings*, which deal with the spiritual problems of his time, are regarded as his best work.

Volta, Count Alessandro (1745-1827) Italian physicist who invented the first electric battery. In the 1780s, GALVANI had found that a frog's leg, hung on a copper hook, twitched when the hook made contact with an iron plate. Volta believed that the contact of metals was generating an electric current, and not the muscle as Galvani thought. He made a 'voltaic pile' of copper and zinc discs, separated by cardboard soaked in salt solution; this was the first battery. He gave his name to the unit of electromotive force, the volt.

Voltaire, François-Marie Arouet (1694-1778) France's universal literary genius, a dramatist, philosopher, poet, novelist, historian and contributor to the *Encyclopédie*. Voltaire spent his life ridiculing, with wit and irony, the vices and injustices of his time. In the best of his philosophical *contes*, such as *Zadig* (1747), *Micromégas* and above all, in *Candide* (1759), Voltaire fused subject matter with style. In *Candide*, a vitriolic work inspired by the Lisbon earthquake and by Voltaire's earlier quarrel with FREDERICK THE GREAT of Prussia, he ridiculed the absurdity of philosophical optimism, especially the theories of LEIBNIZ and POPE. Voltaire spent the years 1726-8 exiled in England, an experience which impressed him considerably and caused him to write his first masterpiece, the *Lettres philosophiques* of 1734, a thinly-veiled onslaught on French institutions, which has been described as 'the first bomb thrown at the *Ancien Régime*'. He also contributed articles to the monument of 18th-century rationalism and scepticism, the *Encyclopédie*. Voltaire was vehemently anti-religious and was in constant conflict with authority for attacking the tyranny of Church and State in France. In his later years, he became renowned for his defence of the victims of persecution and oppression.

Vondel, Joost van den (1587-1679) Dutch poet and dramatist, whose

The Seine at Le Pecq, by Vlaminck, who was influenced by Van Gogh

first important work was *Het Pascha* (1612), a dramatized version of Exodus. *Gijsbrecht van Aemstel*, based on the second book of VIRGIL's *Aeneid*, was written for the opening of Amsterdam's new theatre (1637) and is still acted annually at New Year. Among his other plays are *Lucifer* (1654), *Jeptha* (1659) and *Adam in Ballingschap* (1664).

Vörösmarty, Mihály (1800-55) Hungarian Romantic poet, who wrote 'Appeal' (1836), a patriotic poem that has become one of Hungary's most popular literary works. His work is characterized by a melancholy passion, most effective in his lyric poetry. After the National Theatre's inauguration, he wrote a fairy tale drama inspired by SHAKESPEARE's *Midsummer Night's Dream*, and popular ballads.

Vorster, Balthazar Johannes (born 1915) Prime Minister of South Africa. During the Second World War, Vorster was interned because of his anti-government activities, and so extreme an Afrikaner nationalist that at one time he was refused membership of the National Party. From 1961-6, he was VERWOERD's Minister of Justice, and succeeded him as Prime Minister when the latter was assassinated in 1966. Although as Prime Minister he has encouraged friendly relations with black African countries such as Malawi and Botswana, he has also been responsible for laws which prescribe indefinite detention of political offenders, imprisonment without trial, and the uprooting of whole tribes in the interests of racial segregation.

Voysey, Charles (1857-1941) English domestic architect who rejected contemporary fashion for filling rooms with florid or complex objects and kept them simple and bright. His buildings, with their leaning buttresses and wide eaves, have an appearance peculiar to his style. Within the broad development of Art Nouveau, Voysey stands among the more restrained figures. There are houses by him in Hans Road and Bedford Park, London.

Voznesensky, Andrei Andreevich (born 1933) Russian lyric poet whose poem *Parabolic Ballad* (1960) showed him to be the leader of a new experimental movement with its mixture of startling imagery, puns and unusual vocabulary.

Vries, Hugo de (1848-1935) Dutch geneticist, whose plant-breeding experiments led him to believe that evolution proceeds in large jumps by means of mutations. Studying the

American evening primrose, he showed that each separate character is passed down by means of discrete elements in the nucleus (which he called 'pangenes').

Vuillard Edouard (1868-1940) French painter, whose early work shows affinities with that of GAUGUIN and with Japanese prints. He described himself as an 'intimiste', a term applied also to BONNARD and related to the domestic interiors which were his favourite subjects, and which were often painted in tempera, a muted medium compared with oils. Typical of his work is a fondness for patterned textiles and wallpapers to characterize an environment.

Vyshinsky, Andrei Yanuarevich (1883-1954) Soviet politician and jurist and delegate to the United Nations. He achieved notoriety as the Soviet Union's Public Prosecutor during the treason trials of 1936-8, during which ZINOVIEV, KAMENEV, Tukhachevsky, BUKHARIN, Yagoda and many others were executed. He was Deputy Foreign Minister to MOLOTOV from 1940-9 and from 1945-9 was the permanent Soviet delegate at the United Nations, where he was noted for his disruptive tactics. He was again appointed to the United Nations by MALENKOV in 1953, after serving for four years as Foreign Minister.

Wade, George (1673-1748) British soldier who built a series of strategic roads in the Scottish Highlands for military use. Between 1726 and 1737, he superintended the construction of 250 miles of road, and 40 bridges. He was later promoted Field Marshal.

Wagner, Wilhelm Richard (1813-83) German composer of Romantic, monumental operas. The main influences on Wagner were BEETHOVEN, as the leading symphonist in Romantic music, and GLUCK, whose theory of opera foreshadowed Wagner's idea of 'music drama'. Wagner earned a meagre living in Paris as a music copyist, while writing his first operatic success, *The Flying Dutchman* (1843). Then, as conductor of the Dresden Opera, he turned to the Germanic myths and legends that were to be his main preoccupation, composing *Tannhäuser* (1845) and *Lohengrin* (1850). In 1848, he was implicated in the insurrection in Germany and went into exile in Switzerland, where he began work on his vast cycle of four operas, *The Ring of the Nibelung*, that took 25 years to complete. In his operas,

Wagner aimed at a complete unity between all the components, wrote his own librettos and developed the *leitmotiv* – a recurring theme denoting a specific character or dramatic aspect. To secure control over every facet of production, he built the Festival Opera at Bayreuth, in Bavaria, under Ludwig II's patronage, and it was there, in 1876, that *The Ring* was first performed in its entirety: *The Rhinegold, The Valkyrie, Siegfried* and *The Twilight of the Gods*. Meanwhile, he had written *Tristan and Isolde* a version of sublimated erotic love, and *The Mastersingers* his one comic masterpiece. In the year before he died he completed his 'sacred music drama', *Parsifal*.

Wajda, Andrej (born 1926) Polish film-maker and theatre director of the post-war generation. Wajda interpreted the search for national and political identity and the malaise of those of his countrymen who came to maturity in the war and post-war era, in films such as the trilogy *A Generation* (1954), *Kanal* (1956) and *Ashes and Diamonds* (1958).

Waksman, Selman (born 1888) American microbiologist of Russian origin, who won a Nobel Prize in 1952 for his work in isolating actinomycin, streptomycin, neomycin, candidicin, and other antibiotics from micro-organisms.

Walcott, Derek (born 1930) West Indian poet and playwright. His books include *In a Green Night* (1962) and *The Castaway* (1965).

Waldemar I 'The Great' (c. 1131-82) King of Denmark (1157-82), who brought unity to his country after a long period of civil war. Waldemar became the sole survivor of the royal line when he defeated Sweyn III in battle near Viborg (1157). With his childhood friend Absalon, Archbishop of Lund, as his able chief minister, he established law and order supported by heavy taxes. After ten years of campaigning, he defeated the Wendish pirates who had devastated Denmark's eastern coast and halted commercial progress. Waldemar seized their island stronghold (Rügen), which became the springboard for Denmark's eastward expansion under WALDEMAR II.

Waldemar II 'The Victorious' (1170-1241) King of Denmark (1202-41), who, like CANUTE, created a short-lived Danish Empire. He conquered or was recognized as overlord of territories in northwest Germany, then undertook crusades which swept through the southern Baltic lands from northern Germany to Finland, making the Baltic Sea a Danish lake.

A German revolt (1223-7) ended with Waldemar's defeat at Bornhöved and the abrupt disintegration of his northern empire.

Folklore, medieval legend and Norse mythology provided the source material for the operas of Richard Wagner

Waldemar IV Atterdag (c. 1320-75) King of Denmark (1340-75), who restored Denmark from anarchy and partition among foreign nobles. Elected king, but in fact holding only part of Jutland, Waldemar reconquered the disunited land, solved some of its economic problems by financial reforms, curbed the power of dissident nobles and churchmen, and won back much land that had been lost to Holstein, Schleswig and Sweden. By taking Visby, Waldemar incensed the mighty Hanseatic League of trading towns, which, with Norway and Sweden, forced on him the humiliating Peace of Stralsund (1370). Waldemar's daughter MARGARET began a new phase in Scandinavia's history.

Walden, Paul (1863-1957) Russo-German chemist who discovered an effect now called the Walden inversion (1895), a process which helps to explain the mechanisms governing chemical reactions.

Waldheim, Kurt (born 1918) Austrian diplomat, elected Secretary-General of the United Nations in 1972. Early in his administration, neutral UN troops were required to maintain the cease-fire line between warring Arab and Israeli armies after the 1973 October war.

Waldo, Samuel Lovett (1783-1861) Self-taught American artist, known best for his portraits.

Waldo, Peter (12th cent.) French heretic, founder of the Waldenses. A rich merchant of Lyons, Waldo renounced his wealth to become a mendicant preacher. His theme of voluntary poverty soon won disciples. Known as the 'Poor Men of Lyons', their aim was to imitate the simple life of the Apostles described in the New Testament, which Waldo had translated into Provençal. The movement was excommunicated in 1184.

Waldseemüller, Martin (c. 1470-c. 1518) German cartographer who produced the first map bearing the name *America*, in 1507. Waldseemüller also invented the first printed *gores* – lens-shaped map segments which could be pasted on to spheres and thus mass-produce globes.

Waley, Sir Arthur David (1889-1966) British translator of Chinese and Japanese literature. His first translation, *170 Chinese Poems*, appeared in 1918 and *Japanese Poetry* in 1919. Probably his finest work is his translation of the Japanese masterpiece, *Genji Monogatori* by MURASAKI SHIKIBU. He was also an expert in other aspects of Oriental culture, and his book *Introduction to the Study of Chinese Painting* (1923) remains one of the best and most lucid on the subject.

Walker, John (c. 1781-1859) English apothecary, who invented and sold the first friction matches (1827).

Wallace, Alfred (1823-1913) British naturalist, who evolved the theory of evolution by natural selection. His views, presented jointly with those of DARWIN in 1858, clearly stated the notion of survival of the fittest in the struggle for existence (a phrase of MALTHUS), pointing out that it is the advantage of the stronger and not some effort of the will, as LAMARCK thought, that makes for survival.

Wallace, De Witt (born 1889) American publisher who, with his wife Lila Acheson Wallace, founded *The Reader's Digest* (1922) a magazine noted then as now for its belief in traditional moral values and conservative political viewpoints. On its 50th anniversary the *Digest* was selling 29 million copies a month in 13 languages, aided by the most sophisticated and inventive direct-selling techniques, which it also uses to promote books, records and allied products.

Wallace, George Corley (born 1919) American politician and segregationist Governor of Alabama, elected in 1962 on a programme of opposition to integration 'in the schoolhouse doorway'. He strenuously fought a Supreme Court ruling that racial segregation in public schools was unconstitutional, but was finally forced to give way to Federal authority in 1963. The state's constitution debarred him from serving succeeding terms as governor, so his wife was elected in his place in 1966, though Wallace himself continued to formulate policy. In 1968 he ran as a segregationist candidate in the presidential elections and, although soundly beaten, he won five Southern states and received a larger percentage of popular votes than any third-party candidate since LA FOLLETTE in 1924. An attempt to assassinate him in 1972 left him partially paralyzed.

Wallace, Sir William (c. 1272-1305) Scottish patriot. He made successful attacks on the English troops who were pacifying Scotland after EDWARD I had deposed Scotland's king Baliol, and inspired the Scottish rout of Edward's army at Stirling Bridge (1297). He then pursued the retreating English to Newcastle and briefly ravaged northern England before returning north to govern Scotland. He was defeated at Falkirk by Edward I (1298), but waged war from the hills until he was caught and executed.

Wallenstein, Albrecht von (1583-1634) Austrian general who played a key role during the first half of the Thirty Years' War. With Tilly, he led the emperor FERDINAND II's imperial armies against Protestant forces, defeating CHRISTIAN IV of Denmark in Saxony, forcing on him the Treaty of Lübeck (1629). Later he lost the battle of Lützen (1632), but his Swedish opponent, GUSTAVUS II ADOLPHUS, died in the fighting. After Ferdinand made him Duke of Friedland (1625), Wallenstein became over-ambitious for personal power, and began secret negotiations with Ferdinand's Protestant enemies. Ferdinand denounced him for treason, and one of Wallenstein's own officers stabbed him to death.

Waller, Augustus (1816-70) English physiologist, who carried out much original research, particularly into the nervous system. He was elected a fellow of the Royal Society in 1851.

Waller, Edmund (1606-87) English poet, who was the first to make extensive use of the heroic couplet, the balanced, antithetical verse form later developed by DRYDEN and POPE. A precocious and wealthy youth, he entered parliament at the age of 16.

Wallis, Sir Barnes Neville (born 1887) English aircraft designer. He started designing rigid airships before the First World War and was responsible for the structures of the R80, launched in 1920 and the R100, Britain's most successful airship, which first flew in 1929. Wallis designed two long-range bombers, the Wellesley (1935), and the Wellington (1938) and, during the Second World War, he devised the famous bounce bombs used by a special RAF Squadron in 1943 to breach the Möhne and Eder dams. He was responsible also for the Tallboy, armour piercing and Grand Slam (10 ton) bombs which inflicted enormous damage to Germany during the last year of the war. From 1944-56, he worked on the variable geometry, or swing-wing, concept for supersonic aircraft.

Wallis, John (1616-1703) English mathematician, who did much work in quadratures – that is, finding areas bounded by curves, a precursor of integral calculus. He also helped to clear the ground in mechanics by establishing proper definitions for many of its terms.

Walpole, Horace (1717-97) English wit, letter-writer, art historian and novelist, whose *Castle of Otranto*, a tale of mystery and horror (1764),

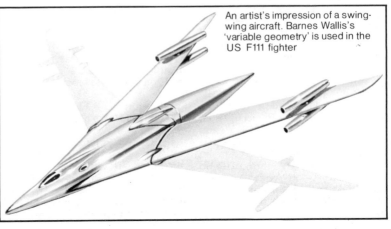

An artist's impression of a swing-wing aircraft. Barnes Wallis's 'variable geometry' is used in the US F111 fighter

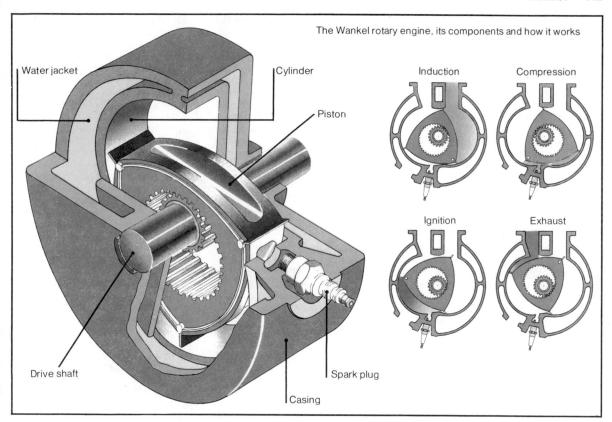

The Wankel rotary engine, its components and how it works

Water jacket · Cylinder · Piston · Drive shaft · Casing · Spark plug

Induction · Compression · Ignition · Exhaust

set the fashion in England for the 'Gothic' romance. Son of Sir Robert WALPOLE, the politician, his enormous number of letters present an invaluable social history of the age, full of gossip and scandal. He collected pictures, set up a private press and printed numerous minor works, including poems by GRAY.

Walpole, Robert, 1st Earl of Orford (1676-1745) Often considered Great Britain's first true Prime Minister (1721-42), an office not officially recognized until 1905. Walpole was instrumental in developing and unifying cabinet government and shifting power from the House of Lords to the House of Commons. He became head of the Whig ministry, at first with Townshend (1721) and then alone (1730). One of his chief aims was to secure the Protestant succession and Hanoverian dynasty by economic prosperity and by avoiding costly conflict with foreign powers, including France (then under the like-minded Fleury). Walpole's popularity began to decline with his attempts to deal with smuggling and his reluctance to fight to end Spain's exclusive claims to the New World and its searching of British vessels. He retired with the title Earl of Orford. 10 Downing Street, the official London residence of the Prime Minister, was Walpole's home, which he bequeathed to the nation.

Walras, Léon (1834-1910) French economist, author of the classic *Elements of Pure Economics* (1874-7). Using mathematical techniques, he pioneered a general equilibrium theory wherein all the individual variables of an economy are mutually interdependent. Elsewhere he urged the nationalization of land and a change in the gold standard to optimum advantage in order to allow the free enterprise system to work.

Walter, John (1739-1812) English journalist and founder of *The Times*. He met the printer Henry Johnson, became interested in printing technology, and in 1784 purchased premises in Printing House Square. An unsuccessful printer of books, in 1785 he started a small newspaper, *The Daily Universal Register*, which, in 1788, became *The Times*. Under his son John Walter II (1776-1847) and the editorship of BARNES, *The Times* established itself as Britain's leading newspaper and daily historical record. It remains an influential newspaper.

Walton, Ernest see COCKCROFT, Sir John Douglas

Walton, Sir William Turner (born 1902) British composer who wrote *Façade* (1923) and the oratorio *Belshazzar's Feast* (1931). The first, musical parodies supporting spoken poems by Edith SITWELL, and the

second, with its barbaric jazz rhythms illuminating an Old Testament text, caused some disturbance in England's conservative musical life between the wars, as did his tense First Symphony.

Wang Mang (33 BC-AD 23) Chinese emperor and reformer, who divided private, tax-free estates among taxpaying peasants, thus antagonizing the powerful landowners, who assassinated him.

Wang Wei (699-759) Chinese painter, calligrapher, poet and musician of the T'ang dynasty, revered in later periods as exemplifying the artist as a man of broad culture. He held a high position in the Imperial Directorate of Music as well as a senior government post, but on the death of his wife became a Buddhist recluse devoted entirely to painting. He is considered the pioneer of monochrome landscape painting and the technique of 'broken-ink'.

Wankel, Felix (born 1902) German inventor and engineer who developed (1934-56) the first viable rotary internal combustion engine. During the Second World War, Wankel worked on the development of fighter planes, and was imprisoned by the French occupation forces. After the war, he refined his engine, which is now used in several production vehicles.

Ward, Artemus (1834-67) Pen-name of C. F. Browne, American writer, whose popular and humorous style was part of the tradition from which Mark TWAIN evolved his style.

Ward, Mrs Humphry (1851-1920) English novelist, author of moral, reforming fiction. Her most famous novel, *Robert Elsmere* (1888), emphasized the social mission of Christianity, playing down faith in miracles. *A Writer's Recollections* (1918) contains interesting accounts of her family; she was grand-daughter of Thomas ARNOLD, aunt of Julian and Aldous HUXLEY.

Ward, Nathaniel Bagshaw (1791-1868) British physician and amateur naturalist who invented the Wardian Case, an airtight glass case which improved the chances of survival of exotic plants found by collectors. It was first used by Robert FORTUNE in China (*c.* 1850) and thereafter by all 19th-century plant collectors.

Wardle, Sir Thomas (born 1912) Lord Mayor of Perth, Western Australia (1967-72). Wardle established a network of 'bargain' stores using old cinema buildings and became known as 'Tom the cheap'. His stores are now found in most major Australian cities.

Warnerius see IRNERIUS

Warren, Earl (born 1891) American judge who presided over the Supreme Court (1953-69) at a time when its decisions led to important changes in race relations. Already known for his liberal views on civil rights, he outraged conservative Southerners by handing down in 1954 the unanimous ruling that racial segregation in public schools was illegal. In 1964 he headed the Commission enquiring into the assassination of President John F. KENNEDY.

Warren, Robert Penn (born 1905) American poet and novelist, who explores the conflicts of the South as universal problems. His main novels are *At Heaven's Gate* (1943), about Southern capitalism; *All the King's Men* (1946), about the rise and fall of a Louisiana demagogue.

Warwick the Kingmaker see NEVILLE, Richard

Washington, George (1732-99) First American President, leader of the American colonists during the War of Independence against Britain. He served in the British army against France in the Canadian War (1755-9), but was afterwards converted to the idea of US independence and became one of its leading advocates.

His principal military feat during the War of Independence was his march, with American and French forces, from the Hudson to Yorktown, where he forced Lord CORNWALLIS, the British commander, to surrender (1781). The Federal Convention of 1787 at Philadelphia, having adopted the Constitution, elected Washington President of the US. He assumed office in 1789 and remained President until 1797.

Wassermann, August von (1866-1925) German bacteriologist who was the inventor of the Wassermann reaction, which remains the standard blood test for syphilis.

Waterman, Lewis Edson (1837-1901) American inventor and industrialist who in 1884, invented the modern type of fountain pen. Self-filling pens were introduced commercially in the early 1900s.

Watkins, 'Gino' (1907-32) English explorer, the first white man to use kayaks for Arctic exploration; he probed Labrador and Greenland and rounded the southern tip of Greenland.

Watson, James (born 1928) American geneticist, who, with Francis CRICK, made the first model of the DNA molecule. Watson and Crick made their discovery while working on nucleic acids, the substances in the nucleus of cells that contain inheritable material. With their colleague Maurice WILKINS they were awarded a Nobel Prize (1962).

Watson, John (1878-1958) American psychologist who was a major proponent of behaviourism. He restricted psychology to the objective study of the relation between stimuli and responses. He believed that each species had a limited repertory of innate reflexes and that learning was a conditioning of these reflexes, as described by PAVLOV. Watson stressed the role of environment in education.

Watson-Watt, Sir Robert Alexander (born 1892) Scottish physicist who led the team which, beginning in 1935, developed the system for the radiolocation of moving aircraft. Radar stations installed around the eastern and southern approaches to Britain, from 1938, played a vital role in its defence against German air attacks during the Second World War. In peacetime, radar has developed a whole range of uses, including the location of hurricane paths.

A celebration in stone at Mount Rushmore, US, of Washington and other Presidents

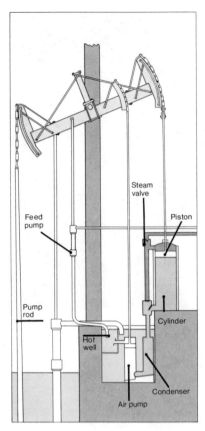

Feed pump

Steam valve

Piston

Pump rod

Hot well

Cylinder

Condenser

Air pump

Coal, iron and inventors such as James Watt (whose vertical pump engine is shown above) were keystones of the Industrial Revolution

Watt, James (1736-1819) Scottish engineer, who improved the efficiency and versatility of steam engines, which powered the Industrial Revolution. To overcome the problem of fuel wastage in each cycle of the cylinder of a NEWCOMEN steam engine, which he was repairing, Watt proposed the introduction of a separate condenser to be kept cool, while the main cylinder could be kept hot, they needed to be connected only when the cylinder was filled with steam. Watt was granted his historic patent for 'a new method for lessening the consumption of steam and fuel in fire engines' in 1769. Six years later, he went into partnership with the Birmingham industrialist Matthew BOULTON, and together they perfected and marketed the steam engine. Watt made a number of other major contributions to the development of steam engines between 1775 and the 1790s: devising the concept of 'horse power', for the measurement of output; a double-acting engine, in which steam expanded and condensed alternately on both sides of the piston; a flying-ball governor by means of which the speed of an engine was used to control it (the first use of feed-back for self-regulation in a machine); and five ways in

which the back-and-forth motion of a piston could be translated into rotary motion – to drive looms, lathes, cable-drums and hoists.

Watteau, Jean-Antoine (1684-1721) French painter, originator of the *fêtes galantes*. His subject matter, epitomized by the *Departure from the Island of Cythera* (1717), emphasized the transitory quality of human happiness. His election to the French Academy was seen as a formal acknowledgment that a new era of light-hearted art to please the senses had ousted the large and formal history paintings of the age of LOUIS XIV. Watteau's delicate cabinet pictures possess a vein of melancholic fantasy and musical lyricism.

Watts, George Frederic (1817-1904) English painter, best known for his allegorical paintings on themes such as *Hope, Destiny* and *Chaos*.

Waugh, Evelyn (1903-66) English novelist, who wrote ironic, witty novels about the English upper-classes in the mid-20th century. In the earlier books, from *Decline and Fall* (1928) to *Put Out More Flags* (1942), Waugh satirizes the foolishness of fashionable society, mixing bitter farce and sharp dialogue, creating an anarchic world. In his later works, *Brideshead Revisited* (1945) and *Sword of Honour* (1965), a rewriting of a war trilogy, his Roman Catholicism and a more tolerant humanity bring nostalgic order to the world he describes.

Webb, Matthew (1848-83) English swimmer, who in 1875 became the first man to swim the English Channel.

Webb, Philip (1831-1915) English architect and an important figure in late 19th-century domestic architecture, who worked with William MORRIS to produce a style of architecture which, although it owed something to PUGIN, went a long way towards creating a kind of domestic Gothic style in red-brick.

Webb, Beatrice (1858-1943) and **Sidney (1859-1947)** English writers and social historians, members of the Fabian Society. Dedicated to socialism, they published prolifically, participated in the establishment of the London School of Economics (1895) and founded the left wing journal *The New Statesman* (1913).

Weber, Carl Maria Freidrich Ernst von (1786-1826) German composer who established a national style in German opera and whose best-known opera is *Der Freischütz* (1821). This story of·humour and

magic in a German village was the first opera in the Romantic style which sought to place emphasis on the music's emotional content. Weber followed it with *Euryanthe* (1823) and *Oberon* (1826), his last opera, commissioned by Covent Garden in London.

Weber, Max (1864-1920) German sociologist and political economist who in the *Protestant Ethic* and the *Spirit of Capitalism* (1904-5) challenged MARX's theory that economic factors are decisive in determining the course of history. He sought to identify some of the origins of capitalism and traced the significance of religious and ethical ideas. In his *Methodology of the Social Sciences* (1922), he argued that scientific methods can be used in the study of sociology, but emphasized that the sociologist cannot be purely objective; he must attempt to put himself in the place of the people he is studying in order to understand their values and motives. Weber contributed almost more than any other scholar to comparative sociology, and, in an effort to find a basis from which comparisons can be made with other civilizations, he evolved the concept of the 'ideal type' or ideal mode of a set of social relationships.

Webern, Anton von (1883-1945) Austrian composer who was, with BERG, one of SCHOENBERG's leading disciples and of whom STRAVINSKY wrote: 'Doomed to failure in a deaf world of ignorance and indifference, he inexorably went on cutting his diamonds.' His music was written painstakingly between his occupations as a conductor at various opera houses and as a teacher of composition. From 1924 he adopted Shoenberg's note-row technique, adapting it to his own highly individual intentions. Webern's work includes a symphony as well as song settings and chamber works, including a string quartet. After surviving years of ostracism imposed by the Nazi régime, he was shot by a sentry of the occupying US army after failing to answer a challenge.

Webster, John (1580-c. 1625) English dramatist, who wrote *The Duchess of Malfi* (c. 1613) and *The White Devil* (1612), both of which are frequently revived. With the exception of his earliest surviving play, *Appius and Virginia* (c. 1609), his dramas are sombre, violent and obsessed with death, but they are informed with poetry of a high order.

Webster, Noah (1758-1843) American lexicographer and compiler of the first *American Dictionary of the English Language* (1828). This compact, comprehensive popular work set out to record current forms of words, pronunciations and accepted meanings. It contained 12,000 words and included over 30,000 new meanings among its definitions.

Weddell, James (1787-1834) English navigator, leader of an Antarctic sealing expedition which (1823) penetrated the Weddell Sea (named after him) to 74°15'S, at that time the farthest south that had been reached.

Wedekind, Frank (1864-1918) German dramatist who was the first to deal outspokenly with sexual themes. His *Awakening of Spring* (1891), which is concerned with adolescent sexual problems, was banned from the London stage until as recently as 1963. In both *Earth Spirit* (1895) and its sequel, *Pandora's Box* (1904), the character of Lulu, a beautiful, uninhibited but soulless woman, is an incarnation of lust and the symbol of Society.

Wedgwood, Josiah (1730-95) English pottery manufacturer who introduced new processes and high standards of design into the ceramic industry.

Wegener, Alfred (1880-1930) German meteorologist, who in 1915 first propounded the theory of continental drift. He contended that evidence of past climates could not be reconciled with the fixed positions of the continents and of the north and south magnetic poles, and that the now-separate continents must at one time have formed a single large mass which later drifted apart. After decades of scepticism, abundant evidence has now come to light to confirm the essence of Wegener's theories.

Weierstrass, Karl (1815-97) German mathematician, who was one of the pioneers in a rigorous approach to the modern theory of functions, both in real variable analysis and functions of complex variables.

Weill, Kurt (1900-1950) German composer who collaborated with BRECHT on *The Threepenny Opera* (1928) and *The Rise and Fall of the City of Mahogonny* (1930). The 'Brecht-Weill' style of song and lyric was one of the most distinctive of the inter-war years. After fleeing from the Nazis to America in 1935, Weill composed several Broadway musicals.

Weismann, August (1834-1914) German biologist, who discovered that the germ cells that transmit the various hereditary characteristics from one generation to the next are formed by a process of division, so as to carry half the genes from each of

the constituent parent germ cells. This is vital in explaining the actual genetic process and forms an important part of modern genetic theory.

Weiss, Ehrich see HOUDINI, Harry

Weizmann, Chaim (1874-1952) Jewish statesman, who became first President of Israel. He was born in Poland but emigrated to Britain, where he became a biochemist and did valuable work in the explosives department of the Admiralty during the First World War. He also became leader of the Zionist movement, whose aim was the establishment of a national home for the Jews. For this aim, he obtained the support of the British government, embodied in the BALFOUR Declaration (1917) and in the League of Nations' mandate for Palestine. As a result of these achievements, he became leader of the World Zionist Organization 1920-31, and head of the Jewish Agency for Palestine (1929-31). He was Provisional President of Israel in 1948 and became the first official President in 1949.

Welch, William (1850-1934) American bacteriologist who discovered the causative bacillus of gas gangrene (1892). After studying in Germany he was appointed to the chair of pathology at Johns Hopkins University, Baltimore, where he remained for 34 years. He was an outstanding teacher.

Weller, Thomas see ENDERS, John

Welles, Orson (born 1915) American actor, director and producer, who once said, 'a film is never really good unless the camera is an eye in the hand of a poet'. His later films

Early tableware made by Josiah Wedgwood's pottery, deep in the heart of England's 'Black Country'

demonstrate the practicality of this remark. *Citizen Kane* (1942), loosely based on the life of William Randolph HEARST, was the first and most famous of the films which Welles directed, wrote and starred in, followed by the masterful *The Magnificent Ambersons* (1942). He has had an equally successful acting career, notably as the black-marketeer Harry Lime in *The Third Man* (1949) and in *Chimes at Midnight* (1966) adapting SHAKESPEARE's *Henry IV* and *Henry V* for the cinema.

Actor-director Orson Welles, major influence on the art of cinema starring here in 'The Stranger'

Wellington, Arthur Wellesley, 1st Duke of (1769-1852) English soldier, who defeated NAPOLEON's armies in the Peninsular War and at Waterloo. He was commissioned in 1787, but from 1796-1805 served as both a soldier and an administrator in India. On his return to England, he became MP for Rye. In 1808, he was given command of the army that was sent to Portugal to fight the French, whom he defeated. For allowing the French to withdraw, he was recalled and court-marshalled, but was exonerated. He returned to his command on the death of Sir John Moore at Corunna (1809), and in a campaign lasting from 1809-14 he drove the French back to the Pyrenees and into France. He was chosen, with CASTLEREAGH, to represent Britain at the Congress of Vienna (1814-15) and brought about the final defeat of Napoleon at Waterloo (18 June 1815). He later became a member of Lord LIVERPOOL's cabinet, and attended the subsequent congresses of Aix-la-Chapelle (1818) and Verona (1822). As Prime Minister (1828-30) his obstinate opposition to parliamentary reform made him unpopular, despite his great services to the country, and on more than one occasion his house was stoned by mobs.

Wells, Herbert George (1866-1946) English novelist and social commentator, whose writings were world famous in the first decades of the 20th century. Wells was the first important writer of science fiction in English and combined scientific interest with social concern in works such as *The Time Machine* (1895), *The Invisible Man* (1897) and *The War of the Worlds* (1898). In many of his works he accurately predicted future events. His early life provided the material for his social comedies such as *Love and Mr Lewisham* (1900) and *Kipps* (1905). After 1911, his novels became social tracts, but he continued to hold an audience with his short stories, his encyclopedic *The Outline of History* (1920) and his revealing *Experiment in Autobiography* (1934).

Welsbach, Baron Carl Auer von (1858-1929) Austrian chemist who in 1885 patented the gas mantle, a woven cotton mesh impregnated with thorium and cerium oxides and fitted over a gas jet. Gas as an illuminant was given a new lease of life by this device to face the growing threat from electricity. Welsbach's second principal invention was the alloy, Auermetal, the cigarette and gas lighter flint.

Welty, Eudora (born 1909) American novelist, whose books have a strong flavour of the Mississippi region, depicting the strangeness and the excesses of Southern life.

Wenceslaus (c. 907-29) Duke of Bohemia who was canonized and became the patron saint of Czechoslovakia. He embraced the Christian faith introduced by his grandfather, Borivoy, and made it the basis for ordered civil life. This antagonized his reactionary younger brother BOLESLAV, whose followers killed Wenceslaus in a brawl. He was subsequently acclaimed as a Christian martyr and is remembered as 'Good King Wenceslaus' in the Christmas carol of that name.

Wentworth, Sir Thomas see STRAFFORD, 1st Earl of

Wergeland, Henrik (1808-45) Norwegian poet, whose rich imagination and gift for language are revealed at their best in *Jan van Huysum's Flowerpiece* (1842) and *The English Pilot* (1844). Although originally destined for the Church, he became involved in politics and disseminated his nationalistic beliefs through periodicals, speeches and pamphlets.

Werner, Abraham (1750-1817) German geologist, whose major contribution was to introduce entirely new methods of mineral description. The most influential teacher of his day, he founded the Neptunist school, which believed (mistakenly) that all rocks, including those we now call igneous, were formed by precipitation out of a solution in water.

Werner, Alfred (1866-1919) German-Swiss chemist who developed a co-ordination theory of chemical bonding. His theory involved the idea of groups of atoms arranged round, and bound to, a single central atom.

Wesley, John (1703-91) English theologian and evangelist founder of Methodism. Wesley spent some time as his parson father's curate, and for a while served as a missionary to the colonists of Georgia. He extended his acquaintance with current mysticism, particularly that associated with the Moravians. In 1738 he began his lifelong work for the conversion of Britain, travelling, writing, preaching regularly and organizing his societies. A staunch Church of England man, he refused to set up a separate Church, but was pushed by hostility and the consequences of his own actions to establish an increasingly independent Connexion of Societies within which a pastoral system was established. Wesley disciplined himself to proclaim his Arminian version of the Gospel, the emphasis of which was the genuine

Mae 'Come up and see me sometime' West in a 1930s production

possibility of Christian perfection for all faithful men.

West, Benjamin (1738-1820) American painter of historical subjects, who worked in England and succeeded Sir Joshua REYNOLDS as President of the Royal Academy in 1792.

West, Mae (born 1893) American actress who began her career on the stage, but made her name in the cinema. In a period of sophistication, she brought a healthy vulgarity to the screen, perfecting the art of the *double entendre* in films such as *She Done Him Wrong* (1933), *I'm No Angel* (1933) and *My Little Chickadee* (1939), in which she co-starred with W. C. FIELDS. Her name became the colloquial term for an inflatable life jacket.

West, Nathanael (1903-40) Penname of Nathan Weinstein, American author who wrote satirically on the neuroses of modern life.

Westermarck, Edward (1862-1939) Finnish anthropologist, philosopher and sociologist who argued that the moral rules of society are based on man's fundamental emotions of approval and disapproval.

Westinghouse, George (1846-1914) American inventor and industrialist, who filed more than 400 patents during his lifetime, mainly concerning railways, the electrical industry and the utilization of natural gas. For railways he invented a device for re-railing derailed steam cars (1865), an air brake (1868) (which he made automatic in 1872, and with it, his fortune) and pneumatic points-switching and signalling systems – which kindled his interest in electricity. From 1883 he pioneered control systems for long-distance natural-gas pipelines and for town distribution networks. In 1886 he formed the Westinghouse Electric Company and started to devise an AC power and lighting system, backing TESLA in his work.

Westmoreland, William C. (born 1914) American general during the escalation of the Vietnam War. In 1968, President JOHNSON transferred Westmoreland to Army Chief-of-Staff amidst disappointment at the progress of the war.

Wettbach, Adrian see GROCK

Wettstein, John Rudolf (1594-1666) Swiss Burgomaster of Basel whose diplomacy helped to achieve the Treaty of Westphalia, which ended the Thirty Years' War, and gained formal recognition throughout Europe of Swiss independence from Germany – an independence which had existed in practice since 1499.

Weyden, Rogier van der (c. 1399-1464) Influential Flemish painter of religious works and some portraits. His most famous painting, which was copied several times in the 15th century, is the *Deposition* altarpiece (*c.* 1435) in which the figures are as if in low-relief sculpture – thrust to the foreground of the picture and seen against a plain gold background. Weyden's technique is as sensitive and luminous as that of van EYCK, but he differs from him in the incisive linear character of his forms, which owe much to Gothic sculpture, and the pathos of his religious scenes.

Wharton,   Edith   (1862-1937) American novelist, who wrote neat, competent portraits of New York and European upper-class society. *The House of Mirth* (1905) and *The Custom of the Country* (1913) are influenced by Henry JAMES. Her best story, *Ethan Frome* (1911), however, deals with bewilderment and pathos in Puritan New England.

Wheatstone, Sir Charles (1802-75) English physicist, who made notable contributions to acoustics and developed his own bridge method for the accurate measurement of electrical resistance. However, his most important work, from 1837, with Sir William Fothergill Cooke, was on the electric telegraph. Its main applications were for alarm systems and railway signalling. The inventors took out a joint patent for the system, which was installed the following year on the Great Western Railway.

Wheeler, Sir Mortimer (born 1890) English archaeologist, who popularized his subject through lectures, books and television. In such books as *Rome Beyond the Imperial Frontiers* (1954) and *The Indus Civilization* (1955) he vividly proved his point that archaeology is about people, not just artefacts: interpreting archaeological finds to reconstruct the patterns of life (and death) in ancient times. The scientific methods of excavation which he developed in England, notably at Maiden Castle, the British Iron Age fort, met with equal success in India, where, during the 1940s, he revitalized Indian archaeology and conducted important excavations of the Indus Valley cities of Mohenjo Daro and Harappa.

Whewell, William (1794-1866) English philosopher who emphasized the need for induction in scientific method, but equally understood the function of framing hypotheses, without which no amount of fact-finding will amount to a theory. In this, he was influenced by the philosophy of KANT and in turn influenced PEIRCE, while coming into conflict with J. S. MILL.

Whinfield, John Rex (1901-66) English chemist who in 1941, with J. T. Dickson, discovered terylene, a polyester fibre made from terephthalic acid and ethylene glycol. After the Second World War, its industrial development by Imperial Chemical Industries in Britain and Du Pont in the US led to a new branch of the textile industry.

Whipple,   George see MURPHY, William

Whistler,   James   (1834-1903) American artist and acid wit. As a painter he sought to impose a harmony on nature rather than faithfully to transcribe her qualities, as is evident in the famous portrait of his mother (1872), whose real title is *Arrangement in Grey and Black*.

Whitaker, Joseph (1820-95) English publisher who founded *Whitaker's Almanac* (1869), the annual reference book on British politics, economics and culture. He also founded *The Bookseller* (1858), the weekly British book trade journal.

White, Gilbert (1720-93) English clergyman, naturalist and nature-writer, whose *Natural History of Selborne* (1789) is a lucid and well-observed record, in the form of collected letters, of the countryside. This work, admired by CONSTABLE, was one of several that helped to prepare the way for the Romantic appreciation of nature.

White, Patrick (born 1912) Australian novelist. His works are long and densely detailed, often creating an oppressive atmosphere, amid which the central characters struggle to survive. His heroes, such as the visionary explorer in *Voss* (1957) or the family in *The Tree of Man* (1955), possess the pioneering fortitude that is part of the tradition of Australian society. He was awarded the Nobel Prize for Literature in 1973.

White, Terence Hanbury (1906-64) English novelist, who retold the Arthurian legend in *The Once and Future King* (1958), a quartet of novels, on which the play and the film of *Camelot* were based.

Whitefield, George (1714-70) English religious revivalist and early Methodist, famed for his preaching. He is said to have preached altogether 18,000 sermons to 10 million people, and had much influence on the revival in America (which he visited seven times) and in Wales. Though he lacked WESLEY's organizing genius, his work nevertheless anticipated many features of Wesleyism. His strict Calvinism, however, led to a breach with Wesley over the problem of predestination.

Whitehead, Alfred (1861-1947) English mathematician and philosopher whose early work on mathematics and logic culminated in his joint authorship, with RUSSELL, of *Principia Mathematica* (1910-14). At Harvard, where he was Professor of Philosophy, he worked on a vast system of mathematics in an attempt to encompass logic, mathematics and physical science on the one hand, with the human element (ethical, aesthetic and religious) on the other.

Whitehead, Robert (1823-1905) English inventor of the naval torpedo. Whitehead at his works at Fiume on the Adriatic developed a self-propelled underwater bomb, powered by compressed air (1866). By 1890 there were torpedoes capable of speeds of up to 30 knots with a half-mile range and a 200-pound warhead. The weapon's effectiveness was demonstrated by the Japanese during their attack on the Russian Fleet at Port Arthur in February 1904.

Whitlam, Edward Gough (born 1916) Australian politician and barrister who became Prime Minister of Australia in December 1972. His government was the first Labour administration in Australia for 23 years.

Whitman, Walt (1819-92) American poet, who wrote with vehemence and audacity of the need for American intellectual independence, of which he became the bardic symbol. After *Leaves of Grass* (1855), his chief works were *Drum Taps* (1865), poems on the Civil War, and the prose *Democratic Vistas* (1871). His poems, on social and moral issues, are unconventionally formed; his language, said Emerson, mixed 'the *Bhagavad Gita* and the *New York Herald*'.

Whitney, Eli (1765-1825) American inventor of the cotton gin (1793). The gin removed the lint from the seeds so easily that even short-fibred cotton – the only kind that could be grown in inland America – became profitable. In 1798, he obtained a contract from the American government for 10,000 muskets, having introduced the technique of making all parts standard and interchangeable, so cutting time and costs. This was one of the early examples of mass production techniques, as later developed on a wide scale by FORD, COLT and others.

Whitney, William Dwight (1827-94) American philologist who studied in Germany under BOPP, later laid the foundations of the scientific study of language in the US and was an important influence on BLOOMFIELD, SAPIR and other American scholars.

Whittier, John Greenleaf (1807-92) American poet, who won a reputation for popular poems and ballads. Coming from a Quaker family, he was a vigorous abolitionist whose obvious sincerity appeared in his anti-slavery poems in *Voices of Freedom* (1846). The popular *Snow-Bound* (1866) recalls his country childhood; his collection *In War Time* (1864) contains the well-known patriotic ballad 'Barbara Frietchie'.

Whittington, Richard (c. 1358-1423) English merchant, three times Lord Mayor of London. As a successful London mercer and husband of the heiress Alice Fitzwaryn, he became rich enough to lend money to HENRY IV and HENRY V. He left a huge sum for charity and for public works, including the rebuilding of Newgate Prison. The popular legend of Whittington as an orphan owning only a cat but rising from poverty to riches, dates from a play printed in 1605.

Whittle, Sir Frank (born 1907) English aeronautical engineer with the Royal Air Force who developed a successful turbo-jet engine for aircraft. Despite German priority in jet propulsion, it was Whittle's engine, supplied to Britain's American and Russian allies in the Second World War for fighter aircraft, that became the prototype of modern jet engines.

A cotton gin. Eli Whitney's invention helped cotton growing to become big business–but increased plantation slave labour

Whitworth, Sir Joseph (1803-87) English mechanical engineer and industrialist, who introduced the machine tools and methods which revolutionized workshop practice. At that time the accepted working tolerance was 1/16th inch, but his equipment enabled it to be reduced to 1/1000th inch, which is still the normal accuracy of conventional machining operations. In 1841, he suggested that a uniform system of screw threads should be introduced and this was eventually adopted, being known as the British Standard Whitworth (BSW).

Whorf, Benjamin (1897-1941) American linguistics theorist and co-formulator of the SAPIR-Whorf hypothesis. Whorf wrote five important articles on the theme that language is the product of a people's experience and culture which therefore limits their thinking. Thus an Eskimo, with four words for 'snow' and an Aztec, with only one word meaning 'snow', 'cold', and 'ice', would differ markedly in what they could say or think about snow.

Whymper, Edward (1840-1911) English explorer, mountaineer and artist and first man to climb the Matterhorn in Switzerland. Between1861 and 1865, he attempted the climb six times and then, in July 1865, his seventh attempt was successful, after ascending the so-called Swiss Ridge. During the climb four men fell to their deaths, but a breaking rope saved Whymper and two guides.

Wicksteed, Philip Henry (1844-1927) British economist and writer on the theory of marginal utility and consumer behaviour, whose most widely known works were *The Alphabet of Economic Science* (1888) and *An Essay of the Coordination of the Law of Distribution* (1894).

Wieland, Christoph (1733-1813) German novelist and poet, author of *The History of Agathon* (1766-7), the first in a series of novels in German

literature concerned with the psychological development of their heroes. He was distrustful of religious enthusiasm, which he saw as a distortion of sensualism, and a belief in a harmony between the spirit and the senses informs most of his mature works. His prose translations of SHAKESPEARE's plays had an important influence on the *Sturm und Drang* movement and helped to popularize Shakespeare in Germany.

Wightman, Mrs George (born 1886) American sportswoman who founded the Wightman Cup competition. She won the US women's tennis singles championships (1909-11) and donated the cup in 1923 to be played for annually by women's teams from Great Britain and the US, thus complementing the men's competition founded by Dwight DAVIS.

Wilberforce, William (1759-1833) English philanthropist, who campaigned for the abolition of the slave trade and slavery. As an MP and a close friend of PITT, who supported his campaigns, Wilberforce devoted all his time and eloquence to denouncing the slave trade. In 1791, he introduced a Bill for its abolition, but had to fight until 1807 to get it on the Statute book. Thereafter, he devoted himself to the complete abolition of slavery in Britain and her dominions. Shortly before his death in 1833, this aim was accomplished during GREY's Whig ministry.

Wilbye, John (1574-1638) English composer who is among the most illustrious of all madrigalists. Wilbye wrote little apart from his madrigals, which belong to the later Jacobean school.

Wilde, Oscar (1854-1900) Irish dramatist, master of the social comedy. *Lady Windermere's Fan* (1892), an immediate success, was followed by *A Woman of No Importance* (1893) and *An Ideal Husband* (1895), which brought Wilde fame and wealth. His best-known play, *The Importance of Being Earnest* (1895), was rated the most elegant and amusing English high comedy for two centuries. A verse-drama written in French, *Salomé* (1892), was produced in France, but banned in England. In 1895 Wilde was imprisoned after being convicted of homosexual practices. In *The Ballad of Reading Gaol* he recorded his prison experiences (1898). He died in poverty and exile.

Wilder, Thornton (born 1897) American playwright and novelist. *The Bridge of San Luis Rey* (1927), a best-selling novel which won the Pulitzer Prize, is an account of life's ironies of fate and providence, and *Ides of March* (1948) is an imaginative reconstruction of the last days of Julius CAESAR. In 1967 he published *The Eighth Day*, his first novel for almost 20 years.

Wiligelmo (11th-12th cent.) Italian Romanesque sculptor who worked in Modena Cathedral (1099-1106), where a school of sculpture appears to have been centred around him. The Genesis reliefs and the prophets on the façade of Modena bear his personal style, which is remarkable for its classicism at this early date.

Wilkes, John (1727-97) English Member of Parliament and political reformer, whose attack on an autocratic speech by the king to Parliament incurred George III's anger and Wilkes's arrest under a general warrant. He was released on the grounds of parliamentary privilege and that general warrants were illegal, both grounds landmarks in British justice. Wilkes was expelled from Parliament, but after a period of exile to avoid a seditious libel action, returned and again became an MP, winning a series of elections whose validity was rejected by the House of Commons, under government pressure. An enraged public (most of whom still had no vote) supported Wilkes in a campaign for parliamentary reform, but Wilkes later abandoned his radicalism and supported the younger PITT.

Wilkie, Sir David (1785-1841) Scottish artist, whose sentimental genre painting won wide popularity,

Wilkinson, Ellen Cicely (1891-1947) English Labour politician, trade unionist, feminist and leader of the 'Jarrow Crusade'. In 1935, she was elected MP for Jarrow, a town that had been ruined by the closure of its shipyard, and in 1936, she organized a march of the yard's unemployed workers from Jarrow to London. She died while in office as Minister of Education (1945-7), the first woman to hold the post.

Willaert, Adriaan (c. 1490-1562) Flemish composer and madrigalist who, as Director of Music at St Mark's, laid the foundations for the Venetian choral tradition that was to culminate in GABRIELI.

William I 'The Pious' (886-918) Duke of Aquitaine, founder of the Abbey of Cluny (910) near Mâcon. Under able abbots (notably Odo, Maieul, Odilo, Hugh the Great, and Peter the Venerable) it developed the Cluniac monastic reforms, which were embraced by a network of western European monasteries.

William I (1027-87) King of England (1066-87), called William the Conqueror, who came to the throne by conquest, and substituted Norman for Anglo-Saxon rule. He was a cousin of EDWARD the Confessor, who supposedly promised him succession to the English throne. On Edward's death, William enforced this claim by landing in England and killing Edward's proclaimed successor HAROLD II in the Battle of Hastings (1066). William completed the conquest of England by 1070, ended HEREWARD's last stand in 1071 and centralized government on feudal Norman lines, allocating big estates and high posts to leading Norman knights and churchmen to hold for the Crown. Under William, and his son Henry I, Norman rule gave England political stability and enriched it with Norman (Romanesque) architecture, and a new language, Norman-French, which eventually combined with Anglo-Saxon to produce the medieval English language.

William I 'The Silent' (1533-84) Count of Nassau, founder of the Dutch Republic. Under the emperor CHARLES V, William became Governor of the northern Netherlands provinces of Holland, Utrecht and Zeeland. Once the territory of the independent French dukes of Burgundy, the Netherlands, through marriages with the Hapsburgs, had become connected with Spain and its empire. Nationalism and Protestantism grew, intensified by the Spanish attempts to suppress them. William became a convinced supporter of both causes. When PHILIP II of Spain sent the Duke of ALVA and Spanish troops to impose Roman Catholic uniformity on the Netherlands, William led stubborn armed resistance in Holland and Zeeland, the Protestant north, and became first Statholder (1579-84) of the northern provinces. By the Union of Utrecht (1579), they were formed into one independent state, variously known as the United Provinces, the Dutch Republic and now the Netherlands. William was murdered by a Burgundian.

William I (1797-1888) King of Prussia (1861-88) and first emperor of Germany (1871-88). He was an autocrat who held extreme conservative views, and during the revolution of 1848 was briefly driven ont of Prussia. After succeeding to the Prussian throne, his appointment of BISMARCK as his chief minister was momentous, for between them they forged the German Empire. William was at first unwilling to fully support Bismarck's policy of conquest, but Prussia's annexation of Schleswig-Holstein in 1864 led him to adjust his vision of Prussia's future. Prussian

domination in Germany was assured by the defeat of Austria in 1866, and the German Empire was founded during the Franco-Prussian War.

William II (1859-1941) Emperor of Germany and King of Prussia (1888-1918). In 1890, two years after his accession, he dismissed BISMARCK from office in order to implement his personal policy of imperialism and industrialization. He sponsored the German challenge to British seapower and by his 'sabre-rattling' forced the other great powers into defensive alliances. His personal responsibility for the war has probably been exaggerated, but the Allies' belief that this was so led them to refuse peace terms until the kaiser's own Officer Corps had forced him to abdicate and leave the country (1918).

William III (1650-1702) Dutch prince of Orange, Statholder of Holland (1672-1702), King of England (1689-1702), whose policies placed a check on the vast powers of LOUIS XIV of France. When Louis XIV invaded Holland (1672), William led the resistance. He suffered defeats, but married Mary, daughter of England's future James II, with whom he opened negotiations, under threat of which Louis reached an agreement with William at Nijmegen (1678). James refused to form an alliance with William, so William turned to the English opposition and supported their disapproval of James's religious policy. After overthrowing James in the so-called Glorious Revolution (1688), William accepted invitations from the Parliaments of England and Scotland to rule the kingdoms jointly with his wife Mary, and made his throne safe by defeating James II, who had retreated to Ireland, at the Battle of the Boyne (1690). He formed two Grand Alliances against France (1689, 1701), the first leading to a war (the War of the League of Augsburg) by which William regained all his possessions taken by Louis XIV.

William IV (1765-1837) King of Great Britain and Ireland (1830-7) the third son of George III. He became king on the death of his brother, GEORGE IV, in 1830. His dislike of extreme measures led him to oppose the Reform Bill, an action by which he incurred popular dislike and which led to a political crisis with GREY, his Prime Minister. His dismissal of MELBOURNE in 1834 and the subsequent invitation to PEEL to form a ministry was the last attempt by an English sovereign to impose a minority ministry on Parliament.

William of Ockham (c. 1300-c. 1349) English scholastic philosopher whose denial of the Pope's temporal power laid the foundations of the modern independence of State from Church. In logic, he held that only singular things exist, while the universals describing these qualities are merely thought. From this arose the dictum known as 'Ockham's razor', which stated that entities ought not to be needlessly multiplied.

William of Sens (c. 1180) French architect of the Choir of Canterbury Cathedral. His style was based on that of contemporary cathedrals in northern France, as well as on Sens Cathedral.

Williams, Roger (c. 1603-83) English-born clergyman, founder of the colony of Rhode Island in America. A Nonconformist, he emigrated to Boston, but antagonized WINTHROP's Puritan régime by urging separation of Church and State, and was banished. He founded Providence on Rhode Island (1636), on land bought from American Indians, where he established religious liberty and democracy by welcoming Christian sects (notably Quakers and Anabaptists) persecuted by the Puritans, and introducing government by popular consent.

Williams, Tennessee (born 1914) American dramatist whose plays for the stage have reached a world-wide audience through the cinema. His first Broadway success, *The Glass Menagerie* (1945), established a pattern for his later plays, with their settings in the southern States, tough heroes, shabby gentility, and confrontations between innocence and passion. These were *A Streetcar Named Desire* (1947), *Summer and Smoke* (1948), *The Rose Tattoo* (1951) and *Cat on a Hot Tin Roof* (1955). Williams has also written some symbolic plays, such as *Camino Real* (1953), and the domestic comedy, *Period of Adjustment* (1961). His most recent plays include *Suddenly Last Summer*, *Baby Doll* and *Small Craft Warnings*.

Williams, William Carlos (1883-1963) American poet who, as he developed, concentrated on objective description and lack of decoration. In his longest poem, 'Paterson' (1946-51), he described the life of a New Jersey town, seeing common events and ordinary people with a cool and appraising view. He also wrote several novels and an *Autobiography* (1951).

Williamson, Henry (born 1895) English novelist and nature writer, whose most famous works are *Tarka the Otter* (1927) and *Salar the Salmon* (1935). He has also written many conventional novels.

Willkie, Wendell Louis (1892-1944) American politician and Republican candidate for the presidency in 1940, when he failed to prevent the election of ROOSEVELT for an unprecedented third term.

Willstätter, Richard (1872-1942) German chemist who investigated the structure of chlorophyll, the green colouring matter in plants.

Wilson, Alexander (1714-86) Scottish astronomer and meteorologist who studied the nature of the Sun and of the Earth's atmosphere. At Glasgow University in 1749 he measured atmospheric temperatures with the help of a kite – so anticipating the use of meteorological balloons developed by Jean Pierre BLANCHARD and Gustave HERMITE. In the same year he discovered the nature of the dark patches on the Sun's photosphere, now known as sunspots.

Wilson, Angus (born 1913) English author and critic, who writes subtle novels that probe, sometimes satirically, the frustrations and weaknesses of intelligent society. Among his books are *Hemlock and After* (1952), *Anglo-Saxon Attitudes* (1956) and *The Old Men at the Zoo* (1961), all lengthy novels with a Dickensian variety of characters.

Wilson, Ernest Henry (1876-1930) British explorer, gardener and botanist who introduced numerous plants from the Far East into Europe and America.

Wilson, James Harold (born 1916) British Prime Minister (1964-70) and the youngest Cabinet Minister (President of the Board of Trade in ATTLEE's government at the age of 31) since PITT. In 1951, Wilson resigned with BEVAN in protest against cuts in social service spending, and he remained a Bevanite throughout the 1950s. He was Prime Minister from 1964-70, but the crisis over Britain's balance of payments and the subsequent devaluation of the pound severely hampered his economic plans. The seeming inconsistency of his views, however, on Britain and the Common Market and on the need for legislation to regulate the conduct of trades unions, has caused him to be regarded in some quarters as a political opportunist. The revolt of Ian SMITH in Rhodesia, and DE GAULLE's intransigence towards Britain's entry into the Common Market, blighted his foreign policy, but he was the first British Premier to face up to the fact of Britain's decline as a world power, while many viewed his efforts to establish a prices and incomes policy as economically sound, though politically unpopular.

Wilson, Richard (c. 1713-82) Welsh landscape artist, who, though he achieved little success in his lifetime, has since come to be regarded with admiration. His absorption of the idyllic calm and atmospheric light of the Roman countryside on a visit to Italy (1750-7), is evident in *Shepherds in the Campagna*.

Wilson, Thomas Woodrow (1856-1924) Twenty-eighth American President, who led the US into the First World War, and helped to found the League of Nations. He was elected President in 1913 in a campaign against Theodore ROOSEVELT and TAFT. He initiated anti-Trust legislation, reformed the national banking system by the Federal Reserve Act, and sent a punitive expedition into Mexico (1916) to put down a border raid by Mexican 'generals', notably Pancho VILLA. Because of his maintenance of US neutrality for the first two years of the First World War, and as a result of his moves to restore peace by mediation, he was elected for a second term. Early in 1917, Germany resumed unrestricted submarine attacks on merchant shipping and, at the same time, tried to arrange that if this provoked Wilson to declare war, Mexico would invade the US. Revelation of these negotiations (the 'Zimmerman telegram') and the sinking of American ships, brought the US into the conflict (April 1917). When he arrived in Europe for the Paris Peace Conference (1919) Wilson was hailed as a saviour, but he was bitterly disappointed by the failure of LLOYD GEORGE and CLEMENCEAU to live up to his own lofty ideals. Overwork led to his collapse in September 1919.

Woodrow Wilson, architect of peace at the end of the First World War

Winckelman, Johann Joachim (1717-68) German art historian who is often called 'the father of archaeology'. While working in Rome, he made a careful study of Greek mythology and also of Roman sculptures and ruins, becoming the first to identify styles in ancient art. His *History of the Art of Antiquity* (1764), showed that it was possible to understand ancient peoples by studying their works of art,

Winckler, Hugo (1863-1913) German archaeologist who established that the Hittites were once a major power. Winckler's finds inspired further excavations, notably by Sir Leonard WOOLLEY, which eventually confirmed that between 1380 and 1230 BC the Indo-European-speaking Hittites had mastered much of Anatolia and Syria.

Wingfield, Walter Clopton (1833-1912) British inventor of lawn tennis. In 1874 he patented an outdoor game called Sphairistike which, in a modified form, was renamed lawn tennis. As such it was adopted by the All England Croquet Club, which organized the first Wimbledon lawn tennis championships in 1877.

Winsor, Frederick Albert (1763-1830) A German company promoter, who after seeing LEBON's demonstration, realized that in a public supply, gas would be piped from the plant to the consumer through a system of mains. Winsor was granted a charter to found a National Light and Heat Company (1812), but was dismissed in the same year for administrative and technical incompetence. Two years later however, the company erected a gas works in London and in April 1814, supplied gas to lamps in the parish of St Margarets, Westminster. Soon, other gas companies were formed in most cities: gas lighting had arrived.

Winstanley, Gerrard (1609-52) English social reformer who led and publicized the Diggers, 20 poor men who seized and cultivated common land at St George's Hill, Cobham, Surrey (1649-50). Winstanley won support for the Diggers in four more counties before mob violence and a hostile government broke up the colony (1650).

Winthrop, John (1588-1649) English Puritan lawyer, first governor of the Massachusetts Bay Colony. He sailed for America as chosen governor of more than 1000 Puritans, who reached Sale and founded settlements, including Boston. As governor almost continuously until his death, Winthrop helped to organize defence against likely English attack

and became first president of the defensive union called the New England Confederation.

Withering, William (1741-99) English physician, who introduced digitalis as a drug for the treatment of heart disease, describing his findings in *An Account of the Foxglove* (1785).

Witte, Count Sergei Yulievich (1849-1915) Finance Minister (1892-1903) and first constitutional Prime Minister of Russia (1905-6), who industrialized Russia and promoted the Trans-Siberian Railway. Despite Russia's backwardness, he forced the country into the industrial era, financing heavy industry with foreign capital (mostly French) and supporting it with foreign expertise. Witte's efforts established the foundations of modern Soviet Russia's industrial position. The Trans-Siberian Railway, begun in 1891 when he was Minister of Communications, was called into service in the Russo-Japanese War of 1904-5.

Wodehouse, Pelham Grenville (born 1881) English humorist, who has created a remarkable and enduring fantasy world of butlers, gentle, foolish aristocrats, country houses and eccentric behaviour. His most popular characters, the bumbling Bertie Wooster, his butler Jeeves and Lord Emsworth, are outstanding comic creations.

Woffington, Peg (c. 1714-60) British actress of Irish extraction, famous in many parts, but especially for her performance in male roles, such as Sir Harry Wildair in FARQUHAR's *The Constant Couple*. She was for some time GARRICK's mistress.

Wöhler, Friedrich (1800-82) German chemist who was the first to synthesize an organic chemical compound from an inorganic one. He heated ammonium cyanate and found that it turned into urea, a substance present in the urine of mammals and therefore organic in nature. This was the first of many setbacks for the then dominant theory of vitalism, which stated that organic compounds could be formed only in living things.

Wolf, Hugo (1860-1903) Austrian-born song composer who is, after SCHUBERT, the finest in the German *Lieder* tradition. Wolf's songs were written in bursts of frenzied activity. He became mentally ill and spent his last days in an asylum.

Wolfe, James (1727-59) British major-general, who added Canada to the British Empire. Fighting in North America in the Seven Years' War, he won the decisive Battle of

Quebec (1759) by making a night landing from the St Lawrence River and scaling supposedly impregnable cliffs with his troops, who reached the Plains of Abraham southwest of Quebec and surprised the city's French defenders under MONTCALM. Wolfe, like Montcalm, died in the battle. His victory was confirmed by the Treaty of Paris (1763), which ended France's American Empire by giving Great Britain Canada and all lands east of the Mississippi.

Wolfe, Thomas (1900-38) American novelist, whose sequence of novels, from *Look Homeward, Angel* (1929), his first and best book, to *You Can't Go Home Again* (1940), follow the thinly disguised author from his Carolina home to his life and loves in New York.

Wolff, Elisabeth (1738-1804) and Deken, Agatha (1741-1804) Dutch novelists, co-authors of *Sara Burgerhart* (1782), a novel in letter form influenced by RICHARDSON. A witty book, wide-ranging and perceptive in its characterization, it immediately achieved European popularity. It was followed by the equally popular *Willem Leevend* (1784-5).

Wolsey, Thomas (c. 1475-1530) English prelate, politician and chief minister to HENRY VIII of England. As Archbishop of York, cardinal and Lord Chancellor, Wolsey virtually ran both Church and State with vigorous efficiency, though with personal extravagance and pomp. He pursued an active foreign policy, endeavouring to utilize to England's advantage the rivalry between FRANCIS I of France and the emperor CHARLES V. His apparent triumphs, like the Field of the Cloth of Gold (1520), were hollow ones, and his personal ambition to be Pope merely resulted in the loss of English influence in Europe in the later 1520s. He failed in his greatest diplomatic test, the annulment of Henry VIII's marriage to Catharine of Aragon (aunt of Charles V), and his dismissal from the chancellorship followed. He died in disgrace, before he could be tried for treason.

Wood, Sir Henry Joseph (1869-1944) English conductor and composer, founder, with Robert Newman, of the annual London Promenade Concerts, which he conducted until his death. He also promoted music festivals.

Wood, John (1704-54) English architect who, with his son John, replanned the city of Bath. Their original designs in an elegant Palladian style for the building of the crescent, circus and parades draw inspiration from the buildings of ancient Rome. Wood senior built Prior Park, Bath, and his son the Assembly Rooms and the Hot Baths.

Woodward, Robert Burns (born 1917) American chemist best known for his syntheses of highly complex organic compounds. Woodward began his remarkable series of syntheses by producing quinine in 1944. Subsequently, he tackled some of the most complex substances in organic chemistry; synthesizing the organic poison strychnine (1954) and the plant pigment, chlorophyll (1960). His techniques have enabled organic chemists to synthesize steroids and hormones.

Woolf, Virginia (1882-1941) English novelist, who was one of the foremost 20th-century experimenters with the technique and form of the novel. She was a member of the Bloomsbury Group (which included STRACHEY, KEYNES and FORSTER), amongst whom many new artistic ideas were discussed. Her novels *Jacob's Room* (1922), *Mrs Dalloway* (1925), *To the Lighthouse* (1927) and *The Waves* (1931) examine in a lyrical flow the myriad impressions of 'an ordinary mind on an ordinary day'.

Woollcott, Alexander (1887-1943) American critic and author who, as drama critic for the *New York Times* and then the *New York World*, had great influence on literary and theatrical taste.

Woolley, Sir Leonard (1880-1960) British archaeologist who awakened widespread interest in the world's first great civilization, the Sumerian. Between 1922-34 he excavated Ur of the Chaldees – the birth place of ABRAHAM – in Iraq. He traced the city's history back to prehistoric times, unearthing richly furnished royal tombs (one 4500 years old), and cuneiform inscriptions which described the daily life of the Sumerians.

Woolworth, Frank Winfield (1852-1919) American merchant, the founder of a five-and-ten-cent store from which grew the international chain of Woolworth stores.

Wordsworth, William (1770-1850) English poet, who believed in a new poetry of simple unadorned language, deriving its inspiration from nature and vivid experiences recalled by memory. After some unsettled years of conflicting experiences Wordsworth devoted himself to the writing of poetry. The *Lyrical Ballads* (1798), written with COLERIDGE, announced a Romantic programme to save the language and forms of poetry from

formality and artifice. 'Intimations of Immortality', 'Michael' and 'The Waggoner' continue this programme with greater profundity. Wordsworth's long, autobiographical poem *The Prelude*, usually considered his masterpiece, begun in 1798, and published posthumously, contains passages of sustained intensity, particularly in Book One, describing his childhood. He was appointed Poet Laureate in 1843.

Worsae, Jens (1821-85) Danish archaeologist whose *Primeval Antiquities of England and Denmark* (1843) was a breakthrough in modern scientific archaeology.

Wren, Sir Christopher (1632-1723) The most famous English Baroque architect, who was equally well known in his own day for his work in astronomy. The main basis of his style, and the mathematical genius that made his daring buildings possible, can be seen in one of his first buildings, the Sheldonian Theatre, Oxford, executed when he was already thirty, and a professor of astronomy. His most famous building, St Paul's Cathedral, London, was built to replace the medieval church destroyed in the Great Fire of 1666. It is a brilliant compromise between the Classical type of architecture which Wren admired, and the Gothic building plan which his patrons demanded. The dome is based on MICHELANGELO's design for St Peter's, Rome, while the medieval-type flying buttresses needed for the roof are hidden behind curtain walls, covered with classical detailing that enhance the bulk of the building. Wren also built 53 churches in London, among the best known being

The man whose name appears in almost every town high street—F. W. Woolworth

Until the appearance of high-rise office blocks, Wren's St Paul's Cathedral dominated London's skyline

St Stephen Walbrook, and St James's, Piccadilly.

Wright, Frank Lloyd (1869-1959) American architect who, both structurally and formally was perhaps the most brilliant American architect of his time. After training as an engineer he worked initially under SULLIVAN in Chicago. The gliding roofs and spatial plans of his early Chicago houses (the Robie House amongst them, which incorporated open plan living space) combined an aesthetic control with a wholly new dynamism and originality of detail that was to prove influential both in the United States and in Europe. Wright's interest in organic structure led in his later years to such projects as the 'mile-high' skyscraper and to the giant mushroom columns and glass tubing of the Johnson's Wax Factory at Racine, Wisconsin.

Wright, Richard (1908-60) American negro novelist and essayist whose books contain passionate outcries against social injustice in the United States. Born on a Mississippi plantation, raised in an orphan asylum, and employed as a clerk in Memphis, Wright saw the tribulations of the poor Southern negro at close quarters and protested angrily in *Uncle Tom's Children* (1935), *Native Son* (1940), *Black Boy* (1945), and his autobiography, *White Man, Listen!* (1957).

Wright, Wilbur (1867-1912) and **Orville (1871-1948)** American aviation pioneers and the first men to fly and control a heavier-than-air machine. They began as bicycle manufacturers in 1892 and became interested in the possibility of flight, experimenting with gliders and kites

until 1903. Then in December of that year, at Kitty Hawk, North Carolina, they made their first flights, the longest being of 852 feet and lasting 59 seconds. By October 1905, they had improved the machine sufficiently to fly a full circle of 24½ miles in 38 minutes at Dayton, Ohio. Their machine was patented in May 1906. The Wright brothers popularized flying in a series of exhibitions in the US and in Europe, winning the Michelin Trophy (1908) with a flight of 77 miles in two hours 20 minutes. Their 1908-9 plane designed for the US army led to the foundation of the American Wright Company to manufacture aircraft.

Wundt, Wilhelm (1832-1920) German psychologist, whose informal laboratory for experimental psychology at Leipzig University was officially established in 1879, becoming the first academic institution of its kind.

Wu Tao-tzu (c. 700-760) Buddhist artist of the T'ang dynasty, revered as the greatest figurative painter in Chinese art. Highly praised in Chinese critical writings of all periods, none of his work now survives except through the medium of stone engravings and copies by later painters. He is reported to have painted 300 murals in the Loyang area (modern Honan), which astounded his contemporaries by their solidity and realism.

Wu Ti (157-87 BC) Chinese Han emperor (140-87 BC) who extended his rule into Korea, Tonkin and Sinkiang, re-opening trade routes and other contacts with the West.

Wyatt, James (1747-1813) English Neo-classical architect who was known as 'the Destroyer' because of his unsympathetic improvements to medieval buildings. In 1796 he became Surveyor-General after a series of successful commissions, including Heveningham Hall, Suffolk, and Heaton Hall, Lancashire. His most famous building was probably Fonthill Abbey, Wiltshire (destroyed in 1825) built in Gothic style for William Beckford the cultivated dilettante.

Wyatt, Sir Thomas (1503-42) English poet and diplomat. On his various embassies to Italy (1526), France (1528-32) and Spain (1537-9), Wyatt learnt the continental verse models, which he helped to establish in English. His best achievements were in lyrics, and Petrarchan sonnets. Wyatt was a lover of Anne BOLEYN.

Wyatt, Sir Thomas (c. 1521-54) English soldier, leader of a revolt against MARY I. He joined a conspiracy to prevent Mary's marriage to PHILIP II of Spain, which the conspirators believed would make England a satellite of the immense Spanish Hapsburg Empire. Wyatt marched on London from Kent at the head of a large force, but failed to capture the capital, surrendered, and was executed.

Wycherley, William (1640-1716) British dramatist, one of the Restoration comedy playwrights whose work is still revived. His fame rests on the popular *The Country Wife* (1674) and *The Plain Dealer* (1676). He learned his theatrical technique from MOLIÈRE in France, but his forthright and robust manner as well as his characters are essentially English.

Wykeham, William of (1324-1404) English Lord Chancellor and Bishop of Winchester, who founded establishments to help poor students and to replace trained clergy killed by the Black Death. Gaining immense wealth and political power under EDWARD II and Richard II, he founded New College, Oxford, and, to supply it with scholars, St Mary's College, Winchester – a school whose members are still called Wykehamists.

X

X, Malcolm (1925-65) American Black Muslim leader, born Malcolm Little. A product of the black ghetto, he joined the Black Muslim Movement and through his preaching of hatred of all white men, became second only to the Muslim leader, Elijah Muhammed. In 1964, however, while on a pilgrimage to Mecca, he became converted to Islam and opposed to the hatred and racialism of the Black Muslims. His conversion to belief in multi-racial action led to his murder by Black Muslims in February 1965.

Xavier, Francis (1506-52) Navarrese Jesuit missionary and saint sometimes called the 'Apostle of the Indies'. Regarded by many as the greatest Christian missionary since the first century AD, Xavier preached in India, the Malay archipelago, Japan and China. He died in Goa.

Xenophon (c. 434-c. 354 BC) Greek historian whose writings reflected a balanced general outlook on society, rather than one of profound and specialized scholarship. His *Hellenica* was a Greek history of 411 to 362 BC. He also wrote memoirs of SOCRATES (*Apology*, *Memorabilia*, *Symposium*), dialogues on tyranny (*Hiero*) and

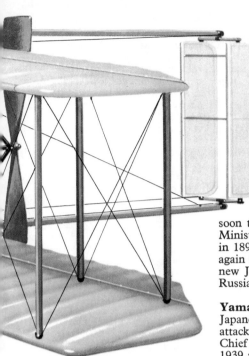

Wood, fabric, wire, a simple engine and the dynamism of the Wright brothers enabled Man to achieve a centuries-old dream with the first controlled, heavier-than-air flight, at Kitty Hawk, North Carolina, in 1903. Within 25 years, fare-paying passengers were being carried, within 50 years, Man was flying faster than the speed of sound

estate-management (*Deconomicus*), treatises on hunting, horsemanship and the constitution of Sparta.

Xerxes I (c. 519-465 BC) King of Persia, whose failure to subdue Greece marked the end of the supremacy of the Persian Empire. In 480 BC he marched approximately 183,000 men (then the biggest army ever known) into Europe, crushed LEONIDAS's Spartans at Thermopylae, and sacked Athens, but THEMISTOCLES destroyed Xerxes's fleet at nearby Salamis. Xerxes returned to Asia Minor and the army and fleet he left in Greece were soon defeated.

Y

Yale, Elihu (1649-1721) American-born Englishman in whose honour Yale University was named. He became an official of the East India Company and was Governor of Fort St George, Madras. A noted philanthropist, in 1718 he sent a cargo of books and East India goods which sold for £560, to the young collegiate school at Saybrook, Connecticut. The college took his name in appreciation of the gift.

Yamagata, Prince Aritomo (1838-1922) Creator of the modern Japanese army. After taking part in the overthrow of the Tokugawa shogunate, he became adviser to the Meiji emperor MUTSUHITO, Minister of War and then Chief of the General Staff. He modernized the Japanese military system and began a programme of mechanization that was

soon to prove itself. He was Prime Minister from 1889 to 1891 and again in 1898, and Chief of General Staff again in 1904, when he directed the new Japanese army in its defeat of Russia in 1904-5.

Yamamoto, Isoroku (1884-1943) Japanese Admiral who planned the attack on Pearl Harbour. He was Chief of the Japanese First Fleet in 1939 and of the Combined Fleet in 1941, and planned the attack on Pearl Harbour in order to destroy American sea power. Though the attack was successful, it sowed the seeds of Japan's defeat: old battleships were sunk, but fuel reserves and aircraft carriers were missed, which forced the US to adopt the fast carrier strategy, by which it ultimately triumphed. Yamamoto, who was privately convinced before the outbreak of war that Japan could not defeat the US, was killed in air action when his plane was intercepted by US aircraft.

Yamashita, Tomoyuki (1885-1946) Japanese conqueror of Malaya and the Philippines in the Second World War. He was responsible for the lightning conquest of Malaya and Singapore (December 1941-February 1942). In March 1942, he was given command of the Japanese forces in the Philippines and by early May had captured Bataan and forced the Americans to surrender at Corregidor. In February 1945, however, MACARTHUR defeated him at Luzon, and a year later he was charged with responsibility for the mass murder of civilians and American prisoners of war, tried and executed as a war criminal.

Yaroslav I 'The Wise' (c. 980-1054) Grand Duke of Kiev, who ruled all southern Russia, though his rule consisted mainly of receiving taxes. Yaroslav tried to strengthen his state by dynastic alliances, marrying his children into European royal families. Although he introduced an order of succession to prevent feuds, his death was soon followed by the breakdown of Russian unity.

Yeats, William Butler (1865-1939) Irish poet and dramatist who wrote a considerable amount of poetry which, for its technical control and a variety and complexity of vision, ranks him among the outstanding poets of the English language. His poetry was haunted by Irish scenery and history and his early poems, influenced by the Gaelic revival, were full of romantic nostalgia. He developed his own mystical system and his own interpretation of history, and slow changes through 'The Green Helmet' (1910), 'Responsibilities' (1914), 'The Wild Swans at Coole' (1917) and 'Michael Robartes' (1920) followed his experience of Irish independence, an obsessive and unhappy love affair, and the Irish literary movement. Yeats wanted to re-introduce verse drama into the theatre, and he directed his plays and those of other Irish writers, including SYNGE, at the newly formed Abbey Theatre in Dublin.

Yesenin, Sergey (1895-1925) One of Russia's most popular poets, whose laments for childhood and the countryside gained a wide response. In 1922 he married Isadora DUNCAN, and achieved literary success with *Confession of a Hooligan* and *Black Man*. Alcoholism and disillusionment with post-revolutionary Russia led to his mental breakdown and suicide in a Leningrad hotel.

Yoritomo (1147-99) Shogun of Japan and founder of the Kamakura shogunate. Eliminating the rivalry of other clans, Yoritomo made the military rule of his Minamoto clan, based at Kamakura, more powerful than the imperial court at Kyoto, so starting Japan's so-called Kamakura shogunate (1185-1333). This was characterized by feudalism, Zen Buddhism, the warrior cult and the rise of the Hojo family.

Yorke, Henry see GREEN Henry

Yoshida, Shigeru (1878-1967) Prime Minister of Japan, who led his country from defeat to economic prosperity. Towards the end of the Second World War, he was imprisoned by the Japanese authorities as a liberal and an advocate of peace. His views commended him, however, to MACARTHUR and, when Yoshida became Prime Minister (1946-7), the two worked closely together. He was again Premier from 1948 to 1954, and adviser in many governments after that. His ability to maintain harmonious relations with the Americans, as well as his intelligent handling of the post-war problems of a defeated nation, enabled Japan to become one of the most competitive industrial powers of the world.

Young, Thomas (1773-1829) English physicist who established the wave nature of light. He studied both NEWTON's particle theory of light and HUYGEN's wave theory, and saw that some effects (such as interference) could be predicted by the wave theory but could not occur if the particle theory were correct. In 1803, Young produced interference fringes on a screen by passing light through a pair of pin-holes in a card. Few other scientists took his work seriously, and not until Arago and FRESNEL produced a mathematical description of light waves, was Young's theory accepted.

Younghusband, Sir Francis Edward (1863-1942) English explorer and author whose Asian expeditions helped to map Central Asia and reopened Lhasa, the forbidden city of Tibet, to Europeans. He marched across the heart of Asia from Peking to Simla, India (1886-7) and later explored extensively in the Karakorum Range and the Pamirs, proving that the Karakorum Range was the watershed between Turkistan and India. Appointed British Commissioner to Tibet (1902), Younghusband led a British mission into Lhasa, and (1904) accomplished an Anglo-Tibetan treaty.

Yukawa, Hideki (born 1907) Japanese physicist who predicted the existence of the meson. In the 1930s he suggested that the powerful forces holding protons and neutrons together in the nucleus of an atom are quite different from any others known. He developed a theory picturing them as arising from a rapid back-and-forth movement between protons and neutrons of a new sub-atomic particle, later identified as a pi-meson. He was awarded the 1949 Nobel Prize for Physics.

Z

Zaydun, ibn- (1003-71) Leading Moorish poet and one of the main exponents of two peculiarly Moorish verse forms – the *muwashsha* and the *zajal* – intended to be sung rather than recited. They were often love poems and from their form and content it seems clear that they influenced the lyrics of the troubadours of Europe.

Zeami, Motokiyo (1363-1443) Japanese dramatist and actor. The master of *Noh* drama, Zeami wrote the majority of the *Noh* plays which are performed today and in a number of crucial essays, laid down the aesthetics of *Noh*.

Zeno (5th cent. BC) Greek philosopher of the Eleatic school. A disciple of PARMENIDES, most famous of his works were the arguments against motion, though only fragments of his work survive.

Zeppelin, Graf Ferdinand von (1838-1917) German army officer who on retiring (1891) concentrated on airship design and manufacture. The first of his dirigible balloons flew in 1900 and commercial services in Germany began 10 years later. Zeppelins carried out the first air raids against civilian London and in East Anglia during the early part of the First World War.

Zermelo, Ernst (1871-1953) German mathematician, who was one of the founders of axiomatic set theory.

Zeromski, Stefan (1864-1925) Polish novelist, poet and dramatist, whose numerous works are concerned with the fate of his native land. The prevailing pessimistic tone of his work reflects Poland's search for national identity and independence.

Ziegfeld, Florenz (1867-1932) American impresario, who created and managed the spectacular Ziegfeld Follies (1907-31), revues famous for their showgirls.

Zimmerman, Dominikus (1685-1766) German Rococo architect who was trained as a stucco-worker and who built the pilgrimage churches at die Wies and Steinhausen. He worked in Bavaria, often in collaboration with his brother, the painter Johann Baptist Zimmerman.

Zinoviev, Gregori (1883-1936) Russian revolutionary and founder, with LENIN and TROTSKY, of the USSR. On Lenin's death (1924), he connived with STALIN and KAMENEV to ensure Trotsky's exclusion from the leadership, but later, was himself tried and executed by Stalin. His name became familiar in Britain when a letter, purporting to be from him, as President of the Third International, urged British Communists to violent revolution. It was published in the press shortly before the General Election of October 1924, and probably contributed to the defeat of Ramsay MACDONALD's Labour government.

Zoffany, Johann (c. 1734-1810) German-born British artist, who painted elegant 'conversation pieces' and informal group portraits. He studied in Italy, and made his name shortly after arriving in England (1761) with the *Farmer's Return* (1762), in which the actor GARRICK, who became his patron, is depicted.

Zola, Emile (1840-1902) French novelist and journalist, author of the *Rougon Macquart* series, 70 inter-related novels documenting the life of a family under the Second Empire. *L'Assomoir* (1882), generally considered to be the model of the naturalist novel and his finest work, was followed, among other works, by *Nana* (1880), *Germinal* (1885), *La Terre* (1889) and *La Débâcle* (1893). Zola later turned to political journalism, defending DREYFUS in the celebrated article *J'Accuse*.

Zoroaster (c. 6th cent. BC) Median prophet, founder of Zoroastrianism, the religion of ancient Persia. He presented life as a struggle between the opposing forces of good and evil, equating evil with darkness and death, and goodness with light and life (personified by the angel Mithras).

Zuckmayer, Carl (born 1896) German dramatist, who wrote *The Captain of Köpenick* (1931). The play ridiculed German militarism and offended the Nazis, which caused Zuckmayer to take refuge in Switzerland (1933). His first success was *The Happy Vineyard* (1923). *The Devil's General* (1946), written after he had emigrated to America (1939), described life in Nazi Germany and was very successful. *The Cold Light* (1955), concerning a defecting nuclear physicist, is among his other plays.

Zurbarán, Francisco de (c. 1598-1664) Spanish painter, best known for the austere devotional pictures he painted for churches and monasteries. His art combines harsh tonal contrasts of CARAVAGGIO with the tactile qualities of Spanish wood sculpture. The *Martyrdom of St Serapion* (1628) shows a soberness of colour and the quiet, spiritual intensity of his work.

Zweig, Stefan (1881-1942) Austrian author known for his biographies of famous writers. In *Master Builders* (1920), on BALZAC, DICKENS and DOSTOEVSKY, and in *Adepts in Self-Portraiture* (1928), on Casanova, STENDHAL and TOLSTOY, he used the methods of psychology to arrive at an understanding of the motivation of his subjects and mainspring of their creativity.

Zwingli, Huldreich *or* **Ulrich (1484-1531)** Swiss religious thinker and leading figure in the Swiss Reformation, though he disagreed with LUTHER on various doctrinal points. Zwingli's chief work was *Concerning True and False Religion* (1525). Zwingli was killed during an attack on Zurich by forces from cantons unsympathetic to his movement.

WHO DID WHAT

A time chart of human achievement

The next 48 pages set in the context of their time the achievements of the people whose biographies appear in this book. They also introduce other people whose achievements were outside the scope of *Who Did What* but who nevertheless played important roles in shaping our world. People whose names appear in small capital letters are fully covered in the body of the book. Abbreviations used are: *c.*, *circa*; d., died; fl., flourished; and r., reigned.

The March of Civilization

Civilizations have come and gone since man first moved from his prehistoric role as a nomadic hunter-gatherer to form stable communities based on agriculture and trade. Science and scholarship together have enabled modern man to establish the bases on which the ancient societies flourished—as he is able to describe the make-up and extent of forests which existed before man himself.

The chart on this page traces the growth and succession of the principal civilizations from the first settlements of the 'Fertile Crescent' in Mesopotamia to the new technological culture that finds its mainspring in the New World of America.

Islam United by Mohammed, the Arabs obeyed his call to Holy War by creating an empire out of the devastation of the wars between Persia and Byzantium. For seven centuries the Arabs occupied most of Spain, and through them was transmitted the learning of the ancient eastern to the medieval western world

Left: Forbidden from representing human form in art, Islamic artists combined representations of flowers and leaves with their decorative Kufic script to create curving, geometric designs on tiles and in sculptures used to ornament their buildings

c. 2500 BC-AD 1974

China The oldest continuous civilization, China was first unified in 250 BC, but took 2000 years to expand her frontiers to their widest extent, during the Ch'ing, the last imperial dynasty

Below: Silks, spices and ceramics gave China a flourishing export trade with the West during the 16th century. Soon, European potters were attempting to reproduce Chinese porcelain and ceramic techniques

India Her past a story of dynastic rivalry and struggle par excellence, India was finally united, after 3000 years, by the Moguls in the 16th century, only to be divided into Hindu and Muslim states of India and Pakistan in 1947, with a further nation, Bangladesh established in 1972

Left: A statue of the Buddha, a symbol of the spirituality of the peoples of the Indian sub-continent

c. 3000 BC-AD 1974

1950 BC-300 BC

Babylon Ancient city state of the Euphrates plain became the hub of an empire under the Amorites, a Semitic race who unified the Mesopotamian kingdoms. Literature and learning flourished under Hammurabi (1728-1686 BC) and later, the neo-Babylonian Empire became the cultural centre of the ancient world

Below: The earliest representations of both the wheel and the chariot were found by archaeologists excavating Babylonian sites. By 1500 BC the horse-drawn cart and chariot were in common use.

c. 550 BC-AD 651

Persia Within a single generation the hitherto obscure Persian tribes arose as a bellicose nation. They overthrew Babylon and Egypt and created an empire which eclipsed all its predecessors in size and strength. Their military superiority won them hegemony over the entire Orient

Below: The ruins of Persepolis, capital of the Achaemenid Persian empire

1400 BC-600 BC

Assyria A North Mesopotamian kingdom on the Tigris, became a great warring state in the 14th century BC, conquering Babylon and creating a vast new empire.

Below: Assyrian standing armies, entirely equipped with iron, included cavalry, charioteer and siege units; all units carried archers

3250 BC-1100 BC

Egypt Thinite Period: Contact with Mesopotamia stimulated Egypt's growth during the third millennium BC. The first dynasty united Upper and Lower Egypt

The Old Kingdom: The classical period of the Egyptian civilization which saw the development of mathematics, astronomy and medicine. This was the great age of pyramid building

Middle Kingdom: An era of expanding trade and influence abroad, after a long period of feudalism

The New Kingdom: Internal division in Egypt was halted by the 18th dynasty which reunited Egypt as a military state and founded the Egyptian empire

Right: Like the Babylonians, whose mathematical lore they inherited, the Egyptians could neither multiply nor divide, but adept at practical mathematics they developed their knowledge to produce the pyramids. They first built step-shaped monuments before discovering how to reproduce a true pyramid shape in stone

3250 BC-1200 BC

Crete The peace-loving Minoan peoples of Crete developed Europe's first Bronze Age culture. Their vivacious art, and their stone-built dynastic palaces like the palace at Knossos, are well known, but their script, which was to influence the Greeks, remains undeciphered to this day

4000 BC-1950 BC

Mesopotamia The world's first city states were created by the Sumerians, mysterious settlers of the Tigris and Euphrates rivers. From their early irrigation culture arose organized temple communities governed by a mixture of theocracy and democracy. Here, the arts of building, writing mathematics and science first appeared and, 2300 years ago Lugalzaggesi built the first empire of the ancient world

Mesolithic (Middle Stone) Age man began to till the soil, and to keep store cattle. The March of Civilization had begun.

8000 BC-4000 BC

America Working through spheres of influence rather than colonization and control, since 1945 the United States has extended the 'Pax Americana' of economic and military aid to a war-scarred Europe and Southeast Asia

AD 1776-AD 1974

Above: The T model Ford exemplifies mass production, an art of technology in which the United States is supreme

AD 800-AD 1974

Europe Overrun by barbarians after the Romans, Europe emerged under Charlemagne as the Christian empire of the West. After the Middle Ages, the pressures of a crowded continent led to the discovery and colonization of hitherto unknown continents

Below: The invention of printing enabled Europe to disseminate the knowledge of past civilizations, as well as to spread new, often heretical ideas

c. 200 BC- AD 1600

AD 1300-AD 1974

Russia From the creation of the Russian state in 1500, to the decimation of her territories after 1918, Russia became the world's largest inter-continental empire. Constantly threatened by internal insurrection or by external harassment through her long, exposed frontiers, she developed one of the most strongly centralized bureaucracies of the modern world

AD 400-AD 1200

The Byzantine Empire Refounded in the 4th century as Constantine's new Rome, Byzantium became the hub of a Christian empire, the first European power, and preserver of the classical heritage. The Byzantine empire retained political and economic supremacy in Europe until the 12th century

The Maya culture once extended through modern Yucatan, Guatemala and Honduras, a loose federation of city states. The Aztecs inherited the mathematical and architectural knowledge of the Maya and evolved rudimentary pictographic writing. By 1500 they controlled colonies in Central America. The Incas founded a great empire in the 14th century, at its height when the Spanish conquered Peru

Above: typical South American stepped pyramid structure, probably an observatory or shrine

c. 900 BC-AD 400

Greece The Greeks developed entirely new forms of political organization, produced the first body of written European literature, and advanced the fund of knowledge about science, astronomy and mathematics. Greek culture was spread east and west during the empire of Alexander the Great. Below: A running girl. The natural simplicity of Greek art appeals to the modern mind

2000 BC-250 BC

Rome The Romans created the largest empire of the ancient world. Their skill in building and engineering was such that later generations of barbarians looked upon their vast monuments, still standing, as the work of giants

Right: A Roman coin

1100 BC-200 BC

Carthage Originally a Phoenician colony, Carthage grew to dominate Phoenicia. With wealth derived from the profits of extensive trade, she founded an empire which was controlled through a mercenary army. Under Hannibal, left, Carthage came near to defeating Rome

1000BC-AD400

Man in prehistory

The single species to which modern man belongs is identifiable from fossils and remains of some 40,000-50,000 years ago. Before that time it is not known whether the remains that have been found form part of the direct ancestry of man, or are extinct offshoots from the main stream. The human beings of the late Old Stone Age (from *c.* 30,000 BC) are set apart from other similar creatures by the development of tools to serve the various activities of hunting, fishing, carving bone and wood, and the evolution of individual, local cultures.

Development took different forms and rates, depending on geographic and climatic variations. Vegetable food was probably plentiful in the broad tundra-like country at the edge of the ice-fields of the last Ice Age (*c.* 30,000-8000 BC), and hunting prosperous. When the ice receded in Europe, forests slowly grew again and large-scale hunting of herds and animals became more difficult. Men settled on the shores of lakes, on river banks and in forests.

Mesopotamia

In warmer climates the process of civilization was more rapid, particularly in such fertile river valleys as the Danube, the Nile, the Euphrates and the Tigris. By 6000 BC the major steps of deliberate cultivation of grain and the domestication of animals had been taken. During the next 1500 years, the working of metals was discovered, and copper came into common use. The communities which were formed lived by farming and hunting.

Communities grew into towns, occupations became specialized, and community leaders emerged with religious and political functions. Migratory groups settled, land was cultivated annually, manured and irrigated. By 3000 BC the art of writing and scientific pursuits were well established. Bronze had been developed and the height of Bronze Age culture in Mesopotamia was reached between 3000 and 2000 BC

As populations grew, waves of migratory groups made for the fertile valleys. Sumerians, Akkadians, Babylonians, Hittites and Assyrians gained, lost and regained sway over the principal cities of Mesopotamia—Ur, Nippur, Babylon, Nineveh, Assur and others.

Egypt and the Mediterranean

The civilization of Egypt formed a separate, parallel centre of human development and it remained independent from Mesopotamian culture (except for brief periods) until 700 BC when ASHURBANIPAL (669-626BC), an Assyrian king, subjected Egypt. The Assyrian empire was, in turn, destroyed by the Medes, Persians and Chaldeans Under CYRUS (*c.* 600-529 BC) the Persian Empire stretched from the Mediterranean far into what is now India.

For about 600 years, from 2000 BC to 1400 BC, a cultured, artistic and scientific civilization flourished in Crete. After that time Crete, along with the Aegean islands and the mainland of Greece, was overrun by invaders from Macedonia, north of Greece. From the middle centuries of the millenium the Phoenicians became renowned as traders over the entire length of the Mediterranean and possibly beyond, to the Scilly Isles, Senegal and, in the east, the Black Sea.

China and India

The civilization of China had also reached an advanced state by 1000 BC. Although it is likely that it developed completely independently of the cultures of western Asia, its progress followed similar lines—villages growing to become city states, settlement around rivers, the invention of writing.

Indian civilization is at least as old as that of western Asia, and achieved a high level of mercantile and political organization and domestic comfort. About 1500 BC, the Aryan people began to conquer

Babylonia and the eastern Mediterranean kingdoms, about 1400 BC

northern India, and eventually spread across the entire continent, settling in small agricultural communities. During this early period of Indian history the Vedic texts, the hymns of the *Rig-Veda,* were first set down.

The pyramids overlook the timeless civilization of the Nile

Bronze ritual wine vessel from Funan, China. 14th-11th century BC

The first section of the Time Chart which begins on the opposite page covers the period in which the use of iron spread from the Middle East across Europe, eventually reaching the extremities of Britain and Ireland about 400 BC. Also included are three of the most important formative influences on western culture—the Greek civilization, the Roman Empire and the birth of JESUS CHRIST. In Asia, the early Vedic religions, the foundation of Buddhism and the empires of ALEXANDER and ASOKA are evidence of civilizations far in advance of that of western Europe and in China, a group of philosophical schools emerged, as wide-ranging, imaginative and subtle as that of the Greeks.

	1000 BC	900 BC		800 BC
Principal Events	**Teutons** (West Germans) spread up the Rhine, displacing the Celts. **Hebrew monarchy founded,** with SAUL as first king (c. 1025). **Reign of** DAVID (d. c. 973) over Israel. He united the 12 tribes, conquered Jerusalem, and brought to it the Ark of the Covenant. **Migration of the Aryan race** to northern India from central Asia. **The Western Chou era,** China. Beginning of cultural unity (c. 1000-771). **Jomon culture** in Japan. Neolithic non-agricultural people who used polished stone tools (c.2500-c.250).	**Reign of** SOLOMON (r. c. 973-933) over Israel. **Phoenician colonization** of western Mediterranean coastlands, including Spain.	**Division of Hebrew kingdom** when the 10 tribes of Israel seceded to the north, and the south became the Kingdom of Judah (935). **New Assyrian Empire** (935-612). **Aramaeans** took over Hittite cities. **Etruscans** first appeared in Italy, possibly from Asia Minor.	**Greek monarchies** replaced by aristocracies, giving power to the nobles. The ascetic, military régime of Sparta probably instituted at this time. **Carthage founded** (814).
Religion	**The Vedic religion** The Indian Aryans worshipped the gods of nature: Indra, God of the air and storm; Agni, the sacrificial fire; Soma, the intoxicating sacrificial juice. The Vedic religion possessed a two-fold divine hierarchy, a complex mythology, elements of cosmology and metaphysical speculation, and an elaborate ritual, including chanting and animal sacrifice, which later gave rise to the important role of the 'brahman', or priest thought to possess magical powers, 'brahma'.	**Primitive Chinese religion** included belief in a spirit world and in a hierarchy of heavenly and earthly deities. Divination using oracle bones was widespread. By 1000 BC the worship of ancestors who could influence the lives of their descendants was practised. During the Chou era, the concept of ti'en, 'heaven' or 'supreme being' evolved.	**Primitive Japanese religion** was a system of ritualistic observances based upon worship of the manifestations of nature. Physical and ritual purity were important, and divination by burning bones was practised. **Expansion of the Aryan race** eastward through Magadha. Beginning of the caste system in India.	
Philosophy	**Egyptian philosophy** was concerned with ethics, and included a concept of an eternal universe.			
Literature	**Vedic literature** The oldest Indian texts, the canon of orthodox Hinduism. The earliest, written in archaic Sanskrit, is the *Rig-Veda*, a collection of sacred hymns; the *Sama-Veda* contains the chants of the Soma sacrifice; the *Yajur-Veda*, sacrificial and exegetic prose and the *Atharva-Veda*, sacrificial hymns.			**Phoenician alphabet** devised in which a separate sign or letter stood for a consonantal or vowel sound.
Art	**Beginning of Iron Age** in Europe. **Geometric period** in Greece, its pottery characterized by lines, dots, key patterns, swastikas and crosses.			
Architecture	**Mesopotamian architecture** Cities were composed of flat-roofed, mud-brick houses with no outward windows, all light being obtained from inner courtyards. Palaces contained many rooms, while religious buildings were centred on the *ziggurat*, a tall, multi-storied rectangular tower, used for worship and astronomy. Arch and vault both used by the Mesopotamians.		**Assyrian architecture** Cities were well-fortified settlements, built around palace complexes, huge areas of courtyards, halls, corridors and royal chambers. The palaces were ornamented with soft limestone bas-reliefs, or frescoes on walls and ceilings of more important chambers. Vaulted rooms, possibly even with domes, indicate a knowledge of barrel vaulting.	
Music	**Egyptian harp** in existence —6 feet high with 10 to 12 strings.	**Vedic chant** Part of the ritual of the Rig Veda, characterized by subtle intonation and differences in pitch, chanted on three notes. Later 5- or 7-note scales were introduced.	**Chinese music,** made with chimes, mouth organs and bamboo pipes as well as stringed instruments, played an important part in agricultural festivals, imperial court ceremonies and religious ritual.	**Greek epic poems** sung by minstrels to the accompaniment of the lyre, in a recitative style. Traditional tunes were used, probably short phrases with variations. **The lyre** probably played chords and interludes rather than melodic accompaniment. It consisted of 3 to 12 strings stretched over a sound-box and cross-bar.
Technology	**The Iron Age** reached its height in Asia. Iron and steel formed into new tools and weapons: hinged tongs, anvils, wire-drawing dies, iron files. Cast iron was produced in China; cast steel in India. Iron ploughshares discovered in Palestine and Syria. The use of iron spread to the west from Greece via Italy to Austria (c. 750 BC).	**Gypsum and limestone** introduced as building materials in Mesopotamia. **Metal keys and locks** commonly used in Egypt; hinges also common. **Olive-oil Presses** in the Mediterranean region worked on the lever principle. **Fermented liquor** from rice and millet produced in China.	**Irrigation developed** in China from the early Chou period—had reached a large scale by the end of the dynasty.	**Bronze pipes** for water supply used by the Phoenicians. **Plough cultivation** and rotation of fields, during Iron Age in Mediterranean area, central and western Europe. Kilns for artificial drying of crops. **Lacquering process** discovered in China. **Open terracotta conduits** in early Greek city states.

	800 BC			700 BC		600 BC
Principal Events	First Olympiad held in Greece (776). **The Eastern Chou era,** China. Decline of central authority as powerful frontier states threatened the Chou (771-256).	Rome founded (753). **Greek colonization,** prompted by food shortage, political or commercial advantage, in N. Africa, Sicily, Nile Delta, S. Italy and S. Gaul. **Kingdom of Kush** founded at Napata by the Ethiopians, or Kushites. Influenced strongly by Egyptian culture, and became a strong military power (c. 750 BC). **Babylonia conquered** by Tiglath Pileser III (r. 745-727).	**First Messenian war** Sparta victorious over Messenia (736-716). **XXVth dynasty** in Egypt—Ethiopian kings (715-656).	**Etruscan predominance** threatened in central Italy by invasions by Celtic tribes into the Po Valley.	**Second Messenian war** when Sparta had to subdue rebellion of Messenian subjects (650-630). **Reign of** ASHURBANIPAL (r. 669-626) in Assyria.	**Neo-Babylonian Empire** (626-333). Chaldean dynasty became a world power under NEBUCHADNEZZAR (r. 605-562).
Religion	**Polytheistic Greek religion** non-ethical; beliefs intended only to explain some of the mysteries of the physical world, and obtain material advantages. Such gods as Zeus, Apollo, Aphrodite and others were believed to be immortal beings with human characters, capable of both good and evil, living on Mt Olympus.			**Progressive Jewish prophets** taught monotheism—that Yahweh was the only god, essentially a god of righteousness. Ritualistic sacrifices were abolished and an ethical sense introduced into the religion.	**Chaldean astral religions** in which gods were identified with planets over whose movements man had no control. The fatalistic belief led to a greater spiritual awareness.	**Jainism** was founded in India by Vardhamana MAHAVIRA (c. 599-527) and spread rapidly to become an independent philosophy. Jainists believe in the goal of liberation from transmigration of the soul, holding that while all matter possesses a soul, inanimate objects are the bodies of souls at the lowest stages of existence. Purification depends upon living a 'balanced life', and observing certain vows, including that of non-violence.
Philosophy					**Milesian school** First significant western philosophical school. Philosophers began to seek rational explanation for natural phenomena. They believed in a single primary constituent, such as water or air, of all material things. Thales (c. 640-546) ANAXIMANDER (6th cent.) Anaximenes (6th cent.)	
Literature	**The Upanishads** Indian metaphysical writings comprising the final stage of the Veda; the basic text of popular Hinduism. The Upanishads are also a basic text of Buddhism.	**Greek epic poetry** Bards, usually minstrels in aristocratic families, sang songs of the exploits of ancient heroes, and the world of the gods. Among the first to be written down were the *Iliad* and *Odyssey* of HOMER (8th cent.).		**Phoenician alphabet** introduced to Greeks, who adapted it and added vowels. **Hesiodic verse** was didactic, full of maxims and discussions of the world's origin. **Homeric hymns** narrated legends of the deities, and were preludes to the epic poems.	**Early classical Chinese literature.** Collections of ancient hymns and poems (*Shih-ching* 'Classic of Songs') and of ancient historical documents (*Shu-ching* 'Classic of History'), thought to have been used by Confucius. The *I Ching* 'Classic of Change' sets out ancient rules of divination.	**The Gilgamesh epic** (dated probably c. 2000 BC) was recorded on tablets and collected with other Babylonian scripts in the Royal Library at Nineveh, under the patronage of ASHURBANIPAL (r. 669-626).
Art	**Assyrian art** Wall paintings and bas-relief in palaces. Stone sculpture in strips glorified the kings and depicted hunting scenes. Sculpture in the round showed great skill in animal art, especially winged bulls.	**Hallstatt period** of the Iron Age (750-450) in central Europe. Produced metal swords, jewellery, knives decorated with scrolls and relief ornamentation with rectilinear, triangular and geometrical motifs. Pottery coloured, its designs symmetrical. Callicrates (5th cent.) ICTINUS (5th cent.) Mnesicles (fl. c. 437)	**Scythian culture** in Europe. Decorative animal themes in art. Dramatic action transformed into pattern.	**Saite art** in Egypt. An attempt to revive the elegant, formal art of the Old Kingdom (2800-2300). Simple, severe sculpture and bas-reliefs, with elongated outlines and angular hieroglyphics, produced in an attempt to restore former brilliance to Egyptian culture.	**Nurarghic art** in Sardinia. Bronze statuettes of deities, funerary ships, warriors and sacred animals, found in the Bronze Age stone fortresses.	**Etruscan art** Frescoes painted on terracotta in burial chambers. Detailed representation of daily life: banquets, dancing, birds, fishes and flowers, as well as depiction of fantastic monsters. Use of precious metals such as gold, silver and bronze. Filigree and elaborate ornament.
Architecture			**Greek temples** were built with timber frames, resting on wooden columns, all on a stone substructure. Roofs were tiled, firstly sloping, then flat. The first temples were no more than developments of the *megaron*, a hall and porch structure used in private houses. The hall was elongated, called a *cella*, and contained the altar.			
Music	**Assyrian music** Court musicians were attached to royal households, playing at banquets. Martial and secular music were important.					**Greek community music** Citizens sang in chorus at all social occasions from religious sacrifices to weddings, accompanied by a professional bard on the lyre or pipes.
Technology	**Pottery-lined wells** built by Greeks; in other parts of the world, wells and mines cased with wood, or, in the East, bamboo. **Glass-making** in Mesopotamia. Vessels cut and shaped from solid pieces of glass.	**Coinage** first used in Mesopotamia.		**Silver coinage** first minted by the Greeks. **Canal from River Nile** to Red Sea cut by Egyptians. **Stone canal and aqueduct** built in Mesopotamia by SENNACHERIB (8th-7th cent.).	**Greek triremes** Boats with three banks of oars.	

600 BC		500 BC		400 BC		
Tyrannies in Greece Individuals overthrew governments, and assumed rule in almost all Greek cities, because the aristocracy would not grant equality to all citizens. Tyrants were popular and successful, responsible for improvement of cultural life. Cleisthenes (c. 600) Periander (r. 625-585) PISISTRATUS (r. 554-527) Polycrates (r. c. 536-c. 522). SOLON (c. 638-c. 558) introduced many judicial and economic reforms in Athens.	CYRUS THE GREAT (c. 600-529). **Babylonian Captivity** Jerusalem fell to the Babylonians, who captured the Jews and carried them to Babylon, where their culture flourished (587-539). **Political fragmentation** in India during which Magadha and Kosala, powerful eastern monarchies, emerged as the political and intellectual centres. DARIUS I (c. 558-486) ruled Persia. Penetrated the northwest of India.	**Judah ruled by Persians** after CYRUS (c. 600-529) took Babylon and released the Jews (539-332). **Roman Republic established** with overthrow of the monarchy (509).	**Rome: conflict** between plebeians and patricians over granting of political rights (500-287). **Ionian wars** against Persia (499-478). Battle of Marathon won by Athenians (490). **Age of PERICLES** (c. 495-429) Period of extensive cultural patronage in Greece. Athenian democracy at its height. Ten generals, elected from each tribe, were chief legislative and executive officials. Ostracism, under which excessively powerful individuals were sent from Athens for 10 years, intended to guard against tyranny.	**Delian League** of Greek states, intended for defence against Persia, based at Delos under leadership of Athens (479-404). **Warring States period,** China. Struggle for hegemony, a time of rapid change (480-221).	**Peloponnesian war** between Athens and Sparta (431-404). Beginning of Spartan hegemony in Greece. **Nanda dynasty** India's first empire builders (c. 413-320 BC).	**Principal Events**
Hinduism The Vedic religion gradually evolved into Hinduism, from a synthesis of the religious beliefs of the Aryans and of the peoples they conquered. The most fundamental of its doctrines are belief in the transmigration of souls, based upon the idea of the essential equality of all living beings; belief in a number of divinities, all subsidiary aspects of one god; mysticism; and support of the caste system.	**Zoroastrianism** Dualistic state religion of Persia, based on concept of the universe as cosmic battleground of semi-personified spirits of good (Ahura-Mazda) and evil (Ahriman). **Confucianism** Chinese theosophy which taught that the 'perfect man', who follows the three universal virtues of wisdom, love and courage, is incomplete unless his knowledge is used to serve society. The ruler at the head of society can, by good example and influence, bring peace and prosperity to the state.	**Taoism** The *Tao-te ching*, The Canon of Way and Virtue', attributed to LAO TZU (c. 604-541), is the basic text of Tao-chia, a Chinese philosophy, which explains the idea of the natural 'way' of harmony with nature-tranquillity and enlightenment. The Tao opposed worldly desires, superficial knowledge, and conventional morality. Organized society was regarded as 'unnatural'. The Taoist religion maintained belief in numerous spirit-gods, and used various forms of divination, including alchemy, among its practices. Chuang-Tzu (c. 370-c. 290).	**Buddhism,** an offshoot of Hinduism, founded by Siddhartha, GAUTAMA BUDDHA (c. 563-c. 483). Buddhism teaches that the means of escape from the cycle of rebirth and human suffering is through renunciation of desire, following the 8-fold Path, the principles of moderate behaviour, and withdrawal from material and religious experience. Salvation is through the achievement of 'nirvana', release from transmigration and the pain of life. Buddhism rejected both the elaborate ritual and asceticism of Hinduism, and the caste system.	**Dissent from Brahmanism** In India many sects sprang up, including the Ajivikas, who believed in total predeterminism, and the Charvakas, who preached total materialism. **First Buddhist Council** 500 disciples met at Rajagriha, India, after the death of GAUTAMA BUDDHA (c. 483), to rehearse his doctrine (*dharma*) and his code of discipline (*vinaya*) for the monastic community (*sangha*) which he founded. **Mohism** Chinese philosophy. In a time of political and social disorder, Mo Ti emphasized the need for discipline and co-ordination in society. In opposition to Confucianism, he believed society to be more important than the individual.	**Cult of Dionysus** (god of wine) developed with increasing cultivation of vineyards. Intoxication was considered divine, and mysticism grew with the worship of Dionysus. **Atomism** Greek belief that matter is composed of an infinite number of indestructible, indivisible atoms of different shapes and sizes. Leucippus (c. 500-430) DEMOCRITUS (c. 460-c. 370)	**Religion**
Pythagoreanism Greek school of mathematics which arose out of the study of music; belief in the universality of numbers led to a religious cult. From the connection between music and arithmetic came the concept of proportion; numerical proportion was established as the basis of ordered forms. Pythagorean beliefs had a profound influence on subsequent mathematical theory, on Plato's 'Ideals' and Aristotle's 'Form'.		**Eleatic school** of philosophy founded in southern Italy. Considered the first metaphysical school. Believed reality was static, immutable and infinite, whereas change and movement were illusory. Xenophanes (c. 570-c. 480); ZENO (c. 490-420); PARMENIDES (fl. c. 450); Melissus (fl. c. 440)			**Sophism** Pragmatic school of thought concerned with teaching such practical subjects needed for public life as oratory, rhetoric and politics. PROTAGORAS (480-410) Gorgias (c. 485-c. 380) Prodicus of Ceos (5th cent.) Hippias of Elis (5th cent.)	**Philosophy**
Greek lyric poetry, accompanied by the lyre, was composed in elegiac metres, on themes of love or patriotism. SAPPHO (fl. c. 600) Alcaeus (fl. c. 600) Tyrtaeus (7th cent.)	**Greek satyr plays** Burlesque or satirical, presented with a tragic trilogy in drama competitions. Hero in conflict with chorus of grotesque satyrs.	**Greek tragedy** Development of dialogue between actors, independent of the chorus. Tragedy concerned with moral problems of man in the universe; later, psychological exploration of an individual. AESCHYLUS (525-456) SOPHOCLES (496-406) EURIPIDES (484-406)	**Greek choral lyric** Development of earlier lyric poetry, accompanied by music, originally religious. Odes celebrating athletic victories or Hellenic glories. SIMONIDES (556-468) PINDAR (c. 518-438) Bacchylides (c. 516-c. 450) **Classical Indian** literature. The sacred literature of the Brahmanical school, consisting of various texts attached to the Vedas.	**Greek historians** First prose descriptions of ancient world and commentaries on contemporary events. Hellanicus (c. 490-c. 405) HERODOTUS (c. 484-424) THUCYDIDES (c. 471-c. 400) **Buddhist scriptures** passed on orally by the followers of GAUTAMA BUDDHA (c. 563-c. 483). Later they were set out in various Asian languages.	**Old Greek Comedy** Witty, parochial drama with formal debate. Parodies of topical social and political events; individuals satirized, often in obscene language. Cratinus (c. 484-c. 420) Eupolis (c. 455-c. 410) ARISTOPHANES (c. 448-c. 380) **Earliest Indian drama** presented Hindu religious stories and legends, using mime, dance and chorus.	**Literature**
Greek sculptured pediments and friezes of temples depicted mythological scenes. Sculpture in the round was generally rigid and restricted.			**Corinthian ceramic art** used several colours in oriental designs and illustrations of daily life.	**Greek sculpture** represented a more rugged physical type as an ideal, in place of the more stylized forms modelled in the archaic period. PHIDIAS (5th cent.) **Argive school** perfected athletic sculpture. POLYKLEITOS (fl. c. 430) MYRON (fl. c. 450)	**Attic vase painting** achieved technical excellence with fine red clay and black glaze depicting mythological scenes. By the end of the century the colours were reversed to enable further experiments, giving red figures on black backgrounds. Euphronius (5th cent.) Douris (5th cent.)	**Art**
Greek Doric order As marble began to be used more generally in Greece, building features, particularly columns, were standardized. The first 'order' was Doric, whose columns had no base, fluted shafts and simple, undecorated capitals.	**Achaemenid architecture** Persian royal cities, such as Persepolis, characterized by their monumental columns, ornamented temples and tombs and stairways.	**Chou dynasty architecture** Early Chinese buildings built with wood, using a beam-frame system. Houses planned round courtyards. Cities symmetrically planned. A high lookout tower built in a park, near an artificial lake, was a classic form of Chou imperial architecture.		**Greek Ionic order** columns had moulded bases, tall, elegant shafts, with flutes separated by fillets and spiralled capitals. Callicrates (5th cent.) Mnesicles (c. 437) ICTINUS (5th cent.) Dinocrates (4th cent.) Pythius (fl. c. 353-334)	**Greek Corinthian order** Columns had high bases, slender fluted shafts and elaborate capitals decorated with acanthus leaves. POLYKLEITOS (fl. c. 430). ICTINUS (5th cent.)	**Architecture**
Chaldean musical theory was associated with astrology and mathematics, resulting in the concept of perfect harmony in the universe.	**Introduction of the octave** attributed to PYTHAGORAS (6th cent.).	**Jewish temple music** was antiphonal and responsorial chant, from which derived many of the psalms. The music of the synagogue had much influence on early Christian music.				**Music**
PYTHAGORAS (fl. c. 530) and his school developed geometrical theorems. **Greek warships** and merchant ships had well-developed keels.	**Papyrus** adopted widely as a writing material in Greece. **Glass** made in Greece by the core-wound technique.	**Pulley and winch** developed by the Greeks for special effects used in the theatre. **Wood-turning lathe,** first used by the Greeks, in common use by the 5th century.	**Veterinary science** flourished in Greece and India—treatises written on treatment of horses and elephants; hospitals for various species of animals. **Greek medical science** Writings on hygiene and preventive medicine, surgery and pharmacy. Clinical records kept. **Egyptian coinage** introduced. Consisted of gold rings or copper weights. **Division of hours and degrees** into 60 parts established by the Babylonians.	**First planned Greek town:** Hippodamus (5th cent.) replanned the Piraeus. **Permanent water supply** in Greek towns: cisterns hewn from rock, built of masonry and concrete; earthenware pipes made in curved sections which fitted together. Lead and bronze also used. **Cloaca maxima** The main drainage system of Rome. The Romans built wooden pipes with iron collars and, later, properly sealed earthenware pipes, embedded in concrete.	**Mechanical devices** known or invented by the Ancient Greeks included the lever, wedge, screw, pulley, winch and inclined plane. The Alexandrian school made an active study of mechanics. **Gearing systems** devised, by Pappus (4th cent.), a Greek. **Greek biremes** built with rib construction, first by the Corinthians: light and elegant, with mast and oars. **The Classic of Astronomy** and other astronomical works produced in China.	**Technology**

	400 BC		300 BC			200 BC
Principal Events	Tyrannies of DIONYSIUS I (430-367) and Dion (c. 408-353) in Sicily. Sicilian wars with Carthage (398-380). Etruscans brought under Roman rule (391).	Downfall of Sparta, defeated by Thebans at Battle of Leuctra (371). Rome: plebeians gain share in government (366). Capital of Kush moved to Meroe (c. 350 BC). The Meroitic civilization had an iron technology, and its political influence stretched south, west and east as far as the Red Sea. Samnite wars in Italy. Rome dominated central Italy (343-290). Celtic expansion in western and central Europe.	Macedonian conquest of Greece at Battle of Chaeronea (338). Ptolemaic dynasty in Egypt (323-30). ALEXANDER THE GREAT (356-323) conquered Asia Minor, Phoenicia, Egypt, Mesopotamia and Persia (333-330). Invaded the Punjab and reached Taxila. Maurya dynasty Chandragupta Maurya (d. c. 286) overthrew the Nandas to control all of India except the southern Tamil kingdoms (c. 321-c. 184).	Seleucid dynasty ruled over Babylonia and Syria (305-30). Rome dominated all Italy after Battle of Beneventum (275). Yayoi culture in Japan. Settled people who cultivated rice in irrigated fields; made wheel-thrown pottery and many different tools.	Punic wars between Rome and Carthage (264-146). La Tène Iron Age people invaded Britain. CATO (234-149). Empire of ASOKA (d.231) extended over India to Kalinga in the south, but, a devout Buddhist, Asoka renounced further conquest. Ch'in dynasty First political unification of China (221-202).	HANNIBAL (247-183) crossed Alps into N. Italy. Defeated Roman army (216). Macedonian wars with Rome Macedonia became a Roman province (215-148). Antiochus III of Syria (286-247) occupied Gandhara, in northwest India (206).
Religion	Orphic and Eleusinian cults Ascetic sects believing in the transmigration of souls. The immortality of the soul depended on behaviour in this life. The Theravada Buddhist sect was the oldest and most orthodox of the sects which sprang up about a century after the death of GAUTAMA BUDDHA (c. 483). It attempted to collect the teachings of the Buddha.	Yin-Yang school in China tried to explain the principles of cosmic creation and destruction in terms of the five elements: wood, metal, fire, water and earth and their interaction with a female force, yin, and a male force, yang.	Epicureanism sought to achieve peace and pleasure (defined as absence of pain) by renunciation of political and family life, and freedom from want and fear. Knowledge had no intrinsic value other than for practical purposes.	Mithraism Indo-European cult which developed in Persia. Mithras was an important deity of Zoroastrianism, a mediator and representative of Ahura-Mazda. A ritual and mystical cult, Mithraism had important influence on Christianity (e.g. 25th December was the birthday of Mithras). Old Testament Books of *Ecclesiastes, Esther* and *Daniel* compiled.	Shinto A hierarchy of deities was presided over by the sun goddess, Amaterasu, and her descendants, the imperial family. Past heroes became mythological figures; each clan venerated its own special deity).	
Philosophy	Cynicism Greek ascetic movement, rejected abstract philosophy, flouted social conventions and advocated a life of simplicity, morality and non-violence. Diogenes (412-323) Antisthenes (c. 444-c. 370) Academic school established in Athens by PLATO (427-347) for philosophical and scientific research.	Mencius (c. 372-c. 289), Chinese Confucian philosopher, who maintained that man is by nature good; all men are essentially equal; evils and failures result from lack of correct training or a poor environment; therefore the state should concern itself with popular welfare.	EPICURUS (c. 342-270) Zeno of Sidon (c. 150-c. 78) Hsun Tzu (c. 300-235 BC) Third in the triumvirate of Confucianists, Hsun Tzu began a major controversy in China by claiming that man's nature is essentially evil. Peripatetic school founded by ARISTOTLE (c. 384-322). Rejected much of the metaphysical nature of Plato's Academy, and taught scientific subjects on the basis of deduction from observed facts. THEOPHRASTUS (c. 372-287); Autolycus (c. 360-c. 300).	Alexandrian school Academy of learning founded (310) by Ptolemy Soter (c. 367-283) and renowned for its grammarians and mathematicians.	Legalists Chinese group which considered society more important than the individual. Believed that a fixed body of written law, firmly and objectively administered, would overcome the dangers inherent in the imperfect natures of rulers and subjects. Stoicism View of the world ruled by universal reason, which led Stoics to believe in brotherhood of man Pacifist and humanitarian movement. Rejected pleasures of physical life, in belief that spirit would control reason. Zeno (335-263); Cleanthes (c. 331-c. 232); Chrysippus (280-207); Posidonius (c. 135-51).	
Literature	Middle Greek Comedy Maintained the satire of Old Comedy, but more controlled, and concentrated on social themes. Oratory and Rhetoric Mastery of the spoken word necessary for social success, so it was developed in Greek literature and education. LYSIAS (c. 456-c. 380) ISOCRATES (436-338) The Jataka Tales Ancient Buddhist folk tales.	New Greek Comedy Comedy of manners, with stock characters. MENANDER (c. 342-290) Philemon (c. 361-c. 263) Sanskrit epic poems In the tradition of the heroic tales of professional minstrels, the *Mahabharata* is the story of a fratricidal war. It contains the *Bhavagad Gita*, in which Krishna claims adoration as an incarnation of Vishnu.	Greek mime Simple drama, improvisations of everyday scenes, often farcical. Stock characters. Later more literary, sometimes topical, sometimes obscene. Song of Songs Hebrew love drama, once attributed to SOLOMON (973-933).	Alexandrian poetry The foundation of the museum and library at Alexandria attracted poets, who made a conscious attempt at a new, subjective style. Aratus (c. 315-c. 245) THEOCRITUS (c. 310-250) The Dharmasastras Treatises on Indian religious law, used as guidelines for civil and religious duties and behaviour.	Roman tragedy Translations of the more violent and melodramatic Greek tragedies. Livius Andronicus (c. 284-c. 204); Quintus Ennius (239-c. 169); Lucius Accius (170-85); SENECA (1-65). Prakrit literature. As an Indian Buddhist teaching dialect, Prakrit became the language of Northern Mahayana Buddhism, and also of Jainism. As a popular form of Sanskrit, Prakrit was used for the dialogue in Sanskrit drama.	Early Pali poetry with its many lyric patterns and metres influenced the later Sanskrit writers. Chinese poetry developed from incantations of the tribal priests into a new form—the rhymeprose style. CH'U YUAN (c. 320-c. 280)
Art	La Tène period of the European Iron Age (400-100). Influenced by the Greek and other Mediterranean cultures, designs included scrolls, spiral patterns, symmetrical decoration, and animal illustration. Pottery imitated metal shapes, and was decorated with geometrical and plant patterns. Sculpture in the round and stone busts were introduced.			Jade assumed a decorative role in Chinese jewellery. Greek sculpture Mythological and idealistic subjects replaced by realism, human portraiture, and expression of humbler aspects of life. PRAXITELES (4th cent.) LYSIPPOS (4th cent.)	Pergamene school Greek sculpture, especially friezes, illustrating history and mythology in a dramatic, exaggerated style, e.g. the Great Altar of Zeus and Athena Nicephorus (197-159).	
Architecture	Trabeated Greek architecture, using beams of limestone and marble instead of arches—fine jointing achieved by grinding the blocks together.	Greek theatres Seats tiered on hillside, circular stage orchestra and proscenium.	Appian Way, the road from Rome to Campania, south Italy, begun in 312.	Greek civic architecture developed. Principal features were the agora (public meeting place), museums and libraries.	Indian stupas, derived from funeral mounds, were Buddhist or Jainist monuments enshrining the relics of saints. They consisted of a large brick dome on a square base and surmounted by a balconied building. The stupa was surrounded by stone walls with four carved gates.	Indian rock architecture Buddhist chapels were tunnelled into rock, with carving imitating earlier wooden chapels. The outer façades had large horseshoe arches; inside, the nave had two sets of columns. Viharas, rock-carved monasteries containing many cells and chapels, were centred on one large square chamber. Great Wall of China begun (221).
Music		Singing and dancing took place as part of Greek drama on the part of the stage called the orchestra.		Mesopotamian music was secular, mostly sensual, entertainment by singing girls in the palaces.	Ctesibius of Alexandria (fl. c. 246-221) invented the water organ. Earliest Japanese music was the Shinto religious chant.	
Technology	Roman agricultural equipment developed. Introduction of the balanced sickle, short-handled scythe and leaf-reaping and lopping knives. Greek bireme improved Oval openings for oars and a narrower and lighter hull gave greater manoeuvrability. Astronomical prediction in the Seleucid Empire. Decimal system in use in China. Piston-bellows used for continuous blast in furnaces in China.	Theory of the lever first explained mathematically in the Greek world. Geometric theory developed. Theaetetus and Eudoxus (4th cent.) developed the geometric theory of irrational numbers and the concept of area. Law of reflection known. Algebra studied by ARISTOTLE (384-322) in Greece. Traction plough in use in China. Canals, dikes and drainage systems constructed to serve Chinese towns. The kite known in China.	The throwing axe was the principal weapon used by the Frankish and Saxon races. The Red Sea Canal rebuilt by PTOLEMY (309-246). Cavalry adopted by the Macedonian army. Torsion engine First recorded use by ALEXANDER (356-323) at the siege of Tyre. Flame-carriers Earthenware pots containing inflammable substances projected from catapults.	Glass-making at Alexandria Development of varied and sophisticated techniques. Mosaic, engraved and enamelled glass produced. Lighthouse at Alexandria built as a navigational aid; one of the seven wonders of the ancient world. The 'gastraphetes' or 'stomach bow' was an elementary form of hand crossbow devised by the Greeks. Greek armour consisted of bronze breast-plates, leg-plates and shield.	The heavy plough introduced into northern Europe. ARCHIMEDES (c. 287-212) calculated mechanical advantage, researched statics, the lever and gravity and defined the law of flotation. The ballista, a two-armed stone-shooting siege engine, invented by the Greeks. Indian astronomical treatises contained measurements and prediction of the movements of Sun, Moon and planets against the background of the stars.	ARISTARCHUS (3rd cent.) stated that the Earth was a globe and calculated its annual revolution round the Sun and daily rotation on its axis. Silk scrolls and the pointed brush adopted as writing materials in China.

Principal Events

Early (Western) Han dynasty Strong, highly centralized dynasty which extended China's boundaries (202 BC-AD 8).
Sunga dynasty in India, founded by Pushyamitra commander-in-chief of the last of the Mauryas, who assassinated his master (c. 185-c. 72).
End of Indian empire A succession of invasions from the west followed the fall of the Mauryas (185 BC) but a new power in the Deccan, the Andhras (c. 100 BC-c. AD 225), prevented the invaders penetrating further south.

King Demetrius of Bactria (fl. c. 206-175) occupied India as far as Pataliputra; established Greek rule in the Punjab.
Jewish revolt against Seleucids (160).
Roman province of N. Africa established after defeat of Carthage (146).

First Servile war Revolt of slaves in Sicily (134-132).
Revolt of the Gracchi in Rome, demanding reform of land and poverty laws (133-121).
Second Servile war (104-43).

Social war Italian cities revolted against Rome (91).
Civil wars in Rome (88) between Marius (c. 155-86) and SULLA (138-78).
The Sakas, from central Asia, conquered the Greeks in Bactria, and controlled the Punjab and Muttra (c. 80 BC).

Belgic invasions of Britain (75).
Third Servile war (73-71) Slave rebellion under SPARTACUS (d. 71) in Sicily.
JULIUS CAESAR (100-44) conquered Gaul and invaded Britain (58-51).
Roman army defeated by Parthians at Carrhae (53).
Vercingetorix rebelled (52) against CAESAR (100-44).
CLEOPATRA (69-30) reigned in Egypt (51-30).
Julian Calendar introduced (46) after reforms by JULIUS CAESAR (100-44).

JESUS of Nazareth born.
Early Roman Empire (31BC-AD192).
Fleet of ANTONIUS (c. 82-30) surrendered to AUGUSTUS (63 BC-AD 14) at Battle of Actium. End of Ptolemaic dynasty in Egypt (30).
AUGUSTUS (Octavius Caesar) (63BC-AD14), Emperor from 27 BC.

Religion

Oracles and prophets, such as the oracle at Delphi, played an important role in political decisions in Greece.

Roman polytheism Romans adopted the Greek Olympian gods, giving them different names (e.g. Zeus became Jupiter; Artemis, Diana).
Tung Chung-Shu (179-104), an outstanding Chinese Confucianist, who combined elements of the Yin-Yang school and Confucian ethics. He taught that Heaven, Earth and man form a triad which the emperor, ruling by the decree of Heaven, must maintain in harmony. This theory was influential throughout Chinese imperial history.

Ritual sacrifice initiated in China by the Han emperor WU TI (157-87) began the practice of sacrificing to Heaven from the sacred mountain, T'ai Shan, and to the Sovereign Earth, to emphasize the unity between the human and spiritual world.

Mystery cults, such as Mithraism and the Egyptian cults of Serapis, Isis and Osiris, infiltrated Europe, and became the chief rivals of early Christianity.

Mahasanghika Buddhist sect was a liberal Indian sect which allowed more freedom in its interpretation of doctrine and practice, and enriched its canonical tradition with legends. This sect flourished in the Punjab and Gandhara.
Sarvastivada Buddhist sect established itself in northern India and eventually in China and Tibet, collecting material in Sanskrit.

Mahayana and Hinayana Buddhism The departures from original Buddhist doctrine among the liberal sects led to a schism in India. During the 1st century BC the Mahayana sect, the 'Greater Vehicle to salvation' arose, which accepts the concept of a bodhisatva, an Enlightened One who forgoes nirvana for the good of mankind. The orthodox sects were called the Hinayana.

Philosophy

The Confucian Classics, the works attributed to CONFUCIUS (c. 551-479) and his followers, together with the three early Classics, constitute the canon of Confucianism. The Ch'un Ch'iu (Spring and Autumn Annals) are thought to have been compiled by Confucius himself, and the Lun Yu is the collection of Confucian analects. The 13 Classics formed the basis of education for entry into the government service in China up to the 19th century.
Roman comedy Derived from Greek New Comedy, tailored to topical Roman themes.
PLAUTUS (c. 254-184)
TERENCE (c. 190-159)

Neo-Pythagoreanism Belief in a transcendental god, outside the comprehension of mortals.

Eclecticism adopted and combined various philosophical systems, especially Stoicism and Scepticism.
CICERO (106-43)
SENECA (1-65)

Literature

Developments in writing The Chinese script was simplified; silk was adopted as a writing material and the pointed brush was introduced.
Maharashtri Prakrit elevated to the status of a literary language in India under the Andhras in the Deccan.

Greek and Roman books written on papyrus rolls and waxed wooden tablets. Roman industry of copying books for private and public libraries.
Sanskrit grammar Arose from a desire to preserve and interpret the sacred texts.
Panini (4th cent.)
Patanjali (fl. c. 150 BC)

The Buddhist scriptures were preserved in India in the Pali language.
Early Tamil literature survives from three bardic assemblies ('shangams'), thought to have been held at Madurai. The Tolkappiyam, the earliest extant Tamil grammar, dates from this period.

Official Chinese histories set the pattern for subsequent official histories. Twenty-six were compiled up to AD 1911.
The codex, a collection of written pages stitched together, replaced the parchment roll and wax tablet in Greece and Rome. Vellum began to replace parchment.

Augustan age Golden age of Roman literature, patronized by AUGUSTUS (63 BC-AD 14), with the intention of inspiring poets with the patriotic ideals of the new age.
VIRGIL (70-19)
HORACE (65-8)
OVID (43 BC-AD 17)

Art

Hellenistic influence on Roman art and sculpture.
Indian relief carving in cave shrines.

Roman pottery Aretine bowls with relief moulding and lead glaze.

Augustan art Emperor AUGUSTUS (63 BC-AD 14) wanted to develop a Roman classical art worthy of its Hellenic model, to demonstrate the glory of his empire.

Architecture

Roman temples based on Greek, with no side colonnades and porticoes at either end. Circular temples also existed, based on Etruscan buildings, such as the Pantheon and the Temple of Vesta in Rome.
Han dynasty houses usually two-storied with walled courtyard, the ground floor used for livestock. Decorated timber-work, such as curved eaves.

Roman secular architecture developed; civil and military engineering, using arches, barrel vaults and semi-circular domes, was aided by invention of concrete. Tiles used for roofing and lining hypocausts, underfloor heating systems.
Kiln-baked bricks, 1½ in. thick, usually covered with marble or plaster veneer. Used by Romans.

Roman roads built of blocks of stone or gravel, on well-prepared beds. Sometimes passed through tunnels or cuttings.
Roman bridges Semi-circular arches, faced of stone blocks, or brick and concrete supported with piers.
Roman concrete Made of volcanic earth. When mixed with lime formed a water- and fire-proof cement. Blended with brick or stone, it made a hard concrete.

Roman fortifications introduced the principle of successive lines of walls and ditches with strategically-placed towers to protect both cities and camps.

Composite order Roman column combining upper part of Ionic column with Corinthian column, plus further elaboration.
Tuscan order Roman column similar to Doric but with a base.

Music

Chinese musical theory based on 12 notes (lü) from which a series of five-note scales were developed. These, not the lü, were used for composition. The foundation note (huang chung) of the 12-note scale assumed a mystical character, representing eternal universal principles. It was standardized by an imperial office established in each dynasty.

Technology

Hjortspring boat of North Europe: early example of clinker-built boat.
Cartography ERATOSTHENES (3rd cent.) estimated the size of the world and used a grid system on maps.
Planispheric astrolabe, for deducing time and latitude from the positions of celestial bodies, thought to have been invented by HIPPARCHUS (2nd cent.).
Breast-strap for horses adopted in China. Replaced neck strap, making it easier for horses to pull heavy loads.

The earliest water-mill Greek or Norse mill with vertical axle operated by a series of scoops.
Alchemy flourished in the Hellenistic culture of Alexandrian Egypt; originated from the work of the Greek metalworkers. Much basic laboratory equipment was invented: stills, furnaces, flasks, beakers.
Chinese alchemy developed under the influence of Taoism. Taoist scientific researches produced works on botany and the natural sciences.

Iron and steel formed into tools and weapons. The Romans used harrows, mallets, iron-shod spades, iron picks and forks, single-handled sheep shears, iron ploughshares, balanced sickles and long scythes, iron files and rasps and saws with raked teeth.
Roman war-galleys built with oars and sail, equipped with ram and hinged, spiked boarding gangway.
Olive oil presses mechanized during Roman times, when the screw principle was applied to them.

Scale armour, of bronze plates sewn on leather, used by the Roman legions.
The pilum, a balanced throwing spear, the principal Roman infantry weapon.
Armoured horses used by the Roman armies.
Horses shod with light iron (but regular shoeing of horses a medieval custom).
Wine introduced into China from Bactria.
Coal-mines in operation in China.
Draw-loom for figured weaves invented in China.

Vitruvian water-mill invented, with horizontal axle and vertical wheel.
Plough with iron share introduced into Europe.
Wagon with steerable wheels developed by the Celts just before the Roman conquest.
Parthians bred the Nesaean horse of Media for bearing heavy armour.
Glass-blowing invented in Syria. By the 1st century AD glass-blowing reached Italy.
Reeling machine for silk-working used in China.

Archimedean screw and scoop-wheel applied to mine drainage by the Romans.
Seed-drill plough with hopper in use in China.
Rotary winnowing-machine with crank handle used in China.
Mat-and-batten sails used in China.
Cable suspension bridges built in China.

Principal Events	**Judaea** became a Roman province (AD 6). **Pontius Pilate**, procurator of Judaea (26-36), ordered crucifixion of JESUS of Nazareth (c. AD 30). **Hsin dynasty** Han dynasty in China temporarily usurped by WANG MANG (33 BC-AD 23), a zealous, reforming emperor. **Later (Eastern) Han dynasty** Internal order in China re-established, but central power declined (25-220).	**Roman conquest of Britain** under Aulus Plautius (43). **Formation of Gothic kingdom** on Lower Vistula (50). **British revolt** (61) against Romans under BOADICEA (d. 62), Queen of the Iceni. **Fire destroyed most of Rome** (64) Emperor NERO (37-68) blamed the Christians. **Axumite civilization** (c. 50-c. 500). Axumite rulers overthrew Kush in the 4th century. Converted to Christianity in early 4th century by Frumentius (d. c. 380). Axumite empire traded with China.	**Revolt in Judaea** against Roman procurators. Jerusalem destroyed (70) by TITUS (c. 39-81). **Roman conquest of Britain** extended to Clyde and Firth of Forth (78-85). **Eruption of Mount Vesuvius** buried cities of Pompeii and Herculaneum (79).	**Roman Empire** at its greatest geographical extent, bounded by Britain in the northwest, Spain and northern Africa in the southwest, Egypt in the south and the River Tigris in the east (98-117). **Parthian war** between Rome and Parthia over Armenia, which was lost to the Romans (113-17).	**Goths migrated** from northern Europe to the Black Sea area. **Jews in Judaea revolted** against Roman colonial government in Jerusalem. Roman suppression depopulated Judaea, completing the denationalization of the Jews (132-35).	
Religion	**Christianity** Religion of those believing in JESUS CHRIST as God in human form, in his resurrection, and in the certainty of an after-life. The Christian god is omnipotent, and will grant redemption from sin to all believers. Christian teaching founded on humanitarian principles. Spread from Asia Minor through the Roman Empire.	**Buddhism** introduced into China by missionaries. **Christianity entered India** from the West. St Thomas is thought to have arrived at Malabar about AD 52 and to have established a number of Syrian churches along the coast. The Syrian church survives in the Malabar region.		**Gnosticism** Early Christian heresy aimed at combining Christian beliefs with mystical oriental religions.	**Montanism** Extreme form of Christianity. Belief in the imminent return to life of JESUS. Ascetic and élitist sect.	
Philosophy			**Roman stoicism** developed more political and ethical theories, particularly in relation to the State. CICERO (106-43) SENECA (1-65) Epictetus (60-140) Marcus AURELIUS (121-80)		**Confucianism** accepted as the official Chinese state philosophy.	
Literature	**The Chinese classics,** proscribed during the severe Legalist era in China, (c. 250 BC) were given official status once again during the 1st century BC. Under the later Han the classics were declared the canon of Confucianism.	**New Testament** Gospels written (48-130). **Roman epic** poetry praised heroic characters, or narrated political memoirs. Naevius (c. 270-c. 201) VIRGIL (70-19) Lucan (39-65) Statius (c. 40-c. 96) Valerius Flaccus (d. c. AD 90)	PLUTARCH (c. 46-c. 120) **Silver age** Latin literature showed disenchantment with the decline of Roman glory and some change in syntactical usage. PLINY THE ELDER (23-79) TACITUS (c. 55-c. 120) JUVENAL (c. 60-c. 140) PLINY THE YOUNGER (62-113)	**Yueh-fu poetry** Chinese folk lyrics and ballads began a new trend of simple poetry, expressing personal sentiments. Ts'ao Chih (192-232)	**The Kavya** Sanskrit epic poetry, written in a new rhetorical style using elaborate metres. Asvaghosa (1st cent.)	
Art	**Roman wall painting** showed landscapes, pastoral scenes and rustic decoration. Painting used to give illusions of size and to suggest perspective in houses.	**Bas-relief** representing glory of Roman Empire on columns and friezes, in a continuous style to show sequence of events, e.g. column of TRAJAN (c. 53-117). **Ming chi** Chinese terracotta statuettes of houses, people, farms and animals, made to accompany the dead in tombs.	**Graeco-Buddhist style** in Afghanistan and Turkestan, later in China and Japan, combined Hellenic motifs with Buddhist traditions. Sculptures of Buddha had Greek and Oriental features. **Brahmanic art** Very highly decorated Indian statues wearing jewellery, usually smiling.		**Roman art** became stagnant, aiming only at formal perfection.	
Architecture	**Roman amphitheatres** Elliptical arena surrounded by tiered seats; used for gladiatorial contests. **Roman aqueducts** used to supply water from distant sources. Water-channel of stone built on arches or sunk in cuttings and tunnels.	**Roman basilicas** built as communal meeting places for political and social functions.			**Japanese Old Tomb** period. Huge man-made mounds surrounded by moats.	
Music			**Buddhist chants** integrated into Chinese music.			
Technology	**Mercury produced** by distillation. Process first discovered in Roman Spain. **Roman wine-growing** developed. Vines were propped or trellised and varied conditions of fermentation allowed for different types of grape.	**Corn ground** by water mills in Italy. HERO OF ALEXANDRIA (1st cent.) designed a fire engine, a slot machine, a steam engine and compressed air catapult.	**First primitive magnet** A lodestone spoon rotating on a bronze plate. Chinese.	**Roman drainage technology** led to beginning of cultivation of marshy areas, including the Netherlands. **Spherical trigonometry** developed by MENELAUS (1st cent.), a Greek mathematician. **Soap** made from goat's tallow and causticized wood ashes treated with salt, referred to by PLINY (23-79). **Wooden cask** with metal hoop replaced earthenware amphora for storing wine. **Deep drilling** for water, brine and natural gas began in China.	**Public medical services** and hospitals in Rome. GALEN (c. 131-200) founded the science of experimental physiology and researched into anatomy. **Craft of locksmith** well-established in Roman world. **Theory of epicyclic motion** of the planets around the Earth developed by PTOLEMY (2nd cent.). **Paper** made in China.	**Quarrying instruments** included wedges, saws of copper fed with sand and emery and water-driven saws. Stone blocks shaped by pounding with stone balls. **Square-pallet chain pump** for raising water, used for irrigation in China. **Edge-runner mill,** for grinding stone for mortar, in use in China. **Rotary fan** for ventilation used in China. **Gimbals** invented in China.

Principal Events

The Three Kingdoms in China. Wei in the north-east; Wu in the south; Shu-Han in Szechuan (220-264). **Indonesian immigrants** arrived on east coast of Africa, and settled on Madagascar.	**Gothic invasions** in eastern Europe. Began to divide into Visigoths and Ostrogoths (220-70). **Sassanid dynasty** established empire in Persia (227-641).	**Germanic tribes** (Franks, Alemanni and Burgundians) crossed the Rhine to the west. **Western Tsin dynasty** Second reunification of China (265-316). **Roman Empire divided** (285) by DIOCLETIAN (245-313) into east and west, for administration purposes. CONSTANTINE (c. 280-337) reunited the Roman Empire under his sole rule. Moved the capital from Rome to Constantinople (330).	**Visigoths** converted to Christianity by Bishop Wulfilas (c. 311-81). Christianity spread among many Germanic tribes. **Eastern Tsin dynasty** in China menaced by barbarians (317-419). **The Sixteen Kingdoms** Non-Chinese kingdoms established conquests in north China (304-439).	**Abyssinians** invaded Yemen, occupying it for 40 years (340). **Picts, Scots and Saxons** began to invade Britain (360-67). **Old Mayan Empire** in central America (320-987). **Roman Empire united** under JULIAN (332-63), and officially reverted to paganism (362). **Tumulus period** Japan's iron age. A period of organization and centralization; characteristic earth and stone tombs discovered, particularly on the Yamato plain.	**Franks** settled in Belgium, with permission of Rome. **Visigoths defeated Romans** at Battle of Adrianople (378). **Roman Empire split** into east and west, after the death of Emperor Theodosius (c. 346-95). **Japanese invasions** of Korea occurred repeatedly during 4th and 5th centuries.

Religion

Manichaeism Dualistic belief based on conflict of light and darkness, God and matter, which advocated refraining from all sensual enjoyment. Founded by Mani (215-273) a religious teacher of the neo-Persian empire.	**Popular Hinduism** in India. Monotheistic cults evolved around a trinity of major gods: Brahma, the creator of the world; Vishnu, the observer, who from the highest heaven descends onto earth incarnate in Krishna or Rama, to preserve men from evil. Shiva personifies the cosmic forces of change; his worship has given rise to a number of fertility cults.	**Monasticism** began to develop in eastern Europe. **Greek Christian writers** Byzantine church fathers, theological commentators and historians. Eusebius Pamphili (263-339) BASIL (c. 330-c. 379) Gregory of Nyssa (c. 331-c. 396) JOHN CHRYSOSTOM (c. 345-407)	**Arianism** Most influential Christian heresy, which denied the divinity of JESUS CHRIST. **Council of Nicaea** met (325) to discuss the Arian controversy. Favoured ATHANASIUS (c. 293-373) against ARIUS (d. 336). **Jain schism** in India. The Digambara, 'Sky-clad', orthodox sect maintained that the original Jain canon was lost; the Svetambara, 'White-clad', interpreted Jainism more liberally.	**St Augustine** (354-430) **Kumarajiva** (344-413), an Indian Buddhist, organized a bureau at the Chinese capital which is said to have translated 94 Buddhist texts into Chinese.	**Christianity established** as official religion of Roman Empire (380) under Theodosius (c. 346-95). **Donatism** Strict purist heresy which doubted the validity of priests to give the sacraments. **Latin Christian writers** adapted Roman judicial ideas to Church organization as well as translating the New Testament and religious commentaries into Latin. TERTULLIAN (c. 160-c. 230) Ambrose (c. 340-97) AUGUSTINE (354-430) JEROME (c. 340-420) PRUDENTIUS (348-c. 410) Sidonius Apollinaris (c. 430-c. 487)

Philosophy

Rationalist Christian philosophers believed reason to be the basis of all knowledge, and affirmed man's free will. ORIGEN (c. 185-c. 254) Clement of Alexandria (c. 150-c. 220) ATHANASIUS (c. 293-373)	**Neo-Platonism** fused the Platonic 'Ideal' with mystical philosophies. PLOTINUS (c. 203-70) Porphyrius (c. 232-c. 304) Iamblichus (c. 250-c. 330)		**Neo-Taoists** in China regarded the sage as a thinker who worked towards social and political reforms. Wang-Pi (226-249) Kuo-Hsaing (d. 312) Hsiang-Hsin (fl. 250) **The Fatalistic Taoists,** such as Yang Chu, saw the universe as mechanical, life as transitory and meaningless, something to be lived as enjoyably as possible.	**The Transcendental Taoists** sought escape from the world in the pleasures of light conversation and unconventional ways of living.	

Literature

			Neo-Taoist literature developed, in which sentences were constructed so that the meanings and sounds of words were balanced in pairs, the *p'ien t'i* style. T'AO CH'IEN (365-427)		

Art

Sassanid art Persian craftsmanship in gold.		**Early Christian art** represented everything in the abstract form of an ideal universe. No concrete reality or perspective.	**Catacomb painting** Symbolic decoration of underground cemeteries in Rome illustrated early Christian ideas of life after death.		

Architecture

Chinese pagodas deriving from the Indian stupa. Multi-storied buildings, usually square, each storey of diminishing proportions, with a protruding roof. Found in India, China and, later, Japan.		**Roman basilicas** used as Christian churches.		**The Mayas** built huge terraced pyramids surmounted by richly carved temples, ascended by wide flights of steps.	

Music

				Psalms were among the first early Christian chants, sung antiphonally or responsorially by priest and congregation.	

Technology

Roman merchant ships built with high stern and through deck beams; broad and round. Carried shrouds, topsail, large and small foresails. **Wheel-barrow** invented in China.	**Catalan furnace** developed in Spain: used two pairs of bellows. **Glass** reached China,from the West—thought to have been regarded as a cheap substitute for jade.	**Eastern padded saddle** adopted by the Romans for riding, in place of primitive horse cloth. **Manufacturing of porcelain** in China achieved the highest standards over the next four centuries. **Fore and aft rig** on Chinese sailing ships.	**Collar replaced yoke** for horses in China. **Helicopter top**, spun by a cord; invented in China.	**Wagon-mill**, which ground corn while travelling, used in China.	**Fire-house** with central hearth common in northern Europe. **Chain mail** used by the Celts. **Edge-runner mill** given water-power drive in China. **Tea** first drunk in China.

Principal Events / Religion / Philosophy / Literature / Art / Architecture / Music / Technology

400-1350

Roman Empire

By AD 400, the Roman Empire, the principal cohesive force in the west in the first three centuries after JESUS CHRIST, was on the wane. The emperor had removed to Constantinople, a fact which eventually split the Empire and, in so doing, led to the rise of the bishopric of Rome as the prime religious power of Christianity and as a political force in its own right. Ascetic reactions to the wealth and worldliness of the Church led, through such men as JEROME (c. 340-420), Ambrose (c. 340-97) and AUGUSTINE (354-430), to the foundation of monasticism.

The failing strength of the Roman borders allowed first Huns and Goths, then Franks and Vandals, to invade the provinces and eventually to sack Rome, which was reduced from its imperial glory to the status of a decrepit provincial town. CHARLEMAGNE (742-814), a Frankish king, was crowned Emperor (800), but his empire, extending over the whole of Europe, except for Britain and Scandinavia, was basically Germanic in character and traditions. The coronation of Charlemagne also caused the definitive break between Rome and the Byzantine half of the empire, ruled from Constantinople, since the eastern Roman Emperor regarded Charlemagne as a usurper. After Charlemagne's death the cohesion of the empire was lost again, this time for ever. Muslims invaded Spain, Scandinavians raided the north, and the empire was divided among the various members of Charlemagne's family.

The Byzantine Empire remained intact, and extended over the whole of the eastern Mediterranean and on into Mesopotamia. Rich, aristocratic, religious, colourful and artistic, it reached its height in the 10th and 11th centuries.

Islam

The Muslim faith was founded in Mecca by MOHAMMED (570-632). To the east Islam spread to Syria and Persia; to the west, along the southern coast of the Mediterranean and, in 711, into Spain.

Great Islamic centres of learning developed. Astronomy, mathematics and alchemy were extensively studied and a House of Knowledge instituted in Baghdad in the 9th

Charlemagne being crowned Holy Roman Emperor by Pope Leo III

century. It became immensely important through its translation and preservation of the works of HIPPOCRATES (c. 460-c. 377 BC), EUCLID (c. 450-374 BC), ARISTOTLE (384-322 BC), GALEN (fl. 2nd cent. AD) and Ptolemy (fl. 2nd cent. AD). Without this store of knowledge and its transmission into modern European culture through Spain, much of the Greek scientific work would have been lost.

In the late 11th century the Christian states of Europe began to attempt to reconquer the lands under Muslim domination. Backed by various popes the movement was blessed with the status of a Holy War and over a period of 200 years a number of Crusades set out to conquer the eastern Mediterranean lands and capture Jerusalem.

The Crusades often caused as much disruption in Europe as they did in the Middle East. Polyglot bands, internecine argument and ineffectual leadership were common, to the detriment of the European countryside through which the Crusaders marched.

Interior of the mosque of Santa Sophia, Istanbul, parts of which date from the 6th century AD

Throughout this period too, the feudal aristocracy of Europe was becoming more powerful and less inclined to bow before monarchs. In 1215 King JOHN of England (c. 1167-1216) was forced to sign the Magna Carta, which subjected the English monarchy to one of the earliest forms of constitutional control in the world.

Asia

As the Crusaders trudged eastwards, so the Mongols were galloping out of Asia towards the west. Under BATU KHAN (d. 1255) they reached Hungary. Previously, with GENGHIS KHAN (c. 1162-1227) at their head, the Mongols had established hegemony throughout Asia and China, failing only to invade Japan.

Genghis Khan captures a Chinese town in 1204-5 (detail)

The threat encouraged a great sense of unity amongst Japanese clans and tribes, which had been divided into shifting, warring factions for centuries. A long period of imitation of Chinese culture, particularly its literature and painting, slowly gave way to indigenous forms, a revival of the Shinto religion and a strong period of Zen Buddhism.

South America

Across the Pacific Ocean, cut off from the rest of the world, developed the main South American civilizations, the Aztecs, the Mayas and the Incas. Although the principle of the wheel and the manufacture of iron were unknown to them, civilization developed to a high degree, particularly in the fields of astronomy, mathematics and building. Complex and elaborate cities were inhabited by a highly-developed hierarchic society. Peasants, soldiers, administrators and priests were subservient to an emperor who claimed divine birth. Eventually they were destroyed by the Spanish.

	400	423	446	469	492	515	538	
Principal Events	**Visigoths** invaded Italy, led by King ALARIC (c. 370-410), and sacked Rome. **Vandals** crossed the Rhine and invaded Roman Gaul (406) and Spain (409). **Roman legions** withdrawn from Britain (410). **The Gupta dynasty** united northern India under CHANDRAGUPTA I in 320. Samudragupta (c. 330-c. 375) extended the empire east and southwards. The reign of Chandragupta II (c. 375-c. 415) marks the zenith of the dynasty's power. **Japan and China** made first direct contact (413).	**Vandals** invaded Roman provinces of northern Africa (429). **Burgundian tribes** settled near Rhône, establishing Burgundian Kingdom (443). **The Southern and Northern dynasties** in China. An era of civil strife and external warfare (420-589).	**Saxons, Angles and Jutes** invaded Britain (449-547). **Vandals** annexed Mediterranean islands (455). ATTILA THE HUN (c. 406-453) invaded Gaul, and was repelled by Roman and Germanic tribes. Invaded northern Italy (452). First invasions into India repelled by Skandagupta (d. c. 480).	ODOACER (c. 434-93) made king of barbarians in Italy after deposing last Roman emperor in the west. Traditional end of Roman Empire (476).	**Defeat of Visigoths** (507) by CLOVIS (c. 466-511) who drove them to Spain. **Italy united** as kingdom of Ostrogoths under THEODORIC the Great (c. 454-526). **Huns** established power in India (510-c. 525). **Rise of new dynasties:** in the west of India, the Maitraka dynasty (c. 490-766); in the north, the Maukhari dynasty (c. 500-606).	**Irish** began to colonize western Scotland (525). **Abyssinians** conquered Yemen (525). **Byzantines** under BELISARIUS (c. 505-65) re-conquered North Africa from the Vandals (534). **The Clan period in Japan** The power of the imperial clan, traditionally based upon religious function through the claim to direct descent from heaven, was threatened by other clans who claimed descent from lesser deities and performed priestly duties. Among the most powerful were the Mimana, Otomo, Soga, Imibe and Nakatomi.	**Principal Events**
Religion	**Nestorianism** Heretical Christian doctrine that JESUS CHRIST had two separate natures, the human and the divine. Idea held by East Syrian Christians, who claimed to have been founded in the Apostolic Age. **Monophysitism** Reaction against Nestorianism, stating that JESUS CHRIST's nature is single, partly divine and partly human.	ST PATRICK (c. 389-c. 461) began his mission in Ireland (432). **Buddhism in China** was at first influenced by Taoist thought. Taoism, equally influenced by the Buddhists, eventually became subordinate to it in terms of its influence on Chinese civilization. Many Indian Buddhist schools were introduced into China during this period.	**Tantrism in India** began with the worship of female deities and was associated with fertility cults. Deriving its name from its literature—'tantras' or 'manuals', its followers engaged in practices considered unorthodox by religious teachers. **The Shakti cult** in India believed that the male god could only be activated by being united with the female.	**Vaishnavas and Shaivas** Practising Hindus became divided into two main sects, each claiming Vishnu or Shiva as the supreme deity. **Six schools of Hindu philosophy** emerged from philosophical debate between the Buddhists and Brahmans: *Nyaya*, analysis or logic; *Vaisheshika*, the idea of a dual universe of souls and matter; *Sankhya*, the 25 principles which gave rise to creation; *Yoga*, a system of control over the body to aid attainment of the knowledge of ultimate reality; *Mimamsa*, systemization of the rules of duty and sacrifice; and the Vedic metaphysical system, which eventually predominated.	CLOVIS (c. 466-511), king of the Franks, converted to Christianity (496). **Irish Church** After the arrival of Christian missionaries following ST PATRICK (c. 389-c. 461), the Church, mainly monastic, flourished. Monks were skilled and scholarly, many of them going on missions to Britain and Europe.	**Benedictine Monastery** founded at Montecassino (529). Benedictine Order, in addition to vows of poverty, chastity and obedience, introduced the idea of stability, whereby monks vowed to remain in the community for life. **St Benedict** (c. 480-c. 543).	**Religion**
Philosophy		**The Ch'an sect** (Zen in Japanese) taught that salvation, oneness with the Buddha-mind, lies through meditation. The Southern Ch'an school believed that salvation is achieved by a sudden and inward enlightenment. Bodhidharma (d. c. 479) Chu Tao-sheng (d. 434)					**Philosophy**
Literature	**Christian ritual drama** Gospel narrative illustrated with dramatic elements. Church responsible for almost all western literary culture at this time. **Japanese adoption of Chinese ideographs** For many centuries prestige was attached to the ability to write in Chinese.	**Classical Sanskrit** literature and the arts flourished under the Guptas. Lyrical and epic poetry, drama, philosophy and scientific and technical literature were produced. The kavya poetic form reached its peak. KALIDASA (fl. c. 5th cent.) Bhavabhuti (fl. c. 700)	**Later Pali** literature. The Mahavihara, the 'Great Monastery' in Ceylon, became the main centre for Theravada Buddhist studies during the 5th century. Commentaries were written on the ancient Pali canon, the Jataka Tales were collected and a history of Buddhism compiled. Buddhaghosa (5th cent.)				**Literature**
Art	**Mosaics** replaced wall-painting of the early Christians. Rich and colourful, combined figurative and decorative art. **Coptic art** Primitive Christian art developed in Egypt, Armenia and Ethiopia. **Gupta art** in India developed sense of composition. Sculptors aware of monumental role of decorative relief carving. More clearly oriental style.				**Barbarian art** of the Germanic tribes. Opulent polychrome jewellery, later with Christian symbols. No human representation, but abstract stylized animal motifs, interlaced geometrical designs.	**Byzantine art** Flat, coloured, stylized patterns, heavily and luxuriously decorated; rigid, ritualistic two-dimensional presentation.	**Art**
Architecture						**Byzantine architecture** Introduction of vaulted church in which the dome was the prevailing characteristic. Smaller domes constructed around large central dome. Development of columns (often brought from ancient ruins), carved with foliage. Cupolas set on arches, semi-circular arches on columns. Interiors heavily decorated with coloured mosaics on gold background. Effect of space and light. Outside, the construction of brick was also used for decoration.	**Architecture**
Music	**Plainsong** Unaccompanied church music, with a single line of melody, usually sung by two voices at intervals of fourths or fifths. Traditional plainsong melodies were for many centuries the basis for western church music.					**Japanese** adopted Chinese and Korean ceremonial music for use in their courts.	**Music**
Technology	**Two-piece, jointed flails** for threshing grain, in Europe. **Coal** used for iron smelting in China.	**Draw-loom** for figure weaves known in Europe.	**Artis Veterinariae** of Vegetius (4th cent.) discussed principles of hygiene and preventive medicine in animals.		**Metal stirrup** copied by Europeans from the Avars of the Asian steppes. **Astronomy** divided from mathematics by Aryabhata (b. 476), a Hindu astronomer, who calculated the length of the solar year and declared the Earth to be a sphere.	**Zero symbol** came into use in Europe as a decimal place-value notation. **Watertight compartments** achieved in ship-building in China.	**Technology**

	538	561	584	607	630	653 / 676
Principal Events	JUSTINIAN (483-565), Eastern Emperor, conquered Italy, reuniting the Roman Empire (535-54). **Persians** made war on Eastern (Byzantine) Empire (539-79). **Turks** defeated White Huns (Avars) (553).	**Lombards** invaded Italy (568). **Avars** conquered Slavs and Hungarian steppes (568). **Persians** overthrew Abyssinian rule in Yemen (575). **Conflict in southern India** continued for three centuries between the Pallava warrior dynasty, the first Chalukya dynasty in Maharashta, and the Pandyas in the extreme south (c. 555-c. 850). **The Sogas** gained power over their rivals by marrying into the Japanese imperial family, and held it by supporting the entry of Buddhism into Japan.	**Christianity accepted** by Visigoths and Lombards. **Sui dynasty** Third reunification of China, a short-lived but prosperous dynasty. (589-618). **Japanese empire** SHOTOKU Taishi (593-621) attempted to adopt the Chinese pattern of centralized government. The constitution he introduced emphasized the importance of Confucian principles and Buddhist philosophy. Missions were sent to the court of the Sui Emperor in China. **First official Japanese embassy** to China (607).	**Persians** conquered Egypt (618-19). **Normans** invaded Ireland (620). **Byzantines**, led by Heraclius (c. 575-641), defeated Persians at Battle of Nineveh (627). HARSHA (c. 590-647) established himself as ruler of northern India. **T'ang dynasty** Period of development and expansion in China. (618-907).	**Kingdom of Mercia** in Britain gained power over Northumbria (642). **Newly united Arabs**, inspired by Islam, began to extend their frontiers. Took Syria, Egypt, Mesopotamia, Persian Empire (636-49). **Downfall of the Soga** in Japan, in a coup d'état by a future emperor, Kotoku (r. 645-54), and Kamatari (d. 669), founder of the Fujiwara clan.	**Umayyad Caliphate** set up in Damascus (661). Arabs attacked Constantinople (674-80). **The Taika reforms** of the Japanese governmental and land distribution system initiated by Kamatari (d. 669) and Kotoku (r. 645-54), along Chinese lines.
Religion	**Buddhism in Japan** The official introduction of Buddhism, from Paekche in Korea, marked the beginning of Chinese influence upon Japan. Buddhism reached Japan as the more advanced culture of two ancient civilizations, with its own institutions, arts and architecture, and as a religion which received support from the court.	**Buddhist sects** Both Hinayana and Mahayana Buddhism flourished in China, but the latter eventually predominated. **The T'ien T'ai sect** believed in the gradual path to salvation in which enlightenment is achieved only after long meditation, concentration, study and discipline. Chi I (531-597) Hui Ssu (d. 577)	**Tamil devotional cults** took the place of Jainism and Buddhism in the south of India. These cults believed in a reciprocal relationship of love between God and man. Hymn chanting, music and dance were an important part of temple ritual. **Manichaeism** Manichaeian temples were built in the centres of Ch'angan and Loyang, and flourished until the 13th century.	**Tantric Buddhism** marked the decline of Buddhism in India. Buddhas and Bodhisattvas were given feminine partners and magical rituals to achieve enlightenment. **Judaism** Jews were in China during the T'ang, but few in number. **Mazdaism** Priests and temples recorded in China during the T'ang.	**Islam** Religion based on divine revelation interpreted by the prophet MOHAMMED (570-632). Its doctrines are based on the Koran, the sacred book believed to have been dictated to Mohammed by God (Allah). They comprise a belief in God, holy books written by the prophets, day of judgement and predestination of good and evil. Islam combines features of paganism, Judaism, Christianity, claiming to have purified them.	**Shi'ites and Sunnites** Schism in Islam resulted from disputes over succession to MOHAMMED (570-632). Sunnites (the majority of Muslims) believe in human appointment of succeeding caliphs. Shi'ites believe that only descendants of Ali, son-in-law of Mohammed, should inherit the caliphate. **Islam** in China: the presence of Muslims recorded during the T'ang.
Philosophy	**Chinese influence on Japan** Through the kingdoms of the Korean peninsula, Confucian ethical and social principles and theories, Taoist metaphysical concepts and elements of the yin-yang philosophy reached Japan.					**Encyclopaedic historians** The most learned men of their period, whose works remained important reference books for several centuries. Bishop Isidore of Seville (c. 560-636) BEDE (673-735)
Literature					**Celtic illumination** of religious texts such as the Book of Kells and the Lindisfarne Gospels.	
Art		**Byzantine mosaic glass** used on walls and ceilings of churches. Stone mosaics on floors.	**Celtic art** Illuminated manuscripts, metalwork, stonework and sculpture, especially high crosses, showing simple Christian symbols, abstract ornamentation and pictorial scenes from gospels.	**Monastic illumination** Decorative embellishment of gospels and such holy books as the Book of Kells, the Lindisfarne Gospels and the Book of Durrow.		
Architecture			**Early Japanese architecture** under Chinese influence. Original single-storied temples with horizontal roofs developed to the grand scale of the pagoda, usually with five storeys, under protruding roofs topped with a steep pinnacle. Much elaborate, delicate ornamentation.	**Chinese town planning** Rectangular walled cities built on a grid plan, e.g. Ch'angan, which was copied in the building of Japan's capitals.	**Islamic architecture** Distinguished by use of domes, horseshoe arches, pointed arches, pierced battlements and arcading. Mosques, minarets, fortifications and sultans' palaces all showed similar characteristics. Decorated with ornate brickwork or tracery in stone and twisted columns in arcaded courtyards.	
Music			**Gregorian chant** ST GREGORY (c. 540-604) revised chants already in use, compiled new melodies, rhythms and modal systems. Still used today in the Roman Catholic Church.	**Chinese ritual music** Confucian melodies, strictly measured music, with instruments and voices participating together. Tone was of more importance than melody, and there was little or no harmony.		
Technology	**The sailing carriage**, invented in China, achieved the first high land speeds.	**Production of raw silk** undertaken in Byzantium under JUSTINIAN (483-565). **Iron chain suspension bridges** built in China.	**Two-storey windmill** with a vertical axle built by the Persians.	**Chinese bridge-building** An-Chi high-level bridge (605) in use until 1954. **Segmental arch bridges** built in China.	**'Greek Fire'** Quicklime, oil and sulphur which exploded on contact with water, used by the Byzantines against the Arabs.	

	676	699	722	745	768	791	814
Principal Events		**The Taiho code** The first codification of Japanese laws (702). **Umayyad Arabs** invaded Armenia (693) and Visigothic Spain (711). **The Arab conquest** of Sind, northwestern India, was the prelude to the Muslim invasions (712).	**The Pala dynasty** (c. 725-1197), in Bengal, in the east, became a major power in India after the death of HARSHA (647). **The Nara period**, named after the first Japanese capital, was a creative period in art, architecture and literature and a time of economic prosperity, but dogged by succession disputes (710-784).	**Pepin** (c. 714-68), king of the Franks, founded Carolingian dynasty. CHARLES MARTEL (c. 689-741) prevented Arab invasion of France at Battle of Poitiers (732) and became ruler of the Franks. **Massacre of Umayyads** resulted in beginning of Abbasid Caliphate (750). Baghdad established as Abbasid capital (762). **An Lu-Shan rebellions** Revolt in the northeast of China (755).	CHARLEMAGNE (742-814) invaded Lombard Italy and made himself king (773-4). **The Gurjara dynasty** united much of northern India. Nagabhata I (r. c. 740-c. 750) defeated the Arabs, and delayed their invasion until the 11th century. **The Rashtrakuta dynasty** destroyed the Chalukya power in India and established their own rule (c. 757-973).	**Viking attacks** on Britain began with sack of Lindisfarne (793). CHARLEMAGNE (742-814) crowned Roman Emperor (800). Revival of Western Empire. Conquered Venetia, Dalmatia and Corsica (805). **The Heian period** in which the Fujiwara clan gained supremacy in Japan as regents, with the power to influence imperial succession (794-1185).
Religion	Nestorian Christianity entered China, and a monastery was built in the capital, Ch'angan. It persisted, through the preachings of missionaries, until the mid-9th century, but depended largely upon foreigners for inspiration and leadership. **Buddhist family altars** ordered to be placed in all households in Japan (685). Buddhism prospered with government support.	**Pilgrimages** to shrines of saints increased in Europe. **Islam in India** Arab traders settled permanently in the coastal regions of south India, where they were free to practise their religion. The Mappillas or Malabar Muslims are descended from these settlers. **Vedanta school** The domination of the Vedanta School after centuries of debate between the Brahmans and Buddhists resulted in a movement to remove obscure and inconsistent doctrines from Hinduism, and to eliminate unnecessary and meaningless ritual. SHANKARA (c. 788-820).	**Iconoclast heresy** Imperial ban on images of JESUS CHRIST or saints for worship, in protest against rising power of the ecclesiastical hierarchy, started the first major conflict between the Byzantine emperor and the papacy (726-843).	**Zoroastrians**, persecuted in Persia by Arab armies, fled from Persia to western India. Given asylum by the Chalukyas, they formed a trading community known as the 'Parsis'. **Construction of the Todaiji**, Japan, the cathedral dedicated to Buddha Lochana, consecrated in the presence of Emperor Shomu, who declared himself a humble slave of Buddha.	**Buddhism and Shinto** said in Japan to be two aspects of the same faith. A slow amalgamation of the two religions followed. **The Nara sects** Six sects of Japanese Buddhism. Ritsu (Vinaya), Jojitus (Hinaya), Kusha (Hinaya), Sanron (Mahayana), Hosso (Mahayana) and Kegon (Mahayana).	**Ryobu Shinto** Kobo Daishi (774-835) provided a theoretical framework for the Ryobu ('Two Aspects') Shinto, the result of the amalgamation of Japanese Shinto with Buddhism. **Bhagavata and Pashupata** cults of devotion to Shiva and Vishnu developed out of Tamil devotional cults in the south of India, and became deeply established.
Philosophy	Nestorians read and translated into Syriac PLATO (427-347), ARISTOTLE (c. 384-322), EUCLID (3rd-2nd cent.), ARCHIMEDES (c. 287-212), SOCRATES (c. 470-399), PTOLEMY (2nd cent. AD), GALEN (c. 131-200), HIPPOCRATES (c. 460-c. 377)					**Carolingian renaissance** Revival of learning in Aachen. Studies concentrated on the seven liberal arts of classical antiquity—arithmetic, geometry, astronomy, music, grammar, rhetoric and logic.
Literature	Translation of Hellenistic texts, among them alchemical works, into Syriac by the Nestorian Christians. **Early Japanese** literature consisted of officially commissioned histories, based upon legend and tradition.	**T'ang Chinese poetry** The, lu-shih, the 'regulated poem', was introduced, which exploited the tonal nature of the Chinese language. LI PO (701-62) TU FU (712-70) Po Shu-i (772-846) HAN YÜ (768-824)	**Chinese vernacular literature** developed from the tales of professional storytellers. Written in popular speech instead of wenyen, the Chinese literary language.	**The kaifuso**, an anthology of Chinese poetry by Japanese poets, marks the decision of the imperial court, the literary centre of the country, to compose in the Chinese language.	**The Waka poetical form** (Japanese) of alternate 5-syllable and 7-syllable lines without rhyme or stress, derived from early folk songs. It became standard in Japan for more than 1000 years. KAKINOMOTO (c. 655-c. 710)	**Carolingian Minuscule** developed—a small, graceful and legible script. **Shoku Nihongi** One of the earliest prose works written in Japanese, this work preserves the Semmyo, the imperial edicts of the 8th century.
Art		**Islamic art** Essentially decorative, due to supposed Koranic ban on representation of living things. However, animal and vegetable motifs were adapted, together with curving linear ornamentation and the use of Kufic script in geometrical decoration.	**Pallava and Chalukya** art in India. Spectacular monuments decorated with sculpture, showing the movement and rhythm of dancers.	**Merovingian art** Very brightly coloured early French illumination of manuscripts, and rich jewellery. **T'ang dynasty** Chinese sculpture was influenced by the movement in Indian sculpture. Either elegant dancers or grotesque figures.	**Iconoclasm** The ban on representation of JESUS CHRIST or saints led to the destruction of many icons throughout Byzantium.	**Carolingian art** tried to return to figurative art of the classical era in reaction to the Barbarians' abstraction. Human figure regained importance. Much manuscript illumination; carving of ivory and jewellery.
Architecture					**Panelling** introduced into domestic architecture as lining and insulation.	**Carolingian architecture** modelled on Roman, Byzantine and Muslim. Extra chapels added to cathedrals for increasing number of pilgrims.
Music		**Classical Arabian school** Elaborate musical traditions under the Umayyad caliphs. Songs were accompanied by lutes. Theory codified by Ibn-Misah (d. c. 715).				**Church organs** introduced to western Europe from Constantinople.
Technology	**Sea-dikes** built to protect the low-lying areas of the Netherlands. **Byzantine warships** fitted with 'Greek Fire': a tube of the combustible substance was fitted with bellows and squirted at the enemy.	**Beginnings of book binding** techniques in Europe. **Paper** gradually began to be used by the Arabs.	**Mining revived** in Europe towards the end of the 'Dark Ages'. Mainly gold and stibnite, the most common ore of antimony. **First record of printing** with wood or metal blocks in China.	**Regular shoeing of horses** with iron in Europe. **Casting of bronze** bells began in Italy. **Stern-post rudder** in use on Chinese junks. **Spread of water-mills** for irrigation. Introduced into Japan from China.	**The Gokstad ship** was the first example of a northern ship with true keel. Clinker-built. **The double-headed axe** was the principal war-weapon of the Vikings. **Rice introduced into Europe** by the Muslims. **Accurate scales** produced in the Middle East. Coiners could weigh to within half a milligram. **Block-printing:** earliest Japanese example.	**Jabir ibn-Hayyan** (fl. c. 721-76) evolved the sulphur-mercury theory of metallic construction. Published The Book of the Composition of Alchemy (810). **Chia Tan** A map of China and Barbarian countries which achieved a high degree of accuracy. **Paper currency** came into use in China.

	814	837	860	883	906	929	952
Principal Events	**Wessex defeated Mercia** for dominance in England at Battle of Ellandun (825) and moved into Kent, Sussex and Essex. **Vikings** established bases in eastern Europe, and began to trade with Byzantium and the Near East (825). **Arab invasion of Sicily** and southern Italy (827-38). **The Yadava dynasty** gained prestige and power in the south of India (c. 825-1312).	**Scotland united** when Kenneth MacAlpin (832-60) became king of the Picts (843). **Vikings** colonized Iceland and took Kiev from Khazars. Beginning of Varangian empire (Danes and Swedes) (850). **Last Japanese embassy** to the T'ang (738).	**Turks** defeated Magyars, ending Khazar control of Russian steppes (c. 860). **Saffarid dynasty** (867-903) established in Persia. ALFRED THE GREAT (849-99) defeated Danes at Edington (878).	**Viking siege of Paris** (885) Charles the Fat (839-88) paid them to leave. **Samanid dynasty** broke the power of the Saffarids in Persia (903). **End of Carolingian dynasty** with death of Charles the Fat (888). **Emperor Uda** (r. 887-97) attempted to rule Japan with the aid of Sugawara Michizane (845-903), a scholar.	**Magyar invasions** of Germany (906-55). **The Chola dynasty** formed a new empire in the south of India, and defeated the Pala king of Bengal. They maintained power until the 12th century, and effectively excluded the Muslims. **The Five Dynasties and the Ten Kingdoms** The collapse of the T'ang was followed by internal division and civil strife in China. Beginning of Mongol threat (907-960). Beginning of Mongol threat in the north. **Fatimid dynasty** founded in Tunisia (909-1171).		**Althing** (general court) introduced in Iceland (930). Oldest parliament still in existence. **Civil strife** in the Japanese provinces as a result of the rise of an independent provincial military class, established in the *shoen*, or country manors (935-941). **Liao dynasty** in China. (937-1125). Inner Mongolian and Manchurian peoples overthrew the enfeebled T'ang.
Religion	**The Chen-Yen** 'True Word', a Chinese Buddhist sect which held that one spirit manifests itself in many forms, and claimed they had a doctrine, the 'true word', which was revealed to members only after a long and gruelling novitiate. A branch of Indian Tantrism. The last indigenous Buddhist sect to be produced in China.				**Cluniac reform movement** endeavoured to revive the strict asceticism of the rule of St Benedict (c. 480-c. 543), with the foundation of the Monastery at Cluny. Later the movement tried to abolish corruption and worldliness from the Church (esp. simony).		**The Bhakti cult** of passionate devotion to Krishna became popular in southern India between the 10th and 13th centuries. Had its basis in the *Bhagavad Gita*.
Philosophy							
Literature	**The Kana**, a phonetic syllabary, invented: form of Japanese writing in which Chinese characters were used in an abbreviated form for their phonetic value only, greatly facilitating the writing of Japanese.	**The Tzu poetic form** developed from songs of popular entertainers and dancing girls. This form influenced Chinese poetry for approximately four centuries. Li Yu (937-978)	**Anglo-Saxon Chronicle** Old English history of England begun under King ALFRED (849-99). Early material adapted from BEDE (673-735). Fragments entered up to 1150. **Earliest Japanese prose** story that survives is *The Tale of the Bamboo Cutter*, a fairy tale; later novels are characterized by greater realism.	**Japanese poetry** developed great refinement and complexity. The *waka* style revived, and poem tales, consisting of *tanka*, short poems, connected by brief prose passages, became popular. ARIWARA NARIHIRA (825-80) KI NO TSURAYUKI (c. 880-946) Ono no Komachi (fl. c. 850) Saigyo (1118-90)			**Icelandic scalds** Elaborate verse, bound by strict rules. Was the principal art of the Viking courts, which recorded and recited history. Egill Skall Grimsson (c. 900-c. 980)
Art			**Mozarabic art** of Spanish Christians. Combination of primitive Visigothic and Islamic art.				**Viking art** Combination of naturalistic animal art and intricate abstract art seen on helmets and swords.
Architecture		**Abassid architecture** Use of brick, ribbed and barrel vaults, and stucco decoration.	**Khmer** architecture (9th-15th cents.). Cambodian stone buildings. Half-vaulted arches, very high towers decorated with motifs and faces.				
Music	**Golden age of Arabic music** Prolific period of Islamic composition, ranging from the Persian romantic style to increasing virtuoso instrumentalism and song, heavily embellished with grace notes and trills. Followers of the classical school migrated to Spain, where their music quickly influenced native traditions. Ishaq al-Mausili (767-850); Ibrahim ibn al-Mahdi (d. 839); Ziryab (9th cent.)		**Organum** introduced: a medieval form of part-writing in which plainsong was harmonized by the addition of up to three new parts.		**Odo of Cluny** (879-942) introduced the letters A-G to represent the notes in an octave.		**Rise of instrumental music** in Europe. Trumpets and kettle drums imported from the Arabs.
Technology	**Copper extracted** from sulphide ores in Moorish Spain. **Astronomical work** of PTOLEMY (2nd cent.) translated into Arabic, as the *Almagest*. **Muslim alchemists** discovered such important new classes of chemicals as caustic alkalis. Improved distillation processes. **Hindu mathematics** codified and recorded. **Baghdad observatory** built (833). **First printed books** in China.	**Viking longboats** used for warfare; similar ships in Europe for many purposes. **The Arabs** had a carrier-pigeon service throughout their empire and produced a geography book of the kingdoms and routes of Asia. Al-Khwarizmi (780-c. 850) compiled astronomical tables and a compendium of medicine. Yuhanna ibn-Masawayh (777-857) wrote *Disorders of the Eye*. A treatise on mechanics, the *Book of Artifices*, was written in 860.	**Coal and water power** slowly adapted to mining in Europe. **Classification** of material substances into animal, vegetable and mineral was made by RHAZES (850-923), a Muslim theologian. **Earliest surviving work** in print, a Chinese translation of the *Diamond Sutra* dated 11 May 868. **Use of gunpowder** in China.	**Manufacturing skills** in textiles, steel, leather-working and tooling and paper production developed throughout Europe. **Cotton and silk industries** established by the Moors in Spain. **The Arabs irrigated fields** by branched channel methods, drained rivers and introduced lifting wheels into Spain. **Man's first attempted flight** with feathers, recorded by ibn-Firnas (888).	**Potter's wheel**, which had fallen into disuse, reintroduced to northern Europe from the south through the Rhineland. **Wine-growing** reintroduced to Europe through Germany. **Hindu-Arabic numerals** used in the West.		**Arabic medicine** Treatises on such diseases as measles and smallpox. Medical examinations introduced in the schools of Baghdad and Persia. **Printing of Confucian canon** in China, with wooden blocks.

952	975	998	1021	1044	1067	1090	
Otto I (912-73) was first Saxon to be crowned Holy Roman Emperor (962). **Fatimid conquest** of Sicily and Egypt (965-72). Capital built at Cairo, which became centre of Shi'ite Empire. **Edgar** (944-75) crowned first king of all England at Bath (973). **Northern Sung dynasty** in China (960-1126). T'ai Tsu (927-76) annexed several of the Ten Kingdoms, but achieved only partial reunification.	ERIC THE RED colonized Greenland (982-85). KING CANUTE of England (994-1035). **Capetian dynasty** (987-1328) established by HUGH CAPET (c. 940-96) in France. **Venice** gained independence in treaties with Byzantine and Western empires (992). **New Mayan Empire** established in central America by Hunac Ceel, under the Cocom dynasty (987-1441). **Fujiwara Michinaga** (966-1027) ruled at the height of Japanese clan power during the greatest period of cultural activity.	**Viking attacks** on southern England (997-99). **Voyage of** LEIF ERICSSON to N. America (Vinland) (c. 1003). **Danish invasions** of England (1003-14). **Raids of Mahmud of Ghazni** (c. 971-1030) succeeded in annexing the Punjab and, by weakening the economy of the Hindu powers, paved the way for Muslim invasion. **Emperor Sanjo II** ruled independently in Japan, attempting to curb the powers of the feudal class (1068-73).	**Byzantine conquest** of Armenia (1045). **Duncan I** (d. 1040) of Scotland murdered by MACBETH (d. 1057). **Hsi Hsia dynasty** in the northwest of China (1038-1227).	**Norman conquest** of England (1066) under WILLIAM (1027-87). **Earlier Nine Years' War** marked the beginning of a period of widespread disorder in Japan (1052-62). **Seljuks**, a Turkish tribe, occupied Persia and Mesopotamia, took over Syria and Palestine and occupied Jerusalem (1055-71).	**Rome sacked** by Normans and Germans (1084). **Domesday Book** in England (1086). **Almoravids**, a Berber tribe, conquered Morocco (1086) and aided Abbasids against Christians in Spain. Revived Mohammedan rule. **Latter Three Years' War** in which the Minamoto clan consolidated its power in the north of Japan (1083-7). **Rule of Retired Emperors** in Japan (1086-c. 1160). Shirakawa (r. 1073-86) was the first emperor to rule after his abdication as a means of avoiding burdensome ritual.	**Principal Events**
				ST ANSELM (1033-1109) Archbishop of Canterbury RAMANUJA (c. 1055-1137), an Indian Vedantist philosopher, believed that only through the saving grace of Vishnu can a human soul realize its divine nature.		**Schism** between the churches of Rome and Constantinople (1054). After the papacy supported the Norman invasion of southern Italy, the controversy over doctrine between the Western and Eastern Orthodox churches came to a head. **Carthusian Order** founded (1084) near Grenoble by ST BRUNO of Cologne (c. 1030-1101). An extremely austere order.	**Religion**
		Nominalism denied the reality of 'universals', considering them abstractions invented to express the common qualities of a group of objects. Anything beyond the observable reality of objects had to be taken on faith, not reason. Berengarius (998-1088) Roscellinus (d. c. 1120)		**House of Learning** established in Cairo to encourage philosophical and scientific study. **Western translators** Arabic scholarship filtered through to European students through the work of learned Jewish translators in Spain. Later, schools were set up to translate into Latin the philosophical and scientific works of the Arabs. Avicebron (1021-c. 1058); MAIMONIDES (1135-1204); Gerard of Cremona (c. 1114-87).	**Humanism** Medieval Christian belief concerned with the expression of human values in relation to theology. Hugh of St Victor (c. 1096-1141) Peter Abelard (1079-1142)	**Philosophy**
Hindi literature sprang from legends and dynastic histories recorded by family bards; the earliest extant chronicle, the *Khumman Raso*, about the deeds of the Chitor rulers, dates from the 10th century. Chand Bardai (12th cent.).	**Tamil** literature, in the far south of India, developed lyric and epic poetry. The *Divakaram*, the oldest dictionary of classic Tamil, was produced during the early part of the period. Tiruvalluvar (fl. c. 900) Kampan (fl. c. 1100)	**Arabic** literature produced *1001 Nights* and love poetry which influenced later medieval European court literature. AL-FIRDAUSI (c. 930-c. 1020) OMAR KHAYYAM (c. 1050-c. 1120) **Decline of Sanskrit** occurred when political fragmentation led to the rise of literary movements in the spoken languages, except in the court literature of various rulers.	**Fujiwara Japanese** literature. The *Genji Monogatari* (c. 1010) by MURASAKI SHIKIBU (978-c. 1025), one of the earliest novels ever written, gives a detailed picture of Japanese court life. The *Majura no Soshi* (*The Pillow Book*) is a collection of notes and observations of a lady-in-waiting to the empress. Sei Shonagon (fl. c. 1000)	**Icelandic sagas** Narratives describing monarchs and legendary heroes of Icelandic and Norwegian tradition. SNORRI STURLUSON (1178-1241) **Official Japanese anthologies** Fifteen were compiled during the later Fujiwara period, of which the *Shinkokinshu* (1205) is most celebrated; its style has since dominated Japanese poetry.	**Goliardic poems** Satirical, bawdy and often blasphemous, written by wandering students, modelled on classical writers such as CATULLUS (c. 84-c. 54 BC). Marbod (1035-1123) Hildebert (1056-1133) Hugo Primas (1095-1160) Gautier de Chatillon (12th cent.)	**Literature**
Persian miniatures and book illustration showed vivid colours, patterns and scenes of courtly life.	**Landscape painting** developed in China. Mostly painted on scrolls, it depicted mountains and forests often shrouded in mists. Ink on silk or paper, with very subdued colours.		**Ottonian art** Otto II's marriage to a Byzantine princess introduced oriental elements into miniatures and manuscript painting in Germany. **Stained glass** introduced into Europe. Windows composed of pieces of glass stained by chemicals when glass was molten, details added later in opaque enamel. Pieces then joined by strips of lead which outlined shapes and separated colours.	**Anglo-Saxon art** Mostly illumination, influenced by Celtic and Viking decoration. **Bayeux Tapestry** A picture chronicle illustrating the story of the Norman conquest of England in 1066.	**Romanesque period** Murals, manuscripts, tapestries and icons showed a trend away from specifically ecclesiastical themes, introducing moral allegories into Old Testament and Gospel subjects. Architects, wanting to build on a grander scale than before, based their plans on the outlines of surviving Roman buildings. New churches were modelled on the Roman basilica, the massive masonry of imperial triumphal arches was copied, and in the north the thick proportions of feudal castles were repeated in religious buildings. Round arches were developed, barrel vaulting replaced flat wooden roofs, followed by groined vaults and the rib vault (c. 1100). Ornament, though simple, was influenced by Celtic, Viking and Byzantine art.	**Art**
Sung period pagodas built on hexagonal or octagonal plans as opposed to the usual square plan. Classic form evolved, using stone and brick, but imitating the decoration of former wooden buildings.		**Indian** Hindu temples were built to even greater proportions with more varied shapes, e.g. pyramid roofs covered by a cupola.	**Motte and bailey castles** Wooden keep, or *donjon*, built on stockaded mound, the motte, surrounded by a moat.	**Stone fortresses**, such as the Tower of London, built with more effective fortifications learned from Arab and Byzantine engineers during the Crusades.		**Architecture**
Chinese orchestras consisted of drums, flutes, reedpipes, pan-pipes, clappers, lutes with plectra.	**Buddhist music**, elegant and graceful, became court music in Japan.		**Church organs** built with pipes of copper or bronze.	**Stave** Four horizontal lines schematized the notation of pitch. Thought to have been introduced in Europe by Guido d'Arezzo (c. 995-c. 1050).	**Polyphony** European plainsong embellished, more voice parts added, often moving independently and at different speeds.	**Music**
Banknotes first used in the western world, a result of the debasement of coinage. **Chinese mathematicians** used the theorem of PYTHAGORAS (fl. c. 530), and a symbol for zero, unknown to the West. **Printing in China** Official banknotes printed for the State during the Sung period.	**Reclamation** of forest land, marshes and rivers in Europe. **Arab astronomy** Al-Khujandi calculated the obliquity of the ecliptic. Astronomical instruments made by Al-Saghani. **Buddhist scriptures** printed in China (972).	**Friesland** protected from the sea by dykes. Seaweed and grass grown on the mudflats provided extra grazing land. **Spherical trigonometry** developed by Muslim mathematicians. Accurate tables for the sin- and tan-function drawn up. **Floating magnet** and the theory of magnetic declination used in China.	**Steel** made in Europe by hearth-carburization; welding common and draw-plate process used for making iron wire. **Hand-crossbow** introduced to the eastern world by invaders. **Lenses**, plane, spherical and paraboloid mirrors discussed in the writings of Alhazen (c. 965-c. 1039) on optics. **Movable earthenware type** used for printing in China.	**Soldering techniques** developed. Wood, pottery and lead pipes were soldered with tin. The **HIPPIATRIKA**, an account of veterinary practice, compiled under Constantine Porphyrogenitus (905-59). **A supernova** observed by the Chinese, in the constellation of Taurus. Later identified as the position of the present Crab nebula.	**Glass industry** established in the West by the 11th century. **Schools of translation** in Europe rendered Arabic texts into Latin. Resulted in a new interest in the sciences, including alchemy. **Chinese mathematics** developed. Properties of the circle defined.	**Technology**

	1090	1113	1137	1150	1173	1196	1219
Principal Events	**Norman conquest of Sicily** completed (1091). EL CID (c. 1040-99) took Valencia from the Moors (1094). **First Crusade** After a disastrous start, Crusaders took Jerusalem; Godfrey of Bouillon elected king (1096-99).	**Saragossa** captured from the Muslims (1118) by Alfonso I of Aragon (d.1134). **Concordat of Worms** Compromise reconciled the Holy Roman Empire and the Papacy over the investiture question (1122). ROGER II of Sicily (1095-1154) took the Zirid emirate of Tunisia (1129), extending the Kingdom of Sicily in North Africa. **Chin dynasty** (1115-1234) in north China. Founded by a Manchurian people, the Juchen. **Southern Sung dynasty** in China (1127-1279) established an unstable peace policy towards the Juchen.	**Civil War** in England (1139-53). **Second Crusade** Emperor CONRAD III (1093-1152) and King Louis VII of France led crusades with little success. (1147-49). FREDERICK BARBAROSSA of Hohenstaufen (c. 1123-90), conquered Roman republic and assumed title of Holy Roman Emperor.	**English invasion** of Ireland (1169). THOMAS À BECKET murdered in Canterbury (1170). **Eric of Sweden** (d. 1160) conquered Finland (1157). **Normans expelled** from North Africa (1160). **Byzantium** allied with Venice against FREDERICK BARBAROSSA (c. 1123-90). **Toltec civilization** in Mexico destroyed by barbarous Aztecs from the north (1168). **Civil War in Japan** erupted over a succession dispute (1156-1180) among the prominent Fujiwara, Minamoto and Taira clans.	**Lombard League** defeated FREDERICK BARBAROSSA (c. 1123-90) at Legnano. Peace of Constance between Holy Roman Empire, Papacy and Lombard towns (1183). **Third Crusade** Led by Barbarossa, RICHARD COEUR DE LION (1157-99) and Philip III of France. Crusaders took Acre and Cyprus, and gained access to Jerusalem (1189-92). **Mohammed of Ghor** (d. 1206) conquered the north of India. **The Kamakura period** (1185-1333) Feudal military rule in Japan by Minamoto YORITOMO (1147-99).	**Magna Carta** signed at Runnymede by King John of England. Guaranteed feudal rights of barons against abuse by the king. Granted concessions to ecclesiastical, agricultural and commercial classes (1215). **The Slave Kings of Delhi** established the Delhi Sultanate (1206-1526). **The first Shogunate** YORITOMO (1147-99) became the first shogun, or political overlord of Japan. **The Mongol invasion** of China (1205). Temuchin (1162-1227), son of a Mongol chief, was acclaimed GENGHIS KHAN.	
Religion	**Cistercian Order** founded at Citeaux (1098) by St Robert (c. 1029-1111), in an attempt to adhere more strictly to the Benedictine Rule. Manual work done by lay brothers. Emphasis on simplicity.	**Papal schism** (1130). Two rival popes, Anacletus II (d. 1138) and Innocent II (d. 1143), elected and held office concurrently until 1138. Innocent had the support of ST BERNARD of Clairvaux (1091-1153). **Neo-Confucianism** The influence of the Buddhist and Taoist philosophies forced the Confucianists to seek metaphysical foundations for their ethics. Chu Hsi (1130-1200) believed that the universe was a dualism, composed of 'law' and material force, which always work together within the 'mind of the universe'. In man, this dualism is seen as moral mind, or nature, and human mind, or desires. Man's goal is to transform human into moral mind.	**Albigensians (Cathari)** Powerful and ascetic movement based in southern France. Believed that material things were evil and that animal instincts should be suppressed. **Waldensians** Followers of Peter WALDO, pledged to poverty and apostolic virtues.	**Carmelite Order** (White Friars) founded in 1156 by St Barthold on Mount Carmel in Palestine. Intended to follow the way of life of ELIJAH (9th cent.) the prophet. Lived as hermits, devoted to prayer, but in 13th century became mendicants.	**Mendicant Friars** practised monastic virtues of chastity, poverty and obedience, but mixed with urban and rural communities. Active in the rise of intellectualism in Europe. **Order of Teutonic Knights** founded (1190).	**Franciscan Order** (Grey Friars) founded in Assisi in 1210 by ST FRANCIS (1182-1226). Originally called Friars Minor, they were pledged to absolute poverty, itinerant preaching and manual labour. **Dominican Order** (Black Friars) founded in Toulouse in 1215 by ST DOMINIC (1170-1221). Primary function to combat heresy, by educating heretics.	
Philosophy	**Realism** Extreme realists held that every individual object derived its characteristics from the 'universal', or category, of which it formed a part. Moderate realists held that the universal was a real quality, the essential nature of an object, apprehended by reason, not by the senses. ANSELM (1033-1109) William of Champeaux (c. 1070-1121)		**Scholasticism** System of thought, based upon logic and authority. Sense experience provided knowledge of material objects, but knowledge of the essential nature of the universe discoverable by reason alone. Conclusions strengthened by recourse to the Scriptures, Church Fathers, PLATO (427-347) and ARISTOTLE (c. 384-322). Purpose was to discover what made up the world, not why it worked. AL GHAZALI (1058-1111); Peter Abelard (1079-1142); Peter LOMBARD (c. 1100-60); Roscellinus (d. c. 1120).		**The new universities** drew students from all over Europe to specialize in particular disciplines, following the failure of the cathedral and monastic schools to provide a thorough education for the layman. Salerno (medicine) (10th cent.) Bologna (law) c. 1120 Paris (theology) c. 1120 Oxford (theology) c. 1160	**Zen Buddhism** became popular in Japan, especially among the military aristocracy, after an initial impetus from Sung China. The Japanese Zen sect held that any incident might lead to enlightenment.	
Literature	**Vernacular literature** Most of the first European literature written in the vernacular took the form of epic-chronicle poems such as the French *chansons de geste*, the German *Song of the Nibelungs*, and the Spanish *Song of El Cid*. **Sanskrit lyric poets** developed intensely erotic, religious verse during the period of the Bhakti cult and Tantric ritual. Jayadeva (fl. c. 1200)	**Courtly literature** Influenced by Celtic, Arabic, Spanish and Islamic lyrical poetry and codes of chivalrous conduct. The concept of courtly love first appeared in the feudal courts of southern France. Troubadours sang of the humble lover, wholly absorbed in admiration for his distant, haughty lady.	**Resurrection plays** and passion plays, in which liturgical passages were dramatized in church, were performed usually at Easter, Christmas and Epiphany. **Japanese historical romance** *Heike Monogatari (Tales of the Heike)* is the most celebrated of a series of military stories written during the Taira period. Such historical romances exerted a wide influence on Japanese literature, including the No drama.	**Provençal** literature reached its peak: the courtly tradition became an elegant, stylized literary pastime.	**Verse romances** Long narrative poems of adventure and romance, related primarily by French poets. Included the Arthurian cycle, the story of Tristan and Iseult and tales of ALEXANDER THE GREAT (356-323 BC). Marie de France (12th cent.) CHRÉTIEN DE TROYES (12th cent.) Geoffrey of Monmouth (c. 1100-54)	**Minnesingers** German poets, in a development similar to the French troubadours, added epic romances and songs and tales of the Crusades to the courtly love themes. HARTMANN von Aue (d. c. 1210) Walter von der VOGELWEIDE (c. 1170-c. 1230) **Marathi** literature developed after religious reforms of RAMANUJA (d. c. 1150).	
Art				**Manuscript illumination** influenced by the use of stained glass.		**Japan** Kamakura art began to demonstrate psychological insight, study of personality of man. Scrolls depicting battles.	
Architecture	**Jaina architecture** (1000-1300). Temples usually in picturesque surroundings. Small square shrines under curved, storied, pyramidal tower. In front, a columned cruciform porch, its columns supporting a pointed dome. Elaborately sculpted interiors, grotesque and symbolic designs.	**Pointed arches** first used in western architecture. **Chalukyan** (central Indian) Hindu architecture. Usually star-shaped plan, low elevation. Richly ornamented throughout with pierced windows.	**Early Gothic** Main features: the pointed arch, flying buttresses and the rib vault. Architecture considered a work of art for the first time in Europe. **Limestone** used for building by the Normans.	**Building of cathedrals** in Europe improved by the introduction of cranes and pulleys powered by treadwheels, and mortar produced by burning lime. **Aztec architecture** Temples consisted of flat-topped pyramids with steps ascending on all sides.	**Early English Gothic** (1190-1300) Church architecture: choirs usually square-ended and richer in ornament than rest. Central towers and, generally, single aisles. **Hammer-beam truss roofs,** usually made of oak, an English architectural innovation.	**Shinden** Japanese architecture. Originally imperial residences, developed in private mansions. Series of rectangular buildings symmetrically planned and joined by corridors overlooking, on the south, a garden containing a pond. Landscape gardening became an important art in Japan.	
Music			**European secular music** Folk songs were handed down through generations, often performed together with dances; strong emphasis on rhythm.	**School of Paris** Notre Dame composers developed, organum, or early polyphony, with complex 3- or 4-part melodic compositions. Leonin (fl. c. 1160-80) Perotin (12th cent.)	**Conductus** The addition of free-moving parts to an existing fixed melody. European innovation.		
Technology	**Alcohol** produced by distillation process by alchemists in Salerno. **Trebuchet** invented. A single-arm, missile-firing machine, powered by a heavy counterpoise. **Chain armour** consisted of iron helmets, usually with nose guard, mail knee-length shirts, leggings, gloves and shield. **Early ripening rice,** introduced into South China, led to a large increase in population.	**Elements of Geometry** by EUCLID (3rd-2nd cent. BC) translated from Arabic by Adelard of Bath (12th cent.). **Deep drilling** for water, natural gas and brine in Europe. **Breast strap** for horses introduced into Europe. **Mariner's compass** used for navigation by Chinese. **Gunpowder** used to fire rockets and fire-lances in China.	**Paper-making** became an industry among the Moors in Spain from where it spread to Christians in Spain, Italy, Germany and the rest of Europe. **Lift-locks** on main European rivers. **Sung ceramists** perfected various new techniques; incised and moulded decoration; high-fired glazes; the ability to control colour; colour-transmutation of pigment.	**Liqueurs** produced from herbs of monastery gardens. **The Hansa cog** A merchant ship built for the northern seas, straight-ended with high freeboard and a deep draught. **Three-cornered 'lateen' sail** introduced to Europe.	**Coal** used for smelting metals in Europe. Water-power applied to bellows and hammers in iron foundries. **Brick-making** techniques, preserved in Byzantium, spread through Italy to northern Europe. **Tile-making** spread through Europe from the Arabs via Moorish Spain. **Rotary disc** to cut jade used in China.	**European windmill** invented, more complex than the earlier Chinese windmill. **Carding and combing** of wool, the latter process using wire-toothed boards, adopted in France and England. **The cross-bow,** known in antiquity, re-introduced into European warfare. **Explosive bombs** used by Chin defenders of Pien-liang in China.	

1219 1242 1265 1288 1311 1334 1350 355

Principal Events

Inca civilization in the Cuzco Valley, Peru (1200-1533)
Period of Hojo rule in Japan. After the death of YORITOMO (1199), power passed into the female branch of the clan, the Hojo (1219-1333).
Tatar (Mongol) tribes under Batu Khan invaded Russia, destroying Moscow and massacring inhabitants of other cities. Founded settlement known as Golden Horde on the Volga. Conquered Poland, Hungary and central Europe. Tatar Mongol Empire permitted safe travel through Asia, initiating European-Chinese contact (1238-42).

ALEXANDER NEVSKI (1220-63), Duke of Novgorod, victorious over Swedes (1240) and Teutonic Knights (1242).
Empire of Mali founded when Sundiata conquered former Ghana Empire (1240).
The Pandya dynasty became powerful in southern India (1251-1310).
Mongols continued to advance westward from Persia. Exterminated Assassins (1256), and captured and sacked Baghdad, ending the Abbasid Caliphate (1258).

Solomonid dynasty (originating from SOLOMON (*c.* 973-*c.* 933) and Sheba) founded in Abyssinia (1270).
First English parliament held by EDWARD I (1239-1307), attended by lords, elected knights and burgesses (1275).
Guelf and Ghibelline wars Rival political factions in Italy derived from feuding German families (Welf and Hohenstaufen). Guelfs supported papacy, Ghibellines the Emperor.
Yuan (Mongol) dynasty A great age under the KUBLAI KHAN (1216-94) was followed by a period of steady decline in China.

French Estates General Series of parliaments held by PHILIP IV (1268-1314).
Sicilian Vespers A rising in Sicily against Normans. Massacre of French in Palermo (1282-1302).
MARCO POLO (*c.* 1254-*c.* 1324) visited southern India (1288).
The Khalji dynasty at Delhi consolidated by Ala-ud-din (1296-1316).
Scotland at war with England (1297-1304).
Mongols finally repelled from India by 1306.
Council of Ten instituted in Venice - an emergency committee of public safety after the rebellion of Tiepolo (1310).

English expelled from Scotland by ROBERT the Bruce (1274-1329) at Battle of Bannockburn (1314).
Salic Law initiated in France, whereby the throne could only pass through male heirs (1317)
Tughluk dynasty in India (1320-1413). The Delhi Sultanate reached its height of its culture.
Moscow became civil and ecclesiastical capital of Russia (1332).
The Imperial restoration in Japan. The Hojo military government overthrown by Emperor DAIGO II (1287-1339).

Hundred Years' War broke out (1337) between Edward III of England (1312-77) and PHILIP VI of France (1293-1350).
Cola di RIENZI (1313-54) attempted to recreate a Roman Republic (1347). Exiled and later murdered.
Black Death ravaged Europe (1348-51).
STEPHEN DUSHAN (*c.* 1308-55) Emperor of Serbs and Greeks.
Ashikaga Takauji (1305-58), a former Japanese Hojo general, revolted against DAIGO II (1287-1339). Civil war between the two courts lasted until 1392.

Religion

Inquisition Instituted by Papal Bull (1233), carried out by Dominican and Franciscan friars authorized to try suspected heretics.
Madhva (*c.* 1199-*c.* 1278) The third of the great philosophers of the Vedanta. His teachings synthesized the ideas of the devotional cults with those of Hinduism.

Islam The invasions of the Arabs, Turks and Afghans brought a proselytizing form of Islam to India. Strictly monotheistic, this religion gained little support from the Hindus. Hinduism was generally tolerated as long as submission was made to the Muslim Caliph, but iconoclasm often served to impress upon the native population the authority of the conquerors.
Jodo Shin sect founded in Japan by Shinran Shonin (1173-1262), who declared that faith alone in Amida gained the believer admission into the Western Heaven. He founded a married priesthood.

Jews expelled from England (1290) and from France (1306).
Acre captured by Mamluks (1291). End of Christian rule in the Near East.
Jubilee instituted by Pope Boniface VIII (*c.* 1235-1303), granting absolution to all pilgrims entering Rome in 1300.
UNAM SANCTAM (Papal Bull, 1302) declared the superiority of the papacy over all other authorities.

'Babylonian Captivity' Exile of the popes from Rome to Avignon (1305-78).

Jews persecuted in Germany (1349).

Philosophy

Franciscan Schoolmen Scholastic philosophers, who all belonged to the Franciscan order.
Roger Bacon (*c.* 1214-94)
St Bonaventure (1221-74)
Duns Scotus (*c.* 1265-*c.* 1308)
William of Occam (*c.* 1300-*c.* 1349)

Oxford school philosophers experimented extensively in alchemy and optics.
Robert Grosseteste (d. 1253)
Roger Bacon (*c.* 1214-94)

Thomist rationalism Belief in a clear distinction between reason and faith: reason gained knowledge through empirical evidence, while faith gained understanding from revelation, using the knowledge provided by reason.

The Bushido philosophy The Japanese feudal military class of the Kamakura period, the bushido warriors, adopted a philosophy of courage and idealism combined with serenity, simplicity, compassion and calm resignation.

Occamist nominalism Development of the earlier nominalist movement.
William of Occam (*c.* 1300-*c.* 1349)

Literature

Sicilian school After the death of FREDERICK II (1194-1250), the lack of courtly life led to the decline of Sicilian poetry into an artificial imitation of Provençal tradition.
Guittone d'Arezzo (*c.* 1235-94)
Jacopo da Lentini (13th cent.)
Pietro della Vigna (*c.* 1190-1249)

Roman de la Rose The most popular and influential work of the 13th century, by Guillaume de Lorris (d. *c.* 1235) and JEAN DE MEUNG (*c.* 1240-*c.* 1305). It treats of love both in chivalric and satirical terms.
Chinese historical romance *San Kuo Chih Yen I (The Romance of the Three Kingdoms)* was the forerunner of many novels based upon historical events.

Dolce stil novo, the 'sweet, new style' of Tuscan lyric poetry. In contrast to the artificiality of the Sicilian court poets, the Tuscans developed a sincere, elegant poetry with few of the stylized subtleties of former years.
Guido Cavalcanti (*c.* 1259-1300)
Guido Guinicelli (*c.* 1235-*c.* 1275)
Cino da Pistoia (*c.* 1270-1336)

Literature of the Five Monasteries A Zen school at Kyoto revived the practice of poetic composition in Chinese.
The Pali chronicle epic The style of the chronicle epic was adapted to narratives during the 13th century, particularly to stories of the life of the GAUTAMA BUDDHA (*c.* 563-*c.* 483).

Dengaku A kind of mime popular in Japan before the appearance of the No theatre.
Popular Chinese drama developed from early court ballets, street entertainment and variety shows. Since dialogue was always in popular speech, however, drama was not respected by intellectuals.

Fabliaux Short humorous tales, derived from oral folk tradition; ribald situation comedies mocking human weaknesses.
Japanese Symbolism The *Tsurezureguša (Essays in Idleness)*, used the Japanese form of symbolism known as *yugen*. This symbolism was important in the No drama.
YOSHIDA KENKOH (1283-1350)

Art

Italian painting broke away from Byzantine rigidity and introduced more humanistic and naturalistic art.
CIMABUE (*c.* 1240-*c.* 1302)

Sienese School added naturalism to formal stylized Byzantine art. Religious narrative painting enlivened by sensitive interpretation, brighter colour, more use of space and perspective.
DUCCIO di Buoninsegna (*c.* 1255-1318)
Simone MARTINI (*c.* 1284-1344)
Ambrogio LORENZETTI (*c.* 1300-*c.* 1348)
Pietro Lorenzetti (*c.* 1280-*c.* 1348)

Architecture

Cathedral building in Europe. Vaulting techniques mastered; the theory of stress and distribution of roof weight understood; pointed arches and flying buttresses used in monumental architecture.

European Gothic Throughout western Europe, pointed arch became more predominant, tracery more flowing, and embellishment and decoration more complicated and sophisticated. Style also used for civic architecture, particularly in Belgium, where the belfry was the most important feature.

Decorated (English Gothic, 1300-80). Further development and elaboration of ribs, producing star-shaped (stellar) pattern of vaulting. Large windows filled with geometrical tracery.

Open timber roofs in English parish churches. Various forms, culminating in 15th century in the hammer-beam roof. Rafters often richly painted, particularly in East Anglia.
Bricks, made in the Netherlands, were used for domestic architecture. Roofing was usually in slate.

Rayonnant French Gothic, characterized by wheel tracery in rose windows.
Segmental arch bridges and cable suspension bridges built in Europe.

Music

Rondels, or catch songs, in which voices sang different parts of the same melody at once. Secular development of European polyphony.

European narrative songs Harmony developed with refined vernacular songs of the troubadours, epic songs of the travelling jongleurs and Latin songs of the Goliards. Instrumental accompaniment increased.
ADAM DE LA HALLE (*c.* 1230-*c.* 1287)

Motet Development of European polyphony, usually 3-part composition in which parts moved separately, often with different words, even different languages. Originally ecclesiastical, later secular.

Dance music often sung. Lyrical compositions such as *ballades* and *rondeaux* originating in France.
Systematic school of musical theorists in Islamic music were principally concerned with intonation.
Safi al-Din (d. 1294)

Meistersingers German craftsmen and traders organized musical guilds. Highly cultured, strict musical regulations.
Ars nova New European style giving freedom from restrictions of *ars antiqua* (the conventions of plainsong and other forms). Greater rhythmic variety, more shapely melodic movement and further development of part-writing. Philippe de Vitry (1291-1361); Guillaume de Machaut (*c.* 1305-77); Francesco Landini (1325-97).

Chinese operas or musical dramas began under the Mongol dynasty.

Technology

Heavy plough with mouldboard for turning the sod, used in northern Europe.
Navigation weirs (staunches) built to maintain the depth of water in navigable waterways. Europe's waterways extended for the use of shipping during this period.
Abacus invented in China, for mathematical calculation.

Spinning-wheel invented in Europe; spindle and distaff had previously been used, the first example of belt power transmission.
Silk-throwing mills in Italy operated by undershot water-wheels. Towards the end of the century, the reeling machine and the twisting and doubling flyer were introduced.
Meteorology The Chinese correlated the sunspot cycle with climatic changes.

Rotary motion, used by the Romans, reintroduced in Europe. The camshaft was applied to hammers and crushers; fulling mills, and bellows and heavy hammers in metallurgy resulted.
Gold coinage became current in the West.
Valley of the Tigris and the Euphrates irrigated by the Mongols.

Gunpowder known in the West.
Iron casting in Europe came into its own with the rise of artillery and the achievement of high-temperature furnaces for cast iron. Iron cast into sand; linked moulding-boxes introduced.
Convex spectacles introduced into Chinese Empire by the Mongols.
The second Grand Canal constructed in China.

Cast cannon became commonplace in Europe. Special stone or iron projectiles were now used, instead of darts.
Water-power applied to silk-working machinery in China.
Printing with movable wooden type in China.
Projectile artillery fired by gunpowder in Europe.

English longbow designed which could pierce mail and tin. An arduous training resulted in the supremacy of English bowmen.
Plate armour introduced as a result of the English longbow. Made of steel, it was a complete covering of articulated plates. Helm was replaced by bassinet.

1350-1600

European Society

The period saw fundamental changes in the structure of European society. The mercantile class grew in strength and political power rested in land and wealth rather than heredity. In 1337 the Hundred Years' War broke out between England and France, precipitated by commercial rivalry.

The Holy Roman Empire ceased to be a monarchy and became instead a collection of federated, individual states. The Moors were driven from Spain and a gradual unification of the Spanish principalities and kingdoms followed. IVAN III (1440-1505) founded the modern Russian state through the conquest of territory and by his marriage to a Byzantine princess, making the Russians custodians of the Eastern Orthodox religion.

The decline of the Byzantine Empire symbolized in this union accompanied the rise of the Ottoman Turks, who, by 1529, had conquered southeastern Europe as far as the walls of Vienna. They fought constantly with the Venetians who were themselves engaged in a struggle for power pursued by the city states and kingdoms of Italy.

The Reformation

Anarchy reigned in Rome. Pope Clement V, a Frenchman, never set foot in Italy, and from 1309 to 1375, the popes held court at Avignon. During this time the rights, privileges and finances of the papacy were reorganized. The papal claim to absolute jurisdiction over clergy of any nationality, abuses of wealth and privilege, internal schisms (which caused two popes to be elected in 1378) promoted adverse reactions throughout Europe.

Such men as HUS (1369-1415), a Bohemian, and WICLIF (c. 1320-84), in England, developed the cause of a vernacular religion free from abuses. The Reformation was openly demanded in 1517 by LUTHER (1483-1546). The critical scholarship of ERASMUS (c. 1466-1536) did much to foster it, and Luther's appeal was echoed by ZWINGLI (1484-1531) and CALVIN (1509-64) in Switzerland, by John KNOX (1505-72) in Scotland and others throughout Europe and Scandinavia.

In 1534 HENRY VIII (1491-1547) was declared Supreme Head of the Church and Clergy of England. Although done for personal motives, it marked a break from Rome which was reinforced under ELIZABETH I (1533-1603) in 1563.

In France, protestantism, clung to by the Huguenots, who formed a large minority, caused a series of intense civil wars. Spain never accepted it. Most rigorous in its persecution was St Ignatius LOYOLA (1491-1556), who founded the Society of Jesus in 1534.

Humanism and the Renaissance

The influence of Erasmus is indicative of the wide spread of the humanistic philosophy which developed out of Italy. Rooted in the philosophy of PLATO (c. 427-347 BC) it was expressed not only in religious and philosophical works, but in the immensely rich activity in painting, sculpture and architecture which developed in Italy and spread throughout Europe. A new respect for the individuality of each human being and a resurgence of the appeal of the classical ideals of harmony and balance reached their height in the artistic and scientific achievements of LEONARDO (1452-1519), MICHELANGELO (1475-1564) and RAPHAEL (1483-1520).

The sciences developed concurrently, particularly in the fields of anatomy, man's examination of himself, and astronomy, his attempt to comprehend the boundaries of the physical universe.

The momentum of the Renaissance was increased by the invention in Europe of the printing press (although similar processes had been used much earlier in China) which enabled the new thoughts and discoveries to be disseminated much more rapidly. Through it, the Bible, translated into the languages of the common peoples of Europe, reached a far wider and more critical audience than ever before.

Raphael's painting of Pythagoras teaching in Athens (detail)

Missions and discoveries

Its word was carried too, out of Europe. Many discoverers, such as HENRY the Navigator (1394-1460), were prompted in their travels largely by religious motives. Henry explored the coast of Africa, Vasco de GAMA (c. 1469-1524) journeyed to India, COLUMBUS (1451-1506) sailed across the Atlantic, searching for the Indies; BALBOA (1475-1519) sighted the Pacific and MAGELLAN (c. 1480-1521) sailed into it.

For such journeys, shipbuilding advanced, new and better navigational instruments were manufactured, and charts drawn up. For those who remained at home, the rapid deforestation of Europe led to a great increase in the coal mining industry. More powerful furnaces led to advances in metallurgy. New crops were introduced from the lands visited by the explorers, and new machines were developed to cultivate those already known.

Navigator's quadrant, for determining the position of a ship at sea

The new technological practice of printing encouraged the publication of many works on the developing scientific and industrial scene. The process was rapidly advanced by Johannes GUTENBERG (c. 1400-67), who developed movable metal type, greatly increasing the speed of setting up books. Alongside, greater accuracy and flexibility in the process of making wood-blocks enhanced the illustrative content. Particularly important printed books of the time were De re aedificora, by Leon Battista ALBERTI (1404-72), which discussed the art and technology of architecture, and Pyrotechnica by Vannocio Biringuccio (1480-1539), which was the first practical textbook on all aspects of metallurgy. De re metallica, by AGRICOLA (1494-1555), was a comprehensive handbook on the mining industry, and dealt not only with the technical aspects, but also the health and social welfare of the miners. It was one of the earliest examples of concern for the social implications of the shift away from simply working the land to an industrial society.

	1350	1358	1366	1375	1383	1391 1400
Principal Events	**The Statute of Labourers** (1351) in England attempted, in face of a shortage of labour after the Black Death, to enforce the feudal authority of landlord over villein. **Swiss Confederation** by 1353 included Zurich, Glarus, Zug and Bern. **Venetian wars:** at sea against Genoa (1353-5); Hungary expelled Venetians from Dalmatia (1358). **The Golden Bull** (1356) regulated elections and constitution of Holy Roman Empire to 1806. **Delhi Sultanate** began to lose its power in India during the reign of Mohammed Tughluk (1325-51).	**Danish at war** with Hanseatic merchant league, who had allied with Norway, Sweden and Teutonic Knights. **The Jacquerie** Peasant uprising in France over war taxes (1358). Ruthless suppression by nobles. **Hapsburgs** made peace with Swiss Confederation (1358). **Peace of Brétigny** (1360) ended the first period of the 100 Years' War. **Crete revolted** against Venetian rule (1364). **Hindu empire** of Vijayanagar founded in southern India (1335-1565). **Muslim dynasty** in Kashmir founded by Shah Mirza (1346-1589).	**Peace of Stralsund** (1370) exempted Hansa towns from customs duties; gave them trading stations throughout the Baltic. **Treaty of Vincennes** between France and Scotland (1372). **Battle of La Rochelle** (1372). Castilian fleet defeated English. Channel thus restored to French. **Alliance of Friendship** (1373) between Portugal and England. TAMERLANE (1336-1405) began his conquest of Asia. **The Ming dynasty** Fourth reunification of China. The Mings were masters of all China: practical, efficient and militarily strong (1368-1621).	**Teutonic Knights** founded Rhein in southeast Prussia (1377). **War of Choggia** between Venice and Genoa (1378-81). Venice's victory led to their control of Levantine trade. **Russian victory** (1380) over Golden Horde of BATU KHAN (d. 1255). Led by Dmitri of Moscow (1359-89). **Mamluk Egyptians** ended the Armenian Empire by capturing Sis, the capital (1375). **Peasants' Revolt** in England. Led by Wat TYLER (d. 1381) in opposition to attempts by landlords to revert to servile tenure (1381).	**Battle of Aljubarrota** Portuguese independence established with defeat of Castilians (1385). **Battle of Sempach** Swiss defended their independence from the Hapsburgs (1386). **Turks** conquered the Balkans. Defeated Serbs and Bosnians at the battle of Kossovo (1389). **Mongols** driven from Karakorum, their capital, by the Chinese (1388). **Autocratic Japanese rule** Yoshimitsu (r. 1367-95), 3rd Ashikaga Shogun, brought the shogunate to its period of greatest power. In 1395 he abdicated and became a monk.	**Richard II** of England (1367-1400) landed in Ireland. Quelled revolt (1394). Married (1396) Isabella of France (1389-1409), extending Anglo-French truce for 28 years. **Union of Kalmar** between Denmark, Norway and Sweden under one king, Eric of Pomerania (1382-1459). TAMERLANE (1336-1405) attacked the Golden Horde and reached Moscow. Conquered Iraq and Persia, sacked Delhi, defeated Egyptians and broke up Ottoman Empire (1393-1405). **Muslim Rajput dynasty** in Gujarat (1396-1572).
Religion	**Zen Buddhism in Japan** Zen monks dominated intellectual and artistic life during the Ashikaga period. They lived and studied in China, and returned to contribute new arts and ideas to the culture of Japan. **The Bhakti movement** became a dynamic force in northern India during the 14th century.	**Islam in India** Conversions to Islam occurred among the lower castes, while the upper castes remained strictly separate. Aspects of Islam were assimilated into both Buddhism and Hinduism.	**Influence of the Sufis,** saints and mystics who came to India with the establishment of Turkish power, preaching mystical doctrine of union with God through the love of God. The Chishti, the Suhrawardi and Firdawsi were the chief Sufi orders in India.	**Lollardry** Movement led by WICLIF (1320-84). Condemned worldliness of friars and secular clergy, temporal power of prelates and celibacy of nuns and priests in England. Reform based on scriptures, preached in the vernacular. Movement sowed seeds of Protestant Reformation. **First English Bible** (1380), translated by WICLIF (1320-84).	**Brethren of the Common Life** Founded by Gerard Groote (1340-84), a German mystic, in the Netherlands. Semi-monastic community of lay men and women carrying out humanistic education and Christian teachings in daily life. **Hussitism** Clerical reform movement influenced by Lollardry but originated from teaching of Jan HUSS (1369-1415). Centred on Utraquism, theory demanding communion of both bread and wine for the laity. Closely allied with revolutionary Bohemian nationalism.	**The Great Schism** Division of the papacy, when two popes were elected, one in Rome, one in Avignon, each with their own cardinals and administration (1378-1417).
Philosophy	**Sung Confucian philosophy** introduced into Japan from China.	**Viyayanagara,** a Hindu Kingdom, became an important centre for Brahman studies. The *Sarva darsana samgraha*, the classic summary of the Brahman philosophies, was written by Madhava (fl. *c.* 1380).				
Literature	**No drama** A non-realistic theatre in which the actors perform formal and symbolic dramas, including rhythmic music and dance. Based upon the ancient *sarugaku-no* entertainment, the No theatre was created in the mid-14th century by Kan-ami (1333-*c.* 1385) and his son, ZEAMI MOTOKIYO (1363-1443), and is influenced by the heroic stories popular at the time. The No plays, generally performed in two acts, are separated by comic interludes, *kyogen*.	**Novelle** Collections of Italian short stories, written in the vernacular, a tradition begun by BOCCACCIO (1313-75). Franco Sacchetti (*c.* 1332-1400) Matteo Bandello (1485-1561) Agnolo Firenzuola (1493-1543)	**Petrarchan sonnets** Poems celebrating love and human individuality in a rhetorical, formal pattern, which became a major form of humanist literature. PETRARCH (1304-74) **Ming literature** The Academy of Letters produced a great many official compilations, including encyclopaedias, histories, dictionaries, bibliographies and commentaries on the Classics.	**English morality plays** Didactic religious plays in the vernacular, essentially a dramatized allegory rather than biblical characterization, in which the protagonists are personifications of vice and virtue. **Chinese drama** was written in simple, everyday language. A new type of theatre evolved in which the plays were accompanied by music.	**Ballade** Traditional Provençal verse form introduced into England during the 14th century. Subjects usually legendary, historical or romantic. Consisted of three stanzas with the final line repeated as a refrain, and a concluding stanza. François VILLON (1431-63) **Bengali literature** Mainly verse originally composed to be sung or recited—narratives, epics and religious verse.	GEOFFREY CHAUCER (*c.* 1340-1400) **Scottish poetry** began to come into its own with patriotic epic poems about such characters as ROBERT THE BRUCE (1274-1329). John Barbour (*c.* 1320-95) **Persian lyric poetry** Form usually used was the *ghazal*, characterized by the *takhallus*, in which the final couplet included the poet's pen-name. HAFIZ (*c.* 1325-89)
Art	**'Four Masters of Yüan Dynasty'** worked at the end of the Mongol period. They were responsible for *wen jen hua*, the literary men's painting, in which painting was personal expression rather than paid work. Huang Kung-wang (1269-1354) Wu Chen (1280-1354) NI TSAN (1301-74) Wang Meng (*c.* 1309-85)	**Giotteschi** Admirers and successors of GIOTTO (1266-1337), who studied human movement and expression, but whose work is softened by the influence of the Sienese School. Master of St Cecilia (fl. *c.* 1300) Bernardo Daddi (*c.* 1290-1349) Taddeo GADDI (*c.* 1300-66) Maso di Banco (fl. *c.* 1350)	**Bohemian school** Not a native school, although much activity took place in the court of Charles IV (1316-78). Peter PARLER (1330-99) Master of Trebon (fl. *c.* 1400) **Chinese lacquer** Red lacquer was applied to furniture in many coats until it was thick enough to carve, generally in designs of flowers or landscapes.	**Icon painting** Mostly in wooden eastern European and Russian churches where fresco and mosaic were impossible. Russian icon painting influenced by Byzantines. Andrei Rublev (*c.* 1360-1430)	**International Gothic** With the increase of European travel, new innovations spread rapidly, and an international style developed. Tapestries, stained glass and illuminations were commissioned by noble and wealthy patrons. Painting was characterized by vivid, rich colour, with dark or gold backgrounds, on religious subjects, often reflecting the rich courtly life. Many paintings were miniatures, used as illustrations, e.g. *Les Tres Riches Heures du Duc de Berry*. Gentile da Fabriano (*c.* 1360-1427); Pisanello (1395-1455); Pol, Hennequin and Herman de Limbourg (fl. *c.* 1410); Stefano da Zevio (*c.* 1375-1451); Jaquemart de Hesdin (d. *c.* 1411); Melchior Broederlam (fl. *c.* 1400).	
Architecture	**Hall churches,** 'Hallenkirchen', with aisles and nave of equal height, common in Germany. Tall spires, often of openwork stone construction, dominated the façade; portals and façades often elaborately decorated.	**Indian architecture** of the Tughluks was more austere than earlier Islamic architecture in India. The fusion of the two cultures continued, but the use of ornament was reduced and stone masonry was used, giving the buildings an appearance of monumentality.	**Ming architecture** in China. Monumental in scale, built in vaulted brick or masonry, and supported by pillars and beams rather than complex bracketing systems. Gave a new appearance of lightness and delicacy to high, steep roofs.		**Japanese shoin-zukari,** 'study-style', architecture evolved as a result of Zen-buddhist emphasis upon simplicity and natural form. The *shoin*, a room for study and meditation in palace and villa, was provided with a bay window for extra light. Dwellings, like temples, were placed among natural or landscaped settings of rocks, pools and trees.	**French flamboyant** style was characterized by the use of the ogee curve (or S-curve) in windows, doorways and panels. Wall surface gave way to window area; geometrical rose windows are typical of this style.
Music				**Laudi** Sacred songs sung in the vernacular in Italy. Probably performed in private houses during services devoted to the Virgin Mary. Written for several voices.		
Technology	**Paddle-wheel** invented in Europe. Applied to various processes such as bellows in blast furnaces, silk-working machinery, hammers to beat iron and textiles, and wiredrawing. **Wind-power** applied to pump machinery for land drainage in Europe, especially in the Netherlands. **Kao-liang,** a cereal crop, grown in northern China from 14th century.	**Steel bow** invented in Europe: a mechanical device for firing arrows, involving pulleys and gears. **Hydraulic hammer** invented and used in forges in the West. Worked on the principle of oscillating lever and ratchets. The same principle was also used for cranes to lift large blocks of stone needed for monumental buildings.	**Iron needles** first produced in Europe. **Ribaudequer** invented: a gun with a number of barrels which could be fired in quick succession. **Practice of paving streets** revived in medieval European towns. Large slabs of stone used.	**Blast furnace** for carburizing and melting iron replaced the bell founder's furnace in Europe. **Breech-loading devices** applied to hand-guns. **Mizzen-mast** common on square-rigged ships by the 14th century; later used on the carrack, a Portuguese galleon.	**The shaduf,** for raising water for irrigation canals, introduced into Flanders from the Middle East via Spain. **Salt glazing** discovered by Rhenish potters. **Mechanical clocks** used in the West, especially in Italy. **Paper manuscripts** in fairly widespread circulation in Europe.	**The flax-breaker,** to break the woody tissues of flax plants, used for making linen, invented in Holland. **Liqueur** distilled from cereals in Europe. **Printing presses** first set up in Europe; used wood or metal blocks. **First printing with movable metal type** carried out in Korea.

	1400	1408	1416	1425	1433	1441	1450
Principal Events	**Scottish invasion** (1402) of England held off by the Percys, who then rebelled against HENRY IV of England (1367-1413). **Civil War in France** between Dukes of Burgundy and Orleans (1405). **Rebellion in Wales** led by Owen Glendower (c. 1359-c. 1416). **Chinese naval expeditions** through the south seas: visited Java, Sumatra, Cambodia, Siam, India and Ceylon. **The Kingdom of Delhi,** India ruled by the Sayyids, occupied only the Jumna, a shadow of the former sultanate.	**Venice at war** with Hungary (1409). **Battle of Tannenberg** Poles and Lithuanians overthrew Teutonic Knights (1410). Lithuanians conquered Ukraine (1412). **Battle of Agincourt** (1415) HENRY V (1387-1422) of England defeated French. **Portuguese** seized Ceuta from the Moors (1415). Marked beginning of their colonization of Africa. **Ottoman Empire** restored by Mohammed I (1387-1421).	**Portuguese** explored Madeira Islands (1418). **Wars of Bohemian Hussites** against the Holy Roman Empire (1419-36). **Normandy captured** from the French by HENRY V (1387-1422), who advanced as far as Paris. At the Treaty of Troyes, English claims to the French throne and conquests as far as the Loire recognized (1420). **Peking** became the Chinese capital under the Ming dynasty (1421). **Turks** besieged Constantinople (1422).	JOAN OF ARC (1412-31) raised the siege of Orleans—a turning point in the 100 Years' War, enabling CHARLES VII (1403-61) to regain Paris. **Philip the Good** (1396-1427) of Burgundy acquired Holland, Hainault and Zeeland. **Portuguese** discovered the Azores (1427). **Swiss Civil war** between Zurich and neighbouring cities (1430-50). **Turks** conquered Albania and Salonika (1430). **Expansion of Aztec Empire** under Itzcoatl (c. 1360-c. 1440)—stretched from Gulf of Mexico to Pacific.	**French regained Paris** from the English (1436). **The Praguerie** French nobles, led by the Dauphin, plotted against the King, but were suppressed (1440).	**End of New Mayan Empire** (1441). **Independence of India,** Persia and Afghanistan gained when the empire of TAMERLANE (1336-1405) disintegrated (1447). **French conquest** of Normandy and Brittany (1450).
Religion	**Conciliar movement** A series of general councils with power over the pope and subject only to a monarch. Originated as a reform movement against the Great Schism. Councils of Pisa, Constance, Basel and Ferrara-Firenze (1379-1448).		**Islam in China** became entrenched in the north and southwest, surviving the downfall of the Mongols.	**Nestorian Christianity,** closely associated with the Mongols, was stamped out from China under the Ming.	**Pragmatic sanction** of Bourges asserted that the Church Council was superior to the pope (1438).	
Philosophy						
Literature	**Alliterative poetry** A tradition of English and Scottish poetry with strict rules of syllabic accents. Began with Old English poetry, revived in the Middle Ages and highly developed in the poems *Sir Gawayne and the Grene Knight* and *Piers Plowman*. **French chronicles** vividly recreated the 100 Years' War. Jean FROISSART (c. 1337-c. 1405)	**Anatolian literature** Strongly influenced by the Persian classics. Mostly romances and mystic poetry, and some chronicles. Sultan Veled (d. 1312) Ashik Pasha (d. 1332) Ahmedi (d. 1413)	**Dance of Death** Theme extremely popular in 15th and 16th centuries throughout Europe, both in literature and art. Dramatized and depicted the concept of death as the ubiquitous leveller.	**Bihari literature** (in Maithili) Lyrics on the life and love of Radha and Krishna, and many popular dramas. Vidyapati Thakkura (15th cent.)		**French mystery and passion plays** developed from medieval Church drama, and became festival affairs, performed spectacularly in all important towns on their festival day.
Art	**Burgundian school** Under the patronage of Philip the Bold of Burgundy (1342-1404), Flemish panel painters and miniaturists flourished. Henri Bellechose (d. 1440) Jean Malouel (d. 1419) Claus SLUTER (d. 1406) Jacquemart de Hesdin (d. c. 1411) **Ming porcelain** Import of cobalt from Persia resulted in the famous blue and white porcelain. Designs were painted on before glazing and were thus protected by the transparent glaze. Speciality of the Ching-te Chen potters.	**Sculpture painted,** which, apart from giving the statue increased naturalism, gave the artist an opportunity to observe the effect of colour in relief, e.g. changing tones in shadows. Practice common in Burgundy.	**Venetian glasswork** Though it had been known to the Romans, the Venetians rediscovered how to produce a 'crystal' glass by using manganese to clarify it. Much coloured glass produced, later decorated with enamel painting, engraving and gilding.	**Perspective** Leone Battista ALBERTI (1404-72) evolved a system which enabled a picture to be geometrically constructed, with the position of the horizon fixed according to the height of the subjects represented. Aerial perspective, a term introduced by LEONARDO (1452-1519), is pictorial depth achieved by scaled changes of tone and colour as objects recede.	**Quattrocento period** (i.e. the 1400s) of the early Renaissance, when the work of painters and sculptors was characterized by the formality of classical art blended with a new interest in the humanity of the individual. Demonstrated in a close imitation of nature, the reappearance of the nude in art (made more naturalistic by the scientific study of anatomy) and the development of perspective. Filippo BRUNELLESCHI (1377-1446); Lorenzo GHIBERTI (1378-1455); DONATELLO (c. 1386-1466); FRA ANGELICO (1387-1455); Antonio Pisanello (c. 1395-c. 1455); Paolo UCCELLO (c. 1396-1475); Luca della Robbia (1400-82); Domenico Veneziano (d. 1461); MASACCIO (1401-28); Bernardo ROSSELLINO (1409-64); Antonio Rossellino (1427-c. 1479); Desiderio da Settignano (1428-64); Mino da Fiesole (1425-84); Antonio POLLAIUOLO (1432-98); Andrea del Verrocchio (1435-88); Piero Pollaiuolo (1441-96); Benedetto da Maiano (1442-97); Sandro BOTTICELLI (1444-1510).	
Architecture	**The Japanese chaseki,** a special apartment or pavilion set aside for the tea ceremony, containing a *tokonoma,* a recess for ink and brush paintings and flower arrangement, the focal point of the room. Screen painting on a large scale developed as a special art. Kano Motonubu (c. 1476-c. 1559)		**Muslim architecture** in India introduced the mosque, with minaret and dome, pointed arch and transverse vault, and the mausoleum. Persian influences prevailed, but Indian craftsmen combined Persian and traditional Indian decorative motifs to produce a modified style.	**Early Renaissance** Inspired by ancient ruins, by recent translations of classical writers and by their own discovery of perspective, the *Quattrocento* architects of Florence attempted to revive the classical spirit. Early Renaissance buildings were elegant, human in scale, based upon simple geometrical shapes, and upon classical form and proportion. Filippo BRUNELLESCHI (1377-1446); Leone Battista ALBERTI (1404-72); Michelozzo di Bartolomeo (1396-1472); Antonio Amadeo (c. 1447-1522).		
Music	**Minstrels of war** were a symbol of a European nobleman's wealth. He employed trumpeters and drummers to give fanfares or danger signals.	**Chamber minstrels** were part of the domestic or court scene—they sang ballads, improvised and set poems to music during banquets or as background to courtly love play. Their instruments were harps, viols, lutes or gitterns.	**Choir schools** established, attached to churches, chapels and hospitals. Taught polyphonic notation and Latin, which enabled a boy to take holy orders. **Cantus firmus mass** By using a common theme throughout the five separate sections of the Ordinary Mass, the *cantus firmus* bound it into a single unit.	**Choral polyphony** Most significant innovation of early Renaissance music. Blended the voices, and instead of producing the accustomed dissonances of medieval music, introduced euphony. John Dunstable (c. 1370-1453)	**Early Franco-Flemish school** First great musical school. Many of its composers were Burgundian court musicians. Introduced many new techniques, particularly in vocal and instrumental counterpoint. Secular songs and rhythms adapted for sacred music. Writing for instruments and instrumental accompaniment increased. Guillaume DUFAY (c. 1400-74); Gilles Binchois (1400-60); Johannes Ockeghem (c. 1425-c. 1495); Josquin DES PRES (1440-1521); Jacob Obrecht (1451-1505).	
Technology	**Mechanical devices** such as the cylinder, in suction and force pumps, flywheel and piston-rods came into use in Europe. **The gig-mill** invented, for raising the nap on cloth.	**Piston pumps** driven by water-wheels in southern Germany. **Weaving loom** for fancy fabrics invented in Europe. **Hopped beer** first produced in England, the process having been carried from medieval Spain through Flanders, Germany and France.	**Cast-iron produced** by a method in which the iron was taken directly from furnace to mould. **Padlocks** widely used; the craft of locksmith became more skilled and intricate. **Drift-nets** for fishing invented by the Dutch.	**Cast-iron water pipes** employed in the improved water supplies of European cities. **Movable metal type** used in printing in Europe. Johannes GUTENBURG (1398-1468)	**Three-masted ships** used by the Portuguese.	**Crank and connecting rod** Important device, found in northern Italy, southern Germany and the Rhine Valley, used to operate a mining pump. **Swivelling cranes** built in western countries.

	1450	1458	1466	1475	1483	1491	1500
Principal Events	**Lodi dynasty,** India, a dynasty of Afghans, was established (1451) by Buhlul Lodi, who ousted the Sayyids and made himself Sultan of Delhi. **Battle of Castillon** (1453) ended 100 Years' War. England renounced all French conquests except Calais. **Cape Verde Islands** claimed by CADAMOSTO (c. 1432-c. 1511) for Portugal. **End of Byzantine Empire** when Turks defeated Constantinople (1453). Turks took Athens (1458).	**Wars of the Roses** (1455-85) English civil war between houses of York and Lancaster. **End of Tatar rule** in Russia (1462). **Polish victory** over Teutonic Knights (1466). **Khanate of Astrakhan** founded (1466). **Songhoi Empire** of W. Africa founded by Sunni Ali, ruler of Gao, when he captured Timbuktu (1468).	**Anglo-Burgundian alliance** (1468) when CHARLES THE BOLD (1433-77) married Margaret of York (1473-1541). **Christian states of Spain** united by marriage (1469) of FERDINAND (1452-1516) and ISABELLA (1451-1504). WARWICK THE KINGMAKER (1428-71) dethroned (1470) EDWARD IV of England (1442-83). **Moscow supreme** in Russia, through IVAN III (1440-1505).	**Turks** conquered the Crimea (1475). At the Treaty of Constantinople Venice agreed to pay tribute to Turks to trade in Black Sea. **Civil strife in Japan** arose over a dispute about succession to the Ashikaga shogunate and resulted in reallocation of land and power. **Battle of Nancy** (1477) ended Burgundian power. Burgundy united under French crown. **Pazzi conspiracy** against the MEDICI in Florence destroyed balance of power in Italy (1478). **Treaty of Toledo** (1480). Spain recognized Portuguese conquest of Morocco.	**Battle of Bosworth Field** (1485), at which RICHARD III (1452-85) of England was killed and HENRY VII (1457-1509) became the first Tudor monarch. **Hungary** conquered Austria (1485). **River Congo** explored by DIOGO CAO (fl. c. 1480). **Cape of Good Hope** rounded (1488) by Bartolomeo DIAS (c. 1450-1500).	**Perkin Warbeck** (1474-99) rebelled against HENRY VII (1457-1509) of England. **Spanish conquest of Granada** completed the Spanish recovery of lands taken by the Moors (1492). **Italian wars** CHARLES VIII (1470-98) of France invaded Italy (1494)—Pope, Holy Roman Emperor, Spain, Venice and Milan—united to expel Charles. **Exploration** COLUMBUS (1451-1506) reached the Bahamas; CABOT (1450-98) North America; DA GAMA (1469-1524) India. A papal bull divided all newly discovered lands between Spain and Portugal.	
Religion	**Buddhist disputes** became common in Japan during the 15th century. Monks of the Enryakuji destroyed the central monastery of the True Pure Land Sect in Kyoto. Rennyo (1415-99) built up a military organization to defend the interests of the sect. **Kabirpanthi** Indian religion founded by the followers of KABIR (1440-1518), independent of Hinduism or Islam. Preached universal love and the simple union of all souls with God. Kabirpanthi later came to be regarded as a Hindu sect.	**Church of Bohemian Brethren** Puritanical sect originated from teaching of Peter of Chelchich, which rejected subordination to Rome.	**Systematic Shinto** philosophies. A monotheistic Shinto was developed by Ichijo Kanera (d. 1481); the Yoshida Shinto of Yoshida Kanetomo (d. 1511) held that the essence of both Shinto deities and Buddhas was identical. **The Amidist Buddhist sects** flourished in Japan despite the domination of the Zen philosophy.	**Spanish Inquisition** A religious court established (1478) by the Spanish monarchy. Often used as a political instrument under TORQUEMADA (1420-98). Victims principally heretics and witches, but often Jews and Muslims as well. Punishment by torture, procedure secret. **Orthodox Neo-Confucianism**, the school of Chu Hsi, was the dominant philosophical system in China during the Ming period; Buddhism and Taoism produced no new ideas. Opposition and stimulation were provided by various syncretist schools and by the scholars of the Tunglin group who sought moral reform of the government and a return to Confucian principles. Wang Yang-ming (1472-1529)	**Witchcraft** Throughout 15th, 16th and 17th centuries, persecution of witches authorised by Church and State. Belief that witches sold their souls to the devil in return for supernatural powers, enabling them to inflict disease or death on man or property. Persecution started with *Summis desiderantes*, the Bull of Pope Innocent (1432-92), and witch hunt manias took place in succeeding centuries. Torture used to extract confessions. **The Ikko uprising** took place in Japan when members of the Ikko (True Pure Land) Sect defeated and killed a local lord north of Kyoto (1488).	**Diet of Worms** settled the problems of the investiture of the Holy Roman Empire (1495).	
Philosophy			**Renaissance Humanism** represented a new interest in the classical heritage and a new confidence and faith in the power of man's ability to comprehend the universe through his own reason. Movement away from the narrow theological conceptions of the previous age. Marsilio FICINO (1433-99) Desiderius ERASMUS (c. 1466-1536) Sir Thomas MORE (1478-1535).		**Italian Renaissance historians** Familiar with the diplomatic world and infused with humanistic critical spirit of the Renaissance, historians attempted to give objective analyses of history and of contemporary society. Lorenzo Valla (1406-57); Niccolò MACHIAVELLI (1469-1527); Francesco GUICCIARDINI (1483-1540); Giorgio VASARI (1511-74). (1511-74).		
Literature	**Gujarati and Rajasthani** literature in India. Jain devotional hymns and poems written after the 15th century. Narasimha (fl. 15th cent.) Mirabai (fl. 16th cent.)	**Scottish Chaucerians** Narrative poems continuing the style of CHAUCER (c. 1340-1400): colloquial and satirical, many animal fables and the *Testament of Cresseid*, an adaptation of one of Chaucer's works. Robert HENRYSON (1430-1506) William DUNBAR (1460-1513)	**First English printed book,** *Rucuyell of the Historyes of Troye* (1474), printed by William CAXTON (1422-91). **Volksbücher** German chivalric novels produced in cheap editions which increased their popularity among the growing reading public.	**Grands Rhétoriqueurs** French school of poetry derived from poets of the Burgundian court, whose work is characterized by elaborate ornament, classical imagery and a formal style. Georges Chastellain (1405-75) Jean Molinet (1435-1507) **Danube school** of painters. The first pure landscape school, which produced naturalistic pictures of the countryside. Rueland Frueauf (1445-1507); Lucas CRANACH (1472-1553); Albrecht ALTDORFER (1480-1538).	**Italian epic poetry,** derived from the chivalric romances of medieval Europe, often dealt with the exploits of CHARLEMAGNE (742-814) or the Arthurian legends. Luigi PULCI (1432-84) Lodovico ARIOSTO (1474-1533)	**Questione della lingua** The problem of the search for a national Italian literary language in a politically divided Italy. Academies instituted throughout Italy to compromise between vernacular literature and the desire for rule and form according to classical precepts. **Aldine Press** established (1494) in Venice by Aldo Manuzio (1450-1515).	
Art	**Trompe l'oeil** Painter's technique of illusion to suggest that the subject of the painting physically exists in the presence of the viewer, e.g. flies on the surface of the painting, mirrors reflecting objects outside the painting. Paolo UCCELLO (c. 1396-1475) Andrea CASTAGNO (c. 1423-57) Petrus Christus (d. c. 1473)	**Early Netherlandish school** Paintings, portraits or altarpieces produced under the patronage of prosperous merchant society as well as that of the Burgundian court. Characterized by close attention to naturalistic detail. Jan van EYCK (c. 1390-1441) Rogier van der WEYDEN (c. 1399-1464) Dieric BOUTS (c. 1415-75) Hugo van der GOES (1440-82) Hans MEMLING (c. 1430-94)	**German woodcarving** Elaborately carved altarpieces showed movement of bodies, folds in clothing. Bernt Notke (c. 1440-1509) **Spanish painting** showed influence of International Gothic and Flemish realism, but connections with Arab art produced flat, graphic and even abstract settings. Bartolomé Bermejo (fl. c. 1485) Jaime Huguet (fl. c. 1475)	**School of Padua** Stiff, severe lines, with elaborate ornamentation such as garlands of flowers and cherubs. Francesco Squarcione (1394-1474); Andrea MANTEGNA (c. 1431-1506). **School of Ferrara** A loosely-connected school, characterized by violent relief and angular aspects. Aggressive expression, strongly influenced by MANTEGNA (1431-1506). Cosimo Tura (c. 1431-95); Francesco del Cossa (c. 1435-c. 1477); Ercole de'Roberti (c. 1448-96); Lorenzo Costa (c. 1460-1535). **Umbrian school** Characterized by symmetry and a sense of balance. Umbrian painters used delicate colours and strong lines. Piero della FRANCESCA (c. 1420-92); PINTORICCHIO (c. 1454-1513); PERUGINO (c. 1445-1523); Melozzo da Forlì (1438-94).		**Printing** developments in Europe allowed the production of illustrated rather than illuminated books. **Copper engraving** A metal plate was capable of finer detail than wood, and the art developed in its own right rather than solely for the illustration of books. Master ES (fl. c. 1460) Martin Schongauer (1453-91) Albrecht DÜRER (1471-1528)	
Architecture	**Indian architecture** of the Lodis introduced the double dome and enamelled tiles as a wall decoration, to produce an elegant architecture. Flourished particularly in Gujarat, Malwa, Bengal and Rajasthan. **Indian Rajput palaces** Enormous constructions guarded by many gateways; monumental in style but less ornamental than the later Muslim palaces.	**The castle,** after the introduction of gunpowder, became a military fortification, with low walls for artillery.	**Massive Spanish architecture** followed upon the reconquest of the Iberian peninsula from the Moors. Gerona was the widest and Seville the largest cathedral in Europe.	**Extremism** in decoration occurred throughout the Iberian peninsula; ogee, or S-curve, arches and figure sculpture on the west front of Spanish buildings; sea-motifs and tropical vegetation in Portugal.		**The Guild- and Town-halls** of England, the Netherlands, the Hanseatic countries and Italy were expressions of a new civic independence.	
Music			**Lute songs** Art of singing to lute accompaniment developed all over Europe. Lutes also used to accompany dances.	**Japanese music** began to show the first signs of developing into a popular native style, having been overshadowed by Chinese music.	**Organ-playing virtuosi** of the Renaissance. Learned instrumental performers, usually of the organ (later the harpsichord), were found in many churches. Arnolt Schlick (1455-1525) Paul Hofhaimer (1459-1537)	**Early German lieder** Choral music, secular or sacred, derived from madrigals. Polyphonic, with the main melody in the top voices. Heinrich Isaac (c. 1450-1517) Ludwig Senfl (1490-1556) Johannes Eccard (1553-1611) Hans Leo Hassler (1564-1612)	
Technology	**Magnetic declination** calculated and incorporated into navigation in Europe. **Movable lock-gates,** with paddles to control the flow of water, invented in Europe. LEONARDO da Vinci (1452-1519) replaced the portcullis lock-gate with the modern mitre-gate.	**Astronomical instruments** manufactured: astrolabes, quadrants, sundials, compasses and rulers. Principally carried out in Oxford and Paris. **The carrack,** a new type of ship with a redesigned forecastle deck, and many more propelling sails, in use in Europe.	**The 'Astronomical Ephemeris'** of Regiomontanus (1436-76), an almanac of navigation, described the principle of determining longitude by lunar distances.	**Hand gun** began to replace the steel bow in Europe as a weapon of attack. **Gunpowder** used in Europe to fire rockets and firelances.	**Advances in metallurgy** led to the manufacture of tinplate, sheet metal and the invention of metal-boring apparatus. **Final development of armour** Great attention paid to design, strength and beauty.	**Pharmacology** Beginnings of scientific preparation and manufacture of medicines and drugs. Philippus PARACELSUS (c. 1493-1541) **Scientific study of anatomy** began. LEONARDO da Vinci (1452-1519) MICHELANGELO (1475-1564) Andreas VESALIUS (1514-64)	

1500 | 1508 | 1516 | 1525 | 1533 | 1541 | 1550

Principal Events

Songhoi Empire at greatest height (1493-1529) under Emperor Askia Mohammed, who took over Mandingo Empire.
Negro slavery introduced into West Indies (1501).
PEDRO CABRAL (1460-*c.* 1526) claimed Brazil for Portugal.
Safavid dynasty founded by ISMAIL the Sufi (1486-1524) in Persia.
Spain conquered Naples (1502).
Mozambique founded by the Portuguese missionaries, who set up posts at Sena and Tete (1505-7).
Treaty of Windsor (1506) concluded a trade war between England and the Netherlands.

English defeated Scots at Flodden (1513).
VASCO NUNEZ DE BALBOA (1474-1517) crossed Panama and sighted Pacific (1513).
Portuguese deposed Muslim ruler of Malacca (1511) and reached China (1513). Established trade headquarters at Goa.
Battle of Chaldiran Turko-Persian war followed Turkish invasion (1514-16).
French expelled from Italy by combined Papal and Swiss forces (1512), but regained supremacy at Marignano (1515).

MAGELLAN (*c.* 1480-1521) circumnavigated the world (1519-22).
Popular revolts in Spain (1520-1) and Germany (1524-5) against feudal authority. Suppressed.
Aztecs defeated by CORTEZ (1485-1547) at Tenochtitlán (1521).
Hapsburg-Valois wars Rivalry between FRANCIS I of France (1494-1547) and CHARLES V (1500-58), Holy Roman Emperor, over succession to Italy. Francis defeated at Pavia (1525).
The Hindu Empire of Vijayanagar, founded on the ruins of the Chola dynasty, reached its zenith under Krishna Deva Raya (1509-29).

League of Cognac FRANCIS I (1494-1547), the Pope, Sforzas, Venice and Florence opposed CHARLES V (1500-58).
Danubian Hapsburg monarchy founded when Hungarian and Bohemian kings united with Austrian Hapsburgs (1526).
Battle of Mohacs Turks defeated Hungarians; ended Hungarian independence (1526).
Sack of Rome by mercenaries of CHARLES V (1527).
Vienna besieged by the Turks (1529).
The Mogul Empire founded by BABER (1483-1530), a descendent of GENGHIS KHAN (1167-1227).

JACQUES CARTIER (1491-1557) sighted coast of Labrador and navigated the St Lawrence river (1534-41).
Pilgrimage of Grace Catholic rebellion in north of England (1535-7).
Spanish conquest of Tunis completed colonization of N. African coast (1535).
PIZARRO (*c.* 1470-1541) conquered Peru (1533).
Venice and Turkey concluded a peace treaty (1540).
Humayun, successor of BABER (1483-1530), was defeated by the Afghan Sher Shah (1539-45) and driven, temporarily, from India.

CORONADO (1510-54) explored land on the west of the Mississippi River (1541).
Peace of Crépy FRANCIS I (1494-1547) agreed to support CHARLES V (1500-58) against Turks (1544).
Turks occupied Tabriz in Persia (1548).
IVAN IV (1530-84) took the title of Tsar of all Russia (1547).
Ethiopia invaded by Muslims led by Ahmed Grañ (d. 1542), using firearms. Expelled with Portuguese aid (1541).
Europeans to the East Portuguese traders established settlements in India (1510), Japan (1542) and Macao (1557).

Religion / Philosophy

The Shi'a form of Islam established in Gulbarga by Yusuf Adil Shah of Bijapur, who annexed the kingdom. This form of Islam was opposed by the Sunnites, who held the élite Muslim posts in India.
The Bhakti Movement became influenced by Islam, particularly by the Sufis, though Sufi mysticism remained unacceptable to the Bhakti leaders, whose aims were to spread the cult throughout all peoples and all castes.
KABIR (1440-1518)
NANAK (1469-1538)

Protestant Reformation Revolutionary movement with profound and far-reaching effects on social, political, economic and intellectual fields. Dissatisfaction with state of the Church, particularly increasing wealth and temporal power of clergy, resulted in anti-clerical and anti-papal opposition. Manifested specifically in the objection of Martin LUTHER (1483-1546) in 1517 to abuses of power in connection with the sale of indulgences. Luther was excommunicated for his heretical ideas, but his reformist principles took root with both peasants and German noblemen, who had begun to fear papal encroachments into temporal power.

Sikhism Indian religion, founded by the followers of NANAK (1469-1538), which rejected the mysticism, caste restrictions, idolatry and ritual of Hinduism.

First complete Talmud published, in Venice. 1520
Vaishnavism remained the dominant orthodox Hindu sect in the north, emphasizing the personal aspects of the Hindu religion.
Ramananda (14th cent.)
CHAITANYA (1486-1533)
Bhakti literature of the Vaishnava saints who propagated the Bhakti doctrine in the regional languages, especially in Bengali and later, Hindi.
Kabir (*c.* 1450-1518)
Chaitanya (1485-1527)
Shankaradeva (15th cent.)

Italian Renaissance comedy Court entertainment, critical of contemporary moral and political standards. Intrigue, satire and representations of everyday life, usually of the lower classes, were common characteristics. Lodovico ARIOSTO (1474-1533); Niccolò MACCHIAVELLI (1469-1527); Pietro ARETINO (1492-1556).

Lutheranism Martin LUTHER (1483-1546) stated that the Bible was the sole authority of faith. It emphasized importance of the sacraments, and stated that justification (salvation) was achieved by faith alone, not by priestly authority.
Calvinism Protestant theology preached by John CALVIN (1509-64) in France, based on same principles as Lutheranism. Additional concept of pre-destination: some souls are destined for salvation, some for damnation.
Zwinglianism Swiss reformation movement adhering to beliefs of Ulrich ZWINGLI (1484-1531). Differed from LUTHER (1483-1546) in the belief that communion was the commemoration of the death of JESUS CHRIST rather than a repetition of the sacrifice.

Act of Supremacy (1535) declared King of England supreme head of English Church. Monasteries dissolved, their property confiscated, abbots executed and buildings pillaged.
Anabaptists Swiss, German and Dutch sect which held that baptism should only be effected when the age of reason had been reached, and could thus be accompanied by confession of faith. Anabaptists denied the necessity of clergy, and were persecuted by Catholics and Protestants.
Capuchin Order A strict reformed order of Franciscan friars, who dressed in a brown habit with pointed hood and wore beards and went unshod in imitation of ST FRANCIS (1182-1226).

Reforming popes attempted to purify the Church, by campaigning against corruption and overhauling the financial organization. Inquisition revived.
PAUL III (r. 1534-49)
Paul IV (r. 1555-9)
Pius V (r. 1566-72)
Sixtus V (r. 1585-90)
Society of Jesus Roman Catholic religious order organized to support the Counter-reformation movement. Founded (1534) by St Ignatius LOYOLA (1491-1556), and answerable to the pope alone, its constitution was military. Jesuit novitiates were required to take the three vows of poverty, chastity and obedience, supplemented by a fourth vow to devote themselves to educating the young.
Jesuit drama Originally part of Jesuit educational curriculum. Written in Latin with Biblical themes.

Literature

Petrarchists Italian lyric poets, who attempted to imitate PETRARCH (1304-74), with elaborate imagery, full of complex and eccentric conceits and metaphors. Petrarch was to be the sole model for verse, BOCCACCIO (1313-75) for prose.
Il Cariteo (*c.* 1450-1515)
Antonio Tebaldeo (1463-1537)
Serafino d'Aquila (1466-1500)
Pietro BEMBO (1470-1547)

Humanist school drama Plays written by Protestant schoolmasters as an educational aid in Latin. Imitated SENECA (*c.* 54 BC-AD 39) and TERENCE (*c.* 190-159 BC).
Willem de Volder (1493-1568)
Joris van Laughveldt (1475-1558)
French farce Broad comic drama based on the *sotie*, a satirical form.
Pierre Gringore (*c.* 1475-*c.* 1538)

Rederijkers Member of Dutch Societies, or Chambers, devoted to producing verse, allegorical ballads and farces. The equivalent of the *Grands Rhétoriqueurs* in France.
Cornelis Everaert (1480-1556)
Anna Bijns (1493-1575)

Commedia dell'Arte Italian popular drama performed by troupes of masked actors. Represented stock characters such as Pulcinella, Pantalone, Arlecchino and Columbine, and spontaneously invented dialogue based on a general synopsis of the play.

Fables Revival in Germany of popular medieval genre, especially the animal epic, used for didactic purposes, often full of social satire.
Burkhard Waldis (*c.* 1490-1556)
Erasmus Alberus (*c.* 1500-53)

Pastoral In imitation of VIRGIL (70-19 BC) and Theocritus (*c.* 310-250 BC), poets and dramatists idealized the rustic life of shepherds and shepherdesses. Jacopo SANNAZARO (1456-1530); Sir Philip SIDNEY (1554-86); Torquato TASSO (1544-95); Gian Battista GUARINI (1538-1612); William SHAKESPEARE (1564-1616); John FLETCHER (1579-1625); John LYLY (1554-1606).

Persian, as the official language of the Moguls, supplanted Sanskrit as the literary language.
Amir Khusrav (d. 1325)
Faidi (d. 1590)
Urfi (d. 1590)
Nau'i (d. 1610)

Ottoman literature's classical period. Turks developed an individual style rather than using Persian models.
Tashlicali Yahya (d. 1573)
Ruhi of Baghdad (d. 1605)

Art

High Renaissance MICHELANGELO (1475-1564), LEONARDO (1452-1519) and RAPHAEL (1483-1520) completed the refinement of all that had gone earlier in the Renaissance, their work characterized by harmony, symmetry and their own individual geniuses.

Late Gothic art continued, mostly in Germany, completely untouched by Renaissance innovations. Characterized by extremely minute detail and pathos in religious paintings.
Bernt Notke (*c.* 1440-1509)
Matthias GRÜNEWALD (*c.* 1475-1528)

Patronage Italian commercial prosperity led to wealthy merchants' encouragement of the arts. In Florence the MEDICI family patronized many artists, while the popes commissioned work through competitions.

Venetian school Artists represented opulent splendour of Venice, with use of warm, subtle colours. More appeal to the senses than to the intellect. Giovanni BELLINI (*c.* 1430-1516); GIORGIONE (*c.* 1476-1510); Palma Vecchio (1480-1528); Sebastiano del Piombo (1485-1547); TITIAN (*c.* 1487-1576).
Japanese priests produced Buddhist subjects and landscapes. Sketches of blossom, birds and misty mountains were more hints of reality than direct representation. Mincho (1352-1431); Sotan (1413-81); Geiami (1431-85); SESSHU (1420-1506); Sesson (1504-89).
Wu school Chinese painters of the northern Ming used powerful brush strokes of delicate colour. A school of professionals founded by Shen Chou (1427-1509).
Wen Cheng-ming (1470-1559); T'ang Yin (1470-1523); Wen Chia (1501-83); Wen Po-jen (1502-75).

Portraiture The developing interest in man himself in Renaissance Europe revived the art of portraiture, particularly in the Netherlands. Portrayal of the physical features often showed an insight into the psychology of the sitter.
Albrecht DÜRER (1471-1528)
Hans HOLBEIN THE YOUNGER (1497-1543)
Jean CLOUET (1510-72)
Antonio Moro (1519-76)

Mannerism In reaction to the balanced perfection achieved by the High Renaissance, the mannerist painters, sculptors and architects created an elegant but complex style in which classical perspective and natural relief were exaggerated by deliberate distortion or elongation. In its later phase, mannerism expressed a new inventiveness and freedom to experiment.
MICHELANGELO (1475-1564)
RAPHAEL (1483-1520)
Baldassare PERUZZI (1481-1536)
Andrea del Sarto (1486-1530)
Jacopo SANSOVINO (1486-1570)
Jacopo Pontormo (1494-1553)
Francesco PARMIGIANINO (1503-40)
Agnolo BRONZINO (1503-72)
Andrea PALLADIO (1518-80)
Giorgio VASARI (1511-74)
EL GRECO (1541-1614)

Architecture

High Renaissance Period in Europe of harmony and balance, massiveness of scale and simplicity of form. Surface decoration was emphasized in high relief. Town planning, inspired by the work of Vitruvius (1st cent. BC) produced radiocentric fortress towns with low star-shaped bastions to withstand artillery. New cities conceived, the old replanned with wide avenues and groups of buildings arranged around a central *piazza*, particularly in southern Europe. Antonio Filarete (d. *c.* 1470); Leone Battista ALBERTI (1404-72); Bernardo ROSSELLINO (1409-64); Donato BRAMANTE (1444-1514); LEONARDO da Vinci (1452-1519); MICHELANGELO Buonarotti (1475-1564); RAPHAEL (1483-1520); Jacopo SANSOVINO (1486-1570); Andrea PALLADIO (1518-80); Vincenzo Scamozzi (1552-1616).

Domestic architecture assumed greater importance during the 15th century in Europe. Residential halls replaced the defensive castle keep.

The staircase developed as a stylistic feature in Spain where the square newel and the T-plan staircase were developed from Italian precedent. The imperial staircase, turning into two arms at an angle of 90° at the first floor, first used in the palace of the Escorial.
Enrique de Egas (d. *c.* 1534)
Diego de Siloē (*c.* 1495-1563)
Juan Bautista de Toledo (d. 1567)

English perpendicular style dominated church architecture of the later Gothic period. Characterized by vertical window tracery, fan vaults and square towers with detailed decoration.
English Tudor style. Large, asymmetrical country houses in patterned brickwork or half-timbering, with groups of bay or rectangular mullioned windows, gabled roofs and oddly-shaped chimneys.

Music

French chanson Music modelled on verse structure of the poetry. Short texts of 8 to 10 lines produced lively rhythmic songs in which the musical form was subordinated to the sense and rhyme scheme.
Claudin de Sermisy (*c.* 1490-1562)
Clement MAROT (1496-1544)

Hymns Reformation prompted much hymn-writing throughout countries affected. In Germany, Lutheran hymns and chorales were composed based mostly on traditional tunes. The *Genevan Psalter* of CALVIN (1509-64) gave metrical versions of the psalms.

Italian madrigal Secular chamber music was shaped by the emotional ideas expressed in the words. Madrigals usually set for unaccompanied voices, with chords used for punctuation. Subjects were often erotic, philosophic or descriptive.

Villanesca A light counterpart to the Italian madrigal, repeating the same melody over again for many verses. Dialects and street songs were used in music and many dance forms evolved.
The violin Great age of the manufacture of violins in Italy by the Amati, Guarneri and STRADIVARI families.

Frottola An Italian choral form founded on popular tradition. Usually sentimental or humorous.
Bartolomeo Trombonchino (d. *c.* 1535)
Marchetto Cara (d. *c.* 1530)
Strambotto A melancholy, single, 8-line, Italian stanza, with similar word treatment to the *frottola*.

Venetian school One of the outstanding Italian music centres. Tradition of polychoral works was founded by Adriano WILLAERT (1490-1562), a Fleming.
Jacques Arcadelt (*c.* 1514-*c.* 1570)
Cipriano de Rore (1516-65)

Technology

Trompe invented in Italy. Forced air into and out of a closed wind-chest by suction created by a water-chute. Replaced bellows.
The cross-staff invented; a navigational device for measuring the angle of elevation of a star or of the Sun.

Mining in Europe profited from improvements in haulage and ventilation machinery and suction pumps.
First road map of Europe appeared, in Germany (1511).
Bridge-building techniques in Europe developed with the improvement of pumping and pile-driving machinery and with the invention of the *caisson*, a watertight compartment for building on the river bed.

Wheel-lock invented to prime guns. Used in Holland and Spain.
Brass identified as a base form of copper.
Reverbatory furnace invented in Europe. Large weights of metal produced. Furnace acted by heat thrown down from a low roof. The piston-bellows was used in furnaces to produce a continuous blast.

New crops Coffee, tobacco, potatoes and maize introduced to Europe from the New World. Maize introduced into China.
Spoons used at table in Europe.
Leather furnishings became fashionable in Europe.

Glass-making began in the Americas—the first industry to be transplanted from Europe in the wake of the conquerors.
The treadle-wheel invented in Europe. Worked from a spinning-wheel by means of a crank-and-connecting rod.
Surveying advanced by the introduction of the principle of triangulation (1533).

Developments in chemistry Stannic chloride, ammonium sulphate, benzoic acid and succinic acid prepared; sulphur was refined and the means of dyeing copper sulphate by saltpetre discovered. Hieronymus Brunschwig (1450-*c.* 1512); Libavius (1540-1616).

Surgery was revolutionized by the appearance of *De Humani Corporis Fabrica*, a work on anatomy by VESALIUS (1514-64). A new school of surgery was founded, its leading surgeon Ambroise PARÉ (*c.* 1517-90).
De revolutionibus orbium coelestium (1543) by Nicolaus COPERNICUS (1473-1543) asserted that the planets move around the stationary Sun.
The screw-press used for the manufacture of coinage in France.

	1550	1560	1566	1575	1583	1591	1600
Principal Events	MARY TUDOR (1516-58) married (1554) PHILIP OF SPAIN (1527-98). **Rebellion** of WYATT (1521-54) against Queen MARY (1516-58) failed (1554). **Religious Peace of Augsburg** (1555) German rulers could choose Lutheranism or Catholicism for faith of the people. CHARLES V (1500-58) resigned Netherlands, Spain and Italy to PHILIP II (1527-98), and the Holy Roman Empire to FERDINAND I (1503-64). **Second Battle of Panipat** AKBAR (1542-1605), grandson of BABER (1483-1530), defeated Hindu resistance and by 1577 annexed the whole of northern India.	**French wars of religion** (1562-98) Civil war resulting from Catholic persecution of the minority Huguenots (French Protestants). **Malta attacked** by the Turks (1565). **Revolt in the Netherlands** (1567-73) against Spanish government of the Low Countries. Religious and economic causes. DUKE OF ALVA (1508-82), with 10,000 Spanish soldiers, imposed a reign of terror.	**Union of Lublin** Formal union of Poland and Lithuania (1569). **Battle of Lepanto** (1571) between Holy League and Turks. In spite of Holy League's victory, the Turks continued to attack western Mediterranean for the next 30 years. **Bornu**, in the central Sudan, at zenith of power under Idris III (c. 1580-c. 1617). **National unification** of Japan. Internal division brought to an end through the skilful strategy of ODA NOBUNAGA (1534-82) and use of newly-introduced firearms.	**Union of Utrecht** (1579) Northern Netherlands provinces formed the Dutch Republic, independent of Spain. SIR FRANCIS DRAKE (1540-96) circumnavigated world (1580). **Portugal conquered** by Spanish (1580). **Gregorian Calendar** (1582) substituted for the ancient Church calendar, which was inaccurate.	MARY, QUEEN OF SCOTS (1542-87) executed on the orders of ELIZABETH I (1533-1603). **Cadiz sacked** (1587) by SIR FRANCIS DRAKE (1540-96). **Spanish Armada** attempted to invade England (1588). **Mogul rule** extended to Kashmir, Baluchistan, Kandahar, Khandesh, parts of Ahmednagar and Orissa. Wise and impartial rule enabled AKBAR (1542-1605) to conciliate his subjects. **Japanese classes** more rigidly defined. Disarming of the peasantry imposed by Hideyoshi (1563-98).		**Songhoi Empire** destroyed by troops from Morocco aided by Portuguese and Spanish mercenaries (1591). **East Indies** explored by the Dutch (1595). **Invasion of Korea** by Hideyoshi (1563-98), who planned the conquest of China. In 1593 he was forced by a Ming army to withdraw to the south coast of Korea.
Religion	**Counter-reformation** Roman Catholic resistance movement in defence against attacks on doctrine made by Protestant reformers. The Council of Trent (1545-63) met to redefine the fundamental doctrines of the Catholic faith in the light of Protestant challenges, and to legislate for the removal of abuses. Succeeding laws were strictly enforced, and papal authority strengthened. ST FRANCIS XAVIER (1506-52) introduced Christianity to Japan. He left behind him two of his followers and a number of Japanese converts. Spread of Christian religion through conversion of the aristocracy and vassals.	**Presbyterianism** First established by CALVIN (1509-64), became the official religion of Scotland in 1560 under John KNOX (1505-72).	**Wars of Religion** between Catholics and Huguenots (Calvinist Protestants) in France. The Huguenots were granted toleration under the Edict of Nantes (1562-98). At the massacre of St Bartholomew (1572) 2000 Huguenots slain after Catholic plot against Protestant leaders. **Macao** became a centre for missionaries trying to reach the Chinese mainland.	**Arminianism** Protestant doctrine of Jacob Harmensen (1560-1609), Dutch theologian who opposed Calvinist idea of predestination. **Decline of Buddhism** in Japan ensued during the reign of NOBUNAGA (1534-82), who began a campaign to deprive the monasteries of political and military power.	**Puritanism** Protestant movement in England which wanted to purify Anglican worship by excluding all material not found in the Bible. Some Puritans objected to the Anglican liturgy, vestments and the episcopal organization. **Spanish Franciscans** in Japan came into conflict with the Jesuits already established.		MATHEO RICCI (1552-1610), a Jesuit, finally achieved entry into Peking and won toleration for the Jesuits. **Persecution of Christians** in Japan. Hideyoshi (1563-98) executed three Jesuits, six Franciscans, and 17 Japanese Christians. The remaining missionaries ordered to leave Japan. **Religious toleration** in India under Akbar (1542-1605).
Philosophy	**Political thought** throughout an age of international and civil strife was concerned with resolving the conflict between Christianity and politics. Theories of tyrannicide or limited monarchy disputed the traditional belief in the divine right of kings. MACHIAVELLI (1469-1527) believed that political beings were governed by their own, not specifically Christian, laws. Theodor BEZA (1519-1605); Juan de Mariana (1536-1624); Jean Bodin (1530-96).		**The Asht Chhap** '8 seals' poets produced devotional poetry in Hindi. Epic ballads about the great rulers of Indian history continued the ancient Hindi and Urdu heroic tradition.	**'Din Ilahi'**, or 'Divine Faith', of AKBAR (1542-1605) was an attempt to create a new universal religion, an eclectic cult influenced by Zoroastrianism and Sufism which also included elements of Hinduism and Islam. Confined to his own court circle during his lifetime, the cult collapsed after his death.	**The Tunglin group** of Chinese scholars sought a revival of ancient Confucianism. Concerned to reform a corrupt government, many were imprisoned and tortured for their ideas.	**Scientific method** The pattern of reasoning common to all empirical sciences, based upon repeated and repeatable observations. A theory can only be presumed true if results from a number of experiments consistently agree. First advocated by Francis BACON (1561-1626) and René DESCARTES (1596-1650), it was firmly established as a working principle by the middle of the 18th century.	
Literature	**Picaresque tale** Spanish satirical genre, which consisted of an episodic series of escapades. Mateo ALEMAN (c. 1547-c. 1614). Miguel de CERVANTES (1547-1616)	**Spanish and Portuguese epic poetry** flowered in the great age of exploration by these two countries. Luis de CAMOES (1524-80) Alonso de Ercilla y Zuniga (1533-94). **Printing in China** increased the circulation of books. Novels became the main vehicle of literary expression and travel diaries became popular. WU CHENG EN (c. 1510-80)		**Spanish drama** Secular plots, romantic and melodramatic. Stagecraft developed quickly, necessitated by constantly changing scenes. Religious plays performed on the feast of Corpus Christi by travelling groups on carts (autos sacramentales). Lope de VEGA (1562-1635); Fray Gabriel TELLEZ (c. 1584-1648); Pedro CALDERON DE LA BARCA (1600-81). **La Pléiade group** of French poets, who sought to revitalize the French poetic language with the alexandrine metre, sonnet form and new classically-based words. Jean Dorat (1508-88); Pontus de Thiard (1521-1605); Joachim du BELLAY (1522-60); Pierre de RONSARD (1524-85); Remy Belleau (1528-77); Etienne Jodelle (1532-73); Jean Antoine de Baif (1532-89).	**Elizabethan English** literature was the outstanding achievement of the Renaissance in England. Its plays were popular, robust, sometimes violent, full of classical allusions, allegory and rhetorical devices. Historical chronicles demonstrated national pride. The essay, a new literary form, discussed such individual subjects as religion, law, education, friendship and ambition. The writings of the University Wits began the tradition of English satire. The English Petrarchan sonnet arrived at its most accomplished form, embodying personal experience, imaginative fancy and intricate wordplay. Raphael Holinshed (d. c. 1580); Edmund SPENSER (1552-99); Richard Hakluyt (c. 1552-1616); Sir Philip SIDNEY (1554-86); John LYLY (1554-1606); Michael DRAYTON (1563-1631); Robert GREENE (1560-92); Christopher MARLOWE (1564-93); William SHAKESPEARE (1564-1616).		
Art	**Antwerp mannerists** Flemish painters, also called Romanists, who visited Italy and first introduced the Renaissance ideas to northern Europe, thus bringing about the transition from Gothic to Renaissance in the north. Quentin MASSYS (1464-1530) Mabuse (d. c. 1533) Barent van Orley (1493-1541) Lucas van LEYDEN (1494-1533)	**First school of Fontainebleau** Italian, French and Flemish artists under the patronage of FRANCIS I (1494-1547). A school of interior decoration, producing ornamental stuccowork and fresco decoration, on mythological and amorous themes. Giovanni Battista Rosso (1494-1540); Francesco Primaticcio (1504-70); Niccolo dell'Abate (c. 1512-71). **Che school** Southern Ming painters in China used ink rather than colour, and strove to achieve atmospheric effect. Tai Chin (15th cent.) Wu Wei (1459-1508) Lan Ying (1578-1660)	**Safavid carpet weaving** Genius of the Persian artists combined with the skill of the wool and silk weavers. Designs were usually central medallions surrounded by garden life.	**Second school of Fontainebleau** Similar decorative tradition to the first school, though less mannered and not so illustrious. Ambroise Dubois (1543-1614) Toussaint Dubreuil (1561-1602) Martin Freminet (1567-1619) **Spanish tenebrism** Artists produced striking contrasts of light and shade in naturalistic and still life painting. Pedro de Campana (1503-80); Francisco Ribalta (1565-1628); Jusepe de Ribera (1591-1652).	**Bolognese school** Influenced by RAPHAEL (1483-1520), the painters idealized nature along the lines of classical works. Lodovico Carracci (1555-1619) Annibale CARRACCI (1560-1609) Guido RENI (1575-1642)		**English miniaturists** An integral part of the courtly love tradition of the court of ELIZABETH I (1533-1603) of England. Vividly detailed, delicately coloured, full-length portraits, full of allusion and symbolism, painted on vellum or playing cards. Nicholas HILLYARDE (c. 1547-1619) Isaac Oliver (c. 1568-1617)
Architecture	**The Loire château school** Italian artists and architects imported into France by the French nobility, and working with French master builders, produced a new form of secular architecture, the château. Renaissance symmetry and decoration was imposed upon an essentially Gothic structure. Francesco Primaticcio (c. 1504-c. 1570)	**The French style of Henry II** (1519-59). A compromise between Italian architects and French masons produced a French mannerist style, characterized by the addition of sculpted figures and ornamentation to the façade, the carved wood and stucco work of the interiors and steeply pitched roofs. Sebastiano SERLIO (1475-1554) Pierre LESCOT (c. 1510-78)	**Dutch and Flemish strapwork** The series of flamboyant curves and classical devices of strapwork decoration, so called because it resembled plaited strips of leather, first evolved by the French and Italian designers of Fontainebleau, became popular throughout northern Europe. Cornelis Floris (c. 1515-75) Hendrik de Keyser (1565-1621)	**Spanish plateresque** (from platero, 'silversmith') A richly ornamental style of decoration of Moorish origin, often added to Gothic buildings. **School of Rome** Revival in popular devotional music, which encouraged prayer and accompanied religious rituals. Giovanni Pierluigi da PALESTRINA (1524-94); Jacobus Kerle (1532-91); Tomás de VITTORIA (c. 1548-1611); Felice Anerio (1560-1614).	**Japanese feudal castles** consisted of moated curtain walls encircling a palace. The walls, built with an inward slope to resist earthquakes, were guarded by wooden watch towers containing living quarters for the garrison.		**Elizabethan English** style. The great country mansions of the aristocracy, still in the traditional Gothic perpendicular style, showed elements of the early Italian Renaissance, the French château style of the Loire valley and the work of Flemish craftsmen.
Music	**Spanish religious music** Composers from Andalusia, Castile and Valencia wrote masses, motets and secular music, most of it characterized by serenity and lyricism. Cristóbal Morales (c. 1500-53) Pedro Fernandez de Castilleja (d. 1547) Francisco Guerrero (1528-99)	**European court dances** originated in folk dances, usually from Italy, such as the pavane and galliard. Other popular dances current in 16th century were the allemande, gavotte, bourrée, chaconne, courante, passacaglia and sarabande. From these grew the suite, lute music based on a series of dances.	**La Pléiade** Music was composed for the French literary movement to accompany their revival of the Greek choral lyric form. Claude Goudimel (1505-72) Claude le Jeune (c. 1527-1600) Guillaume Costeley (c. 1531-1606) Jacques Mauduit (1557-1627)	**English church music** Settings for service in simple counterpoint, with vernacular anthems. Anglican chants used in psalms and canticles. Similar to Gregorian chant but included descant setting to the psalms. Robert White (1510-74); William Mundy (1529-91); Thomas TALLIS (1505-85); William BYRD (c. 1542-1623); Thomas MORLEY (1557-1603); Orlando GIBBONS (1583-1625). **Camerata** Group of Florentine musicians who experimented with putting drama to music. Characters sang their parts while a chorus of shepherdesses or nymphs would explain the plot. Giulio Caccini (c. 1550-1618); Jacopo Peri (1561-1633); Ottavio Rinuccini (1562-1621), librettist.			**English madrigals** Derived from the fashionable Italian madrigal. Lighter in mood—usually settings of 12-line amorous and pastoral poems. William BYRD (c. 1542-1623) John DOWLAND (1563-1626) Orlando GIBBONS (1583-1625)
Technology	**Rotary fan** for ventilation first invented in Europe. **Rotary winnowing machine** invented in Europe. **Comparative anatomy** began with the study of fishes. Pierre Belon (1517-64) Guillaume Rondelet (1507-66)	**Market gardens** first cultivated in England. **Horses** commonly used for ploughing in Europe. **Scythe** supplanted sickle in European farming. **Botany** founded as a separate science. A herbal by Leonhart Fuchs (1501-66) illustrated and described over 400 plants. Otto Brunsfels (1488-1534) Jerome Bock (c. 1489-1554) Konrad von GESNER (1516-65) Andrea CESALPINO (1519-1603)	Gerhardus MERCATOR (1512-94) published his world map for navigators. **The nature of infection** and disease began to be investigated. Infectious diseases such as syphilis, typhus, measles were described and studied. Girolamo FRACASTORO (c. 1483-1553) Guillaume de Baillou (1538-1616) Thomas SYDENHAM (1624-89)	**The wagon-mill**, known previously in China, first used in Europe. **'Gnomonices'**, a summary of knowledge of sundials and chronometers, published by Christopher Clavius (1537-1612). **The Gregorian Calendar** introduced (1582) by Pope Gregory XIII (1502-85) based on astronomical data compiled during the 16th century. Introduced into Spain, Portugal and part of Italy.	**A stocking-frame**, based upon a series of movable hooks, invented in 1589 by William LEE (d. 1610) in England. **Decimal fractions** introduced into arithmetic (1585) by STEVIN (1548-1620), who also investigated the properties of the lever, the inclined plane and falling bodies. Francois VIÈTE (1540-1603) **A supernova** observed by Tycho BRAHE (1546-1601), who produced the first modern star catalogue based upon his own observations.		**Tables of meridinal parts** published in England for cartographers. **'Anatomy of the Horse'**, the first original work on the horse produced for over 1000 years, written by Carlo Ruini. **Physiology** studied. Metabolism, embryology and the blood vessels investigated. Sanctorius (1561-1636) Hieronymus FABRICIUS (1537-1619)

1600-1800

Four revolutions, vital to the present state of the world, occurred during this period. Three were political; one, the most fundamental, was industrial.

The Industrial Revolution

Centred first in the English textile industry, the process of mechanization transformed the lives of the men and women involved. The principal place of work shifted from cottage to factory. As the factories needed more hands, so towns grew up to house them and a long movement of people away from agriculture and the countryside began. Steam power, iron production and engineering advanced rapidly. Transport, by road and canal, and communications were systematically improved. The process of industrialization went on all over western Europe. Important pottery centres, such as those at Delft and Sèvres, were formed, making use of the improvements in furnaces for firing their ware.

A complex network of canals developed in England from 1780 onwards

For those who had to produce the goods, conditions in the expanding towns, often unplanned, frequently promoted disease, distress and an antagonism towards the owners of the industries who were rapidly growing more rich.

The political revolutions

In Britain, America and France, economic, religious and intellectual reasons combined to overthrow the ruling governments. The English Civil War began in Britain in 1642. On one side were parliamentary power, merchant wealth, puritanism and belief in the sovereignty of the individual conscience over institutional authority; on the other, the 'Divine Right' of kings and bishops to rule, and the attempts by CHARLES I (1600-49) to rule and raise money without the authority of Parliament. The King was executed and, after the death of CROMWELL (1599-1658),

the monarchy was restored under Parliament's authority.

Union batteries in Fort Brady, Virginia, USA, preparing for battle

By the 18th century, Britain's American colonies had established an identity of their own. British repression of moves towards more self-governance served to tighten the cohesion of the colonies. The war of 1775-83 bound them together still further, ensuring that independence would be granted to the United States as a whole.

The American success was an important spur to the revolutionaries in France. The widening gap between the extravagant taste for luxury of the king and his court, and the conditions and hopes of the people whose taxes provided his revenue encouraged them to demand a new constitution, and many feudal titles and privileges were abolished. The impetus generated, however, was too strong for moderate reform. The revolution became more extreme and turned bloody: hundreds followed LOUIS XVI (1754-93) to the guillotine.

The dying glow of the French monarchy, in the years leading to the Revolution

Philosophy

A visible link between the American and French revolutions was the work of Thomas PAINE (1737-1809). In 1776 his pamphlet *Common Sense* greatly influenced American public opinion in favour of independence. In 1791, his *Rights of Man* was published, in defence of the aims of

the French Revolution. Paine was one of a number of philosophers of the second half of the 18th century who considered as a whole the situation of man in society. Jeremy BENTHAM (1748-1832) and Adam SMITH (1723-90) respectively dealt with morals and welfare and the economic structure of society. They worked at a time when such men as LOCKE (1632-1704), BAYLE (1647-1706), BERKELEY (1685-1753), VOLTAIRE (1697-1778) and HUME (1711-76) delved into man's capacity for knowledge and reason and their application to his daily life. This intensive, critical examination of man was carried into other fields.

Art and Science

Artists, mathematicians, sculptors, physicists and chemists enquired into the conventions and assumptions that they had inherited. With the work of astronomers, concepts of the universe changed dramatically, throwing into doubt the theologically orientated notions of the mediaeval European world. Heat, magnetism and electricity began to be understood, and, largely through the work of NEWTON (1642-1727), the nature of light and the laws of motion were first explained. Many of the organs of the human body were accurately described for the first time.

Colonization

Such searching energy also found an outlet in territorial expansion through colonization. Spain and Portugal acquired vast areas of South America, destroying such ancient civilizations as the Incas in the process. The Portuguese moved into Ethiopia; Dutch, British and Prussians began to occupy parts of Africa. Trade wars between the European nations were common, and the British and the French competed throughout this period for commerce and territory in India.

Such incursions were made possible by the gradual dismemberment of the Mogul Empire, which broke up after its last great leader, AURANGZEB (1638-1707). The Mongols were eventually driven out of China, whose population was growing rapidly, and who made her own territorial acquisitions by invading Tibet. Farther east, Japan entered a period of strict isolation and political conservatism under the Tokugawa shogunate. Economic decline, internal debt, famine and natural disasters gave rise to fierce riots and social upheaval in 1787.

Principal Events

1600–1605
East India Company granted charter (1600) by Queen ELIZABETH I (1543-1603).
JAMES I of England (James VI of Scotland) (1566-1625) acceded to English throne (1603) after death of ELIZABETH I (1543-1603).
Tomsk founded by the Russians as they began settlement of Siberia (1604).
Persian holy war against the Ottoman Turks (1602-18).
Tokugawa IEYASU (1542-1616) won the battle of Sekigahara; appointed shogun in 1603. Established his headquarters at Edo, later Tokyo.

1605–1610
Gunpowder plot by conspirators to blow up English Houses of Parliament (1605). Guy FAWKES (1570-1606) arrested.
Willem Janszoon (fl. c. 1600) sighted Australia (1606).
Exploration by Henry HUDSON (d. 1611). Discovered Eastern Greenland, Jan Mayen Island and the Hudson River (1607-11)
Quebec founded (1608) by Champlain (c. 1567-1635).
Jamestown, Virginia, founded (1608) by John SMITH (1580-1631).
Benedict de Goez travelled overland from India to China.

1610–1615
Twelve Years' Truce (1609-21) between Spain and the Netherlands. Dutch independence secured.
Russian Cossacks reached north coast of Siberia (1610).
War of Kalmar between Denmark and Sweden (1611).
Romanov dynasty founded in Russia (1613). Lasted until 1917.
Persians recaptured Kandahar during the reign of JAHANGIR (1569-1627) in India.
Western Australia discovered by Dutch (1613-27). Called New Holland.

1615–1620
Fur trading posts founded by the Dutch at mouth of Hudson River (1617).
First American parliament convened in Jamestown, Virginia (1619).
Thirty Years' War began (1618) through Bohemia's claim for independence. Led to general conflict in Europe, pursued by the Protestant CHRISTIAN IV of Denmark (1585-1648) and Albrecht von WALLENSTEIN (1583-1634), Catholic leader of the Holy Roman Empire.
Paul Imbert (fl. c. 1610) of France reached Timbuktu (1618).
Northern Chinese tribes organized into a military force. They later adopted the name 'Manchu' (1652).
Dutch founded Batavia, a post in Formosa (1619).
Spanish and Dutch traders in Japan, encouraged by IEYASU.

1620–1625
Pilgrim Fathers arrived from Plymouth, England, at Cape Cod, Massachusetts, in the *Mayflower*. Founded New Plymouth (1620).
Manchu capital established in China at Liaoyang, after the Ming were expelled from the Liao Basin (1621).
Tokugawa rule consolidated by Iemitsu (1604-51) who adopted a policy of national isolation. Foreigners left or were driven from Japan.

1625–1630
Barbados occupied by English (1627).
Petition of Right granted in English Parliament (1628). Against martial law, arbitrary imprisonment and taxation, billeting of soldiers in private houses.
Siege of La Rochelle (1627) Huguenots besieged by forces of RICHELIEU (1585-1642). Despite English support, Huguenots surrendered, losing what political power they had. Gained religious toleration (1629).
Protestant peasants' revolt in Austria (1626-8).

Religion

1600–1605
Socinianism Italian form of unitarianism proposed by Faustus Socinus (1539-1604). The Scriptures were accepted but the authority of the pope and Church were denied.
Spanish missionaries to eastern Japan were well received by IEYASU (1542-1616) for the economic benefits of trade with Spain, until Spanish merchants ousted the missionaries from their mercantile role.

1605–1610
Dominicans and Franciscans entered Fukien, China, from the Philippines, but Peking remained a Jesuit preserve. The Jesuits began their policy of aiming at the conversion of the aristocracy.

1610–1615
Authorized Version of the Bible issued in England (1611).
Japanese embassy to Spain and the Pope (1613).

1615–1620
Arminians Dutch sect who attacked the Calvinist doctrine of predestination. Condemned at the General Synod of Calvinists (1619).
Jesuit missionaries deported from China to Macao (1616) after being suspected of subversive aims.

1620–1625
Lazarists Order of priests founded (1624) by ST VINCENT de Paul (1581-1660). They evangelized in isolated rural districts of France and trained the priesthood.
Suppression of Christianity in Japan finally achieved by Iemitsu (1604-51).

1625–1630
Jesuit missions to Canadian Indians (1625). Most successful with the Hurons, who were peaceful, settled tribes.

Philosophy

Scientific movement Deductive reasoning had become established as the basis for philosophical enquiry by the early 1600s. The importance of mathematical and scientific discoveries during the Renaissance resulted in emphasis upon reason, based on mathematical models, to investigate natural rather than supernatural phenomena: philosophical thought, like mathematics, should start from axioms which are independent of subjective experience. Nicolas COPERNICUS (1473-1543); Niccolò MACHIAVELLI (1469-1527); Galileo GALILEI (1564-1642); Johannes KEPLER (1571-1630); Baruch SPINOZA (1632-77); Sir Isaac NEWTON (1642-1727).

Literature

1600–1605
English Revenge Tragedy focused on a character who is affected by the murder of a member of his family and moved to revenge. The theme enabled the playwright to explore psychological motives and moral problems, as well as dramatic action.
George Chapman (1560-1634)
Thomas KYD (1558-94)
Cyril Tourneur (1575-1626)

1605–1610
Gongorism Spanish literary style characterized by an emphasis on Latinisms, allusions to obscure classical mythology, and a profusion of hyperbole and metaphors.
Luis de GONGORA Y ARGOTE (1561-1627)
Pedro Soto de Rojas (1585-1658)
Gabriel Bocángel (1608-58)

1610–1615
Marathi literature of the 17th and 18th centuries consisted of erotic lyrics, war ballads and historical and moral tales.
Sivaji (1627-80)
Tukaram (1608-49)

1615–1620
Dutch school Literature reflected the art of the period with realistic genre work. Dutch lyrical poetry influenced German poetical revival.
Pieter Cornelisz (1581-1647)
Gerbrand Brederode (1585-1618)
Joost van den VONDEL (1587-1679)

1620–1625
Middle Hindi literature reached its heights in the reigns of Jahangir and Shah Jahan.
Raja Birbal (16th cent.)
Bihari-Lal (17th cent.)
Tulsi Das (1534-1623)

Art

1600–1605
Caravaggisti Painters in Italy, northern Europe and Spain who were influenced by the *chiaroscuro* techniques of CARAVAGGIO (1573-1610). Attempted to represent psychological reality by the dramatic use of light and shade.
Jusepe de RIBERA (1591-1652)
Moise Valentin (c. 1591-1632)
Georges de LA TOUR (1593-1652)

1605–1610
Utrecht school Dutch, influenced by CARAVAGGIO (1573-1610). Religious paintings and genre scenes showed dramatic contrasts between brilliantly lit and very dark areas, and the effect of candlelight. Influenced HALS (c. 1580-1666), REMBRANDT (1606-69) and VERMEER (1632-75).
Abraham Bloemaert (1564-1651)
Hendrick TERBRUGGEN (1588-1629)

1610–1615
Genre painting Unidealized scenes of peasants at work or leisure. Interiors, particularly tavern scenes, were popular, mainly in Holland.
Pieter BRUEGEL (c. 1525-69)
Jacob JORDAENS (1593-1678)
Adriaen BROUWER (1605-38)
Adriaen van Ostade (1610-85)
Gerard TERBORCH (1617-81)
Pieter de HOOCH (1629-c. 1684)

1615–1625
Baroque artists and architects broke away from the well-defined conventions of classicism. The emotional appeal of subject matter was expressed through dramatic, grandiose, exuberant, opulent work. Influenced by the CARRACCI school, painting became more ornate, theatrical and full of motifs. The architecture often employed tricks of perspective and other optical illusions to produce a symbolic and transcendental style, expressive of the continuing forces of the Counter-Reformation. Characterized by vitality of design and ornate detail. The word 'baroque' was originally a pejorative term signifying a false, decadent and over-emphatic style.
Giacomo VIGNOLA (1507-73); Carlo MADERNO (1556-1629); Guido RENI (1575-1642); Pieter Paul RUBENS (1577-1640); Francesco Albani (1578-1660); Francesco Barbieri (1591-1666); Pietro da CORTONA (1596-1669); Gianlorenzo BERNINI (1598-1680); Diego VELAZQUEZ (1599-1660); Francesco BORROMINI (1599-1667); Martino Longhi the Younger (1602-60); Carlo Rainaldi (1611-91); Guarino Guarini (1624-83); Carlo Fontana (1634-1714); Andrea Pozzo (1642-1709).

1625–1630
Mogul painting in India. Meticulously detailed court painting—palaces, hunting and battle scenes and many portraits, usually painted in profile. Showed Jesuit influence in method.
Rajput painting was court art produced in Hindu States. Varying schools, mostly portraiture, which popularized the cults of the Hindu religion.

Architecture

1620–1625
Mogul architecture The use of native Indian traditions and resources produced monumental Islamic architecture, which combined aesthetic use of decorative stone with intricate and precise carving.

1625–1630
Rajput palaces in India: enormous constructions guarded by many gateways, monumental in style but less ornamental than the contemporary Muslim palaces. Though strongly fortified, the palaces were often set among delicate gardens and lakes.

Music

1600–1605
Basso continuo A 'continuous bass' accompaniment on the keyboard, the first sophisticated harmony. Composer wrote bass and melody lines, but two inner parts were left to the virtuosity of the continuo performer, who had to improvise the chords.
Lodovico Viadana (1564-1627)

1605–1615
Roman opera Earliest opera, centred in Rome after initial Florentine experiments. Distinguished between the emotional arias, and the narrative function of recitative. Themes usually religious or moralistic. Stage settings lavish, often increased by mechanical aids. Stefano Landi (c. 1590-c. 1655); Domenico Mazzocchi (1592-1665); Luigi Rossi (1598-1653).

1615–1620
English masque Court entertainment. Elaborate series of dances, songs and dialogue, lavishly staged, representing mythological and allegorical themes.
Thomas CAMPION (1567-1619)
Ben JONSON (1572-1637)
Inigo JONES (1573-1652)
Henry Lawes (1596-1662)
William Lawes (1602-45)

1620–1625
French court ballet Similar to the English masque. Began with the chorus, followed by dances and mime, concluded by a grand ballet in which the king and his courtiers participated.
Pierre Guedron (1565-1621)
Antoine Boesset (1585-1643)

Technology

1600–1605
De magnete, a study of electricity and magnetism, published by William GILBERT (1544-1603), who also discovered that the Earth is a magnet.
First telescopes built by the Dutch. Astronomical use made public by the discoveries of GALILEO (1564-1642).
Cannon-boring improved the resilience and effect of cannon after 1603.
Heels on shoes became common in Europe.

1605–1610
Elliptical motion of the planets discovered by Johannes KEPLER (1571-1630). His *Tabulae Rudolfinae* made possible the calculation of future positions of the planets.
First compound microscope thought to have been built at this time, by the Dutch.
Improved draw-loom for figured fabrics produced in Lyons, an important step in the mechanization of the weaving process.

1610–1615
Logarithms introduced into mathematics by John Napier (1550-1617).
Converting bar iron into steel, using coal—method discovered in England.
Sulphuric acid produced in Germany by dry distillation of iron or copper sulphate.
Ribbon-loom invented in Danzig; could produce as many as six narrow weaves at one time.
Tea first shipped to Europe by the Dutch East India Co.

1615–1620
Coal-burning glass furnace developed in England after 1615, when wood-fired glass furnaces were banned. The use of coal as a power source encouraged in England as a result of deforestation.
Hydrochloric acid prepared by J. R. Glauber (c. 1603-68) in Germany, who distilled wood to produce tar, acid and spirit.
Fire engines, consisting of a portable cylinder and piston pump, used in Nuremberg.

1620–1625
Medieval German furnaces converted into blast furnaces for smelting iron ore, by the use of water power.
More steel was produced in the works on English, Scottish and Welsh coalfields by the mid-17th century than in the rest of the world.
Spanish explorers in South America used rubber to waterproof soldiers' cloaks.

1625–1630
Circulation of the blood discovered and explained by William HARVEY (1578-1657).
Flintlock for rifles invented in France.
Improvements in printing in Holland included devices to prevent movement of type at the moment of impression. W. J. Blaeuw (1571-1638)
Chinese dynastic calendar reformed (1630) by Johann Schall von Bell (1591-1666).

364 1630 1635 1640 1645 1650 1655 1660

Principal Events

Great Migration More than 16,000 settlers arrived at the Massachusetts Bay Colony (1630-42).
Thirty Years' War in Sweden. GUSTAVUS ADOLPHUS (1594-1632) entered the war to protect Protestants. Capture and massacre of Magdeburg (1631).
Treaty of Polianov 'Eternal peace' concluded between Russia and Poland (1634).
Tokugawa period in Japan. The standard of living increased and the expansion of industry and commerce resulted in the growth of a merchant class. Strict military control over the provinces (1600-1868).

Russian explorers reached Pacific coast, having crossed Siberia (1637).
Emperor Shah Jahan, in attempting to recapture Kandahar, and in his expeditions against Balkh and Badakhstan, led the Mogul Empire into financial crisis.
First English traders arrived in Macao (1637).
Solemn League and Covenant signed (1638) in defence of the Scottish reformed religion, against Scots Church policy of CHARLES I (1600-49).
Scottish Civil War over the introduction of the new Liturgy (1639).

Civil War in England (1642-6). Royalists, known as Cavaliers, supported CHARLES I (1600-49). Consisted mainly of northern and west-central English, the Anglican clergy and peasants. Opposed by Roundheads, parliamentarians led by CROMWELL (1599-1658), mainly from southeast England. Cromwell's victories at Marston Moor (1644) and Naseby (1645) led to the establishment of a Commonwealth in Britain, the abolition of the King's title and the House of Lords, and the execution of Charles

Revolts in Portugal and Catalonia against Spain (1640).
Fronde Revolutionary political party in France which revolted against the absolute power of the crown.
Malacca captured by the Dutch from the Portuguese (1641).
TASMAN (1603-59) discovered Tasmania and New Zealand (1642).

Treaty of Westphalia (1648) ended the Thirty Years' War and concluded peace between Spain and the Netherlands.
Serfdom completely established in Russia under new Code of Laws (1649).

Ch'ing dynasty began, under which the Chinese Empire reached its greatest geographical extent. It achieved an unprecedented level of material prosperity and created the most advanced social institutions of its time in the world (1644-1912).

First Navigation Act (1651) resulted in monopoly for English shipping in foreign trade.
CROMWELL (1599-1658) named Lord Protector in Britain. Ruthlessly suppressed Irish rebellion (1652).
Anglo-Dutch war (1652-4) over the Navigation Act. Act was recognized by Dutch in Peace of Westminster.
Capetown founded by the Dutch (1652).
Brazil taken from Dutch by Portuguese (1654).

Spanish war with England over Jamaica, raided by England (1656).
First Villmergen war In Switzerland, Protestant cantons of Bern and Zurich fought against Catholic cantons (1656).
Candian War between Venice and Turkey arose from Turkish designs on Crete. Initial victory for Venice in Dardanelles, but eventual surrender of Candia to Turks (1645-69).
Treaty of the Pyrenees (1659) between France and Spain settled their mutual borders.

Religion

Laudists followed the theories of Archbishop LAUD (1573-1645), stating that the Roman Catholic and the Anglican Churches were merely two sides of the same Church.
Oberammergau Passion Play first performed (1634) as an act of thanksgiving for the passing of the plague.

Harvard University founded by Puritans to provide education for the ministry (1636).
Shimabara uprising of Christian peasants in Japan. 37,000 peasants who defended themselves against religious and economic persecution were killed (1637-8). Portuguese traders, suspected of complicity, expelled.

Sulpicians and Eudists French orders founded in 1642 and 1643 to educate the clergy. Emphasis on piety rather than learning.
Jansenists French sect who followed tenets of Cornelius JANSEN (1585-1638), who maintained that the teaching of ST AUGUSTINE (354-430) on the subjects of predestination, free-will and grace were directly opposed to Jesuit teaching.

Congregationalists Protestant sect, originating as Brownists. Based on principle of autonomy of each local church, or congregation, to choose its own preachers and ministers. Denied supremacy of the crown.

Quakers (Society of Friends) Protestant movement founded by George FOX (1624-91), who taught that truth comes from the inner light of the Holy Ghost. All believers would be guided to the way of truth without the necessity for ritual, sacraments or the priesthood.

Gallicanism Theory dating from the Pragmatic Sanction of Bourges (1438), which supported the autonomy of the French National Church and its independence from Rome. Its practice intensified under LOUIS XIV (1638-1715), who used the Church to further his political ambitions.

Philosophy

Confucian philosophy in Japan entered a period of growth and popularity during the Tokugawa period, when it was used as a stabilizing force in politics and society by the Tokugawa shoguns.

Rationalism Followers of René DESCARTES (1596-1650), considering sense perception to be incapable of the complete definition of objects, credited Man's reason alone with a thorough knowledge of reality, gained from an analytic progression from one clear idea to another. Material phenomena were held to be of a mechanical nature and hence open to complete understanding. Rationalists believed mind and matter to be fundamentally different entities. Thomas HOBBES (1588-1679); Baruch SPINOZA (1632-1677); Nicolas MALEBRANCHE (1638-1715); Gottfried LEIBNIZ (1646-1716).

Reaction against orthodoxy of the Chinese Ming dynasty took place after the Manchu conquest, as a group of Chinese philosophers sought explanations for the downfall of the Ming dynasty.
Huang Tsung-hsi (1610-95)
Ku Yen-wu (1613-82)
Wang Fu-chih (1619-92)
Yen Yuan (1635-1704)

Literature

The Tokugawa period in Japan produced a reawakening of interest in literature and writers, no longer drawn from the noble or priestly class, included warriors and merchants. The use of printing and more widely available education meant that literature reached a new, larger public.

Cavalier poets Writers of English lyrical poetry mainly at the court of CHARLES I (1600-49). Influenced by Ben JONSON (1572-1637).
Robert HERRICK (1591-1674)
Thomas Carew (*c.* 1598-*c.* 1639)
Sir John Suckling (1609-42)
Richard LOVELACE (1618-58)

Seicentismo Period of Italian literature when freedom of thought and speech was restricted by Spanish rule. Poets resorted to marinism, named after Giambattista MARINO (1569-1625), a literary style characterized by elaboration and ornate conceits, puns and forced artificial images.
Gabriello Chiabrera (1552-1638)
Fulvio Testi (1593-1646)
Francesco Redi (1626-98)

Fables of LA FONTAINE (1621-95). Collections of epigrammatic tales of animals, in witty verse.

German poetry strongly influenced by Lutheranism. Much mystical and lyrical poetry, similar to English metaphysical poets.
Paul Fleming (1609-40)
Andreas Gryphius (1616-64)
Hofmann von Hofmannswaldau (1617-79)
Angelus Silesius (1624-77)

Art

Bambocciata painters Group of painters of genre scenes of low life and peasants, probably named after Pieter van Laer (1592-1642), called Il Bamboccio. Paintings achieved great popularity in Italy, where genre paintings were often disregarded. Michelangelo Cerquozzi (1602-60)
Adriaen BROUWER (1605-38)
Adriaen van Ostade (1610-85)
Jan STEEN (1626-79)

French classicism Movement directed against mannerism, and the realism of CARAVAGGIO (1573-1610). Aimed instead to restore the classical ideals of the High Renaissance. Works characterized by clarity and balanced composition. The style was standardized by the founding of the Royal Academy of Painting and Sculpture in 1648. Nicolas POUSSIN (1594-1665); CLAUDE Lorraine (1600-1682); Philippe de CHAMPAIGNE (1602-74); Laurent de la Hyre (1606-56); Eustache Le Sueur (1616-55).
Flemish portraiture, influenced first by RUBENS (1577-1640) and then Van DYCK (1599-1641), characterized by boldness of brushwork, and a detailed accuracy not seen before in portraits. Caspar de Crayer (*c.* 1584-1669); Cornelis de Vos (1585-1651).

Animal painters Numerous artists painting portraits of animals in a style similar to that of still life.
Sinibaldo Scorza (1558-1631)
Franz Snyders (1579-1657)
Paul de Vos (1590-1678)
Jan Fyt (1611-61)
Paulus Potter (1625-54)
François Desportes (1661-1743)

Dutch marine painting The vogue for representation of marine life reflected the maritime background of the Dutch merchants and explorers.
Hendrik Vroom (1566-1640)
Jan Porcellis (1601-53)
Jan van Cappelle (1626-79)
Ludolf Bakhuysen (1631-1708)
Willem van de VELDE (1633-1707)

Individualists Group of Chinese painters, mostly Buddhist monks, who rejected the formal conventions of the ruling Manchus by painting naturalistic landscapes and nature studies.
Hung-jen (1610-63)
Shih-Ch'ih (1612-80)
Pa-ta Shan-jen (1626-*c.* 1705)
Shih-t'ao (1630-1707)

Architecture

French classicism took as its model the Italian Baroque of VIGNOLA (1507-73). Achieved a monumental but elegant and restrained style, a fusion of classical baroque and national French style.
Salomon de BROSSE (1571-1626)
François MANSART (1598-1666)
Jacques LEMERCIER (*c.* 1584-1654)

Temple architecture of southern India culminated in the development of the temple court. A series of rectangular courtyards guarded the central temple, the entrance to each court guarded by an ornate and successively more colossal gateway. The enclosed courts were later lined with figure-sculpted pillars.

The Japanese house evolved during the Tokugawa period. Of one or two stories, built of wood and paper and roofed in tiles or thatch. Rooms were built up of modules the size of a sleeping mat. Removable sliding screens divided the house into rooms. The entire dwelling, including its landscaped gardens, was enclosed by wooden shutters.

Formal French gardens Symmetrical pathways, avenues and flower beds laid out in the gardens of royal palaces. Terraces, canals and aviaries were common features.
Claude Mollet (1563-1650)
André le Nôtre (1613-1700)

North European Palladianism Inigo JONES (1573-1652) brought a sober and refined version of the Italian Baroque to English towns. Palladian classicism proved adaptable and acceptable to the Protestant countries of northern Europe, where the complexity and emotional appeal of the Roman Catholic baroque was rejected in favour of a more intellectual and restrained spirituality. Pieter Post (1608-69); Elias Holl (1573-1646); Jacob van CAMPEN (1595-1657); Philip Davidsz Vingboons (1607-78).

Ch'ing architecture in China, though prolific, showed little originality or imagination. Monumental and grandiose in style, Ch'ing buildings were boldly decorated with carvings and paintings. The Manchus extended and restored the summer palaces of the emperors.

Music

Brass instruments were first introduced to add colour to hunting scenes, and gradually became accepted as integral parts of the orchestra.

Venetian opera First public opera house opened (1637) and became a common meeting place for all classes. The beauty of the human voice emphasized in maximum use of the aria, and increasing use of *castrati* (male sopranos).
Francesco Cavalli (*c.* 1602-76)
Carlo Pallavicino (1630-88)

Oratorio developed along the same lines as early opera, and was almost indistinguishable except that oratorios had no scenery.
Giacomo Carissimi (*c.* 1604-74)
Bernardo Pasquini (1637-1710)
Alessandro SCARLATTI (1659-1725)

Technology

Copernican system of planetary motion established by GALILEO (1564-1642) as superior to the Ptolemaic.
Principles of falling bodies and of projectile motion propagated by GALILEO (1564-1642).
New illustration techniques, developed in Germany, included 'dry-point' engraving with an iron needle; 'pure' etching, with acid; and the 'mezzotint', using steel engraving tools. L. von Siegen (1609-*c.* 1670).

Analytic geometry developed by René DESCARTES (1596-1650) and Pierre de FERMAT (*c.* 1601-1665).
Paraboloid lens devised by DESCARTES (1596-1650), to avoid aberration of shape in objects observed through a lens.
Lens-grinding machines invented and continually improved in Europe.
Strength of materials examined and theory formulated by GALILEO (1564-1642) after studying the bending of a beam.

Principia philosophiae, by DESCARTES (1596-1650), explained his vortex theory of planetary motion.
Adding machines capable of carrying numbers devised by Blaise PASCAL (1623-1662). A machine able to multiply by repeated additions invented by Gottfried LEIBNIZ (1646-1716).
Coffee first reached Europe.
Semi-metal arsenic, known to the ancient Egyptians (arsenic-bronze), prepared in Europe.

Crops The practice of alternating the planting of cereal crops with roots and green crops originated in the Low Countries. Turnips from the Netherlands and clover from Spain introduced into England.
Jethro TULL (1674-1741)
Charles Townshend (1674-1738)
Evangelista TORRICELLI (1608-47) predicted that the pressure of the atmosphere would fall with increasing altitude. Confirmed experimentally in 1647.

Physiology of respiration and the chemistry of air investigated.
Edmé Mariotte (*c.* 1620-84)
Johann BECHER (1635-82)
Robert BOYLE (1627-91)
Marcello MALPIGHI (1628-94)
Richard Lower (1631-91)
Robert HOOKE (1635-1703)
John Mayow (1640-79)
Human body began to be explained mechanically by philosophers and scientists such as DESCARTES (1596-1650) and BORELLI (1608-79).
Moulded lead shot for cannon produced in Europe by 1650.

Arithmetica Infinitorum (1655), published by John WALLIS (1616-1703), included studies of infinite series and products.
Saturn's rings discovered by HUYGENS (1629-1695).
Science of geology, developing from the work of AGRICOLA (1494-1555), began with investigations into the structure, origin and age of rocks.
Nicolaus STENO (1638-1686)
John Strachey (1671-1743)
Jean Guittard (1715-1786)
Abraham WERNER (1750-1817)

1660 1665 1670 1675 1680 1685 1690 365

Principal Events

British monarchy restored (1660) with the coronation of CHARLES II (1630-85).
Sweden signed treaties (1660-1) with Poland, Denmark and Russia giving Russia all Baltic shores.
English acquired Bombay and embarked upon a long period of rivalry with the French for economic power in India.
AURANGZEB (1618-1707) became Emperor of India after disputing the succession in civil war with his three brothers. Political and religious intolerance against the Hindus characterized his reign.

Great Plague and Fire of London (1665-6).
Second Anglo-Dutch war (1665-7). Holland supported by French and Danes after British had seized New Amsterdam, America (1664), and Dutch towns on African coast.
War of Devolution (1667-8) LOUIS XIV (1638-1715) attacked Spanish possessions in Netherlands, claiming them as the rightful inheritance of his wife, daughter of PHILIP IV of Spain (1605-65). Prevented by Triple Alliance between England, Holland and Sweden (1668).
Portuguese independence recognized by Spain (1668).

Hudson's Bay Company granted royal charter (1670) and gained trade monopoly in Hudson Bay.
Treaty of Dover (1670) Secret Treaty between CHARLES II (1630-88) and LOUIS XIV (1638-1715).
Third Anglo-Dutch war After the Treaty of Dover, England joined by France against Holland (1672-4).
Turkish wars with Poland over the Ukraine, resulting from Cossack and Tatar border raids (1672-6).
Koxinga (Cheng Cheng-kung), a Chinese pirate, opposed the Manchus and took possession of Formosa (1645-83).

Holy Roman Empire declared war against France (1674), in defence of the Dutch, supported by Spain and the Pope. Ended by Treaties of Nijmegen (1678-9).
American Indian attacks on settlers in New England (1675-6).
Popish Plot (1678) Conspiracy in England by Titus OATES (1649-1705) caused persecution of Catholics.
Habeas Corpus Act (1679) Judges in England obliged to produce prisoner in court to show cause for his imprisonment.

French colony established from Quebec to mouth of Mississippi (1680-2).
Sweden became an absolute monarchy (1680) under Charles XI (1655-97).
Royal Charter of Pennsylvania granted (1681).
Vienna besieged by the Turks. Relieved by Germans and Poles (1683).
Rise of Japanese merchants, who held the wealth of the nation and to whom the warrior class had gradually become indebted.

Dominion of New England formed (1686).
Conquest of the Morea (1684-5) Venice, Austria and Poland united against the Turks. Venetians took the Morea and Athens in 1687.
'Glorious Revolution' (1688) deposed James II (1633-1701) and placed WILLIAM of Orange (1650-1702) on the British throne. Bill of Rights (1689) established a constitutional monarchy and barred Catholic succession to the throne.
Treaty of Nerchinsk (1689) between China and Russia: the boundary was defined and commerce formally established.

Religion

Dissenters After the English Act of Uniformity and the introduction of the new Prayer Book, non-conformist Protestants were banned from public performance of their own forms of worship.

Schism of the Old Believers resulted from changes in Russian orthodox ritual which brought it more in line with the Greek orthodox service. Much dissent and subsequent persecution of dissenters *(raskolniks)*.

Prohibition of Hinduism in India by AURANGZEB (1618-1707), who was an orthodox Sunni Muslim. Hindu temples were destroyed, and a tax on non-Muslims imposed. Jat rebellions and Hindu uprisings followed (1659-1660).

Pietism German movement to revitalize the Church after the Thirty Years' War. Practical approach to Christian tenets and less dependence on pomp and ceremony.
P. J. SPENER (1635-1705)
Count von Zinzendorf (1700-60)

Cambridge Platonists were teachers from Cambridge University who believed life to be unintelligible without belief in God, and thought it possible to reconcile reason and mystical faith. Advocated an escape from theological abstractions, and morality based on reason rather than religious dogma.
Benjamin Whichcote (1609-83)
Henry More (1614-87)
John Smith (1616-52)
Ralph Cudworth (1617-88)
Nathaniel Culverwel (1618-51)
Joseph Glanvill (1636-80)

Quietists Ascetic and mystical French sect, following the teaching of Miguel de Molinos (1640-*c.* 1697), who maintained that man should be continuously close to God through contemplative devotion, and unaware of outward senses. Formal religious expression disregarded.
William PENN (1644-1718) founded Pennsylvania (1681), where all religions were granted toleration.

Declaration of Indulgence granted freedom of worship to all denominations in England (1687).
Edict of Nantes in France revoked (1685). All religions except Roman Catholicism forbidden. Emigration was prohibited, though many Huguenots fled to England, Holland, America and South Africa.

Philosophy

Economic nationalism, the doctrine of the mercantile system, evolved among the post-feudal European monarchies during the period of influx of precious metals from the New World. Tending to equate money with wealth, the mercantilists emphasized the desirability of a favourable balance of trade, and supported state intervention to achieve and maintain it. Oliver CROMWELL (1599-1658); Jean Baptiste COLBERT (1619-83); Sir Josiah Child (1630-99); Charles Davenant (1656-1714); FREDERICK THE GREAT (1712-86).

Suika Shinto, in Japan, founded by Yamazaki Ansai (d. 1682). Reconciled two ancient Shinto deities with the Neo-Confucianist 'Supreme Ultimate'. Emphasized the importance of Confucian values—honesty and respect for the emperor.

Confucian Shinto Confucian scholars in Japan aided the revival of Shinto: Hayashi Razan (1583-1657) argued that Shinto, being the 'way' of the ruler, was also the 'way' of Confucianism. Kumazawa Bonza (1619-91)

Literature

French classical drama Heroic drama influenced by the clarity of form and strict regularity of the ancient classics. Adhered strongly to rules of the three unities—time, place and action.
Pierre CORNEILLE (1606-84)
MOLIÈRE (1622-73)
Jean RACINE (1639-99)
Critical writing in India. A period of artifice producing works dealing with rules of poetry and literature.

Heroic English drama, usually tragedy, written in rhymed couplets. In the epic tradition of romance and honour, the protagonist was an exalted hero of great stature. Form influenced by French classicism.
John DRYDEN (1631-1700)
William DAVENANT (1606-1668)

English Restoration drama English theatres, closed since 1642, opened with the restoration of the monarchy (1660). Drama, produced for an élite audience, consisted of heroic tragedy and comedy of manners, the witty and satirical depiction of the customs of court life. Restoration drama first allowed women to act.
John DRYDEN (1631-1700); Sir George ETHEREGE (1634-91); William WYCHERLEY (1640-1716); Thomas Shadwell (*c.* 1642-92); Sir John VANBRUGH (1664-1726); William CONGREVE (1670-1729); Colley CIBBER (1671-1757).

The Ch'ing dynasty in China produced a vast output of scholarly and reference works, collections and works of the history and literature of earlier dynasties.
Chinese fiction Some of China's greatest novels appeared during the Ch'ing period, including satirical novels aimed at official corruption.

Puritan literature dominated early American writing. Poetry was primarily biblical and theological, influenced also by the early British metaphysical poets.
Anne BRADSTREET (*c.* 1612-72)
Michael Wigglesworth (1631-1705)
Edward Taylor (*c.* 1644-1729)
Cotton MATHER (1663-1728)

Art

Style of LOUIS XIV (1638-1715) characterized by pomp and magnificence, to reflect the glory of the king and his country. The Gobelins, a Paris weaving company, were granted the task (1662) of furnishing the royal palaces, not only with tapestries, but also furniture, gold, silver and sculpture. Designs by Charles LE BRUN (1619-90) and Philippe de CHAMPAIGNE (1602-74).

Rubenisme Movement in French art concerning the importance of colour in painting. Those supporting classical and formal arts of design and drawing, stating that colour was necessary for realistic representations, opposed the followers of RUBENS (1577-1640) and TITIAN (1487-1576).

Still life painting became most popular genre of northern European painters. Arrangements of such everyday objects as fruit and flowers, as depicted by CARAVAGGIO (1573-1610), musical instruments or groups of hunting trophies gave an opportunity for brilliant factual representation and experiments with light and composition.

Russian modern painting, resulting from increased contact with European artists, differed radically from icon painting. A brilliant portrait school developed.
Simon Ushakov (1626-86)
A. P. Antropov (1716-95)
P. G. Levitski (1735-1822)

Flemish lace-making Most productive period of the manufacture of bobbin lace in Flanders. Centres at Brussels, Mechelen, Antwerp and Binche.
Luso-Oriental style Portuguese decorative style influenced by Chinese, Japanese and Persian patterns. It appeared in furniture design, tiles and textiles.

Architecture

The 'grand style' of LOUIS XIV (1638-1715), characterized by the open château set in a formal park. Reached its peak in the baroque château of Versailles, a symmetrical palace set among the geometric avenues and hedges of a park by Le Nôtre (1613-1700).
Claude PERRAULT (1613-88)
Louis LE VAU (1612-70)
Jules MANSART (1646-1708)
Charles LE BRUN (1619-90)

French town planning The *places* or royal squares of Paris influenced town plans throughout France and in other European countries. Detached *hôtels* were built for wealthy citizens to a standardized and symmetrical plan.
François MANSART (1598-1666)
Louis LE VAU (1612-70)
Emmanuel Héré (1705-63)
Jacques Gabriel (1698-1782)

English town planning The square was introduced into English town planning by Inigo JONES (1573-1652), who designed the Italian piazza in Covent Garden, London. Sir Christopher WREN (1632-1723) played an important part in the replanning of London after the Great Fire of 1666. Privately owned terraced houses surrounding a central square became a common feature.

Late Baroque churches in Germany and Austria. Largely the work of unprofessional architects—painters, sculptors, stuccoists, gilders—combined ingenious designs with both subtle and sensational effects of lighting and decoration. Produced, also, a secular, palace architecture which was luxurious and monumental, yet light, open and elegant.
J. B. FISCHER VON ERLACH (1656-1723)
Jakob PRANDTAUER (1660-1726)

Churrigueresque style in Spain, though derived in its essentials from the Italian Baroque, incorporated native traditions in an extravagant style which emphasized surface texture and decoration.
Alonso Cano (1601-67)
Eufrasio Lopez de Rojas (d. 1684)
Jose CHURRIGUERA (*c.* 1650-1723)
Pedro de Ribera (d. 1742)

American colonial architecture. The makeshift settlements of the earliest settlers gave way to an architecture of brick and stone or weatherboarding, usually of two stories and reflecting the style of the country of origin of the settlers. Medieval and Renaissance features intermingled.

Music

Vaudeville Originally satirical street songs of Paris. In reign of LOUIS XIV (1638-1715) current lyrics were adapted to well-known melodies and used in the *opéra comique* of the Paris fairs.

Anthems Developed from the Latin motet and from early Anglican anthems into two different styles: choral anthems and verse anthems, which introduced solo passages, recitative and sometimes orchestral instruments.
William Child (1606-97)
John Blow (1648-1708)
Henry PURCELL (1659-95)

Cantata Vocal composition at first for a solo voice, later choral, with continuo, using either sacred or secular texts. Developed further in Germany, adopting dramatic themes with arias and recitative. Giovanni Legrenzi (*c.* 1626-90); Alessandro Stradella (1645-82); Alessandro SCARLATTI (1659-1725).

Suite gradually developed, parallel to the fashion in dancing, from pavane and galliard to allemand, courante, sarabande and gigue.
Johann Froberger (1616-67)
Arcangelo CORELLI (1653-1713)
Henry PURCELL (1659-95)

Chorale prelude Variation or adaptation of chorale, particularly Lutheran hymns, for performance by organ or other keyboard instrument. Elaborate counterpoint.
Franz Tunder (1614-77)
Dietrich BUXTEHUDE (1637-1707)
Johann Pachelbel (1653-1706)
J. S. BACH (1685-1750)

Technology

Great North Road in England first turnpiked to provide funds for its upkeep.
Otto von GUERICKE (1602-86) invented a pneumatic pump and a machine to generate a continuous supply of electricity.
Robert BOYLE (1627-1691) described the relationship between pressure and volume in Boyle's Law.
Mechanization in the European linen industry. First used for the separation of fibres from the flax stalk.

Microscopic analysis developed with the discovery of cells and micro-organisms recorded in *Micrographia* (1665).
Galileo GALILEI (1564-1642)
Marcello MALPIGHI (1628-94)
Antony van LEEUWENHOEK (1632-1723)
Robert HOOKE (1635-1703)
Jan SWAMMERDAM (1637-80)
Nehemiah Grew (1641-1712)
Experiments on reflection, refraction and double refraction of light conducted by BARTHOLIN (1625-1698) and HUYGENS (1629-1695).

Theory of calculus developed by European mathematicians. Isaac NEWTON (1642-1727); Gottfried Wilhelm LEIBNIZ (1646-1716); Jacques BERNOULLI (1654-1705); Guillaume de L'Hôpital (1661-1704); Brook TAYLOR (1685-1731); George BERKELEY (1685-1753); Colin MACLAURIN (1698-1746); Leonhard EULER (1707-83); Joseph-Louis LAGRANGE (1736-1813).

First reflecting telescope, built by NEWTON (1642-1727).
Chromatic aberration, the distortion of colour by a lens, explained by NEWTON (1642-1727).
Pendulum clock invented by HUYGENS (1629-95).
Lead first used for sheathing boats in Europe.

Law of elastic force discovered by Robert HOOKE (1635-1703).
Finite velocity of light discovered in Denmark by Olaus Roemer (1644-1710).
Lead-glass first made in England by George Ravenscroft (1618-71). The casting of plate glass in large sheets developed in Normandy.

Investigation of insects produced a challenge to the previously accepted theory of spontaneous generation (1688).
Jan SWAMMERDAM (1637-1680)
Francesco Redi (1621-1697)
Four satellites of Saturn discovered by Giovanni CASSINI (1625-1712).
Tunnels through rock blasted using gunpowder, by P.-P. Riquet (1604-80) in France.

SIR ISAAC NEWTON (1642-1727) wrote *Philosophiae naturalis principia mathematica* (1687), the first exposition of the theory of gravity and the three laws of planetary motion.
First wind-chart of the trade winds and monsoons produced by Edmond HALLEY (1656-1742).
Botany Systematic classification of plants devised by John RAY (1628-1705). New herbal remedies and drugs introduced into Europe from the New World, including quinine.

	1690	1695	1700	1705	1710	1715	1720
Principal Events	**Salem Witchcraft Trials** (1692). **Massacre of Glencoe** Highlanders defeated by Campbells in Scotland (1692). **League of Augsburg** formed (1686) by WILLIAM of Orange (1650-1702) between Holy Roman Empire, Spain, Sweden, Saxony and the Palatinate (1688). French attacked the Palatinate (1688). French supported by American and Canadian Indians. Treaty of Ryswick (1697) brought French recognition of the limits of her own expansion and of William as King of Britain. **Mongol threat** to China (1690-1727) eventually overcome by the Ch'ing.	**First Partition Treaty** between England, France and Holland over succession to Spain and its possessions (1698). **Treaty of Karlowitz** (1699) Austria received Hungary from Turkey. Venice received the Morea and much of Dalmatia. Poland received Podolia and the Ukraine.	**Great Northern war** between Scandinavia and Russia over Russia's claim for outlet to the Baltic. **Act of Settlement** (1701) established Protestant Hanoverian succession in Britain. **War of Spanish Succession** 1701-13. CHARLES II of Spain (1661-1700) died without offspring. Austria claimed the throne for the son of the Emperor Archduke Charles, but Charles II had named as his heir Philip of Anjou, a Bourbon, and grandson of LOUIS XIV (1638-1715). Involved England, Holland, Savoy, Prussia, France, Portugal.	**Union** between England and Scotland under the name of United Kingdom of Great Britain (1707). Union Jack adopted as national flag. **Battle of Malplaquet** (1709) MARLBOROUGH (1650-1722) defeated the French. **Russian prisoners** first sent to Siberia (1709). **Mogul Empire** disintegrated after the death of AURANGZEB (1618-1707), as provincial governors succeeded in winning independence.	**Second Villmergen war** Supremacy of Protestant cantons established in Switzerland (1712). **Treaty of Utrecht** (1713) ended the War of Spanish Succession. Signed by France, Britain, Portugal, Holland and Savoy. France recognized Protestant succession in Britain and ceded Newfoundland and Nova Scotia. Spanish Netherlands were ceded to Republic of Holland. Savoy received Sicily. PHILIP V (1683-1746) recognized as King of Spain and its colonies. **Asiento Guinea Co.** began the most vigorous period of Britain's slave trade (1713). **Papal Bull** *Unigenitus* condemned the Jansenists (1713).	**First Jacobite rebellion** (1715). Supporters of James Stuart (1688-1766), the Pretender to British throne, rose when he arrived from France, but rebellion dispersed without battle. **Triple Alliance** (1717) and Quadruple Alliance (1718) between Britain, France, Holland and Holy Roman Empire against Spain. **Anglo-Spanish war:** Battle of Cape Passaro (1718) won by English. **Decline of Dutch trade** to Japan. Isolation intensified by limiting to two the number of Dutch allowed to call at Japan each year.	
Religion	**Latitudinarians** Rationalist group of English churchmen influenced by Cambridge Platonists, who tried to reconcile the Church to changing intellectual environment. **Edict of toleration** for the Jesuits in China, in return for scientific services. A quarrel ensued over Jesuit acceptance of Chinese rites concerning heaven, CONFUCIUS (c. 551-479 BC) and the ancestors.	**Sikhs,** under Govind Singh (1666-1708), became a militant movement in India and threatened the Moghuls in the Deccan.	**Shinto revival** in Japan. Kamo Mabuchi (c. 1697-1769) attempted to restore the ancient (pre-Buddhist and pre-Confucian) Shinto, emphasizing in his new philosophy the ideal of simplicity and harmony with nature. Motoori Norinaga (1730-1801)	**Freemasonry** Secret brotherhood, claiming to trace origins to the building of Solomon's Temple, founded in England. Spread rapidly to Europe.		**Camisards** Calvinists from Cévennes who rebelled against LOUIS XIV (1638-1715).	
Philosophy	**The Han Hsueh** 'Han Learning' movement sprang from the critical mood prevalent in China during the period following the Manchu conquest. Reacting against neo-Confucianist eclecticism, philosophers refused to accept theories unsupported by fact and evidence. By close study of the Later Han texts of the Classics, thought to be more authentic than those of the Former Han, scholars hoped to penetrate their real meaning.			**Liberalism** A revolutionary intellectual movement professing belief in the natural dignity of all men, from which springs their inviolable rights. The duty of government is to defend these rights. The American Declaration of Independence (1776) was a landmark in the development of Liberalism. John LOCKE (1632-1704); Louis, Baron de MONTESQUIEU (1689-1755); VOLTAIRE (1694-1778); Jean-Jacques ROUSSEAU (1712-78); Thomas JEFFERSON (1743-1826).	**Empiricism** enquired into the origin and significance of ideas. Believing sense experience to be the source, basis and ultimate testing ground for knowledge, the empiricists led later philosophers to a denial of the reality of matter and to question the feasibility of any metaphysical enquiry. John LOCKE (1632-1704); George BERKELEY (1685-1753); David HUME (1711-76).		
Literature		**The Joruri puppet theatre** in Japan entertained the urban middle classes. In the joruri plays chanters intoned the dialogue of the puppets. The plays were based on historical events and stories, or portrayed modern life. Chikamatsu Monzaemon (1653-1725) Takeda Izumo (1691-1756) Chikamatsu Hanji (1725-83)		**English journalism** A direct consequence of the new middle-class market, the new journals—*The Review* (1704), *The Tatler* (1709), and *The Spectator* (1711)— provided informed criticism of literary, political and social matters. Daniel DEFOE (c. 1660-1731) Richard STEELE (1672-1729) Joseph ADDISON (1672-1719)		**English Augustan poetry** Urbane, witty, pungently epigrammatic, a satirical or mock heroic criticism of man in society. Alexander POPE (1688-1744) Matthew PRIOR (1664-1721)	
Art	**Woodwork** Arts of marquetry, with many different materials, and appliqué, known to the ancient Egyptians, developed during the reign of LOUIS XIV (1638-1715) in France.		**Early American portraits** were family portraits, in a style influenced chiefly by Dutch immigrants. Mostly anonymous.	**Delft pottery** Tin-glazed earthenware strongly influenced by the Chinese blue-and-white style of porcelain, and Chinese and Japanese polychrome porcelains. Scenes represented were of Dutch origin. The import of genuine porcelain from the East caused the decline of Delftware during the 18th century.	**Meissen porcelain** Meissen, in Germany, was the first European centre of hard-paste (true clay, as opposed to a mixture of clay and glass —soft-paste) porcelain. Styles were influenced by China, particularly flower decorations. Manufacture mainly of plates, mugs and figurines.		
Architecture	**Baroque in eastern Europe** The palaces of the Bohemian nobility of the early 17th century were, by the 18th century, built in a curvaceous Bohemian baroque style, later copied in Hungary. Guarino Guarini (1624-83) Johann von HILDEBRANDT (1668-1745) Matthäus PÖPPELMANN (1662-1736) Kilian Ignaz Dientzenhofer (1689-1751)	**Italian town planning** Increasing population necessitated the rebuilding of whole quarters with narrow 'mass-produced' houses of three or four stories, often shared by several families. Fashionable Baroque *palazzi* were given wide roof terraces used to collect rain water. Baldassare Longhena (1598-1682) Giovanni de'Rossi (1616-95) Filippo Juvara (1678-1736) Filippo Raguzzini (d. 1771)	**Western influence** in the architecture of Ch'ing China occurred in the building of the Imperial Summer Palace, with the help of the Jesuits, in an imitation of Italian Baroque style.	**Rococo** style, the last phase of the Baroque, originated in France. It derived its name from the French *rocaille*—'rock' or 'shell-like' decoration. Light and airy, often asymmetrical and abstract in form, rococo was a reaction to the darker and heavier early Baroque. Pierre Lepautre (1660-1744); Nicolas Pineau (1684-1754); Gilles Oppenordt (1672-1742); Juste Meissonier (c. 1675-1750); Jacques Gabriel (1698-1782).		**The Baroque town plan** was influenced by the radiating avenues of parks by Le Nôtre (1613-1700). Karlsruhe was designed in 1715, a star-shaped city with the Ducal Palace as the central feature; in 1791, Washington DC was laid out on a regular axial plan. Domenico Fontana (1543-1607) Pierre Charles L'Enfant (d. 1825)	
Music	**Chorale partita** Similar to the prelude, using hymn tunes, but here each variation corresponded to the theme of each verse. Jan SWEELINCK (1562-1621) Samuel Scheidt (1587-1654) J.S. BACH (1685-1750)	**German passion** Musical setting of Biblical story, influenced by contemporary interest in drama. The narrative was given by the solo voices, and the chorus played the crowd. Heinrich SCHUTZ (1585-1672) J.S. BACH (1685-1750)	**Concerto grosso** Extended composition of three or four movements, for orchestra and a small group of instruments which provided a contrast to the full orchestra. Alessandro Stradella (1645-82); Arcangelo CORELLI (1653-1713); Giuseppe Torelli (c. 1650-1708); Antonio VIVALDI (c. 1676-1741); Tommaso Albinoni (1674-1745).		**Pianoforte** invented (c. 1709). Attributed to Bartolommeo CRISTOFORI (1655-1731). His principal contribution was a lever mechanism allowing greater tonal control in the striking of the strings.		
Technology	**First 'atmospheric engine',** the forerunner of the steam engine, invented by Denis PAPIN (1647-c. 1712), who also designed a pressure cooker. **Global variations** of the magnetic compass, the first isometric map, charted by Edmond HALLEY (1656-1742). **Iatro-chemistry,** the study of diseases assumed to be caused by juices in the body, founded by Franciscus Sylvius (1614-72). George STAHL (1660-1734)	**Fire engine,** an early steam engine built by Thomas Savery (c. 1650-1715), used to pump water for buildings and water wheels. **Glass** Refined and elegant glassware began to appear in Europe, particularly from Venetian factories. Engraving wheels, made of copper, driven by treadle, or water power. **Whale-oil** introduced into the European soap industry which expanded rapidly.	**The 'Opticks'** of Isaac NEWTON (1642-1727) described his investigations into the nature of light. He discovered that all light is refracted when passing from one medium to another. **Berlin Academy** founded 1700. Followed the Accademia dei Lincei, Rome (1603); Accademia del Cimento, Florence (1657); The Royal Society of London (1662); Académie Royale des Sciences, Paris (1666). **First precision lathes** developed by clock-makers in Europe.	**Agricultural improvements** in Europe included the concave curved iron mould-board of the plough and the seed-drill, invented by Jethro TULL (1674-1741). **Coke** used in a blast furnace by Abraham DARBY (1678-1717) in England. **Clinical medicine** began with the work of Hermann BOERHAVE (1668-1738). **Translucent pottery,** a copy of Chinese porcelain, produced in the West.	**Sugar and rice** introduced into the Americas from Europe. THOMAS NEWCOMEN (1663-1729) built an atmospheric engine, which cooled a steam cylinder by introducing cold water inside it through an injection cock. Used to pump water from the Cornish tin mines.	**Probability theory,** proposed by PASCAL (1623-62), Fermat (1601-65) and HUYGENS (1629-93), developed into a branch of mathematics by Jacques BERNOULLI (1654-1705). **Mercury thermometer** and the Fahrenheit thermometric scale introduced (1715) by Daniel FAHRENHEIT (1686-1736). **First table of chemical affinities** constructed (1718) by Etienne F. Geoffroy (1672-1731).	

1720 1725 1730 1735 1740 1745 1750 367

Principal Events

State of Carolina reorganized (1719-29).
Texas occupied by Spaniards (1720-2).
South Sea Bubble (1720). The boom and crash of financial speculation in Britain on the false assumption that extensive British trade concessions would result from the War of Spanish Succession. Similar crash in France.
Treaty of Nystadt between Sweden and Russia (1721).
State of Hyderabad founded (1724) by Chin Kilich Khan (d. 1748) former vizier of the Moghul empire.

BERING (1680-1741) found that Asia was not connected with America. Strait named after him.
Corsica gained independence from Genoa (1729).
Montevideo founded by Spaniards (1726).

War of Polish Succession (1733-5) Augustus III (1696-1763) recognized by Russia and Austria in place of Stanislas (1677-1766), then king, who was supported by France, Spain and Sardinia.
The Maratha government, a Hindu regime, became pre-eminent in India, overrunning Malwa, Gujarat, Bundelkhad and parts of Rajputana.

Tokugawa shogunate in Japan declined. Despite attempts at reform, the Tokugawas were unable to halt the decline, a result of the economic and social ills of the peasant class, financial ruin of the warriors and a series of famines and natural disasters.

Peace of Vienna (1738) formally resolved War of Polish Succession. Stanislas (1677-1766) renounced Polish throne.
War of Jenkins' Ear Capture of Robert Jenkins' ship by the Spanish (1739) and the cutting off of Jenkins' ear was a contributory factor to war between Britain and Spain.
Treaty of Belgrade (1739) Austrians gave up Serbia and Belgrade.
Invasion of northern India by the Persians under NADIR SHAH (1688-1747). Indian forces defeated and the wealth of Delhi pillaged (1739).

War of Austrian Succession (1740-8) started when FREDERICK THE GREAT (1712-86) seized Silesia. Claimants for the Austrian throne included Charles, Elector of Bavaria (1697-1745), PHILIP V, King of Spain (1683-1746), and Augustus III of Saxony (1696-1763).
Treaty of Bavaria (1742) concluded peace between Austria and Prussia.
Treaty of Åbo (1743) between Russia and Sweden. Sweden ceded southern Finland.

Second Jacobite rebellion (1745-6) Charles Edward Stuart (1720-88) landed in Scotland, proclaiming his father, James Stuart (1688-1766), James VIII of Scotland. Jacobites won the Battle of Prestonpans, but beaten at Culloden (1746).
Treaty of Aix-la-Chapelle (1748) ended the War of Austrian Succession. Signed by France, Britain, Spain and Holland.
French captured Madras, under the leadership of Joseph DUPLEIX (1697-1763). French domination of India (1751) was checked when CLIVE (1725-74) seized Arcot, establishing British supremacy.

Religion

Deism, also called natural religion: belief in a personal God who had created the world but intervened no further in the affairs of man. Denounced all forms of organized religion, the idea of revelation, prayers and sacraments. Adhered to by such men as VOLTAIRE (1694-1778), DIDEROT (1713-84), ROUSSEAU (1712-78), POPE (1688-1744), the Earl of SHAFTESBURY (1801-85), Thomas PAINE (1737-1809), Benjamin FRANKLIN (1706-90) and Thomas JEFFERSON (1743-1826). It had strong influences on contemporary literature.

Great Awakening Revivalist period in American religion, encouraged by George WHITEFIELD (1714-70), who revived zeal in languishing denominations.
Eastern Orthodox Church established in Peking.

Convulsionaries Extreme Jansenist movement in France, who were said to perform miracles when they had worked themselves into a frenzied fit.

Methodism Evangelical off-shoot of Protestantism, which aimed at reviving Christian belief throughout Britain. Derisively named methodism because of the methodical regularity of spiritual meetings, fasts, prayers and chapel services. Introduced Sunday school and parish magazines.
John WESLEY (1703-91)
Charles Wesley (1707-88)

Doukhobors Russian sect which arose among Kharkov peasants. Rejected government and Church authority, and opposed war, taxes and the necessity for marriage. Strongly mystical, they claimed that JESUS CHRIST was reincarnated in every generation.

Philosophy

Japanese nationalism took form during the Tokugawa period, when the superiority of Japanese thought and literature was emphasized. The study of ancient Japanese writings was revived during this period.
Kamo Mabuchi (*c.* 1697-1769)
Motoori Norinaga (1730-1801)

The French 'Enlightenment' An intellectual movement, inspired by NEWTON (1642-1727) and LOCKE (1632-1704), which sought social reform based on rational, scientific analysis of society. Exemplified by *l'Encyclopédie* (1747-65), which attempted to gather together all the known information on the arts, sciences and trades. Baron de MONTESQUIEU (1689-1755); VOLTAIRE (1694-1778); Comte de BUFFON (1707-88); Jean-Jacques ROUSSEAU (1712-78); Baron D'HOLBACH (1723-89).

Literature

Arcadia Accademia dell' Arcadia set up in Rome to counteract the excesses of the followers of MARINO (1569-1625) by returning to pastoral simplicity. In effect, it produced another type of affectation—extreme refinement, artificiality, and languid over-sophistication.
Paolo Rolli (1687-1765)
Carlo Frugoni (1692-1768)
Pietro METASTASIO (1698-1782)

English Augustan prose dominated by the essay, used for satirical and didactic social commentary, in factual, colloquial language. A use of literature for public debate of social and moral issues.
Jonathan SWIFT (1667-1745)

Spanish prose Satire and romance heavily influenced by the picaresque tradition. Literary criticism gained importance.

Comédie larmoyante Sentimental French comedy in which the situations were so exaggeratedly tragic they were intended to make the audience weep. Philippe Destouches (1680-1754); Nivelle de La Chaussée (1692-1754).

Social comment in Italy ranged from an influential philosophical survey of social evolution by VICO (1668-1744) to work on penal reform and abolition of torture by BECCARIA (1735-94). Economic and political treatises were directed against the futile and frivolous pursuits of the indulgent and corrupt rich. Pietro Giannone (1676-1748); Gaspare Gozzi (1713-86); Giuseppe Baretti (1719-89); Pietro Verri (1728-95); Giuseppe Parini (1729-99).

French prose dominated by epistolary form, the essay and the short story *(conte)*. Much propagandist political and historical writing, and satirical literary work.
Baron de MONTESQUIEU (1689-1755)

French drama declined from the works of the previous centuries. Usually comedies of situation, sentiment and character, melodrama and didactic tragedies.
Philippe Destouches (1680-1754)
Pierre de MARIVAUX (1688-1763)

French novel Consolidation of formative influences of prose romance and picaresque tradition. Complex social settings and greater individual characterization. Alain-René Lesage (1668-1747); Pierre de MARIVAUX (1688-1763); L'Abbé PREVOST (1697-1763).

Art

Capricci Invented landscapes or townscapes, often dreamlike fantasies set alongside accurate architectural scenes. Similar to *vedute*, imaginary townscapes of existing architectural elements.
Giovanni Battista TIEPOLO (1696-1770)
Francesco Zuccarelli (1702-88)
Francesco GUARDI (1712-93)
Francisco de GOYA y Lucientes (1746-1828)

Rococo Artists and decorators reacted against heavy, elaborate Baroque style and produced light, colourful painting and sculpture. Interior decoration was characterized by scrolls and curves. Subject matter of paintings usually light, intimate scenes of pastoral charm or the artificial elegance of courtly life. Jean WATTEAU (1684-1721) Giovanni Battista TIEPOLO (1696-1770); François BOUCHER (1703-70); Jean FRAGONARD (1732-1806).
Ukiyo-e painting Aimed to serve the new bourgeois society of Japan, who wanted decorative paintings in their houses. Ukiyo-e work was reproduced in polychrome printing, able to print up to 10 colours, and depicted everyday life, historical stories, love scenes and theatrical scenes. Hishikawa Moronubu (1618-95); Kiyonobu I (1664-1729); Okumura Masanobu (1686-1764); Suzuki HARUNOBU (1718-70).

English school of portrait painting, strongly influenced by RUBENS (1577-1640) and Van DYCK (1599-1641), became one of the outstanding schools of portraiture in 18th-century Europe. Sir Peter LELY (1618-80); Sir Godfrey Kneller (1646-1723); Allan Ramsay (1713-84); Sir Joshua REYNOLDS (1723-92); Thomas GAINSBOROUGH (1727-88); Sir Thomas Lawrence (1769-1830).
Chippendale English furniture style, named after Thomas Chippendale (*c.* 1718-79), characterized by Neo-classical form, with much marquetry and inlaid wood pieces.

Architecture

Rationalist architecture of the 18th century evolved in reaction to the decorative excesses of rococo. Simple geometric forms used in diverse combinations resulting in a Baroque architecture of precision and vitality.
Nicholas HAWKSMOOR (1661-1736)
Sir John VANBRUGH (1664-1726)
Jacques SOUFFLOT (1713-80)

English Neo-Palladianism characterized by formal country houses set in parks and landscaped gardens. John WOOD the Elder (*c.* 1704-54) applied Palladianism to the English town square, where terraced houses were unified by the imposition of a palace front.
Giacomo Leoni (*c.* 1686-1746)
Lord Burlington (1694-1753)
William KENT (1684-1748)

Tokugawa period in Japan saw the restoration of temples and the building of pagodas and tombs in an elaborately carved and decorated style, with complex roofing systems.

Russian Baroque marked the westernization of Russia, as Italian and German architects were invited to Russia to design palaces of great luxury and churches.
Andreas Schlüter (*c.* 1660-1714)
Gottfried Schädel (d. 1752)
Domenico Trezzini (1670-1734)
Bartolommeo Francesco Rastrelli (1700-71)

Music

Sinfonia Originally referred to introductory music, or overture, to operatic works. Standardized into three-movement form (fast, slow, fast). To this early form was added a minuet in the second movement, which developed into the classic four-movement form of the symphony.

Opera seria Early serious opera confined to rigid conventions similar to French classical theatre. Emphasis on the virtuosity of singers, particularly *castrati* (male sopranos). Arias commented on the narrative recitative dialogues.
Pietro METASTASIO (1698-1782)
Apostolo Zeno (1668-1750)

Ballad opera English popular dramatic genre, with spoken dialogue and songs. Vehicle for social satire; folk-songs, or the music of PURCELL (1659-95), HANDEL (1685-1759) and others was used with new lyrics.
John GAY (1685-1732)
Charles DIBDIN (1745-1814)
William Shield (1748-1829)

Opera buffa Light-hearted opera, less formal than *opera seria*, dealing with everyday characters. Few characters, music harmonious, dialogue usually spoken.
Baldassare Galuppi (1706-85)
Giovanni PERGOLESI (1710-36)
Niccolò Piccinni (1728-1800)
Domenico CIMAROSA (1749-1801)

Opéra comique French parody of grand opera. Different from *opera buffa*, an idealization in spoken dialogue of common life.
Egidio Duni (1709-75)
François Philidor (1726-95)
Pierre Monsigny (1729-1817)
André Grétry (1742-1813)

Sonata form Three main sections, an exposition, development and recapitulation. Used as the basic structure of sonatas and the first movements of symphonies.

Technology

The shape of the Earth investigated and determined. Isaac NEWTON (1642-1727) Pierre de MAUPERTUIS (1698-1759) Alexis CLAIRAUT (1713-1765)
Flying shuttle invented in England by John KAY (1733-64). Attempt to mechanize the cotton weaving process.
Smelting of zinc established at Swansea and in 1740 at Bristol in England.
René de RÉAUMUR (1683-1757) analysed and described the iron-making processes so far discovered.

Historia coelestis britannica (1725) by John FLAMSTEED (1646-1719) replaced the tables of Tycho BRAHE (1546-1601) as the most accurate catalogue of stars.
Mechanization of figured weaving attempted in France by Jacques de Vaucanson (1709-82).
Aberration of light discovered in England by James BRADLEY (1693-1762).

Navigational quadrant invented by HADLEY (1682-1744). The instrument was not affected by a ship's motion.
Statistics The normal curve of error defined (1733) by Abraham de MOIVRE (1667-1754).
Spirit thermometer invented by RÉAUMUR (1683-1757); an interval of 80° was used between freezing and boiling point of water.
Universal sundials produced in Europe. Adjustable for use in any latitude.

Sulphuric acid manufactured in England by burning a mixture of sulphur and nitre over water which was then distilled. Joshua Ward (1685-1761)
Kinetic theory of gases investigated by Daniel BERNOULLI (1700-1782), a Swiss.
Charles Du Fay (1698-1739) distinguished between two kinds of electricity produced by rubbing—later known as positive and negative.

Ballistic pendulum invented in England for measuring the velocity of a projectile. Enabled greater accuracy in cannon warfare. Benjamin Robins (1707-51)
Cast steel first produced by Benjamin Huntsman (1704-76) in England. Bar iron was purified by intense heat treatment.
First national survey by triangulation carried out in France (1744).
Traité de dynamique (1743) by Jean d'ALEMBERT (1717-1783) solved many problems of mechanics.

Spinning projectile physics explained by B. Rabius; led to the invention of the modern rifle.
Science of bacteriology developed in Europe following the invention of the microscope.
John NEEDHAM (1713-1781)
Lazzaro SPALLANZANI (1729-1799)
Study of natural history laid the basis of evolutionary biology.
Comte de BUFFON (1707-1788)
Chinese lacquer successfully imitated in the West by S. E. Martin, in England.

368 1750 1755 1760 1765 1770 1775

Principal Events

Tibet invaded by Chinese, after intervention in the succession of the Dalai Lama and a series of campaigns against the Tibetan border tribes (1751)
Gregorian Calendar adopted in Britain (1752). Riots over the 'loss' of eleven days.
Anglo-French war in North America (1754).

Earthquake in Lisbon (1755) destroyed the city, caused fire and flood and many thousands of deaths.
Quebec taken by the British (1759).
India Struggle between British and Bengalis for Calcutta. Nawab of Bengal imprisoned 146 British in the 'Black Hole of Calcutta' (1756). British rule established by CLIVE (1725-74).
Seven Years' War between Britain and France over boundary disputes in North America (1756-63).
Maratha forces overran northern India, but were defeated at the third battle of Panipat by Afghans and Muslims (1761).

Treaty of Paris (1763) between Britain, France, Spain and Portugal over colonial possessions. Britain at height of power in the world, receiving St Vincent, Tobago, Grenada, Senegal, Cap Breton and Florida, as well as Nova Scotia and Canada.
Russia and Prussia allied to control Poland (1764).
British victory in India. Affairs for the East India Company were administered by CLIVE (1725-74).

Mason-Dixon Line established between Maryland and Pennsylvania, separating free lands from land where slaves were allowed (1766).
James Bruce (1730-94) explored Ethiopia (1768-73).
HAIDAR ALI (1722-82) usurped the throne of Mysore and forced the British to sign a treaty of mutual assistance (1767).
China at war with Burma. The Burmese recognized Chinese suzeraínty (1769).
JAMES COOK (1728-79) discovered and explored east coast of Australia, calling it New South Wales (1768-71).

Boston Massacre (Massachusetts, 1770). Several people killed after anti-British riots. At the 'Boston Tea Party' (1773), citizens disguised as Indians dumped tea into the harbour in protest against taxes imposed by British.
Peasant revolt in Russia (1773-5) led by Pugachev (d. 1775).
WARREN HASTINGS (1732-1818) became governor of Bengal (1773).
Peace of Kuchuk Kainarji (1774) between Turkey and Russia. Turkey granted free navigation to Russian traders in Crimea. Independence of Tatars recognized.

American Independence Battles of Lexington and Concord (1775) forced British to retreat to Boston, later evacuated. Declaration of Independence, drawn up by JEFFERSON (1743-1826), adopted (1776). War continued, British surrendering to General Gates (1728-1806) at Saratoga. Articles of Confederation proposed the confederacy of the United States (1777).
Viceroyalty of River Plate founded as defence measure by Argentina, Bolivia, Paraguay and Uruguay (1776).

Religion

Moravian Church Revival of Bohemian Brethren, a Protestant sect comparable with Quakers, who rejected the ecclesiastical hierarchy and favoured a direct relationship with God, which they believed would assure their salvation.

Shakers Seceded from the Quakers; founded in England but quickly moved to America. Their name derived from movements made during their religious dances, which were the chief form of worship. Founded by Ann LEE (1736-84), who was considered the 'female Christ'.

Quebec Act guaranteed freedom for Roman Catholicism in Canada (1774).
Evangelist movements Many itinerant evangelists in England, who aroused enthusiasm for crusades against such contemporary evils as the slave trade, and later founded missionary societies.

Wahhabis Puritanical religious revival initiated by Mohammed ibn-Abd-al-Wahhab (d. 1792), who condemned other Muslims for deviation from the Koran. Crusaded against the Turks.

Philosophy

Kogakuhu or Ancient school of Japanese philosophers attempted to return to pre-Sung Confucianism.
Ito Jinsai (1627-1705)
Ogyu Sorai (1666-1728)
Motoori Norinaga (1730-1801)

Political thought The nature of government and national political power preoccupied many philosophers in the years leading to the French Revolution (1789). MONTESQUIEU (1689-1755) classified governments and defined the separation of powers; others discussed democracy, representative government, the rule of numbers, the role of party and the viability of republicanism and federalism. VOLTAIRE (1694-1778); Jean-Jacques ROUSSEAU (1712-78); Edmund BURKE (1729-97); Thomas PAINE (1737-1809); Thomas JEFFERSON (1743-1826).

Literature

English novel Rise of a major literary genre, developing a complex portrayal of individual characters in a detailed social background.
Samuel RICHARDSON (1689-1761)
Henry FIELDING (1707-54)
Laurence STERNE (1713-68)
Tobias SMOLLETT (1721-71)

French poetry A fashionable exercise: verse formal and elegant, following classical Latin style and themes.
VOLTAIRE (1694-1778)

English poetry, while continuing in the Augustan style, began to explore the imaginative, emotional appeal of natural, picturesque scenery.
Thomas GRAY (1716-71)
William COWPER (1731-1800)

Decline of the Commedia dell' Arte After a new but final lease of life by Carlo Gozzi (1720-93), who used fairy tales for basis of improvised farce and satirical drama, the masks and improvisation of the *commedia* tradition were abandoned, and comedy of character and manners introduced. Carlo GOLDONI (1707-93).

Drame bourgeois developed from *comédie larmoyante;* mingled pathos, comedy and moral seriousness.
Denis DIDEROT (1713-84)
Michel Sedaine (1719-97)
Caron de BEAUMARCHAIS (1732-99)
Italian melodrama emerged from opera as a successful literary form, giving equal status to music and poetry.
Apostolo Zeno (1668-1750)
Pietro METASTASIO (1698-1782)

American Revolution Literature almost entirely political, propagandist and emotive. Culminated in the eloquent prose of the Declaration of Independence. Benjamin FRANKLIN (1706-90); Samuel ADAMS (1722-1803); Thomas PAINE (1737-1809); Thomas JEFFERSON (1743-1826); Alexander HAMILTON (1755-1804).
Sturm und Drang 'Storm and Stress'. Upheaval in German thought and literature, promoted by pro-Shakespearean writings of Herder (1744-1803) and his revival of interest in folk-song and history. Instinct, intensity of feeling and a noble savagery of man supplanted rationalism as the cardinal virtues. Influenced by ROUSSEAU (1712-78); precursor of European Romanticism. Johann von GOETHE (1749-1832); Friedrich von Schiller (1759-1805); Gottried Bürger (1747-94); J. M. R. Lenz (1751-92); F. M. von Klinger (1752-1831).

Art

Conversation pieces Usually informal English group portraits of families, depicted in natural settings such as gardens, landscapes, or domestic backgrounds. Subjects in conversation or gentle activity.
William HOGARTH (1697-1764)
Johann ZOFFANY (1734-1810)
Thomas GAINSBOROUGH (1727-88)

Rococo Decorative style introduced by LOUIS XV (1710-74) into his courts. Furniture was often decorated with ormolu (gilded bronze). Juste Aurele Meissonier (*c.* 1695-1750); Pierre Gouthière (1732-*c.* 1813).
Neo-classicism was a reaction against exuberance of baroque and rococo art. Classicists wanted to revive the formal harmony of ancient art. Inspired by archaeological discoveries at Pompeii and Herculaneum, they were able consciously to imitate the qualities of calmness and grandeur of the Greek and Roman sculpture, murals and bas-reliefs. Johann Joachim WINCKELMANN (1717-68); Giambattista Piranesi (1720-78); Anton Mengs (1728-79); Antonio CANOVA (1757-1822); Jacques-Louis DAVID (1748-1825); Jean INGRES (1780-1867).

Sheffield plate Technique of plating other metals with a sheet of silver, discovered by Thomas Boulsover in 1742. Enlarged the market for silver.
Hepplewhite and Sheraton Classical English furniture styles, similar in characteristics of lightness and gracefulness. Usually pale wood, occasionally painted. Sheraton (1751-1806) favoured square chair backs, Hepplewhite (d. 1786), rounded

American painting History painting in the Neo-classical style.
Benjamin WEST (1738-1820)
Charles Willson Peale (1741-1827)
John Turnbull (1756-1843)
Gilbert Stuart (1755-1828)
Sèvres porcelain first manufactured (1772).

Style of LOUIS XVI (1754-93) Reaction against the frivolity of the style of LOUIS XV (1710-74), reflecting the current interest in classicism. Decoration was simple and rectilinear, with much white and gold in place of the varied colours of earlier decades.

Architecture

Spanish colonial architecture. Brought to Spain by a Fleming, Jaime Bort y Melia, the rococo style reached its greatest success in Mexico and Peru.
Ventura Rodriguez (1717-85)

Neo-classicism, inspired by the birth of archaeology and a scientific understanding of Roman and, later, Greek architectural principles, produced no universal style, but solidly linear buildings, churches, monuments and civic buildings, which expressed the Romanticized classical qualities of simplicity and severity. Jacques Gabriel (1698-1782); Jacques SOUFFLOT (1713-80); James Stuart (1713-88); J. J. WINCKELMANN (1717-68); Etienne-Louis Boullée (1728-99); Claude-Nicolas Ledoux (1736-1806); Karl SCHINKEL (1781-1841); Sir Robert SMIRKE (1781-1867); George Basevi (1794-1845); Harvey Elmes (1813-47).

Music

Pre-classical symphony First known symphony in four movements was by Georg Mathias Monn (1717-50). Influenced by the sonata, the concerto grosso and the *opera buffa*, particularly in melodiousness.
Gian Battista Sammartini (1698-1775)
Johann Stamitz (1717-57)

Mannheim symphonists were renowned for their brilliant techniques of orchestral expression. Four-movement symphony established.
Franz Richter (1709-89)
Ignaz Holzbauer (1711-83)
Johann Stamitz (1717-57)
Anton Filtz (1725-60)
Christian Cannabich (1731-98)

Style galant Light, elegant manner of harpsichord musicians. Rhythmically simple, slow chord changes. Stately music which was a basic feature of Viennese classical style.
Georg TELEMANN (1681-1767)
C. P. E. BACH (1714-88)
Josef HAYDN (1732-1809)
Wolfgang MOZART (1756-91)

Singspiele Comic light operatic works in Germany, which developed from fairground theatre and comic drama. Like English ballad opera and *opéra comique*, much spoken dialogue in the vernacular. Sentimental themes developed through fantasy and supernatural tales into German romantic opera. Johann Hiller (1728-1804); J. C. BACH (1735-82); C. D. von Dittersdorf (1739-99); Johann Schulz (1747-1800); Wolfgang MOZART (1756-91); Karl Zeller (1758-1832).

Opera reform GLUCK (1714-87) advocated a return to the classical form: the overture should be a dramatic introduction, arias and recitatives should reflect the development of the plot, and the chorus should regain the importance it had in Greek drama.

Technology

Combustion experiments The phlogiston theory discredited on the discovery of oxygen.
Johann BECHER (1635-82)
George E. STAHL (1660-1734)
Joseph Priestley (1733-1804)
Antoine LAVOISIER (1743-94)
Pierre LAPLACE (1749-1827)
Lathe with a tool-holding carriage invented in England.
Leyden jar invented. Accumulated an electrical charge from a generator.
Pieter van MUSSCHENBROEK (1692-1761)

Pottery industry in Staffordshire, England, based on the local red clays, the availability of lead sulphide for glazing and of abundant coal supplies. Early example of mass production.
Josiah WEDGWOOD (1730-95)
Bridge-building developments in Europe included experiments in gradient, in waterway obstruction, the improvement of centring methods and the enlargement of span.
John RENNIE (1761-1821)
Rubber introduced to Europe from Peru.

Electricity and magnetism studies. Produced the principle of the conservation of the electric charge (1751-4); an account of electric and magnetic attraction and repulsion (1785-9); a theory of 'animal electricity' (1791). Measurements standardized by Alessandro VOLTA (1745-1827). Charles Augustin de COULOMB (1736-1806); Luigi GALVANI (1737-1798).
Earliest canal built in England.
James BRINDLEY (1716-72)
Pit ponies worked in mines.
Science of pathology began with the formulation of its general principles by Giovanni MORGAGNI (1682-1771).
Sextant came into use as an aid to navigation.

Nervous system studied by von HALLER (1708-77).
Luigi GALVANI (1737-98)
Alessandro VOLTA (1745-1827)
Robert Whytt (1714-1764)
James HARGREAVES (*c.* 1720-1778) invented the spinning jenny, a light machine which produced a good weft or hosiery yarn.

Mill to bore cannon invented by John Wilkinson (1728-1808). Used by WATT (1736-1819) to bore cylinders for steam engines.
Obstetrics elevated to a scientific level through the work of William Hunter (1718-83).
Mathematics Advances in the function and solution of equations.
J. LAGRANGE (1736-1813)
Evariste GALOIS (1811-32)
Carl GAUSS (1777-1855)
Hydrogen and oxygen discovered by Karl SCHEELE (1742-1786).

Period of experiment into intensive methods of agriculture.
A. L. LAVOISIER (1743-94)
Sir Humphrey DAVY (1778-1829)
Steam engine built by James WATT (1736-1819) in operation. Faster action possible because of the introduction of a separate cylinder for cooling the steam so that the boiler could be kept hot continuously.
Age of the Earth questioned by the Comte de BUFFON (1707-88).

	1780	1783	1787	1791	1794	1797	1800	
Principal Events	**Gordon Riots** in London against Catholic emancipation (1780). **Armed Neutrality** of the North formed by Russia, Denmark, Sweden and Holland against British (1780). **War of American Independence** British surrendered to George WASHINGTON (1732-99) at Yorktown (1781). **Reforms of** JOSEPH II (1741-90) in Austria (1781-5). **Revolt in Peru** Natives under leadership of Tupac Amaru (1742-81), alleged descendant of Incas, rebelled against the Spanish (1780-2).	**Treaty of Versailles** (1783). Signed by Britain, France, Spain and Holland. Recognized 13 American states as independent. France and Spain recovered colonies from Britain. **Crimea** annexed by Russia (1783). **India Act** of William PITT the Younger (1759-1806) forbade interference in native affairs or declaration of war except in case of aggression (1784). Passed after British involvement in wars against Marathas and HAIDAR ALI (1722-82). **United States** entered into Chinese trade (1784).	**Peasant uprisings** culminated in rice riots in Edo, Japan (1787). **New York** declared Federal capital of United States (1788). **Society for Abolition of Slave Trade** (1787) founded in England. **Russia and Turkey** at war (1787-92). **Convicts** first transported from Britain to Australia. Penal settlements founded outside Sydney (1788).	**Canadian Constitution Act** passed (1791). Divided the country into French-speaking and English-speaking. **French Revolution** Extravagant style of LOUIS XVI (1754-93), based on heavy taxation, caused people of Paris to revolt (1789). Revolution spread throughout country. Louis forced to accept new constitution, but was executed in 1793 when the monarchy was abolished and a Republic declared. Paris ruled largely through the Reign of Terror imposed by ROBESPIERRE (1758-94). **Nepal** invaded by Chinese after the Gurkhas, a new political force, had menaced the Tibetan borders (1792). **Cornwallis Code** in India stabilized the revenue system and reorganized the judicial system along British lines (1793).	**French Revolutionary wars** Austria, Prussia, Holland and Spain declared war on France (1793). Rise of NAPOLEON (1769-1821) led to foreign policy of preserving France's 'natural frontiers', by constantly enlarging its territory. **Toussaint l'Ouverture** (1743-1803) led negro revolt in Haiti (1794). **Cape of Good Hope** taken by British from Dutch (1795). **Ceylon** conquered from the Dutch by the British (1796).	**NAPOLEON** (1769-1821) led the French Revolutionary Army to success in Italy and against Austria and Venice. Intended to invade Britain, but struck instead at her Empire by attacking Egypt. **MUNGO PARK** (1771-1806) explored the Gambia and established that the Niger flowed eastwards (1795-6). **United States' trade** with Japan, on behalf of the Dutch, marked the end of Japan's policy of isolation.	
Religion		**Illuminism** Mystical movement founded in Bavaria in the Middle Ages. Such men as SWEDENBORG (1688-1772) moved towards spiritualism. Influenced writers of the romantic age, and evoked interest in the unknown and infinite, in reaction to 18th-century rationalism.		**Japanese Rangaku school** of Dutch learning thrived despite restrictions and bans upon Christian writings. Liberal, pro-foreign ideas of the 'Dutch scholars' began to spread through Japan from the Dutch trading station at Deshima. Western studies had gained a hold in Japan by the early 19th century.				
Philosophy					**Political economy** Economists who defined and analyzed the problems of the developing industrial nation arrived at the idea of a self-regulating, organized economic life founded upon economic freedom and co-operation. They opposed mercantilist protectionism and advocated free trade. Adam SMITH (1723-90); Thomas Robert MALTHUS (1766-1834); Jean Baptiste SAY (1767-1832); David RICARDO (1772-1823); John Stuart MILL (1806-73).		
Literature	**English drama** Sentimental comedies and a return of the comedy of manners, witty, elegant, with a mastery of stagecraft. Oliver GOLDSMITH (1728-74) Richard SHERIDAN (1751-1816) **Italian purists** Reaction against Gallicisms in Italian language. Antonio Cesari (1760-1828) Pietro Giordani (1774-1848)	**Spanish Neo-classical theatre,** influenced by French classical drama, conformed strictly to the three unities of space, time and action. Leandro de Moratin (1760-1828) **Russian literature** moved from the predominant imitation of French Neo-classical models to more flexible Russian style. G. R. DERZHAVIN (1743-1816) N. M. Karamzin (1766-1826)	**Literary and historical criticism** in England became an important genre, combining stylistic elegance and intellectual clarity. Political writing influenced by French Revolution. Adam SMITH (1723-90) Edmund BURKE (1729-97) Edward GIBBON (1737-94)	**Hartford Wits** One of the first American schools of poetry. Conservative group who wrote satires and mock-heroic epics largely in imitation of English contemporaries. John Trumbull (1750-1831) Timothy Dwight (1752-1817) Joel Barlow (1754-1812)	**Italian patriotism** Literature assumed nationalistic character, and love of liberty in face of political and religious tyranny. A simultaneous intellectual revival resulted in patriotic, idealistic works, often steeped in classical literature and history. Vittorio Alfieri (1749-1803) Vincenzo Monti (1754-1828) Ugo FOSCOLO (1778-1827)	**Gothic novel** English genre characterized by horror and supernatural effects, usually gained from a background of medieval castles, ruins and gloomy landscapes. Horace WALPOLE (1717-97) Ann Radcliffe (1764-1823) Matthew Lewis (1775-1818) Charles Maturir: (1782-1824)	
Art	**Caricature** Portrait representing characteristic features of subject in exaggerated or distorted manner to produce humorous or satirical effect. Used by LEONARDO (1452-1519), developed by the CARRACI brothers and BERNINI (1598-1680). Caricatures were introduced to England by HOGARTH (1697-1764) and employed frequently in 18th century for political and social criticism. Thomas ROWLANDSON (1756-1827); James GILLRAY (1757-1815).		**Fancy pictures** Compositions combining facets of genre and portrait paintings, usually depicting rural scenes with idealized peasant characters. Thomas GAINSBOROUGH (1727-88) Thomas Barker (1769-1847) **Kangra school** combined the meticulous style of Mogul art and the sensuality of Ajanta. Diversified and prolific.	**Bun-jin painting** Japanese form of Chinese wen-jen painting—a visual expression of emotion linked with written verse. Used soft, free brushwork and created an impressionistic style. Yosa Buson (1716-83) Ike-no-Taiga (1723-76) Uragami Gyokudo (1745-1820)			
Architecture	**American colonial architecture** was characterized by projecting doorways flanked by columns, which sometimes extended along the façades. Interiors were influenced by Robert ADAM (c. 1728-92) in a style which became known as 'Federal Adam'. Charles Bulfinch (1763-1844) William Strickland (1787-1854)			**The Romantic movement** revived medieval designs in churches and country houses. Set in picturesque parks with lawns and serpentine lakes, scattered with Gothic- or oriental-inspired follies, and sham ruins. Originating in England, the Gothic rococo became popular in Protestant Europe. Nicholas HAWKSMOOR (1661-1736); Sir John VANBRUGH (1664-1726); Santin Aichel (1667-1723); Lancelot 'Capability' BROWN (1716-83); Horace WALPOLE (1717-97); Richard Mique (1728-94); James WYATT (1747-1813).		**Neo-classical** style in Russia began with European architects in Leningrad. Russians took it up towards the end of the century. Neo-classical styles in Russia were confined to secular architecture, churches continuing to be built in the Russian tradition. Antonio Rinaldi (c. 1709-90) Charles Cameron (c. 1740-1812) Adrian Dmitrievich Zakharov (1761-1811)	
Music	**Chamber music** Usually a sonata or symphony for small groups of instruments. Most important was the string quartet, developed to perfection by HAYDN (1732-1809) and MOZART (1756-91).	**Virtuosi concerti** for solo instruments developed by MOZART (1756-91). The soloist, pitted against the orchestra, was given scope to demonstrate virtuosity of technique.	**Hungarian melodiaria** Collections of popular songs and dances assembled by Kuruc—Hungarian freedom fighters against the Hapsburgs. Distinctive style, played on violin, zymbalom—a dulcimer-like instrument—and taragota, a double-reeded wind instrument.	**Classical symphonies** Final creative expression of the four-movement symphony—a combination of masterful orchestration and intimate knowledge of the effect of each instrument. First movement in sonata form; second usually lyrical and slow tempo; third a dance tempo (development of the original addition of the minuet at this stage); and fourth a long movement in a quick tempo, frequently in rondo form. Wolfgang MOZART (1756-91); Josef HAYDN (1732-1809).		**French Revolutionary songs,** such as La Marseillaise (1792), played and sung in the streets, in the new civic life of the Revolution. Claude Rouget de Lisle (1760-1836) Luigi CHERUBINI (1760-1842)	
Technology	**Developments in astronomy** The concept of the galaxy, the recording of nebulae and star clusters (1771); the discovery of Uranus (1781) and the first binary star system (1783). Thomas Wright (1711-1786) Charles MESSIER (1730-1817) William HERSCHEL (1738-1822) **Organic chemistry** developed after the isolation of carbon, oxygen and hydrogen as the elements of organic substances. Claude BERTHOLLET (1748-1822) Antoine LAVOISIER (1743-94)	**Lightning conductor** invented by Benjamin FRANKLIN (1706-90) to safeguard buildings. **English Channel** crossed for first time by balloon (1785) by J.-A.-C. CHARLES (1746-1823). **First iron bridge** built by Abraham DARBY (1678-1717) at Coalbrookdale in England. **Short-fused shell** for firing from cannon developed by Henry Shrapnel (1761-1842). **Earliest steamships** made by the French; unsuccessful due to insufficient power.	**Chemical composition of water** discovered by Henry CAVENDISH (1731-1810). **Improvements in lighting** Flat-woven wick for lamps, and the circular oil burner with cylindrical wick and glass chimney invented. **Gas generated** from coal. Devised by William MURDOCK (1754-1839). **Theory of calculus,** applied to mechanics and dynamics, explained by Joseph LAGRANGE (1736-1813) in his Mécanique Analytique (1788). Leonhard EULER (1707-83) **Decimal system** of weights, measures and coinage adopted in France.	**Saw-gin,** invented in the US by Eli WHITNEY (1765-1825), removed the seeds from a cotton boll by means of teeth, brushes and fan. **Ordnance Survey** of Great Britain instituted. Led to the mapping of the entire kingdom. **Telegraph stations** using semaphore arms and telescopes initiated by Claude Chappe (1763-1805), a Frenchman.	**Theory of geological change** produced by continuous natural forces published (1795) by James HUTTON (1726-1797). **Photography** Early techniques developed after discovery by Thomas WEDGWOOD (1771-1805) that sunlight caused silver salts to darken. **Preserving food** initiated by François APPERT (1752-1841), who bottled food for the French armies. **Use of artillery** in Europe increased, including the heavy field-gun.	**Gas** produced from wood used for lighting. **Vaccination** first carried out by Edward JENNER (1749-1823), who used a cowpox injection as a vaccination against smallpox. **Public health** Urban improvement acts in Britain; better land drainage reduced the risk of typhoid; many new hospitals built. Jeremy BENTHAM (1748-1832) Edwin CHADWICK (1800-90) **Theodolites** accurate to 1 second at 10 miles built by J. Ramsden (1735-1800).	

1800-1974

Technology

In Europe and America, the period was one of ever-accelerating change in material circumstances. In 1865 an Act of Parliament in Britain restricted the speed of all mechanical road vehicles to four miles per hour or less. Within a hundred years men were orbiting the Earth intent on travelling to the Moon.
Comparable rates of change occurred in many areas of technology, made possible largely by the increased sophistication of machine tools, which enabled more and more complex engineering and manufacturing processes to be carried out rapidly and repeatedly.

The advantages it brought, throughout the 19th century at least, did little for the well-being of the mass of people. The number of people increased more steeply every year and the feelings of anger and frustration at disproportionate wealth and power which had lain behind the English Civil War and the French Revolution manifested themselves frequently. Revolutions occurred throughout Europe, striving to achieve either a more liberal form of monarchy, a more representative government, or the abolition of monarchical and aristocratic rule.

Colonialism

On the basis of the industrial wealth that was being created, the powerful European nations attempted to create and consolidate world-wide colonial empires. During the reign of Queen VICTORIA (1819-1901) British troops were almost permanently engaged somewhere in the world extending or maintaining British influence over the countries which supplied raw materials for British factories. Germans, French, British, Dutch and Portuguese contended for colonies in Africa and the Far East. Russians sought naval access to the Mediterranean and pressed southwards against the British in Afghanistan.

The United States

One principal area of the world was closed to colonization. In 1823 James MONROE (1758-1831), President of the United States, put forward the 'Monroe Doctrine', forbidding further colonization by European powers of the North American continent. During the following century the USA grew in size from the original eastern seaboard states, to cover the entire continent. The Indians were overcome, the northern and southern frontiers defined. The Union itself was given its most severe test in the Civil War of 1861-5. Under the leadership of Abraham LINCOLN (1809-56), the United States was strengthened in the form it has retained ever since.

The Far East

In the Far East, European colonial interest in China vied with the territorial acquisitions of Japan, which continued until the end of the Second World War. Since the revolution in 1911 which overthrew the Manchu dynasty, China has been governed as a republic, first by Nationalists and then, since 1949, by the Communist government created by MAO TSE-TUNG.

Nationalism and Communism

The conflict between Nationalist and Communist was, and still is, a recurrent one in many parts of the world. It was the exaggerated polarization of such political forces which brought HITLER (1889-1945) to power in Germany at the head of a National Socialist regime. Victory for the Communists over the reactionary government of the Russian royal family brought about the foundation of the USSR in 1917, an event which exacerbated international tensions and led, after 1945, to the division of the world into two power blocs.

Internationalism

Out of the nationalistic rivalries of the First and Second World Wars a solution to international conflict was seen to lie in an organisation to which all disputes should be referred. The League of Nations, set up after the First World War, failed to achieve its purpose. The United Nations has been more successful, but international power still resides with the richest and most heavily-armed nations.

Progress

The progression from horse and canal transport to rocket engines and spacecraft, has not altered the nature of international politics but only the machinery. Electronic communications, although they encircle the world, do nothing to feed the majority of the world's population who have less than enough to eat.

Graph of the population of the world projected to the year 2000

527 Europe

992 North and South America

353 USSR

768 Africa

32 Oceania
3458 Asia

392

328

180
222
13
1381

296
156
134
133 6
925

208
64
76
111 2
801

152
31 56
107 2
630

125 18 42
106 2
498

1750   1800   1850   1900   1950   2000

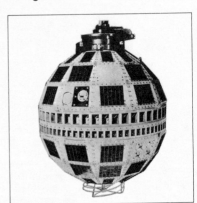

Telstar came into use on 23 July 1962—the first time live television pictures were relayed across the Atlantic

This final section of the Time Chart covers a period of immense technological change, of the theories of DARWIN (1809-82) and FREUD (1856-1939) which revolutionized man's view of himself, and of a constantly-troubled search for a religion, philosophy or morality which will provide some fundamental general principles for human behaviour in our world.

	1800	1804	1808	1812	1816	1820
Principal Events	**Britain and Ireland** formally united in the Act of Union (1801). **Child labour** banned in Britain (1802). NAPOLEON (1769-1821) created first Consul of France for life (1802). **Peace in Europe** (1801-3) Treaty between France and Austria dissolved the Holy Roman Empire. Napoleon made peace with the papacy and gave the German states a new constitution. Hapsburg domination ended. Britain declared war on France again. **Portuguese** crossed Africa from west to east.	NAPOLEON (1769-1821) crowned Emperor in Paris. Against Britain, Austria, Russia and Prussia, French land forces supreme. At the battle of Austerlitz (1805) Austrian and Russian armies defeated. British naval supremacy was ensured by the victory of NELSON (1758-1805). Napoleon became King of Italy (1805), placed his brothers on the thrones of Holland, Naples, Westphalia and Spain, created the Confederation of the Rhine and issued the Berlin Decree (1806) by which he closed Europe to British trade. **Slave trade** abolished in the British Empire (1807).	**Slave trade** abolished in the USA (1808). **Peninsular wars** (1808-14) between Britain and France and Spain. METTERNICH (1773-1859) appointed Austrian Foreign Minister (1809). **Russia** acquired Finland after Russo-Swedish war (1808-9). **Pius VII** (1742-1823) arrested after excommunicating NAPOLEON (1769-1821) who had acquired the papal estates (1809). BERNADOTTE (1763-1844), a French marshal, offered the Swedish crown (1810). **Massacre of the Mamluks** (1811) by Mohammed Ali (1769-1849), emir of Egypt.	**USA declared war** on Britain (1812-14) over Indian and Canadian territorial disputes. NAPOLEON (1769-1821) invaded Russia and occupied Moscow, but was forced to retreat (1812). WELLINGTON (1769-1852) invaded France after victories in Spain, the Austrians defeated the French at Leipzig and Paris fell (1814). Napoleon exiled to Elba. The Congress of Vienna restored the Austrian and Prussian monarchies and established the kingdom of Poland and the Germanic Confederation. Napoleon resumed power but was defeated at Waterloo (1815).	**Protectionism** in trade began in Britain (1815) and USA (1816). **US frontier** with Canada defined (1818). CHAKA (1773-1828) became leader of the Zulu nation (1818). **Boer revolt** broke out in Cape colony, ceded to Britain at the Congress of Vienna. **Indian sub-continent,** except for Nepal and Afghanistan, under British control or influence. **Republic of Colombia** founded by BOLIVAR (1783-1830) who became its first president (1819).	**Egypt** conquered the Sudan (1820). **Greek war of Independence** (1821-30) from Turkish rule. **Insurrections in Italy** put down by Austrians, who ruled the Italian states after 1814. **Liberia** founded (1822) for the repatriation of liberated American negro slaves. **Brazil** declared itself independent of Portugal (1822). **The Monroe Doctrine** closed the USA to colonial settlement by non-Americans. European powers were excluded from interference in the political affairs of the USA (1823).
Religion	**Missionary activity** in the East India Company's territories in India was initially discouraged under a policy of non-interference in Indian cultural affairs.	**Jewish enlightenment** Began in Germany following emancipation and some assimilation in Europe. Rationalist reform movement which criticized and eventually rejected much of Talmudic Judaism. Rejected resurrection and belief in a personal Messiah. Moses Mendelssohn (1729-86); Abraham Geiger (1810-74); Samuel Holdheim (1806-60). **Christian toleration** proscribed in China. In 1815 a Catholic priest was strangled for being in China without permission. **Christian literature** suppressed in China under the Ch'ien Lung Empire.	**Sheikhis** Extreme form of Shi'ite religion, called after Sheikh Ahmad ibn-Zayn-al-Din al-Ahsai (d. 1827), who taught that while the 12 imams (Muslim religious leaders) had no power, they were nevertheless instruments of divine will.	**Southcottians** Followers of Joanna Southcott (1750-1814), who claimed she was going to give birth to a divine son. **Missionaries** allowed for the first time into Indian territories due to the influence of WILBERFORCE (1759-1833) and the evangelicals in the British Parliament. By 1813 five major English missionary societies had been founded.	**Clapham Sect** Group of wealthy, pious and benevolent evangelicals living in Clapham, London, who devoted themselves to such social causes as the abolition of the slave trade. John Venn (1759-1813); William Wilberforce (1759-1833); Henry Thornton (1760-1815); Zachary Macaulay (1768-1838).	**Disciples of Christ** Liberal Protestant sect in USA. Belief in racial equality and Christian unity. **Militant Sikhs** in India, defeated and outlawed by the Mughals, reappeared during British rule in bands under leaders who formed small states. Ranjit Singh (d. 1839) formed a Sikh nation within the Punjab.
Philosophy	**Romantic philosophy of religion** led to emphasis on non-rational and subconscious thought as being the true religious spirit of the human being. Immanuel KANT (1724-1804) Friedrich Schleiermacher (1768-1834) Georg Hegel (1770-1831)	**Transcendental Idealism,** initiated by Immanuel KANT (1724-1804), a germinal figure of modern philosophy, postulated that the summit of man's understanding consisted in being able to discover the conditions that regulate man's knowledge of the world. J. G. FICHTE (1762-1814)		**Influx of western ideas** into China, through merchants, missionaries and diplomats, created a new critical spirit in Chinese thought. Confucianism was considered superior to western philosophical thought, but western learning was used for subjects with practical application.	**Early 'Utopian' socialism** promoted by humanitarian writers of France and Britain who, rejecting the inequalities of capitalist industrial society, sought to establish an economic system based upon collective control of industry and commerce. Early experiments in co-operative and socialist organization were carried out by emigrant communities in America. Comte de SAINT-SIMON (1760-1825); Robert OWEN (1771-1858); Charles Fourier (1772-1837); Etienne Cabet (1788-1856); P. Leroux (1797-1871); Louis BLANQUI (1805-81); J. Reynaud (1806-63); Ferdinand Lassalle (1825-64).	
Literature	**American novel** followed European models, some dealing with adventures of pioneer frontiersmen and Indians, or contemporary social issues. Many sentimental and gothic novels. Hugh H. Brackenridge (1748-1816) William Brown (1765-93) C. B. Brown (1771-1810)	**Weimar classicism** Weimar became the centre of culture in Germany, the main literary theories being those of Schiller (1759-1805) and GOETHE (1749-1832), based on a new idea of poetic humanism. They sought emotional harmony and balance, and were concerned with the spiritual and intellectual development of the individual. J. C. F. HÖLDERLIN (1770-1843)	**Romanticism** in literature was a reaction against stale classicism, combined with the emotional energy of the German *Sturm und Drang* movement and the cult of the individual which arose from the work of ROUSSEAU (1712-78). It covered the whole of Europe, but took on national characteristics. In the poetry of WORDSWORTH (1770-1850), lyrical descriptions of nature expressed personal emotion. FOSCOLO (1778-1827) took up themes of Italian nationalism and liberty. STENDHAL (1783-1842) developed the self-examining, nationalist French novel. The brothers GRIMM in Germany turned to the supernatural for their themes. Dramatists wrote of the glory of the past, high adventure, sweeping emotion and individual heroism. E. T. A. HOFFMANN (1776-1822); Lord BYRON (1788-1824); Victor HUGO (1802-85); Gérard de NERVAL (1808-55).	**Bildungsroman** German novel of ideas, following the development of character. Culmination of long tradition with *Wilhelm Meister* by GOETHE (1749-1832). Christoph WIELAND (1733-1813) NOVALIS (1772-1801) Joseph von EICHENDORFF (1798-1857)	**Historical novel** created by Sir Walter SCOTT (1771-1832), whose picturesque evocation of the past and accurate historical reconstruction had extensive influence on European literature. Alessandro MANZONI (1785-1873)	
Art		**Romanticism** Movement representing the revolt against accepted classical traditions of reason and harmony, and extolling the individualism inspired by, among other things, the French Revolution. Paintings were passionate and sentimental. Their subject matter often included fantasy, exotic scenes, or landscapes with mysterious gothic ruins. History paintings with epic themes were popular, usually representing the growing sense of nationalism. Landscape paintings demonstrated the feeling of self-identification of the artist with an overwhelming force of nature. Henry Fuseli (1741-1825); Francisco GOYA y Lucientes (1746-1828); Caspar David FRIEDRICH (1774-1840); Theodore GÉRICAULT (1791-1824); Eugène DELACROIX (1798-1863).		**Romantic landscape** painters concentrated on the emotive effects of light on their subject, and the changing light of the seasons. Compositions were lyrical, sometimes theatrical. The treatment of light in the work of TURNER (1775-1851) almost completely disregarded any naturalistic form. Caspar David FRIEDRICH (1770-1840); John CONSTABLE (1776-1837); Jean COROT (1796-1875).		**Norwich school** English landscape painting renowned for its range of watercolour techniques and its treatment of outdoor light. John CROME (1768-1821) John Thirtle (1777-1839) John Sell COTMAN (1782-1842) John B. Crome (1794-1842) James Stark (1794-1859) George Vincent (1796-c. 1830) Joseph Stannard (1797-1830)
Architecture	**Rationalism** Amidst the conflicts of the 19th century arose a number of rationalist architects whose work was characterized by a disregard of historical academicism and a free use of form, a development which foreshadowed the new movement in architecture of the 20th century. Sir John SOANE (1753-1837) Friedrich Gilly (1772-1800)					**Romanesque revival** began in Germany with early Christian designs for churches. Byzantine and northern and southern Romanesque styles were reproduced in Germany, England, France and America. Karl SCHINKEL (1781-1841) Jacques Hittorff (1792-1867) Henry RICHARDSON (1838-86)
Music			**Romanticism** In place of ordered, balanced, formal music came intense lyricism and rich harmony, poetically inspired programme music, love songs, massive orchestral works, epic choral works, heroic symphonies, oratorios and requiems. The desire for individual expression led to new freedom of composition, more melody, and new harmonies. Heroic sentiment was expressed in patriotism, from which sprung many national schools of music. Ludwig van BEETHOVEN (1770-1827); Franz SCHUBERT (1797-1828); Frédéric CHOPIN (1810-49); Robert SCHUMANN (1810-56); Anton BRUCKNER (1824-96); Johannes BRAHMS (1833-97); Peter TCHAIKOVSKY (1840-93).		**Programme music** Instrumental music interpreting poetic or narrative subject matter by presenting evocative sounds, either by means of imaginative suggestion or imitation of natural sounds, as in the 'Pastoral Symphony' by BEETHOVEN (1770-1827). Hector BERLIOZ (1803-69) Felix MENDELSSOHN (1809-47)	**German Romantic opera** evolved from the *singspiele* tradition, using fairy-tale legends, themes from medieval history and the supernatural. Scenes were rural, the protagonists humble country people, struggling against supernatural forces. Carl Maria von WEBER (1786-1826)
Technology	**First American suspension bridge** built by James Finley (c. 1762-1828). **Steam carriage** patented by Richard TREVITHICK (1771-1833). Steam engine made more efficient and more safe by James WATT (1736-1819). Oliver EVANS (1755-1819) Arthur Woolf (1776-1837) **Rotary wood-planing** machine invented by Joseph BRAMAH (1748-1814). **Beet sugar** produced in Silesia by Franz Achard (1753-1821).	**First steamboat** to be commercially successful built in US by Robert FULTON (1765-1815). **Railway locomotive** first successfully built by Richard TREVITHICK (1771-1833), in England. **Iron** cables and rigging used on ships. Cast iron barges on rivers and canals in Britain. **Binary stars** studied by Sir William HERSCHEL (1738-1822). **Gas** used for lighting and heating in Europe (1806).	**Chemistry** Quantitative atomic theory established by John DALTON (1766-1844). Amedeo AVOGADRO (1776-1856) distinguished between atoms and molecules. **Geology** Discovery of the volcanic origin of basalt and the uniform theory of the Earth. Foundation of vertebrate palaeontology. James HUTTON (1726-1797); John Playfair (1748-1819); Abraham WERNER (c. 1750-1816); Jean d'Aubisson de Voisins (1769-1819); Georges CUVIER (1769-1832); Alexandre BRONGNIART (1770-1847). **Power-driven printing press** and flat bed press invented. Friedrich Koenig (1774-1833).	GEORGE STEPHENSON (1781-1848) designed his first locomotive (1814). **Transverse wave theory** of light established by Augustin FRESNEL (1788-1827).	**Cast iron plough** invented by Jethro Wood (1774-1834) in the US. **First planing machine** for metal invented. Joseph Clement (1779-1844) Richard ROBERTS (1789-1864) Sir Joseph WHITWORTH (1803-87) **Draisienne,** the forerunner of the bicycle, invented by Freiherr Drais (1785-1851). **Solar spectrum** Principal black lines charted by Joseph von FRAUNHOFER (1787-1826).	**First iron steamship** crossed the English Channel. Assembled from parts prefabricated in Staffordshire ironworks. **Nervous system** studied by Charles BELL (1774-1842), François MAGENDI (1783-1855) and Johannes MÜLLER (1801-58). **Mathematics** studied and developed. Claude BERTHOLLET (1748-1822) Niels ABEL (1802-29) Carl GAUSS (1777-1855) Augustin CAUCHY (1789-1857).

	1824	1828	1832	1836	1840	1844	1847
Principal Events	**Trade Unions** made legal in Britain, after the repeal of the Combination Laws (1824). **First Anglo-Burmese war** (1824-6) broke out after Burmese threat to India. British took Rangoon. **Ashanti wars** between Britain and the Ashanti tribes along the Gold Coast (1824-7). **First Pan-American Congress** at Panama convened (1826) by BOLÍVAR (1783-1830). **Treaty of London** (1827) between Britain, Russia and France, to secure the autonomy of Greece.	**Catholic Emancipation Act** passed in Britain (1829). Catholics admitted to public office. **Revolution in France** (1830) CHARLES X (1757-1836) abdicated; LOUIS PHILIPPE (1773-1850) elected King. **Colombia** divided into New Granada, Venezuela and Ecuador. Abdication of BOLÍVAR (1783-1830). **Uprisings** in Belgium, Poland (1830), Modena, Parma and the papal states (1831). Belgian independence guaranteed by Britain and France, Poland invaded by Russia and Italian states dominated by Austria.	**Egypt's independence** recognized by Turkey (1833). **Reform Act** (1834) in Britain followed increasing and often violent agitation to adjust parliamentary boundaries to give suffrage to new industrial towns. **Liberal government** in Spain and Portugal supported by British, French, Spanish and Portuguese alliance. **South Australia and Victoria** founded (1834-7). Abolition of transportation of convicts. **Great Trek** of the Boer cattlemen in Southern Africa, to settle in the Transvaal (1835-7).	**Texas** formed into an independent republic by American colonists (1836). **Chartist movement** in Britain demanded adult male suffrage. **Austria** evacuated all the papal states except Ferrara (1838). **The Boers** defeated the Zulus at Blood River, Natal (1838). **Britain at war** with China, over the opium trade, and with the Afghans. Kabul occupied to forestall growing Russian influence (1839).	**Convention of the Straits** (1841). Collective guarantee by European powers of Turkish independence. Turkey gained Syria from Egypt. **Webster-Ashburton** treaty further defined the frontier between Canada and the USA (1842). **New British Colonies** Gambia (1843), Natal, after war against Boers (1843), and New Zealand, after Treaty of Waitangi (1840). **Treaty of Nanking** (1842) ceded Hong Kong to Britain and opened Canton, Amoy, Foochow, Ningpo and Shanghai to British trade.	**USA at war** with Mexico (1846-8), who ceded territory to the USA. **Ireland** Strong agitation for repeal of Union and reform of land tenure system. Beginning of Irish potato famine. **Corn Laws** in Britain repealed by PEEL (1788-1850) after widespread distress and agitation (1846). **First segregation** of natives and settlers in Southern Africa—Zulu reserves established in Natal (1846). **Anglo-Sikh wars** in India (1845-8) led to the annexation of the Punjab.
Religion	**Plymouth Brethren** Founded in Dublin by John DARBY (1800-82) who was dissatisfied with the lack of spirituality in the Church. Moved to Plymouth where all who wanted spiritual unity could attend meetings. Rapidly split into many factions, the strictest being exclusive, forbidding contact with non-members. **Foundation** of many European missionary societies.	**Mormons** or Latter-Day Saints. Founded in 1830 in USA by Joseph SMITH (1805-44), who claimed he had been forbidden by two heavenly messengers to join any existing Church, but to prepare to be the prophet of a new one. The Mormon Church is based on a dual priesthood, the spiritual Melchizedeks and the temporal Aaronic priesthood. They believe the *Book of Mormon* to be the Word of God. **Catholic Apostolic Church** (Irvingites) Presbyterian sect following the teaching of Edward IRVING (1792-1834). Founded 1831 after apparently miraculous healing, repetitions of scenes of Corinth as described by ST PAUL (1st cent. A.D.), and speaking in tongues in Scotland and London. Basically orthodox, but very mystical liturgy full of symbolism.		**Oxford Movement** or Tractarians, an Anglican High Church movement originating in Oxford, rejected the increasing secular influence over the Church, and advocated a more Catholic outlook in doctrine and ritual. Also called Anglo-Catholics. John KEBLE (1792-1866) Edward Pusey (1800-82) John Henry NEWMAN (1810-90)	**Christian socialism** English group, though with antecedents in France, committed to reviving Christianity as an aid to social reform, by applying the teachings of JESUS to contemporary industrial problems. Foundation of the Young Men's Christian Association (1844). Robert de Lamennais (1782-1854); Charles KINGSLEY (1819-75); John Ludlow (1821-1911); Thomas Hughes (1822-96). **Babism** Mystical Muslim sect which succeeded the Sheikhis. Founded by the Bab (Ali Muhammad) (1820-50), who considered himself a mirror in which believers could see the image of God.	**Adventists** Group of American sects all of which have faith in the second coming of JESUS CHRIST and the beginning of the millenium. Modern Seventh Day Adventists observe Saturday as the Sabbath.
Philosophy	**Utilitarianism** set forth the principle of Utility— an action is right in so far as it tends to produce the greatest happiness for the greatest number—as the standard by which to determine the value of laws and social institutions. A considerable part of the practical effectiveness of the Utilitarians was due to their alliance with the new political economy of Adam SMITH (1723-90), MALTHUS (1766-1834) and David Ricardo (1772-1823) Jeremy BENTHAM (1748-1832); James Mill (1773-1836); John Stuart MILL (1806-1873).		**Dialectical materialism** stated that all change, and especially historical change, took place in accordance with the law of dialectics, or logical disputation, the final aim of the process being the synthesis of truth and reality. Personal values to be subordinated to the State. Friedrich HEGEL (1770-1831); Karl MARX (1818-83).		**Transcendentalism** Philosophical and literary movement in New England, reacting against the rationalism of science, and advocating intuition and direct experience in order to understand reality. Amos Alcott (1799-1888) R. W. EMERSON (1803-82) Margaret Fuller (1810-50) Henry THOREAU (1817-62)	**Positivism** Auguste COMTE (1798-1857) believed the search for ultimate causes should be abandoned, and that philosophers should focus on the laws of phenomena as the knowledge that is both attainable and useful. He proposed the creation of a new science, sociology, to study, without preconceptions, human phenomena.
Literature	**American literature** began to achieve an international reputation, through the work of William Bryant (1794-1878), Washington IRVING (1783-1859), James Fenimore COOPER (1789-1851) and Edgar Allan POE (1809-49).	**The Kabuki theatre** in Japan provided witty commentary on everyday events using dance, music, mime, sets and costumes. Less formal than the No plays, during the Tokugawa period, Kabuki often used the plays of the puppet theatre, but later accomplished Kabuki playwrights appeared. Chikamatsu Monzaemon (1653-1725) Mokuami Kawatake (1816-1893)	**Costumbrismo** Spanish realistic prose style, ranging from pure descriptive passages to more critical and satirical sketches of customs and individual characters. Fernan Caballero (1797-1877) Serafín Calderón (1799-1867) Mariano de Larra (1809-1837) José de Pereda (1833-1906)	**Jung Deutschland** 'Young Germany'. Radical literary movement in Germany, advocating freedom of thought and expression in political resistance to Romantic idealism. Believed that literature should deal with political and social matters. Heinrich HEINE (1797-1856) Heinrich Laube (1806-84) Theodor Mundt (1808-61) Karl Gutzkow (1811-78) Georg BÜCHNER (1813-37)	**Russian drama** entered a vigorous period with the verse tragedies of PUSHKIN (1799-1837) and LERMONTOV (1814-41), criticizing aristocratic life, and the comic social satire of GOGOL (1809-52) and Griboyedov (1795-1829). Culminated in the psychological, realistic social drama of CHEKHOV (1860-1904). Alexander OSTROVSKY (1823-86)	**English replaced Persian** as the official language in the higher courts of law in India. Schools taught English language and literature. **Chinese theatre** Peking style emerged as the most popular of the regional variations. Developed into a formalized synthesis of movements, dialogue and music. Women's roles played by female impersonators.
Art	**Romantic sculpture** While maintaining classical characteristics, sculptors of the Romantic period, particularly in France, returned to medieval subject matter, inspired by history and literature, and gave animals dramatic importance in their own right. François Rude (1784-1855) Antoine-Louis Barye (1796-1875) Auguste Preault (1810-79)		**Political cartoons** All over northern Europe the cartoon became increasingly used as a weapon of satire. The English magazine *Punch* was founded in 1841. George Cruikshank (1792-1878) Paul Gavarni (1804-66) H. Monnier (1805-77) Honoré Daumier (1808-1879)	**Nazarenes** A community of German artists who wanted to revive German religious art, based on the spiritual inspiration of the medieval Italians. They lived and worked in the deserted monastery of San Isidrio in Rome, and painted frescoes expressing their religious principles. Joseph Koch (1768-1839) P. CORNELIUS (1783-1867) Johann Overbeck (1789-1869)		**Hudson River school** First school of American landscape painting, inspired by the beauty of the New England scenery. The dramatic mountains, forests and rivers of the area were treated in a romantic way, with emphasis on the effect of changing light. Influenced by CONSTABLE (1776-1837). Thomas Doughty (1793-1856) Thomas Cole (1801-1848) Alvan Fisher (1792-1863)
Architecture	**Greek revivalism** in America. Though continuing to follow European precedent during the early 19th century, American architects created a national style, imitating classical architecture for national monuments and government buildings. William Strickland (1788-1854) Ithiel Town (1784-1844) Alexander Davis (1803-92) Thomas Walter (1804-87)	**French Empire style** Baron Georges-Eugène HAUSSMANN (1809-91) planned a development scheme for Paris, consisting principally of a series of *rond points* from which radiate broad, straight avenues. Monuments and civic buildings were built in a style similar to that of the French Early Renaissance. Pierre Vignon (1763-1828) Thomas Walter (1804-87)	**Ancient Russian revival** followed the period of Neoclassicism in Russia, a part of the same revivalist movement which characterized western architecture of the period.	**American rationalism** rejected the impractical nature of the classical revival style for public buildings, in favour of attention to the demands of utility and free use of classical styles. Charles Bulfinch (1763-1844) Benjamin Henry Latrobe (1764-1820) Robert Mills (1781-1855) Horatio Greenough (1805-52)	**Gothic revival** accompanied a strong Anglican religious movement and a search for a new national architectural style in England. Archaeology and historical research gave a more precise understanding of the development of the Gothic style. During the 1830s and 1840s the Neo-Gothic fashion became widespread throughout Europe and spread to America. Franz-Christian Gau (1790-1853); Sir Charles Barry (1795-1860); Sir George Gilbert SCOTT (1811-78); Augustus PUGIN (1812-52); Eugène-Emanuel VIOLLET-LE-DUC (1814-79); William BUTTERFIELD (1814-1900); George STREET (1824-81); Alfred Waterhouse (1830-1905).	
Music	**German lieder** The music assumed as much importance as the lyrics, and the pianist's role became equal to that of the singer. Romantic *lieder* were long, lyrical or dramatic, full of contrasts of mood and atmosphere. Franz SCHUBERT (1797-1828) Robert SCHUMANN (1810-56) Hugo Wolf (1860-1903)	**French grand opera** Written to appeal to the uncultured audiences of the new middle classes. Spectacularly staged, often included ballet; supported by enormous orchestras. Historical subjects. Eugène Scribe (1791-1861) (librettist) MEYERBEER (1791-1864) ROSSINI (1792-1868)	**Russian nationalism** Inspired to patriotic sentiment by the Napoleonic Wars, Russian composers began to turn to their own national heritage. GLINKA (1809-57) was one of the first to incorporate folk themes and local atmosphere into his operas. Alexander Dargomizhsky (1813-60)	**Italian opera** Generally Romantic melodrama, showing some influence of French grand opera, though more elegant and refined in style, and more trivial in content; melodious and dramatic, some of the most popular operas of the 19th century. Giacomo Mayr (1763-1848); Gioacchino ROSSINI (1792-1868); Giovanni Pacini (1796-1867); Gaetano DONIZETTI (1797-1848); Vincenzo Bellini (1801-35); Giuseppi VERDI (1813-1901).		**Virtuosi concerti** Technical improvements of instruments and the Romantic cult of individualism led to spectacular virtuosi performances, often by the composer. Niccolò PAGANINI (1782-1840) Louis Spohr (1784-1851) Franz LISZT (1811-86) Max Bruch (1838-1920) Antonin DVORÁK (1841-1904)
Technology	**Locomotion No. 1** built by George STEPHENSON (1781-1848) for the opening of the Stockton-Darlington railway, first successful passenger service. **Calculating machine** developed by Charles BABBAGE (1792-1871). **Portland cement**, durable and impervious to water, patented by Joseph ASPDIN (1779-1855). **Bonding rubber to cloth** Process developed by Charles MACINTOSH (1766-1843).	**Machine tools** made more accurate by the invention of the standard screw gauge and a machine able to measure to one millionth of an inch. Developed by Sir Joseph WHITWORTH (1803-87). **Horse omnibus**, the forerunner of the tram, in use in Paris and London. **Comparative embryology** founded by Karl von BAER (1792-1876). **Steeple engine**, designed for ocean-going paddle steamers, ensured greater stability by lowering the centre of gravity.	**First horse-tramway car** in New York. In use in Paris (1855) and London (1860-1). **Vapour compressor**, forerunner of the refrigerator, invented by Jacob PERKINS (1766-1849). **Dynamo** invented after studies of electricity and magnetism. André AMPERE (1775-1836) George OHM (1789-1854) Michael FARADAY (1791-1867) **Gravitational astronomy** and the Earth's magnetic field studied by Pierre LAPLACE (1749-1827).	**Revolver** invented by Samuel COLT (1814-62). **Vulcanised rubber** invented by Charles GOODYEAR (1800-60). **Electric telegraph** invented. Samuel MORSE (1791-1872) Sir Charles WHEATSTONE (1802-75) **'Great Eastern'** the first steamship to be fitted with a propeller. Carried enough coal for a voyage to Australia and back. **Daguerreotype** photographic process discovered by Louis DAGUERRE (1787-1851).	**Cunard line** carried transatlantic mails by paddle steamer. **'Railway Mania'** in Britain. Mileage of railways and the traction power of locomotives increased rapidly. **Ice Age** theory devised by Louis AGASSIZ (1807-73). **Breech-loading rifle** invented by J. N. von DREYSE (1787-1867). **Use of steam engine** spread throughout the world.	**Use of ether** as a surgical anaesthetic first demonstrated, in the US, by William MORTON (1819-68). **Rotary printing press** invented by Robert HOE (1812-86). **Planet Neptune** discovered after a study of irregularities in the orbit of Uranus. John ADAMS (1819-92) Urbain LEVERRIER (1811-77) **Heilmann comb**, for combing short wool and cotton fibres, and the Brussels power loom for weaving carpets invented.

	1847	1850	1853	1856	1859	1862 · 1865
Principal Events	**European revolutions** (1848) to set up new republics in France, Naples, Venice, Parma, Milan, Sardinia and Rome. Rebellions the result of poor crops, famine, lack of relief and the increasing hardships of industrialization. Risings in Vienna, Berlin and Poland against aristocratic government. Almost universally suppressed (1849) by French, Austrian and Prussian forces. Prussia enlarged her territory by invading Denmark. LIVINGSTONE (1813-73) crossed the Kalahari desert and reached Lake Ngami (c. 1849).	**France.** Universal suffrage and freedom of press abolished (1850). *Coup d'état* by Louis Napoleon (1808-73), proclaimed **Democratic rights** abolished by the German Diet (1851). **Cuban insurrection** suppressed by Spanish (1851). Emperor NAPOLEON III (1852). **Transvaal** recognized as independent by Britain (1852). **T'ai P'ing** rebellion in China (1850-64) seriously weakened Manchu authority.	**US Republican party** formed (1854). **Crimean war** (1854-6) between Britain, France and Turkey, against Russia, to contain Russian expansion. Russia surrendered after the siege of Sebastopol. **Liberal revolution** in Spain overthrew the government (1854). **Austro-Prussian** alliance in defence against Russia (1854). FERDINAND DE LESSEPS (1805-94) received concession to build Suez Canal (1854). **Anglo-Afghan treaty**, to check Persian designs on Herat (1855).	**Congress of Paris** (1856) established peace in the Crimea, and Turkish independence. Black Sea declared a neutral zone. **Unification of Italy** secretly planned by NAPOLEON III (1808-73) and CAVOUR (1810-61) at the expense of Austria. **British colonial wars** against Persia, forced to recognize Afghanistan, and (with the French) against China. 11 new ports opened, opium trade legalized. **Indian mutiny** (1857-8) put down by British. Government of India transferred to British authority.	**American Civil War** (1861-5) over the right to own slaves. Test of the strength of the Federal government led by Abraham LINCOLN (1809-65). War began when South Carolina attempted to secede from the Union. After four years of fighting, Confederate General LEE (1807-70) surrendered (1865). Slavery abolished. Lincoln assassinated by BOOTH (1838-65). **New Italian kingdom** formed, excluding Venetia, the Marches, Umbria, Naples and Sicily, all conquered by GARIBALDI (1807-82). Unification achieved after Piedmontese defeat of Papal forces. VICTOR EMMANUEL (1820-78) proclaimed king (1861). **Russian serfs** emancipated (1861) under ALEXANDER II (1818-81).	BISMARCK (1815-98) appointed Prussian chancellor (1862). **Revolution in Athens.** Prince William of Denmark became King George I of Greece (1863). **French protectorate** (1863) established over Cambodia and Eastern Cochin China. **Allied expedition** of British, French, Dutch and American troops against Japan (1864).
Religion	**Shinto** folk movements arose towards the end of the Tokugawa period in Japan. Disregarded by the orthodox Shinto priests and scholars, these movements, founded by unknown individuals, appealed strongly to the poor and the lower classes in Japan. Nakayama Miki (d. 1887) Kurozumi Munetada (d. 1849)	**Christadelphians** Organization formed in America claiming to represent the true apostolic faith of the 1st century AD. **Indian Muslim community**, about a quarter of the total population, which had formed the ruling class under the Mughals, found itself in decline as high Muslim officials were replaced by British administrators.	**T'ai P'ing teaching** in China, the 'Heavenly Kingdom of Great Peace' of Hung Hsiu-ch'uan (1812-64), contained elements of Protestant Christianity and native beliefs, giving rise to the Worshippers of Shang Ti, a political and religious sect which attempted to overthrow the Manchu dynasty.	**Confessionalism** Lutheran revival of church discipline, emphasising the use of the sacraments and ritual. Reaction to Romantic emotionalism. Ernst Hengstenberg (1802-69) Gottlieb von Harless (1806-79) **Christian missions** in the interior of China permitted in the Treaties of Tientsin (1858). Rapid growth of missionary activity in China.	**Origin of Species** published (1859) by Charles DARWIN (1809-82). Undermined traditional interpretation of Genesis. Many alienated from orthodox religion, others tried to reconcile both theories, while fundamentalists in America rejected Darwin's theory. **French rights** for Catholic missions to own land in China secured in the Peking conventions (1860).	**Baha'ism** New Muslim system, based on the teachings of the Bab (1820-50), founded by Baha-Allah (1817-92), who claimed to be the manifestation of the divine will foretold by Bab. Influenced by current European liberalism, he added Christian elements to the mystical Shi'ite heritage.
Philosophy	**'Scientific' socialism** evolved in Germany from a combination of Hegelian and French socialist ideas. The *Communist Manifesto* (1848) advanced the theory of the historical inevitability of the revolutionary role of the proletariat in the class struggle. Ludwig Feuerbach (1804-72); Bruno Bauer (1809-82); Moses Hess (1812-75); Karl Grün (1817-87); Karl MARX (1818-83); Friedrich ENGELS (1820-95). **Shinto revival**, which began during Japan's 18th-century transition from a feudal to a unified national state, attempted to redefine the philosophical bases of Shinto. Kamo Mabuchi (c. 1697-1769); Motoori Norinaga (d. 1801); Hirata Atsutane (d. 1843); Matteo RICCI (1552-1610).				**Evolutionists** The publication of the *Origin of Species* by Charles DARWIN (1809-82) brought the living world within materialist laws, challenging social and religious teaching and provoking a revolutionary trend of thought. Herbert SPENCER (1820-1903) Henri BERGSON (1859-1941) C. L. Morgan (1852-1936) S. Alexander (1859-1938)	**Irrationalism** saw the whole world of phenomena to be an objectivization of will: 'We think in order to do'. Arthur SCHOPENHAUER (1788-1860) Friedrich NIETZSCHE (1844-1900)
Literature	**Biedermeier period** of sober resignation, didacticism and social conservatism, rooted in the German middle class. Much nature poetry. Annette von DROSTE-HÜLSHOFF (1797-1848) Eduard MORIKE (1804-75) Adalbert STIFTER (1805-68)	**New England reformers** Writers allied themselves with contemporary reform movements, including better working conditions, female suffrage, temperance and the abolition of slavery. Emotive criticism had a wide effect on legislation. William GARRISON (1805-79) J. G. WHITTIER (1807-92) Wendell Phillips (1811-84) H. B. STOWE (1811-96)	**Victorian English** literature developed two traditions—Romantic and naturalist. Verse ranged from poems of the countryside, firstly as an expression of Romantic ideals, later as an escape from industrial squalor, to Christian religious and neo-medieval works. Novelists were prolific, creating vivid impressions of contemporary life, examining social conditions or reflecting or attacking Victorian middle-class values and attitudes. Poets: TENNYSON (1809-92); BROWNING (1812-89); CLOUGH (1819-61); SWINBURNE (1837-1909); HOPKINS (1844-89). Novelists: Mrs GASKELL (1810-65); THACKERAY (1811-63); DICKENS (1812-70); TROLLOPE (1815-82); the BRONTË family; ELIOT (1819-80); MEREDITH (1828-1909); HARDY (1840-1928).		**American humorists** were particularly successful in portraying local colour, especially those on the western frontier, who told tales of Indians, hunting and pioneering. Later humorists commented on current affairs. Augustus Longstreet (1790-1870) Artemus WARD (1834-67) Mark Twain (1835-1910) Bret HARTE (1836-1902)	**Parnassians** Group of French poets who believed in art for art's sake—a reaction against Romantic subjectivity. Théophile GAUTIER (1811-72) Charles LECONTE DE LISLE (1818-94) Sully Prudhomme (1837-1907) José-Maria de HEREDIA (1842-1905)
Art		**Realism** in visual arts began in France as a reaction to Romantic subjectivity. A desire for truthful representation of commonplace contemporary social life and manners often resulted in scenes of squalor and ugliness, but more usually of unidealized peasants working in the fields, or interiors of taverns or workers' homes. Honoré DAUMIER (1808-79); Jean-François Millet (1814-75); E. Meissonier (1815-91); Charles Daubigny (1817-78); Gustave COURBET (1819-77).		**Barbizon school** Romantic landscape painters based in the village of Barbizon in the Forest of Fontainebleau, near Paris. Specialized in landscape depicted with analytical precision and painted in the open air. V. N. Diaz de la Peña (1807-76) Jules Dupré (1811-89) Theodore ROUSSEAU (1812-67) J.-F. Millet (1814-75) C. F. Daubigny (1817-78)		
Architecture	**Functionalism** The urgent need for cheap and functional buildings to house hospitals, laboratories and factories resulted in the erection of many practical but often ugly buildings. Horatio Greenough (1805-52) saw the possibility of a new architecture in which form and functional purpose would be united. Sir W. Fairbairn (1789-1874) Louis Agassiz (1807-73)	**Iron and glass architecture** The new technology of the Industrial Revolution allowed a new phase of architectural development particularly in Britain. Iron bridges, iron-framed warehouses and iron and glass market halls were followed by iron-framed churches and civil buildings, innovations regarded as alarming by contemporaries. Abraham DARBY (1678-1717); John NASH (1752-1835); Thomas TELFORD (1757-1834); Sir Joseph PAXTON (1801-65); Henri LABROUSTE (1801-75); Robert STEPHENSON (1803-59); I. K. BRUNEL (1806-59); Eugéne-Emanuel VIOLLET-LE-DUC (1814-79); Sir Matthew Wyatt (1820-77); Gustave EIFFEL (1842-1923).		**L'Ecole des Beaux-Arts** in France produced a rationalist architecture, based upon new materials and traditional classical styles to produce elegant utility buildings, economical in use of space, but characterized by the harmony of the Italian High Renaissance. Jacques Hittorff (1792-1867) Henri LABROUSTE (1801-75) Hector M. Lefuel (1801-80) Richard Hunt (1827-95)	**Second French Empire style**, of NAPOLEON III (1808-73), was a massive, monumental Neo-Baroque style, ornate and imposing, an architecture of domes, grand staircases and spacious foyers. Eagerly adopted in Europe and in many colonial countries. Charles GARNIER (1825-98) Sir George Gilbert SCOTT (1811-78) Gottfried SEMPER (1803-79) Joseph Poelaert (1817-97)	
Music	**Piano music** The mechanical improvements in the piano made it capable of the individual technical virtuosity and changes of expression characteristic of Romanticism. Piano recitals became fashionable and popular, but such players and composers as LISZT (1811-86) and CHOPIN (1810-49) avoided superfluous technical showmanship, concentrating on the musical substance. Muzio Clementi (1752-1832); Johann Hummel (1778-1837); John FIELD (1782-1837); Friedrich Kalkbrenner (1784-1849); Sigismund Thalberg (1812-71); Louis Gottshalk (1829-69); Anton RUBINSTEIN (1829-94).		**Symphonic poems** introduced by Franz LISZT (1811-86) were interpretations of themes inspired by, for example, a work of literature. Developed by Richard STRAUSS (1864-1949) as tone poems.	**Conductors** The complexity of symphonic scores necessitated more rehearsals and increased orchestral discipline. Formerly the duty of the keyboard player, and then of the leading violinist, conducting developed into an art in its own right. The baton was introduced. Hans von BÜLOW (1830-94)		**Czech music** Although the Czechs had a background of classical music, it was only with SMETANA (1824-84) that a national school emerged, combining Bohemian folk-music with the grandiose monumental spirit of the Romantics. Antonin DVOŘÁK (1841-1904) Zdenek Fibich (1850-1900) Leoš JANÁČEK (1854-1928)
Technology	**Tool-making machines** which could cut special shapes in a single operation invented by Joseph BROWN (1810-76) in the US. **Human liver** studied by Claude BERNARD (1813-78). **Conservation of energy** principle first proposed. James JOULE (1818-89) Hermann von HELMHOLTZ (1821-94) **Speed of light** in air and water first measured accurately. Jean Foucault (1819-68) Armand FIZEAU (1819-96)	**Photograph of a star** first produced in the US by William Bond (1789-1859). **Wind and current charts** of the North Atlantic produced by M. F. Maury (1806-73). **Crystal Palace**, built for the Great Exhibition in London (1851), was designed by Sir Joseph Paxton (1801-65) and constructed from wrought iron, glass and concrete. Alexandre EIFFEL (1832-1923) **Second law of thermodynamics** introduced by Rudolf Clausius (1822-88)	**Elevator** invented in the US by Elisha OTIS (1811-61). **Turret lathe** in US. Eight tools could be locked into the lathe's turret, so that eight operations could be controlled by one man. **Kerosene** first manufactured by Abraham Gesner (1797-1864). **Celluloid** discovered by Alexander Parkes (1813-90). **First wire cable** suspension bridge in US.	**Atomic particles** studied by Sir Edward FRANKLAND (1825-99) and Friedrich KEKULE (1829-96). **Bessemer process** devised for converting pig-iron into steel, by Sir Henry BESSEMER (1813-98). LOUIS PASTEUR (1822-95) discovered that the fermentation process was the result of the activity of yeast cells. Justus von LIEBIG (1803-73). **Steam plough** invented—able to move along a field as well as drawing the share across it.	**Discovery of oil** at Titusville, Pennsylvania, by Edwin DRAKE (1819-80) began the modern oil industry (1859). **Behaviour of gas** as a collection of molecules subject to the laws of mechanics: theory developed by James MAXWELL (1831-79). **London Underground** railway first constructed. Similar railway systems constructed in Paris (1898) and New York (1900). **First armour-plated warship** produced by the French.	**First railway sleeping car** built in US by George PULLMAN (1831-97). **Modern metallurgy** began with the discovery of the microstructure of steel by Henry SORBY (1826-1908). **Pasteurization of beer**, wine and milk introduced after studies by PASTEUR (1822-95) of micro-organisms of decay. **Internal combustion engine** first recorded attached to a hand cart. Siegfried Markus (1831-99)

	1865	1868	1871	1874	1877	1880	1883
Principal Events	NAPOLEON III (1808-73) agreed to Prussian ascendancy in Germany and to a united Italy, at a secret meeting with BISMARCK (1815-98), (1865). **Prussian alliance** with Italy in preparation for war with Austria (1866). Prussia annexed Hanover, Cassel, Homburg, Nassau and Frankfurt, forming the North German Confederation (1867) and forcing Austria to withdraw from German affairs. GARIBALDI (1807-82) marched on Rome (1867). Defeated by Papal and French troops. **Indians** imported into southern Africa to work on sugar plantations.	**British expeditions** against Ethiopia, to free British prisoners. Basutoland proclaimed British territory (1868). **Suez Canal** opened (1869). **First women's suffrage** introduced in Wyoming, USA (1869). **Franco-Prussian war** resulted from disagreement over succession to the Spanish throne (1870). NAPOLEON III (1808-73) capitulated at Sedan. Revolution in Paris. Third Republic proclaimed (1870). **Papal troops** defeated by Italian forces. Rome declared capital of Italy (1871).	**Trade Union Act** (1871) Unions given full legal recognition in Britain. WILLIAM I (1797-1888) King of Prussia, proclaimed German Emperor at Versailles. France lost Alsace and Lorraine. William, Franz Josef of Austria (1830-1916) and ALEXANDER II of Russia (1818-81) formed the League of the Three Emperors (1872). **Theological faculties** and monasteries abolished in Rome (1873). **First Spanish Republic** founded (1873). **Henry Stanley** (1841-1904) reached LIVINGSTONE (1813-73) on Lake Tanganyika.	**Democrats** won control of US House and southern states. Disenfranchisement of negroes. DISRAELI (1804-81) purchased shares in the Suez Canal for British Government from Khedive ISMAEL (1830-95) of Egypt (1875). **Uprisings against Turks** in Bosnia and Herzegovina. Bulgarians massacred by Turks. Berlin Memorandum (1876) drawn up by Germany, Austria and Russia, pressed for reform. **Serbia and Montenegro** defeated in war with Turkey (1876). **Socialist People's Party** formed in Russia (1876).	**The Balkans** Continued strife over territory and the protection of Christians in Turkey. Russia invaded and defeated Turkey (1877). **Treaty of San Stefano** (1878) Austria to Bosnia-Herzegovina; Russia acquired Bessarabia; Romania, Serbia, Montenegro, Bulgaria gained independence. Britain to administer Cyprus. **Transvaal** annexed by Britain. **Second Anglo-Afghan war** (1878) to secure India's frontier against Russian advances.	**South Africa** gained some independence (1880). KRUGER (1825-1904) became president. Transvaal Boers revolted. **International 3-mile limit** for territorial waters fixed by the Hague convention (1882). **Triple Alliance** formed between Italy, Austria and Germany (1882). **Anti-Catholic measures** in Belgium, France and Germany. **British occupied Cairo** (1882), to subdue nationalist forces rebelling against the Khedive and western control. **Italian colonization** of Ethiopia began (1882).
Religion	**Salvation Army** Originally an offshoot of Methodism, which aimed at preaching the Gospel to those who knew nothing about Christianity. This entailed much social work in addition, such as soup kitchens and help for the poor. Organized along military lines, with uniforms, brass bands and songs.	**Infallibility of the Pope** in decisions regarding faith and morals, declared by Vatican Council (1870). **Tübingen School** was instrumental in the introduction of critical analysis of the text of the Bible, in place of automatic acceptance. Ferdinand Bauer (1792-1860) **Massacre** of French missionaries in Tientsin, China (1870).	**Kulturkampf**, the 'struggle for civilization'. German anti-clerical movement caused by BISMARCK (1815-98), who feared Catholicism as a threat to German nationalism. **Revival of Islam** in India as a reaction against the challenges of Hinduism, Christianity and western domination. Various reform movements founded, both militant and reformist. Sayyid Ahmad Khan of Delhi (1817-98) attempted to reconcile Islam with western thought and founded the Aligarh Muslim College (1875). Mirza Ghulam Ahmad (1838-1908); Aga Khan I (1800-81); Sayyid Amir Ali (1849-1928).	**Theosophical Society** founded in 1875 by Mme BLAVATSKY (1831-91) and developed by Annie Besant (1847-1933). Based on Hindu and Buddhist mystical teachings.	**Christian Science** Founded by Mary Baker EDDY (1821-1910), who believed that disease and evil were illusions of the mind, spiritual healing being the only cure. **Thomism** (i.e. that there is no conflict between true science and true religion) established as centre of Roman Catholic theology by Pope Leo XIII (1878-1903) in encyclical *Aeterna Patris* (1879).	**Shinto**, proclaimed the state religion in 1871, was officially divided into Pure or Shrine Shinto, the orthodox form, and Sect Shinto (1882). The 13 sects, which evolved from earlier folk movements, have been recognized as separate denominations, and emphasize many different aspects of the Shinto beliefs.
Philosophy						**Japanese translations** of the leading English, French and later German philosophers caused a period of intellectual ferment in the Japanese universities. Both liberal and nationalist ideas influenced the drafting of the 1889 constitution.
Literature	**Emancipation of women** was an important theme in much Scandinavian fiction and prose. Other social themes treated are peasant culture and the struggles of rural life. Camilla Collett (1813-95) Jonas LIE (1833-1908) Alexander Kielland (1849-1906) **Detective fiction** introduced in Britain by Wilkie COLLINS (1824-89), who published *The Moonstone* (1868).	**Italian classical revival** combined patriotism and anti-clericalism in the tradition of poets of a century before. Coincided with Italian unification. Giosuè CARDUCCI (1835-1907) Giovanni PASCOLI (1855-1912) **Japanese Noh theatre** was forced into decline after the Meiji Restoration, due to the collapse of the old military rule.	**Landsmål movement** Revival of Norwegian peasant dialects and old Norse language, important to the development of Norwegian literature and Romanticism. Bjørnstjerne BJØRNSON (1832-1910) **Modern Bengali drama** rooted in folk theatre based upon dramatizations of religious legends established with the beginning of professional theatre.	**Realism** Drama and fiction which aimed at depicting, truthfully and objectively, detailed aspects of contemporary life. Artifice and idealistic distortions rejected and replaced by straightforward impersonal and unsentimental treatment of often mundane and ordinary themes. Man is seen as a social being in relation to other people. Honoré de BALZAC (1799-1850); Friedrich Hebbel (1813-63); Theodor STORM (1817-88); Gottfried KELLER (1819-90); Gustave FLAUBERT (1821-80); Alexander OSTROVSKY (1823-86); Henrik IBSEN (1828-1906); August STRINDBERG (1849-1912); Guy de MAUPASSANT (1850-93); G. B. SHAW (1856-1950); Gerhart HAUPTMANN (1862-1946). **Bengali poetry** combined patriotic themes and experiments with new metres, including blank verse, with ancient Sanskrit traditions. Biharilal Cakrabarti (1835-94); Hemcandra Bandyopadhyay (1838-1903); Sir Rabindranath TAGORE (1861-1941).		**Russian novel** ranged from satire and melodrama to documentary, objective chronicles of Russia's cultural and psychological evolution. Detailed, naturalistic style. Nikolai GOGOL (1809-52) Ivan TURGENEV (1818-83) Feodor Dostoyevsky (1821-81) Leo TOLSTOY (1828-1910) Anton CHEKHOV (1860-1904)
Art	**Anecdotal realism** Narrative art became popular throughout Europe. Artists depicted, often in minute detail, historical events, varied incidents of contemporary life and literary themes. Adolf von Menzel (1815-1905) William Frith (1819-1909) Wilhelm Leibl (1844-1900) I. E. Repin (1844-1930)		**Pre-Raphaelites** Group of Romantic painters who formed a secret brotherhood dedicated to returning to the simplicity of the medieval artists before RAPHAEL (1483-1520). Their ideals and religious fervour produced highly symbolic and mystical works, with a meticulous attention to detail. Ford Madox BROWN (1821-93); Thomas Woolner (1823-92); William Holman HUNT (1827-1910); Dante Gabriel ROSSETTI (1828-82); John Everett MILLAIS (1829-96); Edward BURNE-JONES (1833-98); William MORRIS (1834-96).		**Impressionism** Revolutionary movement which marked the beginning of modern painting. Impressionists were concerned with capturing the immediate visual impression of the changing aspect of nature rather than recording a factual image. They often painted out of doors, using fresh, bright colours to reproduce the sense of light and atmosphere of their subject-matter. Camille PISSARRO (1830-1903); Edouard MANET (1832-83); Edgar DEGAS (1834-1917); Alfred SISLEY (1839-99); Paul CÉZANNE (1839-1906); Claude MONET (1840-1926); Berthe Morisot (1841-95); Pierre Auguste RENOIR (1841-1919).	
Architecture				**Back-to-back housing** in England formed the new industrial architecture for the poorer urban classes. Blocks of badly built, two-storey houses with communal sanitary facilities formed growing towns around newly established factories in industrial England. The 1875 Housing Act set a minimum size for urban housing.	**Town planning** ignored the problems of urban housing to devote resources to imposing municipal buildings. Schemes for ideal industrial cities eventually resulted in the construction of estates and new towns, particularly in England. Sir Ebenezer Howard (1850-1928) Sir Raymond Unwin (1863-1940) Lever Brothers Ltd Cadbury's Ltd	**Chicago school** developed the steel-framed commercial building, the forerunner of the skyscraper. A completely new architectural style, it was plain and functional, based on vertical and horizontal lines. William Le Baron JENNY (1832-1907) David H. Burnham (1846-1912) J. W. Root (1850-91) W. Holabird (1854-1923) L. H. SULLIVAN (1856-1924)
Music	**The Mighty Handful** A group of Russian nationalists, also known as 'The Five', who ignored conservatoire conventions, using Russian folklore for inspiration. Alexander BORODIN (1833-87) César Cui (1835-1918) Mily BALAKIREV (1837-1910) M. MUSSORGSKY (1839-81) Nicolas RIMSKY-KORSAKOV (1844-1908)	**Music-drama** refers to the operas of WAGNER (1813-83), in which he wanted to fuse all the arts into an integrated whole. Music became part of the drama itself, not subject to conventional form. Introduced the *leitmotiv*, a phrase which identifies any person or situation with which it is first associated.	**Parisian opéra bouffe** Popular operettas, influenced by earlier French farce, the *opéra comique* and *singspiele*, witty, satirical compositions with topical allusions. Jacques OFFENBACH (1819-80)	**French cosmopolitan movement** Followers of César FRANCK (1822-90), whose music was classically based and inspired by religious idealism. Some harmonic innovations, and the cyclical form of LISZT (1811-86) and SCHUMANN (1810-56) was developed. Henri Duparc (1848-1933) Vincent d'INDY (1851-1931)	**Masses, oratorios and requiems** were composed using full vocal and orchestral resources available with many varied forms and styles, ranging from Gregorian chant or solo recitative to conventional use of aria and orchestra. Giuseppe VERDI (1813-1901) Johannes BRAHMS (1833-97) Gabriel FAURE (1845-1924)	**Impressionism** Like the Impressionist painters, the musicians aimed at capturing a mood or atmosphere in their works. To do so, they used whole tone scales, unusual harmonies, chords fading into one another and sound images. C. DEBUSSY (1862-1918) F. DELIUS (1862-1934) Maurice RAVEL (1875-1937)
Technology	**Red Flag Act** in Britain (1865) restricted all mechanical road vehicles to a speed of 4 mph. **Velocipede**, the first bicycle with cranks and pedals on the front wheel, devised in France. **Antiseptic surgery** first practised by Joseph LISTER (1827-1912). **Theory of genetics** investigated by Gregor MENDEL (1822-84). **Dynamite** first manufactured by Alfred NOBEL (1833-96) after discovery of gelatine.	**United States** More powerful locomotives used compressed air brakes invented by WESTINGHOUSE (1846-1914). First transcontinental railway built. Chicago meat-packing industry began. **Tungsten steel** first manufactured by Robert Mushet (1811-91), in Britain. **Steam tram** introduced into industrial districts in Britain. Ran on flat, grooved rails. **Specialization in ships** Refrigeration ships, passenger liners and oil tankers built.	**Typewriter** invented by SHOLES (1819-90). First manufactured by the Remington Arms Co. in the US. **Oceanography** studied by Thomson (1830-82) and Murray (1841-1914) on a world voyage aboard the *Challenger*. **Coke** substituted for coal to power locomotives in Britain. **Electricity** used to drive machines in Austria.	**Telephone** invented (1876) by Alexander BELL (1847-1922). First telephone exchange installed in New Haven, USA (1877) and an automatic switching system invented (1879). **Electrification of tramways** began in US. System adopted in Germany (1884) and in London Underground (1905). **Arc lamps** used in experimental public lighting in the US. **Practical gas engine** invented by Nicholas OTTO (1832-92).	**THOMAS EDISON** (1847-1931) invented the light bulb and the phonograph. Sir Joseph SWAN (1828-1914) developed a carbon filament light bulb in Britain. **Seismograph** invented by John Milne (1850-1913). **Reinforced concrete** patented by Joseph MONIER (1823-1906). **Cream separator**, worked by centrifugal force, invented by de LAVAL (1945-1913).	**Electricity** Generating station designed by EDISON (1847-1931) for New York City. Electric appliances included iron, stove, sewing machine and washing machine. Storage batteries powered tricycles. **First roll film** invented by George EASTMAN (1854-1932). **Chemical fertilizers** first used to increase yield of farm crops. Chilean sodium nitrate beds exploited from c. 1870.

1883 1886 1889 1892 1895 1898 1901 375

Principal Events

Left wing political movements gained strength all over Europe.
Colonization European powers divided Africa and the Far East into spheres of influence. To Britain: Somali Coast, Nigeria, New Guinea; to France: extension of protectorate in Cochin China; to Germany: south-western Africa, Togoland, the Cameroons, Tanganyika, Zanzibar, northern New Guinea.
Congo Free State established under Leopold II (1835-1909).
GORDON (1833-85) sent to the Sudan. Garrison massacred at Khartoum.

Ireland Agitation against British rule.
Triple Alliance between Italy, Britain and Austria intended to preserve the status quo in the Near East (1887).
Coup d'état attempt by BOULANGER (1837-91) in France failed(1888).
British protectorate established over North Borneo, Brunei and Sarawak. Approval of Royal Charter for the East African Company and the Royal Niger Company. Wars in Nyasaland against slave traders.
Discovery of gold and establishment of De Beers' Diamond monopoly in South Africa(1888).

Organized labour In America, Britain, France and Germany, laws limiting hours and protecting workers passed. In Russia greater centralized, aristocratic control instituted, leading to beginnings of class warfare.
Dismissal (1890)of **BISMARCK** (1815-98) by the young German Emperor, WILLIAM II (1859-1941).
British colonial agreements Exchanged Heligoland for Zanzibar and Pemba with Germany; established limits of influence, with France in Nigeria, and Portugal on the Zambesi. Occupied Sikkim, Uganda and Mashonaland.

US marines overthrew native government in Hawaii, which became a republic (1894).
Trial (1894) of **DREYFUS** (1859-1935) in France.
Congo agreements with Britain and France established its frontiers (1894).
Sino-Japanese war Over Korea (1894-5). China defeated.
SUN YAT-SEN (1866-1925) organized the first of several secret revolutionary societies in China.

WILLIAM II of Germany (1859-1941) visited England.
Balkans Armenians massacred in Constantinople (1895). Insurrection in Crete against Turkish rule.
Jameson Raid (1895) against South African government of KRUGER (1825-1904).
Anglo-French agreements over Siam, Tunisia (1896), Nigeria and Gold Coast (1897). British protectorates established in Sierra Leone and East Africa. France annexed Madagascar.
Italians defeated by Ethiopians. End of Italian protectorate (1896).

Spanish-American war over Cuba. Spain ceded Cuba, Puerto Rico, Guam, Philippines (1898).
First Hague Peace Conference aimed to facilitate settlement of international disputes (1899).
Second Boer War (1899-1902). KRUGER (1825-1904) ordered attack on Cape Colony and Natal, backed by German arms. Eventual victory for British under KITCHENER (1850-1916). Britain annexed Orange Free State and Transvaal.
Boxer rising in China. Nationalist movement against foreign intervention; suppressed (1900).

Religion

Jehovah's Witnesses Organization purporting to have existed since Cain and Abel, which believes that all other religious institutions are the work of Satan. They adhere totally and literally to the Scriptures.

Anticlericalism in France; power of the Church in political and social matters considered a threat to the Republic. Movement culminated in the DREYFUS (1859-1935) affair.
Orthodox Judaism Reformed Judaism did not reach eastern Europe, Africa or the Middle East, so orthodox beliefs survived and were re-promoted.
Samson Hirsch (1808-88)

Rerum Novarum (1891) Encyclical declaring the Church's support of social justice, giving Pope Leo XIII (1878-1903) the title 'the working man's pope'.
Constitutional disestablishment of religion in Japan. Guaranteed freedom of belief. The Russian Orthodox, the Roman Catholic and various Protestant churches successfully established themselves.

Hindu reform movements arose during the 19th century among English speaking Hindus, in response to the influx of western ideas into India.
Ram Mohan Roy (1774-1833) attempted to reconcile Hindu and western ideas in the Brahmo Samaj (1865), a reformed Hindu church.
Dayananda Sarasvati (1827-83)
Mme BLAVATSKY (1831-91)

Anthroposophy School of mystic-religious philosophy based on works of Rudolph STEINER (1861-1925), using special systems of education and medicine intended to enable man to appreciate the spiritual world.
Attempts to encourage Shinto and to reduce the influence of the Buddhist faith in Japan failed, owing to the deep traditions of Buddhism in Japanese life.

Zionism Movement founded by Theodor HERZL (1860-1904) for the establishment of an autonomous Jewish state in Palestine. Zionism is now a major international force concerned with Israeli welfare and influence.
Protestant missionaries in China contributed to the Reform Movement of 1898, but were persecuted during the Boxer Rebellion.

Philosophy

Fabianism advocated social change by using existing institutions to effect a transformation of society by means of social reform and national ownership of industry. The Fabians argued against revolutionary measures in favour of a gradual approach.
Sidney WEBB (1859-1947)
G. B. SHAW (1856-1950)

Chinese Reform movement of 1898 was the culmination of a century of questioning and criticism in Chinese intellectual life. Western subjects were included in Chinese school curricula.
K'ang Yu-wei (1858-1927), described as the 'last of the great Confucianists', questioned traditional interpretations of Confucianism.
Liang Ci-chao (1873-1929)
Ch'en Tu-hsiu (1879-1942)
Hu Shih (1891-1962)

Literature

Southern US writers, such as J. C. HARRIS (1848-1908), described the heat, society and negro culture of the southern states.
Sidney Lanier (1842-81)

Symbolism Reacting against the external realism of the French novel, poets aimed to escape the restrictions of formal verse, and instead evoked and suggested personal experiences rather than described them. Experimental techniques using lyrical language to recreate human consciousness. Highly personalized central symbols and metaphors, image patterns. Followed lead of Charles BAUDELAIRE (1821-67). Stephane MALLARME (1842-98); Paul VERLAINE (1844-96); Arthur RIMBAUD (1854-91).
Russian symbolism strongly influenced by French movement, but more concerned with mysticism and exoticism. Vyacheslav Ivanov (1866-1949); Constantin Balmont (1867-1943); Valeri Bryusov (1873-1924); Alexander BLOK (1880-1921).

Naturalism Extreme form of Realism, mirroring life as photographically as possible. Deterministic, seeing man as victim of heredity and environment. Dialect used extensively in theatre.
Emile ZOLA (1840-1902)
August STRINDBERG (1849-1912)
Maxim GORKY (1868-1936)
Japanese novel gained popularity as western models exerted influence. Vernacular speech polished into a modern literary style.
Tsubouchi Shoyo (1859-1935)
Natsume Soseki (1867-1916)

Victorian drama Naturalistic comedy and satire developed, its success influenced by the lifting of monopolies of the Drury Lane and Covent Garden theatres. Influenced by IBSEN (1828-1906).
Oscar WILDE (1854-1900)
Arthur Wing PINERO (1855-1934)
John GALSWORTHY (1867-1933)
G.B. SHAW (1856-1950)

Verismo Italian school of Realism, characterized by regional idiom, the authors' inspiration rising from life with which they were best acquainted.
Luigi Capuana (1839-1915)
Giovanni VERGA (1840-1922)
Renata Fucini (1843-1921)
Grand Guignol Short French plays of murder, horror, rape and ghosts designed to shock and delight.

Nititalists Swedish literary movement whose works were characterized by a pantheistic, naturalistic, Romantic attitude.
Gustav FRODING (1860-1911)
Generación del '98 Group of Spanish writers who aimed at revitalizing Spanish culture.
Miguel de UNAMUNO (1864-1936)
Piò BAROJA (1870-1956)
Antonio MACHADO (1875-1939)

Art

Symbolism Ideological reaction against Impressionism. Symbolists were more interested in the visual expression of poetic ideas, dreams or allegories than naturalistic representation of the world.
Gustave MOREAU (1826-98)
Henri Fantin Latour (1836-1904)
Odilon REDON (1840-1916)
E. Carrière (1849-1906)
Edouard VUILLARD (1868-1940)

Synthetism Offshoot of the Symbolist movement, centred in Brittany. Process of simplification achieved by painting in flat, bright colours, outlined in black, which, by the elimination of detail, conveyed a concept rather than an actual visual impression.
Paul GAUGUIN (1849-1903)
Paul Sérusier (1863-1927)
Emile Bernard (1868-1941)

Arts and Crafts movement, founded in England by William MORRIS (1834-96), attempted to revive medieval principles of craftsmanship in building, decoration and furnishing. The American Association for the Promotion of Truth in Art adopted Victorian Gothic as a suitable style for civic architecture. Both movements derived their inspiration from the writings of John RUSKIN (1819-1900), and were a strong influence on subsequent book design and interior decoration.
Philip WEBB (1831-1915)
Henry Van Brunt (1832-1903)
W. R. Ware (1832-1915)
William Lethaby (1857-1931)
Charles VOYSEY (1857-1941)
Sir Edwin LUTYENS (1869-1944)

Neo-Impressionism (also called Divisionism and Pointillism). Formal Impressionism in which colour and light were analyzed scientifically. Colours were not mixed in the palette, but applied to canvas in their pure form, in small dots. Their juxtaposition created the overall effect.
C. PISSARRO (1830-1903)
M. Luce (1858-1941)
Georges SEURAT (1859-91)
Paul SIGNAC (1863-1935)

Post-impressionists advocated a return to more formal art, emphasizing the role of the subject.
Paul CEZANNE (1839-1906)
Paul GAUGUIN (1848-1903)
Vincent van GOGH (1853-90)
Graphic arts developed in France with the use of the lithograph. Posters became an important art form.
Gustave DORE (1832-83)
TOULOUSE LAUTREC (1864-1901)
A. Mucha (1869-1939)

Art Nouveau A style of decorative art, design and architecture which spread throughout Europe. Characterized by its flowing curved lines, subtle colours and floral designs and the use of steel, concrete and other unexplored materials. In Germany the movement was known as *Jugendstil*.
William MORRIS (1834-96)
Anatole de Baudot (1834-1915)
Otto Wagner (1841-1918)
Arthur MACKMURDO (1851-1942)
Antoni GAUDI (1852-1926)
Louis SULLIVAN (1856-1924)
James Ensor (1860-1949)
Victor HORTA (1861-1947)
Henry van de Velde (1863-1939)
Hector Guimard (1867-1942)
Charles Rennie MACKINTOSH (1868-1928)
Aubrey BEARDSLEY (1872-98)

Architecture

English domestic revival The English country house assumed numerous styles under Norman SHAW (1831-1912), who designed light and elegant buildings in various period styles.
Eden Nesfield (1835-88)
William MORRIS (1834-96)
Charles VOYSEY (1857-1941)

American domestic revival, inspired by English Victorian cottage architecture, began with the 'stick style' house in which wood was used in a natural, expressive way. The 'shingle style' took its name from the uneven shingles used as surface decoration in open-plan family houses.
W. BUTTERFIELD (1814-1900)
Norman SHAW (1831-1927)
H. H. RICHARDSON (1838-86)
C. McKim (1847-1909)

World's Columbian exposition (1893), for which architects from many schools submitted designs, saw the triumph of the Beaux-Arts tradition in the United States—French and Italian Renaissance revival styles in white stone with spacious plazas and urban gardens.
Richard HUNT (1846-1912)
D. H. Burnham (1846-1912)
C. McKim (1847-1909)
Louis SULLIVAN (1856-1924)

Primitivism A desire to return to original sources of art, resulting in interest in and influence of primitive and children's painting.
Henri ROUSSEAU (1844-1910)
Joán MIRO (b. 1893)

Music

Religious musical revival in Germany and France. Societies formed, pledged to reform church music. Republished PALESTRINA (*c.* 1526-94), revived motets and masses, and wrote in 16th-century manner. New versions of the Gregorian chant, written at Solesmes in France.

Scandinavian nationalism Music based on native folk songs and dances, with their strong rhythms, folk myths and legends of the north.
Niels Gade (1817-90)
Edvard GRIEG (1843-1907)
Christian Sinding (1856-1941)
Carl NIELSEN (1865-1931)
Jean SIBELIUS (1865-1957)

New England Classicists American composers, influenced by BRAHMS (1833-97), who were not concerned with creating a tradition of American music.
Arthur Foote (1853-1937)
George Chadwick (1854-1931)
Horatio Parker (1863-1919)

Märchenoper The interest in fairy-tale opera revived in Germany after WAGNER (1813-83), using both folklore and folk melodies.
Engelbert Humperdinck (1854-1921)

Savoy opera Series of English operettas satirizing grand opera, with light irony, catchy melodies and their adaptability to the amateur stage. The Savoy Theatre was built specially for the operas.
W. S. GILBERT (1836-1911)
Sir Arthur SULLIVAN (1842-1900)

Verismo Italian opera style based on themes of contemporary, everyday situations. Music was simple and lyrical.
Giacomo PUCCINI (1858-1924)
Ruggiero Leoncavallo (1858-1919)
Pietro Mascagni (1863-1945)

Technology

Steam turbine patented by Charles Parsons (1854-1931) in Britain.
High-speed petrol engine, which employed electric ignition, invented in Britain.
Electric trains in common use in Europe and the US.
Penny-farthing bicycle and 'safety' bicycle with chain drive geared to rear wheel invented.
Gasoline engine patented by Gottlieb DAIMLER (1834-1900).

Aluminium obtained from bauxite. Process invented by Charles HALL (1863-1913).
First hydro-electric station built at Niagara Falls (1886).
Pneumatic tyre invented by J. B. DUNLOP (1840-1921).
Hand camera, 'Kodak' produced by George EASTMAN (1854-1932).
Radio waves discovered by Heinrich HERTZ (1857-94).
Alternating current electric motor invented by Nikola TESLA (1856-1943).

Disc records first used, by Emile Berliner (1851-1929), to improve sound reproduction.
Automobile improved in France by René Panhard (1841-1908) and Emile Levassor (d. 1897), who invented a twin-cylinder engine connected by a friction clutch to a 3-speed gear box.
Powered flight Possibilities studied by Otto LILIENTHAL (1848-96) and P. S. Pilcher (d. 1899).
Trans-Siberian railway begun (1891).

Parasitic carriers of disease discovered by Theobald SMITH (1859-1934).
Steam-generator adapted for a steam carriage by Léon Serpollet (1858-1907).
Mechanics of flight and lifting surfaces studied by Chanute (1832-1910), Pilcher (d. 1899), Hargrave (1850-1915) and the WRIGHT brothers.
Heavy oil engine patented by Rudolf DIESEL (1858-1913).

Ford, Wolseley and Lanchester cars first produced.
Physics The electron, the first sub-atomic particle, discovered by Thomson (1858-1940).
Radioactivity discovered in uranium compounds by BECQUEREL (1858-1940).
X-rays discovered by ROENTGEN (1845-1923).
Wireless telegraph invented by MARCONI (1874-1937).
Nobel prizes instituted.

Automatic bottle-making machine invented by M. J. Owens (1859-1923).
Long-distance telephone calls made possible by work of M. I. Pupin (1858-1935).
66 mph World land speed record achieved in an electric car.
Heavy lorry and motor omnibus in wide production in US and Europe.
Zeppelins, the first rigid airships, launched by Count von ZEPPELIN (1838-1917).

1901 | 1904 | 1907 | 1910 | 1913 | 1916 | 1919

Principal Events

US and Canada defined Alaskan frontier (1903).
Britain and France established *Entente Cordiale*, treaty of mutual assistance (1903).
Russian occupation of Manchuria and massacre of 45,000 Chinese. Refused to evacuate Manchuria, defying terms of Russo-Japanese agreement (1903).
Socialist Revolutionary Party in Russia engaged increasingly in terrorist activities.

Swedish-Norwegian union dissolved (1905).
French colonization of Morocco baulked by Germans. Kaiser WILLIAM II (1859-1941) attempted to form league with France and Russia against Britain.
Russians defeated by Japanese (1905).
Russian revolution (1905) General strike after 'Bloody Sunday' in St Petersburg. First Soviet formed. Constitution granted by Tsar.
Sino-British agreement to cut opium imports (1906).

Hague Peace Conference (1907) failed to limit armaments, through opposition of Germany.
Anglo-Russian entente (1907) settling differences over Persia, Afghanistan and Tibet.
Austria annexed Bosnia and Herzegovina (1908). German pressure on Russia to cease support of Serbian claims to Bosnia.
Bulgaria declared her independence from the Ottoman Empire, annexing E. Rumelia (1908).
South Africa Union of Cape Colony, Transvaal and Orange Free State (1909).

International socialism German workers declared themselves against war. Claimed international proletarian solidarity.
Moroccan crisis Germany sent gunboat to Agadir to protect interests threatened by French expansion (1911).
Chinese revolution (1911) Manchu dynasty overthrown and Republic formed.
Italo-Turkish war over Italian policy in Tripoli. Italian victory (1912).
First Balkan war (1912) Serbia, Bulgaria, Greece, Montenegro united against Turks, who massacred Bulgarians.

Balkans partitioned (1913) after second Balkan war.
Irish Home Rule Act passed but Ulster volunteers formed to oppose integration with southern Ireland (1914).

Russian revolution (1917) Tsar NICHOLAS II (1868-1918) abdicated in favour of provisional government. Bolshevik revolution of October 1917 led by LENIN (1870-1924). Tsar executed.

First World War (1914-8) Austrian Arch-Duke Ferdinand (1863-1914) assassinated by Serbs at Sarajevo. Austria attacked Serbia and with Germany declared war on Russia. Germany attacked France and Belgium; Britain declared war on Austria and Germany. Japan declared war on Germany. War fought in Europe, Far East, Africa, at sea and, for the first time, in the air. Italy and Portugal declared war on Germany (1916). Deadlock in trench warfare in northern Europe. Russian army collapsed after Russian revolution (1917). U-boat war against Britain's shipping intensified. US entered war against Germany (1917). Mutinies in French army and German navy. German final offensive in Europe failed. Armistice (1918). Surrender of Austria. Kaiser WILLIAM II (1859-1941) abdicated; Germany and Austria proclaimed republics.

Religion

Muslim League formed in India after the granting of separate electorates for Muslims and other special groups. The Muslim League held a conference with congressional leaders to discuss Hindu-Muslim unity (1911).

Weakening of Confucianism in China due to the influence of missionaries from the West, and the abolition of the Civil Service examinations. The Republic (1912) destroyed the imperial government, with which Confucianism was inextricably connected.

Modernism Movement in Catholic Church formed to try to reconcile new scientific discoveries with religious teaching. Though unacceptable to the Pope, the movement flourished in intellectual circles.
Antonio Fogazzaro (1842-1911)
Alfred Loisy (1857-1940)
George Tyrell (1861-1909)

Theology of Crisis After the optimism of early 1900s, the advent of the First World War brought a return to KIERKEGAARD (1813-55) and an emphasis on faith as the only means to approach God, whose judgement was ultimate over man.
Paul Tillich (1886-1965)
Karl BARTH (1886-1968)
Emil Brunner (b. 1889)
Rudolf Bultmann (b. 1884)
R. Niebuhr (1892-1971)

Muslim leaders called for eventual self-government for India at the annual meeting of the Muslim League in India.

Pentecostal Churches Numerous Christian sects arose in Britain and the US, posing the question whether institutionalized Christianity might be lacking in various necessary qualities of faith and commitment.

Philosophy

Neo-Romantic revival in Denmark in reaction to Realism. Fantasy and emotionalism returned, most themes being religious or mystic.

Bloomsbury Group Number of English writers, artists and philosophers who met together in London on the basis that 'the pleasures of human intercourse and the enjoyment of beautiful objects . . . form the rational ultimate end of social progress'. Bertrand RUSSELL (1872-1970); G. E. MOORE (1873-1958); E. M. FORSTER (1879-1970); Leonard Woolf (1880-1969); Lytton STRACHEY (1880-1932); Virginia WOOLF (1882-1941); John Maynard KEYNES (1883-1946); Duncan Grant (b. 1885).

Pragmatism 'Time is whatever proves itself to be useful.' Thinking is not the reduplication of reality already complete; it is a method of social advance in an ever-changing process. The content of man's knowledge is always dependent upon historical circumstances.
C. S. Pierce (1839-1914)
William JAMES (1842-1910)
John DEWEY (1859-1952)

Chinese 'New Tide' movement marked the passing of the old Confucian orthodoxy as various western schools competed for mastery among Chinese intellectuals, many of whom had returned from periods of study in the West.
Hu Shih (1891-1962)
Chang Tung-sun (b. 1887)
Chin Yueh-lin (b. 1894)
Ts'ai Yuan-p'ei (1867-1940)
Ch'en Tu-hsiu (1879-1942)

Literature

Niels Møller (1859-1941)
Sophus Michaelis (1865-1932)
Johannes Jørgensen (1866-1956)
Helge Rode (1870-1937)

Japanese poetry Traditional forms, the *haiku* and the *tanka*, benefited from an influx of new ideas and free prose forms from the West.
Masaoka Shiki (1867-1902)
Shimazaki Toson (1872-1943)
Yosano Akiko (1878-1942)
Saito Mokichi (1882-1953)

Impressionism German style of writing denoting precision of language, used accurately to describe emotions; much use of symbolist imagery.
Richard Dehmel (1863-1920)
Stefan GEORGE (1868-1933)
Hugo von HOFMANNSTHAL (1874-1929)
R. M. RILKE (1875-1926)
Herman HESSE (1887-1918)

Hindi literature written both in dialect and in High Hindi, a language. Comprised historical tales, novels and verse.
Raja Siva Prasad (1823-95)
Deoki Nandan (1861-1913)
Prem Chand (1880-1936)

American Realism Subject matter was commonplace—love and marriage, domestic problems—or tales of war in Europe and Cuba.
Stephen CRANE (1871-1900)
Theodore DREISER (1871-1945)

New American poetry ranged from the established Victorian style of Robert FROST (1875-1963) to the free verse of Carl SANDBURG (1878-1967) or the dramatic, oral verse of Vachel LINDSAY (1879-1931).
Wallace STEVENS (1879-1955)
Marianne MOORE (b. 1887)
Conrad AIKEN (b. 1889)

Irish Literary Theatre National movement dedicated to the promotion of Irish plays written about Irish subjects, and performed by native actors. Plays drew heavily on Celtic folk history and legend, as well as commenting on the contemporary Irish scene.
Lady GREGORY (1852-1932)
Edward Martyn (1859-1924)
W. B. YEATS (1865-1939)
J. M. SYNGE (1871-1909)

English War Poets early in the First World War wrote with patriotic idealism but later their poetry contained angry and ironic descriptions of the horror at the battlefront. Siegfried SASSOON (1886-1967); Rupert BROOKE (1887-1915); Wilfred OWEN (1893-1918); Robert GRAVES (b. 1895).

Acmeists Russian movement whose adherents advocated precise, clear, concise poetry in opposition to the stylistic vagueness of the symbolists.
Nikolai Gumiliov (1886-1921)
Anna AKHMATOVA (1889-1966)

Art

Nabis (Hebrew for 'prophet') the Nabis were followers of the flat, simplified style of GAUGUIN (1849-1903), which they saw as a new kind of religious illumination. They asserted, like the Symbolists, that art should be a subjective representation of nature.
Pierre BONNARD (1867-1947)
E. VUILLARD (1868-1940)
A. MAILLOL (1861-1944)
Paul Sérusier (1863-1927)
Maurice Denis (1870-1943)

Vienna Secessionists Movement of anti-Realist and Symbolist decorative artists which had close similarities with the Art Nouveau movement.
Gustav KLIMT (1862-1918)

Intimisme An offshoot of the Impressionist movement. The subject matter was usually restricted to interiors and domestic scenes.
Pierre BONNARD (1867-1947)
Edouard VUILLARD (1868-1940)

Fauvism The Fauves (a term given by an outraged critic, meaning 'wild beasts') exhibited together in Paris in 1905, and caused a sensation with their use of violent colour, distortion and simplification of form. Henri MATISSE (1869-1964); Georges ROUAULT (1871-1958); Albert Marquet (1875-1947); Maurice VLAMINCK (1876-1958); Raoul DUFY (1877-1953); André DERAIN (1880-1954).

Der Blaue Reiter An important German movement. The Blaue Reiter group wanted to show the variety of modern artistic expression, and to introduce a spiritual element they found lacking in the Impressionists.
Lyonel Feininger (1871-1950)
Paul KLEE (1879-1940)
Auguste Macke (1887-1914)
Heinrich Campendonck (1889-1957)

Dadaism Deliberately nihilistic movement among some artists and writers, aimed at ridiculing the complacency of accepted values in art and manners.
F. Picabia (1879-1953)
K. SCHWITTERS (1887-1948)
Jean ARP (1887-1966)
Marcel DUCHAMP (1887-1968)
Giorgio de CHIRICO (b. 1888)
Georg GROSZ (1893-1959)

Cubism Movement resulting from the geometrical principles of nature formulated by CEZANNE (1839-1906). Experiments in the structure of form and spatial relationship were conducted. In painting and sculpture, several views of the same object were broken up and superimposed on one another to represent a three-dimensional object in two-dimensional terms. Architecture was characterized by slender columns and thin walls, asymmetrical design and lack of ornament.
Constantin BRANCUSI (1876-1957)
Fernand LEGER (1881-1955)
Pablo PICASSO (1881-1973)
Georges BRAQUE (1882-1963)
Walter GROPIUS (1883-1969)
Juan GRIS (1887-1927)
A. ARCHIPENKO (1887-1964)
LE CORBUSIER (1887-1965)

Architecture

Reaction against Art Nouveau in Europe produced a less ornamental, more rectilinear architecture, featuring rich and elegant interior decoration.
Otto Wagner (1841-1918)
Joseph Maria Olbrich (1867-1908)
Charles Rennie MACKINTOSH (1868-1928)
Adolf LOOS (1870-1933)
Josef HOFFMANN (1870-1956)

Colonial architecture in India The British built churches, houses and office buildings in Indian cities in Neo-Palladian and Greek revival styles. An English adaptation of the French Second Empire style dominated New Delhi. In Portuguese Goa many buildings were in the Iberian Baroque style.
Sir Herbert Baker (1862-1946)
Sir E. LUTYENS (1869-1944)

New domestic architecture in America, influenced by the prairie house of Frank Lloyd WRIGHT (1869-1959) with lines which relate to the surrounding landscape.
Bernard Maybeck (1862-1957).

Tall buildings in concrete were built in America after the discovery of a reinforced concrete in which iron beams could be embedded without risk of erosion. Fire-resistant terracotta and concrete floors, steel beams and high water tanks for fire fighting increased safety.
E. L. Ransome (1844-1917)
Tony Garnier (1861-1948)
A. PERRET (1874-1954)

Music

English revival Influenced by BRAHMS (1833-97) and other Romantics, and the Impressionists, composers used British folk-songs in their choral and orchestral works, oratorios and operas.
Hubert Parry (1848-1918)
Sir Edward ELGAR (1857-1934)
Frederick DELIUS (1862-1934)

Late Romanticism Music in the tradition of the Romantics, such as SCHUBERT (1797-1828) or WAGNER (1813-83), but with technical innovations in harmony and melodic lines, chord structures and unusual combinations of instruments.
Gabriel FAURÉ (1845-1924)
Gustav MAHLER (1860-1911)
Richard STRAUSS (1864-1949)

American music began to make use of such resources of the country as folk-music, blues and jazz.
Charles IVES (1874-1954)

Modern Spanish school, influenced by nationalist ideas of Felipe Pedrell (1841-1922). Used many folk-tunes and syncopated rhythms of flamenco dancing.
Isaac ALBENIZ (1860-1909)
Enrique GRANADOS (1867-1916)
Manuel de FALLA (1876-1947)

New Orleans Jazz Urban negro music for family and public occasions. Rhythmic ensembles based on individual extemporization.
Buddy Bolden (1868-1931)
King Oliver (1885-1938)

Hungarian nationalism As a result of an intense study of the folk-music of Hungary and Rumania there emerged a new idiom, based on Magyar melodies, using authentic instruments, particularly percussion, in quartets, operas and sonatas.
Béla BARTÓK (1881-1945)
Zoltán KODALY (1882-1967)

Technology

Rayon, the first cellulose fibre, patented by Arthur D. Little (1863-1935).
First flight in a heavier-than-air machine made by Orville and Wilbur WRIGHT (1903).
Electrocardiograph, used to diagnose disorders of the heart, invented in Holland by Willem EINTHOVEN (1860-1927).
Rocket-launching studied theoretically by Konstantin Tsiolkovskii.

First aircraft engine specially designed built by Glenn Curtis (1878-1930) in the US.
Neon lamp invented in France by Georges Claude (1870-1960).
Radium and polonium, two radioactive elements, discovered by Marie CURIE (1867-1934).
Theory of relativity proposed (1905) by Albert EINSTEIN (1879-1955).
Vacuum flask designed in Germany by Reinhold Burger.

Model T Ford launched onto the American market by Henry FORD (1863-1947). Conveyor belt mass production introduced (1914).
Tissue cells grown in a culture outside the body by Ross Harrison (1870-1959).
Bakelite, the first polymer, discovered by Leo BAEKELAND (1863-1944).
English Channel first crossed by air (1909) by Louis BLERIOT (1872-1936).

Chromosomes studied in the US by Walter Sutton (1876-1916) and Thomas MORGAN (1866-1945).
First seaplane and deck take-off and landing systems built in the US.
Atomic structure of crystals observed with X-rays by Max von Laue (1879-1960). First nuclear model of the atom built by Ernest RUTHERFORD (1871-1937).
Stainless steel invented by several scientists.

First World War brought the use of tanks and armoured cars. First all-metal monoplanes flown in Germany by Hugo Junkers (1859-1935). Zeppelins bombed England.
New atomic model devised by Niels BOHR (1885-1962).
Continental drift theory proposed by Alfred WEGENER (1880-1930)
Zip fastener invented.
First diesel-electric railway, in Sweden.

FOKKER (1890-1939) invented a mechanism enabling bullets to be fired through a plane's propeller.
First aircraft-carrier, HMS *Argus*, launched.
Quick freezing of food in small containers developed by Clarence BIRDSEYE (1886-1956).
The galaxy Its size and shape and the position of the Sun within it proposed by Harlow SHAPLEY (b. 1885).

1919 1922 1925 1928 1931 1934 1937 377

Principal Events

Paris Peace Conference (1919) Payment of reparations to Germany decided. Lithuania, Finland, Latvia and Estonia proclaimed independent. League of Nations first met (1920). HITLER (1889-1945) founded Nazis in Germany and MUSSOLINI (1883-1945) the Fascists in Italy. **Palestine** established as Jewish state under British Mandate (1920). **Soviet Republic** established (1919). Civil war between Communists and 'white' Russians. Anti-Bolshevik naval mutiny crushed (1921).

French occupied German Ruhr, after German failure to pay war reparations. **USSR** established in Russia (1922). **Egypt** declared independent. Became a hereditary constitutional monarchy. **Turkish Republic** proclaimed (1923) under Mustapha KEMAL (1881-1938). End of Ottoman Empire. **Chinese Nationalist** government set up (1923) by SUN YAT-SEN (1866-1925). **General strike** in England (1926).

League of Nations Great powers agreed to submit disputes to arbitration. Germany admitted to League. Brazil and Spain resigned. **General strike in Vienna,** where the Palace of Justice was burned down. STALIN (1879-1953) gained control of the USSR, defeating TROTSKY (1879-1940), ZINOVIEV (1883-1936) and Radek (b. 1885). **Canberra** founded as federal capital of Australia (1927). **Chinese Communists** hunted and executed by Nationalists.

Kellogg-Briand pact (1928) renounced aggressive warfare. Signed by the Allies, Germany and Japan. **New York Stock Exchange** collapsed (1929). **German reparations** Final settlement demanded. Nazis won 102 seats in 1930 election. GANDHI (1869-1948) began civil disobedience campaign in India. **Jews and Arabs** in conflict in Palestine. CHIANG KAI-SHEK (b. 1887) declared President of the Chinese Republic. MAO TSE-TUNG (b. 1893) and CHU TEH (b. 1886) established soviets in Kiangsi province.

Economic crisis (1931) Special monetary powers granted to ROOSEVELT (1882-1945) in US. National Government formed in Britain. **Disarmament conference** in Geneva and international economic conference in London (1933). HITLER (1889-1945) appointed Chancellor of Germany (1933). **Spanish Republic** declared (1931). Internal split between left and right (1933). **Chinese Soviet Republic** established (1931). Japan occupied Manchuria. War declared by Communists but not by Nationalists.

HITLER (1889-1945) became President of Germany. Reparation payments suspended, conscription re-introduced, Rhineland occupied, and Jews outlawed. Anglo-German naval agreement limited the German navy. German-Japanese treaty against Communism. **Spanish Civil War** after army, led by FRANCO (b. 1892) and supported by Germany and Italy, revolted against the Republic (1936). **Italy invaded Abyssinia** Denounced ineffectively by League of Nations (1936).

Religion

Khalifat movement of GANDHI (1869-1948) attempted to unite Hindus and Muslims in a protest against Allied treatment of the Turks after the First World War. Hindu and Muslim clashes took place during Gandhi's non-co-operation movement (1921-22).

Christianity spread in China. Missionaries opened schools and hospitals, aided the development of agriculture and translated Western writings into Chinese. But reform movements within the ancient Chinese religions, notably Buddhism, and anti-religious groups of sceptics and agnostics halted the spread. Economic depression in the West reduced the flow of missionaries to China.

Russian orthodox theology revived in reaction to Marxism, although persecuted because of its former ties with the Tsarist régime. Renewed interest in the teaching of Vladimir Soloviev (1853-1900) on ethics. Sergius Bulgakov (1871-1944) Nicholas Bedyaev (1874-1948)

Lateran Treaties (1929) restored pope's temporal power, and gave him sovereignty over the Vatican City.

Conflicts between the Muslim League and the All-India Congress after the Government of India Act (1935). The Hindu-dominated Congress won majorities in six provinces. The two nations theory, propagated by Mohammed Ali Jinnah (1876-1948), gained popularity among the Muslim minority.

Philosophy

Nationalism arose in China during the political troubles of the early 20th century and the influx of new ideas from the West. After the First World War, nationalist sentiment was directed against foreign powers in China, notably against Britain. Radical students and young people swelled the ranks of the Kuomintang, the Nationalist Party. SUN YAT-SEN (1866-1925)

Communism A doctrinal-political movement originating from the interpretations by LENIN (1870-1924) of the writings of MARX (1818-83). Lenin held that a small, tightly knit party could bring about the end of capitalism by means of a revolution, and would then rule the state in the name of the proletariat until it was ready to claim its inheritance. Leon TROTSKY (1879-1940).

Traditional Chinese philosophies were revived concurrently with the adoption of Western ideas. Fung Yu-lan (b. 1890) formulated a 'new rationalism' based upon Sung Neo-Confucianism, and Hsiung Shih-li (b. 1885) developed a 'new idealism' from a synthesis of Ming Neo-Confucianism and Buddhist concepts. Ou-yang Ching-yu (b. 1894) T'ai hsu (1889-1947)

New realism Belief that the forms of perception are themselves a true part of the physical world, therefore providing first-hand examples of natural phenomena. Mind is thought of as part of nature, but a nature that, after the theory of relativity, is made to appear much more like mind than ever. A. N. WHITEHEAD (1861-1947) George Mead (1863-1931)

Logical positivism rules out most philosophical problems as meaningless. There is no real logic in so-called 'reality', the logical elements in knowledge being as 'conventional' in character as languages are. Bertrand RUSSELL (1872-1970) Moritz SCHLICK (1882-1936) Rudolph CARNAP (1891-1970)

Literature

Georgian Poetry gathered in anthologies, commercially successful, conventional verse generally describing the English countryside in a Wordsworthian manner. W. H. DAVIES (1871-1940); Gordon Bottomley (1874-1948); W. W. Gibson (1878-1962); Lascelles Abercrombie (1881-1938); John Drinkwater (1882-1937); Rupert BROOKE (1887-1915); Edmund BLUNDEN (b. 1896).
Futurism in Italy advocated new forms in subject matter and style, reflecting the age of machines, aeroplanes and factories. Rejected logical sentence construction; words used more for their sounds than their meaning. War declared a cure for the world; Fascism welcomed as being based on similar doctrines. Influenced Russian poets. Filippo Marinetti (1878-1944); Giovanni Papini (1881-1956); Viktor Khlebnikov (1885-1922); Vladimir MAYAKOVSKY (1893-1930).

Expressionism originated in Germany. Emphasized importance of psychology rather than external physical appearances expressed by naturalistic writers. Main characteristics were pacificism, anti-capitalism and anti-materialism, in support of anarchy, Communism or Socialism. Characters and situations were symbols to represent a view of society. August STRINDBERG (1849-1912); Frank WEDEKIND (1864-1918); Georg KAISER (1878-1945); Sean O'CASEY (1880-1964); Franz KAFKA (1883-1924); Eugene O'NEILL (1888-1953); Karel CAPEK (1890-1938);
Surrealism aimed at expressing subconscious thought by suspending logic and reason, writing automatically and juxtaposing incongruous ideas. Paul ELUARD (1895-1942); André BRETON (1896-1966); Louis ARAGON (b. 1897); Robert Desnos (1900-45).

American theatre Small experimental groups put on new plays with new production methods. Eugene O'NEILL (1888-1953) Elmer Rice (1892-1967) Clifford Odets (1906-63)
Serapion Brothers Group of Russian writers who objected to the encroachment of politics into literature. Yevgeni Zamyatin (1884-1937) Konstantin FEDIN (b. 1892)

Socialist Realism Official Soviet literature and literary criticism, based on depiction of situations shown to be affected by the application of Communist principles, to educate working classes into revolutionary ideals. Emphasis on heroic conduct. Anatoli LUNACHARSKY (1875-1933) Alexander TAIROV (1885-1950) Mikhail SHOLOKHOV (b. 1905)

Art

Futurism Originally Italian movement which aimed to represent the dynamism of the modern machine age by depicting machines or figures in motion by simultaneous portrayal of successive views of the moving form. Carlo Carrà (1881-1966) Umberto BOCCIONI (1882-1916) Gino SEVERINI (1883-1966) Luigi Russolo (1885-1947) Giacomo Balla (1871-1958)

Surrealism Movement in art and literature, which attempted to express the subconscious mind without the preconceptions imposed by tradition, convention or conscious thought. Said to be 'as beautiful as the chance encounter of a sewing machine and an umbrella on an operating table'—Lautréamont (1846-70). Paul KLEE (1879-1940); Pablo PICASSO (1881-1973); Giorgio de CHIRICO (b. 1888); Man Ray (b. 1890); Max ERNST (b. 1891); René MAGRITTE (1898-1967); Yves Tanguy 1900-55); A. GIACOMETTI (1901-66); Salvador DALI (b. 1904)
Expressionism European movement which abandoned the idealization of nature as subject matter, claiming that the representation of emotions should be the prime purpose of art. Painters used strong colours, distortion, and simplified forms. The architects used non-geometric forms, curves and created oddly-shaped skylines in concrete, steel, brick and glass. P. V. Jensen Klint (1853-1930); Hendrikus Berlage (1856-1934); Edvard MUNCH (1863-1944); James Ensor (1860-1949); Emil Nolde (1867-1956); Hans Poelzig (1869-1936); Georges ROUAULT (1871-1958); Fritz Hoeger (1877-1949); Piet Kramer (b. 1881); Walter GROPIUS (1883-1969); Max BECKMANN (1884-1950); Willem Dudok (b. 1884); Oskar KOKOSCHKA (b. 1886); Erich MENDELSOHN (1887-1953); Chaim Soutine (1894-1943); Michel de Klerk (1884-1923).
De Stijl A movement, originating in Holland, concerned with the geometrical appearance of buildings, and geometrical abstraction in painting. The works are characterized by the rectangle and the use of primary colours. Piet MONDRIAN (1872-1944); Theo van Doesburg (1883-1931).

Ecole de Paris The group of young artists living and finding inspiration in Paris, the centre of European artistic activity at this time. A. MODIGLIANI (1884-1920) Jules Pascin (1885-1930) Marc CHAGALL (b. 1887)
New Objectivity German social Realist movement which expressed the disillusionment and despair after the First World War. Max BECKMANN (1884-1950) Otto Dix (b. 1891)

Federal Art Project Idea initiated by President ROOSEVELT (1882-1945) in the depression, aimed at alleviating unemployment. Artists were employed at a small salary to produce, for example, murals on public buildings. Arshile Gorky (1904-48) William de KOONING (b. 1904) Jackson POLLOCK (1912-56)

Constructivism Russian sculptural movement which grew from collage and developed into the construction of abstract forms made from wire, steel, glass or other industrial or man-made materials. Influenced architecture and interior design. Vladimir TATLIN (1885-1953) Antoine PEVSNER (1886-1962) Naum GABO (b. 1890) Richard Lippold (b. 1915) Anthony Caro (b. 1924)

Architecture

Bauhaus School of architecture, craft and design founded in Weimar in 1919 by Walter GROPIUS (1883-1969). Based on the theory that function should control structure, it broke down the distinction between fine and applied arts. Widely influenced art school training and industrial design. Wassily KANDINSKY (1866-1944) Paul KLEE (1879-1940) L. MOHOLY-NAGY (1895-1946)

Japanese architecture was characterized by extreme westernization. European and American architects were invited to teach the techniques of building in brick, glass and iron, steel and concrete. Frank Lloyd WRIGHT (1869-1959) Antonin Raymond (b. 1890) Kunio Maekwa (b. 1905) Kenzo Tange (b. 1913)

Chinese Republican architecture. European styles of architecture, particularly the English Neo-Georgian, were adopted wholeheartedly after 1911 for newly required municipal buildings, government offices, universities, schools and hospitals. During the 1920s a 'Chinese Renaissance' adorned western-style buildings with traditional Chinese decorative techniques.

Post-Revolutionary Russian architecture accepted the most advanced styles of the early 20th century. This short-lived era of modernism was replaced by a revival of classicism for public buildings, often on a monumental scale. Bruno Taut (1880-1938) V. TATLIN (1885-1953) LE CORBUSIER (1887-1965)

Music

Les Six Group of French composers who sought inspiration from the music halls and circuses, music devoid of pointless elaboration and full of wit. Louis Durey (b. 1888) Arthur HONEGGER (1892-1955) Darius MILHAUD (b. 1892) Germaine Tailleferre (b. 1892) Francis POULENC (1899-1963) Georges Auric (b. 1899)

Jazz Virtuosi Star soloists emerged as jazz spread north and centred in Chicago. Louis ARMSTRONG (1900-71); Bix Biederbecke (1903-31).

Neo-classicist movement, initiated by Igor STRAVINSKY (1882-1971), tending towards the principles of the classical composers, e.g. balance, objectivity and small orchestras, as opposed to the subjective, emotional and programme music of the Romantics. Often used phrases or themes from classical composers. Sergei PROKOVIEV (1891-1953); Ferruccio BUSONI (1866-1924); Paul HINDEMITH (1895-1963)

Modern school of Vienna was characterized by the use of atonality, a system using all twelve notes of the conventional scale, with no relation to tonic key. The music was dissonant, with broken melodic lines and uneven rhythms. Arnold SCHOENBERG (1874-1951) Alban BERG (1885-1935)

Young France group formed in 1936, aimed at reviving, in music, spiritual ideas which they considered had been abandoned in post-war composition. Music often inspired by eastern instruments and African rhythms. Yves Baudrier (b. 1906) Daniel Lesur (b. 1908) Oliver MESSAIEN (b. 1908)

Modern English school The revival initiated by ELGAR (1857-1934) and Parry (1848-1918) brought English music to its highest peak for two centuries, in the music of VAUGHAN WILLIAMS (1872-1958) and HOLST (1874-1934). They drew their inspiration from English countryside, and later from folk-songs and poetry.

Technology

Mass communication by radio began with the broadcasts of Frank Conrad (1874-1941) in the US. **Galaxies** Their distances measured by Edwin HUBBLE (1889-1953). **First Atlantic flight** made by Sir John ALCOCK (1892-1919) and Arthur BROWN (1886-1948). **Prediction** by EINSTEIN (1879-1955) that light rays bend near the Sun verified by Sir Arthur EDDINGTON (1882-1944).

Films Technicolor developed by Herbert Kalmus. Synchronous sound system invented by De Forest (1873-1961). **Rocket research** carried out by Hermann Oberth (b. 1894). **Earth's atmosphere** studied utilizing the discovery of Heinrich HERTZ (1857-94) that radio waves can be reflected. **Electrons** discovered to behave like waves as well as like particles.

Machine tools Tungsten carbide cutting tools developed. Hydraulic trace allowed mass reproduction of complex shapes. **Rocket** propelled by liquid fuel first designed by Robert GODDARD (1882-1945). **First flights:** Non-stop New York to Paris (1927) by Charles LINDBERGH (born 1902); across the North pole (1926) by Richard BYRD (1888-1957) **Television** first demonstrated by BAIRD (1888-1946) in Britain.

Electric razor invented by J. Schick. **Computer,** called a differential analyser' produced by Vannevar Bush (b. 1890). **Iron lung** invented in the US by Cecil DRINKER (1887-1956). **Penicillin** discovered by Sir Alexander FLEMING (1881-1955). **Gas turbine** for use in jet propulsion of aircraft developed by Sir Frank WHITTLE (b. 1907).

Cyclotron, a device for accelerating atomic particles, invented by Ernest LAWRENCE (1901-58). **Radio astronomy** began when Karl JANSKY (1905-50) discovered that radio waves are received from space. **Small hearing aids** made possible by the development of miniature electronic valves. **Caterpillar tractor** developed for farming. **Fluorescent lamp** produced, used for flood-lighting and advertising.

Kodachrome, first commercially practicable colour film for still cameras, developed. **Parking meters** invented in the US by C. C. MAGEE (1873-1946). **Bathysphere** of W. Beebe (b. 1877) descended half a mile beneath the surface of the ocean. **Television** broadcast regularly in England (1936) and in the US (1941). **301.7 mph** Land speed record set up by Sir Malcolm CAMPBELL (1885-1948) in a jet propelled car.

1937 | 1940 | 1943 | 1946 | 1949 | 1952 | 1955

Principal Events

HITLER (1889-1945) annexed Austria. European powers agreed at Munich pact (1938) to German seizure of Sudetenland from Czechoslovakia. German invasion of Poland led to declaration of war by Britain, France, Australia and New Zealand.
Japanese invaded China; seized Shanghai and Peking (1937).
Germany formed alliance (Axis) with Italy. Fascist racialism defined. Anglo-German naval agreement denounced (1939).

Second World War As Germany invaded northern Europe, Russia moved into eastern Europe and Scandinavia. France fell to Germany (1940). Invasion of Britain prevented in the Battle of Britain (1940), fought in the air. Italy declared war on Britain and France. CHURCHILL (1874-1965) became Prime Minister of Britain (1940). In Africa, Allies defeated Italians in Ethiopia (1941) and German and Italian (Axis) forces in Tunisia and Libya (1942). Churchill and ROOSEVELT (1882-1945) signed Atlantic Charter. US declared war on Axis Powers after Japanese attack on US navy at Pearl Harbor (1941). Germans invaded Russia and advanced as far as Moscow. Japanese overran southeastern Asia (1942). Greatest extent of Axis powers' acquisitions. RAF began continuous bombing of Germany. National Front for the Liberation of France led by DE GAULLE (1890-1970) from London. Germans defeated in Russia. Italy invaded by Allies. Americans and Australians repelled Japanese in Pacific (1943). Allied landing in Normandy (1944). Russians advanced towards Germany from the east. Germany overrun by Allies; Russians captured Berlin (1945). Japan surrendered after atomic bombing of Hiroshima and Nagasaki. HITLER (1889-1945) committed suicide.

United Nations began its first session in London (1946).
Anglo-US association against Russian expansion. USSR refused to assist economic recovery of Europe. President TRUMAN (1884-1972) proposed military and economic aid to nations subject to Communist influence.
Israel founded (1948). War with Arab League.
India gained independence (1947). GANDHI (1869-1948) assassinated by Hindu extremist.
China split by conflict between Communists and Nationalists.

NATO Defensive alliance by western European Nations, Canada and the US (1949).
Germany divided by creation of German Federal Republic (West) and German Democratic Republic (East).
Comecon founded for mutual economic aid between USSR and Communist States.
Korean War between North Korea and UN forces (1950-1).
Vietnam recognized as independent by France.
Chinese People's Republic proclaimed by MAO TSE-TUNG (b. 1893).

Europe Coal and Steel Community formed by western states. Developed into the EEC (Common Market). Security conference with USSR set up naval bases in Spain.
Anti-Communist riots in E. Berlin.
Mau Mau rebellion against British in Kenya.
Vietnam divided between North and South. Beginning of Communist efforts to dominate South Vietnam.
Racial segregation declared illegal in American schools.

Religion

Persecution of Christians took place in China after the Japanese invasion. As the Japanese moved inland, many Christian missionaries and Chinese converts moved to the West. The depletion of missionaries continued throughout the Second World War.

World Council of Churches Ecumenical organization, inaugurated in 1948 by 147 Churches throughout the world, with the intention of promoting co-operation among its members and fostering Christian unity everywhere.
Dead Sea Scrolls Collection of Hebrew and Aramaic manuscript scrolls discovered in 1947 near the Dead Sea in Palestine. Among them were parts of the Bible and Apocrypha. Considered to have been written by the Essenes between 125 BC and AD 68.
Pakistan Muslims insisted on a separate state. The Indian Independence Bill (1947) called for the partition of India and Pakistan, but the separation was accompanied by violence, and two million refugees were exchanged between the two states.

Chinese Communist régime declared their atheism, but pursued a policy of religious toleration in so far as it did not interfere with their authority. Christianity, however, was denounced as 'cultural imperialism'; missionaries were expelled, financial aid from foreign churches was cut off and religious institutions inside China were closed.

Philosophy

Japanese militarism arose as a result of western opposition to Japanese imperial expansion during the late 19th and early 20th centuries. A revival of interest in Japanese culture took place, accompanied by a mistrust of politicians and the political domination of the army and the navy.

Maoism Though basing his ideas on Marxist-Leninist ideas, MAO TSE-TUNG (b. 1893) differs from the orthodox Communist view in his belief that the revolution must spring from the peasant class as opposed to the industrial proletariat. Mao also opposed doctrine of STALIN (1879-1953) of 'peaceful co-existence' with non-Communist countries, and has placed great emphasis on the idea of 'permanent revolution', first formulated by Leon TROTSKY (1879-1940).

Chinese literature influenced by translations of western works. Movement away from traditional stylization in theatre. New left-wing political writing became the 'revolutionary classics' revered by Chinese Communists. Text books and newspapers rapidly disseminated knowledge and ideas.
Wang Kuo-wei (1877-1927)
Lu Hsun (1881-1936)
Hu Shih (1891-1962)

Political theatre formed an important part of Chinese cultural policy. Theatre intended to be used as a means of raising the political consciousness of the masses. 'Hundred Flowers Campaign', a brief interlude of free expression in 1956, suppressed when criticism of Communist régime was voiced.

Literature

Modern metaphysicals Group of poets using elaborate analogies, metaphors and conceits to express complex philosophical ideas. Showed wide knowledge of European literature and history; borrowed from other languages, poets or cultures.
Ezra POUND (1885-1973)
T. S. ELIOT (1888-1965)
Archibald MACLEISH (b. 1892)
Louise Bogan (1897-1970)

Italian literature emphasized the problems of modern life. Realistic novels of peasant and working-class life, particularly in the south, often with sexual themes. Drama explored the conflict of illusion and reality and themes of non-communication.
Luigi PIRANDELLO (1867-1936)
Carlo LEVI (b. 1902)
Alberto MORAVIA (b. 1907)
Cesare PAVESE (1908-50)

Stream of consciousness English literary form, intended to portray internal reality of character, by presenting thoughts and reactions of protagonists without direct comment or apparent organisation by the author. Influenced by psychological concepts of FREUD (1856-1939). Virginia WOOLF (1882-1941); James JOYCE (1882-1941); William FAULKNER (1897-1962).
Epic Theatre Originally German narrative, didactic theatre, with episodes rather than acts. Employed stylized acting which rejected the idea that drama should represent reality. Instead it aimed to stimulate the intellect of the audience in order to instruct or enlighten on social and moral problems.
Georg KAISER (1878-1945); Erwin Piscator (1893-1945); Bertolt BRECHT (1898-1956).

French novels were mainly concerned with psychological analysis of individual integrity and the individual in French society.
André GIDE (1869-1951)
Marcel PROUST (1871-1922)
François MAURIAC (1885-1970)
COLETTE (1873-1954)

Spanish novel repudiated the cult of the individual by laying emphasis on action. Many novels tried to reiterate Christian values which were threatened by materialism.
Camilo Cela (b. 1916)
Rafael Ferlosio (b. 1927)

Art

Socialist Realism Official style of painting in the USSR and other Communist countries, which aims at producing art for the masses, and at encouraging admiration for the working man. Naturalist techniques.

Biomorphic abstraction of Surrealistic painting and sculpture which uses free forms suggesting living organisms.
Hans ARP (1887-1966)
Joán MIRO (b. 1893)
Henry MOORE (b. 1898)

Photography became an art form in its own right, both influencing and being influenced by surrealist and impressionist painting. Later photographers have developed their own style, and use effects to demonstrate details which the eye might not ordinarily notice.
Laszlo Moholy-Nagy (1895-1946)
Man Ray (b. 1890)

English sculptors sought to break from the past, and experimented with ideas of concavity and flat forms in space. Influenced by BRANCUSI (1876-1957) and ARP (1887-1966).
Jacob EPSTEIN (1880-1959)
Henry MOORE (b. 1898)
Barbara HEPWORTH (b. 1903)

Abstract Expressionism Movement in American painting, also known as action painting, which is a revolt against traditional techniques of representation. It aims at the spontaneous expression of private emotion by, for example, splashing or dripping paint on to canvas, avoiding all conscious composition. Hans HOFMANN (1880-1966); Mark ROTHKO (1903-70); Willem de KOONING (b. 1904); Jackson POLLOCK (1912-56); Robert MOTHERWELL (b. 1915).
Kinetic art Sculptured constructions in motion; based on the Greek idea that movement and light together form a work of art. First used by Naum GABO (b. 1890) in 1920s and developed further with more use of electronics to power moving parts or coloured lights. Alexander Calder (b. 1898); Lynn Chadwick (b. 1914).

Architecture

International Modern style Characterized by generally undecorated Cubist shapes, asymmetry and horizontally grouped windows, the style is essentially functional, light and spatial. It spread through and outside Europe, to develop national and regional variations. Tony Garnier (1869-1948); Frank Lloyd WRIGHT (1869-1959); Adolf LOOS (1870-1933); Josef HOFFMANN (1870-1956); Robert Maillart (1872-1940); Walter GROPIUS (1883-1969); Gunnar ASPLUND (1885-1940); LE CORBUSIER (1887-1965); Sven Markelius (b. 1889); Alvar AALTO (b. 1898); Arne Jacobsen (b. 1902).

South American architecture broke traditional ties with the various mother countries and developed individual styles.
LE CORBUSIER (1887-1965)
Lúcio Costa (b. 1902)
Oscar Niemeyer (b. 1907)
Félix Candela (b. 1910)

Scandinavian architecture avoided the extremism of mainland Europe and retained national styles and regional traditions, principally the native decorative styles, using wood and natural settings.
Ragnar Ostberg (1866-1945)
Gunnar ASPLUND (1885-1940)
Alvar AALTO (b. 1898)
Arne Jacobsen (b. 1902)
Eliel Saarinen (1910-60)

Music

Microtone music Experiments with intervals (the distance between two notes) of less than a semitone (the smallest interval in conventional notation).
Julián Carrillo (1875-1965)
Vittorio Grecchi (1876-1954)
Ernest BLOCH (1880-1959)
Alois Haba (b. 1893)

American musical theatre Light musical stage compositions, without the melodrama or sentimentality of operetta; often with serious social themes.
Frederick Loewe (b. 1901)
Richard Rodgers (b. 1902)
Leonard BERNSTEIN (b. 1918)

American nationalists Influenced by IVES (1874-1954), several composers, many of them pupils of Nadia BOULANGER (b. 1887) used as the basis of their music, Indian tunes, cowboy songs, jazz, some revivalist hymn tunes and central American folk-songs. Douglas Moore (1893-1969); Walter Piston (b. 1894); Virgil Thomson (b. 1896); Roy HARRIS (b. 1898); George GERSHWIN (1898-1937); Aaron COPLAND (b. 1900).
Modern Jazz Big bands were broken up by the war, and smaller groups emerged. 1940s called the bebop generation. Dizzie Gillespie (b. 1917); Charlie Parker (1920-55).

Soviet music was restrained by the ideology of socialist realism and, in fact, many works by the most important composers were denounced as decadent. Ballet flourished.
Igor STRAVINSKY (1882-1971)
Sergei PROKOVIEV (1891-1953)
Aram Khachaturian (b. 1903)
Dmitri SHOSTAKOVICH (b. 1906)

English music Often experimental: operas, choral works, song cycles, some with lyrical qualities, others characterized by distortion and dissonance.
Sir William WALTON (b. 1902)
Sir Michael TIPPETT (b. 1905)
Benjamin BRITTEN (b. 1913)

Technology

Xerography, a dry photographic process, invented in the US by Chester CARLSON (b. 1906).
Nylon first manufactured in the US by Wallace CAROTHERS (1896-1937).
Ball-point pen patented by Ladislao Biro.
Nuclear fission discovered by Otto HAHN (1879-1968) and Lise MEITNER (1878-1968), in Germany.
DDT first produced for use as an insecticide by Paul MÜLLER (1899-1965).

Second World War Parachutes first used as means of attack. Radar developed, to discover enemy aircraft and to pinpoint targets from the air. Rockets and missiles manufactured in Germany, under guidance of Wernher von BRAUN (b. 1912). Atomic bomb developed in the US and used for the first time against Japan.
Oil pipelines of large diameter constructed in the US, after development of welding methods.
Nuclear power Self-sustaining reactor first built in the US by Enrico FERMI (1901-54).
Kidney machine invented in Holland by Willem KOLFF (b. 1911).

Computers First electronic high-speed digital calculating machine built in the US.
DNA molecules studied by Ostwald Avery (1877-1955).
Silicones produced for lubricants, fibreglass water-repellant agents and textiles.

US Atomic Energy Commission founded (1946).
Radiocarbon dating much used in archaeology, developed in the US by Willard LIBBY (b. 1908).
Polaroid Land camera, which developed film inside the camera, invented by Edwin LAND (b. 1909).
Speed of sound first exceeded by a plane in level flight.
Transistor invented by William SHOCKLEY (b. 1910).

Nuclear propulsion introduced into some ships and submarines.
Colour television developed during the 1950s.
Special purpose computers and data processing machines became more widely used.
Poultry mass-produced in battery farms.
Basic-oxygen process for the manufacture of steel developed in Austria.
Milky Way mapped by examining the spectra of the stars.

Solar battery, able to convert sunlight directly into electric power, developed by the Bell Telephone Laboratories in the US.
Cybernetics control and communication in animal and machine, studied with computers by Norbert Wiener.
Structure of DNA discovered by Francis CRICK (b. 1916) and James Watson (b. 1928).

Principal Events

Warsaw Pact, eastern European defence treaty, signed by Communist nations (1955).
Geneva conference on peaceful uses of atomic energy.
KHRUSHCHEV (1894-1971), Soviet leader, declared peaceful coexistence the aim of Russian foreign policy. Russian troops crushed rebellion in Hungary (1956).
Israel attacked Egyptian and Syrian borders (1955). Attacked again (1956) during international crisis following nationalization of Suez Canal by NASSER (1918-70).

DE GAULLE (1890-1970) became President of the 5th French Republic (1959).
Independence gained by Cyprus and Belgian Congo led to fierce internal conflict in both countries.
CASTRO (b. 1927) became President of Cuba. US set up economic blockade. USSR threatened military reprisals (1960).
Chinese Communists bombarded islands held by Nationalists. Although USSR supported Communists, KHRUSHCHEV (1894-1970) criticized Chinese leaders.

East German borders tightened. Berlin wall built (1961).
Nuclear confrontation between US and USSR, who withdrew missiles and bombers from Cuba (1962).
Africa Sierra Leone, Uganda, Zanzibar, Malawi became independent. Organization of African Unity founded. South Africa became a Republic, left the Commonwealth.
Sino-Indian border conflict. US military aid requested by NEHRU (1889-1964).
US began large-scale military operation in Vietnam.

KOSYGIN (b. 1904) became Premier of USSR, after internal conflict in Communist party (1964).
Outer space to be used for peaceful purposes: agreement between US and USSR.
India and Pakistan at war over Kashmir (1965).
Communist coup d'état in Indonesia suppressed by army.
Rhodesia declared independent (1965). Economic pressure by Britain and UN failed to re-establish constitutional government.
Vietnamese war escalated with American bombing of the North.

Six Day war between Israel and Arab allies. Israel occupied Sinai desert, Jerusalem and west bank of the Jordan (1967).
Nigeria split by civil war after secession of Biafra. (1967-70)
Race riots in many American cities. Demonstrations in Paris. Universities and factories taken over by students and workers (1968).
Czechoslovakia invaded by Soviet troops (1968) after liberal reforms of DUBCEK (b. 1921).
Vietnam President NIXON (b. 1913) began policy of 'Vietnamization' of the war.

India at war with Pakistan (1970).
Vietnam Withdrawal of US troops (1971). Cease-fire agreement signed (1973).
China UN General Assembly voted to admit Communist China and expel the Nationalists (1971).
World currency crisis (1972-73) caused many national currencies to be floated.
EEC Britain, Republic of Ireland, and Denmark became members (1973).
Middle East New Arab-Israeli conflict (1973). Largest tank battle ever fought. Cease-fire called by US and USSR.

Religion

Samaritans Voluntary social organization in Britain, giving help and advice to those in trouble, particularly potential suicides.
Confucianism was actively discouraged by the Chinese Communists in the form of attacks upon the traditional and deep-seated family structure, and the substitution of the concept of the 'five loves' for the traditional 'five relations' of the Confucian ethic.

Shinko Shukyo, 'New Religious Sects', which have evolved in Japan since the Second World War, include sub-sects of the older denominations of Sect Shinto, Buddhism, Confucianism and also Christianity. Many are eclectic, and many followers adhere to more than one sect.

Modern Hinduism is considerably influenced by Christianity, nationalism and the ideas of Mahatma GANDHI (1869-1948), who attempted to reform the traditions of caste and social class in India by raising the status of the untouchables and of women, and to adapt their beliefs and practices to modern times.

Ku Klux Klan Secret society of white Protestant fanatics in southern USA. Revival outlawed by President JOHNSON (1908-72) in 1965.
Krishna Worship of the Hindu god revived in the West, in a hypnotic cult.
Archbishop of Canterbury received by the Pope (1966), the first formal relation between the two Churches since the Reformation.

Humanae Vitae (1968) Papal encyclical condemning all methods of contraception.
Jesus movement Young people, disenchanted with eastern mysticism, found fulfilment in the concept of JESUS CHRIST. Began in California; spread to Britain.
Violence in Belfast, Ireland, between Catholics and Protestants, necessitated the presence of British troops (1969).

President TITO (born 1892) of Yugoslavia was the first Communist head of state to be received by a pope (1971).
358 black Churches in South Africa, represented by the African Independent Churches Association, were admitted to the South African Council of Churches (1971).
Persecution of Soviet Jews. By 1971 only 40 synagogues remained from a total of about 3,000 in 1917.

Philosophy

Existentialism Only individuals matter. Existence being individual in character, self-comprehension cannot be achieved by abstract speculation alone but by an ethically engaged existence. Existentialism denies the possibility of general philosophical laws, applicable to every object or being.
S. A. KIERKEGAARD (1813-55)
Karl JASPERS (1883-1969)
Jean-Paul SARTRE (b. 1905)

Literature

Post-revolutionary poetry in Russia mostly dealt with economic or political themes, with the exceptions of PASTERNAK (1890-1960), Tikhonov (b. 1896) and YEVTUSHENKO (b. 1933), all of whom rebel against the dominance of socialist realism.

American literature, largely naturalistic, developed from the novels of social analysis and Freudian character studies of the inter-war years to the picaresque tales of alienated heroes in the works of SALINGER (b. 1919) and BALDWIN (b. 1924). Dramatists such as MILLER (b. 1915) and ALBEE (b. 1928) concentrated on tragedy of the ordinary man. Popular fiction, often sensational crime stories with a high sexual content, and political novels. Gore Vidal (b. 1925) and MAILER (b. 1923) contrast with the laconic, Surrealistic Beat movement, which in the writing of KEROUAC (b. 1922) or GINSBERG (b. 1926), advocates a freedom gained through jazz, sex and drugs.

Theatre of the Absurd expressed playwrights' anxiety at man's apparent lack of purpose, by the rejection of both logical discussion and rational construction. Impression of comedy, though the intent is serious.
Samuel BECKETT (b. 1906)
Arthur ADAMOV (b. 1908)
Jean GENET (b. 1910)
Eugene IONESCO (b. 1912)
Edward ALBEE (b. 1928)
Harold PINTER (b. 1930)

British Neo-Realism Sometimes called kitchen sink drama, or social realism. Written usually from a left-wing standpoint commenting on the social position of the working classes.
Alun Owen (b. 1926)
John OSBORNE (b. 1929)
Arnold Wesker (b. 1932)
Shelagh Delaney (b. 1939)

Protest movement in Russia against the basic principles which rule Soviet literature. Reveals the workings of such Soviet institutions as labour camps and 'special' camps for dissidents.
Alexander SOLZHENITSYN (b. 1918)
Yuri Daniel
Andrei SINYAVSKY (b. 1925)

Art

Social Realism Western paintings depicting contemporary social problems, usually from a left-wing angle. The movement has developed since the Second World War, though is influenced by the realism of COURBET (1819-77), in representing unidealized scenes from the life of peasants or poorer classes. Ben Shahn (b. 1898); Renato Guttoso (b. 1913); Jack Levine (b. 1915); Edward Middleditch (b. 1923); John Bratby (b. 1928); Jack Smith (b. 1928).

Op art Abstract movement inspired by geometric experiments of the Bauhaus. Often using only black and white, the artists seek to produce optical illusions, by careful constructive techniques creating patterns of curved lines or geometric shapes.
Victor Vasarely (b. 1908)
Bridget Riley (b. 1931)

Pop art Painters and sculptors comment on contemporary life by using or reproducing exactly commonplace objects drawn from the world of popular culture. They adapt commercial art techniques such as strip cartoons and advertising posters, and use bright colours, huge canvasses and objects, such as soup tins, to reflect the world of mass production. Roy LICHTENSTEIN (b. 1923); Larry Rivers (b. 1923); Robert RAUSCHENBERG (b. 1925); Andy Warhol (b. 1925); Claes OLDENBURG (b. 1929); Jasper Johns (b. 1930); David HOCKNEY (b. 1937).

Hard Edge Term used to denote abstract painting consisting of clear, sharply-defined, coloured shapes, not necessarily geometric, which are used to explore colour and shape in relation to the shape and size of the canvas.

Architecture

India and Pakistan Western-style architecture has predominated both in India and Pakistan since independence. Often designed by western architects invited for the purpose.
LE CORBUSIER (1887-1965)

Chinese Post-Revolutionary architecture. The imperial residence was taken over for government use; the imperial parks have been opened to the public. Public buildings, predominantly in the International Modern style of the 20th century, have dominated China since 1949, but tall blocks are limited to a height of nine stories.

Music

Skiffle Form of folk-music played on improvised instruments by the poor negroes of Chicago. Led to the development of a new popular music among young people in the US and England.
Lonnie Donegan (b. 1931)
Elvis Presley (b. 1935)

Musique concrète Electronic musical collage, achieved by assembling recordings of fragments of sound (either music, or non-musical sounds like a door slamming, dog barking), distorting them and mixing them on tape.
Pierre Schaeffer (b. 1910)

Avant-garde music has widened the scope of the 12 note system, rejecting repetition or theme-development, instead adapting serial organization (note-row system) to all aspects of music (tone, rhythm, etc.). Other composers combine music from India, primitive or exotic instruments, Gregorian modes or electronically produced sound into their composition. Oliver MESSAIEN (b. 1908); John CAGE (b. 1912); Pierre BOULEZ (b. 1925); Karlheinz STOCKHAUSEN (b. 1928)

Pop music A greater confidence with new electronic effects and instruments and the influence of various folk traditions resulted in energetic, rhythmic, commercial music, with an international audience.
Bob Dylan (b. 1941)
The Beatles (Formed 1961)
Jimi Hendrix (1943-70)

Technology

National Geophysical Year (1957), to study the Earth's atmosphere, shape and magnetic field.
USS Nautilus, a nuclear submarine, passed beneath the ice cap of the North pole.
Violation of the conservation of parity in atomic interactions demonstrated by Chien-shiung Wu (b. 1915).
Sputnik 1, the first man-made satellite, launched by the USSR (1957).

First American satellite, Explorer 1, discovered the Van Allen radiation belts (1958). Explorer 6 and Luna 3 from the USSR photographed the far side of the Moon.
Kidney machine, with tubes small enough to be inserted into an artery, designed in the US.
Laser beam, used for precision cutting, developed by Theodore Naiman.
Hovercraft invented by Sir C.S. COCKERELL (b. 1910).

First manned space flight Yuri GAGARIN (1934-1968) orbited the Earth once in Vostok 1 (1961).
Telstar, first international communications satellite, launched by the US.
JOHN GLENN (b. 1921) first American in space (1962).
Polaroid colour film produced by Edwin LAND (b. 1909).
Concorde, supersonic jet airliner, designed by French and British.

Space flight The first 'space walk' carried out (1965) by the Russian astronaut Alexei Leonov (b. 1934). The Soviet craft Luna 10 became the first satellite to orbit the Moon, and a Russian spacecraft landed on Venus (1966). Rendezvous and docking manoeuvres carried out by US astronauts.
600.6 mph New world land speed record attained in a jet-propelled car.

Space flight Neil ARMSTRONG (b. 1930) was first man to stand on the Moon (1969). Mariner spacecraft (US) photographed the surface of Mars.
Organic molecules discovered to be of non-biological origin. Such molecules found floating freely in space.
First human heart transplant carried out by Dr Christiaan BARNARD (b. 1922) in South Africa.

Skylab, an orbiting space laboratory, launched by the US (1973).
Radiation film, sensitive to heat, used to take photographs of radiation emissions from the Sun (1970).
Organic molecules in a DNA-like spiral discovered in a meteorite in the Ukraine. Revival of the idea of Svante ARRHENIUS (1859-1927) that life on Earth could have been brought from outer space.

Dynasties, Popes and Heads of State

Australia

Governors General

Marquis of Linlithgow	1901-2
Baron Tennyson	1902-4
Baron Northcote	1904-8
Earl of Dudley	1908-11
Baron Denman	1911-4
Viscount Novar of Raith	1914-20
Baron Forster of Lepe	1920-5
Baron Stonehaven	1925-30
Isaac Alfred Isaacs	1931-6
Baron Gowrie	1936-45
Duke of Gloucester	1945-6
William John McKell	1947-53
William Slim	1953-60
Viscount Dunrossil	1960-1
Viscount De L'Isle	1961-5
Baron Casey	1965-9
Paul Meernaa Caedwalla Hasluck	1969-

Austria

Duchy of Austria

OTTOKAR II	1251-76
RUDOLF OF HAPSBURG	1276-91
Holy Roman Emperors	1291-1740

Sovereigns of Austria-Hungary

MARIA THERESA	1740-80
JOSEPH II	1780-90
Leopold II	1790-2
Francis II	1792-1804
Francis II, as Francis I, Emperor	1804-35
Ferdinand I, Emperor	1835-48

Emperors of Austria and Kings of Hungary

FRANCIS JOSEPH I	1848-1916
Charles I	1916-8

Republic (1918-38)

Karl Seitz	1919-20
Michael Hainisch	1920-8
Wilhelm Miklas	1928-38

Second Republic

Karl Renner	1945-50
Theodor Koerner	1951-7
Adolf Schaerf	1957-65
Franz Jonas	1965-

Belgium

Kings

Leopold I	1831-65
Leopold II	1865-1909
ALBERT I	1909-34
LEOPOLD III	1934-51
BAUDOUIN I	1951-

Brazil

Presidents

Manuel Deodoro da Fonseca	1889-91
Floriano Peixoto	1891-4
Prudente José de Moraes Barros	1894-8
Manuel Ferraz de Campos Salles	1898-1902
Francisco de Paula Rodrigues Alves	1902-6
Affonso Augusto Moreira Penna	1906-9
Nilo Peçanha	1909-10
Hermes da Fonseca	1910-4
Wenceslau Braz Pereira Gomes	1914-8
Francisco de Paula Rodrigues Alves	1918-9
Delfim Moreira (acting)	1918-9
Epitacio da Silva Pessôa	1919-22
Arthur da Silva Bernardes	1922-6
Washington Luiz Pereira de Souza (deposed)	1926-30
Getulio Dornelles VARGAS	1930-45
José Linhares (provisional)	1945-6
Enrico Gaspar Dutra	1946-51
Getúlio Dornelles VARGAS	1951-4
Joao Café Filho	1954-5
Nereú Ramos (acting)	1955-6
Jusceline Kubitschek de Oliveira	1956-61
Jânio Quadros	1961
João Belchior Marques Goulart	1961-4
Humberto Castelo Branco	1964-7
Arthur Costa e Silva	1967-9
Emilio Garrastazú Médici	1969-

Canada

Governors General since Confederation

Viscount Monck	1867-8
Baron Lisgar	1869-72
Marquis of Dufferin and Ava	1872-8
Duke of Argyll	1878-83
Marquis of Lansdowne	1883-8
Earl of Derby	1888-93
Marquis of Aberdeen and Temair	1893-8
Earl of Minto	1898-1904
Earl Grey	1904-11
Duke of Connaught	1911-6
Duke of Devonshire	1916-21
Viscount Byng of Vimy	1921-6
Marquis of Willingdon	1926-31
Earl of Bessborough	1931-5
Baron Tweedsmuir	1935-40
Earl of Athlone	1940-6
Viscount Alexander of Tunis	1946-52
Vincent Massey	1952-9
Georges P. Vanier	1959-67
Roland Michener	1967-

China

Early Dynasties

Hsia (mythical)	2205-1766 BC
Shang (or Yin)	1766-1122 BC
Chou	1122-255 BC
Ch'in	255-206 BC
Han, Earlier, or Western	202 BC-AD 9
Han, Later, or Eastern	AD 25-220
Wei	220-64
Three Kingdoms	265-317
Chin, Western	317-419
Chin, Eastern	420-79
Ch'i (Tsi)	479-502
Liang	502-57
Ch'ên	557-89
Sui	589-618
T'ang	618-907
Five Dynasties	907-60
Sung	960-1127
Kin Tatar (in the north)	1127-1234
Southern Sung	1127-1280
Yüan (Mongol) in the north	1206-80
KUBLAI KHAN	1260-94
Yüan (Mongol)	1280-1368
Ming	1368-1644
Ch'ing or Ta Ch'ing (Manchu)	1644-1912

Rulers of Ch'ing (Manchu) Dynasty

Shun Chih	1644-62
K'ANG-HSI	1662-1722
Yung Chêng	1723-35
CH'IEN LUNG	1736-96
Chia Ch'ing	1796-1820
Tao Kuang	1821-50
Hsien Fêng	1851-61
T'ung Chih	1862-75
Kuang Hsü	1875-1908
HSÜAN T'UNG	1908-12

Presidents of the Republic

SUN YAT-SEN	1911-12
Yüan Shih-k'ai	1912-13
Yüan Shih-k'ai	1913-16
Li Yüan-hung	1916-17
Gen. Feng Kuo-chang	1917-18
Hsü Shih-ch'ang	1918-22
Li Yuan-hung	1922-3
Tsao Kun	1923-4
(Civil War)	1924-8
CHIANG K'AI-SHEK (Pres. of Executive Yüan)	1928-45
Lin Sên (Pres. of National Government)	1932-43
CHIANG KAI-SHEK (Pres. of National Government)	1943-9

Presidents of Nationalist Republic

Li Tsung-jen	1949-50
CHIANG KAI-SHEK	1950-

Chairmen of the People's Republic

MAO TSE-TUNG	1949-54
Liu Shao-ch'i	1954-68
MAO TSE-TUNG	1968-

Denmark

Gorm the Old	c.883-c.940
HAROLD BLUETOOTH	c.940-c.985
SWEYN FORKBEARD	c.985-1014
Harold	1014-8
CANUTE II	1018-35
HARDECANUTE	1035-42
Magnus I (of Norway)	1042-7

Estrith Dynasty (1047-1375)

SWEYN II	1047-75
Harold	1076-80
Canute IV	1080-6
Olaf I Hunger	1086-95
Eric I the Evergood	1095-1103
Nicholas I	1104-34
Eric II the Memorable	1134-7
Eric III the Lamb	1137-47
Sweyn III and Canute V (civil war)	1147-57
WALDEMAR I	1157-82
Canute VI	1182-1202
WALDEMAR II	1202-41
Waldemar III (coregent)	1219-31
Eric IV	1241-50
Abel	1250-2
Christopher I	1252-9
Eric V Klipping	1259-86
Eric VI Menved	1286-1319
Christopher II	1320-6 and 1330-2
(Interregnum, 1332-40)	
WALDEMAR IV ATTERDAG	1340-75
(Interregnum, 1375-6)	
Olaf II	1376-87
MARGARET of Denmark, Norway and Sweden	1387-97
MARGARET and Eric VII of Pomerania	1397-1412
Eric VII (alone)	1412-39
(Interregnum, 1439-40)	
Christopher III	1440-8

House of Oldenburg

Christian I	1448-81
John	1481-1513
Christian II	1513-23

Kings of Denmark and Norway

Frederick I	1523-33
(Interregnum, 1533-4)	
Christian III	1534-59
Frederick II	1559-88
CHRISTIAN IV	1588-1648
Frederick III	1648-70
Christian V	1670-99
Frederick IV	1699-1730
Christian VI	1730-46
Frederick V	1746-66
Christian VII	1766-1808
Frederick VI	1808-39

Kings of Denmark

Christian VIII	1839-48
Frederick VII	1848-63
Christian IX	1863-1906
Frederick VIII	1906-12
Christian X	1912-47
Frederick IX	1947-

France

Merovingian kings

Pepin the Short	751-68
CHARLEMAGNE	768-814
Louis I the Pious	814-40
Charles I the Bald	840-77
Louis II	877-9
Louis III	879-82
Carloman	879-84
Charles II the Fat	884-7
Odo, Count of Paris	888-98
Charles III the Simple	893-923
Robert I	922-3
Rudolf, Duke of Burgundy	923-36
Louis IV	936-54
Lothair	934-86
Louis V	986-7

Capetian Line

HUGH CAPET	987-96
Robert II	996-1031
Henry I	1031-60
PHILIP I	1060-1108
LOUIS VI	1108-37
Louis VII	1137-80
PHILIP II	1180-1223
Louis VIII	1223-6
LOUIS IX (Saint Louis)	1226-70
Philip III	1270-85
PHILIP IV	1285-1314
Louis X	1314-6
John I	1316
Philip V	1316-22
CHARLES IV	1322-8

House of Valois

PHILIP VI	1328-50
John II	1350-64
CHARLES V	1364-80
Charles VI	1380-1422
CHARLES VII	1422-61
LOUIS XI	1461-83
CHARLES VIII	1483-98
Louis XII	1498-1515
FRANCIS I	1515-47
HENRY II	1547-59
Francis II	1559-60
Charles IX	1560-74
Henry III	1574-89

House of Bourbon

HENRY IV	1589-1610
Louis XIII	1610-43
LOUIS XIV	1643-1715
LOUIS XV	1715-74
Louis XVI	1774-92
Louis XVII	1793-5

The Republic

National Convention	1792-5
The Directory	1795-9
The Consulate	1799-1804

First Empire

NAPOLEON I BONAPARTE	1804-15

The Restoration

LOUIS XVIII	1814-24
CHARLES X	1824-30
Louis Phillipe	1830-48

Dynasties, Popes and Heads of State

The Second Republic

Louis Napoleon (see NAPOLEON III)	1848-52

The Second Empire

NAPOLEON III	1852-70

The Third Republic

Louis Adolphe THIERS	1871-3
Marshall MACMAHON	1873-9
Jules Grévy	1879-87
Marie François Sadi Carnot	1887-94
Jean Casimir-Périer	1894-5
François Félix Faure	1895-9
Emile Loubet	1899-1906
Armand Fallières	1906-13
Raymond POINCARÉ	1913-20
Paul Deschanel	1920
Alexandre Mulerand	1920-4
Gaston Doumergue	1924-31
Paul Doumer	1931-2
Albert Lebrun	1932-40

Vichy Government

Henri Philippe PÉTAIN	1940-4

Provisional Government

Charles de GAULLE	1944-6
Félix Gouin (Jan. 23)	1946
Georges Bidault (Jun. 19)	1946
Léon Blum (Dec. 12)	1946

The Fourth Republic

Vincent Auriol	1947-54
René Coty	1954-9

The Fifth Republic

Charles de GAULLE	1959-69
Georges POMPIDOU	1969-

Germany

CHARLEMAGNE	768-814
Louis I	814-40
Lothair I	840-3
Louis II the German	843-76
Charles II the Bald	875-7
Holy Roman Emperors	881-1806
Confederation of the Rhine	1806-13
German Confederation	1815-66
North German Confederation	1866-71

Emperors of Germany

WILLIAM I	1871-88
Frederick III	1888
William II	1888-1918

Kings of Prussia

FREDERICK I	1701-13
Frederick William I	1713-40
FREDERICK II THE GREAT	1740-86
Frederick William II	1786-97
Frederick William III	1797-1840
Frederick William IV	1840-61
WILLIAM I	1861-71

Weimar Republic

Friedrich Ebert, President	1919-25
PAUL VON HINDENBURG, President	1925-34
ADOLF HITLER, Führer and Chancellor	1934-45

Presidents of the Federal Republic of Germany (West)

Theodor Heuss	1949-59
Heinrich Lübke	1959-69
Gustav Heinemann	1969

President of the German Democratic Republic (East)

Wilhelm Pleich	1949-60

Chairman of the Council of State

Walter Ulbricht	1960-

Great Britain

Sovereigns of England

Egbert	Saxon	828-39
Ethelwulf	Saxon	839-58
Ethelbald	Saxon	858-60
ETHELBERT	Saxon	860-6
Ethelred I	Saxon	866-71
ALFRED THE GREAT	Saxon	871-99
Edward the Elder	Saxon	899-924
Athelstan	Saxon	924-40
Edmund	Saxon	940-6
Edred	Saxon	946-55
Edwy	Saxon	955-9
Edgar	Saxon	959-75
Edward the Martyr	Saxon	975-8
Ethelred II the Unready	Saxon	978-1016
Edmund Ironside	Saxon	1016
CANUTE	Danish	1016-35
Harold I Harefoot	Danish	1035-40
HARDECANUTE	Danish	1040-2
EDWARD THE CONFESSOR	Saxon	1042-66
Harold II	Saxon	1066
WILLIAM I THE CONQUEROR	Norman	1066-87
William II Rufus	Norman	1087-1100
Henry I Beauclerc	Norman	1100-35
Stephen	Norman	1135-54
Henry II	Plantagenet	1154-89
RICHARD I COEUR DE LION	Plantagenet	1189-99
JOHN LACKLAND	Plantagenet	1199-1216
Henry III	Plantagenet	1216-72
EDWARD I LONGSHANKS	Plantagenet	1272-1307
Edward II	Plantagenet	1307-27
Edward III	Plantagenet	1327-77
Richard II	Plantagenet	1377-99
HENRY IV	Lancaster	1399-1413
HENRY V	Lancaster	1413-22
Henry VI	Lancaster	1422-61
EDWARD IV	York	1461-83
Edward V	York	1483
RICHARD III	York	1483-5
HENRY VII	Tudor	1485-1509
HENRY VIII	Tudor	1509-47
Edward VI	Tudor	1547-53
MARY	Tudor	1553-8
ELIZABETH I	Tudor	1558-1603
JAMES I (VI of Scotland)	Stuart	1603-25
CHARLES I	Stuart	1625-49
(Commonwealth 1649-60)		
CHARLES II	Stuart	1660-85
James II	Stuart	1685-8
WILLIAM III and Mary	Stuart	1689-1702
ANNE	Stuart	1702-14
George I	Hanover	1714-27
George II	Hanover	1727-60
George III	Hanover	1760-1820
GEORGE IV	Hanover	1820-30
WILLIAM IV	Hanover	1830-7
VICTORIA	Hanover	1837-1901
EDWARD VII	Saxe-Coburg	1901-10
GEORGE V	Windsor	1910-36
EDWARD VIII	Windsor	1936
GEORGE VI	Windsor	1936-52
ELIZABETH II	Windsor	1952-

Holy Roman Empire

Frankish Kings and Emperors

CHARLEMAGNE	800-14
Louis I the Pious	814-40
Lothair	840-55
Louis II	855-75
Charles II the Bald	875-7
Charles III the Fat	881-7
Arnulf, King of Germany	887-99
Louis III the Child, King of Germany	899-911
Conrad of Franconia, King of Germany	911-18

Saxon Kings and Emperors

HENRY I THE FOWLER, King of Germany	919-36
Otto I the Great	936-73
Otto II	973-83
Otto III	983-1002
Henry II the Saint	1002-24

Franconian Emperors

CONRAD II	1024-39
Henry III	1039-56
HENRY IV	1056-1106
Henry V	1106-25
Lothair II (or III) of Saxony	1125-37

Hofenstaufen Kings and Emperors

CONRAD III	1138-52
FREDERICK I BARBAROSSA	1152-90
Henry VI	1190-7
Philip of Swabia	1198-1208
Otto IV of Brunswick	1198-1215
Frederick II	1215-50
Conrad IV	1250-54
(The Great Interregnum 1254-73)	

Other Rulers

RUDOLF I OF HAPSBURG	1273-91
Adolf of Nassau	1292-8
Albert I of Austria	1298-1308
Henry VII of Luxemburg	1308-13
WENCESLAUS OF BOHEMIA	1378-1400
Rupert of the Palatinate	1400-10
Sigismund	1411-37

Hapsburg Emperors

Albert II	1438-9
Frederick III	1440-93
Maximilian I	1493-1519
CHARLES V	1519-56
Ferdinand I	1556-64
Maximilian II	1564-76
Rudolph II	1576-1612
Matthias	1612-9
FERDINAND II	1619-37
Ferdinand III	1637-57
Leopold I	1658-1705
Joseph I	1705-11
Charles VI	1711-40
Charles VII of Bavaria	1742-5

Hapsburg-Lorraine Emperors

Francis I	1745-65
JOSEPH II	1765-90
Leopold II	1790-2
Francis II	1792-1806

India

Emperors of Mogul Dynasty

BABER	1526-30
Humayan	1530-56
AKBAR THE GREAT	1556-1605
JAHANGIR	1605-27
Shah Jahan	1628-58
AURANGZEB	1658-1707
Bahadur Shah I	1707-12
Jahandar Shah	1712-3
Farruk-Siar	1713-9
Mohammed Shah	1719-48
Ahmed	1748-54
Alamgir	1754-9
Shah Alam	1759-1806
Mohammed Akbar II	1806-37
Bahadur Shah II	1837-57

Viceroys and Governors General of India

Earl Canning	1858-62
Earl of Elgin	1862-3
Baron Lawrence	1863-9
Earl of Mayo	1869-72
Earl of Northbrook	1872-6
Earl of Lytton	1876-80
Marquis of Ripon	1880-4
Marquis of Dufferin and Ava	1884-8
Marquis of Lansdowne	1888-93
Earl of Elgin and Kincardine	1894-9
Marquis Curzon of Kedleston	1899-1905
Earl of Minto	1905-10
Baron Hardinge of Penshurst	1910-6
Viscount of Chelmsford	1916-21
Marquis of Reading	1921-6
Viscount Halifax	1926-31
Marquis of Willingdon	1931-6
Marquis of Linlithgow	1936-43
Earl Wavell	1943-7
VISCOUNT MOUNTBATTEN OF BURMA	1947-8
Shri Chakravarti Rajagopalachari	1948-50

Presidents of the Republic

Rajendra PRASAD	1950-62
Sarvepalli Radhakrishnan	1962-7
Zakir Husain	1967-9
Varahagiri Venkata Giri	1969-

Italy

Kings of Sardinia and Italy: House of Savoy

Victor Amadeus II	1720-30
Charles Emmanuel III	1730-73
Victor Amadeus III	1773-96
Charles Emmanuel IV	1796-1802
Victor Emmanuel I	1802-21
Charles Felix	1821-31
Charles Albert	1831-49
VICTOR EMMANUEL II	1849-78
Humbert I	1878-1900
Victor Emmanuel III	1900-46
Humbert II	1946

Presidents of the Republic

Enrico de Nicola	1946-8
Luigi Einaudi	1948-55
Giovanni Gronchi	1955-62
Antonio Segni	1962-4
Giuseppe SARAGAT	1964-72
Giovanni Leone	1972-

Japan

Principal Heads of State

(Early (Legendary) Period, 66 BC-AD 710)	
JIMMU TENNO	660-585 BC
Jingo	AD 360
SHOTOKU TAISHI	593-621
Tenchi	662-671
Kwammu	782-805
Fujiwara Clan	858-1156
Sanjo II	1068-72
Taira Clan	1160-85
Kamakura Shogunate:	
YORITOMO	1192-99
Yoriie	1202-04
Sanetomo	1203-19
DAIGO II	1318-39
Ashikaga Shogunate:	
ASHIKAGA TAKAUJI	1338-58
Yoshimitsu	1367-95
NOBUNAGA	1568-82
Hideyoshi	1585-98
Tokugawa Shogunate:	
IYEYASU	1603-16
Hidetada	1616-1623
Iyemiṭsu	1623-1651
Iyetsuna	1651-1680
Tsunayoshi	1680-1709
Yoshimune	1716-45
Iyenari	1793-1837
Komei	1847-67
Hitotsubashi (or Yoshinobu)	1867
Meiji Era: MUTSUHITO	1867-1912
Taisho Era: Yoshihito	1912-26
Showa Era: Hirohito	1926

The Netherlands

Princes of Orange, Stadholders (since 1579)

WILLIAM I	1579-1584
Maurice	1587-1625
Frederick Henry	1625-47
William II	1647-50
(Stadholdership suspended 1650-72)	
Jan De Witt, Grand Pensionary	1653-72
William of Nassau	1672-1702
(Stadholdership suspended, 1702-47)	
William IV	1747-51
William V	1751-95
Batavian Republic	1795-1806

Dynasties, Popes and Heads of State

Kings

Louis Bonaparte	1806-10
Willem Frederick, Prince of Orange, as William I	1815-40
William II	1840-9
William III	1849-90
Wilhelmina	1890-1948
Juliana	1948-

Norway

Haakon the Good	935-61
Harold II	961-970
Earl Haakon	970-95
OLAF I TRYGGVESSON	995-1000
Earls Eric and Sweyn	1000-15
Olaf II	1016-30
Sweyn	1028-35
Magnus I the Good	1035-47
HAROLD III HAARDRAADE	1047-66
Olaf III and Magnus II	1066-9
Olaf III (alone)	1069-93
Magnus III	1093-1103
Olaf IV (d. 1115), Eystein I Magnusson (d. 1122), Sigurd I (joint rule)	1103-30
Magnus IV and Harold Gille	1130-6
Sigurd II and Inge I	1137-61
Eystein II Haraldsson, Haakon II, Magnus V (contenders)	1142-62
Magnus V (alone)	1162-84
Sverre	1184-1202
Haakon III	1202-04
Guthrum	1204-5
Inge II (alone)	1205-17
HAAKON IV THE OLD	1217-63
Magnus VI the Law-Mender	1263-80
Eric Magnusson	1280-99
Haakon V	1299-1319
MAGNUS VII (Magnus II of Sweden)	1319-43
HAAKON VI	1343-80
Olaf V (Olaf II of Denmark)	1380-7
(Norway united with Denmark 1387-1814)	
(Norway united with Sweden 1814-1905)	
Haakon VII	1905-57
Olaf V	1957-

Popes

SAINT PETER	c.41-c.67
Saint Linus	67-c.79
Saint Anacletus	79-c.90
SAINT CLEMENT I	90-c.99
Saint Evaristus	99-c.107
Saint Alexander I	107-c.116
Saint Sixtus I	116-c.125
Saint Telesphorus	125-c.136
Saint Hyginus	136-c.140
Saint Pius I	140-c.154
Saint Anicetus	154-c.165
Saint Soter	165-74
Saint Eleutherius	174-89
Saint Victor I	189-98
Saint Zephyrinus	198-217
Saint Calixtus I	217-22
Saint Urban	222-30
Saint Pontian	230-5
Saint Anterus	235-6
Saint Fabian	236-50
Saint Cornelius	251-3
Saint Lucius I	253-4
Saint Stephen I	254-7
Saint Sixtus II	257-8
Saint Dionysius	259-68
Saint Felix I	269-74
Saint Eutychianus	275-83
Saint Gaius	283-96
Saint Marcellinus	296-304
Saint Marcellus I	308-9
Saint Eusebius	309-c.310
Saint Miltiades	c.310-14
Saint Sylvester	314-35
Saint Mark	336
Saint Julius I	337-52
Saint Leberius	352-66
Saint Damasus I	366-84
Saint Siricius	384-98
Saint Anastasius I	398-401
Saint Innocent I	402-17
Saint Zosimus	417-8
Saint Boniface I	418-22
Saint Celestine I	422-32
Saint Sixtus III	432-40
Saint Leo I, the Great	440-61
Saint Hilarius	461-8
Saint Simplicius	468-83
Saint Felix II (or III)	483-92
Saint Gelasius I	492-6
Saint Anastasius II	496-8
Saint Symmachus	498-514
Saint Hormisdas	514-23
Saint John I	523-6
Saint Felix III (or IV)	526-30
Boniface II	530-2
John II	533-5
Saint Agapetus I	535-6
Saint Silverius	536-c.538
Vigilius	538-55
Pelagius I	556-61
John III	561-74
Benedict I	575-9
Pelagius II	579-90
SAINT GREGORY I THE GREAT	590-604
Sabinianus	604-6
Boniface III	607
Saint Boniface IV	608-15
Saint Deusdedit	615-8
Boniface V	619-25
Honorius I	625-38
Sevennus	640
John IV	640-2
Theodore I	642-9
Saint Martin I	649-55
Saint Eugenius I	654-7
Saint Vitalian	657-72
Saint Adeotatus II	672-6
Donus	676-8
Saint Agatho	678-81
Saint Leo II	682-3
Saint Benedict II	684-5
John V	685-6
Conon	686-7
Saint Sergius I	687-701
John VI	701-5
John VII	705-7
Sisinnius	708
Constantine (I)	708-15
Saint Gregory II	715-31
Saint Gregory III	731-41
Saint Zacharius	741-52
Stephen II (III)	752-7
Saint Paul I	757-67
Stephen III (IV)	768-72
Saint Adrian I (or Hadrian)	772-95
Saint Leo III	795-816
Stephen IV (V)	816-7
Saint Paschal I	817-24
Eugenius II	824-7
Valentine	827
Gregory IV	827-44
Sergius II	844-7
Saint Leo IV	847-55
Benedict III	855-8
Saint Nicholas I	858-67
Adrian II	867-72
John VIII	872-82
Marinus (or Martin II)	882-4
Saint Adrian III	884-5
Stephen V (IV)	885-91
Formosus	891-6
Boniface VI	896
Stephen VI	816-7
Romanus	897
Theodore II	c.897
John IX	898-900
Benedict IV	900-3
Leo V	903
Christopher	903-4
Sergius III	904-11
Anastasius III	911-3
Lando	913-4
John X	914-28
Leo VI	928-9
Stephen VII (VIII)	929-31
John XI	931-6
Leo VII	936-9
Stephen VIII (IX)	939-42
Marinus II (or Martin III)	942-6
Agapetus II	946-55
John XII	955-64
Leo VIII	963-5
Benedict V	964
John XIII	965-72
Benedict VI	973-4
Benedict VII	974-83
John XIV	983-4
Boniface VII	984-5
John XV	985-96
Gregory V	996-9
Sylvester II	999-1003
John XVII	1003
John XVIII	1003-9
Sergius IV	1009-12
Benedict VIII	1012-24
John XIX	1024-32
Benedict IX	1032-45
Gregory VI	1045-6
Clement II	1046-7
Damasus II	1048
Saint Leo IX	1049-54
Victor II	1055-7
Stephen IX (X)	1057-8
Benedict X	1058-9
Nicholas II	1059-61
Alexander II	1061-73
Saint Gregory VII	1073-85
Victor III	1086-7
Urban II	1088-99
Paschal II	1099-1118
Gelasius II	1118-9
Calixtus II	1119-24
Honorius II	1124-30
Innocent II	1130-43
Celestine II	1143-4
Lucius II	1144-5
Eugenius III	1145-53
Anastasius IV	1153-4
ADRIAN IV	1154-9
Alexander III	1159-81
Lucius III	1181-5
Urban III	1185-7
Gregory VIII	1187
Clement III	1187-91
Celestine III	1191-8
Innocent III	1198-1216
Honorius III	1216-27
Gregory IX	1227-41
Celestine IV	1241
Innocent IV	1243-54
Alexander IV	1254-61
Urban IV	1261-4
Clement IV	1265-8
Gregory X	1271-6
Innocent V	1276
Adrian V	1276
John XXI	1276-7
Nicholas III	1277-80
Martin IV	1281-5
Honorius IV	1285-7
Nicholas IV	1288-92
Saint Celestine V	1294
Boniface VIII	1294-1303
Benedict XI	1303-4
Clement V	1342-52
John XXII	1316-34
Benedict XII	1334-42
Clement VI	1342-52
Innocent VI	1352-62
Urban V	1362-70
Gregory XI	1370-8
Urban VI	1378-89
Boniface IX	1389-1404
Innocent VII	1404-6
Gregory XII	1406-15
Alexander V	1409-10
Martin V	1417-31
Eugenius IV	1431-47
Nicholas V	1447-55
Calixtus III	1455-8
Pius II	1458-65
Paul II	1464-71
Sixtus IV	1471-84
Innocent VIII	1484-92
Alexander VI	1492-1503
Pius III	1503
Julius II	1503-13
Leo X	1513-21
Adrian VI	1522-3
CLEMENT VII	1523-34
PAUL III	1534-49
Julius III	1550-5
Marcellus II	1555
Paul IV	1555-9
Pius IV	1559-65
Saint Pius V	1566-72
Gregory XIII	1572-85
Sixtus V	1585-90
Urban VII	1590
Gregory XIV	1590-1
Innocent IX	1591
Clement VIII	1592-1605
Leo XI	1605
Paul V	1605-21
Gregory XV	1621-3
Urban VIII	1623-44
Innocent X	1644-55
Alexander VII	1655-67
Clement IX	1667-9
Clement X	1670-6
Innocent XI	1676-89
Alexander VIII	1689-91
Innocent XII	1691-1700
Clement XI	1700-21
Innocent XIII	1721-4
Benedict XIII	1724-30
Clement XII	1730-40
Benedict XIV	1740-58
Clement XIII	1758-69
Clement XIV	1769-74
Pius VI	1775-99
Pius VII	1800-23
Leo XII	1823-9
Pius VIII	1829-30
Gregory XVI	1831-46
PIUS IX	1846-78
Leo XIII	1878-1903
Pius X	1903-14
Benedict XV	1914-22
PIUS XI	1922-39
PIUS XII	1939-58
JOHN XXIII	1958-63
PAUL VI	1963-

Portugal

House of Burgundy

ALFONSO I	1139-85
Sancho I	1185-1211
Alfonso II	1211-23
Sancho II	1223-48
Alfonso III	1248-79
Denis	1279-1325
Alfonso IV	1325-57
Peter I	1357-67
Ferdinand I	1367-83
(Interregnum 1383-5)	

House of Aviz

John I	1385-1433
Edward	1433-8
ALFONSO V	1438-81
John II	1481-95
Emanuel	1495-1521
John III	1521-57
Sebastian	1557-78
Henry	1578-80

Spanish Domination

PHILIP I (II of Spain)	1580-98
Philip II (III of Spain)	1598-1621
Philip III (IV of Spain)	1621-40

House of Braganza

John IV	1640-56
Alfonso VI	1656-83
Peter II	1683-1706
John V	1706-50
Joseph Emanuel	1750-77
Maria I and Peter III	1777-86
Maria I (alone)	1786-1816
John VI	1816-26
Peter IV (Dom Pedro)	1826
Maria II da Gloria	1826-8
Miguel	1828-33
Maria II (restored)	1833-53

House of Braganza-Coburg

Peter V	1853-61
Louis	1861-89
Carlos I	1889-1908
Manuel II	1908-10

Presidents of the Republic

Teófilo Braga	1910-1
Manuel José de Arriaga	1911-5
Teófilo Braga	1915
Bernardino Luiz Machado	1915-7
Sidônio B. Cardoso da Silva Paes	1917-8
João de Canto e Castro	1918-9
Antônio José de Almeida	1919-23
Manuel Teixeira Gomes	1923-5

Dynasties, Popes and Heads of State

Bernardino Luiz Machado	1925-6
Antonio Oscar de Fragoso Carmona	1926-51
Francisco Higino Craveiro Lopes	1951-8
Américo Deus Rodriguez Thomaz	1958-

Roman Emperors

To the end of the Western Empire

AUGUSTUS (Octavianus)	27 BC-AD 14
TIBERIUS	AD 14-27
Caligula	37-41
CLAUDIUS	41-54
NERO	54-68
Galba	68-9
Otho	69
Vitellius	69
VESPASIAN	69-79
TITUS	79-81
DOMITIAN	81-96
Nerva	96-8
TRAJAN	98-117
HADRIAN	117-38
ANTONIUS PIUS	138-61
MARCUS AURELIUS	161-80
Lucius Aurelius Verus	161-9
Commodus	180-92
Pertinax	193
Didius Julianus	193
Septimius Severus	193-211
Caracalla	211-7
Geta	211-2
Macrinus	217-8
Heliogabalus	218-22
Alexander Severus	222-35
Maximinus	235-8
Gordianus I	238
Gordianus II	238
Balbinus and Pupienus	238
Gordianus III	238-44
Philip the Arabian	244-9
Decius	249-51
Gallus	251-3
Aemilianus	253
Valerian	253-60
Gallienus	260-8
Claudius II	268-70
Aurelian	270-5
Tacitus	275-6
Florian	276
Probus	276-82
Carus	282-3
Carinus and Numerianus	283-5
DIOCLETIAN	284-305
Maximian	286-305
Constantius	305-6
Galerius	305-11
CONSTANTINE THE GREAT	306-27
Constantine II	337-40
Constans	337-50
Constantius II	337-61
JULIAN THE APOSTATE	361-3
Jovian	363-4
Valentinian I (West)	364-75
Valens (East)	364-78
GRATIAN (West)	375-83
Valentinian II (West)	275-92
Thodosius the Great (East)	379-94
Maximus (West)	383-8
Eugenius (West)	392-4
Theodosius (sole emperor)	394-5

Russia

House of Rurik

IVAN III THE GREAT	1462-1505
Basil III	1505-33
IVAN IV THE TERRIBLE	1533-84
Fëdor I	1584-98
BORIS GODUNOV	1598-1605
Fëdor II	1605
Demetrius	1605-6
Basil (IV) Shiuski	1606-10
(Interregnum, 1610-3)	

House of Romanov

Michael Romanov	1613-45
Alexis	1645-76
Fëdor III	1676-82
Ivan V and PETER THE GREAT	1682-9
PETER THE GREAT (alone)	1689-1725
Catherine I	1725-7
Peter II	1727-30
Anna	1730-40
Ivan VI	1740-1
Elizabeth	1741-62
Peter III	1762
CATHERINE II	1762-96
Paul I	1796-1801
ALEXANDER I	1801-25

NICHOLAS I	1825-55
ALEXANDER II	1855-81
ALEXANDER III	1881-94
NICHOLAS II	1894-1917

Chairmen of the Presidium of the Supreme Soviet of the USSR

Mikhail I. Kalinin	1923-46
Nikolai M. Shvernik	1946-53
Kliment E. Voroshilov	1953-60
LEONID I. BREZHNEV	1960-4
ANASTAS I. MIKOYAN	1964-6
Nikolai V. Podgorny	1966-

South Africa

Governors-General

Viscount Gladstone	1910-4
Earl Buxton	1914-20
Duke of Connaught	1920-3
Earl of Athlone	1923-31
Earl of Clarendon	1931-7
Patrick Duncan	1937-43
Gideon Brand van Zyl	1946-50
Ernest George Jansen	1951-9
Charles Robberts Swart	1960-1

Presidents

Charles Robberts Swart	1961-7
Jozua François Naudé (acting)	1967-8
Jacobus Johannes Fouché	1968-

Spain

From the union of Aragon and Castile (1479)

FERDINAND II OF ARAGON AND	
ISABELLA OF CASTILE	1479-1504
Philip I and Juanna	1504-6
FERDINAND V (II OF ARAGON)	1505-16

House of Hapsburg

Charles I	1516-56
PHILIP II	1556-98
Philip III	1598-1621
Philip IV	1621-65
CHARLES II	1665-1700

House of Bourbon

PHILIP V	1700-24
Louis I	1724
PHILIP V	1724-46
Ferdinand VI	1746-59
Charles III	1759-88
Charles IV	1788-1808
Ferdinand VII	1808
Joseph Bonaparte	1808-13
Ferdinand II (restored)	1813-33
Isabella II	1833-68

House of Savoy

Amadeus	1870-3

Republic

Emilio Castelar y Ripoll	1873-4

House of Bourbon

Alfonso XII	1874-85
Alfonso XIII	1886-1931

Presidents of the Republic

Niceto Alcalá Zamora y Torres	1931-6
Manuel AZAÑA	1936-9
(Civil War, 1936-9)	

Chief of the New State

Francisco FRANCO	1938-

Sweden

Folkung Dynasty (1250-1365)

Earl Birger (Regent)	1250-66
Waldemar I	1250-75
Magnus I	1275-90
Birger II	1290-1318
MAGNUS II	1319-65
Eric XII	1356-9
Haakon VI	1362-3
Albert of Mecklenburg	1364-89
MARGARET (Regent)	1389-1412

(Union with Denmark)		
Eric XIII (Eric VII of Denmark)		1412-35
Engelbrekt		1435-6
Karl Knutsson		1436-40
Christopher of Bavaria		1440-8
Charles VIII		1448-57
Christian I of Oldenburg		1457-64
Charles VIII		1464-5
Charles VIII	and	1467-70
Sten Sture the Elder		1470-1503
John II		1497-1501
Svante Sture		1503-12
Sten Sture the Younger		1512-20
Christian II		1520-3

Vasa Dynasty

GUSTAVUS I (Administrator)	1521-3
GUSTAVUS I (King)	1523-60
Eric XIV	1560-8
John III	1568-92
Sigismund	1592-1604
Charles IX (Regent)	1599-1604
Charles IX (King)	1604-11
GUSTAVUS (II) ADOLPHUS	1611-32
Christina	1632-54

Palatinate Dynasty

Charles X Gustavus	1654-60
Charles XI	1660-97
CHARLES XII	1697-1718
Ulrica Eleonora	1718-20
Frederick I of Hesse	1720-51

Holstein-Gottorp Dynasty

Adolphus Frederick	1751-71
Gustavus III	1771-92
Gustavus IV Adolphus	1792-1809
Charles XIII	1809-18
(Sweden and Norway united, 1814-1905)	

Bernadotte Dynasty

CHARLES XIV JOHN	1818-44
Oscar I	1844-59
Charles XV	1859-72
Oscar II	1872-1907
(Norway became independent 1905)	
Gustavus V	1907-50
Gustav VI Adolf	1950-73
Karl Gustav	1973-

United States of America

Presidents

George WASHINGTON	1789-97
John ADAMS	1797-1801
Thomas JEFFERSON	1801-9
James MADISON	1809-17
James MONROE	1817-25
John Quincy ADAMS	1825-9
Andrew JACKSON	1829-37
Martin VAN BUREN	1837-41
William Henry HARRISON	1841
John TYLER	1841-5
James Knox POLK	1845-9
Zachary TAYLOR	1849-50
Millard FILLMORE	1850-3
Franklin PIERCE	1853-7
James BUCHANAN	1857-61
Abraham LINCOLN	1861-5
Andrew JOHNSON	1865-9
Ulysses Simpson GRANT	1869-77
Rutherford Birchard HAYES	1877-81
James Abram GARFIELD	1881
Chester Alan ARTHUR	1881-5
Grover CLEVELAND	1885-9
Benjamin HARRISON	1889-93
Grover CLEVELAND	1893-7
William McKINLEY	1897-1901
Theodore ROOSEVELT	1901-9
William Howard TAFT	1909-13
Woodrow WILSON	1913-21
Warren Gamaliel HARDING	1921-3
Calvin COOLIDGE	1923-9
Herbert Clark HOOVER	1929-33
Franklin Delano ROOSEVELT	1933-45
Harry S TRUMAN	1945-53
Dwight David EISENHOWER	1953-61
John Fitzgerald KENNEDY	1961-3
Lyndon Baines JOHNSON	1963-9
Richard Milhous NIXON	1969-

United Nations

Secretaries General

Trygve LIE (Norwegian)	1946-52
Dag HAMMARSKJÖLD (Swedish)	1953-61
Sithu U THANT (Burmese)	1962-72
Kurt WALDHEIM (Austrian)	1972-

Acknowledgments

Who Did What features work by the following artists and studios

Hussein Abo, Norman Barber, Carol Binch, Sergio Borella, Secondo Bussette, Richard Cole, Roy Coombs, Diagram, Nick Eddison, Michael Embden, Shireen Faircloth, Andrew Farmer, Gilchrist Studios Ltd, Peter Goodfellow, Phil Green, Alan Hood, Eric Jewel, Peter Le Vasseur, Michael Mann Studio, Keith Richens, Colin Rose, Ken Rush, Rodney Shackell, Malcolm Smythe, D.N. Trevellyan, Vladimir Volkonski, John Walsh, John Walton, David Watson

Type setting in Plantin
set by Tradespools Limited,
Frome, Somerset, England
Film setting in Helios
by Quickset Limited, London

Photographs, pictures supplied by:
Page 5, Trinity College, Dublin; 7, Keystone (Adenauer); 8, C.M. Dixon (Oedipus production); 10, Michael Holford (Screen); 13, Transworld (Ali fight); 16, Mansell (Fred Archer); 17, Camera Press (Louis Armstrong); 19, Keystone (Arp sculpture); 20, Mansell (Lady Astor); 20, Keystone (Atlee); 25, Dr. Barnardo's (Barnardo child); 26, Bettman Archive (Barnum & Bailey); 26, David Redfern (Count Basie); 35, Popperfotos (Ernest Bevin); 36, Mansell (Birkenhead & Churchill); 38, Ronan Picture Library (Bleriot); 40, Kobal Collection (Bogart); 43, Michael Holford (Bosch painting); 47, Mary Evans (Genghis Khan); 47, Popperfotos (Roosevelt & Churchill); 53, Rienits (Burke & Wills); 55, Bettman Archive (Byrd); 58, Bettman Archive (Al Capone); 58, John Frost Newspaper Collection (Prohibition issue); 63, Radio Times Hulton Picture Library (Don Quixote); 64, Spectrum (Pagoda at Kew); 64, Kobal Collection (Chaplin *Modern Times*); 66, Mansell (Charles II's death); 66, Mansell (Charles I); 68, Mansell (Belloc); 72, Michael Holford (Claude Lorraine); 75, Magnum (Colette); 79, Mary Evans (Yorktown Surrender); 81, Mander & Mitchenson (*Private Lives*); 82, Mansell (Crippen's arrest); 83, Radio Times Hulton Picture Library (Marie Curie); 85, Camera Press (Salvador Dali); 89, Michael Gee (De Gaulle poster); 91, Mansell (Charles Dickens); 95, Cooper Bridgeman (Francis Drake); 97, Keystone (Isadora Duncan); 98, Michael Holford (Dürer watercolour); 99, Picture-point (Voodoo); 100, Keystone (Edison); 101, Popperfotos (Eichmann); 102, US Airforce (Bikini); 102/3, Picturepoint (Eiffel Tower); 104, Popperfotos (Elgar); 105, Popperfotos (Epstein's studio); 111, National Film Archive (*My Little Chickadee*); 113, Popperfotos (Foch); 115, Mary Evans (Charles James Fox); 120, Novosti (Gagarin); 122, Mansell (David Garrick); 123, Popperfotos (Gauguin's studio); 127, Gillette Industries (early advertisement); 127, Mansell (Poster); 128, Popperfotos (Goering); 131, Popperfotos (Maxim Gorky); 133, Popperfotos (W.G. Grace); 134, Popperfotos (Grieg); 136, Mander & Mitchenson (Grimaldi); 136, Mansell (Grimm); 137, Keystone (Guevara); 139, British Museum (Printing press); 143, Popperfotos (President Harding); 144, Mander & Mitchenson (Hardy); 147, Radio Times Hulton Picture Library (Haydn musical score); 148, H.J. Heinz & Co. (Baked Beans advertisement); 149, Mansell (Henry VIII and wives); 153, John Frost Newspaper Collection (Hillary/Everest ascent); 153, Popperfotos (Himmler); 154, Magnum (Hitchcock); 158, Bettman Archive (Houdini); 160, Mansell (Victor Hugo); 163, Barnaby's (Acropolis); 165, Mansell (Ivan the Terrible); 167, Mansell (Declaration of Independence); 169, Popper-fotos (Augustus John); 170, Keystone (Amy Johnson); 170, Popperfotos (Amy Johnson biplane); 171, Barnaby's (St Paul's); 172, Popperfotos (Joyce); 174, Kobal Collection (Buster Keaton); 175, Bettman Archive (Keller & Mrs. Coolidge); 175, Kobal Collection (Gene Kelly); 176 Ronan Picture Library (Atlantic telegraph); 176, Popperfotos (Kruschev); 177, Popperfotos (Kennedy); 177, Spectrum (Kenyatta); 177, Bettmann Archive (Kennedy family); 179, Patrick Moore (Keppler and Newton); 180, John Frost Newspaper Collection (Luther); 184, Mansell (Kruger); 189, Keystone (Laughton); 193, Mansell (Leonardo flying machine); 194/5, Mansell (Suez Canal); 195, Keystone (Lichtenstein *"Whaam!"*); 199, Popperfotos (Lloyd George); 203, Popperfotos (Low cartoon); 206, Popperfotos (Macarthur); 208, Michael Holford (Magritte); 208, Michael Holford (Magellan Straits map); 212, Mansell (Mahler); 215, Ronan Picture Library (Marconi cartoon); 217, Kobal Collection (Marx Bros.); 223, Mansell (Cook); 224, Patrick Moore (Mercator); 226, C.M. Dixon (David); 231, Mansell (Montgomery); 236, John Frost Newspaper Collection (Mussolini); 238, Popperfotos (Nansen); 238/239, Scott Polar Research (*Fram*); 240, Michael Holford (Royal Pavilion, Brighton); 241, Penguin (A.S. Neill); 242, Michael Holford (*Victory*); 243, Popperfotos (Neruda); 245, Novosti (Nicholas II); 245, Popperfotos (Nietzsche); 247, Barnaby's (Beethoven, Grieg); 247, Mansell (Haydn); 247, Popperfotos (J.S. Bach, Mozart, Wagner); 252, John Frost Newspaper Collection (Mrs. Pankhurst/*Daily Graphic*); 254, Giraudon (Pasteur); 256, Mansell (Samuel Pepys); 256, Michael Holford (Acropolis); 261, Radio Times Hulton Picture Library (Buffalo Bill); 261, Historical Picture Service (General Custer); 261, Western Americana (Calamity Jane, Sitting Bull, Geronimo, Billy the Kid, Wichita, Kansas); 265, Mansell (Madame de Pompadour); 265, Frederick Warne Ltd. (Beatrix Potter); 270, Keystone (Raman and carbon atoms); 276, Keystone (Rockefeller); 277, Barnaby's (Rolls Royce); 277, Keystone (Rommel); 278, Mansell (Rowlandson); 283, Mansell (Lord Salisbury); 287, Keystone (Schweitzer); 288, Michael Holford (Serlio); 289, Mansell Collection (Shakespeare folio title page); 290, Kobal Collection (George Bernard Shaw on film set); 292, Royal Aeronautical Society (Sikorsky); 299, Mansell (Sterne, Stevenson); 300, Magnum (Stravinsky); 302, Keystone (Sutherland's tapestry); 305, Bettmann Archive (Zachary Taylor); 305, Mansell (Tchaikovsky); 306, Mander & Mitchenson (Ellen Terry); 310, Popperfotos (Tolstoy); 311, Mansell (Lautrec poster and locomotive); 312, Popperfotos (Trotsky); 313, Popperfotos (Mark Twain); 315, Kobal Collection (Valentino); 315, Michael Holford (Blenheim Palace); 321, Radio Times Hulton Picture Library (Wagner); 324, Picturepoint (Mount Rushmore); 326, Josiah Wedgwood (Pottery); 326, Kobal Collection (Welles in *The Stranger*); 327, Kobal Collection (Mae West poster); 329, Platt International (Cotton gin); 331, Bettmann Archive (Woodrow Wilson); 338, Michael Holford (Bowmen shooting birds, Buddah, Chinese dish, Pyramid of Chephren); 338, Roger Wood (Frieze of chariot and men, Persia); 339, Ford Motor Co. (1911 Ford); 339, Mary Evans (Gutenberg Press, Hannibal and elephants); 339, Michael Holford (Julius Caesar, Running girl sculpture); 339, Keystone (Pyramid); 340, Keystone (Pyramids); 340, Michael Holford (Bronze vessel); 348, Mary Evans (Genghis Khan); 356, Cooper Bridgeman (Raphael painting); 362, British Waterways Board (Canals); 362, Popperfotos (Union guns); 362, Mary Evans (French salon); 370, United States Information Service (Telstar); 386, Roger Wood (Friday mosque).

STOP PRESS

1974-1975

Politics and power

The period was characterized by many sudden and often violent changes in national leadership, political alignments and styles of government through deaths, resignations and military coups. Localized guerilla warfare and international terrorism continued unabated, especially in support of the cause of Palestinian liberation. Crime and corruption caused many of the world's leading politicians to topple: in the US, President Nixon resigned under the threat of impeachment for his role in the Watergate cover-up, but was pardoned by his successor, Gerald Ford, for anything he might have done while in office; Germany's Willy Brandt stepped down as Chancellor when his personal aide came under suspicion of spying for East Germany; and the Japanese Prime Minister, Kakuei Tanaka, resigned following allegations of irregularities in his private financial dealings. In India, Mrs Indira Gandhi was convicted of corrupt electoral practice, but was allowed to remain as head of state pending her appeal; in the turmoil which followed, she imprisoned many of her political opponents and imposed Press censorship. In Australia, the deputy Prime Minister, Dr Jim Cairns, was dismissed for alleged financial improprieties. Military coups overthrew the Caetano regime in Portugal and Emperor Haile Selassie in Ethopia, and a Turkish invasion forced the temporary withdrawal of President Makarios from Cyprus. King Feisal of Saudi Arabia was assassinated, and the military junta in Greece stood down in favour of republican government. In Niger a military coup overthrew President Diori Hamani. Mrs Golda Meir resigned as Prime Minister of Israel following adverse public reaction to the country's state of preparedness in the October 1973 war.

The oil crisis

A fourfold increase in the price of oil imposed by members of the Organization of Petroleum Exporting Countries (OPEC) underlined worldwide concern over future energy resources and contributed to the inflation and recession being felt through much of the West. Oil was recognized by the Middle East countries as a powerful political weapon and an Arab oil embargo to the US, subsequently lifted, was seen as part of the continuing power-play over the Israeli problem. It was realized that the oil crisis was not simply a consequence of oil being used as a tactical weapon for limited political aims in the Middle East, but that it represented an irreversible change in the balance of world power between previously omnipotent industrial powers and the Third World. The newly rich OPEC members invested much of their surplus revenue in the West but also gave massive aid to less developed parts of the world. In June 1975 the first North Sea oil was landed in Britain, offering some respite from OPEC prices and thereby easing balance of payments problems.

Inflation

Many Western economies reeled under the effects of inflation, coupled with a business recession and rising unemployment. By mid-1975 there were signs of a recovery, although there were still eight million unemployed in the US and a 25 per cent rate of inflation in Britain led to stern economic measures.

Technology

Unmanned US space probes yielded the first detailed, close-up photographs of Mars, Venus, Mercury and Jupiter. Manned space flights became less frequent, but the Skylab 4 astronauts spent a record 2,000 hours in space in 1974.

Principal Events

World energy crisis heightened. Huge oil price increases by producing nations (1974) aggravate worldwide inflation and recession, affect balance of economic power.
India's first nuclear explosion (1974).
Greece Cyprus invaded by Turkey; end of Greek military junta; Greek withdrawal from NATO (1974).
Watergate scandal caused resignation of NIXON (1974).
Indo-China Saigon and Phnom Penh fall to Communist forces (1975).
EEC British membership confirmed by referendum (1975).
Suez Canal reopened to world shipping (1975).

Religion

Vatican reaffirms teaching on insolubility of marriage, after Italian referendum decision in favour of divorce (1974).
New Archbishop of Canterbury Dr Donald Cógan (b. 1909) succeeded Dr Michael Ramsey (1974).
Church of England allowed by Parliament to use alternative services to those laid down since 1662 in Book of Common Prayer (1974).
Growing protest against Vatican ban on contraception.

Philosophy

Central state materialism, which asserts that the mind is only another state within the central nervous system, exercises strong influence on philosophical argument.
Political philosophy reflects revival of the state-of-nature theory first advanced by LOCKE, ROUSSEAU and HOBBES, deriving principles about State from an imagined pre-social condition. Major books include *A Theory of Justice,* by John Rawls, and *Anarchy State and Utopia,* by Robert Nozick.

Literature

Soviet Union expelled ALEKSANDR SOLZHENITSYN (1974).
Black comedy and fantasy writing at a peak, as exemplified by KINGSLEY AMIS in *Ending Up* (1974), PAUL ROTH in *My Life as a Man* (1974), VLADIMIR NABAKOV in *Look at the Harlequins* (1975).

Art

Conceptual art rejects conventional art in favour of experiences and ideas related to ideals. These are communicated by combinations of words, 3-dimensional objects, audience participation, etc. Developed since the 1960s, it is now the foremost international art movement. Yves Klein (1928-62); Diete Roth (b. 1930); Piero Manzoni (1933-63).

Architecture

European Architectural Heritage Year (1975) A campaign launched by the Council of Europe to promote architectural conservation and improvement of design standards. Its activities included conferences, exhibitions, educational projects and special awards.

Music

Reggae Jamaican rhythmic music, evolved from early 1950s New Orleans rhythm and blues. Following success in Britain since the late 1960s, it gains momentum in the US.
Rock music Expansion of world listening audience reached peak (1974), especially in the US, where it had become a billion-dollar industry. Trends included disco revival, rock-classical fusions, teeny-bopper stars.

Technology

Space flight Mercury, Venus, Jupiter and, particularly, Mars photographed in close-up by US unmanned space probes. Skylab 4 Astronauts spent a record 2,000 hours in space (1974).
Artificial blood, suitable for transfusions, developed in the US (1974).
Test-tube (embryo implant) babies The birth of three was claimed at a British Medical Council meeting (1974).
Smallest ever electronic machines made, using microminiature integrated circuits; micro-computer developed in US (1974).

Aiken, Conrad (page 9), died in 1973. He was a member of the American Academy of Arts and Letters.

Ali, Mohammed (page 13), regained the World Heavyweight Championship in 1974 by knocking out George Foreman in Zaire. Later he successfully defended his title against three challengers—Chuck Wepner, Ron Lyle and Joe Bugner.

Bliss, Sir Arthur (page 38), died in 1975, having composed some 130 works during his lifetime.

Blunden, Edmund (page 39), died in January 1974. He was Professor of Poetry at Oxford University from 1966 to 1968.

Brandt, Willy (page 46), resigned as Chancellor of West Germany (1974) after his personal aide, Günther Guillaume, was suspected of spying for East Germany. Brandt remains a member of the German parliament and leader of the Social Democratic Party, on whose behalf he travels widely. He was succeeded by Helmut SCHMIDT.

Bulganin, Nikolai Alexandrovich (page 52), died in February 1975. He retired on a State pension 15 years earlier, but was still to be seen occasionally at Kremlin functions.

Chadwick, Sir James (page 64), died in 1974, four years after being made a Companion of Honour.

Chaplin, Charles (page 65) was knighted in the New Year Honours List, 1975.

Chiang Kai-Shek (page 69), died in April 1975, in Taiwan. The policy of *rapprochement* by President NIXON towards Peking and the subsequent transfer of the UN seat to mainland China dealt a death blow to the aspirations of Chiang's Nationalist government.

Dallapiccola, Luigi (page 85), died in February 1975, in Florence. His most important composition in later years was the opera *Ulysses*, premiered in Berlin in 1968.

Ellington, Edward Kennedy 'Duke' (page 105), died in New York in May 1974. In later years Ellington was only able to keep his beloved orchestra on the road by subsidizing it from record royalties.

Ford, Gerald Rudolf (born 1913) Thirty-eighth President of the US, being inaugurated on August 9, 1974, following Richard NIXON's resignation in the wake of the Watergate scandal. He declined the Vice-Presidential nomination in 1968, but accepted it in December, 1973, following another resignation—that of Spiro AGNEW. Ford graduated from Yale Law School in 1941, saw wartime service in the US Navy and won nomination to the House of Representatives in 1949, becoming minority leader in 1965. He likes to be known as a 'moderate Republican' and has striven hard for the establishment of better relationships between the US and the People's Republic of China.

Gandhi, Indira (page 121), was convicted in June 1975, at Allahabad, of corrupt political practice during the general elections of 1971. She was subsequently allowed to remain head of the government pending her appeal.

Giscard d'Estaing, Valéry (born 1926) Leader of the centre-right Independent Republicans in France, and elected President (1974) following the death of Georges POMPIDOU. He was Minister of Finance under DE GAULLE (1962-6), but took the blame for an unpopular deflationary policy and spent three years in the political wilderness. During this time he built up his own small Independent Republican party and became Pompidou's Minister of Finance in 1969. He is the youngest French president for three-quarters of a century.

Goldwyn, Samuel (page 130), died in Los Angeles in January 1974. He was one of the last of the original American movie magnates.

Haile Selassie (page 140), deposed as Emperor of Ethiopia (1974). Disillusionment with the government's failure to introduce social reforms and its alleged mishandling of aid in the famine of 1973-4 were the prime causes of the coup. Haile Selassie was placed under house arrest and many of his family and members of his government were executed by the Dergue, the provisional military government.

Heath, Edward Richard George (page 147), resigned as Prime Minister of Great Britain (1974) following the general election of February. Less than seven months later, following a second election in which the Conservatives were again beaten, Heath was replaced as leader of the party by Margaret Thatcher.

Hepworth, Dame Barbara (page 150), died tragically in a fire at her home in St Ives, Cornwall, in May 1975. She had designed her own tombstone several years earlier.

Kästner, Erich (page 174), died in a clinic in Munich in July 1974.

Kissinger, Henry (page 181), was awarded the Nobel Peace Prize (jointly with Le Duc Tho of the North Vietnamese Politburo) for his role as mediator during peace talks on the war in Indo-China (1973).

Khan, Mohammed Ayub (page 178), died in April 1974 in Islamabad, where he had lived since his resignation in 1969. He was buried with full military honours.

Krishna Menon, Vengalil Krishnan (page 183), died in October 1974, having worked tirelessly throughout his lifetime for the good of India.

Lagerkvist, Pär Fabian (page 186), died in Stockholm in July 1974. He was described by his friends as 'a believer without a faith, a religious atheist'.

Lindbergh, Charles (page 197), died in August 1974. The final years of his life were devoted to conservation.

Lippmann, Walter (page 198), died in December 1974—still an active and influential columnist and author.

Makarios III, Archbishop (page 212), overthrown as President of Cyprus (1974) in a coup led by Greek officers of the Cypriot National Guard. Makarios fled to Europe and, following the invasion of Cyprus by Turkey, participated in emergency meetings of the UN Security Council. He returned to Cyprus in December 1974 and resumed his presidential functions, although the political situation in the island remained unsettled.

Meir, Golda (page 223), resigned as Prime Minister of Israel in 1974, following a cabinet crisis in the aftermath of the previous year's general election. Her successor was General Itzhak Rabin, the first native-born Israeli to become Prime Minister.

Milhaud, Darius (page 227), died in Geneva in June 1974. In later years he taught composition at the Paris Conservatoire.

Nixon, Richard Milhous (page 245), became the first US president in history to resign. Following months of investigation by a Senate Select Committee, during which three articles of impeachment were brought against him, Nixon finally admitted to withholding knowledge of the Watergate scandal and resigned in August 1974. He was succeeded by Gerald FORD.

Oistrakh, David (page 249), died suddenly in Amsterdam in October 1974. He was the most admired Russian violinist of his generation.

Perón, Juan Domingo (page 257), died of a heart attack in July 1974. His widow succeeded him as President of Argentina in an atmosphere of continuing turmoil.

Plomer, William (page 263), died in September 1973. He was awarded a CBE in 1968 and was President of the Poetry Society of London from that year until 1971.

Pompidou, Georges (page 265), died of cancer in Paris in April 1974. He was succeeded by Valéry Giscard d'Estaing.

Schmidt, Helmut (born 1918) German politician, elected Chancellor of West Germany (1974) following the resignation of Willy BRANDT. A member of the Social Democratic Party since 1946, Schmidt was appointed Minister of Defence in 1969 and three years later became Economics and Finance Minister. Unlike his predecessor, Schmidt advocates close friendship between Germany and the US.

Thant, U (page 306), died of cancer in November 1974. He was succeeded as Secretary-General of the United Nations two years earlier by Dr Kurt WALDHEIM.

Thatcher, Margaret Hilda (born 1925) Leader of the Conservative Party in Britain. Entered Parliament as MP for Finchley, North London, in 1959, having formerly been a research chemist and then a barrister specializing in tax law. She held a succession of senior government and opposition posts and became a Privy Councillor in 1970. After two successive Conservative election defeats, she succeeded Edward HEATH as leader of the party in February 1975.

Warren, Earl (page 324), died in July 1974, having served as Chief Justice

under four presidents. His successor was Abe Fortras.

Wightman, Mrs George (page 329), died in 1974, just over half a century after the first Wightman Cup competition.

Wilson, James Harold (page 331), resumed power as Prime Minister of Great Britain in February 1974. A further election in October 1974 confirmed the Labour government in power, though still with a slender majority.

Wodehouse, Pelham Grenville (page 332), died in New York in 1975, less than two months after receiving a knighthood in the New Year Honours List.

Dynasties, Popes and Heads of State

Australia
Governors-General

Paul Meernaa Caedwalla Hasluck	1969-74
Sir John Kerr	1974-

Austria
Presidents

Franz Jonas	1965-74
Rudolf Kirch Schläger	1974-

Brazil
Presidents

Emilio Garrastazú Médici	1969-74
Ernesto Gaisel	1974-

Canada
Governors-General since Confederation

Roland Michener	1967-74
Jules Léger	1974-

Denmark
Kings and Queens

Frederick IX	1947-72
Margrethe II	1972-

France
The Fifth Republic

Georges POMPIDOU	1969-74
Valéry Giscard d'Estaing	1974-

Germany
Presidents of the Federal Republic of Germany (West)

Gustav Heinemann	1969-74
Walter Scheel	1974-

Presidents of the German Democratic Republic (East)

Wilhelm Pieck	1949-60
Walter ULBRICHT	1960-73
Willi Stoph	1974-

India
Presidents of the Republic

Varahagiri Venkata Giri	1969-74
Fakhruddin Ali Ahmed	1974-

Portugal
Presidents of the Republic

Américo Deus Rodriguez Thomaz	1958-74
Antonio de Spinola	1974
Costa Gomes	1974-

South Africa
Presidents

Jacobus Johannes Fouché	1968-75
Nicolaas Diederichs	1975-

United States of America
Presidents

Richard Milhous NIXON	1969-74
Gerald Rudolf Ford	1974-